Fifty Years of Turmoil and Titles

A History of the Eastern Pennsylvania Interscholastic Basketball League

1926-1975

ISBN: 978-1-965418-09-3
LCCN:

Contents

Preface

In 1982, I joined the Allentown Jaycees and became involved with the LARC Basketball Classic, as it was called at the time. Now, the Via Classic, this event provided extra exposure to the senior high school players in the area from the East Penn Conference, the Centennial League, and the Colonial League. Established in 1976, it quickly became very popular with the basketball community and continues to survive today despite the demise of the Allentown Jaycee organization, which initially sponsored and ran the event. Dave Pfahler, Tom Herrity, and Mike Chomik spearheaded the effort to develop the Classic, a tournament consisting of senior all-star teams: two teams from the East Penn Conference and one each from the Colonial League and the Centennial League. Initially, only involving the senior boys, the tournament expanded to include the senior girls, first with the selectees divided into two teams and then expanding into a four-team setup like the boys. Later, the Lehigh Valley Basketball Hall of Fame was created to honor the outstanding players, coaches, officials, and administrators in the Lehigh Valley area.

The committee assigned me to assist with the Hall of Fame effort. The initial selectees for the Hall of Fame came from a list of names of individuals who made significant contributions to the game in the Lehigh Valley. Being concerned that deserving individuals might be overlooked, I decided to begin research into the local basketball history since I was not a Lehigh Valley native and had little background knowledge of the local leagues and their history. I began my research scanning microfiche of the Morning Call at the Allentown Public Library. Since I worked at PPL up the street from the library, I spent numerous lunch hours tediously reading the microfiche to improve the list of candidates to be considered for selection to the Hall of Fame. In doing some, I became intrigued with the history of the East Penn League and its success with numerous PIAA and PCIAA state titles. I came across many stories of the intense competition between the league members. I felt compelled to compile a history of the league from the research I had been conducting. I initially began to compile a brief synopsis of the league's history in the late 1980s. Unfortunately, other events in my life put the effort in the background for many years. Finally, I decided to reinitiate the effort, but realized that the brevity of my writing efforts did not do justice to the league and its history. I began to review what I had completed and decided to expand the compilation to what has evolved today, over 600 pages. I also decided to keep the history to the 50 years of the league before the area leagues realigned and the East Penn Conference was formed in 1976 with the expansion of the initial league to include some schools from other leagues in the area. This effort became quite the chore when I decided to include capsule writeups of every contest played in the fifty years of the league's competition. It has become a very comprehensive history of one of the outstanding high school basketball leagues in the state of Pennsylvania.

I hope you enjoy the many tidbits of history included throughout the book and appreciate the intense competition which occurred, especially during the early years, and led to numerous state titles.

Enos Martin

Introduction

The Eastern Pennsylvania Interscholastic Basketball League, more commonly known as the East Penn League for much of its existence began league play on December 18, 1925, on the home courts of Allentown, Bethlehem, and Easton. The league's first season included these three teams along with Coatesville, Pottstown, and Pottsville. These six teams would make up the league for the first two years of its existence. Only three of these original six teams would participate in each of the fifty years of the league's existence while known as the East Penn League. Bethlehem, Easton, and Pottsville would retain membership throughout the fifty years.

During the fifty years of the league, sixteen different schools participated as league members.

Allentown, or Allen, as it became known when the Allentown School District split into two high schools for the 1959-60 school year, missed three years from 1948 through 1950 when the PIAA penalized the school for using ineligible players in 1946 and 1947. As a result of the PIAA action, the league expelled the Canaries for three years before allowing the school to reenter the league in 1951. During the 47 years of membership, the Canaries played 640 games including both regular season and playoff matchups to determine league championships. The Canaries won 444 of those contests for a 69.4% winning percentage. Only Dieruff managed to hold a winning record against Allen in league play winning 21 of 39 games played from 1960 through 1975. Allen won 62 of 100 contests against Bethlehem, or Liberty.

Allentown and Bethlehem matched up six times in extra playoff contests to determine the league championship including twice in 1947. After Allentown won the first half title, the two teams tied for the second half title. Bethlehem won that contest forcing a fourth battle between the two schools. Allentown won the overall championship to move into postseason play. A similar scenario occurred in 1952, but this time Bethlehem won the first half title with the teams ending up tied again during the second half. Allentown succeeded in defeating Bethlehem in the first contest forcing an overall league championship contest. This time Bethlehem won the title to move onto district play. In 1953, Allentown won the first half with the teams tying again for the second half. This time Allentown avoided a fourth matchup by winning the playoff for the second half title. The final playoff matchup occurred in 1958. After Bethlehem won the first half, Allentown and Easton tied for the second half. The Canaries won the second half playoff only to be defeated by Bethlehem for the overall title. Overall, the two teams split their six playoff games.

Hazleton, another fierce rival, and Allentown also interestingly played 100 games with the Canaries winning 55 of those contests. The two teams matched up in ten playoff games to determine league titles. The first occurred in 1930 before the league changed to the half format. The two teams tied after the regular season at 12-2. Allentown defeated Hazleton for the league title and the right to move into postseason play. In 1938, the league, for the first time, had moved into the half format. Hazleton ended up winning the first half and Allentown the second half. This time Hazleton won to take the league title.

Two years later in 1940, the two teams tied during the first half with Hazleton winning the title in the playoff. With the Mountaineers winning the second half, they took the overall league championship. Amazingly, the next two years, the two teams squared off in playoff matchups. In 1941, Hazleton won the first half and Allentown the second half. The Canaries won the league title with the defeat of the Mountaineers. The 1942 season saw Hazleton and Allentown tie for the first half title with Hazleton winning the playoff. Hazleton had a disastrous second half going 2-3. Allentown again tied for the second half but this time with Pottsville. The Canaries ended up losing to Pottsville.

The 1944 season saw the two teams play five times with three occurring in the space of a week at the end of the regular season. After Hazleton beat Allentown in the first half, the Mountaineers were upset by Easton to create a first half tie. When no agreement could be reached on a date for the playoff, the league decided to hold it after the regular season ended. In the second half, Allentown defeated the Mountaineers only to be upset by Bethlehem to create a second half tie. After Allentown won the first half playoff in Reading, Hazleton took the second half playoff game three days later, also in Reading. Now, a fifth contest was necessary to decide the league title. Four days later, and again in Reading, Hazleton won the fifth, and deciding contest for the hard-fought league title.

In 1959, Allentown won the first half title in a playoff with Central Catholic. Hazleton finished undefeated in the second half and earned the right to play Allentown for the overall league title. Despite having lost both regular season games to Hazleton, Allentown defeated the Mountaineers in the playoff for the 1959 title. The 1971 season had the Canaries, now known as Allen, tie Dieruff for the first half title. After Allen beat Dieruff, Hazleton went on to win the second half. In the league playoff contest, Hazleton prevailed over Allen.

So, despite holding a winning edge overall, Hazleton took six of the ten playoff contests and four of the seven titles that went to playoffs.

Allentown dominated three teams in league play. They won 77 of 98 over Easton (78.6%), 77 of 97 over Pottsville (79.4%), and 39 of 44 over Tamaqua (88.6%). In a much smaller sample, they also won 20 of 24 (83.3%) over Phillipsburg.

Allentown (Allen) won 19 individual league titles during the 47 years of membership including 7 of 9 from 1951 through 1959. Only Bethlehem interrupted the streak twice in 1952 and 1958. They went on to win state championships in 1935, 1945, 1946, 1947, and 1951. Both the 1946 and 1947 titles were vacated because of the use of ineligible players. The Canaries won seven district titles including 1945, 1946, 1947, 1955, 1957, 1969, and 1975.

Allentown Central Catholic became a member during the 1948 season as a replacement, when Allentown was expelled from the league, and participated in the original league for 28 seasons. Central Catholic won 219 games out of 392 contests (55.9%) which includes playoff results. They only managed to win a single league title which occurred in 1965.

Prior to 1973, the Catholic parochial schools were not members of the Pennsylvania Interscholastic Athletic Association (PIAA). As a member of the PCIAA (Pennsylvania Catholic Interscholastic Association), Central Catholic was not eligible to participate in the PIAA playoffs and instead participated in the PCIAA playoffs. While a member of the league, the Vikings won PCIAA state titles in 1948, 1952, 1956, 1957, and 1964. They also won the title twice before joining the league in 1936 and 1945.

Allentown Dieruff first played in the league during the 1960 season for a total of sixteen years in the league. The Allentown School District split for the 1959-60 school year when Allentown became known as Allen. During the fifty years of the league, Dieruff holds the distinction of having the best winning percentage as the Huskies won 213 of 293 games (72.7%).

Dieruff held winning records over each of their nine league opponents during the sixteen years. The Huskies never lost to either Bethlehem Catholic (18 games) or Phillipsburg (24 games). They also won 25 of 33 contests (75.8%) over Hazleton and 19 of 21 over Tamaqua (90.5%). The Huskies' toughest competition, although still with winning records, included cross-city rival Allen (21-18) and Bethlehem (22-16).

Dieruff won six league titles in sixteen years including three consecutive championships (1966-1968). The Huskies also won four district championships all in consecutive years (1966-1969).

Bethlehem, became known as ***Liberty*** when the Bethlehem school district split and formed Freedom High, remained a member through the fifty years and with the realigned conference. They joined Easton and Pottsville as the only members for the full 50 years of the league.

Bethlehem played 648 contests in the league, most of any member, which was seven more than both Pottsville and Tamaqua. Bethlehem won 402 games (62%) which was second to Allen's 444. In the fifty years, Liberty dominated both Easton and Pottsville winning over 70% against both schools. They won 72 of 100 games against Pottsville and never played any playoff contests with them over the fifty years. Their record against Easton was similar, but Bethlehem had a single playoff game (1972) against Easton, which they lost. Liberty won 72 of the 101 games played. Bethlehem's only losing records were against Allentown, losing 62 of 100 (38%), and Dieruff, losing 22 of 38 (42.1%). They split six playoff games with the Canaries with two each occurring in both 1947 and 1952. In 1947, they lost the second playoff contest which gave Allentown the title. In 1952, they won the second contest to win the title. The following year they lost the playoff game for the league title, but came back in 1958 to win the title with the playoff win.

Bethlehem won seven league titles including 1934, 1948, 1952, 1958, 1961, 1962, and 1963. The 1934 title was a result of eventual forfeits by both Allentown and Hazleton of games won with the use of ineligible players. Liberty won its first district title in 1948 and added titles in 1958 and 1961.

Bethlehem Catholic first joined during the 1967 season and continued its membership in the new conference. In the Hawks nine years in the league, they never posted a winning record. They had three successive seasons (1969-1971) with identical 10-10 records. They did post winning records over Freedom (9-5), Phillipsburg (12-6), and Tamaqua (7-3). They broke even against Easton (9-9).

Bethlehem Freedom made its appearance in the league during the 1969 season and remained in the realigned conference. Freedom was created with the split of the Bethlehem School District and the completion of the high school's construction in the fall of 1967. The Patriots' first season was as an independent prior to joining the league. Freedom struggled in league competition winning only 41 of 132 contests (31.1%). Like Bethlehem Catholic, the best Freedom could do was break even in their first season at 10-10 and 9-9 during 1972. In their seven seasons, their only winning records were against Phillipsburg (10-4) and Tamaqua (5-1).

Coatesville, a charter member, stayed for six years from 1926 through 1931. Coatesville won less than a third of their contests in league competition (23 of 75, 30.7%). They did win 8 of 12 games against Easton. Coatesville joined the Philadelphia Suburban League to avoid the lengthy travel required to play some opponents in the East Penn League.

Doylestown joined in 1928 and played in the league for four years through the 1931 season and left with Coatesville and Pottstown. After a successful 10-4 season to finish third to Hazleton and Allentown, Doylestown could only win nine more league games during their next three seasons. They only won 19 of 56 league contests (33.9%). Doylestown joined the Bux-Mont League to minimize their cost of travel and difficulty in meeting the level of competition in the league.

East Stroudsburg spent four seasons in the league from 1932 through 1935. After a winning inaugural season (6-4) in league play and going 11-17 in 1934 and 1934, East Stroudsburg could not win a contest (0-14) in 1935. They abruptly resigned prior to the 1936 season to join the Lehigh-Northampton League, also known as the Two County League at the time.

Easton, as noted, retained its membership all 50 years and continued in the realigned conference. Participating in 641 contests in league play, tied with Pottsville for second most, the Red Rovers won 269 games while losing 372 (42%). In the first 46 seasons of league play, Easton only had nine seasons with a winning record. During the last four seasons (1972-1975), the Red Rovers finally experienced some significant success winning 62 of 81 contests (77%). Despite this overall record, Easton had tremendous success against Pottsville (63-38, 62.4%) and Tamaqua (28-16, 63.6%). They also went 18-6 against cross-river rivals Phillipsburg. Both Allentown and Bethlehem held dominating records over the Red Rovers. Allen won 77 of 98 and Liberty 72 of 101 contests. Hazleton at 64-32 and Dieruff 24-12 also proved to be difficult opponents.

After 26 years, Easton won its first league title of any kind when they won the first half title only to lose to Allentown, who won the second half, for the league championship. They would not experience another title until the second half of the 1973 season. Central Catholic, Dieruff, and Easton all tied at 8-1 during the second half. Easton won playoff games with both teams to take the league championship for the first time. They went on to win the first district title. Despite not winning the league, they qualified for district play in 1972 and won the district title for the second successive year. In 1975, they won the league title after winning the first half and defeating second half champion Dieruff for the league championship.

Hazleton joined the league for the 1928 season and remained a member of the new conference through the 1982 basketball season. In the Mountaineers first five seasons, they dominated the league with an overall 60-7 record. They won three league titles in 1928, 1929, and 1932. Allentown won the 1930 title in a playoff with Hazleton and won it outright in 1931. Hazleton went on in the 1928 and 1929 seasons to win the Pennsylvania state championship.

During their 48 seasons, Hazleton compiled a record of 377-250 (60.1%) and added a third state championship as a league member in 1938. In their first 23 seasons, they only had two losing records (1934 and 1947). The 1934 campaign became a losing season after they compiled a 13-1 record but had to forfeit eight games because of the use of an ineligible player. From 1961 through 1963, they won only 5 of 40 games including a record of 0-14 in 1963.

In addition to the three state titles, the Mountaineers won thirteen league championships and three district titles. Most of their success happened in their first 25 seasons with only two league titles from 1951 through 1975. As noted in Allentown's writeup, the Canaries and Mountaineers competed fiercely and were bitter rivals over the years. Overall, Hazleton could only win 44 of 100 contests against the Canaries. Bethlehem and Hazleton essentially split their contests with Liberty winning 51 to the Mountaineers 50 games. After Dieruff entered the league, the Mountaineers only could win 8 of 33 contests (24.2%), by far their worst record against any other league opponent.

Mahanoy City became a league member for the 1933 season and spent six years in the league through the 1938 season. During their brief membership, they complied a winning record of 41-37, but never won a league title. They joined the Black Diamond League in 1939. The Maroons had a particularly difficult time with Allentown and Bethlehem with 3 and 9 records against each of them.

Phillipsburg joined the league in 1964. They continued their membership in the realigned league and remained a member until after the 1995 season. During the 12-year stint in the original East Penn League, Phillipsburg never posted a winning league record. The Stateliners best showing was during the 1968 season when they finished 8-10 in league play. Phillipsburg's overall record in league play was 43-173 (19.9%). Tamaqua was the only league member with whom they posted a winning record by taking 10 of 16 contests.

Pottstown, also a charter member, left when Coatesville exited in 1931. In six seasons, Pottstown compiled an overall record of 37-36 and won the league title in the second year 1927. They had lost the league title during the 1926 inaugural season in a playoff with Pottsville. They lost all eight contests with Hazleton and went 4-8 with both Allentown and Bethlehem.

Pottsville, also a charter member and a member for all 50 years, left the East Penn Conference to join the Schuylkill Basketball League beginning with the 1978-79 basketball season. Tied with Easton with the second most contests in league play with 641, Pottsville was only able to win 232 games (36.2%)

in the fifty years. They won the first league championship in 1926 and won it twice more in 1942 and 1964. They won their only district title during the 1942 campaign.

Pottsville had a successful 1970 campaign with a 17-5 record. They tied Central Catholic for the first half but lost the playoff with Vikings. They finished in a four-way tie for the second half title but lost to Allen in the first round of the second half playoff. Pottsville could only achieve winning records over Bethlehem Catholic (14-4), Freedom (12-2), Phillipsburg (20-4), and Tamaqua (26-18). Pottsville's most successful stretch was from 1967 through 1970 when they went 54-25 but could not win a league title.

Tamaqua originally joined the league in 1933 with Mahanoy City and dropped out after the 1944 season only to rejoin in 1962. They joined the Black Diamond league in 1945 when they left the first time. They left again after the 1971 season after another ten years in the league. Tamaqua joined the Tri-County League in 1972. Out of their 230 total games played in the league, the Tams could only win 80 (25.8%). During the two league stints, Tamaqua only had a winning record against one team East Stroudsburg (5-1). Tamaqua had a particularly difficult time against Bethlehem winning only 4 of 44 contests and Allentown 5 of 44. In twenty-two seasons, Tamaqua only compiled a winning record in1936 (8-4) and 1966 (12-4). In 1966, they managed to tie Dieruff for the second half lead only to lose to the Huskies in the playoff for the title.

Beginning with the 1976 season, the league membership changed significantly with the realignment of the three major high school sports leagues. This realignment created an expanded East Penn League which would now become known as the East Penn Conference. The conference would include two divisions with seven schools in each division. Four new schools were added to form the new conference including Emmaus, Northampton, Parkland, and Whitehall.

In addition, both the Lehigh-Northampton League and the Lehigh Valley League were dissolved with the formation of two new leagues: Colonial League and Centennial League. The Colonial League was comprised of Bangor, Catasauqua, Nazareth, Palisades, Pen Argyl, Salisbury, Saucon Valley, Southern Lehigh, and Wilson. The Centennial League included mostly the northern tier schools in the area. East Stroudsburg, Lehighton, Northwestern Lehigh, Notre Dame, Palmerton, Pleasant Valley, Pocono Mountain, Slatington, and Stroudsburg made up the original Centennial League.

In the fifty years of the East Penn League's existence, the members would play 2,457 games with only four scheduled contests not completed. One game between Easton and Pottstown was not played in 1928 and was forfeited to Easton 2-0. The other three games, one in 1928 and two in 1929, were not played and were not forfeited by either team, instead deciding just not to play them. In addition, the teams played an additional 64 contests to decide league championships for an overall total of 2,521 league contests.

During the fifty years, the league won eight state championships with Hazleton winning in 1928, 1929, and 1938. Allentown added five state titles winning in 1935, 1945, 1946, 1947, and 1951. Unfortunately, the 1946 and 1947 titles were vacated by the PIAA when Allentown was found to have used ineligible players. Several players had exhausted their eligibility and played more than the limit of eight semesters of eligibility.

When Central Catholic joined the league, the Vikings were ineligible to participate in the PIAA state playoffs. Instead, they participated in the Pennsylvania Catholic Interscholastic Athletic Association. The Vikings won five PCIAA state championships including 1948, 1952, 1956, 1957, and 1964.

Overall Records of League Members in League Play

Allentown (Allen)	444-196	69.4%
Bethlehem (Liberty)	402-246	62.0%
Bethlehem Catholic	63-105	37.5%
Central Catholic	219-173	55.9%
Coatesville	23-52	30.7%
Dieruff	213-80	72.7%
Doylestown	19-37	33.9%
East Stroudsburg	17-35	32.7%
Easton	269-372	42.0%
Freedom	41-91	31.1%
Hazleton	377-250	60.1%
Mahanoy City	41-37	52.6%
Phillipsburg	43-173	19.9%
Pottstown	37-36	50.7%
Pottsville	232-409	36.2%
Tamaqua	80-230	25.8%

Records Versus League Members

	Allen	BC	CC	Coatesville	Dieruff	Doylestown	ES	Easton
Allen		12-6	19-34	2-10	18-21	7-1	4-4	77-21
BC	6-12		5-13		0-18			9-9
CC	34-19	13-5			11-23			34-23
Coatesville	10-2					2-6		8-4
Dieruff	21-18	18-0	23-11					24-12
Doylestown	1-7			6-2				2-6
ES	4-4							4-4
Easton	21-77	9-9	23-34	4-8	12-24	6-2	4-4	
Freedom	3-11	5-9	2-12		1-13			4-10
Hazleton	45-55	12-6	27-29	8-0	8-25	8-0	7-1	64-32
Liberty	38-62	11-7	33-25	10-2	16-22	2-6	7-1	72-29
MC	3-10						6-0	7-5
Phillipsburg	4-20	6-12	4-20		0-24			6-18
Pottstown	4-8			8-3		5-3		7-5
Pottsville	20-77	14-4	17-41	6-6	12-24	3-5	2-6	38-63
Tamaqua	5-39	3-7	5-15		2-19		5-1	16-28

	Freedom	Hazleton	Liberty	MC	Phillipsburg	Pottstown	Pottsville	Tamaqua
Allen	11-3	55-45	62-38	10-3	20-4	8-4	77-20	39-5
BC	9-5	6-12	7-11		12-6		4-14	7-3
CC	12-2	29-27	25-33		20-4		41-17	15-5
Coatesville		0-8	2-10			3-8	6-6	
Dieruff	13-1	25-8	22-16		24-0		24-12	19-2
Doylestown		0-8	6-2			3-5	5-3	
ES		1-7	1-7	0-6			6-2	1-5
Easton	10-4	32-64	29-72	5-7	18-6	5-7	63-38	28-16
Freedom		4-10	5-9		10-4		2-12	5-1
Hazleton	10-4		50-51	7-5	21-3	8-0	70-27	33-11
Liberty	9-5	51-50		9-3	22-2	6-4	72-28	40-4
MC		5-7	3-9				9-3	8-4
Phillipsburg	4-10	3-21	2-22				4-20	10-6
Pottstown		0-8	4-6				9-3	
Pottsville	12-2	27-70	28-72	3-9	20-4	3-9		26-18

BC = Bethlehem Catholic

CC = Central Catholic

ES = East Stroudsburg

MC = Mahanoy City

League Champions

Year	First Half	Second Half	Overall	
1926			Pottsville	
1927			Pottstown	
1928			Hazleton	State Champions
1929			Hazleton	State Champions
1930			Allentown	
1931			Allentown	
1932			Hazleton	
1933			Allentown	
1934			Bethlehem	
1935			Allentown	State Champions
1936			Allentown	
1937			Hazleton	
1938	Hazleton	Allentown	Hazleton	State Champions
1939			Hazleton	
1940	Hazleton[1]	Hazleton	Hazleton	
1941	Hazleton	Allentown	Allentown	
1942	Hazleton[1]	Pottsville[1]	Pottsville	
1943	Bethlehem	Hazleton[2]	Hazleton[2]	Hazleton District Champions
1944	Allentown[3]	Hazleton[1]	Hazleton[1]	Hazleton District Champions
1945	Allentown[4]	Allentown	Allentown	Allentown District/State Champions
1946	Allentown	Allentown	Allentown	District/State Champions (vacated)
1947	Allentown	Bethlehem[1]	Allentown[2]	District/State Champions (vacated)
1948	Bethlehem	Bethlehem	Bethlehem	Bethlehem District Champions
				Central Catholic PCIAA champions
1949	Hazleton	Bethlehem[5]	Hazleton	
1950	Hazleton	Hazleton	Hazleton	Allentown District Champions
1951	Easton	Allentown	Allentown	Allentown District/State Champions
1952	Bethlehem	Allentown[2]	Bethlehem	Central Catholic PCIAA Champions
1953	Allentown	Allentown	Allentown	
1954	Allentown	Allentown	Allentown	
1955	Allentown	Allentown	Allentown	District Champions
1956	Allentown	Allentown	Allentown	Central Catholic PCIAA Champions
1957	Allentown	Allentown	Allentown	District Champions
				Central Catholic PCIAA Champions
1958	Bethlehem	Allentown[6]	Bethlehem	District Champions
1959	Allentown[5]	Hazleton	Allentown	
1960	Bethlehem[3]	Hazleton	Hazleton	
1961	Bethlehem	Bethlehem	Bethlehem	Bethlehem District Champions
1962	Bethlehem	Bethlehem	Bethlehem	
1963	Bethlehem[5]	Dieruff	Bethlehem	
1964	Pottsville	Dieruff	Pottsville	Central Catholic PCIAA Champions
1965	Central Catholic	Central Catholic	Central Catholic	
1966	Dieruff	Dieruff[7]	Dieruff	Dieruff District Champions
1967	Dieruff[4]	Bethlehem	Dieruff	Dieruff District Champions
1968	Dieruff[2]	Bethlehem[8]	Dieruff	Dieruff District Champions
1969	Dieruff	Allen	Allen	Dieruff District Chanmpions
1970	Central Catholic[4]	Allen[9]	Allen	
1971	Allen[8]	Hazleton	Hazleton	Hazleton District Champions
1972	Central Catholic	Central Catholic	Central Catholic	
1973	Central Catholic[8]	Easton	Easton	Easton District Champions
1974	Dieruff	Dieruff	Dieruff	Easton District Champions
1975	Easton	Dieruff[10]	Easton	Allen District Champions

Notes:
1 – Playoff with Allentown
2 – Playoff with Bethlehem
3 – Playoff with Hazleton
4 – Playoff with Pottsville
5 – Playoff with Central Catholic
6 – Playoff with Easton
7 – Playoff with Tamaqua
8 – Playoff with Dieruff
9 – Four-way playoff (Allen, Dieruff, Pottsville, Hazleton) with Allen defeating Pottsville for title
10 – Playoff with Allen and Pottsville

On Saturday morning, March 20, 1920, representatives from Allentown, Bethlehem, Catasauqua, Easton, Northampton, and Tamaqua met at the Allentown YMCA. They formed a basketball league, the Lehigh Valley Interscholastic Basketball League, with competition to begin in 1921. Alfred C. Lewis, Allentown High School, served as the league's president. Other officers elected included Francis H. Sheckler, Catasauqua, vice president; Clyde S. Frankenfield, Northampton, treasurer; and H.G. Gailey, Easton, secretary. The group decided that a silk banner would be awarded to each year's champion and the team with the best record after three years would receive a silver cup.[1]

Allentown had been a member of the Central Pennsylvania Scholastic League from 1918 through 1920. Other league teams included Reading. Lebanon, York, Harrisburg Central, Harrisburg Technical, and Steelton. The 1918 season was the third for this league. Harrisburg Central dropped out after the 1918 to reduce the league to six teams. Allentown opted out of the league because of the heavy expenses incurred due to long trips to play other league members. In its 3 years in the league, Allentown went 9-22.

1921: With a six-team league, each member played a ten-game schedule with home and away contests with the other league members. As the regular schedule of the inaugural season drew to a close, Northampton and Easton were tied atop the standings both with 7-3 records. Right behind them stood Catasauqua with a 6-3 record with one game to play against 4-5 Tamaqua. Northampton and Easton decided to playoff for the league title ignoring the possibility of a three-way tie should Catasauqua, led by Coach George Bellis, win their game. Northampton defeated Easton 18-16 with forward Bachman scoring 14 of the 18 points. But due to Catty's victory, Northampton now had to play a second playoff match for the league title.

At a league meeting on March 22nd, controversy erupted at a meeting to determine the site of this playoff game. George Bellis and F.C. Scheckler represented Catasauqua at a league meeting at the Allentown YMCA. The league was represented by A.C. Lewis, Allentown, Clyde S. Frankenfield, Northampton, and J.W. Galley, Easton. After a number of heated arguments, Allentown High's gym was selected as a neutral site. The next night in front 500 fans, Northampton outlasted Catasauqua 19-16 to finally take the league title and end the inaugural league season. The Lehigh Valley League continued to exist through 1975.[2]

Northampton entered the Penn State Interscholastic basketball playoffs against Wilkes-Barre in Wilkes-Barre. They were defeated 37-17 to be eliminated from further championship play.[3]

On April 3, 1921, league representatives met at the Hotel Allen. Two new members, Palmerton and Slatington, were added to the league. At the same meeting, A.C Lewis was re-elected as league president. Other elected officers included F.C. Scheckler, Catasauqua, vice president; Clyde S. Frankenfield, Northampton, treasurer; and J. W. Galley, Easton, secretary.[4]

The season records were as follows: Northampton, Catasauqua, and Easton all 7-3, Allentown 5-5, Tamaqua 4-6, and Bethlehem 0-10.***1922:*** The season began in December 1921 with several games played prior to the start of the new year. The school's coaches and captains included:

Allentown: John W. Weimer, coach, and captain Helfrich.

Bethlehem: William H. Emrey, coach, and Donald Dietrich, captain.

Catasauqua: George E. Bellis and Hugh Spang, coaches, and Ray Costenbader, captain.

Easton: W. Etters, coach, and J. Gooves, captain.

Northampton: Austin L. Taggart, coach, and Paul Reiter, captain.

Palmerton: T.C. Cockill, coach, and John Krex, captain.

Slatington: N.E. Smith, coach, and Dale Smith, captain.

Tamaqua: Harold Tracy, coach, and Howard Walker, captain.

In January of 1922, Allentown reacted to the appearance of some overzealous fans who would support the visiting teams to the Allentown gym. A.C. Lewis circulated a letter to the other league members indicating that large groups of fans from the other schools would not be let into the Allentown gym. Because of the letter, Bethlehem threatened to call off their game with Allentown.[5]

Later in the month, Allentown moved its home games to the Allentown YMCA to accommodate more fans at the games. This may also have been a reaction to Catasauqua's use of the YMCA gym to practice. Allentown considered Catasauqua's use of the gym as being poor sportsmanship.

On February 3rd, Catasauqua played Allentown at the YMCA gym in a very eventful match. A thousand people crowded into the gym to see the game while another thousand people congregated outside. This was the largest crowd ever at an Allentown game. Because of the large crowd, the Catasauqua players had a difficult time getting into the gym for the game. The game was almost called off because of Catty's supposed tardiness. During their attempts to get into the gym, they were not initially recognized. Six Allentown policemen were dispatched to the gym to keep the large crowd in order.

Although the game started late at 8:20 pm, the Catasauqua team got off to a quick start. They led the game at one point 14-6. However, they could only muster one more point in the game and lost to Allentown 16-15. At the end of the game, referee Ben Emery from Philadelphia fainted and was actually out for about 8 minutes.[6]

Allentown's one-point victory was due to a technical foul called by the referee when a player scaled the wall of the gym to catch a ball. A player had gotten hurt because of this action. Later in the week, Easton and Palmerton protested the 1-point Allentown win.

On February 10, Allentown defeated Slatington 22–12 at Slatington. Boisterous Slatington fans charged the referee for calling fouls on the Slatington players for scaling the wall.[7]

The next night the league held a meeting to specifically address the wall scaling issue. Due to the calling of technical fouls for scaling the wall, both Palmerton and Easton were expected to protest Allentown's victories since their players had been called for the technical which greatly assisted Allentown in its two victories over the teams. At the meeting, it was decided to charge a personal foul on any player who scaled the wall instead of a technical foul. Palmerton then decided to drop its protest and Easton did the same. At the same time, Referee D'Eliscu was dropped from the roster because of a perceived too strict an interpretation of the rule. He also gained disfavor amongst the league teams by showing up late for games and not allowing time outs in the game because he wanted to leave early.[8]

On March 10th, Coach George Bellis' Catasauqua team avenged its defeat earlier in the season by taking a hard-fought match 22-17. Catasauqua had the advantage since the game was played on their floor, which was much smaller than a regulation floor. Three hundred fans witnessed the game with another 300 gathered outside the building. Allentown led at the half 12-9. However, Catasauqua came on strong and outscored the Canary and Blue 13-5 in the 2nd half. Allentown's Paul Clymer was held to 2 points while Ray Costenbader scored 14 points for Catasauqua. Allentown's loss created a tie for the league lead with both teams having eleven wins and two losses.[9]

Each team had one more game (Allentown with Palmerton and Catasauqua with Tamaqua) and victories by both would mean a tie for the league title and require a rematch for the championship.

In an upset, Tamaqua outscored Catasauqua 24-12 on March 16th in Tamaqua as Ray Costenbader was only able to score 6 points, all on free throws.[10] Astoundingly, the following night, Palmerton also pulled off an upset of Allentown 16-13 at Palmerton. With the game being played on the stage of the school's auditorium, every out of bounds ball would head into the crowd and have to be retrieved. This led to the low scoring game and the ultimate defeat of the Allentown team. The expected victories for both teams became losses requiring a third match between Allentown and Catasauqua for the league title.[11]

On March 31st, Allentown and Catasauqua squared off at the YMCA to determine the league champion. Catasauqua held the advantage after the end of the first half by a score of 9-6. Two players had scored all the points with Ray Costenbader from Catasauqua scoring 9 and Paul Clymer from Allentown scoring 6. Late in the first half, Catasauqua fans began to boo loudly when Clymer tried to shoot a foul shot. Referee Cortwright requested the crowd to stop booing. When they refused, he announced that he would allow Clymer to continue shooting until he made the free throw.

The second half saw Allentown clearly take the game in hand as they outscored Catasauqua 18-8 to win the game 24-17 and take the league championship. Both Clymer and Costenbader ended with 13 points each.[12]

The season records were as follows: Allentown and Catasauqua 11-3, Bethlehem 9-5, Easton 7-7, Palmerton, Tamaqua and Slatington all 5-9, and Northampton 3-11.[11]

The top five scorers in the league for the season were: Kern, Slatington, 156 points; Ray Costenbader, Catasauqua, 146 points; Wolensky, Palmerton, 140 points; Helfrich, Allentown, 138 points; and Shirer, Easton 131 points.

Allentown's coach John Weimer resigned at the end of the season to accept the position of athletic director at York High School.

1922 Allentown High School Basketball Team[12]

John Weimer *coached football, baseball, and basketball at Allentown High School from 1919 through 1921. Weimer starred in football and baseball at Gettysburg College. After college, Weimer played professional baseball, as an outfielder, in the Chicago Cubs minor league organization. Prior to coming to Allentown, he coached football at Bloomsburg University from 1911-1917 finishing with a record of 32-22-6.*

In 1919, he took the position of coach of athletics at Allentown High School. Weimer, along with faculty manager of athletics, A. C. Lewis, conceived the Thanksgiving Day football game between rivals Allentown and Bethlehem High Schools with the first game played in 1921. Weimer, a strict disciplinarian, cancelled the 1919 season after the first two games because the players would not come to practice regularly. He came back with great teams in 1920 and 1921. The 1921 team was hailed as one of the greatest football machines prior to 1945. Following the big gate for the Turkey Day game in 1921 at Taylor Stadium, Weimer requested an increase in salary. When it was not granted, he resigned and left to become coach at York High School and supervisor of recreation at York. He also served as secretary of the Big 15 Conference.

Weimer passed away at the age of 62 on December 1, 1944, of a heart ailment while still serving director of physical education and health in the York schools and as secretary of the Big 15 Conference.[13]

George Bellis *moved to Allentown at an early age. After serving with the National Guard during World War I, Bellis was named Catasauqua playground director. After resigning his coaching position at Catasauqua, he took recreation supervisor positions in Phoenixville and Philadelphia. After coming to Philadelphia in the 1930s, he worked in 52 parochial schools conducting gym classes, coaching football and baseball, and directing activities at several boys' clubs. From 1942 to 1954, he coached football, baseball, and basketball at Norwood Academy while also serving as athletic director. In 1954, he left for Germantown Academy to coach the same three sports.*

In 1930, he was named athletic director for the Pennsylvania American Legion. He was credited with founding the Connie Mack youth program which organized baseball and basketball for teenagers. Nearly 100 ex-Legion players reached the major leagues under his directorship including such players as Stan Musial, Curt Simmons, Roy Campanella, Mickey Vernon, Carl Furillo, Elmer Valo, Vic Wertz, Del Ennis, and Billy Cox. He received the prestigious John B. Kelly Award for promoting athletics among youth and curbing juvenile delinquency.

Bellis passed away at the age of 70 on January 20, 1969, at his home in Wyndmor.[17]

John Weimer[13]

George Bellis[14]

1923: For the third consecutive year, Catasauqua challenged for the league championship. After losing out to Northampton in 1921 and Allentown in 1922 (both in playoff games), Catasauqua prevailed to win the title in convincing fashion. Catasauqua finished the season with a 13-1 league record. Their only loss in the league was to Palmerton 25-21 in its second matchup of the season with them. Overall, the team finished 17-3 with its other two losses to Perkasie and Camden, NJ. After losing to Perkasie 30-24 in the 6th game of the season, they played their last game against them and avenged the defeat 53-26. They outscored their opponents 808 to 371. In their first game against Tamaqua, they did not allow a field goal and only 7 points, all on free throws.

Final league standings were as follows: Catasauqua 13-1, Bethlehem and Palmerton 11-3, Allentown 8-6, Easton 5-9, Slatington and Northampton 4-10, and Tamaqua 0-14.[15]

At the end of the season, Catasauqua's coach George Bellis announced his resignation to accept the position of Recreation Supervisor in Phoenixville. Bellis' three-year record overall was 44-13 and 34-8 with one league championship and two second place finishes. Of the eight losses, three were to Northampton and two to Allentown. Unfortunately, one of the losses to each of those teams was a playoff game loss for the league title.

LEFT TO RIGHT: WILLIAMS, FORWARD; KEAN, CAPTAIN AND GUARD; HORNBECK, FORWARD; GRIM, GUARD; BENNER, GUARD; RICKER, CENTRE; HULICK, CENTER; DAVIS, GUARD; PREBULA, FORWARD; WENNER, FORWARD; F. H. SCHECKLER, FACULTY MANAGER; KOCH, GUARD; GEORGE EARL BELLIS, COACH;

1923 Catasauqua High Basketball Team[16]

1924: The loss of head coach George Bellis had no impact on Catasauqua's basketball fortunes in 1924. Led by new coach Roland Macomber, director of physical education of the Catasauqua schools, Catasauqua easily won its second consecutive title. Catasauqua lost two league games during the season while second place Bethlehem lost five.[18]

Final league records were as follows: Catasauqua 12-2, Bethlehem 9-5, Easton 7-6, Northampton, Allentown, and Slatington all at 7-7, Tamaqua 6-8, and Palmerton 0-13. Apparently, the second Easton-Palmerton game was not played.

Led by team captain James Hornbeck, Catasauqua played Norristown with the winner advancing in the state playoffs. Norristown proved much too strong defeating Catasauqua 25 to 15 at the Bethlehem High School gym. Hornbeck led the team scoring with 6 points.[19]

1925: The eight team Lehigh Valley Interscholastic Basketball League included Allentown, Bethlehem, Catasauqua, Easton, Northampton, Palmerton, Slatington, and Tamaqua.

Bethlehem won the league title and was preparing to move on to the state playoffs. The team had one game remaining at Tamaqua. Bethlehem decided to send its second team to Tamaqua to finish its league schedule. This game was on a Wednesday night, March 29, with the first playoff game scheduled for the following night. During the trip to Tamaqua, the two cars carrying the team took a wrong turn beyond Schnecksville and one of the cars got mired in the road. By the time they got going again, it was too late and they returned to Bethlehem. Meanwhile, Tamaqua waited on court for Bethlehem who would never make it that night. Tamaqua was awarded the win by forfeit.[1]

Bethlehem won its first playoff game the next night against Doylestown 31-29 at Lafayette College's new gym. Wagner, Bethlehem's center, led the scoring with 10 points. Perkasie had won the Bux-Mont League, but since they were not PIAA members, Doylestown, the 2nd place team, played Bethlehem.[2] The Christmas City boys moved on to play Reading at Kutztown. On March 21, Bethlehem defeated Reading 30-29 to win the District I championship. This was the 3rd meeting of the two teams with each team having won on their home court.[2] Nanticoke, the District II champs, then beat Bethlehem 28-21 in Hazleton in front of a packed house of 1600 fans. This was Bethlehem's last game as a member of the Lehigh Valley League.[3]

With the forfeit to Tamaqua, Bethlehem ended its season at 11-3. Easton and Slatington finished second with 9-5 records. Allentown had a disastrous final season in the league and had a bleak outlook for the future. Beginning the year with Ben Ingalls as the head coach, Allentown was tremendously outclassed with little or no morale. One of the key players on the team, team captain Roland Dell, quit in midseason due to the pathetic situation. In desperation, Roy Geary was persuaded to assist coaching the team for the remainder of the season and actually finished as head coach.[4] Several days later, Roland Dell returned to the team.[5] Geary was a local semi-pro player of some renown. His coaching efforts proved beneficial as the team won four games by season's end.

Roy Geary *coached basketball at Muhlenberg for 2 years. Allentown High School for 2 years, and Lehigh University for 13 seasons. Considered as one of the leading professional basketball players in the area, he played for the Hazleton Professionals, Allentown Professionals, Phillipsburg A.C., and Allentown Temperance Society Teams, which won 39 straight games from 1916-1919. He was also a recognized basketball official. He owned Geary Sporting Goods located at W. Fourth Street, Bethlehem. He served as Bethlehem's city inspector of weights and measures from 1940 until his passing on February 15, 1952.*[7]

Despite its success in the Lehigh Valley League, Bethlehem was busy pursuing support for a new broader-ranging, more competitive league. William Emery, Bethlehem coach, had sent invitations to prospective members to attend an exploratory meeting to establish a new league. Representatives from Allentown, Easton, Coatesville, Reading, Pottsville, and Norristown joined Bethlehem on April 3 to discuss the possibility of forming a new league. Lancaster, deciding instead to maintain its independent schedule, declined the invitation to attend.[6]

The new league was born! Bill Emery was elected president with Alfred C. Lewis, Allentown High School's faculty manager of basketball, as league treasurer. The Eastern Pennsylvania Interscholastic Basketball League was now in existence. With seven members, each league member would play a home and away schedule with each fellow league member. The twelve-game schedule would begin in December 1925.

Before the season began, Pottstown replaced Norristown and Reading decided to remain in the Central Pennsylvania Interscholastic Basketball League.

On September 25, 1925, the newly formed Eastern Pennsylvania Interscholastic Basketball League held its first fall meeting to complete the planning for its first season of operation. William Emery, Bethlehem, presided over the meeting at the Reading YMCA. Lansford High School applied for membership at the meeting, but its request was tabled since the league decided to remain at six members for its inaugural season. The season was slated to being on December 19 with Coatesville traveling to Allentown and Pottstown at Bethlehem. Delegates attending the meeting included: William Emrey, Bethlehem HS; Charles W. Richards, Easton HS; D. Edward Atwell, Coatesville HS; W.H. Bell, Pottstown HS; Joseph H. Forrest, Pottsville HS; and Alfred C. Lewis, Allentown HS.[6]

The League Founders from the Lehigh Valley

William H. (Pop) Emrey*, called the "Father of Athletics" in Bethlehem, taught for 41 years and coached for 38 years including 4 years at Mauch Chunk High School prior to coming to Bethlehem High School in 1916. Born in Honey Brook, Chester County, Emrey graduated from Central High School, Philadelphia, and West Chester State College. He coached football, basketball, and track at Bethlehem. He was a founder of the Eastern Pennsylvania Interscholastic Basketball League and served as its first president. He was primarily known for conceiving a triangular track meet between Allentown, Bethlehem, and Easton. He also was instrumental in establishing the "Turkey Day Classic", a football rivalry between Allentown and Bethlehem High Schools. As the head track coach for 38 years, he became known as the "Dean of the Track". Today the Emrey Relays in Bethlehem are named after him. He passed away August 3, 1960.*[8]

Charles W. Richards *served as the business manager for the Easton School District for 18 years beginning in 1947 until his passing on June 24, 1965. A 1922 graduate of Lafayette College, he joined the Easton High School faculty a year later as a math teacher. He served on the faculty for 25 years. Richards was an assistant football coach to head coach James B. (Pat) Reilly, head basketball and baseball coach, and faculty manager of athletics. He served in both World War I and II.*[9]

Alfred C. Lewis *was a teacher at Allentown High School and brought the commercial department at the high school to a high level. He was instrumental in the expansion of the athletic department. As faculty manager of athletics, he boosted both the basketball and football programs. Along with William Emrey, he helped start the annual "Turkey Day Classic" with Bethlehem. He was a very prominent member of the Masonic order and served as the secretary of the Lehigh Consistory for about 20 years. Born in Cardiff, Wales, Lewis came to the US as a child. He died on November 6, 1945.*[10]

Roy Geary[7]

W. H. "Pop" Emrey[8]

Alfred C. Lewis[10]

Eastern Pennsylvania Interscholastic Basketball League

1926

The Inaugural Season

At their April 14, 1925, meeting, the Allentown School Board elected J. Birney Crum, of Alton, IL, as physical director and coach of the boys' teams at a salary of $3000 effective September 1, 1925.[1] Other team coaches included William Emery, Bethlehem, Ed Atwell, Coatesville, Frank Duffy, Easton, Carroll Bechtel, Pottstown, and Randolph "Grubbs" Grimmett, a Muhlenberg graduate, Pottsville. Play in the new league began on December 18, 1925.

Week 1

Allentown 22 Coatesville 14: Allentown, on its home court in a slight upset, captured a win over the taller and supposedly more experienced Coatesville five.

Leading scorers: Allentown – John Koch 6, Bob Gehringer 6; Coatesville – Tim Toomey 5.

Pottsville 33 Easton 27: Game was played at Easton.

Leading scorers: Pottsville – George Dimmerling 13; Easton – Horace Grube 10.

Bethlehem 33 Pottstown 33: On its home court, Bethlehem outscored Pottstown.

Leading scorers: Bethlehem – Ken Kresge 16; Pottstown – Melrose Weidensaul 6, Walter Wentzel 6.[2]

Week 2

Pottstown 33 Coatesville 19: Playing on New Year's Day, Pottstown easily defeated Coatesville.

Leading scorers: Pottstown – Kenneth Leister 21; Coatesville – Tim Toomey 4, William Donnelly 4.[3]

Week 3

Pottsville 35 Bethlehem 33: After leading 18-2 after the first quarter at Pottsville, Bethlehem scored just two points in the second quarter but still held a 20-13 lead at the half. Bethlehem lost the game when Pottsville's forward Earl "Peaches" Greenhalgh sank a shot from half court in the final minutes of the game.

Leading scorers: Pottsville – George Dimmerling 16; Bethlehem - Ken Kresge 10.[4]

Pottstown 47 Allentown 31: According to the newspaper, Allentown missed 20 easy shots in the loss.

Leading scorers: Pottstown – Kenneth Leith 15; Allentown – John Koch 11.

Coatesville 23 Easton 20: Coatesville narrowly defeated Easton on two late field goals by Pottstown's substitute forward Remaley.

Leading scorers: Coatesville – "Lefty" Helmig 7; Easton – Roy Good 7.[5]

Week 4

Bethlehem 40 Coatesville 18: Bethlehem made 16 field goals to Coatesville's 4.

Leading scorers: Bethlehem – Ed Wagner 10; Coatesville – "Doc" Shaneman 7.[6]

Pottsville 34 Allentown 24: Pottsville led 10-3 after a quarter and 21-11 at the half.

Leading scorers: Pottsville – George Dimmerling 18; Allentown – John Koch 10.[7]

Pottstown 26 Easton 24: No box score

Week 5

Allentown 22 Easton 21: Easton's Roy Good missed two foul shots after the game ended to miss the chance for the win for the Red Rovers.

Leading scorers: Allentown – Marlin Shover 8; Easton – Horace Grube 8.[8]

Pottstown 30 Bethlehem 20: With its win over Bethlehem, Pottstown moved past Allentown into sole possession of second place.

Leading scorers: Pottstown – Walter Wentzel 15; Bethlehem – Charles Geyer 5.

Pottsville 44 Pottstown 33: In an early season matchup for the league lead, one-loss Pottstown traveled to meet undefeated Pottsville on January 28. With 4 minutes to play and the score tied at 33, Pottsville scored the last 11 points to solidify its hold on first place.

Leading scorers: Pottsville – George Dimmerling 12, Hugh Cantwell 12, Earl Greenhalgh 12; Pottstown – Walter Wentzel 14.[9]

Allentown 23 Bethlehem 18: The first league game between Allentown and Bethlehem on January 29th resulted in fisticuffs between several players on the two teams. A Bethlehem player, John Hudak, punched Allentown's Marlin "Mibs" Shover in the face slamming his head against the brick wall and opening a bloody gash requiring several stitches to close. Dr. Thomas Weaber, a school board member attending the game, advised that Shover should be taken to Allentown Hospital to close the wound. Bob Gehringer, Allentown's captain, stepped between the two players and ended up flat on his back from a punch by a Bethlehem player. After finally clearing the floor, the first half of the game resumed and no further incidents occurred during the rest of the match.

Leading scorers: Allentown – Walter Moser 4, Charlie O'Brien 4, Marlin Shover 4; Bethlehem – Ed Wagner 4.[10]

Week 6

Allentown 34 Pottstown 32 OT: On February 5, Allentown handed Pottstown its second consecutive loss with an overtime victory to take over second place.

Leading scorers: Allentown – Edwin Lenker 12; Pottstown – Walter Wentzel 20.

Bethlehem 29 Pottsville 14: The Allentown win took on more significance when Pottsville suffered its first loss to Bethlehem in a resounding defeat of the visitors.

Leading scorers: Bethlehem – Frank Bartos 11; Pottsville – Francis Campbell 6.

Easton 21 Coatesville 10: Easton surprised Coatesville for its first league victory.

Leading scorers: Easton - Roy Good 11; Coatesville – "Monk" Remaley 4.[11]

Week 7

Pottstown 42 Easton 22: Pottstown led from start to finish. No box score[12]

Pottsville 41 Allentown 19: Pottsville dashed Allentown's hopes of moving into a tie for first place in a pasting of the Canary and Blue. Allentown players attributed their loss to an unfamiliar slippery floor from a dance the previous night in the Pottsville gym. This solidified Pottsville's hold on the league lead.

Leading scorers: Pottsville – George Dimmerling 14, Earl Greenhalgh 14; Allentown – Edwin Lenker 10.[13]

Bethlehem 30 Coatesville 26: Bethlehem, meanwhile, moved into a tie for third place with Allentown when they defeated Coatesville.

Leading scorers: Bethlehem - Frank Bartos 17; Coatesville – "Doc" Shaneman 8.[14]

Week 8

Pottstown 56 Coatesville 49: The highest scoring game of the season took place on February 19th at Pottstown in a game with Coatesville. Pottstown's home court, considered a band box, contributed to the high scoring. Pottstown scored 56 points to Coatesville 49 for a total of 105 points.

Leading scorers: Pottstown - Walter Wentzel 25; Coatesville - Tim Toomey 21.[15]

Bethlehem 28 Allentown 21: On the same night, Bethlehem avenged its earlier defeat by Allentown and took sole possession of third place behind Pottsville and Pottstown.

Leading scorers: Bethlehem – Austin McCarthy 13; Allentown – Edwin Lenker 9.[16]

Week 9

Pottsville 34 Coatesville 23: Pottsville trailed by a point at halftime before taking charge in the second half.

Leading scorers: Pottsville – Hugh Cantwell 12, George Dimmerling 11; Coatesville – Tim Toomey 8.[17]

Allentown 28 Easton 19: The Canaries led throughout the entire game.

Leading scorers: Allentown – Walter Moser 7; Easton – Roy Good 6.[18]

Week 10

Pottstown 43 Pottsville 34: With 1500 fans crowded into the Armory, Pottstown used the home court advantage to pull out the victory and maintain its hopes of a league title. After holding a one-point lead at the end of the third quarter 31-30, Pottstown outscored the Pottsville 12-4 in the final quarter.

Leading scorers: Pottstown – Kenneth Leister 22, Walter Wentzel 15; Pottsville - George Dimmerling 16, Hugh Cantwell 10.[19]

Easton 40 Bethlehem 28: Easton, with only a single win on the season, surprised Bethlehem at Bethlehem to eliminate them from the championship race. In a hard-fought game, seven players fouled out in a game refereed by "Doggie" Julian. No box score[20]

Coatesville 31 Allentown 30 OT: Coatesville, another team with only a single win, produced the second upset of the night by defeating Allentown in overtime.

Leading scorers: Coatesville – Ed Glauner 10; Allentown – Walter Moser 8.[21]

Coatesville 27 Pottsville 20: On March 12th, Pottsville with a 7-2 record traveled to lowly Coatesville (2-7) needing only a victory to wrap up the league title. Their loss to Pottstown on the previous Friday created the opportunity for a tie between the two schools requiring a playoff to settle the league championship. Pottsville was expected to be able to secure the title with a win. Coatesville, however, had other ideas and tripped up Pottsville with Tim Toomey leading the way with 10 points. No Pottsville player could tally more than 6 points. Coatesville forced Pottsville into a playoff with Pottstown.

Leading scorers: Coatesville – Tim Toomey 10; Pottsville – George Dimmerling 6.

Week 11

Bethlehem 22 Easton 19: Bethlehem led at the half 6-5 with Easton taking the lead early in the third quarter. Bethlehem came back to win the contest.

Leading scorers: Bethlehem – Ed Wagner 8; Easton – William Trumbore 6.[22]

Season Summary

Both the individual and team high scoring totals occurred during the matchup of Pottstown and Coatesville on February 19th. The single game point total for both teams occurred in this game. Wentzel, Pottstown's high scoring forward netted 25 of his team's 56 points in the game. Coatesville scored 49 points to push the game total to 105 points. This was the only game where the combined total exceeded 100 points.

The Lehigh Valley entries had mixed results in the new league. Bethlehem finished with a 6-4 record and third place. Allentown finished with an even 5-5 record to place fourth. Easton placed last with a 2-8 season.

League Championship Playoff

Pottsville 35 Pottstown 22: The new league's first season featured an exciting finish to the thirty-game campaign which would foretell the future of the new league. The regular season ended with Pottsville and Pottstown tied with seven wins and three losses each. Pottsville entered its final regular season game needing a victory over lowly Coatesville to clinch the league's first title. Coatesville had only won two league games all season. Coatesville surprised the Schuylkill Countians and forced them into a playoff with Pottstown. On March 18th on a neutral court in Reading, Coach Grimmett's Pottsville squad prevailed in the playoff with an easy victory to become the inaugural champs of the new league. Pottstown led only once 5-4 during the game in front of 1500 fans at the Reading Armory.

Leading scorers: Pottsville - George Dimmerling 13; Pottstown – Walter Wentzel 15.[23]

Although recognized as a major force in eastern Pennsylvania high school basketball, the league received little respect during post season play for the state championship. Reading, courted as a charter member for the league, stayed in the Central Pennsylvania League. Despite finishing second in their league, Reading declared itself the league representative for post season play since the league champion was not a PIAA member. Reading proceeded to call Pottsville one afternoon to schedule a game for that evening in Norristown. Pottsville was unable to honor the request on such short notice and also protested the playoff site location and was forced to forfeit to Reading. The league protested this action to no avail.[24]

Postseason Play

Reading, the District 1 champions, lost to Nanticoke, the District 2 champs, at Bethlehem Liberty High School on March 23 in a lopsided battle 44-23.[25] Nanticoke moved on to the state playoffs at Penn State and defeated Harrisburg Tech and Erie East to win the state title. As state champs, Nanticoke was invited to participate in the national championship competition in Chicago. After defeating teams from Salt Lake City, NV, and Wheeler, MS, Nanticoke lost its bid to reach the semi-finals when it lost to Fitchburg, MA.[26]

All Star Selections

First team: Forwards – Hugh Cantwell, Pottsville, and Walter Wentzel, Pottstown; Center – George Dimmerling, Pottsville; Guards – Bob Gehringer, Allentown, and Leroy "Doc" Shaneman, Coatesville.

Second team: Forwards – Tim Toomey, Coatesville, and Earl Greenhalgh, Pottsville; Center – Kenneth Leister, Pottstown; Guards – Walter Moser, Allentown, and Frank Bartos, Bethlehem.[27]

Final Standings

Pottsville	7-3
Pottstown	7-3
Bethlehem	6-4
Allentown	5-5
Coatesville	3-7
Easton	2-8

Team Rosters

Allentown: Coach J. Birney Crum, Baer, Leon Cohen, Richard Diehl, Bob Gehringer, Horn, John Koch, Edwin Lenker, Walter "Jackie" Moser, Charles O'Brien, Elmer Roedel, Marlin "Mibs" Shover, William Wackernagle, Joseph Wolfel.

Bethlehem: Coach William Emrey, Frank Bartos, Jerome Beidelman, Lewis Bock, Stephen Borda, Thomas Bowe, Alexander Brougham, Brown, Ken Fluck, John Fuhr, Charles Geyer, Ted Heske, Johnny Howard, John Hudak, Ken Kresge, Robert Leh, Austin McCarty, Ed Wagner.

Coatesville: Coach Ed Atwell, Bob Alexander, William Donnelly, Donald Entrekin, Ed Glauner, Harold "Lefty" Helmig, Orville Holbrook, Harold McWilliams, Walter Miller, George "Monk" Remaley, Walter Russell, Leroy "Doc" Shaneman, Francis Soule, John Teti, Tim Toomey.

Easton: Coach Frank Duffy, Ray Arnold, Edward Epstein, Francis Fuehrer, Roy Good, Horace Grube, Walter Hixon, Harold Morrow, Russell Purdy, Ken Schlabach, Tilghman Schlough, Edgar Smith, Harold Transue, Bill Troxell, William Trumbore.

Pottstown: Coach Carroll "Mush" D. Bechtel, Allen "Bud" Davidheiser, Linwood Drumheller, Carson Elliot, Keiser, Kinser, Kenneth Leiser, Melrose Weidensaul, Walter Wentzel.

Pottsville: Coach Randolph "Grub" Grimmett, Francis Campbell, Hugh Cantwell, George Dimmerling, John Ferrebee, Charles Gould, Earl Greenhalgh, Hubbel, Harold Kinzey, Michael Kovich, Decatur Moore, Harry Reed, F. Reese, Herb Rummel.

Pottsville – 1926 League Champions[28]

Front – Francis Campbell, Hugh Cantwell
Back – Coach Grimmett, Herb Rummel,
George Dimmerling, Earl Greenhalgh

1927

Pottstown's Rebound

Pottsville entered the league's second season having lost most of the members of its championship team. They promptly fell to the bottom of the league's standings. Pottsville did not win its first game until its last game of the season against Easton.

Two new coaches made their debut in the league. Ed Atwell was promoted to the principal position at Coatesville High School. Clyde Mearkle assumed the role of head basketball coach with Atwell's promotion. Apparently, Atwell still prepared the game strategy, but Mearkle would carry out the game plan devised by Atwell. Mearkle had never coached previous to this assignment. His only experience was as a player at West Philadelphia High School and he played for three years on the junior varsity at Penn State College.[1]

With Randolph Grimmett's resignation to take a position at Conshohocken High School, William H. B. Stevens assumed the position of basketball coach, He held the athletic director position as well. He had been hired as a graduate of Gettysburg College where he had earned some recognition as an athlete.[2] Stevens starred for four years on both the football and baseball teams at the college. He also served as president of his senior class.[3]

Week 1

Coatesville 33 Pottsville 17: Coatesville overwhelmed the defending league champions.

Leading scorers: Coatesville - Tim Toomey 11; Pottsville – Thomas O'Reilly 7.[4]

Bethlehem 26 Pottstown 24: No box score

Allentown 39 Easton 22: Allentown led 20-6 at halftime. Easton rallied and only trailed 26-20 after three quarters.

Leading scorers: Allentown - Ed Lenker 20, Walter Moser 12; Easton – Lewis Goldstein 8.[5]

Week 2

Pottstown 48 Coatesville 28: Pottstown converted ten more foul shots (12-2) than Coatesville.

Leading scorers: Pottstown - Walter Wentzel 19, Carson Elliot 18; Coatesville – Leroy "Doc" Shaneman 9.[6]

Allentown 30 Pottsville 23: Allentown handed the defending champions their second straight loss.

Leading scorers: Allentown - Walter "Jackie" Moser 16, Ed Lenker 11; Pottsville – Thomas O'Reilly 11.

Bethlehem 28 Easton 27: With 30 seconds to play, Bethlehem's forward Richard Byington intercepted a bad Easton pass and took it in for the score in the final seconds for the one-point victory.

Leading scorers: Bethlehem – Austin McCarthy 9; Easton – Ray Arnold 8.[7]

Week 3

Pottstown 40 Allentown 30: With the score tied 14-14 in the first half, Allentown lost its flashy guard Richard Diehl to injury for the remainder of the game and Pottstown took advantage of his absence.

Leading scorers: Pottstown - Walter Wentzel 19, Linwood "Red" Drumheller 19; Allentown – Ed Lenker 14.

Bethlehem 46 Pottsville 18: Last year's champions lost their 3rd in a row to start the new season.

Leading scorers: Bethlehem – Richard Byington 12; Pottsville – Thomas O'Reilly 6.[8]

Coatesville 35 Easton 19: Easton lost its 3rd in a row with Coatesville with having six players scoring.

Leadings scorers: Coatesville – Tim Toomey 10: Easton – Ray Arnold 5, Lewis Goldstein 5.[9]

Week 4

Pottstown 24 Bethlehem 23: Pottstown moved into a tie for the league lead. After leading 10-7 after one quarter, Bethlehem lost the lead and Pottstown led the rest of the way to avenge its opening night loss to the Liberty boys.

Leading scorers: Pottstown – Carson Elliot 8; Bethlehem – Richard Byington 9.

Easton 14 Pottsville 11: In a low scoring affair in Pottsville, Easton pulled out the victory after having trailed for the whole game up until the last 20 seconds. Easton's Russell Purdy broke an 11 all tie with a field goal and foul shot in the last 20 seconds to hand Pottsville another loss.

Leading scorers: Easton – Russell Purdy 6; Pottsville – Thomas O'Reilly 8.[10]

Coatesville 38 Allentown 35: After trailing at the end of the third quarter 33-23 in Coatesville, Allentown put on a furious rally in the final period scoring the first 8 points to bring them within 2 points 33-32 only to come up short. Allentown lost its chance to be in a three-way tie for the league lead. With its win, Coatesville became the third team in the three-way tie for the league lead.

Leading scorers: Coatesville – John Teti 10; Allentown – Walter Moser 18.[11]

Week 5

Bethlehem 37 Coatesville 28: Bethlehem knocked Coatesville out of the three-way first place tie.

Leading scorers: Bethlehem - Richard Byington 16; Coatesville – Tim Toomey 12.

Pottstown 39 Easton 37: Pottstown barely averted Easton's upset bid to keep pace with Bethlehem. No box score.

Allentown 36 Pottsville 28: Allentown stayed a game behind the leaders by handing Pottsville its fifth straight loss.

Leading scorers: Allentown - Walter "Jackie" Moser 15, Lew Mantz 11; Pottsville - Thomas O'Reilly 11.[12]

Week 6

Pottstown 54 Pottsville 27: On February 4th, Pottstown easily rolled over the defending champions Pottsville in handing them their sixth consecutive league loss in Pottsville. No box score[13]

Allentown 41 Bethlehem 31: Meanwhile, in Bethlehem, the rivalry between Allentown and Bethlehem was of significant importance for Bethlehem in maintaining a share of the league lead. After leading 20-19 at halftime, Allentown came out on the floor for the second half with renewed intensity. After a very competitive first half, Allentown rolled over Bethlehem 22-11 in the second half to defeat their archrivals with six players contributing to the scoring. Both teams were now tied for second place behind Pottstown.

Leading scorers: Allentown – Lew Mantz 14; Bethlehem – Richard Byington 12.[14]

Easton 38 Coatesville 31: Easton surprised Coatesville to keep them from a three-way tie for second place. Leading scorers: Easton - Russell Purdy 18, Ray Arnold 13; Coatesville – Tim Toomey 15.[15]

Week 7

Pottstown 44 Allentown 27: The previous week's results set up a battle for the league lead between Pottstown and Allentown in Pottstown on February 11. A win by Allentown would pull them into a first-place tie with Pottstown. Pottstown was up to the task and then some as they handed Allentown its worst loss of the season. The loss dropped Allentown to third place behind Bethlehem.

Leading scorers: Pottstown – Walter Wentzel 22, Carson Eliot 17; Allentown – Richard Diehl 11.[16]

Bethlehem 34 Easton 21: Bethlehem and Easton were tied at the half 11-11. However, Bethlehem scored 16 points in the final quarter to win easily.

Leading scorers: Bethlehem – Thomas Bowe 10; Easton – Ray Arnold 7.[17]

Week 8

Bethlehem 43 Pottsville 41: Pottsville, at home, narrowly lost another game to remain winless.

Leading scorers: Bethlehem – Richard Byington 17; Pottsville - Harry "Dicker" Reed 20.

Allentown 32 Easton 24: Allentown stayed a game behind Bethlehem in third place with a victory over Easton with eight Canaries scoring in the game.

Leading scorers: Allentown – Walter Moser 8; Easton – John Smith 10.[18]

Pottstown 42 Coatesville 22: In Coatesville, Pottstown continued its march to the league title with a win over Coatesville. Coatesville lost its two biggest stars, Leroy Shaneman and "Bullet" Soule early due to personal fouls, and was unable to keep up with Pottstown.

Leading scorers: Pottstown – Carson Eliot 17, Walter Wentzel 12; Coatesville – Tim Toomey 9.[19]

Week 9

Allentown 67 Coatesville 34: Allentown set a league record for points in a game on February 26 with their win over Coatesville to avenge their early season loss to Coatesville.

Leading scorers: Allentown –Ed Lenker 29, Walter Moser 17, Joe Wolfel 11; Coatesville –"Bullet" Soule 9.[20]

Pottstown 38 Pottsville 26: In the only other game of the night, Pottstown essentially clinched the league title over the reigning league champs Pottsville 38-26. The loss dropped Pottsville to 0-8 in the league. No box score[21]

Week 10

Pottstown 43 Easton 17: In its final league game of the season, Pottstown easily won its 9th game in a row, clinching the title, after the opening loss to Bethlehem.

Leading scorers: Pottstown - Carson Elliot 16, Walter Wentzel 13; Easton – John Smith 8.[22]

Bethlehem 37 Allentown 29: At the Liberty High School gym, Bethlehem evened the season series with Allentown with a win over the Canaries. Eight players joined the scoring column for the Hurricanes in a well-rounded victory.

Leading scorers: Bethlehem – Frank Bartos 9; Allentown – Edwin Lenker 10, Joe Wolfel 10.[23]

Coatesville 30 Pottsville 25: Pottsville continued its losing ways in a loss to Coatesville.

Leading scorers: Coatesville – John Teti 9; Pottsville – Harry Reed 13.[24]

Week 11

Pottsville 33 Easton 30: The final week of the season finally saw the defending champs win their first league game over Easton. With three minutes to play, Easton led 30-26 only to see Pottsville score the final seven points and secure their first victory.

Leading scorers: Pottsville – Harry Reed 12; Easton – Russell Purdy 15.[25]

Bethlehem 29 Coatesville 26: Bethlehem finished a strong second with its victory over Coatesville.

Leading scorers: Bethlehem – Austin McCarthy 11; Coatesville – Tim Toomey 10.[26]

Season Summary and Highlights

Allentown finished third at 6-4. Allentown accomplished this despite distractions as Shurtleff College attempted to lure Birney Crum, during mid-season, to become an assistant coach in its sports program. Shurtleff was located in Crum's hometown of Alton, Illinois. During his return to his hometown, Crum was rumored as seriously considering a coaching position at Shurtleff. After graduation from high school, Crum had played two years of football under Walter "Punk" Wood at Shurtleff before enrolling at Muhlenberg. When Muhlenberg's Coach Johnny Spiegel tendered his resignation after the 1922 season, Crum strongly recommended Coach Wood as a successor to Spiegel. Wood was hired and coached Crum at Muhlenberg. He later resigned and returned to Shurtleff. When Wood considered leaving Shurtleff for another position in the state of Kansas, Shurtleff contacted Crum about serving as an assistant coach to Wood with the intent to have him take over at Shurtleff when Wood moved on.[27] Crum turned down the offer and lead the team to a 17-5 overall record. The only other loss came at the hands of the Lehigh Valley League champions Slatington by a resounding 43 -25 score at Slatington's gym. Bob Edwards and Bob Davies with 19 and 16 points respectively.[28]

On February 25, Allentown established a league single game scoring record with 67 points in a win over Coatesville in a February contest in the Raub Gym. The Canary and Blue were led by Eddie Lenker's 29 points and Jack Moser's 17 points. Lenker's 29 points set the individual scoring record for the league. Their combined scores did not break the league record of 105 since Coatesville could only tally 34 points against Allentown's defense. Conversely, on January 21 at Pottsville, Easton and Pottsville combined to set the league futility record by only scoring a combined total of 25 points with Easton winning 14-11.

Postseason Play

Postseason competition was short-lived as Pottstown lost its initial playoff game 36-35 to Doylestown, Bux-Mont League champions, at Norristown.[29]

All-Star Selections

First Team: Forwards – Walter "Jackie" Moser, Allentown, and Walter Wentzel, Pottstown; Center – Carson Elliot, Pottstown: Guards – Leroy Shaneman, Coatesville, and Frank Bartos, Bethlehem.

Second Team: Forwards –Ed Lenker, Allentown, and Richard Byington, Bethlehem; Center – Harry Reed, Pottsville; Guards – Ray Arnold, Easton, and Richard Diehl, Allentown.[30]

Team Rosters

Allentown: Coach J. Birney Crum, Joe Blankovitch, Richard Diehl, Dick Duggan, Ambrose Kunkel, Ed Lenker, Lewis Mantz, Bob McDermott (mgr), Walter "Jackie" Moser, Roger Reno, Claude Shell, Lloyd Sterner, Elmer Roedel, Joseph Wolfel.

Bethlehem: Coach Bill Emrey, Frank Bartos, Jerome Beidelman, John Bessemer, Thomas Bowe, Richard Byington, Orel Coursen, Frank Everett, Charles Geyer, John Howard, Austin "Bates" McCarthy, Nobel Siegfried, Joseph Thomas.

Coatesville: Coach Clyde Mearkle, Robert Alexander, "Dump" Entroken, Paul Harey, Charley Herley, Orville Holbrook, Donald Lindsay, Walt Miller, Fullor Patton, Walt Russell, Leroy Shaneman, "Bullet" Soule, Johnny Teti, Tim Toomey, Morris Watson, Warren Yost.

Easton: Coach Frank Duffy, Ray Arnold, Richard Bishop, Jack Burroughs, Oscar Fischer, Charles Glenar, Lewis Goldstein, Ken Hagerman, Alton Marks, Joe Mayrosh, Patsy Mazza, William Ostroff, Russell Purdy, John Smith, Bill Troxell, Ken Worman.

Pottstown: Coach Carroll "Mush" D. Bechtel, Allen "Bud" Davidheiser, Bob Diener, Linwood Drumheller, Carson Elliot, "Herk" Hartman, Joe Horvat, "Lehigh" Kline, Woody Ludwig, Joe Powell, Melrose Weidensaul, Walter Wentzel, Spence Yergey, John "Brownie" Zawaski.

Pottsville: Coach William Stevens, Robert "Ironman" Bell, Dan Brennan, Frank "Joe" Fisher, Joseph Fitzpatrick, Charles "Chuck" Gould, Walter Jones, Decatur "Dick" Moore, Johnny Niece, Arthur Nuss, Thomas "Buck" O'Reilly, Harry "Dicker" Reed, Francis Smedley.

Final Standings

Pottstown	9-1
Bethlehem	8-2
Allentown	6-4
Coatesville	4-6
Easton	2-8
Pottsville	1-9

1927 Pottstown League Championship Basketball Team[31]

1928

League Expansion

At an April 1, 1927, meeting at the Reading YMCA, the league announced its intention to expand the league to eight teams. Three teams were being considered for entry into the league including Doylestown, Norristown, and Hazleton. Each team had won their respective league championships.[1] At the league meeting on May 6m 1927, the league announced its expansion at the Allentown YMCA. Hazleton, the 1927 Anthracite League champions, and Doylestown, the 1927 Bux-Mont League champions, were accepted into the league. Norristown, Philadelphia Suburban League champions, did not join the league. William Emery, the league's president for the first two years, submitted his resignation at the meeting. Bethlehem had recently announced the hiring of Leo Prendergast as its new football coach and Emery indicated that Prendergast may also take over as head basketball coach. A. D. Atwell, Coatesville, took over as president with Frank Duffy, Easton, serving as vice-president. E.A. Rabenold, Allentown's faculty manager of basketball, assumed the secretary-treasurer duties.[2]

Week 1

Allentown 35 Pottstown 24: The opening week, Allentown defeated the defending league champions Pottstown.

Leading scorers: Allentown – Walter "Jackie" Moser 15; Pottstown – Wood Ludwig 9.

Pottsville 19 Bethlehem 12: Pottsville came to Bethlehem to begin the campaign to avenge their disastrous previous season. Coach Leo Prendergast, taking over for Coach Emery, saw his squad lose a low scoring affair.

Leading scorers: Pottsville – Harry Reed 8; Bethlehem – William Reese 4.[3]

Hazleton 52 Coatesville 27: Meanwhile, Hazleton opened its initial league play with a win over Coatesville in front of 800 fans. Another 500 fans had to be turned away.

Leading scorers: Hazleton – Ray Stecker 20, Metro Watson 13; Coatesville – Tim Toomey 16.

Doylestown 39 Easton 15: In the other game, Doylestown opened with a win over Easton in their first game in the league. No box score[4]

Week 2

Allentown 38 Easton 19: Allentown coach J, Birney Crum played his substitutes in the second half of the game.

Leading scorers: Allentown – Walter Moser 16; Easton – unknown.

Pottstown 29 Bethlehem 20: Leo Prendergast's Bethlehem squad lost its second consecutive game.

Leading scorers: Pottstown – Van Jesak 11; Bethlehem - Dudley Wright 15.[5]

Hazleton 44 Doylestown 29: In an early season battle between the two new entries into the league, Hazleton easily bested Doylestown in front of a sold-out home crowd in Hazleton.

Leading scorers: Hazleton – Joe Watkins 14, Ray Stecker 10, Frank Serany 10; Doylestown – Gerald Hennessey 10.[6]

Coatesville 36 Pottsville 22: Coach Lerda's Coatesville team evened its record with a win over Pottsville.

Leading scorers: Coatesville – John Teti 12, Tim Toomey 12; Pottsville – Harry Reed 14.[7]

Week 3

Allentown 33 Coatesville 19: Allentown easily won its third straight over Coatesville after holding a 29-5 lead at the half. Allentown took over possession of first place after Hazleton lost to Bethlehem.

Leading scorers: Allentown – Walter Moser 13, Lloyd Sterner 12; Coatesville – Charlie Forbes 10.

Bethlehem 36 Hazleton 34 3OT: In Bethlehem, the contest required three additional five-minute periods to settle. Bethlehem's Llewellyn "Melon" Musser finally won it with the only score in the 3rd overtime.

Leading scorers: Bethlehem – Van Billiard 8; Hazleton – Joe Watkins 12.

Doylestown 46 Pottstown 34: Doylestown, on its home court, continued their winning streak over Pottstown. No box score[8]

Easton 40 Pottsville 39: With 8 of their 9 players scoring in the game, visiting Easton scored a mild upset of Pottsville on the recently renovated Moose Hall floor.

Leading scorers: Easton – Wren 12; Pottsville – Harry Reed 20, Charles Rummel 11.[9]

Week 4

Hazleton 48 Allentown 24: In a showdown at Hazleton with first place on the line, Hazleton cruised to the victory to pull into a first-place tie with Allentown and Doylestown.

Leading scorers: Hazleton - Ray Stecker 18, Joe Watkins 14; Allentown - Walter Moser 11.[10]

Doylestown 42 Coatesville 20: Doylestown joined Allentown and Hazleton in a three-way tie for the league lead.

Leading scorers: Doylestown – Gerald Hennessey 13; Coatesville – John Teti 9.[11]

Pottsville 39 Pottstown 30: Pottsville rebounded to even its record at 3-3 as Pottstown dropped to 1-3.

Leading scorers: Pottsville – Harry Reed 12, Charles Rummel 11, Decatur Moore 11; Pottstown – Woody Ludwig 11.[12]

Bethlehem 21 Easton 19 OT: Extended to overtime for the second straight game, Bethlehem outlasted Easton.

Leading scorers: Bethlehem – Van Billiard 5, Jim Reynolds 5; Easton – Karl Meixell 7.[13]

Week 5

Allentown 35 Bethlehem 16: Leading the entire game, Allentown crushed archrival Bethlehem in the Steel City.

Leading scorers: Allentown – Walter Moser 13; Bethlehem – Jimmy Quigg 5.[14]

Doylestown 35 Pottsville 22: Doylestown, at home, overwhelmed Pottsville with a 16-4 first quarter lead.

Leading scorers: Doylestown – Jay Richards 14, Gerald Hennessey 11; Pottsville – Charles Rummel 12.[15]

Hazleton 39 Easton 20: In Easton, Hazleton had little trouble with Easton cruising to the win and dropped Easton to 1-4 and a last place tie with Coatesville.

Leading scorers: Hazleton – O'Donnell 12; Easton – Richard Bishop 8.[16]

Pottstown 34 Coatesville 31 2OT: Coatesville lost to Pottstown in two extra periods.

Leading scorers: Pottstown – Jimmie Lynch 14; Coatesville – John Teti 10, Walt Miller 10.[17]

Week 6

Doylestown 33 Allentown 23: During the last week in January, Doylestown defeated the Canaries on Tuesday to move into first place alone on the basis of having played one more game than Hazleton.

Leading scorers: Doylestown – Gerald Hennessey 13, Jay Richards 11; Allentown – Walter Moser 8.[18]

Doylestown 43 Bethlehem 21: Bethlehem led 20-19 early in the second half but were outscored 24-1 after that.

Leading scorers: Doylestown – Gerald Hennessey 13, Jay Richards 11; Bethlehem – Dudley Wright 7.

Allentown 39 Pottsville 31: Allentown rebounded with a win in the Raub Building gym.

Leading scorers: Allentown – Walter Moser 17, Lew Mantz 10; Pottsville – Harry Reed 12.[19]

Hazleton 74 Pottstown 22: In Hazleton, a large contingent of Pottstown fans accompanied their team to no avail when Hazleton broke the single game scoring record. Even with the second team on the floor for most of the second half, Hazleton still outscored Pottstown 34-12 in the half.

Leading scorers: Hazleton –Joe Watkins 27, Ray Stecker 20, Frank Serany 14; Pottstown –Jimmie Lynch 5.[20]

Coatesville 29 Easton 24: In a battle of last place teams, Coatesville beat Easton to escape the cellar.

Leading scorers: Coatesville – Walter Russell 9; Easton – Clair Churchman 8.[21]

Week 7

Allentown 47 Doylestown 25: Allentown turned the tables on Doylestown from their game ten days earlie and knocked Doylestown out of first place. The matchup resulted in a capacity crowd with nearly as many fans turned away. The doors were locked a half hour before the game and three policemen prevented others from entering the building. The game was close until the Canaries went on a 14-1 run in the 4th quarter.

Leading scorers: Allentown – Walter Moser 20, Claude Schell 13; Doylestown – Gerald Hennessey 11, Jay Richards 10.[22]

Hazleton 35 Pottsville 21: Six hundred fans, with 250 from Hazleton, saw Hazleton take over first place.

Leading scorers: Hazleton – Ray Stecker 13, Joe Watkins 10; Pottsville – Harry Reed 8, Charles Rummel 8.[23]

Coatesville 27 Bethlehem 25: Dick Denithorne made a difficult field goal under the basket and Tim Toomey sank three free throws in the final seconds to seal Coatesville's victory.

Leading scorers: Coatesville – Tim Toomey 12; Bethlehem – Louis Bock 7.[24]

Pottstown 44 Easton 26: No box score[25]

Week 8

Hazleton 38 Pottsville 22: In a rare Wednesday game, Hazleton swept the season series with Pottsville with forward Joe Watkins setting a league single game scoring record.

Leading scorers: Hazleton – Joe Watkins 25; Pottsville – Harry Reed 13.[26]

Hazleton 58 Pottstown 23: Two days later in Pottsville, Hazleton's Joe Watkins reset the league scoring record.

Leading scorers: Hazleton – Joe Watkins 31, Ray Stecker 21; Pottstown – Woody Ludwig 12.[27]

Allentown 38 Pottsville 28: In Pottsville, Allentown handed the home team their second loss in as many days.

Leading scorers: Allentown – Lloyd Sterner 15; Pottsville – Harry Reed 13.

Easton 36 Coatesville 28: At Easton, the Red Rovers bested Coatesville to move out of the cellar.

Leading scorers: Easton – Richard Bishop 11; Coatesville – Tim Toomey 15.[28]

Bethlehem 32 Coatesville 23: On Saturday night, Bethlehem handed Coatesville its second loss in two days.

Leading scorers: Bethlehem – Jim Reynolds 11; Coatesville – Dick Denithorne 8.[29]

Week 9

Allentown 38 Bethlehem 32: On Valentine's Day night, Allentown led throughout the whole game except briefly in the fourth quarter 32-31. Bethlehem would not score again.

Leading scorers: Allentown – Walter Moser 15, Lew Mantz 12; Bethlehem – Dudley Wright 10.[30]

Hazleton 72 Easton 23: With 12 players getting court time and nine of them scoring, Hazleton trounced Easton.

Leading scorers: Hazleton – Lloyd Sterner 20, Joe Watkins 20; Easton – Edward Johnson 10.[31]

Doylestown 36 Pottsville 19: Pottsville lost its eighth game out of ten despite the fact that 8 players scored in the game for Pottsville.

Leading scorers: Doylestown – Gerald Hennessey 19; Pottsville – Charles Rummel 5.[32]

Coatesville 42 Pottstown 30: Coatesville moved into fourth place with their win.

Leading scorers: Coatesville – Tim Toomey 21, John Teti 10; Pottstown – Woody Ludwig 16.[33]

Week 10

Hazleton 41 Allentown 30: In front of nearly 1500 fans in the Raub gym, Allentown took on Hazleton in an effort to gain a share of first place. Another 2000 to 2500 fans had to be turned away and twelve policemen were on hand to maintain order both inside and outside the building. Despite leading 8-4 after a quarter and 16-10 at the half, Allentown could not hold up against Hazleton's onslaught during the second half, Hazleton scored the first seven points of the half to take a 17-16 lead. After trading several baskets and the Mountaineers in the lead 23-21, Hazleton poured it on to take a two-game lead over Doylestown with three games to play.

Leading scorers: Hazleton – Joe Watkins 17, Ray Stecker 12; Allentown – Lew Mantz 13, Lloyd Sterner 10.[34]

Doylestown 37 Coatesville 36 OT: Doylestown need an extra period for the win over Coatesville.

Leading scorers: Doylestown – Gerald Hennessey 12; Coatesville – Tim Toomey 16, John Teti 11.[35]

Easton 36 Bethlehem 33: Easton pulled into a tie for 4th place with Coatesville and Pottstown, all with 4-7 records. Bethlehem slipped to 7th place ahead of only Pottsville.

Leading scorers: Easton – Richard Bishop 10; Bethlehem – Dudley Wright 13, Louis Bock 12.[36]

Pottstown 36 Pottsville 27: Pottstown se cured its tie for 4th place with the win.

Leading scorers: Pottstown – Johnny Banjo 11; Pottsville – Charles Rummel 11.[37]

Week 11

Allentown 44 Coatesville 17: Hazleton got a real boost from Allentown when the Canaries put a large dent in Coatesville's expectations of a possible league title. Allentown drubbed Coatesville on their home court.

Leading scorers: Allentown – Walter Moser 16, Lloyd Sterner 11; Coatesville – Tim Toomey 8.

Hazleton 60 Bethlehem 21: Hazleton, behind Ray Stecker, won easily over Bethlehem.

Leading scorers: Hazleton – Ray Stecker 26, Joe Watkins 10; Bethlehem – Dudley Wright 11.[38]

Pottsville 29 Easton 24: Pottsville won its third game of the season.

Leading scorers: Pottsville – Harry Reed 14; Easton – Richard Bishop 7.[39]

Pottstown 27 Doylestown 20: With Doylestown's star forward Gerald Hennessey out of the lineup with an infected foot, Coach Bechtel's Pottstown squad took advantage of his absence to pick up the win.

Leading scorers: Pottstown – Woody Ludwig 6; Doylestown – Phil Waddington 8.[40]

Doylestown 47 Bethlehem 24: The following night in Doylestown, Bethlehem captain Dudley Wright had to be carried off the floor due to injury. No box score[41]

Week 12

Hazleton 32 Doylestown 28: Hazleton wrapped up the title with its victory over Doylestown. Despite leading the entire first half and through the final seconds of the third quarter, Doylestown, on its home court, could not hold on for the victory. They last led 27-26 early in the fourth quarter, but could only score one more point in the loss.

Leading scorers: Hazleton – Ray Stecker 20; Doylestown – Gerald Hennessey 13, Phil Waddington 10.

Allentown 42 Easton 33: Allentown took over second place with its win over Easton.

Leading scorers: Allentown – Lloyd Sterner 13, Walter Moser 12; Easton – Richard Bishop 10.[42]

Pottsville 38 Coatesville 21: Pottsville prevailed over Coatesville to climb out of the league cellar.

Leading scorers: Pottsville – Harry Reed 13; Coatesville – Tim Toomey 12.[43]

Allentown 42 Pottstown 27: Allentown secured second place with its win over Pottstown.

Leading scorers: Allentown – Lew Mantz 14, Lloyd Sterner 14; Pottstown – Woody Ludwig 9.[44]

Doylestown 40 Easton 20: Doylestown finished its season with a victory.

Leading scorers: Doylestown – Jay Richards 11, Gerald Hennessey 10; Easton – Richard Bishop 7.[45]

Pottsville 37 Bethlehem 25: Bethlehem finished its season with five straight losses.

Leading scorers: Pottsville – Harry Reed 10; Bethlehem – Van Billiard 9.[46]

Hazleton 50 Coatesville 33: Led by Frank Serany and Ray Stecker, Hazleton finished with an easy victory.

Leading scorers: Hazleton – Frank Serany 18, Ray Stecker 15; Coatesville – Tim Toomey 14.[47]

Easton 2 Pottstown 0: Pottstown decided on a forfeit rather than play the game.

A game between Bethlehem and Pottstown, which had been postponed by a snowstorm, was not played.

Season Summary

After defeating Allentown in week 4, Hazleton did not relinquish the lead the rest of the season as Hughie McGeehan's Mountaineers breezed through the season with 13 wins in 14 contests. Bethlehem, expected to be among the league leaders, finished last at 3-10.

Postseason Play

Hazleton 48 Mahanoy City 25: With Hazleton as the league's representatives in the state playoffs, Coach McGeehan's wife was quite ill for several days prior to the game. The coaches and players, minus Coach McGeehan, left by train for Bethlehem for the initial playoff game with Mahanoy City. With his wife's condition improving, Coach McGeehan traveled by car to meet the train at the Taylor Gym in Bethlehem. After a close first half with the score tied at one point 14-14, Hazleton outclassed Mahanoy City the rest of the way.

Leading scores: Hazleton – Ray Stecker 20, Joe Watkins 15; Mahanoy City – Len Guaditis 9.[48]

Hazleton 33 Lansdowne 24: Hazleton won its semifinal District 1 contest over the Philadelphia Suburban League champions at Lafayette College.

Leading scorers: Hazleton – Ray Stecker 14; Lansdowne – Elliot Loughlin 13.[49]

Hazleton 50 Lansford 20: After Lansford took a 2-0 lead, Hazleton took the lead for good and won the District 1 title over the Carbon-Schuylkill League champions at Bethlehem in front of nearly 2000 fans.

Leading scorers: Hazleton - Ray Stecker 17, Joe Watkins 12; Lansford – Fuller 8.[50]

Hazleton 25 Scranton 21: The Mountaineers beat Scranton at the Plains gym to put them into the final four grouping in State College, despite an injury to star Joey Watkins, which proved not to be serious.

Leading scorers: Hazleton – Ray Stecker 10; Scranton – Julius Lenchinsky 6, Davis 6.[51]

Hazleton 22 Jersey Shore 19: At the Penn state Armory with 500 Hazleton fans in attendance, Hazleton won the first game with Jersey Shore in tight contest to put them into the state championship game. Trailing 15-14 entering the fourth quarter, Hazleton outscored Jersey Shore 8-4.

Leading scorers: Hazleton - Ray Stecker 8, Joe Watkins 8; Jersey Shore – Delaney 6.[52]

Hazleton 35 Lewistown 31: On March 24, Hazleton defeated Lewistown to capture the title. Forwards Stecker and Watkins led the team to the championship by scoring a combined 145 points our of Hazleton's 213 in six playoff games. In the inaugural season in the league, Hazleton won the Penn State Cup and brought statewide respectability to the league.

Leading scorers: Hazleton – Ray Stecker 13, Joe Watkins 13; Lewistown – Clair Rupp 12.[53]

Postseason Accolades

In a vote by league coaches, a first and second team all-star squad was selected as follow: First team – Ray Stecker and Joe Watkins, Hazleton; Phil Waddington, Doylestown; Walter "Jackie" Moser and Lloyd Sterner, Allentown. Second team – Tim Toomey, Coatesville; Gerald Hennessey, Doylestown; Harry Reed, Pottsville; Metro Watson, Hazleton; and Dick Duggan, Allentown.[54]

Final Standings

Hazleton	13-1
Allentown	11-3
Doylestown	10-4
Pottstown	6-7
Pottsville	5-9
Coatesville	4-10
Easton	4-10
Bethlehem	3-10

Team Rosters

Allentown: Coach J. Birney Crum, Joe Blankowitsch, Dick Duggan, Robert Greenawalt, Hinkle, Edward Judt, Lewis Mantz, William McClellan, Walter "Jackie" Moser, Joe Nagle, Claude "Peanuts" Schell, Francis Sheehan, Bob Schweyer, Lloyd Sterner

Bethlehem: Coach Leo Prendergast, George Baum, Louis Bock, Richard Clark, Gaffner, Michael "Mickey" Glagola, Nathaniel Glazier, Jacoby Koenig, Paul Korin, Austin McCarthy, Llewellyn Musser, Jimmy Quigg, William Reese, Jim Reynolds, Verne Smith, Edward Steers, Harry Van Billiard, Dudley Wright

Coatesville: Coach Louis Lerda, Dick Denithorne, Donald Entreken, Charlie Forbes, Charles Herley, Paul Herley, George Hershey, Donald Lindsay, George Long, Walt Miller, Whitey Pierce, Walter Russell, Johnny Teti, Tim Toomey, Phillip Tuccy, Morris Watson, John Wilson

Doylestown: Coach Bill Wolfe, Tom Bean, Edward Good, Gerald Hennessey, Russell Nash, Walter "Reds" Phillips, Jay Richards, Aloysius Rufe, Ed Slaughter, Arthur Stevens. Phil Waddington

Easton: Coach Frank Duffey, Donald Anderson, Richard Bishop, Clair Churchman, Kenneth Hagerman, Allan Johnson, Edward Johnson, Karl Meixell, James Morrison, Owen, Ronald Pierson, William Ruske

Hazleton: Coach Hugh McGeehan, Albert Audikemow, Angelo Christino, Rocco Christino, Vernard Fegley, John Hildebrand, MacCollum, Charles Murrin, O'Donnell, Andrew Pavlishin, Jack Rothacker, Vincent Santipoli, Frank Serany, Joseph Skurka, Ray Stecker, Ulrich, Joe Watkins, Metro Watson

Pottstown: Coach Carroll "Mush" Bechtel, Johnny Banjo, Harrigan "Joe" Horvat, Jones, Kemp, Woody Ludwig, Jimmie Lynch, Joseph Powell, Maurice Sassaman, Schoenley, Steiner, Van Jesak, Weiss, Harry Yohn

Pottsville: Coach Charles Williams, Robert Bell, Joseph Fitzpatrick, William Gressang, Joe Holt, Edward Kunkle, George Marsden, William Martz, Decatur Moore, John Niece, Harry Reed, Robert Reid, Charles Rummel, George Serfass, Joseph Wilchusky

Hazleton High School – 1928 League and State Champions[55]

Front row: Frank Serany, Vernard Fegley, Metro Watson

Middle row: John Hildebrand, Vincent Santipoli, Joe Watkins, William Ulrich, Joe Skurka

Back row: Faculty Mgr. J. G. McQuaid, Mgr. Jim Provert, Ray Stecker, Dan O'Donnell, Thomas MacCollum, Coach Hugh McGeehan

1929

Hazleton Defends State Title

The 1929 season opened on December 14, 1928. The league membership remained the same as during the 1928 season.

Week 1

Hazleton 40 Coatesville 8: Hazleton, defending state champions, opened their season at Coatesville with a resounding victory. Winning their 19th consecutive game, Hazleton led at halftime 17-7 and allowed only one point in the second half. Coatesville only scored one field goal with the other 6 points on free throws.

Leading scorers: Hazleton –Metro Weston 12, John Hildebrand 11, Frank Serany 10; Coatesville –Ray Pyle 5.[1]

Allentown 51 Pottsville 24: Allentown opened its season in Pottsville with an easy win. Center Lew Mantz outscored the Maroons.

Leading scorers: Allentown – Lew Mantz 30, Francis Sheehan 11; Pottsville – Decatur Moore 14.

Pottstown 34 Bethlehem 13: Coach Bill Emery's Bethlehem team got trounced on the road with the Hurricane being shutout in the final period.

Leading scorers: Pottstown – Woody Ludwig 12, John Banjo 10; Bethlehem – Dudley Wright 7.

Easton 27 Doylestown 10: Homestanding Easton began its season with a victory over Doylestown. The Red Rovers held Doylestown to two foul shots in the first half.

Leading scorers: Easton – Richard Bishop 10; Doylestown – Jay Richards 5.[2]

Week 2

Hazleton 53 Easton 17: With 1600 fans in attendance to open Hazleton's new gym, Coach Hugh McGeehan's team easily handled the visitors from Easton. For the second consecutive game, Hazleton held their opponents to a single field goal which occurred in the second half. Easton's other 15 points were on foul shots.

Leading scorers: Hazleton –Bernard Fegley 14, Frank Serany 13, Metro Weston 13; Easton –Don Anderson 6.[3]

Allentown 57 Coatesville 14: Allentown kept pace with Hazleton in its win over Coatesville. Leading 28-5 at halftime, Coach Crum was able to provide game action for each player on the squad.

Leading scorers: Allentown – Lew Mantz 21, Robert Schweyer 12; Coatesville – Watson 6.

Pottstown 31 Doylestown 29: Pottstown, meanwhile, eked out a 2-point win over Doylestown. Despite having been sick in bed for the past week, Captain Woody Ludwig led the scoring for Pottstown.

Leading scorers: Pottstown – Woody Ludwig 18. No other information available.[4]

Bethlehem 28 Pottsville 24: Bethlehem evened its record at 1-1 by winning over Pottsville. Pottsville was without their coach Charlie Williams who had taken ill after returning from the team's game with Reading.

Leading scorers: Bethlehem – Paul Clay 11; Pottsville – Johnny Niece 8.[5]

Week 3

Pottsville 37 Doylestown 30: After two weeks off for the holidays, Pottsville scored its first victory over winless Doylestown. No box score

Bethlehem 41 Coatesville 20: Playing at home, Bethlehem kept Coatesville winless with a victory in a game they led the whole way.

Leading scorers: Bethlehem – Paul Clay 18, Edward Rice 12; Coatesville – Bob McNelly 5.

Allentown 27 Easton 25: Allentown kept pace with Hazleton in a closely contested match with Easton. Allentown froze the ball over the last few minutes for the win.

Leading scorers: Allentown – Lew Mantz 14; Easton – Ben Gadwell 10.[6]

Hazleton 41 Pottstown 23: In a battle of unbeatens in Pottstown, Hazleton's forwards Vernard Fegley and Frank Serany led their team to a win over Pottsville to remain in the first-place tie with Allentown. Pottsville dropped into a tie for third with Bethlehem.

Leading scorers: Hazleton – Frank Serany 15, Vernard Fegley 14; Pottstown – Jimmie Lynch 7.[7]

Week 4

Bethlehem 29 Doylestown 15: The week began on Tuesday, January 8, as Bethlehem kept Doylestown winless and stayed right behind Allentown and Hazleton in the league race in the Liberty gym.

Leading scorers: Bethlehem – George Gaffney 8; Doylestown – Jay Richards 6, Ed Slaughter 6.[8]

Bethlehem 31 Easton 25: In their second game of the week, Bethlehem pulled away from Easton for the win.

Leading scorers: Bethlehem – George Gaffney 12; Easton – Donald Anderson 13.

Allentown 21 Pottstown 20 OT: Pottstown made a valiant effort to knock Allentown from first place and the ranks of the unbeaten, but lost in the overtime period in a low scoring affair in the Raub gym. After regulation, the score was tied 20-20. Allentown's leading scorer Lou Mantz did not score a single point in regulation, but scored the only point in overtime with a free throw to win the game.

Leading scorers: Allentown – Francis Sheehan 6; Pottstown – Jimmie Lynch 11.[9]

Hazleton 63 Pottsville 21: Led by forward Frank Serany's record-breaking point total, Hazleton pasted Pottsville to retain its first-place tie with Allentown.

Leading scorers: Hazleton – Frank Serany 34; Pottsville – Clifton Cockill.[10]

Doylestown 44 Coatesville 22: Doylestown, on its home court, defeated Coatesville to keep Coatesville winless at 0-4. No box score

Week 5

Allentown 47 Doylestown 36: Prior to the biggest matchup of the season with Hazleton, Allentown took on Doylestown and temporarily took hold of first place in the league with its victory on the Raub floor, With Lou Mantz regaining his scoring touch, the Canaries now assumed a half game lead over Hazleton.

Leading scorers: Allentown – Lew Mantz 18; Francis Sheehan 12, Ed Ohner 10; Doylestown – Jay Richards 11.[11]

Hazleton 52 Allentown 20: On a 23-game winning streak since their last loss in triple overtime to Bethlehem in the 1928 season, Hazleton's gym, which held 1500 fans, was sold out within two days when tickets went on sale three weeks earlier. Apparently, not a single ticket was sold to Allentown fans.[12] On game night, nearly 5000 fans attempted to enter the gymnasium and three hours before game time, any standing room was fully taken. Nearly three times as many counterfeit tickets were presented as were bona fide tickets. Eight people were arrested for using the fake tickets. Unfortunately for the Canaries, the game never met up to its billing as Hazleton raced out to 25-5 halftime lead. The final score showed the Canaries being crushed. Hazleton had 21 field goals to Allentown's six.[13] Allentown's first place hold had lasted less than 3 days.

Leading scorers: Hazleton – Frank Serany 22, Metro Weston 13; Allentown – Lew Mantz 9.

Pottsville 38 Bethlehem 37: Meanwhile, at Pottsville, Bethlehem was surprised with Pottsville taking the lead near the end of the game. Bethlehem had led after each of the first three periods.

Leading scorers: Pottsville – Edward Kunkel 10; Bethlehem – George Gaffney 15, Paul Clay 11[15]

Coatesville 26 Easton 23: No box score.

Pottstown 46 Doylestown 31: No box score[16]

In the case of the fake tickets from the print shop, Lusher and Lusher, where the game tickets were printed, several boys were able to print several hundred extra tickets which were sold to unsuspecting Hazleton fans. The printer of the tickets had left the form of the tickets stand in his printshop. Several boys, who worked for the printer, decided to run off more tickets. However, they forgot to reset the numbering machine. This led to the discovery that the tickets were counterfeit since the numbers went beyond the number first printed plus they were about a half inch different in size. Thirty-five bogus tickets were presented at the doors to the gym. The individuals, who had been arrested, were released and, apparently, the boys were not charged, but severely reprimanded.[14]

Week 6

Hazleton 60 Doylestown 26: During the last week of January, Hazleton solidified its lead with a win over Coach Billy Wolf's Doylestown team. The game had to be postponed one day because another event had been scheduled for the gym. Four hundred loyal fans including the Hazleton band made the 100-mile trip to Doylestown.

Leading scorers: Hazleton – Frank Serany 27, Vernard Fegley 13; Doylestown - Jay Richards 12.[17]

Easton 50 Coatesville 25: Easton avenged its loss to Coatesville the prior week with its relatively easy win on its home court when the Red Rovers took a 16-6 first quarter lead.

Leading scorers: Easton - Benjamin Gadwell 16, Karl Meixell 14; Coatesville – George Long 8.[18]

Allentown 37 Pottsville 22: After trailing 8-2 after a quarter at Pottsville, Allentown fought back led by Lou Mantz to lead 30-11 after three quarters. The Canaries strengthened their hold on second place behind undefeated Hazleton.

Leading scorers: Allentown – Lew Mantz 18, Robert Schweyer 16; Pottsville – George Serfass 8.[19]

Week 7

As play entered the month of February, a new controversy erupted to threaten the existence of the league. Bethlehem and Easton announced they were considering withdrawing from the league unless Coatesville, Pottsville, and Pottstown did not secure larger playing floors. The Coatesville floor was considered one of the "Hat-boxes" of the league. Pottsville and Pottstown had previously agreed to play in their local armories, but still had not made the switch. The Coatesville school board was wrestling with the decision of what to do including the erection of a complete new high school in East Coatesville.[20]

Coatesville 34 Bethlehem 31: On their home court, Coatesville knocked off Bethlehem. No box score.

Doylestown 26 Coatesville 24: In a mild upset, Doylestown defeated Coatesville 26-24. No box score.

Hazleton 54 Pottstown 30: No box score.

Pottsville 27 Easton 17: No box score[21]

Allentown 36 Bethlehem 25: In Bethlehem, Allentown continued its hold on second place with its win over Bethlehem. In the game, Allentown guard "Frannie" Sheehan collided with the elbow of a Bethlehem player resulting in a badly swollen right eye and a bloody nose. He refused to leave the game and played till the end.

Leading scorers: Allentown – Robert Schweyer 12; Bethlehem – Paul Clay 8.[22]

Week 8

Hazleton 30 Allentown 27: On February 9, the second meeting between Hazleton and Allentown was sold out two weeks prior to the matchup. Ticket prices were 25 cents for students and 50 cents for adults. For those who could not attend and had tickets were selling them $7.50 for a pair of tickets. Entering the game on a 26-game winning streak, Hazleton raced out a huge 22-12 first half lead. Although the Canaries outscored Coach Hugh McGeehan's team 15-8 in the second half, they could not overcome the first half deficit in front of over 2000 fans. Allentown was handicapped by the fact that their star guard Sheehan had accidently incurred a broken nose and did not play in the first quarter. When he did appear in the game with a protector over his nose, it was apparent that he was not able to perform to the level necessary. After coming out of the game, he took off the protector and reentered the game and played well the rest of the way. Hazleton now appeared to have a sold lock on the league title.

Leading scorers: Hazleton – Vernard Fegley 9; Allentown – Lew Mantz 7.

Easton 41 Bethlehem 29: In a rough game between old rivals Bethlehem and Easton, Easton pulled off a mild upset. A total of 54 free throws were attempted in the game due to the fouls, but only 19 were made.

Leading scorers: Easton – Russell Purdy 10; Bethlehem – George Gaffney 6.[23].

Doylestown 35 Pottsville 26: Pottsville lost to Doylestown at the Doylestown Armory.

Leading scorers: Doylestown – Jay Richards 17; Pottsville – Johnny Niece 12.[24]

Pottstown 26 Coatesville 24: Pottstown lost both games they played over the weekend. On Friday night, they lost a close match to Coatesville. No box score

Bethlehem 59 Doylestown 52: The following night in Bethlehem, Doylestown lost in a high scoring affair. Bethlehem led at the half 39-32. Gaffney, Bethlehem, and Van Jeski, Doylestown, despite not starting the game, led all scorers.

Leading scorers: Bethlehem - George Gaffney 11; Doylestown – Van Jeski 11.[25]

Week 9

Hazleton 53 Doylestown 20: With a little over two weeks to go in the season, Hazleton continued its cruise to the league title on February 15. Despite losing star Frank Serany in the first half due to fouls, his substitute Vince Santipoli entered the game to start the second half and led all scorers.

Leading scorers: Hazleton – Vincent Santipoli 13. No box score[26]

Allentown 33 Bethlehem 28: Starting out slowly on the Raub floor, Allentown finally took the lead at the end of the first half 18-17. They preserved their slim chance of having a shot at the league title with the win.

Leading scorers: Allentown – Lew Mantz 12; Bethlehem – Paul Clay 12.

Pottstown 26 Easton 25: Easton traveled to Pottstown and started fast with a 10-5 lead at the end of the first quarter. Only scoring 2 points in the 2nd quarter, they fell behind 17-12 by halftime and 23-14 at the end of the third quarter. Despite a furious rally, they could not overcome the deficit in the fourth quarter and narrowly lost the game.

Leading scorers: Pottstown – Joseph Powell 14; Easton – Donald Anderson 11.[27]

Coatesville 34 Pottsville 28: In the other game of the weekend, Coatesville beat Pottsville. No box score

Week 10

Allentown 33 Doylestown 31: On a Tuesday night, February 19, Allentown traveled to Doylestown to take on the last place team. After taking a 21-14 lead at the end of the first half, the Canaries barely pulled out a win at the Doylestown Armory when referee Barfoot ruled that a last second game-tying shot by Doylestown forward Richard occurred after the game had ended. Allentown had barely hung on to second place.

Leading scorers: Allentown –Lew Mantz 9, Robert Schweyer 9; Doylestown –Jay Richards 11. Ed Slaughter 10.[28]

Allentown 43 Coatesville 21: In the weekend, Allentown traveled to Coatesville to record their second victory of the week. Allentown led at the half 24-9.

Leading scorers: Allentown Lew Mantz 15; Coatesville – Watson 7.

Pottstown 57 Pottsville 39: On the road, Pottstown defeated Pottsville to keep its hold on third place. No box score

Easton 24 Doylestown 20: No box score.

Hazleton 53 Bethlehem 25: Hazleton humiliated Bethlehem on their home court to clinch the league title. Hazleton led 17-1 after one period and 34-6 at halftime with the final score ending up with same 28-point deficit.

Leading scorers: Hazleton–Vernard Fegley 17, Frank Serany 11, Metro Weston 10; Bethlehem–Jim Reynolds 6.[29]

Hazleton 46 Coatesville 16: Coatesville traveled to Hazleton the following night and lost badly. No box score.

Pottstown 25 Allentown 23: In their third match of the week, the Canaries came up flat in Pottstown. Their third road game of the week, and possibly the realization that Hazleton had eliminated them from contention for the league title, resulted in a loss to Pottstown. No box score[30]

Week 11

Allentown 47 Easton 23: Entering March and the closing weekend of league play, Allentown finished its season with a victory over Easton. After Easton tied the score at 2-2, Allentown jumped out to a large lead.

Leadings scorers: Allentown – Lew Mantz 15; Easton – Donald Anderson 10.[31]

Pottsville 44 Coatesville 32: At home, Pottsville won with relative ease over Coatesville. No box score.

Hazleton 69 Bethlehem 22: Prepping for its run at another state title, Hazleton closed out its home season by shellacking Bethlehem. The Mountaineers jumped out to a 24-1 lead.

Leading scorers: Hazleton - Frank Serany 23, Metro Weston 10, Tom Powell 10; Bethlehem - Harold Moran 4, Max Connors 4, Riddle 4.

Hazleton 45 Easton 18: The following night, Hazleton traveled to Easton and won easily. No box score[32]

Week 12

Hazleton 78 Pottsville 37: On March 8, in front of 2500 fans in Pottsville's Charlton's Hall, Hazleton easily won, although Pottsville became the first team to score over 30 points against them. At the time, this was the largest crowd ever to witness a basketball game in Schuylkill County.

Leading scorers: Hazleton – Metro Weston 14, Frank Serany 12, Vernard Fegley 12, John Hildebrand 11; Pottsville – Clifton Cockill 14, Johnny Niece 11.[33]

Easton 58 Pottsville 21: The following night, Pottsville traveled to Easton and lost again. Easton led 14-1 after the first quarter and 27-6 at the half.

Leading scorers: Easton – Ronald Pierson 17, Ben Gadwell 13, Don Anderson 12; Pottsville – Decatur Moore 7.

Pottstown 70 Pottsville 41: In a meaningless match, Pottstown handily defeated visiting Pottsville. Pottstown led at the half 27-14.

Leading scorers: Pottstown– Woody Ludwig 25, John Banjo 18, Joe Powell 12; Pottsville– Clifton Cockill 22, Johnny Niece 10.[34]

Easton 33 Pottstown 27: The league play was wrapped up on March 15 when Pottstown traveled to Easton for a makeup of their game postponed due to weather on January 25. No box score[35]

Postseason Play

Hazleton 56 Summit Hill 22: They began their defense of District I title at the Bethlehem Liberty gym with easy victory over Summit Hill' They led at the half 29-15.

Leading scorers: Hazleton - Frank Serany 24, Metro Weston 18; Summit Hill – William Haldeman 12.[36]

Stroudsburg High School filed a protest with District 1 officials over its loss to Tamaqua at Lansford. Stroudsburg's coach Manning Curtis filed the protest late on Tuesday night after the Monday night game. According to the protest, a Stroudsburg player Taylor scored a goal from the floor in the third quarter in their game against Tamaqua. He was fouled on the play. According to Coach Curtis, the official scorer Wolfinger of Nesquehoning did not mark the goal on the official score. On the play, Taylor was awarded two free throws and only made one. Since he was considered in the act of shooting with the two free throws awarded, the goal should have counted. Coach Curtis contended that both referee Roy Geary, of Allentown, and umpire C. A. Bibleheimer, of Easton, had signaled the goal as good but it was inadvertently not entered into the score book. Stroudsburg felt that they should have won the game 35-34 rather than losing 34-33. District 1 officials denied Stroudsburg's protest indicating that it was filed way too late to make the change.[37]

Hazleton 41 Tamaqua 20: Two nights later, again at the Liberty gym, Hazleton tallied its 34th consecutive victory over Tamaqua in front of 2500 fans. Hazleton took an 11-4 lead after the first quarter.

Leading scorers: Hazleton- Frank Serany 20, John Hildebrand 13; Tamaqua – Vincent Norris 6, Joe Pichacolas 6.[38]

Hazleton 69 Lansdowne 33: Three nights later and again in the Liberty gym in Bethlehem, Hazleton led 10-2 after a quarter and 31-14 at halftime. The victory gave the Mountaineers the District 1 title.

Leading scorers: Hazleton - Frank Serany 24, John Hildebrand 14, Metro Weston 11; Lansdowne – Dick Brown 15, Jack Stevenson 13.[39]

Hazleton 29 East Stroudsburg 19: On March 18 at Lafayette College's Memorial Gymnasium, Hazleton met East Stroudsburg, District 2 champions as 3000 fans packed the gym. Another 1000 fans, reportedly, had to be turned away. Fifteen hundred fans made the trip from Hazleton, only to see Hazleton fall behind 11-5 at halftime. Early in the second half, East Stroudsburg lost its center on personal fouls. Hazleton took advantage of his absence and pulled away to advance to the state semifinals to be held at the University of Pittsburgh. At one point, the Hazleton fans made so much noise when their team took the lead that the game had to be halted until the crowd noise subsided since the players could not hear the referee's whistle.

Leading scorers: Hazleton – Frank Serany 11, Vernard Fegley 11; East Stroudsburg – Long 6.[40]

Hazleton 34 Reading 16: Winning its 37th consecutive game with ease, Hazleton moved into the state finals for the second straight year with its win over Reading. After leading 15-8 at halftime, Hazleton took charge in the second half.

Leading scorers: Hazleton – Frank Serany 13, Vernard Fegley 12; Reading – John Kubacki 7.[41]

Hazleton 34 Sharon 22: Over 4000 fans watched Hazleton become the first repeat champion in the ten-year history of the state high school championships. Hazleton beat Sharon for their 38th consecutive victory. Hazleton outscored Sharon 15-4 in the third quarter to put the game away.

Leading scorers: Hazleton - Frank Serany 14, John Hildebrand 12; Sharon – Donald McCamant 8.[42]

Team Rosters

Allentown: Coach J. Birney Crum, Joseph Blankovitch, Richard Duggan, Robert Greenawalt, Wilbur Huber, Edward Judt, James Kunkle, Leibensperger, Ray Lobb, Lewis Mantz, Eddie Ohner, Robert Schweyer, Francis Sheehan, Harry Sherr, Marwood Stark, Kermit Steckel.

Bethlehem: Coach Leo Prendergast, Charles Bedics, Richard Clarke, Paul Clay, Max Connors, Thomas Dickinson, Melvin Fluck, George Gaffney, Gurek, William Koenig, Harold Moran, James Reynolds, Edward Rice, Riddle, George Turek, Dudley Wright,

Coatesville: Coach Louis Lerda, Donald Diffenbaugh, Barty Howe, George Long, Hector McLean, Bob McNelly, Elmer Platt, Ray Pyle, George Rommel, Virgil Sasso, Jake Stark, Harold Steen, Walter Stoneback, Watson

Doylestown: Coach Bill Wolfe, Tom Bean, Edward Good, Ben Kristol, Russell Nash, Peft, Walter "Reds" Phillips, Jay Richards, Aloysius Rufe, Augustine Rufe, Bill Slaughter, Ed Slaughter, Albert Sulak, Van Jeski.

Easton: Coach Frank Duffy, Donald Anderson, Richard Bishop, Benjamin Gadwell, Allan Johnson, Floyd Jones, Parnell Lewis, Karl Meixell, Ronald Pierson, Russell Purdy, Angelo Trumbatore, Ray Williams.

Hazleton: Coach Hugh McGeehan, Albert Audikimow, Angelo Christino, Rex Christino, Vernard Fegley, John Hildebrand, Charles Murrin, Tom Powell, Jack Rothacker, Vincent Santipoli, Frank Serany, Joe Skurka, Metro Weston.

Pottstown: Coach Carroll Bechtel, Johnny Banjo, Hun Eidell, Hendricks, Kemp, Elwood "Woody" Ludwig, Jimmie Lynch, Joseph Powell, Royer, Schoenly, Steiner, Van Jeski, Weiser, Harry Yohn

Pottsville: Coach Charles Williams, Clifton "Mike" Cockill, Nathaniel Cooper, Bill Dimmerling, William Gray. Edward "Ski" Kunkel, Lundy, George Marsden, Meite, Decatur "Dick" Moore, Johnny Niece, Albert Pacenta, Robert Rummel, Herbert Saltzer, George "Gussie" Serfass, Les Sherry.

Final Standings

Hazleton	14-0
Allentown	11-3
Pottstown	8-4
Easton	6-8
Bethlehem	5-8
Coatesville	3-10
Doylestown	3-11
Pottsville	4-10

Note: Two games, Pottstown at Coatesville and Bethlehem at Pottstown, were not played.

1929 Hazleton High School – 1929 League and State Champions[43]

1st Row: Jack Rothacker, Rex Christino

2nd Row: John Hildebrand, Frank Serany, Metro Weston, Vernard Fegley, Joe Skurka

3rd Row: Vince Santipoli, Coach Hugh McGeehan, Charles Murrin, Faculty Manager James McQuaid, Albert Audikimow, Thomas Powell, Student Manager Charles Schaller, Angelo Christino

1930

State Champions Dethroned

During the off season, East Stroudsburg applied for membership in the league. The league met in Allentown on April 1, 1929, to wrap up the just-completed season and plan for the 1929-30 season. The league decided to keep its membership at the current 8 teams and denied the East Stroudsburg application. The league also discussed the concern about Coatesville's small playing floor. The league developed and approved rules specifically for the Coatesville floor. D. E. Atwell, Coatesville, was re-elected league president with W. E. Wolfe, Doylestown, as vice president. E. A. Rabenold, Allentown, was re-elected as secretary-treasurer.[1]

Week 1

Hazleton 51 Coatesville 23: Coach Hugh McGeehan's team began their defense of their league and state titles on their home court in Hazleton. After leading at the half 21-9, they easily disposed of Coatesville to register their 40th consecutive triumph.

Leading scorers: Hazleton – Ken Bommer 17, Woody Gearhardt 13, Jack Rothacker 12; Coatesville – George Long 9.

Allentown 27 Pottsville 15: In Pottsville, Coach Birney Crum's Canaries kept pace with a victory after leading at the half 12-8. The trip to Pottsville was treacherous due to a winter storm.

Leading scorers: Allentown – Eddie Ohner 12; Pottsville – Frederick Falls 7.

Bethlehem 45 Pottstown 8: At home, Bethlehem easily disposed of Pottstown after taking an 18-4 halftime lead. Pottstown only had one field goal and six foul shots.

Leading scorers: Bethlehem – Paul Clay 16, George Gaffney 13; Pottstown – Ricketts 4.[2]

Easton 49 Doylestown 26: Easton polished off Doylestown on their home floor. Easton led at the half 26-12.

Leading scorers: Easton – Ray Williams 20, George Purdy 10; Doylestown – Tom Beans 10.[3]

Week 2

Hazleton 27 Pottstown 16: Hazleton continued its winning streak in Pottstown despite not scoring a point during the third quarter. Having built a 19-9 halftime lead, Hazleton still led heading into the fourth quarter 19-14.

Leading scorers: Hazleton – Jack Rothacker 14; Pottstown – Bologanese 6.

Allentown 43 Doylestown 25: At Doylestown, the Canaries rallied after losing the lead in the third quarter 20-19. Allentown outscored Doylestown 24-5 the rest of the way for an easy win.

Leading scorers: Allentown – Art Leibensperger 14, Eddie Ohner 10; Doylestown – Millard Robinson 9.

Bethlehem 39 Easton 21: Bethlehem took a 6-0 lead early and led at the half 18-3 to hold a share of first place.

Leading scorers: Bethlehem – Paul Clay 12, George Gaffney 10; Easton – Roland Pierson 12.

Pottsville 24 Coatesville 22: In Coatesville, Pottsville won the game on a field goal in the last 30 seconds.

Leading scorers: Pottsville – Frederick Falls 9; Coatesville – George Long 15.[4]

Week 3

Hazleton 48 Allentown 38: Allentown traveled to Hazleton with hopes of knocking off the reigning state champions. Leading most of the first half, Allentown ended up trailing 19-18 on a last second field goal by Woody Gerhardt. In the second half, Hazleton pulled away from the Canaries. Foul shooting helped Hazleton in their margin of victory with Hazleton converting 18 while Allentown only made 10.

Leading scorers: Hazleton – Kenny Bommer 15, Woody Gerhardt 14, Jack Rothacker 10; Allentown – Ken Liebensperger 17.[5]

Bethlehem 40 Coatesville 24: Bethlehem kept pace with Hazleton with the win over Coatesville. After leading 17-12 at halftime, Bethlehem outscored Coatesville 23-12 in the second half.

Leading scorers: Bethlehem – George Gaffney 12, Leslie Polgar 12; Coatesville – George Long 12.

Pottsville 30 Easton 29: After leading at the half 21-10, Easton only scored eight points in the second half.

Leading scorers: Pottsville –George Serfass 15, Easton – Ben Gadwell 8, Roland Pierson 8, Ray Williams 8.[6]

Doylestown 25 Pottstown 16: No box score.

Week 4

Hazleton 30 Easton 25: Easton pressed the Mountaineers and led nearly three quarters of the game before Hazleton tied the game going into the final quarter 18-18. Hazleton rallied for the win in the final quarter.

Leading scorers: Hazleton – Kenny Bommer 14, Jack Rothacker 11; Easton – Roland Pierson 11.[7]

Allentown 39 Bethlehem 23: On the Raub gym floor, Allentown knocked Bethlehem out of the tie for first place. After three quarters, Bethlehem led 22-20, but completely collapsed and were outscored 19-1 in the 4th quarter.

Leading scorers: Allentown – Art Liebensperger 13, Eddie Ohner 12; Bethlehem – George Gaffney 7, Joe Lipsky 7.[8]

Pottsville 38 Pottstown 19: In Pottstown, the home team remained winless in league play.

Leading scorers: Pottsville – George Serfass 13, Albert Pacenta 12; Pottstown – Weiser 5.[9]

Doylestown 30 Coatesville 28: Coatesville also remained winless in league play. No box score.

Week 5

Pottsville 32 Coatesville 21: Coatesville lost its 4th game in a row.

Leading scorers: Pottsville – George Serfass 9; Coatesville – George Long 12.

Hazleton 42 Pottstown 27: Pottstown lost its fifth consecutive league contest while Hazleton rolled to their 45th consecutive victory. After leading 9-8, Hazleton stretched the lead to 32-22 after three quarters.

Leading scorers: Hazleton - Jack Rothacker 15; Pottstown – Johnny Banjo 7, Richard Ricketts 7.

Bethlehem 30 Easton 27: On the Liberty gym floor, the score was tied 24-24 at halftime with Bethlehem then outscoring the Red Rovers 6-3 in the second half.

Leading scorers: Bethlehem – Paul Clay 12; Easton – George Purdy 8.

Allentown 44 Doylestown 23: Allentown led 6-0 after a quarter and 14-7 at halftime. The Canaries scored 30 points in the second to nearly double up Doylestown.

Leading scorers: Allentown – Milton Lipschutz 16, Jimmy Hauze 14; Doylestown – Tom Bean 7.[10]

Week 6

Allentown 42 Hazleton 34: Allentown took a 7-0 lead and never trailed as they shocked the Mountaineers to end their lengthy winning streak. Allentown led 27-10 at the half before Hazleton put on a second half rally but could not overcome the big lead. Hazleton coach Hugh McGeehan blamed the loss on poor officiating by Al "Doggie" Julian.

Leading scorers: Allentown – Jimmy Hauze 11, Art Liebensperger 10; Hazleton – Jack Rothacker 21.

Bethlehem 23 Coatesville 19: Bethlehem pulled into a three-way tie for first place. Leading scorer George Long fouled out of the game for Coatesville.

Leading scorers: Bethlehem – George Gaffney 11; Coatesville – George Long 15.

Easton 39 Pottsville 27: Coach Clyde Notestine's Easton squad knocked Pottsville our of a potential four-way first place tie. Easton led at the half 20-13.

Leading scorers: Easton – Ray Williams 14, George Purdy 12; Pottsville – George Serfass 7.[11]

Week 7

Doylestown 35 Pottstown 29: No box score.

Hazleton 53 Easton 36: Hazleton rebounded with a win at home against Easton to remain tied for first. Easton had led 17-5 early in the game.

Leading scorers: Hazleton – Ken Bommer 16, Jack Rothacker 14; Easton – Benjamin Gadwell 11.[12]

Bethlehem 31 Allentown 25: Bethlehem outplayed Allentown to remain tied for first place with Hazleton. Allentown attributed its loss on their inability to find their shooting range on the larger Liberty floor.

Leading scorers: Bethlehem – Paul Clay 11; Allentown – Art Liebensperger 6, Jimmy Hauze 6.[13]

Doylestown 36 Coatesville 30: After taking an 11-3 first quarter lead, Doylestown kept Coatesville winless.

Leading scorers: Doylestown – Tom Bean 15; Coatesville – George Long 14.[14]

Pottsville 42 Pottstown 22: Pottstown remained without a win in league play. No box score.

Week 8

Easton 41 Pottstown 35: Easton led 28-21 at halftime and kept Pottstown winless in league play.

Leading scorers: Easton – Ray Williams 18, Ben Gadwell 12; Pottstown – John Banjo 20.

Hazleton 38 Pottsville 19: With Pottsville leading 16-10 at the half, Hazleton only allowed 3 points in the second half.

Leading scorers: Hazleton – Ken Bommer 17, Jack Rothacker 11; Pottsville – George Serfass 13.[15]

Allentown 51 Coatesville 29: At the Raub gym, Allentown took 12-6 and 24-10 leads after the first two quarters.

Leading scorers: Allentown – Art Liebensperger 14, Eddie Ohner 13; Coatesville – George Long 16.

Bethlehem 38 Doylestown 24: Bethlehem led 26-13 at halftime and remained tied for first place.

Leading scorers: Bethlehem - Paul Clay 13, Max Connor 10; Doylestown – Tom Bean 13.[16]

Week 9

Pottsville 27 Bethlehem 25: In Pottsville, Pottsville shocked Bethlehem to knock them out of the first-place tie with Hazleton. Although the game was tight the whole way, Pottsville led 16-12 at the half and led all the way.

Leading scorers: Pottsville – George Serfass 9; Bethlehem – George Gaffney 12.

Allentown 50 Pottstown 39: In Pottstown, Allentown only led 13-10 early, but stretched it to 32-16 at the half.

Leading scorers: Allentown – Robert Schweyer 14, Milton Lipschutz 11, Art Liebensperger 10; Pottstown – John Banjo 21.[17]

Hazleton 37 Doylestown 32: Doylestown kept it close, trailing 19-16 at the half, but Hazleton prevailed at the Doylestown Armory.

Leading scorers: Hazleton – Jack Rothacker 14; Doylestown – Tom Bean 10.[18]

Coatesville 47 Easton 23: Coatesville won its first league game. No box score[19]

Week 10

Hazleton 30 Bethlehem 22: On Valentine's Day, Bethlehem took a 7-3 lead after the first quarter only to have Hazleton take an 11-9 lead at halftime. Bill Emery's team took over in the third quarter and led 21-13 going into the fourth quarter. Hazleton dominated Bethlehem in the final quarter outscoring the Hurricane 17-1.

Leading scorers: Hazleton – Jack Rothacker 10; Bethlehem – Paul Clay 9.

Allentown 45 Easton 32: Allentown led 15-4 after a quarter and 25-7 in the second quarter before Easton rallied with ten straight points.

Leading scorers: Allentown – Art Liebensperger 15, Eddie Ohner 10; Easton – Ray Williams 12, Ben Gadwell 12.[21]

Coatesville 26 Pottstown 10: Coatesville won its second game over winless Pottstown. No box score

Doylestown 30 Pottsville 27: After being tied 17-17 at the half, Doylestown took the game to improve to 5-5.

Leading scorers: Doylestown – Tom Bean 17; Pottsville – George Serfass 11.[22]

Week 11

Bethlehem 33 Hazleton 32: Reversing their fortunes from the prior week, the Hurricane shocked Hazleton at Bethlehem. Trailing 17-13 at halftime, Bethlehem rallied in the second half to knock Hazleton out of first place. Hazleton blamed the loss on referee Briody who supposedly wrecked the smooth-running Mountaineer offense by inflicting unjust penalties. A Hazleton paper indicated that Briody would never officiate another Hazleton game.

Leading scorers: Bethlehem – Paul Clay 10; Hazleton – Ken Bommer 10.

Allentown 46 Easton 21: Leading at the half 21-9 on the Raub floor, the Canaries moved into first place.

Leading scorers: Allentown – Art Liebensperger 11, Eddie Ohner 10; Easton – Ben Gadwell 8.

Pottstown 32 Coatesville 25: Pottstown finally cracked into the winner's circle over Coatesville.

Leading scorers: Pottstown – Johnny Banjo 11, Grubb 11; Coatesville – George Long 12.

Pottsville 38 Doylestown 21: Pottsville drubbed Doylestown after taking a 25-8 halftime lead.

Leading scorers: Pottsville – George Serfass 18, Peter Samosky 11; Doylestown – Tom Bean 7.[23]

Allentown 51 Coatesville 21: Allentown led at the half 26-10 and coasted to the victory.

Leading scorers: Allentown – Eddie Ohner 15, Robert Schweyer 12, Art Liebensperger 12; Coatesville – George Long 6.

Easton 53 Pottstown 32: Easton kept Pottstown in the league cellar.

Leading scorers: Easton – Ben Gadwell 24, Laucher 11; Pottstown – Johnny Banjo 10.

Hazleton 42 Pottsville 40: After Hazleton led 13-8 after a quarter, Pottsville surged into the lead at the half 21-20. With the score tied 40-40, John McGeehan, Coach McGeehan's son, made the winning field goal.

Leading scorers: Hazleton – Jack Rothacker 19; Pottsville – George Serfass 16, Albert Pacenta 16.[24]

Bethlehem 41 Doylestown 20: No box score[25]

Week 12

Allentown 64 Pottstown 26: Allentown took a 31-15 halftime lead and extended it to 51-22 after three quarters.

Leading scorers: Allentown – Eddie Ohner 15, Robert Schweyer 12, Art Liebensperger 12; Pottstown – Johnny Banjo 10.[26]

Hazleton 50 Doylestown 27: Leading 22-11 at halftime, Hazleton walloped Doylestown in front of a home crowd of 1800 fans.

Leading scorers: Hazleton – Ken Bommer 16, Jack Rothacker 15, Louis Tarone 10; Doylestown – Tom Bean 11.

Bethlehem 27 Pottsville 17: A game behind the leaders, Bethlehem trailed 6-2 before taking a 9-8 halftime lead.

Leading scorers: Bethlehem – George Gaffney 10; Pottsville – George Serfass 6.

Coatesville 40 Easton 36: Easton led 10-6 after a quarter before Coatesville took the lead at halftime 18-15.

Leading scorers: Coatesville – Roper 12, Hector McLean 10; Easton – Bill Fueher 7.[27]

Week 13

Allentown 67 Pottsville 37: Closing out the regular season on the Raub floor, Allentown led 19-4 after the first period. Pottsville's only lead was 1-0.

Leading scorers: Allentown – Eddie Ohner 19, Jimmy Hauze 16; Pottsville – George Serfass 12.[28]

Hazleton 39 Coatesville 28: At Coatesville, Hazleton took a 20-11 halftime lead. Hazleton's Jack Rothacker outscored Coatesville's George Long to finish as the league's leading scorer.

Leading scorers: Hazleton – Jack Rothacker 16, Louis Tarone 16; Coatesville – George Long 15.

Bethlehem 37 Pottstown 28: Bethlehem clinched third place. After Bethlehem led 10-4 after a quarter, Pottstown closed within 18-16 at halftime.

Leading scorers: Bethlehem – George Gaffney 13, Paul Clay 10; Pottstown – Johnny Banjo 11.

Easton 45 Doylestown 31: The two teams tied for 5th place with 5-9 records. No box score[29]

League Championship Playoff

Allentown 55 Hazleton 26: A one game playoff was scheduled for March 10 at the Penn Palestra in Philadelphia to determine the league champion. Before 10,000 fans, Allentown took a 7-0 lead in the first two minutes and 30-7 at halftime.

Leading scorers: Allentown – Bob Schweyer 14, Milton Lipschutz 12, Eddie Ohner 10; Hazleton – Lou Tarone 11.[30]

PIAA Postseason Play

Allentown 34 Mahanoy City 29: At the Liberty High gym in front of 2500 fans, Allentown ended Mahanoy City's 18 game win streak. The victory stemmed from the Canaries 12-5 second quarter advantage.

Leading scorers: Allentown – Art Liebensperger 13; Mahanoy City – John Zemelavage 6.[31]

Lower Merion 22 Allentown 18: An overflow crowd of 3000 at the Liberty gym witnessed Lower Merion dash the Canaries' hopes for a state title. Allentown's horrendous 6 for 21 foul shooting doomed their chances for victory. Allentown fell behind 6-2 in the first quarter, proving to be the difference in the game.

Leading scorers: Lower Merion – Al Bonniwell 8; Allentown Robert Schweyer 8.[32]

Postseason Accolades

Leading scorers: Jack Rothacker, Hazleton, 185 points; George Long, Coatesville 180; Art Liebensperger, Allentown 158; Tom Bean, Doylestown, 149; George Serfass, Pottsville, 142; Eddie Ohner, Allentown, 137; Paul Clay, Bethlehem, 129; Ken Bommer, Hazleton, 124; Ben Gadwell, Easton, 111; and Ray Williams, Easton, 102.[33]

Final Standings

Allentown	12-2
Hazleton	12-2
Bethlehem	11-3
Pottsville	7-7
Doylestown	5-9
Easton	5-9
Coatesville	3-11
Pottstown	1-13

Team Rosters

Allentown: Coach J. Birney Crum, Eddie Feinour, Al Geschel, Jimmy Hauze, Richard Landis, Art Liebensperger, Milton Lipschutz, Dan McFadden, Eddie "Slim" Ohner, Rodgers, Robert Schweyer, Marwood Stark, Paul Yeakel

Bethlehem: Coach Bill Emrey, Beahm, Joseph Borda, Walter "Wats" Clarke, Paul "Peanuts" Clay, Max Connor, George "Pete" Gaffney, Bernard Glazier, Joseph "Joe" Lipsky, Harold Moran, Leslie Polgar, Bob Taylor

Coatesville: Coach Lou Lerda, Donald Diffenbach, George Long, Hector McLean, Bob McNelly, Albert Morgan, Poff, Raymond Pyle, George Rommel, Roper, Jake Stark, Walter Stoneback

Doylestown: Coach Bill Wolfe, Tom Beans, Edward Good, Ben Kristol, Russell Nash, Nelson, Millard Robinson, Aloysius Rufe, Augustine Rufe, Bill Slaughter, Albert Sulak

Easton: Coach Clyde Notestine, John Bechtel, Thomas Drummond, Wilbur Fuehrer, Benjamin Gadwell, Floyd Jones, Parnell Lewis, McRae Lilly, Roland Pierson, George Purdy, George Robinson, Ray Willaims

Hazleton: Coach Hugh McGeehan, Albert Audikemow, Walter Baker, Kenny Bommer, Angelo Christino, Rex Christion, Woody Gerhardt, John McGeehan, Tom Powell, Jack Rothacker, Louis "Gigi" Tarone

Pottstown: Coach Carroll Bechtel, John Banjo, Bolognesse, Harry Grubb, Langdon, Lawler, Leh, Potts, Richard Ricketts, Hal Royer, Scheffey, Sutter, Warner, Weiser

Pottsville: Coach Ross Hufford, Darlington Bebelheimer, Frederick Falls, William Gray, James Lewis, Albert Pacenta, George "Gussie" Serfass, Les Sherry, Peter Somansky, Victor Tamanosky, Truxton Williams

1931

League Champions Repeat

The 1930 season was a classic struggle between Allentown and Hazleton for the league title. Bethlehem finished a close second and defeated both teams during the season. During the 1931 season, fans witnessed the same three teams in some thrilling matchups. Allentown and Hazleton both continued as powerful forces in the league.

Prior to the start of the season, a controversy from the 1930 season was resolved involving seating arrangements in Bethlehem's Liberty gym. During a Bethlehem-Hazleton game, no provisions were made for the sportswriters covering the matchup. Sportswriters were forced to sit on the floor to score the game. The Hazleton Standard-Sentinel newspaper took issue with these arrangements. To resolve the issue, Bethlehem constructed two tables, each six feet long by fourteen inches wide, to be placed at the center of the bleachers to accommodate game timers, scorers, and sportswriters.[1]

At its spring meeting, in a move to improve the officiating, the league voted to establish a new system of selecting officials for all league games. The league selected H.A. Benfer, a Muhlenberg College faculty member, as commissioner of officials. Later, in the fall, the coaches and faculty managers of the eight schools, reviewed a list of 30 names and pared it down to 22 individuals to serve as approved game officials. Benfer was given the authority to assign officials for each game.[2]

Week 1

Allentown 36 Pottsville 11: Coach Crum's Canaries opened at home in the defense of its league title in its brand new $375,000 gymnasium at the high school. After taking a 14-5 first half lead, Allentown crushed Pottsville allowing only three field goals.

Leading scorers: Allentown – Paul Grim 11, Jim Hauze 11; Pottsville – Charles Howell 4.

Bethlehem 33 Pottstown 13: In Pottstown, Bethlehem took a 13-11 halftime lead and held Pottstown to two free throws in the second half while scoring 20 points of their own.

Leading scorers: Bethlehem – Steve Polgar 12, Bob Taylor 10; Pottstown – Harry Grubb 5.[3]

Hazleton 40 Coatesville 14: Meanwhile, on the road, Hazleton cruised over Coatesville after having taken 14-2 and 27-6 leads after the first two quarters.

Leading scorers: Hazleton – Ken Bommer 15, Hal Lewis 12; Coatesville – Duie Smith 8.

Easton 55 Doylestown 18: Easton traveled to Doylestown and took a 19-9 first half lead and pummeled Doylestown with 36 points in the second half for a resounding victory.

Leading scorers: Easton – Ben Gadwell 18, Ray Williams 17, George Purdy 15; Doylestown – Millard Robinson 8.[4]

Week 2

Bethlehem 43 Pottsville 13: For the second straight game, Bethlehem held an opponent to 13 points in a rare Thursday night matchup in Allentown. The game had been scheduled for Friday night in Pottsville, but their floor was not available and the game was moved to Allentown.

Leading scorers: Bethlehem - Bob Taylor 17; Pottsville – Charles Howell 9.[7]

Hazleton 44 Doylestown 16: Coach Hugh McGeehan's Hazleton team, in its home opener, rolled up a decisive win over Doylestown. Hazleton led at the half 30-5.

Leading scorers: Hazleton - Ken Bommer 17, Louis Tarone 10; Doylestown – Millard Robinson 8.[5]

Allentown 34 Easton 25: Allentown kept pace with its win over homestanding and favorite Easton. Easton had been considered the favorite based on it crushing defeat of Doylestown on the opening night. Coach Crum matched guard Jimmy Hause with Easton's high scoring forward Purdy and kept him scoreless as Allentown won its eleventh consecutive game over Easton.

Leading scorers: Allentown – Bob Meyer 21; Easton – Ben Gadwell 9.

Pottstown 13 Coatesville 12: Despite not scoring a single point in the fourth quarter, Pottstown still held off Coatesville in low-scoring, hard fought matchup in Pottstown. Pottstown held a 13-8 lead after three quarters.

Leading scorers: Pottstown – Harry Grubb 8; Coatesville – Duie Smith 4.[6]

Week 3

Allentown 32 Pottstown 15: After a three-week layoff due to the holidays, Allentown held on to first place with a win over Pottstown. The Canaries held a 23-5 halftime lead and limited Pottstown to a single point in the 2nd quarter.

Leading scorers: Allentown – Paul Grim 13; Pottstown – Harry Grubb 10.[8]

Hazleton 31 Bethlehem 22: With its triumph over Bethlehem, Hazleton continued to hold a share of first place. The Mountaineers built an 18-6 lead at halftime.

Leading scorers: Hazleton - Louis "Gigi" Tarone 14; Bethlehem – Robert "Booby" Long 6, Steve Polgar 6, Lew Ochenhouse 6.

Coatesville 35 Easton 33: Easton again lost a game they expected to win. On its home court, Coatesville eked out a win over the Red Rovers. At halftime, the teams were tied at 5-5 and both offenses exploded in the second half.

Leading scorers: Coatesville – Duie Smith 16; Easton – Ben Gadwell 13.

Pottsville 41 Doylestown 19: Pottsville rebounded from its loss to Bethlehem with an easy win over Doylestown.

Leading scorers: Pottsville – Charles Howell 22; Doylestown - Millard Robinson 7.[9]

Week 4

Allentown 31 Hazleton 13: In a showdown between Hazleton and Allentown, the Canaries decisively won the matchup on the loser's home court. Ahead 19-13 at the three-quarter mark, Allentown held Hazleton scoreless in the final quarter. Guard Jimmy Hauze was given the assignment to guard Hazleton's top scorer Tarone. Just as in the Easton game, he was a defensive wizard holding Tarone to a single point in the game. After the game, Allentown's players celebrated by jumping in the showers in full uniform and hopped around singing "Ring around the rosey" with Coach Crum in the middle.

Leading scorers: Allentown – Jim Hauze 9; Hazleton – Hal Lewis 6.

Bethlehem 27 Easton 25: After being tied at the half 14-14, Bethlehem squeaked out the win to hand Easton its third straight loss in a very physical contest.

Leading scorers: Bethlehem – Steve Polgar 10; Easton – George Purdy 8.

Pottstown 29 Doylestown 23: Pottstown won its first game over Doylestown after taking a halftime lead 13-8.

Leading scorers: Pottstown – Richard Ricketts 11; Doylestown – Albert Sulak 9.

Pottsville 39 Coatesville 36: Coatesville traveled to Pottsville only to lose in a close game.

Leading scorers: Pottsville – Ed Merrick 12, Bill Dimmerling 10; Coatesville – Albert Morgan 11.[10]

Week 5

Allentown 23 Bethlehem 15: In front of a turn-away crowd of 2200 fans in their new home gym, Allentown knocked Bethlehem out of 2nd place. Only leading 9-8 at halftime, Allentown pulled away in the second half.

Leading scorers: Allentown – Jim Hauze 9; Bethlehem – Max Connor 6.

Hazleton 28 Easton 20: Hazleton, handing Easton its fourth straight loss, moved into sole possession of second place with win on the road over Easton. Hazleton led 15-10 at halftime.

Leading scorers: Hazleton – Ken Bommer 13; Easton – Ben Gadwell 6.

Pottstown 25 Pottsville 24: After leading at halftime 15-8, Pottstown, on its home court, barely held on to win at the buzzer over Pottsville.

Leading scorers: Pottstown – Harry Grubb 13; Pottsville – Charles Howell 11.

Coatesville 39 Doylestown 17: After trailing by only five 18-13 at halftime, winless Doylestown was drubbed by Coatesville in the second half. No box score[11]

Hazleton 32 Pottstown 19: Pottstown traveled to Hazleton only to get trounced by the Mountaineers. Hazleton took a 19-8 lead into halftime.

Leading scorers: Hazleton – Louis Tarone 10; Pottstown – Harry Grubb 9.

Easton 44 Pottsville 40: In a hard-fought game in Pottsville, Easton prevailed in a fast-paced game that was nip and tuck throughout and put an end to their four-game losing streak. Easton led 23-19 at halftime.

Leading scorers: Easton – Ralph Williamson 13, Ben Gadwell 12, Ray Williams 11; Pottsville – Charles Howell 19.[12]

Bethlehem 36 Coatesville 16: Bethlehem maintained its third-place position with a win at home over Coatesville. Bethlehem held a 15-6 halftime lead.

Leading scorers: Bethlehem - Steve Polgar 13; Coatesville – Bob McNelly 7.

Allentown 49 Doylestown 25: Jimmy Hauze, who played guard to start the season, was moved to center by Coach Crum and led the Canaries into Doylestown. Leading 25-12 at the half, Allentown stayed unbeaten in league play

Leading scorers: Allentown – Jim Hauze 24; Bobby Meyer 13; Doylestown – Albert Sulak 11.[13]

Week 6

Hazleton 43 Pottsville 23: Hazleton took a 21-15 halftime lead and despite a valiant effort by "Tabby" Howell to keep Pottsville close easily won with a second half surge.

Leading scorers: Hazleton – Ken Bommer 14, Louis Tarone 10; Pottsville - Charles "Tabby" Howell 16.

Allentown 44 Coatesville 25: Still undefeated at the halfway point of the season, Allentown stayed a game ahead of Hazleton by defeating Coatesville. The Canaries held a 22-9 lead at halftime.

Leading scorers: Allentown - Jimmy Hauze 19; Coatesville – Duie Smith 7; Garnett Poff 7.

Pottstown 26 Easton 23: After Pottstown held a 17-12 lead at halftime, Easton came back to take the lead in the third quarter and late into the fourth quarter. Pottstown came back to hand Easton their 5th loss in 7 games.

Leading scorers: Pottstown – Harry Grubb 12; Easton – William Warner 7.

Bethlehem 31 Doylestown 16: Despite keeping the game close at halftime 9-8, Doylestown could not stay with Bethlehem in the second half and remained winless in league play.

Leading scorers: Bethlehem – Bobby Taylor 9; Doylestown – Millard Robinson 9.[14]

Second Half - Week 7

Bethlehem 22 Pottstown 20: Pottstown held a 13-10 lead at halftime, but Bethlehem took down the home team in the second half in Pottstown. Bob Taylor scored all but four of Bethlehem's points.

Leading scorers: Bethlehem – Bobby Taylor 18; Pottstown – Harry Grubb 6.

Easton 62 Doylestown 25: Easton's offense exploded, in their home gym, and the Red Rovers showed the same form as in their earlier matchup with winless Doylestown winning handily.

Leading scorers: Easton - George Purdy 20, Wilbur Fuehrer 14; Doylestown – Millard Robinson 7, Albert Sulak 7.

Hazleton 36 Coatesville 16: At home, after taking a 15-9 halftime lead, Hazleton cruised over Coatesville to keep pace with Allentown.

Leading scorers: Hazleton – Ken Bommer 13, Louis Tarone 12; Coatesville – Garnett Poff 5.

Allentown 45 Pottsville 35: In Pottsville, "Tabby" Howell battled the Canaries' Jimmy Hauze for the league scoring lead with Howell maintaining the lead by a single point. The Canaries led 27-16 at the half.

Leading scorers: Allentown – Jimmy Hauze 20, Paul Grim 14; Pottsville – Charles Howell 15.[15]

Week 8

Hazleton 43 Doylestown 19: Hazleton took a 20-11 halftime lead and kept Doylestown winless.

Leading scorers: Hazleton - Ralph Crocamo 18; Doylestown - Millard Robinson 7.

Bethlehem 34 Pottsville 17: Eleven hundred home court fans saw Bethlehem hold Pottsville scoreless in the first quarter and jump out to a 13-2 lead early in the second quarter when Howell made Pottsville's first field goal.

Leading scorers: Bethlehem - Steve Polgar 20; Pottsville – Charles Howell - 10.

Allentown 40 Easton 16: In a very physical game in the Canaries' gym, Allentown swept the season series with Easton to keep their hold on first place. The rough-housing led to a third quarter altercation which required the on-duty police to call headquarters for additional backup assistance. Jimmy Hauze dribbled the ball up-court only to have Easton's George Purdy charge into him throwing Hauze four feet in the air and landing on his back. More than a hundred fans came onto the floor and mixed with the players in a barrage of fisticuffs. It took 10 minutes to restore order and resume the game.

Leading scorers: Allentown – Bobby Meyers 10; Easton – Ralph Williamson 6.

Coatesville 32 Pottstown 30: Coatesville won over Pottstown in a mild upset. No box score[16]

Week 9

Doylestown 30 Pottsville 25: Doylestown won its first league game over Pottsville. Pottsville's star Tabby Howell scored only three points on his home court and relinquished the league scoring leadership to Allentown's Hauze.

Leading scorers: Doylestown – Millard Robinson 13; Pottsville – Eddie Mader 4, John Moody 4.

Coatesville 24 Easton 23: Coatesville narrowly won its fourth straight contest over reeling Easton. Easton had led at the end of each of the first three quarters and had a 23-18 lead near the end of the 4th quarter when Coach Notestine replaced his starters with the second team. Coatesville scored the last six points for the win.

Leading scorers: Coatesville – Albert Morgan 7; Easton – Wilbur Fuehrer 7.

Hazleton 44 Bethlehem 34: In a matchup of 2nd and 3rd place teams, Hazleton, at home, held off Bethlehem to take a solid hold on second place and maintain its hopes of a league title. Hazleton led at the half 26-17.

Leading scorers: Hazleton - Ken Bommer 27, Ralph Crocamo 10; Bethlehem – Lew Ochenhouse 12, Bob Taylor 11.[17]

Allentown 39 Pottstown 14: Allentown allowed only two field goals and outclassed Pottstown. Allentown held only a slim 5-4 lead after a quarter but increased it to 15-6 at the half. Jimmy Hauze took the league scoring lead.

Leading scorers: Allentown – Jimmy Hauze 16; Pottstown – Charles "Chitty" Guss 3.[18]

Week 10

Coatesville 54 Pottsville 43: Streaking Coatesville led the whole way at Pottsville and won its 5th consecutive match. With Allentown's Jimmy Hauze idle, Pottsville's Tabby Howell retook the league scoring lead.

Leading scorers: Coatesville – Duie Smith 20, Albert Morgan 19; Pottsville – Charles Howell 17, Leroy Shellhammer 13

Pottstown 32 Doylestown 23: Despite holding a 16-7 lead at halftime, Doylestown lost to Pottstown. Pottstown's substitute forward "Chitty" Guss led the second half comeback.

Leading scorers: Pottstown – "Chitty" Guss 12; Doylestown – Millard Robinson 13.[19]

Allentown 24 Hazleton 23: In a high-stakes matchup in Allentown, Hazleton took the floor determined to pull into a first-place tie with the Canaries. In front of 2200 fans, Hazleton looked like the sure winner and held a five-point lead with five minutes to play in the game. Coach Crum removed his starting forwards, Bobby Meyer and Paul Grim, for substitutes Lee Coker and Billy Boyle. A minute later, guard Danny McFadden fouled out and was replaced by "Whitey" Nonnemacher. With a minute to play, the Canaries took a one-point lead and held on to win for their 4th consecutive defeat of Hazleton.

Leading scorers: Allentown – Jimmy Hause 14; Hazleton - Ken Bommer 11.

Bethlehem 27 Easton 18: With neither team scoring in the first five minutes of the game, the first quarter ended in a 5-5 tie. Bethlehem handed Easton its eighth loss against three wins. Easton didn't score a point in the 3rd quarter.

Leading scorers: Bethlehem – Bobby Taylor 10; Easton – George Purdy 6.[20]

Pottstown 29 Pottsville 22: Coach Bechtel's Pottstown team took an 8-6 first quarter lead and led the entire game to defeat Pottsville on its home court.

Leading scorers: Pottstown – "Chitty" Guss 9; Pottsville – Charles Howell 9.

Coatesville 28 Doylestown 25: In a tight contest, Coatesville took a 12-10 halftime lead and turned back Doylestown to win its 6th straight league game.

Leading scorers: Coatesville – Duie Smith 9; Doylestown – Millard Robinson 14.[21]

Week 11

Bethlehem 23 Allentown 19: In a shocking result for the undefeated Canaries, Bethlehem shattered Allentown's 11 game win streak with a low-scoring win in the Liberty gym. Allentown scored only a single point on a free throw in the final stanza to seal the win for Bethlehem. Despite the loss, Allentown still held a one game lead over Hazleton.

Leading scorers: Bethlehem – Bobby Taylor 10; Allentown – Lee Coker 4, Bernard Schwartz 4.[22]

Hazleton 32 Pottstown 16: After having been sidelined for some time with an illness, forward Hal Lewis came back and led Hazleton over Pottstown on its home court and kept hope alive for a league title.

Leading scorers: Hazleton – Hal Lewis 14; Pottstown – Hal Royer 6.[23]

Allentown 41 Doylestown 11: Allentown bounced back by whipping Doylestown, despite Hause fouling out in the third quarter. The Canaries held Doylestown to two field goals in the game, one in each half, and led 24-6 at halftime.

Leading scorers: Allentown – Jim Hause 18; Doylestown – Millard Robinson 7.

Easton 35 Pottsville 28: Easton righted itself with a win over Pottsville at home. Easton led 22-13 at halftime.

Leading scorers: Easton - Wilbur Fuehrer 15; Pottsville – Charles Howell 11.[24]

Bethlehem 19 Coatesville 14: Coach Emrey's Liberty boys won a low scoring game at Coatesville with Bethlehem leading at half time 14-6.

Leading scorers: Bethlehem – Steve Polgar 6; Coatesville – Howard Steen 4.[25]

Hazleton 40 Easton 21: Keeping their slim hopes alive at home, Hazleton whipped Easton. Easton held the lead at the half 14-13.

Leading scorers: Hazleton – Ken Bommer 12, Woody Gerhardt 10; Easton – Wilbur Fuehrer 6.[26]

Week 12

Allentown 34 Coatesville 15: In the final week of the season, Allentown clinched its second consecutive league title with its win over Coatesville after a 3-3 first quarter tie and only leading 11-5 at the half.

Leading scorers: Allentown – Dan McFadden 9; Coatesville – Duie Smith 6.[27]

Hazleton 37 Pottsville 21: Hazleton clinched 2nd place in Pottsville after taking a 21-11 halftime lead.

Leading scorers: Hazleton – Woody Gerhardt 8; Pottsville – Ed Merrick 8.

Easton 32 Pottstown 18: Easton closed out its disappointing season with a win over Pottstown.

Leading scorers: Easton – Wilbur Fuehrer 9; Pottstown – Michael Dezura 4.

Bethlehem 36 Doylestown 23: Bethlehem finished in third place in handing Doylestown its 13th loss. Bethlehem joined Allentown and Hazleton as the only teams with a winning record on the season.

Leading scorers: Bethlehem – Anthony Grebnar 13; Doylestown - Millard Robinson 13.[28]

Postseason Play

Allentown 27 Summit Hill 13: Fresh off its clinching of the league title, Allentown moved on to the post season playoffs. The first matchup pitted Allentown against the Carbon-Schuylkill League champions Summit Hill. The game was held at their fiercest rival Hazleton's home court. Undeterred, the Canaries jumped out to an 8-0 lead after the first quarter and were never headed as they rolled to the win. The Canaries did suffer some misfortune in the game when star Jimmy Hauze received a sharp blow to the nose during the second half and had to be removed from the game. Coach Crum pulled him from the game since he was dizzy and apparently not aware of what was happening. The initial fears that he may have suffered a broken nose proved to be negative.

Leading scorers: Allentown – Bobby Meyer 10; Summit Hill – Charles Melley 4.[29]

Lower Merion 19 Allentown 10: Three thousand fans packed the Lafayette College gymnasium for Allentown's second playoff game with Lower Merion. Lower Merion caused to Canaries play which was by far their worst game of the season. Only scoring 4 points in the first half, Allentown went down 19-10 at the hands of the Philadelphia Suburban League champions in a low scoring affair to end the Canaries' season on a sour note.

Leading scorers: Lower Merion – John Eaton 8; Allentown – Dan McFadden 4.[30]

Postseason Accolades

The league's top ten leading scorers were as follows: Jimmy Hauze, Allentown, 173 points; Ken Bommer, Hazleton, 160; Charles "Tabby" Howell, Pottsville, 159; Bob Taylor, Bethlehem,128; Millard Robinson, Doylestown, 121, Duie Smith, Coatesville, 111, Harry Grubb, Pottstown, 101; Charles "Bobby" Meyer, Allentown, 94; Steve Polgar, Bethlehem, 93; Louis Tarone, Hazleton, 92.[31]

The league all-star selections conducted by the Pottsville Journal included:[32]

First team: forwards- Ken Bommer, Hazleton, and Charles "Tabby" Howell, Pottsville; center - Louis "Gigi" Tarone; Hazleton; and guards - Jimmy Hauze and Danny McFadden, both Allentown. Second team: Forwards - Bob Taylor, Bethlehem, and Harry Grubb, Pottstown; center - Albert Morgan, Coatesville; and guards - Ben Gadwell, Easton, and Millard Robinson, Doylestown.

Final Standings

Team	Record
Allentown	13-1
Hazleton	12-2
Bethlehem	11-3
Pottstown	6-8
Coatesville	6-8
Easton	5-9
Pottsville	2-12
Doylestown	1-13

Team Rosters

Allentown: Coach J. Birney Crum, Alvin Blankowitsch, Billy Boyle, John Burian, Lee Coker, Paul Grim, Jim Hauze, Charles Kemmerer, Dan McFadden, John McFadden, Charles "Bobby" Meyer, Lloyd Moyer, Nevin Nonnemacher, Bernard Schwartz, Morton Sher, Marwood Stark, Harry Weber, Ken Wildonger, Young.

Bethlehem: Coach Bill Emrey, Joe Borda, Max Connor, Tom Garihan, Bernard Glazier, Anthony Grebnar, Harry Greenberg, Horace Hawkey, Robert "Booby" Long, Lew Ochenhouse, Steve Polgar, Harvey Serfass, Bob Taylor, Van Kuren, Jacob White.

Coatesville: Coach Atwell, Henry Cannon, George Hicks, Bob McNelly, Albert Morgan, Garnet Poff, "Dutch" Patton, Bill Roper, "Reds" Slider, Duie Smith, Howard Steen, Walter Stoneback, "Gus" Toomey.

Doylestown: Coach Bill Wolfe, Henry Barrett, Campbell, Gerlach, Martin, Millard Robinson, Rogers, Carl Seiz, Jim Slaughter, Slush, Albert Sulak, George Waddington.

Easton: Coach Clyde Notestine, Irving Bergstein, Harrison Fisher, Wilbur Fuehrer, Ben Gadwell, Hubert Gallagher, Parnell Lewis, George Purdy, Joseph Schmuk, William Warner, Ray Williams, Ralph Williamson, Harry Youngkin.

Hazleton: Coach Hugh McGeehan, Albert "Otto" Audikimow, Walter Baker, Ken Bommer, Ralph Crocamo, Mauro Forte, Woody Gerhardt, Mike Laputka, Joe Lotito, Hal Lewis, Jim Malkames, Harry Schaller, Ken Stecker, Louis "Gigi" Tarone, Charles Woodring.

Pottstown: Coach Carroll Bechtel, Bolognese, Michael Dezura, Grove, Harry Grubb, Charles "Chitty" Guss, Hetrick, Leh, Moody, Pennypacker, Richard Ricketts, Hal Royer, Scheffey, Shellhammer, Vasil, R. Warner.

Pottsville: Coach Ross Hufford, Robert Cole, Wang Devitt, Robert Dietrich, Bill Dimmerling, Harold Freeze, Charles "Tabby" Howell, Eddie Mader, Francis "Moose: McCormick, Ed Merrick, John Moody, Leroy Shellhammer, Les Sherry.

Allentown High School – 1931 League Champions[33]

1932

League Realignment

The new season brought significant changes to the six-year-old league with a new member and several old members gone. Both Pottstown and Coatesville, league charter members, withdrew after six years in the league. Doylestown, after four years in the league, also withdrew and joined the Bux-Mont Basketball League. Coatesville indicated that their decision was based on the lengthy distance from other league members. Doylestown left because of the cost of travel and the high level of competition which made it hard to compete successfully. Pottstown did not give a reason for its decision to withdraw. Coatesville and Pottstown both joined the Philadelphia Suburban League. East Stroudsburg, who had applied to get into the league the previous season, was finally granted admission. These changes left the league with six members and a reduced ten game schedule.

League president David Atwell, from Coatesville, resigned from the office with Coatesville's exit from the league. The league members elected William Emrey, Bethlehem coach, as league president, Charles Richards, faculty manager at Easton, as elected vice-president, and Edgar Rabenold, Allentown, as secretary.[1]

Week 1

East Stroudsburg 29 Easton 15: East Stroudsburg gave notice that they would be a formidable force within the league in its opener at Easton. Leading 13-8 at halftime, they easily took care of a veteran Easton team. An odd occurence during the game, East Stroudsburg's center Pete Peckman accidently put a ball into Easton's basket.

Leading scorers: East Stroudsburg – Tommy Sommers 13; Easton – Wilbur Fuehrer 6.

Hazleton 20 Allentown 15: More than 2000 fans jammed Allentown's gymnasium only to see their favorites lose to Hazleton. In a tough, low-scoring game, Allentown lost its starting guard John McFadden when he fouled out of the game in the first period. Hazleton led at the half 8-6.

Leading scorers: Hazleton – Ralph Crocamo 10; Allentown – Sam Becker 4.[2]

Bethlehem 23 Pottsville 20 OT: Visiting Pottsville extended Bethlehem into an extra period before losing. Bethlehem led at the end of the half 8-7.

Leading scorers: Bethlehem – Lenny Jaeger 10; Pottsville – Bill Dimmerling 7.[3]

Week 2

East Stroudsburg 26 Bethlehem 13: East Stroudsburg, on their home court, continued to send shock waves through the league with another surprise victory over Bethlehem. The Cavaliers led 14-8 at halftime. After two weeks of play, East Stroudsburg, the only undefeated team, had sole possession of first place.

Leading scorers: East Stroudsburg – Tommy Sommers 14; Bethlehem – Eddie Moyer 13.

Easton 31 Hazleton 30: Easton's Red Rovers went into Hazleton and pulled out a surprising win. Samuel "Specks" Cornetto came off the bench and sank two field goals, with the last one being in the air when the buzzer sounded, to pull out the win as time ran out. After leading 17-12, Easton scored the only three points of the third quarter.

Leading scorers: Easton – Wilbur Fuehrer 11; Hazleton – Ralph Crocamo 14.[4]

Allentown 22 Pottsville 12: Allentown evened its record at 1-1 at Pottsville. Allentown led 4-0 to start the game and 13-4 at the half in a game they led the whole way.

Leading scorers: Allentown - Sammy Becker 11; Pottsville – Bob Cole 9.[5]

Week 3

Hazleton 28 East Stroudsburg 22: East Stroudsburg went on the road to Hazleton and suffered its first defeat. The score was close (7-7 at the end of the 1st quarter and 15-13 Hazleton at halftime) until the 3rd quarter when Hazleton took a 24-14 lead. East Stroudsburg came back in the 4th quarter outscoring their opponents 8-4, but could not overcome the big lead.

Leading scorers: Hazleton – Ralph Crocamo 11; Stroudsburg – Bill Kupizewski 8.[6]

Bethlehem 24 Allentown 18: In Allentown, Bill Emrey's Liberty boys took a lead at halftime 12-9. They scored the first six points in the third quarter to take a "so-called" commanding lead only to have Canaries score the next 9 points to knot the score. That was it for Allentown as Bethlehem scored the last six points to win.

Leading scorers: Bethlehem – Bobby Taylor 9; Allentown – Sam Becker 5, Lee Coker 5.

Easton 48 Pottsville 23: Easton took a nineteen-point lead at halftime 30-11 and kept Pottsville winless.

Leading scorers: Easton – Irving Bergstein 15, Wilbur Fuehrer 14, Harry Youngkin 11; Pottsville– Robert Crowe 8.[7]

Week 4

Allentown 25 East Stroudsburg 19: East Stroudsburg lost its second consecutive game as Allentown bumped them out of a tie for the league lead. Kenny Wildonger held East Stroudsburg's high-scoring center Pete Peckman to a single point. The Canaries took an 18-11 lead at the half and the Cavaliers cut it to 22-17 after three quarters.

Leading scorers: Allentown – Neil Boyle 10, Ken Wildonger 9; East Stroudsburg – Tommy Sommers 8.

Bethlehem 26 Easton 21: Meanwhile, Bethlehem tripped up Easton in front of 3000 fans in the Liberty gym. After Bethlehem led 14-9 at the half, Easton tied the score at 18-18 in the third period before the Hurricane forged ahead.

Leading scorers: Bethlehem - Bobby Taylor 9; Easton - Ralph Williamson 8.

Hazleton 32 Pottsville 14: Hazleton kept pace with Bethlehem to remain in a two-way tie for first with and easy win at Pottsville.

Leading scorers: Hazleton –Louis Tarone 10, Mike Laputka 10; Pottsville–Ed Merrick 4, Dean Stevenson 4.

Week 5

East Stroudsburg 25 Pottsville 24: Pottsville hoped to win its first game and run East Stroudsburg's losing streak to three. Pottsville took a 10-5 lead after a quarter, but East Stroudsburg took charge in the second quarter to lead at the half 14-11.

Leading scorers: East Stroudsburg – Tommy Sommers 15; Pottsville - Bill Dimmerling 10.

Hazleton 25 Bethlehem 20: On their home court, Hazleton took sole possession of first place with its win over Bethlehem. Hazleton led from start to finish and led at halftime 12-5. Hazleton had a balanced attack with six players in the scoring column.

Leading scorers: Hazleton – Mike Laputka 7; Bethlehem – Bobby Taylor 10.

Allentown 23 Easton 20: Allentown moved into a three-way tie for second with East Stroudsburg and Bethlehem by handing Easton a loss. It marked the 13th consecutive victory for the Canaries over the Red Rovers. The rowdy Easton crowd lustily booed Allentown's players on foul shots to the point that the officials called two technical fouls on Easton. Easton lost the game on the foul line converting only 6 of 23 free throws.

Leading scorers: Allentown - Neil Boyle 8, Sam Becker 8; Easton – Harry Youngkin 5, Wilbur Fuehrer 5.[9]

Week 6

East Stroudsburg 43 Easton 17: East Stroudsburg regained its early season form with a shellacking of Easton. Easton, the visiting team, did not score a field goal in the first half, but did score on 10 foul shots. They only managed two field goals in the second half.

Leading scorers: East Stroudsburg - Tommy Sommers 18; Easton – Wilbur Fuehrer 4, Roland Henning 4.

Bethlehem 17 Pottsville 15: At home, Pottsville continued to fight to gain its first victory and led 10-2 at halftime over Bethlehem. However, Bill Emrey's Liberty boys outscored Pottsville 15-5 in the second half to win the game. Bethlehem had been held without a field goal and only two foul shots in the first half.

Leading scorers: Bethlehem – Eddie Moyer 8; Pottsville – Ed Merrick 10.

Hazleton 23 Allentown 20: Despite leading 11-6 at the first quarter and 16-13 at halftime, Allentown lost at Hazleton. The score was tied several times in the second half before Hazleton finally went ahead 21-19.

Leading scorers: Hazleton - Jim Malkames 8; Allentown - Neil Boyle 8.[10]

Week 7

Hazleton 32 Easton 21: Hazleton continued its run to the league title in front of a crowd of 2500 fans at Easton's Lafayette College gym. After Hazleton led 6-4 and 11-9 after the first two quarters, Easton briefly jumped ahead 14-11 early in the third quarter. Hazleton scored the next 11 points to lead after three quarters 22-14.

Leading scorers: Hazleton – Louis "Giggy" Tarone 19; Easton – Wilbur Fuehrer 12.

Allentown 24 Pottsville 14: Allentown ran Pottsville's losing streak to seven with its win at home. With the halftime score at 21-9, only a total of 8 points were scored in the second half by both teams. Pottsville lost two players to injury in the second half when forward Bobby Cole suffered a severely sprained ankle and Clarence Freeze received a cut above his eye.

Leading scorers: Allentown – Neil Boyle 11; Pottsville – Bob Cole 5.

Bethlehem 33 East Stroudsburg 23: In Bethlehem, the teams ended the first half in a 12-12 tie. East Stroudsburg briefly took the lead in the third quarter, but Bethlehem forged ahead in the 4th quarter win the game. Late in the 4th quarter, police had to be called in to prevent a small-sized riot. Bethlehem's Eddie Moyer held East Stroudsburg's Tommy Sommer scoreless in the contest.

Leading scorers: Bethlehem – Anthony Grebnar 14; East Stroudsburg – Robert Devore 9, "Pete" Peckman 9.[11]

Week 8

Hazleton 28 East Stroudsburg 20: At East Stroudsburg with Hazleton leading by two points at the end of the third quarter 18-16, the Mountaineers took charge in the fourth quarter to win. Ralph Crocamo, Ken Stecker, Louis Terone, and Frank Appichella scored 26 of Hazleton's 28 points. Coach McGeehan had East Stroudsburg's Tommy Sommers closely guarded which resulted in numerous fouls. Seven of Sommers' nine points were free throws.

Leading scorers: Hazleton – Ralph Crocamo 8; East Stroudsburg – Tommy Sommers 9.[12]

Bethlehem 25 Allentown 18: Twenty-four hundred fans jammed the Liberty gym on Tuesday night to see the rivalry matchup between Allentown and Bethlehem. Allentown came on with a rush early and took a 15-8 lead into the locker room at halftime. Coach Emrey had his boys change from their red and blue jerseys to red and white for the second half. Allentown still led at the end of the 3rd quarter 16-13. Bethlehem outscored the Canaries 12-2 in the final quarter. The win kept them on the heels of Hazleton for the league title. All six players for Bethlehem scored, while Allentown felt the loss of star Neil Boyle who had severely sprained his wrist in practice the day before.

Leading scorers: Bethlehem – Bobby Long 9; Allentown – John Burian 7.[13]

Easton 28 Pottsville 21: At Pottsville, Easton kept Pottsville winless at 0-8.

Leading scorers: Easton – Wilbur Fuehrer 14, Irving Bergstein 10; Pottsville – Bill Dimmerling 9.[14]

Week 9

East Stroudsburg 21 Allentown 13: On Friday night, Allentown, riddled by injuries, continued its late season skid with a loss at East Stroudsburg. Wilbur Gilbert scored the only field goal in the game for the Canaries with the rest of the points on free throws. The Cavaliers led 8-1 after the first period.

Leading scorers: East Stroudsburg – Pete Peckman 7: Allentown – Wilbur Gilbert 8.

Hazleton 38 Pottsville 18: Hazleton kept its league lead with a win over lowly Pottsville and could secure the title with a final game victory over Bethlehem. After Pottsville led 11-5, Hazleton went on a 16-4 to take the lead.

Leading scorers: Hazleton - Ralph Crocamo 17; Pottsville - Bill Dimmerling 10.[15]

Bethlehem 23 Easton 21 2OT: Bethlehem struggled mightily against Easton before the showdown with Hazleton. The Liberty gang needed two extra periods to eke out the win over the Red Rovers. Bethlehem's Walter Lukevics goal with 10 seconds remaining broke the tie. A last second successful shot by Sol Bergstein to tie the game for Easton was ruled after the buzzer and Bethlehem hung on. Easton only made one of ten free throws while Bethlehem only made 3 of 14.

Leading scorers: Bethlehem – Bobby Taylor 10; Easton - Wilbur Fuehrer 9.[16]

Week 10

Hazleton 30 Bethlehem 29 OT: In a see-saw battle at Bethlehem which saw the game tied 11 times with 7 lead changes, Hazleton secured the title in an overtime win. The game attracted five times as many fans as the Liberty gym could hold, according to newspaper reports. With 30 seconds to go in regulation, Hazleton's Jim Malkames tied the score at 26 all with his field goal. Neither team scored until halfway through the extra period. With 30 seconds to go, the Liberty boys led 29-28. Three times Bethlehem tipped the ball out of bounds on the inbound pass under the Bethlehem bucket. Finally, forward Hal Lewis got the inbound pass dribbled down court and made the winning field goal with seconds remaining.

Leading scorers: Hazleton – Ralph Crocamo 11; Bethlehem – Bobby Taylor 16.

East Stroudsburg 38 Pottsville 15: East Stroudsburg finished its season by keeping Pottsville winless in the league with a win in Pottsville and finished in 3rd place in its inaugural season in the league.

Leading scorers: East Stroudsburg –Tommy Sommers 14, Pete Peckman 11; Pottsville –Bill Dimmerling 7.[17]

Allentown 27 Easton 25: Allentown ended its skid and evened its record at 5-5 with win at Easton. After the Canaries led at the half 14-7, the Red Rovers rallied to pull within one in the third quarter 18-17.

Leading scorers: Allentown – Sam Becker 10; Easton – Irving Bergstein 9.[18]

Postseason Play

After the 1931 season, District 1 was split and a new district was formed for the teams to the north of the Philadelphia area. District 11 was formed from teams in the Lehigh Valley and north.

Hazleton 31 Wilson Boro 19: Hazleton's first playoff game took place in Bethlehem against the winners of the Two-County League, Wilson Boro. The Two County League (also called the Lehigh-Northampton County League) was organized in 1930 and included, in addition to Bangor, Coplay, Pen Argyl, Nazareth, Bangor, and South Whitehall. Despite falling behind 5-0 at the outset, Hazleton scored the next eight points and were never headed. Coach McGeehan used nine players in the win.

Leading scorers: Hazleton – Ralph Crocamo 9; Wilson Boro - Storms 11.[19]

Summit Hill 28 Hazleton 20: In their second-round playoff at Allentown's gymnasium, the Mountaineers took on Summit Hill, champions of the Carbon Schuylkill League. Hazleton fell behind early, trailing at the half 17-9 and Coach Turk Gerber's Summit Hill team outclassed the Mountaineers to end their season.

Leading scorers: Summit Hill – Tommy Hiza 10; Hazleton – Louis Tarone 7.[20]

Postseason Accolades

Scoring Leaders: The season was a low scoring one for all the teams. Hazleton, as league champs, averaged only 29.5 points per game. Pottsville, who failed to win a game, averaged only 17.4 points per game. When the league's leading scorers were compiled, the statistics were unimpressive. East Stroudsburg's captain Tommy Sommers and Ralph Crocamo, Hazleton, tied for league honors at 116 points in 10 games for a 11.6 point per game average. Third leading scorer was Easton's center Bill Fuehrer with an 8.6 average. Bobby Taylor of Bethlehem averaged 8.4 points to finish fourth in league scoring.[21]

All-Stars: Birney Crum, Hughie McGeehan, and Pottsville sportswriter Walter Farquhar decided to select their league all-stars and, of course, didn't agree.

Crum selected forwards, Bobby Taylor, Bethlehem; Tommy Sommers, East Stroudsburg; center Bill Fuehrer, Easton; guards, Ralph Crocamo, Hazleton; and his own John McFadden.[22]

McGeehan, Hazleton's outstanding coach, selected forward Bobby Taylor, guard Eddie Moyer from Bethlehem, and his own center "Giggy" Tarone, forward Ralph Crocamo, and guard Jimmy Malkames.[23]

Farquhar selected forwards Tommy Sommers, Ralph Crocamo, and Bobby Taylor, center Wilbur Fuehrer, and guards Louis Tarone, Irving "Sol" Bergstein from Easton, and Bill Dimmerling from Pottsville. At the guard and forward positions, Farquhar selected three each since he could not decide on only two at the position.[24]

The league officially announced its all-star selections later in April. Forwards included Ralph Crocamo, Tommy Sommers, Bobby Taylor, and John Burian, Allentown. The guards were Bill Dimmerling, Irving

"Sol" Bergstein, Eddie Moyer, and Bill Kupizewski, East Stroudsburg. Louis Tarone, Pete Peckman, East Stroudsburg, and Fuehrer were the centers.[25]

Final Standings

Hazleton	9-1
Bethlehem	7-3
East Stroudsburg	6-4
Allentown	5-5
Easton	3-7
Pottsville	0-10

Team Rosters

Allentown: Coach J. Birney Crum, Sam Becker, Neil Boyle, John Burian, Lee Coker, Dick Dewalt, Robert Egan, Wally Forbes, Wilbur Gilbert, Eugene Grossman, Jack McCarthy, John McFadden, Nevin "Whitey" Nonemacher, Irving Perkins, Don Reber, Senger, Serfass, Joseph Milo Sewards, Morton Sher, Ken "Toots" Wildonger.

Bethlehem: Coach William Emrey, Tom Garihan, Anthony Grebnar, Harry Greenberg, Lenny Jaeger, Bobby Long, Walter Lukeivics, Eddie Moyer, Louie Ochenhouse, Steve Polgar, Steve Superka, Bob Taylor, Jacob White.

Easton: Coach Clyde Nothstine, Irving "Sol" Bergstein, Frank Chisesi, Samuel Corneto, James Eakin, Bill Fuehrer, Fisher, William Griffith, Roland Henning, Leroy Knerr, John McIntyre, Ralph "Lefty" Williamson, Harry Youngkin.

East Stroudsburg: Coach Earl Mosier, William Bair, Ed Blewitt, Louis Carmella, Robert Devore, Harice, Edward Harlowe, John Kunkle, Bill Kupizewski, Jack Lantz, Morris "Pete" Peckman, Samuel Puzzio, Tommy Sommers, Robert Smith, Harold Strunk, Eugene Wilson, Albert Zateeny.

Hazleton: Coach Hugh McGeehan, Frank Appichella, Iggy Castura, Warren Cooper, Ralph Crocamo, Pasco "Patsy" DeVecca, Hugh Ferry, Mauro Forte, Mike Laputka, Hal Lewis, Joe Lotito, Jim Malkames, Bobby Pash, "Soup" Santipoli, Harry Schaller, Ken Stecker, Pete Suitch, Louis "Gigi" Tarone, Charles Woodring.

Pottsville: Coach Howard Flack, Leonard Altshuler, Buchinsky, Bob Cole, Conrad, Robert Crowe, Robert Dietrich, Bill Dimmerling, Clarence Freeze, H. Freeze, "Peanuts" McCormick, Ed Merrick, Saul Rosenzweig, Dean Stevenson, Harry Wolfe.

Hazleton High School – 1932 League Champions[26]

Front Row: Pasco DeVecca, Joe Letito

Middle Row: Charles Woodring, Harry Schaller, Mike Laputka, Louis Tarone, Morrow Forte, Ralph Crocamo, Hal Lewis, Jim Malkames

Back Row: Pete Suitch, Bobby Pash, Frank Appichella, T. Turse (student mgr), Warren Cooper, Hugh Ferry, Ken Stecker

1933

Expansion to Eight Teams

At the league meeting on April 1, 1932, the Eastern Pennsylvania Interscholastic Basketball League expanded back to eight teams with the addition of Mahanoy City, the 1932 Anthracite League champions, and Tamaqua. Mahanoy City, coached by John Goepfert for the 15th year, won seven Anthracite League titles and the State Championship twice in the period.

At the same meeting, William Emrey, Bethlehem's basketball coach, was re-elected league president. The principal of Hazleton High School W. G. Davis was elected vice president. E. A. Rabenold, Allentown High School was re-elected as secretary-treasurer. The league also went on record as frowning upon the release of league scoring leaders for fear that it would break up teamwork.[1]

Although no protest was raised at the league meeting, reports surfaced from Hazleton that the Mountaineers were considering resigning from the league due to the acceptance of Mahanoy City into the league. The two schools and the communities were bitter rivals in all sports. Hazleton's bid into the newly organized Northeast Basketball League was rejected along with a similar application from Berwick. The league already had eight formidable members and chose not to add any other applicants. Hazleton had broken off all competition with Mahanoy City after Hazleton defeated Mahanoy City in Bethlehem before a frenzied crowd.[2] The resignation did not occur.

Local officials also raised a concern about two rule changes adopted by national basketball rules committee at a meeting in April. The committee voted to adopt the two new rules to speed up the game. The first change was the requirement for the basketball to be brought across the center court line within 10 seconds after in-bounding the basketball. The second was that a player standing around the free throw line or in the circle with his back towards the basket would have to pass the ball within three seconds.[3] Special meetings were held with local officials to review the rules changes.

John Goepfert's Mahanoy City squad entered the league as a huge favorite to win the regular season title with its strong nucleus of returning players. Several new coaches entered the league. Hugh Hoke, former Gettysburg College star, took over Tamaqua as he succeeded Mooney Welker as the Tams head coach. George Dimmerling, who starred at Pottsville and played at Lafayette College, was hired as a teacher and the new coach at his alma mater, replacing Howard Flack who resigned. Other continuing coaches included Howard Mosier at East Stroudsburg, Bill Emrey at Bethlehem, Hugh McGeehan at Hazleton, Birney Crum at Allentown, and Clyde Notestine at Easton.[4]

Week 1

Mahanoy City 33 Allentown 26: As expected, Mahanoy City, on its home court at Lakewood Park on a bitter cold night, got off to a fast start with a win in their opener over Allentown. The 900 fans in attendance shivered through the four periods of the game because the heating system at the pavilion had failed. After a 7-7 first quarter tie, Allentown was outplayed 12-3 in the second period.

Leading scorers: Mahanoy City – Malcolm Richards 10; Allentown – Harlan Becker 10, Lee Coker 10.

East Stroudsburg 18 Easton 17: Easton lost a heartbreaker on its home court. Easton had thought it pulled out the game with 10 seconds to play when their center Henning converted a field goal only to have it ruled that it did not count since East Stroudsburg had fouled him prior to the shot. East Stroudsburg's captain protested vehemently and received a technical foul. Henning was awarded two free throws, but missed them both and the game was lost.

Leading scorers: East Stroudsburg – Robert Devore 5, John Puzio 5; Easton – Roland Henning 8.[5]

Hazleton 44 Pottsville 20: After losing all ten games during the 1932 season, Pottsville continued its losing ways in Hazleton.

Leading scorers: Hazleton – Charley Brogan 13, Frank Apichella 12; Pottsville – Clyde Spitzner 6.

Bethlehem 30 Tamaqua 19: Tamaqua lost its first league contest.

Leading scorers: Bethlehem – Walter Lukevics 14; Tamaqua – Joe Heisler 11.[6]

Week 2

Mahanoy City 30 Bethlehem 19: Playing its second straight home game to open league play, Mahanoy City sank 16 of 21 foul shots to hand Bethlehem the loss.

Leading scorers: Mahanoy City – Malcolm "Red" Richards 11; Bethlehem – Steve Polgar 6.

Hazleton 31 Tamaqua 25: Coach McGeehan's well-balanced attack, with six players contributing to the scoring, defeated Tamaqua despite trailing at halftime 13-10.

Leading scorers: Hazleton – Frank Apichella 7, Ken Stecker 7; Tamaqua – John Sweeney 10.

Pottsville 28 Easton 17: Pottsville won their first league game since the 1931 season when they surprised Easton on their home court. Easton converted only 5 of 20 foul shots in the game.

Leading scorers: Pottsville – Clyde Spitzner 13; Easton – Bill Barnhart 6.

East Stroudsburg 27 Allentown 26: In East Stroudsburg, Allentown suffered its second consecutive loss despite holding a 17-9 halftime lead.

Leading scorers: East Stroudsburg – John Puzio 12; Allentown – Neil Boyle 12.[7]

Week 3

Mahanoy City 57 Tamaqua 27: Coach John Goepfert's Mahanoy City Maroons continued their early season run through the league. The Maroons second team played most of the second half. No box score,

Allentown 44 Easton 21: The home court found favor with Allentown as the Canaries broke into the win column by crushing Easton. Leading 10-1 after the first period, the Canaries onslaught was led by Wally Forbes, Allentown's Jack McCarthy was banished from the game early in the first quarter for taking a swing at Easton's Russ Servin.

Leading scorers: Allentown – Wally Forbes 21; Easton – Joe Alfero 4, Russ Servin 4, John McIntyre 4.

East Stroudsburg 31 Pottsville 26: Trailing Pottsville 22-20 after three quarters, East Stroudsburg rallied in the fourth quarter to defeat Pottsville and keep pace with Mahanoy City at 3-0.

Leading scorers: East Stroudsburg – John Puzio 10; Pottsville - Clyde Spitzner 10.

Bethlehem 29 Hazleton 27: Bethlehem led at the ends of the first and second periods only to have Hazleton take a lead in the third quarter. Bethlehem came back to tie the game at the end of the quarter. Bethlehem's Walt Lukevicz made a clutch field goal near the end of the game to seal the upset. Four players fouled out of the game including Hazleton's Apichella and Koke and Bethlehem's Croll and Polgar.

Leading scorers: Bethlehem – Walter Lukevicz 10; Hazleton – Charley Brogan 5, Frank Apichella 5, Mike Laputka 5.[8]

Week 4

Tamaqua 29 East Stroudsburg 28: Tamaqua provided the surprise upset of the season so far with its victory in East Stroudsburg. Having won two of their first three games by a point, East Stroudsburg lost this time by a single point despite holding a 20-13 halftime lead.

Leading scorers: Tamaqua – John Sweeney 17; East Stroudsburg – Harold Fusselman 11.

Mahanoy City 43 Hazleton 26: Undefeated Mahanoy City stood alone at the top of the league with a decisive triumph over homestanding Hazleton. It was Hazleton's worst home defeat in recent years.

Leading scorers: Mahanoy City – John Kutz 21, Malcolm Richards 14; Hazleton – Hugh Ferry 7.

Allentown 35 Pottsville 25: Trailing 18-12 at the half, Allentown rallied to pull out the win. The Canaries' third quarter performance, when they outscored Pottsville 15-2, propelled them to victory.

Leading scorers: Allentown – Wally Forbes 16; Pottsville – Matt Whitaker 8.

Bethlehem 29 Easton 13: Easton did not score in the second quarter and trailed 14-5 at halftime.

Leading scorers: Bethlehem – Walter Lukevics 13; Easton – Roland Henning 7.[9]

Week 5

Allentown 34 Hazleton 30: In front of 1200 fans in Hazleton, Allentown dropped Hazleton to 2-3. Despite being outscored from the field 13 to 11, Allentown won the game at the charity stripe by making 12 of 16 attempts to Hazleton's 4 of 11. Wally Forbes made 9 of 10 foul shots.

Leading scorers: Allentown – Wally Forbes 15; Hazleton – Hugh Ferry 12.

Mahanoy City 34 Pottsville 17: With an easy win, Coach Goepfert emptied his bench as 13 players made it into the contest.

Leading scorers: Mahanoy City – Malcolm Richards 18, John Kutz 11; Pottsville – Matt Whitaker 7.

Tamaqua 33 Easton 18: Easton scored only 2 points to Tamaqua's 14 in the third period.

Leading scorers: Tamaqua – Nelson Bassler 10; Easton – Roland Henning 6.

Bethlehem 41 East Stroudsburg 21: East Stroudsburg suffered its second straight loss despite leading 9-2 in the first quarter.

Leading scorers: Bethlehem – Steve Polgar 21; East Stroudsburg – Nelson Bassler 10.[10]

Week 6

Mahanoy City 54 East Stroudsburg 25: After winning three-straight to open league play, East Stroudsburg dropped its third straight to Mahanoy City, who had three players in double figures.

Leading scorers: Mahanoy City – John Kutz 19, Malcolm Richards 17, John Gabuzda 11; East Stroudsburg – Bill Kupiezewski 6, Edward Harlowe 6.

Allentown 36 Tamaqua 14: Allentown rolled to its fourth straight win to tie Bethlehem for second place.

Leading scorers: Allentown – Wally Forbes 10, Wilbur Gilbert 10; Tamaqua – Joe Heisler 5.

Pottsville 22 Bethlehem 19: In Pottsville's new gym, Bethlehem lost the game at the foul line making only 3 of 13 free throws.

Leading scorers: Pottsville – Matt Whitaker 8; Bethlehem – Walter Lukevics 7.[11]

Hazleton 33 Easton 22: After being benched during the game at Allentown the previous week, Hazleton guard Kenny Stecker handed in his uniform and left the team. He was replaced by Charley Brogan.

Leading scorers: Hazleton – Joe Lotito 12; Easton – Roland Henning 7, Russ Servin 7.[12]

Week 7

Mahanoy City 55 Easton 15: Mahanoy City kept its record perfect with their seventh straight win as they handed Easton their seventh straight defeat and remain winless in the league.

Leading scorers: Mahanoy City–Steve Hydock 15, John Kutz 14; Easton–Edwin Folk 3, Richard Bishop 3.[13]

Hazleton 52 East Stroudsburg 32: Hazleton outscored East Stroudsburg 31 -12 in the first and last quarters to hand them their fourth straight loss.

Leading scorers: Hazleton – Frank Apichella 24; East Stroudsburg – John Puzio 9.[14]

Pottsville 36 Tamaqua 31: Pottsville took a 17-14 halftime lead on their way to the victory.

Leading scorers: Pottsville – Matt Whitaker 16; Tamaqua – John Sweeney 10.

Allentown 37 Bethlehem 32: In the key matchup of the week at the Liberty High School gym, Allentown won despite one less field goal than Bethlehem, 13 to 14. Allentown made 11 of 13 foul shots to Bethlehem's 4 of 14.

Leading scorers: Allentown – John Burian 14; Bethlehem – Steve Polgar – 12.[15]

Week 8

Allentown 31 Mahanoy City 22: With the start of the second half of the season, Allentown remained on a tear winning its 6th consecutive game to avenge the season opening loss in front of 2500 frenzied fans at the Allentown High School gym. Lines began to form at 4 pm as twice as many fans appeared as could get into the gym. After a call to police headquarters, eight additional city police were dispatched to the gym in an attempt to maintain control. After two minutes of play, Mahanoy City jumped out to a 6-2 lead, Coach Crum made a lineup change sending in a taller Wilbur Gilbert to replace a smaller good-shooting Earl Repp. The strategy worked for the remainder of the game as Allentown finally took the lead in the third quarter 19-17.

Leading scorers: Allentown – Wilbur Gilbert 10; Mahanoy City – Malcolm Richards 12.

Bethlehem 40 Tamaqua 19: At Tamaqua, Bethlehem took a 17-9 halftime lead and led the entire game.

Leading scorers: Bethlehem – Arpad Kery 12; Tamaqua – John Sweeney 5, Ray Pfeil 5.

East Stroudsburg 48 Easton 18: On their home court, East Stroudsburg broke their losing streak while extending Easton's to eight straight. East Stroudsburg led the whole game and held a 24-11 halftime lead.

Leading scorers: East Stroudsburg – John Puzio 23; Easton – Roland Henning 7.[16]

Hazleton 28 Pottsville 24 OT: Pottsville, in their spacious new gym, provided Hazleton with a scare as they extended the Mountaineers into an extra period. With the score tied at 24 in regulation, Charley Brogan, who took over a starting guard position when Stecker left the team, scored his only two field goals in overtime for the win.

Leading scorers: Hazleton – Frank Apichella 8; Joe Lotito 8; Pottsville – Matt Whitaker 10.[17]

Week 9

Bethlehem 35 Mahanoy City 26: After winning seven straight games to open the league season, Mahanoy City found themselves in a two-game losing streak. In Bethlehem, the Liberty boys shocked the Maroons in front of 2100 fans. Arpad Kery, just promoted to the varsity, led the Bethlehem attack. Mahanoy City led 13-12 during the second quarter, but Bethlehem scored eight straight points to take the lead for good.

Leading scorers: Bethlehem – Arpad Kery 11, Steve Polgar 10; Mahanoy City – Malcolm Richards 10.

Hazleton 33 Tamaqua 24: Guard Charley Brogan continued his outstanding play as Hazleton led from start to finish,

Leading scorers: Hazleton – Charley Brogan 14; Tamaqua – Joe Heisler 11.

Allentown 43 East Stroudsburg 23: Winning their seventh game in a row with 2000 fans in attendance, Allentown moved into a tie for first place with Mahanoy City. Coach Crum played the second team during the entire fourth quarter. Seven players scored in the victory.

Leading scorers: Allentown – Wally Forbes 19; East Stroudsburg – Bill Kupiezewski 9.[18]

Pottsville 34 Easton 8: In their new gym, Pottsville pummeled the Red Rovers. Easton only had two field goals, both in the first quarter by Roland Henning, and only scored on three foul shots in the second half.

Leading scorers: Pottsville - Clyde Spitzner 10; Easton – Roland Henning 4.[19]

Week 10

Mahanoy City 48 Tamaqua 20: Back on the winning track, Mahanoy City took a 10-0 lead to begin the game.

Leading scorers: Mahanoy City – John Kutz 21, Malcolm Richards 16; Tamaqua – Nelson Bassler 7.

Allentown 28 Easton 14: Allentown led 9-1 after a quarter and increased it to 15-4 at halftime.

Leading scorers: Allentown – Lee Coker 8; Easton – Roland Henning 7.

Bethlehem 30 Hazleton 22: With a 6-0 lead to start the game, Bethlehem ended Hazleton's 4-game win streak.

Leading scorers: Bethlehem – Lenny Jaeger 15; Hazleton – Joe Lotito 11.

East Stroudsburg 38 Pottsville 28: East Stroudsburg only led 25-22 at the half, but took charge of the game in the second half.

Leading scorers: East Stroudsburg–Bill Kupiezewski 12, Harold Fusselman 10; Pottsville–Matt Whitaker 7.[20]

Week 11

Mahanoy City 26 Hazleton 16: With both teams making only five field goals, Mahanoy City scored 16 points on free throws for the win.

Leading scorers: Mahanoy City – John Kutz 15; Hazleton – Frank Apichella 5.

Allentown 35 Pottsville 27: Pottsville led 2-0 and 5-4 before the Canaries charged ahead for good 9-5.

Leading scorers: Allentown – Wally Forbes 16; Pottsville – Matt Whitaker 9.

Bethlehem 37 Easton 21: After taking a 19-11 halftime lead, Bethlehem continued Easton's season-long losing streak.

Leading scorers: Bethlehem – Walter Lukevics 13; Easton – John McIntyre 7.

Tamaqua 27 East Stroudsburg 26: Tamaqua won a nailbiter for their third win on the season. No box score

Week 12

Mahanoy City 31 Pottsville 25: Pottsville led early 5-0 before Mahanoy City responded to take the lead for good 8-7 and remain tied with Allentown for first place.

Leading scorers: Mahanoy City – Malcolm Forbes 13, John Kutz 10; Pottsville – Matt Whitaker 13.

Bethlehem 42 East Stroudsburg 29: Although they led 21-18, East Stroudsburg could not keep up with Bethlehem during the second half.

Leading scorers: Bethlehem – Arpad Kery 12, Steve Polgar 10; East Stroudsburg – John Kunkle 9.

Tamaqua 33 Easton 16: Tamaqua handed Easton its 12th consecutive loss, assuring the Red Rovers last place.

Leading scorers: Tamaqua – Nelson Bassler 9, John Sweeney 9; Easton – Ben Griffin 4.

Allentown 43 Hazleton 27: The Canaries raced out to an 8-1 lead at the end of the first quarter and Allentown handed Hazleton a 3rd straight loss. Lee Coker received a standing ovation for several minutes from the fans for his play when Coach Crum took him out of the game.

Leading scorers: Allentown – Lee Coker 13, Wally Forbes 11, Robert Hellerich 10; Hazleton – Robert Yevak 12.[23]

Week 13

Allentown 24 Tamaqua 15: Despite making only 10 of 26 foul shots, Allentown won the game with all six players for the Canaries scoring with no player totaling more than five points.

Leading scorers: Allentown – Lee Coker 5, Wally Forbes 5; Tamaqua – Joe Heisler 7.

Mahanoy City 48 East Stroudsburg 25: Leading at the half 28-11, Mahanoy City handed East Stroudsburg their third loss in a row.

Leading scorers: Mahanoy City – John Kutz 17, Malcolm Richards 12, John Gabuzda 10; East Stroudsburg – John Kunkle 8.

Hazleton 31 Easton 11: Hazleton snapped its losing streak after taking a 17-5 halftime lead.

Leading scorers: Hazleton – Frank Apichella 12; Easton – Frank Bishop 4.

Bethlehem 55 Pottsville 30: Leading 27-7 at halftime, Bethlehem still held hopes for a league title with the win.

Leading scorers: Bethlehem – Lenny Jaeger 17, Walter Lukevics 15, Steve Polgar 13; Pottsville – Clyde Spitzner 10.[24]

Week 14

Mahanoy City 34 Easton 14: Mahanoy City handed the Red Rovers their 14th straight league loss.

Leading scorers: Mahanoy City – Joe Salvadore 13, Malcolm Richards 10; Easton – Roland Henning 6.

Allentown 28 Bethlehem 23: In a mighty struggle, Allentown finally overcame Bethlehem in the last four minutes of the game. Bethlehem led after each of the first three quarters. Guard Milo Sewards and center Lee Coker made critical field goals to put the Canaries in the lead. Allentown made 12 free throws to Bethlehem's 3 for the difference in the victory.

Leading scorers: Allentown – Wally Forbes 7; Bethlehem – Anthony Grebnar 9.[25]

Hazleton 41 East Stroudsburg 33: After falling behind 9-4 early in the contest, Hazleton came back for the win.

Leading scorers: Hazleton – Frank Apichella 16; East Stroudsburg – Harold Fusselman 9.[26]

Pottsville 25 Tamaqua 17: Tamaqua pulled within two points in the third period 15-13 before Pottsville pulled away for the win.

Leading scorers: Pottsville – Matt Whitaker 8; Tamaqua – Joe Heisler 9[27]

League Championship Playoff

Allentown 27 Mahanoy City 26: For the third time in eight years, the league title had to be settled through a playoff. Eighteen hundred fans, well in excess of the 1500 capacity, turned out when Allentown and Mahanoy City met in Pottsville. Except for the opening minutes, Allentown led throughout the game and entered the fourth quarter with a 25-19 lead. Mahanoy City made a desperate fourth quarter rally, but the Canaries held on.

Leading scorers: Allentown – Lee Coker 10; Mahanoy City - John Kutz 11[28]

Postseason Play

Allentown 22 St. Clair 19: Although an overwhelming favorite, Allentown had to battle the Schuylkill County League champions St. Clair in the Pottsville gymnasium. Allentown held one-point leads after the first two quarters and were tied at 15-15 after three quarters. St. Clair took its last lead 17-16 in the middle of the fourth quarter when Wally Forbes and Earl Repp made field goals to put the Canaries ahead for good 20-16.

Leading scorers: Allentown – Wilbur Gilbert 7; St. Clair – George Somers 8, Primo Russavage 8.[29]

Summit Hill 27 Allentown 18: Twenty-five hundred fans packed the Liberty gym in Bethlehem to watch Allentown and Summit Hill battle for a spot in the District XI title game. After being deadlocked at seven after the first period, Allentown took 12-11 halftime lead. Coach "Turk: Gerber's squad outplayed the Canaries in the second half to pull away for the victory.

Leading scorers: Summit Hill – Tom Hiza 11; Allentown – Milo Sewards 5, Wally Forbes 5[30]

Postseason Accolades

Scoring leaders: John Kutz, Mahanoy City, led the league with a total of 176 points foiled by his teammate Malcolm Richards who tallied 166 points. Allentown's Wally Forbes placed third with 147 points. The rest of the top ten included: Steve Polgar, Bethlehem, 127; Frank Apichella, Hazleton, 124; Walter Lukevics, Bethlehem, 114; Matt Whitaker, Pottsville 109; John Puzio, East Stroudsburg, 103; Lee Coker, Allentown, 95; and Joe Lotito, Hazleton, 92.

All-Stars: The ten league all-stars, according to a vote by the league coaches, were forwards Wally Forbes and Lee Coker, Allentown; and John Kutz, Mahanoy City. The centers were Malcolm Richards, Mahanoy

City, and Steve Polgar, Bethlehem. The guards included: John Burian, Allentown; Frank Apichella, Hazleton; Walter Lukevics, Bethlehem; and Joe Salvadore, Mahanoy City.

Final Standings

Allentown	12-2
Mahanoy City	12-2
Bethlehem	10-4
Hazleton	8-6
East Stroudsburg	5-9
Pottsville	5-9
Tamaqua	4-10
Easton	0-14

Hazleton's newspaper compiled a record of all the teams that had participated in the league since its inception. Allentown had the most wins with Hazleton having the best winning percentage. The team records, including playoff games, were as follows: Hazleton 63-13 83.9%; Mahanoy City 12-3 80%; Allentown 77-25 75.4%; Bethlehem 62-38 62%; East Stroudsburg 12-12 50%; Pottstown 36-41 46.7%; Pottsville 35-66 34.6%; Doylestown 18-38 32.1%; Coatesville 24-52 31.6%; Tamaqua 4-10 28.8%; and Easton 27-73 27%.[33]

Team Rosters

Allentown: Coach J. Birney Crum, Harlan Becker, Neil Boyle, John Burian, Lee Coker, Wally Forbes, Thomas Gallagher, Wilbur Gilbert, Eugene Grossman, Robert Hellerich, Jack McCarthy, Nevin "Whitey" Nonnemacher, Irving Perkins, Don Reber, Earl Repp, Salvadore Russiano, Joseph Milo Sewards

Bethlehem: Coach Bill Emrey, Croll, James Gillespie, Anthony Grebnar, Lenny Jaeger, Arpad Kery, Carlton Kresge, Walter Lukevics, Steve Polgar, William Rupert, Bob Taylor, Thomas

East Stroudsburg: Coach Earl Mosier, Ivan Armitage, Ed Blewitt, Louis Carmella, Robert Devore, Edward Harlowe, John Kunkle. Bill Kupiezewski, John Puzio, Harold Fusselman, John Warshefsky, Eugene Wilson

Easton: Coach Clyde Notestine, Joseph Alfero, Bill Barnhart, Frank Bishop, Milton Bricker, Sam Corneto, Edwin Folk, Benjamin Griffin, Roland Henning, Robert Keiber, Carl Martin, John McIntyre, William Metz, Russ Servin, Harry Youngkin

Hazleton: Coach Hugh McGeehan, Anthony Apichella, Frank Apichella, Charley Brogan, Warren Cooper, Pasco "Patsy" DeVecca, Hugh "Steamer" Ferry, Mauro Forte, Stan Kokie, Mike Laputka, Joe "Shorty" Lotito, Harry Schaller, Ken Stecker, Robert Yevak

Mahanoy City: Coach John Goepfert, John Gabuzda, Steve Hydock, Albin Kisieliewski, John Kutz, Paul Petrucha, Malcolm "Red" Richards, Joe Salvadore, Chester Setcavage, Thompson, John Walashunas, John Walchak

Pottsville: Coach George Dimmerling, Frank Boran, Albert Buchinsky, Robert Conrad, Harold Freeze, Robert Koegel, Wayne Lehman, Percy Lokitus, Francis McCormick, Saul Rosenzweig, Clyde Spitzner, Dean Stevenson, Irwin Wagner, Matt Whitaker, Harry Wolfe

Tamaqua: Coach Hugh Hoke, Nelson Bassler, Joe Cutcavage, Donald Dresher, Joe Heisler, George Kleckner, Ray Pfeil, John Sweeney, Joe Tarsavage, E. Waselefsky, Albert Yarish, Leonard Zatoris

Allentown High School – 1933 League Champions[34]

1934

An Unexpected League Title

Unprecedented turmoil would surface during the league's ninth season. The league issues surfaced early in the season with Mahanoy City having to postpone several games for several weeks since their new gymnasium was completed late.

At the wrap-up meeting for the 1933 season in early April, the league members voted to approve an official junior varsity league for the 1934 season. Each league member agreed to field a team. East Stroudsburg had some reluctance because of the extra cost the school would bear to provide this competition, but decided to move forward with a team.[1]

In early May, the league met again to elect officers for the coming season. William Emrey was re-elected president for his seventh consecutive term. James McQuaid, faculty manager at Hazleton High School, was elected vice president. The league elected E. A. Rabenold to his ninth term as secretary-treasurer. In other action, East Stroudsburg and Easton affirmed their participation in the junior varsity circuit. The league also decided that any boy considered as in the top seven of the varsity squad should not play in the junior circuit.[2]

An October preseason meeting cleaned up some open items from the prior meetings. The members decided to have the home team select an official to referee the junior varsity game. Also, each visiting team would be required to notify the home team of the color of their uniforms for the game so that teams would not end up wearing very similar color uniforms.[3]

In early December, an interpretive game was held in the Allentown gym to thoroughly review rules changes for the season. Over 200 coaches, officials, and players turned out for the event. Some of the changes included a redefinition of the 10 second rule to cross mid-court and the allowable number of re-entries of a player into the game. Previously, the 10-second rule applied only to courts which were 60 feet or longer. Now, courts less than 75 feet would have special markings and the 10-second rule would apply on each court. Also, a player was now able to return to the game twice, which would mean he could appear on the court three times unless he had been disqualified by four personal fouls or some other disqualifying foul.[4]

During the offseason, several other schools and a college courted Allentown's coach Birney Crum for positions at their institutions. Muhlenberg College approached Crum about a coaching position when the position became available with the resignation of George R. Holstrum. An unnamed Pennsylvania high school and Passaic, NJ, asked Crum about interests in their schools. Crum turned down all the offers to remain at Allentown.[5]

Week 1

Hazleton 30 Bethlehem 12: Hazleton served notice that they would again be a force in the league. The Mountaineers led 15-5 at the end of the first half.

Leading scorers: Hazleton – Frank Apichella 12; Bethlehem – Joe Freund 6.

Allentown 19 East Stroudsburg 14: In a grueling, low-scoring affair, Allentown took a 4-2 first quarter lead. After leading 7-6 at halftime, the Canaries took a 14-10 lead into the fourth quarter.

Leading scorers: Allentown – "Bumps" Hellerich 8; East Stroudsburg – Sam Puzio 5.

Easton 24 Pottsville 19: After losing all 14 games in 1933, Easton began with a victory. Easton trailed 6-2 after the first quarter, but rallied to tie the game at the half 10-10. After three quarters, the Red Rovers led 19-13.

Leading scorers: Easton – Earl Bishop 12; Pottsville – Matt Whitaker 10.

Mahanoy City 30 Tamaqua 29: At Tamaqua, Mahanoy City scratched out a win over testy Tamaqua. Tamaqua took a 5-point lead 25-20 into the fourth quarter, but could not hold up under the onslaught by Mahanoy City. Coach Goepfert used 12 players to pull out the win,

Leading scorers: Mahanoy City – John Fedorchalk 7, Humanik 7; Tamaqua – John Sweeney 12.[6]

Week 2

Hazleton 22 Easton 20: At Lafayette College's gymnasium, Easton threw a real scare at the Mountaineers. Easton led at the half 10-8, but Hazleton jumped into the lead at the end of the third quarter 16-15. The Red Rovers surged into the lead again 20-18 in the fourth quarter before Hazleton converted two field goals.

Leading scorers: Hazleton – Stan Kokie 8; Easton – Maddock 6.

East Stroudsburg 35 Pottsville 23: Pottsville took a 16-15 lead at halftime, but East Stroudsburg's defense took charge in the second half. The Cavaliers outscored Pottsville 20-7 in the second half.

Leading scorers: East Stroudsburg – Harold Fusselman 10; Pottsville – Matt Whitaker 11.

Bethlehem 24 Mahanoy City 22: At the Liberty gym, Mahanoy City's only lead was 2-0 with the teams tied after the first quarter 4-4 and the half 10-10. After leading 15-14 after three quarters, Bethlehem built the lead to five during the fourth quarter. Foul shooting was shoddy with Bethlehem making 4 of 15 and Mahanoy City 6 of 16.

Leading scorers: Bethlehem – Elmer Gangewere 11; Mahanoy City – John Gabuzda 10.[7]

Allentown 33 Tamaqua 20: After being tied 12-12 at the half at Tamaqua, Allentown outscored the Tams 17-3 in the third quarter. The Canaries only made 5 of 19 fouls shots.

Leading scorers: Allentown – Wally Forbes 11; Tamaqua – John Sweeney 7, Maurice Williams 7.[8]

Week 3

Allentown 28 Pottsville 8: Allentown held Pottsville to a single point in the second half. Although the Canaries only made five field goals, they converted 18 of 31 free throws.

Leading scorers: Allentown – Wally Forbes 15; Pottsville – Matt Whitaker 6.

Bethlehem 22 Easton 18: After taking an 11-4 first quarter lead, Bethlehem hung on for the win. Extremely cold weather kept the attendance very low.

Leading scorers: Bethlehem – Walter Lukevics 6; Easton – Edwin Folk 5.

East Stroudsburg 39 Tamaqua 26: Trailing 18-17 at the half, East Stroudsburg rallied for a comfortable win.

Leading scorers: East Stroudsburg – Harold Fusselman 15, John Kunkle 14; Tamaqua – Joe Cutcavage 11.

Hazleton-Mahanoy City: Since Mahanoy City's gym was still not finished, the game was initially moved to the Tamaqua gym. Hazleton requested a larger floor, but the teams could not come to agreement so the game was postponed to a later date.[9]

Week 4

Hazleton 33 Allentown 25: Sixteen hundred fans in the Hazleton gym witnessed the home team move into sole possession of first place. Allentown converted only 7 of 18 free throws while Hazleton made 11 of 15.

Leading scorers: Hazleton – Frank Apichella 11; Allentown – Wally Forbes 9.

Bethlehem 30 East Stroudsburg 25: With Bethlehem holding a comfortable lead most of the first half, East Stroudsburg came back to tie the game and lead briefly in the second half 22-20. However, East Stroudsburg could only score three more points.

Leading scorers: Bethlehem – Walter Lukevics 16; East Stroudsburg – Harold Fusselman 7.

Easton 23 Mahanoy City 22: Trailing 11-4 at the half, Easton climbed within four 15-11 after three quarters. Earl Bishop made a difficult corner shot at the buzzer for the win.

Leading scorers: Easton – Arnold Ralph 10; Mahanoy City – S. Humanik 13.

Tamaqua 28 Pottsville 20: After trailing 9-8 at the half, Tamaqua rallied to lead 18-11 after three quarters by holding Pottsville to 2 third quarter points. All six players used by Tamaqua scored. Coach Dimmerling suspended two of his starters, Matt Whitaker and Saul Rosenzweig, prior to the game for violating training rules.

Leading scorers: Tamaqua – E. Waselesky 6; Pottsville – Anthony Pacesas 5.[10]

Week 5

Allentown 23 Bethlehem 14: At Allentown's "Little Palestra", Bethlehem took a 1-0 lead and never led again when the Canaries made three foul shots to lead 3-1. Holding only an 8-3 halftime lead, Allentown surged to a 20-8 lead after three quarters.

Leading scorers: Allentown – Wally Forbes 12; Bethlehem – Arpad Kery 4.[11]

Easton 24 Tamaqua 21: Easton took an 11-3 lead in the first quarter and 18-6 at the half. Tamaqua's second half rally fell short.

Leading scorers: Easton – Arnold Ralph 9; Tamaqua – E. Waselesky 7.

Pottsville 25 Mahanoy City 17: Pottsville, after losing the first four games, surprised Mahanoy City. Except for the first few minutes, Pottsville led throughout the game.

Leading scorers: Pottsville – Wayne Lehman 8, Irwin Wagner 8; Mahanoy City – John Gabuzda 5, John Sluzevich 5.

Hazleton 50 East Stroudsburg 29: On their way to their 4th straight win, Hazleton led 27-14 at halftime.

Leading scorers: Hazleton – Frank Apichella 14, Stan Kokie 13; East Stroudsburg – John Kunkle 6.[12]

Week 6

Hazleton 52 Pottsville 12: For the second game in a row, Hazleton scored at least 50 points. Hazleton held Pottsville to three field goals and six foul shots.

Leading scorers: Hazleton – Frank Apichella 15, Stan Kokie 11; Pottsville – Richard Matthews 4.[13]

Easton 27 Allentown 25 OT: Easton's upset of the Canaries pulled them into a second-place tie with Allentown and Bethlehem. No box score

Bethlehem 37 Tamaqua 19: No box score

East Stroudsburg – Mahanoy City: This matchup was postponed.

Week 7

Hazleton 46 Tamaqua 38: Hazleton led from the start and at the half 27-20 to win their 6th straight game.

Leading scorers: Hazleton – Eddie Boyle 15, Stan Kokie 14; Tamaqua – Donald Dresher 10.

Easton 31 East Stroudsburg 21: Easton led from the beginning and held a 14-11 halftime lead.

Leading scorers: Easton – Arnold Ralph 13; East Stroudsburg – Harold Fusselman 8.

Bethlehem 24 Pottsville 17: Pottsville's only lead was at 2-0. Bethlehem led 15-10 at the half and 22-13 after three quarters.

Leading scorers: Bethlehem - George Fidmik 9; Pottsville – Wayne Lehman 5.

Allentown 23 Mahanoy City 8: After leading 4-0 to begin the game, Mahanoy City could only score 4 more points the rest of the way.

Leading scorers: Allentown – Wally Forbes 9; Mahanoy City – Thomas Reing 4, Shadis 4.[14]

Bethlehem 28 Hazleton 26: Bethlehem shocked Hazleton in front of 1800 howling fans. Late in the fourth quarter, Hazleton took the lead 26-24, but the Hurricane's forward Krasowski made a field goal off of a Lawrence Rosati missed foul shot and Arpie Kery made another field goal with less than a minute to play for the win.

Leading scorers: Bethlehem – John Quigg 9; Hazleton – Frank Apichella 9.

Allentown 30 East Stroudsburg 25: East Stroudsburg took the lead early and held it until the middle of the third quarter. Allentown pulled ahead 23-20 after three quarters.

Leading scorers: Allentown – Robert Hellerich 14; East Stroudsburg – John Kunkle 10.[15]

Easton 27 Pottsville 23: At the Lafayette College gym, took a hard fought, close game.

Leading scorers: Easton – Edwin Folk 8; Pottsville – Irwin Wagner 10.[16]

Harold Fusselman, star center of the East Stroudsburg team, was reinstated as a member of the basketball team in late January. He had taken leave of the school to take employment with the National Reemployment Service as requested by his parents. He began work at a flood control project in Pocono Creek. It was determined that he would not be able to work on that project and remain a student at the high school. The situation was resolved when he was reassigned to a school improvement project. He was reinstated and could remain a student and a member of the basketball team as well as continue his employment as desired by his parents.[17]

Week 8

Hazleton 36 Mahanoy City 27: In a game postponed from week 3, Hazleton helped Mahanoy City open and dedicate its new gym. After leading 13-11 at the half, Hazleton sprung out to a 30-25 advantage.

Leading scorers: Hazleton – Frank Apichella 14; Mahanoy City – Shadis 20.[18]

Hazleton 41 Easton 25: After leading by three at the half 15-12, the Mountaineers pulled away in the 2nd half.

Leading scorers: Hazleton – Charley Brogan 12, Stan Kokie 10; Easton – Earl Bishop 13.

Allentown 40 Tamaqua 23: Without Wally Forbes in the lineup due to leg injury suffered against Reading earlier in the week, Karl Meyers picked up the slack to lead the Canaries to a 20-8 halftime lead,

Leading scorers: Allentown – Karl Meyers 16, Robert Hellerich 13; Tamaqua – Donald Dresher 12.[19]

Bethlehem 29 Mahanoy City 20; At Mahanoy City's new gym, Bethlehem handed Maroons their second loss in their new gym. Mahanoy City led 7-6 after a quarter only to see Bethlehem take over from there on.

Leading scorers: Bethlehem – Arpad Kery 12, George Fidmik 11; Mahanoy City – John Gabuzda 7.

East Stroudsburg 23 Pottsville 17: Pottsville led 5-3 with East Stroudsburg tying the game at 10-10 at the half. The Cavaliers continued the rally in the second half to hand Pottsville an 8th loss in nine league contests.

Leading scorers: East Stroudsburg – John Kunkle 10; Pottsville – Irwin Wagner 6, Richards Matthews 6.[20]

Week 9

Mahanoy City 24 Tamaqua 17: No box score.

Mahanoy City 50 East Stroudsburg 32: In a postponed game from week 6, Mahanoy City got their first win their gymnasium. No box score[21]

Prior to their game with Mahanoy City, District 2 of the PIAA informed Hazleton that football and basketball star Pasco "Patsy" DeVecca was ruled ineligible for further play due to his age. West Hazleton had filed a protest with District 2 on the age eligibility of DeVecca. In absence of a birth certificate, Hazleton requested one from the Bureau of Vital Statistics who indicated that there was no certificate on record. West Hazleton, however, did produce a signed birth certificate indicating that he was over the age of 20. It was determined that he had actually reached the age of 20 in May of 1933. Since Hazleton assumed he was of the proper age based on his school attendance dates, the PIAA decided not to censure Hazleton and its record would stand, but DeVecca was no longer eligible.[22]

Allentown 33 Pottsville 14: After holding a slim one-point lead after a quarter 5-4, Allentown built leads of 14-6 at halftime and 23-11 heading into the fourth quarter.

Leading scorers: Allentown – Robert Hellerich 12, Earl Repp 11; Pottsville – Wayne Lehman 5.

Tamaqua 30 East Stroudsburg 28: After holding a 14-11 halftime lead, Tamaqua hung on in the second half.

Leading scorers: Tamaqua – Donald Dresher 12, John Sweeney 11; East Stroudsburg – John Kunkle 7, Ivan Armitage 7.

Bethlehem 32 Easton 18: Bethlehem raced out to a 20-6 halftime lead by holding the Red Rovers to no field goals and only six free throws.

Leading scorers: Bethlehem – Charles Krasowski 11; Easton – Edwin Folk 8.

Hazleton 51 Mahanoy City 23: Despite the absence of DeVecca, Hazleton still took a 29-13 halftime lead and the victory along with sole possession of first place.

Leading scorers: Hazleton – Frank Apichella 18, Charles Brogan 15, Eddie Boyle 10; Mahanoy City – Thomas Reing 9.[23]

Week 10

Hazleton 37 Allentown 28: With the support of a large delegation of fans who traveled to Allentown on a special excursion train, Hazleton showed their superiority with their win over the Canaries with 3000 fans in attendance at the Little Palestra. Hazleton took an early 10-2 lead before the Canaries got within a single point 11-10. Hazleton increased the lead to five points after three quarters 25-20.

Leading scorers: Hazleton – Eddie Boyle 10; Allentown – Robert Hellerich 8.[24]

Bethlehem 24 East Stroudsburg 23: With Allentown's loss, Bethlehem claimed sole possession of second place. East Stroudsburg had led 21-15 going into the fourth quarter. Referee Prendergast was threatened bodily harm by East Stroudsburg students and partisans immediately after the game ended. Only intervention by the Bethlehem players prevented any violence.

Leading scorers: Bethlehem – George Fidmik 9; East Stroudsburg – Eugene Wilson 9.

Mahanoy City 35 Easton 25: Mahanoy City took a 22-5 lead into the half and cruised to the win.

Leading scorers: Mahanoy City - Thomas Reing 11; Easton – Edwin Folk 8.

Tamaqua 30 Pottsville 25: Pottsville and Tamaqua became embroiled in a free-for-all riot with players and spectators both involved. Pottsville's Matthews clipped Tamaqua's Cutcavage to initiate the riot. Both players and fans left fists fly for several minutes before order was restored to the gym. Pottsville led at the half 16-14 with Tamaqua rallying for the win.

Leading scorers: Tamaqua - Donald Dresher 14; Pottsville – Wayne Lehman 11.[25]

Week 11

Allentown 26 Bethlehem 24: A critical game between Allentown and Bethlehem was stopped for 26 minutes as Coaches Crum and Emery argued with referee Chuck Bibleheimer over a double technical foul. Some roughhousing had been occurring during the game. Suddenly, the Allentown bench erupted! Coach Crum used his best tackling techniques to prevent his own player from entering into a fracas and cause more problems. However, the referee called a double technical. Coach Emery loudly disputed the call and won his case as only Bethlehem shot a technical foul. The Canary win diminished Bethlehem's chance of catching Hazleton for the title. Allentown led 23-16 heading into the final quarter.

Leading scorers: Allentown – Karl Meyers 12; Bethlehem – George Fidmik 13.

Easton 35 Tamaqua 30: The Red Rovers ended their three-game skid with a balanced scoring attack. Easton led 21-16 before Tamaqua tied the game at 26-26 at the end of the third quarter.

Leading scorers: Easton – Arnold Ralph 8, Maddock 8; Tamaqua – John Sweeney 11, Donald Dresher 11.

Hazleton 33 East Stroudsburg 22: At Hazleton, the Mountaineers jumped out to a 20-7 lead and cruised to the win to solidify its hold on first place.

Leading scorers: Hazleton – Frank Apichella 10; East Stroudsburg – John Kunkle 6'

Mahanoy City 37 Pottsville 20: Never leading in the contest, Pottsville lost its seventh in a row and 11th of 12 games to visiting Mahanoy City.

Leading scorers: Mahanoy City - Shadis 16; Pottsville - Wayne Lehman 9.[26]

Week 12

Hazleton 45 Pottsville 16: Hazleton won its 12th game in 13 contests in front of 1200 fans in Hazleton.

Leading scorers: Hazleton – Stan Kokie 18; Pottsville – Irwin Wagner 4, George Weissinger 4.

Allentown 20 Easton 16: After taking an early 6-0 lead, the Canaries had to hold off a stubborn Easton team to maintain a hold on second place. Joe "Copper" McFadden joined the varsity with Wally Forbes ineligible due to scholastic difficulties.

Leading scorers: Allentown – Joe McFadden 8; Easton – Arnold Ralph 4, Joseph Alfero 4, Edwin Folk 4, John McIntyre 4.

Bethlehem 22 Tamaqua 17: Although Bethlehem led most of the way, they had to battle hard to hold off Tamaqua and their forward John Sweeney.

Leading scorers: Bethlehem - Charles Krasowski 9; Tamaqua – John Sweeney 13.

Mahanoy City 44 East Stroudsburg 18: Mahanoy City took and early lead and were never threatened.

Leading scorers: Mahanoy City – Thomas Reing 18, Shadis 12; East Stroudsburg – John Kunkle 11.[27]

On February 24th prior to the final weekend of the regular season, the PIAA forced Hazleton to forfeit the eight games won by the Mountaineers during which Patsy DeVecca had participated. Although they were allowed to continue to play, Hazleton was ruled ineligible for state championship play. Hazleton had won 12 of 13 games in the league at the time of the ruling. With the forfeits, their record dropped to 4-9. The re-scrambled league standings now had Bethlehem and Allentown unexpectedly battling for the league crown. Each squad had a record of 11-2 with a game to play.[28]

Week 13

Bethlehem 30 Pottsville 9: Bethlehem responded with a resounding victory over Pottsville. Bill Emrey's boys finally made it to the playoffs after threatening a number of times and falling short. Despite having captured the crown through Hazleton's misfortune, Bethlehem had nonetheless won its first league title. Pottsville could only score three points on three foul shots in the second half of the game.

Leading scorers: Bethlehem – Elmer Gangewere 11; Pottsville – Irwin Wagner 5.

Easton 28 East Stroudsburg 25: After Easton led at the half 14-11, East Stroudsburg rallied for a third quarter lead 21-20. The Red Rovers held the Cavaliers to 4 points in the final quarter.

Leading scorers: Easton – Arnold Ralph 8, Earl Bishop 8; East Stroudsburg - John Kunkle 8.

Mahanoy City 31 Allentown 29 OT: Allentown lost a tough matchup at Mahanoy City and missed a chance to tie with Bethlehem and a playoff for the league title. The Canaries fell behind 22-14 after three quarters, but made a ferocious charge to tie the game in regulation 27-27.

Leading scorers: Mahanoy City – Shadis 9; Allentown – Robert Hellerich 14.[29]

Hazleton 66 Tamaqua 15: Rebounding from a devastating blow of having to forfeit eight wins and be ineligible for postseason play, the Mountaineers made all nine shots to take a 21-0 lead after the first quarter. Tamaqua, on the other hand, did not make a field goal until the final period.

Leading scorers: Hazleton – Stan Kokie 21, Frank Apichella 18, Eddie Boyle 12, Charley Brogan 11; Tamaqua – John Sweeney 5, Joe Cutcavage 5.[30]

Postseason Playoffs

Bethlehem 33 Wilson Boro 18: Bethlehem entered the postseason playoffs for the first time since 1925 when they were members of the Lehigh Valley League. Twenty-five hundred fans, in the Allentown gym, saw Coach Emrey's team crush Wilson Boro, despite Wilson Boro's early 6-4 lead. Wilson came into the game as champions of the Lehigh-Northampton League.

Leading scorers: Bethlehem – Arpad Kery 12; Wilson Boro – A Geffert 8.[31]

Palmerton 33 Bethlehem 21: Thirty-five hundred fans jammed the Allentown gym for Bethlehem's second round game against Bill Braucher's Palmerton team. After staying close at halftime 13-11, Bethlehem could not score a field goal in the second half until late in the fourth quarter. All six of Palmerton's players scored in the game.

Leading scorers: Palmerton – Johnny Fabian 10; Bethlehem – Charles Krasowski 8.[31]

Postseason Accolades

All-Stars: The league all-stars included forwards Frank Apichella and Stan Kokie, Hazleton, Robert Hellerich, Allentown, and John Sweeney, Tamaqua; centers Eddie Boyle, Hazleton, and Karl Meyer, Allentown; and guards Milo Sewards and Earl Repp, Allentown, and Lawrence Rosati and John Quigg, Bethlehem.

Leading scorers: The league's five leading scorers were Frank Apichella, Hazleton, 152 points; Stan Kokie, Hazleton, 136; Eddie Boyle, Hazleton, 118; John Sweeney, Tamaqua, 105; and Robert Hellerich, Allentown, 104 points.[33]

Final Standings

Bethlehem	13-1
Easton	11-3
Mahanoy City	9-5
East Stroudsburg	6-8
Tamaqua	5-9
Hazleton	5-9
Allentown	4-10
Pottsville	3-11

Note: The records for the league include the forfeits for both Allentown and Hazleton for the use of overage players.

At the league wrap-up meeting for the season, Allentown coach Birney Crum volunteered information that star forward Wally Forbes was overage and had turned 20 in November 1933. Allentown voluntarily forfeited all the games the Canaries had won in which Forbes had participated, which was seven games. The forfeits by Allentown and Hazleton drastically changed the league standings.[32]

Team Rosters

Allentown: Coach J. Birney Crum, Ray Bergenstock, Frank Dietrich, William Fahler, Wally Forbes. Robert "Bumps" Hellerich, William Jones, Gene Kirkpatrick, Kulowitch, Ronald Leonard, Joseph "Copper" McFadden, Karl Meyers, Richter, Earl Repp, Milo Sewards, Harvey Weiss

Bethlehem: Coach Bill Emery, George Fidmik, Joe Freund, Elmer Gangewere, James Gillespie, Arpad Kery, Charles Krasowski, Carl Kresge, Walter "Veetz" Lukevics, Joseph McIntyre, John Quigg, William Richter, Lawrence Rosati, William Rupert

East Stroudsburg: Coach Earl Mosier, Drexel Ace, Ivan Armitage, Bensinger, Brodt, Harry Bush, Louis Carmella, Harold Fusselman, Leonard Fusselman, Herring, John Kunkle, Clyde Lessley, Martin, Minor, Sam Puzio, Small, Townsend, John Warshefsky, Eugene Wilson, Zoller

Easton: Coach Clyde Notestine, Joseph Alfero, Earl Bishop, Edwin Folk, Bill Kraus, Maddock, Matthews, Mazza, John McIntyre, Arnold Ralph, William Savitz, Wilson, Ralph Young

Hazleton: Coach High McGeehan, Anthony Apichella, Frank Apichella, Eddie Boyle, Charley Brogan, Pasco "Patsy" DeVecca, Gleim, Karachiewicz, Stan Kokie, Mike Laputka, Michael Roman

Mahanoy City: Coach John Goepfert, Chernock, John Fedorchalk, William Filer, John Gabuzda, Gluzvick, Humanik, Norris, J. Petrucha, Pat Petrucha, Polinchak, Rockatis, Thomas Reing, Schumacher, Shadis, John Sluzevich

Pottsville: Coach George Dimmerling, George Daubert, Dimmerling, Hobbs, Robert Koegel, A. Lefafin, Wayne Lehman, Richard Matthews, Anthony Pacesas, Phlesa, Porlinchak, Saul Rosenzweig, Irwin Wagner, Waite, George Weissinger, Matt Whitaker, Harry Wolfe

Tamaqua: Coach Hugh Hoke, Bresser, Joe Cutcavage, William Devonshire, Donald Dresher, Claire Heisler, Jack Kershner, Melvin Kleppinger, John Sweeney, E. Waselefsky, Paul Wetterau, Maurice William

Bethlehem High School – 1934 League Champions[34]

1935

Another State Championship

For the third consecutive season, the league membership remained the same. With the turmoil of the past season behind it, the league attempted to bring order and reestablish itself as one of the major schoolboy basketball leagues in the state. The task ahead was a difficult one!

The league held its organizational meeting in early April at the Elks Club in Hazleton. The league representatives elected the league officers for the 1935 season. They opted to keep the current officers for the year: William Emrey as president, J. D. McQuaid as vice president, and E. A. Rabenold as secretary/treasurer.[1]

A special committee, consisting of Johnny Goepfert of Mahanoy City, Birney Crum of Allentown, and Earl Mossier of East Stroudsburg, reviewed the player age issue and reported to the league officials at a May meeting in Easton. Based on the committee's recommendation, the league adopted the policy that all players must have a birth certificate filed with the league in order to be eligible to play.[2]

Week 1

Allentown 26 Bethlehem 22: Before a sell-out crowd in Allentown's Little Palestra, Bethlehem's defending league champions took on the Canaries in thrilling opening of the new season. Bethlehem, at one point, held an 8-point lead and threatened to put the game away. At halftime, Coach Emrey's team led by a score of 12-10. Led by Captain Joe McFadden with 7 points in the 3rd quarter, Allentown pulled ahead to win the game.

Leading scorers: Allentown – Joe McFadden 16; Bethlehem – Frank Kovacs 7, Gus Neimeister 7.

Hazleton 59 East Stroudsburg 4: Hazleton opened its season in East Stroudsburg and humiliated the home team with nary a field goal and the four points coming on free throws. The halftime score was 27-2.

Leading scorers: Hazleton - Stan Kokie 23, Homer Knox 14; East Stroudsburg – Beaver 3.

Easton 32 Pottsville 27: Easton traveled to Pottsville and took a halftime lead of 18-14 into the locker room. Pottsville rallied in the 3rd quarter to tie the score at 22 to begin the 4th quarter. Easton outscored Pottsville 10-5 in the final stanza.

Leading scorers: Easton – Epstein 8; Pottsville – Charles Dimmerling 8.

Mahanoy City 30 Tamaqua 17: At Tamaqua, the home team lost to the visiting Mahanoy City Maroons. Mahanoy City rolled to a 14-5 lead at the half. Tamaqua guard Paul Wetterau suffered a severe ankle sprain.

Leading scorers: Mahanoy City – Thomas Reing 8; Tamaqua – Lenny Quather 6.[3]

Week 2

Mahanoy City 37 Hazleton 24: In front of 1400 fans in Hazleton's gym, Mahanoy City shocked the home team. Ahead by only a single point at the half 13-12, the Maroons outscored Hazleton 24-12 in the 2nd half.

Leading scorers: Mahanoy City – Thomas Reing 13; Hazleton - Stan Kokie 10.

Allentown 41 Tamaqua 30: With Tamaqua holding a lead only twice in the game, 17-14 in the first half and 23-22 in the 3rd quarter, Allentown held off the Tams. Coach Crum kept Joe McFadden on the bench during the entire first half. Eight Canaries scored in the game.

Leading scorers: Allentown – Joe McFadden 10; Tamaqua – Art Mohn 9.

Bethlehem 32 Pottsville 18: Bethlehem bounced back from its loss to Allentown with a win over Pottsville at the Liberty gym. The Hurricane led 14-4 at halftime. Coach Emrey used 10 players with seven scoring in the victory.

Leading scorers: Bethlehem – Charles Krasowski 9; Pottsville - Herb Wagner 11.[4]

Easton 35 East Stroudsburg 15: Easton remained undefeated with an easy win over East Stroudsburg in the new Easton gym. East Stroudsburg only had one field goal in the first half and three for the game.

Leading scorers: Easton - Ralph Young 8; East Stroudsburg – John Warshefsky 6.[5]

Week 3

Easton 23 Hazleton 20: At home, Easton handed Hazleton its second straight loss. Hazleton lost the game at the foul line converting only 6 of 15 while Easton countered with 9 of 15.

Leading scorers: Easton – Bill Kraus 9; Hazleton – Tony Apichella 9.[6]

Mahanoy City 72 East Stroudsburg 21: Mahanoy City kept pace with a 72-21 unmerciful shellacking of East Stroudsburg and breaking the league's game scoring record previously held by Hazleton. The Maroons rolled to a 22-0 lead at the end of the first quarter.

Leading scorers: Mahanoy City – Thomas Reing 30, Paul Petrucha 12; East Stroudsburg – Herring 8.

Allentown 39 Pottsville 18: At the Little Palestra, the Canaries rolled over Pottsville after taking a 7-0 lead to start the game. Coach Crum's team saw 10 of the 11 players used in the game score at least a point.

Leading scorers: Allentown – Ronald Leonard 10; Pottsville – Charles Dimmerling 8.

Tamaqua 32 Bethlehem 29: Tamaqua won its first game of the young season and shocked homestanding Bethlehem. Losing 16-11 at the half, the Tams rallied in the 3rd quarter to lead 24-19 to pull out the upset.

Leading scorers: Tamaqua – Art Mohn 8, Clair Heisler 8; Bethlehem – Gus Neimeister 6, Harry Simon 6.[7]

Week 4

Mahanoy City 28 Easton 21: Mahanoy City disposed of Easton to give the Red Rovers their first loss and knock them out of the 1st place tie. Mahanoy City took a 13-3 lead in the 1st quarter to decide the game early.

Leading scorers: Mahanoy City - Paul Petrucha 17; Easton – Bill Kraus 6.

Allentown 62 East Stroudsburg 23: Allentown continued its winning ways against lowly East Stroudsburg and remained tied with Mahanoy City. Allentown led at halftime 33-6

Leading scorers: Allentown - "Copper" McFadden 17, Ronald Leonard 12; East Stroudsburg – Minor 5.

Pottsville 57 Tamaqua 32: After surprising Bethlehem the previous week, Tamaqua got surprised by Pottsville in the upset of the week. Leading 20-16 at the half, Pottsville unleashed its offense in the 2nd half.

Leading scorers: Pottsville – Charles Dimmerling 17, Herb Wagner 12; Tamaqua – Harry Spangler 7, Joseph Kovelesky 7.[8]

Bethlehem 27 Hazleton 25: On the road, Bethlehem won over reeling Hazleton in a game broadcast on the radio. Close all the way, Bethlehem led 12-11 at the half. Hazleton stood at an uncharacteristic 1-3 after 4 weeks.

Leading scorers: Bethlehem – Charles Krasowsky 8, Hazleton – Tony Apichella 7, Homer Knox 7.[9]

Week 5

Pottsville 38 Mahanoy City 33 OT: Mahanoy City unexpectedly lost its perfect record the following week against suddenly surprising Pottsville in overtime. After leading most of the game, Pottsville's Matthews had to make two foul shots in the last 30 seconds to tie up the game in regulation.

Leading scorers: Pottsville – Herb Wagner 17, Charles Dimmerling 12; Mahanoy City – Thomas Reing 14, William Filer 10.

Allentown 30 Hazleton 27: Allentown handed Hazleton an unprecedented fourth consecutive loss. Although the Canaries led the whole game, Hazleton did make several rallies to get close only to fall short. Although neither team was stellar from the foul line, Allentown made six of 15 while Hazleton only made 3 of 11. At 1-4, Hazleton was ahead of only winless East Stroudsburg.

Leading scorers: Allentown – Joe McFadden 11; Hazleton – Homer Knox 7, George Leib 7.

Easton 29 Tamaqua 21: Easton traveled to Tamaqua and won its 4th game to move into a tie with Mahanoy City at 4-1. Easton led the entire game.

Leading scorers: Easton – Edwin Folk 14; Tamaqua – Clair Heisler 6.

Bethlehem 57 East Stroudsburg 11: Bethlehem took its turn rolling up the score against East Stroudsburg. While East Stroudsburg could only muster one field goal during the entire game, Coach Emrey's team had four players in double figures;

Leading scorers: Bethlehem – Harry Simon 14, Charles Krasowski 13, Gus Neimeister 13, Frank Kovacs 10; East Stroudsburg – Herring 5.[10]

Week 6

Hazleton 35 Tamaqua 29: Hazleton broke its losing streak with a determined and gritty win over Tamaqua. After holding a 19-12 halftime lead, Hazleton fell behind the Tamaqua 28-27 in the 4th quarter, but rallied for the win.

Leading scorers: Hazleton - Stan Kokie's 10; Tamaqua – Joe Kovelesky 9.[11]

Pottsville 36 East Stroudsburg 21: Pottsville handed East Stroudsburg yet another loss although the Cavaliers had their best offensive showing of the season.

Leading scorers: Pottsville – Herb Wagner 18; East Stroudsburg – Heller 5.

Allentown 30 Easton 14: Playing solid defense and holding the Red Rovers to a single field goal until late in the 3rd quarter, Allentown trounced Easton in Easton. Five players fouled out of the game with a total of 41 free throws attempted in the game. Easton dropped to third place behind Mahanoy City.

Leading scorers: Allentown – Joe McFadden 14; Easton – Parry 4.

Mahanoy City 33 Bethlehem 19: In Mahanoy City, the Maroons stayed a game behind Allentown with a win over Bethlehem. After leading by one 4-3 after a quarter, Mahanoy City outscored Bethlehem 10-1 in the second quarter.

Leading scorers: Mahanoy City – Paul Petrucha 13, Thomas Reing 11; Bethlehem – Gus Neimeister 7.[12]

Week 7

Allentown 40 Mahanoy City 15: On its home court, Allentown outclassed Mahanoy City in front of 2600 fans. Arriving more than an hour late due to very hazardous roads from ice and snow, the Maroons never got it going at the Little Palestra. Mahanoy City had only three field goals in the game. The Canaries held the league's leading scorer Thomas Reing to three points, all on free throws.

Leading scorers: Allentown – Joe McFadden 20; Mahanoy City – Paul Petrucha 7.

Hazleton 34 Pottsville 21: Hazleton continued its resurgence with a win at Pottsville in a very physical game with 52 fouls called on the players of the two teams. Pottsville made only three field goals in the game.

Leading scorers: Hazleton – George Lieb 13; Pottsville - Herb Wagner 12.

Tamaqua 53 East Stroudsburg 21: Tamaqua became the next team to roll up a big score on East Stroudsburg 53-21. The Cavaliers lost their seventh straight league contest.

Leading scorers: Tamaqua - Art Mohn 13, Lenny Quather 13; East Stroudsburg – Minor 5.[13]

Bethlehem 29 Easton 22: Bethlehem's win over Easton pulled them into a third-place tie with the Red Rovers at 4-3. Easton led 10-5 after a quarter and 11-10 at the half, but Bethlehem tightened its defense and surged ahead early in the third quarter 13-12 and continued to stretch the lead for the victory.

Leading scorers: Bethlehem – Frank Kovacs 8; Easton – Edwin Folk 4, Bill Kraus 4, Parry 4.[14]

Bethlehem 26 Allentown 17: After 12 straight wins, with seven in the league, Allentown lost to Bethlehem. Beating the Canaries for the first time in six tries, Bethlehem led early 6-0 and never surrendered the lead. Gus Neimeister held Joe McFadden to a single field goal and six points.

Leading scorers: Bethlehem – Frank Kovacs 8, John Quigg 8; Allentown – Joe McFadden 6.

Easton 28 Pottsville 20: After trailing for more than three periods, Easton overcame Pottsville with an 12-3 fourth quarter rally. Pottsville led 11-6 at halftime. Six of Easton's eight players scored in the victory.

Leading scorers: Easton – Arnold Ralph 9; Pottsville – Charles Dimmerling 9.

Mahanoy City 48 Tamaqua 25: With its win over Tamaqua, Mahanoy City pulled into second place, a game behind Allentown. Mahanoy City led 17-4 after a quarter and 35-11 at halftime.

Leading scorers: Mahanoy City – Paul Petrucha 17, Thomas Reing 14; Tamaqua – Lenny Quather 10.[15]

Hazleton 52 East Stroudsburg 16: Hazleton continued its dominance over East Stroudsburg with another decisive win after leading at the half 28-2. Twelve of the 13 players in the game scored for the Mountaineers.

Leading scorers: Hazleton – Stan Kokie 10; East Stroudsburg – Minor 6.[16]

Week 8

Hazleton 47 Mahanoy City 21: After falling behind 7-3 in the 1st quarter, Hazleton outscored Mahanoy City 14-1 in second quarter and were never threatened and put a dent in the homestanding Maroons hopes of a league title. Hazleton's Knox took over the league scoring lead from Copper McFadden.

Leading scorers: Hazleton – Homer Knox 22, Stan Kokie 15; Mahanoy City – Thomas Reing 11.[17]

Allentown 60 Tamaqua 37: The following night McFadden tallied 20 points to retake the lead in Allentown's easy defeat of Tamaqua. The Canaries' center Carl Meyers tapped the ball into the basket from a jump ball near the basket. Tamaqua lost one of its starting forwards Spangler in the 1st quarter due to fouls.

Leading scorers: Allentown –Joe McFadden 20, Carl Meyers 16, Harvey Weiss 14; Tamaqua – Art Mohn 12.

Bethlehem 34 Pottsville 29: With Bethlehem leading throughout the game, Pottsville battled back to tie the game at 27 with 4 minutes to go. Bethlehem's guard Krasowski took over the game at this point and led Coach Emrey's team to the win.

Leading scorers: Bethlehem – Charles Krasowski 12; Pottsville – Herb Wagner 11, Charles Dimmerling 10.

Easton 58 East Stroudsburg 21: In Easton's win over East Stroudsburg, it marked the sixth time that a team had scored over 50 points on the Monroe County team. Easton led at the half 28-5.

Leading scorers: Easton – Edwin Folk 17; East Stroudsburg - Clyde Lessig 12.[18]

The starting five Warshefsky, Bensinger, Minor, Herring, and Heller (all seniors) on the East Stroudsburg basketball team handed in their uniforms and quit the team shortly after East Stroudsburg lost its inter-borough match with Stroudsburg. They informed Coach Lew Hastie that it was best for them to quit and allow the underclassmen the opportunity to play and gain experience.[19]

Week 9

Allentown 33 Pottsville 30: In Pottsville, Allentown prevailed despite having one less field goal, 12-13, over the home team. The Canaries won the game at the foul line converting 9 of 13 while Pottsville converted only 4 of 11.

Leading scorers: Allentown – Joe McFadden 12, Lee Dietrick 10; Pottsville – George Dimmerling 12.

Mahanoy City 69 East Stroudsburg 27: Mahanoy City again thrashed helpless East Stroudsburg, reeling from the resignation of the starting five.

Leading scorers: Mahanoy City - Tommy Reing 23, Paul Petrucha 14, William Filer 14; East Stroudsburg – Clyde Lessig 15.

Bethlehem 28 Tamaqua 26 OT: Tamaqua's Blue Raiders, on their home court, forced Bethlehem into an extra period before losing. With Tamaqua leading 21-14 to begin the 4th quarter, Bethlehem scored 7 straight points to tie the game. With a Tamaqua win appearing to be a certainty, Bethlehem's substitute guard scored at the buzzer to tie the game and send it into overtime. Bethlehem's win kept them in a tie for second place with Mahanoy City.

Leading scorers: Bethlehem – Frank Kovacs 10; Tamaqua – Clair Heisler 9.

Hazleton 36 Easton 29: Hazleton won its 5th consecutive game over Easton to pull into a tie with the Red Raiders for fourth place. The game started more than two hours late because a sleet storm made it difficult for Easton to make it over the mountains to Hazleton.

Leading scorers: Hazleton – Stan Kokie 12; Easton – Bill Kraus 10.[20]

Week 10

Allentown 74 East Stroudsburg 13: In holding East Stroudsburg to 13 points, Allentown became the second team to score over 70 points. This marked the most points scored by a team in a game in league history. For some reason with the game well in hand, Coach Crum sent in his first string in the final quarter and they tallied 18 more points. East Stroudsburg played sophomores and juniors as every senior on the team quit the squad earlier in the season.

Leading scorers: Allentown –Bill Fahler 15, Carl Meyers 12, Joe McFadden 12; East Stroudsburg – Puzio 7.

Tamaqua 45 Pottsville 35: Tamaqua lost its center Koveleskie when he quit the team after an argument with Coach Pinky Purnell. Davies, a member of the junior varsity, was promoted as his replacement. Despite this change, Tamaqua beat Pottsville. During the fourth quarter, Matthews of Pottsville and Schaefer of Tamaqua got into a scuffle in the middle of floor and both were ejected from the game. As a result, a riot broke out in the stands involving most of the crowd. Fortunately, no one was injured seriously.

Leading scorers: Tamaqua – Art Mohn 16, Clair Heisler 10, Lenny Quather 10; Pottsville – George Dimmerling 14.[21]

Easton 29 Mahanoy City 26: Easton dashed any hopes that Mahanoy City had for a title with the victory in the Easton gym. Mahanoy City led 8-6 after a quarter, but Easton took the lead at the half 16-14 and led from thereon.

Leading scorers: Easton - Bill Kraus 14; Mahanoy City – Thomas Reing 11.

Bethlehem 24 Hazleton 23: Bethlehem's fifth consecutive win stopped Hazleton's win streak at 5. Bethlehem scored 12 points in the 4th quarter to snatch the win. Down 19-12 with 5 minutes to play, every player on the court contributed points in those minutes to pull out the victory.

Leading scorers: Bethlehem – Charles Krasowsky 6, Jolie Spevak 6; Hazleton – Homer Knox 9.[22]

Allentown 33 Hazleton 30: Playing its second game in the week, Allentown put down Hazleton to even Hazleton's record at 6-6. Down 5-0 on the Mountaineers' home court, Coach Crum's troops rallied to tie the score at 10 in front of 1700 fans. Joe McFadden was held to 5 points by Hazleton's Tomanchek.

Leading scorers: Allentown - Carl Meyers 12; Hazleton – Stan Kokie 8.

Bethlehem 74 East Stroudsburg 17: For the second time in the week, East Stroudsburg gave up 74 points. This time Bethlehem laced the Cavaliers after taking a 32-9 halftime lead.

Leading scorers: Bethlehem – Frank Kovacs 17, Charles Krasowski 17, Jolie Spevak 14; East Stroudsburg – Clyde Lessig 9.

Tamaqua 32 Easton 29: Despite trailing 21-10 during the 3rd quarter on the road in Easton, Tamaqua rallied and took the lead going into the 4th quarter 24-22. Tamaqua maintained the lead to win and shock the Red Rovers.

Leading scorers: Tamaqua – Art Mohn 11; Easton – Ralph Young 10.[23]

Mahanoy City 36 Pottsville 22: Mahanoy City avenged an early season defeat at Pottsville. Pottsville took a 5-4 lead after the first quarter, but it was all Mahanoy City after that.

Leading scorers: Mahanoy City – Paul Petrucha 18; Pottsville – Richard Dietrich 7.[24]

Week 11

Allentown 31 Easton 28: In front of 2500 fans at the Little Palestra, Allentown clinched its 4th league title in the 10 years of the league's existence. Easton pressed the Canaries hard in attempt to avenge a defeat earlier in the season. Easton led for most of the game with Allentown finally taking the lead late 24-23 in the 3rd quarter. With a minute left, Easton tied the game at 28, but the Canaries prevailed to begin the celebration.

Leading scorers: Allentown - Joe McFadden 10; Easton – Meyers 16.

Pottsville 81 East Stroudsburg 21: At Pottsville, East Stroudsburg suffered yet another humiliating defeat. Jumping out to a 20-1 first quarter lead, the 81 points set a league scoring record.

Leading scorers: Pottsville - George Dimmerling 32, Herb Wagner 21, George Daubert 16; East Stroudsburg – Clyde Lessig 9.

Bethlehem 41 Mahanoy City 24: With over 1500 fans in attendance, Bethlehem closed out its home schedule with a win over Mahanoy City. The win secured second place for the Hurricane.

Leading scorers: Bethlehem – Jolie Spevak 16, Frank Kovacs 15; Mahanoy City – Thomas Reing 10.

Tamaqua 25 Hazleton 23: Tamaqua eked out a win in the last minute over Hazleton. Hazleton led 23-21 when Clair Heisler and Lenny Quather each scored a field goal to drop the Mountaineers' record to an uncharacteristic 6-7 and 5th place in the league.

Leading scorers: Tamaqua – Clair Heisler 9; Hazleton – Joe Tomanchek 6.[25]

Week 12

Allentown 36 Mahanoy City 19: Allentown closed out the regular season on the road with victory over Mahanoy City. Coach Paul Clymer, who took over for Coach Crum, played the game with substitutes except for Joe McFadden who was in the running for the league scoring title. The rest of the varsity traveled with Coach Crum to Reading for the Reading-Steelton game.

Leading scorers: Allentown – Joe McFadden 18, Willie Piff 10; Mahanoy City – William File 9.

Hazleton 32 Pottsville 25: After Pottsville held a 20-16 lead at the half, Hazleton rallied to even its record at 6-6 with a win over Pottsville.

Leading scorers: Hazleton – Stan Kokie 10; Pottsville – Herb Wagner 7.

Tamaqua 59 East Stroudsburg 18: Tamaqua rolled over hapless East Stroudsburg after taking a 29-7 halftime lead. Their best showing during the season was a 15-point loss to Pottsville.

Leading scorers: Tamaqua–Art Mohn 16, Lenny Quather 14, Harry Spangler 10; East Stroudsburg-Clyde Lessig 7.

Easton 24 Bethlehem 23: Bethlehem forward Jolie Spevak earned the most dubious distinction for the season when he inadvertently scored a basket for Easton in the 3rd period. After a scramble for the ball near the Easton basket, Spevak lost his sense of location resulting in the basket for the Red Rovers. Bethlehem had rallied to tie the score at 20-20 after trailing most of the game. As it turned out, Spevak's inadvertent basket turned out to be the difference in Easton's win.

Leading scorers: Easton – Bill Kraus 9; Bethlehem – Frank Kovacs 11.[26]

Postseason Play

Allentown 46 South Whitehall 26: Allentown opened post season action against the Lehigh-Northampton League champions South Whitehall at the Little Palestra. Although South Whitehall only led in the first minute 2-0, they battled the Canaries for three periods before succumbing in the first district playoff game. They trailed 33-24 heading into the fourth quarter, during which they were held to two points.

Leading scorers: Allentown - Carl Meyers 14, Joe McFadden 13; South Whitehall – Clarence Grammes 9.[27]

Allentown 31 Frackville 29: In front of 2200 fans in Pottsville, Allentown battled a very game Frackville team, the Schuylkill County League champions. Allentown led at the half 19-11 but Frackville rallied in the second half to make the game close. Leading with 30 seconds left, Allentown was able to hold on over Frackville, whose 19-game win streak was snapped, with no further scoring.

Leading scorers: Allentown – Joe McFadden 10; Frackville – Ed Burchill 11, Cyril Copeland 10.[28]

Allentown 23 Stroudsburg 21: In another thriller at Bethlehem's Liberty gym, Harvey Weiss sunk a field goal in the last 45 seconds against Stroudsburg, the Lehigh Valley League champions, to give the Canaries the District XI crown. Stroudsburg had held the lead at 18-15 at one point during the 3rd period. The score was tied several times in the final period before Weiss won the game with his basket.

Leading scorers: Allentown – Joe McFadden 8; Stroudsburg – Melick 10.[29]

Allentown 30 Steelton 24: Trailing 16-12 before 4500 fans at the Zembo Mosque in Harrisburg, Allentown unleashed a 2nd half offense and stifling man-to-man defense to disappoint Steelton. Steelton scored 2 points, both on free throws, in the 3rd quarter. A special train with 11 coaches and roughly 2000 fans traveled to Harrisburg to cheer on the Canaries. Thirty buses transported the fans from the train terminal to the gym.

Leading scorers: Allentown - Ron Leonard 10; Steelton – Anthony Rozman 7.[30]

Allentown 28 Pottstown 16: Scoring 10 points to Pottstown's 2 points in the second quarter boosted Allentown to the win at the Villanova gym in suburban Philadelphia. The Canaries had defeated Pottstown, the District 1 champions, twice earlier in non-league games.

Leading scorers: Allentown - Joe McFadden 13; Pottstown – Elmer Pollick 7.[31]

Allentown 30 Berwick 28: After leading 16-7 at the quarter and 21-14 at the half, Allentown fought hard to hold off a determined Berwick Bulldog team at the Pottsville gym. The Bulldogs tied the score at 23 in the third period. The Canaries held off the Berwick attack to win the Eastern title. In a balanced offense, no Canary scored in double figures. The Canaries were now off to the state title game for the first time.

Leading scorers: Allentown – Joe McFadden 9; Berwick – Bill Kirk 8, Nick Koch 8.[32]

Allentown 32 Rankin 19: In a matchup at the Penn Palestra in front of 6500 fans, the Canaries faced the Western Regional champions, Rankin High School for the PIAA State Championship. The Canaries trailed at the end of the first quarter 6-4, led at the half 12-8, and were tied 12-12 with the Rabbits of Rankin early in the 3rd period. Allentown outscored Rankin 13-4 in the final period for a relatively easy win. As a result of the win, the High School was given the day off on Monday following the win to allow the students to celebrate and savor the title. This was the 3rd state title during the first ten years of the league's existence.

Leading scorers: Allentown – Carl Meyers 11; Rankin – Toto Campagone 10.[33]

Postseason Accolades

Top scorers were: Joseph McFadden, Allentown, 179 points; Thomas Reing, Mahanoy City, 160 points; Herb Wagner, Pottsville, 145 points; Charles Dimmerling, Pottsville, 142 points; Paul Petrucka, Mahanoy City, 134 points; Stan Kokie, Hazleton, 123 points; Homer Knox, Hazleton, 117 points; Frank Kovacs, Bethlehem, 114 points; Len Quather, Tamaqua, and Charlie Krasowski, Bethlehem, both 102 points.[34]

The all-stars selected by the league include: forwards Joe "Copper" McFadden, Allentown; Stan Kokie, Hazleton; Charles Dimmerling, Pottsville; Homer Knox, Hazleton; and Herbert Wagner, Pottsville; centers Carl Meyers, Allentown; and Thomas Reing, Mahanoy City; guards William Fahler, Allentown; Lee Dietrick, Allentown; Augustine "Gus" Neimeister, Bethlehem; Clair Heisler, Tamaqua; and Bill Kraus, Easton.[35]

Final Standings

Allentown	13-1
Bethlehem	10-4
Mahanoy City	8-6
Easton	8-6
Hazleton	7-7
Tamaqua	6-8
Pottsville	4-10
East Stroudsburg	0-14

Team Rosters

Allentown: Coach J. Birney Crum, Lee Dietrick, William "Fat" Fahler, Walter Jones, Ronald "Chup" Leonard, Joe "Copper" McFadden, Carl Meyers, Arpad Milkovics, Rudolph Rossi, Harvey Weiss

Bethlehem: Coach Bill Emrey, Truman Frey, James Gillespie, Joseph Hochella, Frank Kovacs, Charlie Krasowski, George Melloy, Augustine "Gus" Neimeister, William O'Donnell, John Quigg, Harry Simon, Jolie Spevak, Joseph Zigrai.

East Stroudsburg: Coach Lew Hastie, Beaver, Bensinger, Brocht, Tom Carmella, Heller, Herring, Clyde Lessig, Minor, Sam Puzio, Sommers, Townsend, John Warshefsky

Easton: Coach Clyde Notestine, Joseph Alfero, Epstein, Edwin Folk, Bill Kraus, Maddock, Mazza, Richard Myers, Reinard Parry, Roland Prime. Arnold Ralph, Ralph Young.

Hazleton: Coach Hugh McFadden, Anthony Apichella, Norbert Bechtloff, Dombroski, Dougherty, John Gallagher, Isadore Kline, Homer Knox, Stan Kokie, John Kotch, George Lieb, Joe Moran, Mike Scatton, Walter Strenk, Joe Tomanchek, Robert Wills.

Mahanoy City: Coach John Goepfert, Michael Chernock, William Filer, Wilbert Giles, Paul Petrucha, Stan Pietresiewski, Edmund Rakaitis, Thomas Reing, Larry Ryan, Chester Setcavage, John Simco, Joe Urban, Joe Zukowsky.

Pottsville: Coach George Dimmerling, George Daubert, Richard Dietrich, Charles Dimmerling, George Gregor, James Hobbs, Richard Matthews, Francis Polinchock, Hayden Richard, Harold Sachs, Herbert Wagner.

Tamaqua: Coach Eli "Pinky" Purnell, Sam Davies, Bill Dornblaser, Danny Evans, Elwood Faust, Clair Heisler, Ken Keich, Joseph Kovelesky, Art "Lefty" Mohn, Lenny Quather, Del Schaeffer, Harry Spangler, Paul Wetterau, Don Whitehead, Peter Zatoris.

Leonard Quather was elected captain of the 1935 Tamaqua football team and the 1936 basketball squad. Unfortunately, Lenny contracted pneumonia in late April 1935 and after a two-week illness, died in May 1935.[36]

Allentown High School – 1935 League and State Champions[37]

Harvey Weiss **Rudolph Rossi** **Bill Fahler** **Ronald Leonard**

Carl Meyers Joe McFadden Lee Dietrick Charley Jones

1936

East Stroudsburg Exits

In November after the league had already released its season schedule, East Stroudsburg announced its withdrawal from the league for 1936 season. In their four years in the league, they had managed to win only about a third of their games with an overall record of 17-35. In the 1935 season, they were vastly overmatched by the stiff competition. In their 14 contests, they were outscored 841-249. East Stroudsburg joined the Lehigh-Northampton League, also known as the Two County League. This league became an eight-team league and included Nazareth, Pen Argyl, Bangor, South Whitehall, Coplay, Hellertown, and Wilson Boro.[1]

East Stroudsburg's withdrawal created strange scheduling arrangements which always saw one of the league's teams idle in league action on a league night. Frackville was considered as a replacement for East Stroudsburg, but, to their disappointment, the league opted not to add an 8th team at this late date.[2] The league kept the previously adopted schedule with those teams scheduled to play East Stroudsburg getting an off night in league play.

On December 13, Allentown superintendent of schools Hiram Dodd announced that Captain Joe "Copper" McFadden would not be eligible for play since he had exhausted his four years of eligibility having already played his fourth year of high school basketball during the 1935 championship season. He had previously played two years at Allentown Central Catholic in addition to his two years at Allentown. McFadden had been the starting quarterback on the Allentown football team for the past two seasons in addition to being an honor student and president of his senior class. After having played in three early season non-league contests, McFadden was now lost for the season and it dealt a blow to the Canaries in defense of their title.[3]

Week 1

Tamaqua 32 Hazleton 31: Tamaqua opened the season at Hazleton with a surprising, come-from-behind win over Coach McGeehan's team. Hazleton had led the entire game up to the last minute, including 15-7 at halftime.

Leading scorers: Tamaqua – Ken Keich 11; Hazleton – Joe Podany 14.

Mahanoy City 25 Pottsville 21: On their home court, Mahanoy City disposed of Coach Dimmerling's Pottsville team after jumping out to a 11-2 lead in the first quarter and 15-8 at halftime.

Leading scorers: Mahanoy City – John Gabuzda 11; Pottsville – Herb Wagner 13.[4]

Bethlehem 43 Easton 24: Bethlehem held only a 19-17 lead at the half before their offense exploded for an easy win. No boxscore.[3]

Week 2

Allentown 30 Hazleton 25: On their home court, Allentown opened the defense of its state championship by handing Hazleton a second consecutive league loss. Allentown, led by forward "Shoop" Leonard never trailed in the game.

Leading scorers: Allentown – Ronald Leonard 15; Hazleton – Joe Podany 6, Joe Dobrynio 6.

Tamaqua 42 Easton 31: After Easton led at the half 21-18, Tamaqua rallied to take the lead in the third quarter and hand Easton its second consecutive loss.

Leading scorers: Tamaqua - Sam Davies 17, Ken Keich 13; Easton – Roland Prime 10.[5]

Bethlehem 30 Mahanoy City 22: On a rare Thursday night game, Bethlehem handed Mahanoy City its first league loss to tie Tamaqua for the league lead at 2-0. Frank Kovacs scored all his points in the first half.

Leading scorers: Bethlehem – Frank Kovacs 14; Mahanoy City – John Gabuzda 8.[6]

Week 3

Bethlehem 42 Pottsville 21: Coach Emrey's Liberty boys continued their hot start with a win over homestanding Pottsville. Bethlehem outscored Pottsville 17-1 in the 2nd period to take a 24-5 halftime lead.

Leading scorers: Bethlehem – Frank Kovacs 15, Jolie Spevak 10; Pottsville – Herb Wagner 6.

Allentown 41 Tamaqua 19: Led by forward Willie Piff, Allentown's Canaries easily defeated Tamaqua at the Little Palestra in front of 2500 fans. Allentown captain Bill Fahler and Tamaqua forward Del Schaeffer traded punches at mid-court early in the 4th period and were both ejected from the game. Special police rushed back spectators to their seats when they began to swarm the floor after the scuffle.

Leading scorers: Allentown – Willie Piff 15; Tamaqua – Ken Keich 5, Ed Luckshides 5.

Hazleton 29 Easton 27: Hazleton pulled out its first league victory over Easton. With Easton leading 20-13 at halftime, Hazleton rallied in the 3rd quarter outscoring the Red Rovers 12-2 to take the lead.

Leading scorers: Hazleton - Ed Yevak 12; Easton - Arnold Ralph 9.[7]

Week 4

Allentown 29 Easton 24: Allentown, with a balanced scoring attack with no player scoring more than 8 points, outlasted Easton. With both teams having a total of 9 field goals, the Canaries won the game on the foul line making 11 out of 17 while the Red Rovers only converted 6 of 13. The win moved Allentown into a tie for first with idle Bethlehem, both at 3-0.

Leading scorers: Allentown - Willie Piff 8, Bill Fahler; Easton – Kenneth Fahl 8.

Hazleton 28 Mahanoy City 20: Hazleton won its second game to even their record at 2-2 with a win over Mahanoy City. The Mountaineers took a 16-8 lead at halftime which held up for the win.

Leading scorers: Hazleton – Joe Podany 11; Mahanoy City – John Gabuzda 4, Stan Setcavage 4, John Sluzevich 4, Doro Serano 4.[8]

Tamaqua 44 Pottsville 28: Pottsville lost two of its key players to personal fouls and was not able to hold off Tamaqua. Captain Richard Dietrich fouled out in the 2nd period and center George Daubert fouled out in the 3rd period. Tamaqua's win kept them right behind Allentown and Bethlehem at 3-1.

Leading scorers: Tamaqua – Don Whitehead 10; Pottsville – Herb Wagner 11.[9]

Week 5

Bethlehem 30 Allentown 28: A pivotal matchup between Allentown and its archrival Bethlehem took place in the Liberty gym in front of 2500 fans. Bethlehem prevailed in a game which neither team was ahead by more than two points for most of the game. Harry Simon's last-minute basket won the game. The win gave Bethlehem 8 straight wins with four of them in the league. They were now alone at the top of the standings.

Leading scorers: Bethlehem - Frank Kovacs 11; Allentown - Willie Piff 13.

Hazleton 23 Pottsville 22: Converting 11 of 18 foul shots, Hazleton eked out a win over Pottsville. Pottsville had one more field goal than Hazleton, but three less converted free throws leading to the loss.

Leading scorers: Hazleton – Joe Padony 9; Pottsville - Herb Wagner 16.

Mahanoy City 31 Tamaqua 25: At home, after trailing 15-6 after a quarter, Tamaqua came back to within two points 20-18 at the half and 25-23 after the third quarter only to have Mahanoy City hang on for the win. Tamaqua lost its second consecutive game to fall to third at 3-2.

Leading scorers: Mahanoy City – John Fedorchalk 8; Tamaqua – Ken Keich 8.[10]

Week 6

Hazleton 26 Bethlehem 16: Bethlehem's joy was short lived as Hazleton handed them their first loss of the season. Before an overflow crowd in Hazleton, the Mountaineers held only a one-point lead going into the 4th quarter, but outscored Bethlehem 10-1 in the final stanza to chalk up the victory.

Leading scorers: Hazleton – Joe Podany 11; Bethlehem Frank Kovacs 6.[11]

Allentown 32 Pottsville 18: At the Little Palestra, Allentown, with balanced scoring from six players, pulled even with Bethlehem at 4-1 with its win over Pottsville. The Canaries took a commanding 22-11 lead after three quarters.

Leading scorers: Allentown – Ronald Leonard 9; Pottsville – Herb Wagner 10.

Mahanoy City 27 Easton 25: Despite having four more field goals (10 to 6), Easton lost out to Mahanoy City. Coach Goepert's team converted 15 of 25 free throws to 5 of 13 by Easton to pull out the win. Easton led after the first two quarters only to have Mahanoy City move ahead in the second half.

Leading scorers: Mahanoy City – John Fedorchalk 7; Easton – Al Misero 8.[12]

Week 7

Allentown 34 Mahanoy City 27: On a Tuesday night, Allentown traveled to Mahanoy City and met up with a feisty opponent who held the lead after three periods 21-20. However, Allentown went on a 13-6 run for the win.

Leading scorers: Allentown – Leo Blankowitsch 12, Willie Piff 12; Mahanoy City – Stan Sekula 10.

Easton 35 Pottsville 31: After being tied at 14-14 at halftime, Easton picked up its offense for their first win at winless Pottsville.

Leading scorers: Easton – Al Misero 10; Pottsville - Herb Wagner 13.[13]

Tamaqua 47 Bethlehem 34: Visiting Tamaqua handed Bethlehem a loss as the Tams scored a league record 25 points in the 4th quarter to turn a close game into a rout. Tamaqua led 22-21 after three quarters.

Leading scorers: Tamaqua – Ken Keich 15, Sam Davies 13, Del Shaeffer 13; Bethlehem – Frank Kovacs 10, Walt Kresge 10.[14]

Tamaqua 38 Hazleton 23: Tamaqua dominated Coach McGeehan's team from the start in Hazleton taking a 7-0 lead at the outset and handed the Mountaineers one of their worst defeats in several years. Only once did Hazleton threaten at 20-16, but the Tams suppressed the rally to win.

Leading scorers: Tamaqua - Ken Keich 12, Sam Davies 10; Hazleton – Joe Padony 7.[15]

Easton 35 Bethlehem 23: Meanwhile, Easton won its first league game while handing Bethlehem's its third straight loss. Easton took an early lead and held the lead after every quarter.

Leading scorers: Easton - Bill Kraus 11; Bethlehem – Jolie Spevak 8.

Pottsville 37 Mahanoy City 22: Playing at home, Pottsville also won its first over Mahanoy City in resounding fashion. A stifling defense held Mahanoy City to only three field goals while Pottsville responded with 15.

Leading scorers: Pottsville – Herb Wagner 16; Mahanoy City – John Fedorchalk 10.[16]

Week 8

Hazleton 26 Allentown 20: A total collapse by Allentown in the 2nd half at Hazleton allowed the home team to pick up at a win to knock Allentown out of first place. Leading 19-9 at halftime, the Canaries were outscored 17-1 after the intermission. The single point on a free throw was scored midway through the final period. Late in the game, the Canaries' Willie Piff fouled out and was replaced by Berry, who failed to report his entrance into the game. Hazleton was awarded a technical foul which was converted to add to Allentown's downfall.

Leading scorers: Hazleton – Bill Bechtloff 9, Joe Podany 9; Allentown – Willie Piff 7.

Tamaqua 34 Easton 27: Meanwhile, Tamaqua moved into first place with a 6-2 record with its win over Easton. The Tams rallied from a 20-14 third quarter deficit to lead 22-21 heading into the fourth quarter.

Leading scorers: Tamaqua – Sam Davies 16; Easton – Bill Kraus 10.

Mahanoy City 31 Bethlehem 15: Bethlehem traveled to Mahanoy City and apparently left its offense behind as they were handed a resounding loss. Bethlehem trailed 21-7 at the half.

Leading scorers: Mahanoy City – John Gabuzda 10, Stan Sekula 10: Bethlehem – Jolie Spevak 4.[17]

Week 9

Allentown 36 Tamaqua 24: Allentown regained first place with an easy win at Tamaqua behind 14 points from forward Leonard and 10 from Piff. The win was the 8th straight over the Tams who didn't have a win over the Canaries since they joined the league. At the end of the game, the rival captains, Bill Fahler, Allentown, and Del Shaffer, Tamaqua, exchanged punches in the center of the floor. Fans from both teams rushed onto the floor. Fortunately, Coaches Crum and McGeehan were able to separate the players and restore order.

Leading scorers: Allentown - Ronald Leonard 14, Willie Piff 10; Tamaqua – Sam Davies 9.

Hazleton 34 Easton 22: Hazleton moved into a tie with Tamaqua for second place at 6-3 by defeating Easton. With Hazleton leading 16-13 at the half, Easton took a 17-16 lead before Hazleton went on an 18-5 run to win the game.

Leading scorers: Hazleton – Billy Bechtloft 12; Easton - Bill Kraus 10.

Bethlehem-Pottsville: The only other matchup between Bethlehem and Pottsville was postponed.[18]

In the middle of February, Bethlehem's coach William Emrey suspended four players from the varsity for violating PIAA rules. Joseph Spevak, Michael Karabin, George Zigrai, and Charles Sweigard apparently played using false names to compete on two different teams. Spevak and Karabin played Sunday basketball with the National Sokols and Zagrai played with the Lehigh Croations. All four boys became ineligible to play scholastic basketball. In addition, Bethlehem lost John Kichline due to scholastic ineligibility. Another player, Joseph Hochella, graduated during the school year and became ineligible. The loss of these players left the roster thin and very inexperienced, which compromised Bethlehem's ability to compete with the other league teams.[19]

Week 10

Pottsville 41 Bethlehem 25: Coach Emrey's Bethlehem squad lost its fifth consecutive game due to the inexperienced roster due to the loss of most of his early season starters. On a Tuesday night, Pottsville traveled to Bethlehem for a make up game from the previous Friday when poor road conditions forced the postponement. With a young and inexperienced team, Coach Emrey played all 12 players on the restructured roster.

Leading scorers: Pottsville – Richard Dietrich 9, Richard Striegel 9; Bethlehem – Harry Simon 10.[19]

Pottsville 60 Tamaqua 34: Later in the week, Pottsville won its second game of the week with a lacing of Tamaqua. Pottsville took a six-point lead after a quarter and built it to twelve and seventeen after the next two quarters. The loss dropped Tamaqua into third place behind Allentown and Hazleton.

Leading scorers: Pottsville – Herb Wagner 26; Tamaqua – Sam Davies 11.

Hazleton 33 Mahanoy City 25: Hazleton defeated Mahanoy City after being behind 19-10 at the half and not taking the lead until the end of the 3rd quarter 24-23. Hazleton closed out the game with a 9-2 run.

Leading scorers: Hazleton – Rocco Antinozzi 9; Mahanoy City – Stan Sekula 10.

Allentown 44 Easton 19: Despite losing Wille Piff on personal fouls early in the second quarter, Allentown rolled to an easy win over Easton's Red Rovers. Forward "Chup" Leonard led the Canaries to a 24-8 halftime lead. Easton showed up an hour late due to extremely treacherous road conditions.

Leading scorers: Allentown – Ronald Leonard 15; Easton – Al Misero 9.[20]

Week 11

Allentown 35 Bethlehem 16: In a rematch between Allentown and Bethlehem, Kresge from Liberty and Allentown's Leonard exchanged punches on the court about three minutes before the end of the game. About 100 fans poured onto the floor and traded punches for about 15 minutes before order could be restored by the police by using black jacks. Before the game started, four Bethlehem players opted to warm up at the Allentown basket and not participate with their teammates at their designated basket. Coach Emrey pleaded with the players and they finally joined their teammates at the correct end of the floor.

Leading scorers: Allentown - Willie Piff 14, Ronald Leonard 10; Bethlehem – Walt Kresge 6.

Hazleton 42 Pottsville 29: Hazleton kept pace with the Canaries with their win over Pottsville. Hazleton led throughout the contest and held a 22-13 halftime lead.

Leading scorers: Hazleton –Joe Podany 14, Ed Yevak 11; Pottsville – Richard Dietrich 13, Herb Wagner 10.

Tamaqua 41 Mahanoy City 28: With forward Keich scoring most of his points during the last 4 minutes of the game, Tamaqua, on its home floor, defeated Mahanoy City. Mahanoy City had led the game 24-22 when Tamaqua went on a 19-4 run for the win.

Leading scorers: Tamaqua – Ken Keich 18, Sam Davies 11; Mahanoy City – John Gabuzda 11.[21]

Week 12

Bethlehem 39 Hazleton 26: In the most surprising upset of the season, Bethlehem dashed Hazleton's hopes of overtaking Allentown for the league title. Led by sophomore and junior varsity player, Truman

Frey, Bethlehem shocked Hazleton. Hazleton had led 7-1 early in the game before the Hurricane came alive. Hazleton finished 8-4.

Leading scorers: Bethlehem – Truman Frey 14, Frank Kovacs 10; Hazleton – Bill Bechtloff 8, Norbert Bechtloff 8.

Allentown 41 Pottsville 29: The Canaries led 10-8 after a quarter and increased it to 23-14 at the half. Allentown stood at 9-2 and clinched the title with one game to play after their win at Pottsville.

Leading scorers: Allentown - Willie Piff 15, Ron Leonard 10; Pottsville - Richards 8.

Mahanoy City 35 Easton 31: Easton remained in the league cellar after its 9th loss at Mahanoy City. With the teams even on field goals, Mahanoy City converted 11 free throws to 7 for Easton to seal the win. Easton trailed the entire game.

Leading scorers: Mahanoy City – John Gabuzda 8, Stan Sekula 8, John Sluzevich 8; Easton – Russell Nobel 8.[22]

Week 13

Allentown 32 Mahanoy City 23: Outscoring Mahanoy City 12-0 in the 3rd period, Allentown finished the season at 10-2 with the win at the Little Palestra. Coach Crum played his second string the entire 4th period.

Leading scorers: Allentown – Willie Piff 13; Mahanoy City – John Fedorchalk 8.

Easton 25 Pottsville 23: After trailing 7-3 after a quarter, Easton charged into the lead at the half 11-8 and never lost the lead. Easton pulled into a tie with Pottsville for last place at 3-9. The difference in the win was two more converted free throws for Easton.

Leading scorers: Easton – Bill Kraus 10; Pottsville – George Daubert 6.

Tamaqua 31 Bethlehem 21: After trailing 9-6 after a quarter, Coach Eli Purnell's Tams rallied to defeat Bethlehem and finish a very trying season for Coach Emrey. The win pulled Tamaqua into what turned out to be a very critical tie for second place with Hazleton.

Leading scorers: Tamaqua – Ken Keich 14; Bethlehem – Truman Frey 8, Harry Simons 8.[23]

Disqualification: In a March 6 meeting, Allentown was banned from the state playoffs and could not defend the state title. They were allowed to retain the league title. Although Joe "Copper" McFadden had only played in games against Trenton, NJ, Muhlenberg College freshmen, and Allentown Prep, the PIAA ruled that member schools must abide by PIAA regulations in all games. Hazleton and Tamaqua were tied for second place and were selected to playoff for right to represent the league in the state playoffs.[24]

League Playoff

Tamaqua 27 Hazleton 26: With Allentown disqualified, Eli Purnell's Blue Raiders met McGeehan's Mountaineers at Mahanoy City to decide who would represent the league in the district playoffs. Although Hazleton scored two more field goals (10 to 8), Tamaqua converted 11 free throws to 6 for Hazleton to pull out a one-point victory. Hazleton lost captain Dobrynio at the end of the 3rd quarter on personal fouls.

Leading scorers: Tamaqua – Ed Luckshides 10; Hazleton – Joe Podany 11.[25]

Postseason Play

Tamaqua 33 Catasauqua 20: At the Little Palestra in Allentown, Tamaqua easily handled Catasauqua, the Lehigh Valley League champions, to move to round two against Freeland. Catasauqua had led for most of the first half until Tamaqua wore them down and led for good at 13-11 near the end of the first half.

Leading scorers: Tamaqua – Ken Keich 13; Catasauqua – Frank Mihalik 6.[26]

Freeland 38 Tamaqua 26: Several days prior to the game, three Freeland players were injured enroute to practice in Allentown. However, the Carbon-Schuylkill Champs were still able to best Tamaqua. Tamaqua lost captain Del Shaffer on personal fouls near the end of the first half. Extra police were dispatched to the Little Palestra due to concerns of potential trouble between the fans of the rival schools. The police detail was able to prevent any trouble at the end of the game.

Leading scorers: Freeland – Chappy Boyle 14; Tamaqua – Ken Keich 8.[27]

Postseason Accolades

Leading scorers were: Herb Wagner, Pottsville, 134 points; Willie Piff, Allentown, 123 points; Ken Keich, Tamaqua, 121 points, Sam Davies, Tamaqua, 120 points; Ronald "Chup" Leonard, Allentown, 114 points; Joe Podany, Hazleton, 97 points; Frank Kovacs, Bethlehem, 95 points; John Gabuzda, Mahanoy City, 78 points; and Bill Kraus, Easton, and Stan Sekula, Mahanoy City, 74 points.[28]

The league all-stars included:

Forwards – Willie Piff, Allentown; Herb Wagner, Pottsville; Frank Kovacs, Bethlehem; Ronald Leonard, Allentown; Ken Keich, Tamaqua; and Joe Podany, Hazleton. Centers – Sam Davies, Tamaqua, and George Daubert, Pottsville. Guards: Bill Fahler, Allentown; Bill Kraus, Easton; Norby Bechtloft, Hazleton; and Ed Luckshides, Tamaqua.[29]

Final Standings

Allentown	10-2
Hazleton	8-4
Tamaqua	8-4
Bethlehem	5-7
Mahanoy City	5-7
Easton	3-9
Pottsville	3-9

Team Rosters

Allentown: Coach J. Birney Crum; Robert "Haps" Benfer, Lewis Berry, Leo Blankowitsch, Al Boandl, Joseph Brey, Dick Busby, Bill Fahler, Herman Krevsky, Ronald "Chup" Leonard, Joe "Copper" McFadden, Arpad Milkovics, Karl Meyers; Ralph Perilla, Willie Piff, Donald Praetorius, Leonard Rohn, Robert Reber, Charles Reinsmith, Henry Weider.

Bethlehem: Coach Bill Emrey, Gordon Brandt, William Forrest, Truman Frey, Kenneth Grube, Joseph Hochella, Socrates James, Joseph Karabin, Al Kerchmar, Frank Kovacs, Walter Kresge, Stephen Marchak,

George Melloy, William O'Donnell, Alex Radchuck, Robert Reiss, Harry Simon, Jolie Spevak, Stephen Sweets, Joseph Zigrai.

Easton: Coach Clyde Notestine, Altimer, Kenneth Fahl, Heard, Kraus, Russell Meyers, Albert Misero, Anthony Noble, Roland Prime, Arnold Ralph, Philip Riehl, Schuk.

Hazleton: Coach Hugh McGeehan, Rocco Antinozzi, William Bechtloff, Norbert Bechtloff, Best, Bodoni, Ken "Chief" Brownson, Joe Dobrynio, J. Dombrosky, John Gallagher, Joe Podany, Howard "Cy" Seybert, Ed Yevak.

Mahanoy City: Coach John Goepfert, J, Derosiers, William Dodds, John Fedorchalk, John Gabuzda, Victor Gavanus, Marvin Jacoby, Frank Molisius, Edward Pangonis, Stan Sekula, Doro Serano, Stanley Setcavage, John Sluzevich.

Pottsville: Coach George Dimmerling, Richard Bennie, Bitting, Harry Brecker, George Daubert, Richard Dietrich, Paul Dimmerling, John Furman, John Gorman, Jack Hochgertel, Robert Horn, Jones, Hayden Richards, Harold Sachs, Richard Striegel, Herb Wagner.

Tamaqua: Coach Eli "Pinky" Purnell, Michael Burcin, Sam Davies, Bill Dornblazer, Bruce Fegley, Victor Gigli, Charles Heister, Ken Keich, Leroy Kemery, Lester Lockwood, Edward Luckshides, John Pierson, Sam Saylor, Del Shaeffer, George Tepo, Robert Willauer, Don Whitehead.

After his passing of the ravages of pneumonia in May 1935, the Tamaqua basketball team honored Lenny Quather as a team captain for the 1936 team.

Tamaqua High School – 1936 League Champions[30]

Front Row: Luckshides, Whitehead, Davies, Keich, Shaeffer

Second Row: Saylor, Fegley, Tepo, Dornbalzer

Back Row: Pierson, Coach Purnell, Gigli, Waidell, Lockwood

1937

League Holds at Seven Members

After the 1936 season ended, the league met in April in Pottsville to wrap up business from the just completed season and to reorganize for the 1937 season. Officers elected for the upcoming season included: D. H. H. Lengle, Pottsville, president; H. C. Armour, Mahanoy City, vice president; and Edgar Rabenold, Allentown, secretary/treasurer. Noticeably absent at the meeting was discussion about the addition of an 8th member into the league. The league adopted a schedule with the existing seven league members.[1]

At a preseason meeting in December 1936 just prior to the opening night of the new season, the league members met at the Hotel Allen in Allentown to review player eligibility. To eliminate the many player eligibility problems within the league in the recent seasons, the East Penn League adopted a new rule for the 1937 season. All league players had to file official birth certificates with the league secretary prior to January 31 or would be dropped from league eligibility. The league passed another resolution which required schools to allow scouts admission to their games. Scouts had been refused admission to games by some of the schools. The league operated under their unbalanced arrangement with only seven league members.[2]

Week 1

Bethlehem 46 Pottsville 9: Bethlehem opened with a resounding victory over Pottsville. Playing on their home floor, Pottsville scored only three points in the last three periods of the game against a stingy Bethlehem defense. Leading scorers: Bethlehem - Walter Kresge 20, Frank Kovacs 10; Pottsville – Paul Dimmerling 2, Harold Sachs 2, John Gorman 2.

Hazleton 35 Tamaqua 24: After the teams tied 7-7 at the end of the first quarter, Hazleton, on its home court, pulled away the rest of the game for a win over Tamaqua.

Leading scorers: Hazleton - Joe Podany 16, Bill Bechtloft 10; Tamaqua – Ed Luckshides 11.

Easton 43 Mahanoy City 26: Easton scored 15 points in the 3rd quarter before Mahanoy City registered a single point to put the game away for the Red Rovers. Easton had led by only a single point 19-18 at halftime.

Leading scorers: Easton - Al Misero 14, Roland Prime 10; Mahanoy City – Stan Sekula 11.[3]

Week 2

Hazleton 27 Allentown 20: Allentown opened its league season at home against Hazleton in front of 2500 fans. To the fans' delight, Allentown raced out to a 7-0 lead only to see Hazleton counter by scoring the next 10 points and take the lead in the 2nd quarter. Hazleton led at the half 12-10 and 19-12 after the third period.

Leading scorers: Hazleton – Rocco Antinozzi 7; Allentown – Leo Blankowitsch 7, Willie Piff 7.

Mahanoy City 28 Pottsville 14: In a rough and tumble game at Mahanoy City, a total of 42 fouls were called on the two teams. After trailing 7-4 after a quarter, Mahanoy City took the lead 11-8 and held Pottsville to 3 field goals to win the matchup.

Leading scorers: Mahanoy City – John Gabuzda 9; Pottsville – Harry Brecker 4.

Easton 39 Tamaqua 24: Easton kept Tamaqua winless at Tamaqua's sold-out gym with leads of 12-5, 19-14, and 28-18 after the first three quarters.

Leading scorers: Easton – Russell Noble 11, Roland Prime 10; Tamaqua – George Tepo 7.[4]

Week 3

Hazleton 35 Easton 23: Hazleton and Easton met in Hazleton in a key early season matchup. Easton led early 4-1 and 9-8 at the end of the first quarter. After several ties, Hazleton led at the half 18-15 on the way to the victory.

Leading scorers: Hazleton - Joe Podany 12, Bill Bechtloft 12; Easton – Bill Kraus 10.

Allentown 34 Tamaqua 19: Allentown took a 7-4 lead after a quarter and kept increasing the lead after each quarter as they handed Tamaqua a third loss without a win.

Leading scorers: Allentown - Leo Blankowitch 15; Tamaqua – George Tepo 5.[5]

Bethlehem 29 Mahanoy City 15: On the road, Bethlehem pulled out to a 22-7 lead after the first half and scored a victory over Mahanoy City to remain undefeated at 2-0 and stay right behind Hazleton at 3-0. No box score[6]

Week 4

Hazleton 32 Pottsville 12: The Mountaineers kept up their winning ways against Pottsville, their fourth with no losses. After taking a 6-4 lead after the first quarter, they held Pottsville scoreless in the second while scoring 13.

Leading scorers: Hazleton – Joe Podany 9; Pottsville – Henry Stoner 4.

Bethlehem 51 Tamaqua 19: Bethlehem remained undefeated to stay right behind Hazleton at 3-0 having played one less game. After trailing 7-6 after one quarter, Bethlehem took the lead and never looked back as they crushed winless Tamaqua.

Leading scorers: Bethlehem – Walt Kresge 15, Frank Kovacs 10; Tamaqua – Ed Luckshides 6.

Allentown 33 Easton 31: Allentown took over third place at 2-1 after pulling out a win at Easton. The Red Rovers rushed out to a 10-1 lead only to have the Canaries fight back to take a 19-16 halftime lead and win the game.

Leading scorers: Allentown – Leo Blankowitsch 10, Joe Brey 10; Easton – Bill Kraus 10.[7]

Week 5

Bethlehem 44 Hazleton 26: Bethlehem and Hazleton, both unbeaten, met at Hazleton. After Hazleton had led 10-8 at the end of the first quarter and Bethlehem 18-17 at the half, the Liberty boys outscored Hazleton 14-4 in the 3rd quarter and 12-5 in the final quarter to easily win the contest to take over first place.

Leading scorers: Bethlehem–Frank Kovacs 22, Walt Kresge 12; Hazleton–Joe Podany 10, Billy Bechtloff 10.

Allentown 25 Mahanoy City 22: Allentown struggled against Mahanoy City's zone defense and fell behind 14-6. The Canaries clawed their way back to tie the game at 22 by the end of the 3rd quarter. Although they only scored 3 points in the final quarter, Allentown held Mahanoy City scoreless, won the game, and tied Hazleton for 2nd place.

Leading scorers: Allentown – Willie Piff 8; Mahanoy City – John Gabuzda 6, Stan Sekula 6.

Tamaqua 31 Pottsville 22: In a battle of winless teams, Tamaqua prevailed over Pottsville. After leading by two points after a quarter 8-6 and at the half 15-13, Tamaqua increased the lead to seven 25-18 in the third quarter.

Leading scorers: Tamaqua - Edward Luckshides 12; Pottsville – Harry Brecker 7.[8]

Week 6

Mahanoy City 27 Tamaqua 25: Leading 20-12 at the half, visiting Mahanoy City hung on to defeat Tamaqua. Tamaqua cut the lead to four after three quarters 23-19, but were never able to pull even with the Maroons.

Leading scorers: Mahanoy City - Stan Sekula 14; Tamaqua – George Tepo - 10.

Bethlehem 25 Easton 23: In a game where no player scored in double figures, Bethlehem led after a quarter 8-4 and at the half 11-9. Easton tied the score at 17-17 after three quarters only to have Bethlehem pull out the win.

Leading scorers: Bethlehem – Walt Kresge 8; Easton – Al Misero 9.

Allentown 35 Pottsville 15: Allentown pulled into a tie with idle Hazleton at 4-1 with an easy victory at Pottsville. After being tied 7-7 after a quarter, Allentown outscored Pottsville 10-2 in the second quarter in a game where Coach Crum primarily used the second string throughout the game.

Leading scorers: Allentown – Leo Blankowitsch 10; Pottsville – John Gorman 9.[9]

Allentown 32 Bethlehem 30: At the half way point of the season, Allentown met visiting Bethlehem in front of 2500 fans at the Little Palestra and handed the Liberty boys their first loss. Going into the 4th quarter behind by 8 points 28-20 to Bethlehem, the Canaries scored the first 12 points to take the lead before Bethlehem finally scored with less than 30 seconds left in the game. Both teams and Hazleton were tied for first with 5-1 records.

Leading scorers: Allentown – Leo Blankowitsch 10; Bethlehem – Steve Marchak 7.

Hazleton 28 Mahanoy City 26: Hazleton was able to keep pace despite a scare from Mahanoy City. Leading by 10 points 27-17, Hazleton appeared to have the game in hand only to see the Maroons rally to a one-point deficit 27-26. A foul goal in the last 20 seconds sealed the victory for the Mountaineers.

Leading scorers: Hazleton – Billy Bechtloff 8; Mahanoy City – John Gabuzda 13.

Easton 38 Pottsville 23: Easton, holding a narrow 9-7 lead after the first quarter, took a commanding 21-12 halftime lead and kept Pottsville winless in the first half of the season.

Leading scorers: Easton - Al Misero 17; Pottsville – Henry Stoner 7.[10]

Week 7

Hazleton 34 Tamaqua 24: The Mountaineers took an early 6-1 lead and led at the half 14-9. Hazleton extended the lead to 26-16 after three quarters and cruised to a win.

Leading scorers: Hazleton – Joe Podany 10; Tamaqua – George Zubey 13.

Bethlehem 28 Pottsville 25: Bethlehem trailed winless Pottsville most of the game and into the 4th quarter before rallying to win the game. Pottsville held a three-point lead at the half 17-14 and 24-23 going into the last quarter.

Leading scorers: Bethlehem - Walter Kresge 15; Pottsville - Harold Sachs 7.

Mahanoy City 34 Easton 28: In Mahanoy City, the Maroons led throughout most of the game and stretched it from three points 16-13 at the half to seven 25-18 after the third quarter. Mahanoy City's victory matched them with Easton at 3-4 and tie for 4th place in the league.

Leading scorers: Mahanoy City – John Gabuzda 10, Stan Sekula 10; Easton – Bill Kraus 12.[11]

Week 8

Hazleton 33 Allentown 28: In a battle for first place at Hazleton, the Mountaineers met Allentown in a hard-fought contest. Trailing most of the first half and into the third period, Willie Piff led Allentown into a lead 25-24 at the end of the 3rd quarter. With Piff out of the game on personal fouls late in the 4th quarter, Hughie McGeehan's team prevailed to knock the Canaries out of a share of the league lead. An accidental collision between Allentown's Bob Benfer and Hazleton's Joe Podany knocked the Mountaineer's captain unconscious and held up the game for several minutes. Both players continued in the game. Idle Bethlehem dropped a half game behind Hazleton while Allentown dropped to third place with their two losses.

Leading scorers: Hazleton – Joe Podany 9; Allentown – Leo Blankowitsch 8, Joe Brey 8.

Easton 44 Tamaqua 24: Easton breezed to an easy win over Tamaqua after taking 13-5 and 30-11 leads after the first two quarters to even their record at 4-4.

Leading scorers: Easton – Al Misero 14, Bill Kraus 11; Tamaqua - Ed Quather 13.

Mahanoy City 33 Pottsville 24: Mahanoy City evened their record at 4-4 with a win over lowly Pottsville. With their field goals even at nine, the Maroons converted 15 foul shots to Pottsville's 6 to secure the win.

Leading scorers: Mahanoy City – Stan Sekula 11; Pottsville – Harold Sachs 8.[12]

Week 9

Hazleton 27 Easton 25 OT: Trailing 8-0 to start the game, Hazleton fought hard to tie the game 24-24 at the end of regulation against a feisty Easton Red Rover team. In the extra period, each team made a foul shot, but Hazleton's Joe Podany also made a field goal to win the game and maintain the hold on first place.

Leading scorers: Hazleton – Joe Podany 13; Easton – Al Misero 6, Bill Kraus 6.

Bethlehem 30 Mahanoy City 20: After struggling in the first half and being tied with Mahanoy City 15-15, Bethlehem's offense jelled in the third quarter to propel them to a 10 point which the home team maintained the rest of the game. Bethlehem was twice assessed technical fouls because of malicious booing of the home crowd. The win kept them a half game behind Hazleton.

Leading scorers: Bethlehem – Steve Marchak 11; Mahanoy City – John Gabuzda 16.

Allentown 45 Tamaqua 24: Allentown maintained its hold on third place, a game behind Hazleton, with an easy win over Tamaqua. All eleven players inserted into the game by Coach Crum scored.

Leading scorers: Allentown – Leo Blankowitsch 10; Tamaqua – George Zubey 10.[13]

Week 10

Hazleton 45 Pottsville 19: In Hazleton, the Mountaineers had an easy victory over Pottsville. Hazleton led 18-3 and 30-6 after the first two quarters. Pottsville's Paul Dimmerling was carried off the floor due to a knee injury.

Leading scorers: Hazleton – Joe Podany 14; Pottsville – Harry Brecker 6.

Bethlehem 36 Tamaqua 29: Bethlehem took a 27-6 lead at halftime over the Blue Raiders in Tamaqua and were never headed. Tamaqua fought back in the second half to make the game much closer.

Leading scorers: Bethlehem – Harry Stonum 9; Tamaqua – Ed Luckshides 12.

Allentown 29 Easton 22: The Canaries took a 10-4 first quarter lead and held onto it at the half 19-13 and went on for the victory over Easton in Allentown's Little Palestra.

Leading scorers: Allentown – Leo Blankowitsch 12; Easton – Al Misero 10.[14]

Week 11

Tamaqua 34 Pottsville 19: On their home court, the boys from Pottsville continued their losing ways with a 10th consecutive loss to open the season. Tamaqua used only 5 players in the game and led the entire game.

Leading scorers: Tamaqua – Ed Luckshides 11, George Tepo 10; Pottsville – John Gorman 5.[15]

Allentown 30 Mahanoy City 19: Allentown kept its hopes alive for a title with a triumph over Mahanoy City. Allentown built up a ten-point lead 17-7 at the half and kept extending it the rest of the game.

Leading scorers: Allentown – Bob Benfer 12; Mahanoy City – John Gabuzda 12.[16]

Hazleton 32 Bethlehem 27 OT: Hazleton traveled to the Liberty gym as 200 screaming fans took in this crucial matchup. Bethlehem took a commanding 18-10 lead at halftime only to see if vanish in the third quarter with Hazleton jumping in front 24-20. Bethlehem was able to tie the game at 26 all at the buzzer ending regulation. In overtime, it was all Hazleton with the Mountaineers going home with a win. For Bethlehem, the game was lost at the foul line. Hazleton converted 12 of 24 to Bethlehem's 5 of 19. Bethlehem fell into a tie for second place with the Canaries both at 8-2 and 1 ½ games behind the Mountaineers, both with a very slim chance of catching Hazleton.

Leading scorers: Hazleton – Harry Dorneman 10; Bethlehem – Steve Marchak 12.[17]

Allentown 30 Pottsville 21: Allentown followed up later in the week with a relatively easy win over Pottsville with Coach Crum using his reserves most of the game. The Canaries led 15-6 at the half and 25-13 after three quarters. Allentown was now a game behind with a game to play for both the Canaries and Hazleton.

Leading scorers: Allentown – Leo Blankowitsch 11; Pottsville – Harry Brecker 8.

Easton 28 Bethlehem 27: Bethlehem lost their second game of the week to Easton's Red Rovers to eliminate them from any title hopes. Despite making two more field goals than the Red Rovers, poor foul shooting plagued Bethlehem as they made only 7 of 19. Easton converted 12 of 14 to eke out the win. During the second period, Sternum of Bethlehem and Roberson of Easton engaged in fisticuffs, which resulted each getting a technical foul. Both were allowed to continue in the game.

Leading scorers: Easton – Bill Kraus 15; Bethlehem – Truman Frey 8.[18]

Tamaqua 44 Mahanoy City 24: Tamaqua finished its season by getting its third win, against nine defeats, in an easy triumph over Mahanoy City. The Tams led 23-13 at the half. All 15 players in the game scored.

Leading scorers: Tamaqua – George Zubey 14, Ed Luckshides 13; Mahanoy City – John Gabuzda 7.[19]

Week 12

Mahanoy City 33 Hazleton 20: After a lackadaisical loss to Tamaqua the week before, Mahanoy City easily defeated visiting Hazleton. Leading by three 10-7, Mahanoy City extended the lead to ten at the half 19-9.

Leading scorers: Mahanoy City – John Gabuzda 14, Stan Sekula 13; Hazleton – Billy Bechtloff 11.

Bethlehem 30 Allentown 25: Allentown lost its opportunity to tie Hazleton when the Canaries trailed early 6-0. The Hurricane built up the lead to six 24-18 after three quarters and the Canaries could not recover.

Leading scorers: Bethlehem – Truman Frey 11; Allentown – Leo Blankowitsch 11.[20]

Easton 33 Pottsville 20: Easton evened its record for the season at 6-6 by handing Pottsville its 12th straight loss in the league and keeping them winless, despite the loss of two key players, Jim Noble and Al Misero, who had been suspended for playing in an independent game.

Leading scorers: Easton – Bill Kraus 13, Russell Meyers 12; Pottsville – John Gorman 7.[21]

The league season was over, but the controversy was just to begin. In Easton's match with Bethlehem, the Red Rovers used Jim Noble, who had admitted playing on an independent team. Easton had to forfeit its win over Bethlehem. This threw the Liberty boys into a tie for the title with Hazleton. In what had become a routine occurrence for the league, it held another stormy meeting on player eligibility. Hazleton was voted into the playoffs. Another proposal was made to have Hazleton and Bethlehem play for the league title at such time as Hazleton was eliminated from the state playoffs. Bethlehem's coach Emrey indicated it would be impossible to keep his players together for an uncertain time and that Hazleton should still be awarded the league title.[22]

Postseason Play

Hazleton 54 Barrett Township 16: Hazleton entered the playoffs with a game on its home court against Barrett Township, the Monroe County League champions. Hazleton took 13-3 first quarter and 31-7 halftime leads and used ten players in the contest.

Leading scorers: Hazleton – Joe Podany 19, Billy Bechtloff 12; Barrett Township – Carlton 9.[23]

Northampton 32 Hazleton 18: Next up for the Mountaineers were the Konkrete Kids from Northampton, who were heavy underdogs, at the Little Palestra. The Lehigh Valley League champions made Hazleton's trip to the postseason playoffs end abruptly. Northampton, led by Pete Schneider, outscored the Mountaineers 14-4 in the final period. Early in the 4th period, Hazleton's Bill Bechtloff collapsed at mid-court following a jump ball, at first unnoticed as play continued down the floor. Play was finally stopped only to have Bechtloff's mother faint in the stands near where her son had collapsed. Both were carried off the floor and recovered with no ill effects.

Leading scorers: Northampton – Pete Schneider 10; Hazleton – Frank Famalette 6.[24]

Postseason Accolades

Leading Scorers: The league's leading scorers for the year were: Blankowitch, Allentown, 121 points; Podany, Hazleton, 114 points; Kresge, Bethlehem, 111 points; Gabuzda, Mahanoy City, 110 points; Misero, Easton, and Bechtloff, Hazleton, 95 points; Kraus, Easton, 93 points.[25]

All-Stars: The league coaches selected the league all-stars as follows: Forwards: Blankowitch, Allentown; Podany and Bechtloff, Hazleton; and Kresge, Bethlehem; Centers: Frey, Bethlehem, and Tepo, Tamaqua; Guards: Benfer, Allentown; Lukshides, Tamaqua; Marchak, Bethlehem, and Kraus, Easton.[26]

Final Standings

Team	Record
Hazleton	10-2
Bethlehem	10-2
Allentown	9-3
Mahanoy City	5-7
Easton	5-7
Tamaqua	3-9
Pottsville	0-12

Team Rosters

Allentown: Coach J. Birney Crum, Bob Benfer, Milton Berman, Leo Blankowitch, Walter Boandl, Joe Brey, Edwin Freed, Robert Friedman, Jesse Mair, Willie Piff, Donald Praetorius, James Reber, Marwood Schoedler, Henry Wieder.

Bethlehem: Coach Bill Emery, Peter Berger, Truman Frey, Joseph Karabin, Frank Kovacs, Melvin Kraus, Walter Kresge, Ed Lukievics, Stephen Marchak, Harry Stonum.

Easton: Coach Stan Carney, Norman Andrews, Robert Arnts, Charles Drummond, Joseph Huston, Michael Kapral, Elwood Kindt, Samuel Lipari, Russell Meyers, Russell Noble, Andrew Pribzick, Roland "Beef" Prime, Bill Robertson, Floyd Stem, Jack Yankus

Hazleton: Coach Hugh McGeehan, Rocco Antinozzi, Billy Bechtloff, Maurice Boyle, Harry Dorneman, Frank Famalette, Ross Mainwaring, Larry Marchetti, John Matteo, Joseph Phillips, Joe Podany, Howard "Cy" Seybert, Al Smeraglio, Gordon Stoll, Robert Walk, Fred Wertz.

Mahanoy City: Coach John Goepfert, Peter Deriscavage, Bill Dodds, John Gabuzda, Montonis, Edward Pangonis, Stan Sekula, Serwinski, Joe Setcavage, Simborski, John Sluzevich, Wroblewski,

Pottsville: Coach George Dimmerling, Roy Bowen, Harry Brecker, Paul Dimmerling, John Furman, John Gorman, Robert Lotz, Harold Sachs, Curtis Shellhammer, Henry Stoner.

Tamaqua: Coach Eli "Pinky" Purnell, Jerome Andrukitis, Michael Burcin, Warren Christ, Wesley DeArmit, Joseph Duncavage, Bruce Fegley, Victor Gigli, Robert Hartwick, Charles Heister, Leroy Kemery, Charles Klein, Lester Lockwood, Edward Luckshides, George Mock, John Pierson, Edmund Quather, Samuel Saylor, George Tepo, George Zubey

Hazleton High School – 1937 League Champions[27]

Front row: Robert Walk, Bill Bechtloff, Rex Antinozzi, Joe Podany, Al Smeraglio, Joseph Phillips, Fred Wertz Back row: Larry Marchetti, John Matteo, Gordon Stoll, Harry Dorneman, Joe Pirski (manager), Frank Famalette, Harold Seybert, Ross Mainwaring, Maurice Boyle

1938

Searching for Normalcy

In April 1937, the league met in Bethlehem to elect officers for the following season. The league representatives decided to divide the season into two halves with a champion for each half. D. H. Lengle of Pottsville was re-elected president; W. C. Amour of Mahanoy City vide-president; and E. A. Rabenold of Allentown secretary for the 14th consecutive year. Herb Rathey, representing Freeland High School, attended the meeting to submit an application for his school to become the eighth member of the league. The league opted to remain with the current seven members. After two extremely troubling seasons, the league looked toward 1938 with renewed enthusiasm and a hope that new eligibility rules would prevent the many problems of the recent past.[1]

Week 1

Easton 40 Pottsville 21: Forward Joe Frinzi's 13 points led Easton to a win over a veteran Pottsville team. After being held to an 8 all tie after the first quarter, the Red Rovers' defense held Pottsville to a single point in the second quarter while the offense took off which added up to an easy win.

Leading Scorers: Easton – Joe Frinzi 13; Pottsville – Francis Rehnert 10.

Bethlehem 33 Tamaqua 16: Bethlehem, likewise, had a rather easy time with Tamaqua. Bethlehem took a 14-6 lead after one quarter and cruised to the victory.

Leading scorers: Bethlehem - Paul Adamchik 12, Walter Kresge 10; Tamaqua – Jerome Andrukitis 9.

Allentown 23 Mahanoy City 16: The Canaries also had a relatively easy win as they took a 17-6 lead into the locker room at the half against Mahanoy City. Although Mahanoy City outscored Allentown in the second half, Allentown still triumphed.

Leading scorers: Allentown – Milton Berman 7, Donald Praetorius 7; Mahanoy City – John Sluzevich 6.[2]

Week 2

Hazleton 45 Tamaqua 26: After being idle in the first week, Hazleton traveled to Tamaqua to kick off their league season. Leading 32-14 at the half, the Mountaineers were not threatened throughout the contest. Assistant coaches Fegley and Serany directed the team in the absence of Hugh McGeehan due to his daughter's serious illness.

Leading scorers: Hazleton – Bill Bechtloff 15, George Cheverko 10; Tamaqua – George Zubey 6, Warren Christ 6.

Bethlehem 48 Pottsville 24: Bethlehem chalked up its second straight win by doubling up Pottsville. The Hurricane led at the half 19-9.

Leading scorers: Bethlehem - Walt Kresge 16, Steve Marchak 13; Pottsville – Joe Sage 7, John Gorman 7.[3]

Easton 33 Mahanoy City 30: Easton also won its second in a row at Mahanoy City despite trailing at the end of each of the first three quarters. With both teams having the same number of field goals (11), Easton won the game at the foul line converting three more than Mahanoy City.

Leading scorers: Easton – Philip Rhiel 13, Joe Frinzi 12; Mahanoy City – John Sluzevich.[4]

Week 3

Allentown 37 Easton 27: In front of 2500 fans at the Little Palestra, Allentown handed Easton its first loss in a game that was not as close as the score would indicate. At one point in the 3rd period, Allentown led 27-8 over the visitors. Coach Crum used 12 players and seven of them scored in the game.

Leading scorers: Allentown – Donald Praetorius 7; Easton – Joe Frinzi.

Hazleton 40 Bethlehem 27: In Hazleton, the Mountaineers handed Bethlehem their first league loss. Trailing 10-5 after a quarter, Hazleton outscored Bethlehem 15-4 in the 2nd quarter to take the lead for good.

Leading scorers: Hazleton - Billy Bechtloff 11; Bethlehem – Harry Stonum 8, Walt Kresge 8.

Tamaqua 22 Pottsville 21: Coach Purnell's Tams won their first over still winless Pottsville. Pottsville had every chance to win the game on the foul line, but only converted 9 of 21 attempts.

Leading scorers: Tamaqua – Jerome Andrukitis 10: Pottsville – Francis Rehnert 6.[6]

Week 4

Hazleton 32 Pottsville 24: Hazleton continued its roll with an easy win over Pottsville stretching the lead to 13 points during the third quarter.

Leading scorers: Hazleton – Billy Bechtloff 14; Pottsville – Francis Rehnert 13.

Allentown 36 Bethlehem 26: Allentown, never trailing in the contest, handed Bethlehem their second loss. Bethlehem tied the score at 20-20 in the third period before the Canaries surged ahead to win the game.

Leading scorers: Allentown – Joe Brey 11; Bethlehem – Walt Kresge 12.

Tamaqua 33 Mahanoy City 30: Tamaqua won its second straight over a winless Mahanoy City. After falling behind 22-8, Mahanoy City rallied to make it a close game.

Leading scorers: Tamaqua – Jerome Andrukitis 13; Mahanoy City – Jack Goepfert 8.[7]

Week 5

Hazleton 43 Easton 23: Hazleton invaded Easton and polished off the Red Rovers. They took the lead early and led at the half 25-13.

Leading scorers: Hazleton – Billy Bechtloff 13, Frank Famalette 13; Easton – Al Misero 8.

Allentown 43 Tamaqua 26: Allentown jumped out to a 6-0 lead and went on a 11-1 run in the third period to keep a share of first place with a win over Tamaqua.

Leading scorers: Allentown - Joe Brey 18; Tamaqua – Jerome Andrukitis 11.

Bethlehem 25 Mahanoy City 24: Mahanoy City led at the end of each the first three quarters. Trailing 18-16 at the start of the fourth quarter, Bethlehem rallied to squeak out a one-point win over Mahanoy City.

Leading scorers: Bethlehem - Walt Kresge 12; Mahanoy City - Bill Yext 7.[8]

Week 6

Hazleton 43 Allentown 21: In the most critical game of the first half, Allentown traveled to Hazleton for a battle with the Mountaineers for the top spot. In surprising fashion, Hazleton led from the outset and throughout the game for an easy defeat of the Canaries. Coach McGeehan deployed a man-to-man defense when the Canaries brought the ball up court and then settled into a tough zone defense which the Canaries could not penetrate. Hazleton outscored Allentown 17-7 in the final quarter.

Leading scorers: Hazleton - Billy Bechtloff 16; Allentown – Walt Boandl 6.

Tamaqua 37 Easton 26: Tamaqua pulled its record even at 3-3 with a triumph over Easton. Hazleton took a 12-3 lead in the first quarter and led the rest of the way.

Leading scorers: Tamaqua – George Zubey 12; Easton - Al Misero 15.

Mahanoy City 35 Pottsville 28: In a battle of winless teams, Mahanoy City won at Pottsville. After playing to an 8-all tie at the end of the first quarter, Mahanoy City took a 20-11 lead at the half to secure the win.

Leading scorers: Mahanoy City – Webb 13, John Sluzevich 11; Pottsville – Francis Rehnert 11.[9]

Week 7

Hazleton 41 Mahanoy City 26: Starting out with a 15-6 lead after the first period and 26-11 at the half, Hazleton had an easy time clinching the first half title at Mahanoy City.

Leading scorers: Hazleton - George Cheverko 13, Billy Bechtloff 10; Mahanoy City – Billy Yext 7.

Allentown 44 Pottsville 33: Allentown rolled to a 33-17 lead after three periods. Coach Crum inserted his substitutes and Pottsville cut the lead in half. Coach Crum hastily inserted his starters back into the game when Coach Dimmerling's squad cut the lead to 9 points. Allentown finished with one loss and in 2nd place.

Leading scorers: Allentown – Milton Berman 12, Joe Brey 11; Pottsville – Joe Sage 9.

Bethlehem 32 Easton 27: Bethlehem, after leading only 6-5 after a quarter, stretched the lead to 26-17 after three quarters for the win over Easton and end up in third place with five wins and two losses.

Leading scorers: Bethlehem – Walt Kresge 11; Easton – Al Onarata.[10]

Week 8 – Second Half

Allentown 32 Mahanoy City 26: With Hazleton idle for the first round, Allentown got off to a fast start in Mahanoy City. Mahanoy City battled the Canaries to an 18-18 tie at the end of the 3rd quarter only to see Allentown double them up 14-7 in the final quarter to take the win.

Leading scorers: Allentown – Donald Praetorius 10; Mahanoy City – Billy Yext 9.[11]

Bethlehem 29 Tamaqua 26: At Liberty Hall in Tamaqua, Bethlehem had to battle hard to pull out a triumph over the Tams. Bethlehem won the game at the foul line converting 9 of 11 while Tamaqua made 6 of 14.

Leading scorers: Bethlehem - Walt Kresge 14; Tamaqua – Walter Duncavage 7.

Pottsville 41 Easton 28: Playing at home, Pottsville won its first game in the league over Easton. Pottsville got out to an 11-4 lead at the first quarter mark and increased their lead after each quarter.

Leading scorers: Pottsville – Francis Rehnert 16; Easton – Al Misero 15.[12]

Week 9

Bethlehem 25 Pottsville 14: Bethlehem moved to 2-0 for the second half of the season. Leading 13-6 at the half, Bethlehem scored the only two points of the third period to enter the final period leading 15-6.

Leading scorers: Bethlehem - Walt Kresge 10; Pottsville – Francis Rehnert 7.

Easton 29 Mahanoy City 28: Mahanoy City entered the 4th quarter at Easton with a 22-16 lead, but ended up on the short end of the score when Easton rallied and forward Riehl made a one-handed shot from center court with a half minute left in the game for the Red Rovers.

Leading scorers: Easton – Phillip Rhiel 12; Mahanoy City – Webb 7.

Hazleton 61 Tamaqua 37: Hazleton began second half play with an easy, high-scoring victory over Tamaqua. They led 33-15 at the half. Four Mountaineers scored in double figures in the rout.

Leading scorers: Hazleton – Charles Prokopic 14, George Cheverko 12, Joe Andrejco 11, Billy Bechtloff 10; Tamaqua – George Tepo 9.[13]

Week 10

Hazleton 24 Bethlehem 14: Hazleton remained undefeated in league play in Bethlehem. Coach Emrey's team jumped to an early 3-0 lead, but after that it was all Hazleton and they took a 9-5 lead after a quarter.

Leading scorers: Hazleton – Charles Prokopic 8; Bethlehem – Frank Silvetz 6.

Allentown 40 Easton 23: Allentown stayed with Hazleton at 2-0 as the only two undefeated teams in the second half of play. After the Canaries took a 15-7 first quarter, each team scored 2 points in the 2nd quarter.

Leading scorers: Allentown - Donald Praetorius 14; Easton – James Onorata 11.

Tamaqua 35 Pottsville 15: Half the points were scored in the first quarter with Tamaqua in the lead 16-10. The Tams outscored Pottsville 9-1 in the final period to put the game away.

Leading scorers: Tamaqua – Warren Christ 11; Pottsville – Frank Madara 5.[14]

Week 11

Allentown 47 Bethlehem 26: Allentown took down its archrival Bethlehem in a game where the Liberty boys only threatened to make a game of it during the 2nd period. However, the Canaries put the game away in the third period holding Bethlehem to no points while scoring 13 themselves.

Leading scorers: Allentown - Eddie Freed 12; Bethlehem – Steve Marchak 8.

Hazleton 35 Pottsville 27: After trailing 9-8 after a quarter, Hazleton took command of the game in the second quarter to lead 19-11 by holding Pottsville to two points.

Leading scorers: Hazleton – Billy Bechtloff 17, George Cheverko 10; Pottsville – Frank Madara 7.

Tamaqua 41 Mahanoy City 31: Tamaqua led after one quarter 15-4, but Mahanoy City countered leading at the half 24-19. Tamaqua surged back to lead after three quarters 33-29 and held on for the win.

Leading scorers: Tamaqua – George Tepo 14, Jerome Andurkitis 11, George Zubey 10; Mahanoy City – George Senesky 10.[15]

Week 12

Hazleton 41 Easton 25: Outscoring Easton 14-4 in the first quarter and 11-2 in the third quarter, Hazleton easily defeated visiting Easton.

Leading scorers: Hazleton – George Cheverko 15, Billy Bechtloff 14; Easton – Al Misero 11.

Allentown 37 Tamaqua 28: Allentown traveled to Tamaqua and came home with a triumph over the Tams. Coach Crum's team took an 11-1 lead during the first quarter and 14-3 at the end of the quarter. Tamaqua pulled within four points 23-19 before Allentown pulled away for the win.

Leading scorers: Allentown – Donald Praetorius 15; Easton - George Tepo 10.

Bethlehem 37 Mahanoy City 34: Bethlehem held a slim 16-14 lead over Mahanoy City at halftime. Trailing by 12 points in the third quarter, Mahanoy City rallied in the 4th quarter, but the Hurricane hung on to win.

Leading scorers: Bethlehem – Walt Kresge 20; Mahanoy City – Webb 12.[16]

Week 13

Allentown 32 Hazleton 13: The Mountaineers and Canaries met again in a crucial matchup at Allentown. Over 2500 fans crowded into Allentown's gym and another 4000 fans had to be turned away. The Canaries put on a superior defensive performance and won the game. Allentown held Hazleton to only four field goals for the game and only five points in the second half. The game was held up for 35 minutes at the outset by an argument between the teams' head coaches. Birney Crum wanted to use a new seamless ball, while Hugh McGeehan insisted on a seamed ball. They finally agreed to use the seamed ball in the first half and the seamless ball during the second half. With two minutes left in the contest, someone fired a torpedo from the balcony at the Little Palestra. Both teams, the fans, and the officials initially thought it to be the gun ending the game. Fans swarmed the floor and it took the police several minutes to clear the floor and let the game be finished.

Leading scorers: Allentown – Walt Boandl 11; Hazleton – Billy Bechtloff 4, George Cheverko 4.

Easton 43 Tamaqua 34: Tamaqua led after a quarter 8-7, but Easton charged out to a 21-13 halftime lead on the way to a defeat of Tamaqua.

Leading scorers: Easton – Al Misero 14, Elwood Luckenbach 10; Tamaqua – George Zubey 15, George Tepo 10.[17]

Mahanoy City 36 Pottsville 24: Mahanoy City finally won a second half game by outscoring Pottsville 21-4 in the second half of the game. The win pulled them even with Pottsville at 1-4 for a last place tie.

Leading scorers: Mahanoy City – Jack Goepfert 10; Pottsville – Joe Sage 4.[18]

Week 14

Allentown 17 Pottsville 16: Allentown went into the final week needing only a victory at Pottsville to wrap up an undefeated second half. Pottsville had won only a single league game all season. With two free throws by Walt Boandl with less than 20 seconds left in the game, Allentown barely pulled out the victory. The Canaries trailed by a single point 16-15 with 20 seconds to play when center Walter Boandl was fouled. He calmly dropped in two foul shots to pull out the victory and second half title for the Canaries.

Leading scorers: Allentown – Walt Boandl 8; Pottsville - Russ Bevan 6.

Hazleton 38 Mahanoy City 33: Hazleton also pulled out a somewhat close game against Mahanoy City. Hazleton led 34-21 after three periods only to have Mahanoy City pull close by outscoring Hazleton 12-4 in the final period.

Leading scorers: Hazleton – George Cheverko 19; Mahanoy City – Jack Goepfert 12, George Senesky 10.

Bethlehem 33 Easton 20: Trailing 11-10 at the half, Bethlehem took the lead 21-18 in the third quarter for the triumph over the Red Rovers in Easton.

Leading scorers: Bethlehem - Walt Kresge 18; Easton – Al Misero 8.[19]

With Hazleton having won the first half and Allentown the second half, this set up a playoff for the overall league title between the Canaries and the Mountaineers. After a special meeting held in Pottsville on

Monday night prior to the play of games on Tuesday, D.H. Lengle of Pottsville, the league president, announced that the two teams would play the game at the Penn Palestra. This brought back memories of the 1930 clash between the two at the same site when they finished the season in a first-place tie.[19]

League Championship Playoff

Hazleton 41 Allentown 35: Playing in front of a frenzied crowd of spectators at the Penn Palestra, each paying 50 cents for a ticket, Hazleton won this third meeting of the season between the two teams. Allentown's only lead was 3-2 early in the game. Hazleton won the game on balanced scoring with none of their players scoring in double figures. Eleven double decker buses carried fans to the game in addition to two special trains.

Leading scorers: Hazleton – Charles Prokopic 9, Frank Famalette 9; Allentown – Joe Brey 10.[20]

Postseason Play

Hazleton 46 Summit Hill 35: Summit Hill met Hazleton in the first round of the playoffs in Pottsville. After trailing 11-10 to Wilbur Derby's Black Diamond League champions, Hazleton took the lead in the second period and were never headed. Hazleton played the entire game without starting center George Cheverko who was kept out of the game after having his tonsils removed days earlier.

Leading scorers: Hazleton – Billy Bechtloff 15, Charles Prokopic 10, Frank Famalette 10; Summit Hill – Anthony Piaia 15.[21]

Hazleton 40 Frackville 23: The second-round playoff game was held in Reading with 4200 fans in attendance. With Billy Bechtloff outscoring the opponents by himself, Coach McGeehan's team crushed Frackville in the District 11 semifinal game. This setup a rematch from the prior season between Northampton and Hazleton.

Leading scorers: Hazleton – Billy Bechtloff 26; Frackville – Stan Kubisen 9.[22]

Hazleton 23 Northampton 20: At the new Northwest Junior High School gym in Reading, Hazleton defeated Pete Schneider and his teammates to win the District XI title. Woody Ludwig's Konkrete Kids stumbled out of the gate falling behind 10-3, which proved decisive in the game. Neither team had a player score in double figures in the hard-fought match. Several hundred counterfeit tickets were printed for the game and the gym was packed to capacity two hours before the start of the game. The counterfeit tickets were not discovered until the gym was well filled. The PIAA had only sold 3200 tickets for the game, but several hundred more fans had packed the gym.[23]

Leading scorers: Hazleton – Billy Bechtloff – 8; Northampton – Pete Schneider 6.

Hazleton 30 Steelton 20: Six thousand fans witnessed the first state playoff matchup between Hazleton and Steelton at the University of Pennsylvania Palestra in Philadelphia. Although the District 3 champions Steelton scored first, Hazleton took over from there led by their captain Bechtloff who scored 12 of Hazleton's first 17 points.

Leading scorers: Hazleton – Billy Bechtloff 19; Steelton – Johnny Mahalic 7.[24]

Hazleton 35 Pottstown 33: In the eastern semifinals, Hazleton took on an old league opponent Pottstown in Philadelphia. Center George Cheverko, recovered from his tonsil surgery, led the Mountaineers to a 28-12 lead late in the third period. Pottstown substitute Paul Shaner came off the bench to spark Pottstown. With less than a minute to go, Pottstown pulled to within 2 points, but Hazleton hung on to win the contest.

Leading scorers: Hazleton – George Cheverko 17; Pottstown – Paul Shaner 13.[25]

Hazleton 29 Altoona 27: Hazleton met Altoona at the Penn Palestra in pursuit of its third state title in 11 years. In front of 9500 fans, Hazleton defeated Altoona. The game started out slowly with the score tied at 2 at the end of the first quarter and 10-10 at the half. In third quarter, Altoona briefly took the lead 12-10 only to have Hazleton score the next six points and never relinquish the lead after that. Bill Bechtloff led Hazleton's scoring with 9 points. The East Penn League had its fourth title in 11 years.

Leading scorers: Hazleton – Billy Bechtloff 9; Altoona – Bill Luse 9.[26]

Postseason Accolades

Scoring Leaders: Scoring leaders for the year were: Walt Kresge, Bethlehem, 141 points; Bill Bechtloff, Hazleton, 133 points; George Cheverko, Hazleton, 113 points; Al Misero, Easton, 106 points; Donald Praetorius, Allentown, 86 points: Joseph Brey, Allentown; George Tepo, Tamaqua, 82 points; Francis Rehnert, Pottsville, 80 points; George Zubey, Tamaqua, 77 points; and Charlie Prokopic, Hazleton, 73 points.[27]

All-Stars: The league all-stars included: Forwards: Walt Kresge, Bethlehem; Billy Bechtloff, Hazleton; Joseph Brey, Allentown; and Al Misero, Easton; Centers: George Cheverko, Hazleton, and George Tepo, Pottsville; Guards: Steve Marshak, Bethlehem; Joe Andrejco, Hazleton; Francis Rehnert, Pottsville; and Frank Famalette, Hazleton.[28]

Final Standings

First Half		Second Half		Overall	
Hazleton	6-0	Allentown	6-0	Hazleton	11-1
Allentown	5-1	Hazleton	5-1	Allentown	11-1
Bethlehem	4-2	Bethlehem	4-2	Bethlehem	8-4
Tamaqua	3-3	Easton	2-4	Tamaqua	5-7
Easton	2-4	Tamaqua	2-4	Easton	4-8
Mahanoy City	1-5	Mahanoy City	1-5	Mahanoy City	2-10
Pottsville	0-6	Pottsville	1-5	Pottsville	1-11

Team Rosters

Allentown: Coach J. Birney Crum, Milton Berman, Walter Boandl, Joe Brey, Harry Cawley, Donald Dietrich, Edwin Freed, Robert Friedman, Donald Miller, Donald Praetorius, Richard Rahn, James Reber, Robert Richards, Marwood Schoedler, Henry "Hank" Wieder.

Bethlehem: Coach Bill Emrey, Paul Adamchik, William Healis, Melvin Kraus, Walter Kresge, Ed Lukievics, Frank Majczan, Stephen Marchak, Frank Silvetz, Harry Stonum.

Easton: Coach Clyde Notestine, Tony Amato, Edgar Antrim, Carl Florindi, Joe Frinzi, John Frinzi, Cassidy Gadwell, Frank Gugliuzza, Don Hunt, Richard Johnson, James Kane, Elwood Luckenbach, Russel Meyers, Elwood Miller, Al Misero, Al Onorata, Phillip Rhiel, Edward Schroeder, James Soroko.

Hazleton: Coach Hugh McGeehan, Joe Andrejco, Billy Bechtloff, George Cheverko, Eugene, DeMatt, Frank Famalette, Victor Grusefsky, Robert Hicks, Charles Lotito, Frank Mandart, Bernard McMonigle, Charles Prokopic, Joe Sager, Ed Shimshick, Billy Smith.

Mahanoy City: Coach John Goepfert, Adams, Al Burdanavage, Victor Demborski, Jack Goepfert, Ed Kilkuskie, George Senesky, Silkuski, John Sluzevich, Charlie Urban, Webb, Bill Yext.

Pottsville: Coach George Dimmerling, Russ Bevan, Paul Dimmerling, John Gorman, Charlie Knell, Frank Madara, Francis Rehnert, Joe Sage, Henry Stoner, James Taylor, Walter Thomas.

Tamaqua: Coach Eli Purnell, Jerome "Whitey" Andrukitis, Mike Burcin, Warren Christ, Wes DeArmit, Walter Duncavage, John Heisler, Charles "Fink" Klein, Leonard Miller, George Mock, Edmund Quather, George Tepo, George Zubey.

1938 PIAA State Champions – Hazleton High School[29]

Sitting: Charles Lotito, Joe Sager

Second Row: Joe Andrejco, Frank Famalette, Bill Bechtloff, Charlie Prokopic, George Cheverko

Third Row: Frank Mandart, Bobby Hicks, Bernie McMonigle, Joe Grusefski, Gene DeMatt

Last Row: Manager Al Wagner, Asst Coach Frank Serany, Billy Smith, Coach Hugh McGeehan, Eddie Shimshick, Asst. Coach Vernard Fegley, Team Manager Joe Pape

1939

Mahanoy City Leaves

After six seasons in the league, Mahanoy City withdrew to join the Black Diamond League for the 1939 season. Other Black Diamond League members included Summit Hill, Lansford, Coaldale, Nesquehoning, Shenandoah, Blythe Township, and Mauch Chunk.[1]

The Eastern Pennsylvania League was now left with six teams. After just one season with a format based on halves, the league returned to their old format of competing for a title on a total season setup. With only six members, the league would play its league games in January (5 games) and February (5 games) and abandon the earlier start during the month of December.[2]

At its April 1938 meeting in Tamaqua, Williamsport High School made a plea for admission into the league. It was also understood that if Williamsport was admitted that Freeland High School was prepared to submit it application for admission. The six member schools voted to continue as a six-school circuit and deny Williamsport's request. The league members reasoned that travel costs would be too great for travel to Williamsport. Officers were elected for the upcoming season and included D. H. H. Lengle, Pottsville, as president; Charlie Richards, Easton, as vice president; and for the 14th consecutive term, E. A. Rabenold, Allentown as secretary-treasurer.[3]

Week 1

Hazleton 26 Bethlehem 23: In the first week of the season, Hazleton and Bethlehem engaged in a bench-clearing brawl after Hazleton's Smith and Liberty's Wodzicki exchanged punches. Followers of both teams stormed onto the court and it took four policemen several minutes to clear the floor. Despite Bethlehem having led for over three periods, Hazleton prevailed by outscoring the Liberty boys 10-2, after play was resumed, and came away with a victory.

Leading scorers: Hazleton – George Cheverko 9; Bethlehem – George Moyczan 8.[4]

Allentown 47 Tamaqua 30: Allentown opened the season by traveling to Tamaqua. The Canaries took an early 13-1 lead over the Tams. In the fourth quarter, Tamaqua pulled within 34-25 before Allentown pulled ahead again.

Leading scorers: Allentown – Walt Boandl 17, Dick Rahn 13, Donald Dietrich 11; Tamaqua – George Tepo 10.

Easton 40 Pottsville 22: In Pottsville, Easton led early and put the game away with 15 points in the fourth quarter.

Leading scorers: Easton – James Soroko 10; Pottsville - Joe Sage 13.[5]

Week 2

Hazleton 26 Allentown 17: Hazleton, for the second week in a row, played a tough foe as Allentown came to town for another critical early season matchup. Allentown's arrival was delayed an hour because of difficult traveling conditions in a heavy snowstorm. The Canaries kept the score close through 3 periods trailing Hazleton by two points 16-14, but the Mountaineers outscored Allentown 10-3 in the 4th quarter for the win over its archrival.

Leading scorers: Hazleton - George Cheverko 11; Allentown – Donald Dietrich 6.[6]

Bethlehem 66 Pottsville 31: Bethlehem rebounded with a shellacking of Pottsville after jumping out to a 21-3 first quarter lead. Bethlehem's Rudy Zelko made more field goals (13) than the Pottsville team (12);

Leading scorers: Bethlehem - Rudy Zelko 26. Frank Majczan 12, Al Calvo 11; Pottsville – Joe Sage 15.

Easton 25 Tamaqua 15: Easton won its second straight game to stay in a tie with Hazleton for the early league lead. After scoring 13 points in the first quarter, Easton won a low scoring affair with Tamaqua.

Leading scorers: Easton – James Soroka 8; Tamaqua – Warren Christ 4, Walter Duncavage 4.[7]

Week 3

Allentown 46 Easton 24: Easton's share of first place ended when Allentown hung a decisive loss on the Red Rovers. After Easton tied the game early at 5, the Canaries led at the quarter 11-5 and pulled away to a 23-10 lead at halftime at the Little Palestra.

Leading scorers: Allentown – Walt Boandl 17; Easton – James Soroka 10.

Hazleton 33 Pottsville 12: Meanwhile, Hazleton held on to first place with a victory over Pottsville as nine players contributed to the win. Hazleton led at the half 14-4 and outscored Pottsville 13-3 in the final quarter.

Leading scorers: Hazleton – Frank Smith 10; Pottsville – William Scheerer 3.

Bethlehem 38 Tamaqua 32: Bethlehem moved into a three-way tie for second at 2-1 with Allentown and Easton with its triumph at Tamaqua. Bethlehem held a 12-point lead at halftime. Both Pottsville and Tamaqua were still searching for their first league victory.[8]

Leading scorers: Bethlehem - Paul Marcincin 14; Tamaqua – Jerome Andrukitis 10.

Hazleton-Tamaqua: With the teams scheduled for a second time during the week, Hazleton and Tamaqua played an exhibition match when referee Joe Williams from Wilkes-Barre failed to appear. The schools decided to still play, but as an unofficial matchup. Hazleton won 38-32. The makeup game was played during the last week of the season

Leading scorers: Hazleton – George Cheverko 11; Tamaqua – George Tepo 10, Jerome Andrukitis 10.[9]

Allentown 38 Pottsville 22: Allentown kept Pottsville winless in Pottsville with center Dick Rahn contributing 14 points. Both teams emptied their benches with 11 players on each team seeing playing time.

Leading scorers: Allentown – Dick Rahn 14; Pottsville – Tom Portland 9

Bethlehem 51 Easton 36: Bethlehem handed Easton a second straight loss. Bethlehem stretched a two-point lead 6-4 after one quarter to 14 at halftime 25-11 to take control of the contest.

Leading scorers: Bethlehem – Rudy Zelko 15, Al Calvo 15; Easton – Salvatore Frinzi 7.[10]

Week 4

Hazleton 32 Easton 21: Traveling to Easton, Hazleton took down the home team, despite the benching of forward George Cheverko during the 2nd and 3rd periods due to personal foul trouble. He had committed three fouls during the opening period.

Leading scorers: Hazleton – Charles Prokopic 9; Easton – Salvatore Frinzi 5.

Allentown 51 Bethlehem 41: Allentown knocked off Bethlehem despite trailing at the half 26-21 to take over sole possession of 2nd place behind Hazleton. After Allentown went ahead 34-32, they led the rest of the way. Paul Marcincin played his final game for the Hurricane as he was no longer eligible due to his age.

Leading scorers: Allentown- Walt Boandl 15, Donald Dietrich 14, Dick Rahn 12; Bethlehem– Rudy Zelko 17, Paul Marcincin 12.

Tamaqua 46 Pottsville 29: In a battle of winless teams, Tamaqua prevailed in Pottsville. Tamaqua took charge of the game in the third quarter by outscoring Pottsville 17-8.

Leading scorers: Tamaqua - Jerome Andrukitis 15, Warren Christ 11; Pottsville – Joe Sage 8.[11]

Week 5

Hazleton 48 Bethlehem 37: Hazleton's George Cheverko paced the Mountaineers to a win at Hazleton and remain undefeated in league play. Hazleton took a 14-5 first period lead and were never threatened.

Leading scorers: Hazleton – George Cheverko 17, Billy Smith 10; Bethlehem – Frank Majczan 12, Rudy Zelko 10.

Allentown 38 Tamaqua 19: Allentown put Tamaqua back in its losing ways despite Tamaqua giving the Canaries an early challenge with a 4 all tie after one period and by leading 10-9 right before the half ended. The Canaries upped the lead to ten points in the third quarter 25-15.

Leading scorers: Allentown – Walt Boandl 15; Tamaqua – Leonard Miller 7.

Easton 43 Pottsville 27: After three straight losses, Easton evened its record at 3-3 against winless Pottsville. The Red Rovers took control in the third period with a 15-6 advantage during the period.

Leading scorers: Easton – Salvatore Frinzi 20; Pottsville – Tom Portland 8, William Scheerer 8.[12]

Week 6

Allentown 31 Hazleton 29 OT: Allentown snapped Hazleton's 19 game win streak at the Little Palestra to put the Canaries into first place with a half game lead over the Mountaineers, who played one less game. It was Hazleton's first loss since their game at the Little Palestra the prior season. With five minutes to play in regulation, Hazleton led 24-20. Allentown scored 7 of the next 8 points to take the lead, only to have the Mountaineers tie the game. The Canaries took the lead again 29-27 but Hazleton's Cheverko tied the score with 15 seconds left at 29 all. The Canaries' substitute George Hittinger scored the only goal in the overtime period, and only his 2nd and 3rd points of the game, as Allentown won a thriller.

Leading scorers: Allentown – Dick Rahn 17; Hazleton – Joe Andrejco 8.

Tamaqua 34 Easton 31: Homestanding Tamaqua upset Easton to win only its second game of the season. After trailing 6-2 after a quarter, Tamaqua scored 17 points in the second quarter for a 19-13 halftime lead. The Tams' Andrukitis did not play the first half, but led the Tamaqua charge for the win in the second half.

Leading scorers: Tamaqua – Jerome Andrukitis 14; Easton - James Soroka 11, Salvatore Frinzi 11.[13]

Bethlehem 48 Pottsville 23: Lowly Pottsville was doubled up in the loss to Bethlehem. Bethlehem took the lead in the beginning and never gave it up, despite only leading by 9-6 after one quarter.

Leading scorers: Bethlehem - Frank Majczan 16, Rudy Zelko 16; Pottsville – Tom Portland 6.[14]

Week 7

Allentown 37 Easton 26: Forward Walt Boandl and center Dick Rahn led the Canaries to a triumph over Coach Elmer Carroll's Easton team. Allentown, retaining its half game league lead, led 8-1 early and were never tested in the matchup. Easton did not register a field goal until well into the second quarter.

Leading scorers: Allentown – Walt Boandl 13, Dick Rahn 10; Easton – Frank Gugliuzza 8.

Hazleton 42 Pottsville 20: Hazleton stayed right on the Canaries' tail feathers with Coach McGeehan playing 12 boys in the win over Pottsville. The Mountaineers held a 26-7 lead at halftime.

Leading scorers: Hazleton – Billy Smith 12; Pottsville – William Scheerer 7.

Bethlehem 42 Tamaqua 36: Despite a rally by Tamaqua to pull within a single point as 30-29 in the third period, Bethlehem took control in the 4th period for the win.

Leading scorers: Bethlehem – Frank Majczan 13, Rudy Zelko 12; Tamaqua – Jerome Andrukitis 14, Warren Christ 10.[15]

Allentown 43 Pottsville 27: Playing its second league game in the week, Allentown held on to its thin hold on 1st place by trouncing Pottsville at the Little Palestra. The Canaries shot out to a 17-1 lead in the first six minutes and coasted to a win. Coach Crum played 15 boys in the resounding win.

Leading scorers: Allentown – Dick Rahn 12, Walt Boandl 10; Pottsville – Heller 11.

Hazleton 45 Tamaqua 32: Hazleton also took advantage of one of the weaker league opponents with a win over Tamaqua. The Mountaineers made 19 of 26 foul shots in the victory.

Leading scorers: Hazleton – Joe Sager 10; Tamaqua – Warren Christ 16.

Bethlehem 43 Easton 40: On its home court, Easton held a 27-23 advantage at half time over Bethlehem. Bethlehem finally took the lead in the third quarter, but the game stayed close to the very end with the Liberty boys prevailing 43-40 in the end.

Leading scorers: Bethlehem – Tod Saylor 15; Easton – Salvatore Frinzi 17.[16]

Week 8

Bethlehem 35 Allentown 31: In the final week of the season, Bethlehem and Allentown squared off in the renewal of their series at the Liberty gym with nearly 2000 fans in attendance. With four minutes to play, the Canaries led 30-29 when Bethlehem's Frank Majczan intercepted a pass and took it in for a score and the lead. At that point, a foul was called on Bethlehem, which led to near fisticuffs as the players crowded into each other. George Hittinger made both free throws for the Canaries to tie the score. With Bethlehem taking the lead 34-31 with a field goal and foul shot by Zelko, the Canaries' Don Dietrich committed a foul. Suddenly, the floor was covered with players and spectators swinging at each other. The police cleared the floor only to have two spectators start swinging at each other and another donnybrook ensued. Bethlehem's Majczan converted the foul shot with 20 seconds left. Allentown's Dick Rahn suffered a nasty gash above his eye when he fell to the floor in the first half. The gash required several stitches and he was able to return to the game, but his play was sub-par after the injury. Walt Boandl was also lost in the final minutes of the game due to personal fouls. Bethlehem crushed Allentown's hope for a league title by defeating the Canaries.

Leading Scorers: Bethlehem – Frank Majczan 9, Rudy Zelko 9; Allentown – George Hittinger 12.

Hazleton 57 Easton 19: Hazleton rolled over Easton after taking a 28-9 lead at halftime. With Allentown's loss, the Mountaineers were still in pursuit of the second half title and only needed a win in the final game.

Leading scorers: Hazleton - Charles Prokopic 23, George Cheverko 16; Easton – Salvatore Frinzi 7.

Tamaqua 25 Pottsville 23: Tamaqua won over Pottsville to keep them winless for the league season. After trailing at halftime 12-9, Tamaqua rallied for the win in the third period to take the lead.

Leading scorers: Tamaqua – Jerome Andrukitis 15; Pottsville – William Scheerer 8.[17]

Hazleton 51 Tamaqua 15: Hazleton, with a half game lead over Allentown, made up their postponed match with Tamaqua. After leading 27-6 at the half in Tamaqua, Hazleton trounced "Pinky" Purnell's Blue Raiders to take yet another East Penn championship.

Leading scorers: Hazleton - George Cheverko 17, Joe Andrejco 11; Tamaqua – Jerome Andrukitis 5.[18]

Postseason Play

Hazleton 35 Palmerton 21: Hazleton received a bye during the first round of the District XI playoffs. The Mountaineers opened defense of their state title against Palmerton, the Lehigh Valley League champions at North West Junior High School in Reading with more than 3000 screaming fans in attendance. Coach Bill Wilhelm's Blue Bombers held the lead at half time 11-9. Hazleton took the lead going into the 4th quarter 20-16. During the 4th quarter, Hazleton's experience helped them to outscore Palmerton 15-5 for the win.

Leading scorers: Hazleton – Charles Prokopic 9; Palmerton – John Mlkvy 6.[19]

Hazleton 37 Mahanoy City 33: An old league rival Mahanoy City, who won the Black Diamond League title in their first season in the league, took on Hazleton at the Penn Palestra in Philadelphia with 5000 fans watching the action. Down 10 points at the end of the 3rd quarter, Mahanoy City challenged the Mountaineers with a ferocious rally in the final quarter to pull within 3 points 36-33 with a minute to go. They got no closer as Hazleton scored the final point to win the District XI title for the second consecutive year.

Leading scorers: Hazleton – George Cheverko 8; Mahanoy City – Joe Senesky 15.[20]

Lower Merion 20 Hazleton 17: In the first round of the state playoffs in Hershey, Lower Merion, the District I Champions, ended Hazleton's hopes for a title defense with the victory. In a low-scoring, hard fought game witnessed by 7000 fans, Lower Merion held the lead at the end of each quarter. Despite the loss, the Mountaineer's Bobby Hicks led all scorers with 8 points. The title defense was over.

Leading scorers: Lower Merion – Davis 6; Hazleton - Bobby Hicks 8.[21]

Postseason Accolades

Leading scorers: League scoring leaders were: Rudy Zelko, Bethlehem, 117; Walt Boandl, Allentown, 109; George Cheverko, Hazleton, 102; Dick Rahn, Allentown, 99; Salvatore Frinzi, Easton 96; Frank Majzcan, Bethlehem, 93; Jerome Andrukitis, Tamaqua, 84; James Soroka, Easton, and Warren Christ, Tamaqua, each 67; and Donald Dietrich, Allentown 55.[22]

All-Stars: The "All-League" team included: Guards: Joe Andrejco, Hazleton; Frank Majzcan, Bethlehem; Warren Christ, Tamaqua; and James Soroka, Easton; Centers: Dick Rahn, Allentown and George Cheverko, Hazleton; Forwards: Rudy Zelko, Bethlehem; Walt Boandl, Allentown; Salvatore Frinzi, Easton; and Jerome Andrukitis, Tamaqua.[23]

Final Standings

Hazleton	9-1
Allentown	8-2
Bethlehem	7-3
Easton	3-7
Tamaqua	3-7
Pottsville	0-10

Team Rosters

Allentown: Coach J. Birney Crum, Walt Boandl, Harry Cawley, Donald Dietrich, Willie Domonkos, Ralph Eitner, Bob Friedman, Warren Geyer, George Hittinger, Bill Huskek, Donald Miller, Joseph O'Keefe. Eddie Piff, Dick Rahn, Fritz Sandt, Gene Sterner, Willie Stellar.

Bethlehem: Coach Bill Emrey, Leonard Andrucci, John Bechtel, Bodzack, Alfonso Calvo, Vincent Frisoli, Frank Majczan, Mann, Paul Marcincin, Robert "Babe" McWilliams, George Moyczan, Todd Saylor, Eddie Wodzicki, Peter Venninger, Rudy Zelko.

Easton: Coach Elmer Carroll, Tony Amato, Martin Barnhart, James Crisafulli, Frank Erbio, Carl Florindi, Salvatore Frinzi, Cassidy Gadwell, Frank Gugliuzza, Donald Hunt, Richard Johnson, Russell Meyers, George Pittenger, Robert Rounsaville, James Soroka.

Hazleton: Coach High McGeehan, Joe Andrejco, John Appichella, Richard Brill, George Cheverko, Victor Grushefsky, Robert Hicks, Vincent Parnell, John Price, Charles Prokopic, Joe Sager, Frank Smith, Anthony Valente, William Welliver.

Pottsville: Coach Alfred Sadusky, Becker, Russ Bevan, Robert Cantwell, Robert Fox, Jim Heller, Meyer, Tom Portland, Charles Riehl, Joe Sage, Donald Sandherr, Paul Schartle, William Scheerer, Dan Wazalis.

Tamaqua: Coach Eli Purnell, Jerome Andrukitis, Warren Christ, Walter Duncavage, Clarence Gould, John Heisler, Robert McMichael, Leonard Miller, George Mock, Anthony Morey, Kenny Osenbach, Jack Pauley, Lewis Purnell, George Tepo.

Hazleton High School – 1939 League Champions[24]

Front row: Andrejco, Cheverko, Prokopic, Smith, Welliver, Parnell, Valente, Sager

Back row: Student manager Franzosa, Price, Brill, Apichella, Grushefsky, Hicks, Student manager

1940

Four Titles in a Row

After a season of play using a season long campaign to establish the league champion, the league reversed back to a campaign using a two halves format. The league elected its officers for the upcoming campaign. Pottsville's D. H. H. Lengel was re-elected as president with Easton's Charles Richard as vice president. E. A. Rabenold was elected secretary-treasurer, a position he served in since the league's inception.[1]

The Pennsylvania Interscholastic Athletic Association (PIAA) adopted new rules to be implemented in the upcoming season. Some of the rules included:

- Permitting a team fouled to refuse a free throw and instead keeping possession and inbounding the ball at mid-court with the hope that it might eliminate intentional fouls at the end of close games,
- Allowing a referee to award two foul shots after a made-field goal if the foul appeared to be from the rear or in extreme roughness,
- Establishing a minimum court size of 42 ft. by 74 ft. and the end lines to be between 2 ft. and 4 ft. behind the plane of the backboard,
- Affirming that the team captain is the only player allowed to question a referee about a call or rule,
- Any player is allowed to request a call for a time out or to ask permission to leave the floor as long as the request is made by a player in possession of the ball or the ball is out of play, and
- On a foul shot, the ball must hit the rim and not just the backboard. A violation of this rule awards the ball to the other team.[2]

Week 1

Hazleton 50 Pottsville 15: Opening at home, Hazleton humbled Pottsville and held the Maroons to three field goals. Eight of the 11 players inserted by Coach McGeehan contributed to the scoring outburst.

Leading scorers: Hazleton - Joe Andrejco 10, Carl Welliver 10; Pottsville – Dan Wazalis 6.[3]

Allentown 40 Bethlehem 18: Allentown followed suit with a resounding victory over Bethlehem at the Little Palestra supported by over 2500 howling fans.

Leading scorers: Allentown - Fred Sandt 10, Gene Sterner 10; Bethlehem – Truman Ropos 5.

Easton 44 Tamaqua 36: Easton, at home, built a 18-point lead 31-13 by halftime and held on for the win.

Leading scorers: Easton – Donald Hunt 16; Tamaqua – John Heisler 13.[4]

Week 2

Allentown 31 Hazleton 29: Allentown shocked Hazleton on the Mountaineer's home court. Allentown led at the end of each quarter, but Hazleton pulled even at 29 all near the end of the game. Captain Dick Rahn pulled out the win with a field goal in the last minute for the Canaries, who now had won ten games on the season without a loss.

Leading scorers: Allentown – Fred Sandt 9, Dick Rahn 9; Hazleton – George Cheverko 9.[5]

Bethlehem 29 Easton 27: Bethlehem, on their home court, rebounded to defeat Easton. Despite trailing 17-9 at the half, Bethlehem fought back and outscored the Red Rovers 13-0 in the 3rd period.

Leading scorers: Bethlehem – Leonard Andrucci 8, Ruther Achey 8, George Moyczan 8; Easton – Tony Amato 9.[6]

Tamaqua 34 Pottsville 27: Holding Pottsville scoreless in the second quarter and with a 16-5 halftime lead, Tamaqua handed Pottsville its second loss.

Leading scorers: Tamaqua - Leonard Miller 14, Anthony Morfey 10; Pottsville – Dan Wazalis 11.[7]

Week 3

Allentown 41 Tamaqua 34: After a letdown from the Hazleton game, Allentown battled Tamaqua with the game tied at the half 17-17. Allentown barely moved ahead at the end of the third period 28-26 but outscored the Tams 13-8 in the final period to win the contest.

Leading scorers: Allentown - Willie Stellar 13, Dick Rahn 10; Tamaqua – Leonard Miller 9.

Pottsville 32 Easton 26: Pottsville invaded Easton and surprised the favored Red Rovers. It was Pottsville's first league win since 1936 after they had lost 37 consecutive league games.

Leading scorers: Pottsville – James Kennedy 12; Easton – Anthony Amato 11.[8]

Hazleton 33 Bethlehem 28: Hazleton rebounded from its loss to the Canaries with a triumph in Bethlehem. The Mountaineers held a 9-point lead at the end of three quarters.

Leading scorers: Hazleton - George Cheverko 17; Bethlehem – Bill Hochella 7.[9]

Easton 41 Allentown 37: This week being a two-game week, Allentown traveled to Easton hoping to extend their winning streak and path to the first half league title. The game was close the whole way with the score tied at the half 21-all and with the Canaries leading at the 3rd quarter mark 30-29. Allentown's center Dick Rahn fouled out early in the 4th quarter. The Canaries' lost their leading scorer. He still finished with 15 points in the game despite missing most of the last quarter. Scoring six straight points, Easton took a five-point lead with six minutes to play. However, Allentown came back to take the lead 37-36. Easton scored the last five points to win the game.

Leading scorers: Easton - Tony Amato 13; Allentown – Dick Rahn 15.

Bethlehem 34 Pottsville 18: Scoring 15 points in the third quarter for a 28-13 lead, Bethlehem evened its record at 2-2 with a win over Pottsville.

Leading scorers: Bethlehem - Frank Majzcan 17; Pottsville – Charles Boyer 7.[10]

Hazleton 46 Tamaqua 11: With Allentown's loss, Hazleton moved into a tie for first place with a one-sided victory over Tamaqua. While shutting out Tamaqua in the third quarter, Hazleton scored 15 points.

Leading scorers: Hazleton - George Cheverko 14 points; Tamaqua - Lloyd Jones 5, Purnell Lewis 5.[11]

Week 4

Hazleton 46 Easton 28: In the final game of Joe Andrejco's high school career, since he would turn 20 the following day, Hazleton had an easy game against the Red Rovers. The home fans gave Andrejco a number of gifts including a suit of clothes, hat, shirt, tie, shoes, overcoat, flowers, cake, and a 28-pound turkey wrapped in cellophane.

Leading scorers: Hazleton–George Cheverko 16, Vincent Parnell 11; Easton–Tony Amato 5, Joe Borota 5.[12]

Allentown 36 Pottsville 18: Allentown assured its berth in the playoff by doubling up Pottsville. Coach Crum emptied his bench and had a total of 12 different players in the game.

Leading scorers: Allentown – Dick Rahn 10, Gene Sterner 10; Pottsville – Russ Bevan 3, Clarence McClure 3, Paul Schartel 3.

Bethlehem 45 Tamaqua 11: Bethlehem also had an easy time of it at Tamaqua winning by 34 points. Bethlehem's Frank Majzcan also played his last game for the Liberty boys since he was turning 20.

Leading scorers: Bethlehem – Bill Hochella; Tamaqua – John Heisler 5.[13]

With Allentown and Hazleton tied at 4-1, league officials met in Tamaqua to make arrangements for a playoff. The league voted to hold the playoff at the Penn Palestra in Philadelphia with the ticket price set at 50 cents. Each school was allotted 5000 tickets with special trains being arranged to carry the fans to the game. The rival schools debated the selection of officials with each school vetoing choices made by the opponent. Finally, it was agreed to select two officials from Lancaster, Sherman Hill and A. B. Borger.[14]

First Half Playoff

Hazleton 40 Allentown 28: Playing in front of 6500 fans at the Penn Palestra, Hazleton and Allentown battled to a close game through three periods with Allentown leading 27-24. Hazleton reeled off the first 10 points of the 4th quarter to take a 34-27 lead over the stunned Canaries. The Mountaineers outscored the Canaries 16-1 in the quarter to win the game going away. Vince Parnell and George Cheverko, who had three personal fouls in the first half and still played the entire game, each scored 14 points while Dick Rahn had 15 for the Canaries. Allentown radio station WCBA and Hazleton station WAZL both broadcast the game with Johnny Van Sant handling the Allentown broadcast and Vic Diehm for Hazleton.

Leading scorers: Hazleton – Vincent Parnell 14, George Cheverko 14; Allentown – Dick Rahn 15.[15]

Week 5

Allentown 26 Bethlehem 22: After the playoff loss to Hazleton, Allentown went on the road against archrival Bethlehem. Despite pushing Allentown during the whole game, Bethlehem never led in the game and only tied once 12-12 in the win for the Canaries. No player in the game scored in double figures.

Leading scorers: Allentown – Fred Sandt 6, Dick Rahn 6; Bethlehem – Ruther Achey 8.[16]

Hazleton 55 Pottsville 34: Hazleton began its pursuit of the second half title against Pottsville at home. The visitors held the Mountaineers in check in the first half with Hazleton clinging to a 19-17 lead. The second half was a different story as the Mountaineers outscored the Maroons 36-17 to cruise to the win.

Leading scorers: Hazleton - Vince Parnell 21, George Cheverko 14; Pottsville – James Kennedy 8.

Easton 38 Tamaqua 36: Tamaqua led the whole way until the Red Rovers forged ahead 28-27. John Heisler made a long field goal which would have tied the game, but the officials ruled his shot was after the whistle.

Leading scorers: Easton – Richard Johnson 14, Tony Amato 10; Tamaqua – John Heisler 14.[17]

Week 6

Easton 33 Bethlehem 29: Two weeks into the second half, Easton's Red Rovers surprisingly were tied with Hazleton in first place. After taking a 10-2 lead after one quarter, Easton never trailed in the game in the win over Bethlehem.

Leading scorers: Easton – Tony Amato 12; Bethlehem – Pete Venninger 10.

Hazleton 41 Allentown 37: Hazleton avenged its first half defeat with a victory over the Canaries. The Canaries' loss snapped a 47-game win streak on its home court, the first loss at home since Hazleton won 21-19 in 1936.

Leading scorers: Hazleton – George Cheverko 19, Billy Smith 10; Allentown – Dick Rahn 14, Willie Stellar 10.[18]

Pottsville 33 Tamaqua 27: Pottsville, playing at home, got its second league win of the season by sweeping the two-game series from Tamaqua. Pottsville held Tamaqua to a single point in the second quarter.

Leading scorers: Pottsville – Charles Riehl 11; Tamaqua – Tony Morfey 13.[19]

Week 7

Allentown 41 Tamaqua 28: After a disappointing loss to Hazleton, Allentown traveled to Tamaqua to face the lowly Tams. The Canaries outscored Tamaqua 10-2 in the second quarter to take a commanding lead.

Leading scorers: Allentown - Dick Rahn 19; Tamaqua – John Heisler 16.

Hazleton 43 Bethlehem 32: After trailing 7-6 after a quarter, Hazleton took the lead for good when they outscored Bethlehem 11-3 in the second quarter in Hazleton.

Leading scorers: Hazleton -Vince Parnell 15, Billy Smith 10; Bethlehem -Bill Hochella 9, Pete Venninger 9.

Pottsville 43 Easton 33: After leading by only one at the half 19-18, Pottsville exploded in the second half to improve to a surprising 2-1 with an upset of Easton to take both games of the series from the Red Rovers.

Leading scorers: Pottsville – Charles Boyer 28; Easton – Donald Hunt 12, Tony Amato 12.[20]

Allentown 39 Easton 32: In the second game of the week, forward Fritz Sandt scored all of Allentown's seven points in the first quarter to lead the Canaries to a 7-1 first quarter lead. They were only briefly threatened once in the game when Easton pulled to within one point.

Leading scorers: Allentown - Dick Rahn 13, Fred Sandt 11; Easton – Donald Hunt 10.

Bethlehem 43 Pottsville 29: Bethlehem had to come from behind, as they trailed 11-6 at the end of one quarter, to defeat Pottsville. They took charge of the game by outscoring Pottsville 14-5 in the third quarter.

Leading scorers: Bethlehem - Bill Hochella 16, George Husovsky 10; Pottsville – Charles Boyer 10.[21]

Hazleton 47 Tamaqua 27: Hazleton held Tamaqua scoreless in the second period, while scoring 13 points, as they built a 27-8 half time lead.

Leading scorers: Hazleton - George Cheverko 12, Vincent Parnell 11; Tamaqua – John Heisler 8.[22]

Week 8

Hazleton 37 Easton 23: The Mountaineers traveled to Easton in hopes of winning their fourth consecutive league title. Although they only scored a single field goal in the first half, Hazleton led 10-9 at the half on the way to a title-clinching win. Hazleton made 12 field goals and 13 foul shots in the victory.

Leading scorers: Hazleton – Carl Welliver 13; Easton – Steve Lesko 8.

Allentown 33 Pottsville 31: After trailing 9-4 after a quarter and 20-11 at the half, Allentown pulled out a last-minute win at Pottsville on a long field goal by forward Stellar. With the victory, Hazleton and Allentown were the only teams with more wins than losses in the second half

Leading scorers: Allentown – Dick Rahn 12; Pottsville – James Kennedy 13.

Bethlehem 36 Tamaqua 28: Bethlehem kept Tamaqua winless in the second half of the season. Tamaqua scored only two points in the first quarter as they trailed 12-2 and then only five points in the third quarter. The win put Bethlehem in a three-way tie for 3rd place with Easton and Pottsville all at 2-3.

Leading scorers: Bethlehem – Pete Venninger 11, Bill Hochella 10; Tamaqua – Tony Morfey 12.[23]

Postseason Play

Hazleton 84 Nuremburg 20: Hazleton began its march to a state title with an easy victory over Nuremburg, the Class B Mountain League champions, and set a playoff record for greatest margin of victory and most points scored in a game. They broke their own 1929 record of 69 points versus Lansdowne. Coach McGeehan emptied his bench with 13 players entering the game and 11 of them scoring.

Leading scorers: Hazleton – John Apichella 18, George Cheverko 15, Vincent Parnell 14, Billy Smith 11; Nuremburg – Paul Hoats 7.[24]

Hazleton 58 Palmerton 29: The Mountaineer's roll continued with a win over Palmerton. Palmerton held Hazleton close for one period with the score tied at 11-all to begin period 2. From there on, it was all Hazleton with the Mountaineers taking command by scoring 19 to Palmerton's 9 in the third period.

Leading scorers: Hazleton - George Cheverko 16, Vincent Parnell 14, Billy Smith 10; Palmerton - Charley Fabian 12.[25]

Hazleton 34 Mahanoy City 32 OT: An overtime win over Mahony City allowed the Mountaineers to gain their fifth District XI title in 13 seasons with 9000 fans watching at the Penn Palestra. They saw a thriller. After Mahanoy City took the lead 32-30 with 55 seconds to play, it appeared Hazleton's District XI reign had ended. With five seconds remaining Mahanoy City fouled Vince Parnell. Taking advantage of a new rule for the season, Hazleton elected to take the ball at mid-court. Cheverko missed a field goal attempt but Billy Smith rebounded the ball and put it back in the basket for the tying points at the buzzer. Cal Welliver scored the only points in overtime for Hazleton and move them on to the state playoffs.

Leading scorers: Hazleton – Carl Welliver 13; Mahanoy City – Billy Schuster 11.[26]

Lower Merion 27 Hazleton 25 2OT: Three nights later in front of 10,000 fans at Penn Palestra in Philadelphia, Lower Merion stopped Hazleton's bid for a state title with a two-overtime victory. The crowd was the largest to see a game in Philadelphia since the Penn-Notre Dame game in 1937. With three minutes to play, Hazleton led 24-19 but Lower Merion made two field goals and a foul shot to tie the score. With 46 seconds to play, Cheverko fouled out and Lower Merion made the shot to go ahead by one. With 20 seconds to go, Welliver converted a foul shot and the score was tied once again at 25 all with no further scoring and the game sent into overtime. Lower Merion missed several foul shots in the first overtime which ended with no one scoring. Lower Merion did make a layup in the second overtime for the thrilling win. The classic matchup was officiated by John Heske and Mike Lisetski, two standout Lehigh Valley officials.

Leading scorers: Lower Merion – Nick D'Amora 6, Charles Silvertsen 6; Hazleton – George Cheverko 11.[27]

Postseason Accolades

Leading scorers: George Cheverko, of Hazleton led the league with 124 points for a 12.4 ppg average. He was followed by Dick Rahn of Allentown at 114 points; Tony Amato of Easton, 90 points; Vince Parnell of Hazleton, 86 points; Charles Boyer of Pottsville, 80 points; and Bill Hochella of Bethlehem, 73 points.[28]

All-Stars: The league all-stars included: Forwards: Vince Parnell, Hazleton; Tony Amato and Bill Hochella, Easton; and Charles Boyer, Pottsville; Centers: George Cheverko, Hazleton, and Dick Rahn, Allentown; Guards: Joe Andrejco and Carl Welliver, Hazleton; Frank Majczan, Bethlehem; and Willie Stellar, Allentown.[29]

Final Standings

First Half		Second Half		Overall	
Hazleton	4-1	Hazleton	5-0	Hazleton	9-1
Allentown	4-1	Allentown	4-1	Allentown	8-2
Bethlehem	3-2	Bethlehem	2-3	Bethlehem	5-5
Easton	2-3	Easton	2-3	Easton	4-6
Pottsville	1-4	Pottsville	2-3	Pottsville	3-7
Tamaqua	1-4	Tamaqua	0-5	Tamaqua	1-9

Team Rosters

Allentown: Coach J. Birney Crum, Bob Bender, Ralph Eitner, Jack Ferry, George Hittinger, Clarence Hoehle, Bill Hushkek, Floyd Moschini, Joe O'Keefe, Bob Peters, Ed Piff, Dick Rahn, Fred "Fritz" Sandt, Peter Sass, Willie Stellar, Gene Sterner, Tilberman, Jim Weiss

Bethlehem: Coach Bill Emery, Harry Achey, Leonard Andrucci, Marino Bartera, John Bellew, Jimmy Case, Falkovich, John Gasdaska, Frank Groskovich, Bill Hochella, George "Lefty" Husovsky, Frank Majczan, Ruther Mann, George Moyczan, Truman Ropos, Ben Shaner, Pete Venniger

Easton: Coach Elmer Carroll, Tony Amato, Martin Barnhart, Joe Borota, Carl Florindi, Donald Hunt, Richard Johnson, George Keck, Steve Lesko, Miller, John Vacaro

Hazleton: Coach Hugh McGeehan, Joe Andrejco, Joe Apichella, Dominic Cerullo, George Cheverko, Thomas Molinaro, Vincent Parnell, Frederick Poulmonter, Bill Smith, Robert Steckroth, Thomas Sweeney, Carl Welliver

Pottsville: Coach Al Sadusky, Russ Bevan, Charles "Sonny" Boyer, Marland Boyer, Robert Fox, Kearn, James Kennedy, Andy Kilmurray, Clarence McClure, Charles Riehl, Paul Schartel, Dan Wazalis, William Wintersteen.

Tamaqua: Coach Eli Purnell, Jack Costello, Walter Duncavage, John Heisler, Lloyd Jones, Robert McMichael, Leonard Miller, Anthony Morey, Edward Patrick, Lewis Purnell, Nicholas James Young.

Hazleton High School – 1940 League Champions[30]

Front row: Tom Sweeney, Vincent Parnell, George Cheverko, Joe Andrejco, Carl Welliver, Billy Smith; Back row: George Andrejco, Bob Steckroth, Tom Molinaro, Frank DeFluri, Joe Apichella, Dominic Cerullo, Fred Poulmonter

1941

Hazleton's Streak Ends

At a league meeting held in April 1940 in Allentown, the league reaffirmed its decision to continue with a split season. With no new teams applying for admittance into the league, the league would continue with the current six members. The current league officers were re-elected including D. H. Lengel, Pottsville, president; Charlie Richards, Easton, vice-president; and E. A. Rabenold, Allentown, secretary-treasurer, for the 16th consecutive season.[1]

Week 1

Hazleton 35 Bethlehem 24: Hazleton opened at home against Bethlehem in search of its fifth consecutive league title. Coming into the game as a slight underdog due to some early season losses, the Mountaineers surprised Bethlehem. They jumped out to a first period lead which they never relinquished.

Leading scorers: Hazleton – Billy Smith 9: Bethlehem – Pete Venninger 9.[2]

Allentown 47 Tamaqua 25: Allentown kept pace with a triumph over the Tamaqua Blue Raiders before a capacity crowd at the Little Palestra. Forward Erwin "Moon" Haney, just promoted to the varsity and a starting position, led the Canaries in scoring.

Leading scorers: Allentown - Erwin Haney 10; Tamaqua – Tony Morfey 12.

Easton 35 Pottsville 30: Despite trailing at the end of the second and third periods, Easton started its league season at home with a win over Pottsville.

Leading scorers: Easton - Steve Lesko 10 points; Pottsville - Charles Boyer 12.[3]

Week 2

Allentown 24 Bethlehem 22: At the Liberty gym, Allentown barely hung on to defeat Bethlehem. Trailing the entire game into the 3rd period, Allentown matched its entire first half output with 11 points to take the lead as the period ended 22-18.

Leading scorers: Allentown – Erwin Haney 8; Bethlehem – Bill Hochella 12.

Hazleton 30 Pottsville 17: Pottsville guard Robert Fox scored his team's only two field goals as Hazleton won easily.

Leading scorers: Hazleton – Billy Smith 17; Pottsville – Robert Fox 6.[4]

Easton 33 Tamaqua 32: Easton stayed undefeated with a nail-biting 33-32 win over Tamaqua. The Red Rovers made of 5 of 9 foul shots while Tamaqua made 10 of their 24 attempts.

Leading scorers: Easton - Steve Lesko 13; Tamaqua – Lloyd Jones 12.[5]

Week 3

Hazleton 31 Allentown 25: After both won their first two games, the stage was set for the first confrontation of Hazleton and Allentown. Prior to leaving for Hazleton, Allentown's Coach Crum was stricken with an attack of appendicitis and was not able to accompany the team. Assistant Coach Paul

Clymer assumed the coaching duties for this critical matchup and for several more weeks to follow. Hazleton showed no sympathy to the Canaries.

Leading scorers: Hazleton - Billy Smith 9; Allentown – Willie Stellar 7, John Grainer 7.

Easton 23 Bethlehem 22: Led by Salvatore Frinzi's seven points in the last 5 minutes, his only points of the game, Easton handed Bethlehem its third straight loss to stay in a first-place tie with Hazleton. Despite not scoring till late in the game, Frinzi was the Red Rovers' leading scorer.

Leading scorers: Easton – Salvatore Frinzi 7; Bethlehem – Pete Venninger 8.[6]

Pottsville-Tamaqua: The Pottsville-Tamaqua game was postponed when 42 percent of the Pottsville student body was absent due to illness.[7]

Week 4

Hazleton 39 Easton 31: The battle of the league's only unbeatens took place in Hazleton when Easton came to town looking to rule the league roost. Leading at the end of each quarter, the Mountaineers sent the Red Rovers home with their first loss.

Leading scorers: Hazleton - Robert Steckroth 12, Billy Smith 10; Easton – Steve Lesko 10.

Bethlehem 36 Tamaqua 33: After trailing at halftime 14-12, Bethlehem finally made it into the win column with its victory over Tamaqua.

Leading scorers: Bethlehem – John Gasdaska 10, Bill Hochela 10; Tamaqua - Lloyd Jones.[8]

Allentown 36 Pottsville 29: In a close contest in Allentown, assistant coach Paul Clymer earned his first head coaching victory with the win over Pottsville. Willie Stellar led the Canaries with 10 points and tied Tamaqua's Robert Fox for the game high total.[9] Allentown and Easton were tied for 2nd place at 3-1 behind unbeaten Hazleton.

Leading scorers: Allentown – Willie Stellar 10; Tamaqua – Robert Fox 10.

Hazleton 38 Tamaqua 29: Later in the week, Hazleton traveled to Tamaqua to hopefully clinch the first half title. With seven players in the scoring column, Hazleton had no difficulty with the Tams.

Leading scorers: Hazleton – Billy Smith 9; Tamaqua – Earl Steigerwalt – 9.

Allentown 37 Easton 32: With the Canaries trailing after three quarters 30-26, Allentown ended Easton's first half on a sour note handing them a loss at the Easton gym.

Leading scorers: Allentown – Erwin Haney 10, John Grainer 10; Easton - Jack Rothenhausler 13.

Bethlehem-Pottsville: Prompted by Luzerne County officials' request, Bethlehem postponed its game in Pottsville due to snow and sleet causing treacherous travel over the mountainous highways.[10]

Week 5 – Second Half

Allentown 37 Tamaqua 27: With Coach Birney Crum back at the helm, Allentown traveled to Tamaqua to open the second half. Tamaqua cut the Canaries' 9-point halftime-lead to five points 28-23, but Allentown prevailed.

Leading scorers: Allentown - Bill Huskek 11, John Grainer 10; Tamaqua – Edgar Apanavage 12.

Bethlehem 32 Hazleton 16: Meanwhile, Coach Bill Emrey's Liberty boys crushed Hazleton. Bethlehem built up a 31-9 lead after 3 periods as Hazleton was able to score only a single point in the third period.

Leading scorers: Bethlehem – Pete Venninger 15; Hazleton – Billy Smith 7.

Pottsville 30 Easton 29: At Pottsville, "Sonny ” Boyer led Pottsville with 16 points in their victory over Easton. With the score tied at 29 all, substitute guard Karl Rehnert converted a foul shot with 35 seconds to play. With two seconds to play, the home cr ›wd poured onto the court thinking the game was over. It took 10 minutes to clear the floor to finish the l ıst two seconds of the game.

Leading scorers: Pottsville - Charles Boyer 16; E aston - John Vacaro 11.[11]

Allentown 47 Bethlehem 19: Unleashing its offense during the second period, Allentown outscored Bethlehem 21-2 to cruise to an easy defeat of B ethlehem. Fritz Sandt and Moon Haney led the attack with 8 of the 12 Allentown players who entered the ga me scoring at least a point. Allentown stood atop the league in the second half as the lone undefeated team.

Leading scorers: Allentown - Fred Sandt 13, Erw in Haney 11; Bethlehem – Jim Case 5.[12]

Tamaqua 36 Easton 35: Tamaqua kept Eastor ı winless in the second half. Avenging their one-point loss in their first matchup, the Tams' center Steigerv valt scored two field goals late in the game to pull out the win. Easton was winless in the second half with both losses being by a single point.

Leading scorers: Tamaqua – Lloyd Jones 11, Tor ıy Morfey 11; Easton – John Vacara 8, Joe Borota 8.

Hazleton 28 Pottsville 27 OT: Pottsville force d homestanding Hazleton into an overtime period before the Mountaineers pulled out the victory. Pottsvil le's brief sharing of first place was over.

Leading scorers: Hazleton – Billy Smith 7: Potts ville - Andy Kilmurray 10.[13]

Week 6

Allentown 29 Hazleton 22: Allentown solidifie d its hold on the top spot by holding off Hazleton with a spurt in the 4th period. With no one in double fi gures, the Canaries got balance scoring from all six players that Coach Crum used in the game. After being first half champs, Hazleton was an uncharacteristic 1-2.

Leading scorers: Allentown – Erwin Haney 7; H azleton – Eddie Bresnock 11.

Bethlehem 51 Easton 36: Bethlehem scored 2( ) points in the second quarter and handed Easton its third straight loss to begin the second half of the seas on.

Leading scorers: Bethlehem - Pete Venninger 14, Frank Majzcan 14; Easton – Jack Rothenhausler 8.[14]

Tamaqua 30 Pottsville 21: A rejuvenated Tam aqua team improved to 2-1 with its win over Pottsville to move into a tie for second place with Bethlehem at 2-1.

Leading scorers: Tamaqua – Lloyd Jones 8; Potts ville – Andy Kilmurray 6.[15]

Week 7

Easton 31 Hazleton 30 OT: Easton bounced back from a humiliating defeat by Bethlehem and handed Hazleton a third loss in overtime. In overtim e, Hazleton forged ahead on a technical foul called on Bethlehem only to see Easton forward Jack Roth enhausler score a field goal with 20 seconds to go.

Leading scorers: Easton – Jack Rothenhausler 11 ; Hazleton – John Hospidar 10.[16]

Allentown 35 Pottsville 28: At Pottsville, center Bill Hushkek's 10 points helped lead Allentown to a defeat of the Maroons. At one point in the game, Coac h Crum pulled Fritz Sandt off the court to "cool him off" after a scrimmage with Pottsville's Andy Kilmurr ay.

Leading scorers: Allentown - Bill Hushkek 10; Po ttsville – Charles Boyer 15.[17]

Bethlehem 30 Tamaqua 26: Converting only 4 of 10 foul shots to Bethlehem's 8 of 11, Tamaqua fell to the Liberty boys. The loss dropped Tamaqua out of second place with Bethlehem now alone in second.

Leading scorers: Bethlehem – Bill Hochella 8; Tamaqua – Earl Steigerwalt 9.[18]

Pottsville 47 Tamaqua 23: In a first half makeup game which had no bearing on the first half outcome, Pottsville defeated Tamaqua.

Leading scorers: Pottsville - Charles Boyer 11, Andy Kilmurray 10; Tamaqua - Lloyd Jones 9.[19]

Week 8

Allentown 39 Easton 30: After trailing 11-3 in the first quarter, Allentown fought its way back to win over Easton and clinch the second half title. Moon Haney scored 14 points in the win. Hoping to have him available in the league title game, the Canaries played without Fritz Sandt who was nursing a sore shoulder.

Leading scorers: Erwin Haney 14, John Grainer 10; Easton – Martin Barnhart 8.

Hazleton 36 Tamaqua 23: Jumping out to a ten-point first quarter lead 12-2, Hazleton closed out the second half at 2-3 with its win over Tamaqua.

Leading scorers: Hazleton – Tony Moran 16, Ed Bresnock 12; Tamaqua – Tony Morfey 9.

Bethlehem 42 Pottsville 36: Bethlehem clinched second place at 4-1 with a win over the Crimson Tide after taking a six-point lead at the half and holding it for the rest of the game.

Leading scorers: Bethlehem - Pete Venninger 19; Pottsville – Charles Boyer 14.[20]

Pottsville 48 Bethlehem 39: A final makeup game from the first half of the season was played earlier in the week in Pottsville. Pottsville surprised Bethlehem with the game having no bearing on the outcome of the first half results. Pottsville's Sonny Boyer moved into first place in the league scoring race.

Leading scorers: Pottsville – Charles Boyer 20, Andy Kilmurray 11; Bethlehem – Pete Venninger 12, George Moyczan.[21]

League Championship Game

Allentown 32 Hazleton 24: The league title would again reside in either Allentown or Hazleton as the two squared off at the Penn Palestra for the overall league title. A rousing crowd of 7,500 saw 5'7" forward Willie Stellar lead Allentown to victory as he scored 14 points. Hazleton gave a good account through three periods with the score tied 20-20 heading into the final period. Allentown scored the first 10 points of the 4th period to secure its first title since 1936. Two special excursion trains from Hazleton (6 cars) and Allentown (10 cars) took fans to the game.

Leading scorers: Allentown – Willie Stellar 14; Hazleton – Tony Moran 10.[22]

Postseason Play

Allentown 55 Mauch Chunk 33: Allentown played its initial District XI game on its home court, the Little Palestra. Due to a blizzard, one of the game officials arrived late and delayed the game for more than a half hour. Despite the unpleasant conditions, over 2000 fans crowded into the gym to watch the Canaries win the matchup.

Leading scorers: Allentown – Willie Stellar 16, Bill Hushkek 11; Mauch Chunk – Johnny Watto 10[3]

Allentown 34 Palmerton 23: Allentown traveled to Reading's Northwest Junior High School for the second round of district play against the Palmerton Blue Bombers. Palmerton took and early 4-0 lead, all on foul shots. Allentown came back to take 6-5 first period and 13-8 half time leads. Palmerton did not make a field goal in the first half. The second half was dominated by the Canaries. Ironically, in the second half, Palmerton converted 7 field goals and only a single foul shot.

Leading scorers: Allentown - Bill Hushkek 8; Palmerton – Johnny Harduby 9.[24]

Mahanoy City 32 Allentown 29: Past league foe, Mahanoy City now played Allentown for the district title which was the third consecutive year that Mahanoy City played in the title game. Nine thousand spectators witnessed the District XI title game at the Penn Palestra. The game was a see-saw battle with Allentown leading after one period 10-9, Mahanoy City leading at the half 19-14, and Allentown back in the lead 23-22 after three periods. Foul shots made the difference in the game with Mahanoy City making 10 of 13 and Allentown 7 of 10. After losing the first two title attempts to Hazleton, Mahanoy City finally won their first District XI title as they defeated Allentown. Over 3000 fans traveled to the game from Mahanoy City with many of them arriving by a special train split into two sections with 22 total cars. Mahanoy City moved on to the state playoffs while the Canaries season was over.

Leading scorers: Mahanoy City – Jacubac 9; Allentown – Joe O'Keefe 10.[25]

Postseason Accolades

Leading Scorers: The season's top scorers included: Sonny Boyer, Pottsville, 110 points; Pete Venninger, Bethlehem, 94 points; Billy Smith, Hazleton, 84 points; Lloyd Jones, Tamaqua, 82 points; Erwin "Moon" Haney, Allentown, 80 points; Bill Hochella, Bethlehem, 69 points; Steve Lesko, Easton, 68 points; Bill Hushkek, Allentown, 61 points; Willie Stellar, Allentown, 53 points; and John Hospidor, Hazleton, 50 points.[26]

All-Stars: The Hazleton Plain Speaker published its league all-star team listing four teams:

First team: forwards Charles Boyer, Pottsville, and Stellar, Allentown; center John Grainer, Allentown; and guards Hospidor, Hazleton, and Anthony Morfey, Tamaqua.

Second team: forwards Pete Venninger, Bethlehem, and Lloyd Jones, Tamaqua; center Steckroth, Hazleton; guards Jack Rothenhausler, Easton, and Bill Hushkek, Bethlehem.

Third team: forwards Billy Smith and Anthony Moran, Hazleton; center Steve Lesko, Easton; and guards Frank Majzcan, Bethlehem, and Joe O'Keefe, Allentown.

Fourth team: forwards Erwin Haney, Allentown, and Ed Bresnock, Hazleton; Bill Hochella, Bethlehem, and Joe Borota, Easton.[27]

All-State: Several players from the league were named to the PIAA all-state teams including: center Willie Steller, Allentown, 2nd team; forwards, Fred Sandt, Allentown, Billy Smith, Hazleton, Charles Boyer, Pottsville, and guards Joe O'Keefe, Allentown, and Tony Morfey, Tamaqua, honorable mention.[28]

Final Standings

First Half		Second Half		Overall	
Hazleton	5-0	Allentown	5-0	Allentown	9-1
Allentown	4-1	Bethlehem	4-1	Hazleton	7-3
Easton	3-2	Hazleton	2-3	Bethlehem	5-5
Pottsville	2-3	Tamaqua	2-3	Easton	4-6
Bethlehem	1-4	Easton	1-4	Pottsville	3-7
Tamaqua	0-5	Pottsville	1-4	Tamaqua	2-8

Team Rosters

Allentown: Coach J. Birney Crum, Bob Bender, Eddie Bortz, Mike Chomik, Charles Cohen, John Ferry, Bobby Freed, John Grainer, Roger Graver, Erwin "Moon" Haney, Clarence Hoehle, Bill Hushkek, Ken Moyer, Joe O'Keefe, Bob Peters, Fred "Fritz: Sandt, Pete Sass, Willie Stellar, Jim Weiss.

Bethlehem: Coach Bill Emrey, John Bellew, Jim Case, Roland Correll, Walter Davis, John Gasdaska, Murray Goodman, John Hippenstiel, Bill Hochella, Frank Majczan, Mazzia, Richard McCandless, Emerson Miller, George Moyczan, Ben Shaner, Pete Venninger.

Easton: Coach Elmer Carroll, Martin Barnhart, Joe Borota, Sam Crisafulli, Salvatore Frinzi, George Keck, Steve Lesko, Joseph Marhefka, John Martinkus, Jack Rothenhausler, Rothski, Kenneth Todd, John Vacaro.

Hazleton: Coach Hugh McGeehan, Ed Bresnock, Bushner, Frank DeFluri, John Hospidor, Frank "lefty" McHugh, Anthony Moran, Francis Murphy, Neal Penn, Fred Poulmonter, Billy Smith, Robert Steckroth, Thomas Sweeney.

Pottsville: Coach Al Sadusky, Charles Ashman, Charles "Sonny" Boyer, Marland Boyer, Basil Choman, Robert Fox, Ed Kennedy, Andy Kilmurray, Fred Lennox, Andrew Majeskie, Matt Maley, Clarence McClure, Willard McFee, Karl Rehnert, William Rosenberger, Bruce Young.

Tamaqua: Coach Eli Purnell, Eddie Apanavage, James DeWire, Robert Filer, Lloyd Jones, George Krepak, Tony Morfey, Oosthousen, Arthur ReVak, Earl Steigerwalt, Nicholas James Young.

Allentown High School – 1941 League Champions[29]

Front row: Fritz Sandt, Joe O'Keefe, Jerry Moyer, Bill Huskek, Coach Crum, Bob Hoehle, Jack Ferry.

Back row: Harvey Weiss, Bob Bender, Mike Chomik, Wille Stellar, Asst Coach Clymer, Bob Freed, Roger Graver, Erwin Haney, Eddie Bortz, John Grainer.

1942

Expansion Rejected

In April 1941, the six members schools met in Bethlehem to complete business for the past season and organize for the upcoming season. Three schools applied for membership for the 1942 season and league representatives rejected all three. A proposal to create a Big 15 basketball league split into two divisions was discussed, but no formal action was taken. One of the reasons for not taking action was the league's promise to retain Tamaqua as a league member. Since Tamaqua was not a member of the Big 15, Tamaqua would be dismissed as a member if the proposal had been accepted.

The league received applications for membership from Allentown Central Catholic, Shamokin, and Williamsport High Schools. Since Central Catholic was not a member of the Pennsylvania Interscholastic Athletic Association, the league voted down their application 4-2. The league voted down Shamokin's application due to their lack of a suitable playing floor. Williamsport was rejected again due to similar concerns raised during their previous attempt to enter the league. The six members schools cited the travel distance and cost as their major concern and the application was rejected by a 4-2 vote.

League leadership was re-elected with D. H. H. Lengle, Pottsville, as president, Charlie Richards, Easton, as vice president, and Edgar Rabenold, Allentown, as secretary-treasurer. The members voted to continue the split season arrangement with two halves.[1]

Week 1

Pottsville 42 Tamaqua 29: Pottsville began the season at Tamaqua. Tamaqua was shorthanded with two of the starters, Don Becker and Bud Henne, out ill for the game. After leading at the half 13-11, Pottsville scored 9 straight points to take charge of the contest.

Leading scorers: Pottsville - Ed Kennedy 12, Bruce Young 11; Tamaqua – Earl Steigerwalt 14.

Hazleton 34 Allentown 32: Opening on their home court, Hazleton defeated the previous year's champion Allentown. After trailing 30-19, the Canaries put forth a serious rally to make the game seem much closer than it had actually been. Hazleton used balanced scoring to beat the Canaries with no player scoring in double figures.

Leading scorers: Hazleton – Tony Moran 9, Ed Bresnock 9; Allentown – Kenny Moyer 11.

Bethlehem 35 Easton 27: Traveling to Easton, Bethlehem started out the season fast by taking a 16-4 first period lead on their way to a defeat of the Red Rovers.

Leading scorers: Bethlehem - Charles "Chuck" Bednarik 10; Easton – Francis Tone 6.[2]

Week 2

Bethlehem 30 Hazleton 29: On the road, Hazleton fell to Bethlehem during the second week in a thrilling finish. Hazleton shot out to a 12-2 lead which Bethlehem cut to a single point 17-16 at the half. Three times the score was tied in the final period when Hazleton went ahead 29-28 on a foul shot by Tony "Hunky" Moran. Bethlehem substitute Al Saemmer countered with a long set shot for the win for the Liberty boys.

Leading scorers: Bethlehem – Jimmy Case 10; Hazleton – Frank Apichella 8.

Pottsville 41 Easton 27: After the teams were tied 15-15 at halftime, Pottsville opened the second half on 15-6 run. They remained tied with Bethlehem for the early season lead at 2-0 with Easton now at 0-2.

Leading scorers: Pottsville – Bruce Young 12, Ed Kennedy 10; Easton – Frank Crisafulli 12.

Allentown 39 Tamaqua 23: After holding a slim 15-13 halftime lead, Allentown began the second half on a 14-5 run to build an eleven-point lead at the Little Palestra.

Leading scorers: Allentown – Kenny Moyer 11; Tamaqua – Nicholas James Young 8.[3]

Week 3

Allentown 34 Bethlehem 22: Allentown knocked Bethlehem out of the unbeaten ranks at the Little Palestra in front of 2200 fans. Sprinting out to a 15-5 first period lead, the Canaries went on to win the contest. Early in the 4th period, the officials had to stop the game due to the extreme physical play and called both teams together to order them to stop the rough stuff.

Leading scorers: Allentown - Ervin "Moon" Haney 14; Bethlehem – Al Saemmer 8.

Hazleton 25 Pottsville 18: Meanwhile, Pottsville also lost its first game of the league season to Hazleton. With no player in double figures, the Mountaineers' Ed Bresnock led all scorers with 8 points. After three weeks, Allentown, Bethlehem, Hazleton, and Pottsville were all tied for the league lead at 2-1.

Leading scorers: Hazleton – Ed Bresnock 8; Pottsville – Willard Rosenberger 5, Ed Kennedy 5, Bill McFee 5.[4]

Tamaqua 38 Easton 22: At home, Tamaqua won its first game and kept Easton winless. Tamaqua jumped out to a 10-2 first quarter lead and a 25-9 lead at halftime.

Leading scorers: Tamaqua – Dick Jones 13. Nicholas James Young 10; Easton – Joseph Marks 9.[5]

Pottsville 33 Bethlehem 30: Later in the week in a battle of first place teams, Bethlehem dropped out of the league lead as they lost on the road to Pottsville. The battle was close until the third period when Pottsville took a five-point lead. Bethlehem led at the half 14-13, but Pottsville took the lead after three quarters 27-22.

Leading scorers: Pottsville - Bill Rosenberger 13; Bethlehem – Roland Correll 10.

Allentown 38 Easton 33: Easton took an early 3-0 lead, but Allentown scored the next five to lead 5-3 after a quarter. The Canaries outscored Easton 10-5 in the third quarter to lead 30-21 going into the fourth quarter.

Leading scorers: Allentown – John "Red" Graner 15; Easton – Bill Zwiski 12.

Hazleton 45 Tamaqua 25: Hazleton stayed in the three-way tie with an easy win, leading by 12 points at halftime, over Pinky Purnell's Tamaqua quintet.[6]This led to a scramble for the first half title during the final week of half.

Leading scorers: Hazleton – Al DeGatis 19; Tamaqua – Nicholas James Young 8.

Week 4

Allentown 31 Pottsville 30: At the Little Palestra, Allentown took on Pottsville in a battle to remain in first place and a possible playoff with Hazleton for the first half title. Despite twice leading by seven points and holding a 31-25 lead with five minutes to play, Allentown had to hold on to win the game. Diminutive guard Dick Schmidt, despite not scoring a point, proved to be the hero of the game. Schmidt dribbled the ball up court and out of trouble during the last minutes of the game and prevented Pottsville from getting control of the ball to potentially win the game.

Leading scorers: Allentown - Erwin Haney 13; Pottsville – Bill Rosenberger 9, Bruce Young 9.

Hazleton 36 Easton 18: Hazleton kept the Red Rovers scoreless in the first quarter 9-0 and led at the half 19-1 to easily beat Easton and set up a tie between the Canaries and Mountaineers once again for the first half title.

Leading scorers: Hazleton – Al DeGatis 13; Easton – Theodore Markowitz 7.

Bethlehem 48 Tamaqua 22: After leading 15-4 and 25-12 after the first two quarters, Bethlehem rolled to its win over Tamaqua and finished at 3-2 for the first half.

Leading scorers: Bethlehem – Charles Bednarik 11; Tamaqua – Bob Filer 8.[7]

First Half Playoff

Hazleton 28 Allentown 26 OT: With the Penn Palestra unavailable due to another event, league officials voted to hold the playoff game at Convention Hall in Philadelphia. A special excursion train from Allentown brought 90 band members, drum majorettes, and cheerleaders and over 300 fans to the game. Another train from Hazleton brought several hundred fans. Five thousand fans witnessed another classic confrontation between the two foes with the Canaries jumping out to a 20-9 lead in the first half. Hazleton held Allentown scoreless in the third period and finished the 3rd quarter behind 20-17. With the Canaries ahead 24-22 with a minute and a half to play, Dick Schmidt fouled out of the game when he fouled Hazleton's John Hospidor, who made both foul shots to tie the score at 24 at the end of regulation. In overtime, backup center John Apichella, who had not scored in regulation, made two field goals to pull out the game in overtime 28-26. It was the fifth time the two schools met in a playoff in Philadelphia. Hazleton now had the advantage 3-2.

Leading scorers: Hazleton – Tony Moran 15; Allentown – John Graner 8.[8]

Week 5

Allentown 36 Hazleton 34: Five days after the first half playoff, Allentown and Hazleton played another overtime game to begin the second half at the Little Palestra. The Mountaineers built an almost insurmountable 24-9 halftime lead. By the end of the third quarter, the Canaries cut the lead to 29-21 by outscoring Hazleton 12-5. With 2 ½ minutes to play, Allentown whittled Hazleton's margin to a single point 33-32. By this time, both Red Graner and Ken Moyer had fouled out. After DeGatis made a foul shot for Hazleton, Bill Gower, a Raub Junior High School player on the junior varsity, made a field goal with 20 seconds to play to tie the score. The game ended tied in regulation. Hazleton attempted seven shots in overtime with all missing the mark. Bobby Freed's only goal and points in overtime proved to be the winner and was the only time the Canaries led during the entire game.

Leading scorers: Allentown – John Graner 11; Hazleton – Tony Moran 13, Al DeGatis 12.

Pottsville 38 Tamaqua 22: Pottsville won its second half opener over Tamaqua after racing out to a 21-9 lead.

Leading scorers: Pottsville - Bill Rosenberg 14, Bruce Young 12; Tamaqua – Earl Steigerwalt 7.

Bethlehem 36 Easton 21: Walt Davis scored 14 points in Bethlehem's win over Easton. Bethlehem played ten boys with eight of them scoring points in the game

Leading scorers: Bethlehem – Walter Davis 10; Easton - Frank Crisafulli 10.[9]

Bethlehem 26 Hazleton 23: Bethlehem traveled to Hazleton and handed the Mountaineers their second consecutive loss to start the second half of the season. Despite scoring one less field goal, the Liberty boys won the game on the foul line converting 10 of 12 attempts while Hazleton could only make 5 of 13 tries.

Leading scorers: Bethlehem – Jimmy Case 8; Hazleton – John Hospidar 6.

Allentown 36 Tamaqua 15: Despite holding only a 13-10 advantage at the half, Allentown rolled to a 36-15 defeat of Tamaqua. Tamaqua could only score 5 points in the second half.

Leading scorers: Allentown - Kenny Moyer 13; Tamaqua - Earl Steigerwalt 8.

Easton 36 Pottsville 29: Surprising Easton upset Pottsville in Easton despite trailing after one quarter 12-8. Coach Elmer Carrol used two teams to pull out the win. Five boys played the first and third quarters while a second five played the second and fourth quarters. All but one of the ten players scored for the Red Rovers.

Leading scorers: Easton – Frank Crisafulli 7, Richard Sanguinito 7; Pottsville – Bruce Young 8.[10]

Week 6

Pottsville 24 Hazleton 22 OT: On Friday, the 13th, Hazleton uncharacteristically lost its third straight game at Pottsville in overtime. Pottsville's win broke a 29-game losing streak with Hazleton over 15 years. Hazleton lost the game at the foul line connecting on only 4 of 14 including two misses in the last minute of play.

Leading scorers: Pottsville–Ed Kennedy 8; Hazleton–John Hospidor 4, Ed Bresnock 4, Al DeGatis 4, Patrick McGeehan 4.

Allentown 34 Bethlehem 26: In a battle of unbeatens at Bethlehem's Liberty High School gym, Allentown took sole possession of first place with the victory. Bethlehem held the lead at 4-0 before Allentown to the lead at 6-5.

Leading scorers: Allentown – Erwin "Moon" Haney 12; Bethlehem – Walter Davis 8, Charles Bednarik 8.

Easton 30 Tamaqua 28: At Easton, the Red Rover's John Martinkus scored 14 points as Easton knocked off Tamaqua when Bill Zwiski converted two foul shots in the last minute of play.

Leading scorers: Easton – John Martinkus 14; Tamaqua – Earl Steigerwalt 10.[11]

Week 7

Pottsville 34 Bethlehem 29: After trailing 8-7 after a quarter, the Maroons from Pottsville took the lead at the half 19-15 and went on to knock Bethlehem out of the race for the second half crown in Bethlehem.

Leading scorers: Pottsville – Bill Rosenberg 10, Ed Kennedy 10, Karl Rehnert 10; Bethlehem – Charles Bednarik 9.[12]

Allentown 32 Easton 21: Allentown, although only leading at the first period mark 6-5, handled Easton to knock them out of title contention. Allentown went on to lead 15-9 at halftime and 23-12 after three quarters.

Leading scorers: Allentown - Kenny Moyer 10; Easton - John Martinkus 8.

Hazleton 45 Tamaqua 20: Hazleton finally picked up its first win of the second half at Tamaqua by trouncing the Tams. Coach McGeehan played 10 boys with son Patrick leading the scoring for the Mountaineers.

Leading scorers: Hazleton – Patrick McGeehan 10; Tamaqua – Nicholas James Young.[13]

Week 8

Pottsville 44 Allentown 25: Allentown and Pottsville met with the Canaries only having to defeat the Maroons to clinch the second half title. Coach Al Sadusky's squad surprised the Canaries in an easy win. The Canaries led 8-4 at the first period mark only to see Pottsville move ahead at the half 16-15. Pottsville took over in the second half and their victory created a tie for the second half title between the two teams.

Leading scorers: Pottsville – Bruce Young 15, Ed Kennedy 15; Allentown – Erwin Haney 8.

Hazleton 30 Easton 24: Hazleton took down Easton in a game they led the whole way. They were now in a two-game win streak leading up to their playoff with either Allentown or Pottsville.

Leading scorers: Hazleton – Tony Moran 9; Easton – John Martinkus 8.[14]

Bethlehem 47 Tamaqua 23: Bethlehem kept Tamaqua winless in the second half with a triumph in Tamaqua. Bethlehem led at the half 23-11 and put the Tams away by outscoring them 15-3 in the fourth quarter.

Leading scorers: Bethlehem – Roland Correll 11; Tamaqua – Nicholas James Young 10.[15]

Second Half Playoff

Pottsville 36 Allentown 34: Another playoff was necessary as Allentown and Pottsville squared off at Penn's Palestra. For the second time in 3 days, Pottsville surprised everyone with a victory as Moon Haney's desperation heave bounced off the rim to end the game. With five minutes to play, Allentown led 30-26 only to see Pottsville's Dick McFee and Karl Rehnert each make long field goals from near mid-court. Ed Kennedy made a field goal and foul shot for the win.

Leading scorers: Pottsville – Ed Kennedy 12; Allentown – Erwin Haney 15, John Graner 12.[16]

Season Championship Playoff

Pottsville 34 Hazleton 32: Trailing 11-5 after one quarter, Pottsville, using a fast break, ran their way into the lead 23-15 at the half. Up 10 points early in the 4th quarter, Pottsville hung to outlast the Mountaineers. Seven players scored as Pottsville won its first league title since the first year of league play in 1926!

Leading scorers: Pottsville – Bill Rosenberger 9; Hazleton – Patrick McGeehan 7.[17]

Postseason Play

Pottsville 40 Nuremberg 17: In their opening game of the district playoffs, Pottsville won its first game easily over Nuremberg, the Mountain League champs. They held Nuremberg to two field goals and 2 foul shots in the second half. They held the Mountain League's leading scorer Ken Singley to seven points.

Leading scorers: Pottsville – Ed Kennedy 11; Nuremberg – Ken Singley 7.[18]

Pottsville 56 Port Carbon 26: After leading 18-10 at the half, Pottsville found its stride against Port Carbon in the 3rd quarter to stretch the lead to 38-16. With substitutes playing most of the 4th quarter, the Maroons rolled to an easy victory over Port Carbon.

Leading scorers: Pottsville – Bill Rosenberg 16, Bruce Young 15; Port Carbon – Ralph Miller 9.[19]

Pottsville 49 Catasauqua 34: In the district title game at the Reading Northwest Junior High gym, Pottsville won its first District XI crown with a win over Catasauqua. With Catasauqua leading 31-30 at the end of 3 periods, Pottsville scored 17 points in the last six minutes to pull out the title game.

Leading scorers: Pottsville – Bruce Young 14, Ed Kennedy 12; Catasauqua – Andy Skvoretz 7, Frank Behun 7.[20]

Berwick 30 Pottsville 28: Pottsville's dream of a state title ended in Hershey against an underdog Berwick Bulldog team. The Bulldogs, District 2 champions, took an early 19-7 lead and continued to hold a sizeable lead way into the fourth quarter. Pottsville pulled within three points 29-26, but Berwick spoiled Pottsville's dream season.

Leading scorers: Berwick – Joe "Bells" Colone 11; Pottsville – Jack Stoner 8.[21]

Postseason Accolades

Leading Scorers: Erwin "Moon" Haney, Allentown, finished as the league's high scorer with a total of 97 points. Pottsville's Ed Kennedy finished second with 86 points. Other leading scorers included: Bruce Young, Pottsville, 81 points; Bill Rosenberger, Pottsville, 80; Al DeGatis, Hazleton, 76; Ken Moyer, Allentown, 75; John Graner, Allentown, 74; Charles "Chuck" Bednarik, Bethlehem, and Nicholas James Young, Tamaqua, 68; Earl Steigerwalt, Tamaqua, 57; Anthony Moran, Hazleton, and Walter Davis, Bethlehem, 56; Ed Bresnock, Hazleton, 55; Roland Correll, Bethlehem, 52; and John Martinkus, Easton, 51.[22]

All-Stars: The league's all-stars included:

Forwards: Erwin Haney, Allentown; Bob Young and Bill Rosenberger, Pottsville; and Anthony Moran, Hazleton.

Centers: Ed Kennedy, Pottsville and Earl Steigerwalt, Tamaqua.

Guards: John Graner, Allentown; Willard McFee, Pottsville; Frank McHugh, Hazleton; and Charles Bednarik, Bethlehem.[23]

Final Standings

First Half		Second Half		Overall	
Hazleton	4-1	Allentown	4-1	Allentown	8-2
Allentown	4-1	Pottsville	4-1	Pottsville	7-3
Bethlehem	3-2	Bethlehem	3-2	Bethlehem	6-4
Pottsville	3-2	Hazleton	2-3	Hazleton	6-4
Tamaqua	1-4	Easton	2-3	Easton	2-8
Easton	0-5	Tamaqua	0-5	Tamaqua	1-9

Team Rosters

Allentown: Coach J. Birney Crum, Mike Chomik, Charles Cohen, Charles Epstein, Richard Franklin, Bob Freed, John "Red" Graner, Erwin "Moon" Haney, Michael Melinchok, Kenny Menchin, Kenny Moyer, Dick Schmidt, Gordon "Slim" Slider

Bethlehem: Coach Bill Emery, Charles Baron, Charles "Chuck" Bednarik, Paul Calvo, Jimmy Case, Roland Correll, Walt Davis, Donald Engler, Edward Hoch, Al Saemmer, Ben Shaner

Easton: Coach Elmer Carroll, Frank Crisafulli, Armando Frizo, Santo Gugliuzza, Theodore Markowitz, Joseph Marks, John Martinkus. Charles Musumeci, Ralph Powell, Richard Sanguinito, Donald Smith, James Somers, Leonard Spidale, Francis Tone, Bill Zwiski.

Hazleton: Coach Hugh McGeehan, John Apichella, Louis Belizia, Ed Bresnock, Carmen Chirico, Al DeGatis, John Hospodar, Arthur Johnson, Patrick McGeehan, Frank McHugh, Anthony Moran, James Parpiglia, John Walters.

Pottsville: Coach Al Sadusky, Charles Ashman, Ed Kennedy, Bill Mahall, Andrew Majeskie, Willard McFee, Karl Rehnert, William Rosenberger, Jack Stoner, Bruce Young.

Tamaqua: Coach Eli Purnell, Donald Becker, James DeWire, Bob Filer, Walter Henne, Dick Jones, Raymond Morgans, Tom Rowlands, Earl Stiegerwalt, Nicholas James Young.

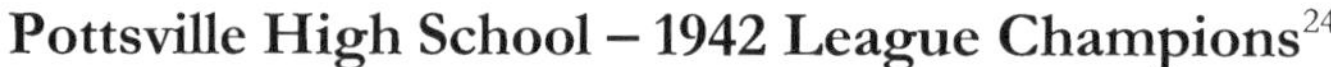

Pottsville High School – 1942 League Champions[24]

Left to Right: Coach Al Sadusky, Harry Johns (mgr), Ed Kennedy, Bruce Young, Karl Rehnert, Andrew Majeskie, Bill Rosenberger, Jack Stoner, Bill Mahall, Willard McFee.

1943

A Champion Returns

League leadership, membership and schedule did not change from the previous several seasons. League representatives re-elected Pottsville's D. H. H. Lengle to his 4th term as president, Easton's Charlie Richards as vice president for a 3rd term, and Allentown's Edgar A. Rabenold for the 17th term as secretary treasurer. War time transportation was discussed at length with some concern about having the junior varsity teams travel with the varsity. No decision on the issue was made at the meeting.[1]

Week 1

Hazleton 54 Pottsville 33: The defending league champions lost their season opener at Hazleton. The Mountaineers dominated the Maroons in the second period outscoring them 22-5 to take a 30-10 half time lead. Hazleton forward Al DeGatis scored the first 12 points in the second period in a resounding victory over Pottsville.

Leading scorers: Hazleton – Al DeGatis 21, Tony Moran 10; Pottsville – Charles Ditmar 9.

Bethlehem 38 Allentown 32: Bethlehem surprised Allentown in Bethlehem. Bethlehem's defense held Moon Haney to 7 points. Allen led early in a game when the lead changed numerous times.

Leading scorers: Bethlehem – Al Saemmer 14; Allentown - Dick Franklin 9.

Tamaqua 42 Easton 37: At Tamaqua, the Tams took an early lead and held it throughout the game.

Leading scorers: Tamaqua - Richard Jones 18; Easton – Richard Sanguinito 11.[2]

Week 2

Allentown 29 Hazleton 28: At the Little Palestra, Allentown bounced back against archrival Hazleton winning a thrilling game. The Mountaineers had their season-opening 8 game win streak snapped. Holding a 26-18 lead at the 3rd quarter mark, Allentown held off a ferocious rally by the Mountaineers. Earlier in the 3rd period, Canary guard Mike Chomik shot at the wrong basket and scored two points for Hazleton. Fortunately, the Canaries held on to win despite Chomik's miscue.

Leading scorers: Allentown – Carl Berger 9; Hazleton – Al DeGatis 11.

Bethlehem 58 Easton 36: Bethlehem was the only undefeated team after two weeks into the season. Leading all the way, Coach Joe Preletz's team trounced the Red Rovers after jumping out to a 14-6 first quarter lead.

Leading scorers: Bethlehem-Al Saemmer 14, Paul Calvo 12, George Gasdaska 10; Easton–Arnold Aiello 10.

Pottsville 50 Tamaqua 24: Pottsville easily knocked off Tamaqua after taking an 8-2 first quarter lead. Tamaqua kept it close at the half 14-9 before Pottsville surged to a 33-15 third quarter lead.

Leading scorers: Pottsville – John Flannery 15, Heber Fisher 14; Tamaqua – Harold Boyer 4, Richard Jones 4.[3]

Week 3

Bethlehem 60 Hazleton 30: On their home court, Bethlehem surprised Hazleton to keep their record unblemished at 3-0. On the losing end of a surprising score, Hazleton's only lead was at 2-0. With the game well in hand, Coach Preletz inserted his second team in the third period as Bethlehem rolled up 60 points on the Mountaineers.

Leading scorers: Bethlehem – Al Saemmer 17, Charles Bednarik 14, Ed Hoch 12; Hazleton – Al DeGatis 9.

Allentown 58 Tamaqua 50: In a high scoring affair in Tamaqua, Allentown prevailed after trailing at the half 30-29. Allentown took the lead in the third quarter by outscoring Tamaqua 15-7.

Leading scorers: Allentown–Moon Haney 15, Carl Berger 11, Mike Melinchok 11; Tamaqua-Richard Jones 15, Paul Lehatto 10.

Easton 46 Pottsville 41 OT: In overtime, Coach Vernon Fegley's Red Rovers took down Pottsville to earn their first league victory. Pottsville had led the game during each of the first three periods before Easton rallied for the win. Easton led 26-17 at the half.

Leading scorers: Easton – Richard Sanguinito 18, Arnold Aiello 10; Pottsville – Heber Fisher 12.[4]

Bethlehem 65 Tamaqua 21: Later in the week, Bethlehem put 60 points on the board again when they swamped Tamaqua. Bethlehem jumped out to 21-3 first period lead in rolling to a 9-0 (4-0 in the league) start to the season.

Leading scorers: Bethlehem - Al Saemmer 14, Ed Hoch 11; Tamaqua – Hubert Becker 11.

Allentown 39 Pottsville 36: Allentown pulled out a close win over a scrappy Pottsville team. Despite leading 37-30 in the fourth quarter, Allentown had to fight off the Maroons as the game ended.

Leading scorers: Allentown – Mike Melinchok 9; Pottsville – Harold Harvey 10.

Hazleton 52 Easton 42: Hazleton took down Easton but not without a struggle. After building a 16-4 first period lead, the Mountaineers scored only a single point in the 2nd period while the Red Rovers scored 17 to take the lead 21-17. Led by Al DeGatis' 16 points, Hazleton rallied in the 3rd period to pull out the win.

Leading scorers: Hazleton – Al DeGatis 16, Carl "Red" Meinhold 10; Easton – Edward Snyder 13.[5]

Week 4

Bethlehem 42 Pottsville 31: Bethlehem traveled to Pottsville through several inches of snow in an attempt to clinch the first half title. After taking the early lead and never relinquishing it, the Liberty boys took the contest and first half title. Al Saemmer played his final game for Bethlehem since he would graduate prior to the start of the second half.

Leading scorers: Bethlehem – Bill Messics 13, George Gasdaska 11, Al Saemmer 10; Pottsville – Heber Fisher 9.

Hazleton 63 Tamaqua 42: Led by DeGatis with 22 points and Meinhold with 17, Hazleton whipped Tamaqua in Tamaqua to finish the first half at 3-2 and in third place.

Leading scorers: Hazleton – Al DeGatis 22, Carl Meinhold 17, James Porpiglia 12; Tamaqua – Richard Jones – 15.

Allentown 59 Easton 46: Coach Birney Crum used his second team the entire 4th period versus Easton when the first five rolled up a 21-point lead at the end of three periods. Allentown finished the first half at 4-1 with the triumph.

Leading scorers: Allentown – Erwin Haney 15, George Krainiak 15, Mike Chomik 11; Easton– Santo Gugliuzza 11.[6]

Week 5

Bethlehem 33 Allentown 32: Despite losing Saemmer, who led the team in scoring with 14 ppg, Bethlehem began the second half with a thrilling win over Allentown. With Allentown leading the game 28-25 in the 4th quarter, Gasdaska was fouled in the act of shooting. Allentown player Dick Franklin protested so vehemently that the referee called a technical. Gasdaska made all three shots to tie the score. Bethlehem took the lead on another foul shot and after a few lead changes, Bethlehem took a 3-point lead and hung on for the win.

Leading scorers: Bethlehem – George Gasdaska 18; Allentown – "Moon" Haney 10.

Pottsville 48 Hazleton 36: Pottsville atoned for its first half loss to Hazleton with a decisive win over the Mountaineers at Pottsville. After holding one-point leads after each of the first two quarters, Pottsville outscored Hazleton 15-8 in the third period.

Leading scorers: Pottsville – Heber Fisher 21; Hazleton – Al DeGatis 12, Carl Meinhold 11.

Easton 59 Tamaqua 40: Building a 28-16 lead at the half, Easton avenged their first half loss to Tamaqua.

Leading scorers: Easton - Richard Sanguinito 15, Bill Zwiski 10; Tamaqua – Paul Lehatto 12, Walter Henne 10.[7]

Bethlehem 60 Easton 52: Easton held the lead three minutes into the third period before finally falling behind the Liberty 36-35. Easton had led at the half 31-28.

Leading scorers: Bethlehem – Charles Bednarik 20, Bill Messics 13; Easton – Arnold Aiello 15, Edward Snyder 11.

Hazleton 36 Allentown 22: At Hazleton, Allentown lost its second in a row and in the week. After falling behind 8-7 after one period, the game was never close for the Canaries. Hazleton held a 16-9 halftime lead.

Leading scorers: Hazleton – Al DeGatis 14; Allentown – "Moon" Haney 12.

Pottsville 60 Tamaqua 42: After trailing 11-8 after a quarter, Pottsville took the lead at halftime 26-20 and defeated the Tams to remain unbeaten in the second half and keep pace with Bethlehem.

Leading scorers: Pottsville – Heber Fisher 14, John Flannery 13, Harold Harvey 11, Charles Dittmar 11, Donald Masteller 11; Tamaqua – Dick Jones 15, Paul Lehatto 11.[8]

Week 6

Hazleton 43 Bethlehem 31: At Hazleton, Bethlehem matched up against Hazleton in a key second half contest. Despite "Chuck" Bednarik's valiant effort, he was unable to carry Bethlehem as Hazleton, led by Al DeGatis, posted an easy victory to give the Hurricane their first loss of the season after 13 victories. Hazleton led at halftime 26-17.

Leading scorers: Hazleton – Al DeGatis 20, Carmen Cherico 11; Bethlehem – Charles Bednarik 13.

Easton 41 Pottsville 34: Pottsville, at home, lost to Easton to create a four team first place tie. Easton led at the end of each of the quarters. Bethlehem, Pottsville, Hazleton, and Easton were all at 2-1.

Leading scorers: Easton – Arnold Aiello 15; Pottsville Charles Dittmar 14.

Allentown 44 Tamaqua 24: Despite not scoring for the first 4 ½ minutes of the game, the Canaries still led after a quarter 10-5. Allentown racked up an easy victory over Tamaqua with Coach Crum using his second team a lot during the contest. Allentown handed the Tams their 3rd straight loss of the second half.

Leading scorers: Allentown – George Krainiak 13; Tamaqua – Dick Jones 8, Paul Lehatto 8.[9]

Week 7

Hazleton 62 Easton 37: At home, Vern Fegley's Easton team got whipped by Hazleton to knock them out of the tie for the second half lead. Hazleton took an 18-12 first quarter lead on their way to the victory.

Leading scorers: Hazleton – Al DeGatis 19, Harry Smith 16, Carmen Cherico 11; Easton Arnold Aiello 12.

Pottsville 39 Allentown 32: Homestanding Pottsville held on to a share of first place by defeating the Canaries. Pottsville won the game on the strength of outscoring Allentown 16-5 in the second quarter. Allentown held an 8-4 first quarter lead.

Leading scorers: Pottsville – John Flannery 13; Allentown – "Moon" Haney 11.

Bethlehem 57 Tamaqua 40: Guard Messics and forward Gasdaska scored 23 and 15 points respectively as Bethlehem stayed in the tie with the win over Tamaqua. The stage was set for a fight for the second half title with three teams still tied of the lead.

Leading scorers: Bethlehem – Bill Messics 23, George Gasdaska 15; Tamaqua – Walter Henne 12, Hubert Becker 10.[10]

Week 8

Bethlehem 53 Pottsville 30: Bethlehem prevented Pottsville from having a chance to defend its title by easily defeating them. By the end of the 3rd quarter, Bethlehem built a 33-17 lead to take complete control of the matchup.

Leading scorers: Bethlehem – Charles Bednarik 11, Bill Messics 11, George Gasdaska 10; Pottsville – Harold Harvey 11.

Hazleton 70 Tamaqua 26: After rolling up a 20-1 first quarter lead, Hazleton ended up with a runaway win over hapless Tamaqua with four players in double figures. Hazleton would play Bethlehem for the second half title.

Leading scorers: Hazleton – Harry Smith 19, Tony Moran 15, Carmen Cherico 13, Al DeGatis 13; Tamaqua – Walter Henne 7.

Easton 37 Allentown 35: Although it had no bearing in the second half race, Easton's triumph over Allentown had much significance. Easton won for the first time at Allentown since 1925. Easton led at the end of each quarter.

Leading scorers: Easton – Richard Sanguinito 16, Arnold Aiello 10; Allentown – Mike Melinchok 11.[11]

Second Half Playoff

Hazleton 46 Bethlehem 43: A Hazleton victory at the Little Palestra in Allentown would force a second matchup between the two teams to decide the overall league title. Although Paul Calvo and Chuck Bednarik had strong performances, Hazleton won to set up a rematch at the Little Palestra. Hazleton led at the end of the first two quarters and Hazleton led 24-20 at the half. Led by Chuck Bednarik, Bethlehem rallied in the 3rd quarter to take a 36-31 lead into the final stanza. With the score tied at 38, Chuck Bednarik fouled out of the game. His replacement Kocsis made a field goal to put Bethlehem into a 42-39 lead. Bethlehem's Gasdaska protested a foul called on him and Hazleton was awarded a technical foul shot in addition to two regular foul shots. Hazleton made all three and tied the game at 42 and went on to win the game.

Leading scorers: Hazleton – Al DeGatis 15, Carmen Cherico 11; Bethlehem– Charles Bednarik 13, Paul Calvo 11.[12]

Season Championship Playoff

Hazleton 36 Bethlehem 35 OT: The rematch at the Little Palestra was a classic! Hazleton defeated Bethlehem in a wild overtime game in front of 2,400 fans. When the game ended after the overtime period, a free-for-all ensued when disappointed Bethlehem fans numbering up to as many as 1,500 individuals stormed referee Eddie Brominski. Brominski ruled George Gasdaska's field goal no good with about 10 seconds to go in overtime. Brominski ruled that Gasdaska had stepped on the line. Since Gasdaska apparently did not hear the whistle, he continued on to score the basket. Fans stormed the floor and one of them struck Brominski. The game was held up briefly at this point until police could clear the floor. Brominski incredulously awarded the ball to Bethlehem on the in-bounds play. Bethlehem, however, could not score. A free-for-all lasted for about an hour after the game. Brominski was held hostage by the fans in a press box behind a cordon of six policemen. He was pelted with oranges, telephone books, and stones. Police Chief Art Yohe had to eventually dispel the crowd with tear gas.

Leading scorers: Hazleton – Tony Moran 14; Bethlehem – Charles "Chuck" Bednarik 11.[13]

Postseason Play

Hazleton 59 Nuremberg 33: For the 3rd time in the last four years, Nuremburg faced the East Penn champion in the first district playoff game, and for the third time they lost. Hazleton took a 19-4 lead and led 39-11 at halftime.

Leading scorers: Hazleton - Al DeGatis 22, Tony Moran 12, Carmen Cherico 11; Nuremberg – Irwin Van Blargen.[14]

Hazleton 47 Palmerton 32: At the Little Palestra, Hazleton defeated Palmerton in the District XI second round game. Palmerton kept the score close with the score being 28-26 Hazleton at one point in the 3rd quarter. Led by captain Anthony "Hunky" Moran, Hazleton put the game away in the 4th quarter.

Leading scorers: Hazleton – Tony Moran 16, Harry Smith 13, Al DeGatis 10; Palmerton – Len Halchevsky 12.[15]

Hazleton 50 Mahanoy Township 29: In the district title game at the Little Palestra, Hazleton easily defeated Mahanoy Township for their 9th district title since 1926. Hazleton took charge of the contest in the second period with a 17-4 run.

Leading scorers: Hazleton - Al DeGatis 14, Tony Moran 14; Mahanoy Township – Joseph Stevens 9.[16]

Hazleton 24 Gettysburg 21: Moving on to the state playoffs, Hazleton took advantage of playing in the familiar confines of Rockne Hall to defeat Gettysburg, District 3 champions. Hazleton trailed 19-15 going into the 4th quarter and rallied in the last four minutes to win the low scoring contest. They had led once before in the second period.

Leading scorers: Hazleton – Al DeGatis 9; Gettysburg – George Boehner 9.[17]

Hazleton 42 Berwick 28: Playing at Rockne Hall in Allentown, Hazleton took on Berwick, District 2 and Wyoming Valley League titlists. Berwick and Hazleton played nip and tuck through the first two periods with both teams in the lead at times. Hazleton led at the half 19-17. In the 3rd quarter, Hazleton blitzed the Bulldogs 18-4 to take command of the game. They held Berwick's all-state center Colone to 3 points with a stingy defense. Hugh McGeehan's squad had reached the Eastern Finals.

Leading scorers: Hazleton – Carmen Cherico 15, Al DeGatis 10; Berwick - Frank Lupashunski 8.[18]

Lower Merion 35 Hazleton 23: Hazleton kept the game within reach for three periods trailing 24-18. In the 4th period, Lower Merion proved too strong for the Mountaineers outscoring them 11-5 and they defeated Hazleton 35-23. Despite the loss, the league demonstrated its strength with Hazleton's showing.

Leading scorers: Lower Merion – Greer Heindel 11; Hazleton - Carmen Cherico 9.[19]

Postseason Accolades

Scoring Leaders: Al DeGatis, Hazleton's outstanding forward, led the league in scoring with 157 points. The rest of the top ten included: Arnold Aiello, Easton, 105; Richard Sanquinito, Easton, 104; Heber Fisher, Pottsville, 99; Charles Bednarik, Bethlehem, 95; George Gasdaska, Bethlehem, 95; Erwin Haney, Allentown, 93; Richard Jones, Tamaqua, 88; Bill Messics, Bethlehem, 85; John Flannery, Pottsville, 82; and George Krainiak, Allentown, 82.[20]

All-Stars: The league all-stars as selected by the Hazleton Plain Speaker[21] newspaper include:

First team: forwards Al Saemmer, Bethlehem, and Erwin Haney, Allentown; center Charles Bednarik, Bethlehem; and guards Tony Moran, Hazleton, and Ed Hoch, Bethlehem.

Second team: forwards Richard Sanquanito, Easton, and George Gasdaska, Bethlehem; center Lou Bellizia, Hazleton; and guards Al DeGatis, Hazleton, and Heber Fisher, Pottsville.

All-State: League selections on the Associated Press All-PIAA basketball team included; Tony Moran, Hazleton, first team; Erwin Haney, Allentown, Al DeGatis, Hazleton, Carmen Cherico, Hazleton, and John Flannery, Pottsville, honorable mention.[22]

Final Standings

First Half		Second Half		Overall	
Bethlehem	5-0	Hazleton	4-1	Bethlehem	9-1
Allentown	4-1	Bethlehem	4-1	Hazleton	7-3
Hazleton	3-2	Easton	3-2	Allentown	5-5
Pottsville	1-4	Pottsville	3-2	Easton	4-6
Tamaqua	1-4	Allentown	1-4	Pottsville	4-6
Easton	1-4	Tamaqua	0-5	Tamaqua	1-9

Team Rosters

Allentown: Coach J. Birney Crum, Carleton Berger, Mick Chomik, Dick Franklin, Bob Freed, Henry Gerhard, Bill Gower, Erwin "Moon" Haney, Bill Kline, George Krainiak, Mike Melinchok, Ken Menchin, Dick Schmidt, Bill Snyder

Bethlehem: Coach Joe "Pickles" Preletz, Charles "Chuck" Bednarik, Paul Calvo, Roland Correll, Ernie DeAngelis, DeDonato, Eddie Finn, Gene Fraley, Frey, George Gasdaska, Ed Hoch, Joyce, Ollie Kocsis, Joe Kozo, Willard Lobb, Bill Messics, John Rollo, Al Saemmer, Smalley, Donald Watson, Yochum

Easton: Coach Vernard Fegley, Arnold Aiello, Richard Blake, John Detwiler, Santo Gugliuzza, Robert Kiefer, Donald Miltenberger, Ralph Powell, Richard Sanguinito, Gerald Smith, Edward Snyder, Willam Zwiski

Hazleton: Coach Hugh McGeehan, John Ballots, Lou Bellizia, Carmen Cherico, Al DeGatis, Gene Gliem, Lenny Kosiak, Carl "Red" Meinhold, Anthony Moran, Danny Parrell, George Patternoster, James Porpiglia, Oronzo Scarcella, Harry Smith

Pottsville: Coach Chet Rogowicz, Charles Dittmar, Heber Fisher, John Flannery, Harold Harvey, Paul LaRoche, Donald Masteller, Bill McClure, Paul Moser, Robert Sheipe, Robert Stoner

Tamaqua: Coach Charles Schaeffer, Donald Becker, Hubert Becker, Harold Boyer, Harry Fetterman, Walter Henne, Thomas Homanick, Richard Jones, William Kasper, Paul Lehatto, Albert Pajakinas, Thomas Rowlands

Hazleton High School – 1943 League and District Champions[23]

1944

Three Playoffs Decide League Title

During its nineteen years of existence, the league displayed an excellent brand of basketball with fierce rivalries and many hotly-contested overtime playoff games to decide the league titles. Despite this record, the 1944 season was to bring some of the most amazing series of matches the league had seen to this point.

At the spring meeting, the league wrapped up its activities for the past season by awarding the league championship trophy to Hazleton. The league opted to continue with the same six current members for the upcoming season but expressed their favor of operating as an eight-club league. However, no new applications had been submitted to the league. League leadership was elected for the upcoming year with Daniel Lengle of Pottsville continuing as president and Edgar Rabenold of Allentown continuing to serve as secretary-treasurer. With Charlie Richards of Easton being called into service with the Navy, Phil Phillipi of Bethlehem was elected vice president.[1]

Week 1

Hazleton 49 Tamaqua 27: Hazleton opened the season at Tamaqua with a resounding victory of the Tams. Various prognosticators questioned Hazleton's outlook after several pre-season losses. Led by center Carl Meinhold, Hazleton served notice to the league as a team to be reckoned with throughout the season.

Leading scorers: Hazleton – Carl Meinhold 29; Tamaqua – Hubert Becker 12.

Allentown 53 Easton 39: With both teams entering the contest unbeaten, each at 7-0, Allentown handed Easton its first loss. Center George Krainiak and guard Billy Kline, an all-state football quarterback, led the Canary attack.

Leading scorers: Allentown – George Krainiak 19, Billy Kline 15; Easton – John Heilman 11.

Bethlehem 44 Pottsville 42: At Pottsville, Bethlehem opened with a thriller with last minute win over the Maroons. Substitute forward Kocsis converted a field goal with 20 seconds remaining to pull out the win. With two minutes to go, Pottsville held a 41-40 lead.

Leading scorers: Bethlehem - Joe Velas 12; Pottsville - Bill McClure 17.[2]

Week 2

Hazleton 45 Allentown 41: In a crucial early season matchup, Allentown traveled to Hazleton for a showdown with the Mountaineers. Held to a single point in the second period, the Canaries fell behind 25-10 at the half. Several rallies in the second half brought the Canaries within three points late in the fourth period 44-41.

Leading scorers: Hazleton – Al DeGatis 18, Carl Meinhold 12; Allentown - Dick Schmidt 13.

Bethlehem 40 Easton 29: After playing to a 13-13 first period tie, Bethlehem gradually pulled away from Easton for the win. Bethlehem outscored Easton 9-3 in the second period to take over the lead.

Leading scorers: Bethlehem - Dick Doster 14, Joe Velas 13; Easton – Bill Zwiski 10.

Pottsville 42 Tamaqua 32: Scoring 17 points in the third quarter, Pottsville took down Tamaqua. Pottsville held the lead at the half 19-18. No player scored in double figures in the contest.

Leading scorers: Pottsville – Robert Scheipe 9; Tamaqua – Thomas Homanick 9.[3]

Week 3

Hazleton 47 Pottsville 32: Three weeks into the season, Hazleton again sat at the top with an unblemished record after its triumph over Pottsville. After a closely contested first half with Hazleton leading 19-17, Hazleton pulled away in the second half.

Leading scorers: Hazleton – Al Degatis 15, Carl Meinhold 13, John Ballots 12; Pottsville – Robert Scheipe 8, Harold Kelly 8.

Allentown 54 Bethlehem 41: Allentown knocked Bethlehem out of a tie for the lead with their win at the Little Palestra. In a fiercely contested match, Bethlehem guard Eddie Hudak received a gash over his eye early in the game and played the rest of the game with a plaster. Both teams were now in a tie for second place at 2-1.

Leading scorers: Allentown – Billy Kline 19, George Krainiak 15; Bethlehem – Joe Velas 12, Dick Doster 11, John Schweder 10.

Easton 59 Tamaqua 26: Easton won its first league game by trouncing Tamaqua. Red Rover center Miltenberger scored 16 points in the first half as Easton led 26-12 at the half. The Red Rovers scored 32 points in the 3rd period.

Leading scorers: Easton – Donald Miltenberger 22, George Terleski 14, Bill Zwiski 11; Tamaqua – Larry Klein 8.[4]

Hazleton 29 Bethlehem 28 OT: Later in the week, Hazleton defeated Bethlehem in overtime. Coach Joe Preletz's Bethlehem quintet led the game most of the way and had a two-point lead with 7 seconds remaining in regulation until Mountaineer center "Reds" Meinhold converted a mid-court set shot to tie the game. Meinhold scored the only point in overtime when he sank a foul shot with 2 seconds remaining for the win.

Leading scorers: Hazleton – Carl Meinhold 9; Bethlehem – Dick Doster 7.

Allentown 47 Tamaqua 33: Allentown kept pace with a win over Tamaqua after taking a 30-16 lead at halftime. They added to the lead by outscoring the Tams 12-5 in the third period.

Leading scorers: Allentown – Billy Kline 18, George Krainiak 18; Tamaqua – Albert Pajakinas 12.

Pottsville 27 Easton 26: At Pottsville, the Maroons defeated Easton to register their first league win. Billy McClure, Pottsville's center, who suffered a number of early season injuries, came off the bench to spark Pottsville to the victory. Easton had led after three quarters 22-18.

Leading scorers: Pottsville – Robert Scheipe 6; Easton – Santo Gugliuzza.[5]

Coach Crum dismissed George Krainiak, Allentown's leading scorer, from the team on January 24th after he informed the coach that he was going to miss a game with Phillipsburg on January 22nd. Krainiak indicated he would miss the game to play with an orchestra that he was a member of since they had an engagement on that night. Coach Crum decided that Krainiak had chosen music over basketball and was no longer a part of the team.[6] However, for the next game against Frackville, his teammates persuaded him to give up the orchestra and rejoin the team. Through the first half of the game, he had been in street clothes as a spectator. Allentown was losing the game entering the locker room for the half. During the 2nd half, he rallied the team to victory and played basketball for the rest of the season rather than participating in the orchestra.[7]

Week 4

Easton 31 Hazleton 29: In a shocker, former Hazleton star and now Red Rover coach Vern Fegley led Easton to a devastating defeat of Hazleton. Easton led the whole game until early in the 4th period when Hazleton finally went ahead 26-24. However, Easton fought back behind guards Gugliuzza and Terlesky to take the lead and upset the Mountaineers.

Leading scorers: Easton – Santo Gugliuzza 7; Hazleton – Al DeGatis 14.

Allentown 50 Pottsville 33: Allentown's triumph over Pottsville tied them for the first half lead with Hazleton necessitating a playoff. Allentown led 23-8 at halftime.

Leading scorers: Allentown – George Krainiak 16; Pottsville – Robert Scheipe 12.[8]

Bethlehem 41 Tamaqua 27: Bethlehem kept Tamaqua winless in the first half with their win at the Liberty gym. Bethlehem held a 22-6 halftime lead.

Leading scorers: Bethlehem - Dick Doster 11; Tamaqua – Hubert Becker 7.[9]

In a meeting at Tamaqua, the league officials ultimately decided to hold the first half playoff at the end of the season after efforts to schedule the game were unsuccessful. Hazleton refused to play the game at Rockne Hall in Allentown and Reading's North West gym was not available for a number of days. Easton refused to change the date of its second half game with Allentown to allow the playoff game to happen. Having no other options, the game was delayed until the end of the regular season.[10]

Week 5

Allentown 51 Easton 36: Although Allentown held relatively small leads 15-10 and 27-21 after the first two periods, the Canaries were never really threatened. Allentown led the whole way.

Leading scorers: Allentown – Billy Kline 21; Easton – Donald Miltenberger 10.

Hazleton 61 Tamaqua 20: Hazleton shellacked Tamaqua to open second half play. The Mountaineers led at the half 23-8. Three players, forwards Ballots, Degatis and center Meinhold, scored 43 of the Mountaineers' points.

Leading scorers: Hazleton – John Ballots 18, Al DeGatis 15, Carl Meinhold 10; Tamaqua – Edwin Kline 7.

Bethlehem 51 Pottsville 41: On their home court, the Bethlehem quintet had an easier time with Pottsville in second matchup with Coach Preletz's team winning. Bethlehem was pressed in the 3rd quarter when the Maroons tied the score at 31-31 before the Liberty gang scored the next five points.

Leading scorers: Bethlehem – Dick Doster 11; Pottsville – Robert Scheipe 14, Harold Harvey 11.[11]

Week 6

Allentown 47 Hazleton 27: Allentown avenged its first half loss to Hazleton with their win at the Little Palestra. The Canaries fell behind early 6-3 and later were tied at 10-10 before they took the lead for good.

Leading scorers: Allentown – Billy Kline 15, George Krainiak 14; Hazleton - Al DeGatis 9.

Easton 44 Bethlehem 35: Easton pulled another surprise with a triumph over Bethlehem. Easton led 38-21 going into the 4th quarter. Despite losing three starters on personal fouls, Bethlehem rallied in the 4th quarter but fell short. Allentown was now at the top as the only undefeated team in the second half.

Leading scorers: Easton – John Heilman 11, Santo Gugliuzza 10; Bethlehem – Joe Velas 11.

Pottsville 59 Tamaqua 33: With center Billy McClure scoring 24 points, Pottsville handed Tamaqua's Blue Raiders their 7th straight league loss with their win in Tamaqua.

Leading scorers: Pottsville– Bill McClure 24, Harold Kelly 12, Robert Scheipe 11; Tamaqua– Hubert Becker 13, Bill Kasper 10.[12]

Week 7

Bethlehem 38 Allentown 25: Bursting out with a 23-10 lead at the half, Bethlehem gave the Canaries their first 2nd half loss. Despite losing star forward Dick Doster late in the first half on personal fouls, Bethlehem's other starting forward Joe Velas led Coach Preletz's team to the unexpected upset of Allentown. Officials halted the hard-fought game with 90 seconds left when a fist fight erupted on the playing floor. After a 10-minute delay, the game resumed with no further incidents. A total of 22 players, 11 for each team, saw action in the contest.

Leading scorers: Bethlehem - Joe Velas 15; Allentown – George Krainiak 15.

Hazleton 36 Pottsville 34: Hazleton held off homestanding Pottsville to remain in contention for the second half title. Trailing 32-22, Pottsville's fourth quarter rally, outscoring Hazleton 12-4 in the quarter, fell just short.

Leading scorers: Hazleton – Jim Munroe 12; Pottsville – Harold Kelly 9.

Easton 51 Tamaqua 42: In Tamaqua, Easton improved to 2-1 over the hapless Tams. After leading 33-26 after three quarters, the Blue Raiders' defense allowed 25 points in the final quarter to give the Red Rovers the win. Again, four teams (Allentown, Bethlehem, Easton, and Hazleton) were tied for the lead at 2-1.

Leading scorers: Easton – Santo Gugliuzza 19, George Terleski 10; Tamaqua – Albert Pajakinas 18, William Kasper 13.[13]

Allentown 69 Tamaqua 26: Later in the week, Allentown became the latest team to benefit from a weak Tamaqua quintet. Registering 30 field goals and 9 foul shots, the Canaries pasted the Blue Raiders.

Leading scorers: Allentown - Billy Kline 18, George Krainiak 17, Bill Wanish 12; Tamaqua – Larry Klein 12.

Hazleton 68 Bethlehem 34: Bethlehem dropped out of the first-place tie when Hazleton dominated the Liberty five. After only holding a 10-7 first quarter lead, the Mountaineers took a 28-15 halftime lead.

Leading scorers: Hazleton - Carl Meinhold 21, John Ballots 12, Al DeGatis 10; Bethlehem – Joe Velas 11.

Easton 50 Pottsville 33: Easton remained in the now three-way first play tie with a victory over Pottsville. After leading by only 2 points 9-7 after one quarter, the Red Rovers outscored Pottsville 26-13 in the 2nd and 3rd periods to secure the win.

Leading scorers: Easton – Donald Miltenberger 13, John Heilman 11; Pottsville – Robert Scheipe 10.[14]

Week 8

Hazleton 54 Easton 33: Hazleton traveled to Easton in a battle for first place. Leading by a score of 13-3 after one period, Hazleton saw the Red Rovers cut the lead to 22-17 at halftime. With a scoring barrage in the third period, the Mountaineers coasted to the victory.

Leading scorers: Hazleton – Carl Meinhold 19, Jim Munroe 11, Al DeGatis 11; Easton – Donald Miltenberger 9.

Allentown 36 Pottsville 30: Allentown maintained its share of first place in Pottsville. Pottsville threatened Allentown in the third period by cutting the lead to four 29-25.

Leading scorers: Allentown – George Krainiak 10; Pottsville – Billy McClure 8.

Bethlehem 38 Tamaqua 33: Bethlehem finished its season by handing Tamaqua its 10th consecutive loss. Bethlehem held the Tams scoreless in the 2nd period on the way to the victory.

Leading scorers: Bethlehem – J Bird 17, Dick Doster 10; Tamaqua – Larry Klein 10, Hubert Becker 10.[15]

First Half Playoff

Allentown 43 Hazleton 31: The first half playoff was held at Northwest Junior High School in Reading. Leading throughout the game, Allentown defeated Hazleton and finally had the first half title two months after it had ended. Center Bill Wanish and guard Henry Gerhard held Hazleton's high scoring center Carl Meinhold to a field goal and 7 points and forward Al DeGatis to 8 points to contribute mightily to the triumph.

Leading scorers: Allentown – George Krainiak 13; Hazleton – Jim Munroe 8, Al DeGatis 8.[16]

Second Half Playoff

Hazleton 34 Allentown 23: Three nights later, the two teams met again on the Northwest JHS gym in Reading to decide the 2nd half title. This time Hazleton prevailed as Allentown could only manage a single point in the final quarter. Hazleton led 24-22 heading into the fourth quarter.

Leading scorers: Hazleton - Carl Meinhold 9; Allentown - George Krainiak 9.[17]

League Championship Playoff

Hazleton 33 Allentown 31: Now the league title would be decided between the two teams for a third consecutive game in Reading four days later. After the first two playoff games each decided by more than a 10-point margin, this battle proved to be more thrilling. Just as in the prior game, Hazleton led 24-22 heading into the fourth quarter. With the score tied over a dozen times throughout the game and 31-31 with 75 seconds to play, Hazleton guard Jimmy Munroe scored the winning field goal. Allentown missed four field goal attempts at the end of the game. In their fifth meeting of the season and third in a week, Hazleton won the league title in a hard-fought victory.

Leading scorers: Hazleton – Al DeGatis 16; Allentown – George Krainiak 10.[18]

Postseason Play

Hazleton 70 Minersville 25: Surviving three intense battles with Allentown, Hazleton entered the PIAA playoffs and crushed Minersville at Allentown's Little Palestra. The Mountaineers led at halftime 42-11.

Leading scorers: Hazleton – Carl "Red" Meinhold 21, Al DeGatis 15, Jim Munroe 13; Minersville – Robert Schofstal.[19]

Hazleton 35 Frackville 29: Playing at Allentown's Rockne Hall, Hazleton took down Frackville, South Schuylkill League champions. Hazleton was never really threatened after jumping out to a 5-0 lead and led 20-13 at halftime.

Leading scorers: Hazleton - Carl Meinhold 12, Al DeGatis 10; Frackville – Dick Hocking 11.[20]

Hazleton 50 Palmerton 29: Four thousand fans, with another 1500 turned away, saw Hazleton take a commanding 21-2 lead over Palmerton after one quarter and cruise to their seventh District XI title. The Mountaineers held Palmerton's high scoring sophomore George Kinek, who was averaging over 20 points a game, to a single goal and two points before he fouled out late in the third period.

Leading scorers: Hazleton – John Ballots 12, Al DeGatis 11; Palmerton – Karl Kummer 9.[21]

Hazleton 52 Swoyersville 21: In their first interdistrict match, Hazleton took an early 11-0 lead while they blanked Swoyersville in the first seven minutes in the second straight game at Rockne Hall. The Mountaineers led at halftime 25-10. With their commanding height, Hazleton dominated the boards throughout the game.

Leading scorers: Hazleton – Carl Meinhold 17, Al DeGatis 16, John Ballots 10; Swoyersville – Joseph Syracuse 9.[22]

Hazleton 59 Lower Merion 31: Coach Hugh McGeehan's squad took on three-time defending state champions Lower Merion in Philly's Convention Hall in front of 9,200 fans. The Mountaineers held the Lower Merion squad to a single field goal in each of the first two periods and finished the half ahead by a 32-12 score with Meinhold scoring 16 points. In defeating Lower Merion, Hazleton handed them one of the most lopsided losses in school history. It was also the first time they had defeated Lower Merion after three previous losses in state tournament play.

Leading scorers: Hazleton - Carl "Red" Meinhold 25, Al DeGatis 15; Lower Merion – Henry "Hank" Belber 10.[23]

Duquesne 43 Hazleton 35: With star center Meinhold on the bench due to a serious knee injury in the Lower Merion contest, Hazleton took on the Little Dukes of Duquesne at Convention Hall for the state title with 8500 fans in attendance. Duquesne held a 14-9 lead after one quarter and led at halftime 22-15. Hazleton lost its dream of a 4th state championship. It was the first loss for Hazleton in a state title game after three consecutive wins. This was the first title for Duquesne after one previous title game loss to Lower Merion in 1941.

Leading scorers: Duquesne – John Kaslak 10, Mike Medich 10; Hazleton – Al DeGatis 17. [24]

Postseason Accolades

Leading Scorers: Allentown's George Krainiak and Billy Kline finished first and second in league scoring with 139 and 129 points. They were followed by Carl Meinhold, Hazleton, 123 points; Al DeGatis, Hazleton, 107; Joe Velas, Bethlehem, 100; Robert Scheipe, Pottsville, 86; Bill McClure, Pottsville, 85; John Ballotts, Hazleton, 80; Dick Doster, Bethlehem, 78; George Terleski, Easton, 74; Santo Gugliuzza, Easton, 72; and Hubert Becker, Tamaqua, 70.[25]

The Hazleton Plain Speaker selected a league all-star team with the following players honored by the newspaper:

All-Stars: First Team: Al DeGatis, Hazleton, and George Krainiak, Allentown, at forward; Carl Meinhold, Hazleton, at center; and Bill Kline, Allentown, and Ed McCluskey, Hazleton, at guard.

Second Team: John Ballots, Hazleton, and Dick Schmidt, Allentown, at forward; Bill McClure, Pottsville, at center; Dick Doster, Bethlehem, and Jim Munroe, Hazleton, at guard.

Honorable Mention: Joe Velas, Bethlehem; George Terleski, Easton; Bill Zwiski, Easton; Robert Stoner, Pottsville; Santo Gugliuzza, Easton; Larry Klein, Tamaqua; Robert Scheipe, Pottsville; and John Heilman, Easton.[26]

All-State: The Associated Press declined to select an all-state team primarily due to the on-going world war.

Final Standings

First Half		Second Half		Overall	
Hazleton	4-1	Hazleton	4-1	Hazleton	8-2
Allentown	4-1	Allentown	4-1	Allentown	8-2
Bethlehem	3-2	Bethlehem	3-2	Bethlehem	6-4
Easton	2-3	Easton	3-2	Easton	5-5
Pottsville	2-3	Pottsville	1-4	Pottsville	3-7
Tamaqua	0-5	Tamaqua	0-5	Tamaqua	0-10

Team Rosters

Allentown: Coach J. Birney Crum, Ray Dini, Henry Gerhard, William Jackson, George Krainiak, Billy Kline, Frank Pfeiffer, Ray Ramella, Dick Schmidt, Julius Schwab, Joe Skurla, William Wanish, Paul Weiss

Bethlehem: Coach Joe Preletz, John Bird, John Check, Paul Correll, Ernie DeAngelis, Richard Doster, Charlie Garcia, Edward Hudak, Oliver Kocsis, Willard Lobb, John Schweder, Joe Velas, Donald Watson

Easton: Coach Vernard Fegley, Richard Blake, Joseph Curzi, Dominic Fimiano, James Gerikonis, Santo Gugliuzza, John Heilman, Robert Kaulius, Donald Miltenberger, John Reaser, Santo Salomone, Edward Snyder, Jay Snyder, George Terleski, Bill Zwiski

Hazleton: Coach Hugh McGeehan, John Ballots, Joe Capece, Neil Cusate, Al DeGatis, Mike DeNoia, Lenny Koziak, James LaMonica, Ed McCluskey, Carl "Red" Meinhold, J. Mihalovic, Jim Munroe, Danny Parrell, J. Rosborough, Tony Sharp

Pottsville: Coach Chet Rogowicz, Irvin Beissel, Walter Gould, Harold Harvey, Harold Kelly, Howard Koons, Joe Majeskie, Bill McClure, Robert Scheipe, Robert Stoner

Tamaqua: Coach John Gildea, William Baer, Hubert Becker, Thomas Homanick, William Kasper, Larry Klein, Edwin Kline, Stanley Meluskey, Albert Pajakinas, Kenneth Reed, Leroy Sembach, Gordon Tonkin, Richard Young

Hazleton High School – 1944 League and District Champions[27]

Front Row: Jim Munroe, Carl Meinhold, Al DeGatis, John Ballots, Ed McCluskey; Back Row: Joe Capece, Lenny Koziak, P Mihalovic, J Rosborough, James LaMonica, Mike DeNoia, Anthony Sharp

1945

Tamaqua Elects to Leave

Tamaqua withdrew from league to join the Black Diamond League for the 1945 season. During the 12 years as a league member, Tamaqua only managed to achieve one winning season (1936) and only won 28% (39-99) of their league contests.

At the league meeting held in April at the Hotel Shankweiler in Fogelsville, the league representatives, in a secret vote, voted down an application from Allentown Central Catholic to join the league as its 6th member. Allentown reportedly abstained during the vote. Williamsport again inquired about membership in the league. As in the past, league members turned down the unofficial application based on the travel distance for the league members. For the 20th year, Edgar Rabenold was elected secretary-treasurer. Phil Phillipi, Bethlehem, was elected to succeed Dan Lengle, Pottsville, as league president. William Breslin, Pottsville, succeeded Phillipi as league vice-president. The league selected the faculty managers of the five member schools to look into the possibility of increasing the league membership to eight schools for the 1946 season. An odd schedule was adopted for the new season with one team always idle in league play.[1]

In December, prior to the start of the 1945 season, the basketball referees requested an increase in fees for officiating the games. Eastern Pennsylvania League representatives protested the requested increase, but decided to pay the higher fees. The league felt that the referees were discriminating against the various leagues and the request to the league for the increase was unjust.[2]

Week 1

Hazleton 38 Easton 32: The defending league champions opened the new season with a win over the Red Rovers in Easton. After trailing 14-9 after one quarter, Hazleton held Easton to a single point in the second quarter to take the lead 18-15 and never relinquished the lead the rest of the game.

Leading scorers: Hazleton - Neil Cusate 12; Easton - John Heilman 15.

Allentown 46 Pottsville 36: Allentown traveled to Pottsville and came home victorious 46-36. Allentown trailed 20-18 after the first half, but took charge of the game by outscoring 22-10 in the third period.

Leading scorers: Allentown – Elmo Jackson 15, Frank Pfeiffer 11; Pottsville - Billy McClure 21, Joe Kelly 10.[3]

Allentown 48 Easton 36: At the Little Palestra, Allentown won its second league game in the first week of the season and its ninth to open the season against Easton. The Canaries took the lead from the outset and were never headed. They led 23-14 at halftime.

Leading scorers: Allentown – Bill Wanish 18, Frank Pfeiffer 13; Easton – John Heilman 11.

Pottsville 45 Bethlehem 38: In Pottsville, Bethlehem could not master the switching zone and man-to-man defenses employed by the Maroons. After leading 14-13 after the first quarter, Pottsville took the lead for good when they outscored the Hurricane 11-4 in the second quarter;

Leading scorers: Pottsville - Billy McClure 16, Jack Kelly 16; Bethlehem - Ed Hudak 13, George Marinkovitch 10.[4]

Week 2

Allentown 47 Hazleton 44: Allentown traveled to Hazleton in a battle for the league lead. Due to a severe snowstorm, the Canaries made the trip via train and stayed the night before traveling back home on the 8:15 am train. Led by forward Harry Hartman's 19 points, the Canaries won their 11th straight game and 3rd league game over the Mountaineers to open the season. Harry Hartman led the Canaries for his first and only time of his career. The day following the game, he left for the Army Air Corp and the war. The game was close and hard fought throughout the matchup. Hazleton led by 3 after one quarter and by one at the half. Allentown took the lead at the third quarter mark. With less than a minute to go, a field goal by the Canaries was disputed by Hazleton. After a lengthy conference between the officials and the two head coaches, the goal was rule valid and the Canaries went on to win the crucial contest.

Leading scorers: Allentown – Harry Hartman 19, Frank Pfeiffer 14; Hazleton – Mike DeNoia 13, Ed McCluskey 10.

Easton-Bethlehem: The severe snowstorm canceled the Easton-Bethlehem contest.[5]

Bethlehem 33 Allentown 30: Bethlehem snatched a victory over Allentown in the last few minutes of the game. With Allentown taking a 24-12 lead into the 2nd half, the Liberty quintet held the Canaries to only six second half points and no field goals. Bethlehem outscored the Canaries 13-1 in the third period to tie the game at 25 all on a field goal by George Marincovich with five seconds before the end of the quarter.

Leading scorers: Bethlehem – Ed Hudak 13; Allentown – Frank Pfeiffer 10.

Pottsville 28 Hazleton 27: Meanwhile, Pottsville's Maroons surprised Hazleton with their victory over the Mountaineers. With Hazleton leading 17-13 at the half, the Maroons outscored Hazleton 15-10 in the 2nd half to capture the win.

Leading scorers: Pottsville – Bill McClure 21; Hazleton – John Ballots 9.[6]

Week 3

Easton 41 Bethlehem 40: Bethlehem made up its postponed match with Easton due to the snowstorm eight days earlier. With Bethlehem still having a shot at gaining a tie for the first half title, Easton knocked them out of contention with their first league win of the season. Despite leading at the end of the 3rd period 33-29, Bethlehem could not hold off Easton in the final period. Frank Weaver had a chance to tie the game for Bethlehem on a foul shot following his field goal to make the score 41-40 but he missed the charity toss. The Red Rovers outscored Bethlehem 12-7 to eliminate the Liberty quintet from the first half race.

Leading scorers: Easton – Joe Curzi 14; Bethlehem – Don Watson 14, Ed Hudak 10.[7]

Pottsville 30 Easton 29: On the road, Pottsville continued its streak with a win over Easton to finish the first half tied with Allentown with a 3-1 record. Despite leading 18-12 at the half and 25-25 after three quarters, Easton could not hold on for the victory.

Leading scorers: Pottsville – Bill McClure 12, Joe Kelly 10; Easton – Joe Curzi 10.

Hazleton 41 Bethlehem 26: After taking a 21-13 halftime lead, Hazleton easily put down Bethlehem to finish the first half at 2-2. Bethlehem and Easton both finished at 1-3.

Leading scorers: Hazleton – Mike DeNois 16; Easton – Frank Weaver 10.[8]

First Half Playoff

Allentown 47 Pottsville 36: In a playoff game refereed by John Heske and Mike Lisetski, the Canaries, behind Frank Pfeiffer's 22 points, took the first half title in front of 3,500 fans at Rockne Hall. After

Pottsville had tied the score at 18 all, Canary guard Bill Wanish went on a scoring rampage to drop in the next seven points and provide Allentown with a 25-18 half time lead. Pottsville never really threatened after that and could only cut the lead to seven points with five minutes remaining.

Leading scorers: Allentown – Frank Pfeiffer 22, Bill Wanish 16; Pottsville – Bill McClure 13.[9]

Week 4

Allentown 47 Pottsville 29: Six days after their first half playoff matchup, Pottsville traveled to Allentown to begin second half play. With Allentown forward Bill Wanish matched up against high-scoring Pottsville center Bill McClure, Allentown easily won the game. Wanish held McClure to five points. McClure's first point was in the 3rd period on a foul shot. Allentown held a 15-12 lead at the half before outscoring the Maroons 16-9 in the third quarter.

Leading scorers: Allentown - Elmo Jackson 16, Dick Hoffman 12; Pottsville – Don Davis 8.

Hazleton 55 Easton 37: With Easton holding a 14-11 first quarter lead, Hazleton unleashed a 21-point barrage in the second period to take a 32-23 lead at halftime.

Leading scorers: Hazleton – John Ballots 21, Mike DeNoia 16 points; Easton – Joe Mazur 10.[10]

Allentown 48 Easton 33: At Easton, Allentown's balanced scoring put down Easton to capture their second win of the week. After keeping the game close at the half with Allentown leading 18-17, the Red Rovers' defense folded in the second half to lead to the lopsided win for the Canaries.

Leading scorers: Allentown – Frank Pfeiffer 10; Easton – Joe Curzi 9.

Pottsville 48 Bethlehem 38: Playing at home, Pottsville rebounded against Coach Preletz's Bethlehem quintet. Pottsville led 23-12 at halftime with Bethlehem surging to cut the lead to four after three quarters 34-30.

Leading scorers: Pottsville - Bill McClure 21; Bethlehem – John Felker 11.[11]

Week 5

Allentown 44 Hazleton 39: At the Little Palestra, Hazleton challenged Allentown for second half superiority with a capacity crowd of 2200 fans. In another typical Allentown-Hazleton tussle, Allentown led at the quarter 8-7, 22-19 at the half, and 30-29 after three periods. All seven players put on the floor by Coach Crum scored in the victory.

Leading scorers: Allentown – Elmo Jackson 12; Hazleton – John Ballots 19.

Bethlehem 47 Easton 37: In handing Easton another loss, the Hurricane sprung out to a 31-15 halftime lead after outscoring the Red Rovers 15-4 in the second quarter. Easton's Bill Filbert scored 12 points in the third quarter.

Leading scorers: Bethlehem - Frank Weaver 17, Ed Hudak 10; Easton - Bill Filbert 18.[12]

Week 6

Allentown 53 Bethlehem 36: Allentown sewed up the second half and overall league title with its triumph over Bethlehem at the Little Palestra. With the Canaries taking a 25-9 first half lead, Bethlehem's first field goal came with less than two minutes left in the second period.

Leading scorers: Allentown – Elmo Jackson 21, Dick Hoffman 11; Bethlehem - Frank Weaver 13, Don Watson 10.

Hazleton 37 Pottsville 31: With the Mountaineers racing out to a 23-12 halftime lead, Hazleton moved into second place with a triumph over Pottsville.

Leading scorers: Hazleton – John Ballots 14; Pottsville – Bill McClure 9, Alfred Burch 9.[13]

Pottsville 56 Easton 34: Easton finished the second half at 0-4 with its loss at Pottsville. Pottsville closed out the season and finished at 2-2 and a three-way tie for second place behind Allentown.

Leading scorers: Pottsville – Bill McClure 24, John Harvey 15; Easton - Joe Curzi 15.

Bethlehem 40 Hazleton 32: Bethlehem joined the tie for second place with Hazleton and Pottsville by handing the Mountaineers a loss at the Liberty gym. The Hurricane held Hazleton to four points in the first quarter and held a 17-11 first half lead.

Leading scorers: Bethlehem – Frank Weaver 9; Hazleton – Mike DeNoia 15.[14]

Postseason Play

Allentown 45 Mahanoy Township 22: Thirty-four hundred fans jammed Rockne Hall to watch Allentown outclass Mahanoy Township. Allentown took a 26-13 halftime lead. Seven of the 11 players for Allentown scored in the game. Fans began to line up a full two hours prior to the opening of the gym doors at 6:30.

Leading scorers: Allentown – Bill Wanish 12, Frank Pfeiffer 12; Dick Hoffman 10; Mahanoy Township – Johnny Kane 8.[15]

Allentown 65 Palmerton 42: In another sellout of 3400 fans at Rockne Hall, Allentown took on the Blue Bombers of Palmerton in a semi-final District XI matchup. After Palmerton forward George Kinek sank a field goal to take an early 4-2 lead, Allentown took command of the game and the Blue Bombers could only get as close as 34-28 early in the third period.

Leading scorers: Allentown - Frank Pfieffer 20, Bill Wanish 11, Elmo Jackson 11, Dick Hoffman 10; Palmerton – George Kinek 11, Russ Krawchuck 11, Karl Kummer 10.[16]

Allentown 57 Weatherly 42: Despite a Rockne Hall individual scoring record by their guard Pete Garber, the Weatherly High Wreckers lost the District XI title to Allentown. After leading 30-19 at halftime, the Canaries scored the first 11 points of the third quarter. Coach Birney Crum arrived at the gym about a half hour prior to the game. Delayed by late trains, Crum was returning from Alton, Illinois, after attending the funeral of his mother.

Leading scorers: Allentown – Frank Pfeiffer 13, Ray Dini 10, Joe Skurla 10; Weatherly – Pete Garber 26.[17]

Allentown 58 Chambersburg 33: After three consecutive playoff games at Rockne Hall, Allentown traveled to Hershey to begin interdistrict play against District 3 champions Chambersburg in the Eastern semi-final. After taking a 12-5 first quarter lead, Allentown was never threatened in the game as the Canaries disposed of Chambersburg rather easily to move to the Eastern Finals. Coach Crum employed all twelve players in the game with seven contributing to the scoring.

Leading scorers: Allentown – Joe Skurla 15, Bill Wanish 13; Chambersburg – Joe Howard 10.[18]

Allentown 38 Radnor 31: Six thousand spectators attended the Eastern final at Convention Hall in Philadelphia. Radnor and Allentown played to 8-8 and 19-19 ties at the end of the first quarter and the half with Radnor taking a one-point lead after three 28-27. The Canaries outscored Radnor 11-3 in the last stanza to prevail and move to the state title game. Coach Crum took his team to Philadelphia and they stayed at the Hotel Philadelphia to get a good rest for the game.

Leading scorers: Allentown – Dick Hoffman 13; Radnor – Vince Colodonato 13.[19]

Allentown 40 Donora 38: The state final with Donora was played at Convention Hall in Philadelphia with a crowd of 8,000 in attendance. In a hard-fought contest, Donora led after both the first period (10-9) and the half (20-15). Allentown forged into the lead at the end of the third period 30-27. After falling behind by seven points in the final quarter 37-30, Donora fought back to within two points 40-38. The game had a bizarre ending as the Canaries had already left to floor and were ready for the showers when they were called back onto the floor. With two seconds left, Dick Hoffman had been called for a foul. The timekeeper left the clock run and time ran out with the Canaries supposedly the victors 40-38. As the Canaries celebrated their way to the locker room, the officials wrangled for several minutes before deciding that one second should be put back on the clock. Donora opted for the ball rather than the foul shots. However, before Donora could get off a shot to tie the game, time ran out and Allentown truly now was the state champion for the second time in state playoff history.

Leading scorers: Allentown - Bill Wanish 13; Donora – Don Fanoni 15, Andrew Lelik 11.[20]

Post Season Accolades

Leading Scorers: The ten leading individual scorers for the season included: Billy McClure, Pottsville, 129 points; Elmo Jackson, Allentown, 99; Mike DeNoia, Hazleton, 87; Johnny Ballots, Hazleton, 86; Frank Pfieffer, Allentown, 79; Joe Curzi, Easton, 73; Bill Filbert, Easton, 70; Frank Weaver, Bethlehem, 68; Joe Kelly, Pottsville, 61; and Bill Wanish, Allentown, 57.

All-Stars: The league all-stars were selected by two different papers, the Hazleton Plain Speaker and the Pottsville Journal. The newspaper selections were not in agreement. An especially intriguing difference was the placement of Bill Wanish, who would be named first team all-state, but second team all-league by the Journal.

The Hazleton paper chose on its first team Johnny Ballots and Mike DeNoia, Hazleton, Elmo Jackson and Bill Wanish, Allentown; and Bill McClure, Pottsville. The Pottsville paper had similar selections except Frank Pfieffer was selected first team over Bill Wanish.

Chosen on the second team by the Plain Speaker were John Hudak and John Heilman, Bethlehem; Ray Dini and Frank Pfieffer, Allentown; Eddie McCluskey, Hazleton. The Journal countered with Bill Harvey, Pottsville; Dick Curzi, Easton; John Hudak, Bethlehem; Bill Wanish, Allentown; Joe Kelly, Pottsville.[21, 22]

All-State: Selections to the PIAA All-State included: William Wanish, Allentown, first team guard; Bill McClure, Pottsville, second team center; and Frank Pfieffer, Allentown, second team guard. Honorable mentions to the all-state team included: Elmo Jackson, Allentown forward; and John Ballots, Hazleton forward.[23]

Final Standings

First Half		Second Half		Overall	
Allentown	3-1	Allentown	4-0	Allentown	7-1
Pottsville	3-1	Pottsville	2-2	Pottsville	5-3
Hazleton	2-2	Bethlehem	2-2	Hazleton	4-4
Bethlehem	1-3	Hazleton	2-1	Bethlehem	3-5
Easton	1-3	Easton	0-4	Easton	1-7

Team Rosters

Allentown: Coach J. Birney Crum, Joseph Casciotti, Paul Clymer Jr, Ray Dini, Bill Elchook, Harry Hartman, Dick Hoffman, Elmo Jackson, Ray Montz, Frank Pfeiffer, Ray Ramella, Jack Ritter, Harold Romig, Joe Schuster, Joe Skurla, Bill Wanish.

Bethlehem: Coach Joe Preletz, William Bollecz, Oran Correll, Ernest DeAngelis, Ralph Deschler, Barry Dietz, John Felker, Richard Getter, Thomas Grund, Ed Hudak, Ralph Kocher, Bill Lobb, Frank Loncar, George Marinkovitch, Don Watson, Frank Weaver, Bill Werpehowski.

Easton: Coach Vern Fegley, Robert Baldwin, Joe Curzi, William Filbert, Earl Hanks, John Heilman, Richard Matthews, Joseph Mazur, Reuben Miller, Donald Murray, Anthony Onorata, James Pacchioli, Robert Richey, Joseph Sanguinito, John Vedomsky, Earl Wallaesa, Robert Wesley

Hazleton: Coach Hugh McGeehan, Johnny Ballots, Jack Broadt, Joe Capece, Pat Capece, Neil Cusate, Michael DeNoia, Emmett Farley, Paul Higgins, Allan Holman, James LaMonica, Ed McCluskey, Don McHugh

Pottsville: Coach Chet Rogowicz, Charles Bretz, John Buck, Alfred Burch, James Campbell, Don Davis, John Harvey, Harold Hausenauer, Joe Kelly, Quentin Koch, Bill McClure, Paul Minchoff

Allentown High School – 1945 League and State Champions[24]

Kneeling: Harold Romig, Bill Wanish, Coach Crum, Ray Dini

Standing: Joe Schuster, Joe Skurla, Ray Weiss, Paul Clymer Jr., Ray Montz, Frank Pfeiffer, Joseph Casciotti, Elmo Jackson, Jack Ritter, Ray Ramella, Bill Elchook, Dick Hoffman

1946

Expansion Rejected Again

At a league meeting April 1945, the league's representatives voted to tentatively remain as a five-team league pending an invitation to Phillipsburg, NJ, to become the sixth member. The 1946 five team schedule was adopted while they awaited an answer from Phillipsburg. Phil Phillipi was re-elected president and Edgar Rabenold as secretary-treasurer. Rabenold was requested to contact PIAA officials relative to the rules for ninth grade students' participation on the varsity squad. In another matter still in question from the previous season, the league voted to approve a $15 stipend for the officials for all league games. Non-league games would remain at $10.[1]

Week 1

Allentown 52 Bethlehem 38: At the Liberty gym, Frank Pfeiffer and Bill Wanish led the Canaries to an opening win over Joe Preletz's Bethlehem squad. Bethlehem tied the score at 12-12 in the second quarter before Allentown took a 24-19 lead at halftime. Allentown scored 20 points to Bethlehem's 8 to take command of the game in the third quarter record their 8th straight win to start the season.

Leading scorers: Allentown – Frank Pfeiffer 20, Bill Wanish 10; Bethlehem – John Felker 13.

Hazleton 33 Easton 25: Despite making only five field goals, Easton made 15 foul shots to keep them in the game with Hazleton. Hazleton led 16-13 at halftime.

Leading scorers: Hazleton – Jim LaMonica 10; Easton – Earl Wallaesa 7, John Vedomsky 7, Robert Baldwin 7.[2]

Week 2

Allentown 41 Pottsville 28: After a slow start by falling behind 11-5 after one period, Allentown rallied to take the lead at the half 19-17. The Canaries extended the lead to 29-21 after three periods and had their 10th straight win to start the season.

Leading scorers: Allentown – Bill Wanish 12, Frank Pfeiffer 10; Pottsville – Harold Hausenauer 7.

Bethlehem 44 Easton 39: At Easton, the Red Rovers challenged Bethlehem for three quarters before finally being outscored in the 4th quarter. The game had been tied at 28 all after three periods.

Leading scorers: Bethlehem – Johnny Felker 18, George Marinkovitch 10; Easton – Joseph Mazur 11, John Vedomsky 10.[3]

Week 3

Allentown 38 Hazleton 20: Although Hazleton took 23 more shots from the floor than Allentown (59 to 36), the Mountaineers only converted 8 while the Canaries made 14. With an 10-3 first quarter lead, Allentown led all the way to register the win and take firm possession of the league lead.

Leading Scorers: Allentown – Elmo Jackson 8, Ray Dini 8, Bill Wanish 8; Hazleton – Neil Cusate 6.

Bethlehem 57 Pottsville 35: After trailing by a point 11-10 after one period, Bethlehem outscored the Maroons 15-2 in the second period on the Pottsville court. After three weeks, only Allentown was unbeaten while Easton and Pottsville were winless.

Leading scorers: Bethlehem – John Felker 15, William Bollecz 14; Pottsville – Alfred Burch 9[4]

Week 4

Easton 53 Pottsville 32: Easton finally won its first game of the league season handily over winless Pottsville. Easton Coach Fegley used 12 players in an effort to keep the score down.

Leading scorers: Easton - John Mazur 11, Robert Baldwin 10; Pottsville – Alfred Burch 10.[5]

Hazleton 35 Bethlehem 32: In a thrilling show at the Liberty gym, Hazleton hit the winning shot with 3 seconds left in the game. With the scored tied at 32, Hazleton guard David Rosborough converted the field goal and a technical called on Bethlehem to pull out the win. In his varsity debut, Nick Scallion led all scorers.

Leading scorers: Hazleton - Nick Scallion 14; Bethlehem – John Felker 10, Richard Getter 10.[6]

Allentown 56 Easton 30: Allentown clinched the first half title by whipping Easton after being tied at 8 after one period. Although they converted only 6 of 17 foul shots, the Canaries made 25 field goals with center Bill Wanish making eleven field goals. Eleven of the 13 players used by the Canaries scored.

Leading scorers: Allentown – Bill Wanish 22; Easton – Earl Wallaesa 10.

Hazleton 45 Pottsville 30: Hazleton took second place at 3-1 by easily outscoring Pottsville, who finished the first half without a win in league play. After leading by only a point in the first quarter 6-5, Hazleton led at the half 20-8.

Leading scorers: Hazleton – Neil Cusate 12; Pottsville - Alfred Burch 9.[7]

Week 5

Hazleton 33 Easton 31: After falling behind by 9 points at the half 20-11, Easton employed a zone defense to check Hazleton in the second half. The Red Rovers' rally fell short as the Mountaineers held on to win.

Leading scorers: Hazleton – Joe Capece 10; Easton – Robert Baldwin 9.

Allentown 51 Bethlehem 38: Allentown registered its 32nd consecutive triumph, with a win over Bethlehem, since their last loss at the hands of the Liberty quintet early in the 1945 season. With only a two point lead after one quarter 10-8, Allentown increased the lead to 29-15 at halftime as the Canaries led all the way to win 51-38.

Leading scorers: Allentown – Elmo Jackson 12, Dick Hoffman 10, Frank Pfeiffer 10; Bethlehem - Richard Getter 11, William Bollecz 10.[8]

Week 6

Bethlehem 56 Easton 33: Bethlehem jumped out to a 22-17 lead after one half of play. As in the first half, Easton started 0-2.

Leading scorers: Bethlehem – Johnny Felker 17, Frank Weaver 10; Easton – Joseph Mazur 10.

Allentown 56 Pottsville 23: At the Little Palestra, Allentown rolled to a resounding win over Pottsville to register their 17th straight win to begin the season. With 10 players scoring for the Canaries, Allentown took an 8-0 lead to start the game and increased it to 30-10 at halftime.

Leading scorers: Allentown – Bill Wanish 17, Frank Pfeiffer 11; Pottsville - Alfred Burch 12.[9]

Week 7

Allentown 36 Hazleton 28: In their third contest of the second half, Allentown continued the recent mastery over Hazleton as they defeated the Mountaineers for the 4th consecutive time. With Hazleton taking the lead several times in the first half, Allentown took charge in the third period to lead by 10 points to register their 36th consecutive win over two seasons.

Leading scorers: Allentown – Bill Wanish 11; Hazleton – Neil Cusate 10.[10]

Bethlehem 80 Pottsville 42: In Bethlehem, Coach "Pickles" Preletz's Liberty gang pasted Pottsville. The Hurricane took a 15-6 lead after a quarter and added 26 more points in the second quarter to lead 41-19 at the half.

Leading scorers: Bethlehem – Frank Weaver 19, Bill Bollecz 18, Frank Loncar 12; Pottsville – Wally Reed 13, Alfred Burch 11.[11]

Week 8

Bethlehem 39 Hazleton 37: Despite holding the lead throughout, Bethlehem's matchup with Hazleton was not decided until the closing minutes of the game on the Mountaineer's home court. With each team sinking 14 field goals, Coach Preletz's team won the game on the foul line converting 11 of 17 compared to Hazleton's 9 of 21.

Leading scorers: Bethlehem - Johnny Felker 14; Hazleton – Neil Cusate 9.

Easton 43 Pottsville 30: In the battle of winless teams during the second half of the season, Easton defeated Pottsville. The Red Rovers jumped out to a 15-2 first quarter lead and maintained that margin throughout the game.

Leading scorers: Easton – Reuben Miller 13; Pottsville – Alfred Burch 15.[12]

Week 9

Allentown 29 Easton 25: Allentown's closest match of the season was against Easton in their last regular league matchup as they won by only a four-point margin. Taking an eight-point lead into the final quarter, Easton rallied to tie with four consecutive field goals before Dini converted two foul shots and Pfeiffer a field goal to close out the game. It was their 40th consecutive win and 23rd for the year and propelled them into the playoffs.

Leading scorers: Allentown – Bill Wanish 15, Frank Pfeiffer 10; Easton – Joseph Mazur 11[13]

Hazleton 27 Pottsville 26: Hazleton evened its second half at 2-2 with a narrow defeat of winless Pottsville. Trailing the game through the late portion of the third quarter and the score tied 20-20, the Mountaineers took the lead on Allan Holman's set shot and prevailed to finish their season with a 15-4 record.

Leading scorers: Hazleton – Neil Cusate 10; Pottsville – Alfred Burch 8.[14]

Postseason Play

Allentown 49 Whitehall 29: Whitehall, the Lehigh Valley League champs, was Allentown's first round opponent. Led by Egypt's Curt Simmons, Whitehall could not handle the Canaries and trailed after one quarter 15-2 and 24-7 at the half.

Leading scorers: Allentown – Elmo Jackson 11, Dick Hoffman 10; Whitehall – Freddie Kimock 6, Andy Palco 6.[15]

Allentown 45 Summit Hill 32: Allentown moved on to the District XI title game against the Black Diamond League champions, Summit Hill. Again, moving out to a big early lead 15-4 after a period, the Canaries won the district title with the defeat of Summit Hill. Summit Hill finished their season at 25-3.

Leading scorers: Allentown– Bill Wanish 13, Frank Pfeiffer 13, Elmo Jackson 10; Summit Hill– George Keister 7, Rich Black 7.[16]

Allentown 29 Williamsport 27: Despite an off night in their next matchup, Allentown was able to put away Williamsport, the District IV champions, at the Kingston Armory. Allentown entered the 4th quarter leading 28-17. The Canaries could only muster a single foul shot in the final quarter but were able to hang on. Although no one scored in double figures, all seven players put on the floor by Coach Crum contributed points in the victory.

Leading scorers: Allentown – Frank Pfeiffer 8; Williamsport – Roy Meyers 8.[17]

Allentown 35 Radnor 29: The Eastern Final was held at Convention Hall and the Canaries faced a repeat matchup from the prior year against Radnor in front of 10,000 fans. After the Canaries led throughout the game, Radnor was able to pull even with Allentown 28-28 halfway through the fourth quarter. Allentown came out victorious to move to the state title game for the second straight year.

Leading scorers: Allentown – Elmo Jackson 16; Radnor – Stu Adams 11[18]

Allentown 45 Homestead 27: Saving their best game of the season for the state title game, Allentown overwhelmed Homestead with Frank Pfeiffer possibly playing the best game of his career. The Canaries put the game away in the third quarter when they scored 14 points and held Homestead to just 3 points on foul shots. Coach Crum inserted all 15 players into the game by the time it ended. Pfeiffer's 24 points was one less than the state championship game record set by Hazleton's Red Meinhold. Allentown had now won 45 consecutive games over two years to tie Hazleton's state record set by the 1928 and 1929 teams. Their 45 points represented to most ever in a state championship game.

Leading scorers: Allentown – Frank Pfeiffer 24; Homestead – Donald Asmonga 10.[19]

Crum's 21 years as head coach had led to an overall 406-96 record. Despite this success, Hazleton still sported a 23-21 winning record over the Canaries in head-to-head competition. Another 20 of those losses came at the hands of Bethlehem, although Allentown had won 28 games against the Liberty boys.

Postseason Accolades

All-State: All five of Allentown's starters were named to the All-Pennsylvania all-star squad. Elmo Jackson and Frank Pfeiffer were named as forward and guard on the 1st Team. Bill Wanish and Ray Dini were named to the second team and Dick Hoffman was selected for the third team. John Felker, Bethlehem was also named to the third team. Five other league players received honorable mention: Pat Capece and Neil Cusate, Hazleton; Alfred Burch, Pottsville; Frank Weaver, Bethlehem; and John Vedomsky, Easton.[20]

All-Stars: The Hazleton Plain Speaker newspaper selected the all-league team with all five Allentown starters named to either the first or second team. Forwards Dick Hoffman and Elmo Jackson and center Bill Wanish made the first team while forward Frank Pfeiffer and guard Ray Dini made the second team. Neil Cusate, Hazleton, and John Felker, Bethlehem also were selected first team while Pat Capece, Hazleton, John Vedomsky, Easton, and Frank Weaver, Bethlehem, were included on the second team.[21]

Leading Scorers: John Felker, Bethlehem finished as the league's scoring champion with 101 points in eight games or 12.6 points per game. The remaining members of top twelve included: Bill Wanish, Allentown, 99; Frank Pfeiffer, Allentown, 85; Alfred Burch, Pottsville, 81; Neil Cusate, Hazleton, 68; Joseph Mazur, Easton, 65; William Bollecz, Bethlehem, 59; Dick Hoffman, Allentown, and George Marinkovich,

Bethlehem, each with 53; Richard Getter, Bethlehem, and Robert Baldwin, Easton, 52; and Elmo Jackson, Allentown, 48.[22]

Final Standings

First Half		Second Half		Overall	
Allentown	4-0	Allentown	4-0	Allentown	8-0
Hazleton	3-1	Bethlehem	3-1	Bethlehem	5-3
Bethlehem	2-2	Hazleton	2-2	Hazleton	5-3
Easton	1-3	Easton	1-3	Easton	2-6
Pottsville	0-4	Pottsville	0-4	Pottsville	0-8

Team Rosters

Allentown: Coach J. Birney Crum, Joseph Casciotti, Paul Clymer Jr., Ray Dini, Dick Hoffman, Elmo Jackson, Ray Montz, Frank Pfeiffer, Ray Ramella, Jack Ritter, Harold Romig, Joe Skurla, Bill Wanish

Bethlehem: Coach Joe Preletz, William Bollecz, Rocco Calvo, Paul Correll, Ernest DeAngelis, Ralph Deschler, Barry Dietz, John Felker, George Geleta, Richard Getter, Thomas Grund, Frank Loncar, George Marinkovitch, Edward Turanchik, Frank Weaver, Bill Werpehowski

Easton: Coach Vern Fegley, Robert Baldwin, Edward Casterlin, Earl Hank, Richard Matthews, Nelson May, Joseph Mazur, Reuben Miller, Donald Murray, John Vedomsky, Earl Wallaesa, Robert Wesley

Hazleton: Coach Hugh McGeehan, Joe Capece, Pat Capece, Neil Cusate, Paul Higgins, Allan Holman, Phil Klocek, Steve Kosiak, Russ Kremer, James LaMonica, Don McHugh, David Rosborough, Nick Scallion, Jimmie Taylor

Pottsville: Coach Chet Rogowicz, Alfred Burch, Don Davis, Bob Ficken, Jack Flanigan, Dick Hasler, Harold Hausenauer, Joe Kelly, Jim Landy, Jerry Laubach, Vic Muncy, Wally Reed, Bobby Unger

Allentown High School – 1946 League and State Champions[23]

Coach Crum, Dick Hoffman, Bill Wanish, Ray Dini, Frank Pfeiffer, Elmo Jackson

1947

Eligibility Questions

At its May 1947 meeting at the Shankweiler Hotel in Fogelsville, the Eastern Pennsylvania Interscholastic Basketball League discussed the issue of eligibility rules of the PIAA at length. They decided to draft another letter to the District XI Committee. A previous letter had questioned the eligibility of junior high students on the varsity team. The meeting included PIAA District XI chairman Roy Stapleton and secretary Edmund Wicht as well as representatives of each of the member schools in the league.[1]

In mid-June 1946, the District XI officials met at the Stephen Palmer High School in Palmerton to address the eligibility issue. Committee members in attendance included: Committee Chairman R. V. Stapleton, Tamaqua; Dr. H. O. Eisenberg, Bangor; C. W. Drumm, Frackville; D. L. Learn, Palmerton; and B. A. Briody, Bethlehem. Briody represented District XI basketball officials. The committee ruled that Elmo Jackson and Bill Wanish had one more year of varsity eligibility and George Montz had two years remaining, all members of the Allentown team.

Week 1

Allentown 43 Hazleton 34: Allentown began its season against it fiercest rival, the Hazleton Mountaineers, in the friendly confines of the Little Palestra. Coach McGeehan collapsed the Mountaineer defense on Bill Wanish and Elmo Jackson. This kept the game close for a time but Canary guard George Montz took advantage of the defense to lead the Canaries to victory. The Canaries now had a 53-game win streak.

Leading scorers: Allentown – George Montz 18; Hazleton – David Rosborough 15.[3]

Pottsville 33 Easton 29: At Easton, Pottsville spoiled the Red Rovers opening contest. With both teams making 10 field goals, Pottsville made 13 foul shots to Easton's 9 to register the victory.

Leading scorers: Pottsville – Bobby Unger 14; Easton – Jim Frawley 8.[4]

Week 2

Bethlehem 46 Hazleton 34: Hazleton uncharacteristically lost its 2nd straight game, at Bethlehem, to start the league season. Although the Mountaineers kept the game close, trailing 33-31 after three quarters, they could not keep pace in the fourth quarter. Bethlehem outscored them 13-3;

Leading scorers: Bethlehem – Cary Smith 13, George Marinkovitch 10; Hazleton – Nick Scallion 11.

Allentown 54 Easton 20: Allentown outclassed Easton with three players in double figures. The Red Rovers attempted 61 field goals and sank only 6.

Leading scorers: Allentown – George Montz 16, Bill Wanish 15, Elmo Jackson 13; Easton – Kohler 6[5]

Week 3

Allentown 49 Bethlehem 43: In a hard-fought game at Lehigh's Grace Hall with 2700 spectators in attendance, Bethlehem challenged Allentown throughout the contest holding the lead from early in the second period until early in the fourth period. Coach Preletz's Liberty quintet held the halftime lead 26-17. Early in the final quarter, Allentown pulled even at 31 all and outscored the Hurricane 23-14 in the quarter for the win.

Leading scorers: Allentown - Bill Wanish 19, Elmo Jackson 14; Bethlehem - George Marinkovich 12.

Hazleton 36 Pottsville 26: After the Mountaineers took leads of 8-4 and 24-10 after the first two quarters, Nick Scallion led Hazleton to their initial league victory.

Leading scorers: Hazleton – Nick Scallion 12; Pottsville – Donald Bretz 7.[6]

Allentown 43 Pottsville 36: Allentown clinched the first half title. Pottsville led the game at 5-2 with the Canaries tying the score at 9-9 before taking the lead for good. Allentown led 26-17 at halftime.

Leading scorers: Allentown - Bill Wanish 13, Elmo Jackson 13; Pottsville – Bob Fey 10.

Bethlehem 58 Easton 42: Bethlehem ended a two-game losing streak as they took a 37-27 lead into the fourth quarter. The Hurricane unleashed a 21-point attack in the fourth quarter.

Leading scorers: Bethlehem - Cary Smith 14, George Marinkovich 14; Easton - Thomas Sparta 12.[7]

Week 4

Bethlehem 66 Pottsville 46: Paul Calvo led Bethlehem to a triumph in Pottsville. Bethlehem led 40-26 going into the fourth quarter during which the teams combined to score 46 points. The win put Bethlehem in second place.

Leading scorers: Bethlehem–Paul Calvo 20, Bill Werpehowski 11, William Bollecz 11; Pottsville–Bob Unger 10, Walter Reed 10.

Easton 39 Hazleton 37: In Easton, the Red Rovers handed Hazleton their third first half defeat in a nip-and-tuck game. Easton led at the half 19-16 with Hazleton moving into the lead 30-26 after three quarters.

Leading scorers: Easton – Thomas Sparta 14, "Flip" Spaziani 10; Hazleton – Nick Scallion 13.[8]

Week 5

Hazleton 48 Allentown 46: Hazleton stunned its archrivals to begin the second half and break the Canaries 17 game league winning streak. It also broke their 60-game winning streak, the state's longest ever. After Hazleton held narrow leads after the first and second periods, the game was all tied at 38 at the third quarter mark. With Elmo Jackson out of the game on personal fouls, the Mountaineers pulled out the upset.

Leading scorers: Hazleton - Nick Scallion 19; Allentown - George Montz 18.

Easton-Pottsville: The Easton-Pottsville game was postponed.[9]

Allentown 39 Easton 31: Allentown rebounded later in the week in Easton. After Easton led early 5-1, the Canaries pulled ahead after a quarter 10-7 and increased the lead to 26-16 at halftime. Easton cut the lead to two points 31-29 before Allentown pulled out the victory.

Leading scorers: Allentown - Elmo Jackson 16; Easton - Jim Frawley 10.

Bethlehem 43 Hazleton 27: After a thrilling victory over the Canaries, Hazleton fell behind Bethlehem 9-0 and could not overcome the deficit. The Mountaineer's leading scorer Nick Scallion was held to 5 points while Bethlehem won with scores from 8 different players.

Leading scorers: Bethlehem – Bill Werpehowski 9, George Marinkovitch 9; Hazleton – Allan Hollman 12.[10]

Week 6

Allentown 48 Bethlehem 47: In a thrilling battle at the Little Palestra, Bethlehem lost to the Canaries by a single point. Allentown's largest lead at any quarter was five 15-10 after the first quarter. Although Allentown led most of the game, they barely held on as a last second shot by Bethlehem's diminutive guard Pete Carril just bounced off the rim as the game ended.

Leading scorers: Allentown – Elmo Jackson 12, Ken Weiss 11; Bethlehem – Bill Werpehowski 15

Pottsville 41 Hazleton 24: Surprising Pottsville upset Hazleton in a rather easy victory. Pottsville held a 17-9 lead heading into the second half.

Leading scorers: Pottsville - Bob Fey 16; Hazleton – Dave Rosborough 8.[11]

Week 7

Pottsville 37 Easton 28: Pottsville made up its postponed game with Easton and moved to 2-0 to set up a battle with Allentown for first place. After leading by only two points 23-21 after three quarters, Pottsville outscored the Red Rovers 14-7 for the win.

Leading scorers: Pottsville - Bob Unger 16, Walter Reed 11; Easton – "Flip" Spaziani 9.[12]

Allentown 55 Pottsville 42: Pottsville fought heartily for three periods to hang onto first place in the showdown. Late in the third period, the Canaries began to turn it on and outscored the Maroons 29-16 in the second half for the win. This clinched at least a tie for the second half title for the Canaries. Allentown finished the half at 3-1 and had to wait for the result of the Bethlehem-Pottsville game to determine their opponent for a second half playoff.

Leading scorers: Allentown – Bill Wanish 18, George Montz 12, Elmo Jackson 10; Pottsville – Bob Unger 12, Donald Bretz 12, Walter Reed 10.

Bethlehem 58 Easton 29: Meanwhile, Bethlehem kept pace by doubling up Easton. After taking an eight-point lead after a quarter 17-9, the Hurricane jumped out to a 31-13 lead at halftime.

Leading scorers: Bethlehem – William Bollecz 15, Don Feist 11, Cary Smith 10; Easton – Al Morello 9.[13]

Week 8

Bethlehem 73 Pottsville 33: Coach "Pickles" Preletz's team left no doubt who should face the Canaries with a whipping of Pottsville to claim the other spot in the second half playoff. Twelve players saw action for Bethlehem with ten of the twelve players scoring for the Liberty boys.

Leading scorers: Bethlehem – William Bollecz 14, Rocco Calvo 13; Pottsville – Bob Unger 10.[14]

Hazleton 53 Easton 41: Hazleton avenged its first half setback by Easton to finish at 2-2 and keep Easton winless in the second half of the season. Hazleton took a ten-point lead 18-8 and held it most of the way.

Leading scorers: Hazleton - Allan Holman 12, Bill Letcher 10, Nick Scallion 10; Easton - Jim Frawley 16.[15]

Second Half Playoff

Bethlehem 57 Allentown 42: The Canaries met Bethlehem in a playoff for the second half title. Playing in the Penn Palestra with more than 5,000 fans, Bethlehem prevailed, as Bill Wanish spent most of the game on the bench with foul trouble after committing 4 fouls in the first half, to force a playoff for the overall league title. Allentown jumped out to 19-7 first quarter and 29-25 halftime leads. In the 3rd period, Bethlehem outscored the Canaries 22-9 to pave the way to the victory.

Leading scorers: Bethlehem - Cary Smith 14, Bill Bollecz 14, Bill Werpehowski 11; Allentown – George Montz, Bill Wanish 11, Ken Weiss 11.[16]

League Championship

Allentown 56 Bethlehem 43: In the rematch two days later, Allentown was able to successfully defend their league title, held again at the Penn Palestra in Philadelphia with over 8000 fans at the game. Despite falling behind 6-0 to begin the game, Allentown outscored Bethlehem in each period of the game to bring home the league title for a record-tying 9th time to match Hazleton.

Leading scorers: Allentown - George Montz 16, Bill Wanish 15, Elmo Jackson 12; Bethlehem - Bill Werpehowski 14.[17]

Postseason Play

Allentown 51 Wilson Boro 36: Allentown began defense of its state title at Allentown's Rockne Hall against Wilson Boro, champions of the Lehigh-Northampton League. Allentown took a 15-3 first quarter lead and maintained a double-digit lead throughout the game. Coach Crum inserted all 15 players on his bench into the game with 10 players contributing to the scoring.

Leading scorers: Allentown - Bill Wanish 19, George Montz 11; Wilson Boro – Elmo Walters 14, Henry Haag 12.[18]

Allentown 37 Catasauqua 36: Catasauqua, the unbeaten champions of the Lehigh Valley League, gave the Canaries all they could handle in front of 8000 fans at the Penn Palestra. Coach Bob Mushrush's Rough Riders never trailed in the game until late in the third period. With 57 seconds to go, Catasauqua led 36-35 when Elmo Jackson took possession of the ball in a scramble under the basket and made the game winning field goal. Allentown escaped to win the District XI title.

Leading scorers: Allentown – Bill Wanish 12; Catasauqua – Kelly McLaughlin 11.[19]

Allentown 68 Chambersburg 48: In the first interdistrict game, Bill Wanish scored 13 points in the first half to lead the Canaries to the win over Chambersburg in their second successive game at the Penn Palestra. After Chambersburg, the District 2 champions, took an early 2-0 lead, Allentown came back to tie the score and take the lead 4-2. Allentown never trailed after that point in the game. Coach Crum nearly emptied his bench again with 13 players seeing playing time.

Leading scorers: Allentown – Bill Wanish 21, Elmo Jackson 14, George Montz 11; Chambersburg – Russ Young 16, Merle Leisher 15.[20]

Allentown 62 Williamsport 45: The Penn Palestra was filled to capacity with 8200 spectators to witness the eastern final between Allentown and the Cherry and White from Williamsport. Coach Crum put Joe Casciotti and Al Cassium, who had not been starters during the year, in the starting lineup because of their height to defend the Williamsport forwards. And it worked to perfection. Williamsport proved to be an easy victim as Allentown had four players in double figure scoring. Allentown was back in the title game for the 3rd year in a row. After holding a 44-35 lead heading into the fourth quarter, the Canaries added ten points to the lead.

Leading scorers: Allentown – Bill Wanish 16, George Montz 16, Elmo Jackson 13, Al Cassium 11; Williamsport – Bob Stine 13, Pete Fortner 12, John Perrotto 10.[21]

Allentown 46 Duquesne 42: Playing their 3rd straight game at the Penn Palestra, Allentown took on the Duquesne Dukes for the state championship. With the game tied six times and the lead changing hand 13 times, each team fought doggedly for the right to be called the state champions. With Allentown leading 42-32 during the final period, Duquesne fought back to close the final margin as the Canaries held on to win their third straight PIAA, and 4th overall, championship.

Leading scorers: Allentown - Elmo Jackson 20, George Montz 10, Bill Wanish 10; Duquesne – James Fulmer 11.[22]

Postseason Accolades

All-League: The Hazleton Plain Speaker's all-league 1st team included: Elmo Jackson, George Montz, and Bill Wanish, Allentown and Cary Smith and Rocco Calvo, Bethlehem. The 2nd team consisted of: Bob Fey, Pottsville; George Marinkovitch and Bill Werpehowski, Bethlehem; Nick Scallion, Hazleton; and Tom Sparta, Easton.[23]

All-State: Elmo Jackson was a repeat selectee at forward on the All-State 1st Team. He was joined on the 1st team by center Bill Wanish, Allentown, and guard George Marinkovich, Bethlehem. Unger from Pottsville was named 3rd team center. Honorable mentions included: Forwards Bill Bollecz, Bethlehem; George Montz, Allentown; Walter Reed, Pottsville; and guard Nick Scallion, Hazleton.[24]

Scoring Leaders: Three Allentown players topped the league in scoring with George Montz leading with 121 points and followed by Bill Wanish with 117 and Elmo Jackson with 113. The rest of the top ten included: Cary Smith, Bethlehem, 96; Bill Werpehowski, Bethlehem, 95; Nick Scallion, Hazleton, and Bill Bollecz, Bethlehem, 82; Rocco Calvo, Bethlehem, 81; George Marinkovitch, Bethlehem, 80; and Bob Unger, Pottsville, 72.[25]

Final Standings

First Half		Second Half		Overall	
Allentown	4-0	Allentown	3-1	Allentown	7-1
Bethlehem	3-1	Bethlehem	3-1	Bethlehem	6-2
Easton	1-3	Hazleton	2-2	Hazleton	3-5
Pottsville	1-3	Pottsville	2-2	Pottsville	3-5
Hazleton	1-3	Easton	0-4	Easton	1-7

Team Rosters

Allentown: Coach J. Birney Crum, Charles Brown, Joe Casciotti, Al Cassium, Paul Clymer, George Fedok, Elmo Jackson, Robert Kurtz, Robert LeVan, George Montz, Walt Schmidt, Fred Schwartz, Joe Snyder, Bill Wanish, Ken Weiss, Roger Williams, Harry Witt

Bethlehem: Coach Joe Preletz, William Bollecz, Rocco Calvo, Pete Carril, James Diefenderfer, Ralph Deschler, Don Fiest, Arthur Guerrieri, Alvin Krause, Edward Krocelic, George Marinkovich, Cary Smith, Bill Werpehowski

Easton: Coach Vern Fegley, Bibighaus, Jack Dixon, John Foster, Jim Frawley, Louis Guadignino, Earl Hank, Rolly Joseph, Jack Kelly, James Kohler, Alfonso Morello, William Nichols, Richard Pasch, Priestley, Joseph Schade, Tom Sparta, Phillip "Flip" Spaziani

Hazleton: Coach Hugh McGeehan, Eddie Beechay, Daniel Dura, Allan Hallman, Anthony "Sonny" Hyde, Bill Letcher, David Rosborough, Nick Scallion, Tom Stich, Jimmy Taylor

Pottsville: Coach Ed Deitch, Donald Bretz, Bob Fey, Jack Flanigan, Harold Hausenaurer, Dick Hasler, Leonard Joyce, Mike Mahall, Walter Reed, Bob Unger, Jim Womer

Allentown High School – 1947 League and State Champions[22]

Front: Al Cassium, George Montz, Walter Schmidt, Ken Weiss, Paul Clymer, Fred Schwartz

Back: Bill Wanish, Coach Crum, Elmo Jackson, Joe Casciotti

1946 And 1947

Titles Vacated

Allentown had barely completed the successful defense of their state championship when charges were leveled against them for the use of several ineligible players. The players in question were Bill Wanish and Elmo Jackson. These charges had initially been raised before the season began. After records at the school were reviewed, the charges were dropped. In March, Hazleton again raised the issue for the second time. An exhaustive search of the records cleared the status of the two players. R. B. Stapleton, from Tamaqua and the District XI Chairman and PIAA President, published a lengthy, detailed statement clearing Allentown. In the days following their championship victory, Stapleton issued another statement supporting Allentown.

Earlier, on March 7, 1947, the District XI Committee met for five hours in Allentown to review a number of issues within the district. Unofficial reports circulated throughout Eastern Pennsylvania indicated that Allentown would be disqualified from the playoffs and all victories would be forfeited because of the reported ineligibility of Bill Wanish and Elmo Jackson. No such ruling was made at the meeting. Instead, Allentown and Bethlehem were each fined $100 for the use of non-PIAA officials at their league championship game played at the Penn Palestra in Philadelphia.[1]

However, a special meeting of the PIAA District XI Executive Committee was called for May 14, 1947, to review the issue once more. Bethlehem cited new evidence that refuted the information reviewed in previous analyses. This evidence supposedly indicated that both Wanish and Jackson had played more than the eight allowable semesters. Edmund Wicht, executive secretary of the PIAA, was sent to review Allentown's records for a third time for the special meeting.

The Executive Committee meeting in Tamaqua reviewed the evidence which indicated that Allentown permitted Ray Dini, Ray Romella, Frank Pfeiffer, and Joe Skurla to participate in at least a 9th semester beyond eighth grade. These infractions occurred during the 1945-46 season. In addition, school records showed Bill Wanish, Elmo Jackson, Ernest Abrahams, Chester Gerulla, Robert Weibl, and Robert Kurtz participated as members of the basketball team after their eighth semester beyond the eighth grade. These infractions occurred during the 1946-47 season just completed. Both these situations violated Rule VIII of the eligibility rule.

As a result, both the state titles garnered by the Canaries were revoked! The PIAA also announced that Allentown would not be able to participate in any athletic competition as a member of the PIAA for the next three years, effective May 14. Although some limited suspensions had been handed out in the past, this was the first of its kind in the history of the PIAA. Despite the suspensions, Allentown's school board announced that it would continue its athletic teams during this period through contests with other non-PIAA member schools and organizations.[2]

1948

Allentown Suspended; Central Catholic Added

Allentown's ban from all PIAA competition reduced the East Penn League to four members. Despite its reputation as one of the best leagues in the state, the league now found itself in a battle for survival. A membership offer to Shamokin was rejected as they decided to remain in the Keystone League. Finally, in January 1948, a new fifth member was found when Allentown Central Catholic accepted an invitation to join. At a meeting held at the Shankweiler Hotel, Bethlehem, Hazleton, and Pottsville voted to accept Allentown Central Catholic. Even though Easton did not attend the meeting, school representatives sent a message indicating their acceptance. However, since it was their first year of membership, Central Catholic would not be eligible to compete in the PIAA playoffs. Central had already scheduled home and away games with the four members. This made scheduling them as a league member easy as the games would now be considered league contests. When membership was granted, Easton had already played Central one time and another match would have to be scheduled which would count as a league contest.[1]

Week 1

Central Catholic 40 Pottsville 36: The 1948 season opened with only a single game in the opening week. Pottsville journeyed to Allentown to take on new league member, the Central Catholic Vikings. Falling behind 23-14 at the half, Coach Eddie Deitch's Maroon quintet rallied to pull ahead 30-29 before Central Catholic scored to take a one-point lead at the end of the 3rd quarter 31-30. Central Catholic held on in the final period to win its inaugural league game. Forward Bobby Pizzolato led the Vikings with 16 points. The loss could be attributed to Pottsville's foul shooting which saw them convert only 14 of 31 foul shots.[2]

Leading scorers: Central Catholic – Bobby Pizolato 16; Pottsville – Walter Reed 9, Bob Fey 9.

Week 2

Bethlehem 67 Pottsville 50: Bethlehem's high scoring machine took on Pottsville at the Liberty gym in Bethlehem and handed the Maroons their second loss of the early season. After leading 14-11 after one period, Bethlehem blitzed Pottsville 24-9 in the second quarter for an insurmountable lead. Bethlehem forward Pete Carril led the charge with 10 of 11 players inserted into the game by Coach Joe Preletz contributing to the scoring.

Leading scorers: Bethlehem – Pete Carril 16, Don Fiest 12; Pottsville – Bob Fey 12, Bob Unger 12, Leonard Joyce 12.[3]

Hazleton 33 Pottsville 30: Playing their third game in the first 10 days of the new season, Pottsville lost to the Hazleton Mountaineers. With a 30-20 lead in the final quarter, Coach McGeehan decided to freeze the ball. The move backfired when Pottsville scored 10 consecutive points to tie the game. Hazleton managed to score the last three points of the game to pull out the win.

Leading scorers: Hazleton - Jack Sipple 10; Pottsville - Bob Unger 10.

Bethlehem 61 Easton 59 OT: Coach Vern Fegley's Red Rovers nearly pulled the upset of the young season when they opened their season against Bethlehem. Easton took Bethlehem into overtime before Coach Joe Preletz's team prevailed. No box score was available for this game. Due to the awkward scheduling from Central Catholic's late entry into the league and a game postponement (Easton-Hazleton due to weather), the standings after the first week and a half had a strange appearance. Three teams had played only a single game while Pottsville played three (all losses) and Bethlehem two (both wins).[4]

Week 3

Central Catholic 57 Easton 19: Central Catholic won its second straight game to start the season in a walloping of Easton. Trailing 12-6 after the first quarter, Easton only made a single field goal in the second quarter, in the last minute of the half. Ten of 13 players inserted in the game by Coach Joe Krajsa contributed to the rout.

Leading scorers: Central Catholic – Russ Meyers 11, Jimmy Elwood 11, Easton – "Flip" Spaziani 5.[5]

Bethlehem 52 Hazleton 39: Meanwhile, Hazleton took on the Liberty quintet in Bethlehem. Coach McGeehan's team succumbed to the Bethlehem squad and were only able to outscore Bethlehem in the final quarter after the game had already been decided. Bethlehem led at the half 27-13.

Leading scorers: Bethlehem -Rocco Calvo 14, Cary Smith 11, Fritz Toner 10; Hazleton –Vince Osadchy 10.[6]

Bethlehem 37 Central Catholic 35: Later in the week, Bethlehem invaded Rockne Hall filled with over 3000 fans in a battle of unbeatens. Bethlehem defeated the Vikings on a field goal by Rocco Calvo with three seconds to play. With 1:50 to play, the Vikings led 34-27. The victory clinched the first half for the Coach Preletz-led team.

Leading scorers: Bethlehem - Rocco Calvo 12; Central Catholic – Russ Meyers 13.[7]

Pottsville 47 Easton 42 OT: In overtime, Pottsville scored its first win, after three losses, over Easton. Easton led at the half 23-22, but they trailed throughout the 4th quarter until a field goal by Easton's Leonard Joyce tied the score at 42-42 at the end of regulation, Pottsville scored 5 in overtime while keeping the Red Rovers scoreless.

Leading scorers: Pottsville – Walter Reed 14, Bob Fey 14, Leonard Joyce 11; Easton – Rolly Joseph 10.[8]

Week 4

Hazleton 57 Central Catholic 41: Central Catholic traveled to Hazleton and suffered their second straight league setback by the Mountaineers. Outscored 14-4 in the first period and trailing at the half 20-13, the Vikings could not overcome the lead. The two teams combined for 65 points in the 2nd half with Hazleton scoring 37.

Leading scorers: Hazleton - Jimmy Mlasgar 12, Anthony Hyde 15; Central Catholic – Bob Pizolato 11, Jim Elwood 11.[9]

Week 5

Hazleton 66 Easton 44: In a makeup for an earlier postponed game, Easton jumped out to a 15-5 lead during the first period at Hazleton before the Mountaineers began a rally which led them to a 26-22 half time advantage. Hazleton won the contest to finish the first half at 3-1.

Leading scorers: Hazleton–Danny Dura 18, Gene Belletierre 14, Nick Ledger 14; Easton–Jimmy Kohler 9.[10]

Bethlehem 61 Central Catholic 44: Bethlehem began the second half at home against Central Catholic. Don Feist with 16 and Pete Carril with 15 points led the Bethlehem scoring attack in a triumph over the Vikings. The Vikings led at the half 22-21 before Bethlehem's high scoring attack scored 40 points in the second half for the win.

Leading scorers: Bethlehem – Don Fiest 16, Peter Carril 15, Cary Smith 11; Central Catholic – Bob Pizolato 11.[11]

Central Catholic 50 Pottsville 41: Playing their second game of the week, Central Catholic traveled to Pottsville and rebounded from their loss to Bethlehem. The Vikings started slow and trailed at the half 27-23. The Vikings rallied in the 3rd period to take a 37-30 lead and cruised to a win.

Leading scorers: Central Catholic - Jimmy Elwood 15; Pottsville – Leonard Joyce 12, Bob Fey 12.[12]

Bethlehem 85 Easton 49: Also playing a second game in the week, Bethlehem rolled over hapless Easton after jumping out to a 26-15 first quarter lead and 46-25 at the half.

Leading scorers: Bethlehem - Pete Carril 19, Cary Smith 15; Easton unknown.[12]

Week 6

Central Catholic 50 Easton 47: In the only league match of the week, Easton, playing at home, provided a stern test for Central Catholic. Playing for the third time with the first contest not considered a league match, the Red Rovers took a 24 -18 lead into the locker room at the half. The Vikings battled back to take a 36-33 lead at the third quarter mark. After Easton closed to within 48-47 with 29 seconds remaining, Central Catholic made the final basket for the win.

Leading scorers: Central Catholic – Pete Krah 12, Bob Pizolato 12; Easton – Louis Guadignino 15, Rolly Joseph 14, Jack Kelly 11.[13]

Week 7

Bethlehem 53 Pottsville 48: Bethlehem avoided a major upset in Pottsville. Pottsville battled Bethlehem throughout the game as the visitors held only a 41-39 lead at the three-quarter mark. With a slim one-point lead early in the fourth quarter, the Hurricane ran off seven points to take a commanding lead.

Leading scorers: Bethlehem – Cary Smith 16, Pete Carril 15; Pottsville – Bob Unger 18.[14]

Hazleton 64 Pottsville 36: Prepping for a big matchup with Bethlehem, Hazleton took on Pottsville at home. Rolling to a relatively easy win after taking a 46-25 third quarter lead, the Mountaineers lost a key player Danny Dura to a severe ankle injury in the final quarter.

Leading scorers: Hazleton - Nick Ledger 17, Jim Mlasgar 10; Pottsville – Leonard Joyce 9.[15]

Bethlehem 44 Hazleton 39: With both teams playing their second game of the week, Bethlehem traveled to Hazleton to settle second half league superiority. Bethlehem handed the Mountaineers their first loss at home after 17 consecutive victories on their home court. Deadlocked at 18-18 at the half, Hazleton went into the final quarter leading 34-30 only to see the Hurricane outscore them 14-5 to pull out the win. Their last loss at home had been to Bethlehem. The win clinched the second half and seasonal titles for Bethlehem.

Leading scorers: Bethlehem – Pete Carril 16, Rocco Calvo 10; Hazleton – Nick Ledger 14, Dan Dura 12.[16]

Week 8

Easton 55 Pottsville 42: Playing at home, Easton avenged a first half loss to Pottsville. Easton led at the half 23-20. It was Easton's first win in the second half. Pottsville suffered their 5th straight setback.

Leading scorers: Easton – Jack Kelly 18, Dixon 14, Rolly Joseph 10; Pottsville – Leonard Joyce 14, Leon Grickis 11.[17]

Hazleton 45 Easton 44: Later in the week, Easton almost pulled off its second victory of the week against visiting Hazleton. Hazleton's largest lead after any quarter was four points. Scoring 7 points in the final two minutes, Easton pulled within a point with twenty seconds to play, but neither team scored after that and Hazleton prevailed.

Leading scorers: Hazleton – Jim Mlasgar 13; Easton – Rolly Joseph 10.[18]

Week 9

Central Catholic 52 Hazleton 44: In a game postponed from the prior week, homestanding Central Catholic defeated the Mountaineers to close out play in the league. In the first half, Central Catholic took a ten-point lead only to have Easton come back and tie the game at 18-18. The win gave the Vikings second place during the second half of the season.

Leading scorers: Central Catholic – Bob Pizolatto, Pete Krah; Hazleton – Nick Ledger 16.[19]

PIAA Postseason Play

Bethlehem 77 Nazareth 36: Bethlehem represented the league in postseason play. At Rockne Hall, Bethlehem easily thrashed Nazareth, Lehigh-Northampton League champions, in their District XI opener. The game was fairly close after one quarter 14-9 in favor of the Hurricane, but Bethlehem opened up a wide lead at the half 40-22.

Leading scorers: Bethlehem – Don Feist 19, Fritz Toner 15, Rocco Calvo 13; Nazareth - Marlin Roth 15.[20]

Bethlehem 61 Palmerton 48: At the Penn Palestra, Bethlehem took on the Palmerton Blue Bombers, Lehigh Valley League champions, who carried a twenty-five-game winning streak into the contest. Palmerton held a 29-25 lead after one half. In the third period, Joe Preletz's team outscored Coach Bill Wilhelm's squad 17-5 to take a commanding lead. Bethlehem handed Palmerton a defeat to end the Blue Bombers win streak and season and gave Bethlehem their second District XI crown.

Leading scorers: Bethlehem - Pete Carril 16, Cary Smith 14, Don Feist 12, Fritz Toner 11; Palmerton - Bill Mlkvy 19, Bob Romig 12.[21]

Norristown 56 Bethlehem 41: Returning to the Penn Palestra, Bethlehem's postseason came to an abrupt end as they lost to the Norristown Timber Toppers 56-41 in their first interdistrict game. Bethlehem kept pace in the first half and were only down two points 21-19 as they headed to the locker room. The game was tied six times in the first half. With Rocco Calvo fouling out in the third period, Norristown was able to take command of the game.

Leading scorers: Norristown – Dom Couno 24, Eugene Cober 13; Bethlehem – Pete Carril 12.[22]

PCIAA Postseason Play

Central Catholic 53 Reading Central Catholic 37: After Reading Central Catholic took a 4-0 lead, Central Catholic came back to lead 10-8 after the first quarter. The Vikings increased the lead to ten at the half 27-17 and thirteen after three quarters 36-23 for an easy first round victory.

Leading scorers: Central Catholic – Henry Schwartz 17, Bob Pizalato 11, Jimmy Elwood 10; Reading Central Catholic – Charles Tulley 18.[23]

Central Catholic 60 Harrisburg Catholic 43: With the score tied 16-16 with two minutes to play in the first half Central Catholic ran off six straight points to lead at the half 22-16. They upped the lead to fourteen points after three quarters 40-26 and cruised to the second-round win at Slatington's Smith Hall.

Leading scorers: Central Catholic – Jimmy Elwood 18, Bob Pizalato 12, Pete Krah 10; Harrisburg Catholic – Tony Rados 17.[24]

Central Catholic 63 St. John's Catholic 48: At West Pittston, Central Catholic ran out to a 15-5 lead after the first five minutes and took complete control of the contest in third period by outscoring their rivals 14-4. Central Catholic played the game under protest contesting the size of the court. The West Pittston court measured 40' by 63' which violated the state playoff required size of 50' by 79'. The court also had a very low ceiling.

Leading scorers: Central Catholic – Bob Pizalato 12, Jimmy Elwood 11, Ray Meyers 11; St. John's Catholic – John Connors 12, Paul Miller 10.[25]

Central Catholic 41 LaSalle Catholic 35: At Rockne Hall, LaSalle Catholic, the Philadelphia city champions, and Central Catholic played a close game the whole way with both teams being tentative from the floor. The Vikings only converted 16 of 56 attempts and the Little Explorers could only convert 13 of 78 attempts. Central Catholic narrowly led after each of the first three quarters 8-7, 16-11, and 26-24. The Vikings were the eastern champs.

Leading scorers: Central Catholic – Henry Schwartz 8; LaSalle Catholic – Charles "Bud" Donnelly 12.[26]

Central Catholic 45 Johnstown Catholic 41: Playing in the friendly confines of Rockne Hall, Central Catholic and Johnstown Catholic waged a ferocious battle with the contest tied eight times with the last being at 39-39. Johnstown Catholic held the first quarter lead 16-12 with the Vikings coming back to take the lead at halftime 21-20. Jimmy Elwood's hook shot with five minutes to play put the Vikings ahead for good 41-39. The Viking were PCIAA champions for the first time since 1945.

Leading scorers: Central Catholic – Jimmy Elwood 11, Bob Pizalato 10; Johnstown Catholic – Leroy Leslie 20, Eddie Salas 11.[27]

Postseason Accolades

All-Stars: At a league meeting in late February, ten all-stars were selected to honor the league's top performers: Jim Elwood and Bob Pizolato, Central Catholic; Cary Smith, Pete Carril, and Rocco Calvo, Bethlehem; Nick Ledger and Sonny Hyde, Hazleton; Jack Kelly and Louis Guadignino, Easton; and Leonard Joyce, Pottsville.[29]

All-State: The All-State team selections included: Pete Carril, Bethlehem, first team forward; and Rocco Calvo, third team guard. Bill Mlkvy, Palmerton's center was named to the first team. Honorable mention selections included: Guard Sonny Hyde, Hazleton; center Louis Guadignino, Easton; guard Leonard Joyce, Pottsville; guard Nick Ledger, Hazleton; and guard Jack Sipple., Hazleton.[30]

Final Standings

First Half		Second Half		Overall	
Bethlehem	4-0	Bethlehem	4-0	Bethlehem	8-0
Hazleton	3-1	Central Catholic	3-1	Central Catholic	5-3
Central Catholic	2-2	Hazleton	2-2	Hazleton	5-3
Pottsville	1-3	Easton	1-3	Pottsville	1-7
Easton	0-4	Pottsville	0-4	Easton	1-7

Team Rosters

Bethlehem: Coach Joe Preletz, Rocco Calvo, Pete Carril, Joe Check, Walter Daniels, William Denofa, Jim Diefenderfer, Don Fiest, Alvin Krause, Bob Lasko, Cary Smith, James Smith, Francis "Fritz" Toner

Central Catholic: Coach Joseph Krajsa, Joseph Billera, Thomas Buck, Jim Elwood, Lou Gernacher, John Hartnett, Pete Krah, Joseph Medl, Raymond Meyers, Ed Novogratz, Bob Pizalato, Joseph Schleder, Henry Schwartz, Richard Weider, William Wolfer, Jim Wukitsch, Richard Yannes

Easton: Coach Vern Fegley, Sam Berkman, Bibighaus, Dixon, Louis Guadignino, Earl Hank, Roland Joseph, Jack Kelly, James Kohler, Alfonso Morello, Joseph Schade, Phillip "Flip" Spaziani

Hazleton: Coach Hugh McGeehan, Gene Belletiere, Jim Brennan, Dan Dura, Gene Gregor, Ed Havrilla, Anthony "Sonny" Hyde, Don Keuch, Harold Kneiss, Nick Ledger, Wassil Masonovitch, Jim Mlasgar, Vince Osadchy, Dan Paisley, Jack Sipple

Pottsville: Coach Ed Dietch, Jim Beissel, Bob Chivinski, Bob Fey, Jim Fox, Leon Grickis, "Corky" Johns, Leonard Joyce, Mike Mahall, Joe Mayberry, Walter Reed, Jim Troilo, Bob Unger

Bethlehem High School – 1948 League and District Champions

Front: Coach Troxell, Fritz Toner, Joe Check, Kleppinger (mgr), Don Feist, Pete Carril, Coach Preletz

Back: Custodian Resetco, Cary Smith, Rocco Calvo, Jim Diefenderfer, Phil Phillippi (faculty mgr)

Allentown Central Catholic High School – 1948 PCIAA Champions[28]

Front: Joe Billera, Bill Wolfer, Ray Meyers, Bob Pizalato, Pete Krah, Henry Schwartz, Jim Wukitsch

Back: Father Daday, Coach Krajsa, Ed Novogratz, Jim Elwood, Joe Medl, Richard Yannes, Joe Schleder, Richard Wieder, Coach Mascavage, Reilly (mgr)

1949

League Icon Lost

Despite a difficult start for the 1948 season with the late addition of Allentown Central Catholic as a new member and replacement for Allentown, the Eastern Pennsylvania Interscholastic League survived! The Central Catholic Vikings helped remove some of the sting felt by Allentown's suspension.

Unexpected news from Hazleton jolted the league in mid-August 1948. Hugh McGeehan, head basketball coach at Hazleton died suddenly prior to a meeting of the school's athletic committee and the school board. The death was attributed to a coronary occlusion. When he arrived at the school building, he noted that he had a slight chest pain and needed to sit briefly. After treatment by a doctor, the ambulance was called to take him to the hospital for further treatment. Unfortunately, he died prior to the arrival of the ambulance.[1] On September 14, 1948, the Hazleton School Board approved the selection of Frank Serany as the head basketball coach. Serany served as Hugh McGeehan's assistant coach for 13 seasons.[2]

Joe Preletz's Liberty squad wanted to give Bethlehem its second consecutive league title. Hazleton, with new head coach Frank Serany, also had aspirations of returning to its elite league status. Central Catholic, after a good showing in its first season, wanted to prove it deserved membership in the league. Hazleton was dealt a setback when its top player Gene Belletiere tore a ligament in his right leg during a practice prior to the opening of the league season.[3]

Week 1

Bethlehem 53 Central Catholic 41: Opening up the season at Bethlehem's Liberty gym, Central Catholic got off to a terrible start. After falling behind 15-7 after one quarter, Coach Preletz's Bethlehem squad caught fire in the second quarter and took the lead for good near the end of the second quarter. The Hurricane led 22-18 at the half and 36-31 after three quarters.

Leading scorers: Bethlehem - Fritz Toner 14 points; Central Catholic – Bill Wolfer 13.

Easton 39 Pottsville 36 OT: In the other opening matchup in Pottsville, Easton took down the Maroons in overtime. Tied at 36 at the end of regulation, Easton blanked Pottsville in overtime while scoring three points to secure the win. Easton had led at halftime 28-25.

Leading scorers: Easton – Roland Joseph 17, Herman Geis 10; Pottsville – Leonard Joyce 13.[4]

Week 2

Easton 40 Central Catholic 37: Playing their second consecutive game on the road to start the season, Central Catholic traveled to Easton. Despite trailing by 10 points 17-7 early in the second period, Vern Fegley's Red Rovers battled back to a 20-20 tie at the half. Guard Joe Sylvester scored 14 of the Red Rover's 20 first half points. Central Catholic entered the 4th quarter with a 31-30 lead. During the quarter, each team held the lead only to see their rivals come back. With one minute to play, the score was tied at 37. With 15 seconds to play, Easton center Rollie Joseph cut under the basket for a layup to take the lead. Easton tallied another foul shot and took the game 40-37.

Leading scorers: Easton – Joe Sylvester 14; Central Catholic – Hank Weider 16, Ray Meyers 11.[5]

Hazleton 38 Pottsville 30: Opening its league season on the road at Pottsville, Hazleton won a hard-fought matchup behind new coach Serany. With three minutes to play, Pottsville had been within a point at 30-29, but could not overcome Hazleton. Hazleton led at the half 18-13 with the score tied after three quarters at 25-25.

Leading scorers: Hazleton – Bobby Obrinsky 10; Pottsville – Leonard Joyce 12.[6]

Bethlehem 53 Easton 34: Later in the week, Bethlehem knocked the Red Rovers out of first place with a convincing triumph. Bethlehem took a commanding 12-5 lead in the opening stanza and were never threatened after that. Bethlehem now shared first-place with Hazleton.

Leading scorers: Bethlehem –Bill Bauder 16, Jim Smith 11, Steve Meilinger 11; Easton –Lou Guadignino 9.[7]

Hazleton 49 Central Catholic 44: Hazleton took a share of the first-place tie by winning its second straight game in league play and 10th straight overall over stumbling Central Catholic. Hazleton took a 10-1 lead to start the game and Central Catholic could never get closer than 4 points the remainder of the game.

Leading scorers: Hazleton - Jim Mlasgar 17, Bobby Obrinski 14; Central Catholic – Bill Wolfer, Ray Meyers 11.[8]

Week 3

Hazleton 53 Bethlehem 48: Bethlehem and Hazleton lived up to their preseason promise. With both teams at 2-0, Hazleton battled Bethlehem on its home court with the winner assuming a commanding league lead. Despite an early 11-2 lead, Bethlehem could not hold on and fell behind 25-22 by halftime. Hazleton would continue to hold the lead until Bethlehem rallied to tie the score at 44 with 2 ½ minutes remaining in the final quarter. Hazleton took charge at that point to pull out the win. Hazleton beat the Hurricane for the first time since 1946.

Leading Scorers: Hazleton – Jim Mlasgar 23, Harold Kneis 16; Bethlehem – Bob Lasko 11, Jim Smith 10.

Central Catholic 70 Pottsville 44: Central Catholic broke out of its slump by pasting Pottsville. Led by forward Wolfer's 21 points, the Vikings took the lead early and won by increasing its lead during each period.

Leading scorers: Bill Wolfer 21, Pete Krah 14; Pottsville – Paul Barnwell 10, Leon Grickis 10.[9]

Week 4

Hazleton 57 Easton 40: Hazleton would only have to defeat Easton to take the first half title. Holding narrow leads 13-11 after a quarter and 32-29 at the half, the Mountaineers ended the five-year drought since their last league title of any kind.

Leading scorers: Don Keuch 20, Jim Mlasgar 18; Easton – Roland Joseph 9, Herman Geis 9.

Bethlehem 61 Pottsville 46: Bethlehem unleashed its attack against winless Pottsville at the Liberty High School gym. After the Hurricane led at the half 26-20, Pottsville tied the game at 26-26 early in the third quarter only to see Bethlehem surge and take a 44-31 third quarter lead. Bethlehem finished second behind Hazleton at 3-1.

Leading scorers: Bethlehem – Bill Bauder 18, Jim Smith 16; Pottsville – Lenny Joyce 20.[10]

Week 5

When Pete Krah was ruled ineligible for further PIAA play, Central Catholic's hopes for second half glory took a major downturn. After playing a Sunday game with St. Aloysius, he was removed from the team.

Central Catholic 59 Bethlehem 38: Despite his ineligibility, the Vikings took the floor against Bethlehem in Rockne Hall in a contest which set a new attendance record of 3200 for an Eastern Pennsylvania Interscholastic League basketball game. After scoring 18 points in the second period, the Vikings led at the half 28-13 and wrapped up with a 21-point fourth period.

Leading scorers: Central Catholic – Bill Wolfer 19, Lou Gerancher 12, Richard Weider 11; Bethlehem – Fritz Toner 10.[11]

Easton 45 Pottsville 27: In Easton, the Red Rovers pressing man-to-man defense kept Pottsville unbalanced and led to an Easton victory. The Red Rovers led 13-5 after a quarter and 21-8 at the half.

Leading scorers: Easton - Rolly Joseph 19; Pottsville – Lenny Joyce 7.[12]

Week 6

Hazleton 52 Pottsville 28: Hazleton opened the second half against Pottsville. After being given a battle by the Maroons during their first matchup, Hazleton came out with a stingy defense holding Pottsville scoreless in the first quarter and allowing only 3 points, all foul shots, in the second quarter. After leading 21-3 at the half, Hazleton cruised with the reserves playing the entire 4th quarter.

Leading scorers: Hazleton - Jim Mlasgar 18, Don Keuch 12; Pottsville – Paul Barnwell 9.

Central Catholic 57 Easton 41: Coach Joe Krajsa's Vikings allowed only one field goal and 9 total points during the first half and avenged their first half loss to Easton with an easy decision. Central Catholic led at the half 26-9.

Leading scorers: Central Catholic - Hank Weider 18; Easton – Rolly Joseph 13.[13]

Week 7

Hazleton 65 Central Catholic 63: Central Catholic traveled to Hazleton seeking revenge for the first half loss to the Mountaineers. In a game which featured the officials calling many fouls, Hazleton prevailed. The officials called 33 fouls on Central Catholic and 26 on Hazleton. The Vikings lost five players to personal fouls while Hazleton lost three. Central Catholic pulled to within two points after trailing by 10 with five minutes to play. Hazleton now had sole possession of first place.

Leading scorers: Hazleton – Bobby Obrinski 17, Emil Wandishin 16; Central Catholic – Bill Wolfer 15, Ray Meyers 15, Bobby Fiertag 15.[14]

Bethlehem 71 Easton 49: After holding a one-point lead 16-15 after the first quarter with Lou Guadignino scoring ten points, Easton fell behind the Hurricane 30-26 at the half. Bethlehem took the game in hand by outscoring Easton 19-10 in the third period.

Leading scorers: Bethlehem –Billy Bauder 16, Jim Smith 11, Len Capuano 10; Easton –Lou Guadignino 18.

Bethlehem 60 Hazleton 53: Hazleton took on Bethlehem at the Liberty gym with an overflow crowd of 2200 fans. With the score tied at 10, Bethlehem ran off eight straight points to lead after a quarter 18-15. Hazleton took the lead 32-29 at the half. Bethlehem outscored Hazleton 15-4 in the 3rd quarter for the upset.

Leading scorers: Bethlehem – Fritz Toner 20, Len Capuano 15, Jim Smith 15; Hazleton – Jim Mlasgar 25, Don Keuch 15.

Central Catholic 59 Pottsville 39: Playing on their home court at Rockne Hall, Central Catholic clinched a tie for the second half title by defeating Pottsville. The Vikings took a 31-15 lead at halftime to take charge of the contest.

Leading scorers: Central Catholic – Bill Wolfer 17, Ray Meyers 11; Pottsville -Lenny Joyce 19.[15]

Week 8

Easton 35 Hazleton 33: Hazleton traveled to Easton intent on earning a tie for the second half title. The Red Rovers shocked the Mountaineers to eliminate them from a second half playoff for the title. Easton held a 12-9 first quarter lead with Hazleton coming back to lead at the half 18-14. After Easton retook the lead after the third quarter 27-25, the Mountaineers charged in front 31-27 before the Red Rovers rallied for the upset win. Easton held the league's leading scorer Jimmy Mlasgar to three points.

Leading scorers: Easton - Rolly Joseph 11; Hazleton - Bobby Obrinski 12.

Bethlehem 63 Pottsville 42: Bethlehem earned its spot in a playoff with Central Catholic with a win at Pottsville. After leading 26-20 at the half, the Hurricane outscored Pottsville 22-8 in the third period.

Leading scorers: Bethlehem – Fritz Toner 16, Jim Smith 11; Pottsville – Jim Beissel 21.[16]

Second Half Playoff

Bethlehem 48 Central Catholic 45: Bethlehem and Central Catholic battled for the second half title at the Penn Palestra with over 4000 fans in attendance. Bethlehem defeated Central Catholic and won the right to battle Hazleton for the overall league championship. Central Catholic led 14-5 after a period and by two points at the half. Bethlehem outscored the Vikings 16-6 in the third quarter to take charge of the game.

Leading scorers: Bethlehem - Bill Bauder 14; Central Catholic – Ray Meyers 14, Bob Feiertag 11, Richard Weider 11.[17]

League Championship

Hazleton 52 Bethlehem 44: Frank Serany, the Mountaineers' first year head coach, led his team into the Penn Palestra in front of more than 5000 fans. Hazleton would enjoy the services of the heralded Gene Belletiere as he returned for the first time since his injury. After a first quarter tie at 12, Hazleton took a one-point lead at the half 24-23. Doubling up the Vikings 16-8 in the third quarter, Hazleton took an insurmountable lead. After a five-year absence, Hazleton had captured its tenth league title.

Leading scorers: Hazleton-Harold Kneis 12, Gene Belletiere 10; Bethlehem-Bill Bauder 12, Fritz Toner 11.[18]

PIAA Postseason Play

Whitehall 50 Allentown 46: Allentown, playing as an independent, had its suspension lifted and was granted the right to enter the postseason playoffs. Allentown would lose its first game to Whitehall as the Zephyrs took the lead in the third quarter by outscoring the Canaries 20-11 after Whitehall trailed 25-23 at the half. Whitehall would now face Hazleton in the second round.

Leading scorers: Whitehall – Mickey Johns 17, Mike Torba 11, Holland 10; Allentown – Kenny Kline 12, Dick Focht 10.[20]

Whitehall 44 Hazleton 43: Surprisingly, Whitehall, the Lehigh Valley League champions, would defeat Hazleton at the Penn Palestra. Coach Bob Steckel's Zephyrs built a commanding 30-16 halftime lead. A fierce Hazleton second half onslaught would fall just short when Gene Belletiere missed a foul shot with seconds to play that would have tied the game. Whitehall would go on to defeat Mahanoy City to capture its first District XI title.

Leading scorers: Whitehall - Mickey Johns 14, Mike Torba 12; Hazleton - Bob Obrinski 9, Harold Kneis 9.[21]

PCIAA Postseason Play

Central Catholic 66 St. Nicholas 26: At Slatington's Smith Hall, Central Catholic held St. Nicholas to 6 points in each of the first two quarters and 3 in the third quarter to take a commanding 42-15 lead. The Vikings' Ray Meyers spent most of the first half on the bench after committing four fouls in the first ten minutes of the game.

Leading scorers: Central Catholic – John Spiegel 12, Bill Wolfer 11; St. Nicholas – Bobby Schuler 8.[22]

Central Catholic 57 DeLone Catholic 41: At Gettysburg, Central Catholic took a 32-17 first half lead and went on to defeat the Squires at the Gettysburg College gymnasium. DeLone Catholic lost three starters in the fourth quarter on fouls.

Leading scorers: Central Catholic – Bill Wolfer 19; DeLone Catholic – Billy Staub 12, Verne Smith 10.[23]

Pittsburgh Central Catholic 54 Central Catholic 42: With the game tied at 12-12 after one quarter, Pittsburgh Central Catholic took a four-point lead at the half 24-20 and then outscored the Vikings 20-13 in the fourth quarter to win the state PCIAA championship. The game was played at the University of Pittsburgh's stadium gymnasium which was directly under the stands of the University's football stadium. Several Viking players were stranded for some time when one of the vehicles broke down. With 42 fouls called in the game, the Vikings lost three players on fouls and Pittsburgh Central Catholic two players.

Leading scorers: Pittsburgh Central Catholic – John Clancy 16, John Killian 14; Central Catholic – Bill Wolfer 12, Bob Feiertag 10.[24]

Postseason Accolades

Leading Scorers: The league's two leading scorers were Jim Mlasgar of Hazleton, 116 points and Bill Wolfer, Central Catholic, 114 points. Other players in the top ten included: Bill Bauder, Bethlehem, 91; Don Keuch, Hazleton, and Roland Joseph, Easton, tied at 87; Leonard Joyce, Pottsville, 86; Jim Smith, Bethlehem, 83; Francis "Fritz" Toner, Bethlehem, 80; Bob Obrinski, Hazleton, 79; and Ray Meyers, Central Catholic, 77.[26]

All-Stars: All-league selectees as noted in the Hazleton Plain Speaker included:

First team: Forwards Jim Mlasgar, Hazleton, and Fritz Toner, Bethlehem; center Ray Meyers, Central Catholic; and guards Harold Kneis and Bob Obrinski, both Hazleton. Second team: Forwards Bill Wolfer, Central Catholic, and Bill Bauder, Bethlehem; center Don Keuch, Hazleton; and guards Jim Smith, Bethlehem, and Emil Wandishin, Hazleton.[27]

All-State: Several players were selected to the Associated Press All Star teams including: Jim Mlasgar, 3rd team; Fritz Toner, Bethlehem, Gene Belletiere, Hazleton, Lou Guadignino, Easton, and Leonard Joyce, Pottsville all honorable mention.[28]

Final Standings

First Half		Second Half		Overall	
Hazleton	4-0	Bethlehem	3-1	Bethlehem	6-2
Bethlehem	3-1	Central Catholic	3-1	Hazleton	6-2
Easton	2-2	Hazleton	2-2	Central Catholic	4-4
Central Catholic	1-3	Easton	2-2	Easton	4-4
Pottsville	0-4	Pottsville	0-4	Pottsville	0-8

Team Rosters

Bethlehem: Coach Joe Preletz, Bill Bauder, Len Capuano, Richard Chuday, Walter Daniels, William DeNofa, Bob Lasko, Steve Meilinger, Pete Meza, Forrest Mutter, Jim Smith, Fritz Toner

Central Catholic: Coach Joe Krajsa, Joseph Billera, Tommy Buck, Benjamin Conto, Bobby Feiertag, Richard Gaal, Lou Gerancher, Pete Krah, Ray Meyers, Joseph Schleder, John Spiegel, Jim Stehlin, Donald Sullivan, John Unger, Hank Weider, Bill Wolfer

Easton: Coach Vern Fegley, Herman Gies, Lou Guadignino, Roland Joseph, Richard Parnell, George Phillips, Lee Smith, Edwin Stipe, Joe Sylvester, Randolph Taylor, John Todaro, Wilbert Werner

Hazleton: Coach Frank Serany, Jimmy Diana, Pat Farace, Lou Fedullo, Gene Gregor, Don Keuch, Harold Kneis, Al Kosiak, Nick Matz, Jim Mlasgar, Charley Murrin, Bobby Obrinsky, Tony Scambia, Pat Walker, Emil Wandishin

Pottsville: Coach Eddie Deitch, Paul Barnwell, Jim Beisel, Joe Fox, Leon Grickis, Leonard Joyce, Mike Mahall, Joe Mayberry, Jim Troilo

Hazleton High School – 1949 League Champions[19]

From left: Asst. Coach Rex Antinozzi, Hal Kneis, Jim Mlasgar, Charley Murrin, Gene Gregor, Tony Scambia, Jimmy Diana, Pat Farace, Nick Matz, Pat Walker, Al Kosiak, Don Keuch, Gene Belletiere, Emil Wandishin, Bob Obrinski, Lou Fedullo, Coach Frank Serany

Allentown Central Catholic – 1949 PCIAA State Runner-up[25]

Front: Richard Weider, Bill Wolfer, Ray Meyers, Coach Krajsa, Pete Krah, Tommy Buck

Back: Bob Feiertag, Joseph Billera, John Speigel, Lou Gerancher, Joseph Schleder

1950

Hazleton Wins 11th League Title

The new season opened with Allentown keeping its independent schedule and the league remaining at five teams. At a December 8, 1949, meeting, the Allentown athletic council decided to accept an invitation to rejoin the Eastern Pennsylvania League in 1950-51 if the league offered it to the school. Three representatives, including School Director and chair of the athletic council chairman Helmut Golatz, high school principal Clifford Bartholomew, and faculty athletic manager Ralph Wetherhold, attended the league meeting.[1]

On December 12, 1949, Allentown's representatives attended the league meeting held at the Shankweiler Hotel, Fogelsville. At the meeting, league secretary Edgar Rabenold read a letter from high school principal Bartholomew that requested Allentown's re-admission to the league for the 1951 season and possibly the 1950 season if the league could work out a schedule. The five members unanimously accepted Allentown's request. Allentown and the league decided that it would be unfeasible to have Allentown play its independent schedule in addition to a league schedule. Such an arrangement would require Allentown to play three games a week over a 3-month period, which was deemed unacceptable for the players.[2]

Week 1

Hazleton 46 Easton 33: In Easton, the Red Rovers kept close to Hazleton for three quarters. After falling behind 10-8 in the first quarter, they finished the middle two quarters only two points behind the Mountaineers 21-19 and 29-27. Led by Don Keuch and Pat Farace, Coach Frank Serany's team outscored Easton 17-6 in the final quarter to go home with the win.

Leading scorers: Hazleton – Pat Farace 17, Don Keuch 17; Easton – Lee Smith 13.

Bethlehem 51 Pottsville 42: In Pottsville, with Bethlehem scoring 14 unanswered points in the last six minutes and with Dick Chuday scoring 8 of them, the visitors, behind 42-37, pulled out a win. Bethlehem had been ahead 37-36 before Pottsville surged ahead.

Leading scorers: Bethlehem – Dick Chuday 14, Len Capuano 10, Bill Bauder 10, Richard, Lawrence 10; Pottsville - Jim Beisel 18, Paul Barnwell 10, Joe Mayberry 10.[3]

Week 2

Central Catholic 70 Bethlehem 35: At Rockne Hall with 2500 cheering fans, Central Catholic took a 14-6 lead after the first quarter. They kept the eight-point lead at the half with each squad bursting out for 21 points in the second quarter. The Vikings led 51-38 after three quarters.

Leading scorers: Central Catholic - Louie Gerancher 23, Bob Feiertag 18, John Spieigel, 14, John Unger 11; Bethlehem - Dick Chuday 19.

Easton 63 Pottsville 44: Coach Vern Fegley's Red Rovers defeated Pottsville in Easton. The Red Rovers led 15-8 and 36-17 at the half to score an easy win over the Maroons.

Leading scorers: Easton - Joe Sylvester 21, Robert Flad 12, Lee Smith 11; Pottsville – Jim Beisel 14.[4]

Week 3

Easton 50 Central Catholic 45: The invading Red Rovers threw a monkey wrench into the Vikings' hopes of a first half title with an unexpected takedown of Central Catholic. The Vikings took a 17-9 lead in the first quarter only to have Easton fight back and take the halftime lead 27-25. Easton never relinquished the lead in the second half.

Leading scorers: Easton -Robert Flad 18, Lee Smith 14; Central Catholic -Lou Gerancher 14, Jim Stehlin 10.

Hazleton 42 Pottsville 24: With 6'5" center Keuch and 5'6" guard Farace leading the way, Hazleton took an easy win over visiting Pottsville. After a low scoring first quarter with the Mountaineers on top 5-2, Hazleton stretched the lead to ten at the half 17-7.

Leading scorers: Hazleton – Don Keuch 17, Pat Farace 15; Pottsville – Joe Mayberry 14.[5]

Hazleton 56 Central Catholic 49: Outscored in field goals 21-20, Hazleton converted 16 of 27 foul shots while Central Catholic made only 7 of 12 attempts to beat the Vikings and take a firm hold on first place. In the third quarter, Central Catholic scored 17 points to Hazleton's 1 to take a 43-37 lead, but the Mountaineers turned the tables in the final stanza 19-6 to pull out the win. Four Central Catholic starters played the fourth quarter with 4 personal fouls.

Leading scorers: Hazleton - Bill Shull 18, Don Keuch 13, Pat Farace 12; Central Catholic – John Spiegel 11, Lou Gerancher 10, Bob Feiertag 10.

Easton 52 Bethlehem 50: In Bethlehem, Easton was outscored from the floor by eight points, but made 18 foul shots to Bethlehem's 8 to eke out a win. With seven seconds remaining, Bethlehem's Bill Bauder missed a shot which would have tied the score. Easton needed Bethlehem to knock off Hazleton in order to tie for the first half title.

Leading scorers: Easton – Lee Smith 14, Joe Sylvester 13, Robert Flad 11; Bethlehem – Billy Miller 14.[6]

Week 4

Hazleton 54 Bethlehem 39: Hazleton dashed Easton's hopes of a first half title despite having Bethlehem take an early 6-0 lead over the visitors. Blanking Bethlehem without a field goal in the second quarter, the Mountaineers rolled to 24-12 halftime lead which proved to be the difference in the game.

Leading scorers: Hazleton – Don Keuch 17, Bill Shull 15, Pat Farace 12; Bethlehem – Bob Lasko 7.

Central Catholic 46 Pottsville 41: Central Catholic pulled their record even at 2-2 despite a fourth period scare from Pottsville. After trailing by 9 at the half, Pottsville pulled to within a point in the final period before finally succumbing to the Vikings 46-41. Pottsville finished 0-4 in the first half of the season.

Leading scorers: Central Catholic – John Unger 16, Lou Gerancher 10; Pottsville – Paul Barnwell 15.[7]

Week 5

Hazleton 64 Easton 43: Bill Shull, who transferred to Hazleton from Sunbury, led Hazleton to victory over Easton in front of 1600 fans in Hazleton. Hazleton led at the half 26-17. Hazleton's defense held the Red Rovers' leading scorer Smith to three points.

Leading scorers: Hazleton – Bill Shull 22, Don Keuch 17, Pat Farace 15; Easton – Joe Sylvester 12.

Bethlehem 65 Pottsville 41: Bethlehem started the half with a win over lowly Pottsville. Bethlehem poured in 28 points in the 2nd period with Billy Miller scoring 12 by himself. Bethlehem led at the half 43-26.

Leading scorers: Bethlehem – Billy Miller 29; Pottsville - Paul Barnwell 17, Joe Mayberry 12.[8]

Easton 40 Pottsville 39: Traveling to Pottsville later in the week after playing on Tuesday night, Easton bounced back with a win, but barely. Ahead by 31-18 entering the 4th quarter, the Red Rovers held on after a desperate last period rally by Pottsville.

Leading scorers: Easton - Lee Smith 18; Pottsville - Paul Barnwell 15, Gus Prahalis 10.

Central Catholic 72 Bethlehem 65: Central Catholic swept the season series from Bethlehem. Bethlehem rallied from an eight-point 37-29 deficit at the half to take the lead 51-46 after three quarters. Trailing by 3 with nearly 3 minutes to play, the Vikings rallied to even their record at 1-1.

Leading scorers: Central Catholic - Lou Gerancher 19, John Spiegel 13, Jim Stehlin 12, John Unger 10; Bethlehem - Bob Lasko, Billy Miller 16.[9]

Week 6

Hazleton 36 Pottsville 35: Pottsville, on their home court, challenged Hazleton the entire night with Hazleton only able to hold single point leads at the end of each of the first two periods, 11-10 and 17-16. Hazleton extended the lead to six points at the three-quarter mark 30-24, but Pottsville rallied in the fourth quarter only to fall short.

Leading scorers: Hazleton - Don Keuch 17; Pottsville – Paul Barnwell 9, Jim Beisel 9, Joe Mayberry 9.

Central Catholic 60 Easton 51: Meanwhile in Easton, Central Catholic kept pace with Hazleton by downing the Red Rovers. Coach Joe Krajsa's Vikings won the game with their second quarter performance outscoring Easton 21-9. Central Catholic and Hazleton shared the second half lead with 2-0 records.

Leading scorers: Central Catholic – Lou Gerancher 17, Bobby Feiertag 17, John Unger 10, John Spiegel 10; Easton – Lee Smith 16, Wilbert Werner 16.[10]

Week 7

Central Catholic 74 Pottsville 53: On a Tuesday night in a game moved ahead of schedule by a week, Central Catholic entertained winless Pottsville at Rockne Hall. The game was never in question after the Vikings scored 12 straight points to take an 18-4 lead during the first quarter. This set up the clash with Hazleton for the second half title on Friday night at Rockne Hall.

Leading scorers: Central Catholic – Lou Gerancher 23, Bob Feiertag 13, John Unger 12, John Spiegel 11; Pottsville – Joe Mayberry 15, Paul Barnwell 14.[11]

Hazleton 62 Central Catholic 54: In front of a crowd of more than 3500 for a new Rockne Hall attendance record, Central Catholic took on Hazleton to decide the second half title. The Vikings were no match for Hazleton. After being tied at 12 after one quarter, Hazleton outscored the Vikings by 15 in the middle to periods to take a commanding lead. Although Central Catholic outscored the Mountaineers 23-16 in the final period, the game belonged to Hazleton. Hazleton now only had to beat Bethlehem the following week to win both halves and to move on to the district playoffs.

Leading scorers: Hazleton–Don Keuch 26, Pat Farace 16; Central Catholic–Lou Geranacher 22. John Spiegel 16, Jim Stehlin 13.

Easton 53 Bethlehem 49: Leading after both the second 26-21 and third periods 38-32, Bethlehem lost the battle with Easton when the Red Rovers scored 21 points to Bethlehem's 11 in the final stanza.

Leading scorers: Easton - Don Flad 19, Joe Sylvester 14; Bethlehem – Bill Bauder 14, Bob Lasko 13.[12]

Week 8

Hazleton 72 Bethlehem 51: Although only a single game remained to be played in the regular season, it was an important one in Hazleton to settle the second half title. Winning their 16th in a row and 18 of 20, Coach Frank Serany's team outclassed Bethlehem. Hazleton took a 28-8 first quarter lead to take charge of the game.

Leading scorers: Hazleton – Don Keuch 25, Bill Shull 16; Bethlehem – Billy Miller 16.[13]

PIAA Postseason Play

Mahanoy City 57 Hazleton 52: Hazleton met longtime foe Mahanoy City in their first playoff game. The game featured 12 ties. Hazleton, however, lost to abruptly end their title hopes. Mahanoy City outscored the Mountaineers 18-12 during the final period for the win. Hazleton had four players in double figures. Twelve seniors would graduate from Frank Serany's squad.

Leading scorers: Mahanoy City – Jimmy Smith 20, Tom Rulis 13, Jack Smigo 11; Hazleton – Pat Farace 14, Don Keuch 14, Emil Wandishin 11, Bill Shull 11.[15]

Allentown 65 Catasauqua 49: Allentown had again entered the playoffs as an independent. The Canaries defeated Catasauqua 65-49 in the first round for their 18th straight win. After Allentown took a 34-18 lead at halftime, Catasauqua made an attempt to get back into the game by cutting the lead to 46-37. However, Allentown took charge in the fourth quarter.

Leading scorers: Allentown – Bill Snyder 19, Bill Adams 11, Ted Glass 11; Catasauqua – Andy Dulik 20, Dick McLaughlin 15.[16]

Allentown 64 Mahanoy City 40: In the district title game at the Penn Palestra in front of a sellout crowd of over 8000 fans, Allentown jumped out to a 34-15 lead at halftime and rolled to an easy win over Mahanoy City for their 5th District XI crown.

Leading scorers: Allentown – Bill Adams 15, Charlie Handwerk 12, Leroy Katz 12; Mahanoy City – Jimmy Smith 11.[17]

Swoyersville 59 Allentown 39: With more than 6500 fans in attendance, Allentown lost their next game, breaking a 19-game winning streak, to Swoyersville at the Kingston Armory to end their championship hopes. Swoyersville opened up with at 31-17 lead at the half and the Canaries never threatened the Sailors.

Leading scorers: Swoyersville – Joe Licata 23, Joe Holup 15, John Holup 10; Allentown – Bill Adams 9.[18]

PCIAA Postseason Playoffs

Reading Central Catholic 67 Central Catholic 47: After five consecutive losses to the Vikings in past playoffs, Reading Central Catholic took a commanding lead early in the game, 30-14 at halftime, to knock Central Catholic out of the PCIAA playoffs in the first round.

Leading scorers: Reading Central Catholic – Johnny Morris 16, Mike DePaul 15, Charles Gehringer 12; Central Catholic – Lou Gerancher 15, John Unger 11.[19]

Postseason Accolades

Leading scorers: Don Keuch, Hazleton, led the league in individual scoring with 149 points in 8 games. Lou Gerancher, Central, finished second with 138 points. They far outdistanced the remaining leaders who included: Pat Farace, Hazleton, 102; Lee Smith, Easton, 94; Robert Flad, Easton, and John Speigel, Central, 89; Bill Shull, Hazleton, and Joe Mayberry, Pottsville, 85; Bob Fiertag, Central, 77; John Unger, Central, and

Bob Lasko, Bethlehem, 75; Bill Miller, Bethlehem, 69; and Jim Biesel, Pottsville, 60 points. Billy Miller scored 29 of his 69 points in a single game, which was also the league high for the season.[20]

All-Stars: The Hazleton Plain Speaker newspaper selected the all-league as follows: First team – Emil Wandishin, Hazleton, and Lou Gerancher, Allentown Central Catholic at forward; Don Keuch, Hazleton, at center; and Billy Miller, Bethlehem, and Pat Farace, Hazleton, at guard. Second team – Bill Shull, Hazleton, and Bob Flad, Easton, at forward; Paul Barnwell, Pottsville at center; and Tom Scambia, Hazleton, and Lee Smith, Easton, at guard.[21]

All-State: The PIAA all-state team included Don Keuch, Hazleton, 4th team, League honorable mention honorees included: Bill Bauder, Bethlehem; Lou Gerancher, Allentown Central Catholic; and Emil Wandishin, Hazleton. Allentown's Bill Snyder was named to the 3rd team.[22]

Final Standings

First Half		Second Half		Overall	
Hazleton	4-0	Hazleton	4-0	Hazleton	8-0
Easton	3-1	Central Catholic	3-1	Central Catholic	5-3
Central Catholic	2-2	Easton	2-2	Easton	5-3
Bethlehem	1-3	Bethlehem	1-3	Bethlehem	2-6
Pottsville	0-4	Pottsville	0-4	Pottsville	0-8

Team Rosters

Bethlehem: Coach Joe Preletz, Patrick Albanese, Dave Arner, Bill Bauder, Don Bittenbender, Leonard Capuano, Dick Chuday, Fred DePretis, Henry Durkop, Charlie Hoydu, Donald Johnson, John "Howie" Johnson, Bob Lasko, Dick Lawrence, Billy Miller, Bill Rodgers, Bob Rohland, Michael Sentelik, Joe Zubia

Central Catholic: Coach Joe Krajsa, Ed Emery, Bob Feiertag, Dick Gaal, Lou Gerancher, John Green, Robert Jezick, William McGuire, Bill McClure, John Spiegel, Eric Spinosa, Jim Stehlin, Don Sullivan, John Unger, Joseph Weber, Walter Yaros

Easton: Coach Vern Fegley, Stanley Butler, Richard Chidsey, Kenneth Fahl, Maurice Feauve, Donald Flad, James Gianopolus, Elmer Hay, Charles Heller, Richard Kline, James Parnell, George Phillips, Glenn Sheats, Lee Smith, Stan Sutphen, Joseph Sylvester, Peter Valieses, Constantine "Gus" Voyagis, Kenneth Werner

Hazleton: Coach Frank Serany, Eddie Boran, Joe Bruno, Pat Farace, Gene Gregor, Don Keuch, Nick Marsicano, Vern Matrese, Nick Matz, Jimmy McGeehan, Tom Mlasgar, Charlie Murrin, Tom Scambia, Ernie Serafin, Bill Shull, Charlie Tarone, Emil Wandishin

Pottsville: Coach Ed Dietch, Paul Barnwell, Jim Beissel, Donald Bevan, Joe Fox, Leon Grickis, Ron Lyons, Mike Mahall, Joe Mayberry, Phil Mascara, Gus Prahalis, Ronald Quinn, Ron Troilo, James Womer

Hazleton High School – 1950 League Champions[14]

Front Row: Tom Mlasgar, Jimmy McGeehan, Ernie Serafin, Pat Farace, Eddie Boran

Middle Row: Don Keuch, Nick Matz, Emil Wandishin, Tom Scambia, Charlie Tarone

Back Row: Nick Marsicano, Bill Shull, Gene Gregor, Charlie Murrin, Joe Bruno, Vern Matrese

1951

Allentown Readmitted

Milo Sewards took over as head coach of the Canaries as Allentown ended its three-year independent stint to rejoin the league. The league was back to its six-team balanced alignment. The season was expected to be exciting and competitive with Allentown, Bethlehem, and Pottsville all entering league play undefeated.

The league officers included Bethlehem's Phil Phillippi, president, and Stanley Steigerwalt from Easton as vice president. The league adopted rules requiring junior varsity games to begin at 6:45 with the varsity games following at 8:15. Immediately after the end of the junior varsity game, the league mandated that the National Anthem and school's Alma Maters be played to avoid unnecessary delays.[1]

Week 1

Easton 60 Allentown 47: Vern Fegley's Easton quintet, led by Don Flad, surprised Allentown. Easton moved ahead at the end of the first quarter 14-8 and 35-21 at halftime and played Allentown even during the second half.

Leading scorers: Easton - Don Flad 21, Lee Smith 18, Ken Werner 13; Allentown - Ed Cahn 13, Bill Snyder 10.

Central Catholic 62 Pottsville 60: At Rockne Hall, Coach Ed Deitch's Maroons held a 19-18 lead after one quarter only to see Central Catholic outscore his team by 6 and 4 points in the next two quarters. Pottsville's starting five, who played the entire game without substitution, fought back during the fourth quarter, but fell short by two points.

Leading scorers: Central Catholic – Ed Emery 25, Bob Feiertag 11, Eric Spinosa 11; Pottsville – Gus Prahalis 23, Phil Mascara 14, Paul Barnwell 12.[2]

Bethlehem 48 Hazleton 28: Bethlehem ran over Hazleton after taking a 15-9 first quarter lead. Hazleton was held to 2 points in the 3rd quarter while Bethlehem scored 14.

Leading scorers: Bethlehem – Joe Zubia 14, Bill Miller 11; Hazleton – Ken Wendel 7.[3]

Week 2

Easton 53 Hazleton 44: Easton traveled to Hazleton looking for its second league win. After a sluggish start which allowed the Mountaineers to hold a 6-point lead at the end of the first quarter 16-10 and 24-22 at halftime, the Red Rovers outscored Hazleton in each of the final three quarters to win going away.

Leading scorers: Easton - Don Flad 14, Ken Werner 13, Jim Parnell 10; Hazleton - Bob Stewart 15.[4]

Central Catholic 52 Allentown 51: With an overflow crowd of over 3500 fans in Rockne Hall, Jack O'Donnell, a late game substitution, sank a foul shot, his only point of the game, after regulation time ran out to defeat the Canaries. The Vikings led at the half 27-26 and held a 6-point lead after three quarters 41-35.

Leading scorers: Central Catholic - Bob Fiertag 13, Ed Emery 12, Eric Spinosa 10; Allentown - Eddie Cahn 16, Bill Snyder 12.

Bethlehem 72 Pottsville 59: Bethlehem's Dick Lawrence scored 20 points in the second half and 17 of those in an incredible 2 minutes as he led his team to a win over Pottsville. Bethlehem trailed 29-28 at halftime.

Leading scorers: Bethlehem - Dick Lawrence 34, Bill Miller 15, Joe Zubia 12; Pottsville - Gus Prahalis 25, Paul Barnwell 14.[5]

Week 3

Bethlehem 59 Central Catholic 43: In a battle of unbeatens in league play, Bethlehem defeated Central Catholic to stretch its winning streak to 11. Coach Joe Preletz kept his quintet fresh all night using at least two substitutes throughout the game. Bethlehem held a one-point lead at the half 23-22 before taking charge in the second half.

Leading scorers: Bethlehem – Dick Lawrence 15, Bob Rohland 12; Central Catholic – Don Guman 10.

Pottsville 48 Easton 46: Meanwhile, Easton was upset by Pottsville. Easton led at the half 26-22. Pottsville took the lead for the first time in the third quarter and never relinquished it. Bethlehem took over first place.

Leading scorers: Pottsville – Gus Prahalis 15, Phil Mascara 10, Paul Barnwell 10; Easton – Lee Smith 15, Ken Werner 13, Don Flad 12.

Allentown 83 Hazleton 61: Allentown garnered its first league victory for Coach Milo Sewards with an easy triumph over winless Hazleton at the Little Palestra. This was the first league action at the Little Palestra after a three-year suspension. The Canaries took leads of 21-10 and 46-27 after each of the first two quarters.

Leading scorers: Allentown – Bill Snyder 22, Bill Adams 16, Ed Cahn 13; Hazleton – Dave Steward 14, Eddie Boran 12, Joe Bruno 11, Ken Wendell 11.[6]

Allentown 76 Bethlehem 46: On Friday night, Allentown trounced Bethlehem after taking 17-11 first quarter and 36-20 halftime leads. The Canaries, by outscoring the Hurricanes in every quarter, snapped Bethlehem's season-long winning streak at 11.

Leading scorers: Allentown – Ed Cahn 21, Bill Snyder 16, LeRoy Katz 16; Bethlehem - Dick Lawrence 14.

Easton 59 Central Catholic 44: Meanwhile, Easton defeated Central Catholic to move into a first-place tie with Bethlehem and deny the Vikings a share of the league lead. Easton led at the end of each quarter with the Vikings briefly tying the game at 14 early in period 2. Fittingly, Easton and Bethlehem were scheduled to meet in their final match of the first half.

Leading scorers: Easton – Lee Smith 18, Ken Werner 16, Don Flad 12; Central Catholic – Don Guman 12, John Unger 12.[7]

Week 4

Easton 48 Bethlehem 39: Easton won the matchup to grab the first half title, which was their first title of any kind in their league history. Jumping out 6-0 at the start of the game and 14-4 at the end of the first quarter, Easton never relinquished the lead in topping Bethlehem.

Leading scorers: Easton - Lee Smith 17; Bethlehem - Bill Miller 11.

Allentown 89 Pottsville 65: In other action, Eddie Cahn set the Little Palestra individual scoring mark besting teammate Bill Snyder's record of 30 earlier in the season against Reading. as Allentown whipped Pottsville. The 89 points also set a team scoring mark for the gym. Cahn made 11 field goals and a remarkable 10 of 10 from the foul line. The Canaries missed only 4 of 27 chances at the foul line. The Canaries took a 25-12 first quarter lead. Gus Prahalis set the visitor individual scoring total in the game.

Leading scorers: Allentown – Eddie Cahn 32 Bill Adams 18, Leroy Katz 15, Bill Snyder 12; Pottsville - Gus Prahalis 29, Paul Barnwell 13.

Hazleton 53 Central Catholic 46: At home, Hazleton won its first game of the league season over Central Catholic. After the two teams tied at 13-13 after a quarter, Hazleton went ahead by three at the half 21-18. With four minutes to play, the Vikings pulled ahead by a point 41-40 before the Mountaineers pulled ahead for the win.

Leading scorers: Hazleton - Ken Wendel 16, Charles Murrin 12, Jim Bruno 11, Don Mitchell 10; Central Catholic – Ed Emery 14, Don Guman 10.[8]

Week 5

Allentown 68 Easton 46: Easton barely had a chance to relish its first title when they met up with Allentown to open second half play. The Canaries served warning that they were a force to be reckoned with during the second half as they beat the Red Rovers. Coach Milo Sewards played his starting five until the near the end of the game. The Canaries jumped out to a 26-10 first quarter lead.

Leading scorers: Allentown - Bill Snyder 17, Bill Adams 16, Ed Cahn 10; Easton - Lee Smith 17.

Central Catholic 65 Pottsville 51: In Pottsville, the two teams were tied four times before the Vikings took a 13-12 first quarter lead. After Pottsville took the halftime lead 31-27, the Vikings' defense stifled Pottsville and held them to only 20 points while scoring 38 themselves.

Leading scorers: Central Catholic – Bobby Feiertag 24, Don Guman 13; Pottsville – Gus Prahalis 20, Paul Barnwell 13.

Bethlehem 47 Hazleton 43: At the Liberty gym, Bethlehem held off a scrappy Hazleton quintet. In a rebuilding mode, Coach Frank Serany started five juniors against Bethlehem. And after trailing by 14 early in the third period, Hazleton closed the gap to four.

Leading scorers: Bethlehem - Charley Hoydu 16; Hazleton – Franny Patton 14, Dave Steward 11.[9]

Allentown 78 Central Catholic 62: Allentown took on Central Catholic at the Little Palestra and the two teams played it tight in the first half with the Canaries taking a 17-16 first quarter lead and 33-32 at the half. Allentown outscored the Vikings 26-14 in the third quarter and took command of the contest.

Leading scorers: Allentown - Bill Snyder 28, Bill Adams 15, Leroy Katz 14, Ed Cahn 12; Central Catholic - Bobby Feiertag 28, Don Guman 15.

Pottsville 62 Bethlehem 44: Coach Eddie Dietsch's Pottsville Maroons shocked visiting Bethlehem with guard Gus Prahalis tallying 19 points. Pottsville led after one quarter 14-8 and never relinquished the lead.

Leading scorers: Pottsville – Gus Prahalis 19, Ron Lyons 14, Paul Barnwell 12; Bethlehem - Dick Lawrence 17, Bill Miller 15.

Easton 52 Hazleton 39: On their home court, the Easton's Red Rovers dropped Hazleton to 0-2 to start second half play. Hazleton had taken a 12-7 first quarter lead, but Don Flad scored Easton's next seven points to even the score at 14. Easton held Hazleton to four points in the second period. Hazleton narrowed Easton's lead to 34-32 after three quarters.

Leading scorers: Easton - Don Flad 18, Lee Smith 11; Hazleton – Franny Patton 12.[10]

Week 6

Easton 46 Pottsville 39: Easton won its second game of the half with a victory over Pottsville and revenged their only first half loss at the hands of the Maroons. Easton led after a quarter 10-7 only to have Pottsville take the halftime lead 25-20. The two teams were tied at 32 after three quarters before Easton rallied in the final quarter.

Leading scorers: Easton - Ken Werner 16, Lee Smith 13, Don Flad 12; Pottsville – Paul Barnwell 12, Ron Lyons 10.

Central Catholic 64 Bethlehem 62: In a thrilling matchup at Rockne Hall, the home team's Ed Emery fired up a long set shot with three seconds left to pull out a win over Bethlehem. After the Vikings took a 23-18 lead, the Hurricane came back to tie the game at 34-34 at the half. Bethlehem took the lead at the three-quarter mark 46-43 before the Vikings rallied for the win.

Leading scorers: Central Catholic - Bobby Feiertag 25, Ed Emery 15, Dick Lawrence 12; Bethlehem -. Bob Rohland 17, Joe Zubia 17, Billy Miller 11.

Allentown 55 Hazleton 54: Allentown stayed undefeated in the second half by pulling out the decision in Hazleton. Hazleton had shot ahead 51-43 in the 4th quarter before Allentown was able to tie the score at 53 all. Bill Snyder sank two foul shots to put the Canaries ahead 55-53. Hazleton's Eddie Boran was fouled with four seconds to go. He converted the first shot, but missed the second to give Allentown its win. The Canaries led at the half 30-27.

Leading scorers: Allentown – Bill Snyder 14, Bill Adams 13, Ed Cahn 11; Hazleton – Eddie Boran 15, Joe Bruno 15, Franny Patton 14.[11]

Week 7

Allentown 77 Bethlehem 61: Eddie Cahn spearheaded Allentown's triumph over longtime rival Bethlehem. Bethlehem took an early 18-11 lead after one quarter only to have the Canaries, led by substitutes Marty Gilbert and Dale Smith, surge to a one-point lead at the half 35-34 The Canaries, undefeated in second half play, continued to pull ahead, leading 55-50 after three quarters, and outscored the Hurricane by 11 in the final quarter.

Leading scorers: Allentown – Ed Cahn 26, Bill Snyder 15, Leroy Katz 11; Bethlehem – Joe Zubia 13, Bill Miller 11, Dick Lawrence 11.[12]

Easton 69 Central Catholic 50: Easton stayed a game off the pace with only a single loss by taking down Central Catholic on the Vikings' home floor. Easton's big second quarter, outscoring the Vikings 24-12, propelled the Red Rovers to the win. Easton led at the half 38-23.

Leading scorers: Easton - Lee Smith 26, Glenn Sheats 14; Central Catholic - Bobby Feiertag 12, Eric Spinosa 11, Dick Lawrence 11.[13]

Hazleton 47 Pottsville 45: Hazleton entered the win column with a narrow victory over Pottsville. Before Hazleton's last quarter rally, Pottsville had led after each of the first three quarters, 14-9, 30-19, and 39-36.

Leading scorers: Hazleton - Joe Bruno 12; Pottsville – Gus Prahalis 11.[14]

Pottsville 76 Allentown 62: Playing their second game of the week, Allentown's title appeared to be a lock. However, Pottsville thought otherwise and led at halftime 38-25. The Canaries narrowed the Maroon's lead to 52-49 when they outscored Pottsville 24-14 in the third quarter. Pottsville blitzed the Canaries 24-13 in the fourth quarter for a decisive win.

Leading scorers: Pottsville - Gus Prahalis 22, Paul Barnwell 22, Ron Lyons 11, Jack Houser 10; Allentown - Bill Adams 22.

Bethlehem 57 Easton 41: Bethlehem knocked off the Red Rovers to give Allentown the 2nd half title. Trailing by four points at the half 26-22, Easton rallied to tie the score at 38 after 3 quarters. However, Easton lost its scoring touch in the final period and could only muster 3 points to Bethlehem's 19.

Leading scorers: Bethlehem – Billy Miller 19; Easton – Don Flad 13.

Central Catholic 83 Hazleton 59: At Rockne Hall, Central Catholic took a 15-point lead into the locker room at halftime and added to it in the second half for an easy win over Hazleton.

Leading scorers: Central Catholic – Ed Emery 21, Bobby Feiertag 19, Eric Spinosa 14, Don Guman 11; Hazleton - Franny Patton 24.[15]

League Championship

Allentown 56 Easton 53: Since Easton won the first half and Allentown the second half, Milo Seward's Canaries met Vern Fegley's Rovers at Rockne Hall for the league title with 3600 fans jammed onto the gym. After trailing 19-10 early in the second quarter, the Red Rovers clawed their way back into the contest reducing the deficit to 3 at the half 27-24. Easton's roll continued early in the 3rd quarter and they took a four-point lead 31-27. By the end of the 3rd quarter, Allen fought back to take a 37-35 edge. The lead seesawed back and forth in the last quarter. The game ended regulation in a 50-50 tie after Easton's Lee Smith missed a last second shot. In the three-minute overtime, the Canaries outscored Easton 6-3 to win their 10th league title. This left Easton still looking for its first league title.

Leading scorers: Allentown – Ed Cahn 15, Dale Smith 12, Bill Adams 11; Easton – Ken Werner 17, Don Flad 12, Lee Smith 11.[16]

Postseason Play

Allentown 74 Palmerton 55: With their league title in hand, the Canaries were pitted against Bill Wilhelm's Palmerton Blue Bombers in district play. With center Bill Snyder playing the entire game, Allentown took an early lead 18-9 after one quarter and never trailed as they defeated Palmerton. The Canaries finished the night by outscoring the Blue Bombers 21-13 in the fourth quarter. This set up a District XI title match with St. Clair at the Penn Palestra.

Leading scorers: Allentown-Bill Snyder 24, Bill Adams 20; Palmerton-Bob Steinmetz 13, Harry Mihalik 11[17]

Allentown 103 St. Clair 55: Billy Adams set an unofficial district scoring record with 30 points to lead the Canaries to a whopping victory. Allentown jumped to a 15-0 lead as they became the first high school or collegiate team to score over 100 points in the Penn Palestra. The Canaries won their second consecutive District XI title and sixth overall.

Leading scorers: Allentown - Bill Snyder 24, Leroy Katz 14, Ed Cahn 12, Don Wentling 12; St. Clair – Anthony Dunlosky 19, George Yanek 17, Emil Platchko 11.[18]

Allentown 50 Radnor 48: Back at the Penn Palestra, Allentown won their first interdistrict match over Radnor. With the score was tied 27 all at the half, Allentown took a one-point lead after three periods. Radnor lost two of its starters, John Queen and Charley Barrick in the closing minutes of the game and Allentown held on to win.

Leadings scorers: Allentown - Ed Cahn 16, Leroy Katz 14; Radnor – Howard Aigeldinger 15, Dave Heller 14.[19]

Allentown 68 Swoyersville 44: The Eastern Final pitted the Canaries against Swoyersville, the North League champions from Luzerne County, in Hershey. After a 4-4 tie early in the first quarter, the Canaries took the lead and outscored Swoyersville in every quarter for a rather easy Eastern final victory. Over 6000 fans including Pennsylvania Governor John S. Fine, watched the Canaries put on a show of basketball skill. Now only Farrell stood between Allentown and its 5th state title.

Leading scorers: Allentown – Bill Snyder 22, Leroy Katz 17, Bill Adams 13; Swoyersville – Joe Holup 17, Stan Schultz 10.[20]

Allentown 66 Farrell 55: Four players scored in double figures as the Canaries handled Jim McCoy and his Farrell teammates. The 66 points eclipsed the prior championship game record of 60 points by Aliquippa in 1949. The game was won on the foul line with Allentown converting 28 of 37 while Farrell only shot 24 and made only 15. Allentown captured its 5th (with two vacated) and the league its 8th state title in 26 years of existence!

Leading scorers: Allentown – Bill Snyder 20, Ed Cahn 16, Leroy Katz 12, Bill Adams 10; Farrell – Julius McCoy 18, Tony Knott 13, Marion Lampkins 10.[21]

Postseason Accolades

Leading scorers: Although Pottsville finished near the bottom of the league, Gus Prahalis, their outstanding guard, won the league scoring title with 196 points averaging 17.7 points per game. Eddie Cahn of Allentown finished second with 163 points. They were followed by: Bob Fiertag, Central, 156 points; Bill Snyder, Allentown, 155 points; Lee Smith, Easton, 152 points; Paul Barnwell, Pottsville, 133 points; Don Flad, Easton, 122 points; Bill Adams, Allentown, 121 points; Dick Lawrence, Bethlehem, 119 points; and Bill Miller, Bethlehem, 116 points. Dick Lawrence's 34 points against Pottsville during the first half matchup was the single game high and tied the league record set by Frank Serany of Hazleton in 1929.[23]

All-State: Several league players received all-state recognition. Bill Snyder, Allentown, was named to the 2nd Team; Gus Prahalis, Pottsville, 3rd team; Ed Cahn, Allentown, 4th Team; and Lee Smith, Easton, 5th Team. Honorable mention included Bill Adams, Allentown; Paul Barnwell, Pottsville; Bob Feiertag, Central; Don Flad, Easton; and Dick Lawrence, Bethlehem.[24]

Final Standings

First Half		Second Half		Overall	
Easton	4-1	Allentown	4-1	Allentown	7-3
Allentown	3-2	Easton	3-2	Easton	7-3
Bethlehem	3-2	Central Catholic	3-2	Bethlehem	5-5
Central Catholic	2-3	Bethlehem	2-3	Central Catholic	5-5
Pottsville	2-3	Pottsville	2-3	Pottsville	4-6
Hazleton	1-4	Hazleton	1-4	Hazleton	2-8

Team Rosters

Allentown: Coach Milo Sewards, William Adams, Edward Cahn, Martin Gilbert, LeRoy Katz, Jerry Kerschner, Arthur McAfee, William Schmidt, James Passaro, Charles Puskas, William Schmidt, William Schuryn, Dale Smith, William Snyder, Robert Stinner, Pat Wanish, Donald Wentling

Bethlehem: Coach Joe Preletz, Patrick Albanese, Don Bittenbender, Henry Durkop, Carmen Gallo, Charley Hoydu, Dick Lawrence, Billy Miller, Bill Rogers, Bob Rohland, Joe Zubia

Central Catholic: Coach Joe Petro, John DiRocco, Peter Ebner, Edward Emrey, Robert Feiertag, Joseph Green, Donald Guman, Joseph Guman, Thomas Hall, Charles Lawrence, Thomas Magill, Harry McAndrew, John McDonald, Bernard McGarr, John O'Donnell, John Schaffer, Connie Spinosa, Ercalo Spinosa, Don Sullivan, John Unger, William Wagner, Joseph Weber, Walter Yaros

Easton: Coach Vern Fegley, Robert Catlin, Dale Dauscher, Kenneth Fahl, Don Flad, Elmer Hay, Charles Heller, David Kline, Jim Parnell, Glenn Sheats, Lee Smith, Stan Sutphen, William Tate, Gus Voyagis, Ken Werner

Hazleton: Coach Frank Serany, Eddie Boran, Joe Bruno, Joe Goffa, Jim Griesing, Joe Grosskettler, Joseph "Chippy" Kender, Jack Kokinda, Joe Lona, Don Mitchell, Charles Murrin, Franny Patton, Joe Polchin, Eddie Richie, Mike Ross, Charlie Schlenker, Louie Smith, Dave Steward, Bob Watro, Ken Wendell

Pottsville: Coach Ed Dietch, Lester Alston, Paul Barnwell, Emerson Carter, Jack Dougherty, Albert "Buddy" Francis, Jack Houser, Bill Keeny, Ron Lyons, Jack McDonald, Joe Motta, Phil Mascarsa, Gus Prahalis

Allentown High School – 1951 League and State Champions[22]

Front: James Passaro, William Adams, William Schmidt, Charles Puskas, William Snyder, Pat Wanish, Martin Gilbert, LeRoy Katz. Back: James Wittman (Mgr), William Schuryn, Edward Cahn, Robert Stinner, Donald Wentling, Coach Sewards, Arthur McAfee, Dale Smith, Jerry Kershner, Asst Coach Paul Clymer

1952

Another State Title (PCIAA)

At the league meeting after the 1951 season, Phil Phillipi, Bethlehem, was re-elected as president of the league. Stanley Steigerwalt, Easton, was re-elected as vice president as well as Edgar Rabenold, Allentown, as league secretary-treasurer.[1] At the pre-season meeting on December 13 at Shankweiler's Hotel in Fogelsville, the league announced that all junior varsity games must start by 6:30 pm followed by the varsity games promptly at 8 pm. Allentown Central Catholic was again ruled ineligible to participate in the PIAA playoffs. If they won the league title, the second-place school would move on to the playoffs. Broadcast rights were also discussed and it was decided that each school to permit broadcasts of games in their building. Bethlehem High School was requested to replace it outmoded scoreboard.[2]

Week 1

Easton 50 Hazleton 42: Opening its season in Easton, Hazleton, a pre-season league favorite, lost to the Red Rovers. The first and third quarters created the winning margin for Easton with the Red Rovers outscoring Hazleton 14-8 and 16-6 in those periods. Easton led 42-31 heading into the fourth quarter. This was Easton's third consecutive victory over Hazleton.

Leading scorers: Easton - Ken Werner 15; Hazleton - Nick Polivka 10.

Bethlehem 61 Allentown 53: Allentown's state champs found little respect in their league opener. Allentown led only once in the game at 6-5. Bethlehem took control of the game by outscoring the Canaries 20-8 in the third period. Bethlehem went into a semi-freeze at the end of the game to preserve the victory.

Leading scorers: Bethlehem – Billy Miller 15, Bobby Gall 15, Henry Durkop 13, Charley Hoydu 10; Allentown – LeRoy Katz 17, Martin Gilbert 12.

Central Catholic 73 Pottsville 60: Central Catholic also had a big 3rd period in outscoring Pottsville 26-12 enroute to a triumph over Pottsville. Pottsville led after the 1st quarter 17-16 before the Vikings took charge.

Leading scorers: Central Catholic - Joe Ludrof 22, Ed Emery 19, John Schaffer 19; Pottsville - Gus Prahalis 16, Bill Keeny 15, Emerson Carter 13.[3]

Week 2

Allentown 65 Pottsville 43: The Canaries bounced back behind Leroy Katz's 22 points as they defeated Pottsville in the Little Palestra in front of a packed house with 2200 fans. Allentown jumped out to a 34-12 lead allowing Pottsville only three field goals in the first half.

Leading scorers: Allentown – Leroy Katz 22, Martin Gilbert 14, Dale Smith 14; Pottsville - Gus Prahalis 12.

Bethlehem 51 Easton 42: Bethlehem won its second game over Easton to keep pace with Central Catholic. The Red Rovers held the lead 33-32 after three quarters only to see Bethlehem outscore them 19-9 in the final stanza.

Leading scorers: Bethlehem – Bobby Gall 21, Charley Hoydu 10; Easton - Ken Werner 19.

Central Catholic 64 Hazleton 49: Central Catholic, on the Rockne Hall floor, took a hard-fought game from Hazleton. An estimated 800 Hazleton students made the trip to cheer on the Mountaineers. After holding a 17-12 first quarter lead, Hazleton could only score 9 points to the Vikings 23 in the second quarter and relinquished a lead that they never got back.

Leading scorers: Central Catholic – Ed Emery 20, Joe Ludrof 13, Harry McAndrew 11; Hazleton – Bob Watro 14, John Ancharski 14.[4]

Week 3

Central Catholic 62 Allentown 51: With two contests scheduled for the league in the week, Central Catholic, despite a 19-4 deficit in the first quarter, roared back to defeat Allentown at the Little Palestra after eight consecutive losses. The Vikings switched into a zone defense to begin the second quarter that led to an amazing second quarter rally and a 31-29 lead at the half.

Leading scorers: Central Catholic - Harry McAndrews 23, Johnny Schaffer 15, Ed Emery 12; Allentown - LeRoy Katz 23.

Bethlehem 54 Hazleton 52: Bethlehem kept pace with a last second thriller at Hazleton. Behind three points, Hazleton's Wendel made a field and a foul shot with 7 seconds left in the game to tie it a 52. Bobby Gall gained control of a jump ball at the Bethlehem foul line and made the shot which went through the hoop as the gun sounded for the two-point win.

Leading scorers: Bethlehem – Bobby Gall 14, Billy Miller 12; Hazleton – Jack Kokinda 18, Bob Watro 15.

Easton 64 Pottsville 35: On their home court, Easton ran over Pottsville by dominating the Maroons in the middle two quarters 36-15. Gus Prahalis scored all 10 points for the Maroons in the first quarter.

Leading scorers: Easton – Glenn Sheats 17, Ken Werner 16, Elmer Hay 11; Pottsville – Gus Prahalis 20.[5]

Allentown 57 Hazleton 55 OT: Allentown traveled to Hazleton and barely escaped with a win. Hazleton led by 18 points with two minutes to play in the third quarter. The Canaries rallied to close the gap. Hazleton lost two starters to fouls, Watro and Ancharski, and Allentown lost center Dale Smith right after he pulled the Canaries within a point 51-50. Barry Wilson replaced Smith and was fouled. He missed the first shot but sank the second to tie the game with 30 seconds to play. Neither team could score and the game went into overtime. Allentown outscored Hazleton 6-4 in the extra period to pull out a miraculous win.

Leading scorers: Allentown – LeRoy Katz 18, Franklin Reinhardt 12, Dale Smith 11; Hazleton – Bob Watro 13, Franny Patton 12, Jack Kokinda 10, John Ancharski 10.[6]

Bethlehem 57 Pottsville 39: Bethlehem continued its winning ways over lowly Pottsville. Tied at 21 at the half, Bethlehem pulled away outscoring the Maroons 19-6 in the third quarter. Pottsville held 10-6 lead after a quarter.

Leading scorers: Bethlehem - Bobby Gall 14, Billy Miller 14, Joe Zaun 11; Pottsville - Gus Prahalis 15, Bill Keeny 10.

Central Catholic 48 Easton 43: Easton employed a deliberate style of play in an attempt to upset Central Catholic. Despite Easton's stalling tactics which kept the score low, 8-6 after one quarter, Central Catholic maintained the lead throughout the game. After the Vikings led 24-12 at the half, the Red Rovers battled back to within four points 36-32 after three quarters. Central Catholic remained unbeaten in league play.

Leading scorers: Central Catholic – Ed Emery 21, Joe Ludrof 12; Easton - Stan Sutphen 14.[7]

Week 5

Bethlehem 62 Central Catholic 55: The first half of the season ended with a match between the two unblemished teams. Trailing 36-25 at the half, Bethlehem dazzled the overflow crowd at the Liberty gym by outscoring the Vikings 25-10 in the third period. Bethlehem went into the lead at 42-41 in the 3rd quarter on Carmen Gallo's two foul shots. The Liberty boys won the first half title with the victory over the Vikings.

Leading scorers: Bethlehem- Billy Miller 22, Bobby Gall 11, Charley Hoydu 10; Central Catholic– Ed Emery 14, Joe Ludrof 12.

Pottsville 54 Hazleton 53: In a battle of winless teams, Pottsville prevailed after trailing 41-36 after three quarters. Pottsville had led after each of the first two quarters 15-11 and 28-25 before Hazleton charged into the lead.

Leading scorers: Pottsville - Gus Prahalis 23, Bill Keeny 12; Hazleton – Mike Melfi 17, Bob Watro 14, Jack Kokinda 11.[8]

Easton 50 Allentown 49: In the remaining game, Easton surprised Allentown at the Easton gym. The Canaries went cold in the 4th quarter and could not score for more than six minutes. Allentown led 43-36 heading into the final quarter. Werner scored 19 for Easton and LeRoy Katz 20 in the loss. The win gave Easton third place over Allentown who finished in fourth place.

Leading scorers: Easton – Ken Werner 19, Ken Fahl 10; Allentown – LeRoy Katz 20, Martin Gilbert 12, Franklin Reinhardt 10.[9]

Week 6

Bethlehem 54 Allentown 53: The second half opened up with a thrilling matchup between Allentown and Bethlehem. Bethlehem prevailed with a one-point victory. Bethlehem held the lead only once briefly in the first half 8-7. Bethlehem trailed 29-22 at the half despite Billy Miller's set shot from at least 43 feet at the buzzer to end the half. On the strength of 11 unanswered points in the 3rd quarter, Bethlehem was able to tie the score at 43 after three quarters. Bethlehem outscored the Canaries 11-10 in the final period to win.

Leading scorers: Bethlehem-Billy Miller 18, Charley Hoydu 12; Allentown-LeRoy Katz 19, Pete Brantley 11.

Central Catholic 69 Pottsville 48: Central Catholic jumped out to a 32-12 halftime lead. Pottsville came back to outscore the Vikings 22-20 in the third period but could get no closer as Central Catholic prevailed.

Leading scorers: Central Catholic- Ed Emery 21, Joe Ludrof 14, Thomas Hall 11; Pottsville– Jack Dougherty 14, Bill Keeny 11.

Hazleton 33 Easton 30: In a low scoring affair, Hazleton managed to win its first game of the league season over Easton. The teams were tied 8-8 after the first quarter with the Mountaineers jumping into the lead 20-14 at the half. Trailing by seven heading into the fourth quarter, Easton rallied but fell short.

Leading scorers: Hazleton – Jack Kokinda 10; Easton - Stan Sutphen 9.[10]

Week 7

Easton 59 Bethlehem 58: Easton surprised the Hurricane with a 59-58 nail biter as Ken Werner scored 20 points to lead the Rovers. Suffering their first league loss of the season, it was Bethlehem's second loss to Easton since the Red Rovers had defeated them in the Lehigh Valley Invitational Tournament over the Christmas holidays. Bethlehem lost four starters to fouls in the second half: Chuck Hoydu, Henry Durkop, Bobby Gall, and Bill Gallo.

Leading scorers: Easton – Ken Werner 20, Elmer Hay 17; Bethlehem – Henry Durkop 16, Bobby Gall 10, Bill Miller 10, Joe Zaun 10.

Central Catholic 67 Hazleton 58: Central Catholic stood alone at the top as they won their matchup with Hazleton. Hazleton took a 6-0 lead in the game before the Vikings came back to tie the game after the first quarter 11-11. The Vikings took the lead in the second quarter and never gave it up.

Leading scorers: Central Catholic – Joe Ludrof 21, Ed Emery 14, John Schaffer 13; Hazleton – Franny Patton 20, Jack Kokinda 11.

Allentown 85 Pottsville 42: At Pottsville, Allentown showed no mercy on the Maroons. After the Canaries rolled out to 19-8 and 36-18 after the first two quarters, they dumped an additional 30 points on Pottsville while holding them to 9 in the third quarter.

Leading scorers: Allentown - LeRoy Katz 31, Pete Brantley 11; Pottsville – Gus Prahalis 19.[11]

Week 8

Allentown 61 Central Catholic 44: Each team played two games during the week. Unfortunately, Central Catholic, in front of 3600 fans at Rockne Hall, was knocked off its lofty perch. The Canaries held the Vikings' Harry McAndrew to five points after having scored 23 in their first matchup. Allentown outscored Central Catholic 17-6 in the final period to seal the victory.

Leading scorers: Allentown – LeRoy Katz 24, Pete Brantley 13; Central Catholic – Ed Emery 14.

Easton 57 Pottsville 53: Although Pottsville was winless, they gave Easton a scare before the Red Rovers won at Pottsville. Leading 46-41 heading into the final quarter, Easton fell behind 49-48 midway through the quarter as Gus Prahalis pumped in 12 points in the quarter to lead the Maroon rally. Pottsville led again 53-51 before Ken Werner put Easton ahead for good 54-53 on a field goal and foul shot.

Leading scorers: Easton - Glenn Sheats 17, Ken Werner 14; Pottsville - Gus Prahalis 20, Jack Dougherty 12, Jack McDonald 10.

Bethlehem 69 Hazleton 62: Bethlehem knocked off Hazleton despite Billy Miller being held scoreless until midway through the third period and only scoring six points in the game. Gallo, Hoydu, and Dorkup picked up the scoring slack with 17, 14, and 12 points respectively. Bethlehem, Easton, Allentown, and Central all had a share of the second half lead.

Leading scorers: Bethlehem – Carmen Gallo 17, Charley Hoydu 14, Henry Durkop 12, Bobby Gall 10; Hazleton – Nick Polivka 18, Joe Polchin 14.[12]

Central Catholic 56 Easton 53: In a "must" game for both teams, Central Catholic knocked Easton out of a share of the lead. The Vikings took a commanding 50-35 lead into the 4th quarter only to see Easton rally, outscoring them 18-6, to make the game close at the end. The Vikings led 32-28 at halftime.[13]

Leading scorers: Central Catholic–Ed Emery 14, Joe Ludrof 11, Harry McAndrew 11, Thomas Hall 10; Easton–Ken Werner 26.

Bethlehem 96 Pottsville 75: In Bethlehem's win over Pottsville, Billy Miller set a new league single game scoring record. With the score at 66-65 in Bethlehem's favor after 3 quarters, Bethlehem outscored the Maroons 30-10 in the final quarter to cruise to the win. Bethlehem took a one-point lead in the first quarter 25-24 with each team scoring 20 and 21 points in the middle two quarters.

Leading scorers: Bethlehem – Billy Miller 38, Bobby Gall 16, Dick Palenchar 11, Carmen Gallo 10; Pottsville – Gus Prahalis 31, Jack McDonald 13, Bill Keeny 10, Jack Dougherty 10.

Allentown 64 Hazleton 49: Hazleton hung with Allentown for three quarters before the Canaries clicked in the 4th period. Allentown led 16-15 after the first quarter with Hazleton tying the score at the half 29-29. Allentown took back a one-point lead before outscoring the Mountaineers by 14 points in the fourth quarter.

Leading scorers: Allentown - LeRoy Katz 18, Dale Smith 14; Hazleton – Franny Patton 17.[14]

Week 9

Bethlehem 82 Central Catholic 57: In the final week of the season, Bethlehem knocked Central Catholic out of the second half title picture with a victory at Rockne Hall with over 3600 fans in attendance. Six Liberty players scored in double figures. Bethlehem outscored the Vikings in all four quarters.

Leading scorers: Bethlehem – Frank Palenchar 17, Billy Miller 13, Carmen Gallo 11, Charley Hoydu 10, Bobby Gall 10, Joe Zaun 10; Central Catholic – Ed Emery 20, Harry McAndrew 12, Thomas Hall 10.[15]

Allentown 67 Easton 39: Allentown won their final second half match over Easton as Leroy Katz set a new league season scoring record. He broke Gus Prahalis's previous mark of 176 points set the previous year. Katz scored 211 points in the 10 league games. The Canaries had a ten-point advantage in the second period and thirteen in the final quarter to roll to the win,

Leading scorers: Allentown – LeRoy Katz 19, Dale Smith 15; Easton – Elmer Hay 11.

Pottsville 61 Hazleton 55: Meanwhile, Prahalis also bettered his own mark as he scored 179 points in only 9 games in the victory over Hazleton. After trailing 49-36 after three periods, Hazleton rallied to trail by four 49-45 before Pottsville sealed the victory. Hazleton was only able to win a single game during the season which easily represented their worst record in league play.

Leading scorers: Pottsville – Gus Prahalis 23, Jack Dougherty 17; Hazleton – Franny Patton 19, Nick Polivka 11.[16]

Second Half Championship

Allentown 58 Bethlehem 53: Since they ended up tied for the second half, Allentown and Bethlehem squared off for the second half title at the Penn Palestra before 7500 fans. Allentown beat Bethlehem to force a second playoff game for the overall league title for the season. Bethlehem led 27-26 going into the second half of the contest. Johnny Wescoe, who replaced starter Franklin Reinhardt when he fouled out near the end of the first half, sparked Allentown's second half offense. In the third and fourth quarters, Allentown scored 16 points in each quarter while Bethlehem scored thirteen in each.

Leading scorers: Allentown - LeRoy Katz 13, Dale Smith 12, Johnny Wescoe 10; Bethlehem – Billy Miller 19.[17]

League Championship

Bethlehem 52 Allentown 44: The league championship game, played at Hershey Sports Arena with 7000 in attendance, saw Bethlehem gain revenge for the league crown. Led by Bobby Gall with 17 points and Billy Miller with 11, Bethlehem led throughout the game and scored their third win in four games against the Canaries. Bethlehem's eight-point margin 16-8 in the first quarter was the difference in the game.

Leading scorers: Bethlehem – Bobby Gall 17, Billy Miller 11; Allentown – LeRoy Katz 20, Johnny Wescoe 10[18]

Postseason Play

Bethlehem 62 Mahanoy City 47: At Rockne Hall, Bethlehem's first opponent in the District XI playoffs was an old league foe, Mahanoy City. Led by Hank Durkop's 20 points, the Hurricane prevailed for the victory. Mahanoy City, the Black Diamond League champs, played Bethlehem on even terms during the first half and trailed by on 4, 29-25, but could not keep pace in the second half.

Leading scorers: Bethlehem–Henry Durkop 20, Bobby Gall 15, Bill Miller 15; Mahanoy City–Titus Puck 14, Joe Troskosky 13'[20]

Catasauqua 56 Bethlehem 52: Catasauqua, with their 16th consecutive win, ended Bethlehem's post season hopes as they won their first District XI title with the victory at the Penn Palestra with 8300 fans in attendance. Coach Bob Mushrush's team was led by guard Bobby Wert who scored 10 points in the first half. The game was close throughout with a 14 all tie at the end of the first quarter and Catasauqua leading 30-28 at the half and 39-38 at the third quarter mark.

Leading scorers: Catasauqua – Bobby Wert 14, Ken James 12; Bethlehem – Henry Durkop 12, Billy Miller 11, Joe Gallo 10.[21]

PCIAA Playoffs

Central Catholic 62 Reading Central Catholic 51: Central Catholic entered the PCIAA playoffs against the defending state PCIAA champions Reading Central Catholic. Scoring 24 points in the third quarter, Reading moved ahead 44-42 heading into the fourth quarter. Central Catholic countered by outscoring Reading 20-13 in the quarter and moved on with its win at Allentown's Little Palestra. Joe Ludrof scored 15 points in the last period.

Leading scorers: Central Catholic – Joe Ludrof 22, Ed Emery 21; Reading Central Catholic – Gerry Kane 14, Jim Larkin 13, Bob Fahlin 11.[22]

Central Catholic 56 Harrisburg Catholic 44: Some 1200 spectators watched Central Catholic take on Harrisburg Catholic at Smith Hall in Slatington. Led by Joe Ludrof's 19 points and Charlie Lawrence's 16, Central easily won the matchup 56-44 despite slowdown tactics used by the Harrisburg area quintet.

Leading scorers: Central Catholic – Joe Ludrof 19, Charlie Lawrence 16, Ed Emery 10; Harrisburg Catholic – Bruno "Pete" DiMartile 16, James Forjan 12, Raymond Naccarrato 10.[23]

Central Catholic 75 St. Rose 45: Coach Joe Petro's Vikings scored 10 consecutive points in the second quarter after having been tied 20-20 early in the quarter and cruised to a win over St. Rose of Carbondale at Rockne Hall in front of 3000 fans. The win gave them the Eastern PCIAA championship. Ed Emery and Joe Ludrof each scored 20 in the rout of the Scranton Diocese champions. St. Rose's center Fran O'Malley, who had over 30 scholarship offers from colleges throughout the nation, led all scorers.

Leading scorers: Central Catholic – Joe Ludrof 20, Ed Emery 20, Charlie Lawrence 13; St. Rose – Fran O'Malley 27, Mike Murnin 10. [24]

Central Catholic 49 Pittsburgh Central Catholic 39: Playing on their home court for the state PCIAA title, Central Catholic struggled for three quarters and trailed Pittsburgh Central Catholic 32-31 at the start of the final period. Tommy Hall, a substitute forward sparked the Vikings in the 4th quarter and scored 10 points in the game, most of them in the final stanza. Holding Pittsburgh to five points in the final quarter, the Vikings scored eighteen to win their fourth PCIAA state title.

Leading scorers: Central Catholic – Joe Ludrof 16, Ed Emery 11, Thomas Hall 10; Pittsburgh Central Catholic – Tom Smith 15, Fran Quinlan 13.[25]

Postseason Accolades

Leading Scorers: In addition to the league record-setting LeRoy Katz, 211 points, other leading scorers included: Gus Prahalis, Pottsville, 179 points; Ed Emery, Central Catholic, 171 points; Billy Miller, Bethlehem, 154 points; Ken Werner, Easton, 146 points; Bobby Gall, Bethlehem, 128 points; Joe Ludrof, Central Catholic, 118 points.[27]

All-Stars: The Hazleton Plain Speaker's all-league team included LeRoy Katz, Allentown; Gus Prahalis, Pottsville; Ed Emery, Central Catholic, Billy Miller, Bethlehem; and Joe Polchin, Hazleton on the first team. The second team consisted of Ken Werner, Easton; Bobby Gall and Charlie Hoydu, Bethlehem, and John Schaeffer, Central Catholic.[28]

All-State: The UPI All-Pennsylvania Scholastic Team included Billy Miller, Bethlehem, 1st team; Leroy Katz, Allentown, 2nd team, and Gus Prahalis, Pottsville, 3rd team[29]

Final Standings

First Half		Second Half		Overall	
Bethlehem	5-0	Allentown	4-1	Bethlehem	9-1
Central Catholic	4-1	Bethlehem	4-1	Central Catholic	7-3
Easton	3-2	Central Catholic	3-2	Allentown	6-4
Allentown	2-3	Easton	2-3	Easton	5-5
Pottsville	1-4	Pottsville	1-4	Pottsville	2-8
Hazleton	0-5	Hazleton	1-4	Hazleton	1-9

Team Rosters

Allentown: Coach Milo Sewards, Don Bearly, Pete Brantley, Melvin Geho, Martin Gilbert, Dick Jones, LeRoy Katz, Art McAfee, Billy Parks, Franklin Reinhardt, Bruce Rodenberger, Willie Shuryn, Dale Smith, Jim Snyder, John Wescoe, Barry Wilson

Bethlehem: Coach Joe Preletz, Henry Durkop, Bob Gall, Joe Gallo, Frank Gerencser, Charley Hoydu, Bill Miller, Dick Palenchar, Joe Zaun

Central Catholic: Coach Joe Petro, Alex DeLucia, John Dugan, Pete Ebner, James Egizio, Ed Emery, Joe Guman, Tom Hall, Bob Hamrick, Charles Lawrence, Joe Ludrof, Harry McAndrew, John McDonald, Jack O'Donnell, John Schaffer, Eric Spinosa, John Unger, William Wagner

Easton: Coach Vern Fegley, Bob Catlin, Kenny Fahl, Wayne "Knobby" Grube, Bob Harling, Watson "Spec" Hart, Elmer Hay, Glenn Sheats, Stan Sutphen, Bill Tate, Gus Voyagis, Kenny Werner

Hazleton: Coach Frank Serany, John Ancharski, Ron Gatski, Jim Greising, Jack Kokinda, Mike Melfi, Don Mitchell, Fred Patterson, Franny Patton, Joe Polchin, Nick Polivka, Eddie Richie, Mike Ross, Charley Schlenker, Bob Watro, Ken Wendell, Charlie Zack

Pottsville: Coach Ed Dietch, John Bender, Emerson Carter, Ken Diehl, William Dougherty, Albert "Buddy" Francis, Jack Houser, William Keeny, Charles Lord, Jack McDonald, Joe Motta, Gus Prahalis, John Sidler

Bethlehem High School – 1952 League Champions[19]

Front: Coach Preletz, Henry Durkop, Charley Hoydu, Bobby Gall, Carmen Gallo, Billy Miller

Back: George Jenkins, Bob Rich, Ed Szvetecz, Dick Palenchar, Joe Zaun, Dave Preletz

Central Catholic High School - 1952 PCIAA State Champions[26]

Left to Right: Coach Petro, John Unger, Eric Spinosa, Charlie Lawrence, Thomas Hall, Joe Ludrof, Edward Emery, Jack O'Donnell, Jack McDonald, John Schaffer, Harry McAndrew, James Harbor (asst coach); Kneeling: Bill Miller (mgr)

1953

Williamsport Seeks League Entry

At the league meeting at Shankweiler's Hotel in Fogelsville, the league representatives elected Edgar Rabenold, an Allentown High School teacher, for a 27th term as the league's secretary and treasurer. Phil Phillippi, Bethlehem High School athletic director, was re-elected to his 11th term as league president. Easton's athletic director Stanley Steigerwalt was re-elected as vice president. During the meeting, Williamsport High School again voiced a desire to enter the league. An off-the-record vote (4-2) turned down their request. No action was taken since Williamsport had not submitted a formal written request. The Lehigh Valley schools opposed their entry due to the travel distance. Pottsville and Hazleton favored their entry as a seventh school in the league.[1] At a pre-season meeting in mid-December, Williamsport filed its formal application to join the league. The league representatives discussed a number of issues including inter-district (since they were members of District 4), travel, and scheduling problems. The application was tabled until the spring meeting.[2]

Week 1

Hazleton 83 Central Catholic 51: On its home court, Hazleton entered league play undefeated with expectation of being a force in the league in 1953. Hazleton jumped out to a 18-9 lead after one quarter, 42-21 at halftime, and were never headed in a thrashing of Central Catholic.

Leading scorers: Hazleton – Nick Polivka 20, Lou Hill 19, Bob Watro 17, Mike Melfi 12; Central Catholic - Alex DeLucia 15, Charlie Lawrence 13.

Easton 46 Bethlehem 42: Easton's Elmer Hay limited Bobby Gall to six points as Easton surprised Bethlehem handing the Hurricanes their first loss of the season. Easton's coach Chuck Brown employed a four-man zone with Hay playing man-to-man on Gall. Gall had four personal fouls in the first half and fouled out with three minutes to play. Hay fouled out a minute later, but had done his duty in throttling Gall for most of the game. Bethlehem had beaten Easton (82-48) in non-league play at the Lehigh Valley Invitational Tournament over the holidays.

Leading scorers: Easton – Elmer Hay 10, Tom Georgaris 10, Watson Hart 10; Bethlehem – Ed Szvetecz 13.

Allentown 64 Pottsville 57: Although it was close the whole way, Milo Seward's Canaries led the whole game and defeated Pottsville. Allentown led at the half 32-22, but Pottsville cut the lead to 48-42 after three quarters.

Leading scorers: Allentown – Melvin Geho 18, Johnny Wescoe 13; Pottsville – Jack Houser 19, Bill Dougherty 14.[3]

Allentown 73 Bethlehem 68: Opening the league season with two games during the first week, Allentown traveled to Bethlehem and handed them their second consecutive loss. John Mascali replaced starter Dale Smith early in the second quarter to lead the scoring attack for the Canaries. The game was not as close as the final score indicated. Bobby Gall bounced back from his off night earlier in the week.

Leading scorers: Allentown – John Mascali 20, Mel Geho 17, Franklin Reinhardt 17; Bethlehem – Bob Gall 24, Ed Szvetecz 10, Jim Bauder 10.

Pottsville 90 Central Catholic 63: In Pottsville, the Maroons routed Central Catholic despite the score being close at the half 38-32. The Vikings were outscored in the second half 52-30.

Leading scorers: Pottsville – Jack Houser 35, Jim Boyer 19, Henry Ludwig 13, Bill Keeny 12; Central Catholic – Alex DeLucia 29, Eric Spinosa 13.

Hazleton 52 Easton 49: Frank Serany's Mountaineers traveled to Easton and chalked up a win over the Red Rovers. Easton had led at halftime 28-21 only to see Hazleton pull into the lead in the third quarter by scoring 20 to the Red Rovers 11 points. Allentown and Hazleton were tied at 2-0 to lead the circuit.

Leading scorers: Hazleton – Bob Watro 22, Nick Polivka 13: Easton – Elmer Hay 18, Watson Hart 10.[4]

Week 2

Allentown 64 Hazleton 55: Allentown and Hazleton squared off at the new St. Joseph's gym in Hazleton, with 3300 screaming fans in attendance, for sole possession of first place. After leading by 15 points in the third quarter, the Canaries had to fight off a closing drive by Hazleton to earn the victory. This snapped Hazleton's 10 game win streak to start the season. Allentown had snapped Coatesville's 10-game streak earlier in the week. Nine Canary players scored in the contest.

Leading scorers: Allentown – Mel Geho 17, Pete Brantley 10; Hazleton – Bob Watro 23, Charlie Zack 11, Jack Kokinda 10.

Bethlehem 88 Pottsville 75: With Bobby Gall scoring 17 points in the 4th quarter and a league record 45 in the game, Bethlehem finally entered the win column in league play over Pottsville. Pottsville led 41-37 at the half.

Leading scorers: Bethlehem – Bobby Gall 45, Dick Palenchar 14; Pottsville – Jack Houser 20, Bill Dougherty 15, Emerson Carter 14, Jim Boyer 12,

Central Catholic 52 Easton 48: Breaking a five-game losing streak (two in league play), Central Catholic took down Easton. Easton led after a quarter 10-6 with the Vikings pulling ahead at the half 21-20.

Leading scorers: Central Catholic – Alex DeLucia 20, Jack Dugan 11, Charlie Lawrence 11; Easton – Elmer Hay 20, Tom Georgaris 10.[5]

Week 3

Pottsville 73 Hazleton 64: The first half of the season culminated with each team playing a pair of games. Hazleton handed Allentown an easy path to the first half title when Pottsville upended the Mountaineers. Hazleton led 37-30 at the half and 51-47 after three quarters. Hazleton went down when Pottsville exploded for 26 points in the fourth quarter.

Leading scorers: Pottsville - Jim Boyer 17, Bill Dougherty 17, Bill Keeney 15, Jack Houser 15; Hazleton – Bob Watro 30, Nick Polivka 15, Lou Hill 14.

Bethlehem 57 Central Catholic 45: Bethlehem pulled their record even at 2-2 with a win over Central Catholic at Rockne Hall. Bobby Gall, the league's leading scorer, upped his four-game total to 100 points. With the Hurricane leading at the half 27-25, they took the contest by outscoring the Vikings 30-20 in the second half.

Leading scorers: Bethlehem – Bobby Gall 25; Central Catholic – Alex DeLucia 15, Charlie Lawrence 12.

Allentown 44 Easton 35: With Hazleton's loss, Allentown sewed up the first half title by defeating Easton. Playing a possession-type game, Easton kept the score close and actually led after three quarters 26-25. The Canaries pulled away for the win by outscoring Easton 19-9 in the fourth quarter.

Leading scorers: Allentown – Dale Smith 15; Easton – Elmer Hay 13.[6]

Allentown 63 Central Catholic 47: To close out the first half of the season, Allentown took on Central Catholic at the Little Palestra. After trailing for most of the game, the Canaries finally took the lead halfway through the third quarter and pulled away from the Vikings for the win. The Vikings led after a quarter 18-11 and at halftime 27-26.

Leading scorers: Allentown – Dale Smith 15, Barry Wilson 13, Pete Brantley 13: Central Catholic – Alex DeLucia 18.

Pottsville 50 Easton 41: After Pottsville took a 10-9 lead after one quarter, Easton took the halftime lead 23-21. Pottsville held Easton to 18 points in the second half and went on to defeat Easton.

Leading scorers: Pottsville - Jack Houser 19, Bill Keeny 12; Easton - Elmer Hay 19, Arthur Kreitz 12.

Bethlehem 56 Hazleton 51: At Hazleton, Bethlehem defeated the Mountaineers with no player scoring in double figures. Hazleton went into the second half leading 25-23 with Bethlehem taking the lead 43-36 after three quarters. With a little over two minutes to play, Hazleton took the lead 49-48 and 51-50 with 1 ½ minute to play. Bobby Gall put the Hurricane ahead and Bethlehem stalled for the last minute of the game.

Leading scorers: Bethlehem – Bobby Gall 9, Dick Palenchar 9; Hazleton - Lou Hill 16.[7]

Week 4

Pottsville 68 Allentown 64: The second half opened up with a thrilling finish and an upset. At Pottsville, the Maroons surprised Allentown to snap the Canaries 9-game win streak and hand them their first league loss of the season. Spurred on by a rousing second quarter with the Maroons scoring 24 points, Pottsville hung on for the victory. Mel Geho's three personal fouls and his benching had a major impact on the Canaries' offense.

Leading scorers: Pottsville – Jack Houser 21, Jim Boyer 16; Allentown – Franklin Reinhardt 16, Dale Smith 14, Mel Geho 12.

Hazleton 52 Central Catholic 50: Substitute JoJo Tarone scored his only basket of the game with two seconds left to lead Hazleton to a win over Central Catholic at Rockne Hall. Central Catholic had led 24-21 at the half and increased the lead to 41-33 after three quarters.

Leading scorers: Hazleton - Bobby Watro 21, Mike Melfi 14; Central Catholic - Charlie Lawrence 16, Alex DeLucia 11.

Bethlehem 55 Easton 48: Easton's defense held Bobby Gall to 11 points, but Bethlehem still pulled out the win avenging a first half defeat by the Red Rovers. Easton trailed by 22 in the 3rd quarter before storming back to make a game of it.

Leading scorers: Bethlehem – Dick Palenchar 12, Bobby Gall 11; Easton – Elmer Hay 18.[8]

Week 5

Central Catholic 61 Pottsville 46: Central Catholic upset the highly favored Pottsville quintet at Rockne Hall. Pottsville lost its 13th consecutive contest against the Vikings at Rockne Hall. Pottsville led early 7-2 before Central Catholic took charge to take the lead for good at the end of the quarter 10-7.

Leading scorers: Central Catholic - Alec DeLucia 18, Charlie Lawrence 16; Pottsville - Jack Houser 16, Bill Dougherty 10.

Allentown 59 Bethlehem 51: Allentown bounced back with a win over Bethlehem. Hampered by a back injury, Bobby Gall only scored 4 points. With Allentown leading most of the way and holding a ten-point lead 31-21, the Hurricane fought back to cut the lead to three 54-51 with 1 ½ minutes to play. The Canaries scored the last 5 points to pull out the win.

Leading scorers: Allentown – Franklin Reinhardt 13, John Mascali 12, Dale Smith 11; Bethlehem – Don Stinner 11, Jim Bauder 10, Ed Szvetecz 10.

Hazleton 83 Easton 44: Meanwhile, Hazleton, now the only undefeated team in the second half after only two games, routed Easton on their home court. The Mountaineers played without Bob Watro due to an ankle injury. The game was decided in the 2nd and 3rd quarters with Hazleton outscoring Easton 39-15.

Leading scorers: Hazleton - Lou Hill 19, Mike Melfi 16, Jack Kokinda 16, Charlie Zack 15; Easton – Elmer Hay 10.[9]

Week 6

Allentown 62 Hazleton 43: Allentown handed Hazleton its first loss of the second half at the Little Palestra in front of 2400 fans. Hazleton suffered its worst defeat at the hands of the Canaries since 1930. Hazleton led after the first two minutes 8-2. The Canaries took the lead 11-10 on a Barry Wilson field goal with two minutes left in the first quarter and led the rest of the way.

Leading scorers: Allentown - Dale Smith 14, Mel Geho 11; Hazleton - Lou Hill 10, Charlie Zack 10.

Bethlehem 67 Pottsville 66: Bethlehem handed Pottsville its second consecutive loss at Pottsville. Pottsville led the entire game until the last two minutes. When Bill Keeney fouled out for Pottsville, a heated argument developed when the Crimson Tide contended that he only had 4 fouls. The official scorer confirmed that he had five. Pottsville led at the time 64-61, but Bethlehem scored the next six points.

Leading scorers: Bethlehem - Frank Palenchar 22, Bob Gall 12, Ed Szvetecz 10; Pottsville - Jim Boyer 17, Bill Dougherty 14, Jack Houser 10.

Central Catholic 55 Easton 52: Central Catholic, meanwhile, moved into a four-way tie for first place along with Bethlehem, Allentown, and Hazleton with a win at Easton. The Vikings led 42-32 entering the fourth quarter when Easton pressed all over the court and pulled within three points of the Vikings.

Leading scorers: Central Catholic - Alex DeLucia 23, Charlie Lawrence 17; Easton - Elmer Hay 16.[10]

Week 7

Bethlehem 65 Central Catholic 63: Bethlehem knocked Central Catholic out of first place with their triumph at the Liberty gym. Trailing by 12 points going into the fourth quarter, the Vikings outscored Bethlehem by 10 points to fall two short of tying the game. After the Vikings led at the half 37-36, Bethlehem outscored Central Catholic 20-7 in the third quarter, just enough to stave off the Viking rally.

Leading scorer: Bethlehem – Bobby Gall 23, Dick Palenchar 17, Dave Preletz 10; Central Catholic - Charlie Lawrence 29, Alex DeLucia 16, Fran Vari 10.

Hazleton 75 Pottsville 56: Hazleton maintained its three-way share of first place with Allentown and Bethlehem with a whipping of Pottsville. Hazleton held the league's leading scorer Jack Houser to 11 points. Hazleton led by three at the half 34-31 before their offense scored 41 points in the second half to 25 for Pottsville.

Leading scorers: Hazleton - Bob Watro 23, Mike Melfi 16, Charlie Zack 15; Pottsville – Bill Keeny 12, Jack Houser 11.[11]

Allentown 46 Easton 42: Easton and Allentown exchanged leads with the Canaries taking the lead after a quarter 12-10. Easton came back for the halftime lead 20-18. The Canaries took a one-point lead 33-32 into the fourth quarter. Easton's Frank Piperato tied the game with a field goal and foul shot at 42-42. The Canaries scored the last four points to garner the win.

Leading scorers: Allentown – Mel Geho 18; Easton – Elmer Hay 13.

Week 8

Allentown 54 Central Catholic 40: Allentown closed out the second half with their victory over Central Catholic and set up a second half playoff with Bethlehem. After holding a slim 25-24 halftime lead, Allentown pulled away in the second half for their share of the second half lead. Central Catholic played without Alec DeLucia, the league's second-leading scorer. A straight A student, DeLucia left his home and traveled south with a companion after a heated family argument.

Leading scorers: Allentown – Franklin Reinhardt 14, Mel Geho 12, Johnny Wescoe 10; Central Catholic – Eric Spinosa 15, Charlie Lawrence 10.

Bethlehem 65 Hazleton 63: Playing at home, Bethlehem battled from behind, trailing 60-55 with about 3 1/2 minutes to play, to defeat Hazleton. Bethlehem escaped with the win, ahead by only two 64-62 with 25 seconds to play, when Hazleton's Charlie Zack, who was fouled, made his first foul shot and missed the second. Hazleton's Ed Novitsky grabbed the rebound and his shot hung on the rim before it fell off and gave Bethlehem the win.

Leading scorers: Bethlehem – Bobby Gall 25, Dick Palenchar 13, Ed Szvetecz 13; Hazleton – Bob Watro 29, Charlie Zack 14.

Easton 55 Pottsville 52: In the lone remaining game, Easton defeated Pottsville. Pottsville dominated the first half to hold a 27-22 lead only to have Easton take the second half 33-25 for the win.

Leading scorers: Easton - Elmer Hay 19, Arthur Kreitz 17; Pottsville – Jack Houser 12, Henry Ludwig 12, Bill Dougherty 10.[12]

League Championship

Allentown 67 Bethlehem 59: For the second consecutive year, Allentown and Bethlehem squared off for the second half title at the Penn Palestra. As in the previous season, Allentown defeated Bethlehem and won their 12th league title since the Canaries had also won the first half. After trailing the Canaries 30-21, Bethlehem came back to lead at the half 32-31 and also led at the end of the 3rd quarter 49-46.

Leading scorers: Allentown - Franklin Reinhardt 17, Mel Geho 17, Dale Smith 15; Bethlehem - Frank Palenchar 19, Bobby Gall 10, Jim Bauder 10.[13]

Postseason Play

Allentown 77 Ashland 64: In the District 11 semi-final game in front of a standing-room-only crowd of 3500 at St. Joseph's Hall in Hazleton, Allentown defeated Ashland. After taking a 2-0 lead, Ashland never led again and were down 23 points at one point in the 3rd quarter. Allentown had 4 players in double figures.

Leading scorers: Allentown - Mel Geho 16, Barry Wilson 16, Franklin Reinhardt 16, Pete Brantley 12; Ashland - Bill Ennis 18, Jim Cuff 16, Dick Wetzel 13.[15]

Allentown 78 Slatington 57: Lloyd Williams' Slatington team, Lehigh Valley League champions, took on Allentown for the District 11 title at the Penn Palestra. With their win over the Slaters, Allentown won its 7th district title. Allentown took a 10-0 lead early and were never threatened in the game.

Leading scorers: Allentown - Mel Geho 21, Dale Smith 13, Johnny Wescoe 11; Slatington - Richard Jones 13, Charlie Sheckler 11, Bill Braerman 11.[16]

Allentown 57 Old Forge 53: Returning to the Palestra in front of 6000 fans, Milo Sewards' Canaries faced Old Forge, Lackawanna League and District 2 champions, in the PIAA Eastern Final. With the score tied at 53-53, forward Frank Reinhardt sparked the victory for Allentown with two last minute field goals. Reinhardt and Center Dale Smith guarded Old Forge's 6'6" center and held him to nine points, well off his average of over 25 points per game. Allentown led at the half 28-27 and after 41-40 heading into the fourth quarter.

Leading scorers: Allentown – Franklin Reinhardt 25, Dale Smith 12; Old Forge – Joe DiSimoni 16, Joe Palmere 14.[17]

Yeadon 60 Allentown 45: Yeadon, the Philadelphia Suburban League champions, pulled off their second straight upset with a decisive victory over the Canaries at the Penn Palestra. They upset Coatesville by 20 points to get to this game. After trailing 10-8 at the first quarter mark and tied 15 all tie early in the second period, Yeadon pulled away for the relatively easy win. Allentown could only score 13 total points in the second and third quarters. Larry Norkas, Yeadon's 6'5" center, led the scoring.

Leading scorers: Yeadon – Larry Norkas 16, Jack Hunter 11, Jack Weissman 11; Allentown – Franklin Reinhardt 11.[18]

PCIAA Playoffs

Central Catholic 51 Pottsville Catholic 42: Central Catholic entered the PCIAA playoffs against Pottsville Catholic at the Little Palestra. A balanced scoring attack with seven players contributing led the Vikings to the victory. Pottsville led at the half 22-17 before being outclassed in the third quarter 16-5. The Vikings scored 34 points to Pottsville Catholic's 20 in the second half.

Leading scorers: Central Catholic– Alex DeLucia 13, Eric Spinosa 10; Pottsville Catholic– Bill Handges 20, John Cielinski 16.[19]

Reading Central Catholic 54 Central Catholic 45: The Reading Central Catholic Cardinals ended Central Catholic's playoff trek at the new Albright College Fieldhouse. After trailing at the end of the initial quarter 21-11, the Cardinals outscored the Vikings 20-6 in the second quarter to spur them on to victory. The Vikings attempted a third quarter rally by outscoring the Cardinals 11-5 but couldn't continue the run through the final quarter.

Leading scorers: Reading Central Catholic - Edward Jablonski 17, Bill Orth 15; Central Catholic – Alex DeLucia 17.[20]

Postseason Accolades

Leading scorers: The league scoring title went to Bobby Gall, Bethlehem's blond bomber, with 184 points despite being hindered by a bad back for several games. Other leading scorers included: Jack Houser, Pottsville, 178 points; Bob Watro, Hazleton, 177 points; Alex DeLucia, Central Catholic, 165 points; Elmer Hay, Easton, 155 points; Charlie Lawrence, Central Catholic, 138 points; Jim Boyer, Pottsville, 117 points; Frank Palenchar, Bethlehem, 114 points; Melvin Geho, Allentown, 113 points; and Bill Dougherty, Pottsville 104 points.[21]

All-Stars: The Hazleton Plain Speaker's all-league team included Mel Geho, Allentown; Jack Houser, Pottsville; Bobby Gall, Bethlehem; and Bob Watro and Ed Novitsky, Hazleton on the first team. The second team consisted of Elmer Hay, Easton; Dale Smith and Frank Reinhardt, Allentown; Bill Keeney, Pottsville; and JoJo Tarone, Hazleton.[22]

All-State: The Associated Press All-Pennsylvania Scholastic Team included Frank Reinhart, Allentown, 2nd team; Bobby Gall, Bethlehem, and Bob Watro, Hazleton, 4th team, and Jack Houser, Pottsville, 5th team. Alex DeLucia, Central Catholic, Melvin Geho, Allentown, and Dale Smith, Allentown were named as Honorable Mention.[23]

Final Standings

First Half		Second Half		Overall	
Allentown	5-0	Allentown	4-1	Allentown	9-1
Bethlehem	3-2	Bethlehem	4-1	Bethlehem	7-3
Pottsville	3-2	Hazleton	3-2	Hazleton	5-5
Hazleton	2-3	Central Catholic	2-3	Pottsville	4-6
Central Catholic	1-4	Pottsville	1-4	Central Catholic	3-7
Easton	1-4	Easton	1-4	Easton	2-8

Team Rosters

Allentown: Coach Milo Sewards, Phil Boger, Peter Brantley, Mel Geho, Robert Hagemes, Richard Jones, John Mascali, Henry Miller, William Parks, Frank Reinhardt, Lee Schweyer, Edward Sedora, Dale Smith, James Snyder, John Wescoe, Barry Wilson, Daniel Zambelli

Bethlehem: Coach Joe Preletz, Ken Bateman, Jim Bauder, Bob Gall, George Jenkins, Stan Kunkle, Charlie Lawrence, Herbie Musselman, Dick Palenchar, Dave Preletz, Jim Slough, Don Stinner, Ed Szvetecz, Jim Williams

Central Catholic: Coach John Wargo, Alex DeLucia, Jack Dugan, Peter Ebner, James Egizio, John Green, Bob Hamrick, Greg Kloiber, Charlie Lawrence, Eric Spinosa, Fran Vari

Easton: Coach Charles Brown, Thomas Bright, John Bulette, Dale Dauscher, Tom Georgaris, Watson "Spec" Hart, Elmer Hay, Arthur Kreitz, Robert Miller, Frank Piperato, Charles Sancinito, Mackey Skinner, Kenneth Warman

Hazleton: Coach Frank Serany, Joe Farace, Lou Hill, Jack Kokinda, Carmen Marnell, Mike Melfi, Ed Novitsky, Nick Polivka, Richie Portland, Richie Reimold, Nat Sando, Joseph "JoJo" Tarone, Bob Watro, Charlie Zack

Pottsville: Coach Ed Deitch, Michael Bender, Jim Boyer, Emerson Carter, Ken Diehl, William Dougherty, Gene Fitzpatrick, Jack Houser, Bill Keeny, Harry Ludwig, Paul Motta, Jack Sidler, Bob Steidle

Allentown High School – 1953 League Champions[14]

Front: Edward Jones, Richard Jones, Lee Schweyer, Daniel Zambelli; Middle: Michael Miller (mgr). Franklin Reinhardt, Mel Geho. Dale Smith, Peter Brantley, John Wescoe, Clarence Broadbent (mgr) Back: Paul Clymer (asst coach), James Snyder, William Parks, Coach Sewards, John Mascali, Robert Hagemes, Barry Wilson, Joe Blankowitsch (trainer)

1954

Williamsport's Entry Tabled

At the league meeting at Shankweiler's Hotel in Fogelsville in May 1953, the league representatives extended a formal invitation to Williamsport High School to join the East Penn Basketball League. At a follow-up meeting on November 16, 1953, Williamsport sent a four-man delegation to accept the earlier invitation. D.L. Learn, the District 11 chairman, also attended the meeting and raised questions about the District 4 team joining a District 11 league. In an effort to resolve these questions, Williamsport's entry into the league was delayed to provide an opportunity for the two district representatives and Williamsport faculty representatives to meet and attempt to resolve these issues.[1]

After a review of the potential conflicts created within the two districts, Williamsport decided to withdraw its application for acceptance into the league. The major conflict appeared to be Williamsport's eligibility to participate in District 4 post-season play if it played the majority of its games in another district.[2] The league formally accepted the withdrawal at its December 14 meeting.[3]

Week 1

Hazleton 53 Easton 52 2OT: The league opened its 29th season on January 8th. At Hazleton, it took two overtimes to determine the winner. Despite trailing by 9 points at the end of each of the first three quarters, Easton tied the score at 47 with a minute remaining in the game. Both teams failed to score and the game went into overtime. Both teams scored 4 points in the extra period to force a second overtime. Neither team scored until Red Rover Tom Wright was fouled and converted only one of two shots to lead 52-51. Hazleton's Joe Tarone then sank a field goal for the win.

Leading scorers: Hazleton – Mike Melfi 20, Joe Tarone 13; Easton - Tom Georgaris 27, Robert Miller 11.

Central Catholic 67 Pottsville 53: Emil Carazo's Vikings equaled the school's longest consecutive win streak at 11 (set in 1941) with its triumph over Pottsville. Trailing 22-20 at halftime, the Vikings took charge in the third quarter to gain the lead at 40-35 and continued to extend the lead in the fourth quarter.

Leading scorers: Central Catholic - Fran Vari 14, Alex DeLucia 12, Ed Mumbert 12, John Dugan 11; Pottsville – Ken Diehl 20, Gene Fitzpatrick 11.

Allentown 64 Bethlehem 56: The Canaries took a ten-point lead in the first quarter 17-7 only to have Bethlehem cut it to six at the half 31-25. Bethlehem continued its surge in the third quarter to reduce Allentown's lead to one-point 32-31 before the Canaries took charge for the remainder of the contest.

Leading scorers: Allentown - John Mascali 16, Dale Horn 14; Bethlehem - Bill Davis 18, Jim Williams 11.[4]

Week 2

Hazleton 67 Central Catholic 58: Hazleton snapped Central Catholic's win streak in Hazleton. The Vikings led after a quarter 15-14 and it was all Hazleton after that except for a short time in the fourth quarter when the Vikings cut the lead to four points 49-45. Hazleton held onto the lead by converting foul shots when Central Catholic attempted to get possession of the ball.

Leading scorers: Hazleton - Charlie Zack 25, Mike Melfi 11, Joe Farace 11, Joe Tarone 10; Central Catholic - Alex DeLucia 22, James Egizio 13, John Dugan 10.

Bethlehem 54 Easton 49: Although Easton led most of the first half, Bethlehem evened its record at 1-1 with a victory over the Red Rovers in Easton. The Red Rovers led 16-11 after a quarter and 22-21 at halftime but the Hurricane jumped into the lead in the third quarter and led 40-37 heading into the final stanza.

Leading scorers: Bethlehem - Jim Bauder 14, Jim Williams 12, Jim Slough 11; Easton - Tom Georgaris 14.

Allentown 64 Pottsville 33: Captain Barry Wilson and Dale Horn were suspended for reporting late for classes on Wednesday following a Tuesday night game in Williamsport. The team was given the approval to report at noon, but Wilson and Horn didn't show till 1 pm. Despite their absence, Allentown easily defeated Pottsville with the Canaries dominating 34-11 in the second and third quarters, allowing only two points in the third quarter.

Leading scorers: Allentown - John Mascali 15, Phil Boger 10, Ed Sedora 10; Pottsville - Ken Diehl 11 [5]

Week 3

Pottsville 58 Hazleton 56: In an early season surprise, Pottsville knocked off Hazleton. Pottsville trailed 17-10 at the end of the 1st period and 32-24 at the half. Despite pulling within two in the third quarter, Pottsville never led until five minutes to go in the game. Pottsville took a five-point lead on foul shots 54-49. Hazleton pulled within two points and had a chance to tie with two foul shots by Mike Nastanovich, but he missed both. Pottsville had its upset!

Leading Scorers: Pottsville – Bill Dougherty 22, Richard Matthews 13, Gene Fitzpatrick 12; Hazleton – Charlie Zack 16, Joe Farace 16, Joe Farace 12, Joe Tarone 10.

Central Catholic 72 Bethlehem 71: Central Catholic bounced back with a win at Rockne Hall over Bethlehem. The Vikings held an 18-point lead in the first half 35-17, but Bethlehem stormed back to lead 62-61 with 3 ½ minutes to play in the game. They extended the lead to 65-61 before Alex DeLucia led an onslaught that led to victory.

Leading scorers: Central Catholic–Alex DeLucia 28, Ed Mumbert 14; Bethlehem-Gary Piff 17, Jim Slough 14, Bob Donchez 10.

Allentown 56 Easton 40: Allentown jumped into sole possession of first place as the only undefeated team with its win over Easton.

Leading scorers: Allentown-Phil Boger 14, John Mascali 10, Edward Sedora 10; Easton-Tom Georgaris 22.[6]

Bethlehem 112 Hazleton 65: Bethlehem shocked Hazleton with an astounding shellacking of the Mountaineers in the Liberty gym and shattered at least five scoring records in doing so. The score was tied after one quarter 22 all, before Bethlehem unleashed its attack. They scored 25 points in each of the next two quarters and 40 in the final period. Scoring records included most points by one team (112), most combined points (177), most points in a period (40), and most points scored for both Bethlehem and in its gym. The game may have set the record for most fouls in a game with 71, 45 by Hazleton and 26 by Bethlehem. Thirteen players scored for Bethlehem

Leading scorers: Bethlehem - Jimmy Bauder 21, Gary Piff 18, Charley Moyer 14; Hazleton - Mike Melfi 19. Joe Farace 14.

Allentown 74 Central Catholic 63: With the Mountaineers' loss, Allentown wrapped up the first half title by turning back Central Catholic. After trailing 20-17 after the first period, the Canaries pulled away, leading at the half 34-31. Alex DeLucia committed three fouls in the first three minutes and missed the rest of the first half.

Leading scorers: Allentown-John Mascali 20, Barry Wilson 14, Bob Benner 12; Central Catholic-Jim Egizio 17, Alex DeLucia 13.

Easton 66 Pottsville 54: Bob Miller scored 22 points to lead Easton over Pottsville. The Red Rovers converted 24 of 28 foul shots to secure the win. Kenny Diehl led Pottsville to an early 13-7 lead only to see Easton outscore them the last three periods.

Leading scorers: Easton – Bob Miller 22, Tom Georgaris 19, Tom Bright 12; Pottsville – Kenny Diehl 19, Gene Fitzpatrick 12, Matt McDonald 10.[7]

Week 4

Bethlehem 81 Pottsville 59: Bethlehem followed up its record-breaking game with another high scoring affair as they rapped Pottsville. Coach Joe Preletz used sixteen players in the romp and played the junior varsity for the last 12 minutes of the game. The Hurricane led at the half 46-20.

Leading scorers: Bethlehem - Jimmy Bauder 17, Mike Preletz 14; Pottsville - Kenny Diehl 22, Gene Fitzpatrick 14, Dick Matthews 10.

Central Catholic 63 Easton 53: After the Vikings led 34-25 at halftime, Easton pulled to within two points in the fourth quarter 47-45. Central Catholic rallied to down Easton to close out the first half of the season.

Leading scorers: Central Catholic-Alex DeLucia 19, Ed Mumbert 14, Jim Egizio 11; Easton-Charles Sancinito 17, Bob Miller 11.

Hazleton 62 Allentown 52: At St. Joseph's Hall in Hazleton, Hazleton handed Allentown its first league loss. Inspired by a pep rally, Hazleton rallied from a 14-10 first quarter deficit to outscore the Canaries in each of the last three quarters. Allentown led at halftime 22-20 before Hazleton scored the first 9 points of the third quarter.

Leading scorers: Hazleton - Joe Tarone 20, Joe Farace 14, Mike Melfi 14, Charlie Zack 11; Allentown - John Mascali 12, Dale Horn 10.[8]

Week 5

Allentown 67 Bethlehem 65: Allentown rebounded from the setback at Hazleton to trim Bethlehem. The Canaries were up eleven points 65-54 when Bethlehem made a charge to pull within 2 with seconds to play. With Bethlehem in-bounding the ball with five seconds to play, Gary Piff attempted a long game-tying shot which missed giving the Canaries the win.

Leading scorers: Allentown – John Mascali 23, Dale Horn 18, Bob Benner 12; Bethlehem - Jimmy Bauder 17, Charlie Moyer 15.

Hazleton 61 Easton 42: Easton only led twice in the contest at 2-0 and 17-15 midway in the second quarter. Hazleton led at the half 27-23 and started the second half of the season by posting a victory over Easton.

Leading scorers: Hazleton - Mike Melfi 16, Joe Tarone 11, Charlie Zack 11; Easton - Tom Georgaris 17.

Central Catholic 72 Pottsville 69: Trailing 67-65 with 2 ½ minutes to play, the Vikings' DeLucia and Egizio scored 7 points combined to pull out the win. In the third quarter, Pottsville scored 9 straight points to take a 53-47 lead before the Vikings rallied to pull out the win. Ken Diehl scored all 11 points for Pottsville in the 4th quarter.

Leading scorers: Central Catholic-Alex DeLucia 20, Jim Egizio 19, Ed Mumbert 16; Pottsville-Ken Diehl 33, Dick Matthews 10.[9]

Week 6

Central Catholic 90 Hazleton 72: Three thousand fans at Rockne Hall saw the Vikings pour in 90 points to outscore Hazleton despite a 34-point performance by Hazleton's Charlie Zack. The victory avenged a first half loss to Hazleton which broke a long Central Catholic win streak. The Vikings scored 31 points in the third quarter.

Leading scorers: Central Catholic - Alex DeLucia 24, Jim Egizio 24, Fran Vari 13, John Dugan 10; Hazleton – Charlie Zack 34, Mike Melfi 20.

Bethlehem 57 Easton 45: Easton led Bethlehem 36-34 after three periods only to see the Hurricane score 17 points in the last five minutes of the game to pull out a victory. Gary Piff was missing from the lineup apparently due to a tiff with Coach Preletz and was demoted to the junior varsity. The teams were tied at the half 21-21.

Leading scorers: Bethlehem - Jim Slough 21; Easton - Bob Miller 15, Tom Georgaris 13.

Allentown 71 Pottsville 57: Trailing 18-14 after the first quarter, Allentown rallied to defeat Pottsville and remain in a tie for first place with Central Catholic. After tying the score at 18 in the second quarter, the Canaries led at the half 29-26.

Leading scorers: Allentown – Dale Horn 21, Baron McElroy 14, Lee Schweyer 11; Pottsville - Ken Diehl 26, Bill Dougherty 14.[10]

Week 7

Allentown 53 Easton 36: Allentown remained undefeated in the half by cruising past Easton. Easton came back to pull the score to within four points 37-33 in the 4th quarter, but the Canaries pulled away for the easy win by outscoring the Red Rovers 20-7 in the final period. Allentown led at the half 21-17.

Leading scorers: Allentown – Dale Horn 19, Bob Benner 14, John Mascali 10; Easton – Tom Georgaris 14, Bob Miller 11.

Bethlehem 90 Central Catholic 74: Bethlehem knocked Central Catholic out of a first-place tie despite a big night from Alex DeLucia, the league's leading scorer. In the second quarter, Bethlehem scored 18 straight points to take a lead from which the Vikings never recovered, although they only trailed 70-66 after three quarters. Gary Piff returned to the varsity after his demotion to the junior varsity.

Leading scorers: Bethlehem - Jim Slough 21, Gary Piff 14, Jim Bauder 11, Jim Williams 10; Central Catholic – Alex DeLucia 30, Fran Vari 21, Jim Egizio 14, John Dugan 11.

Hazleton 82 Pottsville 60: Hazleton trounced Pottsville in front of the home crowd. Hazleton took a 23-14 first quarter lead and extended it to 16 points at halftime 42-26.

Leading scorers: Hazleton - Mike Melfi 30, Charlie Zack 19, Joe Farace 14; Pottsville - Kenny Diehl 25, Gene Fitzpatrick 19.[11]

Easton 56 Pottsville 45: Easton won only its second league game of the season, both over Pottsville. After trailing 23-20 at the half, Easton outscored Pottsville 20-7 in the 3rd period and Tom Georgaris scored 12 of the Red Rovers' 16 points in the final period to carry them to the win.

Leading scorers: Easton – Tom Georgaris 26; Pottsville - Kenny Diehl 18, Bill Dougherty 15.

Hazleton 73 Bethlehem 60: Revenging their humiliating first half loss to the Hurricane, Hazleton kept its second half hopes alive with a win over Bethlehem at St. Joseph's Hall. Bethlehem lost center Charlie Moyer in the third quarter and guard Jim Slough in the 4th quarter on personal fouls. With the game tied at 10, Hazleton took the lead for good 15-10 late in the first quarter.

Leading scorers: Hazleton - Mike Melfi 30, Joe Farace 21, Charlie Zack 17; Bethlehem – Bill Davis 17, Jim Slough 15, Jim Bauder 14.

Allentown 74 Central Catholic 66: Allentown dashed Central Catholic's 2nd half title hopes at Rockne Hall. John Mascali and Bob Benner fouled out of the game as did four Viking starters including Ed Mumbert, Jim Egizio, Fran Vari, and Alex Delucia. The Vikings had led at the half 29-27 with Allentown leading after three quarters 50-44.

Leading scorers: Allentown – Dale Horn 16, John Mascali 15, Lee Schweyer 11; Central Catholic – Alex DeLucia 15, Ed Mumbert 13, Fran Vari 10, John Dugan 10, Bob Potter 10.[12]

Week 8

Allentown 67 Hazleton 54: After falling behind Hazleton 7-2, Allentown charged back to top the Mountaineers and capture their 12th league title. Allentown led at the half 30-22. The win earned Allentown a first-round bye in the District 11 tournament.

Leading scorers: Allentown – John Mascali 17, Baron McElroy 11, Phil Boger 11, Lee Schweyer 10; Hazleton – Mike Melfi 22, Charlie Zack 10.

Easton 74 Central Catholic 66: Tom Georgaris set Easton's scoring mark when he tallied 16 points and 377 for the season, bettering Elmer Hay's mark by 12 points. Easton upset Central Catholic as the Vikings never got closer than five points 71-66 late in the game.

Leading scorers: Easton – Bob Miller 21, Tom Georgaris 16, Charlie Sutphen 13, John Bulette 11; Central Catholic - Alex DeLucia 32, John Dugan 11, Jim Egizio 11.

Pottsville 66 Bethlehem 65: A field goal and foul shot in the last seconds of the game gave Pottsville an upset victory over Bethlehem. With Bethlehem ahead 65-63, Pottsville's high-scoring forward Kenny Diehl missed a shot which was retrieved by Fitzpatrick. Fitzpatrick wheeled and made the shot and was fouled. He converted the foul shot for the one-point win. Pottsville had led at the half 32-28.

Leading scorers: Pottsville – Ken Diehl 19, Gene Fitzpatrick 18, Bill Dougherty 15; Bethlehem – Jim Bauder 20, Gary Piff 15, Charley Moyer 13.[13]

Postseason Play

Slatington 63 Allentown 56: Slatington finally got past an East Penn League team in postseason play with a win over Allentown to advance to the district final. The Slaters took an 18-16 first quarter lead. Allentown only led during the first quarter and last led at 14-12.

Leading scorers: Slatington - Merrill Eckhart 18, Dick Jones 16, Ed Torbey 14, Maurice Schleicher 10; Allentown - Dale Horn 16, Bob Benner 13.[15]

PCIAA Playoffs

Central Catholic 48 Reading Central Catholic 46: In Muhlenberg's new Memorial Hall, Central Catholic took on Reading Central Catholic in the PCIAA playoffs. With a balanced scoring attack with seven players contributing, the Vikings won, avenging a playoff defeat last year by Reading. Trailing 46-45, Jim Egizio made a field goal and foul shot in the last 45 seconds of play to send the Vikings on in the playoffs. Ed Jablonski led Reading in scoring, but could only score two in the second half of the game. The Vikings led at the half 27-25.

Leading scorers: Central Catholic – Alex DeLucia 13; Reading Central Catholic – Ed Jablonski 20.[16]

Central Catholic 78 Scranton Prep 71: Central Catholic opened up a 16-point lead in the third quarter after a close first half and went on to defeat Scranton Prep at Muhlenberg's Memorial Hall. The Vikings led at the half 35-31. Alex DeLucia set the school season record with 505 points. Scranton's fourth quarter pulled them within five points, but the rally fell short.

Leading scorers: Central Catholic – Alex DeLucia 23, Albert Timko 14, John Dugan 12, Jim Egizio 11; Scranton Prep – Bob Kearney 24, Pete Abdalla 16, Ed Cosgrove 15.[17]

Central Catholic 84 Harrisburg Catholic 61: Playing at Harrisburg's Camp Curtin Junior High School, Central Catholic defeated Harrisburg Catholic to propel them into the state PCIAA final. With Harrisburg leading at the half 37-36, the Vikings outscored the Crusaders 26-9, with DeLucia making seven field goals, in the third period to put the game away.

Leading scorers: Central Catholic – Alex DeLucia 29, Jim Egizio 18, John Dugan 13, Ed Mumbert 10; Harrisburg Catholic – John Clark 21, Fran Gorman 15, Frank Salinger 13.[18]

Erie Cathedral Prep 80 Central Catholic 58: Despite having somewhat of a homecourt advantage with the state PCIAA final being played at Muhlenberg's Memorial Hall, Central Catholic could not keep pace with Erie Cathedral Prep and lost in the finals. Erie raced out to an 18-7 first quarter lead and kept adding to the lead in the next three quarters. The Ramblers held Alex DeLucia to a single field goal and five foul shots for a total of seven points. Jim Gross led Erie with 27 points and was supported by Chuck Wittmann's 22. Jim Egizio scored 16 to lead the Vikings.

Leading scorers: Erie Cathedral Prep – Jim Gross 27, Chuck Wittmann 22, Johnny Ruska 12, Joe Savardi 10; Central Catholic – Jim Egizio 16, John Dugan 13.[19]

Postseason Accolades

Leading scorers: Alex DeLucia took the league scoring title with 215 points for a 21.5 ppg average. He was followed by Pottsville's Kenny Diehl, 195 points; Mike Melfi, Hazleton, 191; Tom Georgaris, Easton, 175; Charlie Zack, Hazleton, 162; John Mascali, Allentown, 147; Jimmy Bauder, Bethlehem, 140; Jim Egizio, Central Catholic, 130; Bobby Miller, Easton, 121, and Jim Slough, Bethlehem, 116.[20]

All-Stars: The All-East Penn League first team included Alex DeLucia, Central Catholic; Ken Diehl, Pottsville; John Mascali, Allentown; Tom Georgaris, Easton, and Charlie Zack, Hazleton. The second team consisted of Jim Bauder, Bethlehem; Dale Horn and Bob Benner, Allentown; Jim Egizio, Central Catholic; and Mike Melfi, Hazleton.[21]

All-State: The Associated Press All-Pennsylvania Scholastic Team included Alex DeLucia, Central Catholic, 2nd team; and John Mascali, Allentown, 3rd team. Ken Diehl, Pottsville, Mike Melfi and Charlie Zack, Hazleton, were named as Honorable Mention.[22]

Final Standings

First Half		Second Half		Overall	
Allentown	4-1	Allentown	5-0	Allentown	9-1
Bethlehem	3-2	Hazleton	3-2	Hazleton	6-4
Central Catholic	3-2	Central Catholic	2-3	Central Catholic	5-5
Hazleton	3-2	Bethlehem	2-3	Bethlehem	5-5
Easton	1-4	Easton	2-3	Easton	3-7
Pottsville	1-4	Pottsville	1-4	Pottsville	2-6

Team Rosters

Allentown: Coach Milo Sewards, Bob Benner, Phil Boger, Ken Dornblaser, Dale Horn, Ron Lopczonski, Dick Markowitz, John Mascali, Baron McElroy, Hank Miller, Phil Petrisky, Charles Schimeneck, Lee Schweyer, Eddie Sedora, Leo Stinner, Barry Wilson, Dan Zambelli

Bethlehem: Coach Joe Preletz, Jim Bauder, Jack Cropper, Bill Davis, Bob Donchez, Dave Keen, Lester Lazarowitz, Charlie Moyer, Herb Musselman, Gary Piff, Jim Slough, Jim Williams

Central Catholic: Coach Emil Carazo, Alex DeLucia, Jim DeWar, John Dugan, Bob Egizio, Jim Egizio, Charles Hammer, Gerry Hopper, Greg Kloiber, Clair Miller, Ed Mumbert, Bob Potter, Al Timko, Fran Vari, Tom Wagner, Ed Werner

Easton: Coach Charles Brown, William Anckaitis, Thomas Bright, John Bulette, Tom Greorgaris, Sterling Harvey, Richard Lovell, Sebastian Merlo, Bob Miller, Charlie Ross, Charles Sancinito, Mackey Skinner, Charlie Sutphen, Kenneth Warman

Hazleton: Coach Frank Serany, Joe Bellucci, Jerry Brazzo, Joe Farace, Joe Kokinda, Mike Melfi, Tom Mindick, Mike Nastanovich, Mario Pecile, Joe Petrill, Richie Portland, Nat Sando, Joe Scallion, Dave Shafer, Joe Sinclair, Bob Supowit, Joe Tarone, Ray Yencho, Charlie Zack

Pottsville: Coach Ed Deitch, Tony Barket, Ron Boris, Ken Diehl, William Dougherty, Gene Fitzpatrick, Bill Freed, Dick Matthews, Matt McDonald, Charles Miller, Paul Motta, Jack Rodgers, Vince Schuster, Bob Steidle

Allentown High School – 1954 League Champions[14]

Front: Barry Wildon, Sam Kressly (mgr), Ron Lopczonski; Middle: Ken Dornblaser, Ed Sedora, Coach Sewards, Baron McElroy, Lee Schweyer, Bob Benner; Back: Joe Blankowitsch (trainer), Dan Zambelli, Leo Stinner, John Mascali, Charles Schimeneck, Phil Boger, Hank Miller, Asst. Coach Paul Clymer

1955

Allentown Threepeats

The league's leadership remained intact for another season with Phil Phillippi re-elected to another term as president, Stan Steigerwalt as vice president, and Edgar Rabenold as secretary and treasurer. The elections were held at the Shankweiler's Hotel in Fogelsville in April 1954.[1]

Week 1

Easton 62 Bethlehem 59: The league's 30th season began with Easton upsetting a heavily favored Coach Johnny Howard's Bethlehem squad at the Easton High School gym. Coach Eddie Snyder's Red Rovers took the lead in the first quarter 15-14 and prevailed for the victory despite Bethlehem's valiant 4th quarter rally that cut the margin from 10 to 2 points with 17 seconds left in the game.

Leading scorers: Easton - Bob Miller 18, Charles Sancinito 17, Charlie Ross 12; Bethlehem - Jim Williams 23, Gary Piff 17.

Central Catholic 58 Hazleton 52: Emil Carazo's Viking squad rallied from an eight-point deficit 42-34 in the third quarter to tie the game with Hazleton as the quarter ended. Central Catholic outscored the Mountaineers by six points in the final quarter to open the league season with a victory. Hazleton led at the half 33-31.

Leading scorers: Central Catholic – Jim DeWar 14, Jim Egizio 11, Bob Potter 11; Hazleton – Joe Farace 19, Joe Petrilla 14.

Allentown 79 Pottsville 48: Although Coach Eddie Deitch's Pottsville squad had three players in double figures, Allentown countered with four players scoring 10 points or more. Coach Milo Sewards used all 15 players on his squad in the rout. Allentown held the Maroons to five first-quarter points

Leading scorers: Allentown - Terry German 18, Baron McElroy 16, Joe Berghold 12, Dick Markowitz 10; Pottsville - Dick Miller 18, Dick Matthews 15, Bill Umberger 11.[2]

Week 2

Hazleton 56 Easton 49: With Joe Farace and Dave Shafer scoring 17 of Hazleton's 20 second period points, the Mountaineers took the lead and held on for the win over Easton. Wally Skernolis controlled the backboards with 19 rebounds for the Mountaineers. With the score tied at 11 apiece after the first quarter, Hazleton took charge in the middle two quarters by outscoring Easton 35-28.

Leading scorers: Hazleton – Joe Farace 19, Dave Shafer 13, Wally Skernolis 13; Easton - Bob Miller 22, Charles Sancinito 11.

Central Catholic 59 Pottsville 53: Central Catholic won its second straight league game with their win over Pottsville. Jim Egizio scored 14 points in the first half to lead the Vikings to a 31-19 halftime lead.

Leading scorers: Central Catholic–Jim Egizio 20, Greg Kloiber 15; Pottsville-Charlie Miller 22, Dick Matthews 14, Ken Diehl 13.

Allentown 74 Bethlehem 71: Canary sophomore Bob Heffner broke through with 14 important points to support Baron McElroy and hand Bethlehem their second consecutive loss. Allentown held a 34-30 lead at halftime.

Leading scorers: Allentown – Baron McElroy 20, Bob Heffner 14, Terry German 13; Bethlehem - Gary Piff 20, Jim Bauder 19, Dave Keen 13, Jim Williams 12.

Week 3

Allentown 74 Central Catholic 51: After a romp over Central Catholic, Allentown remained the only undefeated team in the circuit. Winning their 11th game out of 12, the Canaries trailed briefly early 5-4 before pulling ahead for an easy win. The Canaries led 31-21 at the half and scored 27 points in the fourth quarter to the Vikings 11. Viking center Clair Miller experienced some embarrassment when his trunks split in the 2nd quarter. With a new set of shorts, he reentered the game and scored six points in the contest.

Leading scorers: Allentown - Bob Benner 17, Bob Heffner 15, Baron McElroy 13, Ken Dornblaser 12; Central Catholic - Greg Kloiber 15, Bob Egizio 12.

Hazleton 79 Bethlehem 69: Disappointing Bethlehem lost its third straight game in Hazleton. Despite having much smaller players, the Mountaineers out-rebounded Bethlehem 44-39. Bethlehem led at the half 41-40, but, led by Jim Pecile's 9 points in the final quarter, the Mountaineers took down the Hurricane.

Leading scorers: Hazleton - Wally Skerlonis 21, Joe Petrilla 19, Mario Pecile 19, Joe Farace 18; Bethlehem - Gary Piff 22, Jim Bauder 18, Dave Keen 15.[4]

Easton 74 Pottsville 56: Employing a full court press beginning late in the second quarter, Easton won in Pottsville. Easton led at the half 39-28.

Leading scorers: Easton – Charles Sancinito 17, Sterling Harvey 13, Bob Miller 12; Pottsville - Bill Umberger 16, Charlie Miller 15, Dick Matthews 11. Pottsville and Bethlehem both stood at 0-3.[5]

Bethlehem 124 Pottsville 56: Later in the week, Bethlehem unleashed its frustrations when if humiliated winless Pottsville. The scoring outburst established a new scoring record breaking the Hurricane's 112 set last year against Hazleton. Unmercifully employing a full court press almost throughout the first half, Bethlehem led 62-29 at the half.

Leading scorers: Bethlehem - Jimmy Bauder 28 points, Gary Piff 23, Mike Preletz 17, Jim Williams 14, Bob Horvath 10; Pottsville - Bill Umberger 20. Dick Matthews 14, Bob Miller 12.

Central Catholic 55 Easton 39: Central Catholic knocked Easton out of the running for the first half title. The Vikings outscored the Red Rovers 18-9 in both the first and fourth quarters and only allowed six points in the third quarter.

Leading scorers: Central Catholic - Greg Kloiber 16, Jim Dewar 13, Bob Potter 11, Bob Egizio 10; Easton - Charlie Ross 11.

Allentown 72 Hazleton 66: After blowing a 14-point lead in the second period and coming from behind in the fourth quarter, Allentown shut down Hazleton to assure them of at least a first half tie. Baron McElroy paced the Canaries with 21 and Joe Farace had 20 for the Mountaineers. The game was won at the charity stripe with Allentown converting 22 of 36 compared to Hazleton's 14 of 29.

Leading scorers: Allentown - Baron McElroy 21, Terry German 18, Bob Benner 12, Ken Dornblaser 10; Hazleton - Joe Farace 20, Mario Pecile 15, Tom Mindick 12, Tom Grebowski 10.[6]

Week 4

Allentown 53 Easton 52: Allentown had to fight hard to win the first half title at Easton. Ken Dornblaser laid in a field goal with 12 seconds left to pull out the win. Easton employed a tough zone defense in the third period to hold the Canaries to a total of 8 points. Trailing by 12 at the half, the Red Rovers defense allowed them to pull within two after 3 quarters. Easton pulled ahead 52-49 in the last minutes of the game.

After Baron McElroy stole a pass for an easy layup, Easton's erratic pass gave the ball back to Allentown. Set shot artist Bob Benner let go a long shot which missed but was gathered in by Dornblaser for the winning shot. Bob Benner set a school record with 17 consecutive converted foul shots to break LeRoy Katz's record.

Leading scorers: Allentown – Terry German 21, Bob Benner 13; Easton - Charlie Sutphen 17, Sterling Harvey 14, Charlie Ross 12.

Bethlehem 66 Central Catholic 63 OT: Bethlehem, in overtime, won its second straight game by defeating Central Catholic. Bob Egizio scored 21 for the Vikings, while Bethlehem was led by Jim Bauder with 16. Central Catholic fought back from an 11-point deficit at the half to take a 56-54 lead only to have Jim Bauder tie the score with a layup with 12 seconds to go in regulation.

Leading scorers: Bethlehem – Jim Bauder 16, Jim Williams 16, Gary Piff 13, Mike Preletz 12; Central Catholic – Bob Egizio 21, Greg Kloiber 12, Jim DeWar 11, Bob Potter 10.

Hazleton 71 Pottsville 43: Hazleton took a 24-11 first quarter lead on their way to a 36-22 halftime advantage. Hazleton kept Pottsville winless in the first half. Bill Umbarger made 13 foul shots.

Leading scorers: Hazleton - Mario Pecile 16, Mike Nastanovich 14, Dave Shafer 12; Pottsville – Bill Umbarger 19.[7]

Week 5

Allentown 70 Pottsville 41: Allentown began the second half with its 6th straight league win and 16th of 17 overall with a dispatching of Pottsville. With the starters only playing parts of the 1st and 3rd periods, the Canaries held a 38-19 halftime lead and extended it to 30 points in the 3rd stanza. Thirteen of the 14 players who played for Allentown scored in the contest.

Leading scorers: Allentown - Bob Heffner 14, Baron McElroy 10, Ken Dornblaser 10; Pottsville - Dick Matthews 24, Charles Miller 11.

Bethlehem 96 Easton 53: Bethlehem continued its season turnaround with a victory over Easton. The Hurricane took an 8-0 lead to start the game and extended the lead to 49-23 at halftime. Coach Howard used 12 players in the game with 11 of the 12 contributing points to the victory.

Leading scorers: Bethlehem - Gary Piff 25, Mike Preletz 19, Jim Bauder 14, Jim Williams 11; Easton - Bob Miller 12.

Hazleton 70 Central Catholic 59: At Hazleton's St. Joseph Hall, Frank Serany's team handed Central Catholic a loss after having fallen to the Vikings in the first half matchup at Rockne Hall. After Bob Potter tied the score at 15 at the end of the first quarter, Hazleton took the lead for the remainder of the contest.

Leading scorers: Hazleton - Joe Farace 25, Joe Petrilla 20, Mike Nastanovich 13; Central Catholic - Bob Potter 21.[8]

Week 6

Hazleton 59 Easton 57: On a snowy night, Joe Farace converted two foul shots in the last five seconds to pull out a win for Hazleton at Easton. Hazleton froze the ball for most of the last 3 minutes of play before Farace was fouled and made the two shots. Easton then raced down the court and could not tie the score when Charlie Ross's layup rolled off the rim. Hazleton led at the half 36-25 before Easton scored 24 points in the third quarter and took the lead 53-47 with five minutes to play in regulation. Hazleton brought 15 busloads of students to the Easton gym on a treacherous trip. Six hundred of the 900 fans in the Easton gym were from Hazleton.

Leading scorers: Hazleton - Mike Nastanovich 17, Joe Farace 14, Wally Skernolis 13; Easton - Bob Miller 16, Charles Sancinito 14.[9]

Allentown 93 Bethlehem 48: Postponed from the night before, Allentown ended Bethlehem's three-game roll with a walloping of the Hurricane. The 93 points set a new Little Palestra scoring record. The game was decided in the first quarter with Allentown holding a 21-3 lead going into the second quarter. Allentown scored 53 points in the second half to the Hurricane's 32.

Leading scorers: Allentown - Terry German 30, Baron McElroy 29, Bob Benner 14; Bethlehem - Gary Piff 18.[10]

Pottsville-Central Catholic: The game was postponed to later in the month due to the snow.

Week 7

Easton 74 Pottsville 49: A small crowd of 200 fans in Easton witnessed the Red Rovers victory over winless Pottsville. Coach Eddie Snyder inserted his reserves into the contest at the beginning of the second period after the Red Rovers took a 29-13 first quarter lead.

Leading scorers: Easton-Charlie Sutphen 12, Sterling Harvey 12, Bob Miller 12; Pottsville-Charlie Miller 17.

Bethlehem 95 Hazleton 60: Bethlehem bounced back from its loss to Allentown by routing Hazleton on the Liberty gym floor. Leading 18-8 in the first period, Bethlehem scored 18 straight points to put the final result out of question. The Hurricane led at the half 44-22. The game was marred by on-the-floor skirmishes during the rout.

Leading scorers: Bethlehem - Gary Piff 27, Jim Williams 22, Bill Davis 17, Lou Szemenyei 14; Hazleton - Joe Farace 16, Mike Nastanovich 11, Tom Grebowski 11.

Allentown 59 Central Catholic 49: Thirty-three hundred fans packed Rockne Hall to witness a fierce battle between Allentown and Central Catholic. Allentown's triumph was marred by several outbreaks. At the close of the first half, Bob Heffner was fouled in a play questioned by both coaches. Several fans stormed the floor, but police chased them back into the stands. Heffner made a foul shot to tie the game at 27 all at the half. In the last minute of the game, Bob Benner fired a looping pass to Baron McElroy who attempted a shot as he drove toward the basket. Clair Miller lunged into him in a deliberate foul. Fans and players poured onto the floor and started a 10-minute brawl. Fifteen policemen, including 11 called in, attempted to end the brawl. Players were sent to the locker rooms and the game ended prematurely due to the scuffle. The Central Catholic principal, Father Stephen Daday, issued a statement the following day with regrets about the previous night's fracas.

Leading scorers: Allentown – Ken Dornblaser 12, Baron McElroy 11, Terry German 10, Ken Wolfe 10; Central Catholic – Bob Egizio 12, Greg Kloiber 11, Bob Potter 10.[11]

Easton 59 Central Catholic 53: Later in the week, Rockne Hall experienced a much quieter night despite a loss by the Vikings to Easton. The Red Rovers erased a ten-point deficit at halftime 33-23 to a single point 42-41 entering the final quarter. Easton outscored Central Catholic 18-11 in the final period.

Leading scorers: Easton - Charlie Ross 19, Charlie Sutphen 14; Central Catholic - Bob Egizio 12, Bob Potter 10.

Bethlehem 79 Pottsville 48: In front of 1100 fans in Pottsville, Bethlehem showed some mercy in its second matchup with Pottsville, but still routed them, leading at the half 50-17. Bethlehem's Gary Piff and Pottsville's Dick Matthews put on a shooting clinic during the game. Pottsville was still winless in league play.

Leading scorers: Bethlehem – Gary Piff 27, Mike Preletz 10; Pottsville – Dick Matthews 27.

Allentown 55 Hazleton 50: In Hazleton, Allentown assured at least a tie for the second half title with their win over Hazleton. Despite giving the Canaries a tough battle, Hazleton could do no better than pull into a 38-38 tie in the third quarter. Allentown led 30-20 at halftime. Some 300 spectators were forced to pay a second time. Three hundred bogus tickets, for a prior game at the gym but with the same color, were stolen and sold to unwitting fans. Serial numbers were checked and fans with the bogus tickets had to purchase another ticket.

Leading scorers: Allentown – Baron McElroy 18, Ken Dornblaser 14; Hazleton – Joe Farace 12.[12]

Week 8

Central Catholic 60 Pottsville 53: Central Catholic played twice during the week due to a makeup from a snowy night earlier in the month. Pottsville rallied from a 42-31 deficit to start the final quarter to pull within 57-53 with 30 seconds to play, but they could not get any closer.

Leading scorers: Central Catholic – Greg Kloiber 21, Bob Potter 13; Pottsville – Dick Matthews 24.[13]

Hazleton 78 Pottsville 61: In its season finale, Pottsville experienced its 10th straight loss in the season at the hands of arch-rival Hazleton. Only 90 fans at the St. Joseph gym witnessed Joe Farace lead the Mountaineer attack. After taking a 22-12 lead after a quarter, the Mountaineers maintained a similar lead the rest of the way.

Leading scorers: Hazleton – Joe Farace 17, Wally Skernolis 11, Bob Supowit 10; Pottsville – Dick Matthews 24, Ed Embarger 19.[14]

Allentown 75 Easton 49: Allentown sewed up the second half and the season championship with a whipping of Easton. It was the 4th title in five years for the Canaries and pulled their overall record to 22-1. Allentown led 40-20 at halftime

Leading scorers: Allentown-Terry German 26, Bob Benner 13, Ken Dornblaser 12; Easton-Charley Ross 10.

Bethlehem 106 Central Catholic 66: Bethlehem, meanwhile, closed out a very disappointing season with another romp. This time Central Catholic absorbed the humiliation. Gary Piff poured in over half the points to set both a new league game scoring record and a season record of 248 points. Bob Egizio also finished with a fine game with 21 points for the Vikings.

Leading scorers: Bethlehem – Gary Piff 56, Bill Davis 15, Lou Szemenyei 10; Central Catholic – Bob Egizio 21, Greg Kloiber 16, Jim Gianelli 12. [15]

PIAA Postseason Play

Allentown 84 Wilson Boro 40: Allentown opened postseason play at Muhlenberg's Memorial Hall with a mismatch win over Wilson Boro, Lehigh-Northampton League champions. They made their 17th straight victory look easy by taking a 24-7 first quarter lead and employing 14 players in the contest.

Leading scorers: Allentown - Terry German 22, Baron McElroy 18, Bob Benner 10; Wilson Boro - Cal Vogel 22.[17]

Allentown 69 Palmerton 57: Allentown snapped Palmerton's season-long 24-game win streak to take the District 11 Class A title with the victory before 7,247 at Hershey Park Arena. Allentown led after the first quarter 19-6, but Palmerton chipped away and finally pulled within three points 57-54 with two minutes to play. Jim Oravec, hit four of five long shots to tighten the score. However, Allentown fought off the rally in the last two minutes for the win.

Leading scorers: Allentown – Baron McElroy 24, Bob Heffner 13, Terry German 10, Bob Benner 10; Palmerton – Jim Oravec 22, Dave Jones 10.[18]

Reading 69 Allentown 58: Reading, the District 3 champions, upset the favored Canaries at the Hershey arena. Leading 37-30 at the half, Allentown lost Ken Dornblazer and Bob Heffner on fouls and Reading took advantage in the second half. They outscored the Canaries 20-8 in the third quarter to take the lead.

Leading scorers: Reading – Fred Mautino 22, Bob Smith 14, Don Bertram 13, Marty Kemp 12; Allentown - Bob Benner 15, Baron McElroy 14, Terry German 14.[19]

PCIAA Postseason Play

Central Catholic 60 Reading Central Catholic 51: After 15 lead changes during the game, Reading Central Catholic held a one-point lead 46-45 with five minutes to play. The Vikings scored the next 6 points to take the lead and stay in front the rest of the way. Reading Central Catholic had taken a 15-10 lead after a quarter.

Leading scorers: Central Catholic – Greg Kloiber 21, Bill Cramsey 11; Reading Central Catholic – Eddie Jablonski 25.[20]

Central Catholic 62 Pottsville Catholic 40: Coach Emil Carazo started his second team and did not bring in the usual starters until midway through the second quarter. The second team held a 12-9 lead at the end of the first quarter. After holding a 25-20 first half lead, Central Catholic held Pottsville Catholic to four points in the third quarter while scoring 21 to take a commanding lead.

Leading scorers: Central Catholic-Bill Cramsey 13, Bob Egizio 12; Pottsville Catholic-Jimmy Joulwan 15.[21]

Harrisburg Catholic 63 Central Catholic 60: The 20-13 first quarter advantage by Harrisburg Catholic carried them to victory over Central Catholic. The Vikings cut the lead to 32-27 at the half and 50-46 after three quarters. The Vikings fell behind 41-30 in the third quarter before a rally cut the deficit to four points. Late in the fourth quarter, the Vikings lost Bob Egizio and Bob Potter on fouls. With 13 seconds to play, the Vikings' Jim Dewar made a foul shot to cut the lead to 62-60, but the rally ended there.

Leading scorers: Harrisburg Central Catholic – Joe Daylor 16, Frank Salinger 15, John Clark 15; Central Catholic – Greg Kloiber 22, Bob Potter 11.[22]

Postseason Accolades

Leading scorers: Setting numerous scoring records, Bethlehem's Gary Piff easily won the scoring title with the record-setting 248 points. Other top scorers included: Dick Matthews, Pottsville, 171; Joe Farace, Hazleton, and Terry German, Allentown, 160; Baron McElroy, Allentown, 151; Bob Egizio, Central Catholic, 131; Greg Kloiber, Central Catholic, 130; Jim Williams, Bethlehem, 120; Charlie Miller, Pottsville, 115; Jim Bauder, Bethlehem, 113; Bob Miller, Easton 107; and Bob Benner, Allentown 104.[23]

All-Stars: The league's all-stars included: Joe Farace, Hazleton; Gary Piff, Bethlehem; Terry German and Baron McElroy, Allentown; and Bob Egizio, Central Catholic, on the first team. Second team choices included: Bob Benner of Allentown; Jim Williams, Bethlehem; Dick Matthews, Pottsville; and Bob Miller and Charlie Ross, Easton.[24]

All-State: Named to the Associated Press All-State team were Terry German, Allentown, 3rd Team; Baron McElroy, Allentown, 4th Team; Bob Benner, Allentown, and Gary Piff, Bethlehem, 5th Team. Honorable Mention selectees included: Joe Farace, Hazleton; and Dick Matthews, Pottsville.[25]

Final Standings

First Half		Second Half		Overall	
Allentown	5-0	Allentown	5-0	Allentown	10-0
Central Catholic	3-2	Bethlehem	4-1	Bethlehem	6-4
Hazleton	3-2	Hazleton	3-2	Hazleton	6-4
Easton	2-3	Easton	2-3	Easton	4-6
Bethlehem	2-3	Central Catholic	1-4	Central Catholic	4-6
Pottsville	0-5	Pottsville	0-5	Pottsville	0-10

Team Rosters

Allentown: Coach Milo Sewards, Bob Benner, Joe Berghold, John Canzano, Ken Dornblaser, Terry German, Bob Heffner, Carl Johnson, Bill Kesack, Art Kulp, Ed Lesko, Ron Lopsonzski, Dick Markowitz, Baron McElroy, Redfrick "Junior" Quarterman, Dennis Reichard, Charles Schimeneck, Claude Wilson, Ken Wolfe

Bethlehem: Coach John Howard, Jim Bauder, Jim Cropper, Bill Davis, Bob Horvath, Harold Karte, Dave Keen, Lester Lazarowitz, Gary Piff, Mike Preletz, Vince Seaman, Jim Williams, Lou Szemenyei

Central Catholic: Coach Emil Carazo, Tom Brown, Bill Cramsey, Jim DeWar, Jim Egizio, James Gallagher, Jim Gianelli, Wayne Iskra, Bela Kerecz, Greg Kloiber, Clair Miller, Bob Potter, John Redding, Charles Rohrer, George Sheese, Ed Werner, Ed Yost

Easton: Coach Ed Snyder, William Anckaitis, Thomas Bright, Harry Fahl, Sterling Harvey, David Mazzie, Bob Miller, Larry Phillips, Harold Renner, Charles Ross, Charles Sancinito, Charlie Sutphen, Fred Tracy, Kenneth Warman, John Worrich

Hazleton: Coach Frank Serany, Joe Farace, Frank Grebowski, Earl Hunsinger, Joe Kokinda, Tom Mindick, Richie Monks, Mike Nastanovich, Mario Pecille, Joe Pendal, Joe Petrilla. Joe Scallion, Dave Shafer, Norm Shutovich, Wally Skernolis, Herb Skuba, Bob Supowit

Pottsville: Coach Ed Deitch, Merrill Abeshaus, Ron Boris, Tom Devitt, Ronny Diehl, Ron Heckman, Bill Heinbach, Dick Matthews, Charles Miller, Dick Miller, Tom Sanna, Vince Schuster, Bill Umberger, Jimmy Whitaker

Allentown High School – 1955 League Champions[16]

Front: Richard Sterner and Arthur Nagle (mgrs.); Middle: Claude Wilson, William Kesak, Joseph Berghold, Robert Benner, Baron McElroy, Kenneth Wolfe, Dennis Reichard, Arthur Kulp; Back: Charles Schimeneck, Terry German, Joe Blankowitsch (trainer), Dick Markowitz, Coach Sewards, Robert Heffner, Ken Wildonger (asst coach), Kenneth Dornbalser, Ron Lopsonzski

1956

Central Wins Another PCIAA Title

The league representatives decided to retain the same leadership as in the past recent years. Phil Phillippi, Stan Steigerwalt, and Edgar Rabenold were re-elected as president, vice president, and secretary-treasurer for another year in the spring meeting of the league as Shankweiler's Hotel.[1] For the first time in several years, league expansion plans were not brought up and no schools attended the meeting to request consideration.

Week 1

Central Catholic 69 Hazleton 59: Central Catholic opened its season with a scintillating finish at Hazleton. The Vikings held a two-point lead with nearly five minutes remaining in the contest. Center Dick Markowitz and guard Jim Dewar converted what was considered a four-point play to stretch the lead. Jim Dewar was fouled in the act of shooting and made his first attempt. Although he missed his second attempt, Dick Markowitz tapped it in and was fouled on the play. He converted his foul shot and now the lead was six. Twenty seconds later, Markowitz added a hook shot and the Vikings were on to an upset win.

Leading scorers: Central Catholic – Dick Markowitz 31, Jim Dewar 15; Hazleton - Mike Nastanovich 17, Fran Libonati 16, Norm Shutovich 12.

Bethlehem 88 Pottsville 59: In Pottsville, Billy Packer and Gary Piff led the rout of Pottsville with Piff scoring 12 points in the 1st quarter. Bethlehem held a 44-32 lead on their way to their 9th consecutive triumph.

Leading scorers: Bethlehem – Billy Packer 22, Gary Piff 21, John Mika 18, Bob Horvath 11, Rocco Zulli 10; Pottsville – Elmer Umberger 19, Bob Pepe 14, George Joulwan 12.

Allentown 75 Easton 54: Winning its opening game in the league and 10th in a row, Allentown started fast in their quest for a fourth straight league title by downing Easton. After the Red Rovers led at the end of a quarter 13-12, the Canaries took charge of the contest in the second quarter and extended the lead to 57-39 after three quarters.

Leading scorers: Allentown - Ken Wolfe 25, Redfrick Quarterman 16, Bob Heffner 14; Easton - Larry Phillips 13, Dave Mazzie 13, Charlie Ross 11.[2]

Week 2

Allentown 77 Bethlehem 75: Two unbeaten teams squared off with Allentown taking on Bethlehem in front of 4200 fans in Bethlehem's new Memorial Gym. Five hundred fans had to be turned away. In a game that was tied at least seven times, the last one at 51-51 at the start of the fourth quarter, Allentown finally prevailed and remained unbeaten in 11 games. Allentown led at the end of each of the first three quarters 18-13, 31-30, and 51-49. Allentown led 75-67 with a minute and a half to play before Bethlehem's rally fell short. For Bethlehem, Johnny Mika scored 20 points in the 1st half and Gary Piff 25 points in the 2nd half.

Leading scorers: Allentown - Bob Heffner 29, Joe Berghold 20, Ken Wolfe 19; Bethlehem - Gary Piff 27, Johnny Mika 22, Billy Packer 10.

Central Catholic 93 Easton 63: Central Catholic kept pace with Allentown by trouncing Easton. The teams committed 56 personal fouls in the game, 33 by Easton and 23 by the Vikings. The teams shot a total of 75 free throws and the fourth quarter took 37 minutes to play due to the stoppage play due to fouls. After they trailed 11-10 in the first quarter, the Vikings held a 45-28 lead at the half.

Leading scorers: Central Catholic - Dick Markowitz 29, Greg Kloiber 18, Bob Egizio 12; Easton - Charlie Ross 26, Larry Phillips 14, Dave Mazzie 12.

Hazleton 82 Pottsville 67: Hazleton bounced back from its first week loss with a win over lowly Pottsville. The Mountaineers outscored the Maroons 49-28 in the first and third quarters to propel them to the victory.

Leading scorers: Hazleton - Frank Grebowski 21, Mario Pecile 15, Ernie Libonati 14; Pottsville - Bob Pepe 21, George Joulwan 21.[3]

Week 3

Hazleton 83 Easton 72: Hazleton handed Easton its first league loss with their triumph over the Red Rovers. After leading by six at halftime 33-27, Hazleton outscored the Red Rovers 27-18 in the third quarter to take an insurmountable lead.

Leading scorers: Hazleton - Frank Grebowski 25, Fran Libonati 22, Richie Monks 11; Easton - Charlie Ross 24, Harry Fahl 10, Fred Tracy 10, Larry Phillips 10.

Central Catholic 79 Bethlehem 65: Central Catholic avenged its loss to Bethlehem in the Rockne Hall Tournament and handed the Hurricane their second consecutive loss. The Vikings charged out to a 22-7 first quarter lead and kept pouring it on. Central Catholic had five players in double figures.

Leading scorers: Central Catholic - Dick Markowitz 19, Jim DeWar 13, Bob Yost 13, Bill Cramsey 12, Greg Kloiber 11; Bethlehem - Gary Piff 28, Johnny Mika 13.

Allentown 100 Pottsville 72: Allentown outscored Pottsville to tie Central Catholic for the league lead. John Canzano scored the 100th point which set a new team scoring record for the Little Palestra. After taking a 46-35 halftime lead, the Canaries scored 54 points in the second half to hit the century mark.

Leading scorers: Allentown - Bob Heffner 25, Joe Berghold 24, Ken Wolfe 18, Redfrick Quarterman 11, John Canzano 11; Pottsville - Bob Pepe 25, Elmer Umberger 19, George Joulwan 12, Jim Whitaker 10.[4]

Allentown 62 Hazleton 55: Later in the week, the Canaries eliminated Hazleton from the first half championship race at the Little Palestra. Several times throughout the game, Hazleton rallied to keep the Allentown fans anxious. After the Canaries led 36-23 at the half, the Mountaineers cut the lead to 48-41 after three quarters and cut the lead to 59-55 in the 4th quarter before Allentown countered to pull out the victory.

Leading scorers: Allentown - Bob Heffner 22, Redfrick Quarterman 18, Ken Wolfe 16; Hazleton - Frank Grebowski 18, Mario Pecile 13, Fran Libonati 12.

Central Catholic 74 Pottsville 51: Central Catholic kept pace with Canaries to set up a first-place showdown in the final game of the first half. The Vikings easily whipped Pottsville. After leading 40-28 to start the third quarter, the Vikings ran off 12 straight points to start the second half and put the game away.

Leading scorers: Central Catholic - Dick Markowitz 17, Ed Yost 12, Bela Kerecz 10; Pottsville - Bob Pepe 21, George Joulwan 10, Elmer Umberger 10.

Bethlehem 73 Easton 67: Scoring 23 of his points in the second and third quarters, Gary Piff led Bethlehem over Easton. Bethlehem trailed Easton 12-1, 18-5, and 24-14 before battling back to within three points at the half. A nine-point advantage in the 3rd period won the game for the Hurricane.

Leading scorers: Bethlehem – Gary Piff 24, Johnny Mika 15, Billy Packer 14; Easton – Dave Mazzie 21, Charlie Ross 18.[5]

Week 4

Allentown 67 Central Catholic 61: Redfrick "Junior" Quarterman paced the Canaries in a hard-fought triumph over Central Catholic. After the Vikings cut Allentown's third quarter lead to two points 33-31, the Canaries racked up 11 straight points to put them securely in the lead and become the first half champions.

Leading scorers: Allentown – Redfrick Quarterman 24, Bob Heffner 19, Ken Wolfe 14; Central Catholic - Dick Markowitz 18, Jim DeWar 14, Bob Egizio 11 for the Vikings.

Easton 61 Pottsville 58: Easton finally won its first league game over hapless Pottsville. Pottsville led the game at the half 37-28, but Easton rallied and tied the game at 45 early in the fourth quarter.

Leading scorers: Easton - Charlie Ross 24, Larry Phillips 14, Dave Mazzie 13; Pottsville - Jim Whitaker 14, George Joulwan 13, Vince Schuster 12.

Hazleton 67 Bethlehem 59: Hazleton won the contest at the foul line converting 18 of 28 attempts compared to the Hurricane's 9 of 21. Hazleton led at the half 34-31.

Leading scorers: Hazleton - Frank Grebowski 24, Mario Pecile 16, Mike Nostanovich 13; Bethlehem - Gary Piff 21, Billy Packer 16, Bob Horvath 10.[6]

Week 5

Hazleton 76 Central Catholic 66: Despite the Vikings making 18 of 20 foul shots and equalizing Hazleton in field goals with 24, the Mountaineers won the game at Rockne Hall. Hazleton made 28 of 38 foul shots for the ten-point victory. Racking up three personal fouls early, Dick Markowitz was forced to sit early in the first half. He came back in and promptly drew his fourth to force him out again. Eventually, when he came back in the game, he quickly got his fifth plus a technical foul. He scored only 8 points. Hazleton had four players in double figures.

Leading scorers: Hazleton - Frank Grebowski 21, Mario Pecile 17, Mike Nastanovich 14, Norman Shutovich 12; Central Catholic - Bob Egizio 20, Greg Kloiber 14, Bill Cramsey 12.

Bethlehem 81 Pottsville 35: Gary Piff went over the 1000-point mark for his career in Bethlehem's shellacking of Pottsville. Piff scored the last 15 points in the game to put his at a career total of 1,001. With Bethlehem leading 66-28 in the last quarter, Coach John Howard put the first string back in with the purpose of feeding Piff and getting him to the milestone.

Leading scorers: Bethlehem -Gary Piff 34, Billy Packer 16, Bob Horvath 14; Pottsville -George Joulwan 10.

Allentown 64 Easton 50: Allentown opened the second half against a scrappy Easton squad with their 17th straight victory. Easton pulled within 3 points, 46-43 early in the fourth quarter, primarily on the scoring of Dave Mazzie. Mazzie fouled out and Allentown pulled away for the win.

Leading scorers: Allentown - Bob Heffner 18, Joe Berghold 15, Junior Quarterman. 11; Easton – Dave Mazzie 17, Larry Phillips 13, Charlie Ross 12.[7]

Week 6

Central Catholic 78 Easton 53: Central Catholic held only a two-point advantage at the half over Easton 29-27. They unleashed their offense with a 30-point outburst in the third quarter to take a commanding seventeen-point 59-42 lead.

Leading scorers: Central Catholic - Dick Markowitz 17, Bill Cramsey 14, Bob Egizio 10; Easton - Dave Mazzie 15, Charlie Ross 13.

Allentown 87 Bethlehem 53: Despite a big night from Gary Piff, with 16 from the foul line, Bethlehem fell to Allentown. The Canaries' juggernaut offense chalked up a 24-10 first half lead and scored 73 points in the first three quarters of the contest.

Leading scorers: Allentown - Bob Heffner 24, Ken Wolfe 20, Junior Quarterman 17, Joe Berghold 16; Bethlehem – Gary Piff 28, Bob Horvath 12.

Hazleton 90 Pottsville 63: Pottsville absorbed another bruising loss against Hazleton. The Mountaineers led at the half 49-30 and added to the advantage in both the third and fourth quarters.

Leading scorers: Hazleton - Mario Pecile 20, Frank Gebrowski 20, Mike Nastanovich 17; Pottsville - George Joulwan 18, Bob Pepe 17, Elmer Umberger 15.[8]

Central Catholic 70 Bethlehem 62: Gary Piff bettered his own season record for points in a loss to Central Catholic. He bested his season total by 10 to reach 450 with several games to go. No one else scored in double figures for the Hurricane. Bethlehem led 15-12 after the 1st quarter, but the Vikings then took charge.

Leading scorers: Central Catholic-Dick Markowitz 21, Bob Egizio 16, Bill Cramsey 14, Jim DeWar 13; Bethlehem–Gary Piff 25.

Hazleton 68 Easton 61: Hazleton kept pace for the second half title by taking down home-standing Easton. The Mountaineers unleashed their offense in the middle two quarters to outscore the Red Rovers 46-36.

Leading scorers: Hazleton - Frank Grebowski 35, Mario Pecile 14, Mike Nastanovich 13; Easton - Charlie Ross 18, Dave Mazzie 15, Harold Renner 12, Harry Fahl 10.[9]

Allentown 80 Pottsville 65: Allentown traveled to Pottsville and came home with a victory to remain in a first-place tie. Employing a defense determined to continually steal the ball, the Canaries totaled 25 fouls and lost Junior Quarterman, Joe Berghold, and Ken Wolfe on fouls in the 4th quarter. Allentown scored 50 points in the first half to Pottsville's 37 points

Leading scorers: Allentown – Bob Heffner 28, Junior Quarterman 17, Ken Wolfe 12; Pottsville - Jim Whitaker 18, Bob Pepe 18, Elmer Umberger 14, George Joulwan 10.[10]

Week 7

Allentown 91 Hazleton 70: The battle for the second half title took place at the Little Palestra with Allentown getting the upper hand by downing Hazleton. Winning their 21st straight game, they held a one-point lead 19-18 after one quarter and gradually pulled away the rest of the game and led 61-48 after three quarters. The game was delayed for an hour due to bad driving conditions, but the Canaries were undeterred.

Leading scorers: Allentown - Bob Heffner 22, Joe Berghold 22, Junior Quarterman 20, Ken Wolfe 12; Pottsville - Frank Grebowski 19, Mario Pecile 18, Mike Nastanovich 12.

Bethlehem 88 Easton 61: Scoring in spurts of 8 and 12 in the second quarter, Bethlehem took a 43-21 half time lead. In the loss, Charlie Ross raised his season total to 381 points and broke the Easton season record set by Tom Georgaris.

Leading scorers: Bethlehem – Gary Piff 33, John Mika 13, Billy Packer 12, Bob Horvath 12; Easton – Charlie Ross 16, Dave Mazzie 13, Harry Fahl.

Central Catholic 91 Pottsville 70: Central Catholic extended the home team's losing streak to 9 in league play for the season with a mashing of Pottsville. After leading by 40-30 at halftime, the Vikings doubled up the Red Rovers in the third quarter 24-12. Bob Egizio, Jim DeWar, Greg Kloiber, and Dick Markowitz scored 71 of the Vikings' 91 points.

Leading scorers: Central Catholic – Bob Egizio 20, Jim DeWar 18, Greg Kloiber 18, Dick Markowitz 15; Pottsville - Bob Pepe 22, George Joulwan 16, Elmer Umberger 12, Ron Heckman 10.[11]

Week 8

Allentown 92 Central Catholic 53: Allentown (22-0) clinched its fourth straight East Penn League title with its 25th straight league win, a drubbing of Central Catholic (18-4) at the Little Palestra. Allentown scored 16 straight points in the 3rd quarter to build a 30-point advantage and seal the title. Dick Markowitz was the only bright light for the Vikings, scoring a little over half the team's total.

Leading scorers: Allentown - Bob Heffner 28, Joe Berghold 22, Ken Wolfe 22, Junior Quarterman 13; Central Catholic – Dick Markowitz 27.[12]

Easton 67 Pottsville 60: In a battle of second half winless teams, Easton prevailed as Charlie Ross extended the school's season individual scoring record to 403 points. Easton led the entire game with Pottsville scoring six unanswered points to pull within six 60-54, but the rally ended there.

Leading scorers: Easton - Charlie Ross 22, Harry Fahl 13, Larry Phillips 10; Pottsville - Bob Pepe 19, Elmer Umberger 17, George Joulwan 15.

Hazleton 74 Bethlehem 71: In Bethlehem's loss to Hazleton, Gary Piff set an East Penn League scoring record with 271 points in 10 games. Piff also set a school record with 513 points in 22 games and graduated as the Hurricanes' career leader with 1,114 points. After Bethlehem led 18-14 after the first quarter, Hazleton outscored the Hurricane 48-38 in the second and third quarters to build a winning margin.

Leading scorers: Hazleton - Mario Pecile 22, Frank Grebowski 19, Mike Nastanovich 16.; Bethlehem – Gary Piff 30, Billy Packer 11, Bob Horvath 10.[13]

Postseason Play

Allentown 97 Mahanoy City 74: At Muhlenberg's Memorial Hall, Allentown opened district play with a setback of Mahanoy City. Bob Heffner had a record night when his 11 field goals broke LeRoy Katz's school record of 198 points. His total ended at 207. His 535 points established a new season record for the Canaries besting Katz's record of 504. Leading at halftime 40-35, the Canaries broke the game open by outscoring Mahanoy City 26-15 in the third quarter.

Leading scorers: Allentown – Bob Heffner 26, Joe Berghold 22, Ken Wolfe 17, Junior Quarterman 14; Mahanoy City - Pete Ervin 31, Elom Kern 15, Tom Courtney 14.[15]

Palmerton 58 Allentown 57: Bob Mlkvy scored his team's last seven in the final two minutes as Palmerton (22-4) upset previously unbeaten Allentown at the Penn Palestra in the District 11 Class A championship game. It was their first title in 20 years and the Blue Bombers' first win over the Canaries in more than 25 seasons. The Canaries' Joe Berghold had the opportunity for one last shot, but Palmerton's defense prevented him from getting it off. After trailing most of the game, Allentown rallied to lead by five points 56-51 with 2:04 to play. Mlkvy scored two field goals and three foul shots. Before Berghold's last second attempt, Heffner was fouled but converted only one of two foul shots.

Leading scorers: Palmerton-Bob Mlkvy 29, Terry Eckert 17; Allentown-Bob Heffner 22, Junior Quarterman 14, Ken Wolfe 13.[16]

PCIAA Playoffs

Central Catholic 101 Pottsville Nativity 57: Central Catholic began its hunt for another PCIAA title with a whipping of Pottsville Nativity at the Little Palestra. The 101 points topped the Allentown record of 100 points for the gym. With their significant height advantage, the Vikings saw five players reach double figures. The Vikings led at halftime 55-30.

Leading scorers: Central Catholic - Dick Markowitz 24, Bob Egizio 18, Greg Kloiber 13, Bob Yost 10, Bill Cramsey 10; Pottsville Nativity - Jim Joulwan 22, Gerry Powers 11, Tom Liptock 10.[17]

Central Catholic 98 Reading Central Catholic 38: Central Catholic pasted its second straight playoff opponent by rolling over Reading Central Catholic at the Albright College gym in Reading. The game was never in doubt as five Vikings again made double figures. The Vikings held Reading to six first quarter and five third quarter points and led going into the fourth quarter 73-22.

Leading scorers: Central Catholic - Bela Kerecz 24, Bob Egizio 16, Dick Markowitz 14, Greg Kloiber 13, Bill Cramsey 12; Reading Central Catholic - Paul Axbein 21, Michael Yachnik 10.[18]

Central Catholic 99 Bishop Kenrick 44: Bishop Kenrick arrived 30 minutes late for its matchup with Central Catholic for the Philadelphia Diocese title game at the Little Palestra. Central Catholic outclassed an opponent for the third straight playoff game. For the second straight contest, the Vikings held an opponent to single digits in the first, five points, and third period, eight points, to take a substantial lead 74-26 into the fourth quarter.

Leading scorers: Central Catholic – Bela Kerecz 14, Jim DeWar 12, Bob Egizio 12, Bill Dougherty 11, Dick Markowitz 10; Bishop Kenrick - Jim McCrudden 15, Dennis Magee 13, Joe Davis 10.[19]

Central Catholic 56 Harrisburg Catholic 53: After three almost non-contest games, Central Catholic was put to the test and passed against Harrisburg Catholic at Muhlenberg's Memorial Hall to win the Eastern Regional PCIAA title. In a close game all the way and the game tied at 45 at the three-quarter mark, the Vikings had to dig deep to pull out the win. Dick Markowitz scored 7 of the Vikings 11 points in the final quarter. Harrisburg could only tally 8 as the Vikings survived a tough fight.

Leading scorers: Central Catholic – Dick Markowitz 22, Bela Kerecz 14, Bill Cramsey 10; Harrisburg Catholic – Steve Avery 16, Mickey Bekelja 11, Joe Weideman 10.[20]

Central Catholic 68 Pittsburgh Central Catholic 60: On St. Patrick's Day, Bill Cramsey scored six points during a decisive 10-0 run, and Central Catholic (24-5) won its fifth PCIAA Class A state title with a win over Pittsburgh Central Catholic before 2,500 at Muhlenberg's Memorial Hall. Cramsey's points helped the Vikings stretch a 55-53 lead to 65-53 with under three minutes remaining. The Vikings led at the half 37-28.

Leading scorers: Central Catholic – Bill Cramsey 16, Dick Markowitz scored 15, Bela Kerecz 12, Bob Egizio 11; Pittsburgh Central Catholic - Ned Twyman 20, Ray Masa 13, Bill Larkin 12, Tom Powell 11.[21]

Eastern States Catholic Basketball Tournament

As a result of its PCIAA championship, the Eastern States Catholic Invitational Tournament invited Central Catholic to participate in the tournament in Newport, RI.

Central Catholic 85 DeLasalle 53: In the opening round game, the Vikings used its height and speed to defeat DeLasalle of Newport. The Vikings put the game away in the first quarter by building a 24-3 lead. Coach Emil Carazo missed the game due to the birth of his son. Assistant coach John Compardo guided the team to victory.

Leading scorers: Central Catholic - Bobby Egizio 18, Dick Markowitz 18, Jim DeWar 14, Greg Kloiber 14, Bill Cramsey 10; DeLasalle – Terrance Toppa 17, Robert Gibson 16, John Martins 12.[22]

Central Catholic 91 Boys' High School 73: The following night, with Emil Carazo back at the helm, the Vikings took on Boys' High School of Trenton. The game was tied 17 times and was tied at 73 with three minutes to play. The Vikings scored the last 18 points in the game to move on to the title game. Dick Markowitz broke Alec DeLucia's season record for points with 551 to break the old record of 541.

Leading scorers: Central Catholic - Dick Markowitz 22, Bela Kerecz 22, Bob "Pickles" Egizio 15, Greg Kloiber 13; Boys' High – George Kinczel 29, Bob Piotrowski 16, John Samonsky 16.[23]

St. Mary's 50 Central Catholic 49: A buzzer-beating layup denied Central Catholic the Eastern States Catholic Invitational title when St. Mary's of Elizabeth, N.J., pulled out the win in the title game of the eight-team tournament in Newport, R.I. The Vikings led most of the game and had a 49-48 lead on Bill Cramsey's layup with 15 seconds to play. Seconds later, Jim DeWar stole the ball and missed an uncontested layup which would have sealed the victory. St. Mary's got the ball out-of-bounds with three seconds to play. On the in-bound pass, St. Mary's scored at the buzzer to take the hard-fought game.

Leading scorers: St. Mary's – Pat O'Donnell 16, Jim Kenna 13; Central Catholic - Dick Markowitz 19.[24]

Postseason Accolades

Leading Scorers: Gary Piff, Bethlehem, ran away with the scoring title with 271 points. Bob Heffner, Allentown, finished second with 230 points. Others in the top ten included Frank Grebowski, Hazleton, 212; Dick Markowitz, Central Catholic, 202; Charlie Ross, Easton, 184; Bob Pepe, Pottsville, 170; Ken Wolfe, Allentown, 163; Redfrick "Junior" Quarterman, Allentown, 150; Mario Pecile, Hazleton, and Joe Berghold, Allentown 144.[25]

All-Stars: Hazleton's Plain Speaker selected league all-stars for the season. The first team selectees included: Bob Heffner and Ken Wolfe, Allentown; Frank Grebowski, Hazleton; Dick Markowitz, Central Catholic; and Gary Piff, Bethlehem. Members of the second team were Charlie Ross, Easton; Bob Egizio, Central Catholic; Mario Pecile and Mike Nastanovich, Hazleton; and Joe Berghold, Allentown.[26]

All-State: The Associated Press' All Pennsylvania Scholastic Team included Bob Heffner, Allentown, 1st team; Gary Piff, Bethlehem, and Frank Grebowski, Hazleton, 3rd team. The Honorable Mention list included: Bill Cramsey and Dick Markowitz, Central Catholic; Ken Wolfe, Allentown.[27]

Final Standings

First Half		Second Half		Overall	
Allentown	5-0	Allentown	5-0	Allentown	10-0
Central Catholic	4-1	Hazleton	4-1	Central Catholic	7-3
Hazleton	3-2	Central Catholic	3-2	Hazleton	7-3
Bethlehem	2-3	Bethlehem	2-3	Bethlehem	4-6
Easton	1-4	Easton	1-4	Easton	2-8
Pottsville	0-5	Pottsville	0-5	Pottsville	0-10

Team Rosters

Allentown: Coach Milo Sewards, Robert Bauman, Joe Berghold, John Canzano, Bernie Costello, John Donmoyer, Robert Fager, Bob Heffner, Lew Keppel, Bill Kesack, James Kritis, Ed Lesko, John Olsen, Tom Peacock, Redfrick Quarterman, Denis Reichard, Lou Wasser, Ken Wolfe

Bethlehem: Coach John Howard, Bill Chaikowsky, Ross Culligan, Mario Donangelo, Bob Horwath, Harold Karte, Ray Latzo, John Mika, Billy Packer, Gary Piff, Mike Preletz, Don Wilson, Rocco Zulli

Central Catholic: Coach Emil Carazo, Bill Cramsey, Jim DeWar, Bill Dougherty, Bob Egizio, Wayne Ikstra, Bela Kerecz, Greg Kloiber, Dick Markowitz, Tom McHale, Ron Oranczak, Charles Rohrer, Bob Yost

Easton: Coach Ed Snyder, Jerry Amato, Don Anderson, Terry Bartolet, John Evans, Harry Fahl, Mike Griffin, Joe Kohler, Dave Mazzie, Larry Phillips, Harold Renner, Charlie Ross, Fred Tracy, Bruce West, John Worrich

Hazleton: Coach Frank Serany, John Cusatis, Ray DeBalso, Angie Esposito, Lou Farace, Bernie Gatski, Frank Grebowski, Eugene Havrilla, Ernie Libonati, Fran Libonati, Lou Miorelli, Richie Monks, Mike Nastanovich, Mario Pecile, Jim Perneski, Frank Serany Jr, Norman Shutovich, Herb Skuba

Pottsville: Coach Charles "Daw" Miller, Tom Devitt, Bob Edwards, Carl Engleman, Ron Heckman, Bill Heinbach, George Joulwan, John Kendall, Bob Pepe, Tony Roland, Vince Schuster, Bill Sisco, Elmer Umberger, Jim Whitaker, Bob Witcoski

Allentown High School – 1956 League Champions[14]

Front: R. Sterner (mgr), John Olsen, John Canzano, Bill Kesack, Tom Peacock, Lou Wasser, Lew Keppel, Robert Fager, G Werley (mgr): Back: Joe Blankowitsch (trainer), J Kritis, Ed Lesko, John Donmoyer, Redfrick Quarterman, Coach Sewards, Bob Heffner, Ken Wolfe, R Bauman, Joe Berghold, Ken Wildonger (asst coach)

1957

Five Consecutive League Titles

The league representatives retained the same leadership as in the past recent years. Phil Phillippi, Stan Steigerwalt, and Edgar Rabenold were re-elected to the president, vice president, and secretary-treasurer positions for another year in the spring meeting of the league Hazleton.[1]

Week 1

Easton 50 Central Catholic 47: Easton opened the league season at home against Central Catholic and avenged its loss to the Vikings at the Lehigh Valley Invitational Tournament at Rockne Hall over the holidays. Sophomore Terry Bartolet, also quarterback on the football team, led the Red Rovers as they held a lead for the entire game in the victory. After the Vikings got within a point 48-47 with 15 seconds to play, Bartolet made two foul shots to secure the win.

Leading scorers: Easton – Terry Bartolet 22; Central Catholic - Bill Cramsey 16.[2]

Pottsville 69 Hazleton 56: Pottsville fell behind 17-8 in the first period and by 11 points in the third quarter. Bob Pepe, a diminutive 5'9" guard, drilled in 12 points in the third quarter to pull Pottsville ahead of Hazleton for the eventual win. Jim Joulwan, a transfer from Pottsville Catholic, backed up Pepe.

Leading scorers: Pottsville – Bob Pepe 32, Jim Joulwan 16; Hazleton - Fran Libonati 14, Rinaldo Pecile 11, Lou Feola 10.

Allentown 66 Bethlehem 55: Bob Heffner scored two-thirds of the Canaries' 66 points in a league-opening win over Bethlehem. He established a new school scoring record and registered the most points scored by any player at the Little Palestra. Bethlehem had three players in double figures, but could not overcome Heffner's heroics. After the Canaries led by 9 at the half 32-23, the Hurricane stormed back to within a point 50-49. Allentown then scored the next 9 points to build a ten-point lead 59-49 and take charge of the contest.

Leading scorers: Allentown –Bob Heffner 41; Bethlehem -Billy Packer 19, Al Senavitis 14, Dave Sellers 11.[3]

Week 2

Allentown 84 Pottsville 70: Bob Heffner nearly equaled his prior game output in Allentown's drubbing of Pottsville. With Allentown trailing 19-18, the Canaries ran off 16 straight points to lead 34-19. Heffner scored 15 points in the third quarter to keep the Canaries well in front.

Leading scorers: Allentown– Bob Heffner 39, Bob Fager 16, Bernie Costello 12; Pottsville- George Joulwan 25, Bob Pepe 20.[4]

Bethlehem 61 Central Catholic 56: Bethlehem bounced back to hand Central Catholic a 2nd straight league loss. Central Catholic lost the game in the third period when they could only muster 8 points to Bethlehem's 18. The Vikings rallied to within three points 57-54 but could not overcome the cold third quarter.

Leading scorers: Bethlehem - Al Senavitis 17, Dave Seller 14, Billy Packer 11; Central Catholic - Bill Cramsey 18, Bob Yost 11, Charley Rohrer 11.

Hazleton 45 Easton 44: At Easton, the Red Rovers lost by a single point to Hazleton. The referee assessed Easton coach Pete Carril with a technical after an argument with the officials. Hazleton made the shot to put them ahead 45-40. Hazleton led at the half 27-26 and 38-35 after three quarters.

Leading scorers: Hazleton – Fran Libonati 15, Lou Miorelli 14; Easton - Terry Bartolet 19.[5]

Week 3

Pottsville 80 Central Catholic 76: Central Catholic lost its third straight league game to Pottsville at Rockne Hall. Central led at the half 39-35, but Pottsville put on a 26-point third quarter splurge, outscoring the Vikings by 16 in the quarter, to pull ahead. Despite a 4th quarter rally to pull within 3, the lead was too great. Bob Pepe made four consecutive foul shots late the game to pull the Crimson Tide out of danger.

Leading scorers: Pottsville - Jim Joulwan 25, Bob Pepe 21, Bob Edwards 16; Central Catholic – Charlie Rohrer 23, Dick Hollschwander 16, Bob Yost 16, Bill Cramsey 12.

Allentown 74 Hazleton 70: Bob Heffner scored 41 points for the second time in three games setting an individual scoring record for the Hazleton High School gym. He also broke Bill Wanish's all-time school record of 934 total points. Allentown defeated Hazleton to remain as the only undefeated team. Hazleton led after the first two quarters 24-20 and 42-31 before the Canaries rallied behind Heffner's 8 straight points to pull ahead by a point going into the fourth quarter 56-55.

Leading scorers: Allentown– Bob Heffner 41, Bernie Costello 13; Hazleton- Fran Libonati 26, Lou Feola 14, Rinaldo Pecile 10.

Bethlehem 62 Easton 39: After taking a 14-10 first quarter lead, Easton could only score six points in the second quarter and fell behind 26-20 at halftime. The Hurricane's offense took over in the second half as Bethlehem rolled over the Red Rovers.

Leading scorers: Bethlehem - Billy Packer 18, Jim Leslie 14, Al Senavitis 12, Ron Bayak with 11; Easton - Terry Bartolet 13, Fred Tracy 13.[6]

Pottsville 82 Easton 54: Later in the week, Pottsville held Easton to two points in the 1st quarter and jumped out to a 15-2 lead and extended it to 36-12 at halftime. The officials ejected Joulwan in the 4th quarter after a fight with Easton's Dave Griffin. Pottsville established a league record by converting 38 foul shots.

Leading scorers: Pottsville – Bob Pepe 32, George Joulwan 17, Jim Whitaker 10; Easton - Terry Bertolet 20, Fred Tracy 13.

Allentown 70 Central Catholic 66: Central Catholic limited Bob Heffner to 18 points, 12 in the second half, but the Canaries still won the game. John Canzano scored a career high with support from Bob Fager and Bernie Costello to help pull out the win. The Vikings led 18-13 and 36-35 after the first two quarters before the Canaries outscored the Vikings by ten 23-13 in the third quarter on the way to the victory.

Leading scorers: Allentown – John Canzano 18, Bob Heffner 18, Bob Fager 16, Bernie Costello 10; Central Catholic - Bill Cramsey 24, Bob Yost 23, George Kerner 10.[7]

Bethlehem 49 Hazleton 42: In a low-scoring affair, Bethlehem prevailed over Hazleton. A strong first half with the Hurricane leading 28-20 at halftime propelled Bethlehem to the victory. Hazleton could only get within five points in the second half 44-39.

Leading scorers: Bethlehem - Billy Packer 16, Dave Sellers 10; Hazleton - Fran Libonati 17.[8]

Week 4

Allentown 76 Easton 62: Despite a big night from Terry Bartolet (which included 20 of 26 foul shots), Easton could not slow down Allentown as the Canaries won their 30th consecutive league game. Allentown's offense was led by Bob Heffner with support from Bernie Costello, John Canzano, and Bob Fager. Bartolet's 20 converted foul shots set a new individual record for most foul shots made in a game.

Leading scorers: Allentown – Bob Heffner 20, Bernie Costello 14, John Canzano 14, Bob Fager 12; Easton – Terry Bartolet 30, Fred Tracy 14.

Central Catholic 89 Hazleton 87: Bill Cramsey canned two field goals for Central Catholic in the last 57 seconds to capture the victory over Hazleton. Despite fouling out with over five minutes left in the game. Fran Libonati still had a big scoring night for the Mountaineers. His loss severely hindered the Mountaineer's offense. Hazleton led after a quarter 24-20, but the Vikings charged ahead in the second quarter 48-40 by scoring 28 points in the second quarter. Central Catholic held on despite Hazleton tying the score at 85-85 late in the final quarter.

Leading scorers: Central Catholic – Bill Cramsey 33, Dick Hollschwander 17, Bob Yost 17, Charlie Rohrer 10; Hazleton – Fran Libonati 31, Rinaldo Pecile 24, Barney Gatski 14.[9]

Pottsville 66 Bethlehem 65:The Pottsville-Bethlehem game was delayed a day due to bad road conditions. In Pottsville, the home team overcame a five-point deficit 65-60 with two minutes to play for a win over Bethlehem. Bob Pepe dropped in six points in the last two minutes to lead the winning rally. The twin Joulwan brothers led the Maroons in scoring.

Leading scorers: Pottsville - George Joulwan 18, Jim Joulwan 16, Bob Pepe 17; Bethlehem - Al Senavitis 18, Billy Packer 15, Ross Culligan 11, Jim Leslie 10.[10]

Week 5

Allentown 60 Bethlehem 54: Despite a raging snowstorm, nearly every seat was filled with over 3400 fans as Allentown's juggernaut continued on a roll with a come-from-behind victory over Bethlehem. The win marked their 31st consecutive league triumph, 15th straight in the season, and 11th straight defeat of Bethlehem. It did not come easy as Bethlehem jumped out to a 20-7 first quarter lead and kept it until over halfway through the third period. Bernie Costello's foul shot with 3:30 remaining in the third period put Allentown ahead for the first time 33-32.

Leading scorers: Allentown-Bob Heffner 24, Bernie Costello 13, John Canzano 12; Bethlehem-Al Senavitis 18, Billy Packer 13.

Hazleton 72 Pottsville 47: Hazleton began the second half with a surprisingly easy win over Pottsville. The Mountaineers superior height advantage limited Pottsville to single shots. Hazleton held Pottsville to a single field goal and only 11 points in the first half with a stingy defense. Hazleton held Pottsville to single digits in each of the first three periods with 7, 4, and 9 points in mounting a 59-20 lead going into the final quarter.

Leading scorers: Hazleton - Fran Libonati 20, Frank Palermo 16, Lou Miorelli 11; Pottsville - Bob Pepe 16, George Joulwan 11, Frank Prestilio 11.

Central Catholic 64 Easton 55: George Kerner had a breakout night to lead Central Catholic past Easton. He had scored only 30 total points in five first half games. Three other Vikings scored in double figures. After the Vikings held a 29-13 lead midway through the second quarter, Easton nibbled away and tied the game at 36-36 in the 3rd quarter. The Vikings stopped the rally with several baskets to carry them to the win.

Leading scorers: Central Catholic – George Kerner 18, Bob Yost 16, Charlie Rohrer 15, Bill Cramsey 13; Easton - Terry Bartolet 19, Fred Tracy 17.[11]

Week 6

Allentown 73 Pottsville 61: With Bob Heffner scoring 12 of his points in the 4th quarter, Allentown held on to win its 32nd consecutive league match. Pottsville kept rallying to pull within two points 49-47 in the 3rd quarter before the Canaries responded to stretch the lead back to eight points 59-51.

Leading scorers: Allentown – Bob Heffner 25, John Canzano 24, Bernie Costello 14; Pottsville - George Joulwan 25, Bob Pepe 15, Bob Edwards 10.

Hazleton 78 Easton 70 OT: Hazleton kept pace with Allentown with a head-to-head matchup scheduled for the following week. Breaking the foul shot record set by Pottsville three weeks earlier. Hazleton converted 42 in the overtime triumph over Easton. Four of Easton's starters fouled out of the game with only Bill Houston left from the starting five to play in overtime. Despite fouling out with 14 minutes to play, Terry Bartolet still led the Red Rovers in scoring.

Leading scorers: Hazleton – Fran Libonati 28, Lou Miorelli 12, John Yaccino 10; Easton – Terry Bartolet 26, John Worrich 12, Fred Tracy 10.

Bethlehem 60 Central Catholic 54: At Bethlehem, Central Catholic took a 49-44 lead behind third quarter substitute sophomore Tim Marsden. He took a hard hit on the floor on a drive and had to be taken out of the game. The Hurricane took it from there to tie the game at 49-49 and 53-53 before finishing the contest by scoring seven of the last eight points in the game.

Leading scorers: Bethlehem - Dave Sellers 25, Al Senavitis 12, Billy Packer 11; Central Catholic - Bill Cramsey 15, Bob Yost 15, Charlie Rohrer 10.[12]

Week 7

Allentown 83 Hazleton 58: In a battle of the two second half unbeaten teams, the contest was never in doubt. With 2300 fans at the Little Palestra, Allentown took the lead in the first minute and never relinquished it as they demolished Hazleton. The Mountaineers lost two starters, Jim Perneski and Lou Miorelli, in the 3rd quarter and Jerry Olexa with two minutes left in the game on personal fouls. Even though he had to sit half way through the 2nd quarter with three personal fouls, Bob Heffner still was able to lead the scoring. Coach Milo Sewards used 15 players in the game. The Canaries led at the half 43-27.

Leading scorers: Allentown – Bob Heffner 32, John Canzano 17, Bernie Costello 12; Hazleton - John Yaccino 15, Lou Miorelli 10.[13]

Bethlehem 78 Easton 52: Easton started slowly and could not catch up in the loss to Bethlehem. After the Hurricane took a 20-19 first quarter lead, Bethlehem had complete control the game the rest of the way. Terry Bartolet scored 12 points in the 3rd period, all his team's points for the quarter.

Leading scorers: Bethlehem - Ross Culligan 20, Al Senavitis 14, Dave Sellers 12. Billy Packer 12; Easton – Terry Bartolet 16, Fred Tracy 10.[14]

Pottsville-Central Catholic: Due to treacherous travel conditions, the Pottsville-Central Catholic game was postponed a week.

Bethlehem 80 Hazleton 72: Hazleton dropped its second in a row later in the week, when they lost to Bethlehem in front of a home crowd. The Hurricane led after three quarters 70-51. The win kept Bethlehem's hope alive for a second half title.

Leading scorers: Bethlehem - Billy Packer 20, Don Wilson 20, Al Senavitis 17, Jim Leslie 11; Hazleton - Fran Libonati 24, John Yaccino, Rinaldo Pecile 11.

Pottsville 66 Easton 59: Down by 19 starting the 4th quarter, Easton put on a furious rally but fell short to Pottsville. Easton's Fred Tracy scored 12 points in the fourth quarter rally. Pottsville led 48-33 going into the fourth quarter. Easton scored 26 points in the final quarter.

Leading scorers: Pottsville - Bob Pepe 19, Jim Joulwan 16, Frank Prestilio 14; Easton - Fred Tracy 20, Terry Bartolet 13.

Allentown 62 Central Catholic 51: Allentown extended its record to 20-0 as Bob Heffner broke two of Bethlehem's Gary Piff's records. He broke the league seasonal mark with 272 points, bettering Piff by one point with a game to go. He also sank 6 foul shots to break Piff's season foul shot total of 86 by three. The Vikings led after a quarter 13-12 and the Canaries didn't take the lead until they broke a 17-17 tie in the second quarter.

Leading scorers: Allentown – Bob Heffner 30, John Canzano 12; Central Catholic - Bob Yost 23, Charlie Rohrer 10.[15]

Week 8

Allentown 73 Easton 52: Milo Seward's Canaries wrapped up the 35th consecutive league win over Pete Carril's Easton team. The win also secured their 5th straight league title. Bob Heffner broke another Gary Piff-record by tallying six field goals to top his league record of 94. Heffner finished with 99. He increased his season record total to 290 points. He accomplished these feats despite sitting out over 12 minutes in the game with personal foul trouble. He fouled out with nearly six minutes remaining in the game. Allentown led at the half 47-28. Easton finished winless during the second half.

Leading scorers: Allentown – Bob Heffner 18, Bob Fager 18, John Olson 17; Easton - Terry Bartolet 12, John Worrich 11, Fred Tracy 10.

Central Catholic 69 Pottsville 66: In Pottsville, Central Catholic shaded the home team in a makeup game from the week before. The Vikings led 18-8 after the first quarter and 35-23 at the half, then held off Pottsville whose rally could not overcome the first half deficit.

Leading scorers: Central Catholic - Bill Cramsey 25, Charlie Rohrer 18, Bob Yost 14; Pottsville – George Joulwan 18, Frank Prestilio 15, Jim Joulwan 13, Jim Whitaker 10.[16]

Central Catholic 55 Hazleton 49: After trailing for the first three periods, Central Catholic handed Hazleton their third straight loss of the second half. Bill Cramsey scored 13 points in the last stanza as the Vikings outscored Hazleton 24-12 to pull out the win.

Leading scorers: Central Catholic – Bill Cramsey 28, Bob Yost 13; Hazleton - Fran Libonati 17.[17]

Bethlehem 95 Pottsville 66: Bethlehem finished at 4-1 for the second half with a win over Pottsville 95-66. After leading by two after a quarter 19-17, the Hurricane broke away in the second quarter for a 46-30 halftime lead.

Leading scorers: Bethlehem - Al Senavitis 31, Don Wilson 18, Billy Packer 16; Pottsville - Frank Prestilio 18, Bob Pepe 16, George Jouwan 14, Jim Joulwan 11.[18]

Postseason Play

Allentown 75 Nazareth 57: At Bethlehem's Memorial gym, Coach Bob Weiss' Nazareth Blue Eagles tested Allentown in district play but the Canaries prevailed. Bob Heffner continued his record shattering streak to better his own season record for scoring with 580 points, despite having to sit for seven minutes in the second period because of foul trouble. The Canaries outscored the Blue Eagles 39-22 in the first and fourth quarters to propel them to the win.

Leading scorers: Allentown - Bob Heffner 29, John Olson 13, John Canzano 12; Nazareth - Connie Shimer 18, Dick Hunt 15.[20]

Allentown 69 Palmerton 52: Playing the district title game in Hershey, Allentown stunned Coach Win Evan's Palmerton Blue Bombers with close to 9000 screaming fans in attendance. Allentown took an early lead, but Palmerton caught the Canaries to take a 30-27 first half lead into the locker room. Allentown tied the score at 40-40 with a little more than a minute left in the third period. Bob Heffner made a field goal and foul shot to put the Canaries into the lead for good 43-40 as the third quarter ended.

Leading scorers: Allentown–Bob Heffner 20, Bob Fager 20, John Canzano 15, Bernie Costello 10: Palmerton–Bob Mlkvy 23.[21]

Chester 83 Allentown 65: A total of 8.314 fans at the Penn Palestra saw Chester wreck Allentown's 26 game win streak. Billy Wilson scored 28 points while Chester's defense held Bob Heffner to 17 points. Chester took a 27-14 first quarter lead and led the whole game.

Leading scorers: Chester – Billy Wilson 28, Jerry Foster 19, Lou Wade 15, Warren Sutton 12; Allentown – Bob Heffner 17, Bernie Costello 17, John Canzano 13.[22]

PCIAA Playoffs

Central Catholic 74 Pottsville Nativity 65: Central Catholic began defense of the PCIAA title at the Little Palestra against Pottsville Nativity. Showing no signs of a two-week layoff, the Vikings took down their Pottsville foes 74-65. The Vikings took a 26-10 first quarter lead to took charge from the very beginning.

Leading scorers: Central Catholic - Bob Yost 17, Bill Cramsey 12, Charlie Rohrer 10; Pottsville Nativity - Ed Shields 27, Joe Souchak 14, Mike Shovlin 12.[23]

Central Catholic 58 Bishop Kenrick 57: The Vikings met Bishop Kenrick at St. Matthew's High School in Conshohocken for the Philadelphia Diocese title. Despite holding a 12-point half time lead, Central Catholic had to hang on to pull out the victory. The Vikings made their last field goal for a 58-55 lead with two minutes to play. Coach Emil Carazo ordered a freeze in the last two minutes.

Leading scorers: Central Catholic - Bill Cramsey 23, Bob Yost 22; Bishop Kenrick - Jim Bruni 17, Dennis McGee 14, Tom Barrett 13.[24]

Central Catholic 55 Scranton Prep 48: At the Scranton CYO, Central Catholic put forth a strong defensive effort to stop Scranton Prep. After taking an 8-7 lead into the second quarter, Eddie Pfeiffer stole the ball on four consecutive Scranton possessions and triggered a 24-point second quarter rally to break the game open. The Vikings led at the half 32-22.

Leading scorers: Central Catholic - Bob Yost 21, Charlie Rohrer 16, Bill Cramsey 13; Scranton Prep - Mike Abdala 13, Tom McCafferty 13, John Jordan 12.[25]

Central Catholic 66 Harrisburg Catholic 62: Central Catholic qualified for the state final for the second straight season with a defeat of Harrisburg Catholic. The Vikings never trailed and built up an early 12-point lead to allow them to survive Harrisburg's late rally. Bill Dougherty, who averaged 4 points during the season, scored 15 important points for the Vikings.

Leading scorers: Central Catholic – Bill Cramsey 21, Bill Dougherty 15, Bob Yost 15; Harrisburg Catholic - Joe Weideman 20, Ed Siegfried 18.[26]

Central Catholic 60 Johnstown Catholic 46: At the Cambria County War Memorial Arena in Johnstown, Central Catholic garnered it second straight PCIAA state Class A title over Johnstown Catholic. Bill Cramsey scored 27 points to lead the Vikings to their sixth state PCIAA championship, more than any other state parochial school. Falling behind 28-24 at the half, the Vikings parlayed a strong third quarter, outscoring their foes 18-6, to the championship. The Vikings became the first parochial school to win two consecutive titles outright. Reading had won in 1950 and tied for the title in 1951.

Leading scorers: Central Catholic – Bill Cramsey 27; Johnstown Catholic - Jim Burkhardt 14, Jim Kenny 11.[27]

Postseason Accolades

Scoring Leaders: For the second straight year, the scoring leader ran away with the title as Bob Heffner scored 290 points in 10 games for a 29 ppg average. He had finished second to Gary Piff last year with 230 points. Others in the top ten included Fran Libonati, Hazleton, 201; Bob Pepe, Pottsville, 195; Bill Cramsey, Central Catholic, 192; Terry Bartolet, Easton, 190; Al Senavitis, Bethlehem, 161; Bob Yost, Central Catholic, 156; Billy Packer, Bethlehem, 151; George Joulwan, 150, and Jim Joulwan, 130, twin brothers from Pottsville.[28]

All-Stars: The league all-star teams included: Bob Heffner, Allentown, and Billy Packer, Bethlehem, unanimous picks; Terry Bartolet, Easton; Al Senavitis, Bethlehem; Bob Yost, Central Catholic; and Fran Libonati, Hazleton.[29]

All-State: The Associated Press' All Pennsylvania Scholastic Team included Bob Heffner, Allentown, 1st team. Other local players received Honorable Mention including: Billy Packer, Bethlehem; Fran Libonati, Hazleton; Bill Cramsey, Central Catholic; George Joulwan and Bob Pepe, Pottsville; and John Canzano, Allentown.[30]

Final Standings

First Half		Second Half		Overall	
Allentown	5-0	Allentown	5-0	Allentown	10-0
Pottsville	4-1	Bethlehem	4-1	Bethlehem	7-3
Bethlehem	3-2	Central Catholic	3-2	Pottsville	5-5
Hazleton	1-4	Hazleton	2-3	Central Catholic	4-6
Easton	1-4	Pottsville	1-4	Hazleton	3-7
Central Catholic	1-4	Easton	0-5	Easton	1-9

Team Rosters

Allentown: Coach Milo Sewards, Fred Bentelspacher, John Canzano, Bernie Costello, John Donmoyer, Ron Evans, Bob Fager, Tom Greenawalt, Bob Heffner, Ron Katz, Ed Lesko, Joseph Noti, John Olson, William "Rocky" Ruth, Stan Tibensky, Bruce Trotter, Timthy Uhl, Louis Wasser, Brent Werley, Michael Wing, Robert Wahlbach

Bethlehem: Coach John Howard, Clayton Alderfer, Ron Bayak, Ross Culligan, Fred Donatelli, Don Hoydu, Dave Jay, John Kereczman, George Latzo, Jim Leslie, Terry McGee, Eugene Medei, Billy Packer, Dave Seller, Al Senavitis, Don Wilson, Tom Zelko

Central Catholic: Coach Emil Carazo, Allen Berghold, Bill Cramsey, Bill Dougherty, Fred Ehrenstrasser, Tom Groff, Dick Hollschwander, John Hopper, George Kerner, Tim Marsden, Ed Pfeiffer, Tom Reis, Charlie Rohrer, Jim Santee, Bob Spang, Bob Yost

Easton: Coach Pete Carril, G Andrews, Terry Bartolet, Alex Camaioni, Gary Fahl, Jim Gano, Michael Griffin, Bill Houston, Joe Kohler, Charles "Chip" Oldt, Fred Stothoff, Fred Tracy, John Worrich

Hazleton: Coach Frank Serany, Neil Cusate, Angelo Esposito, Lou Farace, Lou Feola, Edmund Ferdinand, Barney Gatski, Bob Leipfert, Fran Libonati, Lou Miorelli, Dave Murrin, Jerry Olexa, Frank Palermo, Rinaldo Pecille, Jim Perneski, Jim Pierson, Jim Senape, John Yaccino

Pottsville: Coach Charles Miller, Tom Devitt, Bob Edwards, Carl Engleman, George Joulwan, Jim Joulwan, Ron Mills, Bob Pepe, Frank Prestilio, Joseph Santor, Jim Whitaker

Allentown High School – 1957 League and District Champions[19]

Front: Ronald Katz, Robert Fager, Joseph Noti, Louis Wasser, Timothy Uhl, Frederick Bentelspacher, John Canzano, John Olson, George Werley (mgr, sitting in front); Back: John Mascavage (asst coach), Edward Lesko, Robert Wolbach, Coach Sewards, Bruce Trotter, Robert Heffner, Ken Wildonger (asst coach), Brent Werley, John Donmoyer, Joe Blankowitsch (trainer)

Central Catholic High School – 1957 PCIAA State Champions

Front: Albert Berghold, George Kerner, Tom Groff, Bill Cramsey, Bob Yost, Dick Hollschwander, Charles Rohrer; Back: Coach Carazo, Tom Reis, Ed Pfeiffer, Bob Spang, Tim Marsden, John Hopper, Jim Santee, Bill Dougherty, Fred Ehrenstrasser, (mgrs.) Carl Hogan, Emil Sos

1958

Bethlehem Ends the Canaries Run

Phil Phillippi, Stan Steigerwalt, and Edgar Rabenold were re-elected to the president, vice president, and secretary-treasurer positions for another year in the spring meeting at the Shankweiler Hotel in Fogelsville.[1]

Before the start of the league season, Pottsville lost their head coach, Charles "Daw" Miller, unexpectedly due to a heart attack. He had conducted a team practice on a Thursday night until 8 pm at the 16th Street Palestra in Pottsville. After not indicating any illness, he went home and died early Friday morning, December 19th at his home in St. Clair. Assistant coach George Dimmerling assumed the interim head coaching position for the rest of the 1959 basketball season.[2]

Week 1

Hazleton 81 Allentown 68: Hazleton abruptly ended Allentown's 35-game league winning streak in Hazleton. The last league loss also occurred in Hazleton at St. Joseph's Hall. With the score tied at 53-53 after three periods, the Mountaineers blew away the Canaries outscoring them 28-15 in the final period. Twice in the first half, Canary Coach Milo Sewards drew technical fouls for vociferously arguing calls made against Allentown's Joe Noti. When Noti fouled out with six minutes to play in the game, Hazleton took off on their ferocious rally.

Leading scorers: Hazleton - Jerry Olexa 32, Tony Farnell 12, Neil Cusate 10; Allentown - Bernie Costello 26, Art Toth 11.

Bethlehem 72 Pottsville 51: At Pottsville, Bethlehem romped over Pottsville. After being down 14-13 after a quarter, Bethlehem took the lead late in the second period and were not threatened after that.

Leading scorers: Bethlehem - Dave Sellers 23, Al Senavitis 23, Billy Packer 17; Pottsville - Tony Roland 14, Garrett Devitt 11, Ron Mills 10.

Easton 58 Central Catholic 45: Central Catholic fell behind by 10 points 17-7 and could not get any closer than 7 points 39-32 in the 3rd quarter. The Vikings' Tim Marsden returned after three weeks with a leg injury.

Leading scorers: Easton - Bill Houston 20, Terry Bartolet 13, Alex Camaioni 10; Central Catholic - Bobby Spang 19.[3]

Week 2

Hazleton 68 Pottsville 46: Hazleton jumped to a 14-4 first quarter lead as Pottsville could only score a single field goal in the first period. Although Jerry Olexa was held in check, the scoring slack was picked up by Barney Gatski, Neil Cusate, and Johnny Yaccino. The Mountaineers led 29-16 at halftime.

Leading scorers: Hazleton - Barney Gatski 16, Jerry Olexa 11, Neil Cusate 10, Johhny Yaccino 10; Pottsville -Tony Roland 10, Frank Prestilio 10.[4]

Bethlehem 63 Easton 56: Bethlehem kept pace with Hazleton with a triumph over Pete Carril's Easton squad. The Red Rovers pulled within a point 53-52 with two minutes left only to have Al Senavitis score six straight points to seal the win for Bethlehem. The Hurricane led 31-23 at the end of the second quarter.

Leading scorers: Bethlehem – Al Senavitis 27, Billy Packer 12; Easton - Terry Bartolet 18, Chip Oldt 15, Alex Camaioni 11.

Allentown 54 Central Catholic 50: Scoring ten points in the final quarter, Canary center Stan Tibensky led Allentown to victory after the Vikings had tied the score at 47-47 with less than two minutes to play. The Vikings had led 17-12 after the first quarter before Allentown moved ahead at halftime 27-25, The score was tied after three quarters 39-39. Tibensky sent the Canaries ahead 41-39 and the Canaries never trailed again.

Leading scorers: Allentown – Stan Tibensky 17, Bernie Costello 10; Central Catholic – Eddie Pfeiffer 18, George Kerner 17.[5]

Easton 65 Hazleton 52: Later in the week, Easton shocked Hazleton with all five starters scoring in double figures. After taking a 15-7 first quarter lead, Pete Carril's team never trailed in the game.

Leading scorers: Easton - Bill Houston 15, Jim Gano 14, Dick "Chip" Oldt 11, Alex Camaioni 11, Terry Bartolet 10; Hazleton - Barney Gatski 16.

Bethlehem 53 Central Catholic 48: Bethlehem took sole possession of first place by downing Central Catholic. With 1:48 to play, a Viking rally pulled them ahead 48-47. However, Dave Sellers scored two baskets and Al Senavitis one to pull out the victory for Coach John Howard. The Vikings' Eddie Pfeiffer held Billy Packer to a single field goal and two points for the night.

Leading scorers: Bethlehem - Al Senavitis 13. Dave Sellers 13, Bernie Medai 11, Ron Bayak 10; Central Catholic - George Kerner 16, Jim Miklos 13.

Allentown 82 Pottsville 71: Allentown traveled to Pottsville and came home with a triumph. The win helped create a three-way tie with Hazleton and Easton all at 2-1. With the score tied at 15 after one quarter, Allentown outscored Pottsville in each of the last three quarters. The Canaries made 26 of 39 foul shots.

Leading scorers: Allentown - Bernie Costello 25, Rocky Ruth 21, Stan Tibensky 21; Pottsville - Frank Prestilio 34, Tony Rohland 10.[6]

Week 3

Bethlehem 74 Allentown 48: Bethlehem scored a decisive victory over Allentown at Bethlehem's Memorial Hall. The win snapped an 11 consecutive game losing streak to the Canaries. The Hurricane took a 17-8 first quarter lead and were never threatened the rest of the way.

Leading scorers: Bethlehem–Al Senavitis 27 Billy Packer 21, Ron Bayak 10; Allentown-Bernie Costello 12, John Canzano 10.[7]

Easton 69 Pottsville 60: At Easton, Pottsville got off to a slow start and trailed 8-0 early and 23-12 after a period. Frank Prestilio, Pottsville's leading scorer, played sparingly due to disciplinary action by Pottsville's Coach Miller and only scored 8 points. The Red Rovers had four players in double figures in points.

Leading scorers: Easton - Terry Bartolet 18, Alex Camaioni 13, Bill Houston 12, Chip Oldt 10; Pottsville – Tony Rohland 26, Garrett Devitt 16.[8]

Central Catholic 64 Hazleton 53: At Rockne Hall, Central Catholic rallied from 4 points down in the 4th quarter by running off 14 straight points to shock Hazleton 64-53. Sixteen busloads of students on a Senior Night trip went home stunned by the unexpected loss.

Leading scorers: Central Catholic - George Kerner 25, Eddie Pfeiffer 14; Hazleton - Neil Cusate 16, Tony Farnell 12.[9]

Week 4

Bethlehem 82 Hazleton 59: Bethlehem handed Hazleton its worst defeat since 1927. With Billy Packer making 14 of his 18 field goal attempts for a game high 32 points and Al Senavitis adding 24 points, the Mountaineers didn't stand a chance. Bethlehem outscored Hazleton 21-7 in the second quarter.

Leading scorers: Bethlehem - Billy Packer 32, Al Senavitis 24, Bernie Medei 12, Ron Bayak 10; Hazleton - Jerry Olexa 26.

Central Catholic 67 Pottsville 63: Central Catholic withstood three rallies that brought Pottsville within two points during the fourth quarter to win. Ed Pfeiffer sat out for most of the second period due to fouls. The Vikings jumped out to a 21-14 first quarter lead. Pottsville threatened the Vikings in the final quarter when they outscored them 19-11.

Leading scorers: Central Catholic - George Kerner 18, Eddie Pfeiffer 13, Bobby Spang 11, Tim Marsden 10; Pottsville - Garrett Devitt 29, Frank Prestilio 15, Tony Roland 12.

Easton 56 Allentown 49: Easton snapped Allentown's 45-game home winning streak to clinch second place for the first half. It was the first loss at home since December 1954 when they lost to Chester in an Eyeglass Fund game. Easton's five-point first quarter margin 16-11 held up for a Red Rover win.

Leading scorers: Easton - Terry Bartolet 25, Jim Gano 10; Allentown - Bernie Costello 14, Joe Noti 11, Rocky Ruth 10.[10]

Week 5

Allentown 64 Hazleton 40: Coach Milo Sewards inserted two first time starters into the lineup against Hazleton. Both made significant contributions in the win over the Mountaineers. Although he only scored six points, Tom Fatzinger ran the offense efficiently which led to the victory. Dave Rooney, a Central Catholic transfer, came off the bench and scored 8 points. Hazleton jumped out to an 18-12 first quarter lead but couldn't hold it when Allentown countered by outscoring the Mountaineers in the 2nd period 20-7.

Leading scorers: Allentown-Bernie Costello 23, Rocky Ruth 12; Hazleton-Barney Gatski 15, Jerry Olexa 10.

Bethlehem 65 Pottsville 44: Pottsville continued winless in league competition with their loss to Bethlehem. About 1300 fans braved sleet and snow to witness Al Senavitis and Billy Packer combine for 49 points for the Hurricane. With Bethlehem leading 36-16 in the second quarter, Coach Howard pulled some of his starters.

Leading scorers: Bethlehem- Al Senavitis 25, Billy Packer 24; Pottsville- Garrett Devitt 14, Frank Prestilio 11, Tony Roland 10.

Easton 53 Central Catholic 52: Easton's Jim Gano scored on a driving layup with seven seconds left in the game to boost the Red Rovers over Central Catholic. Gano scored 14 of Easton's 15 points in the final quarter. The score was tied at 24-24 at halftime with the Vikings leading 40-38 after three quarters.

Leading scorers: Easton–Jim Gano 25, Terry Bartolet 14; Central Catholic-Bob Spang 15, Jim Miklos 11, George Kerner 10.[11]

Week 6

Central Catholic 58 Allentown 47: After 12 consecutive losses to the Canaries, Central Catholic broke the jinx. Diminutive Eddie Pfeiffer at 5'8" led the Vikings' scoring charge, eleven which were foul shots. The Vikings held an 8-6 first quarter lead and bested the Canaries in every quarter except the fourth when both teams scored 19.

Leading scorers: Central Catholic – Ed Pfeiffer 19, Bobby Spang 18, Tim Marsden 10, George Kerner 10; Allentown - Bernie Costello 23, Rocky Ruth 10.[12]

Easton 77 Bethlehem 62: Easton downed the first half champs Bethlehem to move into first place. After holding a narrow 32-30 margin at the half, Pete Carril's quintet scored 12 straight points in the first 2 plus minutes of the second half to take a comfortable lead. Held scoreless in the first half, Terry Bartolet made six field goals and converted ten foul shots in the second half.

Leading scorers: Easton – Terry Bartolet 22, Alex Camaioni 22, Jim Gano 17, Bill Houston 12; Bethlehem - Al Senavitis 24, Billy Packer 16.[13]

Hazleton 73 Pottsville 53: In breaking a five-game losing streak, which was their longest since the 1920s, Hazleton took advantage of lowly Pottsville. All five Mountaineer starters scored in double figures:

Leading scorers: Hazleton - Bernie Gatski 23, Tony Farnell 13, Neil Cusate 11, Jerry Olexa 11, Bob Leipfert 11; Pottsville - Garrett Devitt 26, Frank Prestilio 10.[14]

Easton 64 Hazleton 63: For the second time in three games, Jim Gano scored on a driving layup with seven seconds left to pull out a victory for Easton. Hazleton's Jerry Olexa had a chance to tie the game with one second left. After being fouled, he made the first of a one-and-one situation, but the second attempt fell off the rim and Easton maintained its hold on first place. The Red Rovers pulled it out despite three technical fouls assessed on them (Coach Pete Carril with 2 and Alex Camaioni 1).

Leading scorers: Easton – Jim Gano 15, Terry Bartolet 15, Alex Camaioni 11, Bill Houston 10; Hazleton - Jerry Olexa 20, Barney Gatski 19, Neil Cusate 11.

Bethlehem 67 Central Catholic 57: Billy Packer, held scoreless in the 1st half, hit four field goals and converted 10 of 10 foul shots in the 2nd half in a victory over Central Catholic. Packer's scoring helped erase a 32-27 Central Catholic lead at the half. Bethlehem took the lead for good 41-40 with about 4 minutes left.

Leading scorers: Bethlehem - Al Senavitis 22, Billy Packer 18, Ron Bayak 11; Central Catholic - George Kerner 17, Ed Pfeiffer 15, Jim Miklos 10.

Allentown 62 Pottsville 57: At the Little Palestra, Allentown prevented a scrappy Pottsville squad from getting its first league victory. Pottsville held a one-point first quarter lead and kept the game close the whole way. The game was tied at 57 all with 1:10 to play but the Canaries scored the last five points for the win. Frank Prestilio, Garrett Devitt, and Tony Rohland scored all of Pottsville's points.

Leading scorers: Allentown - Bernie Costello 23, Bruce Trotter 19; Pottsville - Frank Prestilio 23, Garrett Devitt 20, Tony Roland 14.[15]

Week 7

Easton 67 Pottsville 54: Easton fought back with a third quarter rally at Pottsville to win and set up crucial matchup with Allentown for the second half title. Pottsville led 29-26 at the half only to have the Red Rovers outscore them 21-9 in the third period.

Leading scorers: Easton - Alex Camaioni 21, Jim Gano 21, Chip Oldt 12, Bill Houston 10; Pottsville - Frank Prestilio 23, Garrett Devitt 13.

Allentown 69 Bethlehem 61: Allentown took down heavily-favored Bethlehem. Despite fouling out with two minutes to play, Bernie Costello led the Canaries in scoring with 10 field goals and 4 foul shots, Ron Cameron also fouled out after 1:19 into the second half. Al Senavitis was held to six points.

Leading scorers: Allentown – Bernie Costello 24, Rocky Ruth 17, Ron Cameron 12; Bethlehem - Bernie Medei 23, Billy Packer 16, Len Zavacky 10.

Central Catholic 56 Hazleton 47: With George Kerner and Eddie Pfeiffer on the bench after fouling out in the 4th quarter, Central Catholic held on to defeat Hazleton. Tim Marsden and Jim Micklos froze the ball over the last 3:50 to allow the Vikings to hang on for the win.

Leading scorers: Central Catholic - Eddie Pfeiffer 16, Tim Marsden 15; Hazleton - Bernie Gatski 13.[16]

Week 8

Allentown 71 Easton 67: Bernie Costello's brilliant 33 points carried Allentown to an upset victory over Easton to create a tie for the second half title. Easton led at the half 40-31, but the Canaries came out and blitzed the Red Rovers in the third period 19-6 to take the lead which they never gave up. Allentown lost three players on fouls: Joe Noti in the third period and Rocky Ruth and Bruce Trotter in the fourth.

Leading scorers: Allentown – Bernie Costello 33, Rocky Ruth 14, Bruce Trotter 10; Easton - Jim Gano 17, Chip Oldt 17, Bill Houston 12, Alex Camaioni 11, Terry Bartolet 10.

Central Catholic 68 Pottsville 41: Central Catholic kept Pottsville winless in the league for the year. The Vikings held Pottsville to a single field goal in the first quarter and two in the third quarter. Central Catholic scored 18 points in each of the first three quarters for a 54-30 lead heading into the final quarter. The Vikings held Pottsville's scorers Frank Prestilio to 7 points and Garrett Devitt to 4.

Leading scorers: Central Catholic - Tim Marsden 13, Bobby Spang 13, George Kerner 10; Pottsville - Joseph Santor 12.[17]

Bethlehem 68 Hazleton 43: Hazleton finished by losing 8 of the last 9 games when Bethlehem pasted them. Al Senavitis took the league's scoring title with 13 field goals and 3 foul shots in the game. Coach Serany played all 14 of his players.

Leading scorers: Bethlehem – Al Senavitis 29, Billy Packer 18, Ron Bayak 10; Hazleton - Barney Gatski 19.[18]

Second Half Playoff

Allentown 74 Easton 60: Easton and Allentown met at the Penn Palestra to settle the second half title. Playing each other for the second time in a week, Allentown knocked Easton out of any postseason play. With Rocky Ruth sinking six consecutive field goals in the first quarter, the Canaries jumped out to a 14-10 first quarter. Ruth scored 14 points in the first half. Allentown stretched its lead to 42-24 at half time.

Leading scorers: Allentown - Bernie Costello 30, Rocky Ruth 17, Ron Cameron 10; Easton - Terry Bartolet 18, Chip Oldt 12, Jim Gano 12.[19]

League Championship

Bethlehem 60 Allentown 52: Allentown's unexpected run to the league title ended at the Hershey arena with 5,000 fans in attendance. Bethlehem broke Allentown's five-year hold on the league title 60-52, but not without having to hold off a second half rally by the Canaries. Bethlehem held a 31-21 halftime lead, but the Canaries cut the lead to four (49-45) early in the fourth quarter. They would get no closer.

Leading scorers: Bethlehem - Billy Packer 22, Al Senavitis 20, Ron Bayak 10; Allentown - Bernie Costello 20, Bruce Trotter 14, Rocky Ruth 12.[20]

Postseason Play

Bethlehem 77 Wilson Boro 52: At Muhlenberg's Memorial Hall, Bethlehem outscored Wilson Boro in every quarter on the way to the triumph over the Lehigh-Northampton League champions. Wilson Boro's Hal Rice went over the 1000-point mark, finishing at 1,001. The Hurricane led at the half 46-33.

Leading scorers: Bethlehem - Billy Packer 23, Al Senavitis 23, Ron Bayak 16; Wilson - Hal Rice 20, Mike Limberg 12.[22]

Bethlehem 81 Tamaqua 48: In the District 11 title game at the Penn Palestra with over 4000 spectators, Bethlehem took an early 23-8 first quarter lead to an easy 81-48 triumph over Tamaqua, the Black Diamond League champs. Bethlehem used 12 players with 10 of them scoring at least a point in the game.

Leading scorers: Bethlehem - Al Senavitis 22, Billy Packer 19, Bernie Medei 13; Tamaqua - Billy Yelsh 16.[23]

York 55 Bethlehem 48: Bethlehem's foray into inter-district play ended abruptly at the Penn Palestra against the York Bearcats. After leading York by 13 points (39-26) in the third quarter, the Hurricane's offense collapsed in the 4th quarter. They scored their only two points of the quarter in the last 20 seconds on a Billy Packer field goal. York scored 17 points in the 4th quarter. The Hurricane had four players in double figures.

Leading scorers: York - Ron Warner 23, Gene Becker 14; Bethlehem - Packer 14, Al Senavitis 12, Ron Bayak 11, Bernie Medei 11.[24]

PCIAA Playoffs

Central Catholic 63 Reading Catholic 31: Having won the last two PCIAA titles, Central Catholic began its path to another title by downing Reading Central Catholic with ease at the Little Palestra. Building up a 51-21 lead after three quarters, Coach John Compardo showed mercy by inserting his junior varsity squad into the game during the 4th quarter.

Leading scorers: Central Catholic - Eddie Pfeiffer 15, George Kerner 11, Tim Marsden 10, Jim Miklos 10; Reading Catholic - Mike Yacknik 17.[25]

Central Catholic 50 Shenandoah Catholic 41: Shenandoah Catholic presented Central Catholic with a much tougher challenge using a tough 3-2 zone defense. George Kerner and Jim Miklos were held to two points between them in the first half. The Vikings, who led throughout the game, took 9-8 and 23-17 leads after the first two quarters.

Leading scorers: Central Catholic - Tim Marsden 17, Bobby Spang 11, Eddie Pfeiffer 11; Shenandoah Catholic - Bill Hino 12.[26]

Central Catholic 73 Bishop Kenrick 71: Coach John Compardo's Vikings trailed Bishop Kenrick 64-58 with 5:12 left in the 4th quarter. Their captain George Kerner had just been carried off the floor with an injured left ankle. At 2:46 to go, Kerner went back on the floor with a heavily taped ankle and his team still behind 64-58. His inspired teammates made a number of shots to pull even 71-71 with 23 seconds to play. Bobby Spang made three clutch baskets, Tim Marsden two long set shots, and Eddie Pfeiffer the tying basket. George Kerner made the winning field goal with three seconds left. The game had been close until the third quarter when Bishop Kenrick pulled ahead by 10 points going in the final period. With five players in double figures, the Vikings pulled off a miracle win at the Little Palestra.

Leading scorers: Central Catholic - Eddie Pfeiffer 18, Tim Marsden 16, George Kerner 14, Bobby Spang 13, Jim Miklos 10; Bishop Kenrick – Dave Gratz 23, Robert Marshall 13, Frank Matozzo 12.[27]

Bishop McDevitt 71 Central Catholic 64: Bishop McDevitt (previously known as Harrisburg Catholic) put an end to the Vikings pursuit of a third consecutive PCIAA title at the Little Palestra. Central Catholic was hindered by George Kerner's limited action and ability to play caused by his severe ankle injury the previous game. Central Catholic fought back at one point to trail 41-40, but could not maintain the rally. With his injury, Kerner was only able to contribute 9 points in 24 minutes of action.

Leading scorers: Bishop McDevitt – Bill Ludlam 20, Bill Lynch 14, Dennis Dobash 14, Dick Spencer 12; Central Catholic - Bobby Spang 19, Eddie Pfeiffer 17, Jim Miklos 11.[28]

Postseason Accolades

Leading scorers: Bethlehem's Al Senavitis won the scoring title rather easily with his season total of 220 points. Bernie Costello, Allentown, finished second with 188 points. Other leading scorers included Billy Packer, Bethlehem, 176; Frank Prestilio, Pottsville, 155; Terry Bartolet, Easton, 154; Garrett Devitt, Pottsville, 140; Barney Gatski, Hazleton, 139; George Kerner, Central Catholic, 138; Jim Gano, Easton, 135; Tony Roland, Pottsville, Jerry Olexa, Hazleton, and Alex Camiaoni, Easton, all with 126; and Eddie Pfeiffer, Central Catholic, 120.[29]

All-Stars: The league all-star teams included: Bernie Costello, Allentown, and Al Senavitis, Bethlehem, unanimous picks; Billy Packer, Bethlehem; Frank Prestilio, Pottsville; and Jim Gano, Easton.[30]

All-State: The United Press' All Pennsylvania Scholastic Team included Billy Packer, Bethlehem, 2nd team; Bernie Costello, Allentown, 3rd team; and Al Senavitis, Bethlehem, 4th team. [31]

Final Standings

First Half		Second Half		Overall	
Bethlehem	5-0	Allentown	4-1	Bethlehem	8-2
Easton	4-1	Easton	4-1	Easton	8-2
Allentown	2-3	Central Catholic	3-2	Allentown	6-4
Hazleton	2-3	Bethlehem	3-2	Central Catholic	5-5
Central Catholic	2-3	Hazleton	1-4	Hazleton	3-7
Pottsville	0-5	Pottsville	0-5	Pottsville	0-10

Team Rosters

Allentown: Coach Milo Sewards, Ron Cameron, Bill Cooperman, Bernie Costello, Tom Fatzinger, Tom Greenawalt, Joe Noti, Ron Reinhard, Dave Rooney, William "Rocky" Ruth, Don Stermer, Stan Tibensky, Art Roth, Bruce Trotter, Tim Uhl, Mike Wing, Tom Wing, Bob Wolbach

Bethlehem: Coach John Howard, Clayton Alderfer, Ray Bauder, Ron Bayak, Charles Hood, Dave Karvoski, Bernie Medei, Billy Packer, Harry Richter, Dave Sellers, Al Senavitis, Emerson "Skip" Smith, Len Zavacky, Russ Zelko

Central Catholic: Coach John Compardo, Al Berghold, Mike Delisant, Fran Demko, Greg Deutsch, George Kerner, Tim Marsden, Joseph McCafferty, Jim Miklos, Ed Pfeiffer, Tom Reis, Joe Sarmir, Bob Spang, Jack Tate

Easton: Coach Pete Carril, Terry Bartolet, Alex Camaioni, Mario Capecci, Gary Fahl, Jim Gano, Bill Houston, Dean Lowe, Charles "Chip" Oldt, Fred Stothoff, Jack Stothoff

Hazleton: Coach Frank Serany, Neil Cusate, Angelo Esposito, Tony Farnell, Lou Feola, Barney Gatski, Bob Leipfert, Jerry Olexa, Frank Palermo, Rinaldo Pecile, Jim Senape, Bob Shovlin, Bill Subsinsky, Jim Tricoli, John Yaccino

Pottsville: Coach Charles Miller, Garrett Devitt, Ron Emmert, Ron Mills, Andy Palokas, Frank Prestilio, Tony Rohland, Joseph Santor, John Scotnicki, Stan Wilder, Bob Witcoski

Bethlehem High School – 1958 League and District 11 Champions[21]

Front: R, Neiser (mgr), Ron Bayak, Ray Bauder, Billy Packer, Dave Karvoski, Dave Sellers, Charles Hood, T Snyder (mgr); Back: Mr, Resectco, Mr. Fuhr (asst coach), Clayton Alderfer, Al Senavitis, Len Zavacky, Barry Richter, Elsworth Smith, Bernie Medei, Russ Zelko, T. Wolfe (mgr), Coach Howard

1959

The Canaries Regain the Title

Phil Phillippi and Edgar Rabenold were re-elected to the president and secretary-treasurer positions for another year in the spring meeting at the Shankweiler Hotel in Fogelsville. League officials elected Reverend Frank Zavadny, Central Catholic, to succeed Stan Steigerwalt as vice president. [1]

Allentown High School's enrollment required the construction of a second high school to serve the City of Allentown. Construction began in May 1956 and the school, named Allentown Dieruff after a noted educator who served the school district for 44 years, officially opened in September 1959. The school applied for membership into the East Penn League. At a league meeting in December 1958, Allentown Dieruff became a league member for the 1960 basketball season. The league would operate as a seven-team league.[2]

Week 1

Allentown 88 Pottsville 46: Allentown opened its season at home at the Little Palestra with a decisive triumph over Pottsville. Dave Rooney tied the school record for number of field goals in a game with 15. He tied three other former players including Bill Snyder, LeRoy Katz, and Bob Heffner. In the game, he scored 25 points in the first half. Allentown led 25-6 after one quarter.

Leading scorers: Allentown - Dave Rooney 33, Rocky Ruth18, Tom Fatzinger 14, Bruce Wing 10; Pottsville - Joe Santor 17.[3]

Central Catholic 64 Bethlehem 41: In what may have been a league first, Central Catholic scored 16 points in each of the four quarters to down Bethlehem. Almost as incredible, Bethlehem scored 10 in each of the first three quarters, but added an additional point in the fourth quarter for a total of 11. Four of the five starters scored in double figures for the Vikings:

Leading scorers: Allentown - Tim Marsden 18, Bobby Spang 18, Tom Reis 10, Ed Pfeiffer 10; Bethlehem - Charley Marcon 13.

Easton 61 Hazleton 59 OT: At Easton, the Red Rovers nipped Hazleton in overtime. The game ended in regulation tied at 52. "Chubby" Pecile began the overtime with a three-point play only to see Easton score the next six points. In regulation, Hazleton led 52-50 when Terry Bartolet took a rebound with 12 seconds left and raced the length of the court for a layup to tie the game.

Leading scorers: Easton - Chip Oldt 17, Terry Bartolet 13; Hazleton - Rinaldo Pecile 20, Larry Piehota 17.[4]

Week 2

Central Catholic 71 Easton 65: Trailing 53-49 entering the final period and with four starters in foul trouble, Coach John Compardo inserted the four (Ed Pfeiffer, Bob Spang, Joe Sarmir, and Tim Marsden) back into the lineup to lead the Vikings to victory over Easton. Reserves Greg Deutsch, Jack Tate, Al Pappano, and Fran Demko along with starter Tom Reis held the Red Rovers to 10 points in the third period.

Leading scorers: Central Catholic – Ed Pfeiffer 17, Bob Spang 17, Tom Reis 12; Easton – Chip Oldt 18, Dean Lowe 12, Terry Bartolet 12, Bill Houston 11.

Hazleton 87 Pottsville 59: Rushing out to a 21-8 first quarter lead, Hazleton evened its record at 1-1 with a triumph over Pottsville. Hazleton led at the half 42-23.

Leading scorers: Hazleton - Frank Zack 17, Rinaldo Pecile 14, Dale Stewart 12; Pottsville - Joe Santor 23, Ron Emmert 12.

Allentown 53 Bethlehem 49: At Bethlehem, Allentown came back after trailing for nearly three periods to defeat Bethlehem with Rocky Ruth pacing the comeback in the third period. Bethlehem led 16-9 and 30-23 after the first two periods. The Canaries scored 21 points to the Hurricane's 8 in the third period to propel them to victory.

Leading scorers: Allentown – Rocky Ruth 21, Tom Fatzinger 11; Bethlehem – Charlie Marcon 18, Gary Marcus 16.[5]

Allentown 57 Easton 41: Allentown kept rolling later in the week with a victory over Easton at the Little Palestra. The Canaries, who led from start to finish, held a 37-23 lead at halftime. The game was marred by brief fisticuffs between Canary Rocky Ruth and Rover Dean Lowe and a controversial technical assessed on Easton coach Tom Sweeney.

Leading scorers: Allentown - Dave Rooney 21, Tom Fatzinger 14; Easton - Chip Oldt 15.

Central Catholic 75 Hazleton 58: Central Catholic maintained its tie for the league lead with a decisive win over Hazleton at Rockne Hall. After holding a 32-26 lead after two quarters, the Vikings outscored Hazleton 20-8 in the 3rd period to put the game away.

Leading scorers: Central Catholic - Ed Pfeiffer 21, Tim Marsden 20, Bob Spang 13; Hazleton - Rinaldo Pecile 16, Larry Piehota 14, Frank Zack 13.[6]

Bethlehem 70 Pottsville 49: Charley Marcon led Bethlehem to its first league win over winless Pottsville. The Hurricane made 29 field goals to the Crimson Tide's 14. Pottsville made 21 of 28 foul shots.

Leading scorers: Bethlehem - Charley Marcon 23, Pat Gillen 14, Dan Voorhees 10; Pottsville - Ron Emmert 16.[7]

Week 3

Allentown 65 Central Catholic 63: A standing room only crowd at the Little Palestra witnessed a ferocious battle for first place between Allentown and Central Catholic. Angry fans who couldn't get into the game broke several windows at the Little Palestra. No tickets were sold at the door for the game. After Allentown led 41-34 at the half, the Vikings surged in the third quarter and outscored the Canaries 21-9 to take a 55-50 advantage into the final period. With both teams making 24 field goals, Allentown made 17 of 25 foul shots and Central Catholic 15 of 22 for the difference in the final score.

Leading scorers: Allentown - Rocky Ruth 18, Dave Rooney 17, Tom Fatzinger 15; Central Catholic - Ed Pfeiffer 28, Bob Spang 14.[8]

Easton 86 Pottsville 56: Easton evened its record at 2-2 against winless Pottsville. The victory came about with Easton's domination in the second and fourth quarters when they outscored Pottsville 55-28. Easton had five players in double figures.

Leading scorers: Easton - Chip Oldt 20, Dean Lowe 19, Terry Bartolet 19, Dick Dreas 10, Bill Houston 10; Pottsville - Ron Emmert 23, Joe Santor 14.

Hazleton 74 Bethlehem 54: Hazleton walloped Bethlehem to even their record at 2-2. Five Mountaineers scored in double figures with Rinaldo Pecile, named to the Sporting News' Scholastic All-American football team the prior day, leading the attack. Trailing 18-8 after a quarter, Bethlehem got within 8 points after three periods 51-43.

Leadings scorers: Hazleton – Rinaldo Pecile 18, Larry Piehota 17, John Tarone 11, Dale Stewart 10, Frank Zack 10; Bethlehem – Skip Smith 14, Charley Marcon 13, Gary Marcus 11.[9]

Week 4

Hazleton 66 Allentown 58: Hazleton made 26 of 45 foul shots to Allentown's 10 of 20 to knock the Canaries from the ranks of the unbeaten. Although Allentown made four more field goals (24 to 20), the extra 16 foul shot conversions doomed Allentown to defeat. Late in the game, Hazleton's Rinaldo Pecile drove to the basket for a layup and Allentown's Dave Rooney attempted to stop him and Pecile fell heavily to the floor. Hazleton Coach Frank Serany ran onto the floor followed by Allentown coach Milo Sewards with the two tangling on the floor. Fans rushed onto the floor and it took several minutes for policemen and officials to restore order. Although Allentown briefly led in the third quarter 37-36, Hazleton was able to regain the lead which they held for most of the game. Rocky Ruth, Pete Coker, and Mike Wing all fouled out of the game for Allentown.

Leading scorers: Hazleton–Rinaldo Pecile 18, Frank Zack 17, Charlie Unger 10; Allentown-Bruce Wing 10, Tom Fatzinger 10.

Central Catholic 70 Pottsville 62: Meanwhile, Central Catholic, with a bit of a struggle, defeated Pottsville to earn a first-place tie with Allentown, both with 4-1 records, and set up a playoff game for the first half title. Four Vikings scored in double figures. With the Vikings' game ending earlier than Allentown's game, many Viking fans hung around huddled by radios to hear the outcome of that contest.

Leading scorers: Central Catholic - Tim Marsden 19, Ed Pfeiffer 15, Bob Spang 14, Fran Demko 11; Pottsville - Joe Santor 21, Andy Palokas 20.

Bethlehem 66 Easton 65: Bethlehem nipped Easton and both teams finished at 2-3 for the half. After holding a 15-point lead at halftime, the Hurricane had to fight off a Red Rover rally for the win. Despite only winning by a point, Bethlehem never trailed in the game. Trailing the Hurricane 57-43 going into the final period, Easton outscored Bethlehem, 22-9 to fall just short.

Leading scorers: Bethlehem - Gary Marcus 23, Charley Marcon 15, Gene Collins 11; Easton - Chip Oldt 13, Dean Lowe 10.[10]

First Half Playoff

Allentown 48 Central Catholic 42: At Muhlenberg's Memorial Hall with a crowd of roughly 3800 fans, Central Catholic took on Allentown in search of its first East Penn title of any kind. However, the Canaries held Viking star Ed Pfeiffer to 8 points and won a low-scoring game. With a 28-21 first half lead, the Vikings played a tough third quarter defense and outscored the Canaries 8-2 to pull within 1 point entering the 4th quarter. Allentown came back to outscore Central Catholic 18-13 to earn the first half title.

Leading scorers: Allentown- Rocky Ruth 17, Pete Coker 13; Central Catholic- Bob Spang 14, Tom Reis 10.[11]

Week 5

Allentown 68 Pottsville 47: Allentown began the second half by crushing Pottsville. With Dave Rooney out with a virus attack, Bruce Wing led a balanced Canaries offense. Holding a 17-14 lead after the first quarter, the Canaries added six points to the lead in each of the next three quarters.

Leading scorers: Allentown - Bruce Wing 13, Mike Wing 12, Tom Fatzinger 12, Rocky Ruth 11; Pottsville - Mike Palokas 16, Ron Emmert 12.

Central Catholic 65 Bethlehem 52: Central Catholic, led by Eddie Pfeiffer, easily dispersed of Bethlehem and built a 35-19 halftime lead. The Viking defense held Bethlehem's two highest scorers, Gary Marcus and Charley Marcon scoreless in the first half and both finished well under their averages with a combined 16 points in the second half.

Leading scorers: Central Catholic – Ed Pfeiffer 29, Bob Spang 16; Bethlehem - Pat Gillen 14.

Hazleton 87 Easton 84: Terry Bartolet set both a Hazleton gym and an Easton record with 48 points. At one point in the second half, he hit 10 consecutive shots. Despite his scoring prowess, Hazleton defeated the Red Rovers. Foul shots again were a big difference for Hazleton. They converted 43 of 60 while Easton only made 24 of 33.

Leading scorers: Hazleton - Rinaldo Pecile 28, Larry Piehota 22, Bob Barone 11; Easton – Terry Bartolet 48, Chip Oldt 16.[12]

Week 6

Allentown 61 Bethlehem 58 OT: Bethlehem gave Allentown a major scare with the Canaries having to come from behind to tie the game in regulation. Bethlehem took a huge 11-point lead into the locker room at the half by outscoring the Canaries 21-9 in the second period. Bethlehem still led 54-48 with 4:40 remaining in the game, but Allentown scored the last six points to tie at 54 in regulation. In overtime, Allentown outscored the Hurricane 7-4 to pull out a hard-fought triumph.

Leading scorers: Allentown – Tom Fatzinger 18, Rocky Ruth 16, Bruce Wing 14, Pete Coker 10; Bethlehem – Gary Marcus 19, Pat Gillen 18.[13]

Central Catholic 61 Easton 53: Central Catholic kept pace with Allentown by downing Easton. Tim Marsden took offensive and defensive honors in the game when he led the Canaries' scoring attack and held high-scoring Terry Bartolet to only 9 points. Easton led after a quarter 14-11 before the Vikings took the lead at the half 29-26. The lead flipped back and forth several times in the third quarter until the Vikings took the lead for good 41-39.

Leading scorers: Allentown - Tim Marsden 21, Bob Spang 12, Tom Reis 10; Easton - Chip Oldt 22, Dean Lowe 11.

Hazleton 57 Pottsville 52: Hazleton also held on to a piece of first place by hanging on to defeat winless Pottsville. Pottsville had the lead at halftime 33-31. The Mountaineers held Pottsville to 3 points in the third period while scoring 13 to take the lead. Pottsville rallied in the fourth quarter, but fell short.

Leading scorers: Hazleton - Rinaldo Pecile 20; Pottsville - Andy Palokas 13, Jim Sisko 12, Joe Santor 10.[14]

Allentown 60 Easton 56: For the second time in the week, Allentown had to fight off an opponent to remain in first place. Leading by 11 points at the half 39-28, Allentown hung on to win after Easton narrowed the lead to two points 50-48 early in the 4th quarter. The Canaries made 16 foul shots to 10 for the Red Rovers to seal the win.

Leading scorers: Allentown - Pete Coker 18, Rocky Ruth 15, Tom Fatzinger 10; Easton - Chip Oldt 19, Terry Bartolet 19.

Hazleton 63 Central Catholic 53: Hazleton kept its share of first place and they dropped Central Catholic out of it with their win over the Vikings. Hazleton scored 11 points in the last three minutes to break open a tight game 53-51. Hazleton led by a slim one-point at halftime 30-29.

Leading scorers: Hazleton - Rinaldo Pecile 18, John Tarone 15, Bob Barone 13; Central Catholic - Eddie Pfeiffer 20, Bob Spang 13, Tim Marsden 10.[15]

Bethlehem 57 Pottsville 54: Despite making only 16 of 77 field goal attempts, Bethlehem downed Pottsville. They won the game at the foul line by sinking 23 of 34 foul shots. Gary Marcus made only 3 of 17 shots.

Leading scorers: Bethlehem - Gary Marcus 17, Pat Gillen 17, Skip Smith 10; Pottsville - Joe Santor 19, Jack Scotnicki 10.[16]

Week 7

Central Catholic 53 Allentown 49: A sellout crowd of nearly 3,600 fans watched Central Catholic knock Allentown out of a first-place tie with Hazleton for the second half title. Jumping out to a 10-2 lead in the first quarter, the Vikings controlled the game the whole night. They increased the lead to eleven points 28-17 at the half. The Canaries cut the lead to three in the 4th quarter, but the Vikings managed to maintain their lead. The victory avenged the Vikings' only first half loss to the Canaries.

Leading scorers: Central Catholic - Tim Marsden 20, Ed Pfeiffer 17, Bob Spang 10; Allentown - Tom Fatzinger 20.

Hazleton 76 Bethlehem 60: Meanwhile, Hazleton took over sole possession of first place by outlasting Bethlehem. Shooting over 50% from the field, Hazleton never trailed after taking a 20-12 first period lead.

Leading scorers: Hazleton - Dale Smith 26, Rinaldo Pecile 12, John Tarone 11, Charlie Unger 11; Bethlehem - Skip Smith 19, Pat Gillen 12, Gary Marcus 11.[17]

Easton 87 Pottsville 72: Chip Oldt scored 32 points and broke Easton's season scoring record of 406 set by Charley Ross. His total stood at 411 with a game left to add to the record. Easton rolled out to a 49-22 halftime lead and eventually won the game over Pottsville.

Leading scorers: Easton – Chip Oldt 32, Terry Bartolet 22, Dean Lowe 11; Pottsville - Joe Santor 25, Jack Scotnicki 17, Jim Sisko 15.[18]

Week 8

Hazleton 68 Allentown 63: For the first time in 18 seasons, Frank Serany's Hazleton Mountaineers beat Allentown on their home floor to take the second half title. After trailing 51-44 at the end of the third quarter, Hazleton outscored Allentown 24-12 in the final period to take the title. The victory set up a rematch with Allentown, first half champs, at the Hershey Area for the league title. The Canaries lost the game at the foul line converting only 11 of 32 attempts while Hazleton made 18 of 26. Five Mountaineers scored in double figures.

Leading scorers: Hazleton - Charlie Unger 15, Dale Stewart 14, Larry Piehota 13, Rinaldo Pecile 11, John Tarone 10; Allentown - Tom Fatzinger 18, Mike Wing 13, Rocky Ruth 13.

Central Catholic 65 Pottsville 47: With Eddie Pfeiffer scoring 18 points in the first half, the Vikings jumped out to a 40-20 first half lead over Pottsville. One of Pfeiffer's field goals was a halfcourt shot at the buzzer signaling halftime. The Vikings' defense held Pottsville to 15 total points in the 2nd and 3rd periods.

Leading scorers: Central Catholic – Ed Pfeiffer 20, Tom Reis 13, Joe Sarmir 12; Pottsville - Joe Santor 17, Jim Sisko 11.[19]

Bethlehem 67 Easton 53: Bethlehem trounced Easton to close out the season for both teams. Chip Oldt increased his Easton season scoring record to 425 points. Bethlehem led 34-24 at halftime.

Leading scorers: Bethlehem - Charlie Marcon 18, Pat Gillen 15, Gene Collins 13, Gary Marcus 10; Easton – Chip Oldt 14, Terry Bartolet 13, Dick Dreas 10.[20]

League Playoff

Allentown 60 Hazleton 56: After losing to Hazleton twice in the regular season, Allentown took the league title with an avenging victory at the Hershey Arena. After trailing by 13 points at the half, Hazleton put on a furious second half rally to get within two points (55-53 and 57-55) during the last two minutes of the 4th quarter. Allentown converted three foul shots in the last 50 seconds to hang on for the victory.

Leading scorers: Allentown - Rocky Ruth 24, Don Stermer 13; Hazleton - Charlie Unger 20. Larry Piehota 16.[21]

PIAA Playoffs

Allentown 68 Whitehall 55: At Rockne Hall, Allentown began postseason play against Whitehall, the Lehigh Valley League champions. In a very physical game marred by numerous scuffles, Allentown won the contest after taking a 39-28 halftime lead. A total of 79 foul shots were attempted with the numerous fouls assessed during the game. Coach Bob Steckel's Zephyrs lost Bruce Kunkle two minutes into the game with an ankle injury. Ed Folk was assessed three fouls early and sat most of the first half. Two minutes into the second half, Will Pfeifly was ejected for taking swings at the Canaries' Bruce Wing.

Leading scorers: Allentown - Rocky Ruth 15, Pete Coker 14, Tom Fatzinger 10; Whitehall - Paul Harakal 28, John Saganovich 14, Will Pfeifly 10.[23]

Tamaqua 59 Allentown 52: At the Penn Palestra, old league foe Tamaqua stunned the Canaries. The Black Diamond League champions trailed 27-22 at the half, but rallied to outscore Allentown in both the third and fourth quarters to oust Allentown from postseason play. Tamaqua coach Pinky Purnell's defensive strategy of stopping Rocky Ruth worked to perfection. Ruth, despite taking 18 shots, did not score a single field goal and scored only 4 points on foul shots.

Leading scorers: Tamaqua - Bill Yelsh 18, Bill Storch 17, George Willing 10; Allentown - Tom Fatzinger 16, Bruce Wing 11.[24]

PCIAA Playoffs

Central Catholic 77 Bethlehem Catholic 54: Central Catholic entered the PCIAA playoffs seeking its seventh state crown. At Lehigh's Grace Hall, the Vikings dispatched of Bethlehem Catholic outscoring them in all four quarters. The Vikings led 17-6 after the first quarter and 39-23 at the half.

Leading scorers: Central Catholic - Eddie Pfeiffer 21, Bob Spang 16, Tom Reis 11, Joe Sarmir 10; Bethlehem Catholic - Bob Molitoriz 16, Bob Csaszar 15, Bob Bukvics 10.[25]

Central Catholic 59 Reading Central Catholic 29: At Reading's Albright Fieldhouse, Central Catholic displayed a stingy defense by allowing Reading Catholic only 9 points in the second half and 29 for the game in a beat down of Reading Central Catholic. Holding only a two-point lead 15-13 after the first quarter, the Vikings clamped down on the Cardinals.

Leading scorers: Central Catholic - Ed Pfeiffer 17, Joe Sarmir 13; Reading Central Catholic - John McCloskey 13.[26]

Central Catholic 62 Bishop Kenrick 51: At the Norristown High School gym, Central Catholic disposed of Bishop Kenrick 62-51. After being deadlocked at 8 in the first quarter, the Vikings broke loose to outscore their opponents 17-9 at the end of the period. Only four players scored for the Vikings, three in double figures. Joe Sarmir scored the remaining 5 points.

Leading scorers: Central Catholic - Bob Spang 26, Tim Marsden 20, Ed Pfeiffer 11; Bishop Kenrick - Jerry Moran 17, Tom Marshall 15.[27]

Central Catholic 63 Bishop McDevitt 48: At the Farm Show Arena in Harrisburg, the Vikings ended Bishop McDevitt's 20 game win streak to advance to the state finals once again. Trailing 27 -22 at the half, Central Catholic scored 41 points in the second half to stun the Crusaders and the crowd. Tim Marsden played tough defense on the Crusader's Dennis Dobosh, who averaged over 20 points, and held him to six points and only one field goal.

Leading scorers: Central Catholic - Ed Pfeiffer 20, Tim Marsden 19, Bob Spang 13; Bishop McDevitt - Dick Spencer 14, Mike Funk 10.[28]

Pittsburgh North Catholic 83 Central Catholic 67: At the Pittsburgh Fieldhouse, Central Catholic faced defending PCIAA champions, the Pittsburgh North Catholic Trojans. The Trojans jumped out to a 23-7 first quarter lead and led the whole way despite several Viking rallies. The Vikings played the game close after that and were outscored by only one point in the 2nd quarter, three in the third quarter and outscored their opponents by four in the final period. The Vikings were hindered by the loss of Ed Pfeiffer with an injury and Tim Marsden on fouls in the final period.

Leading scorers: Pittsburgh Central Catholic - Matt Szykowny 28, Tom Brown 23; Central Catholic - Tom Reis 20, Bob Spang 17.[29]

Eastern States Catholic Basketball Tournament

St. Peter's Prep 68 Central Catholic 64 OT: After the loss in the PCIAA final, Central Catholic traveled to Newport, RI, to participate in the Eastern States Catholic Basketball Tournament. Trailing by seven at half time (32-25) to St. Peter's Prep of Jersey City, NJ, the Vikings surged into the lead early in the final quarter 55-50 only to see the New Jersey state champions fight back to tie the game at 60-60 in regulation. St. Peter's Prep outscored the Vikings 8-4 in the overtime period for the win.

Leading scorers: St. Peter's Prep – Jim Barry 28, Johnny Massaro 15, Ernie Erwin 10; Central Catholic -Tim Marsden 14, Bob Spang 14, Ed Pfeiffer 11, Tom Reis 10.[30]

DeLasalle 60 Central Catholic 57: In a consolation game at the tournament, Central Catholic bowed to the hosts DeLaSalle. After leading after the first quarter 12-8, the Vikings fell behind in the second quarter 27-22 and could not recover.

Leading scorers: DeLasalle – John Gibson 19, Frank Silvia 17, Andy Anderson 13; Central Catholic - Bob Spang 17, Ed Pfeiffer 14.[31]

Postseason Accolades

Leading Scorers: Chip Oldt, Easton's season scoring record holder, lead the league with 205 points. Other leading scorers included Ed Pfeiffer, Central Catholic, 186; Rinaldo Pecile, Hazleton, 177; Joe Santor, Pottsville, 163; Terry Bartolet, Easton, 147; Tom Fatzinger, Allentown, 142; Tim Marsden, Central Catholic, 140; Bob Spang, Central Catholic, 136; Rocky Ruth, Allentown, 142; Larry Piehota, Hazleton, 131; Gary Marcus, Bethlehem, 129; and Charlie Marcon Bethlehem, 125.[32]

All-Stars: The league all-star first team included: Ed Pfeiffer, Rocky Ruth, and Tom Fatzinger all of Allentown, Rinaldo Pecile, Hazleton, and Chip Oldt, Easton. Second team selections included Terry Bartolet, Easton; Tim Marsden, Central Catholic; Larry Piehota, Hazleton; Gary Marcus, Bethlehem; and Bob Spang, Central Catholic.[33]

All-State: The Associated Press' All Pennsylvania Scholastic Team included Ed Pfeiffer, Central Catholic, Chip Oldt, Easton, and Rinaldo Pecile Hazleton, 2nd team. Honorable Mention status included Rocky Ruth and Dave Rooney, Allentown.[34]

Final Standings

First Half		Second Half		Overall	
Allentown	4-1	Hazleton	5-0	Hazleton	8-2
Central Catholic	4-1	Central Catholic	4-1	Central Catholic	8-2
Hazleton	3-2	Allentown	3-2	Allentown	7-3
Easton	2-3	Bethlehem	2-3	Bethlehem	4-6
Bethlehem	2-3	Easton	1-4	Easton	3-7
Pottsville	0-5	Pottsville	0-5	Pottsville	0-10

Team Rosters

Allentown: Coach Milo Sewards, Peter Coker, William Cooperman, Thomas Fatzinger, Edward Helfrich, Jeff Maier, Charles O'Brien, Ronald Reinard, David Rooney, William "Rocky" Ruth, Donald Saylor, Donald Stermer, Fred Steward, Bruce Wing, Michael Wing

Bethlehem: Coach John Howard, Gene Collins, Bruce Cressman, Buchanan Ewing, David Funk, Pat Gillen, Pat Hoydu, Peter Lake, Charlie Marcon, Gary Marcus, Gary Richter, Skip Smith, Larry Szarko, Robert Vorhees, Donald Wagner, Robert Wisser

Central Catholic: Coach John Compardo, Mike Delisant, Fran Demko, Greg Deutsch, Larry Horinko, Bob Lang, Tim Marsden, Joe McCafferty, Al Pappano, Ed Pfeiffer, Gary Plessl, Tom Reis, Joe Sarmir, Bobby Spang, Jack Tate

Easton: Coach Tom Sweeney, John Avianantos, Terry Bartolet, Ronald Burns, Dick Dreas, Bill Houston, Chuck Lewis, Dean Lowe, Charles "Chip" Oldt, Salvatore Pitino, Solomon Pratt, James Renaldi, John Stothoff

Hazleton: Coach Frank Serany, Robert Barone, Frank Hill, Gene Kapes, Arthur Marsicano, Francis Oravetz, Rinaldo Pecile, Larry Piehota, Jerry Portland, Mike Progansky, Dale Stewart, John Tarone, Charlie Unger, Frank Zack

Pottsville: Coach George Dimmerling, Ron Emmert, George Garrett, John Grazis, Edward Hoffman, Ronald Meagher, Andy Palokas, Joe Santor, Jack Scotnicki, Jim Sisko, Chris Smink, Jim Steidle, Jim Strausser, Stan Wilder, Dick Yuengling

Allentown High School – 1959 League Champions[22]

Front: Donald Stermer, Charles O'Brien, Thomas Gilly (mgr), Fred Steward, Edward Helfrich; Middle: Thomas Fatzinger, Jeff Maier, David Rooney, Joe Blankowitsch (trainer), William Cooperman, Ronald Reinhard, Michael Wing; Back: William Ruth, John Mascavage (asst coach), Bruce Wing, Coach Seward, Peter Coker, Kenneth Wildonger (asst coach), Donald Sailor

1960

Dieruff Enters the League

Phil Phillippi, Rev. Francis Zavodny, and Edgar Rabenold were elected to the positions of president, vice president, and secretary-treasurer positions at the spring meeting at the Shankweiler Hotel in Fogelsville. Applications for entry into the league from Notre Dame-Green Pond and Phillipsburg, NJ, were tabled for discussion until the December meeting. Considerable concern was raised about adding two teams to the league who would not be eligible for postseason play in the district.[1] The decision on the applications from Notre Dame and Phillipsburg were again postponed since neither team was a member of the PIAA and the league officials were reluctant to admit additional non-PIAA members in addition to Central Catholic. A rule was passed to drop any referee from future league officiating if the official drops a league game in order to officiate a collegiate game.[2]

Week 1

Allentown 70 Pottsville 61: Allentown opened the league season by registering the 200th win for Coach Milo Sewards over Pottsville. Pottsville kept the game close trailing at the half 31-30 and trailed by only three points 59-56 with three minutes left in the game. At that point, Pottsville's Ed Hoffman fouled out and Allentown went on to the victory.

Leading scorers: Allentown - Tom Fatzinger 18, Pete Coker 18, Bruce Wing 16; Pottsville - John Grazis 19, Jack Scotnicki 13, Dick Yuengling 11.

Bethlehem 64 Central Catholic 60: Trailing 62-52 with 1:50 remaining, Central Catholic scored 8 straight points to threaten Bethlehem. However, Bethlehem scored the last bucket to win the game. The Vikings had led after a quarter 16-11 but lost the lead by halftime 34-29. Joe Sarmir scored 19 points in the second half for the Vikings.

Leading scorers: Bethlehem - Gary Marcus 22, Charlie Marcon 15, Pat Gillen 11; Central Catholic - Joe Sarmir 24, Larry Horinko 12.

Hazleton 86 Easton 55: Five players scored in double figures as Hazleton drubbed Easton and moved to 9-0 on the season. With only a two-point lead 13-11, the Mountaineers scored seven straight points to take a 20-11 first quarter lead. They put the game away in the 3rd quarter with a 25-11 advantage over the Rovers.

Leading scorers: Hazleton - Dale Stewart 21, Charlie Unger 16, Frank Zack 12, Art Marsicano 10, Mike Progansky 10; Easton - Carl Pitino 13, Jim Renaldi 11, Sal Rizzo 10, Tony Relvas 10.[3]

Bethlehem 74 Easton 50: After leading by a single point after the first quarter 21-20, the Hurricane outscored the Red Rovers 34-15 in the middle two periods to take a commanding lead. During the first period, Easton had led 17-12 before Bethlehem surged into the lead.

Leading scorers: Bethlehem - Pat Gillen 18, Tony Filo 16, Gary Marcus 15, Don Watson 1; Easton -. Sam Pitino 13, Jim Renaldi 11.

Dieruff 63 Pottsville 49: Dieruff made its debut in the league memorable with a victory over Pottsville. Dieruff trailed 35-31 at halftime. The Huskies held Pottsville to a single field goal and 14 total points in the second half. The Huskies scored 21 points in the third quarter to charge ahead of the Crimson Tide.

Leading scorers: Dieruff - Jim Spencer 13, Terry Krause 12, Steve Roth 11; Pottsville – Dick Yuengling 13.

Hazleton 56 Allentown 51: At the Little Palestra, Hazleton edged out Allentown in a typical heated contest between the two rivals. In the 4th quarter, the rival scorekeepers (Allentown's Ron "Pumpkin" Miller and Hazleton's "Chip" Kender) threw punches at each other. The game was held up for five minutes before order was restored and the game could resume. The fracas occurred when Hazleton's Frank Zack fouled out of the game with 5:51 to play. Allentown held a 5-point lead 48-43 with 4:43 to play, but Hazleton scored 7 points in a row to move on to the victory and remain undefeated.

Leading scorers: Hazleton - Dale Stewart 19, Art Marsicano 11; Allentown - Gary Spengler 17, Bruce Wing 13, Tom Fatzinger 11.[4]

Week 2

Hazleton 78 Dieruff 53: At Hazleton, the home team gave an unfriendly league welcome to Dieruff by running over the Huskies. Hazleton scored ten straight in the first period to lead 15-2 and extended the lead to 21-8 at the end of the quarter. At one point late in the fourth quarter, Hazleton led by 33 points 77-44.

Leading scorers: Hazleton - Charlie Unger 19, Dale Stewart 17, Frank Zack 11; Dieruff - Jim Spencer 16.

Central Catholic 62 Easton 44: Easton played even with Central Catholic for nearly three whole periods. With 2:28 left in the 3rd quarter, the score was tied at 38 all. However, the Vikings outscored the Red Rovers 18-6 for the win with Easton only able to make a single field goal in the final period.

Leading scorers: Central Catholic - Joe Sarmir 24, Fran Demko 15; Easton - Chuck Lewis 10.

Bethlehem 56 Allentown 46: Bethlehem stayed tied for the league lead after its takedown of Allentown. After trailing by 20 points in the first half 31-11, the Canaries whittled the lead to 3 points 45-42 with 3:30 to go in the game. Bethlehem led 30-19 at halftime.

Leading scorers: Bethlehem - Gary Marcus 21, Tony Filo 13; Allentown - Jeff Mair 11, Tom Fatzinger 10.[5]

Allentown 69 Easton 57: With both teams sinking 25 field goals, the difference in the game came down to foul shots. Allentown converted 19 of 34 foul shots while Easton only made 7 of 17. Easton had a 42-40 lead in the 3rd quarter, but could not hang on for the victory. Allentown had taken a 29-23 lead at halftime.

Leading scorers: Allentown - Pete Coker 27, Tom Fritzinger 11, Gary Spengler 11; Easton - Sal Rizzo 15, Dick Dreas 14, Sam Pitino 14, Tony Relvas 11.

Bethlehem 73 Dieruff 45: Bethlehem took a half game lead over idle Hazleton with a win over Dieruff. Bethlehem scored ten points in 44 seconds in the 4th quarter while Dieruff could only score a single point in the final four minutes. Bethlehem led at halftime 37-23. The Huskies scored the first nine points of the fourth quarter to cut the Hurricane-lead to 51-44.

Leading scorers: Bethlehem - Gary Marcus 19, Don Watson 17, Charlie Marcon 14, Tony Filo 11; Dieruff - Jim Spencer 16, Steve Roth 11.

Central Catholic 73 Pottsville 58: The Vikings had four players in double figures for Coach John Compardo's Central Catholic quintet as they trounced Pottsville. The Vikings only led by a point 16-15 after the first period and 26-25 with two minutes left in the first half. The teams scored 16 points in the last two minutes of the half with Central Catholic holding the advantage at halftime 37-30.

Leading scorers: Central Catholic - Larry Horinko 19, Fran Demko 18, Joe Sarmir 14, Greg Deutsch 13; Pottsville - Jim Steidle 14, Dick Yuengling 11, Ron Emmert 11.[6]

Week 3

Hazleton 59 Bethlehem 52: Undefeated Hazleton shot out to a 17-2 lead over Bethlehem on their way to the win. After the Mountaineers led 22-6 after a quarter, the Hurricane cut the lead 32-27 at halftime. A crowd of 3600 at Bethlehem's Memorial gym saw the Hurricane fight their way back to a four-point deficit several times in the game including 45-41 at the end of the 3rd quarter.

Leading scorers: Hazleton - Charlie Unger 20, Dale Stewart 15, Larry Piehota11; Bethlehem - Gary Marcus 19, Tony Filo 10, Charlie Marcon 10.

Easton 60 Pottsville 58: Pottsville had Easton down by 15 points in the first half and led at the half 30-19, but the Red Rovers outscored Pottsville by 11 points in the 4th quarter to eke out the win. Easton had cut Pottsville's lead to 47-40 at the end of the third quarter.

Leading scorers: Easton - Tony Relvas 17, Sam Pitino 13, Chuck Lewis 11, Sal Rizzo 10; Pottsville - Dick Yuengling 14, Ron Emmert 14.

Dieruff 52 Central Catholic 45: Dieruff evened their record at 2-2 with a surprising win over Central Catholic. The Huskies led 26-20 at halftime, but the Vikings took a one-point lead 38-37by the end of the third quarter. In the second half, the lead changed hands several times until Dieruff took charge late in the 4th period 43-42 to lead the rest of the way.

Leading scorers: Dieruff - Jim Spencer 18, Steve Roth 15, Terry Krause 11; Central Catholic - Joe Sarmir 16, Fran Demko 12, Greg Deutsch 11.[7]

Central Catholic 50 Hazleton 49: The Vikings' Larry Horinko sank a foul shot with 34 seconds left to stun previously unbeaten Hazleton at Rockne Hall. The loss dropped the Mountaineers into 2nd place, a half-game behind Bethlehem. Central Catholic was down by 10 at the half 30-20, but outscored Hazleton by 14 points in the 3rd quarter. Hazleton led 49-47 with 1:48 left. The Vikings scored the last 3 points for the win.

Leading scorers: Central Catholic-Larry Horinko 20, Joe Sarmir 10, Al Pappano 10; Hazleton-Larry Piehota 12, Frank Zack 12.

Bethlehem 71 Pottsville 57: With Hazleton's loss, Bethlehem took a half game lead with its easy win at Pottsville and clinched at least a tie for the first half title. The contest was tight all the way to the final quarter with Bethlehem leading 17-16 and 35-33 after the first two quarters. Pottsville tied the game after three quarters 52-52. Bethlehem scored 19 points to Pottsville's 5 in the final period.

Leading scorers: Bethlehem - Don Watson 16, Tony Filo 14, Pat Gillen 13, John Matthews 11; Pottsville - Ron Emmert 21, Ed Hoffman 13, Jack Scotnicki 13.

Allentown 62 Dieruff 35: Allentown held Dieruff to two field goals during a 14 ½ minute period from the opening period until late in the 3rd period to defeat their crosstown rivals. As a result, the Canaries extended their 13-9 advantage to 45-19. After a shoving match, Pete Coker and Dieruff sophomore Charlie Noti were ejected with 4 minutes to go in the game. Allentown's Bill Fahler received the same fate with a minute to go for pushing Dieruff's Steve Roth.

Leading scorers: Allentown-Pete Coker 22, Bruce Sauerwine 17, Gary Spengler 16; Dieruff-Jim Spencer 11.[8]

Week 4

Hazleton 80 Pottsville 44: By virtue of a win over Pottsville, Hazleton gained a tie with Bethlehem for the first half championship, necessitating a playoff to decide the first half. After leading by six points 13-7 after 4 minutes of play, Hazleton ran off 16 points to take a commanding 29-7 lead. The Mountaineers extended the lead to 49-18 and cruised to the win with Coach Serany inserting 15 different players into the game.

Leading scorers: Hazleton - Charlie Unger 21, Dale Stewart 13, Frank Zack 12; Pottsville - Ron Emmert 19.

Dieruff 45 Easton 39: Dieruff finished the first half of the season with a victory over Easton. Dieruff led at the half 25-23 with Easton tying up the score to begin the third period. Dieruff scored 7 straight points to take a lead they never relinquished. Easton scored only four points in the third quarter as Dieruff stalled and only scored 9 points.

Leading scorers: Dieruff - Steve Roth 15, Terry Krause 11, Jerry Scheirer 10; Easton – Dick Dreas 16, Sal Rizzo 14.

Allentown 76 Central Catholic 71: Allentown finished at 4-2 with a hard-fought victory over Central Catholic. The Canaries made 20 of 31 first half field goal attempts to take a 45-36 halftime lead. Trailing 64-54 entering the final quarter, the Vikings cut the lead to 74-71 with 1:17 to play, but the Canaries stopped the Vikings rally for the win.

Leading scorers: Allentown - Pete Coker 24, Gary Spengler 19, Bruce Sauerwine 17; Central Catholic - Fran Demko 23, Al Pappano 14, Bob Lang 11, Joe Sarmir 10.[9]

First Half Playoff

Bethlehem 61 Hazleton 55: Bethlehem lost a critical member of the starting five prior to the playoff game with Hazleton. Gary Marcus suffered a dislocated shoulder in the game with Pottsville. Further examination indicated that he would be out for the rest of the season.[9] Despite his loss, Bethlehem outhustled Hazleton at the Penn Palestra to chalk up the win for the first half title. Bethlehem took a 10-point lead into the half 33-23 and held off a furious third quarter rally to pull out the win. Bethlehem rallied from a third quarter tie at 44 to win by six points.

Leading scorers: Bethlehem - Tony Filo 25, Gene Collins 11, Pat Gillen 10; Hazleton - Dale Stewart 17, Frank Zack 11, Charlie Unger 10.[10]

Week 5

Hazleton 85 Easton 52: Hazleton rebounded from its disappointing playoff loss to Bethlehem by manhandling Easton. After holding a 12-8 lead after the first quarter, the Mountaineers outscored the Red Rovers in the middle two periods 46-18 to breeze to victory.

Leading scorers: Hazleton - Dale Stewart 22, Larry Piehota 18, Frank Zack 15, Charlie Unger 11; Easton - Dick Dreas 13, Jim Renaldi 14.

Central Catholic 77 Bethlehem 73: With the lead flip-flopping back and forth, Bethlehem suffered a loss to Central Catholic. The Hurricane led 14-13 after a period with the score being tied at the half at 32-32. Bethlehem took a three-point lead into the fourth quarter. With the game deadlocked at 60 in the final period, the Vikings finished fast to sew up the win after Tony Filo fouled out for Bethlehem with 3:40 left.

Leading scorers: Central Catholic - Joe Sarmir 18. Bob Lang 18, Larry Horinko 17, Fran Demko 10; Bethlehem - Tony Filo 26, Don Watson 17, Pat Gillen 10.

Allentown 74 Pottsville 60: With the game close for nearly three periods, Allentown, leading 50-41, scored 11 straight points in the 4th quarter to secure the win over Pottsville. The Canaries led 29-26 at halftime. It was Pottsville's 29th consecutive loss in league play.

Leading scorers: Allentown - Pete Coker 23, Bruce Sauerwine 14, Bruce Wing 13; Pottsville - Ron Emmert 15, Ed Hoffman 14, Jack Scotnicki 12.[11]

Pottsville 62 Dieruff 41: Pottsville ended its 29-game league losing streak and nine-game season losing streak by surprising Dieruff. Having missed the first matchup with Dieruff, Ron Emmert was the difference in this game as he controlled the boards and tallied 22 points. Pottsville never trailed in the game.

Leading scorers: Pottsville – Ron Emmert 22, Jack Scotnicki 13; Dieruff - Jim Spencer 13, Charlie Noti 10.

Hazleton 76 Allentown 61: Playing without Pete Coker due to an injured ankle, Allentown lost at Hazleton. The game was delayed at the start of the second half when Coach Milo Sewards would not let the Canaries take the court until spectators were moved back at each end of the court. Having traded swings at each other earlier in the game, Allentown's Bruce Wing and Hazleton's Dale Stewart were ejected with 2 ½ minutes to play in the game. Hazleton went into the locker room at the half with a ten-point lead 36-26.

Leading scorers: Hazleton - Charlie Unger 21, Frank Zack 14, Larry Piehota 14, Dale Stewart 12, Frank Hill 12; Allentown - Bruce Wing 16, Gary Spengler 13, Tom Fatzinger 12, Bruce Sauerwine 10.

Bethlehem 72 Easton 49: Bethlehem bounced back by running away from Easton. The Hurricane led at halftime 36-24. Easton pulled within six 45-39 in the third quarter, but the Hurricane pulled away after that for the win.

Leading scorers: Bethlehem - John Matthews 17, Tony Filo 14, Pat Gillen 12 Charlie Marcon 11; Easton - Jim Renaldi 17.[12]

Week 6

Central Catholic 73 Easton 64: Despite registering one more field goal (26-25), Easton lost to Central Catholic as the Vikings made 23 of 39 attempts compared to the Red Rovers 12 of 18. The Vikings jumped out to a 20-9 lead only to have Easton fight back and take a brief lead 42-41 in the 3rd quarter. The Vikings scored 26 points to the Red Rovers 18 in the final quarter in a rally for the win.

Leading scorers: Central Catholic - Joe Sarmir 25, Lang 21, Fran Demko 12, Al Pappano 11; Easton - Jim Renaldi 19, Dick Dreas 16, Tony Relvas 10.

Hazleton 68 Dieruff 50: Hazleton remained unbeaten in the half with a win over Dieruff. The Huskies held a 34-33 lead early in the 3rd quarter only to have the Mountaineers score on a tap-in field goal and seven successive foul shots to take a 42-34 lead. Hazleton outscored Dieruff 24-13 in the final quarter. Don Saylor, a transfer from Allentown, led the Huskies scoring.

Leading scorers: Hazleton - Dale Stewart 18, Larry Piehota 15, Charlie Unger 13, Frank Zack 11; Dieruff – Don Saylor 19.

Allentown 80 Bethlehem 76: Coach Milo Sewards played his starting five the entire game without substitution as the Canaries defeated Bethlehem. Pete Coker did not play due to his injured ankle. The teams battled to a 37 all tie at the half and Bethlehem took a one-point lead 59-58 into the final quarter. The Canaries scored the first eight points of the fourth quarter to take a 66-59 lead they never gave up despite Bethlehem getting within two points 76-74 with two minutes to play.

Leading scorers: Allentown – Bruce Sauerwine 35, Gary Spengler 19, Dale Bartman 12, Bruce Wing 11; Bethlehem - John Matthews 30, Tony Filo 25, Pat Gillen 17.[13]

Central Catholic 55 Pottsville 53: Central Catholic moved into a tie for first with idle Hazleton, each at 3-0, with a last second triumph over Pottsville. Playing on their home court, the Vikings trailed most of the first half, including 27-25 at the half, before taking the lead in the third quarter. Ahead 53-48, the Vikings did not score for 3 ½ minutes as Pottsville was able to tie the game at 53 all. With one second on the clock, Bob Lang made a jump shot to pull out the victory for the Vikings.

Leading scorers: Central Catholic-Bob Lang 19, Joe Sarmir 14, Larry Horinko 12; Pottsville-Jack Scotnicki 17, Ron Emmert 10.

Bethlehem 74 Dieruff 39: Bethlehem employed a full court man-to-man press defense to outclass Dieruff. After the Huskies held a 5-2 lead, Bethlehem reeled off nine straight points and the rout was on. The Hurricane held the Huskies to three field goals in the first half and led 32-15 going into the locker room.

Leading scorers: Bethlehem-Charlie Marcon 25, Tony Filo 12, John Matthews 10; Dieruff-Jerry Scheirer 10.

Allentown 76 Easton 57: Allentown dropped Easton to 0-4 in the second half by downing the Red Rovers. Allentown outscored Easton in every quarter for the easy win. At halftime, the score was still relatively close with the Canaries leading 37-30.

Leading scorers: Allentown - Gary Spengler 21, Tom Fatzinger 19, Bruce Wing 10, Bruce Sauerwine 10; Easton - Jim Renaldi 15, Chuck Lewis 14.[14]

Week 7

Central Catholic 55 Dieruff 45: Central Catholic avenged a first half loss to Dieruff with a win in the Huskies' gym. After a close first quarter with Central Catholic holding a one-point lead 12-11, the Vikings took control of the game to lead at the half 28-20. The Vikings held the Huskies to 17 total points in the second and third quarters.

Leading scorers: Central Catholic - Bob Lang 20, Joe Sarmir 17; Dieruff - Steve Roth 12.

Hazleton 77 Bethlehem 62: Trailing Bethlehem 20-14 after one period, Hazleton rallied to take the halftime lead 29-27. A nine-point surge in the third period put Hazleton in command for the win. The game was held up for 30 minutes after an injury to referee Jim Reese. The teams finally agreed to continue the game with 25-year veteran referee Hal Vowler finishing the game for Reese.

Leading scorers: Hazleton - Charlie Unger 21, Frank Zack 21, Dale Stewart 15; Bethlehem - John Matthews 19, Charlie Marcon 17, Tony Filo 12, Pat Gillen 10.

Pottsville 78 Easton 77: After 29 straight league losses, Pottsville won its second in a row with a defeat of Easton. With the game tied at 75, Pottsville won the game on a foul shot by Ron Emmert and a miss on his second shot which was then tipped in for a field goal by Ed Hoffman.

Leading scorers: Pottsville – Ron Emmert 19, Dick Yuengling 15, Jack Grazis 13, Jim Steidel 12, Jack Scotnicki 11; Easton - Kip Simons 30, Jim Renaldi 14, Dick Dreas 10.[15]

Hazleton 84 Central Catholic 66: At Hazleton, the Mountaineers and Central Catholic met in the crucial battle for the second half title. Avenging a first half loss to the Vikings, Hazleton clinched at least a tie for the title with a trouncing of Central Catholic. Hazleton jumped out to a 21-8 lead in the first quarter. The Vikings could get no closer than 14 points in the game and lost Joe Sarmir on fouls in the third quarter. Heavy snow delayed the Vikings arrival in Hazleton prior to the start of the game.

Leading scorers: Hazleton - Charlie Unger 25, Dale Stewart 21, Frank Zack 11; Central Catholic - Larry Horinko 13, Joe Sarmir 12, Bobb Lang 12.

Bethlehem 85 Pottsville 63: Bethlehem closed out its league season with a rout of Pottsville. Bethlehem was never really threatened after taking an 18-12 lead after the first quarter and 48-34 at halftime, fifty fouls were called in the game with 81 foul shots attempted. Pottsville made 31 0f 40 foul shots.

Leading scorers: Bethlehem - Tony Filo 21, Pat Gillen 16, John Matthews 16; Pottsville - Jock Scotnicki 14, Dick Yuengling 13.

Allentown 76 Dieruff 47: Dieruff took an early 8-5 lead, but Allentown rallied to take the lead at the quarter mark 17-9. The game was never in question after that with Allentown extending the lead to 34-21 at the half. Pete Coker and Bruce Wing each tallied 18 rebounds for the Canaries.

Leading scorers: Allentown - Pete Coker 21, Tom Fatzinger 14, Bruce Wing 14; Dieruff - George Clay 16.[16]

Week 8

Hazleton 76 Pottsville 38: At Pottsville, Hazleton doubled up on Pottsville Coach John Slegeski's home team to take the second half title. Hazleton took a 23-12 lead after one quarter and extended it to 42-19 at halftime. With the win, Hazleton would take on Bethlehem for the league championship.

Leading scorers: Hazleton - Charlie Unger 25, Frank Zack 16, Dale Steward 14; Pottsville - Ed Hoffman 9.

Central Catholic 54 Allentown 46: Down 35-24 early in the third period, Central Catholic rallied to score 11 straight points and tie the game at 35 early in the last quarter. The game seesawed back and forth until Central Catholic went ahead to stay at 46-44. The Canaries lost Pete Coker and Bruce Wing late in the 4th quarter on personal fouls.

Leading scorers: Central Catholic-Fran Demko 14, Bob Lang 12, Joe Sarmir 11; Allentown-Pete Coker 18, Tom Fatzinger 13.

Dieruff 57 Easton 48: Dieruff closed out its first year in the league by downing Easton. Easton lost its last seven league contests. The Huskies scored eight in a row in the first period for a 12-6 and led the rest of the way. Dieruff led at halftime 35-19.

Leading scorers: Dieruff - Steve Roth 21, Don Saylor 14; Easton - Jim Renaldi 11, Tony Relvas 10.[17]

League Playoff

Hazleton 65 Bethlehem 57: At the Hershey Arena, Hazleton won its 12th league title over first half champions Bethlehem. In their fourth meeting of the season, two regular season contests and the first half and league playoffs, Hazleton took three of the four games. Bethlehem took an early 3-0 lead, but Hazleton tied it at 4 and then took the lead for good. Bethlehem closed to within 3 points 52-49, but could not overcome the Mountaineers.

Leading scorers: Hazleton - Dale Stewart 24, Frank Zack 16, Larry Piehota 14; Bethlehem - Tony Filo 16, Charlie Marcon 14, Pat Gillen 11.[18]

PIAA Playoffs

Hazleton 86 Lansford 46: Hazleton deployed a full court press and blew out Lansford in their first District 11 playoff tilt. After blanking the Panthers for the first 2 ½ minutes, the game was never in doubt. The Black Diamond League champions were outscored by 9 points in each of the first three quarters and 12 in the final period. Lansford's center John Hackash was held to 4 points, 15 below his average.

Leading scorers: Hazleton- Dale Stewart 22, Charlie Unger 20; Lansford -Chuck Hanna 14, Mike Baran 11.[20]

Hazleton 62 Mahanoy City 60 2OT: At Muhlenberg's Memorial Hall, Mahanoy City took Hazleton to a second overtime period before losing in a sudden death format. After being tied at the half 27 all, Mahanoy City took a 4-point lead into the fourth quarter only to have Hazleton outscore them by four and tie the game. With the score tied at 60 in the first overtime, Larry Piehota missed a shot to keep the game tied. The second overtime would end with the first points scored. Piehota took a similar shot to the one he missed in the first overtime, but made it this time for the victory. Mahanoy City's loss snapped a 23-game winning streak.

Leading scorers: Hazleton - Frank Zack 18, Larry Piehota 16, Charlie Unger 15; Mahanoy City - Jerry Stefanic 30, Gene Miller 10.[21]

Catasauqua 62 Hazleton 59: With 6000 fans at the Hershey Arena, Bob Mushrush's Catasauqua Rough Riders outplayed Hazleton for the scintillating victory, their 26th without a loss. In a close game the whole way, the score was tied at the half 38 a piece, despite an early eight-point lead by the Rough Riders in the first period. Catasauqua won despite only scoring a single field goal in the final period. Hazleton fans stormed the court after the game to get at the game officials for calling a technical on Hazleton late the game. Police had to escort the officials into the locker room.

Leading scorers: Catasauqua - Gene "Pee Wee" Martz 20, Rich Saylor 12, Ray Laubach 11; Hazleton - Charlie Unger 18, Frank Zack 12, Larry Piehota 12.[22]

PCIAA Playoffs

Central Catholic 69 Pottsville Nativity 49: In a game delayed by snow conditions the previous night, Central Catholic began its PCIAA playoff run at the Dieruff High School gym by defeating Pottsville Nativity. The game was delayed due to the still treacherous roads from the Friday storm. After trailing only by four points 19-15 after one period, Pottsville Nativity could only score 4 points in the second period and fell way behind 37-19.

Leading scorers: Central Catholic - Joe Sarmir 21, Fran Demko 17, Larry Horinko 15; Pottsville Nativity - Jack Ryan 18.[23]

Bishop Kenrick 60 Central Catholic 52: Twin seniors Tom and Denny Marshall ended Central Catholic's season at the Dieruff gym by leading Bishop Kenrick over the Vikings. The twins combined to score 37 points. After trailing by 18 in the third period, the Vikings got within five points 54-49, but that was it. Bishop Kenrick held the Vikings to 16 points in the first half.

Leading scorers: Bishop Kenrick – Tom Marshall 20, Denny Marshall 17; Central Catholic - Joe Sarmir 17, Fran Demko, 15, Larry Horinko 10.[24]

Postseason Accolades

Leading Scorers: The top ten scorers for the league season included: Charlie Unger, Hazleton, 208; Dale Stewart, Hazleton, 191; Tony Filo, Bethlehem, 189; Joe Sarmir, Central Catholic, 178; Pete Coker, Allentown, 171; Ron Emmert, Pottsville, 151; Frank Zack, Hazleton 145; Fran Demko, Central Catholic, 142; Gary Spengler, Allentown, 137; and Tom Fatzinger, Allentown, 136.[25]

All-Stars: The league all-star first team included: Tony Filo, Bethlehem; Dale Stewart, Hazleton; Pete Coker, Allentown; Charlie Unger, Hazleton; and Joe Sarmir, Central Catholic. With a tie vote for the fifth position, six players comprised the second team: Charlie Marcon, Bethlehem; Fran Demko, Central Catholic; Frank Zack and Larry Piehota, Hazleton; Gary Marcus, Bethlehem; and Bruce Wing, Allentown.[26]

All-State: Charlie Unger, Hazleton, was named a third team all-state player. Honorable Mention included: Dale Stewart, Hazleton; Pete Coker, Allentown; Larry Piehota, Hazleton; and Tony Filo, Bethehem.[27]

Final Standings

First Half		Second Half		Overall	
Bethlehem	5-1	Hazleton	6-0	Hazleton	11-1
Hazleton	5-1	Central Catholic	5-1	Bethlehem	8-4
Allentown	4-2	Allentown	4-2	Central Catholic	8-4
Central Catholic	3-3	Bethlehem	3-3	Allentown	8-4
Dieruff	3-3	Pottsville	2-4	Dieruff	4-8
Easton	1-5	Dieruff	1-5	Pottsville	2-10
Pottsville	0-6	Easton	0-6	Easton	1-11

Team Rosters

Allentown: Coach Milo Sewards, Dale Bartman, Neil Boyle, Charles Cohen, Joel Cohen, Pete Coker, Bill Fahler, Tom Fatzinger, Glenn Hall, Jeff Mair, Bob Murtaugh, John Sabo, Bruce Sauerwine, Gary Spengler, Jeff West, Bruce Wing

Bethlehem: Coach John Howard, Eugene Collins, Tom DeNofa, Buchanan Ewing, Tony Filo, David Funk, Brian Garland, Pat Gillen, Charlie Marcon, Gary Marcus, John Matthews, Robert Voorhees, Don Watson

Central Catholic: Coach John Compardo, Fran Demko, Greg Deutsch, Phil Dreisbach, Bernie Grim, Larry Horinko, Bob Lang, Joe Mutis, Al Pappano, Gary Plessl, Joe Sarmir, Jack Tate, Mike Zaia

Dieruff: Coach Dick Schmidt, Mike Bodnar, Jim Carter, George Clay, Gary Edwards, Bob Erie, John Faryniak, Dave Grantham, Alton Heil, Tony Krasnicke, Terry Krause, Charles Noti, Steve Roth, Don Saylor, Gerry Scheirer. Frank Schiavone, Joe Smith, Jim Spencer, Don Tretter, Rudy Zieger

Easton: Coach Tom Sweeney, John Avianantos, Ron DeBona, Dick Dreas, Al Iudicello, Charles "Chuck" Lewis, Barry Miller, Sam Pitino, Tony Relvas, Anthony Renaldi, Jim Renaldi, Ray Rissmiller, Sal Rizzo, David Sales, Kip Simons, Thomas Smith

Hazleton: Coach Frank Serany, Harry Defina, Mike Esposito, Joseph Greco, Frank Hill, Gene Kapes, Bill Nance, Francis Oravetz, Larry Piehota, Tom Pugliese, Dale Stewart, Charlie Unger, Willard Woodring, Frank Zack

Pottsville: Coach John Slegeski, James Beveridge, John Condrack, Ron Emmert, George Garrett, John Grazis, Ed Hoffman, Jack Scotnicki, Chris Smink, Jim Steidle, Tony Weisacosky, Stan Wilder, Dick Yuengling

Hazleton High School – 1960 League Champions[19]

Front: Dale Stewart, Frank Zack, Charlie Unger, Larry Piehota, Frank Hill

Middle: Tom Pugliese, Gene Kapes, Harry Defina, Michael Esposito, Willard Woodring, Francis Oravetz

Back: Coach Serany, William Nance, Joseph Greco, Asst. Coach Murrin

1961

Tamaqua Approved to Rejoin League in 1962

Phil Phillippi, Rev. Francis Zavodny, and Edgar Rabenold were re-elected to the positions of president, vice president, and secretary-treasurer positions for another year in the spring meeting at the Shankweiler Hotel in Fogelsville. Rabenold was unanimously elected to the post permanently and presented with a desk chair for his many years of service. A discussion on doing away with the split season format was tabled for a future league meeting.[1]

After a 16-year absence from the league, Tamaqua received unanimous approval to re-enter the league after having played in the Black Diamond League during those years. They would begin play in the league in the 1962 season.[2]

Week 1

Bethlehem 87 Easton 68: Undefeated Bethlehem traveled to Easton to open the season. The Hurricane took a ten-point lead after a quarter 21-10 and scored 49 points in the second half for any easy victory.

Leading scorers: Bethlehem - Tony Filo 24, Charlie Marcon 15, Don Watson 15, Walt Moore 10; Easton - Kip Simons 20, Tony Relvas 18, Tony Renaldi 11.

Allen 67 Central Catholic 55: Allen, previously known as Allentown, began its league season with a win over Central Catholic. Dave Becker, up from the junior varsity, and John Sabo, a transfer from Hazleton, made significant contributions to Allen's opening league win.

Leading scorers: Allen - Don Eshelman 27, George Nau 13, Dave Becker 11, John Sabo 10; Central Catholic - Bob Zobb 17, Ed Sarmir 16, Bob Lang 12.

Dieruff 82 Pottsville 66: Dieruff jumped out to a 26-16 first quarter lead with Pottsville fighting its way back to trail by seven points after three quarters 64-57. The Huskies stretched the lead in the final quarter to remain unbeaten.

Leading scorers: Dieruff - Jim Spencer 27, Charles Noti 22; Pottsville - Ed Hoffman 23, Dick Yuengling 19, John Condrack 12.[3]

Hazleton 62 Allen 56: At Hazleton, the Mountaineers were down 7 points 54-47 with 4 minutes to play against Allen. Hazleton sophomore Tom Carlyon led a comeback to tie the game at 56 with a foul conversion and a field goal after capturing a rebound from his second missed foul shot. With Allen missing shots and mishandling the ball, Hazleton converted six successive foul shots to win the game. In the 4th quarter, John Sabo, a transfer to Allen from Hazleton when his family moved, and Hazleton's Joe Greco traded punches in a scramble under the basket and were both ejected from the game.

Leading scorers: Hazleton - Bill Nance 18, Tom Pugliese 18; Allen - George Nau 15, Gary Spengler 14, John Sabo 12.[4]

Dieruff 65 Easton 45: Coach Dick Schmidt's Huskies led the whole way in an easy conquest of Easton. Dieruff had three players in double figures: After taking a 12-6 lead going into the second quarter, Dieruff put the game away by halftime leading 34-16.

Leading scorers: Dieruff - Charlie Noti 19, Don Carter 15, Steve Roth 12; Easton - Kip Simons 16.

Central Catholic 69 Pottsville 49: After staying close in the first half trailing by only three at halftime 36-33, Pottsville fell to Central Catholic 69-49. The Crimson Tide could only score 6 points in the final period while the Vikings countered with 15 points.

Leading scorers: Central Catholic - Joe Mutis 18, Bob Zobb 16, Bob Lang 14; Pottsville - John Condrack 12, Jim Steidle 11, Ed Hoffman 10.[5]

Week 2

Bethlehem 67 Dieruff 43: In a battle of two unbeaten teams, Bethlehem had four players in double figures to hand Dieruff its first loss. After leading by eight after a quarter, the Hurricane pushed the lead to 18 points at the half 39-21. Bethlehem held the Dieruff offense to 12 points or less in every quarter.

Leading scorers: Bethlehem - Tony Filo 17, John Matthews 17, Charlie Marcon 12, Don Watson 11; Dieruff - Jim Spencer 14, Don Carter 12.

Easton 59 Central Catholic 56: Trailing by four 39-35 going into the final quarter, Easton rallied to down Central Catholic. The Vikings had held four-point leads at each of the quarter marks only see the Red Rovers pull it out in the final period by outscoring the Vikings 24-17.

Leading scorers: Easton - Tony Relvas 25, Kip Simons 11, Barry Miller 11; Central Catholic - Joe Mutis 19, Bob Zobb 15, Bob Lang 13.

Pottsville 58 Hazleton 56: After coming from behind to take down Allen, Hazleton suffered the same fate at Pottsville when the Crimson Tide squeaked out the win. With 3:30 remaining, Hazleton had a 54-49 lead when Dick Yuengling scored two buckets and John Condrack one to vault Pottsville into the lead 55-54 which they would keep for the win. The Mountaineers held a 10-point lead in the third quarter.

Leading scorers: Pottsville - Ed Hoffman 20, Dick Yuengling 15, John Condrack 13; Hazleton - Frank Zack 16, Bill Nance 12, Tom Pugliese 12.[6]

Bethlehem 93 Allen 69: Bethlehem handed the Canaries their worst loss, by 29 points, in the long history of their competition. Suffering its worst loss at home since Milo Sewards took over as coach, Allen was never in the game as the Hurricane took a 12-point lead after one quarter 30-18. By the end of the third quarter, Hazleton lead by 29. Leading scorers: Bethlehem - Tony Filo 22, Don Rodenbach 21, Don Watson 14, John Matthews 12; Allen - John Sabo 21, Gary Spengler 13, Charles Cohen 10.

Dieruff 61 Central Catholic 56: Dieruff stayed on the tails of unbeaten Bethlehem with a triumph over Central Catholic at Rockne Hall. Dieruff's largest lead was eight points after three quarters.

Leading scorers: Dieruff - Jim Spencer 22, Don Carter 14, Jerry Scheirer 10; Central Catholic - Joe Mutis 15, Bob Lang 13.[7]

Easton 75 Hazleton 66: Easton handed Hazleton its first home loss since December 1958 and 28 consecutive victories. Easton came back from a 32-15 deficit early in the second quarter after Coach Tom Sweeney switched the Red Rovers to a full court press. Easton pulled within two points at the half 39-37. Easton ran off eleven straight points at the end of the third period for a 59-46 lead. Five Easton players hit double figures'

Leading scorers: Easton - Kip Simons 17, Tony Renaldi 17. Tony Relvas 17, Ron DeBona 12, Barry Miller 10, Hazleton - Bill Nance 22, Tom Pugliese 14, Dennis Kozlowski 12, Frank Zack 12.[8]

Week 3

Bethlehem 51 Hazleton 44: Coach Danny Gregoria's Hazleton squad gave unbeaten and home team Bethlehem all it could handle for three periods. Hazleton led 24-23 at the half and trailed by only two points after three quarters 35-33. Early in the 4th quarter, Bethlehem spurted to a 46-34 lead. Hazleton fought back to pull within five before finally losing.

Leading scorers: Bethlehem– Tony Filo 14, John Matthews 13, Charlie Marcon 12; Hazleton– Bill Nance 14, Tom Pugliese 12.

Dieruff 63 Allen 54 OT: Dieruff maintained its 2nd place position at 4-1 with an overtime victory over crosstown rival Allen. The Huskies blew a ten-point half time lead 31-21 with Allen making up 8 in the third period.

Leading scorers: Dieruff – Charles Noti 18, Steve Roth 16, Jim Spencer 15; Allen - Gary Spengler 19, John Sabo 12.

Easton 96 Pottsville 90 OT: With the lead seesawing back and forth, Easton and Pottsville fought to ties in the third quarter and the end of regulation 69-69 and 88-88. Easton pulled out the win in overtime with eight straight points before Pottsville scored its only two points. Five players scored all but six of the Red Rovers points:

Leading scorers: Easton - Barry Miller 25, Tony Relvas 21, Kip Simons 18, Tony Renaldi 16, Joe Creazzo 10; Pottsville - Ed Hoffman 28, John Condrack 14, Dick Yuengling 14, Harry Richter 10.[9]

All three Friday night games were postponed due to hazardous travel conditions. Pottsville and Bethlehem rescheduled their tilt for the following night, while the other two games were rescheduled for the following Friday night.

Bethlehem 83 Pottsville 55: Unbeaten Bethlehem (12-0) clinched a tie for the first half title with a beat down of Pottsville at Bethlehem's Memorial gym. Pottsville kept the score close after one quarter 20-16, but the Hurricane pulled away steadily in the last three quarters.

Leading scorers: Bethlehem - Charlie Marcon 27, John Matthews 21, Tom DeNofa 14; Pottsville - Dick Yuengling 18, Dick Richter 10.[10]

Week 4

Bethlehem 58 Central Catholic 41: Bethlehem clinched the first half title finishing 6-0 with a decisive victory over Central Catholic. Bethlehem jumped out to a 15-5 lead in the first quarter. The Vikings cut the lead to five points at the half 27-22, but Bethlehem pulled away in the last two quarters.

Leading scorers: Bethlehem-John Matthews 23, Tony Filo 11, Don Watson 10; Central Catholic-Bob Lang 13, John Lisicky 12.

Allen 68 Pottsville 62: After leading by as many as 9 points and 33-30 at the half, Pottsville went cold in the 3rd period with Allen outscoring them 23-9. Pottsville's late rally could not bring them back as Allen recorded the win.

Leading scorers: Allen - Gary Spengler 22, Don Eshelman 17, Leo Todd 13; Pottsville - Dick Yuengling 22, Ed Hoffman 17, Jim Steidle 10.

Dieruff 38 Hazleton 31: Shooting only 4 for 39 in the first half, Dieruff fell behind Hazleton 20-11 at the half and still trailed by four after three quarters 27-23. Dieruff's defense clamped down on Hazleton and limited the Mountaineers to four 4th quarter points while scoring 15 to pull out a low-scoring triumph. After 28 straight home court wins, Hazleton now had lost two in a row.

Leading scorers: Dieruff - Steve Roth 13, Jerry Schierer 13; Hazleton – Joe Greco 9.[11]

Hazleton 81 Central Catholic 64: In a postponed makeup, Coach Danny Gregoria's Hazleton squad finished the first half at 2-4 after defeating Central Catholic leaving the Vikings at 1-5. The game was close through the first half with Hazleton leading 32-31 at intermission. Hazleton picked up its offense in the second half to score 49 points while holding the Vikings to 33 points.

Leading scorers: Hazleton-Joe Greco 22, Dennis Kozlowski 20, Billy Nance 14, Frank Zack 11; Central Catholic-Joe Mutis 24.

Easton 78 Allen 61: Easton, finishing third at 4-2, ended Allen's dismal first half (2-4) at the Little Palestra. After Easton led at the half 42-33, the Canaries cut the lead to three points 52-49 heading into the fourth quarter. The Red Rovers' offense poured in 26 points, while the defense held Allen to 12, in the last quarter.

Leading scorers: Easton - Tony Relvas 29, Kip Simons 20, Bob Miller 13; Allen - George Nau 18, Gary Spengler 14.[12]

Week 5

Bethlehem 75 Easton 46: Opening up the second half, Bethlehem remained undefeated as Coach John Howard's Hurricanes took down Easton. With the score not in question with the Hurricane leading 38-20 at the half, Coach Howard inserted his reserves into the game and used 12 players overall.

Leading scorers: Bethlehem - Charlie Marcon 17, Tony Filo 13, Don Watson 11, John Matthews 10; Easton - Tony Relvas 18, Kip Simons 10.

Pottsville 58 Dieruff 48: Pottsville upset Dieruff by extending a two-point halftime lead 25-23 to seven after three quarters 44-37. Pottsville, leading 49-46 in the 4th quarter made 7 free throws and a field goal to extend the lead.

Leading scorers: Pottsville - Dick Yuengling 19, George Garrett 12, Dick Richter 10; Dieruff - Jim Spencer 15, Mike Bodnar 10.

Central Catholic 45 Allen 39 OT: Allen's woes continued when Central Catholic defeated the Canaries in overtime at Rockne Hall. John Sabo tied the score at 39 with 12 seconds to play in regulation. The Vikings scored the only six points in overtime for the win. Allen had led at the end of each of the first three quarters.

Leading scorers: Central Catholic - Joe Mutis 16, Bob Lang 14; Allen - John Sabo 12, Don Eshelman 10.[13]

Hazleton 61 Allen 56: At the Little Palestra, Hazleton dropped Allen to 0-2 with their victory to open their second half. The Mountaineers scored a field goal and four successive foul shots in the last 1:29 to prevent Allen from rallying. It was the 6th consecutive win over the Canaries and third in a row at the Little Palestra. In a hard-fought game, the score was tied six times and thirteen lead changes. John Rosenstock sat out the first half of the season as required by the PIAA after transferring to the Mountaineers from MMI.

Leading scorers: Hazleton - Billy Nance 18, John Rosenstock 12, Frank Zack 11, Tom Pugliese 10; Allen – Gary Spengler 18, Charles Cohen 10.[14]

Easton 69 Dieruff 49: Dieruff dropped to 0-2, after contending for the first half title, and fell out of contention for the second half title, in a drubbing by Easton. Easton led 21-13 after the first quarter and the Huskies never threatened them.

Leading scorers: Easton - Kip Simons 19, Tony Relvas 18, Barry Miller 18; Dieruff - Jim Spencer 12.

The Central Catholic at Pottsville game was postponed.[15]

Week 6

Bethlehem 48 Dieruff 46: Dieruff gave Bethlehem all it could handle before the Hurricane prevailed for a narrow 48-46 win over the Huskies. Dieruff led after the first two quarters 15-11 and 25-24 before

Bethlehem took a one-point lead 37-36 after three quarters. Dieruff had spurts of nine and eight straights in the second half to stay close to Bethlehem. Dieruff had a chance to tie the game when they got off four shots with two being blocked and two missed before the buzzer sounded.

Leading scorers: Bethlehem - John Matthews 23, Don Rodenbach 11; Dieruff - Jerry Scheirer 12, Jim Spencer 11.

Easton 56 Central Catholic 49: Excellent foul shooting, 20 of 24, propelled Easton to a win over Central Catholic. The Vikings led 25-22 at the half, but were held to 6 points in the 3rd quarter by Easton.

Leading scorers: Easton - Kip Simons 20, Tony Relvas 18; Central Catholic - Bob Lang 12, Joe Mutis 11, Bob Zobb 11.

Pottsville 79 Hazleton 62: Pottsville shocked Hazleton with their first victory at the Hazleton gym since 1952. Pottsville, a surprising 2-0 after a 1-5 first half, led by as much as 25 points in the 4th quarter. Pottsville made ten of its thirteen field goal attempts in the second quarter.

Leading scorers: Pottsville - George Garrett 17, Dick Richter 15, Jim Steidle 13, Ed Hoffman 13, Dick Yuengling 12; Hazleton - Frank Zach 23, Tom Pugliese 17.[16]

Easton 61 Hazleton 55: With two players injured, Frank Zack and Dennis Kozlowski, Hazleton battled at Easton before falling to the Red Rovers. Hazleton led narrowly at the end of each of the first three quarters, 11-10, 28-25, and 43-42, before Easton took over in the fourth quarter to pull out the win.

Leading scorers: Easton - Tony Relvas 18, Kip Simons, 17, Barry Miller 14; Hazleton - Billy Nance 14, Tom Pugliese 13, Tom Carlyon 11.[17]

Bethlehem 61 Allen 33: Bethlehem moved a half game ahead of idle Pottsville with a pounding of Allen. Bethlehem held the Canaries to 10 field goals in the game with no Allen players in double figures. Bethlehem's three high scorers outscored the Canaries by themselves. Bethlehem led at the half 31-11 and held Allen to three points in the second quarter.

Leading scorers: Bethlehem-Don Rodenbach 15, John Matthews 15, Tony Filo 13; Allen-Don Eshelman 9.

Dieruff 64 Central Catholic 47: Dieruff won its first second half game with an easy triumph over Central Catholic. The Huskies had four players scoring in double figures. The Huskies led the entire game.

Leading scorers: Dieruff - Steve Roth 19, Charles Noti 17, Jerry Scheirer 14, Jim Spencer 10; Central Catholic - Bill Deutsch 10.[18]

Week 7

Dieruff 63 Allen 61: At the Little Palestra, the new fierce rivalry between Allen and Dieruff was on display with the Huskies taking down Allen. Dieruff had a 13-point lead in the first half 35-22, but Allen fought back twice to take the lead 48-43 in the 3rd quarter and 58-55 in the 4th quarter. The Huskies scored the next six points to lead 61-58 with Steve Roth hitting the clinching field goal with 20 seconds left in the game.

Leading scorers: Dieruff - Steve Roth 25, Jim Spencer 13, Jerry Scheirer 12, Charlie Noti 11; Allen - Don Eshelman 16, John Galliano 14, Gary Spengler 14.

Easton 78 Pottsville 77: At Pottsville, fisticuffs delayed the game with Easton when the Red Rovers' Ron DeBona and Pottsville's Jim Steidle collided going after a free ball with four minutes to play in the game. Other players and fans jumped in the fracas and it took police and officials five minutes to restore order. With the score tied several times in the last minutes, Kip Simons made a foul shot with 8 seconds to play for the win for Easton.

Leading scorers: Easton - Tony Relvas 28, Kip Simons 18, Barry Miller 15, Jim Renaldi 15; Pottsville - Ed Hoffman 28, Dick Yuengling 18, Jim Steidle 12.[19]

Bethlehem 82 Hazleton 53: Bethlehem continued undefeated by drubbing Hazleton for a school record 18th consecutive victory. Leading 18-10 after a quarter, the Hurricane nearly doubled the lead at halftime 37-18. Hazleton's Frank Zack did not play because of a hip injury.

Leading scorers: Bethlehem - John Matthews 24, Charlie Marcon 19, Tony Filo 10, Tom DeNofa 10; Hazleton - Tom Pugliese 23.[20]

Week 8

Bethlehem 99 Pottsville 64: At Pottsville with a standing room only crowd of 1100, Bethlehem clinched the second half title with all five starters in double figures. Bethlehem put the game away in the first period with a 33-15 lead and extending it to 58-34 at halftime.

Leading scorers: Bethlehem - Don Rodenbach 23, John Matthews 22, Charlie Marcon 16, Tony Filo 15, Don Watson 10; Pottsville - Gary Richter 26, Ed Hoffman 17, Dick Yuengling 11.

Allen 68 Easton 54: Allen upset Easton to record their first win of the 2nd half and knock the Red Rovers out of any chance for a 2nd half title. After Allen took a 26-10 first quarter lead, the game outcome was never in doubt.

Leading scorers: Allen - Gary Spengler 25, Jay Borillo 13, John Galliano 12; Easton – Tony Relvas 16, Kip Simons 15, Barry Miller 13.

Central Catholic 76 Hazleton 47: Hazleton lost its game to Central Catholic to fall to 1-4. The Vikings led 27-5 in the second quarter. Coach John Compardo used 17 players in the game with all but three scoring points in the game. Hazleton also used 17 players with 10 of them scoring. In an unusual occurrence, both Hazleton and Allen shared the bottom position in the half, each at 1-4.

Leading scorers: Central Catholic - Bill Deutsch 14, Bill Dreisbach 14, Jack Lisicky 14; Hazleton - Billy Nance 17, Tom Pugliese 11.[21]

Bethlehem 87 Central Catholic 32: Bethlehem closed out the regular season with their 20th victory by rolling over Central Catholic. Central Catholic scored single digit points in each quarter. The Vikings emptied their bench for the second straight game with 17 players being used by Coach Compardo. No player scored in double figures for the Vikings.

Leading scorers: Bethlehem - John Matthews 23, Don Rodenbach 15, Charlie Marcon 14; Central Catholic – Bob Lang 9.[22]

Allen 66 Pottsville 54: Allen won its final game of the season at the Little Palestra to win its final game of the season for the first time since 1951 with a triumph over Pottsville. Ten of Allen's eleven players scored.

Leading scorers: Allen - Gary Spengler 23, Leo Todd 12; Pottsville – Gary Richter 14, Jim Steidle 10, John Condrack 10.

Dieruff 69 Hazleton 57: Dieruff defeated Hazleton to drop the Mountaineers to last place. The Huskies led 37-30 in the third quarter when Hazleton went on a 9-2 run to tie the game. Dieruff countered with 7 straight points for the lead and eventual victory.

Leading scorers: Dieruff - Steve Roth 17, Jerry Scheirer 16, Charlie Noti 12; Hazleton - Tom Pugliese 17, Dennis Kozlowski 10, Joe Greco 10, Bill Nance 10.[23]

Central Catholic 81 Pottsville 75: Pottsville made five consecutive foul shots to pull within two points 77-75 with 40 seconds to play. The Vikings ended the rally with Bill Deutsch's two foul shots and a field goal from John Lisicky. Bob Lang scored 18 points in the 1st half to stake the Vikings to a 16-point halftime lead.

Leading scorers: Central Catholic – Bob Lang 26, Bob Zobb 16, Bill Deutsch 11; Pottsville – Jim Steidle 17, Dick Yuengling 13, George Garrett 12, Ed Hoffman 10, Dick Richter 10.[24]

PIAA Playoffs

Bethlehem 92 Catasauqua 52: Bethlehem opened postseason play at Muhlenberg's Memorial Hall with a rout of Catasauqua. Rusty from a two-week layoff, the Hurricane held only a one-point lead after the first quarter 12-11 and at one point Catasauqua led 11-8. Bethlehem's lead increased to 10 at the half 37-27 as the offense came alive. A 37-point fourth quarter turned the game into a rout. Catasauqua's freshman sensation Larry Miller led the Rough Riders in scoring.

Leading scorers: Bethlehem - John Matthews 22, Charlie Marcon 18, Don Rodenbach 17, Tony Filo 14; Catasauqua - Larry Miller 14.[26]

Bethlehem 82 Tamaqua 57: At the Farm Show Arena in Harrisburg with over 7600 fans in attendance, Bethlehem won the District 11 title over Tamaqua. After leading by only two points 19-17 at the end of the first quarter, Bethlehem's offense kicked in with all five starters ending up in double figures. The Hurricane outscored Tamaqua by 11 in the second quarter and 12 in the 4th quarter. For Tamaqua, four players scored all but six of the team's points.

Leading scorers: Bethlehem - Don Rodenbach 23, Charlie Marcon 17, Don Watson 16, John Matthews 14, Tony Filo 12; Tamaqua - George Tomchick 14, Barry Storch 13, George Barron 12, LaFay Hope 12.[27]

Reading 49 Bethlehem 48: Bethlehem's dream of its first state championship ended at the Farm Show Arena in the first interdistrict game. Hurricane alumnus Pete Carril's Red Knights upset Bethlehem. Trailing 26-19 at the half, Reading fell 11 points behind in the 3rd quarter 35-24. Reading scored 12 straight points in 2 ½ minutes to take the lead 36-35 with 1:10 left in the 3rd quarter. Reading took a 48-43 lead with 2:50 to play and the game appeared over. But Bethlehem ran off five straight points before a Reading foul shot by reserve Grant Jackson, his only point, won the game. Bethlehem had beaten Reading earlier in the season in December by 30 points.

Leading scorers: Reading - Joe Natale 16 points, Dick "Tiger" Graul 13, Bruce Haggerty 10; Bethlehem - Charlie Marcon 18, Don Rodenbach 13, John Matthews 11.[28]

PCIAA Playoffs

Reading Central Catholic 49 Central Catholic 47 2OT: Reading Central Catholic ended Central Catholic's hopes after two overtimes in their initial PCIAA playoff game at Reading's Albright Field House. Central Catholic took an 11-1 first quarter lead when Reading Central Catholic missed all 14 field goal attempts. Central Catholic still held a six-point lead going into the 4th quarter. The Vikings could only score 7 points in the 4th quarter and Reading tied the game with Mike Schorn scoring all 13 points for Reading. He made the final two on foul shots to tie the game in regulation. In the first overtime, Greg Deutsch made a 20-foot jump shot at the buzzer to tie the game at 47. In the second sudden death overtime period, Schorn scored on a layup five seconds into the period to seal the victory for Reading. In the game, Schorn upped his season total to 558 points.

Leading scorers: Reading Central Catholic – Mike Schorn 32; Central Catholic - Bill Dreisbach 10, Bob Lang 10, Greg Deutsch 10.[29]

Postseason Accolades

Leading scorers: For the first time in years, the scoring race was fairly close. The top ten scorers for the league season included: Tony Relvas, Easton 228; John Matthews, Bethlehem, 209; Kip Simons, Easton, 202; Ed Hoffman, Pottsville, 182; Dick Yuengling, Pottsville, 168; Gary Spengler, Allentown, 166; Charlie Marcon, Bethlehem, 159; Tom Pugliese, Hazleton, 158; Tony Filo, Bethlehem, 157; Jim Spencer, Dieruff, and Bob Miller, Easton 149.[30]

All-Stars: The league all-star first team included: Charlie Marcon, John Matthews, and Tony Filo, Bethlehem, Tony Relvas, Easton, and Ed Hoffman, Pottsville. Second team selections included: Jim Spencer, Dieruff, Gary Spengler, Allen, Kip Simons, Easton, Dick Yuengling, Pottsville, and Don Rodenbach, Bethlehem.[31]

All-State: Charlie Marcon, Bethlehem, was named a second team all-state player and his teammate John Matthews made the third team.[32]

Final Standings

First Half		Second Half		Overall	
Bethlehem	6-0	Bethlehem	6-0	Bethlehem	12-0
Dieruff	5-1	Easton	4-2	Easton	8-4
Easton	4-2	Dieruff	3-3	Dieruff	8-4
Hazleton	2-4	Central Catholic	3-3	Allen	4-8
Allen	2-4	Pottsville	2-4	Central Catholic	4-8
Central Catholic	1-5	Allen	2-4	Pottsville	3-9
Pottsville	1-5	Hazleton	1-5	Hazleton	3-9

Team Rosters

Allentown: Coach Milo Sewards, Dave Becker, James Borillo, Neil Boyle, Dick Brobst, Charles Cohen, Don Eshelman, Ed Ferry, John Galliano, Lou Kozloff, George Nau, John Sabo, Gary Spengler, Bill Stephens, Leo Todd

Bethlehem: Coach John Howard, Bill Cvanmen, Tom DeNofa, Tony Filo, Tom Jacoby, Michael Kashner, Tom Kelly, Charlie Marcon, John Matthews, Walt Moore, Paul Pfeiffer, Don Rodenbach, Don Watson

Central Catholic: Coach John Compardo, Bob Andrew, Paul Binder, Jack Callahan, Bill Deutsch, Phillip Dreisbach, Ed Fedok, Pat Gardo, Bernie Grim, Bob Horinko, Bob Lang, John Lisicky, Jim Martin, Joe Mutis, Jim Reisinger, Ed Sarmir, Joe Sarmir, Bill Washychyn, Mike Zaia, Bob Zobb

Dieruff: Coach Dick Schmidt, Mike Bodnar, Jim Carter, George Clay, Tony Krasnicke, Joe Minarovic, Charles Noti, Bob Riedy, Steve Roth, Jerry Scheirer, Joe Smith, Bill Spang, Jim Spencer, Jerry Transue,

Easton: Coach Tom Sweeney, Charlie Bottiglieri, Joe Creazo, Ron DeBona, George Keck, Barry Miller, Tony Relvas, Jim Renaldi, Ray Rissmiller, David Sales, Lew Sigafoos, Kip Simons,

Hazleton: Coach Danny Gregoria, Tom Carlyon, Bruce Carsia, Jerry Gabriel, Don Girard, Joe Greco, Dennis Koslowski, Bill Nance, Gene Olexa, Tom Pugliese, John Rosenstock, Sam Scalleat, Mike Scarcella, Russ Wagner, Richie Yori, Frank Zack

Pottsville: Coach Larry Haberle**,** John Condrack, George Garrett, Joe Grazis, Ed Hoffman, Harry Richter, Jim Steidle, Fred Strausser, Ed Weisacosky, Stan Wilder, Dick Yuengling

Bethlehem High School – 1961 League Champions[25]

Left to Right: Walt Moore, John Matthews, Tom DeNofa, Coach Howard, Tony Filo, Don Watson, Charlie Marcon

1962

League Returns to Eight Teams

Phil Phillippi, Rev. Francis Zavodny, and Edgar Rabenold were re-elected to the positions of president, vice president, and secretary-treasurer positions for another year in the spring meeting at the Shankweiler Hotel in Fogelsville. Tamaqua was recognized as a re-joining member of the league to increase membership to an even eight teams. Tamaqua was a member of the Black Diamond league during their absence from the East Penn League. Eli Purnell continued as their head coach during the period and still remained as the head coach with their re-entry into the league.[1]

Week 1

Central Catholic 84 Hazleton 67: Central Catholic opened at Hazleton and handed the Mountaineers a setback, an unusual third straight loss at home. After a 4-4 tie, Central took the lead and held it the rest of the game. The Vikings led 42-26 at halftime. Hazleton got no closer than nine points early in the 4th quarter.

Leading scorers: Central Catholic - Paul Binder 21, Joe Mutis 19, Ed Sarmir 18, Bill Deutsch 13; Hazleton - Dennis Kozlowski 16, Jerry Gabriel 14, John Barletta 10, Tom Carlyon 10.

Easton 59 Allen 54: In a battle decided by foul shots with the field goals even, Easton defeated Allen. The Red Rovers converted 15 of 23 and the Canaries 10 of 18 to lead to the five-point win. Allen led 13-11 after one quarter, but Easton led at halftime 29-25 and after the third quarter.

Leading scorers: Easton – Tony Relvas 26, Jim Renaldi 14, Kip Simons 14; Allen - Ed Ferry 20, Don Eshelman 13, Jay Borillo 11.

Bethlehem 43 Dieruff 38: With both teams playing possession-style basketball, Bethlehem outscored Dieruff. Dieruff's 14-7 first quarter lead did not hold up as Bethlehem gradually chipped away and took the lead in the 3rd quarter. Dieruff had led at halftime 23-19.

Leading scorers: Bethlehem - Don Rodenbach 16; Dieruff - Bob Reidy 14, Charlie Noti 12.

Pottsville 66 Tamaqua 51: In a close game through three quarters with Pottsville up by four 43-39, the Crimson Tide outscored Tamaqua 23 -12 in the final quarter. Pottsville led the game at the half 30-29.

Leading scorers: Pottsville - Talton Alston 22, Mike Oerther19, George Garrett 13; Tamaqua - Barry Storch 15, Carl Hafer 15, Bill Willing 11.[2]

Week 2

Bethlehem 74 Easton 72 OT: Four thousand fans watched the home team stay unbeaten and hand Easton its first loss of the young season in overtime. Bethlehem was behind after each of the first three quarters, With Easton leading 66-64, Bethlehem threw a long pass that hit official Mike Weber in the face and knocked him to the floor. The ball stayed on the court and the Hurricanes' Walt Moore made a jump shot to tie the score and take the game into overtime. In overtime, Bethlehem's Don Frey made a field goal with 20 seconds to play to win the game. The Red Rovers' Kip Simons took one last shot at five seconds that missed and the game was over. Bethlehem had balanced scoring with five players in double figures.

Leading scorers: Bethlehem - Bill Cvammen 18, Don Rodenbach 17, Barry Frey 12, Walt Moore 12, Tom Kelly 11; Easton - Tony Relvas 23, Kip Simons 22, Tony Renaldi 17.

Dieruff 60 Pottsville 40: Dieruff took a 14-7 lead at the end of the first quarter and doubled the lead at halftime 29-15. The Huskies cruised to a somewhat surprising win over Pottsville.

Leading scorers: Dieruff - Ed Schray 24, Charlie Noti 12; Pottsville - George Garrett 13, Talton Alston 11, Jim Strausser 10.

Central Catholic 59 Tamaqua 50: Down ten points at the half 30-20, Tamaqua scored 21 points to pull within four points of Central Catholic 45-41. However, the Vikings held the Tams to 9 points while scoring 14 in the final quarter for the win.

Leading scorers: Central Catholic - Jeff Mutis 26, Ed Fedok 10; Tamaqua - Bill Willing 14, Barry Storch 13.

Allen 87 Hazleton 65: Coach Milo Sewards employed a full court press against Hazleton and dealt the Mountaineers a defeat. The win snapped Allen's six-game losing streak against Hazleton during the regular season. The game had numerous fouls with the Canaries converting on 25 of 47 and Hazleton 27 for 42. The Canaries took a 28-12 first quarter lead.

Leading scorers: Allen - Don Eshelman 23, Jay Borillo 22, Ed Ferry 12; Hazleton - Ron Hess 18, Tom Carlyon 13.[3]

Central Catholic 67 Allen 40: Central Catholic handed Allen a setback at Rockne Hall. The Vikings held a commanding 37-16 lead at the half to cruise to an easy win. The Vikings made 23 of 30 foul shots.

Leading scorers: Central Catholic - Paul Binder 21, Joe Mutis 21; Allen – Ed Ferry 14, Don Eshelman 10.

Bethlehem 86 Hazleton 65: Bethlehem, running the fast break, took a 23-6 lead in the first quarter which proved to be most of the difference in the game won by the Hurricane. The Hurricane outscored the Mountaineers 63-59 during the last three quarters.

Leadings scorers: Bethlehem - Don Rodenbach 28, Bill Cvammen 18, Barry Frey 17; Hazleton - Dennis Kozlowski 27, Mike Scarzella 14, Tom Carlyon 12.

Easton 75 Pottsville 58: Easton scored 22 points in the second period to take a 38-26 lead at halftime. George Garrett, an all-state football player, led Pottsville in scoring.

Leading scorers: Easton - Tony Relvas 23, Kip Simons 14, Tony Renaldi 14, Pete Wells 11; Pottsville - George Garrett 20, Talton Alston 12, Mike Oerther 11.

Dieruff 59 Tamaqua 53: Dieruff kept Tamaqua winless at 0-3 with a hard-fought win. Dieruff held Tamaqua to eight points in each of the first two periods and led 27-16 at the half. Tamaqua tightened up the contest in the fourth quarter holding Dieruff to a single field goal. However, the Huskies converted 12 of 16 foul shots to maintain the lead and register the win.

Leading scorers: Dieruff - Charlie Noti 23, Pete Sokalsky 21; Tamaqua - Bill Willing 14, George Barron 11.[4]

Week 3

Pottsville 74 Hazleton 58: Pottsville kept Hazleton winless in the league. Pottsville held a 31-29 lead at the end of the first half. Running a fastbreak offense in the beginning of the 3rd quarter, Pottsville pulled ahead of the Mountaineers to stay outscoring them 21-11 in the period.

Leading scorers: Pottsville - Talton Alston 25, George Garrett 21, Jim Harley 11; Hazleton - Dennis Kozlowski 19, Mike Scarcella 14, Tom Carlyon 10.[5]

Bethlehem 70 Allen 55: Bethlehem recorded its 16th straight league win at the expense of Allen. Allen had brief early leads at 9-4 and 15-13 after the first quarter. The Hurricane put on a scoring spurt in the second quarter to take the lead at the half 33-24 and from there on, they never let up.

Leading scorers: Bethlehem - Don Rodenbach 25, Barry Frey 16, Bill Cvammen 15; Allen - Jay Borillo 14, Ed Ferry 13, John Galliano 10.

Easton 63 Tamaqua 58: Winless Tamaqua led at the half 30-29 over Easton and stayed close in the second half only to fall to the Red Rovers. Easton ran off 11 straight points to take a 48-39 lead, but the Tams came back with seven straight points to tighten up the game 48-46. After Tamaqua tied the score at 54-54, Easton went on a 9-4 spurt to pull out the game.

Leading scorers: Easton - Kip Simons 19, Tony Relvas 16, Tony Renaldi 16; Tamaqua - Bill Willing 17, Barry Storch 13, George Barron 13.

Central Catholic 47 Dieruff 41: Central Catholic hung on to defeat Dieruff. In a low scoring first half, the Huskies led 7-4 after a quarter and 16-15 at halftime. Central Catholic held the Huskies to seven points in the 3rd quarter, During the third period, Central Catholic trailed 21-19 but then scored seven straight points to take the lead. Thirteen of the Vikings 19 points in the final period were foul shots.

Leading scorers: Central Catholic - Ed Sarmir 12, Paul Binder 12; Dieruff - Bob Reidy 17, Charlie Noti 10.[6]

Pottsville 59 Central Catholic 56: Central Catholic lost its share of first place when Pottsville upset the Vikings at Rockne Hall. Coach Larry Haberle's Crimson Tide trailed at the half 40-34, but doubled up the Vikings in the 3rd quarter 18-9 to take the lead 52-49. Each team only score 7 points each in the final quarter as Pottsville hung on for the win.

Leading scorers: Pottsville- Talton Alston 27, George Garrett 11; Central Catholic- Paul Binder 15, Joe Mutis 14, Ed Fedok 12.

Bethlehem 72 Tamaqua 55: With the Vikings' loss, Bethlehem took over sole possession of first place with a convincing defeat of Tamaqua. The second and fourth quarters led to the victory with Bethlehem outscoring their opponents 24-14 and 20-12 in those periods. With five minutes left in the game, Tamaqua pulled within four points 52-48, but the Hurricane responded with 10 straight points.

Leading scorers: Bethlehem - Don Rodenbach 24, Walt Moore 15, Barry Frey 11, Tom Kelly 11; Tamaqua - Barry Storch 16, George Barron 13, Bill Willing 10.

Easton 71 Hazleton 65: Hazleton lost its fifth in a row to Easton when the Red Rovers ran off 11 straight points in the 3rd period. The Red Rovers extended their 37-32 lead to 48-32 to take a commanding lead. Easton played without Tony Renaldi who had been suspended for disciplinary reasons. Easton led at the half 29-25.

Leading scorers: Easton–Tony Relvas 23, Kip Simons 21; Hazleton-Dennis Kozlowski 20, Tom Carlyon 18, Mike Scarcella 10.

Allen 55 Dieruff 41: Allen beat crosstown rival Dieruff after taking a 29-16 first half lead using a full court press. The Canary defense held Dieruff's high scoring Bob Reidy to ten points in the game.

Leading scorers: Allen - Jay Borillo 21, John Galliano 14; Dieruff - Pete Sokalsky 11, Bob Reidy 10.[7]

Week 4

Bethlehem 62 Pottsville 52: Bethlehem ran its first half record to 6-0 with a victory over Pottsville. The Crimson Tide held Bethlehem's Don Rodenbach in check with only eight points in the first half and trailed by only five points 26-21. With Rodenbach breaking lose with 19 second half points, the Hurricane pulled away for the win. Pottsville pulled within two points 46-44 with 6:20 to play, but Rodenbach countered with three field goals in a row and Pottsville did not threaten again.

Leading scorers: Bethlehem – Don Rodenbach 27, Walt Moore 12; Pottsville – Jim Strausser 19, Talton Alston 13.

Easton 59 Central Catholic 46: Easton maintained its hold on second place at 5-1 by defeating Central Catholic at Rockne Hall. Easton held an eight-point lead at the half 26-18, but two minutes into the third quarter, the Vikings cut the lead to three points 27-24. Easton responded by scoring seven straight points in a game where the Red Rovers never trailed. Tony Relvas and Kip Simons scored of 17 of the Red Rovers points in the 4th quarter while the Vikings as a team only tallied 13 points.

Leading scorers: Easton - Tony Relvas 21, Kip Simons 21; Central Catholic - Paul Binder 15.

Tamaqua 80 Allen 73: Playing on the road, Tamaqua won its first game with a surprising triumph over Allen. Jumping out 26-12 in the 1st quarter, The Tams never allowed the Canaries to lead in the game. The Canaries pulled within four points 32-28 in the 2nd quarter but the Tams responded to lead at the half 44-33.

Leading scorers: Tamaqua - Barry Storch 25, George Barron 21, Bill Willing 15, Dale Kline 13; Allen - Don Eshleman 23, Jay Borillo 19, Ed Ferry 18, John Galliano 10.[8]

Dieruff 56 Hazleton 39: Hazleton lost six games in a row for the first time in its history by falling to Dieruff. Dieruff held the Mountaineers scoreless for the first 7:23 of the game and held a 12-2 lead at the end of the quarter. Hazleton lost the ball 17 times in the first half without getting a shot. Hazleton cut the lead to six at the half 23-17.

Leading scorers: Dieruff - Charlie Noti 14, Pete Sokalsky 13, Bob Reidy 12, Jerry Transue 10; Hazleton - Tom Carlyon 16.[9]

Bethlehem 84 Central Catholic 53: Bethlehem finished the first half undefeated and clinched the title with a decisive defeat of Central Catholic for their 20th consecutive league win. After trailing 3-0 and tied 5-5, the Hurricane jumped out to a 19-8 lead and were never threatened. They ended the first half leading 42-28. Coach John Howard saw four of his starters hit double figures.

Leading scorers: Bethlehem - Billy Cvammen 19. Barry Frey 17, Walt Moore 16, Don Rodenbach 16; Central Catholic - Paul Binder 20.

Easton 65 Dieruff 48: Easton finished a game behind as a result of a win over Dieruff. The Red Rovers held the Huskies without a field goal for more than 10 minutes and only allowed the Huskies four foul shots in the 2nd period. The score at the half was 29-17 with Easton holding a substantial lead.

Leading scorers: Easton - Tony Relvas 22, Kip Simons 21, Pete Wells 10; Dieruff - Charlie Noti 13, Jerry Transue 10.

Tamaqua 84 Hazleton 64: Hazleton's losing streak was extended to seven by Tamaqua, who won their second consecutive game. Coach Pinky Purnell's team led 10-0 before Hazleton finally scored at the 4:22 mark of the first period. Tamaqua led 65-38 at the three-quarter mark.

Leading scorers: Tamaqua - Barry Storch 19, Bill Willing 17, Carl Hafer 13, Caputo 13; Hazleton - Dennis Kozlowski 25, Tom Carlyon 18.

Pottsville 64 Allen 57: Allen lost its fifth game in seven contests in a loss to Pottsville. Although being tied 32-32 at the half and 42-42 after three periods, Allen never trailed until early in the fourth quarter when Talton Alston made three foul shots as Pottsville took a 45-44 lead. Pottsville never trailed again.

Leading scorers: Pottsville - Talton Alston 19, Jim Strausser 16, George Garrett 10; Allen - Don Eshleman 15, Ed Ferry 10.[10]

Week 5

Dieruff 54 Bethlehem 52: Dieruff broke Bethlehem's 20-game league win streak on the Bethlehem floor. Despite the game being close, Dieruff only trailed during the first 10 minutes with Bethlehem holding a 10-7 first quarter lead. Dieruff led by nine points with 1:49 to play, but Bethlehem cut the lead to one 51-50 with 50 seconds remaining. George Clay added a field goal to put the Huskies in the lead 53-50. With 12 seconds to play, Bethlehem's Bill Boak and Dieruff captain Charlie Noti tangled and both benches emptied. With a double foul called, Bethlehem missed their shot as Dieruff made it for a 54-50 lead.

Leading scorers: Dieruff – George Clay 16, Bob Reidy 14, Charlie Noti 12; Bethlehem - Barry Frey 16.

Central Catholic 68 Hazleton 47: Central Catholic broke their three-game losing streak and extended Hazleton's losing streak to eight with the Vikings' win at Rockne Hall. After the Huskies held the Mountaineers to four first quarter points, Tom Carlyon scored seven points in the last 51 seconds of the second quarter to bring the halftime score to 36-16 in favor of the Vikings. Hazleton outscored the Vikings in the second half 32-31.

Leading scorers: Central Catholic - Joe Mutis 18, Paul Binder 16, Bill Deutsch 12, Ed Sarmir 10; Hazleton - Tom Carlyon 24.

Tamaqua 72 Pottsville 50: Tamaqua continued its roll with a win at Pottsville for their 3rd in a row. After taking a 19-16 first quarter lead, Tamaqua never trailed. Leading 33-28 at halftime, Tamaqua outscored Pottsville 20-5 in the third period to take complete command of the contest.

Leading scorers: Tamaqua - Bill Willing 24, Barry Storch 13, George Barron 15; Pottsville - Talton Alston 17, George Garrett 11, Jim Harley 10.

Easton 76 Allen 57: Easton converted 32 of 36 foul shots in its setback of Allen. After holding a two-point lead after one quarter 17-15, the Red Rovers streaked to lead at half time 41-28 and cruised to an easy victory. Allen took an early 4-0 lead with the game being tied five times, the last at 17-17 at the start of the second quarter, before the Red Rovers took the lead for good. Easton's Kip Simons made 10 of 10 attempts from the foul line.

Leading scorers: Easton – Kip Simons 24, Tony Relvas 19. Tony Renaldi 14; Allen - Don Eshleman 17, Ed Ferry 10.[11]

Week 6

Bethlehem 69 Easton 64: At Easton's new gym, the officials had fans cleared under each basket before the critical second half contest could begin. Bethlehem rebounded from a loss by whipping the Red Rovers. After trailing 25-20, Easton fought back to take a 35-33 first half lead. Barry Frey hit three baskets in a row to give Bethlehem a 49-47 edge after three periods. Early in the 4th quarter, Bethlehem surged ahead 64-54 and the Red Rovers could not recover from the 10-point deficit.

Leading scorers: Bethlehem - Walt Moore 21, Barry Frey 18, Don Rodenbach 13; Easton - Tony Relvas 20, Kip Simons 19.

Tamaqua 80 Central Catholic 68: George Barron powered Tamaqua to another win against Central Catholic. After tying the game early in the second half at 33 all, Barron led a 14-point rally that put the game out of reach for the Vikings. Tamaqua led 31-29 at the half and 56-45 after three quarters with the third quarter rally.

Leading scorers: Tamaqua – George Barron 32, Bill Willing 20, Barry Storch 16; Central Catholic - Joe Mutis 20, Ed Sarmir 15, Dave Pfahler 11.

Pottsville 48 Dieruff 40: Dieruff lost Charlie Noti to an ankle injury late in the 2nd quarter and missed his scoring prowess in a loss to Pottsville. Dieruff still held a 31-29 lead at the end of three quarters, but could not keep up with the Crimson Tide fourth quarter onslaught. Pottsville outscored the Huskies 19-9 in the final quarter.

Leading scorers: Pottsville - Mickey Oerther 16, George Garrett 13, Talton Alston 12; Dieruff - George Clay 13, Bob Reidy 10.

Allen 91 Hazleton 77 OT: Allen took a 14-point lead 37-23 in the second quarter but Hazleton charged back with 12 straight points. Hazleton held a 77-75 lead with five seconds left in regulation. Don Eshleman made two foul shots to send the game into overtime. Allen blanked Hazleton in overtime while the Canaries scored 14. The loss was Hazleton's ninth in a row.

Leading scorers: Allen - Ed Ferry 27, Don Eshleman 26, Leo Todd 11; Hazleton - Dennis Kozlowski 23, Tom Carlyon 22.[12]

Tamaqua 49 Dieruff 43: Surprising Tamaqua maintained its hold on first place as the only unbeaten team in the second half with a victory over homestanding Dieruff. With Charles Noti on the bench with an ankle injury, the Huskies fought hard to lead by two points after three periods 34-32. With the score tied three times in the final period at 36, 38, and 40, Tamaqua scored on a fastbreak layup to take the lead for good. Dieruff hurt its chances by committing five fouls in the last four minutes of the game. Tamaqua made good on seven of the ten foul shots to win the game.

Leading scorers: Tamaqua - Bill Willing 16, George Barron 12, Barry Storch 10; Dieruff - George Clay 12.

Bethlehem 75 Hazleton 49: Tied 13-13 after a quarter, Bethlehem took a 33-24 halftime lead. The Hurricane trounced Hazleton in the 3rd period for their 10th straight loss, outscoring the Mountaineers 21-4.

Leading scorers: Bethlehem-Don Rodenbach 20, Barry Frey 17, Walt Moore 12, Billy Cvammen 10; Hazleton-Tom Carlyon 18.

Easton 66 Pottsville 64 2OT: It took two overtimes, but Easton stayed even with Bethlehem for 2nd place. Pottsville only trailed in the first period during regulation. Pottsville led 60-56 with 3:49 left, but could not score again in regulation as Tony Relvas made two field goals to pull Easton into a tie at the end of regulation. Both teams scored only two points each in the first overtime. In the second overtime, Relvas scored on a layup at the buzzer to give Easton the win.

Leading scorers: Easton – Tony Relvas 26, Kip Simons 20, Tony Renaldi 11; Pottsville - Mickey Oerther 23, Talton Alston 18, George Garrett 12.

Allen 75 Central Catholic 66: Allen avenged a first half loss to Central Catholic. Despite a heavy snowstorm, 1800 fans turned out to watch the contest. After seeing the score knotted eight times in the first quarter, Allen held the Vikings to six third quarter points and pulled away to a 21-point lead after 3 periods 60-39.

Leading scorers: Allen - Ed Ferry 25, Don Eshleman 24; Central Catholic - Ed Sarmir 18, Joe Mutis 13, Paul Binder 13, Jack Lisicky 12.[13]

Week 7

Easton 75 Tamaqua 70: Easton knocked Tamaqua out of its sole possession of the second half lead and into a three-way tie with the Red Rovers and Bethlehem. The victory came about largely on the excellent foul shooting by the Red Rovers, 25 of 28 including 15 in a row. A close game all the way with a 13 all tie after one period and 34-33 lead by Tamaqua at the half, Easton took a four-point lead 52-48 into the final period. With Tamaqua attempting to rally, Kip Simons converted two three-point plays to thwart the comeback. Easton's Tony Relvas made 11 field goals and 11 of 12 free throw attempts to lead the Red Rovers to victory.

Leading scorers: Easton - Tony Relvas 33, Kip Simons 19, Tony Renaldi 11; Tamaqua - Dale Kline 20, Barry Storch 19, George Barron 16.

Bethlehem 86 Allen 47: After destroying Allen in the first half with a 29-point victory, Bethlehem outdid that performance with a 39-point victory at the Little Palestra. In addition to leading his team in scoring, Walt Moore grabbed 25 rebounds and blocked 8 shots for Bethlehem. The Hurricane outscored the Canaries 49-19 in the second half after having led by only seven 37-30 at the half.

Leading scorers: Bethlehem – Walt Moore 22, Don Rodenbach 18, Tom Kelly 16; Allen - Jay Borillo 16, Ed Ferry 11, Don Eshleman 11.

Dieruff 57 Central Catholic 49: Dieruff evened its record at 2-2 at the expense of Central Catholic. The Huskies only trailed once 4-2 as they benefited from the return of Charlie Noti from his ankle injury. Dieruff's Bob Reidy was ejected with 3:28 left for roughing up the Vikings' Paul Binder. The Huskies led 29-20 at halftime.

Leading scorers: Dieruff – Charlie Noti 17, Bob Reidy 15, Jerry Transue 11; Central Catholic - Joe Mutis 13, Paul Binder 11.[14]

Pottsville 74 Hazleton 72: Hazleton's losing streak grew to eleven with Pottsville's victory in Hazleton. Hazleton led by eighteen points 61-43 with two minutes left in the third quarter. Pottsville outscored the Mountaineers 20-2 from that point to tie the game at 63 with 5:44 to play in the game. After Hazleton took the lead 69-65, Pottsville scored 9 straight points to scratch out the win. Hazleton's Dennis Kozlowski was dropped from the squad prior to the game for playing with an independent team. Bob Eigenbrod moved up from the junior varsity to replace him.

Leading scorers: Pottsville - Talton Alston 32, Mickey Oerther 15, George Garrett 14; Hazleton - Tom Carlyon 24, Bob Eigenbrod 20.[15]

Bethlehem 96 Tamaqua 44: On his last appearance on his home court, Don Rodenbach singlehandedly outscored Tamaqua by scoring 59 points in Bethlehem's shellacking of Tamaqua in a battle for a share of first place. His total broke Bethlehem alumnus Gary Piff's record of 56 points set in 1955 against Central Catholic. He scored 17 points in the first half and 42 in the second half. The output set the gym record held by Wilt Chamberlain of 58 points against the Detroit Pistons in January 1960. Coach Eli Purnell's squad battled the Hurricane with the score 16 all after one period and 32-27 after two. The game turned into a massive blowout when the Hurricane outscored Tamaqua 40-6 in the final period.

Leading scorers: Bethlehem – Don Rodenbach 59, Walt Moore 16; Tamaqua - Barry Storch 13, George Barron 12.

Easton 89 Hazleton 58: Easton held to its share of first place by downing Hazleton. In handing Hazleton its 12th straight loss, Easton was led by its big three, Simons, Relvas, and Renaldi, who combined for 71 points. Renaldi also had 28 rebounds in the game. After Easton took a 17-5 first quarter lead, the game was never in question.

Leading scorers: Easton - Kip Simons 28, Tony Relvas 26, Tony Renaldi 17; Hazleton - Tom Carlyon 20.

Dieruff 40 Allen 38: Allen jumped out to a 4-0 lead only to see Dieruff come back and lead the rest of the way. Holding a 9-point lead in the 4th quarter, the Huskies went scoreless for more than 4 minutes to allow the Canaries to trim the lead to one 37-36. Dieruff countered with a foul shot and steal for layup to stymie the Canaries' rally. Allen's Ed Ferry left the game with about 3 ½ minutes to play with an ankle injury.

Leading scorers: Dieruff - Charlie Noti 13, Bob Reidy 12; Allen - Ed Ferry 11.[16]

Pottsville 54 Central Catholic 52: With three seconds to play, George Garrett registered a field goal to give Pottsville a scintillating victory over Central Catholic. Pottsville froze the ball for 42 seconds before the shot went down. The Vikings, who led at the half 28-27, were outscored by three points 12-9 in the 3rd quarter which proved to be the difference in the game.

Leading scorers: Pottsville - George Garrett 17, Mickey Oerther 12, Talton Alston 10, Jim Harley 10; Central Catholic - Jeff Mutis 23, Paul Binder 10.[17]

Week 8

Bethlehem 69 Pottsville 53: Coach John Howard only used his starting five at Pottsville. Pottsville took an early lead in the first quarter 14-13, but Bethlehem doubled up the Crimson Tide 18-9 in the second period to gain an eight-point lead 31-23. After that, the lead was never less than 4 points and the Hurricane took a commanding lead in the 4th quarter for the easy win. Four of the five starters scored in double figures:

Leading scorers: Bethlehem - Don Rodenbach 19, Tom Kelly 14, Barry Frey 14, Walt Moore 14; Pottsville - Mickey Oerther 19, George Garrett 13, Talton Alston 12.

Easton 75 Central Catholic 54: Easton, meanwhile, turned back Central Catholic in Easton. After being down by 3 in the second period 28-25, the Red Rovers scored 16 straight points to take a commanding 41-28 lead. Easton held the Vikings' Joe Mutis to two points. The big three for Easton, Relvas, Simons, and Renaldi led the way.

Leading scorers: Easton - Tony Relvas 31, Kip Simons 21, Tony Renaldi 15; Central Catholic - Ed Sarmir 17, Paul Binder 15, Bill Deutsch 13.

Tamaqua 82 Allen 70: Tamaqua bounced back from its humiliating loss by tripping Allen. Allen held leads the first two quarters 23-17 and 43-35 before Tamaqua put on a second half charge using a full court press. During the last quarter, Coach Milo Sewards complained that youngsters sitting behind the basket were distracting Allen's foul shouting. The game was held up to move them to the main stands. All six players used by Coach Eli Purnell scored in double figures. With Tamaqua leading 50-59 after three quarters, the lead changed four times early in the fourth quarter before Tamaqua took charge.

Leading scorers: Tamaqua - Bill Willing 22, George Barron 14, Dale Kline 14, Barry Storch 12, Angie Caputo 10; Allen - John Galliano 15, Don Eshleman 12, Jay Borillo 12.

Dieruff 61 Hazleton 50: Experiencing their 13th loss in a row, Hazleton dropped the game against Dieruff with the Huskies making 27 of 41 foul shots while Hazleton converted 14 of 26. Hazleton registered one more field goal than the Huskies. Hazleton led after a quarter 13-12 before the Huskies moved ahead 31-25 at the half.

Leading scorers: Dieruff - Bob Reidy 13, Charlie Noti 13; Hazleton - Tom Carlyon 16, Russ Wagner 12.[18]

Dieruff 49 Easton 42: Dieruff spoiled Easton's title hopes when they upset the Red Rovers led by Bob Reidy. The game was close the whole way. With the score tied at 30-30 in the third period, Bob Reidy scored six straight points on two field goals and two foul shots to put the Huskies in the lead by six. After Easton came within two at 41-39, the Huskies countered again with six straight points to put the game out of reach.

Leading scorers: Dieruff – Bob Reidy 20; Easton – Tony Relvas 14.

Allen 68 Pottsville 55: Don Eshleman broke the Little Palestra field goal record for a game with 16 in his final game as a Canary. Eshleman was scheduled to enter the US Naval Academy in March. Although Allen held a commanding lead for most of the game, Pottsville did cut it to one point 37-36 before Allen rallied to take a nine-point lead 52-43 into the final period.

Leading scorers: Allen– Don Eshelman 33, Jay Borillo 12; Pottsville- George Garret 17, Mickey Oerther 16, Talton Alston 10.[19]

Bethlehem 27 Central Catholic 18: Despite a deliberate stall by Central Catholic, Bethlehem broke through in the final period to down the Vikings in a very slow game. Bethlehem successfully defended its league title. The Vikings led 3-2 after one period. Bethlehem had the lead at the half 8-5 and third period 13-8 before finally scoring 14 points in the final period to the Vikings 10. Central Catholic only had one field goal in the first half made by Joe Mutis which gave the Vikings their last lead at 5-4. Vikings' Coach John Compardo dropped Ed Sarmir from the team prior to the game for disciplinary reasons.

Leading scorers: Bethlehem - Don Rodenbach 16; Central Catholic – Paul Binder 6, Bill Deutsch 6.[20]

Tamaqua 78 Hazleton 65: Tamaqua completed its first season back in the league by handing Hazleton its 14th consecutive loss. After trailing by 12 at the half 40-28, Hazleton climbed within three 41-38. Tamaqua finished with a rush in the final period for the win. Both Tamaqua's Bill Willing and Hazleton's John Guydish were ejected from the game after a free-swinging scrap between the two players.

Leading scorers: Tamaqua - Dale Kline 20, George Barron 19, Bill Willing 18; Hazleton – Bruce Carsia 16, Tom Carlyon 15.[21]

PIAA Playoffs

Bethlehem 81 Mahanoy Area 54: At Hershey Arena, Bethlehem opened postseason play against the North Schuylkill League champions, Mahanoy Area. Opening up with a 19-7 first quarter lead, the Hurricane cruised to a trimming of their opponents. The Hurricane made 36 of their 64 (58%) field game attempts. Bethlehem led at the half 42-28. Despite sitting out the entire third period because he had 3 personal fouls, Don Rodenbach still scored over 20 points. The win set up a rematch with Catasauqua for the district title.

Leading scorers: Bethlehem - Barry Frey 22, Don Rodenbach 21, Tom Kelly 13, Walt Moore 11; Mahanoy Area - Frank Millard 14, Dan Friedberg 13, John Alansky 12, Charlie Lawrence 10.[22]

Catasauqua 66 Bethlehem 54: At the Farm Show Arena in Harrisburg with 8,566 fans in attendance, favored Bethlehem met their match in the Roughriders from Catasauqua. After a 13-13 first period tie, the score was again tied at 19-19 when Catasauqua took the lead a 29-23 lead and went to the locker room up 31-27. Bethlehem rallied early in the third period to get within one again 37-36. The Roughriders then broke it open by taking a 44-36 lead at the end of the third period. They built a ten-point lead 50-40 and Bethlehem could not come back as Catasauqua won to move on.

Leading scorers: Catasauqua - Larry Miller 24, Jim Murtaugh 22; Bethlehem - Tom Kelly 20, Don Rodenbach 14.[23]

PCIAA Playoffs

Central Catholic 62 Notre Dame 61 4OT: At Moravian's Johnston Hall, Notre Dame and Central Catholic battled through the fourth overtime before the Vikings prevailed. After leading at the half 37-30, Central Catholic could only score 11 points in the second half and Notre Dame came back to tie the game in regulation at 48-48. Viking co-captain Paul Binder fouled Notre Dame's Zeke Zylwitis at the final buzzer with the game tied, but Zylwitis missed the shot to take the game into overtime. Both teams scored 4 points in the first overtime, none in the second when Notre Dame froze ball for all but ten seconds and missed the shot, and five in the third to take it to the 4th extra period. Central Catholic outscored Notre Dame 5-4 in the period and Joe Mutis converted two fouls with 19 seconds to go for the win.

Leading scorers: Central Catholic - Joe Mutis 25, Bill Deutsch 11, Paul Binder 10; Notre Dame - Rich Baksa 22, John Paukovits 15, Rich Fuisz 15.[24]

Central Catholic 71 Reading Central Catholic 46: At Dieruff's gym, Central Catholic took on the Reading Central Catholic Cardinals for the Allentown Diocese Class A title. The Vikings took a 21-9 first period lead and easily won the game. Reading Central Catholic lost their two big men, Connie Ciesielski and Jerry Twardowski, on fouls early in the third quarter. They both had four fouls in the first half. After the Cardinals cut the lead by one at halftime 37-26, the Vikings pulled way in the second half.

Leading scorers: Central Catholic - Joe Mutis 18, Ed Sarmir 12, Paul Binder 11; Reading Central Catholic - Mike Daley 18, Connie Cieslelski 12.[25]

Central Catholic 60 Scranton Prep 58 4OT: Central Catholic and Scranton Prep met at Dieruff's gym to determine which team would advance to the PCIAA Eastern final. For the second time in three games, Central Catholic had to go into a fourth overtime before the winner could be decided. Scranton Prep to a 14-8 first quarter lead before Central Catholic rallied in the second quarter for a 24-24 half time tie. The Vikings continued its second quarter rally into the third period to take a seven-point lead 38-31 entering the 4th quarter. However, Scranton Prep came back to tie the game 53-53 in regulation with Steve Vacendak's field goal. The Vikings froze the ball up to the last three seconds, but Dave Pfahler missed a shot which left both teams scoreless in the first overtime period. Both teams hit field goals within the first 15 seconds of the period, but those were the only scores as the period ended at 55-55. In the third overtime, both teams made a single foul shot for the only scores and the score remained tied at 56-56 entering a 4th overtime. Both teams converted a field goal in the first minute of the period. Neither team could score until eight seconds left in the period when Ed Sarmir missed a shot but Paul Binder grabbed the rebound and put it up for the winning layup. The Vikings survived another four-overtime game. Scranton Prep's Steve Vacendak set a floor single game scoring record.

Leading scorers: Central Catholic – Ed Sarmir 16, Bill Deutsch 13, Paul Binder 12, Jeff Mutis 10; Scranton Prep – Steve Vacendak 41.[26]

Bishop Egan 60 Central Catholic 50: Bishop Egan and Central Catholic met at the St. Joseph's Memorial Fieldhouse in Philadelphia for the PCIAA Eastern championship. Bishop Egan held the lead after the first two periods 12-10 and 26-19. The Vikings rallied in the 4th quarter to tie the game 44-44 with 3:30 left in the game. Central Catholic kept it close until the final 25 seconds when Bishop Egan scored six straight points. With five seconds left in the game, the Vikings' Paul Binder and Egan's Tom "Moose" Frederick tangled under the basket and both were ejected from the game. Although Bishop Egan only trailed once 4-2 early in the game, the game was tied six times before Bishop Egan won to move on to the PCIAA state title game.

Leading scorers: Bishop Egan - Wade Hartman 15, Bill Coyle 15, Tom Frederick 12, John Kerr 11; Central Catholic - Ed Sarmir 18, Joe Mutis 11, Bill Deutch 11.[27]

Postseason Accolades

Leading scorers: The league's leading scorer was a repeat from the previous season as Tony Relvas, Easton, totaled 323 points, almost 100 more than the year before. He was followed closely by Don Rodenbach, Bethlehem, with 303 points. The rest of the top ten included: Kip Simons, Easton, 280; Talton Alston, Pottsville, 254; Tom Carlyon, Hazleton, 235; Don Eshelman, Allen, 219; Bill Willing, Tamaqua, 214; Joe Mutis, Central Catholic, 212; Barry Storch, Tamaqua, 207; and George Barron, Tamaqua, 196.[28]

All-Stars: The league all-star first team included: Don Rodenbach and Walt Moore, Bethlehem, Tony Relvas and Kip Simons, Easton, Charlie Noti, Dieruff, and Don Eshelman, Allen. Second team selections included: George Barron and Bill Willing, Tamaqua, Paul Binder, Central Catholic, George Garrett, Pottsville, and Ed Ferry, Allen.[29]

All-State: Don Rodenbach, Bethlehem, was named to the third team all-state and Tony Relvas, Easton, was named an Honorable Mention on the team.[30]

Final Standings

First Half		Second Half		Overall	
Bethlehem	7-0	Bethlehem	6-1	Bethlehem	13-1
Easton	6-1	Easton	5-2	Easton	11-3
Central Catholic	4-3	Dieruff	5-2	Dieruff	8-6
Pottsville	4-3	Tamaqua	5-2	Pottsville	7-7
Dieruff	3-4	Allen	3-4	Tamaqua	7-7
Allen	2-5	Pottsville	3-4	Allen	5-9
Tamaqua	2-5	Central Catholic	1-6	Central Catholic	5-9
Hazleton	0-7	Hazleton	0-7	Hazleton	0-14

Team Rosters

Allen: Coach Milo Sewards, Dave Becker, Jay Borillo, Chris "Kit" Bracy, Dick Brobst, Don Canzano, Arnold Chew, Don Eshelman, Ed Ferry, Denny Fritchman, John Galliano, Jim Katz, Dick Moggio, Joe Petro, Larry Seiple, Leo Todd, Charlie Ward.

Bethlehem: Coach John Howard, Bob Bair, Dave Bartholomew, Bill Boak, Bill Cvammen, Barry Frey, Chuck Iobst, Lou Jacoby, Tom Kelly, Fred McGuiney, Walt Moore, Don Rodenbach, Stan Schell, Sal Tavares, Robert Thomas

Central Catholic: Coach John Compardo, Bob Andrew, Paul Binder, Bill Deutsch, Ed Fedok, Frank Gardo, Jack Lisicky, Jim Martin, Joe Mutis, Dave Pfahler, Jim Reisinger, Ed Sarmir, Bill Washychyn

Dieruff: Coach Dick Schmidt, Ron Bauer, Richard Bechtel, George Clay, Joe Marinovic, Charles Noti, Bob Reidy, John Repasch, Ed Schray, Pete Sokalsky, Jerry Transue

Easton: Coach Tom Sweeney, Bob Anckaitis, Karl Bell, Ron DeBona, Thomas Keck, John Kelleher, Frank Nagurney, Don Pyatt, Tony Relvas, Jim Renaldi, David Sales, Kip Simons, Pete Wells

Hazleton: Coach Danny Gregoria, John Barletta, Tom Carlyon, Bob Eigenbrod, Jerry Gabriel, Don Girard, John Guydish, Ron Hess, Dennis Kozlowski, Jerry Petrisko, Richie Prebula, Stan Roslevege, Sam Scalleat, Mike Scarcella, Bruce Scarsia, Russ Stewart, Russ Wagner, Mike Yura

Pottsville: Coach Larry Haberle, Talton Alston, Bevan, David Freeze, George Garrett, Jim Harley, Denny Harris, George Metaxas, Ron Morris, Mike Oerther, Bob Schuetter, Charles Spehrley, Jim Strausser, Ed Weisacosky

Tamaqua: Coach Eli Purnell, George Barron, Angelo Caputo, George Darker, Carl Hafer, John Heitz, Dale Kline, Jim Moyer, Bill Semko Barry Storch, Jack Williams, Bill Willing

Bethlehem High School – 1962 League Champions[20]

1963

Dieruff Reverses its Fortunes

Phil Phillippi, Rev. Francis Zavodny, and Edgar Rabenold were re-elected to the positions of president, vice president, and secretary-treasurer at the spring meeting at the Shankweiler Hotel in Fogelsville. Joe Blankowitsch was named league statistician.[1]

Week 1

Central Catholic 93 Tamaqua 68: Unbeaten Central Catholic won its tenth straight contest over Tamaqua. The teams battled to a 21-21 tie in the first quarter and Central Catholic took a three-point lead at the half 43-40. Tamaqua's 6'4" George Barron, an all-state football player, suffered an ankle injury which the Vikings took advantage of to take the lead. Barron returned to the game and helped keep it close through three quarters. The Vikings broke loose in the final period scoring 27 points to Tamaqua's 11.

Leading scorers: Central Catholic - Dave Pfahler 24, Ed Sarmir 23, Len Kalata 11, Bill Washychyn 11; Tamaqua - George Barron 18, Bill Semko 16, Ed Lyba 11, and Bob Fritzinger 10.

Pottsville 63 Easton 47: Easton took leads of 15-9 and 34-23 at the end of each of the first two quarters. Easton's possession-style of play to begin the second half backfired as Pottsville cut the lead to 39-34. Pottsville limited the Red Rovers to 3 field goals in the second half and scored 29 points, to Easton's 8, in the 4th quarter to defeat the Red Rovers. Mickey Oerther scored 13 points in the 4th quarter for Pottsville. Easton's two leading scorers Bottiglieri fouled with 6:50 to go in the game and Wells fouled out after him.

Leading scorers: Pottsville - Mickey Oerther 24, Talton Alston 17; Easton - Charlie Bottiglieri 17, Pete Wells 14.

Bethlehem 75 Hazleton 43: After Hazleton held an early 6-2 lead, Bethlehem ran off eight straight points to take the lead 10-6. Hazleton fought back for its last lead of the night at 11-10. From thereon, it was all the Hurricane including the third period when Bethlehem outscored Hazleton 20-4. Bethlehem handed the Mountaineers their 15 straight league loss.

Leading scorers: Bethlehem - Barry Frey 30, Sal Tavares 18, Bill Boak 12; Hazleton - Tom Carlyon 18.

Allen 58 Dieruff 57: Allen and Dieruff renewed its crosstown rivalry with a spinetingling finish to the contest. Allen led at half time 27-26 and fell behind by seven points by the end of the third period. The Canaries fought their way back but still trailed 57-54 with 21 seconds remaining in the game. Allen's Charley Haydt hit a field goal with 8 seconds left. On the in-bounds play, Don Canzano stole the pass and laid up the winning shot with four seconds left. Allen had an unbelievable win over the Huskies. Before the last second rally, Dieruff's Tom Young battled Allen's Ted Carls for the ball. Carls deliberately fouled Young who began swinging at Carls. Young was ejected from the game. Both benches emptied and police had to restore order.

Leading scorers: Allen – Ted Carls 16, Charley Haydt 14; Dieruff - Bob Reidy 28 (school record).[2]

Week 2

Bethlehem 74 Tamaqua 51: Bethlehem, stealing the ball and employing a fast break, handled Tamaqua with ease after a relatively close first period 19-15. They broke open the game in the second period outscoring their opponents 15-8, Four Hurricane players were in double figures.

Leading scorers: Bethlehem - Barry Frey 19, Sal Tavares 14, Bill Boak 13, Pat Howlett 13; Tamaqua - George Barron 21, Bill Semko 12.

Central Catholic 77 Dieruff 52: Matching a school record 11th straight win, Central Catholic defeated Dieruff. The Vikings outscored the Huskies 22-8 in the second quarter to take charge of the game after holding only a 19-15 lead after the first quarter. Dave Pfahler held the Huskies' high-scoring Bob Reidy to one field goal in each half.

Leading scorers: Central Catholic –Dave Pfahler 19, Len Kalata 17, Eddie Fedok 11; Dieruff -Bob Reidy 13.

Pottsville 79 Allen 55: Pottsville served notice to the league with its victory over Allen at the Little Palestra. It was their first victory at the Palestra since the 1925-26 season. The Canaries were in the game until half way through the 3rd period when Pottsville finally opened up a ten-point lead. Most of the difference came at the foul line. Pottsville made 31 of 42 free throws while Allen made 11 of 21 attempts. Five of Allen's top six players had 3 fouls by half time. Mickey Oerther and Talton Alston scored over half their team's points.

Leading scorers: Pottsville - Mickey Oerther 22, Talton Alston 21, Denny Harris 16, Jim DeStefano 11; Allen -. Ted Carls 14, Jim Katz 10.[3]

Easton 64 Hazleton 53: At Easton, the Red Rovers opened the game with 10 straight points to take a 17-11 first quarter lead. They closed the half with nine straight points to lead at half time 34-21. The third period was all Mountaineers as they outscored the Red Rovers 16-7 to bring them within 4 points 41-37. Easton took command again to win the contest.

Leading scorers: Easton - Charlie Bottiglieri 21, Pete Wells 18; Hazleton - Tom Carlyon 25.[4]

Hazleton head coach Danny Gregoria resigned on January 7th. He had missed the first game of the season with Bethlehem due to an illness. He was replaced by the junior varsity coach Fran Libonati on an interim basis through the end of the season.[5]

Bethlehem 56 Pottsville 52: Bethlehem won its 10th straight contest in Pottsville. Pottsville led throughout the first half including 17-10 after one period and 34-22 at halftime. With a substantial lead, Pottsville changed to a slower style in the second half. The Hurricane cut the lead in half by the end of the third quarter 42-38. With three minutes remaining, Bethlehem tied the score at 52-52 and went ahead on Bob Thomas's two foul shots. The only scores the remainder of the game were two more foul shots by Barry Frey.

Leading scorers: Bethlehem – Barry Frey 19, Pat Howlett 14; Pottsville – Ron Morris 15, Talton Alston 14.

Central Catholic 62 Hazleton 53: The Vikings set a new school record with a 12th straight win at Hazleton. Converting 26 of 30 foul shots, Central Catholic defeated Hazleton. Hazleton made 7 of 13 free throws. The Vikings first quarter lead of 18-7 turned out to difference in the victory with the Mountaineers battling the Vikings on even terms the rest of the game. Hazleton narrowly outscored the Vikings in both the second and third quarters by one and two points and the Vikings took the final quarter by a point.

Leading scorers: Central Catholic – Ed Sarmir 19, Dave Pfahler 14, Len Kalata 11, Bob Andrew 11; Hazleton – Tom Carlyon 22, Ron Hess 14, Dave Wagner 10.

Easton 54 Dieruff 48: Missing their leading scorer 6'6" Bob Reidy because of an ankle injury the previous game, Dieruff could not handle Easton. Reidy had broken his right ankle in the offseason and missed four early games before coming back with the start of league play. Pete Wells, Easton's 6'2" senior scored all 10 of the Red Rovers' third quarter points. Dieruff only tallied five in the period. Easton scored the first ten points of the game. Dieruff caught Easton late in the 2nd period and led 24-23 with 1:32 to go in the quarter.

Leading scorers: Easton - Pete Wells 31, Charlie Bottiglieri 13; Dieruff – Tim Smith 10.

Allen-Tamaqua: Due to extremely foggy weather, Allen's game with Tamaqua was postponed until late January.[6]

Week 3

Bethlehem 46 Dieruff 31: Bethlehem ran its win streak to 11, and kept a share of first place, with a triumph over Dieruff. The Huskies jumped in front 10-6 but the Hurricane came back to tie the game at 10-10 with Dieruff taking an 11-10 lead at the quarter. The game was tied at 15-15 in the second quarter when Bethlehem reeled off seven straight points to take the lead for good. The Huskies only scored 6, 5, and 9 points in the last three periods. The Huskies played without Bob Reidy, who was still on the injured list. Dieruff fell to 0-4 in league play.

Leading scorers: Bethlehem – Barry Frey 22; Dieruff – Ed Schray 7.

Central Catholic 57 Pottsville 47: The Vikings defeated early season favorite Pottsville to keep their record win streak alive at 13 and stay in a first-place tie with Bethlehem at 4-0. Central Catholic, with a slim 27-25 lead at the half, inserted Bill Washychyn into the lineup and he responded with three field goals early in the quarter to propel the Vikings to a 37-28 lead with a little less than four minutes left in the 3rd quarter. Pottsville pulled with three points with 3:13 left in the game, but the Vikings scored nine straight to stop the rally and pull out the win.

Leading scorers: Central Catholic – Dave Pfahler 14, Ed Sarmir 10; Pottsville – Talton Alston 17, Mickey Oerther 15, Ron Morris 10.

Allen 64 Hazleton 52: Allen handed Hazleton its 23rd consecutive league loss behind the play of 6'2" Jim Katz who was moved from guard to forward earlier in the season. Only in the second quarter did the Mountaineers threaten the Canaries when they pulled within three points 20-17. Allen responded with eight straight points to jump out into a comfortable margin.

Leading scorers: Allen - Jim Katz 19, Ted Carls 14, Don Canzano 13; Hazleton – Tom Carlyon 22, Norb Dudeck 13, Ron Hess 11.[7]

Easton 71 Tamaqua 49: Easton stayed a game behind the frontrunners with a 71-49 pasting of Tamaqua. With Charlie Bottiglieri scoring 15 points in the first half, Easton led after the first half 39-24. They held Tamaqua to 8 points in the third period to roll to an easy victory.

Leading scorers: Easton- Charlie Bottiglieri 21, Pete Wells 20; Tamaqua- Bill Semko 17, George Barron 16.[8]

Allen 71 Bethlehem 63: Twenty-three hundred fans jammed into the Little Palestra to witness the clash between Bethlehem and Allen. With the Hurricane holding a 24-20 lead, Coach Milo Sewards inserted 6'3" junior Charley Haydt into the game at the 4:12 mark of the second period. He led the Canaries to a 28-25 lead at the half. Haydt converted three 3-point plays in the second half all which seemed to stymie Hurricane comebacks. Haydt scored 16 of the Canaries' 24 points in the third quarter. Barry Frey, Bethlehem's leading scorer sat on the bench most of the third period with four personal fouls. Bethlehem cut the Canary lead to four points 61-57 with less than three minutes to play, but Haydt made his final three point play to put the game out of reach. Allen's win knocked Bethlehem out of first place.

Leading scorers: Allen – Charley Haydt 31, Ted Carls, 17, Don Canzano 10; Bethlehem – Bill Boak 18, Barry Frey 16, Pat Howlett 10.

Central Catholic 85 Easton 68: In winning their 14th consecutive game, Central Catholic took sole possession of first place by downing Easton at Rockne Hall with 3,200 in attendance. After holding a slim one-point lead after three quarters, the Vikings steamrolled over the Red Rovers in final period 34-18 for the decisive 17-point win. The Vikings converted 33 of 43 foul shots including 16 of 17 in the final period to contribute to the wide scoring margin. Ed Sarmir picked up three personal fouls in the first 3 ½ minutes of the game and sat out the rest of the half.

Leading scorers: Central Catholic – Dave Pfahler 21, Ed Sarmir 17, Bob Andrew 15, Len Kalata 10; Easton – Pete Wells 27, Charlie Bottiglieri 20.

Tamaqua 69 Pottsville 64: On its home court, disappointing Pottsville lost its third straight league game this time to Tamaqua 69-64. George Darker scored eight points in the first quarter to lead Tamaqua to an 18-13 first quarter advantage. In the final period, Darker scored another eight points to thwart a comeback attempt by Pottsville led by Talton Alston's 16 points in the final period. George Barron grabbed 21 rebounds for Tamaqua. Eight Pottsville players were suspended indefinitely in a disciplinary action by Coach Larry Haberle prior to the game. The players had purchased beer at a Pottsville "speakeasy".[9]

Leading scorers: Tamaqua- George Darker 22, George Barron 16, Ed Lyba 11; Pottsville- Talton Alston 34.

Hazleton 61 Dieruff 56: In a battle to climb out of the cellar, Hazleton snapped its 23-game league losing streak and handed Dieruff its fifth straight loss. After holding a narrow 14-13 lead after one period, Hazleton scored the first ten points of the second quarter to take the lead for the rest of the game. Coach Fran Libonati, who had replaced Danny Gregoria two weeks prior, won his first game as head coach. Bob Tucker, a senior starting his first game and in only his third game, scored 20 points and grabbed 14 rebounds. The Huskies' Bob Reidy was still out with his ankle injury. With a second remaining in the game, Hazleton's John Barletta and Dieruff's George Eichelberger started fighting with both benches emptying. The skirmish was under control after a few minutes and both players were ejected.

Leading scorers: Hazleton - Tom Carlyon 31, Bob Tucker 20, Ron Hess 12; Dieruff – Ed Schray 14.[10]

Week 4

Bethlehem 60 Central Catholic 48: Bethlehem and Central Catholic clashed in a crucial battle for first place with 4,000 fans watching at Memorial Gym in Bethlehem. Coach Johnny Howard employed a zone press to hand the Vikings their first loss of the season, end the Vikings' 14-game win streak, and get a share of first place with both teams now at 5-1. Central Catholic took an 11-4 lead in the first quarter, but Bethlehem cut it to 14-12 at the first quarter mark. In a tight first half, Bethlehem outscored the Vikings 14-12 to end the first half with a 26-26 tie. Bethlehem took the lead in the third quarter and held the Vikings to six points in the final period to win the game. Central Catholic's Dave Pfahler took an elbow in his midsection late in the second quarter and sat the rest of the half. Although he played in the second half, he was hampered by the injury.

Leading scorers: Bethlehem – Pat Howlett 24, Barry Frey 12, Bill Boak 11; Central Catholic - Ed Sarmir 15, Dave Pfahler 12.

Easton 56 Allen 41: In Easton, Allen could not duplicate its success after its upset of Bethlehem and went down to defeat at the hands of the Red Rovers. The Canaries lost Ted Carls to an ankle injury in the first quarter and he was taken to Allentown Hospital for x-rays. Easton played without leading scorer Pete Wells for most of the second quarter and all of the third quarter when he picked up four personal fouls and had to be benched. After an 11-11 tie in the first period, the Red Rovers scored six straight points and did not trail again. Easton's Mike MoDavis tangled with Allen's Charley Haydt in the second quarter and the officials ejected him from the game.

Leading scorers: Easton – Charlie Bottiglieri 15, Pete Wells 15, Frank Nagurney 11; Allen – Charley Haydt 13, Jim Katz 11.

Tamaqua 68 Hazleton 67: Tamaqua scorched Hazleton in the second period by scoring 23 points and taking a 15-point lead at the half 35-20. Hazleton desperately fought back in the second half, but fell a point short. Tom Carlyon singlehandedly led the charge with 13 points and 12 points in each of the last two quarters. George Barron scored 12 points in the final period for Tamaqua to help fight off the rally.

Leading scorers: Tamaqua – George Barron 31, Jack Bassler 17, Ed Lyba 11; Hazleton – Tom Carlyon 35, Ron Hess 14, Bob Eigenbrod 13.

Pottsville 56 Dieruff 43: Dieruff dropped to 0-6 at the hands of Pottsville 56-43. Bob Reidy missed his fourth straight game for the Huskies. Pottsville managed to win despite playing a makeshift lineup due to the continued suspension of eight players from the varsity squad. After leading by only two points 39-37 at the end of the 3rd quarter, Pottsville outscored the Huskies by 11 points as Dieruff could only manage 6 points in the final eight minutes. Pottsville miraculously committed on three fouls during entire game.

Leading scorers: Pottsville – Talton Alston 27, Ron Morris 19; Dieruff – George Daskalakes 16.[11]

Bethlehem 67 Easton 51: Using 1-3-1 zone, Bethlehem managed to keep Easton's high scoring duo of Charlie Bottiglieri and Pete Wells from a big night on the scoreboard. In a closely played first half, Easton took the first quarter lead 9-6 with Bethlehem coming back to take a 26-25 lead at the half. Sal Tavares playing the point in the zone defense kept Bottiglieri at bay and held him to 13 points, well below his average. Bethlehem took a seven-point lead into the final quarter and increased it by nine. The win gave them a tie for the first half with Central Catholic.

Leading scorers: Bethlehem – Barry Frey 22, Bill Boak 13, Sal Tavares 13, Pat Howlett 11; Easton – Pete Wells 16, Charlie Bottiglieri 13.

Central Catholic 65 Allen 53: Without injured Ted Carls in the lineup, the Canaries came out battling to hold slight leads after each of the first three quarters 12-10, 27-25, and 44-43. However, Allen could not keep up with the Vikings speed in the fourth quarter and fell to Central Catholic 65-53 after being outscored 22-9. The Vikings also kept Allen's Charley Haydt scoreless in the second half. The Vikings' Dave Pfahler was still hindered by the stomach injury from a previous game. The win put the Vikings into a playoff game with Bethlehem for the first half title.

Leading scorers: Central Catholic – Ed Sarmir 27, Dave Pfahler 12, Bill Washychyn 10; Allen – Jim Katz 20; Dave Becker 13.

Pottsville 76 Hazleton 75 3OT: With eight players still on suspension, the depleted Pottsville roster played a feisty Hazleton team with the game going to three overtimes. The game was close the whole way. The teams were tied after one period at 17-17 with Pottsville holding a two-point lead at the half 39-37. Pottsville kept the lead after three quarters 52-50. The game was tied at the end of regulation at 64-64. Each team scored six points in the first overtime and only 2 each in the second overtime. Talton Alston scored on a driving layup in the third overtime with 53 seconds left to win the game for Pottsville. Hazleton's Norb Dudeck's shot to win the game in the 3rd overtime hit the rim with one second to play but bounced off.

Leading scorers: Pottsville – Talton Alston 27, Ron Morris 25; Hazleton – Tom Carlyon 33, Ron Hess 16, Bob Eigenbrod 14.

Tamaqua 105 Dieruff 78: Despite being crushed by Tamaqua 105-78, Dieruff, employing a press, fought back early in the third period to within one point 42-41 of Tamaqua after trailing by nine at the half 40-31. Tamaqua set a new league record for points in a half by tallying 65 points in the second half to lead to the rout. Thirty-seven of the points came in the final stanza. The Huskies finished winless in the first half.

Leading scorers: Tamaqua – George Barron 31, Ed Lyba 25, Jack Bassler 15, Bill Semko 13; Dieruff – George Daskalakes 12, Tim Smith 11, George Eichelberger 10.[12]

Allen 85 Tamaqua 63: Allen traveled to Pottsville for a makeup game postponed earlier due to extremely foggy conditions. Without Tamaqua's big George Barron in the lineup on crutches due to an ankle injury received during practice, Allen's Charlie Haydt scored at will to lead the Canaries to the win. Tamaqua actually held a lead 15-13 after one period due to Bill Semko's hot hand as he scored nine points in the quarter. That was it for Tamaqua with the Canaries scoring over 20 points in each of the last three quarters.

Leading scorers: Allen – Charlie Haydt 31, Dave Becker 19, Jim Katz 12; Tamaqua – Bill Semko 29, Ed Lyba 10.[13]

First Half Playoff

Bethlehem 64 Central Catholic 59: At the Hershey Sports Arena, Central Catholic charged out to an early 16-4 lead over Bethlehem, but Bethlehem cut the lead to seven by the end of the quarter 20-13. Bethlehem shaved another point off the lead by the half and still trailed 34-28. With Barry Frey scoring 15 points in the third quarter, Bethlehem, using a zone press defense, caught fire and outscored the Vikings 21-10 in the period to take a 49-44 third quarter lead. The Vikings didn't score a field goal in the period until the 3:16 mark. The Vikings rallied to within two points 57-55 in the 4th quarter, but Bethlehem came back with successive field goals to douse the rally and win the game and the title. The Vikings lost only their second game of the season, both to Bethlehem.

Leading scorers: Bethlehem – Barry Frey 32, Sal Tavares 12, Pat Howlett 10; Central Catholic – Ed Sarmir 17, Bill Washychyn 12, Dave Pfahler 10.[13]

Week 5

Pottsville 63 Easton 50: With the eight suspended players reinstated to the squad by Coach Larry Haberle, Pottsville opened the second half with a win at Easton. For three quarters, the teams played on even terms with Pottsville holding a three-point lead 41-38. Pottsville played without star Talton Alston, benched with four personal fouls, for the last half of the third period. When he returned in the final quarter, he led Pottsville's charge as the Red Rovers were out-scored 22-12 in the final period. Twelve of the points came on 12 of 14 foul shot conversions. Alston made 15 foul shots in 18 tries.

Leading scorers: Pottsville– Talton Alston 23, Ron Morris 14, Jim DeStefano 10; Easton– Pete Wells 20, Charlie Bottiglieri 16.

Dieruff 57 Allen 44: With Bob Reidy playing in his first game since early January, Dieruff snapped its league losing streak at seven with an easy win over crosstown rivals Allen at the Little Palestra. In addition to leading the team in scoring, Reidy grabbed 18 rebounds. Dieruff held the lead at the quarter 15-10 and the half 32-22. Charley Haydt led the Canaries to a two-point lead 38-36 with 1:40 left in the third period. but the Huskies came back to lead at the end of the quarter 40-38. Dieruff's stingy fourth quarter defense limited the Canaries to one field goal and six points in the final period.

Leading scorers: Dieruff – Bob Reidy 23, Ed Schray 10, George Daskalakes 10; Allen – Charley Haydt 17, Jim Katz 11.

Central Catholic 87 Tamaqua 52: Rebounding from a disappointing playoff loss, Central Catholic scored 53 points in the second and third periods to down Tamaqua. With George Barron still out with an ankle injury, Tamaqua could not stop the Vikings' front court. Tamaqua trailed by only 4 points 18-14 before the scoring outburst by the Vikings. Viking sophomore Dave Pfahler only played five minutes still recuperating from an early season stomach injury suffered against Bethlehem.

Leading scorers: Central Catholic – Ed Sarmir 15, Bob Andrew 13, Ed Fedok 12, Bill Washychyn 12; Tamaqua – Bill Semko 24, Ed Lyba 16, George Darker 10.

Bethlehem 63 Hazleton 51: Trailing after the first quarter 16-9, Hazleton rallied behind Tom Carlyon's 13 second quarter points to take a 34-30 half time lead. Bethlehem held Hazleton to eight third quarter points and took a one-point lead into the final period 43-42. After tying the score at 43-43 on a Carlyon free throw, Hazleton fell behind when Bethlehem scored seven straight points and could not recover.

Leading scorers: Bethlehem – Pat Howlett 18, Barry Frey 17, Sal Tavares 10; Hazleton – Tom Carlyon 20, Bob Eigenbrod 11, Ron Hess 11.[14]

Week 6

Pottsville 84 Allen 52: In Pottsville, Allen ran into a motivated Pottsville team and went down to defeat in a drubbing. The second game with the full squad showed the strength of the Pottsville squad as they jumped out to 17-10 and 36-25 first quarter and halftime leads. They never let up in the final two quarters outscoring the Canaries by 7 and 14 points to cement the rout.

Leading scorers: Pottsville – Talton Alston 26, Ron Morris 19, Jim DeStefano 10, Jim Harley 10, Denny Harris 10; Allen – Ted Carls 12, Charley Haydt 12.

Easton 64 Hazleton 61: In Hazleton, the Mountaineers and Red Rovers fiercely battled during all four quarters with Easton getting the best of Hazleton. Easton led at the end of the first quarter 32-12, but Hazleton came back to lead at halftime 31-27. Easton took the lead back heading into the fourth quarter 47-45. The lead seesawed back and forth between the two teams until late in the game when the Red Rovers scored six straight points to take an insurmountable lead. Jack Kelleher was both an offensive and defensive star for Easton. He held Hazleton's Tom Carlyon to 12 points, well below his average. The last minute of the game included some fireworks from both fans and players. With 27 seconds to play, the officials called a deliberate foul on the Mountaineers' Norb Dudeck when he fouled Red Rover Charlie Bottiglieri. Several spectators ran onto the floor to get at Bottiglieri who had to run for cover. Police escorted the fans out of the gym. Then with two seconds to play, Kelleher and Hazleton's Ron Hess were ejected for fighting.

Leading scorers: Easton – Pete Wells 24, Jack Kelleher 19, Charlie Bottiglieri 18; Hazleton – Bob Eigenbrod 18, Ron Hess 17, Tom Carlyon 12.

Dieruff 54 Central Catholic 50: After having lost all their first half contests, Dieruff upset Central Catholic to start 2-0 in the half. In handling the Vikings only their third loss of the year, the Huskies gave up the lead twice both in the first half. Dieruff took a 16-5 first quarter lead only to have the Vikings fight back to only trail by two 24-22. Dieruff increased the lead to six 44-38 at the three-quarter mark. The Vikings fought valiantly to get with a point twice in the last two minutes of the game only to have the Huskies convert foul shots to extend the lead. The Vikings' Dave Pfahler played stellar defense and held Dieruff's Bob Reidy to 7 points, well below his average. Reidy fouled out of the game with three minutes to play.

Leading scorers: Dieruff – Ed Schray 18, Tom Young 14; Central Catholic – Ed Sarmir 13, Ed Fedok 10.

Bethlehem 71 Tamaqua 63 OT: It took an extra period, but Bethlehem stayed in a first-place tie with Dieruff and Pottsville at 2-0 with a 71-63 triumph in Tamaqua. Tamaqua took a 15-9 lead in the first quarter, but Bethlehem fought back to tie it at halftime 31-31. Bethlehem then took a six-point lead after three periods 48-42 only to have Tamaqua reverse the fortunes and tie up the game 57-57 in regulation. Tamaqua's George Barron tapped in a goal in the last ten seconds to create the tie. Overtime was all Hurricane with Bethlehem outscoring Tamaqua 14-6. Eight of the points came on foul shots. Barron scored 10 points in the final period.

Leading scorers: Bethlehem – Barry Frey 26, Bill Boak 11, Dave Bednarik 11; Tamaqua – Bill Semko 21, George Barron 20, George Darker 11.[14]

Bethlehem 60 Pottsville 49: Two of the three league leaders met in Bethlehem when Pottsville traveled to the Memorial Gym. The game was all as it could have been advertised for three quarters. After trailing 18-13 after the first quarter, Pottsville fought back to within one at the half 26-25 and took the lead after three quarters 41-38. A three-point play by Pat Howlett tied the score for Bethlehem. Talton Alston put Pottsville in the lead again with two foul shots. However, that was it for the Crimson Tide as Bethlehem scored seven consecutive points to take a lead they never lost. After Pottsville took its last lead, Bethlehem outscored them 19-6 for the win and a share of first place with Dieruff.

Leading scorers: Bethlehem – Bob Thomas 15, Barry Frey 13, Pat Howlett 13, Bill Boak 11; Pottsville - Talton Alston 20, Jim Harley 15.

Dieruff 60 Easton 54: Meanwhile, Dieruff, the other leader, traveled to Easton and ran its win streak to three with a win over the Red Rovers. Dieruff took an early first quarter lead 17-13 only to have Easton come back to tie at the half 33-33. Both teams scored 13 points in the third quarter to remain tied. Dieruff's Bob Reidy dropped in two fouls shots to give the Huskies their first lead since early in the second quarter. Tom Young scored the next six points on two field goals and two foul shots to give Dieruff a 54-46 lead. Dieruff, who had five less field goals than Easton, made 30 of 35 free throws to lead them to victory and a share of first place.

Leading scorers: Dieruff – Bob Reidy 18, Tom Young 16, George Daskalakes 10; Easton – Pete Wells 17, Bill Eisel 13, Charlie Bottiglieri 13.

Central Catholic 75 Hazleton 68: At Rockne Hall, Hazleton gave Central Catholic all it could handle for 2 ½ periods before the Vikings reeled off nine straight points to turn a two-point 44-42 lead into an 11-point lead during the last four minutes of the third quarter. During the first half, the teams changed leads 14 times and were tied four times. The win kept the Vikings close to the league leaders with a 2-1 record.

Leading scorers: Central Catholic – Ed Sarmir 24, Dave Pfahler 19, Len Kalata 10; Hazleton – Tom Carlyon 29, Ron Hess 11.

Allen 81 Tamaqua 73: At the Little Palestra, Allen's starters all finished in double figures in the defeat of Tamaqua. Allen led all the way and Tamaqua could not get closer than four points 57-53 late in the third quarter. Allen held a thirteen-point lead at the half 46-33. The win was the Canaries' first in the second half.

Leading scorers: Allen – Charley Haydt 24, Ted Carls 16, Jay Borillo 13, Don Canzano 12, Jim Katz 10; Tamaqua – George Barron 17, George Darker 17, Bill Semko 17, Ed Lyba 12.[16]

Week 7

Dieruff 48 Bethlehem 43: The Huskies continued their magical second half with a putdown of Bethlehem to take first place by themselves. Using a slowdown attack and a 1-2-2 zone, Dieruff controlled the pace of the game. Bethlehem led 10-9 after a quarter, but the Huskies took the lead into the locker room 23-21. The Huskies trailed by seven points at one time in the second quarter. In the final quarter with Bethlehem leading 39-38, Coach Dick Schmidt spread out his offense and the Huskies made four baskets to nail the victory. The Huskies' defense held high-scoring Barry Frey to eight points for the night.

Leading scorers: Dieruff – Bob Reidy 19, Tom Young 16, Ed Schray 10; Bethlehem – Pat Howlett 17.

Allen 71 Hazleton 70: At Hazleton, Allen kept the Mountaineers winless in the half with a come-from-behind thriller. After Allen took an early 11-5 lead, Hazleton rallied to take a 19-16 first quarter lead and maintained the lead at the half 40-38. With scored tied at 64 in the 4th period, Don Canzano made a fast break layup and converted foul shot to give Allen a three-point edge 67-64 and the lead for good.

Leading scorers: Allen – Charley Haydt 24, Jim Katz 15, Don Canzano 11; Hazleton – Tom Carlyon 28, Ron Hess 15.[17]

Tamaqua 77 Easton 67: Led by George Barron, who scored eight points in each of the first three quarters and was a perfect 5-5 at the free line in the 4th quarter, Tamaqua, at home, stunned Easton. Tamaqua outscored the Red Rovers in each of the first three quarters to take a 57-44 lead into the final period. Easton and Tamaqua both stood at 1-3 in the second half of play.

Leading scorers: Tamaqua–George Barron 29, Bill Semko 22; Easton–Jack Kelleher 23, Pete Wells 15, Charlie Bottiglieri 12.[18]

Central Catholic 66 Pottsville 60: On its home court, Pottsville lost its second straight in the half to Central Catholic. Pottsville was only able to cop the lead once at 17-16 late in the first period. In the third quarter, Pottsville rallied to within two points only to have the Vikings extend the lead with a Bobby Andrew jump shot. Len Kalata held Pottsville's Talton Alston to nine points. The Vikings' Dave Pfahler played despite having several stitches to close a head wound. The win kept the Vikings tied for second place with Bethlehem a game behind Dieruff.

Leading scorers: Central Catholic – Bobby Andrew 22, Bill Washychyn 12, Ed Sarmir 10; Pottsville – Ron Morris 24, Mickey Oerther 17.[19]

Bethlehem 96 Allen 60: Allen kept it close throughout the first quarter trailing only by a point 16-15 at Bethlehem's Memorial Gym. In the second quarter, Barry Frey took charge of the Hurricane attack and poured in 20 of Bethlehem's 37 points in the quarter. He also converted 17 of 19 foul shots. The game was a rout after that with Bethlehem holding a 53-33 lead at the half. Frey scored 43 points on the night and Coach John Howard took him out of the game with over three minutes left in the contest. Bethlehem employed a press almost the entire game to avenge the first half defeat at the hands of the Canaries with a thrashing of Allen. After scoring 31 in the first half game, Charly Haydt could only manage a field goal and two foul shots in the game for Allen.

Leading scorers: Bethlehem-Barry Frey 43, Sal Tavares 15, Pat Howlett 12; Allen-Jim Katz 20, Ted Carls 14.

Dieruff 76 Hazleton 62: On their home court, the Dieruff Huskies continued their improbable second half run while keeping Hazleton winless in the second half. The win kept them in sole possession of the second half lead with a 5-0 record. Bob Reidy scored 43 points on 10 field goals and converting 23 of 31 foul shots. He set a league record for most converted free throws and a Dieruff individual scoring mark for a single game. Dieruff led 36-16 at the half during which Reidy scored 23 points and George Eichelberger held Hazleton's Tom Carlyon to two field goals in the half.

Leading scorers: Dieruff – Bob Reidy 43, Tom Young 14; Hazleton – Tom Carlyon 19, Ron Hess 11.

Central Catholic 54 Easton 47: Easton held leads after the first three quarters 12-11, 25-22, and 41-38 over Central Catholic. However, playmaker Eddie Fedok scored 14 of the Vikings' 16 points in the 4th quarter to pull out the victory. Fedok scored only three points in the first three periods. The Vikings held the Red Rovers to six points in the final period in a stunning turnaround for Easton. The win kept the Vikings a game behind Dieruff in a second-place tie with Bethlehem at 4-1. Dave Pfahler played sparingly due to his head injury suffered in the previous game.

Leading scorers: Central Catholic – Eddie Fedok 17, Ed Sarmir 16, Len Kalata 11; Easton – Jack Kelleher 16, Pete Wells 11.

Pottsville 90 Tamaqua 75: After trailing 19-14 after the first quarter, Pottsville turned it on in the final three quarters by scoring over 20 points in each to defeat Tamaqua on its home court. Tamaqua's George Barron scored 31 points in the game with 10 coming in each of the first two quarters to keep Tamaqua in the game. Pottsville scored 12 straight points to start the third quarter to build an insurmountable lead.

Leading Scorers: Pottsville – Talton Alston 28, Ron Morris 17, Mickey Oerther 16, Jim Harley 16, Jim DeStefano 12; Tamaqua – George Barron 31, Bill Semko 25.[20]

Week 8

Dieruff 60 Pottsville 58 OT: Traveling to Pottsville, Dieruff clinched at least a tie for the second half title over an aggressive Pottsville squad in overtime. Pottsville took an eight-point lead in the first period 21-13 forcing Dieruff to play catchup the rest of the night. Bob Reidy hit the tying field goal in regulation and the winning goal in overtime for the victory. Dieruff actually took a seven-point lead in the final quarter of regulation but Pottsville rallied to take a 56-54 lead before Reidy's tying field goal.

Leading scorers: Dieruff – Bob Reidy 20, Tom Young 14; Pottsville – Talton Alston 17, Ron Morris 13, Mickey Oerther 12.

Central Catholic 65 Bethlehem 55: With both teams tied a game behind Dieruff, Bethlehem and Central Catholic faced off at Rockne Hall with the winner still having a slim shot at the second half title. After losing the last two contests with the Hurricane, the Vikings found some revenge with a defeat of Bethlehem. Central Catholic took the early lead after the first period 15-12. Bethlehem cut the lead to one at the half 32-31 despite trailing by eight 28-20 midway through the quarter after the Vikings scored 9 straight points. In the second half, the Vikings opened up a 11-point lead early in the final quarter 52-41 and they were on their way to an avenging victory.

Leading scorers: Central Catholic – Ed Sarmir 21, Dave Pfahler 12, Bill Washychyn 10; Bethlehem – Sal Tavares 24, Barry Frey 17.

Easton 77 Allen 75: Easton took a 12-9 lead into the second period at the Little Palestra. However, Allen took charge in the second quarter scoring 25 points and taking a 34-26 half time lead. Entering the 4th quarter leading 58-51, Allen saw Easton catch up and tie the game at 75 with 23 seconds left to play. Easton's Charlie Bottiglieri converted two foul shots after being fouled by Allen's Don Canzano to provide the winning points. Bottiglieri scored 12 points in the final period. A last second layup by Allen's Jim Coker rolled off the rim. Allen's Charley Haydt could not play due to injury.

Leading scorers: Easton – Charlie Bottiglieri 21, Pete Wells 21, Jack Kelleher 12; Allen - Ted Carls 24, Jim Coker 13, Don Canzano 13, Jim Katz 10.

Tamaqua 65 Hazleton 60: Playing without Tom Carlyon due to a virus, Hazleton fell again, this time to Tamaqua. Hazleton was also missing Bob Eigenbrod and Tamaqua was without Barry Fritzinger, both out with the virus. The lead flip-flopped between the two teams at the end of each quarter in the first half with Hazleton leading 36-35 at the half. Tamaqua tied up the game at the end of the third period 48-48, but outscored the Mountaineers by five in the final quarter for the win.

Leading scorers: Tamaqua – George Barron 20, Hafer 13, George Darker 12; Hazleton – Dave Wagner 17, Ron Hess 15, Norb Dudeck 11.[21]

Dieruff 77 Tamaqua 53: After going winless in the first half of the season, Dieruff completely reversed its fortunes going 7-0 in the second half to win the title. With four of the five starters in double figures, Dieruff easily handled Tamaqua. Only in the second period did Tamaqua show some competitive life by outscoring the Huskies 20-17 to cut Dieruff's ten-point first quarter lead to seven points 33-26. In the third period, Dieruff held Tamaqua to six points while scoring 20 to take a commanding lead. Dieruff would move on to play Bethlehem for the overall league title.

Leading scorers: Dieruff – Tom Young 22, Eddie Schray 21, Bob Reidy 14, George Daskalakes 13; Tamaqua – George Barron 20, George Darker 10.

Central Catholic 66 Allen 62: Central Catholic came out fast to take a 22-6 first quarter lead over Allen. With Allen outscoring the Vikings in each of the next three periods, the sixteen-point first quarter lead proved to be the difference in the game. In fact, Allen caught and led the Vikings at 58-57 with 4 ½ minutes left in the game. The Vikings' Eddie Fedok and Bob Andrew responded with a field goal each and a foul shot by Andrew to give them a 62-58 lead which they never gave up the rest of the contest. Central Catholic's victory was marred by the loss of Ed Sarmir for the PCIAA playoffs with a broken wrist. With nearly five minutes remaining in the game, Allen's Dick Brobst upended Sarmir on his drive to the basket. Sarmir landed on the concrete runway behind the basket causing the injury. Brobst was ejected based on the claim that the foul was deliberate.

Leading scorers: Central Catholic – Ed Sarmir 21, Dave Pfahler 15, Bob Andrew 13; Allen – Jim Katz 25, Charley Haydt 15.

Easton 52 Bethlehem 48: Bethlehem did not look anything like it did in the first half in losing its third game of the half to Easton. After Easton took a 12-9 first quarter lead, the Hurricane fought back to lead at the half 22-20 and 39-34 going into the final quarter. Easton scored 10 successive points in the final period and outscored Bethlehem 18-9. Easton took the lead 46-44 with 3:22 left. Early in the quarter, Easton's Charlie Bottiglieri and Bethlehem's Bill Boak were both ejected after a brief tussle.

Leading scorers: Easton – Pete Wells 23; Bethlehem – Barry Frey 12, Stan Shell 10.

Hazleton 77 Pottsville 65: Playing on its home court, Hazleton snatched it first victory of the second half over Pottsville. Pottsville held leads in the first two periods 11-8 and 31-30 before Hazleton took a one-point lead at the end of the third. Hazleton finished big with 30 points in the final period to put the game away. Hazleton made 30 of its 50 field goal attempts. With his 26 points, Hazleton's Tom Carlyon won the league scoring title with 320 points. He set five school records including most career points 843, season points record 468, points per game (ppg) average 23.4 breaking the old mark set by his coach Fran Libonati by over 4 ppg, most field goals in a season, and most field goals in a career.

Leading scorers: Hazleton – Tom Carlyon 26, Bob Tucker 13, Norb Dudeck 12, Dave Wagner 11, Ron Hess 11; Pottsville – Ron Morris 13, Mickey Oerther 12, Jim Harley 11, Talton Alston 11, Jim DeStefano 10.[22]

League Championship Playoff

Bethlehem 81 Dieruff 59: Bethlehem ended Dieruff's miraculous season at Muhlenberg's Memorial Hall with a rout of the second half champions. Bethlehem took a 15-11 lead at the end of the first quarter, but the Huskies played them even in the second period to keep the lead at four 31-27. Shooting a miraculous 17 of 24 from the floor in the second half, the Hurricane outscored the Huskies by identical 25-16 scores in each of the final two periods. Coach John Howard's 2-2-1 zone pestered Dieruff's Tommy Young all night and held him to two points, both on free throws. The Hurricanes' Pat Howlett played after missing the previous two games due to pneumonia.

Leading scorers: Bethlehem – Barry Frey 21, Sal Tavares 20, Pat Howlett 15, Bill Boak 13; Dieruff – Bob Reidy 24, George Eichelberger 11, George Daskalakes 13.[23]

Postseason PIAA Play

Wilson Boro 74 Bethlehem 67: At the Farm Show Arena in Harrisburg with over 5,000 fans in attendance, Lehigh-Northampton League (LNL) champions Wilson Boro stunned Bethlehem. Coach Dick Eckert's Wilson squad enjoyed the first ever win by an LNL team in Class A competition. Bethlehem took a 21-10 first quarter lead only to have Wilson outscore them 22-12 in the second period and take a 35-27 halftime lead. Bethlehem reversed the third period scoring with a 26-18 advantage to tie the game at 53. Wilson's John Smith scored nine straight points to open the fourth quarter to put Wilson into the lead for good.

Leading scorers: Wilson – John Smith 24, Nick Azzolina 21, Gary Laubach 11, Nick Kurilko 10; Bethlehem – Dave Bednarik 16, Barry Frey 15, Sal Tavares 12, Pat Howlett 10 .[25]

Postseason PCIAA Play

Central Catholic 65 Reading Catholic 40: At Dieruff's gym, Central Catholic took on Reading Central Catholic in a semifinal game for the Allentown Diocese Class A title without the services of Ed Sarmir and only a half game performance from Dave Pfahler suffering from the after effects of a virus attack. With underclassmen leading the attack, the Vikings took a 16-9 first period lead and outscored Reading in every period to win the game easily.

Leading scorers: Central Catholic – Tom Kober 20, Dave Pfahler 11, Len Kalata 11; Reading – Mike Raszkiewicz 14, Carmelo Bisbano 12, Mark Braun 10.[26]

Central Catholic 58 Notre Dame 48: Central Catholic took on Notre Dame at Moravian's Johnson Hall for the Allentown Diocese Class A title. Notre Dame gave the Vikings a spirited tussle throughout the game. The Vikings led by two after one quarter 12-10 and three at the half 24-21. The Crusaders held the lead briefly in the third period 33-31 with 2:42 to play, but the Vikings responded to take the lead and extended it to twelve points with two minutes to play 54-42 on their way to the victory.

Leading scorers: Central Catholic – Bill Washychyn 17, Dave Pfahler 14, Len Kalata 12, Ed Fedok 11; Notre Dame – Tony Hanni 20.[27]

Scranton Prep 53 Central Catholic 52 OT: At Wilkes-Barre's Coughlin High School gym Central Catholic and Scranton Prep faced off for the right to play in the Eastern final. Having bowed to the Vikings the year before in four overtimes, Scranton Prep defeated Central Catholic 53-52 in a single overtime period. The Vikings lost the contest because of poor foul shooting making on 4 of 14 while the Cavaliers made 15 of 25. Central Catholic took a 33-26 lead into the locker room at the half. Playing catchup in the second half, Scranton Prep took the lead with 29 seconds to play 50-49. The Vikings' Len Kalata was fouled with a second to play, but made only one of two shots to end the game in regulation 50-50. Despite not wanting to compete in the playoffs and being compelled to play by school officials, the Crusaders were now on their way to the Eastern final with the overtime triumph.

Leading scorers: Scranton Prep – Guida LaPorta 14, Kevin Condron 14, Bobby McGrath 10; Central Catholic – Bob Andrew 12, Bill Washychyn 11, Dave Pfahler 10, Len Kalata 10.[28]

Postseason Accolades

Leading scorers: Despite his Hazleton team only winning two league contests, Tom Carlyon won the league scoring with 320 points in 13 games having missed one due to illness. Pottsville's Talton Alston finished second with 291 points. The rest of the top ten included: Barry Frey, Bethlehem, 276; Pete Wells, Easton, 272; George Barron, Tamaqua, 270; Ed Sarmir, Central Catholic, 240; Bill Semko, Tamaqua, 234; Charlie Bottiglieri, Easton, 211; Charley Haydt, Allen, 204; and Ron Morris, Hazleton, 187.[29]

All-Star: The league all-star first team included: Talton, Alston, Pottsville; Tom Carlyon, Hazleton; Barry Frey, Bethlehem; Ed Sarmir, Central Catholic; and George Barron, Tamaqua.[30]

All-State: Barry Frey, Bethlehem, was named to the third team all-state; Bob Reidy, fourth team; and Talton Alston, Tamaqua, George Barron, Tamaqua, Tom Carlyon, Hazleton, Ed Sarmir, Central Catholic, and Pete Wells, Easton, were named an Honorable Mention on the team.[31]

Final Standings

First Half		Second Half		Overall	
Bethlehem	6-1	Dieruff	7-0	Central Catholic	12-2
Central Catholic	6-1	Central Cath0lic	6-1	Bethlehem	10-4
Easton	4-3	Bethlehem	4-3	Easton	7-7
Pottsville	4-3	Easton	3-4	Dieruff	7-7
Allen	4-3	Pottsville	3-4	Pottsville	7-7
Tamaqua	3-4	Allen	2-5	Allen	6-8
Hazleton	1-6	Tamaqua	2-5	Tamaqua	5-9
Dieruff	0-7	Hazleton	1-6	Hazleton	2-12

Team Rosters

Allen: Coach Milo Sewards, Dave Becker, Jay Borillo, Dick Brobst, Don Canzano, Ted Carls, Jim Coker, Bob Follweiler, Funk, Joe Geschel, Charlie Haydt, Jim Katz, Gene Molovinsky, Mike Sewards, John Washychyn, Jim Wescoe

Bethlehem: Coach John Howard, Bob Bair, Dave Bednarik, Bill Boak, Barry Frey, Jim Heidecker, Charles Iobst, Pat Howlett, Fred McGuiney, Kirk Melloy, Miller, Sal Tavares, Bob Thomas, Dwayne Wartman

Central Catholic: Coach John Compardo, Bob Andrew, Ed Fedok, Len Kalata, Tom Kober, Dave Leber, Rich Kindt, Jim Martin, Dave Pfahler, Ed Sarmir, Anton Schrettner, Bill Washychyn, Steve Zarzeka

Dieruff: Coach Dick Schmidt, Ron Bauer, Richard Bechtel, Ron Berta, Paul Coles, George Daskalakes, Ron Dorshimer, George Eichelberger, Finley, Bob Reidy, Ron Schaeffer, Ed Schray, Tim Smith, Tom Young

Easton: Coach Tom Sweeney, Bob Anckaitis, Karl Bell, Tom Bonstein, Charlie Bottiglieri, Bill Eisel, Ron Farina, Jack Kelleher, Phil Lipkin, Mike MoDavis, Robert Nagy, Frank Nagurney, Don Pyatt, Stan Shell, Pete Wells

Hazleton: Coach Fran Libonati, John Barletta, Mike Berge, Tom Carlyon, Neil Darrough, Norb Dudeck, Bob Eigenbrod, John Guydish, Ron Hess, Tony Moran, Jerry Petrisko, Dave Sell, Bob Solarek, Russ Stewart, Bob Tucker, Dave Wagner

Pottsville: Coach Larry Haberle, Bob Achenbach, Talton Alston, Irv Ambrose, Jim DeStefano, Bill Garland, Jim Harley, Denny Harris, Al Hedeman, Ray Heinley, Bob Lengel, Rich Laubach, George Metaxas, Jack Morris, Ron Morris, Mickey Oerther, Tom Piccioni, Les Price, Roy Shellhammer

Tamaqua: Coach Eli Purnell, George Barron, Jack Bassler, Breiner, George Darker, Bob Fritzinger, Ted Hafer, Allen Lord, Ed Lyba, Don Mikruk, Bill Semko, Fred Valent

Bethlehem High School – 1963 League Champions[24]

Dave Bednarik, Barry Frey, Bill Boak, Pat Howlett,

Sal Tavares (kneeling)

1964

Phillipsburg Enters the League

Edgar Rabenold, who served as secretary-treasurer since the formation of the league in 1926, declined his nomination to the position for the 1964 season. The league representatives elected Joe Blankowitsch to serve in the position. He also served as the league statistician. Phil Phillipi, Bethlehem, and Rev. Francis Zavodny, Central Catholic were re-elected to the positions of president and vice president at the spring meeting at the Shankweiler Hotel in Fogelsville. The league also announced that Phillipsburg NJ would enter the league as its ninth member and be included in the 1964 season schedule. With the addition of a ninth team, league play would begin in mid-December.[1]

Week 1

Central Catholic 66 Pottsville 56: The opening night matched two league favorites at Rockne Hall. With Dave Pfahler holding Pottsville's Talton Alston to seven points, the Vikings held off Pottsville. With Len Kalata and Pfahler scoring 21 of the points, Central Catholic got off to a fast first quarter start 24-14. Pottsville battled back to cut the lead to four at the half 35-31. They cut the lead to two 39-37 early in the third quarter. Len Kalata scored the Vikings first nine points in the third quarter to extend the lead. With Alston on the bench and eventually fouling out with about 4 ½ minutes left in the game, Pottsville's Morris brothers, Ron and John, provided the offensive punch for the visiting team. They scored all twelve of Pottsville's 4th quarter points.

Leading scorers: Central Catholic - Dave Pfahler 23, Len Kalata 28; Pottsville - Ron Morris 28, John Morris 11.

Allen 80 Tamaqua 55: After a closely played first half with Allen leading 16-12 after one and 30-29 at the half, the Canaries broke loose to score 27 points in the third period to only 9 for Tamaqua. Allen went on to extend the lead even further in the 4th quarter in a rout of Coach Eli "Pinky" Purnell's squad. Allen improved to 2-3 overall and Tamaqua dropped to 1-4 in the early season.

Leading scorers: Allen – Charley Haydt 30, Mike Sewards 14, Ted Carls 13; Tamaqua – Ed Lyba 14, Ted Hafer 13.

Bethlehem 94 Phillipsburg 61: Coach Al Senavitis' Phillipsburg team got a tough welcome into the league as Bethlehem thrashed the Garnet. Phillipsburg led 15-12 midway through the first quarter, but Coach John Howard's team scored 11 straight points to take a commanding lead for the remainder of the game. Bethlehem scored over 20 points in each quarter. The Hurricane's Dave Bednarik scored 25 points in the first half which included 13 straight foul shots.

Leading scorers: Bethlehem – Dave Bednarik 38, Tom Szabo 17, Greg Zebrowski 10; Phillipsburg – Mike Zeeman 21, Steve Jeroloman 12.

Dieruff 59 Hazleton 52: At Hazleton, Dieruff jumped out to a ten-point first quarter lead 20-10 and extended to 14 before the Mountaineers rallied to close the score to 38-32 at intermission. Early in the 4th period, Hazleton surged into the lead 50-47 only to have the Huskies answer with six consecutive points. Hazleton could only score a single field goal in the final five minutes of the game. Dieruff finished with six foul shots to win the game.

Leading scorers: Dieruff – Tom Young 19; George Daskalakes 14, Tim Smith 12, Ron Schaeffer 10; Hazleton – Bob Eigenbrod 15, Jim Girard 14.[2]

Allen 74 Phillipsburg 67: At Phillipsburg, Allen handed the home team its second straight loss in its inaugural season in the league. Allen took a nine-point lead into the second quarter 28-19 only to have the Garnet hold the Canaries to nine points while scoring 23 of their own to take a 42-37 half time lead. In the beginning of the 3rd quarter, each team surged with Allen scoring six straight points and Phillipsburg countering with seven in a row to lead 51-45. Allen came back with nine straight to take a 54-51 lead into the 4th quarter. The score was tied six times in the final quarter with the last being 67-67. The Canaries scored the final seven points for the win.

Leading scorers: Allen–Ted Carls 30, Charley Haydt 28; Phillipsburg–Steve Jeroloman 20, Greg Clymer 18, Mike Zeeman 13.

Dieruff 56 Central Catholic 55: In a hard-fought game, Dieruff upset Central Catholic at Dieruff's east side gym. Coach Dick Schmidt's team played a conservative game only looking for a solid shot opportunity. Dieruff took a 14-7 lead into the second quarter only to have the Vikings battle back outscoring the Huskies 24-11 and take a 31-25 lead at the half. During the period, the Vikings outscored the Huskies 18-2 in one stretch. Dieruff reversed the second period results by scoring 21 to the Vikings 11 and take a 46-41 lead into the final stanza. The five-point lead turned out to be just enough to knock off the league's favorites.

Leading scorers: Dieruff - Tom Young 17, Ron Schaeffer 14, George Daskalakes 12; Central Catholic – Steve Zarzeka 17, Len Kalata 13, Dave Pfahler 11.

Pottsville 57 Easton 56: Playing without 6'3" center Talton Alston, Pottsville handed Easton its first loss of the season. Alston had been dismissed from the team by Coach Ken Kline. Despite Alston' absence, Pottsville charged out to a 22-6 first quarter advantage. They continued to hold a large lead at halftime 36-19 and going into the 4th quarter 50-34. With Easton desperately rallying with Jim Marino scoring 14 points in the final period, the big lead was just enough for Pottsville to hang onto the lead.

Leading scorers: Pottsville – Ron Morris 22, John Morris 16, Tom Piccioni 10; Easton – Jim Marino 25, Bill Eisel 10.

Hazleton 86 Tamaqua 59: At Tamaqua, Hazleton exploded with 29 points in the first quarter to take a ten-point lead on the way to a drubbing of Tamaqua to break a 16-game league losing streak on the road. The last road win had been at Allen 88-72 in 1961. The Mountaineers outscored Tamaqua in every quarter except the last, when the game had long been decided.

Leading scorers: Hazleton– Bob Solarek 22, Bob Eigenbrod 18, Neil Darrough 10; Tamaqua– Allan Lord 12, George Krell 12.[3]

Week 2

Allen 80 Bethlehem 69: With Charley Haydt continuing his hot scoring spree, Allen won its third league contest, against no losses, over Bethlehem. Bednarik played tough on the boards as well grabbing 18 rebounds. Leading after one quarter 24-17, Allen held on to enter the locker room with a 43-39 margin. With Dave Bednarik taking the team on his back, Bethlehem took a one-point lead 47-46 in the 3rd period. Joe Ehritz scored a layup to give the Canaries a lead they would not relinquish. Allen shared the early league lead with Dieruff.

Leading scorers: Allen – Charley Haydt 35, Ted Carls 20; Bethlehem – Dave Bednarik 27, Tom Mosser 14.

Central Catholic 64 Tamaqua 50: With Dave Pfahler out of the lineup with a stiff neck, Steve Zarzeka stepped up to lead Central Catholic to a defeat of Tamaqua at Rockne Hall. Tamaqua only held a lead briefly early in the first period as the Vikings were never outscored in any period. An eleven-point run by the Vikings in the second period put the game away. The win put the Vikings at 3-0 to join Allen for the league lead.

Leading scorers: Central Catholic - Steve Zarzeka 16, Tom Kober 14; Tamaqua - Ed Lyba 16, Bob Fritzinger 12.

Dieruff 58 Easton 44: In Easton, Dieruff converted 30 of 37 foul shots for over half their game points in a win over the Red Rovers. Tom Young hit on all 13 of his free throws to extend his streak to 24 consecutive successful shots. Although Easton led briefly in the second period 23-20, the Huskies led at the end of each quarter. With the field goals equal at 14 for each team, the margin of victory was due to the Huskies foul shooting prowess.

Leading scorers: Dieruff – Tom Young 19, Ron Schaeffer 13; Easton – Tom Bonstein 14, Bill Eisel 13.

Hazleton 83 Phillipsburg 63: At home, Hazleton continued its resurgence by disposing of Phillipsburg. The Mountaineers took a ten-point first quarter and were never threatened in the game. With Coach Fran Libonati inserting two sophomores into the lineup in a rebuilding attempt for the program, he saw four players score in double figures. Phillipsburg was still looking for its first league triumph.

Leading scorers: Hazleton – Bob Eigenbrod 22, Jim Girard 22, Joe Tito 12, Bob Solarek 10; Phillipsburg – Steve Jeroloman 17, Greg Clymer 14, Mike Zeeman 10.[4]

Week 3

Bethlehem 55 Hazleton 48: After falling behind 11-9 after one quarter, Bethlehem picked up the pace in the second quarter to outscore the Mountaineers 19-12. The second quarter margin proved enough to give the Hurricane a triumph over Hazleton and give Coach John Howard his 150th win in his ten years as head coach. Bethlehem barely outscored Hazleton by a single point in each of the third and fourth quarters. In achieving the victory, Coach Howard used only his five starters in the game with no substitutions.

Leading scorers: Bethlehem – Greg Zebrowski 13, Jack Wolfe 13, Tom Mosser 12, Kirk Melloy 11; Hazleton – Bob Eigenbrod 20, Bob Solarek 11.

Central Catholic 62 Phillipsburg 50: Central Catholic jumped out to a 17-6 lead in the first quarter only to have the Stateliners cut the lead to 19-14 at the end of the quarter and to two points at the end of the second quarter 29-27. In the final two quarters, the Vikings continued to extend the lead and return home with a win. One of Phillipsburg's leading scorers Greg Clymer hurt his shoulder in the second period and did not return to the game.

Leading scorers: Central Catholic – Dave Pfahler 23, Len Kalata 17, Tom Kober 11; Phillipsburg – Mickey Zeeman 12, Steve Jeroloman 12.

Easton 58 Tamaqua 50: Tamaqua only had a lead once in the game, near the end of the first quarter, and never got closer than three points after that in their loss to Easton. Tamaqua attempted a run at the Red Rovers in the fourth quarter, but it fizzled when Bob Fritzinger fouled out with 2 ½ minutes left in the game. The win was Easton's first in the league for the season.

Leading scorers: Easton – Tom Bonstein 18, Mike MoDavis 14, Bill Eisel 13; Tamaqua – Bob Fritzinger 18, Ed Lyba 11.

Pottsville 76 Dieruff 62: Dieruff took a 32-25 lead into the third quarter on its home court against Pottsville. Pottsville unleashed its offense in the third and fourth quarters scoring 25 and 26 points to send the Huskie fans home disappointed. The comeback gave Pottsville a 76-62 triumph over Dieruff. Pottsville took the lead early in the third quarter 38-37 on a fastbreak layup by Ron Morris. Pottsville never trailed again as Dieruff couldn't get closer than 4 points the rest of the game. Dieruff's loss left Allen as the only undefeated team in league play.[5]

Leading scorers: Pottsville - Ron Morris 25, John Morris 14, Bob Lengel 14, Tom Piccioni 12, Talton Alston 10; Dieruff – Tom Young 25, George Daskalakes 18.[5]

Allen 62 Hazleton 60: At Hazleton, the Mountaineers rallied from 10 points down in the fourth quarter to pull even at 52-52 with about 5 ½ minutes to play in the final quarter. Earlier, the Mountaineers had fallen behind 12-2 in the first quarter when the Canaries scored 12 consecutive points after Hazleton opened the game with a basket. In the second and third periods, the Canaries led by as many as 13 and 12 points. Led by Ted Carls, Allen pulled out the victory to remain undefeated at 4-0 and on top of the league.

Leading scorers: Allen – Charley Haydt 19, Ted Carls 15, Mike Sewards 13; Hazleton – Bob Eigenbrod 26, Bob Solarek 18.[6]

Bethlehem 62 Central Catholic 55: Playing on their home court, preseason favorite Central Catholic fell to Bethlehem to drop to 3-2 in league play. Bethlehem's stingy defense held the Vikings to 17 field goals in 81 attempts. After not scoring a field goal for over four minutes in the first period and trailing 20-12 heading into the 2nd quarter, the Vikings cut the deficit to 20-18 after less than three minutes of play in the quarter. The rally continued through to halftime with the score tied at 28-28. After the Vikings opened with a field goal to take the lead in the 3rd quarter, Bethlehem reeled off 11 points in a row to lead 39-32 and took charge of the game.

Leading scorers: Bethlehem – Dave Bednarik 24, Greg Zebrowski 11, Jack Wolfe 10; Central Catholic – Len Kalata 14, Dave Pfahler 13.

Pottsville 76 Tamaqua 47: Trailing early 5-2, Pottsville poured it on against visiting Tamaqua to take a 15-6 first quarter lead. Pottsville outscored the Tams by 5, 7, and 8 points in the next three periods to win easily. Pottsville kept in the hunt for the first half title with a 3-1 record. Pottsville remained winless at 0-5.

Leading scorers: Pottsville – Ron Morris 30, Tom Piccioni 19, Talton Alston 13; Tamaqua – Jack Bassler 10, Ted Hafer 10.

Easton 105 Phillipsburg 32: Easton showed no mercy in hanging a 105-32 defeat on their cross-river rivals Phillipsburg. The point total broke the school's all-time scoring record of 96 set in an overtime game in 1961 against Pottsville. Easton held the Stateliners to six points in both the second and fourth quarters in the rout. They had scoring streaks of 13, 11, and 16 consecutive points in the game.

Leading scorers: Easton – Tom Bonstein 18, Jim Marino 15, Bill Eisel 14, Mike MoDavis 10; Phillipsburg – George West 8. [7]

Week 4

Central Catholic 75 Allen 70: The chase for the first half title became a four-way race with Central Catholic's defeat of Allen at the Little Palestra. Allen seemed to have the game in hand after the first quarter with a 22-15 lead. The Vikings had other ideas and outscored the Canaries 27-17 to take a 42-39 halftime lead. The Vikings scored 13 straight points in the second period. Trailing by eight in the final period, Central Catholic rallied to take a 63-62 lead and maintained the lead for the victory. Four teams were now tied for the league lead with 4-1 records: Allen, Bethlehem, Dieruff, and Pottsville.

Leading scorers: Central Catholic – Len Kalata 20, Tom Kober 16; Steve Zarzeka 14, Dave Pfahler 10; Allen – Ted Carls 30, Charley Haydt 18.

Bethlehem 63 Easton 60: Although the Easton defense held the Hurricane to only 11 field goals, Bethlehem converted 41 of 61 foul shots to eke out a win over the Red Rovers. Easton had 41 fouls including two technical fouls in the contest. The Red Rovers lost Jim Marino, Bill Eisel, Karl Bell, and Phil Lipkin in the last quarter with five personal fouls.

Leading scorers: Bethlehem– Dave Bednarik 27, Jack Wolfe 10, Kirk Melloy 10; Easton– Mike MoDavis 20, Tom Bonstein 18.[8]

Dieruff 73 Tamaqua 57: Taking advantage of Allen's loss, Dieruff moved into the four-way tie for first place by disposing of Tamaqua. Streaking out early to a 10-2 lead, the Huskies took a 21-12 lead into the second quarter. Dieruff built on the lead in the middle two quarters 37-23 and 56-35 heading into the final stanza. Tamaqua's last period was far from enough with the big lead piled up by the Huskies.

Leading scorers: Dieruff – Tom Young 26, George Daskalakes 20; Tamaqua – Ted Hafer 16, Ed Lyba 15.

Pottsville 71 Phillipsburg 58: Pottsville moved into a first-place tie with its triumph over stubborn, but winless Phillipsburg. The Stateliners battled Pottsville into the third quarter and were tied 32-32 before Pottsville made its move to take a 38-32 lead. After a Phillipsburg foul conversion, Pottsville scored 9 straight points to take a commanding lead. Ron Morris took the league scoring lead with his 32 points in the game.

Leading scorers: Pottsville – Ron Morris 32, John Morris 10, Bob Lengel 10; Phillipsburg – Greg Clymer 14, George West 12, Steve Jeroloman 12, George Hummer 10.[9]

Pottsville 75 Bethlehem 55: In a battle of two of the front runners in Pottsville, Bethlehem lost its share of first place at the hands of Pottsville. Bethlehem tied for the lead three times in the first quarter before Pottsville took the lead for good at 14-12. Bethlehem got close again int the second period 26-25, but Pottsville ran off 12 consecutive points to take a 38-25 lead at the half. The Crimson Tide had a 59-25 rebounding edge in the game.

Leading scorers: Pottsville – Talton Alston 28, Ron Morris 27, John Morris 12; Bethlehem – Dave Bednarik 23, Kirk Melloy 10.

Allen 69 Easton 61: Allen maintained its share of first place with a win over Easton. After being tied at 27-27, the Canaries, led by Mike Sewards and Joe Ehritz, surged to take a 41-29 lead at half time. Easton again committed numerous fouls to allow the Canaries to convert 25 of 44 attempts at the foul line to Easton's 15 of 25, which proved to be the difference in the game.

Leading scorers: Allen – Charley Haydt 23, Ted Carls 14, Mike Sewards 12, Joe Ehritz 10; Easton – Jim Machette 13, Mike MoDavis 11.

Central Catholic 76 Hazleton 64: With Dave Pfahler holding Hazleton's leading scorer Bob Eigenbrod to 12 points, well below his over 20 points per game average, Central Catholic defeated Hazleton. After being tied at 6-6 early in the first period, the Vikings took over and built a 19-point lead midway through the 4th quarter. The Vikings out-rebounded Hazleton 44-33 and held the Mountaineers to single shots at the basket.

Leading scorers: Central Catholic – Tom Kober 18, Steve Zarzeka 18, Dave Pfahler 17, Len Kalata 12; Hazleton – Bob Solarek 24, Jim Girard 14, Bob Eigenbrod 12.

Dieruff 50 Phillipsburg 41: Coach Al Senavitis' Phillipsburg squad fought Dieruff on even terms for 3 ½ quarters only to see the Huskies outscore them 11-3 after they trailed by only one point 39-38. At one point in the second period, Phillipsburg held a seven-point lead 19-12. The Huskies led by only three points at the half 28-25 and Phillipsburg matched the Huskies with each scoring 11 points in the third period.

Leading scorers: Dieruff – Tom Young 19, Ron Schaeffer 13, Tim Smith 10; Phillipsburg – Mickey Zeeman 13, Greg Clymer 10, George Hummer 10.[10]

Week 5

Bethlehem 60 Dieruff 48: Free throws made the difference in this crucial game for Dieruff in the battle for the first half title. Bethlehem converted 20 of 28 while Dieruff made 6 of 12 in Bethlehem's stunning defeat of the Huskies. In a close game till late in the final period, Bethlehem led after one quarter 14-12 only to have Dieruff fight back in a low-scoring second period to lead at the half 20-18. This led to a 36-36 tie after three quarters. Bethlehem pulled away in the final 2 ½ minutes to end the Huskies title hopes.

Leading scorers: Bethlehem – Dave Bednarik 20, Greg Zebrowski 16, John "Sy" Sydorak 10; Dieruff – George Daskalakes 20, Tom Young 18.

Pottsville 80 Allen 68: With Dieruff upset by Bethlehem, this contest became the crucial game for the first half title. Coach Ken Kline's Pottsville squad met the task at hand by defeating the Canaries on their home court. Pottsville's Ron Morris dropped in 42 to points to set a Little Palestra record and lead the Crimson Tide to victory. The game featured a lot of fouls with Pottsville committing 27 and the Canaries 28. After a 17-17 first quarter tie, Pottsville took a 42-33 half time lead. Allen cut it to four 58-54 after three quarters, but Pottsville to command in the fourth quarter.

Leading scorers: Pottsville – Ron Morris 42, John Morris 11; Allen – Ted Carls 21; Charley Haydt 12, Mike Sewards 12, Joe Ehritz 11.

Phillipsburg 63 Tamaqua 57: In a battle of winless teams, Phillipsburg picked up its initial league win over Tamaqua. After trailing at the half 31-28, Phillipsburg coach Al Senavitis switched to a zone defense and took a commanding lead after the third period 50-43 and the Stateliners had their first victory.

Leading scorers: Phillipsburg – George Hummer 19, Steve Jeroloman 15, Mickey Zeeman 12; Tamaqua – Bob Fritzinger 17, Ted Hafer 14, Jack Bassler 10.[11]

Hazleton 84 Easton 69: Holding a two-point advantage at the half 44-42, Hazleton pulled away to take a 62-53 lead after three periods and win the game by a wide margin. Easton's only lead was at 2-0 and Hazleton scored 12 straight to take a 26-13 lead in the second quarter. Hazleton improved to 3-4 while the Red Rovers dropped to 2-5.

Leading scorers: Hazleton – Bob Solarek 31, Bob Eigenbrod 20; Easton – Tom Bonstein 17, Mike MoDavis 15, Phil Lipkin 13, Sal Mentesana 12.[12]

Pottsville 78 Hazleton 63: With Hazleton taking a 16-13 lead into the second quarter, Coach Ken Kline's Pottsville squad answered by outscoring the Mountaineers early in the second period 11-1 to take a 24-17 advantage. Hazleton got no closer than 41-37 during the third period. The win clinched the first half title for the Crimson Tide who would seek their first title since 1942 with a good second half showing.

Leading scorers: Pottsville – Ron Morris 22, Talton Alston 21, Bob Lengel 13, John Morris 12; Hazleton – Bob Eigenbrod 21, Bob Solarek 13, Jim Girard 12.

Central Catholic 65 Easton 62: Easton battled Central Catholic for three quarters taking an 51-44 advantage into the final period. The Red Rovers outscored the Vikings in each of the first three quarters. With Tom Kober scoring five, the Vikings scored six points at the start of the final period to get within one of the Red Rovers. The two teams battled to several ties with the last one at 62-62 before the Vikings went ahead to eke out the win.

Leading scorers: Central Catholic-Tom Kober 19, Len Kalata 16, Dave Pfahler 15; Easton-Mike MoDavis 20, Tom Bonstein 17.

Bethlehem 75 Tamaqua 59: The Hurricane kept Tamaqua winless in the first half with a defeat of the Tams. Tamaqua made it a game and trailed by only five with three minutes left in the game 60-55 after Bethlehem had led by 12 at the half. Deploying a zone defense to start the third period, the switch backfired on the Hurricane as Tamaqua made a comeback.

Leading scorers: Bethlehem – John Sydorak 19, Dave Bednarik 18, Jack Wolfe 14; Tamaqua – Bob Fritzinger 14, Ted Hafer 14, George Krell 13.

Allen 74 Dieruff 69: Trailing by 19 points 64-45 with a little over 6 minutes left in the game, Dieruff put on a fierce rally to narrow Allen's lead to 70-67 with 1:11 left to play. The Canaries then made a couple of free throws to pull out a 74-69 win over the Huskies and claim a tie for second place with Central Catholic and Bethlehem at 6-2.

Leading scorers: Allen – Ted Carls 26, Charley Haydt 20, Rudy Toman 11, Joe Ehritz 10; Dieruff – Ron Schaeffer 20, George Eichelberger 12, George Daskalakes 10.[13]

Second Half - Week 6

Central Catholic 63 Pottsville 62 2OT: Central Catholic, opening the second half at Pottsville, took a double overtime game from the home team to begin its pursuit of the second half title. Both teams rallied from deficits during the hard-fought game. Pottsville rallied in the second and fourth quarters from 5 points down, the last to force the game into overtime. The Vikings trailed by 10 points down in the 3rd quarter. In all, the lead changed 11 times and the game was tied nine times throughout the contest. With four seconds left in the second overtime, Jerry Guman made only his second field goal of the night, but it was the winner.

Leading scorers: Central Catholic – Steve Zarzeka 15, Len Kalata 13, Tom Kober 10, Tom Herrity 10; Pottsville – Ron Morris 20, Talton Alston 15, John Morris 14.

Dieruff 85 Hazleton 48: Dieruff scored the most points in its brief league history in the defeat of Hazleton. Dieruff employed a 2-2-1 full court press, forcing Hazleton into losing the ball 27 times without getting a shot, in the overwhelming victory over the Mountaineers. No Hazleton player was able to score in double figures. Hazleton managed only 15 field goals on 65 shots while the Huskies registered 38 field goals.

Leading scorers: Dieruff – Tom Young 21, George Daskalakes 17, Ron Schaeffer 14, Tim Smith 14; Hazleton – Jim Girard 9.

Allen 76 Tamaqua 67: Tamaqua stayed close throughout the game and was only two points behind Allen with a little over 5 minutes left in the third period. The game was tied after one period 14-14 and Allen took a 35-32 lead into the locker room. Tamaqua was hindered by injuries to Ed Lyba with a pulled back muscle and Bob Fritzinger who was shaken up in a mad scramble and saw only limited action. In their absence, sophomore George Krell had a breakout night in the loss to the Canaries. After the injury to Lyba, Allen took command of the game.

Leading scorers: Allen – Charley Haydt 26, Ted Carls 17, Rudy Toman 12; Tamaqua – George Krell 32, Bob Fritzinger 12, Main 10.

Bethlehem 90 Phillipsburg 61: After playing a close first quarter with Bethlehem holding a slim one-point lead 18-17, Phillipsburg fell behind in the second quarter by 11 points 43-32, during which Bethlehem scored 10 straight points. Bethlehem continued to pour it on in the last two quarters on their way to 90-61 pasting of the Stateliners.

Leading scorers: Bethlehem – Dave Bednarik 33, Greg Zebrowski 15, Tom Szabo 12; Phillipsburg – Mickey Zeeman 19, Steve Jeroloman 15, Greg Clymer 10.[13]

Week 7

Allen 80 Phillipsburg 43: Allen took an early 22-6 lead into the second quarter and expanded the lead to 38-15 by holding the Stateliners to only 9 points in the second period. Coach Milo Sewards used his starters only sparingly in the easy win over Phillipsburg.

Leading scorers: Allen-Charley Haydt 22, Scott Beeten 10, Mark Nissenbaum 10; Phillipsburg-Dan Roble 11, George West 10.

Hazleton 95 Tamaqua 48: Everyone one of the twelve players used by Coach Fran Libonati got into the scoring column in a shellacking of Tamaqua. Bob Eigenbrod scored 12 points in a row as the Mountaineers jumped out to a 14-0 lead to start out the contest. Tamaqua fought back to score 13 of the next 21 points to end the first half trailing 21-13. Hazleton scored over 20 points in each quarter.

Leading scorers: Hazleton – Bob Eigenbrod 28, Bob Solarek 13, Jim Girard 13, Neil Darrough 13, Jim Dietrich 10; Tamaqua – Bob Fritzinger 16, Ted Hafer 10.

Dieruff 53 Central Catholic 51: Dieruff continued its mastery, winning 7 of the last 10 games in the rivalry, of Central Catholic with a win over the heavily favored Vikings. Using a zone press, the Huskies lengthened their early 22-21 second quarter lead with a 10-2 spurt. Central Catholic caught the Huskies with 4:49 left in the third quarter at 36-36. Dieruff froze the ball for the last five minutes of the final quarter to perfection holding the Vikings to a single field goal. The Huskies scored a field goal and two foul shots by Tom Young with 45 seconds to go which proved to be the winning points.

Leading scorers: Dieruff – Tom Young 14, George Daskalakes 14, Tim Smith 10; Central Catholic – Len Kalata 15, Steve Zarzeka 11, Dave Pfahler 11.

Pottsville 85 Easton 56: After a tight first quarter with Pottsville holding a 20-18, the Crimson Tide scored 7 points in a row to start the second quarter and then had another 10-point spurt to take a commanding lead at the half over Easton 41-24. The loss was Easton's sixth in a row.

Leading scorers: Pottsville - Ron Morris 27, Talton Alston 22, John Morris 14, Tom Piccioni 12; Easton – Bill Eisel 12.[14]

Week 8

Allen 63 Bethlehem 62: With a slim one-point lead 13-12 going into the second quarter, Allen outscored Bethlehem 13-2 right before the half to take a 36-25 lead into half time. Allen added one point to the lead to move ten points ahead with a quarter to play. They needed every point of that margin as Bethlehem clawed back to tie the score at 59. Scott Beeten, coming off the bench due to Teddy Carls' foul trouble, scored the last four points for an Allen triumph.

Leading scorers: Allen – Charley Haydt 26; Bethlehem – Greg Zembrowski 22, John Sydorak 17, Dave Bednarik 11.

Dieruff 45 Easton 42: Dieruff won its third straight game of the second half with a defeat of Easton, who lost its seventh in a row. Despite only hitting on 11 of 54 field goal attempts, the Huskies pulled out the game by converting 23 of 27 foul shots. The Huskies did not have a field goal in the final quarter scoring all 13 points on foul shots. Dieruff held the Red Rovers to one first quarter field goal and led 13-5 after one period. They scored nine straight points to lead 22-5 before Easton fought back valiantly to tie the game at 34 in the fourth quarter. Dieruff made 11 critical foul shots to pull out the win. Dieruff tied Allen for the league lead both with 3-0 records.

Leading scorers: Dieruff– Ron Schaeffer 13, Tom Young 12, George Eichelberger 12; Easton– Bill Eisel 15.

Central Catholic 89 Tamaqua 68: Tamaqua lost their 16th game out of 17 on the season in its loss to Central Catholic. The Vikings took a 13-point lead after one period 24-11 and outscored the Tams again by 13 points in the third period 27-14 to cruise to the win. Tamaqua made a run in the second period and again in the final period but could get no closer than 9 points.

Leading scorers: Central Catholic – Tom Kober 23, Dave Pfahler 22, Jerry Guman 10; Tamaqua – Bob Fritzinger 17, George Krell 17, Ed Lyba 12, Ted Hafer 11.

Hazleton 80 Phillipsburg 41: Hazleton held Phillipsburg to five field goals in the first half and charged out to a 37-16 half time lead. Phillipsburg only made 5 of 35 field goal attempts in the first half and 14 for 75 in the game. Hazleton converted 32 of their 71 field goal attempts. Hazleton grabbed 55 rebounds to the Stateliners 27. Hazleton's George Sanko scored all of his 12 points in the final period.

Leading scorers: Hazleton – Bob Solarek 19, Jim Girard 13, George Sanko 12, Tony Moran 12; Phillipsburg – George West 17, Mickey Zeeman 10.[15]

Week 9

Dieruff 73 Pottsville 63: With Allen idle, Dieruff, at 4-0, took a half game lead over the Canaries with an upset of Pottsville on their home court. Dieruff took a 42-34 lead in the first half on the strength of a remarkable 20 of 33 from the field and a tough zone press. Pottsville held a 22-19 lead at the end of the first quarter only to see the Huskies score 12 straight points to take a 40-29 lead with about 2 ½ minutes left in the second quarter. Pottsville cut the lead to three in the fourth period 56-53 when Dieruff employed a spread offense forcing the Crimson Tide to come after the ball. Dieruff countered by making the all-important foul shots.

Leading scorers: Dieruff –Tom Young 29, George Eichelberger 16, George Daskalakes 11; Pottsville – Ron Morris 24, Talton Alston 17, John Morris 14.

Hazleton 65 Bethlehem 63: At St. Joseph's gym in Hazleton, Bethlehem lost its second game in a row to Hazleton on a last second field goal by Bob Solarek. Despite playing shorthanded with the suspension of several players including two starters, the Mountaineers pulled out the victory in a very close game. Hazleton took an eight-point lead in the final quarter only to have Bethlehem tie the score at 61 with less than two minutes to play. With the teams exchanging foul shots, the score was tied again at 63-63 before Solarek sank his field goal for the win.

Leading scorers: Hazleton – Bob Solarek 25, Jim Dietrich 12, Bob Eigenbrod 11, Jim Girard 11; Bethlehem – Dave Bednarik 19, Greg Zebrowski 18.

Easton 70 Tamaqua 56: Easton broke its seven-game losing streak and won its first game of the second half over Tamaqua. Bill Eisel's 11 first quarter points led Easton to a 19-10 advantage after a period. Holding a 13-point lead at intermission, Easton played on even terms in the second half to gain the victory. Easton made only 19 of 64 field goal attempts.

Leading scorers: Easton – Tom Bonstein 19, Jim Marino 16, Bill Eisel 14; Tamaqua – Ed Lyba 16, George Krell 11, Bob Fritzinger 10.

Central Catholic 74 Phillipsburg 53: At Rockne Hall, Central Catholic charged out to 22-6 lead over Phillipsburg. Tom Kober led the first quarter charge with 13 points. The Stateliners played the Vikings on equal terms in the second period with each scoring 17 points. The Vikings added seven points to their lead in the third and cruised comfortably to the win.

Leading scorers: Central Catholic – Tom Kober 21, Dave Pfahler 18, Tom Herrity 10; Phillipsburg –Mickey Zeeman 10, George West 10.[16]

Bethlehem 68 Central Catholic 57: Bethlehem evened its record at 2-2 and severely damaged the Vikings' second half chances dropping them to 3-2. Both teams missed key players in the game with Bethlehem's Greg Zebrowski out of the game as well as the Vikings' Len Kalata. Bethlehem put the game away early with a ten-point lead after one quarter 20-10 and extending it by 3 and 4 points in the next two quarters. The Vikings tried to comeback in the final period, but the lead was too great and Bethlehem prevailed.

Leading scorers: Bethlehem – John Sydorak 20, Dave Bednarik 18, Kirk Melloy 12, Jack Wolfe 10; Central Catholic – Dave Pfahler 13, Fran Bolez 12, Tom Herrity 11, Jerry Guman 11.

Hazleton 68 Allen 65: Hazleton, again playing shorthanded because of player suspensions, knocked Allen from the ranks of the unbeaten in the second half 68-65. After Allen took a 17-16 first quarter lead, Hazleton played strongly in the middle two periods and took a 51-43 lead into the final period. Allen, trailing by nine points with a little over 4 minutes left in the game, came back to tie the game at 64-64 only to see the lead slip away with Hazleton's Jim Girard scoring four points for the win. The loss put Dieruff into first place as the only undefeated team at 4-0.

Leading scorers: Hazleton – Bob Solarek 24, Bob Eigenbrod 15, Jim Dietrich 11, Jim Girard 10; Allen – Charley Haydt 22, Jim Coker 13.

Easton 88 Phillipsburg 48: Easton used a full court press to run up a 24-10 lead in the first quarter. Phillipsburg's many turnovers against the Red Rover defense led to many easy Easton baskets. Easton finished off the Stateliners 26-8 in the final period. With Easton holding a 71-44 lead in the fourth, they scored 11 straight points to crush Phillipsburg.

Leading scorers: Easton – Bill Eisel 20, Tom Bonstein 18, Jim Machette 14, Jim Marino 10; Phillipsburg – Greg Clymer 14.

Pottsville 109 Tamaqua 62: Pottsville crushed Tamaqua in a record-breaking performance for the team and Ron Morris. Morris set a new league scoring standard with 20 field goals and 7 of 7 foul shots for 47 points. He also broke the league's season scoring record held by Easton's Tony Relvas and the Pottsville single game record of 44 set by Gus Prahalis in 1950. Morris's 12 points helped the Crimson Tide take a 29-13 lead after one period and the rout was on.

Leading Scorers: Pottsville –Ron Morris 47, Talton Alston 23, Lou Chervanek 12; Tamaqua – Bob Fritzinger 16, Ed Lyba 16, George Krell 12.[17]

Week 10

Dieruff 83 Tamaqua 51: Dieruff took advantage of a weak opponent in Tamaqua to remain undefeated in the half at 5-0 and maintain its hold on first place. Tamaqua held a 10-8 lead in the first quarter when the Huskies reeled off 12 straight points to lead after one quarter 20-12. The Huskies extended the lead to 42-25 at the half and Coach Pinky Purnell's squad got no closer than 12 points in the second half. Tom Young handed out 11 assists and scored 25 points to extend his school record season total to 361 points.

Leading scorers: Dieruff –Tom Young 25, George Daskalakes 19, Ron Schaeffer 10, Don Burkert 10; Tamaqua – Ed Lyba 20, Bob Fritzinger 12, George Krell 10.

Bethlehem 71 Easton 61: Taking a 20-4 lead over Easton, the point difference turned out to be critical in Bethlehem's victory. Easton made only 2 of 14 field goal attempts in a very poor first period. After that, the Red Rovers outscored the Hurricane 57-51 but could not get over the first quarter margin. Easton lost the ball six times in the first period before they got their first shot.

Leading scorers: Bethlehem – John Sydorak 18, Tom Mosser 18, Kirk Melloy 14, Dave Bednarik 13; Easton – Jim Marino 18, Len Machette 10, Bill Eisel 10.

Central Catholic 74 Allen 63: Central Catholic handed the Canaries their second consecutive loss to damage their hopes of a second half title. Allen's Charley Haydt took an elbow in the midsection in the second period and returned to action in the third period at less than full speed. The Vikings' Tom Herrity left in the fourth period with a knee injury. After taking a 19-13 first period lead, the Vikings were only briefly threatened in the third period when Allen pulled within 39-36 but the Vikings countered by taking a 59-45 lead by the end of the period.

Leading scorers: Central Catholic – Dave Pfahler 25, Steve Zarzeka 15, Fran Bolez 12, Tom Herrity 10; Allen -Ted Carls 18, Rudy Toman 10.[18]

Pottsville 86 Phillipsburg 61: After Phillipsburg held Pottsville to a 11-11 tie part way through the first period, Pottsville took off to take a 22-16 lead after one period. Coach Ken Kline played many of his bench players during the second and fourth quarters.

Leading scorers: Pottsville – Bob Lengel 24, Ron Morris 21, Talton Alston 17; Phillipsburg – Mickey Zeeman 19, Greg Clymer 16.[19]

Dieruff 76 Phillipsburg 46: Dieruff took advantage of its second straight hapless opponent and improved to 6-0 with a win over Phillipsburg. Dieruff held a significant lead over the rest of the league with every other team having at least two losses. After taking a 15-11 first quarter lead, Dieruff held the Stateliners scoreless from the floor in the second period and outscored them 23-3. With the game never in question, both coaches used 15 players in the game.

Leading scorers: Dieruff – Tom Young 21, George Daskalakes 13, Tim Smith 11, George Eichelberger 11; Phillipsburg – George Hummer 10.

Easton 80 Allen 55: Allen dropped its third in a row, this time to Easton. Easton outscored the Canaries in every period. Both teams stood at 3-3 after Easton's win. Easton scored 31 points in the final period to put an exclamation mark on the victory.

Leading scorers: Easton – Jim Marino 21, Tom Bonstein 17, Bill Eisel 14, Jim Machette 11, Mike MoDavis 10; Allen – Ted Carls 13, Scott Beeten 10.

Pottsville 69 Bethlehem 61: After Bethlehem took a 17-12 lead in the first quarter, Pottsville fought back to take a 26-25 lead with 30 seconds left in the second period. Bethlehem never held the lead again but managed five ties in the third quarter. Bethlehem last tied the game at 55-55 after rallying for six points after trailing 55-49 and the Crimson then took the lead for good.

Leading scorers: Pottsville – Ron Morris 23, Bob Lengle 18, Talton Alston 15; Bethlehem – Dave Bednarik 17, Kirk Melloy 12, John Sydorak 11.

Central Catholic 74 Hazleton 69: Central Catholic made 19 of 27 field goal attempts in the first half to take a 45-33 lead into the locker room. Cutting the lead to four after three periods 57-53, Hazleton pulled even at 57-57 a minute into the 4th quarter, Central Catholic held a 61-59 lead when Hazleton went almost four minutes without a score. The Vikings converted 6 of 8 foul shots in the final 1 ½ minutes for the win.

Leading scorers: Central Catholic – Dave Pfahler 22, Fran Bolez 18, Len Kalata 15, Steve Zarzeka 11; Hazleton – Bob Eigenbrod 23, Bob Solarek 15, Tony Moran 12, Jim Dietrich.[20]

Week 11

Dieruff 80 Bethlehem 55: Lacking height, with the tallest player being 6'1", Dieruff hustled its way to the second half title with an easy victory over Bethlehem. After leading 17-12 with a minute to play in the first quarter, the Huskies held Bethlehem scoreless in the final minute of the quarter and the first 6 ¾ minutes of the second quarter while scoring 16 points of their own to take a 33-12 lead. Bethlehem recovered to trim the Huskies' lead to 38-30 at the half. That was it for the Hurricane as the Huskies came out firing in the third quarter to outscore their opponents 24-12.

Leading scorers: Dieruff – Tom Young 24, George Daskalakes 20, George Eichelberger 15, Ron Schaeffer 15; Bethlehem – John Sydorak 23.

Allen 68 Pottsville 63: In Pottsville, Allen handed the first half champions their third loss of the second half. Pottsville held a lead in each of the first two periods to head into half time with a 38-33 advantage. Allen outscored the Crimson by eight to take a three-point lead into the final quarter. With both teams having high hopes for the second half title hunt, they both stood a 4-3 with a game to play.

Leading scorers: Allen – Charley Haydt 26, Joe Ehritz 11; Pottsville – Ron Morris 24, John Morris 18, Talton Alston 14.

Easton 87 Hazleton 49: Easton continued its resurgence with a 4th straight victory by defeating Hazleton. After the game, both teams stood at 4-3 and were tied with Allen and Pottsville in a four-way tie for third place. Easton took a 24-8 lead in the first quarter and the contest was never in question from that point on.

Leading scorers: Easton – Tom Bonstein 31, Mike MoDavis 15, Bill Eisel 11; Hazleton – Bob Eigenbrod 20.

Phillipsburg 90 Tamaqua 86: Despite scoring 34 points in the fourth quarter, Tamaqua could not overcome the lead built by Phillipsburg over the first three quarters. Easton took a four-point lead 19-15 which proved to be the winning margin as Phillipsburg won the contest. Both teams scored 21 points in the second quarter with Phillipsburg outscoring Tamaqua by 11 in the third period. Tamaqua allowed Phillipsburg to score 23, enough to ensure the victory.

Leading scorers: Phillipsburg – Mickey Zeeman 25, Greg Clymer 21, Steve Jeroloman 18, George Hummer 17; Tamaqua – Bob Fritzinger 24, Ed Lyba 23, George Krell 14, Jack Bassler 10.[21]

Dieruff 82 Allen 81: Dieruff finished off the second half unblemished with their eighth straight victory by squeaking by Allen. The Huskies fell behind 16-3 in the first quarter and had to battle back the rest of the game. Finally, with 2:14 left in the third quarter, The Huskies had their first lead at 55-54. Dieruff fell behind by six 65-59 in the final period before finally taking the lead for good with 1:43 left in the game. Allen finished at 4-4 in the second half.

Leading scorers: Dieruff – Tom Young 29, Ron Schaeffer 15, George Daskalakes 14, George Eichelberger 14; Allen – Joe Ehritz 25, Charley Haydt 20, Ted Carls 19.

Easton 66 Central Catholic 59: Easton fell behind the Vikings 11-0 after the first two minutes of play. After allowing Central Catholic to build this big lead, the Red Rovers worked their way back to only a five-point deficit after the first period 19-14. Trailing by a point after three periods 46-45, Easton took its first lead after 27 seconds of the last quarter 49-48. The lead bounced back and forth until it was tied for the last time at 56-56. Easton outscored the Vikings 10-3 the rest of the way to win 66-59. Both teams finished at 5-3 to tie Pottsville for second place in the half.

Leading scorers: Easton – Tom Bonstein 23, Bill Eisel 16, Jim Marino 13, Phil Lipkin 10; Central Catholic – Dave Pfahler 24, Len Kalata 11.[22]

Bethlehem 70 Tamaqua 41: Visiting Tamaqua lost its eighth contest in the second half to Bethlehem. After trailing 4-2, Bethlehem scored eleven points in a row to take a commanding lead 13-4 later in the first quarter. Tamaqua made only four field goals in the second half. Tamaqua finished with only one league win, which occurred in the first half of the season. Jim Heidecker and Dave Bednarik combined for 25 points in the first half for Bethlehem, two more than Tamaqua as a team was able to score. Twelve players scored for Bethlehem in the game.

Leading scorers: Bethlehem- Dave Bednarik 17, Jim Heidecker 14; Tamaqua- Ed Lyba 14, George Krell 10.

Pottsville 68 Hazleton 63: Coach Ken Kline's Pottsville squad tuned up for the league title game with Dieruff with a come-from-behind victory over Hazleton. Hazleton took a 24-14 lead going into the 2nd quarter. Pottsville battled back to take a lead in the 3rd period only to see Hazleton wipe out the lead and go ahead 63-60. The Mountaineers were held scoreless from that point on as Pottsville scored the last eight points for the win. Ron Morris finished league play with 443 points and a 27.7 points per game average.

Leading scorers: Pottsville– Ron Morris 29, John Morris 16, Talton Alston 12; Hazleton– Bob Eigenbrod 30, Bob Solarek 10.[23]

League Playoff

Pottsville 71 Dieruff 58: At Bethlehem's Memorial Gymnasium, Pottsville ended a 22-year league championship drought to end Dieruff's season. The Huskies essentially lost the game in the first period when Pottsville outscored them 20-8. After trimming the lead to 42-37 midway through the third period,

Ron Morris led a burst to increase the lead to 48-37. The period ended with Pottsville leading 52-40. Pottsville had its first title since 1942.

Leading scorers: Bethlehem – Barry Frey 21, Sal Tavares 20, Pat Howlett 15, Bill Boak 13; Dieruff – Bob Reidy 24, George Eichelberger 11, George Daskalakes 13.[24]

Postseason PIAA Play

Catasauqua 77 Pottsville 69: Returning to Bethlehem's Memorial Gym, Pottsville's Ron Morris battled Catasauqua's Larry Miller in the District 11 semi-final. Catasauqua rolled to an early 17-5 lead but Pottsville held the Roughriders scoreless for about four minutes and narrowed the lead to 17-15 at the quarter. Catasauqua recovered to stretch the lead to 39-33 at the half and 60-51 after three quarters. Pottsville's season ended with the loss to the Roughriders.

Leading scorers: Catasauqua – Larry Miller 25, Walt Panik 18, Ron Crayoski 18; Pottsville – Ron Morris 30, Talton Alston 23, John Morris 11.[25]

Postseason PCIAA Play

Central Catholic 76 Pottsville Nativity 53: Central Catholic began its almost annual foray into the PCIAA playoffs against Pottsville Nativity in the Dieruff gymnasium. Central Catholic held the Pottsville squad to seven and nine points in the first two periods to take a 33-16 half time lead. Pottsville Nativity showed some fight in the 3rd period outscoring the Vikings by three points, but could get no closer than 10 points 37-27.

Leading scorers: Central Catholic – Dave Pfahler 20, Tom Kober 14, Tom Herrity 11, Len Kalata 10; Pottsville Nativity – Ron Matalavage 11.[26]

Central Catholic 61 Notre Dame 45: As in the previous season, Central Catholic took on Notre Dame, this time at the Dieruff gym, for the Allentown Diocese Class A title. Notre Dame battled the Vikings on even terms in the first half and held an 11-8 lead after one period and 25-24 at the half. Central Catholic regrouped in the locker room and came out to outscore the Crusaders 16-5 and take command of the game in the third period. The Crusaders also lost Matt Kacsar, their 6'6 ½" center who was jamming the middle, to personal fouls with three minutes remaining in the third period. The Vikings won the game move into state PCIAA semi-final contest.

Leading scorers: Central Catholic – Dave Pfahler 19, Len Kalata 17; Notre Dame – Len Kelly 12, Woody Badway 11, Denny Posivak 11.[27]

Central Catholic 65 Scranton Prep 52: Central Catholic and Scranton Prep faced off in the Eastern final matchup at Muhlenberg's Memorial Hall. Scranton Prep outscored the Vikings by a single point in each of the first two quarters to take a 27-25 lead at the half. With Steve Zarzeka, who sat for a long period in the first half after getting three quick fouls, leading the Vikings after half time, Central Catholic took a four-point lead at the end of the third quarter. The score was tied three times in the period before the Vikings jumped in front. In the first three minutes of the final period, Central Catholic extended the lead to 10 points and the Vikings cruised into the state final with the win.

Leading scorers: Central Catholic – Len Kalata 18, Tom Herrity 15, Dave Pfahler 10, Fran Bolez 10; Scranton Prep – Joe Cronkey 16, Pat Clark 10.[28]

Central Catholic 59 Pittsburgh Central Catholic 57 2OT: Pittsburgh Central Catholic traveled east to Muhlenberg's Memorial Hall to take on Central Catholic for the PCIAA State Championship. The contest was close all the way with the Vikings taking a 12-10 lead after the first quarter. Pittsburgh cut the lead to one at the half 29-28. With Dave Pfahler getting his fourth personal foul with nearly 4 minutes left in the third, Pittsburgh took advantage of his absence to build a six-point lead heading into the final period. Early in the 4th, the lead was extended to ten 51-41 much to the chagrin of Viking fans. After the Vikings scored to pull within eight 51-43, Dave Pfahler fouled out with six minutes remaining. However, in his absence, Central Catholic scored nine points to move ahead 52-51. With Pittsburgh ahead 54-52 after a foul shot and a field goal, Len Kalata scored the tying basket with seven seconds to play. In the first overtime, the Vikings held the ball for 2 ¼ minutes and then missed a shot. Pittsburgh grabbed the rebound and a long heave at the basket was unsuccessful. The Vikings converted five foul shots out of six attempts in the second overtime to overcome a field goal and foul shot by Pittsburgh to win its seventh state PCIAA title.

Leading scorers: Central Catholic – Len Kalata 17, Steve Zarzeka 16, Dave Pfahler 10; Pittsburgh Central Catholic – Bob Kroner 21, John "Junior" Kennedy 12.[29]

Postseason Accolades

Leading Scorers: Finishing over a hundred points ahead of the closest challenger, Ron Morris scored 443 points and averaged 27.7 points per game. The remaining top ten scorers included: Charley Haydt, 342; Tom Young, Dieruff, 324; Dave Bednarik, Bethlehem, 320; Bob Eigenbrod, Hazleton, 295; Ted Carls, Allen, 262; Dave Pfahler, Central Catholic, 256; Bob Solarek, Hazleton, 252; Tom Bonstein, Easton, 243; and Talton Alston, Easton 231.[30]

All-Star: The league all-star first team included: Ron Morris, Pottsville; Tom Young, Dieruff; Dave Bednarik, Bethlehem; Dave Pfahler, Central Catholic; and Charley Haydt, Allen. The second team consisted of: Talton Alston, Pottsville; Bob Eigenbrod, Hazleton; Ted Carls, Allen; Tom Bonstein, Easton; Len Kalata, Central Catholic; and George Daskalakes, Dieruff.[31]

All-State: Ron Morris, Pottsville, was named to the first team all-state. No other league players were recognized on the all-state team.[32]

Final Standings

First Half		Second Half		Overall	
Pottsville	7-1	Dieruff	8-0	Dieruff	13-3
Central Catholic	6-2	Central Catholic	5-3	Pottsville	12-4
Allen	6-2	Easton	5-3	Central Catholic	11-5
Bethlehem	6-2	Pottsville	5-3	Allen	10-6
Dieruff	5-3	Bethlehem	4-4	Bethlehem	10-6
Hazleton	3-5	Allen	4-4	Hazleton	7-9
Easton	2-6	Hazleton	4-4	Easton	7-9
Phillipsburg	1-7	Phillipsburg	1-7	Phillipsburg	2-14
Tamaqua	0-8	Tamaqua	0-8	Tamaqua	0-16

Team Rosters

Allen: Coach Milo Sewards, Scott Beeten, Ed Boner, Ted Carls, Jim Coker, Joe Ehritz, Bob Follweiler, Joe Geschel, Charlie Haydt, Jim Kozloff, Marc Nissenbaum, Mike Sewards, Rudy Toman, Jim Wescoe

Bethlehem: Coach John Howard, Balutis, Dave Bednarik, Fran Horvath, Jim Heidecker, Jim Kennedy, Walt Kovacs, Gary Lavelle, Kirk Melloy, R. Miller, Tom Mosser, Smith, John Sydorak, Tom Szabo, Paul Taglang, Dwayne Wartman, Wilgruber, Jack Wolfe, Greg Zebrowski

Central Catholic: Coach John Compardo, Julius Amici, Fran Bolez, Rich Deutsch, Ed Ellwood, Jerry Guman, Tom Herrity, Len Kalata, Tom Kober, Dave Pfahler, Steve Zarzeka, Joe Zellin

Dieruff: Coach Dick Schmidt, Jeff Arbogast, Don Burkert, George Daskalakes, George Eichelberger, Jim Finley, John Hanasits, Rich Kindt, Bob Lowe, Ron Schaeffer, Tim Smith, Tom Young

Easton: Coach Tom Sweeney, Karl Bell, Tom Bonstein, Bill Eisel, Dave Kemmerer, Kummer, Phil Lipkin, Jim Machette, Jim Marino, Sal Mentesana, Mike MoDavis, Dave Norwood

Hazleton: Coach Fran Libonati, Chandler, Neil Darrough, Jim Dietrich, Bob Eigenbrod, Richie Fuddy, Jim Girard, Tony Moran, George Sanko, Joe Scitney, Bob Simmons, Bob Solarek, Joe Tito, Joe Ulichny

Phillipsburg: Coach Al Senavitis, Greg Clymer, George Hummer, Steve Jeroloman, Ed Maslonka, B. Miller, R. Miller, Murphy, Dan Roble, Shields, Shive, Snyder, Vega, George West, Mike Zeeman

Pottsville: Coach Larry Haberle, Talton Alston, Ambrose, Lou Chervanek, Ray Heinley, Bob Lengel, John Morris, Ron Morris, Mull, Tom Piccioni

Tamaqua: Coach Eli Purnell, Jack Bassler, Art Connely, Bob Fritzinger, Ted Hafer, George Krell, Allen Lord, Ed Lyba, Art Main, Lee Shafer, Bob Toth, Fred Valent

1965

Dieruff Gets First PIAA Playoff Berth

Week 1

Central Catholic 69 Dieruff 43: Dieruff held a slim one-point lead 10-9 in the opening period of the new season against Central Catholic. The Vikings began to take charge of the game in the second period and moved in front 28-23 at the half. The Vikings dominated the 3rd quarter 13-4 to take 41-27 lead. In a four-minute stretch of the 4th quarter, Central Catholic shutout the Huskies 16-0 to take a whopping 30-point lead. The Viking's Dave Pfahler held the Huskies' high scoring Skip Kintz to 10 points in the game.

Leading scorers: Central Catholic- Dave Pfahler 14, Len Kalata 14, Steve Zarzeka 11, Jerry Guman 10; Dieruff– Skip Kintz 10.

Allen 68 Phillipsburg 55: Phillipsburg took on Allen in the Little Palestra and was only able to stay with the Canaries during the first period with Allen in the lead 15-12. Allen held the Stateliners to eight points in the 2nd period to take a double-digit lead 33-20. With Rudy Toman providing both scoring and rebounding, the Canaries expanded the lead through the late stages of the final period when they took their largest lead 68-49. Phillipsburg finished the game with six straight points. Toman hauled down 26 rebounds for Allen.

Leading scorers: Allen - Rudy Toman 23, Marc Nissenbaum 16; Phillipsburg – Steve Samson 11, George Hummer 10, Bill Dukett 10, Jim Chicerelli 10.

Easton 75 Pottsville 44: After winning the league title last year, Pottsville dropped its fifth game in a row to open the season with its defeat by Easton. With many of the championship squad having graduated, Pottsville could not stay with the Red Rovers despite holding an early 10-9 lead in the first quarter. Easton scored 14 points in a row to take the lead 23-10 and outscored the Crimson 27-7 in the second quarter.

Leading scorers: Easton – Tom Bonstein 20, Sal Mentesana 15, Jim Marino 11, Bill Eisel 10; Pottsville – Tom Shaffer 16, Jack Dolbin 11.

Hazleton 79 Tamaqua 55: At Hazleton, the Mountaineers outscored Tamaqua in every period and led from start to finish. It was Hazleton's fourth win in five games in the early season.

Leading scorers: Hazleton – Bob Solarek 18, Carmen Chandler 17; Joe Tito 17, Neil Darrough 11; Tamaqua – Rich Fritzinger 12, Rich Krepak 12, George Krell 10.[1]

Week 2

Allen 66 Bethlehem 59: Although Bethlehem made six more field goals (24-18), Allen won the game on its performance at the free throw line. The Canaries made 30 of 43 attempts. Bethlehem shot only 17 free throws and made 11 of them. Bethlehem left the floor for half time with a 34-31 lead in a very close half that saw ten lead changes and seven ties. With the game tied in the 4th quarter 57-57, Allen, led by John Washychyn and Rudy Toman, took charge with a 9-point run.

Leading scorers: Allen – Rudy Toman 23, John Washychyn 23, Marc Nissenbaum 11; Bethlehem – Greg Zebrowski 14, John Sydorak 11.

Central Catholic 92 Tamaqua 71: After taking a 20-17 first quarter lead on Gerry Guman's six straight points, Central Catholic saw the lead cut to one 20-19 at the start of the second period. Dave Pfahler went on a scoring rampage with 14 points in the period to give the Vikings a 50-32 halftime lead. Near the end of the third quarter, Pfahler scored on a layup to reach the 1,000-career scoring total.

Leading scorers: Central Catholic – Dave Pfahler 26, Len Kalata 19, Tom Herrity 16, Gerry Guman 10; Tamaqua – George Krell 22, Ed Tomchick 18, Rich Fritzinger 16.

Dieruff 51 Easton 47 OT: Dieruff held a six-point halftime lead 27-21 with Easton never holding a lead. In the third quarter, Easton made a run at the Huskies and cut the lead to one 34-33. The Red Rovers finally took their first lead with about 5 ½ minutes left in the final quarter 39-38. Easton increased the lead to five 45-40 with a little over three minutes left in the game. Easton went into a freeze and the move backfired as the Huskies scored five straight points to tie the game at 45-45. Easton's Tom Bonstein had a chance to win the game in regulation with two foul shots from a foul at the buzzer. After going 5 for 5 at the line, Bontein stunningly missed both shots and the game went into overtime. Huskies went on to win in overtime.

Leading scorers: Dieruff – Skip Kintz 17, George Eichelberger 12; Easton – Tom Bonstein 17.

Hazleton 65 Phillipsburg 53: On its home court, Phillipsburg rallied in the second and third periods but could not overcome the leads built up by Hazleton. In the first quarter with the score tied at 8-8, Hazleton's Rich Fuddy scored the last 9 points of the period for a 17-8 Hazleton lead. Phillipsburg never recovered from this scoring burst. Despite the rallies of eight straight points in the second period and nine straight in the third period by the Stateliners, Hazleton large leads held up for a 65-53 win.

Leading scorers: Hazleton – Bob Solarek 16, Rich Fuddy 15, Neil Darrough 10, Carmen Chandler 10; Phillipsburg – Bill Dukett 15, George Hummer 12.[2]

Week 3

Bethlehem 81 Hazleton 73: At Hazleton's St. Joseph's gym, Bethlehem fought through Hazleton's full court press to take home a surprising 81-73 victory over the Mountaineers. Hazleton lost for the first time after opening the season with eight wins. Hazleton's only leads were early in the first quarter. Bethlehem's Fran Horwath scored six straight points after Hazleton led for the last time 4-3, for a 9-4 lead. Bethlehem increased to lead to 32-17 in the second period before Hazleton rallied back to cut the lead to seven points at the half 44-37. After the Hurricane pulled out to a 52-39 lead in the third quarter, Hazleton rallied with 11 straight points, with Bob Solarek scoring 8 of the points, to make the score 52-50. The Hurricane outscored Hazleton by seven in the final period for the win.

Leading scorers: Bethlehem –Tom Szabo 21, Fran Horwath 16, John Sydorak 14; Hazleton – Bob Solarek 29, Rich Fuddy 14.[3]

Central Catholic 64 Phillipsburg 34: At Rockne Hall, Central Catholic defeated Phillipsburg for its eighth straight win to open the season. After taking a 16-6 first quarter lead, the Vikings outscored Phillipsburg 6-4 in a very slow second quarter. Central Catholic scored 21 points in the last two periods to roll to an easy victory. After Phillipsburg scored the first basket, the Vikings ran off ten straight and Coach John Compardo's team rolled to the easy victory.

Leading scorers: Central Catholic – Dave Pfahler 17, Steve Zarzeka 12; Phillipsburg – Steve Samson 11, Bill Dukett 10.[4]

Dieruff 63 Pottsville 42: In Pottsville, the defending league champions dropped to 0-2 in the league and 1-8 overall with Dieruff's win. Pottsville kept it close for a period, trailing only 15-12, before the Huskies began to roll in the next two periods to hold a 49-28 commanding league going into the final period. In addition to being the game's high scorer, Skip Kintz also grabbed 17 rebounds.

Leading scorers: Dieruff – Skip Kintz 31, Mike Lopsonzski 11, Greg Schmidt 10; Pottsville – Norm Waters 17, Tom Shaffer 13.

Easton 72 Tamaqua 58: After Tamaqua was tied with the Red Rovers in the first period 13-13, Easton ran off a 9-2 streak to end the period and lead 22-15. Easton streaked again in the second period with a run of 14 points to bust out to a 38-16 lead. Tamaqua did outscore Easton in the second half 36-30, but the game was well in Easton's hands at the half.

Leading scorers: Easton – Jim Marino 18, Bill Eisel 14, Tom Bonstein 11, Mike MoDavis 10; Tamaqua – George Krell 26.[5]

Allen 65 Hazleton 61: With the lead changing hands six times in the first period, Allen finally went ahead for good and ended the first period in the lead 18-14. Hazleton made numerous attempts to pull themselves close to the Canaries to no avail. The halftime score was 35-30 in Allen's favor. A seven-point run put the Canaries ahead 59-50 early in the 4th quarter, but the Mountaineers fought back to 61-60. With 17 seconds left in the game, Hazleton had possession of the ball and trailed by two 63-61. They missed their shot at the basket and Allen had the victory. Hazleton's Rich Fuddy pulled down 18 rebounds in his efforts to keep Hazleton close.

Leading scorers: Allen – Rudy Toman 20, Marc Nissenbaum 10, Jim Kozloff 10, John Washychyn 10; Hazleton –Bob Solarek 26, Rich Fuddy 13.

Central Catholic 68 Bethlehem 67: Bethlehem employed a zone defense in their efforts to keep the basketball away from Dave Pfahler and Len Kalata. Coach John Howard's tactics kept Bethlehem close the whole way and propelled them to a 41-39 half time lead. The Vikings trailed by five 50-45 late in the 3rd quarter, but they battled back to take their first lead since the start of the 2nd quarter 53-50. With 1:55 to play, the Vikings led 68-61 to appear to have the game in hand, but the Hurricane scored three quick goals in the last 39 seconds only to lose by a point.

Leading scorers: Central Catholic – Dave Pfahler 17, Steve Zarzeka 17, Len Kalata 13, Gerry Guman 13; Bethlehem – Greg Zebrowski 24, Tom Szabo 12, Paul Taglang 11.

Easton 76 Phillipsburg 63: Easton took command in the first half with leads of 21-12 and 43-25 after the first two quarters. Although Phillipsburg outscored the Red Rovers 38-33 in the second half, the outcome of the game was never in doubt with Easton traveling back across the river with the win. The Stateliners made their second half run by using a pressing defense.

Leading scorers: Easton – Tom Bonstein 17, Mike MoDavis 14, Bill Eisel 13, Jim Marino 13; Phillipsburg – Steve Samson 22, George Hummer 20.

Tamaqua 57 Pottsville 55: Tamaqua won its first league game in four starts and kept Pottsville winless in three starts. Pottsville seemed well on the way to its first victory with leads through each of the first three periods: 18-7, 36-26, and 48-35. Using a press in the fourth quarter, Tamaqua fought back to tie the game at 51-51. At the 55 second mark, Gary Wetterau tapped in a field goal and Tamaqua had the lead for good for a stunning 57-55 win.[5]

Leading scorers: Tamaqua-George Krell 21, Rich Fritzinger 12, Ed Tomchick 11; Pottsville-Tom Shaffer 19, Jack Dolbin 14.[6]

Week 4

Phillipsburg 72 Pottsville 68 OT: Pottsville dropped to 0-5 at the hands of Phillipsburg in overtime. Phillipsburg jumped out to a 21-7 first quarter lead and needed every one of those points to down Pottsville. Pottsville whittled away at the big lead in each of the next three quarters to tie the game with 57 seconds to play in regulation 64-64. George Hummer and Bill Dukett each scored a basket in the final two minutes of overtime for the win. It was Phillipsburg's first win in league play.

Leading scorers: Phillipsburg – Steve Jeroloman 26, Bill Dukett 17, Steve Samson 11, George Hummer 10; Pottsville – Tom Shaffer 21, Norm Waters 20, Jack Dolbin 12.

Central Catholic 82 Allen 46: Central Catholic took sole possession of first place as the league's last unbeaten team. In the trouncing of the Canaries, handing them their first league loss, the Vikings held the Canaries to 10, 10, and 9 points in the first three quarters while they scored seventy points to take a 41-point lead into the final quarter. Coach John Compardo played his second unit during the entire 4th quarter. The Vikings' Dave Pfahler and Len Kalata pulled down 20 and 12 rebounds and both scored in double figures.

Leading scorers: Central Catholic – Len Kalata 13, Dave Pfahler 26; Allen – Rudy Toman 15.

Dieruff 80 Tamaqua 50: Dieruff got off to a 19-9 start after a quarter and doubled up Tamaqua 46-23 at the half. The Huskies' George Eichelberger defended Tamaqua's high-scoring George Krell and held him well below his 20 points per game average at 13 points. With Coach Dick Schmidt using his second unit for most of the 3rd and 4th periods, the Huskies downed Tamaqua to stay in the first half title chase.

Leading scorers: Dieruff – Skip Kintz 22, Jeff Arbogast 13, Greg Schmidt 12, Mike Lopsonzski 10; Tamaqua – Ed Tomchick 14, Rich Fritzinger 13, George Krell 13.

Easton 79 Bethlehem 71: Easton and Bethlehem played a very close game into the fourth quarter with Bethlehem holding two-point leads 13-11 and 30-28 in the first two quarters. Easton took the lead at the three-quarter mark 50-48. With the score tied at 35 in the 3rd quarter, Easton ran off six points. Bethlehem came back to tie the score at 48-48. In the 4th quarter, Easton made 10 of 15 field goal attempts and seven free throws to take the game from Bethlehem.

Leading scorers: Easton – Bill Eisel 21, Mike MoDavis 17, Tom Bonstein 16, Jim Marino 14; Bethlehem – Greg Zebrowski 19, Paul Taglang 19, John Sydorak 13.[7]

Hazleton 71 Central Catholic 65: Coach Fran Libonati's Hazleton squad stunned Central Catholic 71-65 to hand them their first overall and league loss of the season. The Mountaineers took an 18-17 first quarter lead and never trailed despite the game being close the rest of the way. Hazleton's Rich Fuddy held Dave Pfahler to a season-low 11 points. In the third period, Hazleton took an eight-point lead, but the Vikings tied it at 57-57. Hazleton took the lead for good 63-61 with four minutes left in the game.

Leading scorers: Hazleton – Bob Solarek 17, Rich Fuddy 16, Carmen Chandler 15, Joe Tito 14; Central Catholic – Len Kalata 20, Steve Zarzeka 12, Dave Pfahler 11, Fran Bolez 10.

Bethlehem 74 Pottsville 58: Bethlehem used a half court press and fast break to keep Pottsville winless in league play. Pottsville could only convert 4 of 19 foul shots. Pottsville led early 3-2 when Bethlehem ran off 8 points to take a 10-3 lead that they never gave up. Greg Zebrowski scored in double figures and grabbed 20 rebounds in the win.

Leading scorers: Bethlehem – Greg Zebrowski 15, Tom Szabo 12, Fran Horvath 12; Pottsville – Norm Waters 14, Ray Heinly 13, Jack Dolbin 10, Charles Snowell 10.

Dieruff 72 Phillipsburg 50: With Skip Kintz scoring at least 30 points for the fourth game, Dieruff defeated Phillipsburg. Phillipsburg was able to get within five points in the third quarter 33-28, but the Huskies pulled away and a few minutes later ran off seven straight points to put the game away.

Leading scorers: Dieruff – Skip Kintz 30, Mike Lopsonzski 17; Phillipsburg – George Hummer 15, Bill Dukett 14, Steve Sampson 11.

Allen 82 Easton 73: Fifty-seven fouls and several fights marred the contest at the Little Palestra between Allen and Easton. The officials whistled a total of thirty-seven personal fouls and two technical fouls on the Red Rovers, Allen had 20 fouls called. Allen made 30 of 57 foul shot attempts. With 2:45 left in the game, both teams ran onto the floor with fists flying and fans joined in. The police and coaches got the situation under control, but with 11 seconds left, another fight broke out in the stands with the police also halting this altercation. Five Red Rovers fouled out of the game; Bill Eisel left in the third quarter and Dave Kemmer, Mike MoDavis, Tom Bonstein, and Sal Mentesana in the fourth quarter. Allen's John Washychyn played sparingly with a face shield to protect a broken nose suffered in the Central Catholic game. With the score tied 61-61 entering the fourth quarter, Allen made 13 foul shots to pull out to a ten-point lead.

Leading scorers: Allen - Jim Kozloff 23, Barry Nagle 19, Jim Hinman 15, Rudy Toman 14; Easton – Tom Bonstein 25, Mike MoDavis 12, Jim Marino 12, Bill Eisel 10.[8]

Week 5

Allen 71 Pottsville 67: Despite being winless, defending champion Pottsville, on its home court, gave Allen all it could handle for three periods. After playing to a 16-16 tie in the first period, Pottsville took a two-point lead at half time 40-38. Norm Waters made 9 of 10 free throws and a field goal for eleven points in the third period as Pottsville outscored the Canaries 20-13 to take a 60-51 lead into the final quarter. Allen battled hard in the final period and with 24 seconds left in the game, Rudy Toman laid in a shot to give Allen a 69-67 lead. Jim Kozloff converted two foul shots in the final seconds for the win for the Canaries. The win tied them for first place with idle Central Catholic, both at 5-1. Pottsville lost its seventh without a win.

Leading scorers: Allen – Rudy Toman 21, Joe Moore 15, Jim Kozloff 14; Pottsville – Norm Waters 21, Tom Shaffer 19, Lou Chervenak 10, Jack Dolbin 10.

Easton 73 Hazleton 54: After taking a one-point lead into the second quarter, Easton poured it on in the middle quarters outscoring Hazleton 24-14 and 25-9 to take an insurmountable 58-31 lead into the final period. With a slim chance at the first half title, the Red Rovers kept their hopes alive with the domination of the Mountaineers.

Leading scorers: Easton – Bill Eisel 25, Tom Bonstein 19, Jim Marion 11, Mike MoDavis 10; Hazleton – Bob Solarek 17, Carmen Chandler 15, Rich Fuddy 10.

Bethlehem 75 Dieruff 68: Dieruff lost out on its opportunity to share first place with Allen and Central Catholic with a loss to Bethlehem. Dieruff held leads after the first two quarters 20-17 and 37-31. In the third period, the Hurricane put it all together to wipe out the Huskies lead and take a lead of their own 57-52. With 15 seconds left, the Huskies pulled within two points and had possession for an in-bound play. John Sydorak tied up Skip Kintz and Bethlehem won the jump ball to secure the victory.

Leading scorers: Bethlehem – John Sydorak 17, Jack Wolfe 14, Tom Szabo 12; Dieruff – Skip Kintz 21, Don Burkert 17, Mike Lopsonzski 15.[9]

Tamaqua 87 Phillipsburg 68: With each team in search of a second league win, Tamaqua took charge in the second half to improve their record to 2-4. Tamaqua had a ten-point lead in the third period when Phillipsburg ran off eight points to reduce the lead to two 44-42. Tamaqua countered with their own eight point run to regain their 10-point lead 52-42. On their way to the win, Tamaqua led throughout the contest.

Leading scorers: Tamaqua – George Krell 19, Rich Fritzinger 17, Ed Tomchick 16, Long 13; Phillipsburg – Bill Duckett 21, Steve Jeroloman 16, George Hummer 15, Steve Samson 12.[10]

Bethlehem 91 Phillipsburg 51: Bethlehem, with six players in double figures, rolled over Phillipsburg. The Hurricane jumped out to an 8-2 lead and Phillipsburg never got any closer than five points after that, which was 16-11 after one quarter. Bethlehem improved to 4-3 while the Stateliners fell to 1-7.

Leading scorers: Bethlehem – Jack Wolfe 17, John Sydorak 16, Paul Taglang 14, Gene Moore 11, Fran Horwath 11, Tom Szabo 10; Phillipsburg – Steve Samson 14, Bill Dukett 13, Steve Jeroloman 10.

Allen 72 Tamaqua 69: For the second game in a row, Allen faced a test against a lesser opponent in Tamaqua. After falling behind early 12-3, Allen cut the lead to four 17-13 after one quarter. With Barry Nagle scoring 11 points in the second period, Allen rolled to a 38-30 led at the half. After building a 14-

point lead in the third period, Tamaqua fought back to within two points 69-67. Allen held on to win the contest 72-69 and maintain a share of first place with Central Catholic at 6-1.

Leading scorers: Allen – Rudy Toman 19, Joe Moore 17, Barry Nagle 15, Jim Hinman 11; Tamaqua – Rich Fritzinger 21, George Krell 14, Ed Tomchick 11, Gary Wetterau 11.

Central Catholic 80 Pottsville 58: Dave Pfahler scored a personal high of 34 points as Central Catholic rolled to the win over homestanding Pottsville. Pottsville led early 5-3 and 11-10 before the Vikings started to roll. Pottsville did cut the lead to four in the second period 25-21, but the Vikings took charge to lead at the half 39-30. At 6-1, the Vikings shared the lead with Allen. Pottsville remained winless at 0-7.

Leading scorers: Central Catholic – Dave Pfahler 34, Len Kalata 14, Tom Herrity 13; Pottsville – Tom Shaffer 21, Norm Waters 17.

Dieruff 75 Hazleton 49: Prepping for a crucial game with Allen, Dieruff employed a zone defense to take down Hazleton. Holding a 38-30 first half lead, the Huskies put the game away with a 19-6 advantage in the third period. The Huskies scored the last 13 points of the period. Don Burkert thrilled the crowd with a buzzer-beater 60-foot heave to end the half.

Leading scorers: Dieruff – Skip Kintz 24, Don Burkert 15, Greg Schmidt 13; Hazleton – Bob Solarek 19, Dan Gallagher 11.[11]

Week 6

Hazleton 84 Pottsville 72: Hazleton handed Pottsville its eighth loss without a win in the first half. Although Hazleton never trailed, Pottsville did tie the score four times in the third period. After the last tie, Hazleton rallied to take a 13-point lead in the 4th quarter. Pottsville came with six points with 1 ½ minutes to play, but Hazleton prevailed for the win to even their record at 4-4.

Leading scorers: Hazleton – Carmen Chandler 23, Dan Gallagher 19, Bob Solarek 16, Rich Fuddy 15; Pottsville – Tom Shafer 24, Norm Water 19, Ray Heinly 13, Jack Dolbin 10.[12]

Central Catholic 64 Easton 56: Central Catholic won its first league title of any kind with a 4th quarter comeback over Easton. Easton held a 19-16 lead after one period with the Vikings coming back to lead at the half 34-30. Easton assumed the lead after three periods 49-46. The Vikings took the lead 54-53 on a Tom Herrity field goal. Taking advantage of several steals, Central Catholic built the lead to 62-54 on a steal and layup by Herrity.

Leading scorers: Central Catholic –Dave Pfahler 18, Len Kalata 12, Fran Bolez 11, Gerry Guman 10; Easton – Tom Bonstein 15, Dave Kemmerer 12.

Bethlehem 89 Tamaqua 49: Bethlehem cruised to a fourth straight win to finish at 5-3 in the first half with a blistering of Tamaqua. Tamaqua took a 1st quarter lead 13-12 with Bethlehem overtaking them at the half 33-29. In the 3rd period, George Krell cut the Hurricane lead to 37-34, but Bethlehem finished the quarter by scoring the last 28 points for an overwhelming 65-34 advantage.

Leading scorers: Bethlehem – Tom Szabo 19, Jack Wolfe 15, Greg Zebrowski 14, Walt Kovacs 11, Paul Taglang 10; Tamaqua – George Krell 13.

Dieruff 73 Allen 61: In the intracity rivalry, Dieruff came from a seven-point deficit to lead by eight on the strength of Jeff Arbogast's 12 points in the quarter. Allen cut the lead to five 34-29 by half time. Dieruff outscored the Canaries by three in the third and four in the fourth period to win the game. Dieruff's win dropped Allen into a tie for second place. With the expanded PIAA playoffs, the two teams had to play an extra game to decide who would represent the league as the first half second-place team.

Leading scorers: Dieruff – Jeff Arbogast 20, Skip Kintz 19, Don Burkert 17; Allen – Jim Kozloff 18, Barry Nagle 15, Rudy Toman 15.[13]

First Half Playoff

Dieruff 56 Allen 54: Dieruff and Allen met to determine the league representative in the PIAA playoffs as the second-place team in the first half of league play. Dieruff took a 33-25 lead into the locker room at the half. They expanded the lead to nine after three quarters. The Canaries rallied fiercely in the final quarter to finally pull even at 54-54 on field goals by Joe Moore and Jim Kozloff in the final seconds of the game. With Dieruff bringing the ball up court, Jeff Arbogast got off a desperate two-hand shot from 40 feet at the buzzer that bounced twice on the rim before it dropped in for an exasperating victory for the Huskies.

Leading scorers: Dieruff – Skip Kintz 23, Jeff Arbogast 15; Allen – Rudy Toman 21, Jim Kozloff 11, Joe Moore 10.[14]

Second Half - Week 7

Hazleton 71 Pottsville 65: In Pottsville, Hazleton handed the Crimson their 9th consecutive league loss. Pottsville's overall record dropped to 1-14 while Hazleton improved to 10-5. Pottsville stayed even with the Mountaineers in the first half. They held a 14-13 lead after a quarter, but dropped a point behind at the half 33-32. Hazleton maintained the one-point lead through most of the third quarter with the score being 46-45 late in the period. Hazleton ran off six points to take a seven-point lead after three quarters 54-47.

Leading scorers: Hazleton – Bob Solarek 19, Dan Gallagher 18, Joe Tito 13; Pottsville – Tom Shaffer 31, Jack Dolbin 15.[15]

Bethlehem 69 Tamaqua 67: Bethlehem's Jack Wolfe converted two foul shots with six seconds to play to secure the win. After leading 19-15 after one period, Tamaqua took the lead 24-23 five minutes into the second period. Bethlehem fought back for a six-point lead at the half 39-33. Tamaqua cut the lead in half 52-49 entering the final quarter. After trailing by nine 60-51, Tamaqua tied the game at 67-67 with 30 seconds left in the game.

Leading scorers: Bethlehem – John Sydorak 18, Greg Zebrowski 16, Jack Wolfe 14, Tom Szabo 10; Tamaqua –Bob Fritzinger 22, Rich Krepak 17, George Krell 13.

Central Catholic 74 Easton 61: Although the game was tight through three quarters, Easton last held a lead at 14-13 in the first quarter. The Vikings led at the end of the quarter 19-16. The Red Rovers shaved a point off the lead at the half with the score 35-33. With the Vikings leading 49-44, they ran off six straight points to begin the fourth period and Easton did not threaten again.

Leading scorers: Central Catholic – Steve Zarzeka 21, Dave Pfahler 14, Len Kalata 14, Gerry Guman 11; Easton – Bill Eisel 21, Tom Bonstein 20, Jim Marino 10.[16]

Dieruff 79 Allen 47: Playing each other for the third time in five days, Dieruff defeated Allen by a lopsided score of 79-47. Dieruff fired out to a 20-6 first quarter advantage only to have the Canaries fight back to cut the lead to 31-26 at the half, fueled by a 13-2 run. Dieruff opened the third quarter with six straight points and Allen did not threaten after the Huskies took an eleven-point lead 37-26. With Skip Kintz scoring a career-high, he gave the Canaries fits causing Joe Moore to foul out of the game in the third period.

Leading scorers: Dieruff – Skip Kintz 36, Jeff Arbogast 16; Allen – Rudy Toman 13.[17]

Week 8

Hazleton 86 Tamaqua 68: Hazleton ran its second half record to 2-0 with a defeat of Tamaqua. Tamaqua held a first quarter lead 23-19 before Hazleton came back to tie it at the half 33-33. In the third quarter, the Tams took a one-point lead 41-40, but Hazleton surged to take a 61-49 advantage into the final period. Tamaqua's 6'4" center Ed Tomchick did not play due to injury and Bob Fritzinger sat out a full quarter due to foul trouble.

Leading scorers: Hazleton – Bob Solarek 23, Carmen Chandler 18, Joe Tito 14, Rich Fuddy 13; Tamaqua – Bob Fritzinger 15, Gary Wetterau 16, George Krell 15, Rich Krepak 13

Central Catholic 45 Dieruff 36: In an effort to slow down the fast-breaking Vikings, Dieruff maintained a methodical pace which kept them in the game. The Huskies were within two points 28-26 on the third period, but went scoreless for eight minutes at the end of the 3rd quarter and well into the final quarter allowing the Vikings to pull out the win. In the second quarter, driven by Skip Kintz's scoring, Dieruff had built a five-point lead before the Vikings rallied to take a 21-17 half time lead.

Leading scorers: Central Catholic – Gerry Guman 15, Tom Herrity 13; Dieruff – Skip Kintz 14.

Easton 76 Pottsville 67: After staying with Easton through the first half 34-30, Pottsville could not keep up with the Red Rovers in the third period and were outscored 23 to 11. Pottsville tried to rally in the fourth but could not overcome the 16-point lead built in the third quarter. Easton handed Pottsville its tenth straight loss in league play.

Leading scorers: Easton – Jim Marino 23, Tom Bonstein 22, Bill Eisel 11, Mike MoDavis 10; Pottsville – Tom Shaffer 21, Norm Waters 19, Jack Dolbin 13.[18]

Allen 75 Phillipsburg 68: Allen evened its record at 1-1 in the second half with a relatively easy victory. Early in the game with Allen holding a slim one-point lead 11-10, the Canaries scored 15 straight points and another string of 9 points to take the sizeable advantage into the locker room. Allen held a 45-28 half time lead. Against Coach Milo Sewards' reserves in the 4th quarter, Phillipsburg ran off a string of 16 points to make the score more respectable. Rudy Toman and Joe Moore each grabbed 17 rebounds each in the game.

Leading scorers: Allen – Rudy Toman 19, Marc Nissenbaum 14, Joe Moore 12; Phillipsburg – Steve Jeroloman 25, Bill Dukett 14, Bob Miller 11.

Bethlehem 88 Allen 58: At the Little Palestra, Bethlehem surprised Allen with a pasting of the Canaries to move to 2-0 in the second half. Allen found Bethlehem's zone defense to be impenetrable while their own man-to-man defense couldn't stop the Hurricane. Leading 24-21 early in the second period, Bethlehem ran off 11 straight points to take an insurmountable lead. In the final quarter, they strung together another 8 points to go up 71-45.

Leading scorers: Bethlehem – John Sydarak 22, Jack Wolfe 16, Fran Horwath 15, Paul Taglang 12, Tom Szabo 10; Allen – Rudy Toman 26, Joe Moore 12.

Dieruff 80 Easton 60: At Easton, Coach Dick Schmidt's Huskies trailed Easton 28-25 with two minutes to play in the second quarter. They scored the next seven points to take a 34-30 lead into half time. Dieruff's assault continued in the second half with the Huskies scoring 46 points to the Red Rovers 30 to give Dieruff the win and improve to 2-1 in the second half. Skip Kintz continued his drive towards the Dieruff season scoring record of 456 held by Tom Young, finishing nine points short.

Leading scorers: Dieruff – Skip Kintz 27, Greg Schmidt 15, Don Burkert 13, Jeff Arbogast 10, George Eichelberger 10; Easton – Tom Bonstein 23, Sal Mentesana 13.

Central Catholic 50 Tamaqua 36: Playing on their home court, Central Catholic got an early scare from Tamaqua when the Tams took a first quarter lead 13-12. Central Catholic took the lead by half time 28-23.

The Vikings resorted to a possession slowdown-type offense to pull out the game. The Vikings held the Tams to three points in the final period while only scoring ten. Tamaqua played the game without Bob Fritzinger due to illness, while the Vikings used Dave Pfahler very sparing also due to illness. The win tied the Vikings with Hazleton for first place, both at 3-0.

Leading scorers: Central Catholic – Fran Bolez 14, Len Kalata 12; Tamaqua – George Krell 17.

Hazleton 91 Phillipsburg 58: Hazleton held Phillipsburg to three foul shots in the first quarter to take charge of the game early with a 20-3 lead after a period. Phillipsburg finally scored a field goal 12 seconds into the second quarter. Hazleton led 40-18 at the half. Rich Fuddy grabbed 20 rebounds along with scoring in double figures. The Mountaineers 3-0 start tied them with Central Catholic for the second half lead with Bethlehem a half game behind at 2-0.

Leading scorers: Hazleton – Bob Solarek 28, Joe Tito 19, Rich Fuddy 14, Carmen Chandler 10; Phillipsburg – George Hummer 17, Steve Jeroloman 15, Bill Dukett 15.[20]

Week 9

Dieruff 68 Pottsville 47: Playing on his home court, Skip Kintz broke the school's single season scoring record by boosting his total to 478 points. Kintz hit 10 of 18 field goals and 11 of 12 free throws along with 14 rebounds. Winless Pottsville scored the first 6 points in the contest before the Huskies got it going with 8 straight points to take a lead they never lost. The Huskies held Pottsville to 7 points in the second period.

Leading scorers: Dieruff – Skip Kintz 31; Pottsville – Tom Shaffer 21.

Bethlehem 65 Hazleton 65: In a battle crucial to the second half title chase, Bethlehem eked out a one-point win over Hazleton. Jack Wolfe made two free throws with 15 seconds left to improve the Hurricane's record to 3-0. Hazleton dropped to 3-1. Hazleton led early in the first period only to see Bethlehem take a nine-point lead in the second period. With Bethlehem leading most of the game, Hazleton charged in front again at 60-58 with 2:15 to play when Bob Solarek dropped in two foul shots. They led again at 62-60 before Bethlehem countered with foul shots of their own to produce the victory.

Leading scorers: Bethlehem – Tom Szabo 24, John Sydorak 14, Fran Horwath 12; Hazleton – Bob Solarek 23, Rich Fuddy 14, Dan Gallagher 12.

Easton 79 Tamaqua 70: Easton kept Tamaqua winless in the second half of league play. After trailing 17-16 due to a George Krell half-court shot at the buzzer, Easton burst out with 26 points in the second period to take 42-35 half time lead. Tamaqua pulled within seven points 73-66 when Bob Fritzinger went to the bench with an injured wrist and Gary Wetterau fouled out.

Leading scorers: Easton – Bill Eisel 25, Tom Bonstein 20, Mike MoDavis 13, Sal Mentesana 12; Tamaqua – Rich Krepak 15, George Krell 15, Ed Tomchick 13, Bob Fritzinger 10, Long 10.

Central Catholic 76 Phillipsburg 46: At Phillipsburg, Central Catholic took a half game lead over Bethlehem with a 4-0 record by defeating the Stateliners. With the Vikings taking 21-12 lead after one period, they rolled to the victory in a game where Phillipsburg never really threatened. The Vikings also defeated Phillipsburg by 30 points in first half play.

Leading scorers: Central Catholic – Dave Pfahler 31, Tom Herrity 13, Len Kalata 12; Phillipsburg – Steve Jeroloman 24, Steve Samson 10.[21]

Hazleton 86 Allen 79: At Hazleton, in a hard-fought game, Allen held the lead over the Mountaineers until the third period. The Canaries held a slim 41-39 lead at the half. After three quarters, the score was tied at 42-42. With Hazleton leading 79-77 with 45 seconds to play, Rich Fuddy and Bob Solarek each scored a field goal and Solarek added a foul shot.

Leading scorers: Hazleton – Bob Solarek 25, Joe Tito 17, Rich Fuddy 14, Carmen Chandler 11; Allen – Joe Moore 21, Rudy Toman 17, John Washychyn 10.[22]

Central Catholic 59 Bethlehem 58: Both undefeated in second half play, Central Catholic took on Bethlehem for sole possession of first place with a 5-0 record. With the Vikings leading by ten points 50-40 in the fourth quarter, Bethlehem roared back outscoring the Vikings 14-2 to take a 58-55 lead with 41 seconds left in the game. Dave Pfahler drained a shot with 19 seconds left. Bethlehem's down court pass went out-of-bounds. Gaining possession of the ball, the Vikings took the victory when Tom Herrity fed Len Kalata driving to the basket for the winning layup and the game 59-58.

Leading scorers: Central Catholic – Dave Pfahler 19, Len Kalata 19, Jerry Guman 11; Bethlehem – Fran Horwath 16, Greg Zebrowski 11, Tom Szabo 11, Paul Taglang 10.

Easton 79 Phillipsburg 61: After being tied 6-6, Easton scored 14 consecutive points on their way to a 22-8 lead after a period and rolled to a triumph over winless Phillipsburg. The Red Rovers had eight-point runs in the 2nd and 3rd periods to take a 62-39 lead into the final period. Easton improved to 3-2 in league play.

Leading scorers: Easton – Tom Bonstein 21, Mike MoDavis 18, Dave Kemmerer 15; Phillipsburg – Bill Dukett 20.

Tamaqua 70 Pottsville 57: In a battle of winless teams in second half play, Tamaqua pulled out of a three-way tie for last place by keeping Pottsville winless. Pottsville was held to eight points in the second period and never recovered. Tamaqua took a 57-33 lead into the final period.

Leading Scorers: Tamaqua – George Krell 17, Ed Tomchick 17, Bob Fritzinger 11; Pottsville – Tom Shaffer 22, Norm Waters 10.[23]

Week 10

Dieruff 83 Tamaqua 63: On their home court, Tamaqua took a four-point lead 20-16 in the opening period and held onto it at the half 42-38 over Dieruff. The Huskies finally pulled even at 48-48 with a little over three minutes gone in the third period. With the score tied at 50-50, Skip Kintz scored five straight points for a 55-50 lead and the Huskies led for good. The Huskies scored ten points in a row in the final period to move in front 65-50. At the four-minute mark of the period, the Tams lost Bob Fritzinger, Ed Tomchick, and George Krell on fouls in the space of 20 seconds. The Huskies won to move to 6-0.

Leading scorers: Dieruff –Skip Kintz 35, Don Burkert 13; Tamaqua – Ed Tomchick 10, Bob Fritzinger 10, George Krell 21.

Bethlehem 67 Easton 66: In Bethlehem, Easton made a gallant effort against Bethlehem only to lose the game in the last three seconds. The Red Rovers held leads at the end of each of the first three quarters with a 13-point lead at the half and a 10-point lead early in the 4th quarter. Bethlehem furiously rallied to cut the lead to one-point 64-63 and 66-65 with under a minute to play. Fran Horwath made two free throws with three seconds to play to the frustration of Easton. After the foul shots, benches emptied in a short-lived fight with fans joining in. Police dispersed the crowd and had to escort the Easton bus out of Bethlehem.

Leading scorers: Bethlehem – Greg Zebrowski 16, Paul Taglang 16, Joe Moore 13; Easton – Tom Bonstein 19, Mike MoDavis 16, Jim Marino 13, Dave Kemmerer 10.

Central Catholic 92 Allen 79: Central Catholic dropped Allen to 1-4 while extending their own record to 6-0 with a put down of Allen at the Little Palestra. After taking a 24-16 lead after one quarter, Allen cut the lead to 42-38 at the half. From late in the first period into the second period, Allen outscored the Vikings 13-1 to take a brief 29-27 lead. The Vikings outscored Allen 50-41 in the second half.

Leading scorers: Central Catholic – Dave Pfahler 37, Fran Bolez 13, Gerry Guman 12, Tom Herrity 11; Allen -Joe Moore 16, Jim Hinman 14, Jim Kozloff 12, Rudy Toman 11.[24]

Phillipsburg 82 Pottsville 70: Phillipsburg moved out of the league basement with its triumph over Pottsville, the only remaining winless team. Phillipsburg won the game due to a 25-14 advantage in the 3rd period.

Leading scorers: Phillipsburg – Bill Dukett 26, Steve Jeroloman 16, Bob Miller 16; Pottsville – Tom Shaffer 22, Jim Walters 20, Jack Flannery 17.[25]

Dieruff 78 Phillipsburg 64: Despite having on a single victory in the second half, Phillipsburg showed some fight against Dieruff. Despite never holding a lead, Phillipsburg kept the game close and forced the Huskies to battle them for the win. The win kept Dieruff's slim hopes alive for a second half title.

Leading scorers: Dieruff – Skip Kintz 31, Jeff Arbogast 13, Don Burkert 12; Phillipsburg – George Hummer 16, Steve Jeroloman 16, Bill Dukett 12.

Easton 93 Allen 61: Easton routed Allen to drop the Canaries to 1-5 and improve their record to 4-3. With Easton leading 12-10, Coach Tom Sweeny's team went on a 12-1 outburst to take a commanding 24-11 first quarter lead. Easton expanded the lead in each quarter to avenge a first half loss to the Canaries.

Leading scorers: Easton – Jim Marino 10, Dave Kemmerer 10, Tom Bonstein 20, Mike MoDavis 20, Bill Eisel 21; Allen – Rudy Toman 25, Jim Kozloff 12.

Bethlehem 81 Pottsville 69: Bethlehem handed the defending league champions their 14th consecutive league loss in league play. Bethlehem improved to 5-1. Pottsville stayed close trailing by only two points at the half 38-36. The Hurricane extended the lead to 56-42 late in the third period.

Leading scorers: Bethlehem – John Sydarak 17, Fran Horwath 16, Jack Wolfe 12, Joe Moore 10; Pottsville – Jim Walters 27, Jack Dolbin 19, Tom Shaffer 11.[26]

Central Catholic 88 Hazleton 50: Central Catholic avenged its only loss of the season on its home floor by outclassing Hazleton and moved to 7-0 with a game to go against winless Pottsville. After holding a 4-point lead after a quarter, the Vikings outscored the Mountaineers 41-17 in the middle quarters to put the game out of reach. In the 4th quarter, the Vikings doubled the score 88-44 before Hazleton scored the last six points of the game.

Leading scorers: Central Catholic – Dave Pfahler 24, Fran Bolez 19, Len Kalata 14, Tom Herrity 14, Gerry Guman 11; Hazleton –Bob Solarek 17.[27]

Week 11

Dieruff 66 Bethlehem 61: Down six points in the final period, Skip Kintz scored 15 of his game-high 36 points to pull out a win for Dieruff over Bethlehem. After trailing 20-12 after the first period, Bethlehem held the Huskies to six second quarter points to take a 28-26 lead into the locker room. Leading 47-43 heading into the final period, they extended the lead to six on a Jack Wolfe field goal. The Huskies scored the next eight points to take the lead and go on to the victory.

Leading scorers: Dieruff-Skip Kintz 36, Jeff Arbogast 10; Bethlehem-Greg Zebrowski 17, John Sydorak 13, Fran Horwath 11.

Allen 87 Pottsville 70: After losing four in a row, Allen snapped its losing streak against winless Pottsville. Allen took the first quarter lead and led to the finish. Pottsville got within six points in the second period when the Canaries went nearly three minutes with only one foul shot to show for their efforts.

Leading scorers: Allen – Joe Moore 23, Rudy Toman 18, Barry Levine 12, Jim Kozloff 11; Pottsville – Norm Waters 21, Jim Walters 18, Jack Dolbin 10.

Hazleton 69 Easton 67: In Hazleton, the Mountaineers pulled out a narrow victory over Easton. The Red Rovers held a nine-point lead 25-16 in the second period when Hazleton scored 15 of the next 19 points to take a 31-29 lead. Easton recovered and went into half time with a 36-34 lead. The teams played even in the third period with each scoring 16 points. Rich Fuddy scored six points late to put Hazleton in the lead and his two foul shots with 57 seconds left won the game.

Leading scorers: Hazleton – Joe Tito 17, Carmen Chandler 17, Bob Soloarek 16, Rich Fuddy 14; Easton – Tom Bonstein 22, Mike MoDavis 20, Bill Eisel 15.

Tamaqua 71 Phillipsburg 50: In a low-scoring first half, Tamaqua and Phillipsburg played to a 23-23 tie with neither team holding more than a three-point lead. Coming out of the locker room, Tamaqua ran off the first 8 points. After Steve Jeroloman scored four straight points for the Stateliners, Tamaqua ran off six more points to take third quarter lead to 35-25. The game was never close after that.

Leading scorers: Tamaqua – George Krell 20, Rich Krepak 15, Bob Fritzinger 15, Ed Tomchick 10; Phillipsburg – Steve Jeroloman 14, Bill Dukett 12, Jim Chicerelli 12.[28]

Allen 64 Tamaqua 59: Senior Jim Kozloff, scoring 19 points in the first half of his last game for the Canaries, led Allen to a fast start out-of-the-gate as the Canaries took 21-6 first quarter and 39-21 first half leads over Tamaqua. Tamaqua responded in the second half outscoring Allen 20-9 in the third period and 18-15 in the final period. The lead was too great with the Tams falling to the Canaries. Tamaqua played without George Krell, who injured his ankle in practice.

Leading scorers: Allen – Jim Kozloff 25, Rudy Toman 12; Tamaqua – Ed Tomchick 15, Rich Krepak 14.

Central Catholic 73 Pottsville 51: With an eighth straight win in the second half over winless Pottsville, Central Catholic won its first league title in the seventeen years in the league. The win had to be earned as Pottsville rallied from a 12-point deficit in the second quarter to lead at half time 31-30 over the Vikings. After regrouping at half time, Central Catholic outscored Pottsville 22-9 and 21-11 in the last 2 quarters to win the game and their first league title.

Leading scorers: Central Catholic - Len Kalata 25, Dave Pfahler 17, Steve Zarzeka 11; Pottsville - Jim Walters 17, Norm Waters 14.

Bethlehem 80 Phillipsburg 41: Bethlehem held Phillipsburg to eleven points in each of the first three quarters and eight in the final period to defeat the Stateliners. Bethlehem led at half time 45-22. Coach Johnny Howard used 15 players in the game with all but two of them scoring in the game. Bethlehem finished the season at 16-6 overall and 12-4 in the league.

Leading scorers: Bethlehem – Greg Zebrowski 13, Fran Horwath 12; Phillipsburg – Steve Jeroloman 8, Bill Dukett 8.

Dieruff 54 Hazleton 52 4OT: With Central Catholic ineligible for PIAA play, Dieruff captured its first ever PIAA playoff berth. The Huskies needed 4 overtimes to defeat Hazleton. In the second period, Dieruff trailed by eleven at one point 24-13 and were behind 31-28 at the half. The Huskies finally caught Hazleton with 3:39 to play in the third period and went ahead 41-39. With 1:20 to play, the Huskies led by four but Joe Tito's two foul shots and a Carmen Chandler field goal with five seconds to play tied the game at 50-50. Neither team scored in the first and third overtime. In the second overtime, Joe Tito made two free throws, but Skip Kintz hit a field goal to tie the game again at 52-52. Greg Schmidt scored the only points in the fourth overtime with a tap-in of a missed shot at the buzzer.

Leading scorers: Dieruff – Skip Kintz 22; Hazleton –Bob Solarek 13, Carmen Chandler 12, Rich Fuddy 10, Joe Tito 10.[29]

Postseason PIAA Play

Mahanoy Area 71 Dieruff 63: Dieruff's first ever playoff opportunity was short-lived. The Huskies took on Mahanoy Area at Muhlenberg's Memorial Hall. In their sixth straight appearance in the District 11 playoffs, Mahanoy Area defeated the Huskies to make it to the district championship game for the first time. The game was close with Mahanoy Area leading at half time 34-32. Dieruff did tie the game briefly in the third period 40-40. Mahanoy Area pulled away at the end of the third period when they scored five points in 32 seconds to lead heading into the fourth quarter 51-44. Dieruff finished the season at 20-4.

Leading scorers: Mahanoy Area – Stan Wlodarczyk 23, Billy Pilconis 16, Whitey Markosky 14; Dieruff – Skip Kintz 22, Greg Schmidt 14, George Eichelberger 13.[30]

Postseason PCIAA Play

Central Catholic 69 Notre Dame 35: Central Catholic opened postseason PCIAA play against Notre dame at Bethlehem Catholic's new gymnasium. With a week off, the Vikings started slowly as they did not score a field goal for nearly four minutes and had trouble handling the ball. Once they got going, Notre Dame was no match for the Vikings. After taking a 17-10 first quarter lead, Central Catholic held the Crusaders to 6 points in the second period and 5 in the third. The Vikings held Notre Dame to three field goals in the second half with two coming in the last 14 seconds of the game.

Leading scorers: Central Catholic – Len Kalata 23, Dave Pfahler 18; Notre Dame – Steve Polaha 8.[32]

Central Catholic 96 Pottsville Nativity 53: At the Pottsville High gym, Pottsville Nativity did not have much more success against Central Catholic than Notre Dame did the previous game. The Vikings took off with a 20-9 first quarter lead and increased it to 51-19 at the half. The Vikings had 18 steals in the game and made 36 of 54 free throw attempts.

Leading scorers: Central Catholic – Fran Bolez 22, Len Kalata 21, Dave Pfahler 15, Jack Johnson 14; Pottsville Nativity – Dale Clouser 16.[33]

Central Catholic 67 Kingston Catholic 51: Central Catholic and Kingston Catholic Queensmen faced off in the Eastern final Scranton's Catholic Youth Center. Although the Vikings led the game the whole way, Kingston Catholic constantly kept pressure on the Vikings. Gerry Guman held the Queensmen high scorer Dan Green without a field until near the end of the third quarter. He was then assigned to guard Kingston's Jim Williams who had scored 20 points in the game and he blanked him the rest of the way. The Vikings had leads of 18-10, 28-21, and 46-35 in the first three quarters leading the win and a spot in the state PCIAA finals yet again.

Leading scorers: Central Catholic – Dave Pfahler 22, Gerry Guman 18, Len Kalata 10; Kingston Catholic – Jim Williams 20.[34]

South Hill 64 Central Catholic 60: At the Pitt fieldhouse, South Hills took on Central Catholic for the PCIAA State Championship. Taking a 21-14 first quarter lead, the South Hills advantage from the first quarter led them to the championship win over the Vikings. The Vikings outscored South Hills 46-43 the rest of the way, but the seven-point first period lead was enough for the victory. Early in the second quarter, the Vikings pulled with a point 21-20 after scoring six straight points to open the quarter. But the Vikings could not score another field goal for 4 ½ minutes and the Viking threat ended. Although he only scored seven points in the game, Dave Pfahler ended his Viking career with a school record 1,327 points.

Leading scorers: South Hills – Hank South 30, Dave Litz 10; Central Catholic – Len Kalata 23.[35]

Postseason Accolades

Leading scorers: The scoring race was another runaway with Dieruff's Skip Kintz scoring 406 points for a 25.4 points per game (ppg) average and an 83 point and 5.2 ppg lead over the second-place scorer Bob Solarek of Hazleton who scored 323 points on the season. He was the only other player to average over 20 ppg with a 20.2 average. The remaining top ten scorers included: Dave Pfahler, Central Catholic, 315; Tom

Bonstein, Easton, 307; Rudy Toman, Allen, 291; Tom Shaffer, Pottsville, 277; George Krell, Tamaqua, 256; Len Kalata, Central Catholic, 225; Bill Dukett, Phillipsburg 220; Norm Waters, Pottsville, and Steve Jeroloman, Phillipsburg, 208.[36]

All-Stars: The league all-star first team included: Skip Kintz, Dieruff; Tom Bonstein, Easton; Dave Pfahler, Central Catholic; Len Kalata, Central Catholic; and Charley Haydt, Allen. The second team consisted of: Greg Zebrowski, Bethlehem; Jim Kozloff, Allen; Jeff Arbogast, Dieruff; Bill Eisel, Easton; Rich Fuddy, Hazleton; Mike MoDavis, Easton; and Norm Eaters, Pottsville.[37]

All-State: Dave Pfahler, Central Catholic, and Skip Kintz, Dieruff, were named to the third team all-state. Tom Bonstein, Easton, was named to the fourth team. Bob Solarek, Hazleton was named Honorable Mention.[37]

Final Standings

First Half		Second Half		Overall	
Central Catholic	7-1	Central Catholic	8-0	Central Catholic	15-1
Allen	6-2	Dieruff	7-1	Dieruff	13-3
Dieruff	6-2	Bethlehem	6-2	Bethlehem	11-5
Bethlehem	5-3	Hazleton	5-3	Allen	9-7
Easton	5-3	Easton	4-4	Easton	9-7
Hazleton	4-4	Allen	3-5	Hazleton	9-7
Tamaqua	2-6	Tamaqua	2-6	Tamaqua	4-12
Phillipsburg	1-7	Phillipsburg	1-7	Phillipsburg	2-14
Pottsville	0-8	Pottsville	0-8	Pottsville	0-16

Team Rosters

Allen: Coach Milo Sewards, Berger, Crum, Heffner, Jim Hinman, Jim Kozloff, Barry Levine, Joe Michael, Joe Moore, Barry Nagle, Marc Nissenbaum, Sarmir, Rudy Toman, John Washychyn, Tim Weeg, Ken Wildonger

Bethlehem: Coach John Howard, Hartzell, Fran Horvath, Kennedy, Walt Kovacs, Gary Lavelle, Gene Moore, Smith, John Sydorak, Tom Szabo, Paul Taglang, Jack Wolfe, Greg Zebrowski

Central Catholic: Coach John Compardo, Fran Bolez, Pete Bucha, Ricco Caggiano, David Egge, Ed Ellwood, Gerry Guman, Tom Herrity, Jack Johnson, Len Kalata, Dave Pfahler, William Samer, Walt Witkowski, Steve Zarzeka, Joe Zellin

Dieruff: Coach Dick Schmidt, Jeff Arbogast, Bauer, Blount, Don Burkert, Carl, George Eichelberger, Jim Finley, Dan Kemeter, Skip Kintz, Mike Lopsonzski, Saylor, Greg Schmidt

Easton: Coach Tom Sweeney, Tom Bonstein, Bill Eisel, Matt Ewadinger, Hartman, Steve Hutnik, Karam, Dave Kemmerer, Jim Marino, Sal Mentesana, B Meyers, Charlie Meyers, Miller, Mike MoDavis

Hazleton: Coach Fran Libonati, Bast, Carmen Chandler, Neil Darrough, Lou Fiore, Rich Fuddy, Dan Gallagher, Mike Glezman, Joe Scitney, Bob Solarek, Joe Tito, Joe Ulichny, Williams

Phillipsburg: Coach Al Senavitis, Jim Chicerelli, Greg Clymer, Bill Dukett, George Hummer, Steve Jeroloman, Bob Miller, Murphy, Steve Samson, Shane, Dick Spears

Pottsville: Coach Ken Kline, Lou Chervanek, Keith Curtier, Jack Dolbin, Jack Flannery, Joseph Garland, Ray Heinley, Robert Mull, Tom Shafer, Doug Snowell, Thomas Waite, Jim Walters, Norm Waters, William Weber

Tamaqua: Coach Hugh Hoke, Baddick, Ed Brode, Art Connely, Bob Fritzinger, George Krell, Rich Krepak, Davel Long, Art Main, John Mateyak, Lee Schafer, Ed Tomchick, Bob Toth, Gary Wetterau

Central Catholic High School – 1965 League Champions[31]

Front: Steve Zarzeka, Fran Bolez, Len Kalata, Dave Pfahler, Tom Herrity, Gerry Guman

Back: Dave Egge (mgr), Pete Bucha, Walt Witkowski, Ed Ellwood, Joe Zellin, Jack Johnson, Rico Caggiano, William Samer (mgr), Coach Compardo

1966

Dieruff Cops First League Title

First Half - Week 1

Tamaqua 81 Central Catholic 70: Tamaqua took on the defending league champions at Rockne Hall to open league play. The Vikings took a six-point lead into the second period. Tamaqua came back to tie the game at 36-36 at half time. The game, still close at the end of three 53-52, saw eleven lead changes and eleven ties. Central Catholic led 59-58 with six minutes to play in the game. George Krell, who averaged 36 ppg coming into the contest, was held to only four field goals in the first three quarters. He suddenly got hot in the final quarter and hit five decisive field goals in the 4th quarter to lead Tamaqua to the victory.

Leading scorers: Tamaqua – George Krell 20, Rich Krepak 17, Art Connely 13, Paul Long 12, John Mateyak 10; Central Catholic – Ed Ellwood 25, Jack Johnson 23, Joe Kramer 12.

Bethlehem 80 Allen 67: After going 1-2 in the preseason, Bethlehem opened league play against Allen at the Little Palestra. After a close first period with Bethlehem in the lead 17-16, the Hurricane took command of the game in the second period to hold a 38-30 lead at the half. Midway through the third period, Bethlehem built the lead to 17 before Allen came back to cut the lead to six with 3:22 to go in the game. Bethlehem halted Allen's comeback to win the game.

Leading scorers: Bethlehem – Fran Horwath 34, Paul Albino 24; Allen – Joe Moore 16, Barry Levine 16, Barry Nagle 12.

Dieruff 80 Easton 51: Easton took a first quarter lead, but the rest of the game was all Dieruff with the Huskies taking charge in the second by outscoring the Red Rovers 22-10. In the middle of the second period, Easton took a short-lived 22-21 lead before the Huskies reeled off eleven points in a row to take a 32-22 half time lead. Dieruff really put the game away in the final period by scoring 30 points to Easton's 13.

Leading scorers: Dieruff – Skip Kintz 28, Mike Lopsonzski 15, Greg Schmidt 14, Jan Kapcala 11; Easton – Tom Fisher 11, Charlie Meyers 10.[1]

Hazleton 96 Phillipsburg 61: Hazleton's Joe Marnell scored the game's first eight points on three field goals and two foul shots to propel the Mountaineers to a 25-9 first quarter lead over Phillipsburg. With six players in double figures, Hazleton easily downed Coach Al Senavitis' squad. Coach Fran Libonati used 13 players in the game and played many of the substitutes beginning in the second quarter.

Leading scorers: Hazleton – Rich Fuddy 17, Joe Tito 14, Joe Marnell 14, Dan Gallagher 14, Jim Williams 10, Mike Glezman 10; Phillipsburg – Bill Dukett 21.[2]

Bethlehem 73 Hazleton 56: Bethlehem's superior height proved too much for Hazleton to overcome as the previously unbeaten Mountaineers lost to the Hurricane. Bethlehem took a 23-12 lead into the second quarter and kept increasing the lead throughout the game. Early in the third period, Hazleton attempted a comeback but got no closer than ten points. The Mountaineers' fate was sealed by a Bethlehem run of 10 points in the period to increase the lead to 60-40.

Leading scorers: Bethlehem-John Lehman 23, Paul Taglang 19, Fran Horwath 19; Hazleton-Rich Fuddy 19.

Tamaqua 66 Easton 64: Neither team led by more than three points at the end of any of the four quarters. Tamaqua, playing at home, took a three-point lead after one quarter 20-17, Easton tied the game at halftime 36-36. Tamaqua went ahead by two after the third period 49-47, which proved to be the winning margin when each team scored 17 points in the final period. Tamaqua won the game at the foul line in converting 18 of 37 attempts while Easton only shot 13 free throws and made 9 of them. After missing his last three foul shots, Paul Long made the two that counted as the winning margin with 90 seconds to play.

Leading scorers: Tamaqua – George Krell 28, Ed Tomchick 11, Paul Long 10; Easton – Tom Fisher 18, Joe Braido 13, Matt Ewadinger 12.

Dieruff 77 Pottsville 64: Using its height advantage, Dieruff handed Pottsville its 17th consecutive league loss since winning the league title in 1964. The Huskies hit their first six shots from the floor and took a 22-10 advantage into the second period. Although Pottsville kept pace with Dieruff over the last three periods, they were never able to get closer than ten points. At one point in the fourth quarter, the Huskies' Skip Kintz scored 13 consecutive points.

Leading scorers: Dieruff – Skip Kintz 35, Jeff Arbogast 14, Greg Schmidt 10; Pottsville – Norm Waters 31, Tom Shaffer 11.

Phillipsburg 65 Central Catholic 55: Winless on the year, Phillipsburg, on its home court, surprised the defending league champions for the first win ever over the Vikings. Trailing 17-16 early in the second period, Phillipsburg switched to a full court press and outscored the Vikings 19-2 to stake them to a 36-23 lead. Although Central Catholic outscored Phillipsburg 32-29 in the second half, the big second quarter carried Phillipsburg to the surprising victory.

Leading scorers: Phillipsburg – Jack Shane 16, Jim Suydam 13, Steve Samson 12, Bill Dukett 12; Central Catholic – Ed Ellwood 19, Jack Johnson 13.[3]

Week 2

Bethlehem 64 Central Catholic 56: Highly-favored Bethlehem had to fight hard to pull out a triumph over the smaller, but scrappy Viking squad. Tied at 14 after the first period, Bethlehem took an eight-point lead into the locker room at the half. Fired up in the third quarter, the Vikings took a three-point lead into the final period when they scored 18 points to Bethlehem's 7. Coach John Howard switched to a press in the final period and forced the Vikings into many mistakes and violations to hold the Vikings to ten points while this Bethlehem squad scored 21.

Leading scorers: Bethlehem –Paul Albino 32, Fran Horwath 13; Central Catholic – Ed Ellwood 18, Jack Johnson 14.

Phillipsburg 69 Easton 56: Phillipsburg stunned Easton for their second consecutive upset. After only two league wins in their first two years in the league, Coach Al Senavitis' squad snapped an 8-game losing streak to the Red Rovers. Led by center Bucky Spear with 18 points in the first half, Phillipsburg went into half time with a commanding 37-24 lead. In a low-scoring 3rd period, Easton cut the lead to eight by outscoring their cross-river rivals 12-7. Phillipsburg rebounded in the final period with 25 points to Easton's 20 to secure the win.

Leading scorers: Phillipsburg – Dick "Bucky" Spear 28, Jack Shane 11, Bill Dukett 11; Easton – Joe Braido 16, Tom Fisher 14.

Tamaqua 63 Pottsville 58: Pottsville extended its frustrating league-losing streak to eighteen when Tamaqua took a come-from-behind victory. Unbeaten Tamaqua went to 3-0 in the league after trailing at the half 31-30. With the game tied after three periods 40-40, Tamaqua tallied 23 points in the final period including seven foul shots to gain the victory.

Leading scorers: Tamaqua – George Krell 23, Paul Long 17, Ed Tomchick 14; Pottsville – Jack Dolbin 18, Norm Waters 17, Tom Shaffer 12.

Allen 74 Hazleton 60: Hazleton dropped to 1-2 on its home court with a loss to Allen, who ended a three-game losing streak to the Mountaineers. Allen held the lead after each quarter, but Hazleton closed in trailing Allen 52-49 in the fourth period. Allen ran off 9 straight points to win the game. Joe Moore led the scoring attack and grabbed 15 rebounds and blocked 5 shots.

Leading scorers: Allen – Joe Moore 20, Jim Hinman 19, Barry Levine 11, Glenn Angelino 10; Hazleton – Rich Fuddy 19, Joe Tito 14, Jim Williams 10.[4]

Week 3

Allen 93 Central Catholic 73: Allen, at the Little Palestra, won its first matchup with Central Catholic since February 1962 with surprising ease. The Vikings went to 0-4 in league play. Allen went out to an 8-0 lead over coach Mike Koury's squad and had the game in hand the rest of the way. Six Canaries scored in double figures to improve Allen's league record to 2-1.

Leading scorers: Allen – Glenn Angelino 20, Joe Moore 17, Jim Hinman 16, Phil Miller 11, Barry Nagle 10, Ray Peters 10: Central Catholic – Joe Kramer 20, Ed Ellwood 15, Walt Witkowski 11.

Easton 68 Bethlehem 56: Bethlehem handed Easton its fourth consecutive loss to start league play while improving to 4-0. Despite taking a 9-2 lead, Easton trailed at the end of the first quarter 16-12. Easton registered four more field goals than Bethlehem 23-19, but the Hurricane took advantage of shooting 43 foul shots, making 30 of them. They made 15 in the last period to hold off the Red Rovers. Tempers flared in the last period with several fist fights including one requiring police to restore order. Bethlehem's Paul Albino and Easton's John Cappellano and Bob Keiber were ejected as a result.

Leading scorers: Bethlehem – Fran Horwath 19, Paul Albino 12; Easton - Steve Hutnik 13, Tom Fisher 12, Joe Braido 11, Charlie Schramm 10.

Pottsville 88 Phillipsburg 75: Pottsville snapped its 18-game league losing streak at the expense of Phillipsburg. After the teams exchanged leads several times in the first period, Pottsville took a 20-18 lead. After Phillipsburg tied the score at the start of the second period, Pottsville countered with three field goals to take a six-point lead and never trailed again. Pottsville extended the lead and Phillipsburg could get no closer than seven points.

Leading scorers: Pottsville – Jack Dolbin 18, Tom Shaffer 16, Norm Waters 14; Phillipsburg – Jim Suydam 17, Steve Samson 15, Dick Spear 14, Bill Dukett 13, Jack Shane 12.

Dieruff 82 Tamaqua 62: Dieruff improved to 3-0 when they handed a loss to Tamaqua. After trailing 19-15 after a period, Ed Tomchick's field goal put Tamaqua ahead 23-21 in the second period. Dieruff responded to take the half time lead 33-30. After three periods, Dieruff hung on to their three-point lead 53-50 before the Huskies surged in the final period to outscore the Tams by 17 points.[5]

Leading scorers: Tamaqua– George Krell 21, Rich Fritzinger 12, Ed Tomchick 11: Pottsville– Tom Shaffer 19, Jack Dolbin 14.[5]

Bethlehem 84 Pottsville 71: Bethlehem ran its record to 5-0 and a half game lead in the league standings with a win at Pottsville. After Bethlehem built up a nine-point lead in the second quarter 25-16, Pottsville trimmed it to four points 32-28 at the half and three points after three quarters 55-52. The fourth quarter was all Bethlehem as they outscored Pottsville by ten points. Bethlehem's Fran Horwath broke lose in the second half scoring 26 points. For the game, he made 15 of 16 foul shots including 13 in a row. Bethlehem won the game at the foul line converting 24 of 31 while Pottsville made 11 of 27.

Leading scorers: Bethlehem – Fran Horwath 39, Paul Taglang 20, John Lehman 14; Pottsville – Norm Waters 28, Tom Shaffer 16, Jack Dolbin 10.

Allen 54 Easton 48: At Easton, the Red Rovers jumped out to an 8-0 lead before Allen scored 13 of the next fifteen points to take a 13-10 lead. Hitting a shot at the buzzer, Easton tied the game a 13-13 to end the quarter. The tie was short-lived when the Canaries surged to a 27-14 advantage with Glenn Angelino hitting four jump shots during the rally. Early in the fourth quarter, Easton, led by Tom Fisher, cut the lead to 43-40. Allen scored the next six points to put the game away.

Leading scorers: Allen – Glenn Angelino 15, Joe Moore 13, Jim Hinman 12; Easton – Tom Fisher 20, Charlie Meyers 10.

Dieruff 82 Phillipsburg 57: Dieruff improved to 4-0 with a thrashing of Phillipsburg and stayed a half game behind Bethlehem in the first half title chase. Dieruff kept the lead from the start of the game, but Phillipsburg stayed within striking distance through nearly three quarters. Extending the lead to eleven 55-44 entering the final period, Dieruff dropped 27 points on the Stateliners to win going away.

Leading scorers: Dieruff –Skip Kintz 28, Mike Lopsonzski 12, Jeff Arbogast 12, Jan Kapcala 12, Greg Schmidt 10; Phillipsburg – Dick Spear 14, Steve Samson 10.[6]

Hazleton 68 Central Catholic 47: Central Catholic lost its fifth game with no wins in league play when Hazleton downed them at Rockne Hall. After the Vikings held a slim two-point lead 11-9 after a period, Hazleton scored 10 straight points in the second quarter with the game tied at 17 to take a 27-77 lead. They maintained the ten-point lead at the half 33-23 and continued to add to it the rest of the way. Hazleton held the Vikings' Ed Ellwood ten points below his 19 ppg average.

Leading scorers: Hazleton – Mike Glezman 21, Rich Fuddy 20; Central Catholic – Jack Johnson 12.[7]

Week 4

Pottsville 72 Allen 65: Pottsville traveled to the Little Palestra with an undersized squad when compared to Allen. Pottsville's tallest starter, Jim Walters at 6 feet, was five inches shorter than Allen's Joe Moore. Walters scored 22 points including 10 of 14 foul shots, making ten in a row after missing his first four shots. He held Moore to five points. Pottsville took the early lead 16-10 after a quarter. Allen cut the lead to two at the half 35-33, but Pottsville increased it to twelve in the third quarter 55-43 which led to the victory.

Leading scorers: Pottsville – Jim Walters 22, Norm Waters 19, Tom Shaffer 16, Jack Dolbin 13; Allen – Jim Hinman 37, Barry Nagle 11, Phil Miller 10.

Hazleton 92 Easton 61: Easton remained winless in league play in Hazleton. Hazleton held the Red Rovers scoreless for over the first four minutes of the opening period and did not allow a field goal until the last minute of the period to take a 16-5 lead. Although Easton picked up its offense in the last three periods, Hazleton scored 24 points or more in each of periods to overwhelm Easton.

Leading scorers: Hazleton – Joe Tito 26, Dan Gallagher 23, Lou Fiore 17; Easton – Tom Fisher 14.

Dieruff 63 Bethlehem 55: In a battle for the league lead, Dieruff invaded Bethlehem's Memorial Hall with nearly 4000 fans in attendance. Coach Dick Schmidt had his Husky squad play a control game to neutralize Bethlehem's running game. His players perfected the strategy to take sole possession of first place in the title race. After the teams were tied at 23-23 in the 2nd quarter, Dieruff moved out to take a 34-27 half time lead. They extended the lead to 12 early in the 4th period with a 10-2 run before Bethlehem tightened the score.

Leading scorers: Dieruff – Skip Kintz 23, Mike Lopsonzski 14, Jeff Arbogast 12; Bethlehem – Fran Horwath 17, John Lehman 15, Paul Albino 12.

Tamaqua 59 Phillipsburg 56: Tamaqua improved to 4-1 in Phillipsburg with a win over the Garnet. The game was tight the whole way with Phillipsburg holding a slim one-point lead at the half 27-26. Tamaqua took the lead heading into the fourth quarter 41-40 and took a commanding 52-43 lead on a 11-3 run. Phillipsburg's late surge fell short.

Leading scorers: Tamaqua – Long 18, George Krell 17, Ed Tomchick 11; Phillipsburg – Bill Dukett 18, Dick Spear 14.[8]

Bethlehem 78 Phillipsburg 60: Bethlehem moved out to a 6-0 early lead before Phillipsburg rallied to tie the score at 12-12. Bethlehem responded to take a 19-17 lead at the quarter and never trailed in the game, although it was close the entire first half. The score was tied three times in the second period, but Phillipsburg never grabbed the lead. Bethlehem outscored the Garnet by 14 in the second half for the win and remained a half game behind league leader Dieruff.

Leading scorers: Bethlehem – Paul Albino 24, Paul Taglang 20, Fran Horwath 14, John Lehman 10; Phillipsburg – Bill Dukett 20, Jim Suydam 13, Jack Shane 10.

Allen 71 Tamaqua 62: Playing at home at the Little Palestra, Allen took a 15-7 lead after a quarter and extended it to ten at the half 36-26. Tamaqua cut the lead to two 52-50 after three quarters and took a brief lead early in the final quarter 54-52. Allen rallied with several field goals and foul shots to spurt into the lead and win the game.

Leading scorers: Allen –Barry Nagle 27, Jim Hinman 14, Joe Moore 11, Glenn Angelino 10; Tamaqua – George Krell 25, Ed Tomchick 10, John Mateyak 10, Rich Krepak 10.

Pottsville 62 Central Catholic 49: Central Catholic dropped its sixth straight game to Pottsville at Rockne Hall. Pottsville held the Vikings' leading scorer Ed Elwood scoreless in the contest. Pottsville employed a switching zone defense to baffle Central Catholic's offense. After taking an 18-12 first quarter lead, Pottsville maintained the lead throughout the game to even their league record at 3-3.

Leading scorers: Pottsville – Jim Walters 18, Tom Shaffer 16, Norm Waters 13, Jack Dolbin 11; Central Catholic – Jack Johnson 15, Joe Kramer 14, Walt Witkowski 11.

Dieruff 75 Hazleton 54: Dieruff traveled to Hazleton looking to maintain its league lead. The two teams tussled in the first half with Hazleton coming out on top at the half 33-32. Dieruff regrouped at half time to hold the Mountaineers without a field goal for over 4 ½ minutes while scoring 9 unanswered points to take a 41-33 lead. They put the game on ice 75-54 with 14 straight points late in the last period. The Huskies handed Coach Schmidt his 100th victory as head coach and improved to a 6-0 record and maintained a lead over Bethlehem (6-1) by a half game.

Leading scorers: Dieruff – Jeff Arbogast 21, Skip Kintz 19, Jan Kapcala 13, Mike Lopsonzski 12; Hazleton – Joe Tito 13, Dan Gallagher 13, Rich Fuddy 10.[9]

Week 5

Hazleton 75 Pottsville 72: Despite Hazleton taking a 24-15 lead in the second quarter, Pottsville fought back to tie the game at the half 28-28. Hazleton went into the final quarter with a two-point lead 49-47 and extended it to 67-60 with two minutes to play. Pottsville made two field goals and converted two foul shots to get within one 67-66. Hazleton's Mike Glezman was fouled by Pottsville's Jim Walters, which Coach Fran Libonati argued, to no avail, that it should have been called flagrant. Glezman made one of the shots for a two-point lead 68-66. Pottsville's Tom Shaffer drove for the bucket, was fouled, and tied the game at 68 with his two shots. With 17 seconds to play, Hazleton went ahead 70-68 on Joe Marnell's two foul shots only to have Tom Shaffer tie it 70-70 with a jump shot to send the game into overtime. Hazleton won the game in overtime on the conversion of five foul shots. Pottsville's points were also from foul shots.

Leading scorers: Hazleton –Rich Fuddy 19, Joe Tito 17, Jim Williams 16; Pottsville – Jack Dolbin 23, Norm Waters 20, Tom Shaffer 14.[10]

Easton 60 Central Catholic 51: Central Catholic and Easton battled to determine which team would exit the league cellar. Easton took a 30-21 lead into the locker room. The Vikings cut the lead to three points heading into the final period 41-38. The Vikings' Joe Kramer made a driving layup as he was fouled. He converted the foul shot to tie the game at 41-41. Jack Johnson followed with a foul shot to give the Vikings their first and only lead of the night. The Red Rovers followed with seven straight points to take a commanding lead.

Leading scorers: Easton – John Cappellano 13, Steve Hutnik 11; Central Catholic – Jack Johnson 26.

Bethlehem 81 Tamaqua 53: Bethlehem stayed on the tails of Dieruff by improving its record to 7-1. After trailing by three-points in the first quarter 15-12, Tamaqua pulled within two points 19-17 in the second period. Bethlehem took off on an eleven-point spurt to take a 30-17 lead. At the half, the Hurricane had a fourteen-point lead 38-24. Bethlehem added to the lead in both the third and fourth quarters to win convincingly and squash any hopes Tamaqua had for a first half title.

Leading scorers: Bethlehem–Paul Albino 22, Paul Taglang 19, Fran Horwath 10; Tamaqua–George Krell 21, Ed Tomchick 12.

Dieruff 66 Allen 49: Allen invaded the Dieruff gym hoping to put a dent in the Huskies' drive to a first half title. Allen began the game using a stall strategy in an attempt to halt the Huskies run. Instead, the Huskies jumped out to a 14-4 lead after the first quarter. Allen's first field goal didn't come until about 1 ½ minutes left in the quarter. Allen cut the lead to three 24-21 at the half. Rejuvenated in the locker room, Allen came out and hit eight straight points to take a 29-25 lead. The third quarter ended with Dieruff holding a slim two-point lead 40-38. The fourth quarter doomed the Canaries as the Huskies went on a rampage to outscore Allen 26-11 clinch at least a tie for the first half title.

Leading scorers: Dieruff – Skip Kintz 26, Jeff Arbogast 16, Greg Schmidt 16; Allen – Joe Moore 24, Barry Nagle 16.[11]

Tamaqua 77 Hazleton 66: Trailing twice in the first quarter, Tamaqua rallied to take a 20-16 lead into the second stanza. With both teams scoring 17 points, Tamaqua held onto the lead at half time. Tamaqua's George Krell went to the bench late in the second quarter and all of the third quarter with four personal fouls. Hazleton took advantage of Krell's absence to move in front 51-47 when they scored 10 straight points. Krell returned for the fourth quarter and scored 14 points to lead a ferocious comeback. The Tams humiliated the Mountaineers 23-5 and allowed them only a field goal and three foul shots in the final period.

Leading scorers: Tamaqua – George Krell 25, Art Connely 14, Paul Long 14, Rich Krepak 10; Hazleton – Mike Glezman 17, Joe Tito 16, Rich Fuddy 13, Jim Williams 13.

Dieruff 83 Central Catholic 49: Dieruff won its eighth straight and handed the Vikings their eighth straight loss. Dieruff took control from the beginning with a 22-14 first quarter lead and outscored the Vikings by a least seven points in every quarter. Skip Kintz finished the contest just 14 points shy of hitting the 1,000 total for his career.

Leading scorers: Dieruff – Skip Kintz 21, Greg Schmidt 15, Jan Kapcala 13, Jeff Arbogast 12; Central Catholic – Jack Johnson 11, Walt Witkowski 10.

Allen 79 Phillipsburg 50: With four of Phillipsburg starters fouling out in the third period, Allen cruised to an easy victory at Phillipsburg. The game was over early with Allen outscoring the Stateliners 24-5 during an eight-minute period of the first and second quarters. The result left Allen at 5-3 and Philipsburg at 2-6.

Leading scorers: Allen – Glenn Angelino 17, Barry Nagle 13, Barry Levine 13, Joe Moore 10; Phillipsburg – Bill Dukett 12.

Pottsville 93 Easton 64: Employing a tight pressing defense, Pottsville buried the Red Rovers after starting out with a 23-14 lead after the first quarter. Four Pottsville players scored in double figures while three players scored all but eight of Easton's points. Easton finished the half at 1-7 while Pottsville evened its record at 4-4.

Leading scorers: Pottsville – Jim Walters 22, Norm Waters 22, Tom Shaffer 16, Bob Devlin 12; Easton – Tom Fisher 28, Joe Braido 16, Steve Jefferson 12.[12]

Second Half - Week 6

Hazleton 78 Phillipsburg 73: Although Phillipsburg outscored Hazleton 44-36 in the second half, the Stateliners could not overcome a really poor start in the first half and lost to Hazleton to open up second half play. Hazleton used 15 players in the game.

Leading scorers: Hazleton – Joe Tito 22, Mike Glezman 16, Jim Williams 14; Phillipsburg – Bill Dukett 27, Steve Samson 18, Jim Suydam 12, Jack Shane 10.

Bethlehem 64 Allen 52: John Lehman led a staunch Bethlehem defense with seven blocks in the first half in a win over Allen. Allen fell behind at the half 31-22 and 44-36 after three quarters. Allen narrowed a ten-point lead in the fourth quarter to one 51-50 with 3:48 left to play. Bethlehem would have no part of a further Canary rally and outscored them 13-2 for the victory.

Leading scorers: Bethlehem – Paul Taglang 16, Fran Horwath 15, Paul Albino 14; Allen – Joe Moore 13, Barry Nagle 12, Jim Hinman 11.

Tamaqua 68 Central Catholic 61: In Tamaqua, Central Catholic fought hard to pick up its first league win of the season. Despite holding a commanding 36-24 lead at the half, Tamaqua had to fend off a determined Viking squad in the second half. Leading by 17, Coach Pinky Purnell substituted freely and the large lead began to evaporate with the Vikings trimming the lead in the last two quarters, but finally losing and still had no league win.

Leading scorers: Tamaqua – George Krell 17, Paul Long 17, Art Connely 13, Ed Tomchick 10; Central Catholic – Jack Johnson 27.

Dieruff 77 Easton 43: Dieruff continued its roll to start the second half with an easy win over Easton. Skip Kintz hit the 1,000-career point mark with a tap in of a missed foul shot and make him the first Husky to score over a thousand points. Dieruff held the Red Rovers to 13 first half points and 24 after three quarters while taking a 57-24 lead.

Leading scorers: Dieruff – Skip Kintz 29, Dan O'Donnell 14, Greg Schmidt 13, Jack Conrad 10; Easton – Tom Fisher 11.[13]

Week 7

Hazleton-Bethlehem: This contest was postponed and was played in late February due to a snow storm.

Phillipsburg-Central Catholic: This contest was postponed and played the following week due to a snow storm.

Dieruff 77 Pottsville 71: In Pottsville, Dieruff and Pottsville squared off after a postponement for a day due to a snow storm. Although Pottsville pressed Dieruff throughout the game, the Huskies used their superior height to hold off the Crimson. Dieruff led at the end of the first and second quarters by two points and a single point 20-18 and 39-38. They opened up an eight-point lead 57-49 and extended to thirteen 68-55 with 3 ½ minutes left. Pottsville countered by outscoring the Huskies 14-4 to get within three points 72-69, but could get no closer.

Leading scorers: Dieruff – Skip Kintz 27, Mike Lopsonzski 16, Jeff Arbogast 15, Greg Schmidt 11; Pottsville –Norm Waters 28, Tom Shaffer 20.

Tamaqua 75 Easton 29: Tamaqua humiliated homestanding Easton to move to 2-0 in the second half of play. Tamaqua ran off eight points before Easton scored and then scored another twelve points to take a

20-2 lead after a quarter. It didn't get much better in the next two quarters with the Red Rovers being outscored 18-4 and 21-9 to give Tamaqua a 59-15 lead. In the final period, Easton went nearly seven minutes without a field goal.

Leading scorers: Tamaqua – George Krell 24, Rich Krepak 12; Easton – Joe Braido 9.[14]

Allen 83 Hazleton 74: Hazleton traveled to the Little Palestra looking for its second victory and stay undefeated in second half play. Allen built up a sixteen-point lead at the half 46-30 using the fast break. After the Mountaineers cut the lead to nine, Allen's Joe Moore went on a scoring rampage scoring 14 points in the third period and ten in a row at one point of the quarter. The Canaries extended the lead to 18 to begin the final quarter 68-50. Despite Hazleton's 4th quarter rally, Allen hung on to win. Both teams were now at 1-1 for the second half of play.

Leading scorers: Allen – Joe Moore 28, Jim Hinman 20, Barry Nagle 16, Phil Miller 12; Hazleton – Joe Tito 23, Rich Fuddy 16, Joe Marnell 11, Phil Andras 11.

Easton 70 Phillipsburg 48: After a devasting defeat by Tamaqua, Easton traveled to Phillipsburg and routed the Stateliners to win their first game of the second half. After a close first quarter with the Red Rovers leading 16-12, Easton extended the lead by 16 points over the next two quarters to head into the final quarter with a 49-29 lead.

Leading scorers: Easton – Bob Keiber 21, Joe Braido 16, Matt Ewadinger 12; Phillipsburg – Jim Suydam 20.

Bethlehem 78 Central Catholic 52: Still searching for its first league win, Central Catholic lost decisively to Bethlehem to suffer its second loss of the second half. Without two starters, Ed Elwood and Walt Witkowski, due to illness, the Vikings could not keep pace with the Hurricane. The closest the Vikings could get was 17-13 late in the first period.

Leading scorers: Bethlehem – Fran Horwath 19, John Lehman 15, Paul Taglang 11, Paul Albino 11; Central Catholic – Jack Johnson 15, Joe Kramer 12.

Tamaqua 83 Pottsville 77: Tamaqua improved to 3-0 to take a half game lead over Bethlehem and Dieruff both at 2-0. With George Krell needing 44 points to join the 1,000-career scoring mark, he scored exactly that to lead Tamaqua to a triumph over Pottsville. Krell scored 20 of the points in the second period as Tamaqua took a 53-33 lead at the half. He was a perfect 12 for 12 at the foul line.

Leading scorers: Tamaqua – George Krell 44, Ed Tomchick 11, John Mateyak 11; Pottsville – Tom Shaffer 25, Norm Waters 24, Bill Devlin 14.[15]

Week 8

Phillipsburg 69 Central Catholic 55: Phillipsburg and Central Catholic made up a postponed game from the week before at Rockne Hall. After playing a tight first quarter with Phillipsburg holding a one-point lead, the Garnet went on a 9-2 run late in the second quarter to take a 40-26 half time lead. After a low-scoring third period with only 16 total points, the Vikings made a run to get within six points twice in the fourth quarter, 54-48 and 56-50. Phillipsburg then outscored the Vikings 13-5 for the win. It kept the Vikings winless for the year in league play and they suffered their 11th consecutive loss. Phillipsburg won its first game of the half.

Leading scorers: Phillipsburg – Jim Suydam 24, Steve Samson 18, Bill Dukett 10; Central Catholic – Jack Johnson 21, Ray Bazylak 12.[16]

Dieruff 75 Tamaqua 53: After George Krell scored 44 points in Tamaqua's previous game, Dieruff's Greg Schmidt held him way below his season average when he was able to score only 18 points in Dieruff's triumph over the Tams. Dieruff outscored Tamaqua in all but the third quarter. Dieruff's Skip Kintz also finished below his average mainly due to sitting out the entire fourth quarter due to personal fouls and Dieruff's large lead. The win kept the Huskies tied with Bethlehem for the 2nd half lead with both at 3-0.

Leading scorers: Dieruff – Mike Lopsonzski 22, Jeff Arbogast 20, Skip Kintz 19, Jan Kapcala 10; Tamaqua – George Krell 18, Ed Tomchick 12, Paul Long 10, Art Connely 10.

Bethlehem 76 Easton 72 OT: It wasn't easy and took an extra period, but Bethlehem kept pace with Dieruff with an overtime win over Easton. A close game in the first half with the Hurricane in the lead 35-32, Bethlehem added to the lead for 58-48 lead after three quarters. Late in the 4th quarter, Bethlehem was up 68-60 with the game in hand until shockingly Easton scored 8 straight points to tie the game in regulation 68-68. Bethlehem prevailed in overtime by converting several foul shots.

Leading scorers: Bethlehem – Fran Horwath 29, Paul Taglang 19, Paul Albino 18; Easton – Tom Fisher 18, Joe Braido 17, John Cappellano 13, Matt Ewadinger 13.

Allen 59 Central Catholic 54: In a low-scoring first half, Allen held a 22-19 lead over a winless, but battling Central Catholic squad. Surprisingly, the Vikings had jumped out to a first quarter lead 15-9. Early in the 3rd period, the Canaries held only a one-point lead 28-27 over Coach Mike Koury's squad. With Allen's backcourt getting hot late in the period, they jumped out to a ten-point lead heading into the fourth quarter. Central Catholic fought back, but could not get any closer than five points and lost their 12th straight contest in league play.

Leading scorers: Allen – Joe Moore 19, Jim Hinman 14, Barry Nagle 12; Central Catholic – Joe Kramer 16, Jack Johnson 12, Ray Bazylak 12, Walt Witkowski 10.[17]

Pottsville 83 Phillipsburg 59: After a roughly played first quarter which saw Pottsville hold a three-point lead 15-12, the Crimson took the game in hand with a 28-point outburst in the second period and led at half time 43-22. Pottsville's Jim Walters scored eight points in a row at the start of the third period to put the game away for the Crimson. The loss kept Phillipsburg winless in the second half and tied with Central Catholic in the cellar at 0-3. Pottsville won its first after two losses in the second half.

Leading scorers: Pottsville – Tom Shaffer 24, Jim Walters 16, Jack Dolbin 11, Dan Guers 10; Phillipsburg – Dick Spear 15, Bill Dukett 14, Al Pianelli 11.[18]

Allen 96 Easton 64: At the Little Palestra, Allen took a six-point lead after one period 23-17 over Easton. Early in the second period, the Red Rovers cut the lead to four points 26-22. The Canaries then put on an 11-2 spurt which gave them a thirteen-point lead. They expanded the lead to eighteen at the half 53-35. Allen dominated Easton in the second half and won the game handily. The win kept Allen a game behind undefeated Dieruff and Bethlehem at 3-1.

Leading scorers: Allen – Barry Levine 25, Joe Moore 24, Barry Nagle 17; Easton – Tom Fisher 27, John Cappellano 18, Joe Braido 12.

Bethlehem 67 Pottsville 49: Pottsville started slowly and fell behind 16-7 to Bethlehem after a period. Pottsville cut a point off the lead at the half with Bethlehem entering the locker room with a 33-25 lead. The second half was all Bethlehem with the Hurricane winning the contest to improve to 4-0 and share first place with Dieruff.

Leading scorers: Bethlehem– Paul Taglang 24, Paul Albino 13, Fran Horwath 10; Pottsville– Norm Waters 16, Jack Dolbin 14.

Dieruff 91 Phillipsburg 27: Although Phillipsburg held high-scoring Skip Kintz to nine points, they could not contain the rest of the team as the Stateliners got pummeled by Dieruff. After Phillipsburg took a 2-1 lead, Dieruff held them scoreless the rest of the first period and only gave up eight in the second period, and three in the third period to take a 66-13 lead into the final quarter. They scored 14 in the final period, but gave up 25 to the Dieruff reserves.

Leading scorers: Dieruff – Danny O'Donnell 24, Greg Schmidt 13, Jeff Arbogast 10: Phillipsburg – Bill Dukett 6, Joe Liro 6.

Hazleton 82 Central Catholic 72: Continuing their season long slump, Central Catholic dropped their 13th in a row losing to Hazleton. With the Mountaineers starting slowly, the Vikings took a 20-6 lead after one period. Hazleton cut the lead in half 36-29 as both teams headed into the locker room. The third period was devastating with Hazleton scoring seven straight points to tie the score at 36-36 and continuing to surge to lead at the end of the quarter 56-47. Although the Vikings offense clicked in the final period scoring 25 points, Hazleton still outscored the them by a point to send the Vikings to the defeat.

Leading Scorers: Hazleton – Rich Fuddy 22, Joe Tito, 20, Jim Williams 20, Mike Glezman 10; Central Catholic – Ray Bazylak 21, Jack Johnson 20, Joe Kramer 10.[19]

Week 9

Dieruff 66 Bethlehem 58: In a battle of second half unbeatens, Dieruff won a 13th consecutive league win and 18 of 19 overall in a hard-fought victory over Bethlehem. The Huskies took a 18-12 lead into the second period, but Bethlehem rallied to take a one-point lead 20-19. The Huskies came right back with Greg Schmidt hitting 2 shots to put the Huskies into the lead for good. Bethlehem made a run in the middle of the final period and got within five 50-45 with 5 ½ minutes to play. Jeff Arbogast singlehandedly squashed the rally by scoring ten points from that point on to lead the Huskies to victory. Dieruff was now alone in first place with a 5-0 record. Bethlehem fell into a tie for second with Tamaqua at 4-1.

Leading scorers: Dieruff –Skip Kintz 21, Jeff Arbogast 19, Greg Schmidt 10, Jan Kapcala 10; Bethlehem – Fran Horwath 18, John Lehman 16, Paul Taglang 13.

Hazleton 72 Easton 68 OT: In Easton, Hazleton rolled into the fourth quarter with a seemingly secure 49-41 lead. Easton surprised the Mountaineers by outscoring them 20-12 in the final period to tie the score at the end of regulation at 61-61. Hazleton, however, took charge in the overtime period, scoring eleven points to the Red Rovers seven to win the game 72-68. Hazleton improved to 3-1. Easton dropped to 1-5.

Leading scorers: Hazleton – Joe Marnell 16, Rich Fuddy 14, Joe Tito 14, Lou Fiore 12, Jim Williams 11; Easton – Joe Braido 18, John Cappellano 15, Matt Ewadinger 11.

Pottsville 75 Allen 71: Allen traveled to Pottsville, got off to a slow start in the first period, and fell behind 23-15 which proved to be the difference in a loss to the Crimson. Allen tried desperately to rally in the last seconds of the game. A last shot play went astray and Pottsville added 2 foul shots to win the game by 4.

Leading scorers: Pottsville – Tom Shaffer 30, Jim Walters 15, Norm Waters 11; Allen - Barry Nagle 20, Joe Moore 17, Jim Hinman 14, Barry Levine 10.

Tamaqua 87 Phillipsburg 57: Phillipsburg visited Tamaqua only to head home with a decisive loss to the Tams, despite hitting 21 of 30 foul shots. After the score was tied 6-6, Tamaqua's George Krell led his team to a 21-12 first quarter lead and it only grew from that point on until Phillipsburg outscored Tamaqua in the last period 16-15. Tamaqua stayed on the tails of Dieruff at 4-1. Phillipsburg fell to 1-5 in the second half.

Leading scorers: Tamaqua – George Krell 28, Rich Krepak 14, Ed Tomchick 11, Paul Long 10, John Mateyak 10; Phillipsburg – Jack Shane 14.[20]

Bethlehem 75 Phillipsburg 63: Phillipsburg, playing at home, played its best game of the season against Bethlehem. In a very close game, Phillipsburg never trailed in the first half and held 59-56 lead midway through the final period. Bethlehem ran off 9 points at that point to take the lead and travel home with a victory. Bethlehem made 25 of 30 free throws, the difference in the contest. The Hurricane improved to 5-1 in the second half.

Leading scorers: Bethlehem – Fran Horwath 23, Paul Taglang 19, Mike Rosko 14, Paul Schreiber 12; Phillipsburg – Bill Dukett 29, Jack Shane 10.[21]

Tamaqua 76 Allen 70: Allen took a 17-11 lead into the second period only to have Tamaqua's George Krell go on an eleven-point splurge in the second quarter which led the Tams to 41-38 half time advantage. After playing even in the third quarter with each team scoring 12 points, Tamaqua held off the Canaries to send them home with a loss. Tamaqua improved to 5-1 while Allen's record evened out at 3-3.

Leading scorers: Tamaqua – George Krell 33, Rich Krepak 14, Paul Long 10; Allen – Joe Moore 17, Barry Nagle 13, Barry Levine 12, Jim Hinman 10.

Pottsville 86 Central Catholic 65: Central Catholic took a one-point lead after a quarter. Homestanding Pottsville countered to lead by five at the half 43-38. Earlier in the period, the Vikings held a 38-36 lead, but the Crimson Tide reeled off seven straight points and took the lead for good. Pottsville improved to 3-3 while the Vikings dropped their 14th straight in league play.

Leading scorers: Pottsville –Tom Shaffer 26, Norm Waters 19; Central Catholic – Jack Johnson 16, Ed Ellwood 14.

Hazleton 30 Dieruff 28: Playing on Dieruff's home court, Hazleton went into a deliberate stall right from the beginning in an attempt to neutralize the Huskies' running game. In the four regulation periods and the two overtime periods, neither team scored in double figures. The first quarter ended 2-2 and Dieruff took a single point lead at the half 10-9. The third period ended with Dieruff in front 16-13. Dieruff led 21-19 with 25 seconds to play, when Lou Fiore stole the ball. After a timeout, Hazleton held for the last shot which Joe Tito made to tie the score for Hazleton in regulation. Both teams scored four points in the first overtime to knot the score at 25-25. Dieruff took a 27-25 lead only to have Joe Tito make a three-point play on a layup and a foul to take the lead 28-27. Dieruff's Greg Schmidt only made one of two foul shots to tie the score again at 28-28. Hazleton worked the ball until nine seconds were left and Rich Fuddy hit the game-winning field goal. The loss dropped Dieruff into a three-way tie with Bethlehem and Tamaqua in the second half race, all at 5-1.

Leading scorers: Hazleton – Lou Fiore 10; Dieruff – Greg Schmidt 9.[22]

Week 10

Dieruff 75 Allen 73: Dieruff took a 39-30 half time lead and expanded it to 55-40 with about 2 ½ minutes left in the third period. Skip Kintz scored 15 points in the second quarter. Allen's Joe Moore did not play at all in the second period after picking up three fouls in the first period. The Canaries put on a fierce rally from late in the 3rd period and into the fourth to catch the Huskies and tie the score at 69-69 with 2:24 to play. The Huskies' veteran experience took over and they were able to prevail and remain in a first-place tie at 6-1 with Tamaqua.

Leading scorers: Dieruff – Skip Kintz 31, Jeff Arbogast 14, Mike Lopsonzski 14, Greg Schmidt 13; Allen – Joe Moore 20, Barry Nagle 14, Jim Hinman 13.

Hazleton 82 Pottsville 69: Hazleton kept its second half title hopes alive by downing Pottsville. Pottsville took a first quarter lead 14-12 before the Mountaineers put on a second quarter show outscoring Pottsville 24-11. Hazleton led for the first time 22-20 and led at the half 36-25. Pottsville trimmed the Hazleton lead to 36-30 after the half, before Hazleton's Dan Gallagher went on a scoring rampage with seven straight successful field goals to help drive the lead to 60-39.

Leading scorers: Hazleton – Dan Gallagher 24, Joe Tito 17, Phil Andras 16, Rich Fuddy 15, Lou Fiore 10; Pottsville – Jim Walters 26, Jack Dolbin 12.

Central Catholic 65 Easton 57: At Rockne Hall, Central Catholic snapped its 14-game league losing streak with a win over Easton. Three teams were now tied at 1-6 in the league's cellar: Easton, Central Catholic, and Phillipsburg. Although the game was close throughout, the Vikings never trailed after the latter stages of the first period when they were behind 15-14. The Vikings led after one 18-15, at the half 32-30, and after three 48-43.

Leading scorers: Central Catholic – Jack Johnson 24, Ray Bazylak 12, Bob Neff 11, Joe Kramer 10; Easton – Tom Fisher 22, John Cappellano 17, Joe Braido 11.

Tamaqua 64 Bethlehem 62 OT: Tamaqua invaded Memorial Hall in a battle with Bethlehem to remain in a tie for the second half lead. And a battle it was, with the game going into overtime before Tamaqua finally prevailed 64-62. With Bethlehem outscoring Tamaqua 15-14 in the first period and Tamaqua doing the same in the second period, the teams went into the locker room tied at 39-39. Tamaqua took a three-point lead after three only to have Bethlehem turn the tables in the fourth and deadlock the game at 56-56 in regulation. Tamaqua's Rich Krepak tapped in a missed shot with 20 seconds to play to win the game 64-62.

Leading scorers: Tamaqua – George Krell 22, Rich Krepak 14, Paul Long 11, Ed Tomchick 10; Bethlehem – Fran Horwath 26, Paul Taglang 13, Paul Schreiber 11.[23]

Tamaqua 74 Hazleton 70: With the second half title on the line, Tamaqua visited Hazleton and came away with a victory based on huge 1st and 4th quarter performances. Tamaqua took an 18-8 first quarter lead only to have Hazleton catch them after three periods at 50-50. They outscored the Mountaineers by 4 in the final period for the win. The Tams won the contest on the foul line by converting 32 of 42 tries while Hazleton connected on 18 of 26.

Leading scorers: Tamaqua - George Krell 24, Paul Long 15, Rich Krepak 14; Joe Tito 23, Phil Andras 11, Dan Gallagher 10.[24]

Allen 96 Phillipsburg 64: Allen handed Phillipsburg its seventh loss in eight second half games which evened the Canaries record at 4-4. Allen outscored Phillipsburg by at least six points in every quarter. Senior Joe Moore scored 29 points and grabbed 12 rebounds in less than three periods of play.

Leading scorers: Allen – Joe Moore 29, Glenn Angelino 14, Barry Levine 13; Phillipsburg – Al Pianelli 21, Dick Spear 15.

Dieruff 71 Central Catholic 41: Dieruff cruised to a win over Central Catholic to finish the second half at 7-1 and in a tie with Tamaqua for first place at 7-1. Dieruff put the game out of reach after the first period by outscoring the Vikings 21-5 and by the half led by 41-15. The Vikings finished the league season with only one win in 16 games.

Leading scorers: Dieruff – Skip Kintz 18, Jeff Arbogast 16, Greg Schmidt 14, Mike Lopsonzski 12; Central Catholic – Joe Kramer 8.[25]

Pottsville 72 Easton 68: Pottsville essentially won its game with Easton in the first period by outscoring the Red Rovers 26-9. Easton played catchup the rest of the night and trimmed the lead to two points 67-65. Pottsville's Tom Shaffer made four foul shots in the last 25 seconds to win the game for Pottsville. The win evened Pottsville's record at 4-4 in the half and dropped Easton to 1-7 which kept them in a last place tie with Central Catholic and Phillipsburg.

Leading scorers: Pottsville – Norm Waters 20, Jack Dolbin 20, Jim Walters 16, Tom Shaffer 10; Easton – Tom Fisher 27, Steve Hutnick 11, Jack Pearson 10, Joe Braido 10.[26]

Hazleton 85 Bethlehem 84 OT: In a makeup game postponed due to snow earlier in February, Hazleton closed out its season with an overtime win over Bethlehem. Bethlehem held leads in each of the first three quarters before the Mountaineers tied the game in regulation 78-78. It was the sixth time in the fourth period that the game was tied. Hazleton prevailed in overtime to improve its record to 6-2 in the second half to finish third. Bethlehem finished at 5-3.

Leading scorers: Dieruff – Skip Kintz 22; Hazleton –Bob Solarek 13, Carmen Chandler 12, Rich Fuddy 10, Joe Tito 10.[27]

Second Half Playoff

Dieruff 74 Tamaqua 58: At Bethlehem's Memorial gym, Dieruff and Tamaqua squared off to decide the second half title. The two teams battled in the first half with both teams holding leads. Tamaqua jumped out to a four-point lead 28-24 with better than five minutes left in the first half. The Huskies came back to take a narrow lead 35-34 into the locker room. Despite picking up three personal fouls in the first quarter, Tamaqua's George Krell was able to play the rest of the game without getting disqualified. Dieruff expanded the lead to three at the end of the third period 52-49. With the Huskies leading 57-54, Dieruff scored the next 13 points to expand the lead to 70-54 and sew up the second half and the school's first ever league title.

Leading scorers: Dieruff – Skip Kintz 38, Jeff Arbogast 13; Tamaqua – George Krell 22, Ed Tomchick 13, Rich Krepak 10.[28]

Postseason PIAA Play

Dieruff 71 Nazareth 36: Dieruff entered postseason play for the 2nd year in a row at Muhlenberg's Memorial Hall against Nazareth. Nazareth came into the game at a disadvantage with two starters, Lou Schrenko and Jerry Lilly, ailing with a virus. After a low-scoring first quarter with the Huskies leading 9-7, Dieruff began to pull away from the Lehigh-Northampton League champions and held a 29-17 half time lead. The final two quarters were more of the same as Dieruff outscored Nazareth by 10 and 13 points to easily win the district semi-final game

Leading scorers: Dieruff – Skip Kintz 31, Greg Schmidt 14; Nazareth – Ken Shiffert 9.[29]

Dieruff 55 Catasauqua 50: With more than 9,000 fans in attendance at the Harrisburg Farm Show Arena, Dieruff faced Catasauqua for the District 11 title. After losing to Catasauqua in a preseason contest by 19 points, the Huskies had revenge on their mind. The Roughriders put up a tough zone defense to take a 1st quarter lead 16-11. Dieruff finally took the lead at 19-18 in the 2nd quarter and maintained the lead at half time 31-30. Catasauqua controlled the third quarter to take a 44-39 lead. The lead increased to six points 48-42 with a little more than six minutes to play. Dieruff changed from a man-to-man defense to press the Roughriders in the final six minutes of the game. The pressure led the Huskies to go on a 13-2 run to close out the game and win the district title.

Leading scorers: Dieruff - Skip Kintz 26, Jeff Arbogast 12; Catasauqua - Dave Harakal 17, Tom Burkholder 14.[30]

Chester 55 Dieruff 50: Dieruff returned to the Farm Show Arena for a matchup with Chester in inter-district play. Despite turning over the ball six times, the Huskies prevailed in the first quarter to take an 11-8 lead. Chester countered by outscoring Dieruff by five to take two-point lead 23-21 at the half. Dieruff continued its strong play in the third quarter to retake the lead 33-32. With the fourth quarter less than a minute old and the score tied at 33-33, Chester stole an in-bounds pass to start a run of 12 points and stake them to a 45-33 lead. The Huskies fought back to get within three 50-47, but could get no closer.

Leading scorers: Chester – Mike Marshall 24, John McLean 18; Dieruff – Skip Kintz 26.[31]

PCIAA Postseason Playoff

Bethlehem Catholic 63 Central Catholic 50: At the Dieruff gym, Bethlehem Catholic avenged an early season defeat by 22 points 65-43 at the hands of Central Catholic. Employing an aggressive 2-3 defense, the Hawks defeated the Vikings to win the Allentown Diocese championship. Trailing 15-14, the Hawks tapped in a missed foul shot early in the second period and never trailed again after 11 minutes into the contest.

Leading scorers: Bethlehem Catholic – Dan Dougherty 22, Jim Chassar 12, Greg Falkenbach 10; Central Catholic – Ray Bazylak 15, Jack Johnson 12.[32]

Postseason Accolades

Leading Scorers: Three players cracked the 300-point mark for the season with Tamaqua's George Krell leading the pack with 398 points for a 24.8 ppg average. Dieruff's Skip Kintz finished second with 364 points and a 22.8 ppg average, the only other player averaging over 20 ppg. Fran Howorth, Bethlehem, finished third with 319 points followed by Pottsville's Norm Waters with 304. The remaining top ten scorers included Joe Moore, Allen, 283; Joe Tito, Hazleton, Tom Shaffer, Pottsville, and Jack Johnson, Central Catholic, all with 263 points; Paul Taglang, Bethlehem, 241; and Tom Fisher, Easton, 239.[33]

All-Stars: The league all-star first team included: Skip Kintz, Dieruff; George Krell, Tamaqua; Fran Horwath, Bethlehem; Jeff Arbogast, Dieruff, and Norm Waters, Pottsville. The second team consisted of: Joe Moore, Allen; Tom Fisher, Easton; Rich Fuddy and Joe Tito, Hazleton; Jack Johnson, Central Catholic; Greg Schmidt, Dieruff; and Paul Taglang, Bethlehem. Fisher, Johnson, Schmidt, and Taglang were tied in the voting for the final spots on the second team.[34]

All-State: George Krell, Tamaqua, and Skip Kintz, Dieruff, were named to the second team all-state. Jeff Arbogast, Dieruff, and Fran Horwath, Bethlehem, were named Honorable Mention.[35]

Final Standings

First Half		Second Half		Overall	
Dieruff	8-0	Dieruff	7-1	Dieruff	15-1
Bethlehem	6-2	Tamaqua	7-1	Tamaqua	12-4
Allen	5-3	Hazleton	6-2	Bethlehem	11-5
Tamaqua	5-3	Bethlehem	5-3	Hazleton	10-6
Hazleton	4-4	Allen	4-4	Allen	9-7
Pottsville	4-4	Pottsville	4-4	Pottsville	8-8
Phillipsburg	2-6	Central Catholic	1-7	Phillipsburg	3-13
Easton	2-6	Easton	1-7	Easton	3-13
Central Catholic	0-8	Phillipsburg	1-7	Central Catholic	1-15

Team Rosters

Allen: Coach Milo Sewards, Glenn Angelino, Larry Belford, Vic Berliant, Joe Bierman, Heffner, Jim Hinman, Kerstetter, Leh, Barry Levine, Mike Mess, Phil Miller, Joe Moore, Barry Nagle, Neil Pendry, Ray Peters, Charlie Steckline, Bob Ulaner, Ken Wildonger, Ziegler

Bethlehem: Coach John Howard, Paul Albino, Bob Biggs, Hartzell, Fran Horvath, Hudak, Inman, John Lehman, Mike Rosko, Paul Schreiber, John Sotzing, Paul Taglang, Vanic

Central Catholic: Coach Mike Koury, Ray Bazylak, Pete Bucha, Ricco Caggiano, Ed Ellwood, B. Hetzel, Jack Johnson, Joe Kramer, Bob Neff, Fred Payonk, William Samer, John Sass, Leo Seier, Denny Williams, Walt Witkowski

Dieruff: Coach Dick Schmidt, Jeff Arbogast, Jack Conrad, Ron D'Argenio, Jan Kapcala, Skip Kintz, Mike Lopsonzski, Dan O'Donnell, Bob Repp, Greg Schmidt, Rudy Trinkle. Dan Waelchi

Easton: Coach Tom Sweeney, Joe Braido, John Cappellano, Matt Ewadinger, Tom Fisher, Bob Huffstettler, Steve Hutnik, Steve Jefferson, Bob Keiber, McNabb, Charlie Meyers, Miller, Jack Pearson, Charlie Schramm

Hazleton: Coach Fran Libonati, Phil Andras, Carmen Chandler, Lou Fiore, J Fuddy, Rich Fuddy, Dan Gallagher, Mike Glezman, Joe Marnell, Joe Moran, Perry, Bob Solarek, Joe Tito, Jim Williams

Phillipsburg: Coach Al Senavitis, Edwin Clymer, Bill Dukett, G Hanisak, Joe Liro, Al Pianelli, Bill Rodenbough, W Rowe, Steve Samson, Scherer, Jack Shane, Dick Spear, Jim Suydam

Pottsville: Coach Ken Kline, Frank Deitz, Bill Devlin, Jack Dolbin, Dan Guers, Robert Lewis, Karl Lombel, Al Portland, W Rowe, K Scherer, Tom Shaffer, Doug Snowell, Jim Walters, Norm Waters, Nelson Womer

Tamaqua: Coach Eli Purnell, Ed Brode, Art Connely, Dobroski, Rich Fritzinger, George Krell, Rich Krepak, Paul Long, John Mateyak, Schoener, Ed Tomchick

1967

Possible Playoff Dilemma

In April 1965, the league announced that Bethlehem Catholic would begin play and expand the league to ten teams in the 1967 season. The admission of Bethlehem Catholic brought the total of non-PIAA schools competing in the league to three. This created the distinct possibility that the league could enter a fourth-place team in the post-season playoffs if Central Catholic, Phillipsburg, and Bethlehem Catholic all finished in the top three in league play.[1]

First Half - Week 1

Bethlehem Catholic 64 Allen 53: Coach Paul Calvo's Bethlehem Catholic squad successfully opened play in the league with a triumph over Allen in its debut contest despite committing 22 turnovers in the game. After playing to a 13-13 tie after one quarter, the Golden Hawks to a 10-point lead at half time 33-23. This proved to be the winning margin after the teams played evenly with each scoring 11 points in the third period and Bethlehem Catholic taking the final quarter 20-19. This was the Golden Hawks first win since 1959 over Allen and only the second in 10 contests.

Leading scorers: Bethlehem Catholic – Tom Coyle 28, Greg Falkenbach 10; Allen – Tom Kerstetter 12, Glenn Angelino 10, Bob Ulaner 10.

Pottsville 58 Dieruff 55: Pottsville's full court press led Coach Ken Kline's team to a 58-55 win over Dieruff. Dieruff led after one period 13-11, but Pottsville outscored the Huskies 11-2 at one stretch of the second period to take a 28-24 half time lead. Pottsville stretched the lead to 43-36 heading into the final period. In the final minute, Dieruff missed two foul shots, two field goals and threw a pass away negating any chance for a comeback win.

Leading scorers: Pottsville – Bill Devlin 16, Jim Glenn 12, Norm Waters 11; Dieruff – Jan Kapcala 17, Danny O'Donnell 14, Ross Moore 12.

Easton 72 Tamaqua 53: Easton ran off two spurts of eight points each to take a 24-12 first quarter lead. They continued to pour it on during the next two periods to hold a 65-35 lead heading into the final period. Tamaqua outscored the Red Rovers 18-7 in the final period to make the score more respectable.

Leading scorers: Easton – Tom Fisher 27, Joe Braido 11, Bob Keiber 10; Tamaqua – Rich Krepak 19.

Central Catholic 73 Phillipsburg 48: Central Catholic opened its season in an effort to forget the 1966 season. Coach Mike Koury's squad defeated Phillipsburg decisively. The Vikings got their first field goal after more than three minutes of play. Although they did not get a field goal until a little less than three minutes to play in the quarter, Phillipsburg held an 11-8 lead. In the second quarter, Central Catholic took over and the game was essentially over.

Leading scorers: Central Catholic – Ray Bazylak 16, Jim Booros 10, Bob Neff 10; Phillipsburg – Art Russo 11, George Stamets 10.

Bethlehem-Hazleton: This contest scheduled for Hazleton was postponed due to a heavy snowstorm.[2]

Bethlehem 79 Central Catholic 48: After the postponement of their opening game against Hazleton, Bethlehem opened its season with Central Catholic. Spotting the Vikings early leads of 6-2 and 8-3, Bethlehem trailed Central Catholic after one quarter 12-11. Bethlehem took the lead at 13-12 to begin the second quarter and led at the half 29-26. Bethlehem's offense came to life in the third and fourth periods when they scored fifty points while holding the Vikings to 22.

Leading scorers: Bethlehem-John Lehman 23, Mike Rosko 20, Bob Bear 10, Bill Wescoe 10; Central Catholic-Ray Bazylak 20.

Pottsville 77 Tamaqua 76: Pottsville improved to 2-0 to start the season with a win over Tamaqua 77-76. Pottsville built up ten-point lead at the half 43-33 seemingly in command against winless Tamaqua. Tamaqua burst out in the third quarter to score 27 points and pull within four of Pottsville 64-60. The Tams continued to fight and trailed by a single point 73-72 with 90 seconds to play. The teams traded baskets in the last minute as Pottsville escaped with a narrow victory.

Leading scorers: Pottsville – Norm Waters 32, Jim Glenn 14, Bill Devlin 11, Dan Guers 10; Tamaqua – Jim Knoblauch 24, Rich Krepak 21, John Forys 14, John Mateyak 11.

Dieruff 68 Bethlehem Catholic 49: Dieruff's press defense buried Bethlehem Catholic 24-6 in the first period and cruised to the win. Jan Kapcala scored 11 points for the Huskies in the opening period. The Golden Hawks made only 17 of 76 shots from the floor in the loss. After the first period, Bethlehem was outscored by only a single point in the last three quarters.

Leading scorers: Dieruff – Jan Kapcala 22, Dan O'Donnell 14, Jack Conrad 10; Bethlehem Catholic – Greg Falkenbach 13.

Hazleton 96 Allen 88 OT: At the Little Palestra, Allen and Hazleton, reminiscent of past years, battled hard with the game going into overtime after an 84-84 tie in regulation. Hazleton's Tony Kinney made a layup with 33 seconds left to create the tie. Allen had led the game 84-80 with 90 seconds to play. Eleven lead changes and ten ties highlighted the contest. Hazleton led after one period 22-18 only to have Allen take a half time lead 41-39. The score was tied after three periods 66-66 and both teams scored 18 points in the final period. Hazleton dominated the Canaries in overtime to head for home with a 2-0 record and left the Canaries at 0-2.

Leading scorers: Hazleton - Joe Marnell 27, Joe Moran 20, Phil Andras 16, Tony Kinney 14, Ron Sube 10; Allen – Glenn Angelino 30, Dan Helman 19, Bob Ulaner 14.[3]

Easton 84 Phillipsburg 58: Easton built up a 19-8 lead in the first period. and increased it to 38-21 at half time. Phillipsburg cut the lead to 11 in the third period 58-47, only to see the Red Rovers add to it in the final period for a 26-point win.

Leading scorers: Easton – Joe Braido 23, Tom Fisher 21, Bob Keiber 18; Phillipsburg –Steve Samson 15, Al Pianelli 13, Don Samson 10.[4]

Week 2

Bethlehem 94 Easton 67: Undefeated Easton took an early lead 6-0 before Bethlehem reeled off six in a row to tie the score. Bethlehem went on to take a first quarter lead 20-12 and took a commanding lead in the second quarter 46-26. Easton could get no closer than 12 points 62-50 in the third period in suffering their first loss of the season after winning four straight games.

Leading scorers: Bethlehem – Mike Rosko 25, John Lehman 24, Paul Schreiber 19, Paul Albino 12; Easton – Tom Fisher 27, Bob Keiber 15, Joe Braido 10.

Dieruff 96 Tamaqua 59: Led by sophomore Ross Moore's twelve points, Dieruff took a 23-15 lead into the second quarter. Dan O'Donnell scored ten points in the third quarter to increase the Huskies' lead to 71-48. Dieruff set home court records with the 96 points and 39 field goals scored in the game. Coach Pinky Purnell's squad dropped to 0-3 in league play.

Leading scorers: Dieruff – Ross Moore 30, Jan Kapcala 18, Dan O'Donnell 16, Jack Conrad 12; Tamaqua – John Mateyak 23, John Forys 18.

Hazleton 81 Bethlehem Catholic 42: Connecting on only 12 of 62 from the floor, Bethlehem lost its second straight league game to Hazleton. The unbeaten Mountaineers took a modest 13-10 lead in the first quarter before their offense started to click. They held the Golden Hawks to seven points in the second quarter while they scored 20. Hazleton outscored Bethlehem Catholic 48-25 in the second half.

Leading scorers: Hazleton – Joe Marnell 12, Ron Sube 12, Darrell Farkus 12, Phil Andras 12, Joe Moran 10; Bethlehem Catholic – Tom Coyle 11.

Allen 58 Central Catholic 53: Playing a zone defense and falling behind after a quarter 18-11, Coach Milo Sewards switched to a man-to-man defense and Allen recovered to take a 32-31 half time lead. The Canaries expanded the lead to 50-41 after three quarters and fended off the Vikings for their first league victory.

Leading scorers: Allen – Dan Helman 14, Tom Kerstetter 12; Central Catholic – Ray Bazylak 13, Rico Caggiano 10.[5]

Pottsville 93 Phillipsburg 43: At Pottsville, the Crimson more than doubled up winless Phillipsburg to remain tied with Bethlehem for the league lead at 3-0. Pottsville hit on 41 field goals with Phillipsburg getting only 18.

Leading scorers: Pottsville – Dan Guers 22, Norm Waters 17, Jim Glenn 14, Bill Devlin 14; Phillipsburg – Al Pianelli 10.

Bethlehem 89 Hazleton 82: In a snow makeup game in Hazleton, with six ties and four lead changes in the first period, Bethlehem came away with a 24-22 lead. Scoring 30 points in the second quarter to the Mountaineer's 26, Bethlehem expanded the halftime-lead to six 54-48. In the third period, Hazleton put on a rally which cut the lead to one early in the final quarter 67-66 before the Hurricane scored five in a row to end up with an 89-82 win.

Leading scorers: Bethlehem – John Lehman 22, Paul Albino 22, Paul Schreiber 17, Mike Rosko 17; Hazleton – Joe Marnell 19, Joe Moran 18, Ron Sube 14, Darrell Farkus 13.[6]

Week 3

Easton 70 Allen 63: Allen took a 19-16 lead into the second quarter, but Easton came back to take a one-point lead into halftime 33-32. Parttime starter Vic Berliant scored 20 of the Canaries first 26 points with 15 of them in a row. Easton took an eight-point lead 50-42 late in the third quarter, but Allen fought back to tie the game at 58-58 with a little more than four minutes left in the game. Tom Fisher rallied Easton in the last few minutes for the win.

Leading scorers: Easton – Tom Fisher 22, Bob Keiber 18, Bob Huffstettler 13; Allen – Vic Berliant 35.

Pottsville 79 Bethlehem 77: With Pottsville holding a 17-12 lead after a quarter, Bethlehem rebounded to take a half time lead 33-29. The Hurricane took off early in the third period to build a seventeen-point lead 48-31 and the game seemed in hand. Outscoring Bethlehem 12-2, Pottsville cut the lead to 75-69 with less than two minutes to play. Pottsville tied the score at 77-77 with 25 seconds to play. Norm Waters hit a field goal with two seconds left to send the Hurricane to first league loss. Pottsville improved to 4-0 in league play and 8-0 overall.

Leading scorers: Pottsville – Norm Waters 30, Dan Guers 18; Bethlehem – Mike Rosko 22, John Lehman 20, Paul Albino 12, Paul Schreiber 11.

Tamaqua 52 Bethlehem Catholic 41: Tamaqua ended its seven-game losing streak at the expense of Bethlehem Catholic. In a low-scoring first half, the Golden Hawks took an 18-16 lead heading into the locker room. Tamaqua came out in the third quarter and hit two shots to take a 20-18 lead and eventually expanded it to 13. After missing all five first half foul shots, Tamaqua hit on 14 of 17. Jim Chassar scored 19 of the Golden Hawks first 29 points.

Leading scorers: Tamaqua – Rich Krepak 16, John Mateyak 14, Ron Forys 10; Bethlehem Catholic – Jim Chassar 24.

Dieruff 93 Phillipsburg 49: Dieruff, after taking a 19-12 first quarter lead, tied a school record with 29 points in the second quarter to jump out to a 48-23 half time lead. Pottsville lost its fourth straight league contest and had never beaten Dieruff. Dieruff improved to 3-1 in league play.

Leading scorers: Dieruff – Jack Conrad 22, Jan Kapcala 20, Dan O'Donnell 15, Jerry Houser 11; Phillipsburg – Steve Samson 19, George Stamets 13.[7]

Hazleton 108 Central Catholic 73: At Hazleton, the Mountaineers scored 25 points or more in each of the four quarters in a pouncing of Central Catholic and set a school record for points in a game. Hazleton burst out to a 10-1 first quarter lead and were never threatened.

Leading scorers: Hazleton – Joe Marnell 23, Joe Moran 19, Tony Kinney 12, Ron Sube 11; Central Catholic – Fred Payonk 14, Jim Booros 13, Bob Neff 12.[8]

Pottsville 73 Allen 69: At Pottsville, Allen took a 14-9 lead over the home team with 2:15 to play in the first period only to see the Crimson Tide score 18 straight points and surge into a 27-14 lead with a little less than six minutes to play in the second period. They maintained the lead into half time 38-25. With six minutes to play in the game, Allen trailed 60-45. Glenn Angelino sparked a comeback which brought the Canaries to within five 70-65 with 44 seconds to play. Pottsville prevailed to win the game and remain unbeaten at 5-0.

Leading scorers: Pottsville – Dan Guers 22, Bill Devlin 20, Norm Waters 19; Allen – Glenn Angelino 24, Vic Berliant 12.

Easton 67 Hazleton 59: Easton controlled the first half of the game against Hazleton taking a 15-7 first quarter lead and extending it to 35-24 at the half. In the 3rd period, Hazleton closed the gap to 39-37. With Easton leading 41-38, the Red Rovers went on an 8-2 run to take a 49-41 lead into the final period. With a little over three minutes to play, Hazleton took their first lead 53-52. Hazleton increased the lead to 59-54 with a 1:41 to play. From here, Bob Keiber took over for the Red Rovers with a field goal and foul conversion and a steal and layup to tie the game in regulation 59-59. Easton then held Hazleton scoreless in overtime.

Leading scorers: Easton – Bob Keiber 23, Tom Fisher 22, Bob Huffstetler 11; Hazleton – Darrell Farkus 15, Joe Moran 14.

Dieruff 84 Bethlehem 57: Dieruff went on a 21-4 spurt over a 7 ½ minute period from late in the first period through most of the second period. The Huskies led 32-18 going into half time. Bethlehem could not get any closer than 11 points and the Huskies scored 30 points in the final period to win handily.

Leading scorers: Dieruff –Dan O'Donnell 27, Jan Kapcala 21, Ross Moore 12, Jack Conrad 11; Bethlehem – John Lehman 15, Andy Lukevics 12.

Bethlehem Catholic 65 Central Catholic 51: Bethlehem Catholic ended its three-game league losing streak at the expense of Central Catholic. The Golden Hawks' superior height prevented Central Catholic from getting much more than a single shot each time down the court. The Vikings pulled within two in the third period 38-36, but the Golden Hawks went on a small run and took a 44-37 lead into the final period.

Leading scorers: Bethlehem Catholic – Jim Chassar 17, Tom Coyle 14, Len Eddinger 12; Central Catholic – Jim Booros 10.

Tamaqua 63 Phillipsburg 59: Phillipsburg took a five-point lead 18-13 into the second period and held on to the lead through the third period 44-31. Tamaqua finally took the lead in the game with 2:11 to play 57-56. An eight-point run in the last two minutes gave Tamaqua a triumph over the Stateliners.

Leading scorers: Tamaqua – Jim Knoblauch 17, Rich Krepak 17, Jim Mateyak 14, Ron Forys 10; Phillipsburg - Dave Leone 16, Steve Samson 14, Don Jean 11, George Stamets 10.[9]

Week 4

Tamaqua 85 Allen 76: After losing their first seven contests, Tamaqua won its third in a row with a win over Allen to even their league record at 3-3 as Allen fell to 1-5. Tamaqua took a 20-13 lead after one quarter, but Allen fought back in the second period to take a 29-27 lead with 3:11 left in the second quarter. That was the only lead the Canaries had in the contest as Tamaqua charged out in front again at the half 42-36. Tamaqua's man-to-man defense worked to perfection in forcing the Canaries to numerous turnovers.

Leading scorers: Tamaqua – Rich Krepak 23, Jim Knoblauch 22, Ron Forys 14, Jim Mateyak 10; Allen – Tom Kerstetter 25, Glenn Angelino 23, Vic Berliant 12.

Dieruff 96 Hazleton 56: Dieruff, improving to 5-1, dropped Hazleton to 3-3 with an easy victory at the East Side gym. The 96 points matched the school single game record set earlier in the season. Dieruff led 45-20 at the half and Hazleton coach Fran Libonati, frustrated with the situation, pulled his starting five and inserted an entire new lineup. The strategy had no impact as the Huskies continued to build the lead.

Leading scorers: Dieruff – Jan Kapcala 27, Dan O'Donnell 19, Jack Conrad 16, Ross Moore 14; Hazleton – Joe Moran 11, Bob O'Donnell 11, Bob Farnell 10.

Bethlehem 86 Phillipsburg 44: Using superior height, Bethlehem jumped out to an eleven-point half time lead 36-25 over Phillipsburg, winless in league play at 0-6. The Hurricane put the game out of reach with a 29-point outburst in the third period and built the lead to 65-36. In the fourth quarter, Bethlehem held the Stateliners to a mere 8 points to complete the rout.

Leading scorers: Bethlehem – John Lehman 26, Mike Rosko 20, Bill Wescoe 10; Phillipsburg – Steve Samson 14, Dave Leone 11.

Bethlehem Catholic 61 Easton 55: Through three periods, Easton appeared well on its way to victory with a 49-42 lead over Bethlehem Catholic. With Tom Coyle scoring ten and Jim Chassar seven points in the fourth quarter, the Golden Hawks outscored the Red Rovers 19-6 in the final period to upset Easton.

Leading scorers: Bethlehem Catholic-Jim Chassar 19, Tom Coyle 18, Len Eddinger 10; Easton-Joe Braido 20, Tom Fisher 18.

Pottsville 87 Central Catholic 53: Pottsville remained undefeated in league play and held on to first place with a pasting of Central Catholic. Tied after a period 16-16, Pottsville's Norm Waters and Bill Devlin converted 14 of 15 free throws in the second period to take a 40-28 half time lead. Pottsville expanded the lead in the second half by outscoring the Vikings 47-25. The Vikings lost their 5th straight in league play after opening the season with a win. Pottsville kept the Vikings' leading scorer Ray Bazylak scoreless.

Leading scorers: Pottsville – Norm Waters 24, Bill Devlin 17, Dan Guers 13, Bob Wilson 11; Central Catholic – Jim Booros 22.[10]

Bethlehem 86 Tamaqua 53: Bethlehem snapped Tamaqua's modest three-game win streak and improved to 5-2. Tamaqua hung in with the Hurricane in the first period trailing by a point 19-18. Bethlehem took charge in the second period and continued to add to the lead in each period of the second half. In the fourth quarter, Bethlehem went on a 14-2 spurt to take a 75-42 lead.

Leading scorers: Bethlehem–John Lehman 29, Mike Rosko 21, Paul Albino 16; Tamaqua–Rich Krepak 14, Jim Knoblauch 12.

Dieruff 70 Allen 53: With a 32-25 halftime lead, Dieruff allowed Allen to pull within a point 32-31 before going on a 12-2 run in the middle of the third period and take an eleven-point lead 48-37 into the final quarter. With Pottsville's loss to Hazleton, the victory put the Huskies into a tie for the league lead with Pottsville, both at 6-1. Allen dropped to 1-6 and fell into a three-way last place tie with Central Catholic and Phillipsburg.

Leading scorers: Dieruff - Dan O'Donnell 17, Jack Conrad 16, Ross Moore 13, Jan Kapcala 13; Allen – Vic Berliant 19, Glenn Angelino 14, Tom Kerstetter 10.

Hazleton 89 Pottsville 77: For the third year in a row, Hazleton knocked a team out of the ranks of the unbeaten by handing them their initial league loss. Two years prior, it was Central Catholic and one-year prior Dieruff. On their home court, the Mountaineers stayed close with Pottsville in the first half with one-point leads at the end of each quarter 19-18 and 39-38. Down 42-41 in the 3rd period, Hazleton strung together 10 points to jump into the lead 51-42 and built it to 17 in the 4th quarter 72-55. Pottsville dropped into a tie for the league lead with Dieruff.

Leading scorers: Hazleton – Joe Marnell 28, Darrell Farkus 18, Tony Kinney 18, Joe Moran 16; Pottsville – Norm Waters 29, Dan Guers 22.

Phillipsburg 61 Bethlehem Catholic 57: Phillipsburg won its first league game in a closely contested matchup with Bethlehem Catholic. In a game that was hardly ever more than four points apart, Phillipsburg took a four-point lead in the first quarter 19-15, saw it reduced to three in the second quarter 31-28, and ended up tied after three 45-45. When Al Pianelli fouled out in the middle of the last quarter, Don Samson replaced him and he hit a key field goal to put Phillipsburg in the lead for good.

Leading scorers: Phillipsburg – Al Pianelli 18, Steve Samson 16, George Stamets 11; Bethlehem Catholic – Tom Coyle 16, Len Eddinger 14, Gary Kardos 10.

Easton 80 Central Catholic 73: Central Catholic fell behind Easton 43-32 at the half with the Red Rovers' Tom Fisher scoring 17 points. Employing a press to start the third quarter, the Vikings struck quickly to take the lead 50-49 with 3 ½ minutes left in the quarter. They ended the quarter still holding a one-point lead 58-57. Easton regained the lead 69-68 for good when Allen missed three layups in the space of a minute.

Leading scorers: Easton – Tom Fisher 30, Bob Keiber 13, Joe Braido 12, Phil Schramm 11, Miller 10; Central Catholic – Jim Booros 25, Stan Bushner 14, Bob Neff 10.[11]

Week 5

Hazleton 93 Tamaqua 56: Tamaqua led Hazleton 18-15 after one period, but then the Mountaineers employed a press in the second quarter and held them to eight points. Hazleton scored 21 to take a 36-26 lead. Joe Moran led the way with eleven points in the quarter as Hazleton dumped 36 on Tamaqua to take a commanding lead. The Mountaineers added on to the lead in the 4th quarter to crush Tamaqua.

Leading scorers: Hazleton –Joe Moran 24, Phil Andras 17, Joe Marnell 14, Tony Kinney 11; Tamaqua – John Forys 21, John Mateyak 11.

Dieruff 39 Central Catholic 37: Although it was not a slow-down, Dieruff had to fight hard through a Viking staunch defense to register the win over the Vikings. Both teams played a conservative defensive-minded game with both the first and last quarters ending up with both teams scoring in the single digits. The Vikings took the first quarter lead 7-6 with the half ending in a 20-20 tie. After three quarters, the game was still tied at 32. Dieruff won the game on a Jan Kapcala follow-up of a missed layup with four seconds to go and preserve their first-place tie.

Leading scorers: Dieruff – Jan Kapcala 21; Central Catholic – Jim Booros 19.

Bethlehem Catholic 58 Bethlehem 53: Jim Chassar scored 22 points in the second half including ten consecutive points and Bethlehem Catholic surprised Bethlehem. Bethlehem's only lead of the night was at 2-1. After a low-scoring first quarter with the Hawks taking an 8-5 lead, the scoring picked up in the final three periods. The Hurricane came within one at 50-49 but the Hawks responded to close out the victory with several foul shots and a tap-in goal.

Leading scorers: Bethlehem Catholic – Jim Chassar 25, Gary Kardos 14; Bethlehem – John Lehman 26, Mike Rosko 12.

Phillipsburg 66 Allen 61: In a battle to get out of the league cellar, Coach Al Senavitis' Phillipsburg squad prevailed for their first win ever over the Canaries in seven tries. Phillipsburg did not substitute in the game until Al Pianelli fouled out with 2 ½ minutes to play and was replaced by Don Samson. The lead seesawed back and forth with Allen leading after one period 16-10, Phillipsburg after two 30-23, and Allen after the third 48-43. In the second period, Phillipsburg trailed 20-10 when they ran off 20 straight points to take the lead. With Allen ahead in the 4th period, Phillipsburg scored 10 straight points to take the lead 60-55. Allen responded with six points to lead 61-60. With Don Ramson scoring four of the points, Phillipsburg scored the last six points for the win.

Leading scorers: Phillipsburg – Don Jean 19, Al Pianelli 14, George Stamets 11, Steve Samson 10; Allen – Jim Wildonger 14, Glenn Angelino 14, Tom Kerstetter 10.

Pottsville 78 Easton 68: Pottsville kept pace with Dieruff for first place by downing Easton. Trailing 38-29 at the half, Easton came out and scored 26 points in the third period to take the lead 55-52. With Easton leading 57-56, Pottsville scored ten points in a row to take the lead for good. With each team making 25 field goals, Pottsville won the game at the foul line by making 28 of 35 while Easton only shot 26 and converted 18.

Leading scorers: Pottsville – Norm Waters 22, Bill Devlin 15, Dave Bechtel 12, Karl Lombel 12; Easton – Tom Fisher 27, Bob Huffstettler 10.[12]

Phillipsburg 74 Hazleton 63: Phillipsburg won its third consecutive game after six losses with its upset of Hazleton. Phillipsburg outscored Hazleton in every quarter but the fourth and never trailed in the game. The Stateliners took a 17-8 first quarter lead and increased it to 15 points 56-41 heading into the final quarter. Despite not pressing in the game, Phillipsburg still came up with 13 steals which led to easy baskets.

Leading scorers: Phillipsburg – Steve Samson 17, Al Pianelli 17, Dave Leon 16, Don Jean 12, George Stamets 12; Hazleton – Joe Moran 14, Phil Andras 12, Darrell Farkus 10, Bob Farnell 10.

Tamaqua 85 Central Catholic 71: Tamaqua outscored Central Catholic by 12 in the first period and 7 in the third period and held off the Vikings. The Vikings strong second and fourth quarters could not overcome the large lead built up by Tamaqua. The closest the Vikings could get was ten points 73-63 early in the 4th quarter. Central Catholic dropped to 1-8 for the first half and a tie for last place with Allen.

Leading scorers: Tamaqua – Rich Krepak 26, John Mateyak 17, Jim Knoblauch 12; Central Catholic – Jim Booros 27, Fred Payonk 11, Rico Caggiano 10.

Bethlehem 64 Allen 52: Allen finished the first half at 1-8 with a loss to Bethlehem. Allen's only lead was at 1-0 and could get no closer than six points later in the game. Bethlehem led at the half 32-25 and outscored the Canaries in every quarter.

Leading scorers: Bethlehem– Mike Rosko 23, John Lehman 23; Allen– Glenn Angelino 21, Vic Berliant 15.

Dieruff 72 Easton 59: Dieruff built up a big first half lead which at one time reached fifteen points. They led by eleven at the half 35-24. Early in the 4th quarter, the Red Rovers cut the lead to four at 52-48 before Dieruff rose to the occasion to extend the lead and win the game. For a six-minute stretch from late in the first period and into the second period, Dieruff outscored Easton 18-2. Dieruff's win set them up for a first half title playoff with Pottsville.

Leading scorers: Dieruff – Dan Waelchi 19, Dan O'Donnell 19, Jan Kapcala 14, Jack Conrad 12; Easton – Tom Fisher 21, Joe Braido 14, John Cappellano 10.[12]

Pottsville 90 Bethlehem Catholic 56: Pottsville earned its way into a first half playoff with Dieruff by routing Bethlehem Catholic. Two players, the Hawks' Tom Coyle and Pottsville's Norm Waters went over the 1000-point mark for their high school careers. Waters achieved the milestone in the second period and Coyle in the third. After the Hawks tied the game at 11 right at the beginning of the second quarter, Pottsville blitzed Bethlehem Catholic with thirty-nine points in the quarter to take a commanding 50-25 halftime lead.

Leading scorers: Pottsville – Dan Guers 22, Bill Devlin 19, Karl Lombel 15; Bethlehem Catholic – Tom Coyle 16.[13]

First Half Playoff

Dieruff 68 Pottsville 48: After trailing 25-18 to end the first half with Dieruff scoring only 9 points in each of the first two periods, Coach Dick Schmidt squad came out of the locker room and outscored Pottsville 24-13 to take the lead. Jan Kapcala scored 15 points in the period. The Huskies scored 26 more points in the final period to win the first half title and avenge their only first half loss.

Leading scorers: Dieruff - Jan Kapcala 26, Ross Moore 14, Jack Conrad 13; Pottsville – Norm Waters 16.[14]

Second Half - Week 6

Bethlehem 71 Hazleton 54: Bethlehem scored the last eight points of the first period and the first four of the second period for a 19-8 margin early in the second quarter over Hazleton. The Mountaineers never got within nine points during the rest of the game. The Hurricane also ended the second quarter with a seven-point run and scored ten in a row in the final period to hand Hazleton a decisive loss. Coach John Howard won his 200th game as head coach.

Leading scorers: Bethlehem-John Lehman 22, Andy Lukevics 18, Mike Rosko 13; Hazleton-Joe Marnell 22.

Bethlehem Catholic 61 Allen 58: Bethlehem Catholic began the second half of play with a stunning upset of Allen. Scoring only 14 points in nine previous games, guard Mark Cacciatore scored 10 big points in the Hawks second upset of the Canaries in league play. Allen took a 17-9 lead part way through the first quarter, but Bethlehem Catholic tightened up the game to within two points at the end of the quarter 19-17. Both teams scored 10 points in the second quarter and the Hawks outscored the Canaries by three in the third to take a 32-31 lead. The lead changed 8 times and the game was tied 8 times in a very tight contest. Bethlehem Catholic outscored the Canaries by 13-4 in a 2 ½ minute stretch of the final quarter to pull out the win.

Leading scorers: Bethlehem Catholic – Tom Coyle 17, Greg Falkenbach 15, Mark Cacciatore 10.; Allen – Glenn Angelino 25, Vic Berliant 15.

Phillipsburg 81 Central Catholic 73: After being down 40-19 at halftime, Central Catholic fought back in the second half. Battling the Stateliners on a nearly equal basis in the third quarter, the Vikings came on with a rush by outscoring Phillipsburg 31-17 in the fourth quarter to make the final score much more respectable despite the loss.

Leading scorers: Phillipsburg – Steve Samson 22, Dave Leone 19, George Stamets 17, Don Jean 14; Central Catholic – Jim Booros 19, Stan Bushner 14, Rick Weider 13.

Dieruff 58 Pottsville 47: Playing Pottsville for the second time in a week, Dieruff fought off a scrappy Crimson Tide quartet to start the second half. Dieruff held nine-point leads after the first quarter 17-8 and at the half 31-22. A determined Pottsville squad cut the lead to 38-33 heading into the final period, but clutch field goals by Jack Conrad headed off Pottsville's rally.

Leading scorers: Dieruff-Jack Conrad 17, Dan O'Donnell 14; Pottsville-Norm Waters 16, Dave Bechtel 11.[15]

Tamaqua 66 Easton 59: Easton took a slim two-point lead after a quarter 17-15 only to have Tamaqua outscore the Red Rovers 27-12 in the second quarter and take the lead 40-27. Easton held the Tams to eight points in the third quarter to trim the lead to 48-43. In the final quarter, the Red Rovers tied the score 55-55 but Tamaqua bounced back for the win.

Leading scorers: Tamaqua – Jim Knoblauch 19, John Forys 18, John Mateyak 15; Easton – Tom Fisher 24, Joe Braido 11.[16]

Week 7

Bethlehem 90 Central Catholic 57: Central Catholic coach Mike Koury used his sophomore lineup and their supposed shooting prowess against a taller Bethlehem quintet. The strategy failed as the more experienced Hurricane led after one quarter 19-9. The Vikings made a push in the second quarter but were still outscored 21-18. The Hurricane made 37 of 62 field goal attempts to roll to the triumph.

Leading scorers: Bethlehem – Andy Lukevics 23, Paul Schreiber 19, Paul Albino 15, John Lehman 15, Mike Rosko 11; Central Catholic – Jim Booros 17.

Easton 74 Phillipsburg 53: Tom Fisher scored ten points in the first quarter as Easton took an eight-point lead 18-10. Phillipsburg rebounded in the second quarter to outscore the Red Rovers 16-14, but still trailed by six at the half. The Stateliners would get no closer. Easton took the contest by nineteen points and ended Phillipsburg's four-game win streak.

Leading scorers: Easton – Tom Fisher 27, Steve Jefferson 18, Joe Braido 10, Phil Schramm 10; Phillipsburg – Al Pianelli 15, Steve Samson 13, Dave Leone 10.

Pottsville 86 Tamaqua 49: Tamaqua hung with Pottsville early in the 1st period, but Pottsville took off with Norm Waters hitting ten points in the quarter to lead his team to a 24-15 lead. It only got worse for Tamaqua as Waters scored eight more points in the 2nd quarter for a commanding Pottsville lead at the half 44-27. The 3rd quarter was all Pottsville as Ken Kline's squad outscored Tamaqua 25-9 to trounce the Tams.

Leading scorers: Pottsville – Norm Waters 35, Dan Guers 12, Jim Glenn 11, Bob Devlin 11; Tamaqua – Rich Krepak 21, Jim Knoblauch 10.

Dieruff 54 Bethlehem Catholic 53: Despite the suspension of Jim Chassar due to academic issues, Bethlehem Catholic gave Dieruff all it could handle with Dieruff never having more than a five-point lead in the contest. Paul Calvo's quintet trailed by five at the half 26-21, but then the Hawks came out in the third quarter to go on a 10-1 spurt and take a 31-27 lead. The third quarter ended in a 38-38 tie. With Dieruff leading 52-51 and 12 seconds to play, the Hawks fouled Jack Conrad in an attempt to get the ball back. Conrad calmly made both ends of a 1 and 1 foul shot opportunity to hold off Bethlehem Catholic.

Leading scorers: Dieruff – Jan Kapcala 21, George Isaacson 12, Dan O'Donnell 10; Bethlehem Catholic – Tom Coyle 15, Greg Falkenbach 14.

Hazleton 88 Allen 86: Allen traveled to Hazleton, looking for its first victory of the second half. Allen fell for the eighth straight time despite five more field goals 35-30 than Hazleton. Hazleton ran off nine straight points to lead at the half 47-38. The Canaries came back with a furious third quarter rally to take the lead 66-64 heading into the final quarter. Allen still held the lead 82-79 when Rick Wehr was injured and had to be taken to the hospital for examination. At that point, the Mountaineers went on to score six points in a row for the win.

Leading scorers: Hazleton – Joe Marnell 29, Joe Moran 22, Phil Andras 16, Tony Kinney 12; Allen – Glenn Angelino 36, Vic Berliant 17, Phil Miller 10.[17]

Hazleton 71 Bethlehem Catholic 70: For the second consecutive contest, Bethlehem Catholic dropped a contest by a single point, this time to Hazleton. Playing to a 16-16 tie after one period, the Hawks charged out to a ten-point lead 36-26 at the half. Hazleton cut the lead to seven 45-38 in the third period. The Hawks still held the lead 70-66 with 33 seconds to play. Two walking violations led to five points by Joe Marnell with two field goals and a foul shot to put Hazleton in the lead and hand the Hawks a frustrating loss.

Leading scorers: Hazleton – Darrell Farkus 26, Joe Marnell 23, Joe Moran 10; Bethlehem Catholic – Tom Coyle 25, Len Eddinger 14, Mark Cacciatore 10.[18]

Bethlehem 85 Easton 62: After holding small leads early in the first quarter, Easton was unable to stay with Bethlehem's scoring machine with four players in double figures. The Hurricane held the half time lead 41-24. Easton scored the first bucket of the second half to cut the score to 41-26 and that would be the closest Easton would get for the rest of the game. Despite having three players in double figures, Easton lost the game.

Leading scorers: Bethlehem – John Lehman 22, Mike Rosko 19, Andy Lukevics 18, Paul Albino 10; Easton – Phil Schramm 14, Tom Fisher 12, Joe Braido 11.

Allen 100 Central Catholic 75: With both teams at 0-2 in the second half, Allen broke an eight-game league losing streak in a rousing manner with the triumph over Central Catholic. The loss was the Vikings eleventh straight in league competition. The result was never in doubt with Allen taking 23-10 and 48-25 leads in the first two quarters. The Canaries scored 35 in the third period to extend the lead to 83-55.

Leading scorers: Allen – Vic Berliant 33, Dan Helman 19, Dick Zellickson 13, Tom Kerstetter 12, Glenn Angelino 10; Central Catholic – Jim Booros 25, Stan Bushner 12, Mike Pfahler 12, Bob Neff 11.

Pottsville 87 Phillipsburg 57: Phillipsburg committed 30 turnovers in the game and Pottsville outscored the Stateliners 26-8 in the second period. As a consequence, Pottsville trounced Phillipsburg. Pottsville's press defense forced Phillipsburg into the many turnovers including 20 in the first half.

Leading scorers: Pottsville – Dan Guers 21, Norm Waters 20, Jim Glenn 12, Bill Devlin 11; Phillipsburg – Al Pianelli 18, Don Jean 15.

Dieruff 85 Tamaqua 58: With five players in double figures, Dieruff decisively put away Tamaqua. After the Huskies moved in front 8-0, Tamaqua fought back to trail 14-12 partly due to Jim Knoblauch's six straight points. With a big third quarter in favor of the Huskies 25-8, coach Dick Schmidt turned the game over to the bench.

Leading scorers: Dieruff – Jan Kapcala 24, Dan O'Donnell 19, Jack Conrad 14, George Isaacson 12, Ross Moore 10; Tamaqua – Rich Krepak 20, Jim Knoblauch 12, John Forys 12, John Woodring 11.[19]

Week 8

Hazleton-Central Catholic: This game was postponed and scheduled for the following week on Monday.

Bethlehem-Pottsville: The game was postponed to the following week on Wednesday.

Dieruff 92 Phillipsburg 39: Coach Dick Schmidt played his starters for less than two periods against Phillipsburg after jumping out to 30-8 first period and 51-16 half time leads. Dieruff scored 49 points before Phillipsburg could score 10. In the second quarter, Dieruff's regulars scored 17 straight points and held the Stateliners without a field goal until 1:40 in the period.

Leading scorers: Dieruff – Dan O'Donnell 22, Jan Kapcala 17, George Isaacson 11, Ross Moore 11; Phillipsburg – George Stamets 20.

Tamaqua 82 Bethlehem Catholic 73: Bethlehem Catholic started out well to take a 21-20 lead over Tamaqua. Tamaqua came back to lead at the half 39-36. After Tamaqua took a 13-point lead in the third quarter, the Hawks wiped out most of the lead to get within a single point 58-57. Tamaqua's Rich Krepak and Jim Knoblauch then took charge to lead the Tams to an 82-73 triumph and even their record at 2-2.

Leading scorers: Tamaqua – Jim Knoblauch 20, Rich Krepak 20, John Forys 17, John Mateyak 15, John Woodring 10; Bethlehem Catholic – Tom Coyle 18, Greg Falkenbach 15, Len Eddinger 14.

Easton 74 Allen 65: Scoring 16 of their final 26 points on free throws, Easton handed Allen another loss. Allen led several times in the third period 36-33, 38-35, and 39-37 before the Red Rovers took a 49-41 lead to take command of the game.

Leading scorers: Easton – Tom Fisher 27, Bob Huffstettler 20; Allen – Glenn Angelin0 26, Vic Berliant 15.[20]

Allen 87 Pottsville 84: After only winning two of the past twelve league contests, both over Central Catholic, Allen shocked Pottsville with the upset victory in a game in which they trailed only three times, all in the first period. Entering the fourth period with an eight-point lead 51-43, the Canaries increased it to 79-69 with 3:50 to play in the game. Pottsville stormed back to within a single point with 12 seconds left to play 85-84 when Pottsville fouled Allen's Vic Berliant. He calmly made both foul shots with three seconds to play to seal the victory.

Leading scorers: Allen – Vic Berliant 27, Dan Helman 26, Glenn Angelino 14; Pottsville – Dan Guers 19, Bob Wilson 14, Jim Glenn 13, Bill Devlin 10.

Phillipsburg 60 Tamaqua 53: Coach Al Senavitis' squad broke a three-game losing streak with a triumph over Tamaqua. Phillipsburg's stingy defense held Tamaqua to eleven first half points while scoring 35. Although Tamaqua outscored the Stateliners 24-8 in the 3rd period, they could not overcome the big first half lead.

Leading scorers: Phillipsburg – Don Samson 15, Steve Samson 15, George Stamets 10, Don Jean 10, Dave Leone 10; Tamaqua – Rich Krepak 21, John Mateyak 10.

Easton 87 Hazleton 76: Hazleton took a nine-point lead 25-16 after a quarter with Easton cutting the lead to one at the half 40-39. Coach Tom Sweeney's club forged into the lead entering the final period 65-62. The Red Rovers retained the lead at 69-66 when they held Hazleton scoreless for four minutes in the final period while scoring only six points. The six points was sufficient for an Easton victory. Hazleton played without Joe Marnell who was out with a virus.

Leading scorers: Easton – Tom Fisher 24, Joe Braido 18, Bob Huffstettler 12, John Pearson 12; Hazleton – Darrell Farkus 25, Tony Kinney 18, Phil Andras 13.

Bethlehem 60 Dieruff 53 OT: In a battle for sole possession of first place, Bethlehem ended Dieruff's 12-game win streak in overtime. Dieruff took a 9-point lead after the first quarter. Bethlehem chipped away in the next three periods to tie the game in regulation. Bethlehem's Andy Lukievitz hit a desperation heave from 47 feet at the buzzer to end the first half. Bethlehem tied the score at 53 with 2:21 left in regulation. Neither team could score after that to send the game into overtime. Bethlehem held Dieruff scoreless in overtime. Paul Albino led the Hurricane with four points in overtime and give his team sole possession of first place in the second half.

Leading scorers: Bethlehem – John Lehman 19, Andy Lukevics 14, Mike Rosko 13; Dieruff – Jan Kapcala 18, Dan O'Donnell 16, Dan Waelchi 10.

Bethlehem Catholic 51 Central Catholic 42: Bethlehem Catholic kept Central Catholic winless in the second half with the win over the Vikings. The Hawks led 13-3 after one period. The Vikings narrowed the lead to two twice in the third period 29-27 and 34-32, but got no closer than six points in the final period.

Leading Scorers: Bethlehem Catholic – Len Eddinger 14, Gary Kardos 12, Greg Falkenbach 10; Central Catholic – Bob Neff 13.[21]

Week 9

Hazleton 84 Central Catholic 71: Postponed from a week earlier, Hazleton traveled to Rockne Hall and handed the Vikings their 13th consecutive league loss since their season-opening win over Phillipsburg. The Vikings held a four-point lead early in the first quarter and were tied at 16, 18, and 20 before the Mountaineers moved ahead for good. Hazleton's Tony Kinney scored 14 points in the third quarter.

Leading scorers: Hazleton – Tony Kinney 28, Darell Farkus 22, Phil Andras 15; Central Catholic – Stan Bushner 16, Bob Neff 13, Jim Booros 11.[22]

Allen 75 Tamaqua 64: Allen evened its second half record at 3-3 with the triumph over Tamaqua. The Canaries only trailed in the first period when Tamaqua went out to a 6-0 lead to start the game and still held the lead at 11-10. Thereafter, Allen took the lead and never relinquished it. Tamaqua narrowed the lead to six in the 4th period 57-51, but Allen countered again to take a safe lead on a Glenn Angelino goal.

Leading scorers: Allen – Dan Helman 22, Glenn Angelino 19, Dick Zellickson 11, Vic Berliant 11; Tamaqua – Rich Krepak 25, John Woodring 11, Jim Knoblauch 10.

Bethlehem 95 Phillipsburg 35: Bethlehem held Phillipsburg to six points in the first and third periods and four in the second to enter the final period with a 68-16 lead. Despite scoring 19 points in the final period, the Stateliners still lost by sixty points 95-35. Every player on both benches made it into the game.

Leading scorers: Bethlehem – John Lehman 20, Andy Lukevics 14, Mike Rosko 12, Paul Schreiber 11; Phillipsburg – Art Russo 10.

Bethlehem Catholic 52 Easton 50: Both teams evened their records at 3-3 with Bethlehem Catholic's win over Easton. The teams were evenly matched in three of the four periods with each team scoring 9 points in the first, 12 in the third, and 21 in the final period. Bethlehem Catholic outscored the Red Rovers 10-8 in the second period which was the difference in the game. The Hawks led 48-42 on the strength of six straight foul shots by Tom Coyle. Easton scored the next eight points to surge into the lead 50-48. The Hawks' Don Meder tied the score at 50 and soon after Easton missed a go ahead shot. Greg Falkenbach grabbed the rebound, later was fouled, and made two foul shots with two seconds to play for the win.

Leading scorers: Bethlehem Catholic – Tom Coyle 20, Len Eddinger 14, Greg Falkenbach 12; Easton – Tom Fisher 21, Bob Huffstettler 12, Joe Braido 11.

Pottsville 74 Central Catholic 62: Central Catholic took a lead 39-36 into the third quarter in an attempt to break their long league losing streak. Pottsville took the lead in the third period 53-52. After a field goal by Bob Neff, Central had its last lead at 54-53. Pottsville outscored the Vikings 21-8 down the stretch for the triumph and the Vikings' 14th consecutive league loss.

Leading scorers: Pottsville – Norm Waters 27, Dan Guers 19; Central Catholic – Bob Neff 19, Jim Booros 17, Fred Payonk 14.[23]

Pottsville 70 Bethlehem 62: In a game postponed from the week before, Pottsville dropped Bethlehem into a tie for first place at 6-1 with Dieruff with the defeat of the Hurricane. Pottsville led after a period 18-11 with Bethlehem cutting the lead to 32-31 at the half. Pottsville surged to a ten-point lead after three quarters 56-46 and Bethlehem could not overcome the lead. Pottsville improved to 4-2.

Leading scorers: Pottsville – Norm Waters 19, Bill Devlin 17, Dan Guers 16, Dave Bechtel 10; Bethlehem – Paul Albino 24, Andy Lukevics 10.

Dieruff 76 Hazleton 59: Dieruff rolled into Hazleton looking to stay right behind Bethlehem for the league lead. After taking down the Mountaineers, the Huskies found themselves in a first-place tie with Bethlehem's loss to Pottsville, both at 5-1. After one quarter, Dieruff fell behind 22-4 and defeat stared them in the eyes. A 23-9 spurt in the second period pulled Dieruff within four points. Before the half, Phil Andras heaved a 75-foot shot at the buzzer that went in for the Mountaineers. With 4:50 remaining in the third period, Dieruff finally went ahead 36-35. Dieruff pulled away to secure an unlikely win after the miserable first period.

Leading scorers: Dieruff – Dan O'Donnell 20, Jan Kapcala 18, Jack Conrad 18; Hazleton – Darrell Farkus 18, Tony Kinney 14.[24]

Allen 45 Dieruff 44: Dieruff's shared possession of first place lasted only two days when Allen invaded their home court and shocked the Huskies in their intracity rivalry. Allen charged out of the gate with an 18-9 first quarter lead. Dieruff reduced the lead to four at the half 24-20 and took a four-point lead 34-30 in the third period. Allen scored the next six points to head into the final period ahead 36-34. With a little more than five minutes to play, the Huskies had scored six in a row to lead 40-36. Allen outscored Dieruff 9-4 the rest of the way to pull out the one-point win.

Leading scorers: Allen – Vic Berliant 19, Glenn Angelino 14; Dieruff - Jack Conrad 14, Ross Moore 12.

Pottsville 60 Hazleton 58: After a 2-1 lead at the outset of the game, Pottsville did not take the lead again until three seconds to play when Norm Waters dropped in a field goal to escape with an unlikely victory over Hazleton. Hazleton led at the end of each of the first three quarters 17-12, 18-17, and 17-14 and held a 52-43 going into the final quarter. With their lead cut to 58-56, the Mountaineers lost the ball on a walking call and Pottsville's Dave Bechtel tied the score at 58. Hazleton's Dale Farkus missed two foul shots with Pottsville getting the rebound to set up the last shot for the victory.

Leading scorers: Pottsville – Norm Waters 20, Bill Devlin 15, Dave Bechtel 14; Hazleton – Phil Andras 20, Darrell Farkus 13, Tony Kinney 10.

Bethlehem Catholic 55 Phillipsburg 52: In a low-scoring first half, Bethlehem Catholic held a 19-15 lead over Phillipsburg before increasing it to nine points or more during the third period. With a ten-point lead at the start of the fourth period, the Hawks were able to hold on for the victory despite being outscored by Phillipsburg 24-17 in the final period. Don Meder scored ten points for the Hawks to spark the big lead.

Leading scorers: Bethlehem Catholic – Greg Falkenbach 14, Don Meder 12, Tom Coyle 11; Phillipsburg – George Stamets 18, Steve Samson 13, Don Samson.

Bethlehem 96 Tamaqua 79: Bethlehem regained sole possession of first place with a win over Tamaqua. Bethlehem led after one period 28-19, but Tamaqua attempted to make a game of it in the second period outscoring the Liberty boys 23-22. With two key players in foul trouble, John Forys with four and John Mateyak with three, Tamaqua could not keep pace with them on the bench. Hindered with these players in foul trouble and no one to stop John Lehman, Bethlehem pulled ahead for a 96-79 triumph over Tamaqua.

Leading scorers: Bethlehem – John Lehman 38, Mike Rosko 19, Paul Schreiber 15, Paul Albino 12, Andy Lukevics 10; Tamaqua – Jim Knoblauch 24, Rich Krepak 24, John Mateyak 15.

Easton 85 Central Catholic 57: Central Catholic gave Easton a tough fight in the first half and trailed only 32-31 going into the locker room. The second half was a different story with the Red Rovers outscoring the Vikings 53-26 to win easily and hand the Vikings their 15th straight loss in the league. Easton improved to 4-3 for the second half.[25]

Leading scorers: Easton – Tom Fisher 20, Steve Jefferson 19, Joe Braido 19, Bob Huffstettler 15; Central Catholic – Stan Bushner 19, Jim Booros 14, Bob Neff 12.

Week 10

Allen 74 Phillipsburg 63: Allen continued its second half surge to improve to 5-3 with their defeat of Phillipsburg. With Glenn Angelino scoring only a single field goal in the first half, Allen held on to a one-point lead at the half 31-30. Phillipsburg only made two second quarter field goals but converted on 12 foul shots to stay close to the Canaries. Phillipsburg continued to stay close at 41-40 in the third period before Allen moved ahead by ten points. Phillipsburg could get no closer than six points the rest of the game.

Leading scorers: Allen – Vic Berliant 23, Dan Helman 17, Glenn Angelino 15; Phillipsburg – George Stamets 15, Dave Leone 12, Steve Samson 11.

Easton 83 Pottsville 77 2OT: It took two overtimes, but Easton took Pottsville out of the running for a second half title with the win. Pottsville led throughout the game until Easton's Tom Fisher tied the game at 71 with 1:50 left in regulation. Joe Braido put Easton ahead 73-71 before Norm Waters tied it 73-73 for Pottsville with four seconds left. The score remained tied at 75-75 after the first overtime. The score was again tied at 77-77 when Tom Fisher took over for Easton to score the final six points on four foul shots and a field goal for the win.

Leading scorers: Easton – Tom Fisher 34, Bob Huffstettler 16, Steve Jefferson 15, Joe Braido 12; Pottsville – Norm Waters 25, Carl Lombel 13, Dave Bechtel 11.

Dieruff 76 Central Catholic 44: After Dieruff took a 10-0 lead four minutes into the game, they cruised into half time with a 31-10 lead. Central Catholic only made five of 23 field goal attempts in the first half with Jim Booros going scoreless on eight missed shots. Jan Kapcala, Dieruff's high scorer only played 5 minutes because of a sore hip.

Leading scorers: Dieruff – Ross Moore 23, Jack Conrad 14, Dan O'Donnel 14; Central Catholic – Jim Booros 14, Bob Neff 12, Fred Payonk 10.

Bethlehem 69 Bethlehem Catholic 42: In Coach John Howard's last home game, his Bethlehem team took down Bethlehem Catholic. Liberty took off on 12-0 run to start the game and came back with a 15-point run to go ahead 27-4. Bethlehem took its biggest lead in the third quarter 46-18, but the Hawks came back to reduce it to 51-29 at the third quarter mark.

Leading scorers: Bethlehem – John Lehman 19, Paul Schreiber 17, Andy Lukevics 10; Bethlehem Catholic – Len Eddinger 11, Tom Coyle 10.

Tamaqua 87 Hazleton 84 OT: After first quarter tied at 19, Hazleton pulled ahead of Tamaqua 44-35 at the half. Tamaqua cut the lead to 58-55 going into the final period. Jim Knoblauch and Rich Krepak led a charge to put Tamaqua ahead 75-69 with a minute and a half to play. Joe Marnell scored five points and Darrell Farkus three points as Hazleton tied the game at 78-78 with 10 seconds to play. The lead changed hands eight times in the last 3 ½ minutes. Tamaqua won in overtime to put both teams at 3-5.

Leading scorers: Tamaqua – Jim Knoblauch 29, Rich Krepak 25; John Mateyak 12, John Forys 12; Hazleton – Joe Marnell 21, Phil Andras 20, Darrell Farkus 19, Kennedy 16.[26]

Pottsville 60 Bethlehem Catholic 59 OT: Dan Guers converted two foul shots with seven seconds left in overtime to pull out the win over Bethlehem Catholic. Pottsville had led through most of the first three quarters until the Hawks broke a full court press to take the lead at the end of the quarter 40-39. Pottsville surged ahead again 47-40, but Bethlehem Catholic overcame the lead to tie in regulation 53-53. In overtime, Tom Coyle had given the Hawks the lead 59-58 with a layup prior to Guers' foul shots.

Leading scorers: Pottsville – Norm Waters 20, Jack Dolbin 20, Jim Walters 16, Tom Shaffer 10; Easton – Tom Fisher 27, Steve Hutnick 11, John Pearson 10, Joe Braido 10.

Bethlehem 74 Allen 71: Allen gave Bethlehem everything it had and made the Hurricane earn their second half title. Allen led after a quarter 15-14 and at the half 34-31. They increased the lead to eleven points with 1:29 to go in the third period. Bethlehem forced Allen into four turnovers to make up the difference and tied the score at 51-51 heading into the fourth quarter. With the score tied at 55-55 in the final quarter, Bethlehem ran off ten consecutive points to take a commanding lead 65-55 and pull out the win. Bethlehem would now move on to play first half champions Dieruff for the overall league title.

Leading scorers: Bethlehem – Mike Rosko 21, John Lehman 16, Andy Lukevics 15, Paul Albino 12, Paul Schreiber 10; Allen – Vic Berliant 30, Glenn Angelino 25.

Easton 75 Dieruff 67: In a very physical contest, Dieruff held narrow leads throughout the game: 16-14 after one quarter; 35-32 at the half; and 50-45 after 3 periods. Dieruff had held a 14-point lead 47-33 in the third period after they had run off 12 points in a row. Led by Tom Fisher, Easton fought back to narrow the advantage to five. After Bob Huffstettler put Easton in front 63-61 in the fourth quarter, a fight erupted mid-way through the quarter when Husky Dan Waelchli and Red Rover Charlie Schramm jostled under the basket. A free-for-all erupted between players and spectators joined the fracas. After a ten-minute delay, game resumed only to have Easton's Steve Jefferson and Dieruff's Jan Kapcala crashed onto the floor after going after a rebound. Kapcala appeared to injure his neck. Before play resumed, Coach Dick Schmidt sent his starting five into the locker room and finished the game with the second team.

Leading scorers: Easton – Tom Fisher 31, Bob Huffstettler 16, Steve Jefferson 11; Dieruff – Ross Moore 18, Jack Conrad 16.[27]

Tamaqua 73 Central Catholic 71: Tamaqua ran Central Catholic's league losing streak to seventeen with a last second shot in overtime for the victory. Tamaqua's seven-point lead from the first quarter 20-13 held up until the final minutes of regulation. Jim Booros, who scored 13 points in the final period, led the Vikings from a 51-47 deficit entering the fourth quarter. Booros hit a long jump shot with 17 seconds remaining to tie the game at 65-65. In overtime, Tamaqua took the lead only to have the Vikings tie the score until John Forys hit a 15-foot jumper with three seconds left in overtime to win the contest for the Tams.

Leading scorers: Tamaqua – Jim Knoblauch 30, John Forys 13, Rich Krepak 12, John Mateyak 10; Central Catholic – Jim Booros 24, Bob Neff 17, Fred Payonk 15.

Hazleton 79 Phillipsburg 69: Hazleton closed out its season with the triumph over Phillipsburg. After building a 24-point lead 64-40 in the third period, Hazleton had to fight off the Stateliners who closed the gap to 73-69 with 1:50 to play. Hazleton scored the last six points for the win and an 11-10 overall record for the season.

Leading scorers: Hazleton – Phil Andras 21, Joe Marnell 16, Daryl Farkus 15, Tony Kinney 10; Phillipsburg – George Stamets 23, Dave Leone 21, Steve Samson 10.[28]

League Playoff

Dieruff 58 Bethlehem 56: At Muhlenberg's Memorial gym, Dieruff and Bethlehem met to determine which team would be crowned as the league champions. The game was nip-and-tuck the whole way. Huskie Coach Dick Schmidt stayed with his starting five the whole way and his counterpart, John Howard, only used one extra player. Dieruff took a one-point lead after the first quarter 17-16 and increased it another point in the second 29-27. Bethlehem erased the lead the third quarter with the game tied at 44-44. With four minutes left in the final quarter, Dieruff trailed 50-46. Jan Kapcala tied the score for Dieruff at 50 with a field goal and foul shot. He also scored the Huskies' last four points as Dieruff outlasted Bethlehem for the title.

Leading scorers: Dieruff – Jan Kapcala 24, Dan O'Donnell 17, Ross Moore 10; Bethlehem – Mike Rosko 16, Paul Albino 12, John Lehman 10, Andy Lukevics 10.[29]

Postseason PIAA Play

Dieruff 90 West Hazleton 77: At the St. Joseph's gym in Hazleton, Dieruff took on West Hazleton in a semi-final district contest. With the Huskies scoring 33 points in the opening period to take a 15-point lead, it looked like the game would be a runaway for Dieruff. The second quarter slowed down quite a bit with Dieruff outscoring West Hazleton by a single point 14-13. In the third quarter, the Huskies scored six more points than West Hazleton to enter the final period with a 22-point lead. Suddenly, West Hazleton went on a 16-3 run in the first 3 ½ minutes to reduce the lead to 68-59. The Huskies increased the lead back to 15 points 76-61 with 2 ½ minutes left.

Leading scorers: Dieruff – Jan Kapcala 23, Jack Conrad 23, Dan O'Donnell 20, Ross Moore 11; West Hazleton – Jim Platukis 25, Dennis Mummey 17, Stan Komosinsky 14.[30]

Dieruff 57 Mahanoy Area 49: Dieruff took on Mahanoy Area, North Schuylkill League champions, for the District 11 title at the Harrisburg Farm Show Arena. Playing a more controlled offense, the Huskies took a three-point lead into the second quarter and Mahanoy shaved a point off the lead going into half time 24-22. With seventeen seconds to play in the second quarter, Dan O'Donnell converted a three-point play that gave the Huskies the lead for good. Early in the third period, the Huskies had an eight-point run to move ahead by nine points 33-24. Mahanoy bounced back to reduce the lead to 37-30 going into the final period. Outscoring Mahanoy 20-19, the Huskies hung on for the win. With both teams making 21 field goals, Dieruff won the game at the foul line converting a phenomenal 15 of 16 compared to Mahanoy's 7 of 10.

Leading scorers: Dieruff – Jan Kapcala 23, Dan O'Donnell 16; Mahanoy Area – Mickey Holland 11, Butch Mack 10, Mickey Wargo 10.[31]

Dieruff 45 Central Dauphin 43: Back at the Farm Show Arena for the eastern semi-final matchup with the Central Dauphin Rams, Dieruff spurted out to a 21-8 first quarter lead. In the second quarter, the Rams scored nine straight points to reduce Dieruff's lead to 23-20. Dieruff fought back to increase the lead to 33-26 at the half. In the third quarter, Dieruff missed all eleven field goal attempts and scored only four points while the Rams scored ten. One point separated the teams going into the final quarter 37-36. In another low scoring quarter, Central Dauphin finally tied the game at 43 with 2:33 to play. Dieruff went into a freeze and held the ball the rest of the game. Almost losing the ball several times, Dieruff won the game on a desperation shot by Dan Waelchi with two seconds to play that miraculously went in for the game winner.

Leading scorers: Dieruff – Ross Moore 15, Jan Kapcala 10: Central Dauphin – Ted Knauss 13, Al Rafferty 12.[32]

Chester 65 Dieruff 51: Playing their third game in a row at the Farm Show Arena in Harrisburg, Dieruff took on Chester for the PIAA Eastern championship. Dieruff started fast by taking a 22-14 first quarter lead. Early in the second quarter, Dieruff increased the lead to nine only to go into a cold spell and not score a point for nearly six minutes. Chester ran off twelve straight points to take a 29-28 lead into the locker room. The Huskies retook the lead in the third quarter 35-33, but that was their last lead. Chester led at the end of three quarters 41-39. The fourth quarter was all Chester as the Huskies shooting went cold again and they were outscored 24-12. The final score was not entirely indicative of the closeness of the game for over three periods. Dieruff's season was over.

Leading scorers: Chester – Paul Williams 18, Harry McLaughlin 15, Steve Powell 12, Ken Shamberger 12; Dieruff – Dan O'Donnell 18, Jan Kapcala 13.[33]

PCIAA Postseason Playoff

Bethlehem Catholic 59 Central Catholic 48: Bethlehem Catholic and Central Catholic squared off in an Allentown Diocese semi-final matchup. The Hawks took a modest two-point lead 10-8 into the second quarter only to see the Vikings overtake them at the half 22-20. Bethlehem Catholic surged ahead again after three periods 36-33. The Vikings scored first in the final quarter to cut the lead to one, but the Hawks came back with three baskets to lead 42-37. At the 2:15 mark of the final period, Bethlehem Catholic froze the ball forcing the Vikings to foul. The Hawks made seven foul shots in the final two minutes to win the game.

Leading scorers: Bethlehem Catholic – Tom Coyle 20, Gary Kardos 15, Greg Falkenbach 13; Central Catholic – Bob Neff 17, Jim Booros 13.[34]

Shamokin Lourdes 72 Bethlehem Catholic 68: Bethlehem Catholic traveled to Selinsgrove to take on Lourdes of Shamokin in an Eastern semi-final matchup. The Hawks played catchup all night after falling behind by three points after one quarter 20-17 and seven points at the half 37-30. Lourdes finished the quarter scoring ten in a row and added two more to start the third quarter. Playing a full court press in the fourth quarter, the Hawks finally went ahead 68-67 with 45 seconds to play. However, the only points scored from that point on were five foul shots by Lourdes to pull out the victory.

Leading scorers: Lourdes – Joe Smith 23, Barry Boblick 22, Gryzbowski 12; Bethlehem Catholic – Tom Coyle 21, Gary Kardos 16, Jim Chassar 13, Greg Falkenbach 10.[35]

Postseason Accolades

Leading Scorers: Tom Fisher, Easton, led the league in scoring with 435 points in 18 games for a 24.1 points per game average. Only four other players cracked the 300-point mark. John Lehman, Bethlehem, scored 386 points and was followed closely by Norm Waters of Pottsville with 379 points. Glenn Angelino, Allen, had 337 points with Rich Krepak, Tamaqua, the only other player over 300 with 323 points. The sixth through tenth leading scorers included: Jan Kapcala, Dieruff, 296; Mike Rosko, Bethlehem, 289 points; Vic Berliant, Allen, 285 points; Dan Guers, Pottsville, 284 points; and Jim Booros, Allen, 278 points.[36]

All-Stars: The league all-star first team included: Jan Kapcala, Dieruff; Norm Waters, Pottsville; John Lehman, Liberty; Tom Fisher, Easton; and Glenn Angelino, Allen. The second team consisted of: Mike Rosko, Bethlehem; Rick Krepak, Tamaqua; Tom Coyle, Bethlehem Catholic; Jack Conrad, Dieruff; and Joe Marnell, Hazleton.[37]

All-State: The only league players on the all-state team were mentioned as honorable mention. They included: Tom Fisher, Easton; Jan Kapcala, Dieruff; John Lehman, Bethlehem; and Norm Waters, Pottsville.[38]

Final Standings

First Half		Second Half		Overall	
Dieruff	8-1	Bethlehem	8-1	Dieruff	14-4
Pottsville	8-1	Dieruff	6-3	Pottsville	14-4
Bethlehem	6-3	Easton	6-3	Bethlehem	14-4
Easton	5-4	Pottsville	6-3	Easton	11-7
Hazleton	5-4	Allen	5-4	Hazleton	9-9
Bethlehem Catholic	4-5	Bethlehem Catholic	4-5	Bethlehem Catholic	8-10
Tamaqua	4-5	Hazleton	4-5	Tamaqua	8-10
Phillipsburg	3-6	Tamaqua	4-5	Allen	6-12
Allen	1-8	Phillipsburg	2-7	Phillipsburg	5-13
Central Catholic	1-8	Central Catholic	0-9	Central Catholic	1-17

Team Rosters

Allen: Coach Milo Sewards, Glenn Angelino, Vic Berliant, Joe Bierman, Everett, Dan Helman, Tom Kerstetter, Phil Miller, Ray Peters, Bill Snyder, Bob Ulaner. Rick Wehr, Jim Wildonger

Bethlehem: Coach John Howard, Paul Albino, Bob Behr, Bob Biggs, Grimes, Inman, Kaufman, John Lehman, Andy Lukevics, Tom Partridge, Randy Peto, Mike Rosko, Paul Schreiber, Joe Tavares, Rich Wescoe

Bethlehem Catholic: Coach Paul Calvo, Mark Cacciatore, Jim Chassar, Tom Coyle, Len Eddinger, Greg Falkenbach, Dave Griffith, Gary Kardos, John Kearney, Tom Leary, Larry Lynch, Don Meder, Rich Metzger

Central Catholic: Coach Mike Koury, Ray Bazylak, Jim Booros, Stan Bushner, Rico Caggiano, Phil Cech, Bob Neff, Fred Payonk, Mike Pfahler, Ernie Thoma, Rick Weider, Denny Williams,

Dieruff: Coach Dick Schmidt, Jack Conrad, Jerry Houser, George Isaacson, Jan Kapcala, Don Knerr, Ross Moore, John Nyemscek, Dan O'Donnell, Jay Radio, Rudy Trinkle, Dan Waelchi, Mike Witkowski

Easton: Coach Tom Sweeney, Gary Betts, Joe Braido, Terry Briggs, John Cappellano, Tom Fisher, Bob Huffstettler, Steve Hutnik, Steve Jefferson, Bob Keiber, Tom Meier, Miller, Bob Nelson, T Nelson, John Pearson, Charlie Schramm, Daryl Woodring

Hazleton: Coach Fran Libonati, Phil Andras, Rich Babon, Darrell Farkus, Jim Fuddy, Bob Farnell, Tony Kinney, Anthony Lucadamo Joe Moran, Joe Marnell, Bob O'Donnell, Chris Perry, Ron Sube, Steve Yencho

Phillipsburg: Coach Al Senavitis, Gary Farmer, Gordon, Don Jean, Dave Leone, Long, Al Pianelli, Race, Rodenbaugh, Art Russo, Don Samson, Steve Samson, George Stamets, Touchton, Bucky Utley

Pottsville: Coach Ken Kline, Clyde Baskerville, Dave Bechtel, Bill Devlin, Jim Glenn, Dan Guers, Frank Mills, Bob Seiberling, Tom Shaffer, Mark Spector, Jim Walters, Norm Waters, Bob Wilson

Tamaqua: Coach Eli Purnell, Barron, John Forys, Walt Henne, Jim Knoblauch, Rich Krepak, John Mateyak, Ruggeri, Richard Southam, George Wenzel, Williams, John Woodring, Kevin Young

1968

The Little Palestra Era Ends

In early December 1967, Allentown School Board announced that the Allen's basketball team would play all its home games at Muhlenberg College's Memorial Hall. Built in 1930, the Allen's gym and the court size (78' X 44') was considered outdated and too small. The switch to the new "home" court would begin on January 3, 1968, with league opponent Pottsville. Pottsville had been Allen's (then known only as Allentown) first opponent at the Little Palestra when it opened on December 12, 1930.[1]

First Half - Week 1

Allen 71 Hazleton 62: Coach Milo Seward's Allen quintet opened the 1968 season against one of its longest archrivals Hazleton. The Canaries opened league play with a fast start in the first half by outscoring the Mountaineers by twenty-two points 41-22. Coach Fran Libonati found the right lineup combination in the second half with his squad scoring 43 points while holding the Canaries to 30. The first half lead proved to be too much to overcome as Allen took the contest 71-62.

Leading scorers: Allen – Tom Kerstetter 26, Glenn Angelino 20, Bob Ulaner 10, Mark Schultz 12; Hazleton – Bob O'Donnell 14, Tony Kinney 14, Darrell Farkus 14, Bob Farnell 10.

Dieruff 76 Bethlehem Catholic 50: With a slim one-point lead over Bethlehem Catholic after one quarter 12-11, Dieruff opened up an eleven-point lead 33-22 heading into the locker room, despite 17 points by the Hawks' Jim Chassar. Dieruff demonstrated more of the same in the second half as the taller Bethlehem Catholic squad could not keep up with the faster Huskies. In the third period, the Huskies held the Hawks without a point for nearly five minutes to put the game out of reach 66-33. The Hawks scored eleven points in a row in the final period, but Dieruff still prevailed in a rout 76-50.

Leading scorers: Dieruff – Jan Kapcala 22, Ed Benson 20, Ross Moore 13, Mike Witkowski 11; Bethlehem Catholic – Jim Chassar 28.

Pottsville 69 Tamaqua 75: Pottsville led after a quarter 16-14 and stretched the lead to 34-22 at the half. Both teams scored 16 points in the 3rd quarter. Pottsville put the game well out-of-reach by outscoring the Tams by eight in the final period for a 69-49 triumph.

Leading scorers: Pottsville – Jim Berrang 20, Bill Devlin 16, Jim Glenn 13, Bill Yaag 13; Tamaqua – Jim Knoblauch 12.

Bethlehem 83 Central Catholic 75: Central Catholic opened its season hoping to end a 17-game losing streak in league play. First-year head coach Fritz Toner's Bethlehem squad took an eleven-point lead 22-11 in the first quarter. Despite outscoring the Hurricane in the next three periods 64-61, the Vikings could not overcome the 1st quarter advantage built up by Bethlehem and lost their 18th consecutive league game 83-75.

Leading scorers: Bethlehem – Mike Rosko 24, Tim Fisher 16, Bill Wescoe 16, Dan Yocum 16; Central Catholic – Bob Neff 27, Phil Cech 15.

Easton 80 Phillipsburg 73: Phillipsburg used a zone press to stay in the game against Easton. Except for a poor third quarter showing, the strategy worked. The game was close at the half 33-32 in Easton's favor. An eight-point run near the end of the third period gave Easton a ten-point lead 57-47 heading into the last quarter. Despite scoring 26 points in the quarter, Phillipsburg could not overcome Easton's lead.

Leading scorers: Easton – Bob Huffstettler 27, Steve Jefferson 17, Bob Pilz 14; Phillipsburg – Dave Leone 21, Brian Dominic 18, Al Pianelli 11.

Bethlehem 71 Easton 55: Dan Yocum scored 18 points and grabbed 19 rebounds to lead Bethlehem to a 71-55 win over Easton. The Hurricane committed only three turnovers during the game. After trailing by 34-18 at the half, Easton came out of the locker room to outscore Bethlehem 23-16 in the third quarter and cut the lead to 50-41. Bethlehem reeled off seven straight points to start the fourth period and put the game out of reach. Bethlehem won to go to 2-0 in league play.

Leading scorers: Bethlehem – Dan Yocum 18, Tim Fisher 15, Mike Rosko 14, Paul Schreiber 10; Easton – Steve Jefferson 16, Bob Huffstettler 15, Bob Pilz 11.

Dieruff 111 Tamaqua 86: Visiting Dieruff ran all over Tamaqua in the first period putting up 38 points to the Tams 13. The offensive explosion continued in the second quarter with Tamaqua countering by scoring 25 points for a half time score of 55-38. The offensive onslaught continued in the second half with both teams scoring 21 or more points with Dieruff finishing with 32 in the 4th quarter. In winning the game 111-86, Dieruff set both a school record and a Tamaqua floor record. Eight players scored in double figures.

Leading scorers: Dieruff – Jan Kapcala 30, Mike Witkowski 19, George Isaacson 17, Ross Moore 16, Ed Benson 13; Tamaqua – Jim Knoblauch 36, John Forys 16, Dan Truskey 12.

Hazleton 88 Bethlehem Catholic 74: Hazleton erupted for 32 points in the second quarter on their way to an 88-74 win over Bethlehem Catholic. The 18-point second quarter advantage was the difference in the game. Bethlehem Catholic led by three after one quarter 16-13 and outscored the Mountaineers in the 4th quarter 30-21. The Hawks could not get closer than 16 points in the final period.

Leading scorers: Hazleton – Bob Farnell 31, Darrell Farkus 27, Joe Duda 11, Tony Kinney 11; Bethlehem Catholic – Greg Falkenbach 25, Jim Chassar 16, John Kearney 13.

Allen 53 Central Catholic 48: At the Little Palestra, Allen rallied late to thwart an upset bid by Central Catholic. The Vikings started fast with an 18-7 first quarter lead. Allen reduced the lead to five at the half 22-17 as they held the Vikings to four points. The Vikings entered the last period with a 36-30 lead. The Canaries finally pulled even at 42-42 with about five minutes to play. In the last four minutes, the game was tied twice and the lead changed hands six times before Allen pulled ahead in the last minute of the game.

Leading scorers: Allen - Tom Kerstetter 21, Glenn Angelino 18, Dan Helman 19; Central Catholic - Bob Neff 26, Stan Bushner 10.

Pottsville-Phillipsburg: This game was postponed to the following week.[3]

Week 2

Allen 67 Easton 61: Allen moved to 3-0 with a 67-61 win over Easton at the Easton gym. After trailing 32-26 at the half, Easton made several runs at the Canaries in the second half. The first cut Allen's lead to 45-43 after three periods. In the fourth quarter, the Canaries held a 53-45 lead with seven minutes to play. In less than two minutes, the Red Rovers tied the score at 53-53 with Bob Huffstettler making three field goals and Tom Meier adding one. After the score was tied again at 55-55 and 57-57, Allen moved ahead for good on four points by Rick Wehr and George Zellickson's two free throws.

Leading scorers: Allen – Glenn Angelino 21, Rick Wehr 17, Tom Kerstetter 11, Dick Zellickson 11; Easton – Bob Huffstettler 26, Daryl Woodring 14.

Bethlehem Catholic 80 Tamaqua 56: With Jim Chassar's twelve points in the first quarter, Bethlehem Catholic took a 20-17 lead after Tamaqua had jumped out to an early lead. The Hawks scored ten points in a row after Tamaqua opened with a point in the 2nd quarter to take a commanding lead into half time 41-31. The Hawks expanded the lead and held the Tams to ten points in the final period to win handily 80-56.

Leading scorers: Bethlehem Catholic – Jim Chassar 43, Greg Falkenbach 16; Tamaqua – Jim Knoblauch 22, Walt Henne 13.

Hazleton 68 Central Catholic 64: Central Catholic started slowly on their home court falling behind Hazleton 35-22 at the half. In the last four minutes of the third quarter, the Vikings jelled and cut the lead to 55-46. In the 4th quarter, the Vikings pulled within four points 64-60, but could get no closer as Hazleton took the contest 68-64. The Vikings lost their 20th in a row in league play.

Leading scorers: Hazleton-Bob Farnell 22, Darrell Farkus 18, Tony Kinney 17; Central Catholic-Stan Bushner 23, Bob Neff 22.

Dieruff 72 Phillipsburg 42: Dieruff missed their first seven shots allowing Phillipsburg to take a 10-8 lead into the second period. The Huskies countered by holding Phillipsburg to six points and scoring 17 straight points late in the second period to open up 32-16 lead into the half. The second half was no better for the Stateliners as they were outscored 40-26 in the 72-42 loss to the Huskies.

Leading scorers: Dieruff - Ross Moore 23, Jan Kapcala 23, George Isaacson 13; Phillipsburg - Steve Samson 8.

Bethlehem 73 Pottsville 56: Traveling to Pottsville, Bethlehem came home with an easy 73-56 win over the Crimson. Pottsville took an early 4-3 lead before the Hurricane scored six straight to take the lead for good. Holding Pottsville to eight points and scoring twenty themselves, Bethlehem had an almost insurmountable 55-34 lead going into the final quarter. Pottsville made a valiant attempt to comeback by scoring 15 consecutive points but came up quite a bit short due to Bethlehem's large lead. Bethlehem improved to 3-0 to tie Dieruff and Allen for the league lead.

Leading scorers: Bethlehem – Mike Rosko 22, Bill Wescoe 18, Tim Fisher 14; Pottsville – Bill Devlin 29, Bill Yaag 10.[5]

Phillipsburg 64 Pottsville 40: Rescheduled from the previous week, Pottsville lost in Phillipsburg 64-40. Phillipsburg outscored the Crimson 25-6 in the 2nd quarter to take a 39-17 lead and control of the game.

Leading scorers: Phillipsburg – Al Pianelli 19, Dave Leone 17, George Stamets 13; Pottsville –Jim Glenn 10, Bill Devlin 11.[6]

Week 3

Allen 68 Pottsville 64: Pottsville came into Muhlenberg's Memorial Hall seeking to upset Allen in the first league game in the Canaries' new home. Pottsville took a 22-19 lead after one quarter with the Crimson scoring the last five points in the quarter. Allen scored six straight points at the start of the 2nd quarter only to see Pottsville retaliate with 12 in a row to help build a 42-38 lead going into half time. Allen's Tom Kerstetter and Mark Schultz each scored four points during a crucial stretch of the 3rd quarter driving Allen to a 54-49 lead after three periods.

Leading scorers: Allen– Mark Schultz 22, Tom Kerstetter 21; Pottsville– Jim Berrang 17, Bill Devlin 16, Claude Baskerville 14.

Dieruff 63 Bethlehem 46: In a battle of two early season unbeaten teams, Dieruff's stingy defense held Bethlehem to nine points in the first quarter and eight in the third quarter on the way to a 63-46 triumph. The Huskies defense limited the Hurricanes' Mike Rosko to 9 points for the game and forced Bethlehem into 21 turnovers. Allen and Dieruff now shared the league lead, both at 4-0.

Leading scorers: Dieruff – Ross Moore 19, Jan Kapcala 17, Ed Benson 16; Bethlehem – Tim Fisher 13, Paul Schreiber 13.

Phillipsburg 81 Tamaqua 62: Taking an incredible 100 shots from the floor, Phillipsburg made only 31 in the Stateliners' 81-62 victory over Tamaqua. The missed shots led to 25 offensive rebounds and numerous easy layups. Phillipsburg's shooting woes did not flow over to the foul line as they converted 19 of 23 foul shots. Tamaqua's Jim Knoblauch suffered through a tough first half with only two points, but recovered after halftime to add twenty points to his game total.

Leading scorers: Phillipsburg – Don Jean 20, Brian Dominic 15, Al Pianelli 13, Dave Leone 13, George Stamets 10; Tamaqua – Jim Knoblauch 22, Gary Williams 16.

Central Catholic 64 Bethlehem Catholic 42: Central Catholic rode its fast start, 15-6 after one quarter, to register its first win in league play after 20 consecutive losses. They added to the lead in each of the following quarters to defeat Bethlehem Catholic 64-42. The Hawks made only 19 of 72 field goal attempts. Both teams were at 1-3 in league play.

Leading scorers: Central Catholic – Stan Bushner 12, Phil Cech 11; Bethlehem Catholic – Jim Chassar 11.

Hazleton-Easton: This contest was postponed and rescheduled for late January.[7]

Allen 90 Tamaqua 70: At Muhlenberg's Memorial Hall, Allen ran its early season league win streak to five in a row with an easy 90-70 triumph over Tamaqua. After a 26-17 first quarter lead, Allen ran off ten straight points late in the second period to extend the lead to 45-25. After Tamaqua played the Canaries tough in the third period outscoring them 18-16, Allen scored nine in a row to extend the lead to 23 points.

Leading scorers: Allen – Glenn Angelino 21, Dick Zellickson 17, Mark Schultz 15, Rick Wehr 12; Tamaqua – Jim Knoblauch 24, John Forys 10, Gary Williams 10.

Dieruff 82 Hazleton 59: Roaring out of the locker room to take a 20-6 first quarter lead over Hazleton, the Huskies cruised to an 82-59 triumph to maintain a tie with Allen at 5-0 for the league lead. Jan Kapcala scored 12 points in the dominating first period. Dieruff took a 67-37 lead into the final period. Hazleton went on a 12-3 run in the final period to make the final score a little closer.

Leading scorers: Dieruff – Jan Kapcala 32, Ross Moore 20; Hazleton – Tony Kinney 12, Daryl Farkus 10, Bob O'Donnell 10.

Bethlehem 93 Phillipsburg 89 2OT: Despite losing three key players to fouls and trailing by 13 points in the third period, Bethlehem persevered in two overtimes to take the game from Phillipsburg 93-89. Phillipsburg went into half time with a 52-41 lead. Bethlehem cut the lead to three 66-63. With about 3 ½ minutes to play, Bethlehem took its first lead since the first period 73-70. Phillipsburg scored the next eight to lead 78-73 with 1 ½ minutes to play. At this point, Phillipsburg's George Stamets was ejected for punching Bethlehem's Bill Wescoe. With the Stateliners' leading 81-78, Ruyak made a field goal and Tim Fisher converted a free throw to send the game into overtime. Both teams scored four points in the first overtime. Tim Fisher and Jim Pavel made layups late in the second overtime to secure the win for Bethlehem.

Leading scorers: Bethlehem – Tim Fisher 23, Paul Schreiber 21, Dan Yocum 18, Mike Rosko 13; Phillipsburg – George Stamets 28, Al Pianelli 20, Dave Leone 19, Don Jean 13.

Pottsville 60 Central Catholic 57: After breaking its long league losing streak, Central Catholic could not maintain the momentum and lost to Pottsville at Rockne Hall 60-57. Trailing throughout the 1st half and at the half 27-24, the Vikings took a 42-38 lead into the final eight minutes. With the game tied at 55-55, Pottsville made critical foul shots on their way to the victory. Pottsville made 12 foul shots in the final period.

Leading scorers: Pottsville – Jim Glenn 18, Jim Berrang 16, Bill Devlin 13; Central Catholic – Rick Weider 18, Bob Neff 12.

Bethlehem Catholic 63 Easton 61: Jumping out to a 10-0 lead, Bethlehem Catholic left Easton catch up and tie the game at 15-15 and 17-17 before scoring seven in a row for a 24-17 first quarter lead. Scoring eight in a row in the second period, they extended the lead to 34-20 and finished the half ahead 40-27. After the Hawks scored the first bucket of the 4th quarter, Easton went on a 16-point run to tie the game at 57-57. Steve Jefferson made another field goal for Easton's only lead of the game 59-57. Jim Chassar and Greg Falkenbach then took over to pull out the game for the Hawks 63-61.

Leading scorers: Bethlehem Catholic - Jim Chassar 20, Greg Falkenbach 17, Allan Calvo 15; Easton – Bob Huffstettler 24, Steve Jefferson 18.[8]

Week 4

Allen 58 Dieruff 53 2OT: Cross-city rivals Dieruff and Allen, both undefeated in league play, met to determine which team would take command of first place. For three quarters, Dieruff took charge of the contest, although their advantage was not overwhelming at 41-33. Allen went on a 12-4 run to start the fourth quarter and tie the game at 45-45 with 3:15 left to play. Mark Schultz made four straight foul shots to give Allen the lead at 49-47 only to have Ross Moore connect from the corner with 10 seconds to play and tie the game in regulation 49-49. Each team scored two points in the first overtime with Mark Schultz making two foul shots and Ross Moore connecting for a field goal. The Canaries took charge in the second overtime with seven points to Dieruff's two for the Allen victory 58-53 and sole possession of first place.

Leading scorers: Allen – Mark Schultz 16, Tom Kerstetter 14, Glenn Angelino 11, Rick Wehr 11; Dieruff – Jan Kapcala 23, Ross Moore 16.

Bethlehem Catholic 77 Phillipsburg 64: Bethlehem Catholic stormed out to 10-0 and 12-2 leads, but Phillipsburg came right back with ten straight points to tie the game at 12-12. The Hawks took the first quarter lead 22-18 only to have Phillipsburg tie up the game at the half 39-39. Bethlehem Catholic broke the game open in the 3rd quarter outscoring Phillipsburg by ten and increased the lead by four more in the fourth for a 77-64 win.

Leading scorers: Bethlehem Catholic – Jim Chassar 29, Greg Falkenbach 16, Mark Cacciatore 14, John Kearney 10; Phillipsburg – George Stametz 19, Don Jean 15, Al Pianelli 14.

Bethlehem 92 Tamaqua 78: Tamaqua took an early 9-2 lead, but Bethlehem strung together 13 straight points to take a 28-22 first quarter lead. After Tamaqua cut the lead to four points 42-38, the Hurricane came out of the locker room to blitz Tamaqua 30-19 and take a commanding lead into the last quarter. Jim Knoblauch, the Tam's leading scorer, fouled out early in the third quarter.

Leading scorers: Bethlehem – Mike Rosko 25, Bill Wescoe 22, Dan Yocum 16, Paul Schreiber 11; Tamaqua – John Forys 20, Jim Knoblauch 14.

Easton 64 Central Catholic 61: In a closely contested game with few personal fouls, five by Central Catholic and eight by Easton, the Red Rovers prevailed over the Vikings 64-61. The Vikings trailed by 12 points with three minutes to play, but rallied back within two points 63-61 with 35 seconds to play. Central Catholic had two opportunities go awry. After a steal, they missed a layup and a follow-up tap-in rolled off the rim. Easton's Bob Huffstettler made a foul shot for the final point.

Leading scorers: Easton – Steve Jefferson 19, Bob Huffstettler 18, Bob Nelson 12; Central Catholic – Bob Neff 18, John Gaspar 16, Rick Weider 10.[9]

Hazleton 67 Pottsville 65: Despite being outshot from the floor with Pottsville hitting 30 to Hazleton's 20 field goals, Hazleton won a close contest with numerous lead changes 67-65. Foul shots made the difference in the game as Hazleton converted 27 of 33 foul shots while Pottsville only shot 9 and made 5. Neither team had more than a six-point lead, which Pottsville held twice in the 2nd quarter. With the score tied at 61-61, Bob Farnell put the Hazleton ahead with a field goal 63-61 and Hazleton converted 4 foul shots.

Leading scorers: Hazleton – Darrell Farkus 21, Steve Yenchko 15, Tony Kinney 15, Bob Farnell 11; Pottsville – Jim Glenn 17, Bill Devlin 14, Jim Berrang 12, Karl Lombel 12.[10]

Bethlehem 74 Bethlehem Catholic 30: Without top scorer Jim Chassar and playmaker Al Calvo, both suspended for disciplinary reasons by Coach Paul Calvo, Bethlehem Catholic could not muster any offense in a 74-30 rout by Bethlehem. The Hawks only scored in double figures in the second quarter, 11 points. With Allen's loss, Bethlehem joined a three-way tie for the league lead with Allen and Dieruff, each at 6-1.

Leading scorers: Bethlehem – Mike Rosko 24, Bill Wescoe 12, Paul Schreiber 11; Bethlehem Catholic – John Kearney 9.

Dieruff 64 Central Catholic 57: Central Catholic continued to provide stiff competition despite having won only a single game in the league. The Vikings took a half time lead 36-33 over Dieruff on the strength of Rick Weider's six consecutive field goals. With the score tied at 49-49 with 6:40 to go in the game, Jan Kapcala made a field goal to put the Huskies in the lead for good and pull out a 64-57 over Central Catholic.

Leading scorers: Dieruff: Jan Kapcala 26, Ross Moore 16; Central Catholic – Rick Weider 15, Bob Neff 15, John Gaspar 11, Stan Bushner 10.

Hazleton 81 Tamaqua 71: With each team successful on 31 field goals, Hazleton defeated Tamaqua by converting 19 of 24 foul shots. Tamaqua made 9 of 14 foul shots. After the score was tied at 19-19 after a quarter, Hazleton surged ahead by eight at halftime 43-35 primarily on the scoring of Tony Kinney with 10 points in the second quarter. Tamaqua came within four points 75-71 in the 4th quarter before Hazleton made six successive foul shots for the win 81-71.

Leading scorers: Hazleton – Tony Kinney 22, Darrell Farkus 18, Steve Yencho 17, Bob O'Donnell 14; Tamaqua – Jim Knoblauch 27, John Forys 17, Walt Henne 12.

Phillipsburg 73 Allen 62: Phillipsburg stunned unbeaten Allen 73-62. Phillipsburg took the first quarter lead 15-11, but Allen came back to tie the score at the half 35-35. Allen only led once in the first half. Allen took an early second half lead 42-38, but Phillipsburg went on a 20-2 run during the last half of the third period. Phillipsburg went into the final quarter with a 60-46 lead. The closest Allen got was 60-53 with five minutes left, but Phillipsburg made eleven free throws to put the game in the win column for the Stateliners.

Leading scorers: Phillipsburg – Dave Leon 25, George Stamets 14, Steve Samson 11, Don Jean 11, Al Pianelli 10; Allen – Tom Kerstetter 18, Dick Zellickson 12.

Pottsville 66 Easton 58: Easton trailed through the whole first half. The Red Rovers fell behind 16-11 after a quarter before reducing the lead to three at the half 29-26. After Pottsville entered the 4th quarter up 45-43, Easton tied the score at 49-49 and then again at 51-51. Pottsville forged ahead 60-52 on a 9-1 run with a little more than two minutes remaining. With both teams equal in field goals, Pottsville won the game by converting 22 of 36 foul shots while Easton made 14 of 31 for the final eight-point difference 66-58.

Leading scorers: Pottsville – Jim Berrang 16, Karl Lombel 14, Don Hill 11; Easton – Bob Huffstettler 24, Steve Jefferson 15.[11]

Week 5

Bethlehem 74 Allen 60: Bethlehem Liberty and Allen met at Muhlenberg's Memorial Hall to determine which team would continue to at least share first place. The two teams battled fiercely through three quarters with Bethlehem holding a slim one-point lead early in the last quarter 55-54. Coach Fritz Toner's squad went on a tear to outscore the Canaries 19-6 during the last four minutes and knocked Allen out of the first-place tie with a 74-60 triumph. Liberty outrebounded the Canaries 40-19 during the game.

Leading scorers: Bethlehem – Mike Rosko 21, Bill Wescoe 18, Paul Schreiber 14, Tim Fisher 12; Allen – Glenn Angelino 18, Tom Kerstetter 17, Daryl Tollinche 10.

Dieruff 50 Easton 46: Despite not scoring a single point in the first four minutes of the last quarter, Dieruff hung on to defeat Easton 50-46. During the first quarter, Coach Dick Schmidt benched George Isaacson because of his wild offensive play. When Coach Schmidt reinserted him into the lineup, Isaacson scored ten of the Huskies' 12 points in the third period to keep Dieruff in the lead going into the 4th quarter 44-38. Although they never led, the Red Rovers came within two points on three occasions 44-42, 46-44, and 48-46. Steve Jefferson fouled out with a little over four minutes left and his absence impacted the Red Rovers offense. The last quarter saw the teams score only 14 points combined with Easton scoring eight of the points to draw within 4 at buzzer. The win kept the Huskies in a first-place tie with Bethlehem.

Leading scorers: Dieruff – Jan Kapcala 20, George Isaacson 15; Easton – Steve Jefferson 18, Bob Huffstettler 17.[12]

Pottsville 72 Bethlehem Catholic 36: Bethlehem Catholic's offense continued to sputter with single digit points in three of four quarters. Pottsville outscored the Hawks 19-5 in the second quarter to spring out to a 32-14 lead. Despite a strong third period with the Hawks scoring two more points than their counterparts, they collapsed again in the last quarter and scored only eight points in a 72-36 loss to Pottsville.

Leading scorers: Pottsville – Jim Glenn 20, Karl Lombel 19, Claude Baskerville 16; Bethlehem Catholic – Jeff Jennings 8, Bob Alpago 8.

Central Catholic 89 Tamaqua 65: Central Catholic snapped its three-game losing streak by downing winless Tamaqua decisively 89-65. After struggling with Tamaqua's defense and the score tied at 6-6, the Vikings suddenly went on a 16-6 run to finish off the first quarter. The Vikings converted 36 of 65 field goal attempts. The Vikings improved to 2-6.

Leading scorers: Central Catholic – Bob Neff 21, John Gaspar 12, Stan Bushner 11, Phil Cech 10; Tamaqua – Jim Knoblauch 21, John Forys 15.[13]

Phillipsburg 82 Hazleton 78: With all five starters scoring in double figures, Phillipsburg defeated Hazleton to even their record at 4-4. Hazleton dropped to 4-3 with a makeup game to play. Hazleton trailed 18-4 in the first quarter and 35-17 in the second quarter before they began to chip away at the lead in the second half. Despite scoring 54 points to Phillipsburg 44 in the second half, they could not overcome their first half deficit.

Leading scorers: Phillipsburg – George Stamets 24, Dave Leone 22, Al Pianelli 13, Steve Samson 12, Don Jean 11; Hazleton – Bob Farnell 21, Tony Kinney 13, Darrell Farkus 12, Bob O'Donnell 12[14]

Bethlehem 68 Hazleton 50: Despite having Hazleton play them even during the first and third periods, Bethlehem used strong second and fourth periods to put away the Mountaineers 68-50. Early in the last quarter, the Mountaineers got within six points 49-43 before Mike Rosko scored eight points to stretch the lead back to over ten points.

Leading scorers: Bethlehem – Mike Rosko 22, Paul Schreiber 16, Tim Fisher 12, Bill Wescoe 10; Hazleton –Darrell Farkus 13, Tony Kinney 10.

Central Catholic 80 Phillipsburg 72: After Central Catholic held a 42-31 halftime lead, Phillipsburg came back to within four points twice in the third quarter 49-45 and 51-47. The Vikings ran off nine points in a row at the start of the last quarter only to have Phillipsburg drop eight in a row to bring the score to 60-55. Phillipsburg missed six crucial foul shots near the end of the game to end the rally and give the Vikings their second win in a row 80-72.

Leading scorers: Central Catholic – Rick Weider 20, Bob Neff 20, Phil Cech 19, John Gaspar 14; Phillipsburg – Al Pianelli 22, Dave Leone 21, Don Jean 12, Steve Samson 10.

Allen 69 Bethlehem Catholic 54: Bethlehem Catholic took a 15-13 first quarter lead and still hung on to the lead 26-23 in the second period. Allen scored nine straight points and took a 38-32 halftime lead. Bethlehem Catholic's Jeff Jennings scored the last six points in the third period as Allen led 51-45 going into the last quarter. Jennings scored the Hawks first six points in the 4th quarter to bring the Hawks within four points 55-51. Allen then scored eight in a row to put the game away and give them a 69-54 triumph.

Leading scorers: Allen – Tom Kerstetter 15, Daryl Tollinche 13, Dick Zellickson 13, Glenn Angelino 12; Bethlehem Catholic - Jeff Jennings 14, Jim Chassar 11, Greg Falkenbach 10.

Dieruff 68 Pottsville 54: Dieruff built up a big lead through the first three quarters 55-35 to cruise to an easy victory and secure a spot in the playoff against Bethlehem for the league's first half title. They increased the lead to 22 points with about three minutes to play 65-43. Pottsville closed out the game with an 11-3 run to make the final score much tighter 68-54.

Leading scorers: Dieruff– Ross Moore 26, George Isaacson 14, Don Knerr 12; Pottsville– Claude Baskerville 16, Bill Devlin 14.

Easton 88 Tamaqua 81: Winless Tamaqua held leads in each of the first three periods 21-17, 41-39, and 61-60. Easton drew even with the Tams 77-77 with 90 seconds to play and went ahead on a three-point play by Tom Meier and never surrendered the lead in an 88-81 win.

Leading scorers: Easton – Steve Jefferson 24, Bob Huffstettler 23, Tom Meier 18; Tamaqua – Jim Knoblauch 26, John Forys 23, Walt Henne 17.[15]

Hazleton 83 Easton 60: In a makeup from the third week of the season, Tony Kinney set a school record for points in a game to break the old record of 35 held by Tom Carlyon and Frank Grebowski. He scored 30 of the points in the second half of the game. The game was close in the first half with the Mountaineers holding a 33-31 lead. Hazleton scored eight straight in the opening minutes of the last quarter to stretch the lead to 64-44.

Leading scorers: Hazleton – Tony Kinney 37, Bob O'Donnell 15, Stever Yenchko 10; Easton – Bob Huffstettler 19, Steve Jefferson 19.[16]

First Half Playoff

Dieruff 66 Bethlehem 43: Once again, Dieruff saw itself in a playoff to determine the title-winner for the first half of the season. With two players, Dan Yocum and Mike Rosko, playing with effects of the flu, Dieruff moved ahead of Bethlehem after one quarter 18-7 and maintained the lead at the half 31-20. In the third quarter, the Huskies went on a 16-3 run to build up a 47-24 lead. The first half title went to the Huskies with the decisive 66-43 triumph over the Hurricane.

Leading scorers: Dieruff- Jan Kapcala 21, Ross Moore 12, George Isaacson 10; Bethlehem- Tim Fisher 11.[16]

Second Half - Week 6

Allen 62 Hazleton 57: Hazleton took a 19-11 lead into the second quarter with Allen fighting back to cut the lead to three at halftime 29-26. The Canaries continued their rally in the third period to take the lead 47-42. They opened the last quarter by scoring seven straight points to take a commanding 54-42 lead over the Mountaineers. Allen went into a scoring drought with several turnovers allowing Hazleton to tie the score at 54. That's when Daryl Tollinche took over, with 90 seconds to play, by canning a jumper and making a steal and feed to Tom Kerstetter for another basket and propel the Canaries on to victory 62-57.

Leading scorers: Allen - Tom Kerstetter 14, Daryl Tollinche 14; Hazleton - Steve Yenchko 17, Bob O'Donnell 15, Daryl Farkus 10.

Dieruff 67 Bethlehem Catholic 38: Hindered by the loss of their top scorer and rebounder Jim Chassar to a broken foot suffered in practice, Bethlehem Catholic began the second half of play against Dieruff on the losing end 67-38. Without Chassar, the Hawks had very little offense and were able to tally only 15 total points in the second and third quarters. After missing their first five shots in the game, the Huskies hit 8 of their next 9 to begin their dominance of the contest. The game marked the debut of Jim Booros, who had just become eligible after transferring from Central Catholic to Dieruff.

Leading scorers: Dieruff – Jan Kapcala 21, George Isaacson 14, Ross Moore 12; Bethlehem Catholic –Greg Falkenbach 13.

Bethlehem 69 Central Catholic 51: Central Catholic played on even terms with Bethlehem in the first half and took a 20-19 lead two minutes into the second quarter. They upped the lead to 28-23 before Bethlehem scored the last two buckets of the half to cut the Vikings' lead to 28-27 at the half. The Hurricane came storming out of the locker room to take a 44-33 lead during the third period. The Vikings could not stay with the Hurricane in the 4th quarter as Bethlehem stretched the lead for the final score of 69-51.

Leading scorers: Bethlehem - Bill Wescoe 20, Mike Rosko 12; Central Catholic - Stan Bushner 14, Phil Cech 11.

Pottsville 87 Tamaqua 67: Winless Tamaqua made a game of it during the first half of their contest with Pottsville. The lead changing six times in the first quarter, but Pottsville led 22-17 going into the 2nd quarter. Tamaqua responded by cutting the lead to three at half time 37-34. During the 3rd quarter, Pottsville scored ten in a row and took a decisive lead 66-50 after three quarters on their way to an 87-67 triumph.

Leading scorers: Pottsville – Karl Lombel 16, Bob Wilson 15, Bill Devlin 15, Claude Baskerville 15, Jim Glenn 11; Tamaqua – Jim Knoblauch 18, Gary Williams 13, John Forys 13, Kevin Young 10.

Phillipsburg 80 Easton 74: Easton led after the first two quarters 19-16 and 36-32 and built the lead to 47-39 in the third period. Phillipsburg switched to a full court press and scored the next nine points to take a 48-47 lead. Phillipsburg led 58-57 going into the last quarter and then reeled off six straight points early in the quarter to take a 66-59 lead and go on to win the contest.

Leading scorers: Phillipsburg – Don Jean 26, George Stamets 21, Al Pianelli 13, Dave Leone 10; Easton – Steve Jefferson 27, Bob Huffstettler 25, Bob Nelson 10.[17]

Week 7

Allen 93 Central Catholic 89: Despite playing another close, competitive game, Central Catholic lost another disappointing contest to Allen 93-89. After Allen took a 23-15 lead in the first quarter, Central Catholic came back to tie the game at the half 36-36. Allen jumped out to a fifteen-point lead in the third quarter only to have the Vikings rally to tie the score at 72-72 with five minutes left in the game. The Canaries went on an 11-2 run in the next 2 ½ minutes to pull out Coach Milo Sewards' 300th win 93-89.

Leading scorers: Allen – Glenn Angelino 31, Tom Kerstetter 18, Dick Zellickson 16, Mark Schultz 11; Central Catholic – John Gaspar 24, Phil Cech 21, Rick Weider 15.

Bethlehem 71 Easton 66: Bethlehem took a 22-16 lead into the second quarter, but Easton ran off eight straight points to take a 24-22 lead. Easton held the lead at the half 33-31. After the score was tied five times in the third quarter, Liberty scored six straight to take a slim 52-51 lead entering the last quarter. Bethlehem took charge in the final quarter to secure the victory.

Leading scorers: Easton – Tom Fisher 27, Steve Jefferson 18, Joe Braido 10, Phil Schramm 10; Phillipsburg – Al Pianelli 15, Steve Samson 13, Dave Leone 10.

Dieruff 92 Tamaqua 67: With Dieruff focused on getting Jan Kapcala to the 1000-point career total, Dieruff cruised to a 31-11 first quarter outburst as Kapcala reached the coveted total with three minutes left in the second quarter. The first quarter advantage led the Huskies to the triumph over the winless-in-league play Tamaqua squad. Tamaqua's Jim Knoblauch, the league's leading scorer, had 30 points, but was overshadowed by Kapcala's milestone achievement.

Leading scorers: Dieruff – Jan Kapcala 32, Mike Witkowski 14, Ross Moore 13, Don Knerr 12; Tamaqua – Jim Knoblauch 30, John Forys 10, Walt Henne 10.

Hazleton 63 Bethlehem Catholic 52: Although Bethlehem Catholic put on a better offensive performance and held a 13-7 lead in the first quarter, Hazleton came back to score 23 points in the second period to take a 38-27 half time lead. The Hawks shaved three points off the lead in the third quarter 47-39.

Leading scorers: Hazleton – Tony Kinney 23, Darrel Farkus 14, Bob Farnell 14; Bethlehem Catholic – Greg Falkenbach 12, Mark Cacciatore 11, John Kearney 10.[18]

Pottsville 75 Phillipsburg 69: Pottsville trailed Phillipsburg 17-12 after a quarter and battled back to tie the game with six minutes left in the second period 20-20. They took the lead at the half 34-26. Down 50-35 in the third quarter, Phillipsburg rallied to within 52-45 at the end of the third quarter and continued their rally to tie the score at 52-52. With 4:40 left in the final period, Pottsville's Claude Baskerville and Phillipsburg's George Stamets were ejected from the game for overly aggressive play. Pottsville broke the tie with several foul shots.

Leading scorers: Pottsville – Bob Wilson 17, Jim Glenn 16, Bill Devlin 15, Jim Berrang 12, Karl Lombel 10; Phillipsburg - Don Jean 16, Dave Leone 16, George Stamets 13, Al Pianelli 11.[19]

Bethlehem Catholic 44 Tamaqua 42: Bethlehem Catholic won its first game of the second half 44-42 over Tamaqua. In the first half, the Hawks outscored Tamaqua 26-12, holding the Tams to single digits in each quarter with five in the first and seven in the second. Both teams scored ten points in the third period to give the Hawks a 14-point lead 36-22 heading into the last quarter. After switching to a press. the fourth quarter saw a different Tamaqua squad on the floor. Tamaqua held Bethlehem Catholic to eight points in the final period while scoring 20 to pull within two points at the buzzer.

Leading scorers: Bethlehem Catholic–John Kearney 16, Greg Falkenbach 14; Tamaqua–Jim Knoblauch 17.

Bethlehem 65 Pottsville 44: With neither team sharp in the first half, Pottsville took a one-point lead 12-11 over Bethlehem into the second period only to score a mere five points in the second quarter. They fell behind 25-17. The night only got worse for Pottsville in the second half as Bethlehem pulled ahead decisively in the 4th quarter by scoring eleven points in a row to win the game 65-44. The loss dropped Pottsville to 2-1 while Bethlehem stayed undefeated in the half at 3-0 and tied for first place with Dieruff.

Leading scorers: Bethlehem – Bill Wescoe 18, Dan Yocum 16, Tim Fisher 10; Pottsville – Bob Wilson 16.

Easton 63 Allen 54: Easton won its first game of the second half by handing Allen their first loss 63-54. Easton outrebounded Allen 52-26. The first half ended with Easton holding a 31-30 lead over the Canaries. They added six points to the lead in the third quarter. Easton's Bob Huffstettler scored 12 consecutive points from the third quarter into the fourth quarter and scored 18 of the Red Rovers final 23 points. The Canaries could get no closer than 53-49 with Easton adding six foul shots in the final minutes of play.

Leading scorers: Easton – Bob Huffstettler 29, Daryl Woodring 12, Steve Jefferson 11; Allen –Glenn Angelino 17, Dick Zellickson 13, Tom Kerstetter 12.

Dieruff 66 Phillipsburg 63: Phillipsburg, trailing by nine points 43-34 in the third period, scored nine points in a row to tie the score. In the first four minutes of the last quarter, Phillipsburg outscored Dieruff 15-2 to take an eleven-point lead 60-49 with 3:50 to play. From that point on, Phillipsburg only scored on a 3-point play by Steve Samson. Dieruff rallied and took the lead on foul shots by Jan Kapcala to avoid the upset.

Leading scorers: Dieruff – Jan Kapcala 21, Ross Moore 10; Phillipsburg – George Stamets 23, Al Pianelli 14, Dave Leone 14.

Central Catholic 75 Hazleton 68: Central Catholic came out of the locker room fast to take a 16-12 first quarter lead and 40-30 at halftime. In the third quarter, they increased the lead to 44-30 before Hazleton began a rally to pull within two points 64-62 with three minutes left to play. The Vikings then made several field goals and foul shots and the Mountaineers rally ended with the Vikings winning the game 75-68.

Leading scorers: Central Catholic – Phil Cech 21, Rick Weider 18, Bob Neff 17; Hazleton – Bob Farnell 20, Darrel Farkus 16, Tony Kinney 16.[20]

Week 8

Pottsville 74 Allen 58: With Glenn Angelino hitting his first three shots, Allen took an early 6-5 lead before Pottsville rallied 15-5 to take a 20-11 first quarter lead. Pottsville added to the lead in each of the next three quarters outscoring the Canaries by two, three, and two points to take the contest 74-58. Allen's eleven turnovers in the first half alone contributed to Pottsville's victory.

Leading scorers: Pottsville – Bob Wilson 19, Jim Glenn 15, Karl Lombell 14, Jim Berrang 13; Allen – Glenn Angelino 22, Rich Wehr 10, Dick Zellickson 10.

Bethlehem 56 Dieruff 55: In a battle for first place by the last two unbeaten teams, Dieruff missed their first ten shots to fall woefully behind 14-1 after one quarter. Bethlehem increased the lead to 17 points at the half 37-20. Late in the third quarter, Bethlehem built the lead to 19 as Bill Wescoe scored 18 points in the half. Late in the third quarter, Dieruff came alive with a furious rally which continued into the fourth quarter. Dieruff cut the lead to a single point 54-53 with 1:03 remaining in the contest, but Bethlehem withstood the rally to win the game 56-55.

Leading scorers: Bethlehem- Bill Wescoe 24, Mike Rosko 13; Dieruff- George Isaacson 18, Jim Booros 14.[21]

Phillipsburg 102 Tamaqua 78: In a high-scoring contest in Tamaqua, Phillipsburg, led by Dave Leone's 41 points, routed the Tams 102-78. Leone scored only two points in the first period, but blistered the nets the rest of the game. With the Stateliners taking a first quarter lead 26-14, Tamaqua's Jim Knoblauch scored 12 of his team's 14 first quarter points. Tamaqua's only lead was at 2-0 on the opening tap.

Leading scorers: Phillipsburg – Dave Leone 41, George Stamets 15, Don Jean 15, Steve Samson 11, Al Pianelli 11; Tamaqua – Jim Knoblauch 32, John Forys 17.

Central Catholic 60 Bethlehem Catholic 48: A strong first half propelled Central Catholic to victory over Bethlehem 60-48. They ended the first half with a thirteen-point lead 33-20 and held on in the second half to even their record at 2-2. The Vikings converted 20 of 26 foul attempts which was the difference in the contest since both teams had 20 field goals.

Leading scorers: Central Catholic – John Gaspar 19, Bob Neff 14, Rick Weider 14; Bethlehem Catholic – Greg Falkenbach 13, John Kearney 11.

Easton 75 Hazleton 64: Easton scored four points to end the first quarter to take the lead 15-14 and then scored eleven more to open the second period and take a 26-14 lead on their way to a 36-23 half time advantage. Hazleton charged twice in the fourth quarter to pull with 60-53 and 67-60 but could get no closer as the Red Rovers evened their record at 2-2 with a 75-64 triumph.

Leading scorers: Easton –Bob Huffstettler 29, Steve Jefferson 22, Daryl Woodring 10; Hazleton – Bob Farnell 17, Tony Kinney 16, Tony Manfriedi 11.[22]

Allen 93 Tamaqua 67: The scoring leaders for Allen and Tamaqua both put on strong performances with banner scoring nights as Allen outscored the Tams 93-67. Glenn Angelino poured in 43 points for the Canaries. Jim Knoblauch chalked up nearly half his team's points with 31 including 15 of 16 foul shots. Allen improved to 3-2 while Tamaqua remained winless at 0-5.

Leading scorers: Allen – Glenn Angelino 43, Dick Zellickson 12, Mark Schultz 11, Rick Wehr 10; Tamaqua – Jim Knoblauch 31, Gary Williams 11.

Bethlehem 80 Phillipsburg 53: Phillipsburg took an early 14-10 lead after the opening quarter before undefeated Bethlehem began to roll late in the second quarter. The Hurricane took the lead at the half 27-24 and continued to add to it in the second half on their way to an 80-53 romp. Phillipsburg was hindered by the limited play of center Al Pianelli who committed his fourth foul in the middle of the second period, He did not play again until two minutes left in the third quarter and then fouled out 30 seconds later.

Leading scorers: Bethlehem – Bill Wescoe 17, Mike Rosko 15, Paul Schreiber 11, Dan Yochum 10; Phillipsburg – Dave Leone 16, Brian Dominic 11, George Stamets 10.

Dieruff 79 Hazleton 52: Hindered by the absence of their center Darrel Farkus, Hazleton fell behind Dieruff by 15 points in the second period but battled their way back to within three points 38-35 midway through the third period. Dieruff responded with a 10-2 run and scored 31 points in the final quarter to easily take the game.

Leading scorers: Dieruff – Ross Moore 20, Jan Kapcala 20, Jim Booros 10; Hazleton – Bob Farnell 13.

Easton 51 Bethlehem Catholic 48: Bethlehem Catholic took a 10-2 lead with Easton not scoring its first points until almost four minutes into the opening period. The Hawks held leads in each of the first three quarters 13-10, 27-24, and 35-34. Easton came back to take the lead for good at 45-43.

Leading scorers: Easton- Bob Huffstettler 21, Steve Jefferson 10; Bethlehem Catholic- Greg Falkenbach 19.

Pottsville 76 Central Catholic 65: Pottsville remained a game behind Bethlehem at 4-1 by taking down Central Catholic 76-65. Pottsville took an early 14-1 advantage in the first period and led 19-6 at the end of the quarter. This margin proved to be the difference in the game as the Vikings outscored the Crimson 51-49 over the last three quarters.

Leading Scorers: Pottsville – Bob Wilson 22, Bill Devlin 18, Karl Lombel 14, Jim Glenn 10; Central Catholic – Bob Neff 17, John Gaspar 11.[23]

Week 9

Central Catholic 70 Easton 61: After a slow start and trailing 14-9 in the opening period, Central Catholic picked it up and outscored Easton 21-12 in the second quarter to take a four-point halftime lead 30-26. They increased the lead to ten points 51-41 heading into the fourth quarter. With Easton's coach Tom Sweeney and high-scoring forward Bob Huffstettler both getting technical fouls in the fourth quarter, the Vikings took the contest 70-61.

Leading scorers: Central Catholic – John Gaspar 16, Bob Neff 15, Rick Weider 14, Phil Cech 13; Easton – Steve Jefferson 32, Bob Huffstettler 20.

Bethlehem 83 Tamaqua 46: Bethlehem improved to 6-0 for sole possession of first place with a win over Tamaqua 83-46. Bethlehem held Tamaqua to 13 or less points in each quarter While the Hurricane scored over at least 20 points in each quarter to cruise to the win. Tamaqua never led in the game.

Leading scorers: Bethlehem – Bill Wescoe 19, Mike Rosko 18, Paul Schreiber 13, Dan Yochum 11, Tom Partridge 10; Tamaqua – Jim Knoblauch 12, Dan Truskey 12.

Phillipsburg 57 Bethlehem Catholic 49: Phillipsburg took a 12-9 lead after one quarter, but Bethlehem Catholic came back to tie the game at the half 20-20. Phillipsburg scored 12 straight points at the start of the second half. The Hawks closed the gap to four points after three quarters 38-34. Halfway through the final quarter, Phillipsburg went on another 10-2 run to put the game away 57-49 and even their record at 3-3.

Leading scorers: Phillipsburg – Dave Leone 12, Don Jean 12, George Stamets 12; Bethlehem Catholic – Greg Falkenbach 26.

Dieruff 64 Allen 63: Allen gave Dieruff a tussle after taking a 21-16 first quarter lead. Dieruff reduced the lead to three points 34-31 by halftime. The Huskies first lead was at 39-37 in the third period and they increased it to five points 58-53 in the final quarter. The Canaries came back to take a brief one-point lead 61-60 with 1:39 left to play. An Allen turnover led to two foul shots and the win for the Huskies. Glenn Angelino had a chance to win the game for Allen but his 20-foot jumper just missed the mark and fell off. Dieruff stayed a game behind Bethlehem at 5-1.

Leading scorers: Dieruff – Ross Moore 35, Jan Kapcala 17; Allen – Glenn Angelino 17, Paul Budline 13, Rick Wehr 12, Daryl Tollinche 10.

Pottsville 60 Hazleton 47: Hazleton fell behind in the first half 27-18, but fought back early in the third quarter to trim the lead to three points 37-34. Pottsville stretched the lead to six points by the end of the quarter 41-35. Hazleton committed 21 turnovers which contributed greatly to the loss to the Crimson. Pottsville improved to 5-1 for second place tie with Dieruff.

Leading scorers: Pottsville – Bob Wilson 19, Bill Devlin 14, Jim Glenn 13, Karl Lombel 10; Hazleton – Tony Kinney 19.[24]

Hazleton 81 Tamaqua 66: Down 42-30 at the half, Hazleton switched to a zone press coming out of the locker room to hold Tamaqua to nine points in the third quarter while the Mountaineers countered with 25 to take the lead 55-51. Tamaqua's Jim Knoblauch scored 21 points to help push the Tams into the lead. Hazleton got their first lead at the 3:30 mark of the third period 47-46. Hazleton outscored Tamaqua by eleven points and win the matchup easily 81-66.

Leading scorers: Hazleton – Tony Kinney 27, Bob Farnell 20, Daryl Farkus 13; Tamaqua – Jim Knoblauch 30, John Forys 14, George Wenzel 12.[25]

Allen 94 Phillipsburg 82: Despite making 34 of 44 foul shots in the game, Phillipsburg lost to Allen 94-82. The Canaries' duo of Tom Kerstetter and Glenn Angelino poured in 34 points each to lead the attack against the Stateliners. Phillipsburg led only three times in the game at 1-0 and 7-6 during the first quarter and 58-57 late in the third quarter. Allen took the lead at the end of the third quarter 64-58 on their way to the win.

Leading scorers: Allen – Glenn Angelino 34, Tom Kerstetter 34, Daryl Tollinche 10; Phillipsburg – George Stamets 33, Dave Leone 22, Al Pianelli 16.

Easton 57 Pottsville 51: After being tied after a quarter 17-17, Easton could only score four points in the 2nd period and fell behind 34-21. After intermission, Easton played a stingy defense and held Pottsville to nine points in the 3rd quarter and eight in the final quarter to pull out the game. With the game tied at 43-43 at the end of the 3rd quarter, Easton outscored the Crimson 11-3 in the last 3 ½ minutes for the win.

Leading scorers: Easton- Bob Huffstettler 21, Steve Jefferson 16; Pottsville- Bill Devlin 13, Bob Wilson 10.

Bethlehem 53 Bethlehem Catholic 35: With Bethlehem Catholic only able to make 14 of 55 field goal attempts in the game, the Hawks were held to single digit points in three of four quarters and scored only ten in the other quarter, the third. Although Bethlehem only hit 21 of 70 shots, the Hurricane prevailed easily 53-35. The Hawks also made only 7 of 19 foul shots. The win kept the Hurricane undefeated at 7-0 in the second half and in sole possession of first place.

Leading scorers: Bethlehem – Bill Wescoe 16, Tim Fisher 10; Bethlehem Catholic – Greg Falkenbach 15.

Dieruff 64 Central Catholic 52: Central Catholic gave Dieruff a tussle before the Huskies pulled away in the final quarter for a 64-52 triumph. Dieruff took the first quarter lead 15-13, but the Vikings kept pace with the Huskies with each team scoring 14 points to give Dieruff a 29-27 halftime lead. The Vikings hung tough in the third period but Dieruff was able to add three points to the lead 45-40. Dieruff held Central Catholic to two field goals in the final six minutes with the last one coming with 12 seconds left. A stingy defense led to the Husky win.

Leading scorers: Dieruff – Jan Kapcala 21, Ed Benson 14, Ross Moore 13; Central Catholic – Rick Weider 16, Bob Neff 15, Phil Cech 12.[26]

Week 10

Bethlehem 72 Allen 58: At the end of the first quarter, Bethlehem appeared to have the game under control after taking an 8-point lead 18-10. Allen had other plans as they came back with a strong second period 20-12 to tie the game at 30-30 at the half. Bethlehem took a slim one-point lead into the final quarter 48-47. The Canaries took a three-point lead at the 4:05 mark of the quarter. That was it for Allen as Bethlehem finished the contest with 17 consecutive points with Paul Schreiber scoring eleven of the 17 points. The final score was not indicative of the severe test that the Canaries provided Bethlehem throughout the first 3 ½ quarters of the game.

Leading scorers: Bethlehem – Mike Rosko 20, Paul Schreiber 19, Bill Wescoe 17; Allen – Glenn Angelino 2, Tom Kerstetter 13, Daryl Tollinche 10.

Dieruff 80 Easton 56: Easton stayed with Dieruff through the early part of the third quarter despite having been outscored 21-9 in the first quarter. Easton pulled with four points at the beginning of the third period 35-31 before Dieruff unleashed its offense. By the end of the quarter, the Huskies led 57-40. With three of Easton's starters fouling out of the game (Bob Nelson, Steve Jefferson, and Bob Pilz), Dieruff went on a 22-9 run to win the game.

Leading scorers: Dieruff – Jan Kapcala 30, Ross Moore 15, Jim Booros 10; Easton – Bob Huffstettler 29, Steve Jefferson 11.

Central Catholic 75 Tamaqua 63: Tamaqua opened its new gymnasium with much fanfare but unfortunately the results on the court took away from the euphoria. After playing to an 8-8 tie after the first quarter, Central Catholic did not treat the Tams kindly as they outscored them 33-19 in the 2nd quarter for a 41-27 lead. They increased the lead to 20 points after three quarters 61-41 on their way to victory 75-63.

Leading scorers: Central Catholic – Bob Neff 16, Phil Cech, Rick Weider 13, Den Williams 10; Tamaqua – Jim Knoblauch 19, Walt Henne 11.

Pottsville 58 Bethlehem Catholic 48: With Bethlehem Catholic able to score only two foul shots and a field goal in the first quarter, Pottsville moved out to a 13-4 lead. The Hawks then tallied only eight points in the second quarter as the Crimson led 31-12 at halftime. With the game outcome decided, both teams substituted freely in the final quarter as the Hawks scored 26 points, after scoring only 22 in the first three periods, to make the final score closer at 58-48.

Leading scorers: Pottsville – Bob Wilson 15, Karl Lombel 10; Bethlehem Catholic – Greg Falkenbach 11.

Phillipsburg 87 Hazleton 68: Phillipsburg outscored Hazleton by three and four points during the first two quarters to take a 39-32 lead into the second half. After the game was tied at 2-2, Phillipsburg scored the next eight points to take a 10-2 early lead. Hazleton never led in the game. Phillipsburg put the game away by scoring eight in a row to open the second half. At one point, the Stateliners held a 21-point lead 61-40 in the third period.

Leading scorers: Phillipsburg – George Stamets 31, Al Pianelli 20, Dave Leone 15, Don Jean 12; Hazleton – Bob Farnell 20, Tony Kinney 18, Dan Yenchko 12.[27]

Easton 93 Tamaqua 67: Eli "Pinky" Purnell wrapped up his 26-year coaching career with another setback 93-67 to Easton. Despite Tamaqua losing 21 of 22 games during the season, Purnell wound up his career with a 284-270 career coaching record. He did see his scoring ace Jim Knoblauch win the league's scoring title with 426 points. Easton's Bob Huffstettler finished second with 421 points. Other than the second period when Tamaqua outscored Easton 22-21, the Red Rovers rolled over the Tams in every other quarter.

Leading scorers: Easton – Steve Jefferson 34, Bob Huffstettler 34; Tamaqua – Jim Knoblauch 28, Dan Truskey 14.

Hazleton 66 Bethlehem 60: After taking a 17-14 first quarter lead, Bethlehem fell behind Hazleton 30-26 at the half. Hazleton increased the lead to as many as eleven points in the third quarter only to have Bethlehem rally to within three points 61-58 with 1:27 to play in the final quarter. Hazleton's Bob Farnell was fouled deliberately by Bob Partridge and received a technical foul with a second technical assessed when the Bethlehem bench protested. Farnell missed both foul shots but made both technical foul shots as Hazleton stunned Bethlehem 66-60.

Leading scorers: Hazleton – Bob Farnell 18, Darrel Farkus 16, Dan Yochum 14; Bethlehem – Bill Wescoe 24, Mike Rosko 14, Paul Schreiber 12.[28]

Dieruff 66 Pottsville 57: With Bethlehem's loss to Hazleton, Dieruff earned a spot in a second title playoff with the Hurricane by downing Pottsville 66-57. The first quarter proved to be the difference in the contest with the Huskies taking a 19-8 lead. Pottsville outscored the Huskies in the final three quarters 49-47.

Leading scorers: Dieruff – Jan Kapcala 19, Ross Moore 14, Jim Booros 13; Pottsville – Bob Wilson 18, Bill Devlin 16.

Central Catholic 63 Phillipsburg 54: After leading 10-8 after a period, Central stretched the lead to nine points 31-22 at the half. Trailing 47-32, Phillipsburg went on a 15-4 run to cut the lead to 51-45 with a little over four minutes to play. They cut the lead to five points 55-50 with 1:45 to play only to see the Vikings pull away.

Leading scorers: Central Catholic – Bob Neff 18, Phil Cech 15, John Gaspar 15, Rick Weider 10; Phillipsburg – George Stamets 13, Dave Leone 12.

Allen 58 Bethlehem Catholic 56: After almost missing the team bus due to an automobile accident, Allen's Glenn Angelino suffered through a difficult three periods as he missed all ten field goal attempts with no points. With Allen trailing 46-42 with five minutes to play in the game, Angelino went on a tear to make six field goals and four foul shots to lead the Canaries to a 58-56 triumph over the Hawks.

Leading scorers: Allen–Glenn Angelino 16, Dick Zellickson 12, Tom Kerstetter 10; Bethlehem Catholic–Greg Falkenbach 19.[29]

Second Half Playoff

Bethlehem 45 Dieruff 41: At Muhlenberg's Memorial Hall, Bethlehem moved out to a 13-8 first quarter lead, which proved to be decisive as the Hurricane stunned Dieruff with a 45-41 win. Bethlehem's defense stifled both Ross Moore and Jan Kapcala. Moore ended up with two points on a woeful 1 for 15 from the field. Jan Kapcala scored only seven points and took only two shots in the second half. Dieruff held the lead twice in the fourth quarter 34-32 and 37-36 but fell behind 40-37 on two field goals by Bill Wescoe. Mike Roscoe made a clean steal with 1:10 left and went in for the layup to seal the win for Bethlehem.

Leading scorers: Bethlehem – Mike Rosko 25, Paul Schreiber 10; Dieruff – Ed Benson 14, Jim Booros 10.[30]

League Playoff

Dieruff 67 Bethlehem 49: Playing each other for the second time in three days at Muhlenberg's Memorial gym, and for the fifth time in the season, Dieruff and Bethlehem met to decide the league championship. The two clubs had split the four prior games with Dieruff winning the first two and Bethlehem the last two games. After Bethlehem led 13-10 after one period, Dieruff's offense took off in the second period with an 11-2 run to put the Huskies up by six points 21-15. They increased the lead to ten points 29-19 in the second quarter before Bethlehem cut it to 31-24 at the half. After having a woeful shooting game in the second half title playoff, Ross Moore hit 12 of 16 shots for the Huskies. The Huskies outscored Bethlehem in each of the last three quarters to cruise to the win and the league championship.

Leading scorers: Dieruff – Ross Moore 26, Jan Kapcala 15, Jim Booros 12; Bethlehem – Tim Fisher 19, Mike Rosko 12.[31]

Postseason PIAA Play

Dieruff 77 Northampton 53: In a District 11 semifinal matchup, Dieruff took on Northampton at Muhlenberg's Memorial Hall. After the Huskies entered the second quarter with a 15-12 lead, they went on a 17-2 run, including 13 points in a row, to start the second quarter. Northampton never got closer than 12 points the rest of the night.

Leading scorers: Dieruff – Ross Moore 20, Jan Kapcala 19, Ed Bensen 14, Jim Booros 12; Northampton – Dan Marakovits 16, Joe Steffie 15, Steve Gabryluk 10.[32]

Dieruff 68 Freedom 52: Bethlehem Freedom and Dieruff matched up for the District 11 title at the Farm Show Area in Harrisburg. Freedom, under coach Charlie Dubbs, was in its first year of play. The Patriots gave the Huskies a first half tussle with Dieruff holding a one-point lead at the half 26-25. Dieruff ran off 17 points while limiting Freedom to two field goals to start the second half. They increased the lead to seventeen points 62-45 with two minutes to play and won easily 68-52.

Leading scorers: Dieruff – Jan Kapcala 20, George Isaacson 15; Bethlehem Freedom – Tom Hussar 17, Joe Morris 16, Andy Lutkieicz.[33]

Dieruff 67 Williamsport 57: Dieruff's defense caused several Williamsport turnovers and helped the Huskies take a 14-9 first period lead. They extended the lead to 14 points near the end of the half before the Millionaires fought back to cut the deficit to 32-24. Early in the 4th quarter, Williamsport cut the lead to five 51-46, but Ed Bensen followed with a field goal and foul shot to extend the lead again and the Huskies went on to the win.

Leading scorers: Dieruff – Ed Bensen 21, Ross Moore 14, Jan Kapcala 11, Jim Booros 10; Williamsport – Greg Spotts 18, Joe Walker 18, Bob Peterson 11.[34]

Cheltenham 52 Dieruff 46: For the second year in a row, Dieruff was denied a shot at the state title game with a loss in the Eastern final, this time to Cheltenham 52-46. Cheltenham's sliding man-to- man defense caused 20 turnovers by the Huskies. Despite the turnovers, Dieruff played Cheltenham even at the half 28-28 and after three quarters 38-38. However, Cheltenham scored seven straight points to start the fourth quarter and Dieruff could not recover and lost the opportunity for the state title game 52-46.

Leading scorers: Cheltenham - Chuck Schectman 14, Craig Littlepage 12, Bill Haff 12; Dieruff – Ross Moore 13.[35]

PCIAA Postseason Playoff

Central Catholic 48 Bethlehem Catholic 43: Central Catholic squared off against now league foe Bethlehem Catholic for the Class A Allentown Diocese title. Bethlehem Catholic had leads through each of the first three quarters 16-8, 27-22 and 36-35. With 6:06 to play, the Hawks' Jim Chassar, who had missed the last nine games due to a broken bone in his foot, was injured and had to leave the game. Central Catholic had the lead 41-39 with 3:15 remaining when the Hawks' Greg Falkenbach fouled out of the game.

Leading scorers: Central Catholic – Bob Neff 17, John Gaspar 15; Bethlehem Catholic – Jim Chassar 13, Jeff Borda 11.[36]

Scranton Prep 68 Central Catholic 61: At the Easton gym, Central Catholic's path in the PCIAA playoffs ended with a 68-61 loss to Scranton Prep. With game tied 30-30 at the half, Scranton Prep came out in the second half and outscored the Vikings in both periods for the 68-61 victory.

Leading scorers: Scranton Prep – John Reddington 29, Steve Dougherty 25; Central Catholic – Bob Neff 19, John Gaspar 15, Rick Weider 10, Phil Cech 10.[37]

Postseason Accolades

Leading scorers: Jim Knoblauch, Tamaqua, led the league in scoring with 426 points in 18 games, nine points shy of the league record set by Easton's Tom Fisher the previous season. Easton's Bob Huffstettler also scored over 400 points with 419 to finish second. Five players scored over 300 points including Jan Kapcala, Dieruff, 385; Glenn Angelino, Allen, 346; Steve Jefferson, Easton, 331, Bill Wescoe, Bethlehem 317; and Dave Leone, Phillipsburg, 309.Bob Neff, Central Catholic, 298; Mike Rosko, Bethlehem, 297; and George Stamets, Phillipsburg, 296, finished out the top ten scorers.[38]

All-Stars: The league all-star first team included: Jan Kapcala, Dieruff; Mike Rosko, Liberty; Bob Huffstettler, Easton; and Glenn Angelino, Allen; Jim Knoblauch, Tamaqua; and Ross Moore, Dieruff. The second team consisted of: Steve Jefferson, Easton; Bob Neff, Central Catholic; Jim Chassar, Bethlehem Catholic; Ed Bensen, Dieruff; Tom Kerstetter, Allen; Dave Leone, Phillipsburg; and Bill Wescoe Liberty.[39]

All-State: The only league players on the all-state team were mentioned as honorable mention. They included: Tom Fisher, Easton; Jan Kapcala, Dieruff; John Lehman, Bethlehem; and Norm Waters, Pottsville.[40]

Final Standings

First Half		Second Half		Overall	
Dieruff	8-1	Bethlehem	8-1	Bethlehem	16-2
Bethlehem	8-1	Dieruff	8-1	Dieruff	16-2
Allen	7-2	Pottsville	6-3	Allen	12-6
Hazleton	5-4	Allen	5-4	Pottsville	10-8
Pottsville	4-5	Central Catholic	5-4	Central Catholic	8-10
Phillipsburg	4-5	Easton	5-4	Easton	8-10
Easton	3-6	Phillipsburg	4-5	Hazleton	8-10
Bethlehem Catholic	3-6	Hazleton	3-6	Phillipsburg	8-10
Central Catholic	3-6	Bethlehem	1-8	Bethlehem Catholic	4-14
Tamaqua	0-9	Tamaqua	0-9	Tamaqua	0-18

Team Rosters

Allen: Coach Milo Sewards, Glenn Angelino, Fred Bechtel, Paul Budline. Dan Hellman, Tom Kerstetter, Mark Schultz, Daryl Tollinche, Bob Ulaner, Rick Wehr, Dick Zellickson

Bethlehem: Coach Fritz Toner, Ed Cunningham, Tim Fisher, Grimes, Tom Partridge, Jim Pavel, Randy Peto, Mike Rosko, Paul Schreiber, Shaffer, Bill Wescoe, Dan Woodard, Dan Yocum

Bethlehem Catholic: Coach Paul Calvo, Jeff Borda, Mark Cacciatore, Al Calvo, Jim Chassar, Ed Chladny, Christ, Degnan, Greg Falkenbach, Dave Griffith, Paul Grube, Jeff Jennings, John Kearney, Tom Leary, Dick Metzger, George Yasso

Central Catholic: Coach Mike Koury, Paul Bucko, Stan Bushner, Phil Cech, Dan Damweber, Tony DaRe, John Gaspar, Bob Kasper, Bob Neff, John Susko, Rick Weider, Denny Williams

Dieruff: Coach Dick Schmidt, Ed Benson, Lou Benson, Jim Booros, Jerry Houser, George Isaacson, Dan Joseph, Jan Kapcala, Don Knerr, Ross Moore, John Nyemscek, Bogdan "Bucky" Paraszczak, Hamp Smith, Mike Witkowski

Easton: Coach Tom Sweeney, Gary Betts, Gary Bond, Joe Braido, Terry Briggs, Don Dickey, Rick Feauve, Bob Huffstettler, Steve Jefferson, Bob Keiper, Rick Lehr, Ed McIntyre, Tom Meier, Bob Nelson, Bob Pilz, Phil Schramm, Daryl Woodring

Hazleton: Coach Fran Libonati, Joe Duda, Darrell Farkus, Bob Farnell, Tony Kinney, Anthony Manfredi, Tony Manfredi Jr., Bob O'Donnell, Greg Persico, Dave Pikna, Joe Portland, Fillmore Williams, Steve Yenchko

Phillipsburg: Coach Al Senavitis, Brian Dominic, Bruce Exley, Gary Farmer, Gordon, Hancewicz, Don Jean, Dave Leone, Al Pianelli, Steve Samson, George Stamets, Touchton, Bucky Utley

Pottsville: Coach Ken Kline, Claude Baskerville, Jim Berrang, Bill Devlin, Jim Glenn, Jim Heller, Don Hill, Jim Lengel, Karl Lombel, Frank Mills, Bob Wilson, Bill Yaag

Tamaqua: Coach Eli Purnell, John Forys, Walt Henne, Jim Knoblach, Joe Ruggerio, Dennis Sabol, Dan Truskey, Mike Weidell, George Wenzel, Gary Williams. John Woodring, Kevin Young

1969

Another League Expansion

The league expanded to eleven teams with the addition of Bethlehem Freedom. The addition gave the league two schools from both Allentown and Bethlehem with the Allentown schools being referred to as Allen and Dieruff and the Bethlehem schools as Liberty and Freedom. League officials admitted Freedom at its Spring meeting in March 1967 at a meeting at the Village Inn. At the time, officials were uncertain when Freedom would begin play in the league.

At the same meeting, Phil Phillippi, Liberty, was re-elected league president and Rev. Francis Zavodny as vice president. Bob Stimmel was elected secretary-treasurer and Joe Blankowitsch as statistician.[1]

First Half - Week 1

Allen 82 Pottsville 68: Pottsville's pressing defense forced Coach Milo Seward's Allen team into a number of turnovers during the first half. With the game tied 17-17 after one period, Pottsville took a slim lead 37-35 into the locker room. In the third period with the score tied at 45-45, Allen ran off eight straight points, but Pottsville came back to within two points 57-55 in the fourth quarter. An 11-2 run by Allen put the game out of reach for the Crimson.

Leading scorers: Allen – Mark Schultz 23, Tim Schmeidel 22, Dick Zellickson 21; Pottsville – Claude Baskerville 16, Pete Marchetti 15, Barry Kelly 12.

Bethlehem Catholic 52 Phillipsburg 44: With Jim Chassar scoring 15 points in the first half, Bethlehem Catholic took 20-9 and 35-20 leads in each of the first two quarters. Although Phillipsburg outscored the Hawks in the second half 24-17, they could not overcome Bethlehem Catholic's large first half advantage.

Leading scorers: Bethlehem Catholic – Jim Chassar 24, Paul Grube 12; Phillipsburg – Bruce Tibbit 15.

Dieruff 87 Tamaqua 56: Dieruff ran Tamaqua's league losing streak to nineteen. Dieruff's pressing man-to-man defense held Tamaqua scoreless for the first five minutes enroute to a 20-9 first quarter advantage. The Huskies expanded the lead to twenty points 39-19 at the half and the rout was on when Dieruff outscored the Tams 29-18 in the third quarter.

Leading scorers: Dieruff – Jim Booros 19, Lou Bensen 15, Dan Joseph 14, Ross Moore 12, Bob Stellar 10; Tamaqua – Steve Sassaman 13, Dennis Sabol 10.

Easton 63 Liberty 60: After Easton took an eight-point lead 21-13, Liberty came back to cut it to three at halftime 33-30. Easton increased the lead to 50-42 in the third quarter. Liberty whittled away at the lead and caught the Red Rovers at 60-60. Easton's Gary Betts hit a field goal and foul shot for the win and hand Coach Al Senavitis his first loss as coach at Liberty. Both Senavitis and Easton Coach Tom Sweeney were assessed two technical fouls for violating the new jumping off the bench rule.

Leading scorers: Easton – Gary Betts 16, Rick Feauve 14, Ed McIntyre 11; Liberty – Ed Ruyak16, Tim Fisher 15, Dan Woodard 13.

Freedom 61 Hazleton 50: In Freedom's league debut, the Patriots took an early 5-0 lead on their way to a 13-4 first quarter advantage. With a good second quarter, Hazleton pulled within three at the half 24-21. In the third quarter, Hazleton closed to within a point 28-27 with 5:50 left when Freedom scored nine points in a row. Freedom expanded the lead to 42-29 in the third period on their way to their first league win.

Leading scorers: Freedom – Joe Morris 18, Tom Husser 18, Ken Bedics 12; Hazleton – Tony Kinney 18, Joe Duda 12, Fillmore Williams 10.[2]

Bethlehem Catholic 60 Easton 53: Coach Paul Calvo's Hawks never trailed, although Bethlehem Catholic and Easton were tied at 17-17 with less than three minutes left in the second quarter. After taking an 11-7 lead after one quarter, the Hawks pulled out to a 25-17 lead when they scored eight straight points to break the second quarter tie. After trailing by fourteen in the third quarter 33-19, Easton rallied to within four points later in the period 35-31. The Hawks went on a 7-2 run to pull away for the victory

Leading scorers: Bethlehem Catholic – Jim Chassar 28, Jeff Jennings 16; Easton – Gary Betts 19, Ed McIntyre 15.

Dieruff 79 Liberty 54: Despite committing 9 turnovers in the first period, Liberty held a one-point lead over Dieruff 19-18. With a little over three minutes left in the second quarter and leading 25-24, the Huskies exploded for fifteen points to take a 40-26 halftime lead. After the teams played an even third quarter with each team scoring 17 points, Dieruff erupted again in the last quarter by outscoring Liberty 22-11.

Leading scorers: Dieruff – Jim Booros 24, Ross Moore 20, Dan Joseph 15; Liberty – George Korpics 14, Dan Woodard 13.

Allen 78 Hazleton 77: Trailing by 20 points 66-46 entering the final quarter, Hazleton rallied furiously to pull ahead by a point 77-76 over Allen with 15 seconds remaining in the game. After a timeout, the Canaries' Dick Zellickson made a jumper near the foul line to salvage the victory. Hazleton's brief lead was the only one for Mountaineers in the contest.

Leading scorers: Allen – Mark Schultz 30, Dick Zellickson 24, Tim Schmeidel 14; Hazleton – Tony Kinney 20, Ed Parsons 19, Fillmore Williams 15.

Central Catholic 81 Tamaqua 51: At Rockne Hall, Central Catholic won its opening match in league play and handed Tamaqua its 20th straight league defeat. In the first 5 ½ minutes, the Vikings took a 12-2 lead when Tamaqua missed its first nine shots. After leading by 20 points at the half, the Vikings opened up a 36-point lead 74-38 in the fourth quarter.

Leading scorers: Central Catholic – John Gaspar 21, Bob Neff 18, Tony DaRe 11; Tamaqua – Gordon Tonkin 14, George Wenzel.[3]

Pottsville 83 Phillipsburg 41: Pottsville held Phillipsburg to nine points in the 2nd quarter and five points in the 4th quarter while scoring a combined 45 points in the two quarters to crush the Stateliners. The game was tied at 6-6 in the first quarter before Pottsville took a 16-11 first quarter lead and took a commanding lead in the second quarter.

Leading scorers: Pottsville – Jim Berrang 21, Dave Wilson 14, Pete Marchetti 12, Claude Baskerville 10; Phillipsburg – Bob Clymer 13, Brian Dominic 11[4]

Week 2

Pottsville 58 Easton 39: After an early 3-3 tie, Pottsville scored the next fifteen points for an 18-3 first quarter lead and take complete control of the contest. Easton only made 1 of 15 field goal attempts in the first quarter. Only Pottsville's futile third quarter when they scored four points to Easton's eleven points kept the score from being more lopsided.

Leading scorers: Pottsville – Jim Berrang 15, Dave Wilson 14; Easton – Rick Feauve 11.[5]

Dieruff 85 Bethlehem Catholic 52: Despite 17 second quarter points by Dieruff's Ross Moore, Bethlehem Catholic held a one-point lead 33-32 over the Huskies at the half. The Hawks had led at the end of the first quarter 16-8. After halftime, Coach Dick Schmidt switched the Huskies' defense to a 1-3-1 and Dieruff outscored the Hawks 21-9 to take the lead for good. Dieruff added 12 points to the lead in the fourth quarter.

Leading scorers: Dieruff – Ross Moore 34, Jim Booros 19; Bethlehem Catholic – Jim Chassar 17, Bob Alpago 12, Jeff Jennings 10.

Hazleton 83 Phillipsburg 61: In Phillipsburg, the Stateliners took a 19-12 lead in the first quarter and increased it to 30-18 midway through the second period. Hazleton stunned Phillipsburg by scoring the next 17 points and took a 37-32 lead into the locker room at the half. The Mountaineers increased their lead by five and twelve in the final two quarters for an easy win.

Leading scorers: Hazleton – Ed Parsons 19, Joe Duda 17, Tony Kinney 17, Tony Manfredi 11; Phillipsburg – Brian Dominic 16, Rich Easterly 14, Bob Clymer 10.

Central Catholic 68 Liberty 56: Liberty dropped its third straight to open league play to Central Catholic, which was Coach Mike Koury first win over Liberty after six losses. With John Gaspar scoring 20 of the team's 32 points in the second quarter, Central Catholic took a 47-31 lead at halftime. The Vikings took a 10-0 lead in the first quarter before Liberty scored. Liberty fought back to take a 14-13 lead before Bob Neff made a field goal to put the Vikings in the lead after a quarter. The Vikings scored 23 points and added ten points to the margin on their way to an easy win and a 2-0 start in league play.

Leading scorers: Central Catholic – John Gaspar 23, Tony DaRe 12, Rick Weider 11, Dan Damweber 10; Liberty – Dan Woodard 32, Ed Ruyak 11.

Allen 68 Freedom 56: Allen took an early 8-0 lead and a 19-15 lead at the end of the first quarter, but Freedom came back to lead at the half 34-32. Coach Milo Sewards switched to zone defense in the second half and the Canaries responded by outscoring the Patriots 21-12 and 15-10 in the final two periods to cruise to the win and a 3-0 start to the league season.

Leading scorers: Allen – Mark Schultz 21, Tim Schmeidel 16, Jay Haines 12, Dick Zellickson 10; Freedom – Tom Husser 21, Joe Morris 18.[6]

Freedom 63 Phillipsburg 50: Winless Phillipsburg hustled to stay within reach of Freedom for most of the game. However, midway through the 4th period, the Patriots went on six-point run to stretch the lead to 13 points where it stayed through the end of the contest. The Stateliners played Freedom evenly in the middle two periods with both teams scoring 30 points each.

Leading scorers: Freedom- Tom Husser 22, Joe Morris 19, Dan Gilbert 11; Phillipsburg- Rich Easterly 19.

Central Catholic 75 Bethlehem Catholic 66: Bethlehem Catholic outscored Central Catholic in the opening and closing quarters 36-33; however, the Vikings took an eight-point advantage 24-16 in the 2nd period and four more in the 3rd period 18-14 to hold off the Hawks. The entire starting five for the Vikings scored in double figures which countered the Hawks' Jim Chassar's outstanding 31-point performance with 25 points in the second half.

Leading scorers: Central Catholic - Bob Neff 17, Tony DaRe 16, John Gaspar 14, Dan Damweber 13, Rick Weider 13; Bethlehem Catholic – Jim Chassar 31, Jeff Jennings 12.

Dieruff 67 Pottsville 55: With Lou Benson hitting his first six shots, Dieruff led at the quarter 22-15 and the half 34-28. Jim Booros, Lou Benson, and Hal Stermer totaled 51 points enabling the Huskies to take charge of the game despite having a height disadvantage. The Huskies moved to 4-0 for the season while Pottsville dropped to 2-2.

Leading scorers: Dieruff - Jim Booros 23, Lou Benson 18, Hal Stermer 10; Pottsville - Pete Marchetti 21, Claude Baskerville 14, Jim Berrang 12.

Hazleton 68 Easton 53: Hazleton scored 23 points in each of the first two quarters and held Easton to a mere 16 points for a 30-point halftime lead. In the 2nd half, Hazleton Coach Gene Evans substituted freely. Easton took advantage to cut the half time lead in half. Hazleton only scored four points in the 3rd quarter.

Leading scorers: Hazleton – Tony Kinney 16, Joe Duda 14, Ed Parsons 11; Easton – Rich Lehr 17, Gary Betts 12, Rick Feauve 12.

Liberty 59 Tamaqua 54: Liberty won its first game while keeping Tamaqua winless in league play. A big first quarter, with Liberty grabbing a ten-point lead 22-12, spelled victory for the Hurricane. After trailing at the half 32-21, Tamaqua made a run and got within four points 47-43 early in the 4th quarter, but could get no closer.

Leading scorers: Liberty – Jim Pavel 16, Tim Fisher 15, Dan Woodard 15; Tamaqua – Steve Sassaman 20, Dan Truskey 13, Dennis Sabol 11.[7]

Week 3

Allen 76 Phillipsburg 69: Bruce Merkle scored 14 points and grabbed 13 rebounds in less than three periods to help boost the Canaries to a 20-point lead over Phillipsburg after three periods. Coach Pete Tomaino's Stateliners took early 4-0 and 12-11 leads before the Canaries vaulted into a 24-13 first quarter lead. Phillipsburg outscored the Canaries 26-13 in the final quarter, but the lead was too large to overcome.

Leading scorers: Allen – Mark Schultz 18, Dick Zellickson 17, Bruce Merkle 14, Tim Schmeidel 13; Phillipsburg – Rich Easterly 14, Brian Dominic 12, Bob Clymer 11, Barry Coopersmith 11.

Dieruff 81 Hazleton 71: Jim Booros had a career night scoring 42 points, one off the school record, and pulling down 17 rebounds to lead the Huskies to victory. His 19 field goals, out of 28 shots, set the school record. Dieruff took a 61-46 lead into the final quarter only to see Hazleton rally to pull within three points 74-71. The Huskies scored the final seven points.

Leading scorers: Dieruff – Jim Booros 42, Ross Moore 16, Lou Benson 12; Hazleton – Tony Kinney 16, Joe Duda 14, Fillmore Williams 11, Wally Kisthardt 11.

Bethlehem Catholic 77 Tamaqua 55: Bethlehem Catholic opened up a 20-8 first quarter lead and followed it up by another 20-12 quarter to take a 20-point lead at the half 40-20. They extended the lead to 26 points after three quarters and held their biggest lead early in the 4th quarter 65-36. The loss was Tamaqua's 22nd consecutive loss in league play.

Leading scorers: Bethlehem Catholic – Jim Chassar 25, Jeff Borda 14, Jeff Jennings 12; Tamaqua – George Wenzel 13.

Pottsville 80 Central Catholic 78: Central Catholic turned the ball over 19 times in the first half and made only 10 of 30 field goal attempts as Pottsville took a 39-24 at the half. The Vikings cut the lead to 56-49 by the end of the 3rd quarter and got within two points with 19 seconds to play. Dave Wilson then made two foul shots to seal the upset victory for Pottsville.

Leading scorers: Pottsville – Claude Baskerville 26, Dave Wilson 22, Pete Marchetti 14, Jim Berrang 10; Central Catholic – Tony DaRe 22, Stan Bushner 18, Rick Weider 14, Bob Neff 12.

Freedom 58 Easton 53: Although they made only 14 of 43 field goal attempts, Freedom converted 30 of 43 foul shots to pull out the win. Freedom made just four field goals in the second half. Freedom led most of the game but Easton pulled ahead 51-48 with 2:40 remaining in the game. The Patriots made a field goal and six foul shots in the final 1:19 of the game.

Leading scorers: Freedom – Joe Morris 18, Tom Husser 16, Ken Bedics 14, Dan Gilbeert 10; Easton – Gary Bond 19.[8]

Allen 92 Easton 55: Allen went on a 14-2 run during the first quarter to take a 27-10 lead at the quarter's end. The Canaries increased the lead to 50-24 by halftime and to 30 points after three quarters 70-40. Four Canaries scored in double figures.

Leading scorers: Allen – Tim Schmeidel 24, Dick Zellickson 21, Jay Haines 18, Mark Schultz 15; Easton – Don Dickey 15, Rich Lehr 11.

Dieruff 55 Freedom 54: Freedom led 20-15 after the first period and increased it to 22-15 at the start of the second period for their biggest lead of the game. Dieruff cut the lead to two points at the half 32-30. The Huskies took the lead in the third quarter and increased it to 12 points before settling for a ten-point lead to begin the fourth quarter 53-43. Coach Charlie Dubbs' Patriots employed a tight man-to-man defense in the final quarter and limited the Huskies to two points, a field goal. The two points was enough as the Patriots rally fell short. A short brawl broke out when Jim Booros grabbed a rebound for Dieruff. A player from each team was ejected.

Leading scorers: Dieruff – Ross Moore 29, Lou Benson 11; Freedom – Tom Husser 18, Joe Morris 16, Dan Gilbert 14.

Liberty 68 Bethlehem Catholic 61: Liberty's starting five played the entire game with four of them scoring in double figures. The first quarter ended in a 15-15 tie with Liberty taking a three-point lead at the half 33-30. The Hawks could not cut into the Patriots lead as they widened it to 54-47 entering the final period. Each team scored 14 points in the fourth quarter.

Leading scorers: Liberty – Ed Cunningham 20, Dan Woodard 16, Tim Fisher 14, Ed Ruyak 12; Bethlehem Catholic - Jim Chassar 25, Jeff Jennings 11.

Pottsville 62 Tamaqua 42: In a low-scoring first half, Pottsville took a 27-19 lead. The Crimson, led by Claude Baskerville's ten points, took a commanding lead in the third period 47-28. The loss was the Tams' 23rd straight in East Penn League play. Pottsville improved to 4-2.

Leading scorers: Pottsville – Pete Marchetti 20, Claude Baskerville 13, Jim Berrang 12; Tamaqua – Steve Sassaman 10.

Hazleton 76 Central Catholic 70 OT: Central Catholic made only 26 of 79 field goal attempts, while Hazleton converted 29 of 58 attempts throughout the game. Hazleton was also 18 of 20 from the foul line. The Vikings ineffective shooting led to Hazleton's 13-point lead 51-38 midway through the third quarter. The Vikings began a rally which pulled them even and then gave them the lead 67-65 with 17 seconds left in regulation. Hazleton's Tony Manfredi hit a jumper from the foul line to force overtime. In overtime, the Mountaineers made five of six foul shots for the win.

Leading scorers: Hazleton -Fillmore Williams 17, Ed Parsons 15, Joe Duda 15, Wally Kisthardt 10; Central Catholic – Tony DaRe 24, Bob Neff 13, John Gaspar 11, Rick Weider 10.[9]

Week 4

Hazleton 87 Tamaqua 60: Tamaqua's league losing streak reached 24 games at Hazleton's St. Joseph gym. Coach Nick Young's Tams never led in the game as Hazleton continued to increase the lead through the game. Hazleton shot a blistering 52% from the field as five Mountaineers scored in double figures.

Leading scorers: Hazleton – Joe Duda 18, Tony Kinney 13, Tony Manfredi 12, Fillmore Williams 11, Wally Kisthardt 11; Tamaqua – Gerry Watto 13, Gary Williams 13, Steve Sassaman 11, Tony Forte 11.[10]

Dieruff 69 Allen 57: The only two undefeated teams in league play met in the East Side gym. Allen took a slim one-point lead after the first quarter. With Allen still leading by a point 32-31 late in the second quarter, Dieruff ran off eleven straight points to end the quarter to take a 42-32 lead into the locker room. The Canaries pulled within four points early in the 3rd quarter 44-40 and five points 57-52 halfway through the final quarter only to have the Huskies respond to increase their lead. Dieruff scored its last ten points of the game from the foul line to take over sole possession of first place.

Leading scorers: Dieruff – Ross Moore 23, Lou Benson 18, Jim Booros 13; Allen – Jay Haines 21, Mark Schultz 14, Tim Schmeidel 10.

Easton 55 Phillipsburg 48: Easton (2-5) snapped a five-game losing streak and they kept Phillipsburg winless (0-6) in league play. After three first period ties, Easton ran off six straight points to take an 18-13 lead. In a low-scoring 2nd period, Phillipsburg outscored the Red Rovers 8-6 to cut Easton's lead to three points 24-21 at the half. Early in the 3rd quarter, the Stateliners came within a single point 28-27 only to have Easton run off seven in a row. Phillipsburg got no closer than 6 points the rest of the game.

Leading scorers: Easton – Gary Betts 16; Phillipsburg – Rich Easterly 16, Brian Dominic 13.

Central Catholic 54 Freedom 50: With the lead changing eight times in the first 12 minutes of the game, Freedom led at the quarter 14-10. They continued to lead 22-21 with 2 ½ minutes to play in the second quarter when the Vikings went on a spurt to lead at the half 27-24. The Vikings won the game in the third quarter by outscoring the Patriots 16-7 to take a 43-31 lead. Despite scoring 19 points to the Vikings 11 in the final period, Freedom could not overcome the big lead.

Leading scorers: Central Catholic – Bob Neff 20, Tony DaRe 17, John Gaspar 11; Freedom – Tom Husser 15, Joe Morris 15.

Pottsville 88 Liberty 74: Employing a full court press, Pottsville made 24 steals in the game to thwart the Liberty offense. Liberty led most of the first quarter only to see Dave Wilson make a basket to give Pottsville a 16-14 first quarter lead. The Crimson took advantage of the many steals to lead 64-47 after three quarters. Despite scoring 27 points in the final quarter, Liberty only shaved three points from the lead as Pottsville countered with 24 points.

Leading scorers: Pottsville – Barry Kelly 27, Jim Berrang 18, Bill Yaag 15, Dave Wilson 15; Liberty – Dan Woodard 17, Tim Fisher 17, Mike Hartenstine 11, John Priestas 10.[11]

Bethlehem Catholic 56 Pottsville 42: Bethlehem Catholic put on a stingy defensive performance during the first half, including a six-point second period, to take a commanding 29-16 halftime lead. With 3:10 left in the first period, the Hawks took the lead 10-8 and never relinquished it the rest of the game. The second half was played evenly with Bethlehem Catholic outscoring the Crimson 27-26 to complete the stunning upset of Pottsville.

Leading scorers: Bethlehem Catholic – Jim Chassar 16, Jeff Jennings 12, Ed Chladny 10; Pottsville – Claude Baskerville 10.

Dieruff 66 Phillipsburg 44: Dieruff improved to 8-0 by successfully overcoming a slow-down strategy by Phillipsburg. With Phillipsburg leading 4-3, the Huskies went on an 11-1 run to take a first quarter lead 15-5. Beginning the third period, Phillipsburg attempted the same strategy with result nearly the same. Dieruff outscored the Stateliners 19-6 to jump into the lead 51-23 after three quarters.

Leading scorers: Dieruff- Jim Booros 19, Ross Moore 11, Lou Benson 11; Phillipsburg– Brian Dominic 18.

Hazleton 79 Liberty 67: Liberty went ahead 6-4 in the first period and held the lead into the third period. With the Hurricane ahead 37-26 later in the second period, Hazleton took a thirteen-point run into the third period to grab the lead 39-37. The Hurricane fought back to take a lead 49-46 and the teams swapped baskets before Hazleton went ahead for good 66-64 with 3:14 to play. Hazleton went on a second 13-point run to extend the lead to 79-64 and seize the contest.

Leading scorers: Hazleton – Tony Kinney 25, Tony Manfredi 20, Ed Parsons 13, Joe Duda 10; Liberty – George Korpics 19, Dan Woodard 14, Mike Hartenstine 14, Tim Fisher 13.

Allen 85 Central Catholic 74: Allen took an early seven-point lead after one quarter. Central Catholic came on strong in the second quarter to come within a point of the Canaries three times. Allen responded and headed into the half with a 49-39 lead. The Vikings cut the lead to six after three quarters 65-59 and again 69-63 with 2:50 to play. The Vikings lost Bob Neff on fouls and the Canaries went on to improve their record to 6-1.

Leading scorers: Allen – Jay Haines 24, Bruce Merkle 14, Tim Schmeidel 14, Dick Zellickson 13; Central Catholic – Bob Neff 27, Tony DaRe 16, Rick Weider 11.

Tamaqua 50 Freedom 44: After scoring only four points in the third period and trailing 36-31, Tamaqua rallied against Freedom to snap their 24-game league losing streak. The Tams scored 19 points in the final period while they held the Patriots to 8. George Wenzel, who sat out the first three quarters nursing an injury, came off the bench in the 4th quarter to score 11 points to lead the Tams to victory.

Leading scorers: Tamaqua – George Wenzel 11, Steve Sassaman 10; Freedom – Dan Gilbert 9.[12]

Week 5

Allen 86 Tamaqua 55: Allen held Tamaqua to 13 points or less in each quarter to cruise to an easy win and keep their first half title hopes alive. The Canaries took the game out of reach in the middle two periods by scoring 50 points to the Tams 25.

Leading scorers: Allen – Dick Zellickson 27, Tim Schmeidel 19, Mark Schultz 12, Jay Haines 12; Tamaqua – Tony Forte 28.

Dieruff 79 Easton 44: Even though Dieruff played a somewhat sloppy game, the Huskies had little trouble with the hapless Red Rovers. The Huskies outscored Easton by eight points in each of the first three quarters. After Dieruff's starters ran off 12 straight points to begin the final quarter, Coach Terry German inserted the reserves to finish of the 35-point triumph.

Leading scorers: Dieruff – Ross Moore 25, Lou Benson 15, Jim Booros 12, Bob Stellar 12; Easton – Rick Feauve 14.

Bethlehem Catholic 56 Hazleton 55: Although each team held seven points leads, Bethlehem Catholic at 8-1 and Hazleton at 38-31 in the third period, the game was tight throughout. The Hawks led after one quarter 15-14 with Hazleton taking the lead at the half 29-28. Each team scored 16 points in the third period. With Hazleton leading 55-54, the Hawks' Bob Alpago was fouled and missed both free throws. However, Alpago grabbed the rebound on his last missed free throw and passed it to Jim Chassar who made the game-winning shot with six seconds left.

Leading scorers: Bethlehem Catholic - Jim Chassar 32, Al Calvo 10; Hazleton - Ed Parsons 22, Tony Kinney 15.

Central Catholic 89 Phillipsburg 43: After a slow start in the first period, Central Catholic handed Phillipsburg their tenth straight defeat with eight being in the league. In the first period, the Vikings went through a 6 ½ minute period when they made only 3 of 19 field goals and fell behind 9-8. But after they pulled their game together, the rest of the game was a romp for the Vikings. Central Catholic held Phillipsburg to four points in the third quarter while scoring 28.

Leading scorers: Central Catholic – Bob Neff 26, Tony DaRe 12, John Gaspar 11, John Susko 11, Tom Williams 10; Phillipsburg – Brian Dominic 19.

Freedom 53 Liberty 49: In a very close contest, Freedom went into the final quarter with a four-point lead 40-36. Liberty rallied early in the quarter by scoring eight points while holding the Patriots scoreless for almost four minutes to take the lead 44-40. With two minutes to play Liberty held a five-point lead 49-44 but would score no more as Freedom tallied the final nine points to pull out the victory.

Leading scorers: Freedom – Tom Husser 16; Liberty – Dan Woodard 12, Ed Cunningham 11.[13]

Allen 83 Liberty 74: In a game in which they never trailed, Allen survived several scares with Liberty coming within several points in the second and third quarters. After Allen took 19-12 lead after a quarter, Liberty outscored the Canaries 43-41 in the second and third quarters to keep within reach of Allen. The Canaries pulled away in the final three minutes of the game for the win.

Leading scorers: Allen – Tim Schmeidel 27, Mark Schultz 16, Jay Haines 16, Dick Zellickson 14; Liberty – Tim Fisher 23, Bob Mohylsky 23.

Central Catholic 67 Easton 47: After Central Catholic held 14-11 first quarter and 31-23 halftime leads, Easton cut the Vikings lead to one 43-42 to open the fourth quarter. The Vikings responded by scoring the next 18 points to put the game in the win column.

Leading scorers: Central Catholic – Bob Neff 19, John Gaspar 16, Tony DaRe 11; Easton – Ed McIntyre 10, Gary Betts 10.

Bethlehem Catholic 56 Freedom 44: Freedom took charge of the game in the first half with leads of 13-10 and 28-21 in each of the first two periods. Bethlehem Catholic came out of the locker room with a stingy defense and allowed Freedom only single digits in each quarter and sixteen points total. The Hawks offense rallied to score 35 points in the half and improve their league record to 7-3 for the first half.

Leading scorers: Bethlehem Catholic - Jeff Jennings 13, Jim Chassar 13, Greg Falkenbach 10; Freedom – Tom Husser 11, Steve Pecsek 11, Ken Bedics 10.

Phillipsburg 59 Tamaqua 57: Winless Phillipsburg won its first contest in league and overall play by defeating Tamaqua, who lost for the 25th time in 27 outings in league play. With Tamaqua leading at the half 34-32, Phillipsburg outscored the Tams by five in the third quarter 16-11 which eventually led to the victory. Tamaqua could only trim the lead by one in the final period.

Leading scorers: Phillipsburg – Brian Dominic 20, Bob Clymer 11, Doug Maczko 11; Tamaqua – Tony Forte 17, Steve Sassaman 12.[14]

Pottsville 59 Hazleton 48: With Hazleton hitting only 19 of 69 from the floor and 10 of 21 from the foul line, Pottsville overcame an early first quarter lead by the Mountaineers 14-7. The score was tied three times in each of the second and third periods. Pottsville took a 42-38 lead into the final period only to have Hazleton tie it at 43-43. Pottsville took the lead on a foul shot and two field goals and the Mountaineers could not stage a comeback as Pottsville improved to 6-3.

Leading scorers: Pottsville – Barry Kelly 18, Dave Wilson 16, Bill Yaag 12, Claude Baskerville 11; Hazleton – Tony Kinney 16, Ed Parson 14.[15]

Week 6

Dieruff 65 Central Catholic 61: Dieruff finished the first half with a perfect 10-0 record despite an effort by Central Catholic hand the Huskies their first league loss. After taking the lead for good in the second period, the Huskies increased the lead to ten points to start the fourth quarter. With Dieruff leading 54-45, the Vikings made four straight field goals to come within one at 54-53. Ross Moore made two clutch field goals to give Dieruff a cushion and ultimately the win. Dieruff made 19 of 20 foul shots in the game.

Leading scorers: Dieruff - Ross Moore 15, Jim Booros 13, Bob Stellar 12, Lou Benson 11, Dan Joseph 10; Central Catholic – Tony DaRe 17, John Gaspar 14, Dan Damweber 12, Rick Weider 10.

Allen 102 Bethlehem Catholic 57: Using their superior height, the Canaries routed the Hawks after a close first period with Allen ahead 18-16. The last three periods the Canaries outscored Bethlehem Catholic 84-

41 with little resistance from the Hawks defense. With an 18-18 tie to start the second period, Allen began the onslaught with a 15-point run. Allen finished second to Dieruff with a 9-1 record.

Leading scorers: Allen – Mark Schultz 25, Tim Schmeidel 23, Dick Zellickson 22, Jay Haines 10; Bethlehem Catholic – Jim Chassar 37.

Pottsville 62 Freedom 60 OT: Pottsville improved to 7-3 by defeating host Freedom in overtime. After Freedom led 12-11 at the end of the first period, Pottsville outscored the Patriots in the next two quarters to take a 40-38 lead into the final quarter. With the Crimson leading 56-54, Joe Morris scored on a driving layup with 20 seconds to play to tie the score and send the game into overtime. In overtime with the score tied at 60-60, Freedom missed a layup and Jim Berrang was fouled on the rebound by Ken Bedics with two seconds remaining. Berrang connected on both shots to give Pottsville the victory.

Leading scorers: Pottsville – Jim Berrang 19, Barry Kelly 14; Freedom – Joe Morris 24, Tom Husser 18.

Liberty 53 Phillipsburg 51: After Phillipsburg scored the first two points of the game, they never regained the lead. The score was tied numerous times with the two teams trading baskets. Liberty took a ten-point lead 30-20 at the half, but Phillipsburg scored the first eight points of the 3rd period to tighten up the game.

Leading scorers: Liberty-Tim Fisher 20, Ed Cunningham 10; Phillipsburg-Brian Dominic 14, Bruce Exley 14, Bob Clymer 13.

Tamaqua 49 Easton 36: Tamaqua defeated Easton to win its second game in the league and third on the season. Easton led at the half 20-17 when Tamaqua could only score six points in the quarter, all by Dennis Sabol. Tamaqua took the lead in the third quarter and then held Easton to six points in the final quarter while scoring 18 of their own.

Leading scorers: Tamaqua – Dennis Sabol 15, Gary Williams 13; Easton – Gary Betts 13.[16]

Second Half - Week 7

Allen 79 Pottsville 72: After Allen took an 18-9 lead during the 1st quarter while Pottsville shot 4 of 20 from the floor, the Crimson got hot in the middle two periods to outscore the Canaries 48-30 and took a 47-38 lead into the final quarter. Allen cut the lead to 68-65 before scoring 10 points in a row to take a 75-68 lead.

Leading scorers: Allen – Daryl Tollinche 22, Jay Haines 16, Dick Zellickson 13, Mark Schultz 13, Tim Schmeidel 10; Pottsville – Jim Berrang 21, Pete Marchetti 18, Dave Wilson 14, Claude Baskerville 12.

Bethlehem Catholic 52 Phillipsburg 45: In a sloppy contest, Bethlehem Catholic had 22 turnovers and Phillipsburg 17 with neither team shooting well. The Hawks lost a six-point lead in the 1st quarter and trailed 13-12 when it was over. Bethlehem Catholic recaptured the lead by half time 22-19 and held it into the 4th quarter when the Stateliners tied them at 36-36. The Hawks scored on five fastbreaks in the last six minutes to pull out the win.

Leading scorers: Bethlehem Catholic – Jim Chassar 20, Jeff Borda 17; Phillipsburg – Brian Dominic 18.

Liberty 71 Easton 64: Easton opened the game scoring the first seven points before Liberty went on a 12-2 run to go ahead 12-9. Easton had its own run 12-1 for a 21-13 lead. Easton scored seven points in a row to start the 2nd period to go ahead 28-15, but Liberty narrowed the lead to 37-31 at the half. Liberty went into a tight man-to-man press to start the 3rd period and retook the lead 47-44. Easton responded by getting the lead back early in the 4th quarter 55-51. Liberty ran off 7 points to take the lead and, after a bucket by Easton, went on an 8-1 spurt to put the game away.

Leading scorers: Liberty – Tim Fisher 24, Dan Woodard 21; Easton – Bob Renaldi 15, Rick Feauve 14, Don Dickey 13, Ed McIntyre 12.

Dieruff 73 Tamaqua 45: Dieruff caused three turnovers in the first minute on their way to an 8-0 lead and 17-5 first quarter lead. Tamaqua scored only one field goal in the quarter which was six minutes into the game. After that, the game was not much of a contest with Dieruff's bench getting a lot of playing time.

Leading scorers: Dieruff – Dan Joseph 19, Jim Booros 17, Lou Benson 11, Ross Moore 10; Tamaqua – Gary Williams 15.

Hazleton 71 Freedom 50: Falling behind 7-0 and 15-8 during the first period, Freedom rebounded to cut the deficit to 15-14 early in the 2nd period. Hazleton went on a 15-3 run in the last six minutes of the quarter and took a 30-17 half time lead. Hazleton continued to add on in the final two quarters for a decisive win.

Leading scorers: Hazleton– Tony Kinney 21, Ed Parsons16, Jim Famalette 12; Freedom- Tom Husser 12, Steve Pecsek 10.[17]

Week 8

Allen 75 Hazleton 74: At the Little Palestra, Allen fell behind Hazleton midway through the first quarter and trailed by as many as 12 points in the game. Hazleton led at the half 41-33 and at the end of the third quarter 58-55. Allen continued to trail up until a minute to play in the game when Dick Zellickson hit a jumper to put Allen ahead 73-71. They had finally tied Hazleton at 71-71 on two free throws and a field goal by Tim Schmeidel.

Leading scorers: Allen – Dick Zellickson 28, Tim Schmeidel 18, Daryl Tollinche 11, Mark Schultz 10; Hazleton – Tony Kinney 18, Tony Manfredi 15, Fillmore Williams 14, Joe Duda 12.

Bethlehem Catholic 63 Easton 60 OT: In a close game separated by no more than a point after each quarter, Easton led after one 9-8. Bethlehem Catholic tied it up at the half 24-24 and took the lead after three quarters 38-37. The Hawks moved to a 50-45 lead with 2:50 remaining only to have Easton move ahead 56-54. Jim Chassar sank a desperation shot at the buzzer to send the game into overtime. With Bethlehem Catholic ahead 62-60, Easton missed a shot to tie and Hassar took the rebound and was fouled. He converted one of two for the win.

Leading scorers: Bethlehem Catholic-Jim Chassar 32, Jeff Borda 17; Easton-Rick Feauve 25, Gary Betts 15.

Dieruff 78 Liberty 65: After Liberty scored 24 points to take a 24-18 lead in the first quarter, Dieruff held them to six points in the second quarter to take over the lead 35-30. Dieruff managed to hold nine-point leads three times in the third period at 39-30, 41-32, and 43-34. Liberty came back to tie the game at 56-56 with a little under six minutes to play. The Huskies responded with a foul shot and two field goals to move ahead for good.

Leading scorers: Dieruff –Ross Moore 23, Jim Booros 17, Lou Benson 14, Bob Stellar 13; Liberty – Tim Fisher 23, Dan Woodard 20, Ed Cunningham 12.

Central Catholic 75 Tamaqua 35: Central Catholic held Tamaqua to single digits in each of the first three periods on the way to 39-14 half time and 57-23 third quarter leads. After Tamaqua took a 4-2 lead, Central Catholic ran off 10 straight points and another eight in a row after a Tamaqua field goal. The Vikings played the second team for the entire final quarter and still outscored the Tams 18-13.

Leading scorers: Central Catholic – John Gaspar 12, Tony DaRe 10, Bob Kasper 10; Tamaqua – George Wenzel 9.[18]

Pottsville 83 Phillipsburg 52: Pottsville jumped out to a 10-0 lead and 22-10 at the end of the first quarter on the way to a romp over Phillipsburg. Pottsville moved ahead 70-35 after three quarters and Coach Ken Kline inserted the second team for the final quarter.

Leading scorers: Pottsville – Pete Marchetti 17, Jim Berrang 16, Dave Wilson 10; Phillipsburg – Brian Dominic 17, Bob Clymer 17.[19]

Hazleton 88 Phillipsburg 46: Hazleton Coach Gene Evans used twelve players, with eleven of them scoring, against an overmatched Phillipsburg squad. Hazleton had little trouble as the Mountaineers ran up leads of 9, 17, 33, and 42 points after each of the quarters. In the third quarter alone, Hazleton added 16 points to the lead outscoring the Stateliners 26-10 and doubling the game total at the end of the quarter 65-32.

Leading scorers: Hazleton – Tony Kinney 18, Tony Manfredi 18, Joe Duda 17, Sam Mumaw 10; Phillipsburg – Brian Dominic 16, Bob Clymer 12.[20]

Dieruff 34 Bethlehem Catholic 32: In a classic defensive struggle, both teams deployed strategies to neutralize each team's top scorers: Bethlehem Catholic's Jim Chassar and Dieruff's Ross Moore and Jim Booros. And the strategy worked with those players scoring well below their game averages. Chassar fared best with 13 points while Moore scored 6 and Booros 9 points. In the first quarter, Dieruff scored the last ten points to take a 12-3 lead. The Hawks cut the lead to 19-13 in the second quarter. The third quarter saw both teams score in double digits with Dieruff outscoring the Hawks 13-11. Coach Dick Schmidt had his team employ the freeze at the beginning of the final period with his team ahead 32-26. The move nearly backfired as Bethlehem Catholic made four field goals while the Huskies made only two foul shots during the entire period. The Huskies hung on to win and remain undefeated in league play.

Leading scorers: Dieruff – Jim Booros 9; Bethlehem Catholic – Jim Chassar 13.

Central Catholic 94 Liberty 70: Liberty put Central Catholic to the test in the 1st period and only a buzzer-beater by Bob Neff gave the Vikings the lead 22-21. Central Catholic then took charge in the final three quarters to remain undefeated in the second half of play. The Vikings ran off ten straight points early in the 2nd quarter and followed with another 8-point run later in the quarter. Taking advantage of Liberty's aggressive play, the Vikings converted 30 of 40 foul shots. Liberty's Mike Hartenstine, their top rebounder, fouled out late in the 3rd quarter.

Leading scorers: Central Catholic – Bob Neff 18, John Gaspar 18, Dan Damweber 16, Tom Williams 16, Tony DaRe 14; Liberty - Tim Fisher 13, Bob Majczan 12.

Allen 63 Freedom 52: Allen and Freedom battled on even terms through the first three periods. Freedom did take an eight-point lead in the first quarter and led by four with 1:39 left in the third quarter 40-36. Allen took charge in the final period with a 17-2 run which began late in the third period to take a commanding lead 53-42. The Patriots never threatened the Canaries after that.

Leading scorers: Allen –Tim Schmeidel 23, Mark Schultz 15, Dick Zellickson 12; Freedom – Tom Husser 16, Joe Morris 13, Steve Pecsek 11.[21]

Pottsville 68 Easton 39: With a woeful first half, Easton fell behind Pottsville 37-10 with an atrocious shooting night. Although they played Pottsville fairly even in the second half with Pottsville only outscoring them by two points 31-29, they could not overcome the massive lead held by the Crimson.

Leading scorers: Pottsville – Jim Berrang 16, Pete Marchetti 15, Barry Kelly 13; Easton – Ted Tyson 7, Don Dickey 7.[22]

Week 9

Pottsville 90 Dieruff 64: At Pottsville, the Crimson stunned visiting Dieruff in snapping the Huskies 13 game league winning streak. Pottsville made a statement in the first quarter jumping out to a 27-12 lead. Pottsville outscored Dieruff in all four quarters. The loss dropped the Huskies into a three-way tie with Hazleton and Pottsville for 3rd place at 3-1 and a half game behind Central Catholic and Allen, both at 3-0.

Leading scorers: Pottsville– Jim Berrang 28, Claude Baskerville 19, Pete Marchetti 14, Barry Kelty 14; Dieruff– Jim Booros 31.

Liberty 95 Tamaqua 80: In Bethlehem, Liberty won the contest in the first quarter by scoring 32 points to the Tams 8. Despite outscoring Liberty in each of the final three quarters, the 24-point first quarter advantage held up easily as Liberty still won the contest by 15 points. Early in the second period, Liberty built the lead to 44-10 before Tamaqua ran off 13 points in a row to narrow the gap. The closest Tamaqua got all night was 10 points 89-79 with a little over a minute left in the game.

Leading scorers: Liberty – Tim Fisher 36, Dan Woodard 18, Mike Hartenstine 14, Ed Ruyak 12, Ed Cunningham 10; Tamaqua – Steve Sassaman 19, Mike Weidell 17, Dan Truskey 16, Dave Reed 14, George Wenzel 13.

Freedom 47 Phillipsburg 41: The second period doomed Phillipsburg when they only were able to score five points to Freedom's thirteen. Freedom scored 13 points in each of the first three periods to build a 39-27 lead. The Stateliners did hold early leads in the first quarter 7-4 and 10-8 before Freedom took the lead for good late in the first quarter. Phillipsburg outscored the Patriots 14-8 in the last quarter but the lead was too great to overcome.

Leading scorers: Freedom – Joe Morris 21; Phillipsburg – Brian Dominic 17.

Central Catholic 77 Bethlehem Catholic 49: Central Catholic scored 27 points in both the first and fourth quarters. The Vikings held a 20-point lead after the first quarter when they held the Hawks to seven points. The Hawks tried to come back and outscored the Vikings 26-23 in the middle periods. However, the Vikings retaliated by pouring in 27 points to the Hawks 16.

Leading scorers: Central Catholic – Bob Neff 23, Dan Damweber 16, Tom Williams 13, Tony DaRe 10; Bethlehem Catholic – Jim Chassar 20.

Hazleton 70 Easton 56: Hazleton kept Easton winless in the second half while staying in a tie for third place at 3-1, a half-game behind Allen and Central Catholic, both at 3-0. After holding the Red Rovers to five points while scoring 16 points in the first quarter, Hazleton built the lead to 31-8 before Easton fought back to cut the lead to 33-21 at the half. Easton's only lead on the night was 2-1 in the first quarter.

Leading scorers: Hazleton – Ed Parsons 18, Joe Duda 18, Tony Manfredi 12; Easton – Gary Betts 12, Rick Feauve 10.[23]

Hazleton 71 Dieruff 67 OT: In Hazleton, the Mountaineers started fast with 16-9 first quarter and 36-23 halftime leads. Early in the third quarter, Hazleton led by as many as 15 points. Dieruff fought back to cut the lead to three 47-44 when Jim Booros severely hurt his knee and sat out the rest of the contest. Dieruff actually led the game by a point five different times in the final quarter. Hazelton's Tony Manfredi tied the score at 65 with 1:40. But despite opportunities, neither team could convert and the game went into overtime. Hazleton's Tony Kinney hit two field goals and a free throw to win the game in overtime for the Mountaineers. Tony Kinney broke Hazleton's season scoring record of 849 points and finished the game with 864 points.

Leading scorers: Hazleton – Tony Kinney 29, Ed Parsons 16, Tony Manfredi 13, Joe Duda 10; Dieruff - Ross Moore 38, Lou Benson 11.[24]

Allen 91 Phillipsburg 61: Allen scored 25 or more points in each of the first three quarters to build a 53-24 lead at the half and 78-48 lead after three quarters. The loss left the Stateliners still winless in the second half while Allen improved to 4-0. Allen had a number of easy layups due to steals by Daryl Tollinche early in the game to build the big lead.

Leading scorers: Allen – Tim Schmeidel 24, Dick Zellickson 19, Mark Schultz 16, Jay Haines 13; Phillipsburg – Brian Dominic 15, Rich Easterly 11.

Tamaqua 72 Bethlehem Catholic 61: Tamaqua won its first game of the second half with four players scoring in double figures. The Tams outscored the Hawks in all but the second quarter. The Hawks dropped to 2-3 in the second half. Late in the game, Bethlehem Catholic could get no closer than six points.

Leading scorers: Tamaqua – Steve Sassaman 20, Dave Reed 13, Gary Williams 12, Dan Truskey 11; Bethlehem Catholic – Jim Chassar 27, Jeff Borda 12.

Freedom 62 Easton 43: Freedom's defense allowed the Red Rovers to make only five of 27 field goal attempts in the first half. Freedom jumped out to a 32-18 lead and increased it to 52-30 after three quarters to cruise to an easy win. Freedom evened its record at 2-2 and Easton remained winless at 0-4

Leading scorers: Freedom – Joe Morris 18, Steve Pecsek 12, Dan Gilbert 12; Easton – Rick Feauve 16.

Central Catholic 77 Pottsville 63: Central Catholic remained tied for first place with Allen at 4-0. Being down by a point after a quarter 20-19, the Vikings took the lead at the half 37-36. They had a 12-point lead in the second quarter 35-23 before Pottsville cut it to one at the half. The Vikings took a 14-point lead into the fourth quarter and were only challenged once in the fourth quarter when Pottsville cut the lead to eight.

Leading Scorers: Central Catholic – Dan Damweber 17, John Gaspar 15, Rick Weider 13, Tom Williams 13, Tony DaRe 10; Pottsville – Jim Berrang 19, Claude Baskerville 16.[25]

Week 10

Allen 54 Easton 32: With Easton Coach Tom Sweeney employing slowdown tactics in an effort to slow down the Canary offense, Allen Coach Milo Sewards played his starting five the entire game against Easton. Despite using this strategy, the Red Rovers only briefly kept themselves in the contest. After Allen took a 9-4 lead after a quarter, Easton hit their first two field goals in the 2nd quarter to pull within 9-8. The Canaries ran off nine points in a row to extend the lead to 19-8 and 21-11 at the half. Both teams played at a faster pace in the 2nd half as Allen continued to increase the lead and remain tied for 1st place with Central Catholic.

Leading scorers: Allen – Tim Schmeidel 18, Dick Zellickson 15; Easton – Gary Betts 9.

Pottsville 87 Tamaqua 77: After Tamaqua took a 2-0 lead, Pottsville ran off 14 straight points on their way to a 23-10 first quarter lead with Pete Marchetti scoring 10 of the points in the quarter. Pottsville built the lead to 50-28 at the half and increased to 30 in the third quarter before the bench took over. Tamaqua outscored the Crimson 49-37 in the second half but could not overcome Pottsville's first half margin.

Leading scorers: Pottsville – Jim Berrang 25, Pete Marchetti 20, Bill Yaag 11; Tamaqua – Gary Williams 21, Dave Reed 15, Steve Sassaman 14, Tony Forte 13, Dan Truskey 12.

Bethlehem Catholic 78 Liberty 59: Liberty led for the only time at 2-0 and tied the game at 3-3 before Bethlehem Catholic ran off nine points for 12-3 lead. The Hawks' Jim Chassar led all scorers and rebounders with 35 points and 24 rebounds. Bethlehem Catholic evened its record at 3-3 while Liberty fell to 2-3.

Leading scorers: Bethlehem Catholic – Jim Chassar 35, Jeff Jennings 22; Liberty – Tim Fisher 21, Dan Woodard 11.

Dieruff 68 Freedom 56: After two consecutive league losses and with Jim Booros out with an injury, Dieruff rebounded behind Ross Moore to defeat the Patriots. Ken Fedor took Booros' spot in the Husky lineup. After falling behind 15-14, Dieruff held Freedom to 7 points in the 2nd quarter to take the lead for good 30-22 at the half.

Leading scorers: Dieruff – Ross Moore 31, Lou Benson 11, Bob Stellar 10; Freedom – Steve Pecsek 13, Ken Bedics 11, Joe Morris 10.[26]

Central Catholic 65 Hazleton 57: In Hazleton, Central Catholic avenged a first half loss to the Mountaineers to remain in a tie for first place. After holding the lead briefly in the second quarter and falling behind at the half 34-31, Hazleton came back to tie the game at 48-48 and 50-50. The Vikings scored eight in a row to lead 58-50 and maintained the lead the rest of the way

Leading scorers: Central Catholic – Tom Williams 19, Bob Neff 16, John Gaspar 14; Hazleton – Tony Kinney 19, Wally Kisthardt 10.[27]

Hazleton 87 Tamaqua 73: After a close first period with Hazleton in the lead 15-12, the Mountaineers took charge in the second quarter with a 43-27 lead. Hazleton continued to add on in the third period to extend the lead to 25 points 71-46. Tamaqua, by scoring 27 points in the final period, cut the lead but the game had already been decided at that point.

Hazleton – Tony Manfredi 21, Joe Duda 15, Wally Kisthardt 12, Ed Parsons 10; Tamaqua – Gary Williams 19, George Wenzel 17, Dan Truskey 15.[28]

Allen 84 Dieruff 67: With Dick Zellickson scoring 28 points and grabbing 23 rebounds, Allen continued undefeated at 6-0 in the second half. The Huskies fell to 4-3. After falling behind 17-14 in the first quarter, Allen took control of the game from the second period on as Dieruff missed the rebounding presence of Jim Booros, still healing from a knee injury.

Leading scorers: Allen – Dick Zellickson 28, Tim Schmeidel 24, Mark Schultz 14, Daryl Tollinche 12; Dieruff – Ross Moore 18, Bob Stellar 14, Lou Benson 13, Bob Racosky 11.

Pottsville 75 Liberty 64: After Liberty took a 4-2 lead and led the rest of the 1st quarter, Pete Marchetti scored 18 points in the middle two periods to take Pottsville from an 18-17 deficit to a 58-44 lead after three quarters. Liberty had led 14-9 at one point in the opening quarter. Pottsville improved to 5-2 with Liberty at 2-4.

Leading scorers: Pottsville – Pete Marchetti 26, Jim Berrang 20, Bob Wilson 10; Liberty – 17, Dan Woodard 14, Mike Hartenstine 13, Ed Ruyak 10.

Phillipsburg 53 Easton 52: With Phillipsburg winning its first game of the second half, they dropped Easton into sole possession of the cellar at 0-6 and handed them their 10th straight loss. Down eleven points in the second quarter, Phillipsburg cut the Red Rovers lead to three at the half 30-27. After Easton extended the lead 39-31, Phillipsburg scored ten in a row to take the lead 41-39. Easton led 49-48 with 2:42 to play, but Phillipsburg scored two field goals to lead 52-49. The score was tied again at 52-52 when Easton's Harry Keller made three free throws. With 28 seconds left Brian Dominic sank a foul shot for the Stateliner's win.

Leading scorers: Phillipsburg- Brian Dominic 27, Rich Easterly 11; Easton- Gary Betts 12, Rich Feauve 10.

Central Catholic 83 Freedom 71: After leading 16-12 after one quarter, Freedom extended the lead to seven points several times in the second quarter with the last being 23-16. The Vikings cut the lead to 34-32 at the half. Coach Mike Koury switched the Vikings' defense to a press to start the second half. Central Catholic responded by making nine straight shots, went on to victory, and remained tied for the league lead with Allen.

Leading scorers: Central Catholic – Bob Neff 28, Tony DaRe 26, Dan Damweber 13; Freedom – Joe Morris 25, Tom Husser 21.[29]

Week 11

Allen 82 Central Catholic 80 OT: In a showdown for first place at Rockne Hall, the matchup between Allen and Central Catholic lived up to its pre-game billing. The first quarter ended in a tie 23-23 with Allen taking a one-point lead into the locker room at the half. The Canaries attempted to break away in the third period and held as much as a twelve-point lead before taking 62-52 lead at the end of the quarter. Allen still held an eleven-point lead with 5 ½ minutes to play. The Vikings rallied to outscore the Canaries 17-6 in the final 4:49 of regulation to tie the contest at 76-76 on Tony DaRe's three straight field goals. Daryl Tollinche scored Allen's six points in the stretch with three jump shots. Tim Schmeidel's field goal with seven seconds left in overtime won the game for the Canaries and gave them sole possession of 1st place in the second half.

Leading scorers: Allen – Tim Schmeidel 19, Daryl Tollinche 16, Jay Haines 15, Dick Zellickson 14, Mark Schultz 14; Central Catholic - Bob Neff 26, Dan Damweber 19, Tony DaRe 16, John Gaspar 12.

Dieruff 77 Phillipsburg 51: Dieruff took the lead from the outset and never left Phillipsburg lead or tie the game. The Huskies held Brian Dominic, the Stateliners' leading scorer, to nine points with four coming near the end of the 4th quarter. The closest that Phillipsburg got to Dieruff was four points 25-21 midway through the 2nd quarter.

Leading scorers: Dieruff – Ross Moore 19, Ken Fedor 17, Bob Stellar 13; Phillipsburg – Bob Clymer 16.

Freedom 80 Tamaqua 61: Coach Charlie Dubb's Patriots had a hot shooting night as Freedom hit 30 of 53 field goal attempts and 20 of 26 free throws. Tamaqua took an early lead 13-9 into the 2nd quarter only to see the Patriots score 25 points and take a 34-28 lead at the half, a lead they never lost.

Leading scorers: Freedom – Steve Pecsek 18, Dan Gilbert 16, Tom Husser 13, Joe Morris 12; Tamaqua – Dan Truskey 23, Gary Williams 10, Steve Sassaman 10.

Pottsville 59 Bethlehem Catholic 40: Despite a tight defense, Jim Chassar still scored 23 points and pulled down 26 rebounds for Bethlehem Catholic. Even with his heroics, the Hawks still lost the game. Pottsville took a 16-7 first quarter, never trailed in the game, and improved to 6-2.

Leading scorers: Pottsville – Pete Marchetti 15, Bob Wilson 14; Bethlehem Catholic – Jim Chassar 23.

Hazleton 73 Liberty 71: Liberty held a four-point lead with 3:40 to go and decided to freeze to ball. The strategy backfired as Hazleton countered with two field goals to tie the game at 71-71. Liberty missed the front end of two one-and-one foul shot opportunities. Hazleton's Tony Manfredi missed a shot with six seconds left but was fouled. He made both free throws for the win.

Leading scorers: Hazleton – Tony Kinney 26, Tony Manfredi 15; Bethlehem – Tim Fisher 21, Mike Hartenstine 15, Dan Woodard 14.[30]

Central Catholic 76 Phillipsburg 51: Central Catholic rebounded after its disappointing loss to Allen with a defeat of Phillipsburg to retain its chance of a second half title. The Vikings took the floor and promptly took 20-10 and 41-29 leads after the first two quarters. Playing without team captain Bob Neff and Rick Weider, the Vikings easily outplayed the Stateliners.

Leading scorers: Central Catholic – Tony DaRe 22, Dan Damweber 13, Tom Williams 12; Phillipsburg – Brian Dominic 17, Charlie Morgan 12.[31]

Allen 100 Tamaqua 64: Allen and Tamaqua battled to a 16-16 tie after one quarter with Allen moving into the lead at the half 37-31. Responding to Coach Milo Sewards' halftime tongue-lashing, the Canaries took the floor and scored 63 points to Tamaqua's 33 to turn the game into a rout. The second half outburst set a school record for most points in a half. Tamaqua held the league record with 65 against Dieruff in 1963.

Leading scorers: Allen – Dick Zellickson 21, Jay Haines 17, Mark Schultz16, Tim Schmeidel 14, Daryl Tollinche 10; Tamaqua – Steve Sassaman 14, Dan Truskey 14.

Bethlehem Catholic 65 Hazleton 63: With neither team being able to grasp a big lead, Hazleton led after one quarter 14-12 with Bethlehem Catholic tying the game at the half 30-30. The game stayed close the rest of the way with neither team getting more than three points ahead. The Mountaineers tried freezing the ball with 2:43 remaining and leading by two points 61-59. With 58 seconds left, Jim Chassar tied the score for the Hawks. After the teams traded baskets, Hazleton lost the ball out-of-bounds. With three seconds left, Chassar shot and missed but Mark Halbreiner tapped in the missed shot for the win.

Leading scorers: Bethlehem Catholic – Jim Chassar 21, Jeff Jennings 18; Hazleton – Tony Kinney 19, Fillmore Williams 14.

Dieruff 69 Easton 37: After a low-scoring first quarter with Dieruff taking an 11-5 lead over Easton, the Huskies outscored the Red Rovers 20-9 in the second quarter and the rout was on. The score was only close early in the first period at 2-1 and 6-5 in the Huskies' favor as Easton never held the lead in the game.

Leading scorers: Dieruff – Ross Moore 25, Bob Racosky 11; Easton – Rick Feauve 12, Hank Godown 12.

Freedom 79 Liberty 59: Freedom held Liberty to a single basket in the first six minutes of the game as the Patriots went on a 10-point scoring spree and a 19-10 first quarter lead. Liberty got no closer than five points the rest of the game. At the start of the 4th quarter, the Patriots made 10 of their first 11 field goal attempts.

Leading scorers: Freedom – Tom Husser 26, Dan Gilbert 20, Joe Morris 13, Steve Pecsek 11; Liberty – Tim Fisher 19, Dan Woodard 10.[32]

Week 12

Allen 95 Liberty 74: Allen ensured itself of at least a tie for the second half with an easy win over Liberty. Allen led 24-17 after a quarter and 47-34 at the half. After Liberty opened with a basket in the second half, Allen ran a streak of eight straight points to put the game in the win column.

Leading scorers: Allen – Tim Schmeidel 23, Dick Zellickson 22, Jay Haines 17, Mark Schultz 14, Daryl Tollinche 11; Liberty – Dan Woodard 21, John Priestas 13, Mike Hartenstine 10, Tim Fisher 10.

Central Catholic 78 Easton 57: With Easton registering only two foul shots in the first period to fall behind 19-2, the Red Rovers recovered to score 22 in the second period and shave five points off the Vikings' lead 36-24. Bob Neff increased his career total to 1,024 points.

Leading scorers: Central Catholic – Rick Weider 23, Bob Neff 18, John Gaspar 11, Stan Bushner 11; Easton – Bob Renaldi 12, Rick Feauve 11, Hank Godown 10.

Freedom 61 Bethlehem Catholic 56: Although Jim Chassar had another big scoring night, he could not lead Bethlehem Catholic to victory. Going into the fourth quarter, Chassar had scored all but four of his team's 37 points. Despite holding a 46-37 lead going into the final quarter, Freedom only led 56-54 with a minute and a half to play. A field goal by Dan Gilbert and Joe Morris's two free throws ensured a victory for the Patriots.

Leading Scorers: Freedom – Steve Pecsek 21, Tom Husser 14; Bethlehem Catholic – Jim Chassar 40, Jeff Jennings 10.[33]

Hazleton 73 Pottsville 68: Pottsville led after a quarter 19-15 with Hazleton rallying to tie the score at 23-23 and 25-25 in the second quarter. Hazleton kept its rally going to take a half time lead 41-36. Pottsville brought the score within four points 50-46, but Hazleton countered to take a 57-49 third quarter lead. Hazleton improved to 7-3 while the Crimson stood at 6-3.

Leading scorers: Hazleton – Joe Duda 24, Ed Parsons 20, Wally Kisthardt 10; Pottsville – Pete Marchetti 16, Dave Wilson 14, Claude Baskerville 13, Jim Berrang 13.

Tamaqua 64 Phillipsburg 63: Phillipsburg staked Tamaqua to a seven-point lead after a period 17-10 and Tamaqua parlayed this margin into a narrow win over the Stateliners. Phillipsburg finally went into the lead 53-52 only to see Tamaqua recover and hang on for a one-point win.

Leading scorers: Tamaqua – Gary Williams 13, Steve Sassaman 12, Gerry Watto 11, Dave Reed 10; Phillipsburg - Rich Easterly 17, Brian Dominic 14, Barry Coopersmith 13, Bucky Utley 11.[34]

Allen 59 Bethlehem Catholic 53: Bethlehem Catholic stunned Allen by taking an early 6-0 lead at the outset of the game and held on for a 13-12 first quarter lead. After Allen came into the third quarter with a 29-24 lead, Jim Chassar scored 13 of the Hawks' 15 third quarter points and pulled them into a 38-37 lead with 1:43 left in the quarter. After Allen took the lead again, the Hawks led once more in the final quarter 43-41 on two Chassar free throws. With Allen getting the lead again, Chassar once more put the Hawks in the lead 48-47, their last lead of the game. Foul shooting in the final minutes pulled out the win for Allen.

Leading scorers: Allen – Jay Haines 17, Tim Schmeidel 14, Dick Zellickson 11, Daryl Tollinche 10; Bethlehem Catholic – Jim Chassar 35.

Dieruff 70 Central Catholic 67 OT: After a low-scoring first period with Dieruff holding a 9-7 lead, both teams picked it up in the second quarter with the Huskies extending their lead to 30-25. Dieruff increased the lead to 41-33 before the game tightened at the end of the third quarter when the Vikings cut the lead to 45-42. Central Catholic continued its surge to take the lead 57-55 with 2 ½ minutes to play. Allen tied the game and both teams added a couple field goals to tie the game at the end of regulation 61-61. In overtime, the Canaries made seven free throws to outlast the Vikings 70-67.

Leading scorers: Dieruff – Ross Moore 32, Bob Stellar 13, Lou Benson 12, Bob Racosky 11; Central Catholic – John Gaspar 20, Bob Neff 13, Tom Williams 13, Dan Damweber 10.[35]

Phillipsburg 80 Liberty 74: With Brian Dominic scoring fourteen points in the fourth quarter, Phillipsburg surprised Liberty by making their first half advantage hold up. The Stateliners took a 17-13 lead in the first quarter and extended it to 37-31 at the half. After Phillipsburg extended the lead to twelve during the third quarter, Liberty fought back to take a brief three-point lead in the fourth quarter. However, Dominic's scoring burst in the final quarter brought Phillipsburg back for the victory. The Stateliners made 33 of 57 shots from the floor.

Leading scorers: Phillipsburg – Brian Dominic 33, Rich Easterly 12; Liberty – Dan Woodard 21, Tim Fisher 18, Mike Hartenstine 12, Ed Ruyak 12.

Freedom 62 Pottsville 55: Freedom led at the half 24-21; however, Pottsville scored the first five points of the third quarter to take a 26-24 lead. Freedom countered with a 14-3 run for a 38-29 advantage. Pottsville never caught the Patriots as both teams ended up with 6-4 records for the second half.

Leading scorers: Freedom – Tom Husser 18, Joe Morris 16, Ken Bedics 12; Pottsville – Jim Berrang 14, Frank Messina 11.

Tamaqua 59 Easton 48: Tamaqua kept Easton winless in the second half while the Tams picked up their third win. After taking a 14-6 lead at the end of the first quarter, Tamaqua increased it to 20-8 early in the second quarter before the Red Rovers cut the lead back to 29-21 at the half. Tamaqua surged again in the second half to take an eighteen-point lead 50-32 before Easton rallied to trim the lead to 11.

Leading scorers: Tamaqua-Gary Williams 17, Steve Sassaman 15, George Wenzel 13; Easton-Rick Lehr 15.[36]

League Playoff

Allen 81 Dieruff 78: After the first two periods, Allen appeared to have the league championship well in-hand with 21-16 and 40-30 leads. They extended the lead to sixteen points at one time. The Huskies press helped them climb back within five points 66-61 with five minutes to play. Allen countered with an eight-point run to take the score to 74-61. Dieruff came back again to within three 77-74 with 1:14 left. However, Allen held on to win its 8th league title in Coach Milo Sewards' 19 years as head coach.

Leading scorers: Allen – Tim Schmeidel 25, Jay Haines 17, Mark Schultz 16, Dick Zellickson 13; Dieruff – Ross Moore 30, Lou Benson 18, Bob Stellar 13.[37]

Postseason PIAA Play

Both Allen and Dieruff qualified for post season play.

Allen 71 Mahanoy Area 65: At Muhlenberg's Memorial Hall, Allen took on an old league nemesis Mahanoy Area in a semi-final matchup for the District 11 title. Playing their fourth game in a week, the Canaries built an eleven-point lead after three periods. The Canaries held a 20-point lead with 3:22 left in the third period after a 16-2 run to start the second half.

Leading scorers: Allen – Jay Haines 22, Tim Schmeidel 17, Dick Zellickson 11, Daryl Tollinche 10, Mark Schultz 10; Mahanoy Area – Bob Galetz 19, Dave Holland 15, Russ Miller 15, Joe Whitaker 14.[38]

Dieruff 75 Emmaus 72: After Emmaus took an 18-13 lead over Dieruff in the first quarter, the Huskies came back in the second quarter to cut the lead to 44-42. Midway through the third period, Emmaus increased the lead back to eight points 54-46. After Coach Dick Schmidt called a timeout, his Huskies responded by scoring 12 points in a row to take a 58-54 lead with a little over four minutes left in the third period. The lead was cut to three at the quarter's end 63-60, but Emmaus could not get any closer. Both teams scored 12 points in the fourth quarter. Emmaus's Roy Stauffer ended his career with 1,778 points. Ross Moore brought his career total to 1,237 points

Leading scorers: Dieruff - Ross Moore 31, Jim Booros 22, Lou Benson 12; Emmaus – Roy Stauffer 35, Bruce Wieder 14.[39]

Dieruff 75 Allen 68: Allen and Dieruff met for the fourth time in the season, this time in a semi-final District 11 Class A contest, in a battle of the "small guys" against the "big guys". The hard-fought matchup saw the two teams play to a 17-17 tie after a quarter with Allen taking a three-point lead into the locker room 38-35. The Huskies then took the lead after three quarters 54-52 when Lou Benson hit a push shot with 15 seconds left in the quarter. The Huskies began the final quarter on a 7-1 run for an eight-point advantage. The Canaries got to within two 63-61, but Dieruff responded with the next four points. Allen could not counter and the Huskies won its third and most important game of the four with the Canaries.

Leading scorers: Dieruff – Ross Moore 35, Bob Stellar 15, Lou Bensen 11; Allen – Tim Schmeidel 18, Daryl Tollinche 18, Dick Zellickson 15.[40]

Dieruff 79 West Hazleton 57: At the Farm Show Arena in Harrisburg, Dieruff took on West Hazleton in search of their 4th consecutive district title. After taking a 20-17 first quarter lead, the Huskies went on a 12-3 run to close out the second quarter for a twelve-point advantage 42-30. Lou Benson and John Smurda, filling in for the injured Jim Booros, anchored the Huskies' defense which limited West Hazleton to seven points in the third quarter. It gave the Huskies an insurmountable 58-37 lead entering the final period. The win gave the Huskies an unprecedented four-year championship run and moved them into inter-district play. John Smurda, playing in place of the injured Jim Booros, helped keep West Hazleton's high scoring offense below their season average.

Leading scorers: Dieruff – Ross Moore 24, Bob Racosky 12, Lou Benson 11, Dan Joseph 10; West Hazleton – Tom Smith 16, LaVerne Mummey 10, George Petrylak 10.[41]

Penncrest 25 Dieruff 12: At the Penn Palestra, Coach Dick Schmidt opted to employ a deep freeze in an effort to knock off the undefeated Penncrest team. With Penncrest fans reacting with a loud chorus of boos, Dieruff scored with four seconds left in the first quarter for a 2-0 lead. At the half, the Huskies trailed 6-4 still with a chance against the much taller Penncrest team featuring 6'9" Gene Armstead and 6'8" Dan Tarr. Penncrest extended the lead to 13-6 entering the final period. Dieruff took only one shot in the first period, three in the second, one in the third period. Penncrest also only got one shot in the first period. Dieruff finally opened up the offense with a little over 3 ½ minutes left in the game. They took eleven shots, but only scored six points to Penncrest's 12 points. Dieruff's season had ended finishing with a 21-6 record.

Leading scorers: Penncrest – Gene Armstead 11; Dieruff – Bob Stellar 3, John Smurda 3.[42]

PCIAA Postseason Playoff

Central Catholic 61 Bethlehem Catholic 39: Facing each other for the third time, Central Catholic defeated the Hawks for the third time to take the Allentown Diocese title. The Vikings took a 13-10 lead into the second quarter and promptly went on a 15-2 run for a 26-12 lead after the first five minutes of the quarter. After Bethlehem Catholic closed the lead a bit to 28-19 at the half, Central Catholic held the Hawks to four 3rd quarter points to take a commanding 47-23 lead.

Leading scorers: Central Catholic – John Gaspar 13, Tony DaRe 13, Tom Williams 10; Bethlehem Catholic – Jim Chassar 18.[43]

Central Catholic 61 Scranton Prep 60: At Scranton University's Long Center, Coach Mike Koury's Vikings took on undefeated Scranton Prep in a PCIAA Eastern semi-final matchup. After a 13-13 first quarter tie, Scranton Prep built an 18-13 lead early in the second quarter. The Vikings came back to lead at the half 30-28 and held a 9-point lead 55-46 with four minutes to play in the game. Scranton Prep fought back to within a point 61-60 with possession under their basket and six seconds to play. Tony DaRe picked off the in-bounds pass to preserve the Vikings' win.

Leading scorers: Central Catholic – Tony DaRe 18, John Gaspar 14, Bob Neff 12; Scranton Prep – Joe Ruzbarsky 25, Bob Nape 14, Steve Dougherty 11.[44]

Central Catholic 61 Bishop McDevitt 58: Central Catholic took on Bishop McDevitt for the PCIAA Eastern title at Liberty's Memorial Gym. Leading 18-11 after a quarter, the Viking stretched the lead to 32-18 with four minutes to play in the second quarter only to hit a cold spell shooting-wise the last two minutes of the quarter and the first five minutes in 3rd quarter. The Vikings came back for an eleven-point lead 51-40 heading into the final period. With a minute left to play, Bishop McDevitt had made a game of it trailing by a single point 59-58. The Vikings scored the last basket to preserve the win.

Leading scorers: Central Catholic – Tom Williams 16, Bob Neff 15, Dan Damweber 12; Bishop McDevitt – Bob Sebastian 22, Ed Wintergrass 13.[45]

Pittsburgh Canevin 80 Central Catholic 57: At the University of Pittsburgh Fieldhouse, Central Catholic took on a taller Canevin team and held its own through the first two periods by taking a 16-13 first quarter lead and falling behind by two points at the half 33-31. Height prevailed in the third quarter as Canevin added ten points to the lead 52-40, outscoring the Vikings 10-1 to start the second half. Canevin had the game easily in hand after the first 3 ½ minutes of the half. Bob Neff finished his career with 1,098 points.

Leading scorers: Canevin – Jack Wojdowski 21, Jim Bolla 15, Tom Clements 14, Tom Rosepink 10, Tom Pipich 10; Central Catholic – John Gaspar 12, Bob Neff 11.[46]

Postseason Accolades

Leading scorers: Jim Chassar, Bethlehem Catholic, scored 125 more points than his closest competitor for the league scoring title with 514 points. The rest of the top ten included: Ross Moore, Dieruff, 389 points; Tim Schmeidel, Allen, 369 points; Dick Zellickson, Allen 354 points; Tim Fisher, Liberty, 342 points; Tony Kinney, Hazleton, 331 points; Brian Dominic, Phillipsburg, 324 points; Mark Schultz, Allen, 314 points; Dan Woodard, Liberty, 305 points; and Jim Berrang, Pottsville, 301 points.[47]

All-Stars: The league all-star first team included: Jim Chassar, Bethlehem Catholic; Bob Neff, Central Catholic; Ross Moore, Dieruff; Dick Zellickson, Allen; and Tony Kinney, Hazleton. The second team consisted of: Jim Booros, Central Catholic; Jim Berrang, Pottsville; Tim Schmeidel, Allen; Joe Morris, Freedom; and Mark Schultz, Allen.[48]

All-State: Jim Chassar, Bethlehem Catholic, was named to the All-State first team. Other members included: Ross Moore, Dieruff, 2nd team; and Dick Zellickson, Allen, 3rd team. Honorable mention team members included: Bob Neff, Central Catholic, and Tony Kinney, Hazleton.[49]

Final Standings

First Half		Second Half		Overall	
Dieruff	10-0	Allen	10-0	Allen	19-1
Allen	9-1	Central Catholic	8-2	Dieruff	17-3
Pottsville	7-3	Hazleton	7-3	Central Catholic	14-6
Bethlehem Catholic	6-4	Dieruff	7-3	Pottsville	13-7
Central Catholic	6-4	Pottsville	6-4	Hazleton	12-8
Hazleton	5-5	Freedom	6-4	Freedom	10-10
Freedom	4-6	Bethlehem Catholic	4-6	Bethlehem Catholic	10-10
Liberty	3-7	Tamaqua	3-7	Liberty	5-15
Easton	2-8	Liberty	2-8	Tamaqua	5-15
Tamaqua	2-8	Phillipsburg	2-8	Phillipsburg	3-17
Phillipsburg	1-9	Easton	0-10	Easton	2-18

Team Rosters

Allen: Coach Milo Sewards, Jay Haines, Burt Horowitz, Ron Hahn, Mark Kreindel, Bruce Merkle, Tim Schmiedel, Mark Schultz, Daryl Tollinche, George Whary, Don Wieand, Dick Zellickson

Bethlehem Catholic: Coach Paul Calvo, Bob Alpago, Jeff Borda, Stan Bushner, Al Calvo, Jim Chassar, Ed Chladny, Greg Falkenbach, Don Jean, Jeff Jennings, Paul Grube

Central Catholic: Coach Mike Koury, Stan Bushner, Dan Damweber, Tony DaRe, John Gaspar, Bob Kasper, Tim McGorry, Bob Neff, Mike Pfahler, John Susko, Rick Wehr, Rick Wieder, Tom Williams

Dieruff: Coach Dick Schmidt, Lou Benson, Jim Booros, Jerry Dzerens, Don Eck, Dan Joseph, Steve Michelerya, Ross Moore, Bogdan "Bucky" Paraszczak, Bob Racosky, Dave Slider, John Smurda, Bob Stellar, Hal Stermer

Easton: Coach Tom Sweeney, Gary Betts, Gary Bond, Don Dickey, Rick Feauve, Don Gentzle, Hank Godown, Tom Keller, Tom Lacey, Rick Lehr, Ed McIntyre, Bob Pilz, Bob Renaldi, Bill Smereczynski, Don Sterner, Ted Tyson

Freedom: Coach Charlie Dubbs, Ken Bedics, Steve Bucko, Mike Freundel, Dan Gilbert, Tom Hussar, Fred Mendoza, Joe Morris, John Pecsek, Steve Pecsek, Mike Pietrouchie, Phil Turton, Glenn Warkala

Hazleton: Coach Gene Evans, Joe Duda, Jim Famalette, Tony Kinney, Wally Kisthardt, Bruce Lieb, Charlie Liott, Tony Manfredi, Sam Mumaw, Ed Parsons, Dave Pikna, Fillmore Williams

Liberty: Coach Al Senavitis, Ed Cunningham, Tim Fisher, Mike Hartenstine, George Korpics, Bob Majczan, Bob Mohylsky, Jim Pavel, John Priestas, Ed Ruyak, Dan Woodard

Phillipsburg: Coach Pete Tomaino, Bob Clymer, Barry Coopersmith, Brian Dominic, Rich Easterly, Bruce Exley, Doug Maczko, Charlie Morgan, Bruce Tibbit, Bucky Utley

Pottsville: Coach Ken Kline, Claude Baskerville, Jim Berrang, Fred Brokhoff, John Cantwell, Jim Heller, Barry Kelly, Jim Lengel, Pete Marchetti, Jim McGowan, Frank Mussina, Jim Siket, Dave Wilson, Bill Yaag, Joel Yob

Tamaqua: Coach Nick Young, Tony Forte, Dave Reed, Dennis Sabol, Steve Sassaman, Gordon Tonkin, Dan Truskey, Gerry Watto, Mike Weidell, George Wenzel, Gary Williams

1970

New League Scoring Record Set

First Half - Week 1

Allen 71 Bethlehem Catholic 65: Under first year coach Bob Bukvics, Bethlehem Catholic battled Allen on even terms for most of the opening night of the season. The Hawks led 14-13 after a quarter with Allen clawing back to take a 32-27 halftime lead. The lead remained five points heading into the final quarter, but Bethlehem Catholic pulled within two points 65-63 with a little over two minutes left in the game. Allen responded with a field goal and two free throws and the Canaries had their opening night victory.

Leading scorers: Allen – Bruce Merkle 17, Don Wolfe 13, Tim Schmiedel 11, Daryl Tollinche 11, Phil Boandl 10; Bethlehem Catholic – Bob Alpago 18, Rich Kearney 12, Jeff Jennings 10, Paul Grube 10.

Central Catholic 72 Dieruff 70: Central Catholic and a rebuilding Dieruff squad battled each other hard throughout the game. Early in the second period, Dieruff had a five-point lead as result of running off eight straight points. The Vikings countered by going on a 14-4 run to lead at the half 32-27. In the 4th quarter, Dieruff cut a seven-point Viking lead 69-62 to two points 72-70. With 13 seconds to play, Tom Williams stole a Dieruff inbounds pass and the Vikings held on to win.

Leading scorers: Central Catholic – Tony DaRe 21, John Gaspar 17, Dan Damweber 17; Dieruff – Bob Stellar 19, Ken Fedor 16, Brad Leibensperger 15.[1]

Liberty 75 Phillipsburg 55: After trailing early 6-1 and 8-4, Liberty scored eight consecutive points to lead 12-8 and never trailed again. Coach Al Senavitis saw all five of his Hurricane starters score in double figures.

Leading scorers: Liberty – Dan Woodard 19, John Priestas 15, Ed Ruyak 13, Mike Hartenstine 11, George Korpics 11; Phillipsburg – Charlie Morgan 14, Brian Dominic 14.

Easton 63 Tamaqua 26: In his coaching debut, Stan Sutphen's Easton squad held Tamaqua without a field goal until a little over a minute into the second quarter. The Red Rovers led the Tams 16-4 after a period and 33-17 at the half. Tamaqua could only score 9 points total in the second half. Sutphen used 12 players in the rout.

Leading scorers: Easton – Tom Lacey 18, Don Dickey 16, Hank Godown 10; Tamaqua – Gerry Watto 8.

Pottsville 55 Freedom 51: Pottsville jumped put to a 17-7 first half lead and increased it to fourteen 25-11 in the second quarter before Freedom rallied to cut it to 29-22 at the half. Freedom came all the way back to tie the game at 39-39 with a little over a minute to play in the third quarter. With 5:21 to play, Freedom took a 44-41 lead only to have Pottsville charge ahead 45-44. Freedom countered with a field goal for its last lead in the game 46-45. Pottsville held on for the win despite turning over the ball 26 times in the game.

Leading scorers: Pottsville – Jim Berrang 20, Pete Marchetti 16, Dave Wilson 11; Freedom – Dan Gilbert 21, Mike Freundel 14.[2]

Freedom 61 Hazleton 56: Hazleton held leads through the first three quarters 14-10, 30-25, and 39-36 and 50-43 with five minutes to play in the game, Suddenly the Patriot offense came to life and outscored the Mountaineers 18-6 to snatch a victory over Hazleton.

Leading scorers: Freedom – Dan Gilbert 20, Jim Lees 12; Hazleton – Sam Mumaw 17, Jim Famalette 16, Wally Kisthardt 15.[3]

Liberty 88 Easton 50: Liberty's defense forced Easton into a poor shooting performance as the Red Rovers converted only 18 of 74 shots from the floor. Easton took a 21-15 lead into the second quarter, but the Hurricanes stormed back outscoring Easton 31-8 to take a 46-29 halftime lead. Liberty cruised to the victory in the second half doubling up Easton 42-21.

Leading scorers: Liberty – Dan Woodard 26, Ed Ruyak 20, Mike Hartenstine 11; Easton – Harry Keller 18.

Dieruff 66 Tamaqua 50: Dieruff opened by scoring the first eleven points and held a 22-8 lead after a quarter. The Huskies could only manage two field goals in the second quarter and Tamaqua cut the lead to 30-22 at the half. Dieruff again got hot in the third period and took a 20-point lead into the final quarter. Tamaqua rallied to cut the lead to eight 54-46 with about 3 ½ minutes to play. However, the Huskies responded by outscoring the Tams 12-4 for the victory.

Leading scorers: Dieruff- John Smurda 18, Bob Stellar 17, Brad Leibensperger 11; Tamaqua- Tony Forte 16.

Pottsville 70 Allen 69: At Pottsville, Allen rallied to wipe out a 16-10 first quarter deficit to take the lead 21-20 and 31-28 in the second quarter. Jim Berrang made three straight field goals to put Pottsville in the lead at the half 34-31. In a seesaw battle, Allen wiped out an eight-point lead by the Crimson to take a six-point lead 59-53 with about three minutes left in the game. Ron Lombel made a field goal and three foul shots to pull Pottsville into the lead and garner a satisfying win over the Canaries.

Leading scorers: Pottsville – Jim Berrang 26, Ron Lombel 18, Pete Marchetti 13; Allen – Tim Schmiedel 26, George Whary 16, Bruce Merkle 10.

Phillipsburg 71 Bethlehem Catholic 50: Bethlehem Catholic took a slim one-point lead 17-16 after a quarter only to grow cold in the second quarter and score but four points. The Stateliners scored 18 in the second quarter to lead at the half 34-21. The Hawks would get no closer than 11 points the rest of the way.

Leading scorers: Phillipsburg – Brian Dominic 19, Barry Coopersmith 13, Doug Maczko 13, Charlie Morgan 11; Bethlehem Catholic – Paul Grube 16, Bob Alpago 13.[4]

Week 2

Pottsville 76 Phillipsburg 45: After Phillipsburg took an early 7-6 lead, Pottsville scored the next 20 points beginning with three minutes left in the first period and the first 2 ½ minutes of the second period. Pottsville finished the half with a 36-18 halftime lead. Pottsville continued the onslaught in the second half to cruise to an easy victory.

Leading scorers: Pottsville – Jim Berrang 22, Pete Marchetti 20, Dave Wilson 11; Phillipsburg – Brian Dominic 11, Barry Coopersmith 10.

Dieruff 59 Liberty 44: Dieruff and Liberty battled back-and-forth with Dieruff holding leads 13-9 and 29-26 after the first two quarters. Liberty tied the game by the end of the 3rd quarter at 39-39. Although the Huskies employed a press most of the game, its effectiveness really impacted the game in the fourth quarter. They forced eight turnovers and held Liberty scoreless for the first four minutes of the final quarter. The Huskies went on to outscore Liberty 21-6 to run away with the contest in its final minutes.

Leading scorers: Dieruff – Brad Leibensperger 17, John Smurda 14, Bob Stellar 12; Liberty – George Korpics 21, Dan Woodard 14.

Hazleton 76 Allen 69: At the Little Palestra, Hazleton surprised Allen by taking a 16-3 lead in the first 4 ½ minutes of the game and a 23-14 lead at the end of the quarter. Allen cut into Hazleton's lead at the half 40-36 and 73-69 with 20 seconds left in the game, but Hazleton came back to beat back the Canaries' rallies.

Leading scorers: Hazleton – Jim Famalette 18, Wally Kisthardt 17, Sam Mumaw 14, Bruce Leib 14, Ed Parsons 11; Allen – Tim Schmiedel 24, Daryl Tollinche 13.

Central Catholic 101 Tamaqua 62: Tamaqua played Central Catholic nearly even during the second quarter only being outscored 19-17. However, the Vikings scored 24 points in the first quarter, 26 in the third, and 32 in the final quarter in the thrashing of the Tams.

Leading scorers: Central Catholic – Dan Damweber 23, Tony DaRe 20, John Gaspar 16, Tom Williams 13; Tamaqua – Tony Forte 14, Bill Stickler 12, Dennis Pastucha 10.

Bethlehem Catholic 61 Easton 58: Easton lost its 20-15 lead in the second quarter as Bethlehem Catholic held the Red Rovers to eight points and took a 29-28 lead at the half. The Hawks extended the lead 46-42 after three quarters and 58-51 with a minute to play. Easton scored the next six points to pull within one 59-58 before the Hawks sank two foul shots to hold off the Red Rovers.

Leading scorers: Bethlehem Catholic – Paul Grube 19, Bob Halbreiner 19, Rich Kearney 11, Jeff Jennings 10; Easton – Tom Lacey 24, Don Sterner 11.[5]

Allen 70 Freedom 53: Although Allen led at the end of the first quarter 14-12, the Canaries trailed for most of the first 2 ½ quarters. Allen took a 37-36 lead in the third quarter and scored eight more points in a row to take a 45-36 lead. After Freedom made a foul shot, Allen upped the lead to twelve 49-37 and the Patriots never got closer than 10 points the rest of the game.

Leading scorers: Allen – Tim Schmiedel 32, Ron Kahan 10; Freedom – Dan Gilbert 17, Mike Freundel 13.

Central Catholic 68 Liberty 55: With a balanced offense with four players in double figures, Central Catholic outscored Liberty in each of the four quarters. The Vikings pulled away from a 22-22 tie in the second quarter to take a ten-point lead 51-41 at the end of the third quarter.

Leading scorers: Central Catholic - John Gaspar 17, Tony DaRe 16, Dan Damweber 10, Tom Williams 10; Liberty – Dan Woodard 15, George Korpics 13, Mitch Lukevics 10.

Dieruff 59 Bethlehem Catholic 58: Dieruff hopelessly trailed by 19 points in the third period with many fans leaving and conceding defeat. Trailing 52-38 going into the final period, the Huskies cut the lead to 54-46 in the first two minutes of the period. Brad Leibensperger tossed in a jumper and converted a foul shot with 2:25 to play for the lead 57-56. The Huskies hung on for a stunning victory.

Leading scorers: Dieruff – Al Sincavage 10, Kay Finley 10; Bethlehem Catholic – Paul Grube 24, Jeff Jennings 14.

Hazleton 52 Phillipsburg 50: Despite being missing Sam Mumaw with a broken hand, Hazleton took a 13-point lead during the second quarter. They led by three going into the final quarter 40-37. The Mountaineers added to the lead 52-46 with 50 seconds to play. Phillipsburg made two field goals to close the lead but didn't score again.

Leading scorers: Hazleton – Wally Kisthardt 16, Bruce Leib 12; Phillipsburg – Brian Dominic 21.

Pottsville 56 Easton 34: Pottsville remained undefeated at 4-0 after fighting back an Easton rally that cut the 23-9 first quarter to 23-20 in the middle of the second quarter. Pottsville shut down the Red Rovers without a field goal in the final period and outscored them 13-2 for the win.

Leading scorers: Pottsville – Jim Berrang 18, Pete Marchetti 14; Easton – Harry Keller 10.[6]

Week 3

Freedom 54 Phillipsburg 44: After Phillipsburg took a 11-10 lead into the 2nd quarter, they scored the next four points to build a 15-11 lead a minute into the quarter. Freedom went on a 16-5 run in the last seven minutes to lead at halftime 26-20. Freedom never fell behind again and evened their league record at 2-2.

Leading scorers: Freedom – Mike Freundel 17; Phillipsburg – Bob Clymer 13, Brian Dominic 10.

Hazleton 59 Easton 50: In Easton, Hazleton's Larry Kovatch came off the bench to score ten points in the final quarter to lead the Mountaineers to victory. Easton played a slowdown, deliberate game in the first half and held the lead going into the locker room 20-18. The two teams were tied five times in the third quarter with Hazleton taking the lead 37-33 into the final quarter. With Easton within two points 48-46, Kovatch went on a tear which led to the Mountaineers victory.

Leading scorers: Hazleton- Wally Kisthardt 20, Jim Famalette 18, Larry Kovatch 10; Easton- Jim Haney 12.

Liberty 76 Tamaqua 35: After Tamaqua took a 2-0 lead on the opening tap, Liberty went on outscore Tamaqua 40-13 in the first half. The rout continued in the third quarter with the Hurricanes building a 39-point lead 62- 23. Liberty coach Al Senavitis played reserves for most of the final half. The loss kept Tamaqua winless in league play at 0-4.

Leading scorers: Liberty – Dan Woodard 12, Mike Hartenstine 11, Mitch Lukevics 10, Ed Ruyak 10; Tamaqua – Dennis Pastucha 11.

Pottsville 75 Dieruff 38: Pottsville scored the first nineteen points in the game before Dieruff scored and the Crimson Tide led 21-1 after one quarter. Dieruff scored their first field goal three minutes into the second quarter. Dieruff missed their first twelve shots and turned the ball over seven times in the first quarter. The Huskies outscored Pottsville in the fourth quarter 16-15 but the game had long been decided. Pottsville improved to 5-0 for a half game lead over Central Catholic at 4-0.

Leading scorers: Pottsville – Pete Marchetti 25, Jim Berrang 16; Dieruff – Ken Fedor 11.

Central Catholic 68 Bethlehem Catholic 56: Central Catholic and Bethlehem Catholic played to a 32-32 at the half. The Hawks took a four-point lead early in the third quarter 38-34 before the Vikings rallied to take 48-45 lead at the end of three quarters. Although Central Catholic never lost the lead again, the Hawks came within two points 52-50 and the Vikings stole the ball twice within 18 seconds and scored easy layups to wrap up the game.

Leading scorers: Central Catholic-Tom Williams 15, Tony DaRe 14, John Gaspar 13, Dan Damweber 10, John Susko 10; Bethlehem Catholic-Jeff Jennings 16, Bob Alpago 12, Rich Kearney 10, Bob Halbreiner 10.[7]

Hazleton 68 Dieruff 42: After falling behind Dieruff 12-10 in the first minute of the second quarter, Coach Dave Shafer's Hazleton squad scored the next eight points to take a lead they would not relinquish the rest of the night. The Mountaineers kept increasing their lead and the Huskies could not get any closer than eight points 37-29 in the third quarter. Hazleton improved to 4-1 while Dieruff dropped to 3-3.

Leading scorers: Hazleton -Charlie Liott 15, Jim Famalette 14, Wally Kisthardt 12; Dieruff – Bob Stellar 10.[8]

Allen 91 Phillipsburg 60: Allen took a 16-9 at the end of a quarter, but Phillipsburg stormed back to tie the game at 16-16. Allen ran off 30 points to the Stateliners' six points to take a 30-21 halftime lead. Tim Schmiedel scored 24 points in the second and third quarters to lead the Canaries in the rout of Phillipsburg.

Leading scorers: Allen – Tim Schmiedel 28, Daryl Tollinche 12, Ron Kahan 10, Burt Horowitz 10; Phillipsburg – Brian Dominic 16, Doug Maczko 16.

Freedom 61 Easton 40: Freedom jumped out to a 5-0 lead and Easton never got closer than 10-7, the score at the end of the first quarter. Freedom outscored the Red Rovers in every period to register an easy win and improve to 3-2. The Red Rovers fell to 1-4.

Leading scorers: Freedom – Dan Gilbert 19, Jim Lees 14; Easton – Harry Keller 10.

Bethlehem Catholic 73 Tamaqua 39: Tamaqua's Allen Smith hit a field goal after three minutes of the game for a 2-0 lead. Bethlehem Catholic scored the next ten points for a 10-2 lead after a quarter. The Hawks increased to lead to 38-25 after three periods before breaking loose and scoring 35 points in the final period.

Leading scorers: Bethlehem Catholic – Paul Grube 17, Jeff Jennings 15; Tamaqua – Ron Ritsick 9.

Central Catholic 87 Pottsville 73: In a battle of league unbeatens, Central Catholic played its strongest game of the season. In the first period, the Vikings ran off nine points in a row when Pottsville came within a point. In the 2nd quarter with the score tied at 34-34, Central Catholic went on another nine-point spurt to take a 43-34 lead at the half. The Vikings stood at 5-0 while Pottsville fell a half game behind at 5-1.

Leading scorers: Central Catholic – Tony DaRe 26, Dan Damweber 21, John Gaspar 17, Tom Williams 12; Pottsville – Jim Berrang 19, Pete Marchetti 17, Joel Yob 11, Dave Wilson 10, Ron Lombel 10.[9]

Week 4

Central Catholic 72 Easton 40: Central Catholic took a 4-0 lead to start the game and Easton got no closer than 6-4 the rest of the game as the Vikings led 17-9 after a quarter. In the third quarter, Easton scored only six points as the lead grew to 54-27. Easton fell to 1-6 while the Vikings remained undefeated and in sole possession of first place at 6-0

Leading scorers: Central Catholic – Dan Damweber 19, Tom Williams 14, Tony DaRe 13, John Gaspar 12; Easton – Tom Attinello 13.

Allen 106 Liberty 79: In a very physical contest with 53 total personal fouls, Liberty ended the first half with Dan Woodard, Mike Hartenstine, and George Korpics on the bench with three fouls. At the start of the second quarter, Liberty closed within two points 24-22 before Allen went on an 18-2 run for a 42-24 lead. With Allen leading 50-37, the Canaries went on another 17-3 spurt. Liberty only led once in the game 4-3 in the opening period.

Leading scorers: Allen – Tim Schmiedel 33, Daryl Tollinche 23, Bruce Merkle 15, Ron Kahan 10; Liberty – John Priestas 22, Dan Woodard 20, George Korpics 13.[10]

Phillipsburg 74 Tamaqua 49: With the scored tied 6-6, Phillipsburg went on a 10-0 run to take command of the game in Tamaqua. Tamaqua only converted 9 of 27 shots in the first half and 8 of 29 in the second half. Tamaqua only matched the Stateliners in the third quarter when each team scored 12 points.

Leading scorers: Phillipsburg – Brian Dominic 25, Barry Coopersmith 12, Jim Oberley 10; Tamaqua – Gordon Tonkin 10.[11]

Bethlehem Catholic 51 Freedom 48: After Freedom took a 12-8 1st quarter lead, Bethlehem Catholic held the Patriots to eight points in the 2nd quarter and took a 23-20 lead into the locker room. The second quarter lead held out throughout the game. Freedom dropped to 3-3 while the Hawks improved to 3-4.

Leading scorers: Bethlehem Catholic – Bob Alpago 17, Bob Halbreiner 11; Freedom – Jim Lees 12.

Pottsville 81 Hazleton 59: Hazleton took a 17-12 first quarter lead and still led at halftime 35-33, but could not maintain the pace in the second half against Pottsville at Hazleton's 16th Street Palestra. After Hazleton built a four-point lead in the third quarter, Pottsville went on a 17-3 run to take charge of the game.

Leading scorers: Pottsville – Pete Marchetti 31, Joel Yob 17, Jim Berrang 14, Ron Lombel 10; Hazleton – Sam Mumaw 15, Wally Kisthardt 13, Jim Famalette 11.[12]

Week 5

Bethlehem Catholic 78 Liberty 62: Liberty dominated the first 1 ½ quarters of the contest holding a 20-16 lead after a period and extending it to 30-24 half way through the second quarter. Bethlehem Catholic held Liberty to one field goal the rest of the half while scoring 18 for a 44-32 lead. Liberty pulled within three by the end of the third quarter 57-54. The Hawks took a commanding lead in the final quarter by outscoring the Hurricane 17-2 in the first 2 ½ minutes.

Leading scorers: Bethlehem Catholic – Jeff Jennings 24, Bob Alpago 15, Paul Grube 14; Liberty – Dan Woodard 29.

Dieruff 52 Freedom 49: With Dieruff holding comfortable leads 12-7, 29-17, and 41-34 after the first three quarters, Freedom came back in the final quarter to make a game of it. The Patriots pulled within a point twice at 41-40 early in the period and 50-49 with 56 seconds left. Freedom had a chance for the win, but a Patriot pass was intercepted by the Huskies with 14 seconds. Bob Stellar added two foul shots with four seconds left in the game.

Leading scorers: Dieruff – Bob Stellar 21, Ken Fedor 16; Freedom – Dan Gilbert 29.

Hazleton 60 Central Catholic 56: Central Catholic seemed well on the path to its seventh victory with leads of 20-10 and 35-25 after the first two quarters. The Vikings held a 13-point lead 42-29 in the third quarter when Hazleton began to cut the lead. By the end of the quarter the lead was down to eight 49-41. Hazleton scored the first ten points in the final quarter to take a 51-49 lead. After the Vikings tied the game, Jim Famalette scored on a jumper and added two free throws a minute later and the Mountaineers stunned the Vikings with their first league loss.

Leading scorers: Hazleton – Sam Mumaw 19, Ed Parsons 14, Jim Famalette 14; Central Catholic – Dan Damweber 17, John Gaspar 16, Tony DaRe 10.

Allen 81 Easton 54: Easton took a 2-1 lead, its only of the game, before Allen went on a 13-2 spurt in the last four minutes of the quarter for a 24-9 lead. They did the same in the last five minutes of the 2nd quarter with a 16-4 run to take a commanding half time lead 44-21. Allen played substitutes most of the second half.

Leading scorers: Allen – Tim Schmiedel 27, Phil Boandl 11, Daryl Tollinche 10; Easton – Tom Lacey 15, Hank Godown 10.

Pottsville 89 Tamaqua 50: Pottsville took advantage of Central Catholic's loss to Hazleton to take a half game lead over the Vikings by improving their record to 7-1. Pottsville led from start to finish and scored over 20 points in each quarter. Tamaqua remained winless (0-7) in league play.

Leading scorers: Pottsville – Pete Marchetti 18, Jim Berrang 14, Dave Wilson 14, Joel Yob 12; Tamaqua – Gerry Watto 12.[13]

Allen 99 Dieruff 60: Allen scored 32 points in each of the last two quarters to hand the Huskies their worst defeat in their short history. Eight players, four on each team, had three fouls called on them in the first half with thirty fouls called in the half. Dieruff held a first quarter lead 16-15 prior to Allen's offensive outburst.

Leading scorers: Allen – Tim Schmiedel 31, Daryl Tollinche 19, Burt Horowitz 14, Phil Boandl 10; Dieruff - Bob Stellar 19.

Easton 41 Phillipsburg 40: Both Phillipsburg and Easton had off nights shooting with the Red Rovers making only 28% of their field goal attempts and the Stateliners being even worse at 22%The most points scored in a quarter was 13 with Easton doing it in the second and Phillipsburg in the third. The score was deadlocked at 40 with 2:11 to play in the game when Don Sterner made a free throw to win the game for the Red Rovers. Neither team scored after that.

Leading scorers: Easton – Harry Keller 11; Phillipsburg – Brian Dominic 16, Barry Coopersmith 13.

Hazleton 62 Tamaqua 53: Hazleton took a 14-13 first quarter lead only to see Tamaqua take the lead at the half 21-20, one of the few times they had led in a league game in the season. Hazleton ran off six points to start the second half and Tamaqua could not counter and lost its eighth lead contest. Outscored from the field 24 field goals to 21 for the Tams, Hazleton made 20 of 29 free throws to win the game.

Leading scorers: Hazleton – Wally Kisthardt 23, Sam Mumaw 14, Jim Famalette 12; Tamaqua – Gerry Watto 14, Gordon Tonkin 12, Dennis Pastucha 10

Central Catholic 68 Freedom 63: In a game that was tied 18 times, Freedom led after a quarter 21-18 and at the half 33-31. Central took the lead at the end of three quarters 49-48, but Freedom ran out to a five-point lead early in the fourth quarter 56-51. The Vikings switched to a press in the last five minutes of the game and came back to tie the game at 61-61. John Gaspar made two field goals and three foul shots to wrap up the win.

Leading scorers: Central Catholic –Tony DaRe 19, John Gaspar 19, Dan Damweber 14; Freedom – Jim Lees 17, Mike Freundel 15, Dan Gilbert 11.

Pottsville 68 Liberty 50: With Liberty leading only twice early in the first quarter 2-0 and 4-3, Pottsville ran out to a 42-20 lead at the half. Liberty pulled within 49-35 in the third quarter and outscored Pottsville 30-26 in the second half, but Pottsville's first half advantage was too great to overcome. The win kept Pottsville a half game ahead of Central Catholic.

Leading scorers: Pottsville – Jim Berrang 16, Dave Wilson 16, Ron Lombel 14, Joel Yob 14; Liberty – Mitch Lukevics 11.[14]

Week 6

Hazleton 62 Liberty 46: After Mike Hartenstine scored off of a rebound to keep Liberty within three points 24-21, Hazleton held the Hurricane scoreless for nearly the next five minutes running from late in the second quarter into the early third quarter. The 31-21 lead at the half turned in a 42-21 lead at the end of the run. Liberty never got any closer than fifteen points the rest of the game. Both teams had an off-shooting night from the floor with both teams making less than 1/3 of their shots in the game.

Leading scorers: Hazleton – Tony Manfredi 15, Sam Mumaw 15, Wally Kisthardt 10; Liberty – Mike Hartenstine 10.

Central Catholic 80 Allen 78: Allen fought valiantly in an effort to upset Central Catholic and held lead in each of the first three quarters 20-13, 46-38, and 61-59. At one point the Vikings had trailed by 12 points. The Vikings finally took the lead 64-62 with over 6 ½ minutes left. After that, the lead changed six times before Central Catholic took the lead for good with less than 2 minutes to play. A win in the final game of the first half would tie them with Pottsville forcing a first half playoff for the title.

Leading scorers: Central Catholic – Dan Damweber 24, John Gaspar 24, Tony DaRe 13; Allen – Phil Boandl 23, Daryl Tollinche 19, Tim Schmiedel 17, Burt Horowitz 11.

Pottsville 86 Bethlehem Catholic 55: Pottsville finished the first half at 9-1 and clinched at least a tie with Central Catholic for the first half crown. Pottsville scored the first 12 points of the game and never allowed Bethlehem Catholic any closer than eight points. In the third quarter, Pottsville put the game away by outscoring the Hawks 25-10.

Leading scorers: Pottsville – Jim Berrang 30, Pete Marchetti 16, Joel Yob 15; Bethlehem Catholic - Jeff Jennings 17, Bob Alpago 10.

Dieruff 90 Phillipsburg 49: Dieruff took an 18-12 first quarter lead and put the game away by outscoring Phillipsburg 23-9 in the second quarter for a twenty-point lead at the half. The onslaught continued in the second half with the Huskies holding the advantage 49-28. Phillipsburg never led as Dieruff ran off seven straight points to start the game.

Leading scorers: Dieruff – Bob Stellar 24, Mike Reiter 19, Hamp Smith 12; Phillipsburg – Brian Dominic 15, Bob Clymer 11, Barry Coopersmith 10.

Freedom 69 Tamaqua 44: Taking an 18-5 first quarter lead, Freedom cruised to victory over winless Tamaqua. The Patriots stretched the lead to 21 points at the half 38-17. Tamaqua did outscore the Patriots in the third period 15-14.

Leading scorers: Freedom – Dan Gilbert 27; Tamaqua – Alan Smith 9.[15]

Easton 60 Dieruff 58 2OT: Dieruff started the game on an 11-0 run before Easton scored and the Huskies led after the first quarter 12-7. Both teams scored 18 points in the second period as the Huskies maintained their five-point lead. Easton grabbed a brief lead near the end of the third quarter, but the teams ended up tied 39-39 going into the last quarter. With Dieruff leading 50-49, Don Dickey stole the ball with six seconds to play. He passed the ball to Tom Attinello who was fouled. He converted one shot for a 50-50 tie in regulation. In the first overtime, Dieruff's Bob Stellar stole an inbounds pass and made a 20-foot shot with two seconds to go and tied the game again at 56-56. In the second overtime, Don Sterner sank a layup with 15 seconds left for the victory.

Leading scorers: Easton-Don Dickey 16, Don Sterner 12, Jim Haney 11, Harry Keller 10; Dieruff-Bob Stellar 15, Ken Fedor 14.

Allen 102 Tamaqua 74: Tim Schmiedel set both a Little Palestra and Canary single game scoring record with 49 points as Allen rolled to an easy win over Tamaqua. After taking a 22-14 lead in the first quarter, Allen went on an 18-2 run to extend their lead to 44-19. The quarter ended with the Canaries leading 48-24. Both teams went on a scoring spree in the 2nd half with Allen outscoring Tamaqua 54-50. Daryl Tollinche handed out 18 assists.

Leading scorers: Allen – Tim Schmiedel 49, Chuck Strzelecki 11; Tamaqua – Gerry Watto 19, Al Smith 14, Dennis Patucha 13, Bill Stickler 10.

Liberty 57 Freedom 53: Mike Hartenstine grabbed 22 rebounds as the Hurricane outrebounded Liberty 46-19 in a close game with the biggest lead being six points by Liberty in the fourth quarter. Freedom then pulled within a point 54-53 with 40 seconds to play before Liberty pulled out the win on several free throws.

Leading scorers: Liberty – Mike Hartenstine 15, Dan Woodard 13, John Preistas 12; Freedom – Dan Gilbert 22, Mike Freundel 11.

Central Catholic 75 Phillipsburg 55: Despite playing their poorest game of the season, Central Catholic held off Phillipsburg to gain a tie with Pottsville for the first half title. The Vikings took a 42-24 lead into the third quarter and promptly committed nine turnovers, but still held on to their big lead. Each team scored only nine points in the quarter. The Vikings outscored the Stateliners 24-22 in the final quarter.

Leading scorers: Central Catholic – Tim McGorry 17, John Gaspar 15, Dan Damweber 11, Tom Williams 10; Phillipsburg – Brian Dominic 12.

Bethlehem Catholic 66 Hazleton 65: Jeff Jennings 15-foot jumper with 15 seconds to play stunned Hazleton. Hazleton's Ed Parsons was fouled with two seconds to play and missed the opportunity for the win when he missed both shots. The Hawks trailed most of the first half and trailed by two points heading into the third period. With Jeff Jennings scoring 11 points, the Hawks took the lead in the third quarter 48-45 and held on for the win.

Leading scorers: Bethlehem Catholic – Jeff Jennings 17, Paul Grube 15, Bob Halbreiner 12, Bob Alpago 11; Hazleton – Ed Parsons 15, Sam Mumaw 15, Jim Famalette 15, Wally Kisthardt 11.[16]

First Half Playoff

Central Catholic 64 Pottsville 61: At Muhlenberg's Memorial Hall, Pottsville and Central Catholic battled to determine the first half champions. After Central Catholic took a 2-0 lead, the Vikings did not get it back until midway during the second period. Pottsville took a 19-15 first quarter lead, but the Vikings took it back at the half 31-28 after holding the Crimson to nine points in the quarter. Going into the final quarter, the Vikings led 46-45 and scored 18 points to Pottsville 16 to win the game and the first half title.

Leading scorers: Central Catholic – John Gaspar 19, Tony DaRe 12, Dan Damweber 12, Tom Williams 10; Pottsville – Jim Berrang 19, Pete Marchetti 12, Joel Yob 12, Ron Lombel 11.[17]

Second Half - Week 7

Allen 85 Liberty 65: Dan Woodard scored 22 of Liberty's first 24 points to keep the Hurricane in the game with Allen during most of the first half. Woodward turned his ankle late in the half and could contribute little the rest of the game. With Allen up by only seven mid-ways through the final quarter, the Canaries scored 16 straight points to finally put the game in the victory column.

Leading scorers: Allen – Tim Schmiedel 32, Phil Boandl 20, Bruce Merkle 11; Liberty – Dan Woodard 30.

Bethlehem Catholic 74 Freedom 69: Freedom took a 21-17 lead after a quarter before Bethlehem Catholic turned on its offense and outscored the Patriots 41-25 in the middle quarter to take a 12-point lead into the second half. They added six to the lead in the third quarter and needed the extended lead as Freedom rallied in the final quarter, but fell short.

Leading scorers: Bethlehem Catholic – Jeff Jennings 26, Bob Alpago 14, Bob Halbreiner 12; Freedom – Dan Gilbert 21, Mike Freundel 18, Mike Pietrouchie 13, Jim Lees 10.

Central Catholic 83 Easton 64: Trailing by two 32-30 at the half, Central Catholic dropped 33 points on Easton in the third quarter while holding the Red Rovers to 11. The third quarter proved the difference in the game as the Vikings outscored the Red Rovers 19-1 to start the second half.

Leading scorers: Central Catholic – John Gaspar 26, Dan Damweber 20, Tony DaRe 12; Easton – Tom Lacey 24, Jim Haney 17, Harry Keller 10.

Phillipsburg 64 Tamaqua 54: Brian Dominic tied the Phillipsburg single game high with 43 points in leading the Stateliners to victory. Behind 13-10 after a quarter with the rest of his squad shooting poorly from the floor, Coach Pete Tomaino had them feed Dominic most of the night. Tamaqua held a 44-41 lead early in the final quarter, but the Stateliners ran off 12 straight points and were never headed.

Leading scorers: Phillipsburg – Brian Dominic 43; Tamaqua – Tony Forte 20, Gerry Watto 14, Gordon Tonkin 11.

Hazleton 55 Pottsville 50: After Pottsville fell to Central Catholic in the first half playoff, Hazleton handed them a surprising loss to start the second half. Pottsville took an 11-8 first quarter lead but were outscored by the Mountaineers 36-26 in the middle quarters which led to their defeat. Pottsville turned the ball over 20 times in the contest. Pottsville lost for only the third time in the season with both first two losses to Central Catholic.

Leading scorers: Hazleton – Wally Kisthardt 17, Sam Mumaw 13, Tony Manfredi 12; Pottsville – Jim Berrang 20, Pete Marchetti 17, Joel Yob 11.[18]

Allen 75 Bethlehem Catholic 61: Tim Schmiedel scored all 14 first quarter points as Allen took a 14-10 lead over Bethlehem Catholic at the Little Palestra. The Hawks only lead was 5-2 in the first quarter. They could not get any closer than the halftime score with Allen on top 31-27.

Leading scorers: Allen – Tim Schmiedel 31, Daryl Tollinche 12, Don Wolfe 11, Charles Strzelecki 10; Bethlehem Catholic – Paul Grube 14, Jeff Jennings 12, Bob Alpago 12, Mike Halbreiner 10.

Easton 66 Tamaqua 39: Tamaqua converted only 4 of 23 field goal attempts in the first half as Easton went out to a 20-11 lead at the end of the first quarter. Tamaqua's only scores in the second period came on four free throws as the Red Rovers took full command of the contest with a 31-15 halftime lead. Tamaqua dropped its 12th in a row in league play.

Leading scorers: Easton – Harry Keller 17, Don Dickey 11, Tom Lacey 11; Tamaqua – Tony Forte 9.

Liberty 62 Phillipsburg 55: With the game tied at 53-53 with 2:25 left to play, Phillipsburg lost Bob Clymer and Barry Coppersmith, a few seconds later, on fouls. Liberty converted two of four foul shots, but that was sufficient to take them to victory. The game was tied after a quarter 14-14 with Liberty taking a seven-point lead at the half 35-28. Liberty was down by ten points 24-14 in the second period before Liberty rallied to take the lead. Phillipsburg came back to tie the game after three quarters 44-44.

Leading scorers: Liberty - Dan Woodard 21, Ed Ruyak 13; Phillipsburg - Brian Dominic 22, Charlie Morgan 10.

Central Catholic 61 Dieruff 47: Dieruff's only lead of the night came in the second quarter 17-16, a period where John Smurda scored all twelve of his team's points. After making the first two field goals in the third period, he ran his streak to 16 points in a row prior to Bob Stellar's jump shot with 5:23 left in the third quarter. The Huskies had gone 10:52 without anyone other than Smurda scoring. In the final quarter, the Vikings scored 14 straight points, to put the game away, while Dieruff went scoreless for over 4 ½ minutes.

Leading scorers: Central Catholic – John Gaspar 24, Tony DaRe 13, Dan Damweber 12; Dieruff - John Smurda 19.

Pottsville 70 Freedom 69: Visiting Freedom charged out of the locker room to take 22-17 and 41-29 leads at the end of the first two quarters. The Patriots extended the lead to 44-29 before Pottsville scored the next 11 points to trim the lead to four points. Pottsville continued its comeback with Dave Wilson putting them ahead for the first time 51-49 with twenty-three seconds left in the third period. The two teams went into the final quarter tied at 51-51. With 51 seconds left, Pete Marchetti converted a three-point play for the lead 68-67, but Mike Freundel answered to put Freedom on top 69-68. Ron Lombel made a bucket with four seconds left and Pottsville avoided its 4th overall loss and the upset bid by the Patriots.

Leading scorers: Pottsville – Pete Marchetti 26, Dave Wilson 13, Jim Berrang 11, Ron Lombel 11; Freedom – Dan Gilbert 27, Mike Freundel 17.[19]

Week 8

Hazleton 77 Freedom 74: After Freedom took their only lead 2-0 to start the contest, Hazleton ran off ten straight points, and held the Patriots scoreless for four minutes, on their way to a 20-10 first quarter advantage. The Mountaineers increased the lead to 40-27 at the half. The Patriots fought valiantly in the second half to claw back into the contest as they outscored Hazleton 47-37, but could not overcome the big first half lead.

Leading scorers: Hazleton – Sam Mumaw 21, Wally Kisthardt 18, Ed Parsons 17, Jim Famalette 12; Freedom – Dan Gilbert 21, Mike Freundel 16, Mike Pietrouchie 11.

Dieruff 92 Tamaqua 44: With five starters in double figures, Dieruff easily handed Tamaqua its thirteenth consecutive league loss. The Huskies outscored the Tams in the second and fourth quarters combined 48-15. Tamaqua had stayed with the Huskies through much of the first period with the game tied four times, the last one at 8-8, before Dieruff went on a five-point run to pull away from the Tams.

Leading scorers: Dieruff – John Smurda 19, Ken Fedor 18, Brad Liebensperger 16, Al Sincavage 15, Bob Stellar 12; Tamaqua – Gerry Watto 9.

Easton 59 Liberty 57: Easton took an 18-12 first quarter lead and continued to increase the lead in the 2nd and 3rd quarters. The Red Rovers led at the half 31-23 and increased it to 12 points 45-33 before Liberty began its comeback. The Hurricane took the lead 50-48 with a 10-point rally only to have Easton score six in a row and move ahead 54-50. Liberty tied the score at 54-54 before the Red Rovers converted 4 foul shots and a field goal.

Leading scorers: Easton – Tom Lacey 20, Don Sterner 14, Harry Keller 11; Liberty – Dan Woodard 17, George Korpics 14, John Priestas 14.

Allen 99 Pottsville 72: Allen remained undefeated in the second half at 3-0 with a resounding win over Pottsville at the Little Palestra. The outcome of the game was settled in the 2nd quarter after the Canaries scored 27 points to Pottsville's eleven for a 46-26 halftime lead. Allen's defense forced Pottsville into 31 turnovers in the game. The Canaries held the Crimson's two top scorers, Jim Berrang and Pete Marchetti, to 19 points combined.

Leading scorers: Allen –Tim Schmiedel 27, Daryl Tollinche 14, Don Wolfe 11, Bruce Merkle 10; Pottsville – Ron Lombel 20, Joel Yob 12, Jim Berrang 12.

Phillipsburg 59 Bethlehem Catholic 58: After scoring ten points in a row in the second period, Bethlehem took the biggest lead of the night 26-19. Phillipsburg came back to lead at the half 31-29. With the score tied at 45-45 after three periods, the Hawks scored six in a row for a 51-45 advantage. The lead flip-flopped in the last minute before Brian Dominic made two free throws to seal the victory for Phillipsburg.

Leading scorers: Phillipsburg – Brian Dominic 22, Bob Clymer 22; Bethlehem Catholic – Paul Grube 16, Rich Kearney 14, Bob Alpago 12, Jeff Jennings 10.[20]

Pottsville 90 Phillipsburg 69: Phillipsburg led the game several times along with five ties in the first period, the last one at 18-18. Pottsville took the lead at the end of the period 21-19 and led the rest of the way. Jim Berrang and Peter Marchetti scored 21 of Pottsville's 26 points in the third period when the Crimson took a commanding 69-53 lead. Both teams were 2-2 in the half.

Leading scorers: Pottsville – Jim Berrang 31, Pete Marchetti 17, Dave Wilson 15, Joel Yob 15; Phillipsburg – Bob Clymer 21, Brian Dominic 11, Doug Maczko 11, Barry Coopersmith 11.

Central Catholic 98 Tamaqua 42: Surprisingly, Tamaqua jumped out to an 8-0 lead at the start of the game only to have Central Catholic come back to take the lead at the end of the quarter 22-20. Tamaqua hit on 10 of 11 shots from the field in the quarter. Just as surprising, Tamaqua only scored two points in the second period while the Vikings poured in 26 points. The Tams dropped their 14th consecutive league contest.

Leading scorers: Central Catholic – Dan Damweber 30, Bob Kasper 10; Tamaqua – Charlie Connely 10.

Dieruff 45 Liberty 43 OT: In a very low-scoring game, Dieruff and Liberty tied after a quarter 6-6 with Liberty taking the halftime lead 20-19. Dieruff came back to take a five-point lead after three quarters 35-30. Liberty's Dan Woodard made two field goals to put Liberty ahead 39-37 with 3:16 to play. Dieruff's Brad Leibensperger tied it with a little over a minute left with his field goal as the last score in regulation. Bob Stellar missed a foul shot with 38 seconds left. In overtime, Stellar came back to hit two free throws to win the game for the Huskies.

Leading scorers: Dieruff – Al Sincavage 15, John Smurda 12; Liberty – Dan Woodard 17, Bill Hemmerly 16.

Bethlehem Catholic 61 Easton 57 OT: Easton, led by Tom Lacey's 9 points, ran off a 13-3 spurt to take a one-point lead 50-49 after having trailed by nine points in the fourth period. The Hawks had the lead at 51-50 with nine seconds to play when Easton's Don Sterner had two foul shots to win the game but only made one for the tie in regulation. With the game tied at 53-53, Bethlehem Catholic won the game on an 8-2 spurt in the overtime period. During the contest, the Hawks's Bob Halbreiner scored a goal for Easton.

Leading scorers: Bethlehem Catholic – Jeff Jennings 20, Bob Alpago 19; Easton – Tom Lacey 29, Don Sterner 10.

Hazleton 65 Allen 55: With both teams unbeaten, Hazleton led almost the whole way as Allen only led once early in the first period 4-2. Hazleton increased its one point first quarter lead to five at the half 31-26. The teams played even in the third period with both teams scoring 13 points. Hazleton took over in the fourth for the win and a first-place tie with Central Catholic.

Leading scorers: Hazleton – Wally Kisthardt 16, Ed Parsons 14, Tony Manfredi 13, Jim Famalette 12, Sam Mumaw 10; Allen – Tim Schmiedel 22.[21]

Week 9

Hazleton 69 Phillipsburg 53: On the road, Hazleton took a 12-2 lead, but Phillipsburg countered by scoring the next nine points. Hazleton then scored five in a row for 17-11 first quarter lead. The Stateliners scored the first two points of the 2nd quarter, but the Mountaineers scored the next eight to lead 25-13 and the game was never in question. Hazleton went on another 9-point spurt from the 3rd into the 4th quarter to remain tied for first place.

Leading scorers: Hazleton – Sam Mumaw 28, Wally Kisthardt 13; Phillipsburg – Brian Dominic 22, Bob Clymer 15.

Allen 83 Freedom 65: Allen took a ten-point lead during the first quarter only to have Freedom cut the margin to two points at the end of the quarter 23-21. The Canaries added nine points to the lead at the half 44-33. During the third quarter, the Patriots cut the lead to seven 55-48 but Allen scored 14 points in a row from late in the third quarter into the fourth quarter. The win kept the Canaries, at 4-1, a half-game behind Central Catholic and Hazleton, both at 4-0.

Leading scorers: Allen – Tim Schmiedel 28, Phil Boandl 15, Bruce Merkle 11, Daryl Tollinche 11; Freedom – Mike Pietrouchie 23, Jim Lees 15, Dan Gilbert 10.

Dieruff 58 Bethlehem Catholic 52: In a game close the whole way, the score was tied seven times in the first half including 28-28 at half time. Three ties and seven lead changes occurred in the second half. After a final tie at 51-51, the Huskies ran off seven straight points to take the victory and improve to 3-1, a game behind the league leaders. Al Sincavage scored 11 points in the final quarter to lead the Huskies to the win.

Leading scorers: Dieruff – Al Sincavage 18; Bethlehem Catholic – Bob Alpago 14, Jeff Jennings 12.

Pottsville 65 Easton 46: Despite being tied at 1-1 and 3-3 in the first period, Easton only made one of twenty field goal attempts in the first quarter to fall behind 19-3. Pottsville scored the last 16 points of the quarter. The Red Rovers recovered somewhat in the second period, but still trailed at the half 29-19. Easton again went cold from the floor in the third quarter making on 3 of twelve shots.

Leading scorers: Pottsville – Jim Berrang 15, Peter Marchetti 14, Joel Yob 14, Dave Wilson 10; Easton – Tom Lacey 14.

Central Catholic 58 Liberty 57: Upset-minded Liberty led Central Catholic at the end of the first quarter 15-14, trailed at the half 31-29, and took the lead after three quarters 45-43. Liberty's aggressive play put the Vikings on the line 31 times to only 12 for the Hurricane. The Vikings converted eleven free throws in the final period to pull out the victory and remain undefeated in the second half.

Leading Scorers: Central Catholic – Dan Damweber 16, Tony DaRe 16, Roger Worman 10; Liberty – George Korpics 13, Bill Hemmerly 12, Gary Fejes 10.[22]

Hazleton 62 Easton 51: With Sam Mumaw and Wally Kisthardt each scoring 8 points in the 1st quarter, Hazleton took a 23-8 lead against Easton. The closest Easton got was seven points in the second quarter as the Mountaineers picked up an easy win. They took over first place with a loss by Central Catholic.

Leading scorers: Hazleton – Sam Mumaw 21, Wally Kisthardt 13; Easton – Tom Lacey 17.

Liberty 52 Tamaqua 51: Liberty traveled to Tamaqua shorthanded with four regulars missing from the lineup. Bill Hennerly was ill, Bob Ruyak was injured, and Dan Woodard and George Korpics were not active because of disciplinary actions. The only remaining starter, Mike Hartenstine grabbed 21 rebounds and led the team in scoring as the Hurricane pulled out a last second victory. After Liberty built an eleven-point lead at the half 29-18, Tamaqua came back to take a 51-48 lead with 1:50 remaining in the game. A Hartenstine field goal and a Rich Wescoe steal and layup with three seconds pulled out the victory.

Leading scorers: Liberty – Mike Hartenstine 18, Ed Ruyak 10; Tamaqua – Gordon Tonkin 17, Tony Forte 15, Gerry Watto 11.

Bethlehem Catholic 70 Central Catholic 67: Jeff Jennings scored sixteen points in the final quarter to spearhead an amazing comeback by Bethlehem Catholic to hand Central Catholic their first loss of the second half and knock them out of first place. After the Vikings entered the final quarter with a 55-47 lead which grew to ten points in the first ten seconds of the quarter, the Hawks, led by Jennings' offensive outburst, scored the next 18 points to take a commanding 65-58 lead with three minutes to play.

Leading scorers: Bethlehem Catholic – Jeff Jennings 41, Rich Kearney 11, Bob Alpago 10; Central Catholic – Dan Damweber 21, John Gaspar 12, Tom Williams 12, Tony DaRe 10.

Phillipsburg 65 Freedom 60: Phillipsburg held the lead most of the game until Freedom pulled even at 42-42 late in the third period. In the fourth quarter, the Stateliners led 59-53 when the Red Rovers scored seven in a row to take the lead 60-59. Phillipsburg finished the game with six foul shots while the Patriots were held scoreless.

Leading scorers: Phillipsburg – Brian Dominic 18, Bob Clymer 18, Doug Maczko 13, Barry Coopersmith 12; Freedom – Mike Csizmadia 14, Joe DeAngelis 14, Mike Pietrouchie 11, Jim Lees 10.

Pottsville 44 Dieruff 42 OT: In a hard-fought game that was tied 13 times, Dieruff led at the half 27-22. With the scored tied at 42-42 and nearly four minutes to play in the game, the Huskies held the ball for over two minutes and then missed a shot. Pottsville could not score and the game went into overtime. With neither team having scored in the overtime, Ron Lombel made a field goal with ten seconds to play for the only overtime points and the win for Pottsville

Leading scorers: Pottsville – Jim Berrang 17, Joel Yob 12; Dieruff – John Smurda 16, Bob Stellar 10.[23]

Week 10

Dieruff 67 Hazleton 65: Dieruff surprised Hazleton, undefeated in the second half, by taking a 17-5 lead in the first quarter. Hazleton countered with a high scoring second period to tie the contest a 28-28 at the half. Dieruff held the Mountaineers to seven points in the third quarter and took a 46-35 lead into the final quarter and extended it to 16 with six minutes left in the game. The Huskies fought off a ferocious Hazleton rally to escape with a two-point win and drop Hazleton into a tie with Allen for first place, both at 5-1.

Leading scorers: Dieruff – John Smurda 22, Bob Stellar 15, Al Sincavage 14; Hazleton – Tony Manfredi 21, Joe Duda 15, Wally Kisthardt 12, Ed Parsons 10.

Allen 96 Phillipsburg 66: With Phillipsburg holding a 7-6 lead in the first quarter, Allen reeled off ten straight points to take the lead for good. Only in the third period did Phillipsburg give the Canaries a fight when they outscored them 23-22. Allen came back to score 34 in the final quarter to complete the rout and move into a tie for first with Hazleton. With nearly four minutes left in the third period to a little over three minutes into the fourth period, Brian Dominic scored all 20 of Phillipsburg's points.

Leading scorers: Allen – Tim Schmiedel 33, Phil Boandl 22, Daryl Tollinche 22; Phillipsburg – Brian Dominic 42.

Pottsville 50 Central Catholic 48: Central Catholic took a 17-14 lead at the end of the first quarter. Pottsville opened the second quarter with two field goals to take their last lead until less than two minutes left in the fourth quarter. The Vikings held a 44-38 lead with less than six minutes left in the game. At this point, Jim Berrang re-entered the game after sitting due to foul trouble, and led the Crimson to a stunning win over the Vikings. His layup with four seconds left sealed the victory for Pottsville.

Leading scorers: Pottsville – Jim Berrang 14, Dave Wilson 11, Ron Lombel 10; Central Catholic – John Gaspar 18, Dan Damweber 13.

Bethlehem Catholic 90 Tamaqua 46: Tamaqua suffered its 16th consecutive loss in league play with Bethlehem Catholic scoring 50 points in the second half while holding the Tams to just 21 in the rout. With four players in double figures, the Hawks improved to 4-3 in the second half.

Leading scorers: Bethlehem Catholic – Jeff Jennings 19, Paul Grube 19, Mick Halbreiner 13, Rich Kearney 12; Tamaqua – Charles Connely 15, Gordon Tonkin 12.[24]

Freedom 60 Easton 55: With the game close through 2 ½ periods, Freedom broke a 36-36 tie with a 12-4 run and a 48-40 lead. Then, with Freedom holding a 53-44 lead, Coach Stan Sutphen's Red Rovers went on their own run 11-5 to get within three points with less than a minute to play. Several Freedom free throws put the game in the win column for the Patriots.

Leading scorers: Freedom – Mike Pietrouchie 14, Jim Lees 12; Easton – Tom Lacey 24, Don Sterner 18.[25]

Allen 100 Easton 46: A tie game at 8-8 midway through the first quarter, Allen went on a 15-3 run the rest of the quarter for a 23-11 lead. Although the Canaries held a 42-22 advantage at the half, they took no mercy on Easton as they outscored the Red Rovers 30-10 in the fourth quarter. Canaries, listening on transistor radios, heard that Hazleton lost to Central Catholic to put the Canaries in sole possession of first place and the fans chanted "We're number 1".

Leading scorers: Allen – Tim Schmiedel 26, Daryl Tollinche 20, Bruce Merkle 14, Pat Sewards 12, Phil Boandl 10; Easton – Tom Attinello 12, Tom Lacey 11.

Dieruff 48 Freedom 35: Both teams played a deliberate offense, but Dieruff's shooting touch was better than Freedom. After trailing 7-6 in the first quarter, the Huskies took the lead and held it 13-8 after a quarter. Freedom got no closer than four points, both times in the third quarter, 29-25 and 34-30. Dieruff held the Patriots to only five points in the fourth quarter to garner their fifth win and stay a game behind Allen for the second half title.

Leading scorers: Dieruff – John Smurda 17, Kay Finley 13; Freedom – Mike Pietrouchie 9.

Pottsville 87 Tamaqua 35: Pottsville held Tamaqua to twelve points in the first half and rolled to a thirty-point lead 42-12. Pottsville then added 31 points in the third quarter and the lead was at 73-22. Tamaqua entered the game with a revamped lineup with a number of regulars benched for the start of the contest.

Leading scorers: Pottsville – Pete Marchetti 21, Jim Berrang 17, Ron Lombel 14, Dave Wilson 11; Tamaqua – Glen Behr 12.

Bethlehem Catholic 73 Liberty 68: Liberty led after the first quarter 16-13, but Bethlehem Catholic came back to lead at the half 32-29. With Bob Halbreiner scoring ten points in the third quarter, the Hawks lead grew to eight 51-43. Liberty rallied to within two points twice in the final quarter 60-58 and 64-62, but Paul Grube with ten points helped the Hawks thwart the Hurricane rally.

Leading scorers: Bethlehem Catholic – Bob Halbreiner 23, Paul Grube 19, Bob Alpago 14, Jeff Jennings 11; Liberty - Dan Woodard 24, Rich Wescoe 11, Ed Ruyak 10.

Central Catholic 52 Hazleton 51: In a sloppily played contest, Hazleton took a two-point lead into the second quarter 14-12 and maintained the lead at the half 25-25. After falling behind by six in the third quarter on turnovers, the Vikings came back to tie the game at 31-31. They fell behind by five again only to score eight straight points and take a 41-38 lead at the end of the third period. The Vikings opened up a seven-point lead in the final quarter, but turned over the ball five straight times allowing the Mountaineers to tie the game at 47-47 and briefly take the lead 50-49. Tom Williams made a field goal for a 51-50 lead, but Jim Famalette made one of two foul shots to tie the game at 51, Tim McGorry made a foul shot for the win and Hazleton lost its share of first place. The Vikings and Hazleton were now both a game behind Allen.

Leading scorers: Central Catholic – John Gaspar 22, Tim McGorry 11; Hazleton – Sam Mumaw 16, Tony Manfredi 11, Jim Famalette 10.[26]

Week 11

Central Catholic 87 Freedom 68: Central Catholic led Freedom 25-20 after a quarter, but Freedom battled back to take a 29-28 lead in the second quarter. The lead flip-flopped back and forth several times before the Vikings took a 40-36 lead into the locker room. Tony DaRe took charge for the Vikings in the third quarter handing out four assists and making a steal to extend the lead to 65-52 heading into the final quarter. The Vikings held off the Patriots in the fourth quarter and improved to 6-2, a half-game behind league leader Pottsville at 7-2.

Leading scorers: Central Catholic – Dan Damweber 24, Tony DaRe 13, John Gaspar 12, Tom Williams 11; Freedom – Mike Pietrouchie 18, Mike Csizmadia 12, Fred Mendoza 12, Mike Freundel 10.

Dieruff 56 Allen 50: Dieruff scrambled the race for the second half crown with a defeat of Allen at the East Side Gym. The Huskies started fast for a 20-9 first quarter lead and still held the lead at the half 30-26. Dieruff extended the lead to 50-39 heading into the final period. The Canaries rallied to score ten points in a row and tie the game at 50-50. The Huskies played keep away and Allen fouled in an attempt to get the ball back. Dieruff scored the final six points all on foul shots. Bob Stellar made 15 of 17 foul shots for Dieruff. In his team's heart-breaking loss, Tim Schmiedel went over the 1000-point mark for his career.

Leading scorers: Dieruff – Bob Stellar 35; Allen – Tim Schmiedel 27.

Easton 58 Phillipsburg 49: With Phillipsburg missing the first eight shots of the game, Easton took an 18-11 lead. Both teams had a dismal second quarter with Easton outscoring the Stateliners 8-7 for a 26-18 halftime lead. When Phillipsburg came within two points 27-25 in the third quarter, Easton had an 8-1 run to pull away. Both teams shot poorly with Phillipsburg hitting only 16 of 59 from the floor with Easton not much better hitting 23 of 67 shots.

Leading scorers: Easton– Harry Keller 19, Tom Lacey 15, Don Dickey 10; Phillipsburg– Brian Dominic 25, Charlie Morgan 13.

Pottsville 69 Liberty 60: Pottsville took an early 6-0 lead and held onto it until midway through the second quarter when Liberty tied the game at 18-18 and at 25-25. In the last three minutes of the quarter, Pottsville outscored Liberty 10-3 to take a 35-28 lead. After Liberty pulled within three points in the third quarter, Pottsville rebuilt its lead to 13 points with less than two minutes left in the game. The win gave Pottsville, with a 7-2 record, a half game lead over Hazleton, Central Catholic, Allen and Dieruff, all at 6-2.

Leading scorers: Pottsville – Pete Marchetti 26, Dave Wilson 15, Joel Yob 10; Liberty – Mike Hartenstine 14, Ed Ruyak 13, Dan Woodard 10.[27]

Hazleton 86 Tamaqua 49: Hazleton handed Tamaqua coach Nick Young's team their eighteenth consecutive league loss at the Hazleton gym. After Tamaqua took an early 4-1, Hazleton came back to lead 5-4 and never fell behind again. Hazleton extended its leads to 5, 14, 22, and 37 at the end of each quarter.

Leading scorers: Hazleton – Sam Mumaw 23, Ed Parsons 18; Tamaqua - Dennis Pastucha 9.[28]

Dieruff 67 Phillipsburg 65: With Dieruff holding a slim two-point lead at the half 30-28, Phillipsburg's Brian Dominic scored 13 points in the third quarter to give the Stateliners an 50-42 lead going into the final quarter. Phillipsburg extended the lead to eleven points 55-44 after 1:20 of the quarter. Dieruff scored 12 of the next 13 points to tie the game at 56-56 on a field goal by Kay Finley. After two more ties, the Huskies went ahead 61-60 only to have Dominic score four straight points to give Phillipsburg the lead 64-61. After Dieruff tied the game at 65-65, Bob Stellar sank two free throws to win the game and keep Dieruff in the running for the second half title.

Leading scorers: Dieruff – Bob Stellar 14, Ken Fedor 12, Kay Finley 11, Al Sincavage 11, John Smurda 11; Phillipsburg - Brian Dominic 37.[29]

Allen 74 Central Catholic 70: Allen and Central Catholic battled at the Little Palestra to determine which team would remain in the second half title race. The game lived up to its billing with 19 ties and the winner decided in the last seconds of the matchup. The two teams were tied after the first quarter 17-17 with Tim Schmiedel scoring 15 of the Canaries' points. Despite John Gaspar's 21 points in the first half, Allen took a 23-17 lead early in the second quarter and held the lead at the half 39-35. The Vikings tied up the game after three quarters 53-53. Allen fell behind by four points with 6 ½ minutes to play. Allen rallied to tie the score at 70 and took the lead when Don Wolfe made both free throws in a one-and-one situation. During the contest, Schmiedel became the league's leading all-time scoring leader.

Leading scorers: Allen – Tim Schmiedel 25, Daryl Tollinche 18, Don Wolfe11; Central Catholic – John Gaspar 28, Tony DaRe 18, Tim McGorry 10.

Pottsville 58 Bethlehem Catholic 52: Despite a valiant effort from Bethlehem Catholic, Pottsville assured itself at least a spot in the second half playoffs in the game played in Bethlehem. Pottsville led at the half 34-19 and after three quarters 47-32. The Hawks fought back to within six 54-48 in the final quarter to threaten the Crimson, but could not overcome Pottsville's huge advantage.

Leading scorers: Pottsville – Jim Berrang 19, Dave Wilson 12, Pete Marchetti 10, Joel Yob 10; Bethlehem Catholic – Paul Grube 22, Jeff Jennings 11.

Freedom 68 Tamaqua 59: After trailing by only a point after the first quarter 15-14, Tamaqua could not stay with Freedom as the Patriots took a 28-22 lead at the half and 50-35 after three quarters. Tamaqua made an attempt to comeback in the final quarter by outscoring the Patriots 24-18, but fell well short.

Leading Scorers: Freedom-Mike Pietrouchie 24, Mike Freundel 12; Tamaqua-Tony Forte 17, Bill Stickler 13, Gordon Tonkin 11.

Hazleton 78 Liberty 66: Hazleton took an 8-0 lead, but Liberty roared back to tie the game at 13 and take a 17-13 first quarter lead. Hazleton took the lead at halftime 41-37. Liberty remained close to the Mountaineers until about five minutes remained in the game. Liberty's Dan Woodard took a hard blow to the face and, although he stayed in the game, he was no longer a scoring force for the Hurricane. Hazleton pulled away for the victory and remain in the running for the second half title.

Leading scorers: Hazleton– Sam Mumaw 22, Wally Kisthardt 20, Tom Cerasaro 12; Liberty– Dan Woodard 23, Ed Ruyak 16.[30]

Week 12

Allen 90 Tamaqua 50: With Tim Schmiedel setting a new league season scoring record with 574 points in 20 games and a new school record for points in a season, Allen easily handled winless Tamaqua. The Canaries held the Tams to ten points in each of the first three quarters as they built a 74-30 margin. Tamaqua lost its 20th in a row over two league seasons. The win kept Allen in the playoff hunt for the second half title.

Leading scorers: Allen- Tim Schmiedel 45, Daryl Tollinche 15, Phil Boandl 12; Tamaqua- Gerry Watto 10.

Dieruff 51 Easton 35: Dieruff entered into a four-way tie for the second half title although the first half of the contest was a struggle. Neither team scored much in the half with the halftime score 17-11 in favor of the Huskies. Dieruff scored 17 points in each of the last two quarters to pull away from the Red Rovers. Easton did not make a field goal in the last quarter until 2:26 remained in the game.

Leading scorers: Dieruff – Al Sincavage 15, John Smurda 11, Ken Fedor 10; Easton – Tom Attinello 8.

Central Catholic 97 Phillipsburg 59: Phillipsburg provided little opposition for Central Catholic as the Vikings took a 20-10 first quarter lead. The win gave the Vikings a 7-3 second half record as they waited for the results of the playoff to determine who they would play for the overall league title. John Gaspar scored 30 of this game high 41 points in the middle two quarters and finished eight points shy of 1000 for his career.

Leading scorers: Central Catholic – John Gaspar 41, Dan Damweber 18; Phillipsburg – Brian Dominic 29.

Liberty 71 Freedom 61: The teams played to an 18-18 tie after a quarter and Liberty took a three-point lead into halftime 37-34. In a low-scoring third period, Liberty outpointed the Patriots 12-7 for an eight-point lead and held on in the fourth quarter for the win to pick up their third win in the second half.

Leading scorers: Liberty-Dan Woodard – 27, Mike Hartenstine 11, Ed Ruyak 10; Freedom-Mike Freundel 16, Joe DeAngelis 15.

Hazleton 66 Bethlehem Catholic 55: After a tight first period with Hazleton on top 13-10, the Mountaineers took charge in the second quarter and increased their lead to 12 points 34-22. The Hawks spotted Hazleton a 20-point lead midway through the third quarter and any hopes to stage a comeback disappeared when five of the top six Hawks fouled out in the last period of the contest. The win put Hazleton into the four-team playoff for the second half title.

Leading scorers: Hazleton – Wally Kisthardt 14, Sam Mumaw 14, Charlie Liott 10; Bethlehem Catholic – Jeff Jennings 13.[31]

Second Half Playoffs

Allen 68 Dieruff 61: At the Farm Show Area in Harrisburg, Allen stunned Dieruff in the first quarter as the Canaries took 24-11 lead and followed it up with a halftime lead of 41-24. Dieruff switched to a man-to-man defense to start the second half and cut the Canary lead to seven points after three quarters 54-47. Dieruff forced the Canaries into 14 turnovers in the second half. Dieruff could get no closer as both teams scored 14 points in the fourth quarter.

Leading scorers: Allen – Tim Schmiedel 27, Daryl Tollinche 12, Phil Boandl 11; Dieruff – Al Sincavage 19, Bob Stellar 17, John Smurda 10.

Pottsville 64 Hazleton 54: In the second game of the doubleheader at the Farm Show Arena, Jim Berrang scored 16 of Pottsville's first 22 points as Pottsville took early commanding leads after the first two quarters 14-7 and 33-16. The onslaught continued into the fourth quarter with Pottsville holding a 20-point lead with a little more than five minutes left in the contest. But with 54 seconds left, Hazleton cut the lead to six points 60-54. Berrang responded again with a field goal and two foul shots to cut Hazleton's rally short.

Leading scorers: Pottsville – Jim Berrang 25, Ron Lombel 15, Joel Yob 14; Hazleton – Wally Kisthardt 16, Ed Parsons 12, Sam Mumaw 11.[32]

Allen 74 Pottsville 73: At Rockne Hall, Pottsville took a two-point lead after one quarter 20-18. With about 2 ½ minutes left in the second quarter, Tim Schmiedel twisted his ankle and had to be helped off the floor. Allen trailed by eight at the time and finished the quarter trailing by ten points 39-29. Schmiedel re-entered the game with about four minutes left in the third period and the Canaries down by ten points. With 2:49 left in the game, the Canaries were still down 70-62. Allen outscored the Crimson 12-3 in the final 2 ½ minutes to win the second half title. However, Bruce Merkle had to score the final two points on foul shots with no time left on the clock. With seven seconds left, Pottsville's Pete Marchetti made one of two foul shots to put his team ahead 73-72.

Leading scorers: Allen – Tim Schmiedel 34, Daryl Tollinche 15; Pottsville – Pete Marchetti 24, Jim Berrang 21, Joel Yob 12.[33]

League Playoff

Allen 73 Central Catholic 72: Allen and Central Catholic met for the league title at Muhlenberg's Memorial Hall. Central Catholic took a two-point lead after one quarter 15-13. Allen trimmed the lead to one at the half 38-37. The Vikings held ten point leads four times in the third quarter only to have Allen come back to trail by only one going into the final quarter 61-60. With 3:45 left in the game, the Vikings scored their last field goal and were up by five points. Allen rallied to tie the score at 71. With 2:02 left, Don Wolfe stole the ball and fed Burt Horowitz for the field goal which proved to be winner. The only score the remainder of the game was by the Vikings' Dan Damweber on a foul shot but he missed a second game-tying attempt. In the game, the Vikings' John Gaspar went over the 1000-point mark for his career.

Leading scorers: Allen – Tim Schmiedel 26, Daryl Tollinche 17, Phil Boandl 11; Central Catholic – Tony DaRe 24, John Gaspar 15, Tim McGorry 12, John Susko 10.[34]

Postseason PIAA Play

Both Allen and Pottsville qualified for post season play.

Allen 72 Parkland 59: At Muhlenberg's Memorial Hall, Allen took on Parkland, from the Lehigh-Northampton League, in a quarter-final contest in District 11 play. Allen took a 15-point lead during the first quarter and held a 23-10 lead going into the second quarter. After Parkland cut the lead to seven points in the second quarter, the Canaries went into the locker room at the half leading 39-25. During the second half, Parkland outscored Allen by a point 34-33, but could not overcome Allen's first half advantage.

Leading scorers: Allen – Tim Schmiedel 24, Daryl Tollinche 20, Phil Boandl 14; Parkland – Frank Posocco 25, Scott Huber 15.

Pottsville 75 Palmerton 53: In another District 11 quarter-final, Pottsville led 14-12 after a quarter and held Palmerton to six points in the second quarter to take charge of the contest 32-18. Pottsville ended the quarter by scoring the last seven points and started the second half on a 16-5 run to put the game out of reach for Palmerton. Pottsville's Jim Berrang went over the 1000-point career mark in the game.

Leading scorers: Pottsville – Jim Berrang 21, Pete Marchetti 16; Palmerton – Reggie Hernandez 10.[35]

West Hazleton 68 Allen 64: West Hazleton solved the Allen 2-1-2 zone defense in the first half by scoring 45 points while holding the Canaries to 28 points. Allen appeared to be on its way to another thrilling finish when the Canaries, using a press defense, rallied to within two points 64-62 with about 2 ½ minutes left in the final quarter. With four of their starters fouling out of the game, including Tim Schmiedel early in the final quarter, Allen could not pull off another miracle finish. West Hazleton remained as one of two unbeaten teams in the state at 23-0.

Leading scorers: West Hazleton – Bill Pavlik 14, Laverne Mummey 14, Tom Smith 13, Dave Scripko 12; Allen – Tim Schmiedel 19, Daryl Tollinche 16.

Pottsville 70 Catasauqua 54: Pottsville took a 4-0 lead to start the game and steadily increased the lead in the first half while holding the Roughriders to 14 points in each first half quarter. Pottsville held a 43-28 lead at the half. Catasauqua made a run at the Crimson in the 3rd quarter and outscored Pottsville 16-10 to reduce the lead to 53-44. Pottsville recovered in the 4th quarter to squash the Catasauqua comeback attempt.

Leading scorers: Pottsville – Pete Marchetti 21, Jim Berrang 16, Ron Lombel 15; Catasauqua – Bob Superka 19, Rich Gemmel 17, Walt Winch 11.[36]

West Hazleton 76 Pottsville 54: West Hazleton, with four players in double figures, easily dispensed of Pottsville for the District 11 Class A title. Pottsville could only convert 23 of 76 field goal attempts. In addition, Pottsville made only 8 of 21 foul shots. After falling behind 4-0, West Hazleton ran off 8 points and led after a quarter 15-11. They continued to increase the margin throughout the next three quarters.

Leading scorers: West Hazleton – Dave Scripko 16, Tom Smith 16, Laverne Mummey 14, George Petrylak 11; Pottsville – Jim Berrang 17, Joel Yob 12, Pete Marchetti 10, Dave Wilson 10.[37]

PCIAA Postseason Playoff

Central Catholic 70 Bethlehem Catholic 50: Early in the first quarter, Bethlehem Catholic held the lead several times and were tied at 8-8 with Central Catholic before John Susko put the Vikings ahead to stay at 10-8. The Vikings held the Hawks to ten points in each of the first two quarters and took a 39-20 lead at the half. The teams played even in the second half and the Vikings took the Allentown Diocese title.

Leading scorers: Central Catholic – Dan Damweber 21, Tony DaRe 18, John Gaspar 11; Bethlehem Catholic – Jeff Jennings 12, Paul Grube 12.[38]

Central Catholic 91 Bishop McDevitt 76: Central Catholic made 23 of 31 field goal attempts in the first half as they took a 53-33 halftime lead. They did not let up in the second half as they continued their hot shooting making 16 of 27 attempts. Bishop McDevitt outscored the Vikings 43-38, but could only cut the final margin by five points.

Leading scorers: Central Catholic –Dan Damweber 23, John Gaspar 21, Tony Da Re 20, Tim McGorry 15; Bishop McDevitt – Bob Sebastian 20, Little 10.[39]

Bishop Guilfoyle 76 Central Catholic 74: At the Farm Show Arena in Harrisburg, Bishop Guilfoyle took a nine-point first quarter lead 26-16. Central Catholic cut the lead to four 41-37 at the half. The Vikings continued their strong play in the third quarter to rally to a six-point lead going into the final quarter 60-54. They took the lead 51-50 in the third quarter with a little over two minutes to play. They continued to hold the lead late into the final quarter 74-70 with 2:11 to play. With the score tied at 74, Bishop Guilfoyle made the winning field goal with 4 seconds left for the PCIAA Class A state title.

Leading scorers: Bishop Guilfoyle – Bob Landolfi 25, Tim Lambour 22, Dennis Tomasetti 15; Central Catholic – John Gaspar 23, Dan Damweber 23, Tony DaRe 13.[40]

Postseason Accolades

Leading scorers: Tim Schmiedel, Allen, set a new league season scoring standard with 574 points and averaged 28.7 points per game, also a league record. The rest of the top ten included: Brian Dominic, Phillipsburg, 431 points; John Gaspar, Central Catholic, 368 points; Jim Berrang, Pottsville, 360 points; Dan Woodard, Liberty 340 points; Dan Damweber, Central Catholic, 334 points; Pete Marchetti, Pottsville, 326 points; Jeff Jennings, Bethlehem Catholic, 307 points; Sam Mumaw, Hazleton, 290 points; and Wally Kisthardt, Hazleton, 281 points.[41]

All-Stars: The league all-star first team included: Brian Dominic, Phillipsburg; Tim Schmiedel, Allen; Jim Berrang, Pottsville; John Gaspar and Tony DaRe, both of Central Catholic. The second team consisted of: Dan Gilbert, Freedom; Pete Marchetti, Pottsville; Daryl Tollinche, Allen; Bob Stellar, Dieruff; and Wally Kisthardt, Hazleton.[42]

All-State: The league did not have any player named to the three all-state teams. The following players received honorable mention status: Tim Schmiedel, Allen; Jim Berrang, Pottsville; John Gaspar, Central Catholic; Tony DaRe, Central Catholic; and Bob Stellar, Dieruff.[43]

Final Standings

First Half		Second Half		Overall	
Pottsville	9-1	Hazleton	8-2	Pottsville	17-3
Central Catholic	9-1	Allen	8-2	Central Catholic	16-4
Hazleton	7-3	Dieruff	8-2	Allen	15-5
Allen	7-3	Pottsville	8-2	Hazleton	15-5
Bethlehem Catholic	5-5	Central Catholic	7-3	Dieruff	13-7
Dieruff	5-5	Bethlehem Catholic	5-5	Bethlehem Catholic	10-10
Freedom	4-6	Liberty	3-7	Liberty	7-13
Liberty	4-6	Phillipsburg	3-7	Easton	6-14
Easton	3-7	Easton	3-7	Freedom	6-14
Phillipsburg	2-8	Freedom	2-8	Phillipsburg	5-15
Tamaqua	0-10	Tamaqua	0-10	Tamaqua	0-20

Team Rosters

Allen: Coach Milo Sewards, Phil Boandl, Burt Horowitz, Ron Kahan, Bruce Merkle, Tim Schmiedel, Pat Sewards, Charles Strzelecki, Daryl Tollinche, George Whary, Don Wolfe

Bethlehem Catholic: Coach Bob Bukvics, Bob Alpago, Becker, Dennis Butler, Gary Cacciatore, Tom Eddinger, Paul Grube, Bob Halbreiner, Mike Halbreiner, Ed Hartigan, Jeff Jennings, Rich Kearney. John O'Boyle, Michael Saliba

Central Catholic: Coach Mike Koury, Ron Caldarelli, Dan Damweber, Tony DaRe, John Gaspar, Bob Kasper, George Kinek, Tim McGorry, Jerry Schleder, Bob Stano, John Susko, Tom Williams, Roger Worman

Dieruff: Coach Dick Schmidt, Ken Fedor, Kay "Bo" Finley, Jerry Dzerens, Brad Leibensperger, Steve Michalerya, Bogdan "Bucky" Paraszczak, Mike Reiter, Al Sincavage, Hamp Smith, John Smurda, Bob Stellar, Mike Zambelli

Easton: Coach Stan Sutphen, Tom Attinello, Don Dickey, Robin Farina, Don Gentzle, Hank Godown, Jim Haney, Harry Keller, Tom Lacey, Kerry Myers, S Myers, Don Sterner, Dave Troxell

Freedom: Coach Charlie Dubbs, Mike Csizmadia, Joe DeAngelis, Mike Deschler, Mike Freundel, Dan Gilbert, Jim Lees. Fred Mendoza, Mike Pietrouchie, Pete Pozefsky, Bill Werpehowski, Wiesenberg

Hazleton: Coach Dave Shafer, Tom Cerasaro, Jim Chapman, Jim Famalette, Wally Kisthardt, Larry Kovatch, Bruce Leib, Charlie Liott, Tony Manfredi, Manfred Marotta, Sam Mumaw, Ed Parsons, Jack Temchatin,

Liberty: Coach Al Senavitis, Ed Cunningham, Dave DiGiacinto, Easterling, Gary Fejes, Jack Harrington, Mike Hartenstine, Bill Hemmerly, George Korpics, Mitch Lukevics, John Preistas, Ed Ruyak, Bob Ruyak, Dan Woodard

Phillipsburg: Coach Pete Tomaino, Bob Clymer, Barry Coopersmith, Brian Dominic, John Freeman, Pat James, Tom James, Doug Maczko, Charlie Morgan, Jim Oberley, Dennis Staples, Bruce Tibbott, Eric Weisel, Walter Wrede, Jim Ziegenfuss

Pottsville: Coach Ken Kline, Ken Bailey, Jim Berrang, Jerry Evans, Chris Higgins, Ron Lombel, Pete Marchetti, Sergio Ramirez, Paul Shellhammer, Jim Siket, Dave Sydnor, Dave Wilson, Joel Yob

Tamaqua: Coach Nick Young, Glen Behr, Charles Connely, Ron Eva, Tony Forte, Craig Krause, Mike Miller, Dennis Patucha, Ron Ritsick, Alan Smith, Bill Stickler, Gordon Tonklin, Jeff Truskey, Gerry Watto, Matt Welsh

1971

Hazleton's Final League Title

First Half - Week 1

Central Catholic 66 Easton 32: After Central Catholic scored the first five points, Easton ran off three in a row. The Vikings put on a 10-1 spurt and led after a quarter 20-8. It didn't get much better for the Red Rovers in the second quarter as they again scored only eight points as Central Catholic scored 16. Easton's third quarter was worse as they could only muster four points and now trailed 49-20.

Leading scorers: Central Catholic – Tim McGorry 17, Mike Busolits 15, George Kinek 12; Easton – Tom Lacey 17.

Allen 71 Liberty 45: With five new starters from the previous year, Allen began the season with an easy victory over Liberty. Liberty did not score its first field goal until 20 seconds were left in the first quarter and trailed as the quarter ended 13-6. The Canaries outscored Liberty in all four quarters.

Leading scorers: Allen – Pat Sewards 23, Warnell Lamb 15; Liberty – Mike Hartenstine 14.

Freedom 71 Bethlehem Catholic 51: Freedom's shorter, but more aggressive, squad took command of the game after the first two periods by holding the Hawks to 15 points while pouring in 36 of their own. Bethlehem Catholic scored the first 8 points of the third quarter to cut the lead to 13, but Freedom bounced back with five straight points by Jeff Hoydu to cut off the Hawks rally.

Leading scorers: Freedom – Jim Lees 16, Carl Pietrouchie 16, Mike Deschler 12; Bethlehem Catholic – Rick Cacciatore 17, Tom Eddinger 12, Dennis Butler 12.[1]

Hazleton 61 Pottsville 45: Hazleton scored the first eight points and led 14-2 on their way to a 24-10 first quarter lead. After trailing by 19 at the half 40-21, Pottsville had a brief comeback in the third period to cut the lead to 12 points 45-33.

Leading scorers: Hazleton - Tom Cerasaro 15, Jerry Fallabel 14, Wally Kisthardt 12; Pottsville - Ron Lombel 19.[2]

Phillipsburg 64 Tamaqua 59: Tamaqua lost its 21st consecutive league contest. Phillipsburg led after each of the first two quarters 20-14 and 37-30, but Tamaqua held the Stateliners to six points in the third quarter and took the lead 45-43. Phillipsburg bounced back in the final quarter to hand the Tams yet another defeat.

Leading scorers: Phillipsburg – John Freeman 26, Tom James 10, Dennis Staples 10; Tamaqua – Dennis Pastucha 21.[3]

Week 2

Allen 82 Bethlehem Catholic 62: In a very sloppily played game, each team committed ten turnovers in the first quarter and Hawks turned the ball over 32 times in the game with the Canaries close behind at 30. In addition, each team committed 25 personal fouls. Allen made 18 of 38 foul shots while Bethlehem Catholic on converted 10 of 36. In another oddity, Allen was assessed a technical foul before the start of the game when a Canary player slapped the backboard. The Hawks missed the foul shot but began the game with the possession of the ball. Allen took charge of the game in the second quarter by outscoring the Hawks 23-10 and cruised to the victory.

Leading scorers: Allen – Warnell Lamb 17, Chuck Strzelecki 17, Pat Sewards 13; Bethlehem Catholic – Dennis Butler 15, Rick Cacciatore 14.

Dieruff 62 Central Catholic 50: Dieruff raced out to a twelve-point lead 17-5 after the first quarter which turned out to be the final margin of victory. The Vikings played the Huskies even the rest of the night. Poor foul shooting helped doom the Vikings when they were only able to convert 14 of 34 attempts.

Leading scorers: Dieruff – Ken Fedor 23, Al Sincavage 13, Bo Finley 13; Central Catholic – Joe Pfahler 23.[4]

Liberty 70 Phillipsburg 34: Liberty took an 8-6 lead in the first period before going on an 11-1 run to close out the first period for a 19-7 lead. Liberty did not score a point in the first four minutes of the second period, but Phillipsburg could only score five points to narrow the gap to 19-12. Liberty then went on a tear and outscored the Stateliners 18-5 in the last four minutes of the period to take a commanding 37-17 lead. Liberty cruised to an easy victory and outscored Phillipsburg 21-7 in the final period to complete the rout.

Leading scorers: Liberty – Mike Hartenstine 14 Jack Harrington 12; Phillipsburg – Dennis Staples 10.

Easton 71 Tamaqua 34: After scoring the first ten points of the game, Easton took a 16-5 first quarter lead and extended it to 23 points at the half 40-17. They finished off the game by outpointing the Tams 21-5 as Tamaqua suffered its 22nd consecutive league defeat.

Leading scorers: Easton – Tom Lacey 25, Hank Godown 14, Mark Betts 14; Tamaqua – Lew Erbe 10.

Pottsville 64 Freedom 58: Neither team took more than a four-point lead in the first half. With Pottsville holding a 28-24 lead at the half, the Crimson employed a full court press in the third period to hold the Patriots without a field goal. The Patriots made only four foul shots as Pottsville extended the lead to 43-32. Although Freedom ran off eight straight points in the final period and cut the lead to six points, they could not overcome the Crimson Tide's third period advantage.

Leading scorers: Pottsville- Chris Higgins 24, Dave Sydnor 12; Freedom- Jim Lees 20, Carl Pietrouchie 19.[5]

Hazleton 67 Freedom 50: After Freedom's only lead 2-0, Hazleton raced out to a 20-16 first quarter lead and extended it to 35-22 at the half. Freedom cut the lead to four points with a little over two minutes left in the first half, but the Mountaineers countered with 9 straight points. The Patriots never threatened again.

Leading scorers: Hazleton – Jerry Fallabel 18, Wally Kisthardt 12, Tom Cerasaro 10; Freedom – Jim Lees 16, Jeff Hoydu 10.

Liberty 59 Easton 40: Liberty held Easton to 17 points in the first three periods and held a 48-17 advantage entering into the fourth quarter. Although Easton outscored Liberty 23-11 in the final period, the Hurricane still held on for an easy victory.

Leading scorers: Liberty – Jack Harrington 17; Easton – Dave Troxell 10.

Dieruff 82 Tamaqua 55: Dieruff handed Tamaqua its 23rd consecutive league loss as they outscored the Tams in each period. The Huskies built leads of 23-11, 43-27, and 64-39 at the end of each of the first three periods to roll to an easy victory.

Leading scorers: Dieruff – Al Sincavage 13, Kay Finley 13, Brad Leibensperger 12, Hamp Smith 11; Tamaqua – Dennis Pastucha 30, Lew Erbe 10.

Allen 75 Pottsville 51: At Pottsville, Allen ruined the dedication of the new Pottsville gymnasium. After playing to a 15-15 first quarter tie and still tied at 24-24 with three minutes left in the second quarter, Allen ran off 12 straight points to take a 36-24 halftime lead. They didn't let up until they had built a 26-point lead late in the final quarter.

Leading scorers: Allen – Pat Sewards 18, Joe Thompson 18, Chuck Strzelecki 17; Pottsville – Leo Ostrosky 16, Joel Yob 11.[6]

Bethlehem Catholic 49 Phillipsburg 47: Phillipsburg held the lead 10-9 after a period, but Bethlehem Catholic outscored the Stateliners 26-16 in the second quarter to take a 35-26 halftime lead. At the end of three quarters, the Hawks led by eight points 38-30 only to have to hang on for the win after Phillipsburg closed in to within two points at the final buzzer.

Leading scorers: Bethlehem Catholic-Bob Halbreiner 16; Phillipsburg-John Freeman 22, Dennis Staples 11.[7]

Week 3

Dieruff 48 Liberty 45: Dieruff led 14-9 after one quarter and 18-11 early in the second period for the largest lead of the game. Liberty fought back to cut the lead to 23-21 at the half. The score was tied six times and the lead changed hands six times throughout the contest. Liberty took the lead early in the fourth quarter 41-40. The Huskies made six foul shots in the final minutes of the game to pull out the win. Dieruff made 14 of 18 foul shots while Liberty only made 3 of 11.

Leading scorers: Dieruff – Bo Finley 14, Al Sincavage 13; Liberty – John Priestas 12, Gary Fejes 12.

Hazleton 85 Allen 58: With both teams unbeaten in early league play, Allen traveled to Hazleton only to return home soundly beaten by the Mountaineers. Hazleton took a 29-18 lead into the locker room at the half and continued to extend the lead in the final two quarters. The Mountaineers scored 37 points in the final quarter. The win improved Hazleton to 3-0 while Allen dropped to 3-1.

Leading scorers: Hazleton – Jerry Fallabel 16, Tom Cerasaro 14, Charlie Liott 14, Wally Kisthardt 13, Jim Munley 11; Allen – Pat Sewards 21, Chuck Strzelecki 15.[8]

Pottsville 51 Phillipsburg 49: Phillipsburg took a 10-6 lead after a quarter, Pottsville cut the lead to a point 25-24 at the half. Phillipsburg added two to the lead after three periods 37-34. With Phillipsburg ahead 47-45, the Stateliners committed a backcourt violation and Joel Yob tied the game with a field goal from the corner with 28 seconds to play. With 10 seconds left, Yob scored on a fast break layup to win the contest.

Leading scorers: Pottsville-Joel Yob 20; Phillipsburg-John Freeman 14, Cliff Oberley 13, Dennis Staples 12.

Central Catholic 85 Tamaqua 47: Central Catholic took 22-16 lead after the first quarter and outscored Tamaqua by 9, 9 and 14 points in the last three quarters to hand the Tams their 24th straight lead loss. Tamaqua never led at any time in the game. The Vikings improved to 2-1 in league play.

Leading scorers: Central Catholic – Joe Pfahler 21, Jerry Schleder 12, Jeff McGeehin 12, Ron Caldarelli 10, Tim McGorry 10; Tamaqua – Ed Hromyak 12, Dennis Pastucha 11, Tom Yelito 10.

Bethlehem Catholic 54 Easton 51: Easton led 14-11 going into the second period only to have Bethlehem Catholic score the first ten points of the period and take a 21-14 lead. The Hawks scored seven straight points at the end of the quarter to lead 28-24 at the half. Bethlehem Catholic padded the lead by five in the third period 43-34. With the Hawks leading 49-34, Easton scored 12 points in a row to narrow the lead to three. They cut the lead to two 53-51, but could not score again.

Leading scorers: Bethlehem Catholic – Casey Eddinger 24, Rick Cacciatore 10; Easton – Tom Lacey 19.[9]

Hazleton 79 Phillipsburg 44: After taking a 12-8 lead after the first quarter, Phillipsburg could not hold up to the scoring onslaught by Hazleton. Hazleton outscored the Stateliners 23-11 in the second quarter and it only got worse from there for Phillipsburg. In the fourth quarter, Hazleton poured 23 points on Phillipsburg while holding the Stateliners to only six points. Hazleton remained undefeated at 4-0 while Phillipsburg dropped to 1-4.

Leading scorers: Hazleton – Charlie Liott 19, Wally Kisthardt 11, Jerry Fallabel 10; Phillipsburg – John Freeman 14.[10]

Allen 103 Freedom 64: Allen bounced back with a vengeance after its whipping by Hazleton to thrash Freedom and improve their record to 4-1. Allen took a 20-9 lead after the first quarter and scored 22 or more points in each quarter after that. The score at the half was 44-41. In an unusual streak, Bob Handschue scored the 100th point for the Canaries in the game. It ran his streak to four games over the past two years where the Canaries went over 100 and he scored the basket each time for the 100th point.

Leading scorers: Allen – Bill Frederick 27, Pat Sewards 21, Tom Donley 11, Chuck Strzelecki 10, Joe Thompson 10; Freedom – Jeff Hoydu 15, Carl Pietrouchie 13, Mike Deschler 12.

Liberty 78 Central Catholic 59: Liberty took an 11-9 lead into the second quarter but Central Catholic ran off six straight points to go ahead 17-13 early in the quarter. After Liberty tied the score at 17-17, the Vikings took their last lead 19-17 on a tap in by Ron Caldarelli. Liberty took control the rest of the way.

Leading scorers: Liberty – Mike Hartenstine 19, Jack Harrington 17, Rich Wescoe 14, Gary Fejes 10; Central Catholic – Joe Pfahler 21, Tim McGorry 17.

Dieruff 72 Bethlehem Catholic 51: Dieruff maintained its share of first place at 4-0 with a victory over the Hawks. The Huskies took a 14-7 first quarter lead and increased it to 18 in the second quarter before Bethlehem Catholic cut it to twelve at the half 33-21. Dieruff added 9 points to the lead in the second half.

Leading scorers: Dieruff – Al Sincavage 22, Kay Finley 12, Mike Zambelli 12, Ken Fedor 10; Bethlehem Catholic – Bob Halbreiner 26.

Easton 59 Pottsville 44: Easton held Pottsville to nine points in each of the first three quarters to build a 50-27 lead over the Crimson Tide. Both clubs stood at 2-3 as a result of the Red Rovers' victory.

Leading scorers: Easton – Tom Lacey 15, Jim Haney 11, Dave Troxell 11, Tom Attinello 10; Pottsville – Jim Berrang 18, Pete Marchetti 14, Hal Bertsch 11.[11]

Week 4

Due to a snowstorm. The entire week 4 schedule was postponed at least a week with three games rescheduled the week after Christmas and two other contests to the first week of January.[12]

Hazleton 63 Easton 50: Hazleton ran its league record to 5-0 with the eleven-point victory over Easton. The Mountaineers built the eleven-point lead in the first half 32-21. Easton had a mild comeback in the third period, but Hazleton responded in the fourth quarter to maintain the lead.

Leading scorers: Hazleton – Jerry Fallabel 18, Wally Kisthardt 12, Charlie Liott 10; Easton – Tom Lacey 20, Jim Haney 12.

Liberty 84 Tamaqua 56: Liberty pushed Tamaqua's league losing streak to 25 games at Tamaqua. After Liberty took an 18-8 lead after a quarter, Tamaqua outscored Liberty 20-19 in the second quarter. The Hurricane put the game away in the third quarter by dropping 27 points on Tamaqua and adding 16 points to their advantage. Liberty improved to 4-2.

Leading scorers: Liberty – Mike Hartenstine 15, Gary Fejes 14 Jack Harrington 12, Rich Wescoe 10; Tamaqua – Dennis Pastucha 16.[13]

Week 5

Allen 94 Phillipsburg 62: Allen jumped out to a 6-0 lead ending the 1st quarter in front 22-10. They nearly duplicated the feat in the 2nd quarter to lead at the half 45-21. Allen placed 5 players in double figures in the rout.

Leading scorers: Allen – Pat Sewards 20, Tom Donley 20, Joe Thompson 14, Chuck Strzelecki 13, Bill Frederick 10; Phillipsburg – Dennis Staples 18, John Freeman 17.

Bethlehem Catholic 87 Tamaqua 60: Bethlehem ran off 12 points in a row to take a 48-22 lead and had streaks of 5, 8, and 10 points in the third period to build the lead to 73-32. Tamaqua narrowed the advantage slightly in the final quarter but still suffered its 26th consecutive game in league play.

Leading scorers: Bethlehem Catholic – Tom Eddinger 27, Bob Halbreiner 17, Rick Cacciatore 14, Gary Cacciatore 11; Tamaqua – Dennis Pastucha 26.

Easton 60 Freedom 50: After Freedom held a 16-15 lead after a quarter, Easton scored the last seven points of the first half and added a 9-2 run to start the second. With Freedom missing its first eight shots in third period, Easton stretched the lead to twelve points 41-29 and picked its third victory of the first half against four losses.

Leading scorers: Easton – Tom Lacey 19, Dave Troxell 15, Jim Haney 11, Mark Betts 10; Freedom – Carl Pietrouchie 14, Jeff Hoydu 13.[14]

Dieruff 59 Hazleton 49: In a battle of unbeatens with Hazleton at 5-0 and Dieruff at 4-0, the Huskies gave coach Dick Schmidt his 200th career win. Dieruff's deliberate strategy played off with the Huskies taking 13-11 and 27-23 leads after the first two quarters. Dieruff padded the lead in the third to 44-33 and held off the Mountaineers in the final quarter to take sole possession of first place. Hazleton dropped into a tie for second with Allen, both at 5-1.

Leading scorers: Dieruff – Kay Finley 22, Ken Fedor 16; Hazleton – Jim Ceresaro 16, Jerry Fallabel 10.

Central Catholic 57 Pottsville 45: With Central Catholic converting 21 of 27 foul shots compared to Pottsville's 1 of 7, the Vikings overcame a 22-18 field goal disadvantage. The teams went into the final quarter tied at 40-40. The Vikings defense shut down Pottsville and held them to 5 fourth quarter points.

Leading scorers: Central Catholic – George Kinek 19; Pottsville – Joel Yob 12, Ron Lombel 12.[15]

Freedom 57 Phillipsburg 50: The teams exchanged leads with Phillipsburg taking an 11-8 lead after the first quarter. Freedom countered and took the lead at the half 25-21. The Stateliners rebounded to take a 43-39 lead after three quarters. Freedom then held Phillipsburg to seven points in the fourth quarter to pull out the win behind Carl Pietrouchie's nine points during the quarter.

Leading scorers: Freedom-Carl Pietrouchie 22, Jim Lees 16; Phillipsburg-John Freeman 12, Mike Kline 10.[16]

Central Catholic 55 Bethlehem Catholic 40: Central Catholic scored 18 of its 22 points on foul shots in the fourth quarter to pull out its win over Bethlehem Catholic. The Vikings entered the final quarter with a slim two-point lead 33-31, but held the Hawks to nine points. With the Viking's lead at 40-36 early in the final quarter, they scored ten consecutive points to put the game in the win column.

Leading scorers: Central Catholic – Tim McGorry 17, Jeff McGeehin 15, Joe Pfahler 12; Bethlehem Catholic - Casey Eddinger 12, Bob Halbreiner 10, Dennis Butler 10.

Dieruff 53 Pottsville 31: In the 1st period, the two teams battled to ties at 13-13 and 15-15 before Dieruff kept Pottsville without a field goal in the 2nd period and took a 23-17 lead into halftime. Dieruff cruised to an easy victory by outscoring the Crimson Tide by 8 points in each of the last two quarters. The Huskie defense held Pottsville's top two scorers to a combined 4 for 31 from the field. Dieruff held on to sole possession of first place.

Leading scorers: Dieruff– Al Sincavage 15, Kay Finley 12, Brad Liebensperger 10, Ken Fedor 10; Pottsville-Chris Higgins 7.[17]

Week 6

Liberty 55 Bethlehem Catholic 39: Bethlehem Catholic held a 19-12 lead after two minutes of the second quarter, but did not score another point in the next five minutes. Liberty scored nine unanswered points to take the lead into halftime 23-21. With Mike Hartenstine and Jack Harrington both on the bench for the entire third quarter, the Hurricane increased their lead to six 39-33 in the quarter. Both returned for the final quarter and helped break the game wide open as Liberty improved to 5-2.

Leading scorers: Liberty- Mike Hartenstine 13, Mitch Lukevics 10; Bethlehem Catholic- Rick Cacciatore 14.

Dieruff 54 Freedom 40: Dieruff remained unbeaten at 7-0 and hold a game lead over second place Allen. Pesky Freedom stayed within striking distance of the Huskies throughout the game until the fourth quarter. They trailed Dieruff 39-34 in the third quarter, but the Huskies put on a 10-2 spurt in the final period to jump into a 49-36 lead and secure yet another victory.

Leading scorers: Dieruff – Kay Finley 15, Mike Reiter 14, Al Sincavage 13; Freedom – Carl Pietrouchie 16.

Central Catholic 77 Hazleton 76: Central Catholic stunned Hazleton to hand coach Mike Koury his 100th victory. At Rockne Hall, the Vikings built a 59-48 lead after three quarters. Although the Vikings never trailed, Hazleton climbed with two points 74-72 with 37 seconds to play. Hazleton then intercepted the Vikings in-bounds pass and immediately called a time out. Since they had none left to take, a technical was called, which Tim McGorry converted, and Central Catholic received the ball at mid-court. Joe Pfahler was fouled and converted both shots for the winning points despite two last second baskets by the Mountaineers.

Leading scorers: Central Catholic – Tim McGorry 21, Joe Pfahler 19, George Kinek 13, Jerry Schleder 12, Jeff McGeehin 10; Hazleton – Jerry Fallabel 18, Wally Kisthardt 18, Jim Munley 12, Tom Cerasaro 11.

Allen 64 Easton 48: Easton blitzed Allen in the first quarter by taking a 23-14 lead. Allen fought back to tie the game at the half 32-32. However, the Red Rovers could only score 18 points in the second half as the Canaries pulled away with a 9-1 run and another seven straight points in the third period. The win kept the Canaries a game behind Dieruff and set up a key matchup with the Huskies in their next contest.

Leading scorers: Allen – Bill Frederick 16, Warnell Lamb 15, Pat Sewards 13; Easton – Tom Lacey 19, Jim Haney 14.[18]

Pottsville 68 Tamaqua 47: Tamaqua kept within reach of Pottsville during the first half and trailed by only six at the half 29-23. However, Pottsville exploded for 28 points in the third quarter to put the game away and hand the Tams their 7th loss without a win and their 27th straight league loss over the last two seasons.

Leading scorers: Pottsville – Joel Yob 17, Ron Lombel 13, Chris Higgins 13, Dave Sydnor 12, Jerry Evans 11; Tamaqua – Dennis Pastucha 19.[19]

Hazleton 79 Tamaqua 32: Hazleton held Tamaqua to 16 points in the first half to take a commanding 45-16 lead at halftime. The loss was Tamaqua's 31st straight overall and 28th in league play.

Leading scorers: Hazleton – Jerry Fallabel 21, Jim Chapman 13; Tamaqua – Ed Hromyak 12.[20]

Allen 49 Dieruff 47: In front of a standing room-only crowd, Dieruff and Allen battled with first place on line. Dieruff took the lead after a quarter 15-12 and built as much as an eleven-point lead in the first half. The Canaries kept pecking away at the lead and, after trailing by five at the half, tied the game at 38-38 going into the final quarter. Allen took a 46-42 lead with 3 ½ minutes left only to have Dieruff tie the score at 46-46 with 54 seconds to play. Tom Donley hit a field goal, which proved to be the game-winner, with 41 seconds to play. Both teams were now tied for first with 7-1 records with two games to play.

Leading scorers: Allen – Bill Frederick 21, Pat Sewards 11; Dieruff – Al Sincavage 17, Kay Finley 12, Ken Fedor 10.

Phillipsburg 56 Easton 53: With four seconds left to play, Phillipsburg's Tom James completed a three-point play to break the Stateliners' six-game skid in league play. Coach Pete Tomaino's squad trailed most of the game before pulling out the last second victory. Stan Sutphen's Easton squad led by eight in the first half and five in the second half but could not hold on for the win.

Leading scorers: Phillipsburg – Dennis Staples 18, Tom James 15, Cliff Oberly 13; Easton – Tom Lacey 29.

Central Catholic 64 Freedom 52: Central Catholic took their first lead at 9-8 in the 1st period and never trailed after that in the contest. The Vikings built the lead to ten points at the half 30-20 and stayed in command the rest of the way.

Leading scorers: Central Catholic – Joe Pfahler 25, Jeff McGeehin 14; Freedom – Carl Pietrouchie 20, Jeff Hoydu 11.

Liberty 54 Pottsville 51: Liberty led at the half 30-19 after outscoring Pottsville 18-9 in the second quarter. The eleven-point lead was just enough to hold off the Crimson Tide who dominated the second half 32-24. Liberty improved to 6-2 while Pottsville dropped to 3-6.

Leading scorers: Liberty – Jack Harrington 18, Mitch Lukevics 15, Rich Wescoe 14; Pottsville – Joel Yob 16, Chris Higgins 14, Ron Lombel 13.[21]

Week 7

Hazleton 71 Liberty 54: With both teams at 6-2, each had slim hopes for a first half title. The game was close throughout the first half with Liberty taking a 14-8 after a quarter only to have the Mountaineers come back to tie the game at the half 25-25. With Liberty trailing 40-37 and two seconds remaining in the third quarter, the Hurricane threw a full court pass that went out of bounds and gave Hazleton the ball under their own basket. On the in-bounds play, Hazleton scored to extend the lead. Liberty never got closer than five points after that and their first half hopes were dashed.

Leading scorers: Hazleton – Wally Kisthardt 19, Jerry Fallable 18, Tom Cerasaro 10; Liberty – Rich Wescoe 15, Mike Hartenstine 11.

Allen 91 Central Catholic 77: Two separate spurts carried Allen to victory over Central Catholic. The Canaries trailed by five points in the second quarter when they ran off 16 straight points to build an eleven-point lead. Then after the Vikings cut the lead to six at the end of the third quarter 65-59, Allen scored five straight baskets for a 16-point lead to thwart any hopes of a Viking win.

Leading scorers: Allen – Bill Frederick 32, Warnell Lamb 19, Tom Donley 16, Pat Sewards 13; Central Catholic – Joe Pfahler 31, Tim McGorry 16.

Pottsville 63 Bethlehem Catholic 54: After trailing 40-32 at the half, Bethlehem Catholic opened the third quarter with a field goal and four foul shots and the lead was two 40-38. Pottsville ran off eight straight points to lead by ten but the Hawks came back to within four entering the final quarter 49-45. After Pottsville hit two baskets for a six-point lead, they froze the ball the rest of the way and continued to extend the lead.

Leading scorers: Pottsville – Chris Higgins 22, Ron Lombel 17, Dave Sydnor 10; Bethlehem Catholic – Casey Eddinger 14, Bob Halbreiner 13, Rick Cacciatore 10.

Dieruff 60 Phillipsburg 43: Dieruff took an early 11-1 lead and held Phillipsburg to twelve points in the first half to take a 29-12 lead. The third quarter was not much better for the Stateliners when they could only score nine points and the lead grew to 42-21 and the Huskies cruised to the win and maintain its tie for the league lead with Allen.

Leading scorers: Dieruff – Al Sincavage 17, Mike Zambelli 11, Brad Liebensperger 11; Phillipsburg – John Freeman 17, Mike Fichera 10.

Freedom 85 Tamaqua 63: Tamaqua took Freedom by surprise with an early 14-6 lead before the Patriots recovered in the second quarter with twelve straight points to take a 22-15 lead that they never gave up. Tamaqua suffered its 29th consecutive loss in league play.

Leading scorers: Freedom – Carl Pietrouchie 24, Jim Lees 20, Jeff Hoydu 11; Tamaqua – Dennis Pastucha 28.[22]

Dieruff 47 Easton 39: Dieruff hung on to its share of first place in a surprisingly tough struggle with Easton. Easton tied the Huskies at 15-15 and Dieruff went on a 10-2 spurt to put some distance between them and the Red Rovers. In the third quarter, Easton came within a point 29-28 and the Huskies went on an 11-3 spurt to end the third quarter. Dieruff slowed play in the final quarter and scored their only field goal with 17 seconds left.

Leading scorers: Dieruff – Kay Finley 13, Al Sincavage 10; Easton – Jim Haney 14, Tom Lacey 12.

Allen 103 Tamaqua 41: Allen thrashed Tamaqua to hand the Tams their 30th straight league loss, a league record. Allen fell behind early 8-5, but reeled off 16 straight points and were well on their way to a rout of the Tams. After building a 70-31 lead after three quarters, the Canaries poured in 33 points in the 4th quarter.

Leading scorers: Allen – Bill Fredericks 19, Tom Donley 16, Pat Sewards 14, Chuck Strzelecki 14, Joe Thompson 12, Warnell Lamb 11; Tamaqua – Ed Hromyak 13, Dennis Pastucha 11.

Liberty 68 Freedom 48: Freedom hung in against a taller Liberty team in the first two quarters with the Hurricane leading at the half 29-24. The size advantage took its toll as Liberty outscored the Patriots 15-4 in the third quarter to take a commanding lead.

Leading scorers: Liberty – Mitch Lukevics 18, Mike Hartenstine 15, Jack Harrington 12; Freedom – Jeff Hoydu 11, Carl Pietrouchie 10.

Central Catholic 60 Phillipsburg 53: Central Catholic and Phillipsburg played to a 31-31 tie at halftime. The Vikings made field goals on seven of the Stateliners' eight turnovers in the third period to take a seven-point lead at the end of the quarter. Central Catholic froze the ball in the final quarter and both teams were able to score only six points each.

Leading scorers: Central Catholic – Joe Pfahler 24, Tim McGorry 17; Phillipsburg – Dennis Staples 16, Tom James 14, John Freeman 11.

Hazleton 89 Bethlehem Catholic 58: Hazleton outscored Bethlehem Catholic in each quarter by nine points or more except in the second quarter when the Hawks played the Mountaineers nearly even at 16-15. Hazleton's Jerry Fallabel scored 15 points in the third quarter and nine in a row.

Leading scorers: Hazleton – Jerry Fallabel 24, Charlie Liott 19, Tom Cerasaro 13, Jim Chapman 10; Bethlehem Catholic – Casey Eddinger 16.[23]

First Half Playoff

Allen 52 Dieruff 47: At Muhlenberg's Memorial Hall, Allen built a significant lead in the first half and led 29-16. The Canaries established an eleven-point lead before the Huskies made their first field goal. Although they never led in the game, Dieruff came within four points with two minutes left before Allen rallied to take the first half title.

Leading scorers: Allen– Warnell Lamb 24, Bill Frederick 12, Pat Sewards 11; Dieruff– Brad Liebensperger 18, Kay Finley 11.[24]

Second Half - Week 8

Allen 72 Liberty 63: After winning the first half playoff, Allen came out flat against Liberty and trailed after each of the first three quarters 14-11, 36-25, and 51-45. Trailing by as much as twelve points, the Canaries made a furious comeback beginning in the fourth quarter. They scored 16 straight points and went on a 20-2 spurt to snatch a victory after a sluggish start.

Leading scorers: Allen – Pat Sewards 29, Jim Emery 10; Liberty – Jack Harrington 17.

Bethlehem Catholic 48 Freedom 45: Bethlehem Catholic never trailed in the game, but Freedom gave the Hawks a struggle throughout the game. The difference in the victory came in the second period when the Patriots could only score five points and the Hawks built the lead to eight points at the half 22-14. Despite outscoring the Hawks 31-26 in the second half, Freedom could not overcome the first half deficit.

Leading scorers: Bethlehem Catholic- Rick Cacciatore 14, Bob Halbreiner 12; Freedom- Carl Pietrouchie 15.

Easton 54 Central Catholic 53: Central Catholic began the contest by building a 16-9 lead after a quarter. Easton came on in the middle two quarters to cut the lead to five at the half 28-23 and then take the lead after three quarters 40-39. Easton added to the lead 48-45 with almost five minutes left to play. The lead grew to five 53-48 with 87 seconds to play. The Vikings cut the lead to one 54-53 with six seconds to play and had a chance for the win with a last second shot bouncing off the rim.

Leading scorers: Easton – Tom Lacey 27; Central Catholic – Jeff McGeehin 17, Tim McGorry 10.[25]

Phillipsburg 59 Tamaqua 57: Tamaqua made a valiant effort to end their 30-game league losing streak. After a first period tie at 13-13 and halftime tie at 29-29, the Tams took the lead at the end of the third quarter 44-43. Although they had leads of up to six points and still by two 57-55 with a minute left, Phillipsburg finished with a field goal and two foul shots to extend the Tamaqua losing streak to 31 games.

Leading scorers: Phillipsburg – Dennis Staples 18, Jim Oberley 17; Tamaqua – Dennis Pastucha 22, Ed Hromyak 13.[26]

Pottsville 49 Hazleton 47: Pottsville took a 13-4 lead during the 1st quarter and led 16-9 at the quarter's end. With a strong 2nd quarter, Hazleton took the halftime lead 28-26 and extended it to 36-30 entering the final quarter. Pottsville took a 5-point advantage on a goaltending call 46-41, but Hazleton came back to tie the game at 47-47. Ron Lombel's driving layup with 7 seconds left gave the Crimson Tide their upset win.

Leading scorers: Pottsville – Joel Yob 19, Dave Sydnor 14; Hazleton – Jerry Fallabel 13.[27]

Bethlehem Catholic 77 Allen 71: After Bethlehem Catholic took an early first quarter lead 10-2, Allen came back to trail by one 18-17 at the end of the quarter. They took the lead 35-34 at halftime. The Hawks outscored the Canaries 20-15 in the third quarter to take the lead 54-50. With 5 ½ minutes left, Allen's Warnell fouled out with the Canaries trailing 59-57. The Hawks then began to pull away to break Allen's ten-game winning streak.

Leading scorers: Bethlehem Catholic – Bob Halbreiner 25, Casey Eddinger 16; Allen – Pat Sewards 26, Warnell Lamb 19.

Easton 62 Tamaqua 40: Easton won its second game of the half to stay in a first-place tie. After taking a 10-6 lead in the first quarter, the Red Rovers never trailed in handing Tamaqua its 32nd straight league loss. Nine different players scored for Easton.

Leading scorers: Easton – Jim Haney 18, Tom Lacey 14; Tamaqua – Tom Yelito 12.

Liberty 76 Phillipsburg 63: On a layup by Dennis Staples, Phillipsburg went into the locker room at the half with a 32-30 lead. They extended the lead to five 35-30 to start the second half, but Liberty scored the next seven points to take a 37-35 lead that they never relinquished. Liberty stretched the lead to 72-52 late in the final quarter before the Hurricane bench played the rest of the game.

Leading scorers: Liberty – Mitch Lukevics 20, Jack Harrington 18, Rich Wescoe 13, Mike Hartenstine 12; Phillipsburg – Dennis Staples 20, Cliff Oberley 17, John Freeman 12.

Dieruff 44 Central Catholic 42 OT: Dieruff seemed well in command with a ten-point lead with 6:46 to play in the contest. Central Catholic, using a pressing defense, forced the Huskies into numerous errors to tie the game in regulation at 42-42. The only shot taken in overtime by either team handed the victory to the Huskies when Brad Liebensperger made Dieruff's first field goal in over nine minutes.

Leading scorers: Dieruff – Mike Zambelli 13, Al Sincavage 11; Central Catholic – Tim McGorry 10.

Pottsville 70 Freedom 69: Pottsville remained undefeated in second half play despite playing sluggish basketball for three periods. After a 7-7 tie after a period, Pottsville slowly built leads the rest of the game and led at halftime 24-21. Their offense came alive in the final quarter when they outscored Freedom 29-19.

Leading scorers: Pottsville – Joel Yob 15, Jerry Evans 15, Chris Higgins 14, Dave Sydnor 11; Freedom – Curt Kemmerer 16, Jim Lees 13.[28]

Week 9

Hazleton 59 Freedom 48: Freedom took a 12-10 lead in the first quarter at Hazleton and trailed by only three 23-20 heading into the second half. Hazleton switched to a man-to-man defense in the second half. After scoring the last four points in the half to take the lead, the Mountaineers scored the first eight points of the second half and Hazleton cruised to the win,

Leading scorers: Hazleton – Charlie Liott 21, Jerry Fallabel 12, Wally Kisthardt 11; Freedom – Mike Deschler 14, Steve Bilan 11.

Dieruff 86 Tamaqua 60: Dieruff started out with an 8-0 lead on their way to a 22-8 lead after a quarter. They scored over twenty points in the next three quarters to roll to an easy win and hand Tamaqua a 33rd consecutive league loss.

Leading scorers: Dieruff – Brad Liebensperger 21, Mike Zambelli 18, Kay Finley 15, Al Sincavage 12; Tamaqua – Dennis Pastucha 21, Ed Hromyak 11, Glen Behr 10.

Liberty 72 Easton 47: Liberty took a slim one-point lead 14-13 into the second quarter and were up 23-19 when the Hurricane scored two baskets in seven seconds to extend the lead to eight points. Liberty built the lead to 40-25 at the half on their way to a rout of the Red Rovers, their first loss in the second half.

Leading scorers: Liberty – Mike Hartenstine 17, Mitch Lukevics 11, Jack Harrington 11, Gary Fejes 10; Easton – Tom Lacey 16, Dave Troxell 10.

Allen 91 Pottsville 61: Allen handed Pottsville its first loss of the second half at the Little Palestra. The Canaries took a thirteen-point lead 24-11 in the first quarter and breezed to an easy victory.

Leading scorers: Allen –Bill Frederick 29, Pat Sewards 22, Tom Donley 16; Pottsville – Chris Higgins 21, Jerry Evans 13, Ron Lombel 10.

Bethlehem Catholic 46 Phillipsburg 45 OT: In a deliberate first quarter, the teams were tied at 5-5 going into the second period. Bethlehem Catholic took a four-point lead at the half 22-18 and still led after three quarters 38-35, The Hawks tied the game 45-45 in regulation on a foul shot by Rick Cacciatore after he had missed the first shot and was awarded a second shot on a foul line violation by Phillipsburg. John Majczan made the only point in overtime on a foul shot midway through the overtime period.

Leading scorers: Bethlehem Catholic–Rick Cacciatore 19; Phillipsburg-John Freeman 14, Tom James 12, Denny Staples 11.[29]

Pottsville 59 Phillipsburg 58: Pottsville led by eleven points three times in the contest but each time Phillipsburg went on seven-point runs to cut the lead to four points, the final one at 52-48. With the Crimson Tide holding a 59-52 lead with 90 seconds to play, Phillipsburg scored the final six points and had a chance to tie the game on a foul shot by Tom James, but he missed it.

Leading scorers: Pottsville – Joel Yob 19, Chris Higgins 13; Phillipsburg – Cliff Oberley 16, Dennis Staples 13, Tom James 12.

Central Catholic 84 Tamaqua 61: Tamaqua dropped their 16th game in a winless season and their 34th straight league loss as Central Catholic took a 16-2 lead during the first quarter. Leading 69-44 after three quarters, Coach Mike Koury put his substitutes in for the entire fourth quarter.

Leading scorers: Central Catholic – Joe Pfahler 26, George Kinek 14, Tim McGorry 14; Tamaqua – Dennis Pastucha 16, Ed Hromyak 12, Harry Krapf 12.

Liberty 66 Dieruff 56: After taking a 31-28 lead at the half and extending it to 50-40 after three quarters, Coach Al Senavitis' Liberty squad handed Dieruff their first loss of the second half. Dieruff did take a 36-33 lead during the first two minutes of the third quarter, before Liberty scored five field goals to take the lead for good.

Leading scorers: Liberty–Mike Hartenstine 17, Rich Wescoe 15, Jack Harrington 12; Dieruff–Al Sincavage 19, Mike Reiter 12.

Bethlehem Catholic 56 Easton 49: Brothers Rick and Gary Cacciatore scored a combined 12 points in the first quarter to lead Bethlehem Catholic to a 17-5 lead after a quarter. Then later in the fourth quarter, they combined to freeze the ball to prevent any Easton rally as the Hawks cruised to victory.

Leading scorers: Bethlehem Catholic – Rick Cacciatore 16, Gary Cacciatore 13, Bob Halbreiner 12; Easton – Tom Lacey 15, Mike Kadjeski 13, Dave Troxell 12.

Hazleton 62 Allen 60 OT: Allen held an eight-point lead with 2:48 left to play in the game. Hazleton took the lead 54-52 on Joe Novotnak's field goal before Bill Frederick tied the game with three seconds left by converting two foul shots. Bill Frederick scored all six Allen points in overtime. With the score tied at 60-60, Wally Kisthardt rebounded a missed shot for the winning goal in the overtime period.

Leading scorers: Hazleton – Wally Kisthardt 23, Jerry Fallabel 15, Charlie Liott 11; Allen – Bill Frederick 25, Chuck Strzelecki 11.[30]

Week 10

Allen 81 Freedom 54: With the score tied 15-15 after one quarter, Allen scored 16 straight points during the second quarter to a 41-25 halftime lead over Freedom. Freedom never got any closer than 12 points during the rest of the game.

Leading scorers: Allen - Bill Frederick 16, Pat Sewards 16, Tom Donley 15; Freedom – Mike Deschler 12.

Dieruff 67 Bethlehem Catholic 52: Dieruff and Bethlehem Catholic were tied five times during the first quarter and a half. Al Sincavage broke a 23-23 tie with a field goal and the Huskies led the rest of the way. The Hawks suffered their first loss of the half and dropped into a three-way tie for first with Pottsville and Liberty at 4-1. Sincavage scored 13 points in the second quarter.

Leading scorers: Dieruff – Al Sincavage 31, Mike Hersch 12, Kay Finley 10; Bethlehem Catholic – Rick Cacciatore 12, Bob Halbreiner 11, Dennis Butler 10.

Pottsville 63 Easton 37: After one quarter, Easton held a 7-6 lead. But a minute into the second quarter, Pottsville took the lead 14-13 and led at the half 30-20. Easton could only score four points in the third and the game was a rout after that.

Leading scorers: Pottsville – Chris Higgins 24, Joel Yob 14, Ron Lombel 11; Easton – Tom Lacey 13.

Liberty 53 Central Catholic 42: Falling behind 9-1 in the first quarter, Liberty went on a 16-2 run to take the lead 17-11 after a quarter. They maintained the six-point lead at the half 31-25 and added five points to it in the third period to defeat Central Catholic and remain in a first-place tie in the second half race at 4-1.

Leading Scorers: Liberty – Mike Hartenstine 13, Gary Fejes 12, Jack Harrington 11; Central Catholic – Tim McGorry 10.[31]

Hazleton 81 Phillipsburg 61: Hazleton led early 6-0 before Phillipsburg scored the next seven points to lead 7-6. Hazleton regained the lead at the end of the quarter 14-10 and increased it every quarter the rest of the way to improve to 3-1 and move to a half game out of first place.

Leading scorers: Hazleton – Charlie Liott 17, Jerry Fallable 17, Wally Kisthardt 12; Phillipsburg – Dennis Staples 13, John Freeman 11, Cliff Oberly 10.[32]

Hazleton 71 Easton 47: Hazleton held Easton without a field goal for the first six minutes of the game and the Mountaineers took a 14-4 lead after one quarter. Hazleton continued its dominance in the second quarter by allowing the Red Rovers only nine points to hold a commanding 31-13 lead at the half. Hazleton improved to 4-1 to stay a half game behind Liberty and Bethlehem Catholic, both at 5-1.

Leading scorers: Hazleton–Wally Kisthardt 15, Jerry Fallabel 12, Charlie Liott 12, Steve Falatovich 10; Easton–Tom Lacey 25.

Liberty 96 Tamaqua 48: Tamaqua extended its league winless streak to 35 games after another rout, this time at the hands of Liberty. Coach Al Senavitis played his reserves a greater part of the game after his starters scored 32 points in the first quarter for a nineteen-point lead. Tamaqua could only put up 16 points in the middle two quarters. Liberty improved to 5-1 to share first place with Bethlehem Catholic.

Leading scorers: Liberty – Dick Packer 22, Bill Frey 15, Mike Hartenstine 11, Jack Harrington 10; Tamaqua – Dennis Pastucha 17, Harry Krapf 12.

Bethlehem Catholic 49 Central Catholic 46: Bethlehem Catholic relied on its rebounding ability of Bob Halbreiner and Casey Eddinger in its contest against the Vikings at Rockne Hall. Nine times a man broke downcourt to make an easy field goal from their outlet passes. The Viking's Joe Pfahler severely bruised his hand in the previous game and was mostly ineffective. Central catholic made only 17 of 52 field goal attempts. A strong 3rd quarter, outscoring the Hawks 14-9. kept the Vikings in the game.

Leading scorers: Bethlehem Catholic – Rick Cacciatore 15, Gary Cacciatore 12; Central Catholic – Jeff McGeehin 12, Ron Caldarelli 10, Mike Busolits 10.

Phillipsburg 55 Freedom 54: Freedom led 47-40 entering the 4th quarter and led by nine points early in the quarter 51-42. Phillipsburg closed the gap to 54-49 with four minutes left. Freedom would not score again as the Stateliners rallied with Denny Staples making a layup with three seconds left for the comeback win.

Leading scorers: Phillipsburg – Cliff Oberley 18, John Freeman 13, Doug Maczko 11; Freedom – Mike Deschler 12, Jeff Hoydu 10, Jim Lees 10.

Dieruff 48 Pottsville 47: Dieruff took the 1st quarter lead 12-5 only to have Pottsville take the halftime lead 24-21. With the Huskies outscoring Pottsville by four in the third quarter 13-9 and taking a one-point lead 34-33, this advantage proved to be the game winner as both teams scored 14 points in the final period. With the scored tied at 46, Ron Lombel put Pottsville ahead with 25 seconds to play. Brad Liebensperger pulled out the game for the Huskies with a field with 15 seconds to play. Pottsville's shot to win the game bounced off the front of the rim.

Leading scorers: Dieruff – Al Sincavage 15, Brad Liebensperger 11; Pottsville – Ron Lombel 14, Chris Higgins 11, Hal Bertsch 10.[33]

Week 11

Hazleton 66 Dieruff: Dieruff took a seven-point lead after a quarter 17-10 and held the lead through the next two quarters 36-32 and 54-49. Hazleton tied the game at 63-63 with a little over three minutes left to play on Charlie Liott's field goal. Hazleton got the ball back and went into a stall. Charlie Liott made another field goal and was fouled. He converted the shot for a 66-63 lead. Dieruff got within a point on a field goal and had the ball with 31 seconds to play with a chance to win the game, but they never got a shot off. The loss hurt the Huskies' chances, now 4-2, of a second half title with Hazleton still in the running at 5-1.

Leading scorers: Hazleton–Wally Kisthardt 21, Charlie Liott 19; Dieruff–Brad Leibensperger 34, Ken Fedor 14, Al Sincavage 10.

Allen 92 Phillipsburg 63: The second quarter proved the undoing of Phillipsburg when Allen outscored the Stateliners 26-8 to hold a 44-22 lead. The lead grew to 76-42 after three periods. Five players scored in double figures for the Canaries in the rout.

Leading scorers: Allen – Warnell Lamb 25, Pat Sewards 21, Tom Donley 15, Joe Thompson 10, Chuck Strzelecki 10; Phillipsburg – John Freeman 20, Cliff Oberley 12, Doug Maczko 12.

Pottsville 59 Central Catholic 54: The two teams exchanged leads during the first two quarters with Pottsville in front 14-12 after one and Central Catholic taking the lead at the half 25-24. With both teams scoring 12 points in the third quarter, the Vikings went into the fourth quarter leading 37-36 and held a 52-49 lead with two minutes to play. Pottsville made a field goal and converted two foul shots to take the lead 53-52. The Vikings fouled in an effort to get the ball and Pottsville made the shots to pull out the win.

Leading scorers: Pottsville – Ron Lombel 19, Chris Higgins 16, Joel Yob 14; Central Catholic – Tim McGorry 21, Mike Busolits 11.

Bethlehem Catholic 70 Tamaqua 50: In handing Tamaqua their 36th consecutive league loss, Bethlehem Catholic improved to 6-1 for a half game lead over Liberty and Hazleton for first place. The Hawks took a 40-24 lead at the half and cruised to the win.

Leading scorers: Bethlehem Catholic – Rick Cacciatore 21, Bob Halbreiner 16, Gary Cacciatore 10; Tamaqua – Charles Connelly 13, Dennis Pastucha 12, Ed Hromyak 12.

Easton 44 Freedom 40: In a low-scoring contest, Easton took a 12-9 lead into the second quarter. With both teams scoring only 18 points each in the middle two quarters, Easton added a point to the lead in the final quarter. Freedom dropped to 0-6 in the second half while the Red Rovers improved to 3-4.

Leading scorers: Easton – Tom Lacey 15, Jim Haney 12; Freedom – Ron Donchez 12, Steve Bilan 11.[34]

Allen 77 Easton 61: Allen took the lead for good after Easton took a brief 1-0 lead in the first quarter. The Canaries led 18-14 after a quarter and increased the lead through the next three quarters to improve to 5-2. Tom Donley held the Red Rover's high-scoring Tom Lacey to five points through the first three quarters.

Leading scorers: Allen – Pat Sewards 25, Bill Frederick 15, Chuck Strzelecki 11, Tom Donley 11; Easton – Tom Lacey 15, Mark Betts 13, Jim Haney 12.

Dieruff 64 Freedom 37: After playing to a 13-13 tie in the first quarter, Dieruff held Freedom to six points in the second quarter and again in the fourth quarter in a rout of the Patriots. Coach Charlie Dubbs' team remained winless in the second half while the Huskies improved to 5-2.

Leading scorers: Dieruff – Al Sincavage 20, Brad Leibensperger 13; Freedom – Carl Pietrouchie 12.

Pottsville 72 Tamaqua 55: Despite 27 points from Dennis Pastucha, Tamaqua dropped its 19th game of the season and 37th in a row in the league. After a slim two-point lead 14-12, Pottsville extended the lead to 12 points at the half to improve to 6-2 in the second half.

Leading scorers: Pottsville – Chris Higgins 19, Joel Yob 16; Tamaqua – Dennis Pastucha 27.

Liberty 66 Bethlehem Catholic 58: In a battle for a share of first place, Bethlehem took an early 7-4 lead only to see Freedom score seven points in a row and then take a 17-13 lead after a quarter. The Hurricane kept adding to the lead the rest of the game. The Hawks got within four points 34-30 early in the third quarter, but Liberty went on an 8-1 spurt to pull away for the win.

Leading scorers: Liberty – Mike Hartenstine 15, Mitch Lukevics 14, Rich Wescoe 13; Bethlehem Catholic – Bob Halbreiner 21, Rick Cacciatore 12, Casey Eddinger 10.

Hazleton 71 Central Catholic 56: Hazleton held onto its share of first place, along with Liberty, as the Hurricane led the whole game. After the Mountaineers took a 48-38 lead in the third quarter, they added four to the lead and the Vikings never got any closer than ten points after that.

Leading scorers: Hazleton – Jerry Fallable 22, Wally Kisthardt 18, Jim Munley 12, Charlie Liott 10; Central Catholic – Mike Busolits 14, Joe Pfahler 14, Tim McGorry 10.[35]

Week 12

Freedom 68 Central Catholic 57: Freedom surprised Central Catholic to pick up its first win of the second half. In a game that changed the lead fifteen times including the start of the fourth period 48-48, the Patriots scored six straight points to start the final period and pulled away for the win. The Vikings dropped to 1-7 in the second half.

Leading scorers: Freedom – Bill Werpehowski 17; Central Catholic – Mike Busolits 18, George Kinek 16.

Allen 59 Dieruff 57: Despite not registering a field goal in the final 6 ½ minutes, Dieruff built a ten-point lead 54-44 in the final quarter. With Dieruff making a couple of more free throws, Allen was able to rally and tie the game 57-57 with 1:30 to play. Bill Frederick made two free throws with four seconds to play to pull out the big comeback.

Leading scorers: Allen – Pat Sewards 23; Dieruff – Al Sincavage 16, Ken Fedor 16.

Phillipsburg 58 Easton 57 OT: Easton took a 9-8 first quarter lead only to fall behind by six at the half 26-20 and seven after three quarters 41-34. Easton rallied to take a 52-51 lead, but John Freeman hit a foul shot to tie the game in regulation. With five seconds left in overtime, Tom James hit a short jumper to win the game for the Stateliners.

Leading scorers: Phillipsburg – Tom James 19, Dennis Staples 17; Easton – Tom Lacey 23, Kadjeski 12.

Liberty 65 Pottsville 56: Pottsville and Liberty battled to an 11-11 tie after a quarter. Joel Yob put Pottsville up 13-11 to begin the second quarter, but Liberty ran off the next nine points and led the rest of the way. After Liberty extended the lead to 61-46 in the final period, Pottsville scored ten in a row to get within five, but Liberty scored two fast break baskets to put the game away.

Leading scorers: Liberty – Jack Harrington 21, Gary Fejes 15, Mitch Lukevics 11; Pottsville – Chris Higgins 15, Ron Lombel 10, Joel Yob 10.

Hazleton 105 Tamaqua 65: Hazleton poured in sixty-five points in the middle two periods to rout Tamaqua. Hazleton Coach Dave Shafer emptied his bench midway in the third quarter. Tamaqua lost its 41st consecutive game overall and 38th in league play.

Leading scorers: Hazleton - Jerry Fallabel 21, Tom Cerasaro 19, Jim Munley 16, Jim Cipriano 14; Tamaqua – Harry Krapf 13, Ed Hromyak 10.[36]

Dieruff 64 Phillipsburg 46: Leading 31-29 at halftime, Dieruff fell behind Phillipsburg 35-34 early in the 3rd period. Dieruff scored the next 13 points with Al Sincavage scoring seven of them on the way to a Huskie 46-36 lead after three quarters. Dieruff added 8 points to the lead in the 4th quarter to improve to 6-3.

Leading scorers: Dieruff – Al Sincavage 21, Brad Leibensperger 20, Ken Fedor 10; Phillipsburg – Dennis Staples 21.

Allen 62 Central Catholic 56: Allen led in each of the first three periods 20-10, 30-24, and 45-35. They extended the lead to 56-42 with the game well in-hand when the Vikings ran off seven points to pull within striking distance of the Canaries. Allen countered with two free throws and a field goal to thwart the Viking rally. Allen improved to 7-2 while the Vikings fell to 1-8.

Leading scorers: Allen - Pat Sewards 20, Tom Donley 11; Central Catholic - Tim McGorry 14, Mike Busolits 10.

Pottsville 62 Bethlehem Catholic 55: Bethlehem Catholic took a 9-3 lead in the first quarter, but Pottsville scored the last nine points to take a 12-9 lead. The Hawks took a point off the lead in each of the next two periods and trailed 42-41 going into the fourth quarter. Pottsville made two early baskets in the fourth quarter to build a five-point lead and take the game.

Leading scorers: Pottsville – Joel Yob 20, Ron Lombel 12, Chris Higgins 11; Bethlehem Catholic – Bob Halbreiner 15, Rick Cacciatore 14, Casey Eddinger 13.

Freedom 68 Tamaqua 59: Freedom took a slim one-point lead 15-14 and increased it to nine at the half 38-29. Tamaqua fought back in the third quarter but could not overcome the second quarter deficit and experienced its 39th straight league loss.

Leading Scorers: Freedom – Carl Pietrouchie 25; Tamaqua – Dennis Pastucha 23, Ed Hromyak 17.

Hazleton 64 Liberty 58: In the battle for the sole possession of first place, neither team was able to take a commanding lead. Hazleton led 12-10 after a period and by one at halftime 26-25. Hazleton's six-point dominance 15-9 proved to be the difference in the game and gave Hazleton sole possession of the second half lead.

Leading scorers: Hazleton – Wally Kisthardt 24, Jerry Fallabel 15; Liberty – Mike Hartenstine 16, Rich Wescoe 13, Mitch Lukevics 10.[37]

Week 13

Allen 139 Tamaqua 72: Pat Sewards and his teammates set league scoring records in a romp over winless Tamaqua. Sewards scored 62 points in 2 ½ quarters to break Liberty's Don Rodenbach's record of 52. The 139 points broke Liberty's previous high of 124 in 1955. The 211 total points set a new record. The Canaries led by 67-29 at the half and 108-48 after three quarters. Tamaqua's lost its 40th straight in league play.

Leading scorers: Allen – Pat Sewards 62, Warnell Lamb18, Bill Frederick 14, Joe Thompson 13; Tamaqua – Dennis Pastucha 28, Glenn Behr 10, Tom Yelito 10.

Dieruff 70 Easton 55: With the score tied 6-6, Dieruff took the lead and never trailed the rest of the way. They led 13-8 after one quarter and 30-17 at the half. The Huskies held the red Rovers for nearly five minutes from late in the first quarter and into the second quarter.

Leading scorers: Dieruff – Al Sincavage 23, Ken Fedor 13, Mike Hersch 12, Kay Finley 10; Easton – Tom Lacey 16, Jim Haney 14.

Central Catholic 86 Phillipsburg 74: Central Catholic won only its second game of the second half after dominating the Stateliners in three of the four quarters. The Vikings took a 29-20 lead only to have Phillipsburg come back to take the lead at the half 47-43. They outscored Phillipsburg 43-27 to pull away.

Leading scorers: Central Catholic – Joe Pfahler 29, Tim McGorry 26; Phillipsburg – Dennis Staples 19, Cliff Oberley 16, Tom James 15, Doug Maczko 15.

Liberty 77 Freedom 72: In a close contest, Liberty led 16-15 and 35-30 after the first two quarters. Entering the 4th quarter, Liberty led 57-51, only to have the Patriots get to within a point twice late in the game 71-70 and 73-72. Mike Hartenstine grabbed a missed free throw for a field goal and Liberty added two free throws.

Leading scorers: Liberty – Mitch Lukevics 21, Rich Wescoe 16, Hack Harrington 13; Freedom – Carl Pietrouchie 19, Mike Deschler 13.

Hazleton 66 Bethlehem Catholic 55: Hazleton clinched the second half title with a 9-1 record but not without a struggle against Bethlehem Catholic. The Hawks jumped out to a 17-8 first quarter lead with Hazleton taking a 31-30 lead into the locker room. Bethlehem Catholic kept it close through three quarters 44-42. Led by Jerry Fallabel, who broke his nose and missed some of the game early, Hazleton outscored the Hawks 13-2 in a six-minute stretch of the final quarter to take the second half title.

Leading scorers: Hazleton – Jerry Fallable 25, Charlie Liott 17, Wally Kisthardt 16; Bethlehem Catholic – Casey Eddinger 19, Rick Cacciatore 16.[38]

League Playoff

Hazleton 74 Allen 63: In Pottsville's new gymnasium, Allen took early 11-1 and 14-4 leads on their way to a 16-12 first quarter lead. The Canaries turned the ball over seven times in the second period as Hazleton took charge of the game with a 17-point advantage in the period. They increased their 39-26 lead at the half to 55-37 entering the fourth quarter.

Leading scorers: Hazleton – Tom Cerasaro 20, Charlie Liott 17, Steve Falatovich 13, Wally Kisthardt 10; Allen – Bill Frederick 20, Pat Sewards 12, Warnell Lamb 10.[39]

Postseason PIAA Play

Both Hazleton and Allen qualified for post season play.

Palmerton 74 Allen 62: After Allen took a 20-12 first quarter lead, the rest of the contest was all Palmerton. Palmerton took the lead at halftime with a 25-point outburst in the second quarter. Allen was never in the game after that and four Canaries fouled out in the final quarter.

Palmerton: Glenn Levandusky 31, Randy Stubits 12, Reggie Hernandez 11, Rick Costenbader 10; Allen – Bill Frederick 22, Warnell Lamb 17, Pat Sewards 11.[40]

Hazleton 69 North Schuylkill 45: At Pottsville, Hazleton got 14 players into the game with 12 of them scoring in an easy win in its District XI quarterfinal match. Hazleton led 38-15 at the half and 56-27 after three quarters.

Leading scorers: Hazleton – Wally Kisthardt 14, Jerry Fallable 11, Jim Munley 10; North Schuylkill – Jim Roadermel 10.[41]

Hazleton 57 West Hazleton 55: At Pottsville, Hazleton led the game five times by five points and West Hazleton led by no more than two points during the game. The score was tied at 11 after a period with Hazleton taking the lead at the half 29-28. The game was tied again going into the last quarter at 42-42. With four minutes to play, it was tied again at 47. A field goal and a technical gave Hazleton a 50-47 lead. After a West Hazleton field goal, Jerry Fallabel was fouled and West Hazleton's Ron Bason punched Tom Cerasaro.

A two-shot technical was awarded to Hazleton. Hazleton made 2 of the four foul shots to lead 52-49. Later, with the score tied at 55-55, Hazleton's Wally Kisthardt intercepted a West Hazleton pass. He was fouled and another player jumped on him. Both benches emptied and a scuffle ensued. Hazleton converted fouls shots to pull out the game.

Leading scorers: Hazleton – Tom Cerasaro 15, Jim Munley 13, Jerry Fallabel 10; West Hazleton – Brian Minnig 14, Kluck 10.[42]

Hazleton 65 Northampton 60: Northampton built a nine-point lead in the first half and led at half time 33-27. Hazleton took a seven-point lead in the third quarter 46-39 only to have Northampton roar back to tie the game at 46-46 early in the final quarter. The lead changed hands several times with Northampton holding its last lead at 54-53. Hazleton took command from that point on to win the District 11 A title.

Leading scorers: Hazleton – Jerry Fallable 27, Wally Kisthardt 13, Tom Cerasaro 11; Northampton – Ed Groller 22, Greg Vogel 15.[43]

Norristown 54 Hazleton 49: Hazleton surprised Norristown by taking the first quarter lead 17-14. They had the lead 25-22 near the end of the first half before Norristown scored six straight points for a 28-25 lead at the half. With a little less than five minutes left in the third quarter, Hazleton still led 32-30, but Norristown came on to take the lead and never gave it up.

Leading scorers: Norristown – Henry Williams 23, Wayne Butler 14; Hazleton – Jerry Fallabel 15, Wally Kisthardt 13, Charlie Liott 11.[44]

PCIAA Postseason Playoff

Central Catholic 70 Bethlehem Catholic 52: Bethlehem Catholic led at the end of the first half 32-30 after the score had been tied after a quarter 15-15. In the third quarter, the Vikings rallied to take a two-point lead 42-20. In the final quarter, Coach Mike Koury employed a pressing defense which led the Vikings to victory.

Leading scorers: Central Catholic – Mike Busolits 20, Tim McGorry 15, George Kinek 13; Bethlehem Catholic – Bob Halbreiner 15, Casey Eddinger 12, Dennis Butler 10.[45]

Central Catholic 51 Bishop McDevitt 45: Central Catholic held slim leads after each of the first two quarters 13-12 and 27-24 before holding Bishop McDevitt to five points in the third quarter. With a 38-29 lead heading into the fourth quarter, the Vikings held off Bishop McDevitt to advance to the state final.

Leading scorers: Central Catholic – Tim McGorry 23, Mike Busolits 18; Bishop McDevitt – Bob Sebastian 22, Charlie O'Donnell 11, Tony Abate 10.[46]

Erie Cathedral 65 Central Catholic 64: At St. Vincent's College in Latrobe, Erie Cathedral took a nine-point first quarter lead 22-13, but Central Catholic cut the lead to five 39-34 at the half. In the third quarter, the Vikings continued their comeback and went into the final period behind by two points 50-48. In the fourth quarter, they came all the way back to take a 64-63 lead with 41 seconds to play. Erie's John Reynders rebounded a missed shot with seconds to play and finished with a layup to win the game.

Leading scorers: Erie Cathedral – Will Cardot 22, Joe Cook 14, Don Bukowski 14; Central Catholic – George Kinek 21, Mike Busolits 18, Joe Pfahler 16.[47]

Postseason Accolades

Leading scorers: Pat Sewards, Allen, led the league with 412 points and 21 ppg, the rest of the top ten included: Tom Lacey, Easton, 358 points; Dennis Pastucha, Tamaqua, 342 points; Jerry Fallabel, Hazleton, 327 points; Al Sincavage, Dieruff 320 points; Bill Frederick, Allen, and Joe Pfahler, Central Catholic, 284 points; Tim McGorry, Central Catholic, and Dennis Staples Phillipsburg, 268 points; Chris Higgins, Pottsville, 263 points.[48]

All-Stars: The league all-star first team included: Pat Sewards, Allen (MVP); Jerry Fallabel and Wally Kisthardt, Hazleton; Bill Frederick, Allen; and Al Sincavage, Dieruff. The second team included: Bob Halbreiner, Bethlehem Catholic; Brad Leibensperger, Dieruff; Charlie Liott, Hazleton; Mike Hartenstine, Liberty; Joe Pfahlerm Central Catholic; and Dennis Pastucha, Tamaqua.[49]

All-State: The league only had one player named to the all-state teams. Wally Kisthardt, Hazleton, was named to the third team. The following players received honorable mention status: Jerry Fallabel, Hazleton; Bob Halbreiner, Bethlehem Catholic; and Bill Frederick, Allen.[49]

Final Standings

First Half		Second Half		Overall	
Allen	9-1	Hazleton	9-1	Allen	17-3
Dieruff	9-1	Allen	8-2	Hazleton	17-3
Hazleton	8-2	Liberty	8-2	Dieruff	16-4
Liberty	7-3	Pottsville	7-3	Liberty	15-5
Central Catholic	7-3	Dieruff	7-3	Pottsville	11-9
Pottsville	4-6	Bethlehem Catholic	6-4	Bethlehem Catholic	9-11
Freedom	3-7	Phillipsburg	3-7	Central Catholic	9-11
Bethlehem Catholic	3-7	Easton	3-7	Easton	6-14
Easton	3-7	Central Catholic	2-8	Freedom	5-15
Phillipsburg	2-8	Freedom	2-8	Phillipsburg	5-15
Tamaqua	0-10	Tamaqua	0-10	Tamaqua	0-20

Team Rosters

Allen: Coach Milo Sewards, Tom Donley, Jim Emery, Bill Frederick, Bob Handschue, Warnell Lamb, Steve Miller, Pat Sewards, Charles Strzelecki, Joe Thompson

Bethlehem Catholic: Coach Bob Bukvics, Greg Adams, Becker, Dennis Butler, Gary Cacciatore, Rick Cacciatore, Tom Chladny, Tom "Casey" Eddinger, Griffin, Bob Halbreiner, Mike Harvilla, John Majczan, Steirer

Central Catholic: Coach Mike Koury, Mike Busolits, Ron Caldarelli, Tom Gallagher, George Kinek, Jeff McGeehin, Tim McGorry, R Miller, Bob Muthard, Joe Pfahler, Jerry Schleder, Bob Stano, Roger Worman, Mike Yannes

Dieruff: Coach Dick Schmidt, Frank Brucker, Ken Fedor, Kay "Bo" Finley, Joe Groller, Mike Hersch, Doug Kistler, Brad Leibensperger, Rick Miller, Mike Reiter, Al Sincavage, Hamp Smith, Gene Sweeney, Mike Zambelli

Easton: Coach Stan Sutphen, Tom Attinello, Mark Betts, Farina, Hank Godown, Jim Haney, Jim Hutnik, Mike Kadjeski, Brian Kelly, Tom Lacey, Kerry Myers, Dana Parr, Sino, Dave Troxell

Freedom: Coach Charlie Dubbs, Steve Bilan, Mike Deschler, Ron Donchez, Jeff Hoydu, Kemmerer, Jim Lees, Tom Panik, Peters, Carl Pietrouchic, Pete Pozefsky, Phil Subits, Bill Werpehowski

Hazleton: Coach Dave Shafer, Tom Cerasaro, Jim Chapman, Jim Cipriano, Steve Falatovich, Jerry Fallabel, Joe Gavio, Wally Kisthardt, Charlie Liott, Manfred Marotta, Joe Mingo, Jim Munley, Joe Novatnack, Jerry Provizzi, Jack Temchatin

Liberty: Coach Al Senavitis, Dave DiGiacinto, Gary Fejes, Bill Frey, Jack Harrington, Mike Hartenstine, Mitch Lukevics, John Majczan, Frank Olshefski, Dick Packer, Jose Perna, John Priestas, Kevin Wescoe, Rich Wescoe

Phillipsburg: Coach Pete Tomaino, Mark Bennett, Mike Fichera, John Freeman, Tom James, Mike Kline, Doug Maczko, Cliff Oberley, Dennis Staples, Jim Ziegenfuss

Pottsville: Coach Ken Kline, Ken Bailey, Jim Berrang, Hal Bertsch, B Brown, Jerry Evans, Chris Higgins, Robert Liddle Ken Kline, R Liddle, Ron Lombel, Pete Marchetti, J McNulty, Leo Ostrosky, Al "Chip" Raczka, Dave Sydnor, Joel Yob

Tamaqua: Coach Nick Young, Glen Behr, Bohannon, Charles Connelly, Lew Erbe, Ed Gernavage, Ed Hromyak, Harry Krapf, Bill Milot, Dennis Patucha, Mark Truskey, Tom Yelito

1972

Tamaqua Drops Out Again

At its spring meeting at the close of the 1971 season, the East Penn League elected a new president and vice president. Bethlehem Liberty's Phil Phillippi, who served for over 30 years, retired in June 1971 after serving as Liberty's athletic director after 41 years in the position. John Maitland, Easton's athletic director, succeeded Phillippi. Reverend Francis Zavodny, from Central Catholic, also stepped down as vice president and was succeeded by Larry Haberle from Pottsville. Allen's athletic director Bob Stimmel was re-elected as secretary treasurer of the league. Tamaqua dropped out of the league and joined the Tri-County League, reducing league membership back to ten teams.[1].

First Half - Week 1

Central Catholic 55 Freedom 53: Central Catholic took a 19-12 first quarter lead and extended it to 13 points in the second quarter 27-14. Freedom rallied later in the quarter to trail by only two at the half 33-31. Going into the final quarter, the Vikings held a four-point lead 44-40, but Freedom came back to tie the game at 49-49 with less than five minutes to play. After two Viking field goals, Freedom added a field goal to reduce Central Catholic's lead to two again 53-51. A Joe Pfahler-steal and layup by Mark Trinkle produced the winning bucket as the Vikings won a hard-fought contest.

Leading scorers: Central Catholic – Joe Pfahler 25, Jeff McGeehin 12, Mike Busolits 10; Freedom – Phil Subits 20, Phil Sedlock 13.

Liberty 77 Allen 64: Allen led after a quarter 16-10 and at the half 37-32, but Liberty came out after halftime to take a five-point lead before Allen came back to trail by only a single point after three quarters 53-52. With five minutes left in the game, Liberty put on a 16-2 spurt including ten in a row to take a commanding lead with a minute left to play.

Leading scorers: Liberty – Rich Wescoe 22, Jose Perna 18, Steve Farkus 15, Dick Packer 12; Allen – Joe Thompson 22, Doug Snyder 14, Jeff Kreindel 11.

Dieruff 57 Bethlehem Catholic 53: After taking a 20-10 lead into the 2nd quarter, Dieruff maintained at lead at the half 33-25. They expanded by scoring the first 5 points in the 3rd quarter for a seemingly safe 13-point lead 38-25. With Doug Kistler on the bench with four fouls with five minutes to play in the 3rd quarter, the Hawks rallied to get within a point 41-40. Dieruff held off the Hawks to pick up the win with the return of Kistler in the final quarter.

Leading scorers: Dieruff – Doug Kistler 20, Jim Mates 18; Bethlehem Catholic – Rick Cacciatore 19, Mike Godboldt 15.

Hazleton 54 Pottsville 51: The teams battled to a 23-23 tie at the half after Pottsville had held a four-point lead 23-19 late in the second quarter. Hazleton took a two-point lead into the final quarter 37-35 and led by five 46-41 late in the quarter. Pottsville fought back to within one 50-49 before the Mountaineers made a field goal and two foul shots for the win.

Leading scorers: Hazleton - Joe Novatnack 20, Jack Temchatin 17; Pottsville - Chris Higgins 24, Hal Bertsch 15.

Easton 50 Phillipsburg 39: Holding Phillipsburg to only four points in the second period, Easton went into the half with a 21-14 lead. The Stateliners reduced the lead to four points 29-25 heading into the 4th quarter. Easton scored the first 5 points in the final period to go ahead 35-25, but Phillipsburg quickly cut the lead to three 39-36 with a little over three minutes to play. The Red Rovers scored the next seven points to hold on to the win.

Leading scorers: Easton – Jim Hutnik 13, Dave Troxell 12; Phillipsburg – Dennis Staples 16, John Freeman 12.[2]

Week 2

Allen 89 Bethlehem Catholic 57: Despite turning over the ball ten times in the first period, Allen still took a 21-4 lead. They extended the lead to 37-7 in the second quarter and led at the half 48-18. Coach Bob Bukvic's Hawks committed 28 turnovers in the game and top scorer Rick Cacciatore, who was averaging 20 points a game, could only score two points all night.

Leading scorers: Allen – Joe Thompson 24, Doug Snyder 20, Gene Saverese 10; Bethlehem Catholic – Bob Gallagher 11, Greg Adams 11.

Central Catholic 64 Pottsville 53: Central Catholic made nine foul shots in a row in the first quarter, and 22 of 24 overall, to take a 19-6 first quarter lead. Pottsville outscored the Vikings 31-29 in the second half but could not overcome Central Catholic's first quarter advantage.

Leading scorers: Central Catholic – Mike Busolits 19, Joe Pfahler 18. Tom Gallagher 10; Pottsville - Hal Bertsch 17, Al Holtzer 14, Dennis Ebling 12.

Easton 65 Dieruff 50: Easton held a ten-point lead after the first quarter after converting 9 of its first 10 field goal attempts. When Easton did not score a field goal for over 4 ½ minutes in the second quarter, the Huskies took the lead 27-26 before the Red Rovers took a 31-28 lead at halftime. Dieruff held its only other lead of the night in the third quarter 39-38, but Easton countered to take the lead 41-39 after three quarters and scored 24 points in the final quarter for the win and a 2-0 start in the league.

Leading scorers: Easton – Dave Joseph 22, Jim Hutnik 15, Dave Troxell 12; Dieruff - Mike Hersch 12, Mike Zambelli 11, Doug Kistler 10.[3]

Liberty 66 Phillipsburg 61: Liberty held a 17-6 lead after a quarter and 39-20 at halftime. They increased the lead to 20 points 53-33 going into the fourth quarter. Phillipsburg scored 28 points in the final quarter and pulled within four points 64-60 with 20 seconds to play. Barry Frey made two free throws with ten seconds left to wrap up the game for Liberty.

Leading scorers: Liberty – Dick Packer 18, Barry Frey 14, Steve Farkus 13; Phillipsburg – John Freeman 19, Dennis Staples 13, Mark Bennett 12.

Freedom 57 Hazleton 55: Hazleton lead throughout the 1st half and until the final shot of the third quarter when Phil Sedlock put the Patriots ahead 41-40. The Mountaineers moved ahead by five points 53-48 with a little over two minutes to play. Freedom went ahead with 30 seconds to play to hand Hazleton the loss.

Leading scorers: Freedom – Gary Kesack 21; Hazleton – Joe Novatnack 22, Ron Portanova 10.[4]

Central Catholic 64 Hazleton 62: At Hazleton, Central Catholic ended the first quarter with an eleven-point lead 21-10 and extended it to 13 in the second quarter. By the end of the second quarter, the Mountaineers had cut the lead to six 33-27. Hazleton took another point off the lead in the third quarter 45-40. With a little over two minutes left in the game, the Vikings were down to a one-point lead 55-54. Mike Busolits then scored the next seven points to put an end to Hazleton's upset hopes.

Leading scorers: Central Catholic – Joe Pfahler 18, Mike Busolits 18, Tom Gallagher 14; Hazleton – Joe Gavio 15, Ron Portanova 11 Jack Temchatin 10.

Liberty 58 Bethlehem Catholic 47: Bethlehem Catholic owned the first half taking leads of 17-11 and 30-19 in the first two quarters. In the second half, Liberty came roaring back led by John McCaffery, who Coach

Al Senavitis recruited in the school's hallway and had never played basketball. From late in the third quarter and through the fourth quarter, McCaffery scored eight points, grabbed six rebounds, and blocked three shots as Liberty outscored the Hawks 39-17 to win the game.

Leading scorers: Liberty – Rich Wescoe 16, Jose Perna 12, Dick Packer 11; Bethlehem Catholic – Rick Cacciatore 17, Mike Harvilla 11.

Freedom 62 Dieruff 54: Dieruff took an 11-10 lead after one quarter and remained in the lead until Gary Kesack put the Patriots into the lead with a field goal with 2:22 left in the second quarter. The Patriots led from that point on despite never taking a commanding lead.

Leading scorers: Freedom – Phil Sedlock 11, Curt Kemmerer 11, Phil Subits 11, Ron Donchez 10, Gary Kesack 10; Dieruff – Tom Stellar 13, Jim Mates 11, Mike Hersch 10.

Allen 104 Phillipsburg 63: Allen took a 27-12 lead into the 2nd quarter with Phillipsburg trimming it to ten points at the half 45-35, After the Stateliners scored the first 4 points in the 3rd quarter, Allen went on a 17-2 tear to take a commanding lead. The Canaries poured it on in the final quarter scoring 35 points to turn the game into a rout.

Leading scorers: Allen – Joe Thompson 29, Jeff Kreindel 26, Doug Snyder 21; Phillipsburg – John Freeman 17, Mark Bennet 15, Mike Fichera 10.

Easton 44 Pottsville 39: Playing at home, Pottsville led after each of the first three quarters 11-6, 23-16, and 33-28. Easton charged back behind Dave Troxell to take the lead for the first time at 39-38 with 57 seconds to play in the game. Troxell scored 14 of Easton's 16 points in the fourth quarter. Easton improved to 3-0 while Pottsville dropped to 0-3 in league action.

Leading scorers: Easton – Dave Troxell 27; Pottsville - Hal Bertsch 18.[5]

Week 3

Dieruff 61 Liberty 44: Liberty lost its share of first place with a loss to Dieruff in the East Side gym. After taking the lead late in the first quarter, Dieruff held the lead the rest of the contest. The Huskies used only six players and added to the lead after each quarter. Liberty's Jose Perna had three fouls in the first quarter and sat the rest of half which greatly impacted their offense.

Leading scorers: Dieruff – Jim Mates 20, Doug Kistler 14, Mike Zambelli 12; Liberty – Jose Perna 12, Dick Packer 11.

Allen 84 Hazleton 76: At the Little Palestra, Hazleton held a 13-point lead one minute into the second quarter 33-20. Allen finally took the lead with a little less than three minutes to play in the third quarter. Going into the fourth quarter, the teams were tied at 60-60. Allen took the lead 75-70, but Hazleton came back to move in front 76-75. The Mountaineers would not score again as Allen scored the last nine points of the game for the win.

Leading scorers: Allen – Joe Thompson 28, Doug Snyder 17, Jeff Kreindel 16; Hazleton – Jerry Provizzi 24, Ron Portanova 14, Jack Temchatin 13, Joe Gavio 10.

Central Catholic 73 Phillipsburg 51: Central Catholic took a commanding 17-4 lead after a quarter and cruised to victory the rest of the way. All eleven players used by Mike Koury scored as the Vikings were able to increase the lead in each of the quarters. Central Catholic held high-scoring John Freeman to a single point in the game. The win kept the Vikings in a share of first place at 4-0 with Easton.

Leading scorers: Central Catholic – Joe Pfahler 17, Tom Gallagher 12; Phillipsburg – Dennis Staples 12.

Freedom 49 Pottsville 47: Freedom did not score its first field goal until the last minute of the 1st quarter and trailed at the end of the quarter 13-7. Despite 10 turnovers in the first half, Freedom's defense held

Pottsville to only 20 points in the first half and the Patriots rebounded in the 2nd quarter to tie the game at 20-20 at the half. Freedom took a five-point lead into the 4th quarter 35-30. With a minute and a half to play, Pottsville trailed by two points 45-43, but Freedom's Ron Donchez sank a field goal with 30 seconds to play to pull out the victory

Leading scorers: Freedom – Phil Subits 11; Pottsville – Hal Bertsch 12.

Easton 48 Bethlehem Catholic 39: Easton remained undefeated in league play and tied for first place with Central Catholic with its win over Bethlehem Catholic. After Easton took a 17-10 lead after one quarter, the Hawks came back to tie the game at 28-28. The Red Rovers took the half time lead 28-24 and then held the Hawks to a single field goal over 12 ½ minutes during the second half.

Leading scorers: Easton – Dave Troxell 14, Dave Joseph 12; Bethlehem Catholic – Rick Cacciatore 14, Mike Harvilla 13.[6]

Dieruff 55 Hazleton 44: After Hazleton held a four-point lead in the first quarter, Dieruff ran off six in a row and the first quarter ended in an 11-11 tie. Dieruff led 18-13 in the second quarter, but the Mountaineers clawed back to trail by a point at the half 21-20. With Mike Zambelli scoring 12 points in the third quarter, the Huskies outscored Hazleton 18-7 to take charge of the contest.

Leading scorers: Dieruff - Mike Zambelli 21, Doug Kistler 10; Hazleton – Jack Temchatin 15.

Liberty 58 Freedom 46: With a minute left in the first half, Freedom led by seven points only to have Liberty go on a 20-6 run in the next ten minutes to take their own seven-point lead. The rally continued through the final quarter as Liberty improved to 4-1.

Leading scorers: Liberty – Dick Packer 20, Rich Wescoe 16, Steve Farkus 10; Freedom – Phil Sedlock 17.

Central Catholic 74 Easton 52: In a battle of the two remaining unbeaten teams, Easton and Central Catholic battled to a 12-12 tie after the first quarter. The Vikings employed a full court press part way through the second quarter and charged into the lead 35-20 before settling for a 35-23 half time lead. The Vikings added on to the lead in the third and fourth quarters to take sole possession of first place at 5-0

Leading scorers: Central Catholic-Mike Busolits 23, Joe Pfahler 20, Jeff McGeehin 14; Easton-Dave Troxell 13, Jim Hutnik 12.

Bethlehem Catholic 57 Phillipsburg 42: Bethlehem Catholic picked up its first win of the first half and kept Phillipsburg winless. The Hawks held the Stateliners to six points in each of the first two quarters while scoring 28 to take charge of the game early. The teams played even throughout the second half with Phillipsburg outscoring the Hawks 30-29, but the first half lead doomed Phillipsburg.

Leading scorers: Bethlehem Catholic- Mike Godbolt 20, Rick Cacciatore 15; Phillipsburg- John Freeman 19.

Allen 60 Pottsville 55: Allen took a 12-10 first quarter lead and built it up to ten points 24-14 before Pottsville countered with seven straight points to cut the lead to 26-23 at the half. Pottsville came out after halftime and took the lead 27-26 and held it until Joe Thompson put the Canaries in front 32-31. The lead changed hands several times and Pottsville then took a 45-40 lead before Allen made a field goal to end the quarter. A seven-point run midway through the final period pulled out the win for the Canaries.

Leading scorers: Allen – Joe Thompson 23, Bill Ent 11; Pottsville – Chris Higgins 21, Hal Bertsch 14.[7]

Week 4

Hazleton 81 Bethlehem Catholic 73: At Hazleton, Bethlehem Catholic took early 11-6 and 15-10 leads before Hazleton cut the lead to 17-15 at the end of the first quarter. Hazleton took the lead in the second quarter and held leads of 36-33 and 55-44 at the ends of the second and third quarters. The Mountaineers increased the lead to 64-52 midway through the fourth quarter only to have the Hawks score the next eleven points to come within a point 64-53. Hazleton beat back the Hawks rally by scoring the next seven points to take the victory.

Leading scorers: Hazleton – Jack Temchatin 22, Joe Novatnack 20, Ron Portanova 14, Jerry Provizzi 13; Bethlehem Catholic – Rick Cacciatore 32, Mike Godbolt 14.

Liberty 54 Easton 52: After four straight wins to open league play, Easton lost its second straight contest in a nail-biter with Liberty. Liberty led going into the final quarter 44-41, but Easton tied the game at 44. The contest was tied three more times at 46, 48, and 50 when Liberty decided to freeze the ball with 2 ½ minutes left to play. Liberty went ahead by two at 49 seconds, but Easton countered to tie the game eight seconds later at 52. Liberty held the ball for the final shot with seven seconds left with Rick Cacciatore hitting a field goal for the win.

Leading scorers: Liberty – Rich Wescoe 13, Steve Farkus 13; Easton – Dave Troxell 11, Mike Young 10.

Pottsville 76 Phillipsburg 56: Pottsville held a slim one-point lead at the half 32-31 and Phillipsburg was still within striking distance with a little more than a minute to play in the 3rd quarter 44-40. In the next three minutes, Pottsville scored 13 straight points to take a commanding 57-40 lead two minutes into the 4th quarter.

Leading scorers: Pottsville - Chris Higgins 21, Hal Bertsch 17, Al Holtzer 14, Dave Snyder 13; Phillipsburg - John Freeman 15, Dennis Staples 12.

Freedom 76 Allen 65: Freedom started the contest by taking a 20-8 lead after the first quarter. Allen countered to cut the lead to 39-32 at the half and 55-53 after three quarters. Allen pulled within two points again 61-59 on a Doug Snyder three-point play with about 5 ½ minutes to play. The Patriots rallied to take a 75-63 lead and put the game out-of-reach for the Canaries.

Leading scorers: Freedom – Ron Donchez 26, Gary Kesack 18, Tom Panik 13, Phil Sedlock 12; Allen – Joe Thompson 20, Jeff Kreindel 12, Bob Frederick 10.

Central Catholic 57 Dieruff 49: Central Catholic improved to 6-0 after taking a 28-21 lead at the half and then fighting off a Dieruff rally which put the Huskies briefly in the lead 44-43 with 4 ½ minutes left in the contest. The Vikings countered with a 10-2 run to secure the victory,

Leading scorers: Central Catholic – Tom Gallagher 18, Jeff McGeehin 16; Dieruff – Doug Kistler 18, Mike Zambelli 11.[8]

Central Catholic 83 Allen 75: Central Catholic charged out to a ten-point lead in the second quarter and settled for a 36-32 lead at the half. Allen came back to take a seven-point lead in the second half. The Vikings tied the score at 64 with 4 ½ minutes to play. In the next two minutes, Central Catholic scored eleven points in a row to hand the Canaries the loss. Joe Pfahler made only four of 16 field attempts, but he made 20 of 26 free throws.

Leading scorers: Central Catholic – Joe Pfahler 28, Mike Busolits 25, Jeff McGeehin 14, Tom Gallagher 10; Allen – Doug Snyder 30, Joe Thompson 17, Jeff Kreindel 14.

Dieruff 87 Phillipsburg 63: Dieruff kept Phillipsburg winless in league play despite giving the Huskies a very competitive challenge for three periods. Dieruff only led by a single point going into the final period 59-58. Halfway through the period, Dieruff was up six points 69-63 and closed out the game by scoring the next 18 points.

Leading scorers: Dieruff – Mike Zambelli 26, Doug Kistler 22, Mike Hersch 16, Jim Mates 13; Phillipsburg – Dennis Staples 21, Mike Fichera 14, John Freeman 12.

Easton 57 Freedom 35: Freedom did not make a field goal until 2 ½ minutes into the second period and missed its first 15 shots as Easton took a 13-1 first quarter lead. Freedom recovered in the second period to cut the lead to 27-18 at the half. Easton added 13 points to the lead in the second half.

Leading scorers: Easton – Jim Hutnik 13, Dave Troxell 10, Dana Parr 10; Freedom – Tom Panik 9.

Liberty 64 Hazleton 62: Liberty traveled to Hazleton and won its sixth game in seven outings to stay in the first half race. After falling behind 23-16 after a quarter, Hazleton took a nine-point lead into the final quarter 53-42. In less than three minutes of the fourth quarter, Liberty hustled to an 11-1 spurt to pull within a point 54-53. With a little over three minutes to play, Liberty went ahead for good 59-58 and added three foul shots to extend the lead and travel home with the win.

Leading scorers: Liberty – Dick Packer 16, Rich Wescoe 14, Steve Farkus 12, Barry Frey 11; Hazleton – Jack Temchatin 18, Ron Portanova 11.[9]

Pottsville 64 Bethlehem Catholic 50: Pottsville held the lead after the first two quarters 15-9 and 29-20. Bethlehem Catholic came out of the locker room to score the first 13 points of the 2nd half to take a 33-29 lead and increased it to 38-33. Pottsville rallied to score nine straight points to retake the lead going into the final quarter 40-38. Scoring the first four points of the fourth quarter, Pottsville was not threatened again.

Leading scorers: Pottsville – Al Holtzer 20, Chris Higgins 12, Dennis Ebling 10; Bethlehem Catholic – Mike Godbolt 19, Rick Cacciatore 13.[10]

Week 5

Hazleton 95 Phillipsburg 80: Phillipsburg dropped to 0-8 in league play, although it played Hazleton even for three periods. Phillipsburg led at the half 36-35. Hazleton held a two-point lead 61-59 entering the final period. After the Stateliners tied the score at 61, Hazleton ran off the next 10 points and Phillipsburg could not come back.

Leading scorers: Hazleton – Joe Gavio 20, Joe Novatnack 17, Jerry Provizzi 16, Jack Temchatin 14, Ron Portanova 13; Phillipsburg – John Freeman 23, Dennis Staples 20.

Freedom 65 Bethlehem Catholic 50: Freedom held Bethlehem Catholic to 28 points over the first three periods to take an 11-point lead 39-28. The Patriots never trailed in the game after taking an early 3-0 lead.

Leading scorers: Freedom – Phil Sedlock 16, Ron Donchez 12, Curt Kemmerer 11; Bethlehem Catholic – Rick Cacciatore 15.

Easton 66 Allen 53: Easton took an early 4-0 lead and never fell behind Allen on the way to their sixth victory against two defeats. In earning their first victory over Allen in four years, the Red Rovers led by as many as 14 points and the Canaries could get no closer than seven points in the 2nd half.

Leading scorers: Easton – Dave Troxell 19, Jim Hutnik 15, Mike Kadjeski 14; Allen – Jeff Kreindel 17, Doug Snyder 17.

Pottsville 63 Dieruff 56: Pottsville held a 32-26 lead at the half, but Dieruff rallied in the third quarter to take a one-point lead 38-37. After Pottsville regained the lead at 39-38, the Crimson Tide extended the lead to 56-45 during the 4th quarter and dropped the Huskies to 4-4 in league play. Pottsville improved to 3-5.

Leading scorers: Pottsville – Chris Higgins 14, Ken Bailey 14, Al Holtzer 12, Dave Sydnor 11; Dieruff – Mike Hersch 15, Doug Kistler 15, Mike Zambelli 11,

Central Catholic 56 Liberty 55: Central Catholic clinched the first half with a win over its closest challenger Liberty, but not without a challenge from the Hurricane. After falling behind by a point 13-12, Liberty took it to the Vikings in the 2nd quarter to go into halftime with a 34-25 advantage. The Vikings trimmed the lead to seven points after three periods 48-41. After Central Catholic went into the lead 54-53, Liberty came back with a basket to retake the lead. Joe Pfahler fed Mike Busolits for the winning layup with 11 seconds left.

Leading scorers: Central Catholic-Joe Pfahler 28, Jeff McGeehin 10; Liberty-Barry Frey 16, Dick Packer 14.[11]

Phillipsburg 68 Freedom 66: Phillipsburg stunned Freedom to win its first game in the first half of play. Phillipsburg dominated the middle two quarters of the contest to win the game. After Freedom took a 17-12 first quarter lead, Phillipsburg outscored the Patriots 38-24 in the third and fourth quarter to take an unexpected 50-41 into the final quarter. Trailing 66-50 with a little less than three minutes to play, Freedom switched to a full court press and scored the next 16 points to tie the game. Phillipsburg could only get the ball to midcourt because of the press and Mark Bennett made the miraculous shot with a second on the clock to shock the Patriots.

Leading scorers: Phillipsburg – Mike Fichera 19, Dennis Staples 14, John Freeman 14, Mike Kline 10; Freedom – Phil Sedlock 16, Gary Kesack 13, Ron Donchez 12, Tom Panik 12.

Central Catholic 77 Bethlehem Catholic 68: Despite leading the whole way, Central Catholic had to battle Bethlehem Catholic through the entire contest to finish the first half undefeated. Each time the Vikings took a seven or eight-point lead, the Hawks would respond to cut the deficit to only several points.

Leading scorers: Central Catholic – Mike Busolits 26, Tom Gallagher 20, Jeff McGeehin 11, Joe Pfahler 10; Bethlehem Catholic – Rick Cacciatore 15, Mike Godbolt 12.

Liberty 64 Pottsville 63: Liberty fell behind 18-7 after a quarter and still trailed at halftime 32-28. Liberty took the lead with less than two minutes to play in the third quarter 40-39 and increased it to 45-41. After trailing at the beginning of the 4th quarter 45-43, Pottsville tied the game at 46. The game was tied three times, the last time at 59, before Liberty converted several foul shots and a tap-in on a missed free throw to pull out the win.

Leading scorers: Liberty – Dick Packer 19, Rich Wescoe 14, Jose Perna 13, Barry Frey 10; Pottsville – Chris Higgins 20, Al Holtzer 12, Hal Bertsch 11.

Easton 74 Hazleton 61: With the victory over Hazleton, Easton tied Liberty for second place and would play the Hurricane to determine the league's first half representative in the state playoffs since the first half champions were ineligible for PIAA play. A big 2nd quarter with 25 points and a twelve-point advantage in the period led to the victory for the Red Rovers. The two teams played nearly even in the other three periods.

Leading scorers: Easton – Dave Joseph 23, Dave Troxell 19, Mike Kadjeski 12, Jim Hutnik 12; Hazleton – Ron Portanova 16, Joe Novatnack 16.

Allen 73 Dieruff 60: After seeing the game tied eight times and the lead changing nine times in the first three quarters, Allen took the lead for good with a minute left in the third period. The win for Allen evened the series at 15 wins a piece since Dieruff was established.

Leading scorers: Allen – Bob Frederick 16, Doug Snyder 16, Jeff Kreindel 13, Joe Thompson 11; Dieruff – Mike Zambelli 18, Doug Kistler 16, Mike Hersch 11.[12]

First Half Playoff

Easton 53 Liberty 48: With Central Catholic ineligible to play in the PIAA state playoffs, Liberty and Easton, both tied at 7-2, for second place squared off at Muhlenberg's Memorial Hall to decide the league representative. Liberty took the first quarter lead 14-10, but Easton countered in the second quarter by holding the Hurricane to six points and taking a 24-20 lead at the half. Although Easton never relinquished the lead, Liberty kept within striking distance the rest of the game. The win gave Easton its first opportunity ever to play in the postseason.

Leading scorers: Easton – Jim Hutnik 23, Dave Troxell 11; Liberty – Jose Perna 15, Dick Packer 12.[13]

Second Half - Week 6

Dieruff 60 Bethlehem Catholic 56: Dieruff and Bethlehem Catholic played to a 27-27 tie with Mike Godbolt making a layup with ten seconds to go in the half to create the tie. The Hawks led twice early in the second half, but Dieruff took control after that and led the rest of the way. Mike Zambelli scored 13 points in the second half to lead the Huskie charge.

Leading scorers: Dieruff – Mike Zambelli 19, Doug Kistler 14, Mike Hersch 13; Bethlehem Catholic – Mike Godbolt 22, Greg Adams 10.

Freedom 52 Central Catholic 50: Central Catholic led throughout the first half and took a 28-24 lead into the locker room. Freedom tied up the contest after three quarters 36-36 only to see the Vikings take a 50-42 advantage with 2:41 to play in the game. Phil Sedlock hit a field goal to tie the game at 50-50 and converted a foul shot for the lead 51-50 and hand the Vikings the first blemish in the league for the season. The Vikings made only 18 of 34 free throws in the loss.

Leading scorers: Freedom – Phil Sedlock 18; Central Catholic – Mike Busolits 18, Jeff McGeehin 12.

Easton 61 Phillipsburg 51: Easton outscored Phillipsburg three out the four quarters on their way to the victory. Phillipsburg held a 9-7 first period lead until Easton scored the last nine points to head into the second quarter up seven points. In the third period, Phillipsburg closed to within 42-41 before Easton ran off the next eight points to take an insurmountable lead.

Leading scorers: Easton - Dave Troxell 16, Dave Joseph 10; Phillipsburg - Dennis Staples 19, John Freeman 16.[14]

Liberty 78 Allen 77: With 4:34 left in the contest, the Allen-Liberty basketball game was suspended due to a bomb threat. Without indicating the reason, Allen principal John McHugh calmly announced that the 1700 fans would have to empty the gym. Within 7 ½ minutes, everyone had left the gym. Allen led at the time 70-61. Liberty led by a point after the first quarter 16-15, but the Canaries took a 39-33 halftime lead before Liberty cut it to 58-55 after three quarters. The game was resumed the following week. Liberty employed a zone press as the Hurricane outscored the Canaries 15-3 in the final two minutes of the game for a shocking come-from-behind win.

Leading scorers: Liberty–Rich Wescoe 27, Steve Farkus 11; Allen–Joe Thompson 19, Bob Frederick 18, Jeff Kreindel 18.[14, 15]

Hazleton 61 Pottsville 59: Trailing for most of the contest, Hazleton rallied in the final period to score 20 points while holding Pottsville to six for the win. Hazleton scored the first five points of the final quarter to take the lead 46-44 and increased the lead to 57-49. Pottsville rallied to take the lead 59-58 only to not score again as Hazleton converted three foul shots to pull out the win. After the game ended, several players on each team fought after the intense finish.

Leading scorers: Hazleton – Joe Gavio 15, Joe Novatnack 14; Pottsville – Chris Higgins 15, Hal Bertsch 11.[16]

Week 7

Freedom 72 Hazleton 56: With Jeff Hoydu scoring 18 points in the first half, Freedom took a 31-26 lead over Hazleton. After the Patriots took the lead at 21-20 in the second quarter, they never trailed again in the game. Freedom held the Mountaineers to eight points in the third period while scoring 20 to take full command of the contest.

Leading scorers: Freedom – Jeff Hoydu 20, Ron Donchez 15, Tom Panik 14; Hazleton – Joe Gavio 22.

Allen 70 Bethlehem Catholic 69 OT: After three quarters, Allen led Bethlehem Catholic 52-43 and still held a nine-point lead 64-55 with a little over 2 ½ minutes to play. The Hawks scored the last nine points in regulation to tie the contest. After missing a last second shot which would have won the game, Joe Thompson scored four of the six Canary points in overtime. The last two were two free throws with six seconds left to lead Allen to victory.

Leading scorers: Allen – Joe Thompson 30, Doug Snyder 16, Jeff Kreindel 12; Bethlehem Catholic – Mike Godbolt 20, Greg Adams 10, Rick Cacciatore 10.

Dieruff 41 Easton 39: Easton took a five-point lead in the first quarter 13-8 only to have Dieruff cut the lead to one at the half 20-19. With Mike Zambelli scoring 12 points in the third quarter, the Huskies jumped into the lead 37-31. The Red Rovers tied the score at 37 and again at 39. Dieruff took the lead 41-39 on a Doug Kistler lay-up with 4:13 to play. Neither team scored after that as the Huskies finished the game with a very deliberate offense.

Leading scorers: Dieruff – Mike Zambelli 14; Easton – Dave Troxell 9.

Central Catholic 54 Pottsville 53: Central Catholic missed 14 of 26 foul shots and turned the ball over 24 times and still hung on to win and even their record at 1-1 for the second half. The Vikings trailed 40-38 entering the fourth quarter and finally took the lead for good 47-46. Jeff McGeehin's two foul shots with 19 seconds left sealed the victory for the Vikings.

Leading scorers: Central Catholic–Joe Pfahler 18, Mike Busolits 11; Pottsville–Al Holtzer 17, Hal Bertsch 12, Chris Higgins 10.

Liberty 80 Phillipsburg 63: Liberty started the second quarter with a 17-13 lead and then scored ten straight points to start the quarter which led to a 45-28 lead at halftime. Phillipsburg cut the lead to 12 points at the start of the third period, but Liberty came back to lead by 16 and cruise to victory over the Stateliners.

Leading scorers: Liberty – Barry Frey 33, Rich Wescoe 16; Phillipsburg – John Freeman 25, Dennis Staples 13, Barry Stocker 11.[17]

Central Catholic 78 Hazleton 70: Central Catholic scored the first ten points of the game on their way to a 21-8 first quarter lead. The Vikings increased the lead to 14 points at the half 41-27. Although Hazleton outscored Central Catholic 43-37in the second half, the Mountaineers could not overcome the Vikings first half advantage.

Leading scorers: Central Catholic – Mike Busolits 26, Tom Gallagher 20, Joe Pfahler 20; Hazleton – Jack Temchatin 25, Ron Portanova 14.

Phillipsburg 78 Allen 74: Allen trailed four times in the first quarter before taking an 18-14 lead going into the second quarter. Allen maintained a four-point lead 34-30 at the half and increased it to 58-51 after three quarters. Dennis Staples scored 13 points in the final quarter to spearhead a major comeback by the Stateliners and upset the Canaries.

Leading scorers: Phillipsburg – Dennis Staples 27, Mark Bennett 15, Mike Kline 14; Allen – Joe Thompson 29, Bob Frederick 12, Doug Snyder 11.

Liberty 63 Bethlehem Catholic 56: Bethlehem Catholic jumped out to a 16-6 lead after a quarter and increased to 22-8 with 5:45 left in the second quarter. The rest of the quarter the Hawks committed 11 turnovers and Liberty outscored the Hawks 25-10 to take a 33-32 halftime lead. Liberty took a seven-point lead in the third quarter, but Bethlehem Catholic went on 9-2 run to tie the game going into the final period. Liberty took charge in the fourth quarter and outscored the Hawks 15-8 to win the contest.

Leading scorers: Liberty – Dick Packer 18, Rich Wescoe 14, Terry Marcincin 12; Bethlehem Catholic – Mike Godbolt 16, Bob Gallagher 14, Rick Cacciatore 14.

Dieruff 48 Freedom 34: Dieruff outscored Freedom 13-8 in each of the first two quarters to lead by ten points at the half. They maintained the lead after three quarters as both teams were only able to score six points each. The win improved the Huskies to 3-0 and stayed tied with Liberty for first place in the 2nd half.

Leading scorers: Dieruff – Mike Zambelli 17, Mike Hersch 11, Joe Groller 10; Freedom – Ron Donchez 8.

Easton 49 Pottsville 42 OT: After leading by eight points after three quarters 36-28, Pottsville increased the lead to ten points seven seconds into the final quarter. Easton went to a full court press and scored the next eight points to get within two 38-36. Pottsville went ahead by four, but the Red Rovers came back to score and get within two points. Pottsville stalled, but then missed a shot with the Red Rovers gaining possession. Jim Hutnik made a jumper to tie the game in regulation. Easton dominated the overtime period with Mike Young scoring the first five points to take the lead.

Leading scorers: Easton – Dave Troxell 20; Pottsville – Chris Higgins 18.[18]

Week 8

Easton 58 Bethlehem Catholic 50: Despite only one successful field goal in the fourth quarter and scoring only eight points, Easton defeated Bethlehem Catholic to improve to 4-1. The Red Rovers went on a 12-1 run in the last four minutes of the third quarter to build a 50-34 heading into the fourth quarter. Easton took a 14-8 lead in the first quarter and the Hawks never got any closer than four points the rest of the contest.

Leading scorers: Easton – Dave Joseph 14, Jim Hutnik 13, Mike Kadjeski 12; Bethlehem Catholic – Rick Cacciatore 12, Dan Sinnott 11.

Allen 86 Hazleton 68; At Hazleton, Allen improved to 2-2 after taking a commanding lead in the first quarter 22-4. They scored the last 18 points of the first quarter after a 4-4 tie. Hazleton never got any closer than 16 points after the first quarter. Hazleton dropped to 1-3 for the second half of league play.

Leading scorers: Allen – Joe Thompson 26, Bob Frederick 20, Doug Snyder 17, Jeff Kreindel 15; Hazleton – Jack Temchatin 25, Charlie Craig 14.

Liberty 55 Dieruff 53: Rich Wescoe hit a jumper at the buzzer to stun Dieruff and remain alone atop the league standings at 4-0. Liberty took an eight-point lead 15-7 after a quarter and maintained the lead through three quarters 43-35. In the fourth quarter, Dieruff rallied to tie the score at 47 and led 53-51 with 1:20 to play. With 45 seconds left, Steve Farkus tied the score at 53 before Wescoe hit the winner for the Hurricane.

Leading scorers: Liberty – Dick Packer 16, Rich Wescoe 13, Barry Frey 12; Dieruff – Doug Kistler 16, Mike Zambelli 13, Rich Schmidt 12.

Central Catholic 77 Phillipsburg 71: After a tight first half with neither team leading by more than three points and with the score tied at the half 36-36, Central Catholic took charge in the final minutes of the third period to open up a six-point lead. Phillipsburg came back to within two points 63-61 before the Vikings ran off 9 straight points late in the final quarter and hold off the Stateliners to improve their record to 2-2.

Leading scorers: Central Catholic – Joe Pfahler 17, Mike Busolits 17, Tom Gallagher 16, Tom Kern 10; Phillipsburg – John Freeman 22, Barry Stocker 19, Mark Bennett 10.[19]

Pottsville 61 Freedom 48: Freedom led 13-12 after the first quarter with Pottsville surging into the lead at halftime 30-26. With the score tied at 30 with five minutes to play in the third period, Pottsville went ahead for good and opened up a 38-31 lead.

Leading scorers: Pottsville – Chris Higgins 20, Hal Bertsch 17, Chip Raczka 10; Freedom – Jeff Hoydu 13, Gary Kesack 11.[20]

Pottsville 84 Allen 77: After Allen took a 7-2 lead, Pottsville came on to take the lead at the end of the quarter 16-12. The Canaries only managed one other lead 24-22 in the second quarter, but Ken Kline's Pottsville squad went on a 10-3 spurt to take the lead for good. Both teams stood at 2-3 after the contest.

Leading scorers: Pottsville – Chris Higgins 31, Dennis Ebling 20, Chip Raczka 11, Hal Bertsch 10; Allen – Doug Snyder 28, Joe Thompson 18, Bob Frederick 14, Bill Ent 11.

Bethlehem Catholic 84 Phillipsburg 83 OT: Bethlehem Catholic led most of the contest with leads of 17-12, 38-29, and 63-59 through the first three quarters. Phillipsburg tied the score at 77 before Mike Godbolt put the Hawks ahead 79-77. Dennis Staples tied the game with a hook shot with four seconds left. Rich Cacciatore scored all five points in overtime for the Hawks.

Leading scorers: Bethlehem Catholic – Rick Cacciatore 19, Mike Harvilla 19, Mike Godboldt 15, Bob Gallagher 14; Phillipsburg – Mark Bennett 28, John Freeman 16, Mike Fichera 12, Barry Stocker 10, Dennis Staples 10.

Central Catholic 53 Easton 52: Easton took a four-point lead after a quarter with Central Catholic cutting it to a point at halftime 25-24. The teams played even in the 3rd period with both teams scoring 13 points. In the final quarter, Easton built an 8-point lead by scoring ten points in a row with 3 ½ minutes to play. The Vikings followed the Easton spurt with a 12-3 run of their own to improve to 4-1. The winning bucket was scored with 1:25 to play.

Leading scorers: Central Catholic – Mike Busolits 15, Joe Pfahler 15; Easton – Mike Young 14, Dave Troxell 12, Dave Joseph 12.

Liberty 68 Freedom 41: Liberty only allowed Freedom one field in the first 11 minutes and jumped out to a 35-15 lead at halftime. Undefeated in second half play, Liberty continued to add to the lead during the last two quarters.

Leading scorers: Liberty – Rich Wescoe 15, Steve Farkus 15, Dick Packer 12, Barry Frey 12; Freedom – Jeff Hoydu 8.

Hazleton 55 Dieruff 46: After bolting out to a 12-2 lead, Hazleton led 17-8 after a quarter and increased the lead to 12 at halftime 31-19. Dieruff went on a 14-2 run to start the 3rd period and tie the game at 33. Hazleton countered to take the lead 36-33 entering the final quarter and the Huskies could not get any closer the rest of the game.

Leading scorers: Hazleton – Jack Temchatin 21, Ron Portanova 10; Dieruff – Mike Zambelli 12, Doug Kistler 12.[21]

Week 9

Bethlehem Catholic 61 Hazleton 60: Bethlehem Catholic took an 11-5 lead midway through the first quarter before Hazleton ran off eight straight points. The Hawks came back to lead 19-17 at the end of the quarter, but Hazleton wiped out the lead and went into the locker room ahead 29-27. The Hawks took the lead going into the fourth quarter 57-53 and held on to win the game.

Leading scorers: Bethlehem Catholic – Rich Cacciatore 20, Mike Godbolt 15, Mike Harvilla 12; Hazleton - Ron Portanova 19, Joe Gavio 14, Joe Novatnack 13, Jack Temchatin 10.

Easton 55 Liberty 53 3OT: Easton handed Liberty its first loss of the half in a defensive struggle. Easton scored 12 points in each of the four quarters and led 36-28 going into the final period. Both teams were awarded a double technical with 1 ½ minutes to play with Liberty making both and Easton missing both to make the score 48-44. Liberty made a field goal and two foul shots to tie the game in regulation, the first time they had not been behind the entire game. After being tied after each of the first two overtimes, Dave

Troxell scored on a layup a minute into the third overtime to win the game with neither team being able to score the rest of the overtime.

Leading scorers: Easton – Dave Troxell 20, Jim Hutnik 12; Liberty – Dick Packer 17.

Allen 94 Freedom 89 2OT: Allen took a commanding 20-6 lead after the first quarter, but Freedom fought its way back, especially in the third period when they outscored the Canaries 27-16, to tie the game in regulation at 75. With four of its starters having fouled out, the Patriots took a four-point lead in the first overtime only to have Allen come back to tie the contest. Allen took a quick lead early in the second overtime and never allowed Freedom to make a comeback.

Leading scorers: Allen – Joe Thompson 25, Doug Snyder 22, Bill Ent 19, Jeff Kreindel 18; Freedom – Charlie Pescek 20, Tom Panik 19, Phil Sedlock 11, Ron Donchez 10.

Central Catholic 61 Dieruff 59 2OT: In a defensive battle, Central Catholic took a 15-12 lead into the second quarter and maintained the lead at halftime 29-26. Dieruff took the lead in the third quarter 40-38 and led by as many as five points in the fourth quarter before the Vikings tied the game in regulation. After each team scored two points in the first overtime with Dieruff missing an opportunity to win when Doug Kistler missed two free throws, the Vikings took the game in the second overtime. Dieruff made only 19 of 34 free throws while the Vikings connected on 27 of 39. With Liberty's loss, the Vikings tied the Hurricane for the second half lead at 5-1. The Huskies' Mike Zambelli collapsed from exhaustion during the last overtime period.

Leading scorers: Central Catholic – Jeff McGeehin 14, Tom Gallagher 13, Joe Pfahler 13, Mark Trinkle 12; Dieruff – Mike Hersch 20, Mike Zambelli 11.[22]

Pottsville 81 Phillipsburg 62: Pottsville held Phillipsburg scoreless for 4:19 in the first period in rolling to a 20-8 lead. They increased it to 28-18 at the half, before the Stateliners cut the lead to fourteen 56-42 going into the final period. Early in the final quarter, Phillipsburg cut the lead to 13 before Pottsville beat back any attempt at a rally by the Stateliners.

Leading scorers: Pottsville – Chris Higgins 22, Hal Bertsch 10, Al Holtzer 10, Jim Sweeney 10; Phillipsburg – Mike Kline 11, John Redos 10.[23]

Hazleton 80 Liberty 77: Hazleton handed Liberty its second consecutive loss in a stunning upset in Bethlehem. Hazleton took a 19-11 lead in the first period and made the eight-point advantage hold up the rest of the game. The eight-point lead held up at halftime 39-31, but Liberty went into the lead in the final 1 ½ minutes of the third period 56-55. With the scored tied at 77, Joe Novatnack made two free throws with 12 seconds to go for the win,

Leading scorers: Hazleton – Jack Temchatin 26, Ron Portanova 16, Joe Gavio 15, Tom Donahue 10; Liberty – Dick Packer 33, Rich Wescoe 20.

Dieruff 82 Phillipsburg 57: After leading 22-8 after a quarter, Dieruff stretched the lead to 45-20 at the half. With six players scoring in double figures, Coach Dick Schmidt took all his starters out of the game by the end of the third quarter.

Leading scorers: Dieruff – Doug Kistler 16, Mike Hersch 12, Richie Schmidt 11, Jim Mates 11, Tom Stellar 10, Joe Groller 10; Phillipsburg – Dennis Staples 15, John Redos 13.

Easton 56 Freedom 34: Easton held Freedom to single digits in three of the four periods in cruising to an easy win and improve to 5-2 and a tie for second place with Liberty.

Leading scorers: Easton – Dave Troxell 16, Dave Joseph 12, Jim Hutnik 10; Freedom – Phil Sedlock 13.

Central Catholic 64 Allen 55: Allen battled Central Catholic for three periods and held a halftime lead 30-27 before the Vikings took the lead after three quarters 44-43. In the final two minutes of the fourth quarter, the Vikings went on 10-3 run to wrap up the victory. The win kept the Vikings in sole possession of first place in the second half of play.

Leading scorers: Central Catholic – Mike Busolits 18, Jeff McGeehin 12, Tom Gallagher 11, Joe Pfahler 10; Allen – Doug Snyder 17, Joe Thompson 15.

Bethlehem Catholic 59 Pottsville 57 2OT: Pottsville built a six-point lead after three quarters 41-35 only to have Bethlehem Catholic battle back to tie the game in regulation with nine seconds to play on two free throws by Mike Godbolt. The Hawks forced a second overtime when Dan Sinnott tapped in a missed shot with two seconds to play. In the final period, John Majczan scored his only two points of the night with two seconds left on a 10-foot jumper for the win.

Leading scorers: Bethlehem Catholic – Rick Cacciatore 17, Mike Godbolt 12, Bob Gallagher 11; Pottsville – Al Raczka 17, Dave Sydnor 13, Chris Higgins, 12, Hal Bertsch 12.[24]

Week 12

Hazleton 109 Phillipsburg 56: With Hazleton's starters playing less than a full half, the Mountaineers still built a 57-19 lead at the half. During the third period, the lead was more than 50 points. The scoring outburst set a school record for points in a game. Hazleton's Tom Donahue went 8 for 8 from the field and 3 of 3 from the foul line to complete a perfect night.

Leading scorers: Hazleton – Tom Donahue 19, Ron Portanova 14, Jack Temchatin 13, Craig 11; Phillipsburg – Dennis Staples 14.

Central Catholic 90 Liberty 75: In clinching the second half title, Central Catholic registered only its second overall league title since joining the league in 1947. The game was essentially over after the first half when the Vikings held 51-36 lead. The loss was the third in a row for the Hurricane after having won the first five games of the second half.

Leading scorers: Central Catholic – Joe Pfahler 27, Mike Busolits 26, Mark Trinkle 10; Liberty – Rich Wescoe 23, Dick Packer 17, Terry Marcincin 12.

Dieruff 60 Pottsville 54: After Dieruff and Pottsville tied after the 1st quarter 15-15, Pottsville took a two-point lead into halftime 33-31. Dieruff came out with a big third quarter to take a seven-point advantage 49-42. Despite making only a single field goal in the final quarter, the Huskies held off the Crimson Tide by making ten free throws.

Leading scorers: Dieruff – Doug Kistler 17, Mike Zambelli 14, Tom Stellar 11; Pottsville – Ken Bailey 11, Chris Higgins 10.

Freedom 55 Bethlehem Catholic 44: Freedom broke a 6-6 tie and scored eight points in a row to take the lead it never lost. Bethlehem Catholic went without a field goal for the first six minutes of the third quarter as Freedom rolled to a 32-19 lead. As a result, both teams were at 3-5 during the second half of play.

Leading scorers: Freedom – Tom Donchez 13, Tom Panik 13, Phil Subits 12; Bethlehem Catholic - Rich Cacciatore 18, Greg Adams 12, Mike Godbolt 10.

Allen 67 Easton 64: Coach Stan Sutphen opened the game with his second team, but the strategy backfired as Allen took a 17-9 lead after one quarter. With the starting five on the floor, Easton still got no closer than five points the rest of the way. The game was played in front of many of the school's all-time greats in possible the last game at the Little Palestra.

Leading scorers: Allen – Joe Thompson 25, Jeff Kreindel 15, Doug Snyder 13, Bob Frederick 10; Easton – Jim Hutnik 14, Dave Troxell 14, Dana Parr 10.[25]

Freedom 65 Phillipsburg 55: With Phillipsburg taking a 2-0 lead on free throws, Freedom came back with eight straight points and never lost the lead. The Patriots led 17-8, 31-25, and 49-38 after each of the first three periods. The Stateliners closed to within 58-50 in the final quarter but could get no closer.

Leading scorers: Freedom-Tom Panik 18, Ron Donchez 17, Phil Subits 11; Phillipsburg-Dennis Staples 15, John Freeman 13.

Central Catholic 66 Bethlehem Catholic 59: Central Catholic only led by four points at the half 35-31 before breaking away from Bethlehem Catholic in the third period to open up a 14-point lead 56-42 going into the final quarter. Not eligible for PIAA post season play, the Vikings would play the Hawks again in the PCIAA playoffs.

Leading scorers: Central Catholic – Joe Pfahler 19, Tom Gallagher 11, Mark Trinkle 11, Mike Busolits 10, Jeff McGeehin 10; Bethlehem Catholic – Greg Adams 14.

Easton 72 Hazleton 62: Trailing 18-16 in the second quarter, Easton went on a 12-1 spurt to take the lead for good. With a 30-25 lead at the half, the Red Rovers increased it to 50-38 on their way to qualifying for a playoff spot with Dieruff and Liberty to determine the league's second half qualifier for the state playoffs.

Leading scorers: Easton – Dave Troxell 25, Jim Hutnik 14; Hazleton - Jack Temchatin 26.

Liberty 67 Pottsville 57: Liberty took a 50-43 lead into the fourth quarter, but Pottsville battled back to within a point 56-55 with 1:51 remaining. Rich Wescoe countered by scoring nine points to hold off the Crimson Tide and help the Hurricane qualify for the playoff against Dieruff and Easton to determine the second half league representative in the PIAA playoffs.

Leading Scorers: Liberty – Rich Wescoe 25, Dick Packer 17, Barry Frey 12; Pottsville – Chris Higgins 16, Al Holtzer 10.

Dieruff 72 Allen 62: Dieruff capitalized on a big second period against Allen to qualify for the second half playoffs. With Allen leading after a period 18-15, the Huskies outscored the Canaries by ten points in the second quarter 17-7. Dieruff outscored the Canaries 40-37 in the second half.

Leading scorers: Dieruff – Mike Hersch 18, Doug Kistler 18, Mike Zambelli 13, Rich Schmidt 11; Allen – Doug Snyder 21, Bill Ent 10.[26]

Second Half Playoff

With Central Catholic ineligible for PIAA play, the three teams, Liberty, Dieruff, and Easton, tied for second place in the second half which required a playoff to determine the league representative in the post season playoffs. Dieruff and Liberty played in the first game with the winner taking on Easton.

Dieruff 66 Liberty 53: The game was close in the first half with Dieruff holding a three-point lead after one quarter 16-13. Liberty closed the gap to two points at the half 25-23. The Huskies expanded the lead to 42-33 in the third quarter. Dieruff connected on 26 of 31 free throws to take command of the game.

Leading scorers: Dieruff – Mike Hersch 21, Mike Zambelli 17, Doug Kistler 10; Liberty – Dick Packer 18, Jose Perna 10, Rich Wescoe 10.[27]

Easton 69 Dieruff 46: After Dieruff jumped out to an 18-12 lead after a quarter, Easton held the Huskies to only 13 points in the middle two quarters on their way to a rout of the Huskies. The Red Rovers outscored Dieruff 57-26 in the last three quarters. As a result of the win, Coach Stan Sutphen was able to choose his seeding in the playoffs and he decided to be the number 2 team to enable his team to play at Muhlenberg's Memorial Hall. Dieruff became the number 1 seed as a result of Easton's choice.

Leading scorers: Easton – Dave Troxell 19, Dave Joseph 15, Mike Kadjeski 14; Dieruff – Doug Kistler 12, Mike Hersh 11.[28]

Postseason PIAA Play

Easton 65 Mahanoy Area 47: Easton opened up with an 8-0 lead before Mahanoy Area got on the board. The Red Rovers took a 16-9 lead in the first quarter and extended the lead to 29-16 at the half. Easton cruised to the win to move on to the district finals.

Leading scorers: Easton – Dave Troxell 20, Jim Hutnik 15, Dave Joseph 11; Mahanoy Area – John Linckhorst 12, John Fletcher 12, Fran Kane 11.

Dieruff 76 West Hazleton 57: Playing at Hazleton, Dieruff ran out to a 10-0 lead in the quarterfinal District 11 matchup with West Hazleton. The Huskies kept extending the lead in the next two quarters, leading at the half 32-18 and at the end of the third quarter 56-33.

Leading scorers: Dieruff – Rich Schmidt 17, Mike Hersch 12, Mike Zambelli 10, Tom Stellar 10; West Hazleton – Ron Bason 13, Ed Kluck 11.[29]

Northampton 63 Dieruff 55: Dieruff took a 12-5 first quarter lead and went into halftime with a 25-19 lead over Northampton. Coach Bob Nemeth switched the Konkrete Kids defense to a combination man-to-man defense to shut down the Huskies attack. By the end of the third quarter, Northampton took the lead 42-36 after going on a 15-1 run during the quarter. After Northampton built the lead to 12 points, Dieruff came back to within five points with less than two minutes to play before Northampton extended their lead again and better their record to 23-2 with the victory.

Leading scorers: Northampton - Greg Vogel 16, Jim Schneider 14, Mike Schneider 14, Jim Spitzer 10; Dieruff - Mike Zambelli 19.[30]

Easton 77 Parkland 51: At Pottsville, Easton reached its first ever district title game with a victory over Parkland, the Lehigh Valley League champions. Easton took a 17-8 first quarter lead and expanded it to as much as 18 points in the second quarter before going into halftime with a 40-25 lead. Easton held Parkland to six points in the third period and went into the final quarter with a 56-31 advantage.

Leading scorers: Easton – Dave Troxell 19, Jim Hutnik 16, Mike Kadjeski 14, Dave Joseph 10; Parkland – Bernie Anderson 13, Mike O'Boyle 13.[31]

Northampton 60 Easton 57: Northampton took the early lead after a quarter 13-8 only to have Easton rally in the second quarter to go into halftime with a 29-25 advantage over the Konkrete Kids. Northampton's Mike Schneider was ejected from the contest in the second quarter for taking a punch at an Easton player. Easton extended the lead to 36-30 early in the third quarter, but Northampton halted the Red Rover offense and held a 44-41 lead going into the final quarter. Northampton extended the lead to 57-48 with a little less than three minutes left in the game. Late Easton baskets brought the final margin to three.

Leading scorers: Northampton – Jim Schneider 20, Greg Vogel 16, Carl Christman 13; Easton – Dave Troxell 22, Kerry Myers 11, Jim Hutnik 10.

Dieruff 60 Parkland 57: Dieruff took third place in district play despite starting the contest with a woeful 4 of 22 in field goal attempts in the first half. The Huskies trailed 13-6 and 27-21 after the first two quarters, but rebounded in the third quarter to take a three-point lead 45-42. Parkland roared back to take a 57-56 lead with 1:23 to play, but Doug Kistler made a layup and two free throws to pull out the win for the Huskies.

Leading scorers: Dieruff – Doug Kistler 21, Mike Hersch 18; Parkland – Brant Flax 21, Dave Posocco 17.[32]

PCIAA Postseason Playoff

Central Catholic 83 Bethlehem Catholic 69: At Liberty's Memorial Gym, Central Catholic won its fifth consecutive Allentown Diocese Class A title. The Vikings held a 16-10 lead after a quarter, but the Hawks came back to cut the lead to three at the half 33-30. Going into the fourth quarter, the Vikings led 53-46 and then scored nine straight points later in the quarter to take a commanding 67-50 lead,

Leading scorers: Central Catholic – Joe Pfahler 30, Mike Busolits 18, Jeff McGeehin 10; Bethlehem Catholic – Rich Cacciatore 18, Mike Godbolt 18, Bob Gallagher 14.[33]

Central Catholic 66 Lancaster Catholic 51: Central Catholic took a 17-2 lead after the first five minutes on the way to an 18-8 first quarter lead. A minute into the second quarter, a bomb scare forced the game to stop with the 3000 spectators evacuated from Muhlenberg's Memorial Hall. When firemen found no threat, the Vikings continued their assault to take a 35-18 lead into halftime. The Vikings lost two key players in the second quarter when both Joe Kalata and Mike Busolits suffered knee injuries could not continue. Despite their loss, Central Catholic maintained a commanding lead the rest of the way for the win.

Leading scorers: Central Catholic – Joe Pfahler 16, Mark Trinkle 14, Tom Gallagher 13, Jeff McGeehin 11; Lancaster Catholic – John Boyer 21, Beichler 12.[34]

Central Catholic 52 Kingston Catholic 42: At the Farm Show Arena, Kingston Catholic held leads after each of the first two quarters 11-8 and 22-20. Central Catholic did not get the lead until about two minutes into the third quarter and led by three at the end of the quarter 33-30, The Vikings scored six quick points to start the fourth quarter and maintained the lead the rest of the way to advance to the state final. The Kingston fans stopped play several times when items were thrown out onto the gym floor.

Leading scorers: Central Catholic – Joe Pfahler 16, Tom Kern 12; Kingston Catholic – Frank Britt 13.[35]

South Hills 69 Central Catholic 53: South Hills held Central Catholic to 14 points in the first half and led by 18 going into the third quarter. The Vikings rebounded to outscore South Hills 39-37 in the second half, but could not mount the rally necessary to get back into the contest.

Leading scorers: South Hills – Mark Albert 25, Greg McBride 18, Bob Del Greco 14; Central Catholic – Joe Pfahler 26, Jeff McGeehin 12.[36]

Postseason Accolades

Scoring Leaders: Joe Thompson, Allen, led the league with 369 points and 21.7 ppg, The rest of the top ten included: Joe Pfahler, Central Catholic, 317 points; Doug Snyder, Allen 300 points; Mike Busolits, Central Catholic, 291 points; Dick Packer, Liberty, 288 points; Rich Cacciatore, Bethlehem Catholic, 280 points; Dave Troxell, Easton, 276 points; Jack Temchatin, Hazleton, 274 points; Rich Wescoe, Liberty, 273 points; and Chris Higgins, Pottsville, 268 poionts.[37]

All-Stars: The league all-star first team included: Joe Pfahler, Central Catholic; Joe Thompson, Allen; Dave Troxell, Easton; Chris Higgins, Pottsville; and Jack Temchatin, Hazleton.[38]

All-State: With no players named to the three all-state teams, the following league players received honorable mention status: Joe Pfahler, Central Catholic; Joe Thompson; and Dave Troxell, Easton.[39]

Final Standings

First Half		Second Half		Overall	
Central Catholic	9-0	Central Catholic	8-1	Central Catholic	17-1
Liberty	7-2	Dieruff	6-3	Liberty	13-5
Easton	7-2	Liberty	6-3	Easton	13-5
Freedom	5-4	Easton	6-3	Dieruff	10-8
Allen	5-4	Allen	4-5	Allen	9-9
Dieruff	4-5	Hazleton	4-5	Freedom	9-9
Hazleton	3-6	Freedom	4-5	Hazleton	7-11
Pottsville	3-6	Pottsville	3-6	Pottsville	6-12
Bethlehem Catholic	1-8	Bethlehem Catholic	3-9	Bethlehem Catholic	4-14
Phillipsburg	1-8	Phillipsburg	1-8	Phillipsburg	2-16

Team Rosters

Allen: Coach Milo Sewards, Bill Ent, Bob Frederick, Frizzell, Jeff Haas, Hoch, Rick Krause, Jeff Kreindel, Steve Miller, Numbers, Mark Pessina, Gene Saverese, Doug Snyder, Joe Thompson, Todd, Tom Ward, Jim Wills

Bethlehem Catholic: Coach Bob Bukvics, Greg Adams, Rick Cacciatore, Tom Chladny, Bob Gallagher, Mike Godbolt, Mike Harvilla, Leary, John Majczan, Shannon, Dan Sinnott

Central Catholic: Coach Mike Koury, Mike Busolits, Tom Gallagher, Tim Johnson, Joe Kalata, Tom Kern, Rich Lang, Joe Ludrof, Jeff McGeehin, Bob Muthard, Joe Pfahler, Mark Trinkle

Dieruff: Coach Dick Schmidt, Len Brantley, Joe Groller, Mike Hersch, Doug Kistler, Jim Klusaritz, Jim Mates, Mark Mazziotti, Jim Noti, Rich Schmidt, Tom Stellar, Gene Sweeney, Mike Zambelli

Easton: Coach Stan Sutphen, Brantley, Jim Hutnik, Dave Joseph, Mike Kadjeski, Bruce Kelly, Bryan Kelly, Don Lehr, Kerry Myers, Dana Parr, Willard Stem, Dave Troxell, Mike Young

Freedom: Coach Charlie Dubbs, Ron Donchez, Jeff Hoydu, Curt Kemmerer, Steve Kondor, Jay Johnson, Gary Kesack, Tom Lees, Tom Panik, Charlie Pecsek, Noel Rituper, Phil Sedlock, Mike Sell, Phil Subits

Hazleton: Coach Dave Shafer, Charlie Craig, Tom Donahue, Jerry Dymek, Joe Gavio, Carmen Gugliemini, Steve Lazar, Dave Nance, Joe Novatnack, Ron Portanova, Jerry Provizzi, Rick Rogers, Greg Saul, Jack Temchatin

Liberty: Coach Al Senavitis, Steve Farkus, Jack Ferri, Bill Frey, Bruce "Skip" John, Kovacs, Tom Ludwig, Terry Marcincin, John McCaffrey, Dick Packer, Jose Perna, Rich Wescoe

Phillipsburg: Coach Pete Tomaino, Mark Bennett, Conine, Mike Fichera, John Freeman, Mike Kline, McGinnis, Parent, John Redos, Dennis Staples, Barry Stocker, Weisel, Weiss

Pottsville: Coach Ken Kline, Ken Bailey, Hal Bertsch, Dennis Ebling, Larry Haberle, Chris Higgins, Al Holtzer, Ken Kline, Jamie Lightstone, Leo Ostrosky, Al "Chip" Raczka, Mike Sanders, Bob Scheipe, Roy Snowell, Dave Snyder, Dave Sydnor, Jim Sweeney

1973

Central Catholic Eligible for PIAA Postseason Play

The Spring meeting for the wrap-up of the 1972 season and reorganization for the 1973 season was held at the Village Inn. John Maitland, Easton, was re-elected as president for the second consecutive year as well as Larry Haberle of Pottsville as vice president. Bob Stimmel, of Allen, and Joe Blankowitch were re-elected as secretary-treasurer and statistician. Gene Hartzell was elected to the position of league commissioner succeeding the Reverend Francis Zavodny, who had served for eight years in the position. Bob Perugini, Reading's athletic director, officially requested admission into the league. The request was taken under advisement by the league.[1]

First Half - Week 1

Central Catholic 73 Bethlehem Catholic 55: With each player in the starting five scoring in double figures, Central Catholic started the defense of the league title on a positive note. Taking a 20-8 first quarter lead, the Vikings increased it to 36-20 at halftime and cruised to the victory. Only in the 3rd quarter did Bethlehem Catholic show some life when they outscored the Vikings 16-12. In the 4th quarter, the Vikings made 15 of 20 foul shots.

Leading scorers: Central Catholic – Jeff McGeehin 15, Mike Busolits 14, Mark Trinkle 13, Joe Ludrof 12, Tom Kern 11; Bethlehem Catholic – Bob Gallagher 17, Mike Godbolt 16.

Dieruff 88 Allen 46: Dieruff took off with a 20-5 first quarter lead enroute to the most lopsided victory in the intracity series history. Dieruff outscored the Canaries by at least eight points in each quarter. Dieruff had three scoring streaks of 10, 12, and 10 points in the game.

Leading scorers: Dieruff – Rich Schmidt 27, Foo Belfield 17, Doug Kistler 11; Allen – Bob Frederick 15, Bill Ent 10.

Pottsville 77 Liberty 65: Undefeated Pottsville, playing on their home court, got 32 points from Al Holtzer. After the two teams played to a 16-16 tie after one quarter, Pottsville dominated the middle two quarters by scoring 44 points to Liberty's 24. Al Holtzer scored 13 points in the second quarter alone.

Leading scorers: Pottsville– Al Holtzer 32, Mike Sanders 13, Tom Francavage 12; Liberty– Terry Marcincin 23, Ken Houser 19.

Freedom 75 Phillipsburg 63: After the teams tied at the end of the first quarter 14-14, Freedom outscored Phillipsburg by eleven in the second quarter to take a 45-34 halftime lead. The teams had been deadlocked at 27-27 in second quarter before the Patriots went on an 18-7 run to end the first half. Phillipsburg narrowed the gap to seven points 68-61 in the final quarter.

Leading scorers: Freedom - Spence Pierce 17, Steve Kondor 12, Charlie Pescek 11; Phillipsburg – Mark Bennett 19, Dennis Staples 13, Gary Carhart 12.[2]

Easton 58 Hazleton 49: In Easton, the Red Rovers took an 18-13 lead in the first quarter and maintained the lead at halftime 32-27. After Hazleton pulled within three points in the third quarter 38-35, Easton ran off six straight points to forge in front for the rest of the game.

Leading scorers: Easton – Jim Hutnik 16, Don Griffin 11, Bill Sweeney 11; Hazleton – Charlie Craig 12, Rick Rogers 10, Ron Portanova 10, Tom Donahue 10.[3]

Week 2

Allen 74 Liberty 58: With Bob Frederick scoring 14 points in the 2nd quarter, Allen extended its 18-15 lead after one quarter to 38-28 at halftime. Both teams had numerous turnovers with Allen committing 38 and Liberty 25.

Leading scorers: Allen – Bob Frederick 23, Bob Freed 18, Steve Carl 10; Liberty – Terry Marcincin 20.

Central Catholic 48 Freedom 39: After falling behind 8-6 in a lackluster first period, Central Catholic turned it on in the middle two periods to outscore Freedom 31-15 to cruise home with the 100th win for Coach Mike Koury.

Leading scorers: Central Catholic – Jeff McGeehin 16, Mike Busolits 14, Mark Trinkle 10; Freedom – Steve Kondor 10, Tom Lees 10.

Easton 71 Phillipsburg 45: Phillipsburg stayed close throughout the first half and had the lead 28-24 before Easton went on an 11-1 run to end the half. After leading only by six points 35-29 at halftime, Easton employed a tight zone in the second half and turned the game into a rout by outscoring the Stateliners 36-16 after halftime.

Leading scorers: Easton – Jim Hutnik 14, Mike Young 12, Dave Joseph 11; Phillipsburg – Mark Bennett 21.

Dieruff 57 Bethlehem Catholic 39: Although Bethlehem Catholic never led in the game, the Hawks pressured Dieruff in the first half with the Huskies gaining a four-point lead 20-16 after a quarter. The Hawks stayed four back at the half 30-26. Bethlehem Catholic's undoing occurred in the third quarter when Dieruff took a commanding lead by outscoring the Hawks 18-4.

Leading scorers: Dieruff – Rich Schmidt 19, Doug Kistler 15, Tom Stellar 10; Bethlehem Catholic – Bob Gallagher 17, Mike Godbolt 10.[4]

Pottsville 58 Hazleton 57: With Hazleton leading 57-56, the Mountaineers; Steve Lazar was called for traveling which gave the ball to Pottsville. Al Holtzer took the in-bounds pass and dribbled once before putting up a hook shot with two seconds left that went in for the winning score for Pottsville. Pottsville led most of the first half before Hazleton caught up and went ahead by six points in the third period. Pottsville knotted the score at 46 and the teams battled back and forth the rest of the way with the Crimson Tide winning on a last second shot.

Leading scorers: Pottsville – Al Holtzer 28, John Burch 14; Hazleton – Ron Portanova 14, Sam Monticello 14, Charlie Craig 12, Tom Donahue 10.[5]

Central Catholic 58 Pottsville 40: Central Catholic went out to a 15-5 first quarter lead and extended to 13 points at the half 34-21. Jeff McGeehin made several long full-court passes for field goals by his teammates as the Vikings handed Pottsville their first loss. Central Catholic never trailed in the contest after taking a 7-0 lead to start the game.

Leading scorers: Central Catholic–Tom Kern 16, Jeff McGeehin 15, Mike Busolits 13; Pottsville–Al Holtzer 12, John Burch 11.

Bethlehem Catholic 61 Allen 57: Playing to a 12-12 tie after a quarter, Bethlehem Catholic took control of the game in the second and third periods and built leads of 32-27 at the half and 46-35 after three quarters. Allen rallied in the fourth quarter but could not overcome the Hawks big lead.

Leading scorers: Bethlehem Catholic – Dan Sinnott 18, Mike Harvilla 14, Bob Gallagher 12; Allen – Bob Frederick 16, Tom Ward 12, Bill Ent 10, Steve Carl 10.

Dieruff 56 Easton 45: In a 14-14 tie after the first quarter, Easton took a 24-18 lead into the locker room at the half. After halftime, Dieruff's offense came to life as they outscored the Red Rovers 38-21 in the last two periods. The Huskies' use of the zone defense triggered the second half outburst.

Leading scorers: Dieruff – Tom Stellar 16, Joe Groller 13, Rich Schmidt 11; Easton – Jim Hutnik 10, Dave Joseph 10.

Hazleton 68 Freedom 49: Hazleton hit on 29 of its first 39 field goal attempts in the game to take a 23-6 first quarter lead and extend to 53-34 after three periods. Freedom never got any closer than seven points which happened early in the third quarter.

Leading scorers: Hazleton – Rich Rogers 18, Ron Portanova 15, Charlie Craig 14; Freedom – Spence Pierce 12, Tom Lees 10,[6]

Week 3

Dieruff 70 Freedom 52: Just four games into the season, Dieruff stood alone as the only unbeaten team in league play. Leading 18-11 after a quarter, the Huskies kept building the lead after each of the four quarters to cruise to the win. With Dieruff employing a press often in the game, Freedom committed 28 turnovers.

Leading scorers: Dieruff – Rich Schmidt 22, Foo Belfield 17, Tom Stellar 15; Freedom – Gary Kesack 19, Steve Kondor 10.

Allen 93 Phillipsburg 70: Allen raced out to a 19-8 first quarter lead, but Phillipsburg responded to cut the lead to six points at halftime 46-30. With six players scoring in double figures, Allen took command of the game in the final two quarters for an easy win.

Leading scorers: Allen – Tom Ward 17, Bill Ent 15, Steve Carl 14, Bob Frederick 14, Bob Freed 11, Dave Korfin 10; Phillipsburg – Dave Smith 13, Dennis Staples 11, John Redos 10.[7]

Hazleton 43 Central Catholic 40: Central Catholic made only 1 of 13 field goal attempts in the second quarter as Hazleton took a 24-15 lead at halftime. The Vikings rallied early in the third quarter to cut the lead to 26-24, but could never take over the lead despite getting within a point 28-27 at the end of the third quarter. Hazleton rallied to build the lead to 40-27 three minutes into the fourth quarter

Leading scorers: Hazleton - Ron Portanova 14, Charlie Craig 10; Central Catholic – Joe Ludrof 10.[8]

Liberty 52 Bethlehem Catholic 43: Bethlehem Catholic sprung out to a 16-8 first quarter lead only to have Liberty outscore the Hawks 16-8 in the second quarter for a 24-24 halftime tie. After a 30-30 tie with 3:20 left in the third quarter, Liberty took the lead for good

Leading scorers: Liberty – Terry Marcincin 18, Jack Ferri 16; Bethlehem Catholic – Mike Godbolt 21.[9]

Easton 49 Pottsville 40: After Pottsville took a 14-13 first quarter lead, the two teams tied at 18-18 in the second quarter before Easton rallied and took a six-point lead into halftime 26-20. Easton took a commanding 19-point lead 49-30 in the 4th quarter before Pottsville scored the final ten points in the contest.

Leading scorers: Easton – Dave Joseph 14, Mike Young 13, Dana Parr 10; Pottsville - Al Holtzer 13, John Burch 12.[10]

Dieruff 68 Liberty 48: Scoring just nine points in the first quarter, Dieruff's offense got gradually better as the scored 13, 19, and 30 points in the next three quarters. Liberty took a 9-6 lead after a quarter and the teams were tied at halftime 19-19, but the Hurricane could not keep pace with the Huskie offense the rest of the game.

Leading scorers: Dieruff - Doug Kistler 28, Al Blount 11; Liberty – Jack Ferri 15, Skip John 10.

Pottsville 53 Freedom 43: Freedom took its only lead at the first quarter buzzer 8-7 on a Spence Pierce jumper. The teams were only tied once in the game at 14-14 during the second quarter. Otherwise, it was all Pottsville as the Patriots at one point went nearly 12 minutes without a field goal.

Leading scorers: Pottsville – John Burch 18, Al Holtzer 16; Freedom – Gary Kesack 11, Steve Kondor 11, Spence Pierce 10.

Central Catholic 97 Phillipsburg 48: Central Catholic's offense exploded as they scored 24 points in the first quarter and followed that up with 25 in the second quarter. After taking a 49-24 lead at the half, they came out of the locker room and held the Stateliners to four points in the third quarter while scoring 25 points of their own. The second string scored 23 points in the 4th quarter as the Vikings improved to 4-1.

Leading scorers: Central Catholic – Jeff McGeehin 21, Mark Trinkle 18, Mike Busolits 16, Tom Kern 11; Phillipsburg – Mark Bennett 14.

Easton 63 Bethlehem Catholic 42: Bethlehem Catholic kept it close in the first half and led 20-19 with 1:49 left in the second quarter. Easton scored the next six points to take a 25-20 lead at the half. The Red Rovers took a 35-25 lead with nearly five minutes to play in the third quarter. They put the game away by scoring the last 14 points to head into the final quarter with a 49-25 lead. At 4-1, Easton tied Central Catholic for second place behind undefeated Dieruff.

Leading scorers: Easton – Jim Hutnik 21, Dana Parr 12, Mike Young 10; Bethlehem Catholic – Mike Godbolt 10.

Hazleton 75 Allen 51: With Allen never leading in the game, Hazleton took 16-10 after a quarter. After the Mountaineers came out of the locker room with a 28-23 lead, they scored the first eight points of the third quarter for a thirteen-point lead. Allen made a field goal and Hazleton promptly ran off eight more points in a row and the lead grew to nineteen points.

Leading scorers: Hazleton – Charlie Craig 18, Rick Rogers 15, Tom Donahue 11; Allen – Bill Ent 22, Steve Carl 10.[11]

Week 4

Dieruff 64 Hazleton 50: Dieruff, who scored 13 points in each of the first three quarters, took a 26-22 lead at the half and extended it to 34-23 midway through the third period. Hazleton came roaring back to tie the game going into the final quarter 39-39. The Huskies regrouped in the fourth quarter to take a 54-50 lead and then scored the last ten points of the contest.

Leading scorers: Dieruff – Doug Kistler 20, Tom Stellar 14; Hazleton – Charlie Craig 14.

Allen 83 Pottsville 81: Allen took a 21-14 lead heading into the second quarter only to have Pottsville storm back to take a 41-39 halftime and 65-58 lead after three quarters. With six minutes left to play, Pottsville still led 71-62 before Allen outscored the Crimson Tide 14-2 to take a 76-73 lead which they never relinquished.

Leading scorers: Allen – Bill Ent 21, Bob Frederick 20, Doug Snyder 19; Pottsville - Al Holtzer 33, John Burch 16, Tom Francavage 12.[12]

Freedom 67 Liberty 50: Liberty held only one lead in the game, but kept it close until the fourth quarter. Freedom held early leads of 17-13 after a quarter and 33-31 at the half. The score was still only 46-41 after three quarters before the Patriots outscored the Hurricane 21-9 in the final period.

Leading scorers: Freedom – Gary Kesack 19, Tom Lees 18, Spence Pierce 14, Steve Kondor 11; Liberty – Terry Marcincin 30, Skip John 14.

Bethlehem Catholic 65 Phillipsburg 62: Phillipsburg held its first lead 10-9 with three minutes to play in the first period and held the lead until 7 ½ minutes remained to play in the game when Bethlehem Catholic took 50-49 lead. Phillipsburg held the lead again at 62-59, but the Hawks scored the last six point of the game to pull out the win over the Stateliners, winless in the league.

Leading scorers: Bethlehem Catholic – Bob Gallagher 19, Mike Godbolt 18, Dan Sinnott 14; Phillipsburg - Dennis Staples 17, John Redos 15.

Central Catholic 47 Easton 44: The second quarter proved pivotable for Central Catholic as they outscored Easton 16-11 as both teams played nearly even the rest of the game. Easton took a one-point lead after a quarter 16-15 and outscored the Vikings 7-6 in the final period, but Central Catholic's five-point second period advantage took them to victory, both teams scored ten points in the third period.

Leading scorers: Central Catholic-Mike Busolits 16, Jeff McGeehin 10, Tom Kern 10; Easton-Dana Parr 13.[13]

Freedom 72 Allen 61: With teams tied at 13-13 at the end of the first quarter, they knotted the score again at 21-21 midway through the second quarter. Freedom moved ahead at the half 32-27 only to see the Canaries tie the score at 32-32 in the beginning of the third quarter. In the next three minutes, the Patriots went on a 16-2 run to take charge of the contest. The closest Allen got was 65-59 late in the final quarter.

Leading scorers: Freedom – Tom Lees 27, Gary Kesack 19, Spence Pierce 12; Allen – Doug Snyder 26, Bob Frederick 14.

Central Catholic 63 Dieruff 54: Central Catholic halted Dieruff's ten-game overall win streak and six in the league to take a share of first place with the Huskies. When Dieruff took a 9-8 first quarter lead, the Vikings struck back to take the lead at the half 28-23. At the end of three quarters, Central Catholic still led by five, but Dieruff narrowed the lead to four points 54-50 with 3 ½ minutes left. The Vikings stretched the lead in the final minutes of the contest.

Leading scorers: Central Catholic – Joe Ludrof 16, Mark Trinkle 16, Jeff McGeehin 13, Tom Kern 10; Dieruff – Rich Schmidt 16, Foo Belfield 14, Doug Kistler 12.

Easton 57 Liberty 44: Despite committing 22 turnovers and making only 12 of 23 foul shots, Liberty held its own in the contest until early in the fourth quarter when they trailed by only four points 41-37. Liberty took an early lead 15-14 going into the second quarter. Easton scored the first six points in the second quarter and never trailed after that, although Liberty threatened several times including 34-33 early in the third quarter. Easton scored the next seven points and Liberty could get no closer than four points.

Leading scorers: Easton – Jim Hutnik 21, Dave Joseph 13; Liberty – Ken Houser 13, Jack Ferri 10.

Hazleton 70 Bethlehem Catholic 58: Both teams began the contest with lengthy scoring runs. Hazleton scored the first 13 points only to have Bethlehem Catholic counter with an 11-point run to complete the scoring in the first quarter. Hazleton's second quarter won the game for the Mountaineers when they outscored the Hawks 23-12 for a thirteen-point first half advantage. Although the Hawks tallied one more point in the second half 35-34, the game had been decided by halftime when Bethlehem Catholic could not make a serious run at Hazleton.

Leading scorers: Hazleton – Charlie Craig 23, Richard Rogers 11; Bethlehem Catholic – Dan Sinnott 17, Mike Godbolt 10, Joe Zubia 10, Bob Gallagher 10.[14]

Pottsville 69 Phillipsburg 36: While Pottsville improved to 4-3, Phillipsburg remained winless in league play at 0-6. Al Holtzer and John Burch, with 40 combined points, outscored the Stateliners total points for the game. After holding a 31-18 lead at the half, Pottsville turned the game into a rout when they scored 26 points in the third quarter.

Leading scorers: Pottsville – Al Holtzer 22, John Burch 18, Tom Francavage 10; Phillipsburg - Dennis Staples 11.[15]

Week 5

Dieruff 92 Phillipsburg 46: Using a pressing defense and a fast-break offense, Dieruff ran up 46-19 halftime lead. Coach Dick Schmidt used his starters only half way through the third quarter and inserted his bench for the rest of the contest. Despite not having starter Tom Stellar available due to an injury, the Huskies easily took the contest over the winless Stateliners.

Leading scorers: Dieruff – Joe Groller 15, Rich Schmidt 13, Jack Booros 13, Al Blount 13, Doug Kistler 10, Jim Noti 10; Phillipsburg – Sandy McGinnis 13, Gary Carhart 11.

Central Catholic 69 Allen 57: With a fast 21-9 start in the first quarter, Central Catholic used the large advantage to hand Allen its fifth loss in eight league contests. The Canaries played the Vikings on even terms the rest of the way with each team scoring 48 points in the final three quarters.

Leading scorers: Central Catholic – Jeff McGeehin 22, Mike Busolits 18, Tom Kern 11; Allen – Bill Ent 19, Bob Frederick 13.

Easton 46 Freedom 43: Freedom appeared to be on the way to victory for most of the contest and built as much as a 32-25 lead late in the third quarter. Easton narrowed the gap to a single point 34-33 before the Patriots rallied for a five-point lead 40-35. But Easton scored the next six points to take their first lead of the night with two minutes to play 41-40. Freedom tied the score at 41-41 before the Red Rovers ran off the next five points for the victory.

Leading scorers: Easton – Mike Young 16; Freedom – Tom Lees 12, Gary Kesack 10.[16]

Hazleton 64 Liberty 52: Despite playing only half the game because of foul problems, Charlie Craig still scored 20 points to lead Hazleton to the win over Liberty. Liberty took a 5-0 lead to start the contest, but they committed 10 turnovers the rest of the quarter as Hazleton took a 14-7 lead into the second quarter, The Mountaineers increased the lead to 34-19 at the half. Hazleton extended the lead to 40-21 at the start of the second half before the Hurricane ran off 11 straight points. Unfortunately, Liberty's rally ended as the Mountaineers cruised to the win.

Leading scorers: Hazleton- Charlie Craig 20, Tom Donahue 15; Liberty- Jack Ferri 12, Terry Marcincin 11.[17]

Pottsville 66 Bethlehem Catholic 64: Bethlehem Catholic held a two-point lead 12-10 with Pottsville coming back to lead at the half 24-22. Pottsville increased the lead to four points after three quarters and held a ten-point lead 59-49 with five minutes to play. The Hawks rallied to tie the score at 64. Pottsville turned the ball over to the Hawks on a traveling violation with three seconds to play. Pottsville's Bruce Heffner intercepted the in-bounds pass for an easy lay-up at the buzzer, his only points of the night, for the thrilling victory.

Leading scorers: Pottsville – Al Holtzer 35, John Burch 20; Bethlehem Catholic – Mike Harvilla 18, Mike Godbolt 12, Bob Gallagher 11.[18]

Bethlehem Catholic 56 Freedom 47: In a ragged, physical contest which had 46 turnovers and five players foul out of the game, Bethlehem Catholic jumped out to a 14-8 after a quarter. With Joe Zubia scoring his team's first nine points of the second quarter, the Hawks took a 23-9 lead to take control of the game. The Patriots had a 10-2 run in the fourth quarter to cut the lead to 51-42, but that was as close as they would get.

Leading scorers: Bethlehem Catholic – Joe Zubia 18, Mike Godbolt 13, Bob Gallagher 10; Freedom – Gary Kesack 22.

Central Catholic 87 Liberty 56: Central Catholic rolled over Liberty to maintain a share of first place and force a first half title playoff with Dieruff. Central scored 35 points in the second quarter and held Liberty to five points in the third quarter in an easy win over the Hurricane.

Leading scorers: Central Catholic–Joe Ludrof 18, Jeff McGeehin 16, Chris Johnson 13, Tom Kern 10; Liberty–Kirk Shelley 19.

Dieruff 81 Pottsville 44: Dieruff settled the matter early as they ran off 12 straight points on their way to a 24-6 first quarter lead. Preparing for their playoff with Central Catholic for the first half title, the Huskies led by as much as 41 points in the third quarter.

Leading scorers: Dieruff – Foo Belfield 18, Rich Schmidt 16, Joe Groller 13; Pottsville – Al Holtzer 20, John Burch 18.

Easton 59 Allen 50: After trailing 32-21 at the half, Allen saw the Easton's lead increase to 19 points early in the third quarter 42-23. The Canaries switched to a man-to-man defense and fought back to within four points three times in the 4th quarter before the Red Rovers recovered to hand Allen its 6th loss in nine first half league games.

Leading scorers: Easton – Dave Joseph 22, Dana Parr 13, Jim Hutnik 11; Allen – Doug Snyder 20.[19]

Week 6

Two make up contests were played in what was originally an off week for the teams prior to the begin of second half play.

Liberty 83 Phillipsburg 53: Liberty won its second contest in league play with a win over hapless Phillipsburg. Liberty scored 20 points in each the first three quarters and held the Stateliners to nine points in the third quarter to roll to the victory.

Leading scorers: Liberty – Skip John 17, Tom Ludwick 14, Jack Ferri 12, Terry Marcincin 12; Phillipsburg – Dennis Staples 16, Sandy McGinnis 14.[20]

Hazleton 83 Phillipsburg 55: Hazleton took a 10-0 lead before Phillipsburg scored its first points as they held a 28-7 lead after the first quarter. Coach Dave Shafer substituted as early as the second quarter in the romp over the Stateliners, who finished winless in the first half of league play.

Leading scorers: Hazleton – Charlie Craig 16, Rick Rogers 10; Phillipsburg – John Redos 13, Dennis Staples 11, Sandy McGinnis 11, Gary Carhart 11.[21]

First Half Playoff

Central Catholic 56 Dieruff 52 OT: Dieruff suffered only two losses in the first half of league play, both to Central Catholic. The Huskies build up a five-point lead over the first three quarters 36-31 only to have the Vikings rally in the final period to tie the game in regulation. The Vikings trailed by seven points with two minutes left in regulation. Viking Rich Lang replaced Jeff McGeehin after he fouled out with a little over four minutes left. Lang converted a crucial one and one foul opportunity to tie the game at 50-50 and send it to overtime. After missing twelve straight field goal attempts, Mike Busolits made one when it counted in overtime for the winning field goal.

Leading scorers: Central Catholic – Joe Ludrof 16, Mark Trinkle 12; Dieruff – Joe Groller 13, Foo Belfield 12, Doug Kistler 10, Rich Schmidt 10.[22]

Second Half - Week 7

Dieruff 89 Allen 68: Dieruff never trailed in the contest as the Huskies built an eleven-point lead at the half 43-32. Dieruff scored the first eight points of the fourth quarter before Allen ran off eleven straight points. Despite the run, the Canaries never threatened the Huskies' lead.

Leading scorers: Dieruff – Tom Stellar 28, Foo Belfield 16, Doug Kistler 15, Rich Schmidt 12; Allen – Doug Snyder 23, Bob Frederick 19, Bill Ent 14.

Freedom 62 Phillipsburg 46: Because of Tom Lees injury, Dave Tomaszlewski got a rare start and responded with 25 points as the Patriots handed Phillipsburg its tenth league loss and dropped to 1-12 overall. After Phillipsburg took a 4-2 lead, Freedom ran off eight straight points to lead 12-6 at the end of the first quarter. The Patriots eventually stretched the lead to 23 in the third period.

Leading scorers: Freedom – Dave Tomaszewski 25, Gary Kesack 10; Phillipsburg – Gary Carhart 10.

Easton 50 Hazleton 39: Easton held Hazleton to four points in the second quarter on their way to a 22-16 halftime lead. Although the Red Rovers never trailed after the first period, the Mountaineers pulled within two points in the 4th quarter 36-34 before Easton responded with several field goals to pull away for the win.

Leading scorers: Easton – Dave Joseph 17, Mike Young 150; Hazleton – Charlie Craig 10.

Central Catholic 66 Bethlehem Catholic 53: After their thrilling win two nights earlier for the first half title, Central Catholic responded by taking a 33-19 first half lead and expanding it to 24 points 58-34 heading into the fourth quarter.

Leading scorers: Central Catholic–Mark Trinkle 18, Jeff McGeehin 13, Chris Johnson 12; Bethlehem Catholic–Joe Zubia 13.[23]

Pottsville 80 Liberty 51: After several first quarter ties with the last at 10-10, Pottsville ended the quarter with three field goals to lead 16-10. Pottsville's second quarter settled the contest when the Crimson Tide outscored the Hurricane 21-9. Pottsville kept command of the 2nd half for an easy second half opening win.

Leading scorers: Pottsville – Al Holtzer 23, Tom Francavage 12, Ed Mady 10; Liberty – Terry Marcincin 23, Kirk Shelley 10.[24]

Week 8

Central Catholic 66 Freedom 53: Sixth man Rich Lang, who played for Mark Trinkle suffering from a back injury, responded with nine rebounds, nine points, and three assists to help lead Central Catholic to its seventh straight win. Freedom's only lead came with less than 30 seconds to play in the first quarter 14-12. The Vikings tied the score 14-14 at the end of the quarter and used a strong second quarter, outscoring the Patriots 23-14, on their way to the win.

Leading scorers: Central Catholic – Mike Busolits 20, Chris Johnson 14, Jeff McGeehin 10; Freedom – Spence Pierce 27, Gary Kesack 12.

Allen 59 Liberty 56: Allen took a 13-10 first quarter lead, but Liberty charged back in the second quarter to lead at the half 31-25. Allen cut the lead to 47-37 after three quarters. The Canaries rallied in the final quarter and took the lead 54-53 only to see Liberty take the lead 56-54 with 11 seconds to play. Doug Snyder drove down the lane and was fouled in a controversial call. Liberty coach Al Senavitis was called for a technical for protesting the call. Allen went ahead on the technical and Steve Carl stole the in-bounds pass, was fouled, and made the foul shots as the Canaries pulled out the win.

Leading scorers: Allen - Doug Snyder 18, Bob Frederick 17; Liberty – Terry Marcincin 22, Skip John 12.

Dieruff 81 Bethlehem Catholic 49: With the score tied at 12-12 in the first quarter, Dieruff ended the quarter with 12 straight points and went on a 10-2 run in the second quarter to lead at the half 41-28. When Dieruff was able to score only one field goal over an eight-minute period, the Hawks fought back to within seven points in the third period. The Huskies went on a 12-2 spurt to pull away for the win.

Leading scorers: Dieruff – Rich Schmidt 17, Tom Stellar 15, Joe Groller 14, Doug Kistler 13; Bethlehem Catholic – Mike Godbolt 19, Joe Zubia 16,

Easton 67 Phillipsburg 53: Phillipsburg went into the second period tied with Easton 12-12 only to have the Red Rovers charge to a 33-20 halftime lead. Easton added 24 points in the third quarter as they rolled to the victory to start 2-0 in the second half. Easton scored 14 consecutive points in the second quarter while the Stateliners went scoreless for almost 5 ½ minutes.

Leading scorers: Easton – Dana Parr 17, Don Griffin 12, Mike Young 12; Phillipsburg – Rich Weiss 11, Gary Carhart 10, Denny Staples 10.[25]

Hazleton 65 Pottsville 57: Pottsville raced out to an 18-8 first quarter lead, by scoring the last ten points of the quarter, only to have Hazleton cut the lead to one at the half 29-28. Hazleton finally tied the score at 37-37 in the third quarter and took a three-point lead into the final quarter. Hazleton took command of the contest in the fourth quarter.

Leading scorers: Hazleton – Tom Donahue 18, Steve Lazar 13, Charlie Craig 11; Pottsville – Al Holtzer 20, John Burch 11.[26]

Central Catholic 62 Pottsville 43: Leading 20-17 with 39 seconds to play in the first half, Central Catholic turned four steals into three baskets and a 26-17 halftime lead. The Vikings kept wearing down Pottsville with a stingy defense in the second half to win the eighth in a row and share first place with Easton at 3-0.

Leading scorers: Central Catholic – Mike Busolits 14, Joe Ludrof 12, Jeff McGeehin 12, Tom Kern 10; Pottsville – Al Holtzer 12, John Burch 12.

Allen 85 Bethlehem Catholic 72: Tom Ward moved into a starting role after serving as 6th man and scored 22 points to help spark Allen to its win over Bethlehem Catholic. The Canary offense scored 21 or more points in each quarter.

Leading scorers: Allen – Tom Ward 22, Doug Snyder 20, Bob Frederick 18, Steve Carl 10, Bill Ent 10; Bethlehem Catholic – Mike Godbolt 26, Dan Sinnott 16, Joe Zubia 10.

Liberty 83 Phillipsburg 57: Phillipsburg took a 6-3 lead in the first quarter only to have Liberty outscore them 27-1 the rest of the quarter for a commanding 30-7 lead. Phillipsburg committed 16 turnovers in the period and went three minutes without a shot. The teams played nearly equal the rest of the way with the Hurricane outscoring the Stateliners 53-50.

Leading scorers: Liberty – Terry Marcincin 20, Skip John 11, Kirk Shelley 10; Phillipsburg – Sandy McGinnis 13, Gary Carhart 10.

Hazleton 47 Freedom 45: Finishing the first quarter with five ties and a 14-13 Freedom lead, Hazleton was not able to score for the first four minutes of the second quarter. Freedom had as much as a 14-point lead in the quarter on the way to a 31-23 halftime lead. Freedom could only score seven points in each of the third and fourth quarters as the Mountaineers rallied for the win.

Leading scorers: Hazleton – Charlie Craig 13, Paul Shershen 10; Freedom – Spence Pierce 10, Dave Tomaszewski10, Charlie Pescek 10.

Easton 64 Dieruff 41: Easton parlayed strong 1st and 4th quarters to a win in a battle for a share of first place with Central Catholic. Easton led 10-2 after a period and outscored the Huskies 26-13 in the final period for a relatively easy win. Dieruff was 1 for 13 in the first quarter, 5 for 24 at the half, and 16 for 50 on the night from the field.

Leading scorers: Easton – Dana Parr 23, Dave Joseph 12, Jim Hutnik 10; Dieruff – Rich Schmidt 17.[27]

Week 9

Bethlehem Catholic 67 Liberty 60: Bethlehem Catholic built a 33-24 lead at halftime after trailing early in the first quarter 6-3. Both teams saw several starters sitting on the bench for extended periods of time due to foul issues. The teams combined for 66 foul shots.

Leading scorers: Bethlehem Catholic – Mike Harvilla 14, Dan Sinnott 13, Mike Guman 12, Mike Godbolt 10; Liberty – Skip John 14, Terry Marcincin 12, Kirk Shelley 10, Jack Ferri 10.

Allen 100 Phillipsburg 69: Allen took a 53-21 lead while making 23 of 37 field goal attempts. The Canaries held the Stateliners to only eight points in the first quarter. Allen's starters only played during the first half as sixteen players got into the game with fourteen scoring.

Leading scorers: Allen – Doug Snyder 25, Tom Ward 14, Bob Frederick 14, Steve Carl 10; Phillipsburg – John Weisel 14, John Redos 12, Jim Vaughn 11, Gary Carhart 10.

Dieruff 59 Freedom 45: Trailing 13-10 after a quarter, Dieruff rolled to a 32-23 lead at the half. Freedom pulled within 40-35 near the end of the 3rd quarter, but Dieruff came on in the 4th quarter to secure the win.

Leading scorers: Dieruff – Joe Groller 16, Rich Schmidt 14, Doug Kistler 10; Freedom – Spence Pierce 13, Charlie Pescek 12, Gary Kesack 10.

Central Catholic 56 Hazleton 51: In a deliberate first half, Hazleton took the lead after a quarter 8-6 with Central Catholic coming back to tie the game at the half 17-17. Both teams scored 18 points in the 3rd quarter to remain tied going into the 4th quarter. Four times the Vikings took 6-point leads in the final quarter but could not pull away. The Vikings sealed the win on Jeff McGeehin's rebound and long downcourt pass for a lay-up by Mike Busolits.

Leading scorers: Central Catholic –Mike Busolits 17, Mark Trinkle 17, Jeff McGeehin 12; Hazleton – Tom Donahue 18, Sam Monticello 12.

Easton 66 Pottsville 49: Easton maintained its share of first place with big 1st and 3rd quarters against Pottsville. They outscored the Crimson Tide by 11 in the first and 10 in the third. Easton never trailed in the contest.

Leading scorers: Easton – Dave Joseph 18, Mike Young 13, Jim Hutnik 12, Dana Parr 11, Don Griffin 10; Pottsville – Al Holtzer 11.[28]

Pottsville 58 Freedom 50: Freedom could only score 15 points in the first half while Pottsville scored 34 points. Freedom trailed 21-15 in the second quarter when the Crimson Tide scored the final 13 points of the half. Even though the Patriots outscored Pottsville 35-24 in the second half, they could not overcome the 19-point first half advantage.

Leading scorers: Pottsville – Al Holtzer 20, John Burch 13, Tom Francavage 10; Freedom – Gary Kesack 19, Spence Pierce 16, Tom Lees 10.

Easton 69 Bethlehem Catholic 54: Easton made 16 of its 25 shots but trailed Bethlehem Catholic going into halftime 34-33. The Hawks, trailing the Red Rovers 12-2 in the first quarter hit the next seven shots to tie the score at 24-24. Easton went scoreless while Bethlehem Catholic ran off 10 straight points. The Red Rovers scored seven points to close out the half. Easton took the lead early in the 3rd quarter when the Hawks' gym had a power failure. Undeterred, the Red Rovers continued their 3rd quarter run to outscore the Hawks 17-5. Easton scored ten points in a row late in the 3rd quarter to take an insurmountable 52-39 lead.

Leading scorers: Easton – Mike Young 17, Don Griffin 14, Dave Joseph 14, Dana Parr 11, Jim Hutnik 10; Bethlehem Catholic – Joe Zubia 15, Mike Guman 10, Mike Godbolt 10.

Central Catholic 91 Phillipsburg 50: Taking a 17-6 lead after a quarter, Central Catholic scored at least 22 points in each of the last three quarters in the romp over Phillipsburg. All twelve players used by Coach Mike Koury managed to score in the game. While the Vikings improved to 17-2 overall, Phillipsburg dropped its 16th game in a row after a season-opening victory.

Leading scorers: Central Catholic – Chris Johnson 19, Jeff McGeehin 18; Phillipsburg – Rich Weiss 11, Gary Carhart 10.

Dieruff 81 Liberty 61: Dieruff scored the first nine points of the game and took a 17-point lead in the second quarter before going into halftime with a 41-29 lead. Dieruff improved to 4-1, a game behind the leaders, while Liberty dropped to 1-4.

Leading scorers: Dieruff – Foo Belfield 22, Joe Groller 16, Doug Kistler 13, Jack Booros 12, Rich Schmidt 11; Liberty – Skip John 21, Kirk Shelley 16, Terry Marcincin 15.

Hazleton 78 Allen 72: With seven ties and six lead changes during the first three periods, Allen led Hazleton by a point 62-61 going into the 4th quarter. The Canaries went into a scoring drought in the first 2 ½ minutes of the quarter while the Mountaineers converted three field goals, a lead from which Allen could not recover.

Leading scorers: Hazleton – Tom Donahue 19, Ron Portanova 14, Charlie Craig 11, Sam Monticello 10; Allen – Steve Carl 16, Bill Ent 14, Bob Frederick 13, Tom Ward 13, Doug Snyder 10.[29]

Week 10

Dieruff 71 Hazleton 60: Dieruff held a 34-24 lead going into the third quarter, but Hazleton pulled within three points midway through the quarter. In the next eight minutes, the Huskies outscored the Mountaineers 22-5 to take charge. Dieruff's win tied them with Easton for second place, a game behind Central Catholic.

Leading scorers: Dieruff – Doug Kistler 15, Tom Stellar 15, Rich Schmidt 15, Foo Belfield 11; Hazleton - Ron Portanova 14, Rick Rogers 12, Charlie Craig 11.

Freedom 67 Liberty 45: After Liberty had taken a 12-10 lead after a quarter, Freedom scored the first five points of the second quarter to take the lead which they never lost. Freedom took a commanding lead in the quarter by outscoring the Hurricane 20-8. Freedom ran off 14 straight points from the last 35 seconds of the first half through the first few minutes of the third quarter.

Leading scorers: Freedom – Spence Pierce 22, Tom Lees 12, Steve Kondor 10; Liberty – Jack Ferri 12, Terry Marcincin 11.

Allen 73 Pottsville 60: Allen dominated the first and fourth quarters to defeat Pottsville and improve their second half record to 4-2. After leading the Crimson Tide 29-23, Allen gave up the lead 34-33 early in the third period. Allen recovered and took a six-point lead into the fourth quarter 48-42 and then pulled away.

Leading scorers: Allen – Bob Frederick 21, Bill Ent 16, Tom Ward 13, Steve Carl 11, Doug Snyder 10; Pottsville - Pat Flannery 20, Al Holtzer 13.

Central Catholic 66 Easton 64: In the battle for sole possession of first place, Easton took a 16-14 first quarter lead. Central Catholic tied the contest at 23-23 in the second quarter and took a lead they never relinquished on a Tom Kern layup. With the Vikings holding a 62-53 lead with 3:48 to play, Easton fought back to within five points when Mike Busolits stole an in-bounds pass and converted it into a layup to seal the win for the Vikings.

Leading scorers: Central Catholic – Mike Busolits 24, Jeff McGeehin 19, Tom Kern 12; Easton – Jim Hutnik 19, Dana Parr 17, Dave Joseph 17.

Bethlehem Catholic 84 Phillipsburg 52: Led by freshman Mike Guman's ten first period points, Bethlehem Catholic took a 22-7 first quarter lead over Phillipsburg. Phillipsburg remained winless in league play while the Hawks improved to 2-4.

Leading scorers: Bethlehem Catholic – Mike Guman 18, Dan Sinnott 18, Joe Zubia 10; Phillipsburg – John Fritts 11.[30]

Dieruff 66 Central Catholic 53: Dieruff and Central Catholic battled for first place at the East Side Gym. Dieruff took a slim one-point lead in the first quarter 31-12. They increased it to six at the half 31-25 and seven after three periods 43-36. The Huskies held a five-point lead midway through the fourth quarter and went on a ten-point run to take a commanding 15-point lead. The win created a three-way tie at the top with Easton, Central Catholic, and Dieruff with two games to play.

Leading scorers: Dieruff – Doug Kistler 22, Jack Booros 15, Tom Stellar 11; Central Catholic – Jeff McGeehin 19.

Easton 64 Liberty 38: Easton held on to its share of first place with a victory over Liberty. The Red Rovers ran off 16 straight points and held Liberty scoreless for almost 6 ½ minutes in the second quarter. Liberty had a 7-6 lead when Easton went on its run.

Leading scorers: Easton – Jim Hutnik 23, Dave Joseph 10; Liberty – Skip John 10.

Freedom 68 Allen 58: After a tight first half with Freedom on top 30-28, Allen rallied in the third quarter for a 34-30 lead. Freedom took the lead again, but the game was tied five times in the period before Freedom ran off six points to take the lead for good.

Leading scorers: Freedom – Spence Pierce 20, Gary Kesack 16, Steve Kondor 15; Allen – Doug Snyder 18, Steve Carl 11, Tom Ward 10.[31]

Hazleton 67 Bethlehem Catholic 63: With the score tied three times in the opening period, Hazleton took a 14-12 lead going into the second quarter. After another tie to start the quarter, Hazleton spurted to a 22-14 lead and led the rest of the way. The Mountaineers led by nine at the half 38-29, but the Patriots cut the lead to two 54-52 heading into the final period. Hazleton held off Freedom during the last few minutes. Hazleton's Steve Lazar grabbed 30 rebounds in the game.

Leading scorers: Hazleton Rick Rogers 22, Tom Donahue 18, Steve Lazar 13, Charlie Craig 10; Freedom – Mike Godbolt 28, Dan Sinnott 12, Joe Zubia 10.[32]

Pottsville 93 Phillipsburg 48: Pottsville took leads of 24-7 and 50-24 after the first two periods and cruised to victory over Phillipsburg. Phillipsburg lost its 22nd consecutive game in league play.

Leading scorers: Pottsville – Al Holzer 33, Pat Flannery 14, Lance Haberle 11, John Burch 10; Phillipsburg – John Redos 12.[33]

Week 11

Hazleton 75 Liberty 57: Liberty jumped out to a 12-9 lead before Hazleton went on a 13-2 run to lead after a quarter 22-14. The Mountaineers added nine points to the lead in the second quarter to go into the locker room ahead 43-26. They cruised to the win to improve to 5-3 in the second half of the season.

Leading scorers: Hazleton – Steve Lazar 14, Sam Monticello 11; Liberty – Terry Marcincin 20.

Central Catholic 75 Allen 63: Central Catholic held Allen to eight points in each of the first and third quarters to a 55-36 lead after three quarters. With the Vikings taking a 12-8 lead in the first quarter, the Canaries never led in the game. The loss evened Allen's record at 4-4 while the Vikings remained tied for first place with a game to go in the second half.

Leading scorers: Central Catholic–Jeff McGeehin 33, Chris Johnson 13; Allen–Doug Snyder 16, Bob Frederick 14, Bill Ent 12.

Dieruff 81 Phillipsburg 42: Dieruff continued its winning streak over Phillipsburg with its 23rd straight triumph. The Stateliners lost their 23rd in a row in league play. Despite some lackluster play, the Huskies held Phillipsburg to 10 points in each of the first two quarters and 11 in each of the final two quarters to roll over their opponents.

Leading scorers: Dieruff – Foo Belfield 17, Rich Schmidt 14, Tom Stellar 13, Joe Groller 10, Doug Kistler 10; Phillipsburg – John Weisel 6, Rich Weiss 6, Gary Carhart 6.

Bethlehem Catholic 50 Pottsville 42: The teams were tied at the half at 22-22, when Bethlehem Catholic moved ahead 32-27 heading into the final period. With 3:38 to play, Pottsville came within a point of the lead 38-37 only to have the Hawks score ten straight points to seal the win.

Leading scorers: Bethlehem Catholic – Mike Harvilla 21, Mike Godbolt 10; Pottsville – Al Holtzer 11, Bruce Heffner 10.

Easton 62 Freedom 47: Easton retained its share of first place with its win over Freedom. After leading by 10-2 during the first quarter, Easton extended its lead to as many as 19 points in the fourth quarter.

Leading scorers: Easton – Dave Joseph 22, Jim Hutnik 16; Freedom – Gary Kesack 15, Spence Pierce 14.[34]

Hazleton 77 Phillipsburg 55: Hazleton took a 22-10 first quarter lead which included a 10-point run. By halftime, the lead was up to 20 points 44-24. Phillipsburg showed some life in the third period when they outscored the Mountaineers 18-12. The Stateliners lost their 24th consecutive league contest dating back to the second half of last season.

Leading scorers: Hazleton – Charlie Craig 24, Rick Rogers 14, Ron Portanova 12; Phillipsburg – John Redos 22, Gary Carhart 14, Rich Weiss 10.

Central Catholic 56 Liberty 51: Coach Al Senavitis decided to use a slow-down offense as Liberty took a 13-9 first quarter lead and expanded it to 17-9 early in the second quarter. Then, the Vikings went on a 22-2 run the rest of the quarter to take a 31-19 lead at the half. Early in the fourth quarter, Liberty rallied to cut the lead to two points 45-43, but the Vikings beat back the Hurricane rally to maintain its share of first place and qualify for a second half playoff.

Leading scorers: Central Catholic - Mark Trinkle 17, Mike Busolits 14, Jeff McGeehin 13, Chris Johnson 10; Liberty – Dave McKellin 11, Terry Marcincin 10.

Easton 66 Allen 46: Easton also qualified for a second half playoff with an easy win over Allen. After taking a 14-6 lead into the second quarter, they increased the lead to 20 points before Allen came back to cut it to 34-20 at the half. The Red Rovers outscored the Canaries 30-24 in the second half.

Leading scorers: Easton - Dave Joseph 15, Don Griffin 14, Jim Hutnik 13, Dana Parr 10; Allen - Doug Snyder 12, Bob Frederick 12.

Dieruff 65 Pottsville 50: In a slow first quarter, the teams tied at 7-7 before Dieruff took a 30-25 lead over Pottsville. In the third quarter, Dieruff increased the lead to 39-29 with a little under four minutes left in the quarter. The Huskies held off the Crimson Tide in the 4th quarter and qualified for the second half playoff with Central Catholic and Easton.

Leading Scorers: Dieruff – Doug Kistler 20, Rich Schmidt 15, Foo Belfield 14; Pottsville – Bruce Heffner 17, Al Holtzer 10.

Bethlehem Catholic 68 Freedom 52: Bethlehem Catholic took charge in the game by outscoring Freedom 14-3 in the first quarter and 24-14 in the third quarter for a 49-31 lead. During the fourth quarter, they increased their lead 20 points 55-35 and coasted to the win.

Leading scorers: Bethlehem Catholic – Mike Godbolt 24, Mike Harvilla 16, Dan Sinnott 12; Freedom – Gary Kesack 22, Spence Pierce 18.[35]

Second Half Playoff

Three teams, Dieruff, Easton, and Central Catholic, tied for first place, all at 8-1, for the second half title. With Central Catholic eligible for the first time to participate in the PIAA post season playoffs, the Vikings qualified for their first PIAA playoff by virtue of winning the first half title. Dieruff and Easton faced off in the first round with the winner to face the Vikings. If Easton defeated Dieruff and Central Catholic, the Red Rovers would join the Vikings as the league representatives. If Easton beat Dieruff and lost to the Vikings, Dieruff and Easton would have to play again to decide the second league representative.

Easton 56 Dieruff 40: Easton took control of the contest from the very beginning with a 17-10 lead after the first quarter and added five points to the lead at the half 31-19. Easton's stifling defense allowed the Huskies to convert only 7 of 30 field goals in the first half and 14 of 58 for the game. Easton grew the lead to 18 points early in the fourth quarter to prevent Dieruff from making a final charge in the game.

Leading scorers: Easton – Don Griffin 17, Dave Joseph 10; Dieruff – Rich Schmidt 14.[36]

Easton 37 Central Catholic 35: In a low scoring, defensive contest, the teams battled to a 4-4 tie after one quarter. Central Catholic took charge in the second and third quarters. They had built a five-point halftime lead. They added four more points to the lead in the third quarter 27-18 to seemingly have control of the contest. Easton switched to a man-to-man defense in the fourth quarter and forced the Vikings to numerous turnovers. With over three minutes left in the contest, the Vikings had a six-point lead 31-25. After exchanging baskets, Easton scored six straight points to tie the game at 33-33. The Vikings went ahead again on a Jeff McGeehin layup, but Dave Joseph made two foul shots to tie the game at 35. Jim Hutnik then stole the inbounds pass and fed Dana Parr for the winning, driving layup with four seconds left in the contest.

Leading scorers: Easton – Jim Hutnik 10; Central Catholic – Jeff McGeehin 10.[37]

Postseason PIAA Play

Easton 43 Whitehall 36: At Kutztown State's Keystone Hall, Whitehall employed a slow-down offense and a strong inside defense in an effort to overcome Easton's strengths. Easton took a two-point lead 8-6 into the second quarter and increased it to 21-14 at the half. Once in the third period and twice in the fourth, Whitehall trimmed the lead to one only to have Easton counter and move on in the playoffs.

Leading scorers: Easton – Jim Hutnik 14, Dave Joseph 12; Whitehall – Jim Mates 12.[38]

Central Catholic 88 West Hazleton 57: Central Catholic made its initial appearance in PIAA postseason play at Kutztown's Memorial Hall a memorial one with a romp over West Hazleton. The Vikings took a 28-10 first quarter lead and increased it to 48-27 at the half. After holding West Hazleton to only eight points in the third quarter, the Vikings emptied their bench with all 12 players getting into the contest.

Leading scorers: Central Catholic – Joe Ludrof 17, Rich Lang 10; West Hazleton – Joe Callen 17, Dave Ruminsky 10.[39]

Easton 61 Nazareth 38: In Pottsville, Easton and Nazareth played to a 10-10 tie after a quarter before Easton dominated the middle two quarters and took a 39-20 lead into the final quarter. Easton held Nazareth to ten total points in the second and third periods.

Leading scorers: Easton – Mike Young 15, Jim Hutnik 12, Don Griffin 11, Dave Joseph 10; Nazareth – Keith Schlamp 11.[40]

Northampton 58 Central Catholic 53: At Pottsville, Central Catholic led 15-6 over Northampton after a quarter. They increased the lead to thirteen points at the half 33-20. Northampton went to a ball-hawking defense in the third period and outscored the Vikings 13-1 in one stretch to narrow the lead to only two points. The Vikings rallied to take a seven-point lead early in the fourth quarter but the Konkrete Kids countered with a 9-1 streak to tie the game at 44-44. After six lead changes, the Vikings took a 53-50 lead with two minutes to play. They would not score again as Northampton closed with several foul shots and field goals to upset the Vikings.

Leading scorers: Northampton – Jim Spitzer 19, Carl Christman 18, Jim Schneider 15; Central Catholic – Jeff McGeehin 14, Joe Ludrof 12, Mark Trinkle 12.[41]

Central Catholic 66 Nazareth 39: At Muhlenberg's Memorial Hall, Central Catholic took on Nazareth to determine the third team to enter the PIAA playoffs from District 11. Taking an early 4-0 lead, the Vikings were never threatened in the contest. They held leads of 17-7, 33-21, and 49-31 after the first three quarters.

Leading scorers: Central Catholic – Jeff McGeehin 20, Chris Johnson 12, Rich Lang 10, Mike Busolits 10; Nazareth – Keith Schlamp 15.[42]

Easton 56 Northampton 46: In the District 11 championship contest in Pottsville, Easton won its first ever district championship in a battle for over 3 ½ periods before taking command of the contest. Easton led 24-21 heading into the second half, but Northampton came back to take the lead twice in the 3rd quarter. After taking a one-point lead 35-34 to the 4th quarter, the Red Rovers pulled away to a nine-point advantage to win their first crown.

Leading scorers: Easton Dana Parr 17, Don Griffin 13, Mike Young 12, Dave Joseph 10; Northampton – Jim Schneider 20.[43]

Reading 72 Central Catholic 53: At the Farm Show Arena, Central Catholic met its match in Reading and its star player Stu Jackson. After battling Reading in the first quarter and trailing by only two points, Reading took charge in the second quarter to lead at the half 39-28. In the third quarter, the Vikings held Reading at bay and were outscored by only a point. Reading again took charge in the fourth quarter to knock the Vikings out of the playoffs.

Leading scorers: Reading – Mike Garman 26, Wentzel 18, Stuart Jackson 16; Central Catholic – Jeff McGeehin 23, Mike Busolits 10.

Easton 49 Williamsport 41: In Pottsville, Easton took on Williamsport from District 4 in the first round of the PIAA interdistrict playoffs. Despite giving up a season high 15 points in a quarter, Easton took an 18-15 lead into the second quarter. The Red Rovers limited Williamsport to 8 points in each of the two middle quarters to increase their lead to 39-31. Each team scored ten points in the fourth quarter as Easton moved onto the second round of the state playoffs.

Leading scorers: Easton – Dave Joseph 12, Don Griffin 12, Dana Parr 11; Williamsport – Bob Janeski 13, Dave Patton 12.[44]

Easton 57 Pottstown 48: In Pottsville, Pottstown took a slim one-point lead into the second period 9-8 before Easton countered to take the lead at the half 21-18. With the referees allowing the teams to play a physical game, Easton's Dave Joseph suffered a cut over his eye which required several stitches, but he still finished as the Red Rovers' top scorer. In the third quarter, Easton burst out with 20 points to increase the lead to nine 41-32. Both teams scoring 16 points in the final period and Easton moved onto the third round of championship play.

Leading scorers: Easton – Dave Joseph 19, Dana Parr 13, Jim Hutnik 10; Pottstown – Mike Missimer 19, Ken Slotter 13.[45]

Chester 55 Easton 47: Easton battled Chester for three quarters with the Red Rovers taking a first quarter lead 12-10 before Chester took the halftime lead 27-26. The teams battled hard again in the third period with Chester adding a single point to its lead 37-35. Chester's Herman Harris turned the slim lead into a game-deciding advantage when he hit four jump shots in the first two minutes of the final period. Chester took a 46-37 lead. Easton could not overcome the lead and missed its opportunity to advance to the Eastern finals.

Leading scorers: Chester – Herman Harris 19, Phil Mann 14; Easton – Dana Parr 11, Mike Young 11.[46]

Postseason Accolades

Scoring Leader: Al Holtzer, Pottsville, lead the league in scoring with 364 points and an 18-2 points per game average.

All-Stars: The league all-star first team included: Jeff McGeehin, Central Catholic (Most Valuable Player); Al Holtzer, Pottsville; Jim Hutnik, Dave Joseph, Dana Parr, all from Easton. The second team consisted of: Rich Schmidt and Doug Kistler, Dieruff; Mike Busolits, Central Catholic; Tom Donahue, Hazleton; and Bob Frederick, Allen.[47]

All-State: Jeff McGeehin, Central Catholic, was named to the Second Team All-State. The following league players received honorable mention status: Jim Hutnik and Dana Parr, Easton; Al Holtzer, Pottsville; Rich Schmidt, Dieruff; and Mike Godbolt, Bethlehem Catholic.[48]

Final Standings

First Half		Second Half		Overall	
Central Catholic	8-1	Central Catholic	8-1	Central Catholic	16-2
Dieruff	8-1	Dieruff	8-1	Dieruff	16-2
Easton	7-2	Easton	8-1	Easton	15-3
Hazleton	6-3	Hazleton	6-3	Hazleton	12-6
Pottsville	5-4	Allen	4-5	Pottsville	8-10
Allen	3-6	Bethlehem Catholic	4-5	Allen	7-11
Bethlehem Catholic	3-6	Pottsville	3-6	Bethlehem Catholic	7-11
Freedom	3-6	Freedom	3-6	Freedom	6-12
Liberty	2-7	Liberty	1-8	Liberty	3-15
Phillipsburg	0-9	Phillipsburg	0-9	Phillipsburg	0-18

Team Rosters

Allen: Coach Milo Sewards, Berner, Steve Carl, Bill Ent, Bob Frederick, Bob Freed, Dave Korfin, Rick Krause, Numbers, Powell, Rabenold, Smith, Doug Snyder, Spiegel, Scott Stephens, Todd, Tom Ward

Bethlehem Catholic: Coach Bob Bukvics, Gus Concilio, Bob Gallagher, Mike Godbolt, Mike Guman, Mike Harvilla, Leary, Dan Sinnott, Joe Zubia

Central Catholic: Coach Mike Koury, Mike Busolits, Rick Eddinger, Chris Johnson, Tim Johnson, Tom Kern, Joe Kiehstaller, Rich Lang, John Legath, Joe Ludrof, Jeff McGeehin, John Stein, Mark Trinkle, Bob Wootsick

Dieruff: Coach Dick Schmidt, Saunders "Foo" Belfield, Al Blount, Jack Booros, Joe Groller, Doug Kistler, Landis, Mark Mazziotti, Jim Noti, Rich Schmidt, Tom Stellar

Easton: Coach Stan Sutphen, Dave Cardell, Dan Finocchio, Don Griffin, Jim Hutnik, Steve Jones, Dave Joseph, Kelly, Lucey, Mike Miller, Dana Parr, Bill Sweeney, Mike Young

Freedom: Coach Charlie Dubbs, Barry Correll, Joe Hudak, Gary Kesack, Steve Kondor, Tom Lees, Bill Matz, Charlie Pescek, Spence Pierce, Mike Sell, Dave Tomaszewski

Hazleton: Coach Dave Shafer, Bajda (Vadja), Charlie Craig, Tom Donahue, Jeff Fierro, Steve Lazar, Sam Monticello, Nance, Ron Portanova, Rick Rogers, Paul Shershen

Liberty: Coach Al Senavitis, Chuck Alexander, Alex DeAngelis, Wayne Edwards, Jack Ferri, Ken Houser, Bruce John, Skip John, Kozero, Tom Lasko, Tom Ludwig, Terry Marcincin, Dave McKellin, Bryant Perry, Dennis Roebuck, Kirk Shelley

Phillipsburg: Coach Pete Tomaino, Mark Bennett, Gary Carhart, John Fritts, Sandy McGinnis, Rob Pianelli, Pyrek, John Redos, Dave Smith, Snyder, Dennis Staples, Jim Vaughn, John Weisel, Rich Weiss,

Pottsville: Coach Ken Kline, John Burch, Tom Derfler, Pat Flannery, Tom Francavage, Larry Haberle, Bruce Heffner, Al Holtzer, Charlie Jonathon, Todd Kline, Ed Mady, Gary McClure, Mike Sanders, Roy Snowell, Jim Sweeney, Howie Wilson

1974

Easton Defends Its District Title

First Half - Week 1

Central Catholic 57 Liberty 55: Central Catholic took a 14-11 lead after the 1st quarter and increased it to 20-11 early in the 3rd quarter. First year coach Dave Pfahler's Vikings looked like they would take commanding lead in the contest. Liberty fought back to trail at the half by three 32-29. Liberty tied the score twice at 34-34 and 36-36, but Jeff McGeehin put the Vikings ahead for good as they led 46-38 with less than a minute to play in the third period.

Leading scorers: Central Catholic – Jeff McGeehin 15, Chris Johnson 15, Joe Kiehstaller 13, Bob Wootsick 12; Liberty – Kirk Shelley 16, Alex DeAngelis 14, Ken Houser 14.

Easton 64 Allen 52: Coach Stan Sutphen had his Easton squad's defense continue where it had left off in last season's league play. The Red Rovers held the Canaries to 32 points in the first three quarters while putting up 54 points of their own to easily down Allen.

Leading scorers: Easton – Mike Young 17, Don Griffin 11, Butch Brantley 11, Ed Geosits 11; Allen – Doug Snyder 19, Steve Carl 14, Eric Marshall 12.

Dieruff 66 Pottsville 46: Dieruff ran out to an 18-6 lead after a quarter and increased to 37-17 at halftime in Pottsville. The Crimson Tide helped the Huskies' cause with 31 turnovers in the game. The Huskies maintained their 20-point lead at the end of the game.

Leading scorers: Dieruff – Tom Stellar 14, Jack Booros 14, Foo Belfield 10; Pottsville – Ed Mady 13, Pat Flannery 13, John Burch 10.

Hazleton 54 Phillipsburg 53: New first year coach Mike Koury, after moving from Central Catholic, took over the helm at Phillipsburg. The Stateliners continued their league losing streak as the lost their 25th consecutive league contest. For most of the game, it appeared that Phillipsburg might end the streak when they led 40-36 entering the final period. With two seconds to play in the game, Hazleton's Sam Monticello hit a jumper to squeak out the win and hand Phillipsburg yet another loss.

Leading scorers: Hazleton – Sam Monticello 20, Joe Polchin 18, Tom Mundie 14; Phillipsburg – Stan Dyrek 14, Dave Smith 10, Gary Carhart 10.

Freedom 59 Bethlehem Catholic 45: Bethlehem Catholic was unable to put a point on the board during two different 6 ½ minutes stretches in the game. Freedom outscored the Hawks 19-8 in the first quarter and 13-6 in the third quarter during the scoreless streaks. Bethlehem Catholic outscored Freedom by slim margins in the other two periods, but the large advantage in the first and third periods doomed the Hawks.

Leading scorers: Freedom – Spence Pierce 20, Dave Tomaszewski 13, Bill Matz 12; Bethlehem Catholic – Joe Zubia 18.[1]

Week 2

Dieruff 72 Allen 55: Allen opened the game by taking a 17-10 first quarter lead and led in the second quarter by as many as eight points. Using a pressing defense, Dieruff rallied to take a one-point lead at halftime 34-33. Allen took the lead 43-42 lead in the third quarter, but the Huskies hit three straight field goals to take the lead for good 48-43. Dieruff kept rolling in the fourth quarter to take a commanding lead.

Leading scorers: Dieruff – Foo Belfield 28, Rich Schmidt 14, Jack Booros 11; Allen – Doug Snyder 17, Bob Frederick 11, Eric Marshall 10.

Central Catholic 73 Bethlehem Catholic 61: Bethlehem Catholic held an 18-12 lead after a quarter and stretched it to 13 points in the second quarter 30-13 before Central Catholic cut it to seven at the half 34-27. Coach Dave Pfahler employed a pressing halfcourt defense after halftime and took the lead with 27 seconds to play in the third quarter 50-48. The Vikings' roll continued in the final period as they outscored the Hawks by nine points for the win,

Leading scorers: Central Catholic – Jeff McGeehin 25, Bob Wootsick 20, Chris Johnson 11; Bethlehem Catholic – Mike Guman 27, Joe Zubia 24.

Freedom 42 Phillipsburg 36: For the second straight contest, Phillipsburg made a valiant attempt to break its league losing streak which extended over three seasons. The Stateliners led 23-18 with a minute to play in the second quarter, but turnovers resulted in three quick baskets as Freedom took the halftime lead 24-23. Both offenses went cold in the third period with the Patriots outscoring Phillipsburg 6-3. Freedom took a 36-26 lead early in the final quarter. The Stateliners rallied to within three points 39-36 but could not sustain the spurt and lost their 26th straight in the league.

Leading scorers: Freedom – Spence Pierce 16, Dave Tomaszewski 11; Phillipsburg – Gary Carhart 12.

Easton 44 Hazleton 40 2OT: At Hazleton, Easton and Hazleton battled to ties in each for the first two quarters 9-9 and 19-19. Easton had led 19-13 before the Mountaineers rallied for a tie at the half. Hazleton took a two-point lead into the final quarter 28-26 after having led 26-20 during the quarter. After Easton tied the game 36-36 in the last minute of regulation, Hazleton missed a free throw and field goal attempt to send the game into overtime. East team scored two points in the first overtime with Easton making a field goal with ten seconds left to send it to a second overtime. The Red Rovers' Mike Young hit the winning jumper to send the Red Rovers home with the hard-earned victory and improve to 2-0.

Leading scorers: Easton – Butch Brantley 11; Hazleton – Tom Mundie 14.

Pottsville 66 Liberty 64: Pottsville took a seven-point advantage in the first period 15-8 and held on to defeat Liberty as a result of the first half lead. They maintained the lead at the half 33-26 and increased it to eleven early in the third period. Liberty then began its rally to attempt a comeback win. The Hurricane cut the lead to four at the third quarter mark 49-45. Pottsville led 66-60 with 30 seconds to play and Liberty closed to within two points on Crimson Tide turnovers but Pottsville ran out the clock for the win.

Leading scorers: Pottsville – Ed Mady 18, John Burch 17, Todd Kline 12, Tom Francavage 12; Liberty – Bruce John 22, Kirk Shelley 16, Ken Houser 13.[2]

Central Catholic 68 Freedom 41: After taking a 14-10 first quarter lead, Central Catholic held Freedom to seven points in the second quarter on their way to a 37-17 halftime lead. With eleven players scoring in the contest, the Vikings cruised to the win in the second half.

Leading scorers: Central Catholic – Jeff McGeehin 24, Bob Wootsick 12, Chris Johnson 10; Freedom – Joe Hudak 10.

Dieruff 75 Bethlehem Catholic 45: Bethlehem Catholic led early 6-2, but Dieruff's full court press caused 20 turnovers in the first half and led to 16-11 and 36-22 advantages in the first half. The onslaught continued in the third quarter as the Huskies stretched the lead to 58-31. Dieruff improved to 3-0 to tie Central Catholic and Easton for the first half lead.

Leading scorers: Dieruff – Foo Belfield 20, John Landis 13; Bethlehem Catholic – Mike Guman 12, Joe Zubia 11.

Easton 56 Phillipsburg 34: Phillipsburg, after two efforts to break their losing streak, could not stay with Easton as they fell for the 27th straight time in league play. Holding a 21-15 lead at the half, the Red Rovers made 8 of 11 field goal attempts in the third quarter for a 37-21 lead and a rout of the Stateliners.

Leading scorers: Easton – Don Griffin 14, Butch Brantley 13; Phillipsburg – Gary Carhart 11.

Pottsville 59 Hazleton 52: Pottsville took a 27-22 lead into the third quarter and hit 6 of its first 7 shots in the third period to take an overwhelming lead after three quarters 48-33. A Hazleton rally in the final quarter could only cut the lead to seven points.

Leading scorers: Pottsville – Pat Flannery 16, Todd Kline 16, Ed Mady 13; Hazleton – Joe Polchin 12.

Allen 63 Liberty 57: Allen took an early 6-0 lead only to see Liberty rally to lead after a quarter 17-15. Allen grabbed the lead at halftime 29-27, but Liberty owned the third quarter as the Hurricane took a 43-33 lead during the period on their way to a 45-38 lead at the end of the quarter. Doug Snyder scored the last nine points of the game to lead Allen's comeback to win the game in the final quarter and their first in league play.

Leading scorers: Allen – Chris Nunan 17, Doug Snyder 16, Eric Marshall 10, Steve Carl 10; Liberty – Bruce John 14, Alex DeAngelis 13, Kirk Shelley 10.[3]

Week 3

Dieruff 48 Easton 38: Using a controlled offense and pressing defense, Dieruff took a 9-6 first quarter lead and extended it to 23-17 at the half. With a 36-28 lead going into the 4th quarter, Dieruff had to battle in the final minutes when Easton pulled within three points with 2 ½ minutes to play. Despite only attempting 11 field goals in the second half, and making 9, the Huskies held off the Red Rovers by converting free throws. The win over previously unbeaten Easton, and Pottsville's upset of Central Catholic, gave Dieruff sole possession of first place.

Leading scorers: Dieruff – Foo Belfield 14, Jack Booros 13, John Landis 10; Easton – Mike Young 12.

Allen 75 Bethlehem Catholic 57: Bethlehem Catholic trailed 17-9 after a quarter, but went on a 20-4 run to take a 29-25 advantage in the 2nd period and kept the lead 30-29 at the half. With two minutes to go in the 3rd period, Allen led 44-42 and rallied during the first three minutes of the fourth quarter to take a commanding 61-46 lead.

Leading scorers: Allen – Doug Snyder 24, Bob Frederick 21, Steve Carl 12; Bethlehem Catholic – Mike Guman 17, Pat Haney 16, Joe Zubia 10.

Pottsville 64 Central Catholic 62: At Rockne Hall, Pottsville used strong showings in the second and third periods to build a 48-40 lead heading into the fourth quarter. Central Catholic fought back to tie the contest on two Jeff McGeehin foul shots in a one-and-one situation to tie the game at 64-64. With two seconds to play, Mike Smink, off of a rifle pass from Pat Flannery, hit the winning field goal to upset the Vikings and knock them out of first place. McGeehin scored his 1000th career point in the game.

Leading scorers: Pottsville – Pat Flannery 18, Todd Kline 14, Ed Mady 12; Central Catholic – Jeff McGeehin 17, Joe Kiehstaller 16, Chris Johnson 14.

Liberty 64 Phillipsburg 58: First year coach Len Zavacky won his first game after four losses by a total of four points as Liberty handed Phillipsburg yet another loss. Liberty trailed 27-23 heading into the third period when the Hurricane blitzed the Stateliners 22-7 to take the lead, the only quarter that Liberty outscored Phillipsburg in the contest.

Leading scorers: Liberty – Ken Houser 27, Bruce John 14, Kirk Shelley 13; Phillipsburg – Gary Carhart 17,

Hazleton 78 Freedom 70: Despite Spence Pierce's school record-setting scoring night on 11 field goals and 11 free throws, Freedom could not overcome the exploits of Hazleton's sophomores Tom Mundie and Bob Gabriel. The two scored 44 total points in the contest as Hazleton took a 23-16 first quarter lead and was never headed.

Leading scorers: Hazleton – Bob Gabriel 26, Tom Mundie 18, Joe Polchin 16, Sam Monticello 15; Freedom – Spence Pierce 33, Dave Tomaszewski 11.[4]

Bethlehem Catholic 53 Liberty 45: Bethlehem Catholic center Gary Falkenbach took advantage of the absence of Liberty's Ken Houser due to a sprained ankle and scored 11 points in the first period to give the Hawks a 19-8 first quarter lead. The 11-point advantage held up through the rest of the contest as they won their first contest in league play. Liberty climbed to within three points during the second quarter when the Hawks went cold.

Leading scorers: Bethlehem Catholic – Gus Concilio 13, Joe Zubia 13, Mike Guman 12, Gary Falkenbach 11; Liberty – Kirk Shelley 16, Bruce John 13.[5]

The other four contests were postponed due to the weather and were played in the week during the break between the first and second halves of the season.

Week 4

Dieruff 70 Liberty 59: Taking an 11-2 lead in the first quarter and 15-7 at quarter's end, Dieruff played lethargically the rest of the game. Although Liberty got within five points in the third period 39-34, the Huskies were never threatened as they retained sole possession of first place.

Leading scorers: Dieruff – Jack Booros 20, Foo Belfield 16, Rich Schmidt 13, Tom Stellar 10; Liberty – Kirk Shelley 27, Ken Houser 11.

Allen 77 Hazleton 66: Allen fell behind 14-10 after a quarter and 25-17 with 2 ½ minutes left in the 2nd quarter. The Canaries finished the quarter by outscoring the Mountaineers 13-2 to take the halftime lead. After Allen led by 14 points in the fourth quarter, Hazleton rallied to within five points 59-54 before Allen put the game away.

Leading scorers: Allen – Doug Snyder 27, Eric Marshall 22, Bob Frederick, Steve Carl 10; Hazleton – Mike Caparell 19, Bob Gabriel 15, Sam Monticello 11.

Pottsville 61 Freedom 57: With five players in double figures and a 13-point lead 50-37 going into the fourth quarter, Pottsville seemed well on its way to an easy victory. Freedom went on a 16-6 run to start the quarter to pull within three points 56-53 with four minutes to play. Pottsville responded with six points to hang on for the win.

Leading scorers: Pottsville – Todd Kline 12, Pat Flannery 12, John Burch 12, Ed Mady 12, Tom Francavage 12; Freedom – Spence Pierce 21, Dave Tomaszewski 10.

Central Catholic 71 Phillipsburg 35: Central Catholic ended the first period with a 17-4 lead and rolled to the victory against their old head coach Mike Koury. The Vikings led going into the fourth quarter 57-25.

Leading scorers: Central Catholic – Bob Wootsick 20, Jeff McGeehin 11, Joe Kiehstaller 10, Kevin Lloyd 10; Phillipsburg – Gary Carhart 13.

Easton 41 Bethlehem Catholic 38: Easton outscored Bethlehem Catholic by a point in the second quarter and two in the third quarter to make the difference in the win. Each team scored ten points in both the first and fourth quarters. Butch Brantley made a pair of foul shots with three seconds to play to seal the win for the Red Rovers.

Leading scorers: Easton – Butch Brantley 15, Dave Cardell 10; Bethlehem Catholic – Joe Zubia 12.[6]

Freedom 54 Liberty 51: Freedom held a five-point lead 28-23 heading into the second half and opened up the third quarter with two quick baskets to take a comfortable lead. Liberty fought back to within a point 36-35 with 90 seconds left in the third period. In the next 5:45 of the game, Freedom went on a 16-6 run to open an eleven-point lead 52-41. Liberty's late game 10-2 rally fell just short as the Patriots hung on to win.

Leading scorers: Freedom – Spence Pierce 2, John Majczan 10; Liberty – Ken Houser 12, Kirk Shelley 11, Paul Rosko 10.

Central Catholic 54 Easton 32: Central Catholic's smothering defense kept Easton scoreless for the first 14 ½ minutes of the game as the Red Rovers scored only two points in the entire first half. With Jeff McGeehin scoring 10 points and grabbing 11 rebounds in the first period alone, the Vikings blanked Easton 12-0 in the first quarter and held an insurmountable 22-2 lead at the half.

Leading scorers: Central Catholic – Jeff McGeehin 27; Easton – Dave Cardell 14.

Bethlehem Catholic 54 Phillipsburg 51: Phillipsburg took a 14-12 first quarter lead and battled Bethlehem Catholic the entire game before Joe Zubia converted both ends of a one-and-one foul situation to seal the win for the Hawks. Bethlehem Catholic held the lead at the halfway mark 24-22, but the Stateliners came back to tie the score at 30. The Hawks then took the lead for good, but Phillipsburg came back to within a point 52-51 with 20 seconds to play.

Leading scorers: Bethlehem Catholic – Gary Falkenbach 15, Joe Zubia 13, Pat Haney 10; Phillipsburg – Stan Dyrek 16, Chris Fichera 11.

Dieruff 68 Hazleton 47: Dieruff remained unbeaten in league play at 6-0 with a big second quarter when they outscored the Mountaineers 23-12. The Huskies took an eighteen-point lead into the fourth quarter.

Leading scorers: Dieruff – Jack Booros 18, Rich Schmidt 17, John Landis 12, Tom Stellar 10; Hazleton – Sam Monticello 12.

Pottsville 75 Allen 67: Ken Kline's Pottsville team took a 24-14 first quarter lead and added a point to the lead at the half 45-34. Although Allen got to within two points 58-56 late in the third quarter, the Canaries could not overtake the Crimson Tide who improved to 5-1, a game behind the leaders Dieruff.

Leading scorers: Pottsville – Pat Flannery 23, Todd Kline 18, Tom Francavage 14, John Burch 11; Allen – Doug Snyder 25, Bob Frederick 17, Steve Carl 12, Eric Marshall 10.[7]

Week 5

Dieruff 62 Central Catholic 49: Dieruff handed Central Catholic its second loss in league play. Central Catholic took the early lead 12-11 after a quarter, but Dieruff held the Vikings to only seven points in the second period to assume the lead at the half 31-19. The Huskies went on a 16-2 run in the period to build the lead. After trailing going into the fourth quarter 50-36, the Vikings rallied to within four points before Dieruff ended their hopes with two quick layups.

Leading scorers: Dieruff – Foo Belfield 26, John Landis 15, Tom Stellar 10; Central Catholic – Jeff McGeehin 18, Joe Kiehstaller 14, Bob Wootsick 10.

Allen 81 Freedom 50: Freedom committed 22 turnovers in the first half to allow Allen to build up a 38-24 lead heading into the locker room. Allen continued the onslaught using a full court press and triangle and two defense on the way to the rout of the Patriots.

Leading scorers: Allen – Doug Snyder 24, Eric Marshall 17, Bob Frederick 15, Steve Carl 10; Freedom - Spence Pierce 22.

Easton 56 Liberty 51: Liberty led Easton 24-22 at halftime and maintained the lead at 43-42 with 5:45 to play in the game. Bill Sweeney and Steve Jones scored the next nine points for Easton to take a 51-43 lead.

Liberty came right back with an 8-1 run to get within a point 52-51 with 50 seconds to play. Sweeney made a game-clinching layup to end the Liberty rally.

Leading scorers: Easton – Mike Young 17, Steve Jones 14; Liberty – Kirk Shelley 18, Alex DeAngelis 11, Gordon Smith 10.

Hazleton 79 Bethlehem Catholic 58: Hazleton took a seven-point lead 15-8 and expanded it to eleven at the half 38-27. A brief Hawk rally to begin the second half cut the lead to nine before Mike Caparell scored seven straight points. Hazleton put the game out of reach with 29 points in the third period while the Hawks scored only 13. Gary Falkenbach had a career scoring night and also pulled down 22 rebounds.

Leading scorers: Hazleton – Sam Monticello 17, Mike Caparell 17, Bob Gabriel 14, Billy Cortese 10, John Portland 10; Bethlehem Catholic – Gary Falkenbach 24, Mike Guman 13, Joe Zubia 10.

Phillipsburg 59 Pottsville 57: Coach Mike Koury's Phillipsburg's quintet broke a 30-game league losing streak by pulling out the win with five seconds to play on a Chris Fichera layup. Phillipsburg took a 14-9 first quarter lead only to see Pottsville explode for 25 points in the second period for a 34-26 halftime lead. Phillipsburg cut the lead in half in the third quarter and took the lead midway through the fourth quarter 55-54. Ed Mady's three-point play put Pottsville ahead 57-55 before Dave Smith tied the score for Phillipsburg and set up the winning field goal to break the Stateliners' string of frustrating losses.

Leading scorers: Phillipsburg – Dave Smith 14, Chris Fichera 11, Stan Dyrek 10, Gary Carhart 10; Pottsville – Pat Flannery 18, Ed Mady 15, John Burch 10.[8]

Pottsville 64 Bethlehem Catholic 43: Pottsville built a large first half lead 29-18 aided by 13 first half turnovers by Bethlehem Catholic. After a mild resurgence by the Hawks in the third quarter, Pottsville put the game away with 26 points in the final quarter. Pottsville improved to 6-2.

Leading scorers: Pottsville – Todd Kline 16, Pat Flannery 15, John Burch 14; Bethlehem Catholic – Mike Guman 17, Gus Concilio 13.

Allen 57 Central Catholic 56: Allen held a 28-23 lead at the half and led 38-31 in the third period when Central Catholic scored 10 consecutive points to take a 41-38 lead. With five minutes left to play, the Vikings held the lead 50-45. Allen pulled within a point 56-55 with 44 seconds to play. Central Catholic failed to get the ball inbounded with 23 seconds to play and turned the ball over. Allen missed with an air ball with seven seconds to play. The Vikings missed a one-and-one foul situation with five seconds to play. Doug Snyder took a desperation 25-foot jumper which missed but was tapped-in by Steve Carl at the buzzer for the game winner, despite protests from Viking coach Dave Pfahler that it did not beat the clock.

Leading scorers: Allen – Doug Snyder 20, Steve Carl 17, Bob Frederick 10; Central Catholic – Jeff McGeehin 26, Joe Kiehstaller 12, Chris Johnson 10.

Dieruff 74 Phillipsburg 48: Dieruff ended Phillipsburg's winning streak at one game and clinched the first half title in Phillipsburg. The Huskies took a 27-9 lead in the 1st quarter and the game was never in question.

Leading scorers: Dieruff – Foo Belfield 16, Rich Schmidt 15, Jack Booros 11; Phillipsburg - Gary Carhart 16, Dave Smith 11.

Easton 57 Freedom 45: Freedom led 25-18 with a little less than five minutes left in the second quarter before Easton rallied for a 29-27 halftime edge. Easton opened the second half with eight straight points and put the game out of reach for the Patriots. Easton played without the services of Mike Young and Butch Brantley who were under a one-game suspension.

Leading scorers: Easton – Dave Cardell 24, Don Griffin 19; Freedom – Spence Pierce 19.

Liberty 62 Hazleton 59: At Hazleton, the Mountaineers took an 18-6 first quarter lead before Liberty began to climb back into the contest. Still trailing 34-24 at the half, the Hurricane cut the lead to 49-45 in the third period behind Gordon Smith's eight points. Liberty finally took the lead with four minutes to play in the game 54-51. Hazleton retook the lead 59-58 before Kirk Shelley made a layup for the winning basket and the upset of the Mountaineers.

Leading scorers: Liberty – Alex DeAngelis 15, Kirk Shelley 14, Bruce John 12, Gordon Smith 10; Hazleton – Sam Monticello 16, Dave Caparell 15, Billy Cortese 10.[9]

Week 6

Four make up contests were played which were postponed during the third week of league play in December.

Allen 77 Phillipsburg 67: With junior Dave Smith making 9 of 13 shots for 18 points in the first half, Phillipsburg trailed by only five points 45-40. Eric Marshall hit 4 of 5 field goal attempts in the third period as Allen moved away from the Stateliners to build a 15-point lead.

Leading scorers: Allen – Bob Frederick 25, Doug Snyder 19, Eric Marshall 16; Phillipsburg – Dave Smith 20, Gary Carhart 18, Stan Dyrek 11.

Hazleton 78 Central Catholic 73: Hazleton stunned Central Catholic and handed the Vikings their third straight loss. Central Catholic went into the third quarter with a 31-29 lead, but the Mountaineers outscored the Vikings 21-16 to take the lead for the rest of the game.

Leading scorers: Hazleton – Sam Monticello 19, John Portland 13, Billy Cortese 11, Tom Mundie 10, Mike Caparell 10; Central Catholic – Jeff McGeehin 27, Chris Johnson 13, Bob Wootsick 12.

Dieruff 70 Freedom 48: Freedom stayed with Dieruff until the Huskies went on a 13-point streak beginning late in the first quarter and into the second quarter. Still with only a ten-point lead, Dieruff finally took a commanding lead late in the third and early in the final quarter.

Leading scorers: Dieruff – John Landis 17, Foo Belfield 13, Tom Stellar 11, Rich Schmidt 10; Freedom – Spence Pierce 22.

Easton 71 Pottsville 37: Easton held Pottsville to two points in the first quarter on their way to a 17-2 lead going into the second quarter. Pottsville could not get much more offense in the next two periods as they only added 13 points and trailed 52-12 entering the fourth quarter.

Leading scorers: Easton – Mike Young 18, Don Griffin 14, Ed Geosits 10; Pottsville – Pat Flannery 8.[21]

Second Half

Dieruff 79 Pottsville 56: Foo Belfield converted 13 of 17 field goal attempts in leading Dieruff to a sixteen-point halftime lead 44-28 and their 14th straight win overall, ten in a row in league play. Belfield along with John Landis almost outscored the Pottsville team with 52 points between them. Before the Huskie scoring onslaught, they had only led by three 15-12 after a quarter.

Leading scorers: Dieruff – Foo Belfield 31, John Landis 21, Tom Stellar 15; Pottsville – Todd Kline 19, Pat Flannery 14, Ed Mady 12.

Hazleton 56 Phillipsburg 48: Phillipsburg battled Hazleton for the first three quarters and held a 20-18 lead during the second quarter. They trailed going into the second half 25-22 and tied the game at 32 in the third quarter. Hazleton scored the first six points of the fourth quarter to propel the Mountaineers to victory,

Leading scorers: Hazleton-Dave Caparell 12, Billy Cortese 10; Phillipsburg-Gary Carhart 13, Dave Smith 11.

Allen 62 Easton 53: Allen converted 22 of 27 free throws, and made twelve in a row, to contribute to the Canaries' 400th career win for coach Milo Sewards. Allen took an early 9-2 lead and never trailed.

Leading scorers: Allen – Doug Snyder 21, Bob Frederick 13, Steve Carl 12, Eric Marshall 11; Easton – Don Griffin 16, Mike Young 12, Steve Jones 11.

Central Catholic 71 Liberty 54: With a career high 28 points, Chris Johnson sparked Central Catholic to victory over Liberty. Liberty trailed 31-12 at halftime.

Leading scorers: Central Catholic – Chris Johnson 28, Jeff McGeehin 19, Joe Kiehstaller 10; Liberty – Alex DeAngelis 14, Kirk Shelley 11.

Bethlehem Catholic 51 Freedom 49: Bethlehem Catholic raced out to a 12-2 lead before Freedom rallied with 22 points in the second quarter for a 28-28 halftime tie. The Hawks led after three quarters by a single point 41-40. The game was tied four times in the fourth quarter, the last time at 49, before Joe Zubia took an in-bounds pass up court and hit a 15-foot jumper for the win.

Leading scorers: Bethlehem Catholic – Joe Zubia 14, Gary Falkenbach 10; Freedom – Spence Pierce 20.[11]

Week 7

Central Catholic 70 Bethlehem Catholic 53: With Central Catholic's defense causing numerous first quarter turnovers, the Vikings took a 16-2 lead into the second quarter against Bethlehem Catholic. By halftime, the lead was 43-17 as the Vikings cruised to the win over the Hawks.

Leading scorers: Central Catholic –Chris Johnson 20, Joe Kiehstaller 12, Dan Kendra 11; Bethlehem Catholic – Joe Zubia 18, Mike Guman 13.

Pottsville 60 Liberty 54: Ed Mady and John Burch scored 15 of Pottsville's 21 first quarter points as the Crimson Tide took a 21-6 lead. Pottsville stretched the lead to 28- 7 before the Hurricane fought their way back. The first quarter advantage carried Pottsville to victory despite Liberty outscoring Pottsville in the second and fourth quarter and each team with 14 points in the third quarter.

Leading scorers: Pottsville – John Burch 17, Ed Mady 12, Mike Smink 10; Liberty – Ken Houser 16, Gordon Smith 12, Kirk Shelley 11.

Dieruff 67 Allen 62: The two cross-city rivals battled through four quarters with Allen leading after one 16-15. Dieruff came back for the halftime lead 31-28. Allen took the third quarter by five points to take the lead into the fourth quarter 47-45. Four times the Huskies had eight-point leads only to see the Canaries battle back. Dieruff scored 10 straight points early in the 4th quarter, but Allen clawed back to tie 60-60. A technical foul call on Coach Milo Sewards halted the Canaries rally as the Huskies took a 63-60 lead and the win.

Leading scorers: Dieruff – Rich Schmidt 15, Foo Belfield 14, Tom Stellar 13, John Landis 12; Allen – Doug Snyder 18, Bob Frederick 18, Eric Marshall 12.

Freedom 55 Phillipsburg 44: After Freedom took a 14-7 first quarter lead, Phillipsburg came back to cut the lead to three points 22-17. The Stateliners' rally was halted in the third quarter with the Patriots holding Phillipsburg to six points.

Leading scorers: Freedom – Spence Pierce 23, Bill Matz 11; Phillipsburg – Gary Carhart 18, Dave Smith 10.

Easton 64 Hazleton 55: Easton held a slim 33-30 lead at the half when Don Griffin scored 11 points in the third period to lead the Red Rovers to a 48-36 advantage. Hazleton pulled within six 57-51, but Steve Jones stole an in-bounds pass and passed to Mike Young for an easy layup to seal the win for the Red Rovers.

Leading scorers: Easton–Don Griffin 23, Butch Brantley 15, Mike Young 12; Hazleton–Dave Caparell 13, Sam Monticello 12.[12]

Central Catholic 50 Freedom 48: Central Catholic and Freedom played a half of stall ball with the halftime score 16-15 in favor of the Patriots. In the 2nd half, both teams opened up the offenses which led to a thrilling finish. With a minute to play, Freedom led the Vikings 46-41 when Central Catholic scored six points, with four of them on Patriot turnovers, in 24 seconds to take the lead 47-46. After Freedom's Spence Pierce converted both ends of a one-and-one foul opportunity to take the lead back, Chris Johnson made the first of two foul shots to tie the score at 48. He missed the second free throw. Freedom rebounded the ball, moved it up court, and called a timeout. On the in-bounds pass, Jim Trinkle stole the inbounds pass and drove for the winning layup for the Vikings.

Leading scorers: Central Catholic – Chris Johnson 18, Jeff McGeehin 14; Freedom – Spence Pierce 29.

Allen 72 Liberty 58: With Liberty leading 12-10, Allen went on a 12-2 run to take the lead 22-14. Liberty scored six in a row to close to within 22-20 and Allen again came back with an 11-2 run to increase the lead to 33-22. With seven minutes left to play in the game, Allen had its biggest margin at 50-38 and still led by 13 points with three minutes to play. Liberty's 12-2 run cut the Canary lead to three points. Coach Milo Sewards reinserted his starters to counter the Liberty rally and pull out the win for Allen.

Leading scorers: Allen – Doug Snyder 25, Steve Carl 15, Bob Frederick 12; Liberty – Ken Houser 16.

Easton 63 Phillipsburg 45: Easton led Phillipsburg by two points 12-10 with two minutes left in the first quarter. The Red Rovers scored the next sixteen points to take a commanding lead 28-10 and a 35-21 halftime lead. Easton held the Stateliners to eight points in the third period to cruise to the easy victory.

Leading scorers: Easton – Dave Cardell 20, Don Griffin 11; Phillipsburg – Gary Carhart 17, Stan Dyrek 10.

Pottsville 60 Hazleton 58 OT: After the officials made a controversial call to add a second to the time remaining in regulation to increase it to 3 seconds, Hazleton led 54-52 with Pottsville to inbound the ball. John Burch took a desperation shot which was short but Mike Smink picked it out of the air and sank a shot at the buzzer to tie the game. Smink made the Crimson Tide's first two buckets in overtime, but Hazleton tied the score at 58 and lost the ball with 10 seconds to play. They fouled John Burch and he made both free throws for the win for Pottsville.

Leading scorers: Pottsville – Tom Francavage 19, John Burch 12, Pat Flannery 10, Todd Kline 10; Hazleton – Dave Caparell 19, Sam Monticello 16, Joe Polchin 11.

Dieruff 49 Bethlehem Catholic 29: Missing two of its starters, Bethlehem Catholic used a stall offense. The Hawks led only once in the game 4-2. The Huskies led at the quarter mark 7-4 and 21-16 at the half. The third quarter put the game out of reach for the Hawks when they were outscored 10-3. Dieruff, at 3-0, remained tied with Central Catholic for the second half lead.

Leading scorers: Dieruff – John Landis 13, Foo Belfield 10; Bethlehem Catholic – Joe Zubia 10.[13]

Week 9

Allen 71 Bethlehem Catholic 44: Allen held a slim 9-8 lead after a quarter, but began to pull away in the second quarter when they took a 28-19 lead into the locker room. The added six and twelve points to the lead in the third and fourth quarters in an eventual rout of the Hawks.

Leading scorers: Allen – Doug Snyder 29, Eric Marshall 12; Bethlehem Catholic – Mike Guman 14, Paul Golden 12.

Liberty 85 Phillipsburg 59: Liberty won its first game of the second half while Phillipsburg dropped to 0-4. With an offensive outburst in the first quarter, Liberty took a 30-12 lead. Liberty made small comeback in the second period to cut the lead to 45-33. The second half was all Liberty as they turned the game into a rout by outscoring the Stateliners 40-26. The game, somewhat haggard, saw a total of 55 fouls with almost as many turnovers.

Leading scorers: Liberty – Bruce John 17, Wayne Edwards 17, Alex DeAngelis 10, Kal Illyes 10; Phillipsburg – Gary Carhart 16, Chris Fichera 10.

Dieruff 74 Easton 58: Behind the play of their three guards, Rich Schmidt, Tom Stellar, and Foo Belfield who combined for 51 points, Dieruff won its 17th consecutive game and moved to 4-0 for sole possession of first place in the second half. Outscoring Easton 16-8 in each of the first two quarters, the Huskies took a 16-point lead into the second half of the game. After the Red Rovers cut five off the lead in the third quarter, Dieruff added the five back in the final quarter.

Leading scorers: Dieruff – Tom Stellar 20, Rich Schmidt 20, Foo Belfield 11, Jack Booros 10; Easton – Mike Young 18, Don Griffin 16.

Pottsville 47 Central Catholic 45: Ed Mady grabbed a rebound and put it back up for a field goal to upset Central Catholic and knock them out of the first-place tie with Dieruff. After trailing 23-19 at the half, the Vikings had rallied to the third quarter lead 35-29.

Leading scorers: Pottsville – Pat Flannery 15, Tom Francavage 12, John Burch 11; Central Catholic – Jeff McGeehin 15.

Hazleton 53 Freedom 44: Dave Tomaszewski and Spence Pierce combined for 16 points to lead Freedom to a 24-23 lead at halftime. After scoring 14 points in the 1st half, Sam Monticello led Hazleton's running game as the Mountaineers took the lead 41-34 after three quarters and held on to it in the final quarter to even their second half record at 2-2.

Leading scorers: Hazleton – Sam Monticello 18, Joe Polchin 14; Freedom – Spence Pierce 23.[14]

Easton 58 Pottsville 51: Pottsville trailed by 15 points with four minutes to play in the third period and still trailed by nine 49-40 with seven minutes to play in the game. Pottsville scored eight in a row to pull within one 49-48 when Easton's Steve Jones wiped out the Crimson Tide comeback by making a field goal and converting six free throws to lead the Red Rovers to victory.

Leading scorers: Easton – Steve Jones 17, Mike Young 12, Dave Cardell 12, Don Griffin 10; Pottsville – Pat Flannery 18, Ed Mady 10.

Bethlehem Catholic 71 Liberty 53: Despite being ill and having to be rested periodically, Joe Zubia still scored 23 points to lead Bethlehem Catholic to the win over Liberty. The Hawks led by three 30-27 at the half but pulled away for a commanding lead in the third period 51-35.

Leading scorers: Bethlehem Catholic – Joe Zubia 23, Gary Falkenbach 15, Mike Guman 14; Liberty – Kirk Shelley 15, Bruce John 14.

Central Catholic 58 Hazleton 45: Chris Johnson and Jeff McGeehin scored 18 of Central Catholic's 22 points in the final quarter to break away from a slim three-point lead 36-33 to defeat Hazleton. Hazleton had held the lead at the half 25-22. The Vikings improved to 4-1, a game behind Dieruff and tied with Allen for second place in the second half of the season.

Leading scorers: Central Catholic – Jeff McGeehin 20, Chris Johnson 18; Hazleton – Dave Caparell 15, Sam Monticello 12.

Dieruff 82 Freedom 47: Dieruff's starting five played less than a half as the Huskies built a 43-22 lead at halftime. They held the Patriots to eight points in the second quarter. Ten of the eleven players used by Coach Dick Schmidt scored in the contest.

Leading scorers: Dieruff – John Landis 15, Jack Booros 13, Rich Schmidt 12, Tom Stellar 11; Freedom – Spence Pierce 10.

Allen 94 Phillipsburg 52: The game was tied at 8-8 until Allen scored eight straight points and take a 20-10 lead after a quarter. They added seven to the lead in the second quarter and turned the game into a rout in the third period by outscoring Phillipsburg 25-8

Leading scorers: Allen – Doug Snyder 25, Eric Marshall 20, Bob Frederick 14; Phillipsburg – Dave Smith 20, Gary Carhart 18.[15]

Week 10

Liberty 70 Dieruff 67: Liberty shocked Dieruff by handing the Huskies their first loss of the season after 18 wins. With the Hurricane taking a 21-9 first quarter lead, the Huskies did not make their first field goal until 1:40 was left in the first period. Although Dieruff outscored Liberty 58-49 in the last three quarters and got within a point 64-63 with 2:10 to play, the Huskies could not overcome the huge first quarter deficit. Kirk Shelley made several critical foul shots to pull out the upset win for Liberty. The loss dropped the Huskies into a three-way tie with Central Catholic and Allen for first place.

Leading scorers: Liberty – Kirk Shelley 18, Ken Houser, Paul Rosko 12, Alex DeAngelis 12, Bruce John 12; Dieruff – Rich Schmidt 18, John Landis 15, Foo Belfield 14.

Pottsville 83 Freedom 61: Pottsville took a 6-0 lead on their way to a 17-10 first quarter advantage. After leading by eleven at the half 37-26, Pottsville added 13 more to the lead in the third quarter 64-40 enroute to their fourth victory against two losses in the second half.

Leading scorers: Pottsville – Pat Flannery 17, John Burch 16, Ed Mady 14, Tom Francavage 14; Liberty – Spence Pierce 22, Bill Matz 12.

Allen 70 Hazleton 63: Doug Snyder scored 36 points and topped the career 1000-point milestone and ended with 1,011 at the night's end. The Canaries led at the end of each of the first three quarters with Hazleton pulling within four points 65-61 in the fourth quarter before the Canaries converted two free throws and a field goal to seal the win.

Leading scorers: Allen – Doug Snyder 36, Bob Frederick 11; Hazleton – Mike Caparell 23, John Portland 12, Joe Polchin 10.

Central Catholic 66 Phillipsburg 42: Central Catholic had a safe eight-point lead 32-24 at the half and pulled away in the last two quarters to keep Phillipsburg winless in the second half. The Vikings outscored the Stateliners 34 -18 in the second half.

Leading scorers: Central Catholic – Chris Johnson 22, Joe Kiehstaller 13, Jim Trinkle 10; Phillipsburg – Jim Vaughn 14.

Easton 68 Bethlehem Catholic 56: Taking an early 10-2 lead, Easton led by at least four points the rest of the way. Easton led 12-8 after the first period and scored the first six points of the second quarter to lead at the half 28-16. After scoring only 31 points in the first three quarters, the Hawks scored 25 points in the final period.

Leading scorers: Easton – Dave Cardell 14, Ed Geosits 13, Don Griffin 12, Steve Jones 11; Bethlehem Catholic – Joe Zubia 15, Mike Guman 12.[16]

Dieruff 62 Hazleton 60: Dieruff, leading 20-8 with 1:45 left in the first period, went ahead by sixteen 26-10 early in the second quarter. The Huskies went cold in the second quarter allowing Hazleton to pull within three points at the half 30-27. The Mountaineers then tied the game at 39-39 in the middle of the third period. The Huskies grew the lead to nine points with 37 seconds left 62-53, but had to hang on for the win as Hazleton scored the last seven points.

Leading scorers: Dieruff – Jack Booros 21, Rich Schmidt 20, Tom Stellar 11; Hazleton – Mike Caparell 16, Ned McNelis 12, Sam Monticello 10.

Easton 44 Central Catholic 39: Easton held Central Catholic to 13 points in the first half to take a 24 -13 lead at halftime. Despite holding the Red Rovers to five points in the 3rd quarter, Easton was able to hold on to a slim two-point lead 29-27 going into the final eight minutes of the contest. Easton began the final quarter with two quick field goals and used their defense to hold on for the upset of the Vikings and knock them out of the first-place tie.

Leading scorers: Easton – Ed Geosits 12, Dave Cardell 12, Mike Young 12; Central Catholic - Jeff McGeehin 13, Chris Johnson 12.

Liberty 52 Freedom 50: Freedom began a rally in the second period which they continued into the third quarter to take a ten-point lead 34-24. Freedom scored only a single field goal in the next nearly eight minutes while Liberty scored ten points to tie the game at 34-34. The game stayed close with several ties with the last being 50-50. Liberty rebounded a missed Patriot free throw and went the length of the court with Kirk Shelley missing a jumper. Paul Rosko rebounded the miss and laid it in for the game winner.

Leading scorers: Liberty – Kirk Shelley 12; Freedom – Spence Pierce 24.

Phillipsburg 62 Bethlehem Catholic 52: Trailing 20-17 after the first quarter, Phillipsburg went into a matchup zone defense and held Bethlehem Catholic to sixteen points in the middle two quarters to take the lead 44-36 into the final quarter. The win was their first of the second half and matched their first half total.

Leading scorers: Phillipsburg – Jim Vaughn 16, Dave Smith 16, John Williams 12, Stan Dyrek 10; Bethlehem Catholic – Mike Guman 19, Joe Zubia 16.[17]

Week 11

Easton 75 Liberty 54: With Ed Geosits scoring 12 points in the second quarter, Easton took a 46-19 lead at the half and held on for an easy win. Liberty outscored the Red Rovers 35-29 in the second half.

Leading scorers: Easton-Ed Geosits 21, Don Griffin 19, Mike Young 12, Steve Jones 12; Liberty-Kirk Shelley 14, Kal Illyes 10.

Dieruff 83 Central Catholic 68: Dieruff handed Central Catholic their third loss of the second half and knocked them out of contention for the 2nd half title. After taking a 40-35 lead into halftime, the Huskies held the Vikings to eight points in the third quarter to extend their lead to 18 points 61-43 and cruised to victory in the final period.

Leading scorers: Dieruff – Rich Schmidt 21, John Landis 18, Foo Belfield 16, Tom Stellar 15, Jack Booros 13; Central Catholic – Jeff McGeehin 25, Chris Johnson 13, Jim Trinkle 12.

Pottsville 63 Phillipsburg 59 OT: Pottsville took a five-point lead 12-7 after a quarter. The two teams played even in the middle periods with each team scoring 30 points in the two periods. Phillipsburg was down four points with 23 seconds to play and rallied to tie the game. In overtime, John Burch made four foul shots and Ed Mady and Mike Smink one each to win the game for Pottsville.

Leading scorers: Pottsville – John Burch 18, Todd Kline 14, Ed Mady 12, Pat Flannery 11; Phillipsburg – John Williams 24.

Bethlehem Catholic 60 Hazleton 55 OT: Hazleton led after a quarter 17-11, but ran into a cold spell in the second quarter as Bethlehem Catholic took the lead 25-23. The lead flipped back to Hazleton 40-35 after three quarters. Hazleton led 50-48 with eight seconds to play when the Hawks came up with a loose ball in a scramble and fed it up court to Pat Haney for the layup and tie the game in regulation. Mike Guman scored six points in overtime to led the Hawks to the win.

Leading scorers: Bethlehem Catholic – Mike Guman 22, Joe Zubia 12, Pat Haney 10, Gary Falkenbach 10; Hazleton – Sam Monticello 19, Joe Polchin 10.

Allen 65 Freedom 55: Despite 30 points from Spence Pierce, Freedom could not stay with Allen despite leading the Canaries 46-44 after three quarters. After13 ties and eight lead changes in the contest, Allen went ahead for good 50-48 and outscored the Patriots 15-8 in the final minutes of the contest. The win kept the Canaries tied with Dieruff for first place.

Leading scorers: Allen – Eric Marshall 18, Doug Snyder 16, Steve Carl 16, Bob Frederick 11; Freedom – Spence Pierce 30.[18]

Allen 79 Pottsville 63: In a makeup game from the prior week, Allen grabbed a ten-point lead 40-30 at the half and extended it to sixteen after three quarters 58-42. Each team scored 21 points in the final quarter as Allen kept pace with Dieruff for first place at 7-1.

Leading scorers: Allen - Doug Snyder 32, Bob Frederick 16, Steve Carl 14, Eric Marshall 11; Pottsville – Pat Flannery 24, John Burch 15.[19]

Dieruff 65 Phillipsburg 32: Phillipsburg battled Dieruff in the first half and trailed by only five points 24-19. Dieruff scored the first 17 points of the third period to outscore the Stateliners 23-5 and followed it up in the 4th quarter with an 18-8 advantage and an overwhelming victory and the second half title with Allen's loss to Central Catholic.

Leading scorers: Dieruff – Rich Schmidt 21, John Landis 17, Tom Stellar 13; Phillipsburg – Bud Baxter 10.

Central Catholic 65 Allen 44: Central Catholic crushed Allen's hopes of a second half title at Rockne Hall. The Vikings held ten-point leads throughout the game as Allen never threatened after the first quarter.

Leading scorers: Central Catholic – Jeff McGeehin 22, Chris Johnson 15, Joe Kiehstaller 10; Allen – Eric Marshall 15, Doug Snyder 11.

Easton 56 Freedom 43: Easton took a slim one-point lead 9-8 into the second period and extended it to six 26-20 at the half. Easton added six more to the lead in the third quarter for an easy win over the Patriots.

Leading scorers: Easton - Don Griffin 17, Mike Young 17, Ed Geosits 15; Freedom – Spence Pierce 21, Bill Matz 10.

Liberty 70 Hazleton 65: Hazleton led Liberty 38-24 after a half of play. Liberty's offense took over in the second half to score 46 points and hand Hazleton a stunning loss.

Leading Scorers: Liberty – Kirk Shelley 19, Bruce John 14, Alex DeAngelis 13, Paul Rosko 12; Hazleton – Sam Monticello 14, Bob Gabriel 11.

Pottsville 51 Bethlehem Catholic 49: Pottsville held a slim three-point lead 31-28 in the first half and lost a point in the third quarter to lead by two 39-37. In the final minute of the game, the score was tied at 47 when Ed Mady was fouled on a successful field goal and made the foul shot to give Pottsville the win.

Leading scorers: Pottsville – Ed Mady 13, Pat Flannery 10, Tom Francavage 10; Bethlehem Catholic – Joe Zubia 18, Mike Guman 16.[20]

District 11 Postseason Play

Five league teams qualified for the expanded district playoffs. The seedings for the playoffs were as follows: 1st - Dieruff; 2nd - Easton; 3rd – Allen; 4th – Central Catholic; and 5th – Pottsville.[21]

First Round

Dieruff 59 Nazareth 49: At the Allen Phys Ed Center, Dieruff took leads at the end of each of the first three periods 16-10, 26-18, and 45-30. They rode the 15-point lead to an easy win over the Blue Eagles.

Leading scorers: Dieruff – Tom Stellar 15, John Landis 14, Rich Schmidt 12, Jack Booros 10; Nazareth – Mike Kraemer 18, Rich Bickert 11, Jamie Fry 10.

Central Catholic 69 Pottsville 54: The two league teams were matched up in the first round with Central Catholic avenging its two losses in the regular season with the win over Pottsville at the Allen Phys Ed Center. Strong showings in the first period (17-9) and the fourth period (27-16) led to the win over their league rivals. Going into the final quarter, Pottsville had climbed to within four points 42-38.

Leading scorers: Central Catholic – Chris Johnson 28, Jeff McGeehin 21, Joe Kiehstaller 12; Pottsville – Todd Kline 27, Pat Flannery 16.[22]

Easton 41 Whitehall 27: At Liberty's Memorial Gym, Easton used Whitehall's deliberate game plan to move into the second round of the District 11 playoffs. Whitehall took an 11-10 lead only to have Easton respond to lead 22-17 at the half. Easton held Whitehall to six points in the second period, only four in the third period, and six again in the fourth period to hand Whitehall the loss.

Leading scorers: Easton – Dave Cardell 10, Steve Jones 10; Whitehall – Randy Kemmerer 12.

Allen 46 Parkland 44: Bob Frederick and Steve Carl scored Allen's last nine points to lead the Canaries to the win over Parkland. After Allen took a 34-30 lead after three quarters, Parkland took the lead 38-37 and 40-39 in the 4th quarter. Allen finally took the lead for good 41-40 and moved on to the second round.

Leading scorers: Allen – Eric Marshall 12, Doug Snyder 11, Bob Frederick 11; Parkland – Mike O'Boyle 19, Randy Seltzer 14.[23]

Second Round

Dieruff 53 Central Catholic 50: The two league foes met for the third time in the season in the second round of the District 11 playoffs. For the third time, Dieruff defeated the Vikings on the strength of their second quarter performance. Central Catholic took a two-point lead after the first quarter, but the Huskies came back to outscore the Vikings by seven and take the halftime lead 33-28. Playing even in the third quarter with both teams scoring 12 points, Central Catholic attempted a comeback in the fourth quarter, but fell short. The Vikings got within a point 51-50 with 55 seconds to play, but the Huskies scored off their four-corner offense to take the game.

Leading scorers: Dieruff – Jack Booros 21, Rich Schmidt 11, Foo Belfield 10; Central Catholic – Chris Johnson 18, Jeff McGeehin 13.[24]

Easton 56 Allen 45: Easton pressured the Allen guards throughout the contest on their way to their second victory over Allen in three contests. Easton took a 16-8 lead after a quarter only to experience a bad period with five turnovers and only three field goals. Allen got within three twice, 16-13 and 22-19, before the Red Rovers recovered to lead at the half 26-19. Easton outscored the Canaries 30-26 and prevented any hope of a comeback by Allen. Allen was hindered by the absence of Bob Frederick who had the flu.

Leading scorers: Easton - Don Griffin 20, Steve Jones 13; Allen – Doug Snyder 16.[25]

Third Round

Allen 62 Central Catholic 53: At Muhlenberg's Memorial Hall, Allen took on Central Catholic in a consolation game to determine the third entry into the PIAA playoffs from District 11. Allen dominated the first and fourth quarters to defeat the Vikings. With Bob Frederick back in the lineup, the Canaries exhibited a balanced lineup with four players in double figures. The Vikings lost Jeff McGeehin in the middle of the final quarter when he dove to attempt a steal and hurt his thigh and was lost for the game.

Leading scorers: Allen – Eric Marshall 15, Doug Snyder 14, Steve Carl 14, Bob Frederick 13; Central Catholic – Jeff McGeehin 14, Chris Johnson 11, Dan Kendra 11.[26]

Easton 48 Dieruff 41: In Pottsville, Easton committed 19 turnovers in the first half and fell behind Dieruff by as many as 13 points before cutting the lead to ten at the half 28-18. With 5 ½ minutes left in the third period, Easton still trailed by 12 points. The Red Rovers scored ten points in a row to cut the lead to two. They still trailed by three 33-30 entering the fourth quarter. With 3 ½ minutes left in the game, the Red Rovers finally took the lead on successive field goals by Don Griffin and Steve Jones. They closed out the win by converting 10 of 14 foul shots in the last few minutes. Both teams entered the PIAA playoffs along with Allen as the third-place team.

Leading scorers: Easton – Don Griffin 15, Steve Jones 14, Mike Young 10; Dieruff – John Landis 11, Tom Stellar 11.[27]

PIAA Playoffs

Easton, Dieruff and Allen qualified for PIAA post season play from District 11 in the expanded playoff format.

First Round

Williamsport 68 Allen 55: On Williamsport's home court, Allen battled Coach Charlie Blackburn's Millionaires on even terms during the first half and most of the third quarter with the Canaries holding a 12-8 lead after a quarter and tied at the half 30-30. With the score tied at 48-48 late in the third quarter, Williamsport scored the last four points to lead 52-48 going into the final stanza. The Millionaires held the Canaries without a field goal for the first five minutes of the fourth quarter and held Allen to 7 points to eliminate the Canaries from further playoff action.

Leading scorers: Williamsport – Sam Washington 30, Dan Fuller 15, Willie Manville 10; Allen – Doug Snyder 20, Eric Marshall 14, Bob Frederick 10.

Dieruff 70 Harrisburg 68: In Pottsville, Tom Stellar sank two foul shots with six seconds left to take down Harrisburg. Dieruff led by as many as nine points in the first half before Harrisburg cut the lead to three at the half 37-34. Dieruff added a much needed two points to the lead in the third quarter 51-46. Stellar's two free throws ended Harrisburg's comeback attempts after they had tied the game three times in the fourth quarter at 51-51, 66-66, and 68-68.

Leading scorers: Dieruff – John Landis 26, Foo Belfield 14, Jack Booros 13, Rich Schmidt 10; Harrisburg – Wilkerson 17, Clarence Jones 15, Fulwiley 13.

Easton 64 Dallastown 46: Dallastown battled Easton for three quarters and held a first quarter lead 15-14 with Easton coming back at the half to lead 28-25. Dallastown cut the lead by one 39-37 going into the 4th quarter, but the Red Rovers overpowered York County team by scoring 25 points while only giving up 7.

Leading scorers: Easton – Ed Geosits 21, Don Griffin 16, Steve Jones 14; Dallastown – Smith 16, Gifford 10, Bill Rutecki 10.[28]

Second Round

Nanticoke 65 Dieruff 48: Dick Schmidt's Dieruff squad battled Nanticoke for three quarters and trailed by only three 44-41 going into the final period. Dieruff played without Jack Booros who was injured in the contest against Harrisburg earlier in the week. Dieruff missed its first 13 shots of the fourth quarter and finished making just 2 of 16 and scoring only 7 points in the final quarter. The loss ousted Dieruff from further play in the post season.

Leading scorers: Nanticoke – Mark Voshefski 17, Rick Pincofski 15, Gary Verazin 12; Dieruff – Foo Belfield 14, Rich Schmidt 10, Tom Stellar 10.

Easton 64 Chester 50: After falling to Chester in each of the past two seasons in post season play, Easton took charge from the very beginning and kept adding to the lead throughout the game. With leads of 10-4 after a quarter and 28-19 at the half, Easton expanded their margin to as much as 15 points in the third quarter. Chester cut the lead to six early in the fourth quarter. The Red Rovers fought back on several easy drives to the basket to seal the satisfying win.

Leading scorers: Easton – Don Griffin 14, Steve Jones 14, Butch Brantley 12, Ed Geosits 10; Chester – Hank Mann 13, Burton 12.[29]

Third Round

Abington 49 Easton 45: Easton charged out to a 14-9 first quarter lead, but the Red Rovers were caught by Abington at the half as the two teams were tied going into the locker room 21-21. The Red Rovers opened the third quarter with two quick field goals, but Abington came back to lead by four points. Easton trailed by only two going into the fourth quarter 35-33. Abington went into a stall with 2 ½ minutes left and a 44-41 lead. Easton only managed two shots after that as Abington eliminated the Red Rovers.

Leading scorers: Abington – Rick Reed 15, Rick Wright 11, Bob Harvey 10; Easton – Don Griffin 14, Mike Young 11.[30]

Postseason Accolades

Leading scorers: Doug Snyder, Allen topped the season league scoring list with 405 points and a 22.6 point per game average. He outscored Spence Pierce, Freedom, by 18 points, who finished with 387 points and a 21.5 ppg average. The resto of the top ten included: Jeff McGeehin, Central Catholic, 334 points; Foo Belfield, Dieruff, 259 points; Pat Flannery, Pottsville 253; Kirk Shelley, Liberty, 241; Joe Zubia, Bethlehem Catholic, 239; Sam Monticello, Hazleton, 238; Chris Johnson, Central Catholic, 236; and Rich Schmidt, Dieruff, 235 points.[31]

All-Stars: The league all-star first team included: Jeff McGeehin, Central Catholic (Most Valuable Player for the second consecutive year); Doug Snyder, Allen; Tom Stellar, Dieruff; Spence Pierce, Freedom; and Don Griffin, Easton. The second team consisted of: Rich Schmidt and Foo Belfield, Dieruff; Mike Young, Easton; Pat Flannery, Pottsville; and Bob Frederick, Allen.[32]

All-State: Jeff McGeehin, Central Catholic, was named to Third Team All-State. The following league players received honorable mention status: Doug Snyder, Allen; Rich Schmidt, Dieruff; Don Griffin, Easton; and Pat Flannery, Pottsville.[33]

Final Standings

First Half		Second Half		Overall	
Dieruff	9-0	Dieruff	8-1	Dieruff	17-1
Easton	7-2	Allen	7-2	Easton	14-4
Allen	6-3	Easton	7-2	Allen	13-5
Pottsville	6-3	Central Catholic	6-3	Pottsville	12-6
Central Catholic	5-4	Pottsville	6-3	Central Catholic	11-7
Hazleton	4-5	Liberty	4-5	Hazleton	6-12
Freedom	3-6	Bethlehem Catholic	3-6	Liberty	6-12
Bethlehem Catholic	2-7	Hazleton	2-7	Bethlehem Catholic	5-13
Liberty	2-7	Freedom	1-8	Freedom	4-14
Phillipsburg	1-8	Phillipsburg	1-8	Phillipsburg	2-16

Team Rosters

Allen: Coach Milo Sewards, Steve Carl, Bob Frederick, Bob Freed, Bob Lerner, Eric Marshall, Rick Middleton, Chris Nunan, Powell, Mark Smith, Nate Smith, Doug Snyder, Scott Stephens

Bethlehem Catholic: Coach Bob Bukvics, Ahearn, Gus Concilio, Gary Falkenbach, Paul Golden, Mike Guman, Leroy Halleman, Pat Haney, Sean Lynch, Jim Machain, Bob Nuno, Jeff Traupman, Joe Zubia

Central Catholic: Coach Dave Pfahler, Chris Johnson, Joseph Keeney, Dan Kendra, Joe Kiehstaller, John Legath, Kevin Lloyd, John Luchansky, Jeff McGeehin, George Roman, Al Sodl, J Stein, Jim Trinkle, Bob Wootsick, Worman

Dieruff: Coach Dick Schmidt, John Banks, Saunders "Foo" Belfield, Jack Booros, Fred Fischer, John Landis, Ray Lucknicki, Keith O'Brien, Sarmir, Rich Schmidt, Tom Stellar, Jim Thompson

Easton: Coach Stan Sutphen, Butch Brantley, Dave Cardell, Dan Finocchio, Ed Geosits, Don Griffin, Jake Hepp, Steve Jones, Dave Mazzie, Mel Ransom, Rod Simmons, Bill Sweeney, Mike Swint, Mike Young

Freedom: Coach Charlie Dubbs, Close, Barry Correll, Mark Dorrah, Bill Hochstetler, Joe Hudak, Kidd, John Majczan, Bill Matz, Spence Pierce, Kirk Shelley, Dave Tomaszewski

Hazleton: Coach Dave Shafer, Mike Caparell, Billy Cortese, Jeff Fierro, Joe Gabriel, Bob Gabriel, Ned McNellis, Sam Monticello, Tom Mundie, Mike Palumbo, Perry, Joe Polchin, John Portland, Ernie Serafine, Dave Vilushis

Liberty: Coach Len Zavacky, Ed Barreiro, Ray Crouthamel. Alex DeAngelis, Wayne Edwards, Ken Houser, Kalman Illyes, Bruce John, McKellin, Bryant Perry, Dennis Roebuck, Paul Rosko, Kirk Shelley, Gordon Smith

Phillipsburg: Coach Mike Koury, Bud Baxter, Gary Carhart, Carl Corpora, Richard DeWire, Stan Dyrek, Chris Fichera, Kormandy, Tom Marzano, Anthony Ritz, Jack Searfoss, Dave Smith, Jim Vaughn, John Williams

Pottsville: Coach Ken Kline, John Burch, Jerry Flannery, Pat Flannery, Todd Francavage, Todd Kline, Ed Mady, McClure, Irv Schappel, John Sencak, William Solan, Mike Smink, Robert Umbenhauer

1975

A Final Season Before League Realignment

The league reorganization was held in April 1974. Larry Haberle was elected to succeed John Maitland as league president. Maitland was elected to succeed Bob Stimmel, the retiring Allen athletic director, as secretary treasurer of the league.[1]

First Half - Week 1

Allen 58 Central Catholic 45: Allen opened up the season by giving new Coach John Donmoyer a victory over Central Catholic. Donmoyer took over for the retired Milo Sewards. Allen took the lead in the first minute of the game and never trailed. The Canaries led 10-6 after a quarter and the Vikings trimmed a point off the lead at halftime 26-23. Allen scored the first five points of the fourth quarter to extend their third quarter lead 41-33 to 13 points and the Vikings did not threaten the rest of the way.

Leading scorers: Allen-Eric Marshall 19, Roy Schuetz 16, Rick Middleton 11; Central Catholic-Ed Topper 18.

Easton 49 Freedom 33: Coach Stan Sutphen's Easton squad trailed early in the first quarter 6-4 before running off 10 straight points and take a 19-8 first quarter lead. Leading at halftime 29-17, the Red Rovers saw Freedom score the first five points of the third period before they ran off their second long scoring streak, 11 points, to take a commanding 40-22 lead.

Leading scorers: Easton – Ed Geosits 22, Dave Lutz 10; Freedom – Rocky Calvo 13.

Bethlehem Catholic 55 Pottsville 54 OT: Pottsville's Todd Kline and Bethlehem Catholic's Joe Zubia each scored 10 points in the opening quarter as the teams played to a 16-16 tie. Bethlehem Catholic built a four-point lead over the next two quarters to lead 41-37 heading into the fourth quarter. With the Hawks leading 41-37, Kline hit two jumpers to send the game into overtime. Zubia made two jump shots in the last 1:43 to pull out the upset win for the Hawks in overtime.

Leading scorers: Bethlehem Catholic – Joe Zubia 24, Mike Guman 12; Pottsville – Todd Kline 27, Tom Francavage 12.

Dieruff 58 Phillipsburg 42: Phillipsburg missed its first five shots of the game and scored its first basket with five minutes left in the first quarter. Six turnovers by Dieruff allowed the Stateliners to tie the Huskies 8-8 before Coach Terry German's squad made two field goals for a 12-8 first quarter lead. Phillipsburg trailed 20-16 in the second quarter when the Huskies scored the final six points for a 26-16 halftime lead. Dieruff took charge of the game in the third period by building the lead to 41-24.

Leading scorers: Dieruff – Jack Booros 20, Foo Belfield 12, Keith O'Brien 10; Phillipsburg – Jim Vaughn 8.

Hazleton 52 Liberty 30: Mike Palumbo scored eight first quarter points to lead Hazleton to a 20-8 first quarter advantage. Liberty fought back to trail by three points at the half 25-22. Hazleton's defense shutdown Liberty in the second half with the Hurricane scoring only four points in each of the quarters. Hazleton's man-to-man defense resulted in 16 steals with Joe Polchin getting five.

Leading scorers: Hazleton – Joe Polchin 13; Liberty – Gene Kent 9.[2]

Week 2

Dieruff 60 Pottsville 57: Despite Foo Belfield's eleven straight field goals and 33 points for Dieruff, Pottsville nearly pulled out the victory at the East Side Gym. Dieruff held a 57-50 lead with about three minutes left in the contest. Pottsville ran off the next seven points to tie the contest with 34 seconds left in the game. Belfield passed up a shot and fired a pass to Jack Booros for the game winning layup and foul shot for the win.

Leading scorers: Dieruff – Foo Belfield 33, Mike Timmons 10; Pottsville – Todd Kline 17, Pat Flannery 17, Tim Siket 16.

Central Catholic 69 Liberty 55: Liberty put a scare into Central Catholic with a big first quarter lead 21-10 which kept the Hurricane in the lead through the second and third quarters 29-21 and 41-37. Central Catholic exploded for 32 points in the final quarter, with Chris Johnson scoring half of them, to pull out the win, more difficult than the final score indicated.

Leading scorers: Central Catholic – Chris Johnson 23, Lou D'Annibale 13, Joe Kiehstaller 12, John Wootsick 11; Liberty – Kirk Shelly 10, Paul Rosko 10.

Hazleton 56 Phillipsburg 52: After Hazleton took a 12-11 first quarter lead, Phillipsburg tied the score at 18-18 only to see the Mountaineers run of the next 11 points on their way to a 28-20 halftime lead. Phillipsburg could not get any closer than three points in the second half, which they finally did at 55-52 with ten seconds left.

Leading scorers: Hazleton-John Portland 14, Andy Fierro 11; Phillipsburg-Gary Carhart 25, Chris Fichera 11.

Easton 52 Allen 50: Easton scored ten in a row in the first quarter on their way to a 16-9 first quarter lead. Allen came back in the second quarter to lead 20-18 and 22-21 before Easton scored four points to lead at the half 25-22. With 5:35 to play in the game, Easton led 46-35 but scored only four points in the next five minutes as Allen stormed back to lead 50-49. Ed Geosits drove the lane and scored to put Easton ahead with 27 seconds to play and added a free throw at seven seconds to ice the win for the Red Rovers. Allen's Eric Marshall missed the game due to a two-game suspension.

Leading scorers: Easton – Ed Geosits 17, Rod Simmons 12, Dave Mazzie 11; Allen – Steve Carl 14.

Bethlehem Catholic 53 Freedom 37: Bethlehem Catholic held Freedom to two first quarter points as they took an 11-2 lead. The Hawks grew the lead to twelve points 24-12 at the half. Bethlehem Catholic had its own two-point quarter in the 3rd quarter to allow Freedom back into the game and trail by only a point 26-25. In the 4th quarter, the Hawks had an eight-point run early and ended the game by scoring the last nine points.

Leading scorers: Bethlehem Catholic – Joe Zubia 19, Nick Sable 10; Freedom - Rocky Calvo 11.[3]

Central Catholic 69 Bethlehem Catholic 59: Central Catholic used the two middle periods to propel the Vikings to victory over Bethlehem Catholic. The Hawks played the Vikings to a 10-10 tie after a quarter. Central Catholic outscored Bethlehem Catholic 41-24 to take charge of the contest. During the fourth quarter when the Hawks made a small run and cut the lead to eight points 62-54, Chris Johnson pumped in five points on a free throw, an impossible layup, and subsequent intentional foul for two more free throws to put a stop to the Hawk rally.

Leading scorers: Central Catholic – Chris Johnson 21, Lou D'Annibale 14, John Wootsick 11, Ed Topper 10; Bethlehem Catholic – Mike Guman 28, Joe Zubia 10.

Allen 71 Dieruff 69 5OT: After 5 overtimes and two hours and forty-five minutes, Tom Stenack hit a 15-foot jump shot to pull out the win for Allen. The Canaries had led by ten points in regulation with three minutes to play when the Huskies rallied back to tie the game with 16 seconds to play 49-49. Jack Booros' field goal tied the game in the first overtime 53-53 with three seconds to play. In the third overtime, Roy Schuetz hit a field goal at the buzzer to tie the game again at 63-63. An Allen field goal by Jace Wagner at the end of the fourth overtime was disallowed and the game carried on to a fifth overtime. Dieruff was called for a three seconds lane violation with 23 seconds to go which turned the ball over to Allen for the dramatic finish.

Leading scorers: Allen – Steve Carl 21, Roy Schuetz 16, Chuck Bachert 11; Dieruff – Jack Booros 24, Foo Belfield 13, Mike Timmons 10.

Easton 52 Hazleton 43: Four teams were tied for first at 2-0 to start the night. Only Easton survived to sit alone in the lead at 3-0. With over three minutes remaining in the second quarter, Hazleton led 17-12, but could not score the rest of the quarter as the Red Rovers charged into the lead 20-17. Easton led during the third period 30-21, but Hazleton clawed back to trail by only three early in the final period. The Red Rovers outscored the Mountaineers 17-11 the rest of the way to secure the win.

Leading scorers: Easton – Ed Geosits 19, Rod Simmons 12; Hazleton – Andy Fierro 10, Joe Polchin 10.

Pottsville 67 Liberty 52: Pat Flannery scored 13 points in the second quarter to lead Pottsville to a 34-29 lead at the half after Liberty held the first quarter lead 14-12. Liberty was only able to get within three the remainder of the game 38-35 with a little more than five minutes to play in the third quarter.

Leading scorers: Pottsville – Pat Flannery 22, Tom Francavage 18, Todd Kline 11, Jerry Flannery 10; Liberty – Kirk Shelly 20, Ed Barreiro 10.

Phillipsburg 54 Freedom 41: Phillipsburg held Freedom to four field goals in the first half to take a 29-14 lead into the locker room. Freedom battled to within seven in the fourth quarter 39-32, but Gary Carhart scored nine points late in the final quarter to lead Phillipsburg to their first league victory.

Leading scorers: Phillipsburg-Gary Carhart 23; Freedom-Rocky Calvo 12, Jose Maldonado 11, Jim Garcia 10.[4]

Week 3

Easton 43 Phillipsburg 33: Phillipsburg took a 4-1 lead on a Jim Vaughn field goal with four minutes left in the first period. The Stateliners would not convert another field goal until more than three minutes into the third period. Easton led by only 5-4 after the initial quarter, but grew the lead to 23-14 in the third period when Dave Smith finally hit a field goal for Phillipsburg. Dave Lutz's three-point play stretched the lead to ten and the Stateliners got no closer than eight points the rest of the game.

Leading scorers: Easton – Rod Simmons 12, Ed Geosits 12, Dave Lutz 11; Phillipsburg – Gary Carhart 7.

Dieruff 63 Bethlehem Catholic 53: Foo Belfield scored 15 points in the first half and Dieruff took a 30-26 lead into the locker room. Bethlehem Catholic trailed by only three heading into the fourth quarter. With Bill Edwards scoring nine points in the final quarter, the Huskies pulled away for the victory.

Leading scorers: Dieruff – Foo Belfield 17, Jack Booros 15, Bill Edwards 11, Keith O'Brien 11; Bethlehem Catholic – Joe Zubia 16, Mike Guman 12, Paul Golden 12.

Central Catholic 43 Freedom 42 OT: Central Catholic led 27-22 at the half and increased it to seven points after three periods 35-28. Coach Rich Baksa had his Patriots employ a deliberate offense in the second half and they used it to make up the seven-point deficit and force an overtime period. With the Patriots trailing 39-38, Rocky Calvo made only one of two free throws with 16 seconds left to tie the game. Chris Johnson scored the Vikings' four overtime points while Rocky Calvo had a chance to tie the game in overtime, but made only one of two foul shots to give the Vikings the win and keep the Patriots from the upset.

Leading scorers: Central Catholic – Chris Johnson 15, Lou D'Annibale 10; Freedom – Rocky Calvo 14, Jose Maldonado 12.

Liberty 67 Allen 55: Coach Len Zavacky used his three big men, Ken Houser, Paul Rosko, and Gene Kent, to control the boards against Allen and they provided 38 points on offense to propel the Hurricane to victory. With Liberty leading 11-10, the Hurricane outscored the Canaries 17-4 from late in the first quarter into the second quarter. After Liberty was up 34-25 at the half, Allen scored the first six points of the third period to pull within three points. Liberty followed by running of the next ten points to rebuild the lead and they were not threatened the rest of the game.

Leading scorers: Liberty – Kirk Shelley 21, Paul Rosko 11, Ken Houser 10; Allen – Eric Marshall 14, Roy Schuetz 14.

Hazleton 77 Pottsville 57: Pat Flannery scored eight points in a Pottsville 10-point run leading the Crimson Tide 16-9 advantage before Hazleton closed it to 16-13 by the end of the quarter. Hazleton took the lead in the 2nd quarter and led 32-26 at the half. Starting the 4th quarter with an even larger lead 50-41, Joe Polchin scored 14 fourth quarter points to turn the game into a rout as Hazleton added 27 points to their total.

Leading scorers: Hazleton – Joe Polchin 29, Andy Fierro 20, Ernie Serafine 12; Pottsville - Todd Kline 20, Pat Flannery 11.[5]

Allen 62 Bethlehem Catholic 60: Allen built a ten-point lead during the second quarter only to see it cut to two points at the half 30-28 when Bethlehem Catholic outscored the Canaries 10-2 to end the quarter. The Hawks got off to a 13-3 run to start the third period and take an eight-point lead 41-33. With the Hawks leading by five 55-50 with a little less than four minutes to play, Steve Carl led a final rally to tie the contest at 60 and the win on his field goal with eight seconds to play.

Leading scorers: Allen – Roy Schuetz 17, Eric Marshall 15, Steve Carl 11, Jeff Trainer 10; Bethlehem Catholic – Mike Guman 14, Jim Machain 12, Joe Zubia 11, Paul Golden 10.

Easton 52 Dieruff 50: Coach Stan Sutphen's Easton quintet could only manage 25 points in the first 24 minutes of the game against Dieruff's defense and fell behind 38-25 heading into the fourth quarter. The Red Rovers used a pressing defense creating eight Husky turnovers to rally from behind. They scored 27 points in the quarter to hand Dieruff their second defeat of the first half. After Greg Kowalick hit a jumper to give Easton the lead 51-50, Dieruff turned the ball over for the final time on an errant pass to give the Red Rovers the victory to stand alone atop the league at 5-0.

Leading scorers: Easton – Dave Lutz 16, Greg Kowalick 12; Dieruff – Jack Booros 16, Bill Edwards 13.

Pottsville 84 Central Catholic 59: Running out to an 18-6 lead after 5 minutes of play, Central Catholic turned the ball over 11 times in the first quarter to allow Pottsville to cut the first quarter lead to 20-18. Pat Flannery scored 16 points in the second quarter to continue the Pottsville assault on the Vikings and produce a 43-32 halftime lead. After the Vikings cut the lead to five 51-46, Pottsville came on to score 25 points in the fourth quarter while holding Central Catholic to 9 and turn the game into a rout.

Leading scorers: Pottsville – Pat Flannery 26, Todd Kline 21, Jerry Flannery 13; Central Catholic – Chris Johnson 15, John Wootsick 15.

Hazleton 46 Freedom 42: Hazleton scored the first 12 points of the game and Freedom did not score until 35 seconds were left in the first quarter as Hazleton took a 14-2 first quarter lead. The Mountaineers held a 46-36 lead in the fourth quarter before a number of turnovers allowed the Patriots score the last six points.

Leading scorers: Hazleton- Andy Fierro 22, Joe Polchin 10; Freedom- Rocky Calvo 10, Jose Maldonado 10.

Liberty 57 Phillipsburg 46: With the lead changing hands in the first ten minutes, Kirk Shelley made four free throws and a field goal to put the Hurricane into a lead they would not lose. Phillipsburg did manage to tie the score at 20-20 in the second quarter. Liberty scored the last six points of the quarter to lead at the half 26-20. Despite forcing Liberty into 27 turnovers, Phillipsburg committed 26 fouls which led to 19 successful free throws and the Liberty victory.

Leading scorers: Liberty – Paul Rosko 13, Kirk Shelley 12, Wayne Edwards 12; Phillipsburg – Gary Carhart 14, John Williams 12.[6]

Week 4

Dieruff 65 Freedom 46: Dieruff took a 19-8 first quarter lead, but Freedom continued to stay within touch early in the third period when they were down by only eight 30-22. In the next 2 ¼ minutes, the Huskies ran off 12 straight points to expand the lead to 20 points and stay in command the rest of the way.

Leading scorers: Dieruff – Foo Belfield 20, Jack Booros 17, Mike Pletz 11; Freedom – Rocky Calvo 14.

Hazleton 63 Central Catholic 48: Hazleton took early leads of 15-6 after a quarter and 33-18 at the half. They increased the lead to 41-26 before Central Catholic scored the next eight points to cut the lead to 41-34. Early in the final quarter, the Vikings got within nine points 49-40 only to see the Mountaineers score the next 14 points. The Vikings scored the last eight points of the game.

Leading scorers: Hazleton – Andy Fierro 18, John Portland 15, Mike Palumbo 12; Central Catholic – Joe Kiehstaller 13.

Easton 71 Pottsville 69 OT: Easton took a 14-7 first quarter lead and still held the lead at the half 30-26 over Pottsville. Pottsville cut the lead to two after three periods 44-42 and took the lead in the fourth quarter. They held a seven-point lead 61-54 with a little over three minutes to play in the game. Easton rallied to tie the game at 63 on a Greg Kowalick jumper. In overtime, Easton jumped out to a 68-62 lead and Rod Knighton made two clutch free throws for the winning points.

Leading scorers: Easton – Kevin Fitzpatrick 18, Ed Geosits 12, Rod Knighton 12; Pottsville – Jerry Flannery 19, Pat Flannery 16, Todd Kline 12.

Phillipsburg 46 Allen 43 OT: Phillipsburg held a 17-12 lead in the second quarter when Allen rallied for 10 straight points to take a 22-17 halftime lead. After Phillipsburg regained the lead by four 39-35 late in the fourth quarter, Allen tied the score in regulation on four straight free throws by Roy Schuetz. In overtime, the Stateliners scored the first seven points and hung on for the upset win over the Canaries.

Leading scorers: Phillipsburg – Gary Carhart 14, Dave Smith 13; Allen – Roy Schuetz 14.

Liberty 48 Bethlehem Catholic 47: Liberty trailed 15-8 after a quarter and 26-24 at the half before finally grabbing the lead in the third quarter 30-29 with three minutes to play. With the lead changing hands five time in the final period, the two teams were knotted at 45 with a minute to play, Liberty scored the next three points on a field goal and foul shot and hung on for the win to even their record at 3-3.

Leading scorers: Liberty-Kirk Shelley 13, Mike Rosko 12, Ken Houser 10; Bethlehem Catholic-Joe Zubia 20.[7]

Week 5

Liberty 63 Dieruff 61: Liberty took an early 10-4 lead, but had to connect on a Kirk Shelley jumper to tie the score after one period 12-12. Liberty scored the last six points of the second quarter to take a 35-26 halftime lead. Dieruff rallied in the second half to eventually tie the score at 61-61. Ken Houser dropped in both ends of a one-and-one to win the contest for Liberty.

Leading scorers: Liberty – Kirk Shelley 20, Ken Houser 16, Wayne Edwards 13, Kal Illyes 10; Dieruff – John Banks 20, Foo Belfield 13, Jack Booros 12, Mike Timmons 10.

Central Catholic 42 Phillipsburg 40: After a quarter, Central Catholic led 10-4, but Phillipsburg fought its way back to trail by only a point at the half 21-20. The Stateliners took the lead after three quarters 31-29. Jim Trinkle took a rebound the full length of the court for a layup to give the Vikings a 42-38 lead and they held on for the win.

Leading scorers: Central Catholic – Ed Topper 11, John Wootsick 10; Phillipsburg – Gary Carhart 11, Chris Fichera 10.

Easton 76 Bethlehem Catholic 36: Easton took a 15-point lead 17-2 in the first quarter and rolled to victory to remain as the only undefeated team in league play at 7-0. The Hawks dropped to 2-5 in league play. Easton used 15 players in the game with 12 of them scoring at least a point. Mike Guman wasn't available to play for the Hawks.

Leading scorers: Easton – Dave Mazzie 15, Dave Lutz 14, Kevin Fitzpatrick 11; Bethlehem Catholic – Joe Zubia 16.

Hazleton 50 Allen 49 OT: In Hazleton, Allen led only four times in the contest with three in the fourth or overtime period. Allen trailed by a point at the end of three quarters 37-36 and trailed 43-38 when they scored three straight field goals to lead 44-43. After a Hazleton three-point play, Chuck Bachert tied the game at 46 for Allen in regulation. In overtime Allen led 49-48 only to have Mike Palumbo hit a field goal to win the contest for the Mountaineers.

Leading scorers: Hazleton – Mike Palumbo 18, Joe Polchin 14; Allen – Eric Marshall 18, Roy Schuetz 11.

Pottsville 81 Freedom 39: Ken Kline's Pottsville team took a 13-9 first quarter lead and held Freedom to nine points over the next two quarters to take 56-18 lead. They finished the rout of Freedom by pouring in another 25 points in the fourth quarter. Pottsville used 14 players with all but one scoring a point.

Leading scorers: Pottsville-Pat Flannery 22, Todd Kline 15; Freedom-Rocky Calvo 12, Jose Maldonado 10.[8]

Dieruff 49 Hazleton 48: Dieruff led Hazleton by 13 points in the second quarter only to have the Mountaineers go on a 13-4 run and take a 32-29 lead in the third quarter. With Hazleton leading 44-40 with 5 ½ minutes to play, Jack Booros tied the score on two field goals. Hazleton went ahead 48-46 on an Andy Fierro field goal. Foo Belfield made a free throw and followed it up with a field goal at the buzzer after a missed shot was batted back to him as the Huskies pulled out the win and knocked the Mountaineers out of first half title contention.

Leading scorers: Dieruff – Foo Belfield 21, Jack Booros 20; Hazleton – Ned McNelis 15, Andy Fierro 12.

Allen 69 Pottsville 62: Roy Schuetz hit a field goal in the final minute of the first period as the Canaries took the lead 18-16 at quarter end and would not trail again. Allen scored the first eight points of the second quarter on their way to a 34-25 halftime lead. When Pottsville pulled within ten points 52-42 with six minutes to play, Allen went on a 13-2 spurt to put the game safely in the win column.

Leading scorers: Allen – Steve Carl 22, Roy Schuetz 16, Eric Marshall 14, Jeff Trainer 12; Pottsville – Pat Flannery 23, Jerry Flannery 10.

Easton 68 Central Catholic 57: Easton made 20 of its 27 shots from the field in the first half to take a 49-33 halftime lead over Central Catholic. In the second half, the Red Rovers went into a controlled offense to down the Vikings and clinch the first half title with Hazleton's loss to Allen.

Leading scorers: Easton – Rod Simmons 17, Ed Geosits 16, Dave Mazzie 12, Kevin Fitzpatrick 11; Central Catholic – Joe Kiehstaller 12, Lou D'Annibale 12.

Bethlehem Catholic 44 Phillipsburg 42: Phillipsburg held leads after each of the first three periods 14-7, 23-21, and 38-32. After making 7 of 11 shots in the third period, Phillipsburg could only convert 2 of 9 in the fourth quarter and did not score in the last two minutes. With the Stateliners leading 42-40, Mike Guman made two free throws to tie the score for the Hawks with 1:35 to play. Bethlehem Catholic held the ball until Joe Zubia put the Hawks ahead with a field goal with 12 seconds to play. Phillipsburg attempted two field goals with both rolling in and out as time ran out.

Leading scorers: Bethlehem Catholic – Mike Guman 15, Joe Zubia 12; Phillipsburg – Gary Carhart 16.

Liberty 47 Freedom 37: Liberty held a 24-18 lead at halftime and increased it to 35-22 in the third quarter. Freedom rallied in the opening minutes of the fourth quarter to cut the deficit to 38-32. Liberty held off the Patriots the rest of the way for the win.

Leading scorers: Liberty – Ken Houser 13, Kirk Shelley 12; Freedom – Jose Maldonado 10.[9]

Week 6

Hazleton 49 Bethlehem Catholic 45: The teams battled to an 8-8 first quarter tie with Hazleton taking charge of the contest in the second period with a 24-18 lead at the half. The Hawks were only able to score eight points in each of the first three quarters as the Mountaineers built an eleven-point lead 35-24 going into the fourth quarter. With Hazleton suddenly turning the ball over frequently in the final quarter, the Hawks narrowed the lead to three points 48-45 near the end of the game.

Leading scorers: Hazleton – Joe Polchin 14, Andy Fierro 13, Mike Palumbo 11; Bethlehem Catholic – Mike Guman 21.

Dieruff 72 Central Catholic 62: Central Catholic stretched its 16-14 first quarter lead to seven points 29-22 in the second quarter before Dieruff recovered to tie the Vikings at the half 31-31. The Huskies exploded for 26 points in the third period led by sixth man Bill Edwards 11 points in the quarter. The Huskies rode the 57-43 third quarter lead to the victory over the Vikings. Central Catholic played without Chris Johnson, who was considered a potential league all-star, when he decided to transfer to Dieruff High School after a disagreement with Viking coach Dave Pfahler.

Leading scorers: Dieruff – Bill Edwards 20, Foo Belfield 16, John Banks 15, Jack Booros 12; Central Catholic – Bob Wootsick 14, Lou D'Annibale 12, Ed Topper 12, Joe Kiehstaller 12.

Pottsville 78 Phillipsburg 57: Pat Flannery hit 9 of 13 shots and combined with Todd Kline to score 28 of Pottsville's 32 first half points. The Crimson Tide built a 12-point lead. With Irv Schappel scoring 11 points in the fourth quarter, Pottsville added 28 points to turn the game into a rout.

Leading scorers: Pottsville-Pat Flannery 32, Todd Kline 16, Irv Schappel 15; Phillipsburg-Gary Carhart 22.

Easton 61 Liberty 45: Easton finished the first half of league play unbeaten with an easy victory over Liberty. The Red Rovers took 28-20 first half and 49-33 third quarter leads to coast to the win. The loss snapped Liberty's five game league winning streak.

Leading scorers: Easton – Ed Geosits 19, Dave Lutz 14, Dave Mazzie 12; Liberty - Kirk Shelley 9.

Allen 60 Freedom 51: Allen grabbed a 16-9 first quarter lead and saw it sliced to a single point at halftime 30-29. Freedom took the lead in the third period 37-34 before the Canaries ran off ten straight points to take the lead for the rest of the game.

Leading scorers: Allen – Steve Carl 21, Roy Schuetz 16; Freedom – Rocky Calvo 14, Jose Maldonado 10.[10]

Second Half - Week 7

Dieruff 49 Phillipsburg 46: Dieruff took a 13-7 first quarter lead before Phillipsburg exploded for 23 second quarter points to lead at the half 30-23 aided by Randy Swift's 10 first half points. Dieruff moved ahead late in the fourth quarter 46-43 with Phillipsburg coming back to tie the game at 46 with under two minutes to play. Foo Belfield hit a 20-foot jump shot and Bill Edwards converted a free throw to complete the scoring and sew up the contest for the Huskies.

Leading scorers: Dieruff –Foo Belfield 13, Bill Edwards 10; Phillipsburg –Gary Carhart 21, Dave Smith 11.

Allen 75 Central Catholic 67: The Vikings held a 16-14 lead after a quarter with the Canaries tying the game at 20-20 early in the second quarter. Allen held Central Catholic to only eight points in the second quarter and moved out to a 39-24 halftime advantage. The Vikings tightened their defense in the second half and trailed by only three points 70-67 with 78 seconds to play. Allen closed out the game with the last five points to halt the Viking threat.

Leading scorers: Allen – Steve Carl 17, Roy Schuetz 13, Jeff Trainer 12, Eric Marshall 10; Central Catholic – Bob Wootsick 22, Lou D'Annibale 14, Joe Kiehstaller 12.

Easton 63 Freedom 42: Despite missing starters Ed Geosits and Dave Lutz due to sickness, Easton rolled to its 10th straight league win on the season. Easton took a 19-4 first quarter lead after Freedom had scored the first two points of the game. Easton ran the lead to 20 points early in the second quarter 26-6 and 22 points 56-34 in the fourth quarter.

Leading scorers: Easton - Kevin Fitzpatrick 16, Rod Simmons 15, Rod Knighton 10; Freedom - Rocky Calvo 10, Lou Strubeck 10.

Pottsville 81 Bethlehem Catholic 77: Bethlehem Catholic could not overcome a seven-point first quarter. Pottsville took a ten-point lead despite Bethlehem Catholic scoring 28 points in the second quarter. Pottsville scored 22 points in the second quarter. The Hawks also scored 25 points in the last quarter but the total was matched by the Crimson Tide.

Leading scorers: Pottsville – Tom Siket 23, Todd Kline 20, Tom Francavage 16, Pat Flannery 13; Bethlehem Catholic – Joe Zubia 26, Mike Guman 23, Pat Haney 11, Jim Machain 10.[11]

Pottsville 62 Dieruff 61: Jerry Flannery scored 16 points and held Foo Belfield to six points as Pottsville improved to 2-0 in the half. Pottsville took a first quarter lead 19-14 but Dieruff took the lead after the second quarter 34-31 and kept it after the third quarter 49-45. The lead seesawed back and forth several times before Dieruff took the lead 61-57. Dieruff would score no more and Todd Kline made a basket with five seconds remaining to give the win to Pottsville.

Leading scorers: Pottsville – Jerry Flannery 16, Tim Siket 16, Todd Kline 14, Tom Francavage 11; Dieruff – Jack Booros 28.

Hazleton 45 Phillipsburg 43: For the fourth time in five outings, Phillipsburg held the lead going into the fourth quarter only to suffer a frustrating defeat. The Stateliners led Hazleton at the end of each of the first three quarters, 13-9, 27-22, and 37-33, but the Mountaineers moved ahead 42-40 in the 4th quarter. Gary Carhart completed a three-point play to put the Stateliners in front only to have Hazleton's Mike Palumbo make a field goal deep in the corner to pull out the win for the Mountaineers.

Leading scorers: Hazleton-Mike Palumbo 12, Ned McNelis 11, Joe Polchin 10; Phillipsburg-Dave Smith 10.

Allen 47 Easton 46: Allen held Easton to 16 first half points while unleashing 18 in the second period for a 25-16 halftime lead. Easton fought back to within a point in the third period 35-34. With the score tied at 44 with 1:21 to play, Easton Coach Stan Sutphen received a technical foul for his vociferous response to what he thought was a goaltending call. Allen made the technical and followed it up with a field goal by Nate Smith to upset the Red Rovers and hand them their first loss in league play.

Leading scorers: Allen – Eric Marshall 15, Roy Schuetz 10; Easton – Dave Mazzie 16.

Central Catholic 61 Liberty 58: Central Catholic took the first quarter lead 18-15 and expanded it to 34-24 at the half. Early in the third quarter, the lead had grown to 38-26 before Liberty went on a 12-4 run to tighten the score to 44-38 going into the final quarter. With Joe Kiehstaller scoring 12 points in the quarter, the Vikings held off the Hurricane.

Leading scorers: Central Catholic – Joe Kiehstaller 24, John Wootsick 16; Liberty – Kirk Shelley 13.

Bethlehem Catholic 64 Freedom 52: Freedom dominated the game in the first half to take 17-9 and 34-28 leads into the second half. Bethlehem Catholic's offense clicked int the second half and they scored 18 points in each of the quarters while holding the Patriots to eight in the third quarter and taking the lead for good 38-36 during the middle of the third quarter.

Leading scorers: Bethlehem Catholic – Mike Guman 23, Joe Zubia 20; Freedom – Rocky Calvo 17.[12]

Week 8

Bethlehem Catholic 68 Central Catholic 63: Joe Zubia and Mike Guman scored 29 of Bethlehem Catholic's points as the Hawks took a 41-34 lead into the locker room over Central Catholic. Bethlehem Catholic held on to the lead through the third 58-52 and fourth quarters to improve to 2-1 and stay a game behind Allen at 3-0.

Leading scorers: Bethlehem Catholic – Joe Zubia 25, Mike Guman 23, Pat Haney 12; Central Catholic – Bob Wootsick 18, John Wootsick 15, Lou D'Annibale 12.

Liberty 66 Pottsville 59: Liberty had a ten-point run in the first quarter on their way to a 20-10 lead. Pat Flannery led a Pottsville charge that got the Crimson Tide to within a point several times in the second quarter but Liberty built the lead up to four at the half 35-31. Liberty's defense shut down Pottsville in the third quarter and held them to four points to take a commanding lead in the game 53-35.

Leading scorers: Liberty – Kirk Shelley 18, Ken Houser 14, Wayne Edwards 12, Paul Rosko 11; Pottsville – Pat Flannery 21, Jerry Flannery 16, Todd Kline 14.

Allen 63 Dieruff 61: Dieruff took a 19-8 lead in the first quarter and increased it to as many as 15 points before Allen cut it to eleven 35-24 at the half. Allen outscored Dieruff 18-8 in the first 6 ½ minutes of the third period to cut the lead to a single point. Dieruff finished the third quarter up three points 47-44. Trailing 59-58, Allen made two free throws with 1:37 to play, two more at 13 seconds and one at six seconds to pull out the win.

Leading scorers: Allen – Roy Schuetz 20, Steve Carl 10, Jace Wagner 10; Dieruff – Foo Belfield 28, Jack Booros 15, John Banks 10.

Freedom 56 Phillipsburg 54 OT: Phillipsburg took the lead at the end of the first 12-10 and third quarters 38-37 with Freedom leading at halftime 29-27. The two teams tied in regulation at 50-50. In overtime, Phillipsburg scored on a field goal and a layup to go up 54-50, but Rocky Calvo scored on a field goal and four free throws to score the last six points of the game for the winning margin for the Patriots. Phillipsburg lost its fifth game by three points or less and lost eight games overall by a total of 21 points.

Leading scorers: Freedom – Rocky Calvo 17, Jim Garcia 17; Phillipsburg – Gary Carhart 14, Dave Smith 12, Jim Vaughn 12.

Hazleton 45 Easton 38: For three quarters, the two teams managed a combined total of 41 points with Hazleton holding the lead after three quarters 25-16. Easton made only 2 of 23 field goal attempts in the first half with both successful attempts in the first quarter. The Red Rovers managed only two free throws in the second quarter. In the fourth quarter alone, the teams combined for 42 points. Easton could not overcome the dreadful first half and fell to 1-2. It was the first time since the 1972 season that the Red Rovers lost back-to-back games.

Leading scorers: Hazleton-Mike Palumbo 15; Easton-Rod Knighton 12, Dave Lutz 10, Dave Mazzie 10.[13]

Central Catholic 58 Freedom 52: Central Catholic held a slim one-point lead after the first quarter, but fell as many as 13 points behind Freedom in the second quarter. The Patriots led at the half 36-26. The Vikings' man-to-man defense in the third period caused steals and turnovers and when the period was over, the Vikings led 45-43. They continued the domination in the fourth quarter on their way to evening their second half record at 2-2.

Leading scorers: Central Catholic – John Wootsick 14, Bob Wootsick 13, Lou D'Annibale 12; Freedom – Lou Strubeck 16, Mike Petruny 11, Jim Garcia 10.

Liberty 73 Allen 67: Three teams shared first place at 3-1 with the upset of Allen by Liberty. Pottsville also stood at 3-1. Kirk Shelley and Wayne Edwards combined for 50 points. Allen held a 15-13 lead going into the second quarter. After Allen extended the lead to four points, Liberty had runs of seven and six straight points to take a 31-23 lead. Allen scored the last six points of the half to trail 31-29. After Liberty opened up a ten-point lead 43-33 in the third quarter, Allen chipped away at the lead and finally tied the game at 55 with 4 ½ minutes remaining. With Allen trailing 62-61, Liberty ran off eight in a row to complete the stunning win.

Leading scorers: Liberty – Kirk Shelley 29, Wayne Edwards 21, Ken Houser 12; Allen – Roy Schuetz 19, Eric Marshall 16, Steve Carl 12, Jeff Trainer 10.

Phillipsburg 46 Easton 40: After a 14-14 first quarter tie, Phillipsburg took the lead at the half 24-10. Easton came back in the third quarter to take a 32-30 lead. After losing so many close games, Phillipsburg was finally able to take the lead in the fourth quarter with four minutes remaining and hold on for the win.

Leading scorers: Phillipsburg – Chris Fichera 13, Gary Carhart 12, Randy Swift 11, Dave Smith 10; Easton – Dave Mazzie 16, Kevin Fitzpatrick 10.

Pottsville 60 Hazleton 50: With Hazleton leading 9-8 in the first quarter, Pottsville answered with eight straight points to take the lead for the rest of the contest. The Crimson Tide held the Mountaineers to six points in the second quarter to build a twelve-point lead. A fourth quarter comeback by Hazleton fell way short due to the big first half advantage.

Leading scorers: Pottsville – Tom Francavage 16, Todd Kline 15, Tim Siket 12, Jerry Flannery 11; Hazleton – Dave Vilushis 9.

Dieruff 71 Bethlehem Catholic 62: The Huskies took a 32-26 lead into the third quarter and extended it to 46-34 with three minutes to play in the third period. By the time the quarter ended, the lead was back to six 48-42. The Hawks ended up tying the game at 50-50 with 5:15 to play on a 16-4 run. Dieruff countered with 15-4 streak to pull out the win. Coach Schmidt did not start two of his starters, Banks and Booros, for disciplinary reasons.

Leading scorers: Dieruff – Foo Belfield 19. John Banks 17, Jack Booros 10, Keith O'Brien 10; Bethlehem Catholic – Mike Guman 27, Joe Zubia 12.[14]

Week 9

Allen 80 Bethlehem Catholic 56: With Bethlehem Catholic attempting to handle Allen with a man-to-man defense, the Canaries shredded the defense by hitting 9 of 10 field goal attempts in the quarter on their way to a commanding 23-7 lead. The Hawks were impacted by the loss of Joe Zubia who missed the game because of personal problems. In the second quarter, the Hawks scored eight straight points but got no closer than 14 points, which is the closest they got the rest of the contest. The win kept the Canaries tied for first with Pottsville.

Leading scorers: Allen-Eric Marshall 13, Roy Schuetz 13, Gary Ginter 12, Steve Carl 11; Bethlehem Catholic-Mike Guman 28.

Phillipsburg 50 Liberty 40: Liberty entered the night tied for first place, but fell to the Hurricane after Phillipsburg took a 14-6 first period lead and were never threatened by Liberty. After numerous heartbreaking losses, Phillipsburg exhibited the impact it could have in the league the rest of the season.

Leading scorers: Phillipsburg- Gary Carhart 20, Chris Fichera 10; Liberty- Ken Houser 13, Kirk Shelley 10.

Dieruff 58 Easton 49: Dieruff handed Easton its fourth consecutive loss after going into the final period trailing 42-41. Dieruff scored the first seven points of the quarter to take a 48-42 lead. After Easton cut the lead to three, the Huskies went on a 10-2 spurt to put the game in the win column. Foo Belfield set a Husky record with his 231st career assist.

Leading scorers: Dieruff – Jack Booros 20, Foo Belfield 15, John Banks 11; Easton – Mike Young 18, Don Griffin 16.

Pottsville 74 Central Catholic 70: Pottsville made 20 of 25 free throws, while the Vikings missed six critical foul shots in the final quarter, to defeat Central Catholic and remain tied for first place with Allen. The Vikings trailed 59-57 going into the fourth quarter, but took a 66-61 lead behind Joe Kiehstaller's three field goals. Central Catholic made only one field goal and missed needed free throws the rest of the way as the Crimson Tide rallied to the win.

Leading scorers: Pottsville – Todd Kline 22, Jerry Flannery 20, Pat Flannery 13; Central Catholic – Joe Kiehstaller 22, John Wootsick 18, Bob Wootsick 16.

Hazleton 58 Freedom 40: Joe Polchin scored ten points as Hazleton took a 16-6 lead in the first quarter. The Mountaineers scored the first six points of the second quarter, but did not score again until the last five seconds of the quarter, enough to hold a 23-18 halftime lead. Hazleton put the game away in the fourth quarter scoring twenty points while holding the Patriots to 9.

Leading scorers: Hazleton – Joe Polchin 19, Mike Palumbo 11, Andy Fierro 10; Freedom – Rocky Calvo19.[15]

Easton 65 Pottsville 63: Easton traveled to Pottsville to battle the Crimson Tide with a share of first place on the line for Pottsville. In a back-and-forth contest, Pottsville led after the first period 20-16 only to see the Red Rovers go into the locker room with a 36 33 advantage. Pottsville rebounded to go in front 49-44. With Pottsville leading 62-60, Chris Myers hit a tying field goal with 18 seconds left in regulation. Ed Geosits, who had missed four games due to mononucleosis, put in an offensive rebound and a free throw in the overtime period to upset the Crimson Tide and drop them out of the first-place tie.

Leading scorers: Easton – Dave Lutz 17, Ed Geosits 14, Kevin Fitzpatrick 14; Pottsville – Todd Kline 19, Tom Francavage 15, Pat Flannery 11, Tim Siket 11.

Liberty 79 Bethlehem Catholic 70: Liberty built a 39-17 first half lead when the Hawks could only make 7 of 31 field goal attempts in the first half. After Bethlehem Catholic rallied to pull within nine points in the third period, Liberty answered with ten straight points. Liberty made 31 of 41 free throw attempts to contribute largely to the outcome.

Leading scorers: Liberty – Kirk Shelley 20, Wayne Edwards 12, Ken Houser 12; Bethlehem Catholic – Mike Guman 31, Joe Zubia 21.

Hazleton 68 Central Catholic 54: Hazleton pulled away methodically over all four quarters and earned a spot in the post season playoffs with the win over the Vikings. Central Catholic pulled within 54-48 with 3 ½ minutes to play, but Hazleton pulled away for the win.

Leading scorers: Hazleton – Andy Fierro 20, Mike Palumbo 14, John Portland 10; Central Catholic – Lou D'Annibale 13, John Wootsick 12, Bob Wootsick 12.

Dieruff 58 Freedom 49: The two teams exchanged leads several times throughout the contest with Dieruff leading after a quarter 14-11 and Freedom, after leading 19-18, tied it at the half at 25. Dieruff led early in the third quarter by as much as four 33-29 before the Patriots took 38-36 edge. After the teams tied at 41, Dieruff went ahead 54-45 and cruised to the win.

Leading scorers: Dieruff – Jack Booros 26, Foo Belfield 16; Freedom – Mike Petruny 14, Lou Strubeck 12, Rocky Calvo 10.

Allen 46 Phillipsburg 42: Phillipsburg battled Allen hard for four quarters only to lose another close game. Dave Smith tied the game at 42 with a 20-foot jump shot with 32 seconds to play. With 23 seconds to go, Jeff Trainer missed a shot which Roy Schuetz grabbed and put up for the deciding field goal in the game and keep Allen in first place alone with the loss by Pottsville.

Leading scorers: Allen – Eric Marshall 14, Steve Carl 10; Phillipsburg – Dave Smith 14.[16]

Week 10

Dieruff 64 Liberty 47: John Banks scored 17 points and grabbed 18 rebounds as Dieruff defeated Liberty to qualify for District 11 post season play. The Huskies led at the half 35-28 and 47-36 after three quarters. Leading 51-40 early in the final quarter, the Huskies went on a 11-point run to put the contest in the win column for Dieruff.

Leading scorers: Dieruff – Foo Belfield 24, John Banks 17; Liberty – Kirk Shelley 13, Ken Houser 10.

Pottsville 68 Freedom 57: Freedom gave Pottsville a battle the whole way trailing by three after a quarter 16-13, four at the half 35-31, and six 52-46 at the three-quarter mark. Freedom pulled within three 57-54 with 3 ½ minutes to go before the Crimson Tide made several baskets to wrap up the win.

Leading scorers: Pottsville – Pat Flannery 25, Jerry Flannery 10, Todd Kline 10; Freedom – Mike Petruny 14, Lou Strubeck 11, Greg Terleski 10.

Allen 56 Hazleton 40: In a slow start, Allen led Hazleton 4-2 after one period. Hazleton followed by scoring 17 points each in the second and third periods to lead going into the fourth quarter 36-33. The Canaries stunned the Mountaineers in the final quarter by exploding for 23 points while holding Hazelton to a mere four points.

Leading scorers: Allen – Steve Carl 13, Jeff Trainer 12, Eric Marshall 10; Hazleton – Andy Dwyer 15, Mike Palumbo 10.

Phillipsburg 52 Central Catholic 41: Phillipsburg coach Mike Koury came back to Rockne Hall to defeat his old team. After the Stateliners led at halftime 24-17, the Vikings held Phillipsburg to only seven points in the third period, but could only score nine themselves. The win was the first for Koury over his old team.

Leading scorers: Phillipsburg – Gary Carhart 14, Chris Fichera 14; Central Catholic – Joe Kiehstaller 16 Bob Wootsick 12.

Easton 81 Bethlehem Catholic 72: Easton led after the first two quarters 40-36 with Rod Simmons scoring 14 points in the half. Bethlehem Catholic scored the first five points in the third quarter to give the Hawks their only lead of the game. Making several easy steals, Easton ran off nine straight points to retake the lead 49-41 and take control of the game.

Leading scorers: Easton – Rod Simmons 22, Ed Geosits 15, Dave Mazzie 14, Dave Lutz 10; Bethlehem Catholic – Mike Guman 26, Joe Zubia 22, Jim Machain 10.[17]

Pottsville 75 Allen 64: In Pottsville, the Crimson Tide ran Allen out of the house by taking a 24-14 lead in the first quarter. After trailing 37-26 at the half, the Canaries managed to pull within five points 43-38 before the Crimson Tide ran off six points to hold off an Allen rally. The loss dropped Allen into a three-way tie for first with Pottsville and Dieruff.

Leading scorers: Pottsville – Pat Flannery 17, Jerry Flannery 16, Tom Francavage 15, Todd Kline 14; Allen – Steve Carl 15, Rick Middleton 13, Eric Marshall 11.

Dieruff 59 Hazleton 58: Hazleton went into the second period with a 18-16 lead and led 24-20 with 4 ½ minutes to play in the second quarter. The Mountaineers would not score for the next eight minutes while Dieruff poured in 18 points to take a 14-point lead. Dieruff held a 51-38 lead with 5 ½ minutes to play. Hazleton outscored the Huskies 20-8 the rest of the way and had a chance to win the game, but a Hazleton shot rolled off the rim and Dieruff grabbed the rebound to escape with the win.

Leading scorers: Dieruff – Jack Booros 21, Rich Schmidt 20, Tom Stellar 11; Hazleton – Mike Caparell 16, Ned McNelis 12, Sam Monticello 10.

Easton 69 Central Catholic 48: The return of Ed Geosits to the lineup after his illness turned the second half around for the Red Rovers. The victory at Rockne Hall was the first for Easton in four years. After leading by five 31-26, the Red Rovers broke the game wide open in the third period by adding nine to their lead 49-35 and adding to it in the final quarter.

Leading scorers: Easton – Kevin Fitzpatrick 18, Dave Mazzie 13, Ed Geosits 12, Rod Simmons 11; Central Catholic – Bob Wootsick 15, Lou D'Annibale 13, Joe Kiehstaller 12.

Liberty 57 Freedom 54: Kirk Shelley scored nine straight points in the second period to lead Liberty to a 26-18 lead at the half. After adding a point to the lead in the third quarter 41-32, the Hurricane escaped a fierce Patriot rally, which cut the lead to two 49-47, when Shelley scored six more at the end of the game.

Leading scorers: Liberty- Kirk Shelley 26; Freedom- Mike Petruny 18, Simmie Griffin 11, Rocky Calvo 10.

Phillipsburg 69 Bethlehem Catholic 46: Phillipsburg held high-scoring Joe Zubia without a field goal in the first half on their way to a 32-20 lead. Playing their best game of the season, the Stateliners outscored Liberty in every quarter and evened their second half record at 4-4.

Leading scorers: Phillipsburg – Gary Carhart 15, Randy Swift 14, Dave Smith 12, Chris Fichera 12; Bethlehem Catholic – Mike Guman 16, Joe Zubia 10.[18]

Week 11

Easton 63 Liberty 57: After a 12-12 tie after a quarter, Liberty took a one-point lead at the half 30-29. With Kevin Fitzpatrick scoring ten points, Easton took the lead in the third period and had a 43-38 advantage heading into the final quarter. The loss eliminated the Hurricane from post season play.

Leading scorers: Easton – Ed Geosits 20, Kevin Fitzpatrick 19, Mike Young 12, Steve Jones 12; Liberty – Kirk Shelley 20, Ken Houser 13, Paul Rosko 12.

Dieruff 56 Central Catholic 51: Contending for the second half title, Dieruff fell behind Central Catholic 24-23 at the half and 26-23 when the Vikings hit the first field goal of the second half. Foo Belfield then hit three consecutive field goals to give the Huskies the lead 29-26, a lead they did not lose. Dieruff opened a 35-28 lead in the 3rd quarter, but the Vikings went on a 10-4 run to get within a point 39-38. The Huskies fought off the rally to make it to the playoffs for the second half title. Foo Belfield broke the 1000-point career mark finishing with 1,012.

Leading scorers: Dieruff – Jack Booros 19, Foo Belfield 17; Central Catholic – Joe Kiehstaller 16, John Wootsick14.

Pottsville 60 Phillipsburg 34: Led by the Flannery brothers 10 points in the 1st period, Pottsville took a 12-4 lead and extended it 28-14 at the half. The victory kept Pottsville in the playoffs for the 2nd half title.

Leading scorers: Pottsville – Pat Flannery 15, Jerry Flannery 14, Todd Kline 12, Tim Siket 10; Phillipsburg – Gary Carhart 8.

Hazleton 73 Bethlehem Catholic 55: Andy Fierro and John Portland combined for 18 of Hazleton's 22 points in the second quarter as the Mountaineers took a 36-25 halftime lead. Midway through the 3rd quarter, Hazleton increased the lead to 50-26 on their way to an easy victory and a 5-4 record in the second half.

Leading scorers: Hazleton – Sam Monticello 19, Joe Polchin 10; Bethlehem Catholic – Mike Guman 22, Joe Zubia 12, Pat Haney 10, Gary Falkenbach 10.

Allen 65 Freedom 44: Big advantages in the first (14-5) and third quarter (17-8) gave the Canaries an easy win over Freedom. They qualified to participate in the playoff for the 2nd half title with Pottsville and Dieruff.

Leading scorers: Allen – Jeff Trainer 16, Eric Marshall 12, Roy Schuetz 12, Steve Carl 11; Freedom – Rocky Calvo 15, Lou Strubeck 10.[19]

Second Half Playoffs

Dieruff 65 Pottsville 56: Pottsville jumped out to a 28-16 lead while making 9 of 12 field goal attempts during a stretch in the first half. In the last five minutes of the second quarter, the Huskies went on an 18-4 run to explode into the lead 34-32. Dieruff's frontcourt scored 27 of the Huskies' 31 second half points to hold off the Crimson Tide and move on to play Allen for the second half title.

Leading scorers: Dieruff – Jack Booros 26, Foo Belfield 10; Pottsville – Pat Flannery 20, Jerry Flannery 18.[20]

Dieruff 66 Allen 65: At Muhlenberg's Memorial Hall, Dieruff and Allen squared off to determine the second half title. After Allen led 16-15 after a quarter, Dieruff, led by Keith O'Brien's ten points, took the half time lead 35-29. The Huskies increased the lead to 39-31, but Allen scored the next seven points to get within a point 39-38. Despite making only two field goals in the last 11 minutes of the game, Dieruff made six clutch field goals in the final period to hold off the Canaries for the second half title and the right to face Easton for the overall league title.

Leading scorers: Dieruff – John Banks 21, Foo Belfield 14, Jack Booros 10, Keith O'Brien 10; Allen – Steve Carl 25, Jeff Trainer 16, Roy Schuetz 14.[21]

League Championship

Easton 75 Dieruff 51: At Lafayette's Kirby Field House, Easton left no doubt in the league championship contest as they routed Dieruff after a slow start in the contest. Trailing 12-11 after a quarter, Easton held the Huskies to eight second quarter points and took a 27-20 halftime lead. The Red Rovers exploded for 24 points in each of the quarters in the second half. Dave Lutz held Jack Booros scoreless in the game, which was the first time that occurred in 61 games.

Leading scorers: Easton - Ed Geosits 17, Dave Lutz 17, Dave Mazzie 13, Rod Simmons 13, Kevin Fitzpatrick 10; Dieruff – Foo Belfield 20, John Banks 18.[22]

District 11 Postseason Play

Five league teams qualified for the expanded district playoffs. The seedings for the playoffs were as follows: 1st - Easton; 2nd - Dieruff; 3rd – Allen; 4th – Pottsville; and 5th – Hazleton.[23]

First Round

Hazleton 50 Nazareth 45: In Pottsville, Hazleton took leads after the first two quarters 11-9 and 23-15. Nazareth trailed 36-25 going into the final quarter, but rallied back to within a point 46-45. Ernie Serafine came off Hazleton's bench in the final minute to score field and convert two free throws to put an end to the Blue Eagle rally

Leading scorers: Hazleton- Andy Fierro 17, Joe Polchin 11, John Portland 10; Nazareth- Todd Quinter 14.

Pottsville 72 West Hazleton 69: In Hazleton, Pottsville fell behind West Hazleton 20-18 and 36-29 after the first two periods. Cutting the lead to two 52-50 after three quarters, Pottsville took the lead with 3:20 to play and sank six free throws to take a 68-63 lead. West Hazleton went back ahead with 37 seconds to play 69-68. Todd Kline hit a field goal and Tim Siket was fouled when he stole an inbounds pass and converted both for the winning points.

Leading scorers: Pottsville – Jerry Flannery 25, Pat Flannery 13, Tom Francavage 12, Todd Kline 10; West Hazleton – Alan Lonoconus 26, Dave Ruminski 17.[24]

Quarterfinal Round

Easton 68 Emmaus 61: In Pottsville, Emmaus battled Easton for four periods with Easton taking a six-point first quarter lead 14-8. Emmaus cut the lead in half 26-23 at halftime, The Red Rovers got the three points back in the third quarter to go into the final quarter with a 43-37 lead. In a high scoring final quarter with 49 points scored, Easton added another point to its winning margin.

Leading scorers: Easton – Ed Geosits 21, Kevin Fitzpatrick 21, Dave Mazzie 11; Emmaus – Hoppes 19, Keith Dorney 18.

Allen 68 Parkland 59: Whitehall took an 18-11 lead after a quarter and increased it to ten points 24-14 in the second quarter. Allen held the Zephyrs without a field goal for five minutes during a 14-2 run to take a 28-26 lead. At halftime, Allen led 34-33. In the second half, Allen hit 12 of its first 13 field goals from the outside to build a ten-point and hold on for the victory.

Leading scorers: Allen – Roy Schuetz 19, Eric Marshall 14, Jeff Trainer 13, Steve Carl 11; Whitehall – Dave Boandl 28.

Pottsville 59 Northampton 55: At Kutztown's Keystone Hall, Pat Flannery scored 16 points in the first half to keep the Crimson Tide in the game as Northampton to a 30-28 lead. Northampton added to the lead early in the third period 34-30 when Pottsville ran off eight straight points to take the lead for good 38-34. Pottsville led 49-44 going into the fourth quarter with the Konkrete Kids battling back for a 53-53 tie. Pottsville, behind baskets from Flannery and Todd Kline, held on for the win.

Leading scorers: Pottsville – Pat Flannery 19, Jerry Flannery 14, Tim Siket 14; Northampton – Andy Onkotz 19, George Crawford 14, Jim Filipovits 14.

Dieruff 64 Hazleton 52: In a battle between two league teams, Dieruff used an eight-point advantage (18-10) and a sixteen-point advantage in the fourth quarter to defeat Hazleton. Hazleton had taken a 42-38 lead after the third quarter when the Mountaineers had their own big quarter (18-6).

Leading scorers: Dieruff – Jack Booros 24, Foo Belfield 16, John Banks 12; Hazleton – Ned McNelis 14.[25]

Semifinal Round

Dieruff 70 Pottsville 62: At Keystone Hall on the Kutztown campus, Dieruff and Pottsville played even in the first and third quarters with 17 points each in the first and 14 in the third. The contest came down the second and fourth quarters and Dieruff prevailed by four points in both to knock off the Crimson Tide. With Pottsville trailing 51-50, Dieruff scored eight in a row to take a 59-50 lead only to have Pottsville rally to within five points before the Huskies snuffed the rally.

Leading scorers: Dieruff – Jack Booros 25, John Banks 23, Foo Belfield 10; Pottsville – Pat Flannery 17, Jerry Flannery 16, Tim Siket 14;

Allen 51 Easton 44: Easton took the early lead 14-12, but Allen outscored Easton by identical 12-9 scores to take a 36-32 lead into the final quarter. At one point in the third quarter, Allen had built the lead to eleven points, only to see the Red Rovers cut the lead to four.

Leading scorers: Allen – Jeff Trainer 16, Eric Marshall 14, Roy Schuetz 11; Easton – Ed Geosits 22.[26]

Pottsville 60 Easton 57: In a consolation game to determine the third district team for the PIAA playoffs, Pottsville opened a nine-point lead and hung on in the second half to oust Easton. Pottsville only made four field goals in the second half but made 13 of 15 at the foul line to pull out the third seed from the district in the state tournament.

Leading scorers: Pottsville – Todd Kline 17, Pat Flannery 17, Jerry Flannery 10, Tom Francavage 10; Easton - Rod Simmons 15, Dave Mazzie 13, Ed Geosits 10.[27]

District Championship

Allen 74 Dieruff 68: In the fourth meeting between the two in the season, the teams battled fiercely with Dieruff taking the first quarter lead 19-14, but with Allen battling back for the half time lead 35-34. Allen held a seven-point advantage in fourth quarter, but the Huskies scrambled back to tie the game at 58 with 2:45 left. The Canaries ran off eight in a row to win the title

Leading scorers: Allen – Eric Marshall 20, Rick Middleton 19, Jeff Trainer 16, Steve Carl 14; Dieruff – Foo Belfield 26, Jack Booros 15, Keith O'Brien 11.[28]

PIAA Playoffs

Allen, Dieruff, and Pottsville qualified for PIAA post season play from District 11 in the expanded playoff format.

First Round

Pottsville 67 Williamsport 62: At Bloomsburg, Pottsville took a 34-26 lead at the half and outlasted Williamsport to win the first-round matchup. With 10 minutes left to play, Pottsville held 12-point lead 47-35 before Williamsport cut the lead in half by the end of the game. Williamsport's only lead was 2-0.

Leading scorers: Pottsville – Pat Flannery 16, Jerry Flannery 16, Todd Kline 14, Tom Francavage 12; Williamsport – Fred Brown 14, Ed Llewellyn 14, Willie Manville 14, Cohick 14.[29]

Reading 48 Dieruff 41: In Pottsville, Dieruff held a 21-14 lead with 4 ½ minutes left in the second quarter and by five at the half 23-18. Reading's defense clamped down on the Huskies in the 2nd half and only allowed 7 field goals in the half. In the early minutes of the third quarter, Reading went on a 15-4 run to take a 33-29 lead. Even though they got within two points twice in the final quarter, they could not sustain the rally against Reading.

Leading scorers: Reading – Henry Merritt 13, Branch 13; Dieruff – John Banks 15, Foo Belfield 11.

Ephrata 64 Allen 59: Allen took a 30-18 lead with Ephrata cutting the lead to 30-24 at the half. Ephrata switched from a zone defense to a man-to-man in the second quarter and it had an immediate impact. After they scored the last six points of the second quarter, Ephrata outscored the Canaries 24-12 to take a commanding lead into the final quarter. Ephrata held an eleven-point lead at one point in the third quarter.

Leading scorers: Ephrata – John Bucher 23, Mike Matto 20, Bob Gunselman 14; Allen - Eric Marshall 15, Jeff Trainer 14, Steve Carl 14, Roy Schuetz 10.[30]

Second Round

Plymouth-Whitemarsh 81 Pottsville 62: Pottsville was only one-point behind after the first quarter 12-11. Plymouth-Whitemarsh broke away during the next two periods with seven and eight-point advantages to take a 57-41 lead into the final quarter and cruised to victory.

Leading Scorers: Plymouth-Whitemarsh – John Wisniewski 19, Cameron 18, O'Donnell 11, Steve Tees 10; Pottsville – Todd Kline 14, Tim Siket 13, Pat Flannery 10.[31]

Postseason Accolades

Leading Scorers: Mike Guman, Bethlehem Catholic, topped the season league scoring list with 342 points and a 20.2 point per game average. The rest of the top ten included: Foo Belfield, Dieruff, 306 points; Jack Booros, Dieruff, 296 points; Pat Flannery, Pottsville, 293 points; Kirk Shelley, Liberty 290 points; Todd Kline, Pottsville, 287 points; Joe Zubia, Bethlehem Catholic, 281 points; Gary Carhart, Phillipsburg, 247; Roy Schuetz, Allen, 238 points; and Steve Carl, Allen, 228 points.[32]

All-Stars: The league all-star first team included: Ed Geosits, Easton (Most Valuable Player); Pat Flannery, Pottsville; Jack Booros, Dieruff; Saunders "Foo" Belfield, Dieruff; and Mike Guman, Bethlehem Catholic. The second team consisted of: Kirk Shelley, Liberty; John Banks, Dieruff; Todd Kline, Pottsville; and Steve Carl and Roy Schuetz, both Allen.[33]

All-State: Pat Flannery, Pottsville, was named to Third Team All-State. The following league players received honorable mention status: Ed Geosits, Easton; Jack Booros, Dieruff; Roy Schuetz, Allen; and Dave Mazzie, Easton.[33]

Final Standings

First Half		Second Half		Overall	
Easton	9-0	Dieruff	7-2	Easton	14-4
Hazleton	7-2	Allen	7-2	Dieruff	13-5
Dieruff	6-3	Pottsville	7-2	Hazleton	12-6
Allen	5-4	Easton	5-4	Allen	12-6
Liberty	5-4	Hazleton	5-4	Pottsville	11-7
Central Catholic	4-5	Liberty	5-4	Liberty	10-8
Pottsville	4-5	Phillipsburg	4-5	Phillipsburg	6-12
Bethlehem Catholic	3-6	Bethlehem Catholic	2-7	Central Catholic	6-12
Phillipsburg	2-7	Central Catholic	2-7	Bethlehem Catholic	5-13
Freedom	0-9	Freedom	1-8	Freedom	1-17

Team Rosters

Allen: Coach John Donmoyer, Charles Bachert, Steve Carl, Scott Gehringer, Gary Ginter, Bob Hrebik, Eric Marshall, Rick Middleton, Roy Schuetz, Nate Smith, Tom Stenack, Jeff Trainer, Jace Wagner

Bethlehem Catholic: Coach Bob Bukvics, Mario Alexio, Jim Altimaro, Bill Czar, Gary Falkenbach, Paul Golden, Mike Guman, Leroy Halleman, Pat Haney, Jim Machain, Pete O'Leary, Noel Rodriguez, Nick Sabie, Joe Zubia,

Central Catholic: Coach Dave Pfahler, Mike D'Annibale, A Feiertag, Chris Johnson, Joe Kiehstaller, Paul Lloyd, John Luchansky, Joe Polaha, Ed Topper, Jim Trinkle, Jim Waterbury, Bob Wootsick, John Wootsick

Dieruff: Coach Terry German, John Banks, Saunders "Foo" Belfield, Paul Belfield, Jack Booros, Bill Cassium, Bill Edwards, Fred Fischer, Glen Kocher, Keith O'Brien, Mike Pletz, Rich Schmidt, Tom Stellar, Jon Thompson, Mike Timmons, Tyrone Wright

Easton: Coach Stan Sutphen, Brown, Diacount, Kevin Fitzpatrick, W Fitzpatrick, Ed Geosits, Don Griffin, Steve Jones, Rod Knighton, Len Kobylus, Greg Kowalick, Dave Lutz, Maciejcyk. Dave Mazzie, Myers, Rod Simmons, James Spagnola, Mike Swint, Mike Young

Freedom: Coach Rich Baksa, Jim Albert, Rocky Calvo, Close, Jim Garcia, Simmie Griffin, Tom Hooker, Jeff Kasander, Jose Maldonado, Morgan, Mike Petruny, Lou Strubeck, Greg Terleski

Hazleton: Coach Dave Shafer, Joe Bruno, Mike Caparell, Ray Chulock, Andy Dwyer, Tony Fadule, Andy Fierro, Ron Fierro, Carl Manfredi, Ned McNelis, Sam Monticello, Mike Palumbo, Joe Polchin, John Portland, Brian Reber, Ernie Serafine, Dave Vilushis

Liberty: Coach Len Zavacky, Ed Barreiro, Ray Crouthamel, Wayne Edwards, Ken Houser, Kal Illyes, Bobby Jones, Gene Kent, Dave McKellin, Dennis Roebuck, Paul Rosko, Kirk Shelley, Gary Shunk, Smith, Jim Villani

Phillipsburg: Coach Mike Koury, Robert Baxter, Gary Carhart, Carl Corpora, Richard DeWire, Chris Fichera, Tom Marzano, Anthony Ritz, Jack Searfoss, Dave Smith, Randy Swift, Jim Vaughn, Russell Viscomi, John Williams

Pottsville: Coach Ken Kline, Bob Carter, Paul Davis, Jerry Flannery, Pat Flannery, Tom Francavage, Ernie Haynes, Dennis Kline, Todd Kline, Irv Schappel, Tim Siket, Mike Smink

League Coaches

The following is the list of coaches for each of the league schools during the years of the school's membership in the East Penn League:

Allentown

J. Birney Crum (1926-1950)

Born in Alton, Illinois, Crum graduated from Alton High School and briefly attended Shurtleff College in Alton prior to transferring to Muhlenberg College. A star football, basketball, and baseball athlete, Crum graduated from Muhlenberg College in 1923. Prior to coming to Allentown HS, he coached and taught briefly in Somerville NJ and Carnegie PA. An extremely successful football and basketball coach at Allentown High School, Crum's football teams compiled a 186-48 record including six undefeated seasons. On the court, his teams won state titles in 1935, 1945, 1946, and 1947 while compiling an overall record of 490-106. After retiring from Allentown HS, Crum briefly coached the Muhlenberg College basketball team. Beginning in 1954, he led the team to a 78-70 record. He was elected to the Pennsylvania Sports Hall of Fame in 1975. He passed away on Christmas Day 1981 at the age of 82.[1]

J. Milo Sewards (1951-1974)

Milo Sewards, a graduate of Allentown High School, attended Muhlenberg College and received a bachelor of philosophy degree. He played football and basketball at Muhlenberg College. Prior to Muhlenberg, he attended Pennsylvania Military College where he won three varsity letters. He began his teaching and coaching career at Allentown High School in 1940. During World War II, he served as head basketball coach at Union College in Schenectady, NY. He returned to Allentown in 1945. He served as an assistant to J. Birney Crum and became the head basketball coach in 1951 with the retirement of Coach Crum. He served as head coach until 1974 when he was appointed athletic director at Allen High School. He was a Navy veteran of World War II. He passed away in July 2003.[2]

John Donmoyer (1975)

John Donmoyer earned letters in football, basketball, and track at Allentown High School prior to his graduation in 1957. Donmoyer experienced a winning tradition as player on several outstanding teams coached by his predecessor Sewards. The 1956 team won the East Penn Championship. The 1957 team won both the East Penn and District XI titles. Those two teams finished with a combined record of 51-2.

He attended the University of Pennsylvania before transferring to and graduating from Muhlenberg College. He taught mathematics at William Allen High School. He began his coaching career as an assistant football coach at Muhlenberg College for four years and at Allen (Allentown) for seven years. He later served as the junior varsity basketball coach for eight years at Allen High School.

When Milo Sewards retired in 1974, Donmoyer took over as head basketball coach and served in the role for 23 years winning 423 games in the position. His teams won East Penn titles in 1979, 1980, 1984, 1985, and 1990. Six of his teams continued on to win District XI championships including 1975, 1979, 1980, 1984, 1988, and 1993. In two successive years, he led the Canaries to PIAA Eastern Championships only to suffer defeat in the state title games. Donmoyer's success earned him four "Coach of the Year" honors. After retiring from teaching at Allen, he continued his coaching career at Moravian Academy for another 17 years. Donmoyer passed away in August 2014.[3]

J Birney Crum[4] **J Milo Sewards**[5] **John Donmoyer**[6]

Bethlehem (Liberty)

William "Pop" Emery (1926-1927, 1930-1942)

William H. (Pop) Emrey, called the "Father of Athletics" in Bethlehem, taught for 41 years and coached for 38 years including 4 years at Mauch Chunk High School prior to coming to Bethlehem High School in 1916. Born in Honey Brook, Chester County, Emrey graduated from Central High School, Philadelphia, and West Chester State College. He coached football, basketball, and track at Bethlehem. He was a founder of the Eastern Pennsylvania Interscholastic Basketball League and served as its first president. He was primarily known for conceiving a triangular track meet between Allentown, Bethlehem, and Easton. He also was instrumental in establishing the "Turkey Day Classic", a football rivalry between Allentown and Bethlehem High Schools. As the head track coach for 38 years, he became known as the "Dean of the Track". Today the Emrey Relays in Bethlehem are named after him. He passed away August 3, 1960.[7]

Leo Prendergast (1928-1929)

Leo Prendergast was a star athlete at Easton High School and lettered in football, baseball, basketball, and track. After attending Allentown Prep and Kiski, Prendergast attended Lehigh University and starred on the football team. He left Lehigh for St. John's College. He was a four-sport letterwinner at St. John's including football, baseball, basketball, and swimming. He began his coaching career at St. John's before coming to Bethlehem to coach football, baseball, basketball, and track. Later, he coached football at Lehigh University from 1943-45. He passed away in October 1969.[8, 9]

Joseph Preletz (1943-1954)

Joe "Pickles" Preletz was born and raised on Bethlehem's south side where he was often found raiding the pickle barrel at his parents' restaurant. He was an outstanding athlete at Bethlehem High School in basketball, football, baseball, and track graduating with the class of 1925. He continued to play football, basketball, and baseball at Rutgers. He graduated from Rutgers in 1929 and also obtained a master's degree at Lehigh University.

He began his teaching and coaching career at Washington Junior High School before moving on to Bethlehem High School as head basketball coach in 1942 and also served as assistant football coach. During his twelve years, he never had a losing season and finished with a 74% winning percentage as he won 196 games with only 69 losses. His 1948 team won the District XI Class A championship. He passed away in 1980 in California.[10]

John Howard (1955-1968)

A 1927 graduate of Bethlehem High School, John Howard played for the late Bill Emery. After graduating from Perkiomen Prep, where he had gained stature in baseball, basketball, and soccer, he enrolled at

Gettysburg College for what proved to be a successful college career. Howard's versatility as an athlete was exemplified in his receiving nine consecutive letters in basketball, baseball, and football. He was captain of the basketball team his senior year, and he also served as president of the student body.

He began his varsity coaching career at Bethlehem Catholic in 1950, winning the Philadelphia Suburban Catholic League Championship each of the five years he coached there. His Becahi teams also captured the PCIAA Class B Eastern Championships in 1950, 1953, and 1954. In his short career at Becahi, his team compiled an impressive 115-31 record. Returning to his alma mater in 1954, he began a 13-year career as coach of the Hurricane team. His teams won District XI championships in 1958 and 1961 and four East Penn League titles. His Bethlehem Liberty squad of 1955 holds the team high scoring record with 124 points against Pottsville. Howard's 18-year career totals as a head coach include 322 wins against 116 losses for an enviable 74% winning percentage.

He served as head coach at St. Francis Academy and coached the Northampton Area Community College women's basketball team. He passed away in August 1985 in Bethlehem.[11]

Francis "Fritz" Toner (1968)

Fritz Toner, a three sport-athlete at Bethlehem High School, also became a standout basketball player at Moravian College. In addition to Bethlehem High School, he also coached basketball at Moravian College and Northampton Community College. He died in April 2018.[12]

Al Senavitis (1970-1973)

An All-State performer in both basketball and track at Bethlehem High School, Al Senavitis started for three seasons at Seton Hall University. In 1958, he teamed with Billy Packer to lead Bethlehem to both the East Penn League and District XI titles. In addition to Liberty, he also coached at Phillipsburg and Moravian College.

At Liberty High School, Senavitis taught special education which later motivated him to became heavily involved with the Special Olympics. He served as chairman of the Special Olympics Pennsylvania for many years and stayed involved with the organization for 40 years. Senavitis passed away in November 2010.[13]

Len Zavacky (1973-1975)

Len Zavacky graduated from Bethlehem Liberty High School in 1958 and Moravian College in 1962. He played basketball at both Bethlehem and Moravian College. Prior to his head coaching position, Zavacky had served as an assistant basketball coach at Bethlehem. He also served as a reading and drafting teacher in the school district.[14]

Bill Emrey[15]

Leo Prendergast[16]

Joe Preletz[17]

Fritz Toner[12]

Al Senavitis[18]

Len Zavacky[19]

Bethlehem Catholic

Paul Calvo (1967-1969)

Paul Calvo graduated from Bethlehem Vo-Tech in 1943. While in high school, he played both football and basketball for Bethlehem High School. After serving with the US Army in World War II from 1943-1946, he attended Moravian College and graduated in 1952. He played basketball at Moravian College. After graduation from Moravian, Calvo taught in the Bethlehem School District for 32 years.

Calvo coached basketball at Bethlehem Catholic High School from 1954 through 1969. He compiled a record of 260 wins against 155 losses. Bethlehem Catholic won the 1960 and 1962 Pennsylvania Catholic (PCIAA) state championships under his direction. He also served as an assistant football coach at Moravian College from 1954 through 1972. He passed away in March 2012.[20]

Bob Bukvics (1970-1975)

An outstanding basketball player at Bethlehem Catholic, Bob Bukvics graduated in 1960 after leading the Hawks to the 1960 Class B Pennsylvania Catholic state championship and finishing with a school record 1,485 points. Bukvics earned first team all-state honors for his performance. He attended Villanova University and earned a degree in secondary education. He taught at Bethlehem Catholic and served as head basketball coach from 1969 to 1980. He also served as the school's athletic director.

Paul Calvo[20]

Bob Bukvics[21]

Central Catholic

Joe Krajsa (1948-1950)

Joe Krajsa graduated cum laude in 1939 from East Stroudsburg University where he played varsity basketball, football and baseball. He joined the faculty at Allentown Central Catholic and served as the school's athletic director and director of health and physical education. He served as head basketball coach from 1940-42 and 1947-50. His teaching and coaching career was interrupted by his service in the Navy during World War II from 1942-46. He also served as head football coach from 1946-1949. He posted a record of 104-37 as head basketball coach. He led the team to the 1948 Pennsylvania Catholic championship. He died in June 1998.[22]

Joe Petro (1951-1952)

Joe Petro graduated from Central Catholic in 1935. He attended St. Joseph's College and received All-American honorable mention as a football player. When St. Joseph's discontinued its football program, Petro transferred to Muhlenberg College and was named All-State and Little All-American. He graduated from Muhlenberg with a bachelor's degree in social studies. He played semi-professional football with the Wilmington Clippers and Bethlehem Bulldogs. He taught and coached at St. Joseph's Preparatory School prior to teaching and coaching at Central Catholic. He coached the basketball team in the 1951 and 1952 seasons. He also coached and taught at Muhlenberg College and Kutztown State College. He was a veteran of World War II, serving in the Navy. He passed away in March 1975.[23]

John Wargo (1953)

John Wargo graduated from Newport Township High School, Wanamie, PA (near Nanticoke), Bucknell University (BS in Education), and the University of Scranton (MS). Prior to being hired by Central Catholic, he taught and coached at Shickshinny High School. Later, he also taught physical education and coached football and basketball in the Crestwood and Northwest Area School Districts before retiring in 1970. He served in World War II with the Marines. He resigned after one year at the helm when he was called back into active duty with the US Marine Corps. He died in January 2003.[24, 25]

Emil Carazo (1954-1957)

Emil Carazo joined the Central Catholic faculty as a teacher and head basketball coach in 1953. He led the Vikings to two PCIAA state championships (1956 and 1957). He graduated from Palmerton High School in 1943 and starred in football, baseball, and basketball. He graduated from East Stroudsburg State Teachers College in 1948. He coached and taught for five years at Davenport High School prior to Central Catholic. Carazo passed away in January 1984.[26, 27]

John Compardo (1958-1965)

John Compardo assumed the role of head basketball coach in 1958, with the resignation of Emil Carazo, and served through 1965. He also served as the head football coach. He had served as an assistant basketball coach under Carazo. In 1965, he joined the Allentown College (now DeSales University) staff as athletic director and Director of Physical Education. He retired in 1989 from those positions. Compardo graduated from Pen Argyl High School, Springfield College (BS), Moravian College (MS), and Lehigh University (Doctorate). He served in the Navy for three years and was discharged in 1945. He died in January 2018.[28, 29]

Mike Koury (1966-1973)

Mike Koury graduated from Easton Catholic High School and Moravian College (1959). Prior to Central Catholic, Koury spent four years at Pottstown's St. Pius X High School as head basketball coach and social studies teacher. He served as athletic director at Central Catholic for 10 years and as head basketball coach. He taught social studies at Central Catholic and later at Phillipsburg NJ (4 years). Koury passed away in October 1997.[30]

Dave Pfahler (1974-1975)

Dave Pfahler graduated from Central Catholic High School in 1965 as the school's all-time leading scorer with over 1000 points. He helped lead the Vikings to the PCIAA state championship in 1964. He received a bachelor of arts degree in marketing at St. Joseph's University. As a varsity letter winner, he helped lead the Hawks to MAC and Big Five championships. From 1969-73, he taught and served as the head basketball coach at Reading Central Catholic High School. He died in June 2012.[31]

Joe Krajsa[32] Joe Petro[33] John Wargo[25] Emil Carazo[34]

John Compardo[35] Mike Koury[36] Dave Pfahler[31]

Coatesville

Ed Atwell (1926, 1931)

Born in Townsend, Delaware, and a graduate of West Chester Normal School, Atwell served as a basketball and track coach and taught math at Coatesville High School from 1919 until 1940. He also served as principal at Coatesville and later as the first principal at Scott High School in Coatesville. He retired in 1943. He passed away on March 1, 1972.[37]

W. Clyde Mearkle (1927)

Clyde Mearkle graduated from Penn State in 1921 where he was the captain of the baseball team. He taught for ten years at Coatesville and Aliquippa High Schools. Mearkle briefly played baseball with Seattle in the Pacific Coast League and managed Shamokin in the New York-Pennsylvania League. He passed away in October 1968 in Illinois.[38]

Lou Lerda (1928-1930)

Lou Lerda served as Coatesville head basketball coach from 1928 through January 1943 when he accepted an assignment with the armed forces during World War II. He grew up in the Nanticoke area and graduated from the Bloomsburg Normal School in 1924. He played football and basketball at the school and was named captain of the basketball team. He came to Coatesville from the Bloomsburg Normal School.[39]

Clyde Mearkle[38]

Louis Lerda[40]

Dieruff

Richard Schmidt (1960-1974)

Dick Schmidt graduated from Allentown High School in 1944 and served as captain of the basketball team as a senior. He went on to earn a bachelor's degree from East Stroudsburg State Teachers College and a master's degree at Lehigh University. He served in the Korean War with the US Army. He taught and coached in the Allentown School District for 39 years. During his tenure as head basketball coach at Dieruff, he compiled an overall record of 271 wins against only 100 losses. His teams earned four East Penn League titles and four consecutive District XI championships. Prior to Dieruff, he served as an assistant basketball coach at Muhlenberg College for head coach Birney Crum. He also served as athletic director at Dieruff High School from 1975-1986. He finished his coaching career as the girls' head coach at Bethlehem Catholic with a very successful record of 142-75 and retired in 1995. He died in June 2011.[41, 42]

Terry German (1975)

After failing to make the varsity basketball roster at Allentown High as a sophomore and a junior, German finally found daylight as a senior. German led Allentown to an undefeated East Penn League and District 11 championship in 1955 and was first team all-league, third team all-state. As a four-year starter at West Chester State, German scored 1,679 points and was named All-Pennsylvania Conference each year. He was a four-year member of the Philadelphia All-Small College Team and was Honorable Mention Little All-American in 1959.

He played in various city leagues and spent a year as a professional with the Allentown Jets. German began his varsity coaching career at Parkland (1969-74) and finished up at Dieruff (1975-82) after taking over for former mentor Dick Schmidt. He chalked up a 98-36 record at Parkland and went 149-60 at Dieruff. He was EPC Coach of the Year twice and his 1978 team went undefeated in the conference, the first team to do so since 1960.[43]

Dick Schmidt[41]

Terry German[43]

Doylestown

Bill Wolfe (1928-1931)

Bill Wolfe went to Lebanon High School and Lebanon Valley College prior to assuming the head basketball coach position at Doylestown. He served as basketball coach through 1943 and later became the athletic director for Central Bucks High School. He was a teacher in the Doylestown School District from 1925 through 1962. He passed away in April 1969.[44, 45, 46]

Bill Wolfe[47]

East Stroudsburg

Earl Mosier (1932-1934)

Earl Mosier succeeded Frank McGuire for the 1932 season when McGuire was ruled out because he was not a certified faculty member at East Stroudsburg High School. He graduated from both Syracuse and New York Universities. During World War II, he left the East Stroudsburg faculty to serve in the Air Force. After the war, he joined the Newark and Glen Ridge school districts and the Essex County Vocational School in New Jersey. He died at the age of 60 in July 1965.[48]

Lew Hastie (1935)

Lewis Hastie served as East Stroudsburg's coach during their last season in the league. Hastie served as the coach through the 1937 season. He led the Cavaliers to the Lehigh Northampton League championship during their initial season in the league in 1936. He served as a biology teacher at East Stroudsburg for many years. He passed away in July 1987.[49]

Earl Mosier[50]

Lew Hastie[51]

Easton

Frank Duffy (1926-1929)

Duffy served as physical education teacher and football and basketball coach at Easton High School from 1924 until 1929. In 1929, he became a teacher and coach at Dunmore High School in Lackawanna County, PA. He retired in 1962 and died on December 27, 1975.[52]

Clyde Notestine (1930-1936, 1938)

W. Clyde Notestine graduated from East Stroudsburg State Teacher's College where he excelled in both basketball and football. He began his teaching and coaching career at Easton in the late 1920s and taught at both the junior and senior high school levels. He passed away in July 1966 at the age of 61,[53]

Stan Carney (1937)

Stan Carney served as a school teacher in the Wilson School District for 40 years and retired in 1973. In addition to Easton, he also coached at Wilson Boro for a number of years. He graduated from Muhlenberg College with both bachelor's and master's degrees. He starred in both basketball and baseball for Muhlenberg. He passed away in February 2001 at the age of 93.[54]

Elmer Carroll (1939-1942)

Elmer Carroll coached the basketball team from 1939 through the 1942 season. He also served as Easton's football coach from 1935 to 1946 when he resigned to take the coaching position at Abington High School. He also served as a history teacher at Easton. Before coming to Easton, he coached at football, basketball and track at Greensburg High School, Greensburg, PA, and at Wilkinsburg High School, in Wilkinsburg, PA. He graduated from Washington and Jefferson College in 1920. He passed away in August 1982 at the age of 86 in Florida.[55, 56]

Vernard Fegley (1943-1952)

Vernard Fegley assumed the head coaching position with the resignation of Elmer Carroll, who would concentrate on football. Fegley graduated from Hazleton High School in 1930 and graduated from Grove City College where he also played basketball. After serving for seven years as an assistant at Hazleton, he accepted the coaching and teaching position at Easton. He left Easton after ten years for similar positions at Abington High School. He died in 1967.[57]

Charles Brown (1953-1954)

Charles Brown took over as head coach with the resignation of Vern Fegley. Brown graduated from Muhlenberg College and coached and taught at Hellertown High School for eleven years prior to taking the Easton position. After two years in the position, he left to take a teaching and coaching position at Pottstown High School. He passed away in June 1998.[58]

Ed Snyder (1955-1956)

Ed Snyder was named to succeed Charles Brown when he resigned to take a similar position at Pottstown High School. He graduated from Easton High School in 1944 and Lafayette College in 1950. At Easton, he played basketball for Coach Fegley in 1943 and 1944. He served in the Navy during the latter part of World War II. He had previously coached at Wilson Boro. In addition to basketball, he coached varsity basketball at Easton for 11 seasons and won three East Penn League and two District 11 titles. He also taught social sciences at the high school. He died unexpectedly at the age of 40 after suffering a heart attack while speaking at a sports dinner in Easton in January 1967.[59, 60]

Pete Carril (1957-1958)

Pete Carril served as the assistant coach to Ed Snyder for two years at Easton, When Snyder resigned, Carril was hired immediately to succeed Snyder as head coach. He graduated from Bethlehem High School in 1948 and helped lead the team to the District 11 title in 1948. He graduated from Lafayette College and was the top scorer on the 1952 team. His coaching career included four years at Easton High School, eight years at Reading High School, a year at Lehigh University, 29 years at Princeton, and ten years with the Sacramento Kings of the NBA.[61]

Tom Sweeney (1959-1969)

Tom Sweeney took over the Easton head basketball position from Pete Carril when Carril resigned to take the same position at Reading High School. Sweeney graduated from Hazleton High School in 1941. He graduated from Bucknell University with a Bachelor of Science degree in Education. After serving for four years in the US Air Force, Sweeney took a coaching and teaching position at Hazle Township High School. He played semi-profession basketball during the 1948-49 season for the Sunbury Mercuries of the Eastern League.[62]

Stan Sutphen (1970-1975)

Stan Sutphen served as Easton Area High School head basketball coach from 1969 through 1993 after having served as junior high, junior varsity, and varsity assistant at Easton for 10 years previously. Stan also was a varsity player at Easton from 1949 through 1952, serving as team co-captain in 1952. As Easton's head coach, Sutphen achieved an outstanding record of 378 wins against 267 losses in his 24 years. His teams won 20 or more games in seven different seasons. Easton won East Penn titles in 1973, 1975, 1976 and 1991 and District XI titles in 1973 and 1974. His teams had 18 winning seasons and qualified for District XI post season play 17 times. After teaching and coaching for 34 years, Stan retired at the end of the 1992-93 school year.[63]

Frank Duffy[64] **Clyde Notestine**[65] **Stan Carney**[66] **Elmer Carroll**[67] **Vernard Fegley**[68]

Charles Brown[69] **Ed Snyder**[70] **Pete Carril**[71] **Tom Sweeney**[62] **Stan Sutphen**[63]

Freedom

Charlie Dubbs (1969-1974)

During his 25 years as a high school coach (18 at Fountain Hill and 7 at Freedom), Charlie Dubbs' teams won 370 games against 228 losses. Dubbs returned to his alma mater as head basketball coach in 1948. His college career at East Stroudsburg State was interrupted while he served in the US Army during World War II in the European Theatre. He graduated from East Stroudsburg State in 1948 and was immediately appointed head coach at Fountain Hill. Under his reign, the Hillers won the District XI Class B championship seven times in the eleven years that they qualified. In the mid-fifties, Dubbs achieved honors that most coaches only dream about. In a three-year span, his teams were runners-up in the Class B State Finals in 1955 and captured the State Title in 1956 and 1957. In 1966, the great tradition of Fountain Hill basketball came to an end as the school was merged with the Bethlehem School District. Dubbs was appointed head coach of the new Freedom High School, which was under construction. During the year before Freedom was opened, Dubbs served on the Liberty coaching staff and was freshman basketball coach at Lafayette College under head coach George Davison. He finished his coaching career at Freedom in 1974, and was appointed Athletic Director. He passed away in August 2006.[72]

Rich Baksa (1975)

Rich Baksa graduated from Notre Dame High School in 1963 and Moravian College in 1967. In May 1970, Baksa was named head basketball coach at his alma mater. He served as an assistant for three years prior to being named head coach. In 1973, became an assistant basketball coach at Freedom and took over the head coaching position with the retirement of Charlie Dubbs. He spent 16 years at Freedom with 15 years as head coach. He resigned in February 1989. In June 1990, he accepted the head coaching position at Central Catholic. He stepped down as the Vikings head coach in 1995.[73, 74, 75, 76]

Charlie Dubbs[72]

Rich Baksa[76]

Hazleton

Hugh McGeehan (1928-1948)

Hugh McGeehan attended St. Gabriel's High School and Villanova College. As a freshman at Villanova, his team shocked Army in football. He had the opportunity to quit college and play professional baseball, at the urging of John McGraw, of the New York Giants, but decided to finish college. After graduation, he coached at Villanova Prep for a year and at Aquinas Institute in Rochester, NY. He came to Hazleton in September 1925 to teach and coach. He served as head basketball coach until his sudden passing in August 1948.[77]

Frank Serany (1949-1960)

Frank Serany served as an assistant to Hugh McGeehan for thirteen seasons and as a teacher in the high school. At the time of his appointment, Serany was head of the commercial department. He served as head coach until 1960. He graduated from Hazleton High School in 1929 and from Duquesne University where he also starred in basketball. He passed away in 1982.[78]

Danny Gregoria (1961-1963)

Danny Gregoria graduated from St. Gabriel's High School in 1929. He received all-state Catholic Class A first team honors in 1929. He graduated from East Stroudsburg Teacher's College with a Bachelor of Science degree in physical education. He enlisted in the US Navy in 1942 and served for 3 ½ years. Upon discharge, he began his teaching and coaching career at Hazleton High School and later at St. Gabriel's High School. He took the head basketball coach position at Hazleton in 1960 and served till January 1963 when he resigned. He retired from teaching in 1975. He passed away on July 26, 1977.[79]

Fran Libonati (1963-1968)

Fran Libonati took over as the interim coach with the resignation of Danny Gregoria on January 9, 1963, before being named permanently to the position. He graduated from Hazleton High School in 1957. He set the single season scoring average record and was named all-East Penn League First Team in 1957. He attended St. Francis College where he majored in history. Upon graduation, he taught history at Hazleton High School. He passed away in November 2020.[80]

Gene Evans (1969)

Gene Evans held the head coach position for one year prior to resigning at the end of the 1969 season to return to Carlisle High School. Prior to Hazleton, he had served as head basketball coach at Carlisle High School for 17 years from 1953 to 1962 and 1970 to 1976. He moved on to Bucknell University as head basketball coach for two years (1963-1964). He left Bucknell to take an assistant football coaching position at the University of Pennsylvania under head coach Bob Odell. He came to Hazleton from Penn. He graduated from Plymouth (PA) High School and Dickinson College. After ending his second stint as Carlisle HS coach, he took the Dickinson College head coaching position for 13 years. As a high school teacher, he taught mathematics. Evans passed away in January 2010.[81]

Dave Shafer (1970-1975)

Dave Shafer graduated from Hazleton High School in 1955. He attended both Dickinson and Lycoming College and graduated from Lycoming in 1961 with a degree in secondary education. Prior to Hazleton, he served as a teacher and coach at Solanco High School in Lancaster for two years and Mining and Mechanical Institute (MMI) in Freeland (PA) for four years. He retired from the Hazleton position in 1976.[82]

Hugh McGeehan[83]

Frank Serany[84]

Danny Gregoria[79]

Fran Libonati[80]

Gene Evans[85]

Dave Shafer[86]

Mahanoy City

John Goepfert (1933-1938)

John Goepfert coached for 35 years at Mahanoy City with a record of 807-139. In 1922, Mahanoy City won the state championship. After returning from World War I in 1919, he began his teaching and coaching career at his alma mater. For the first 17 years, he was not paid to coach. He retired in 1957 from his positions as head of the physical education department and athletic director. He was the first inductee into the Pennsylvania Basketball Coaches Association Hall of Fame. He died in February 1974.[87]

John Goepfert[87]

Phillipsburg

Al Senavitis (1964-1968)

Al Senavitis took over at Phillipsburg from Gene Quinn. He resigned as a special education teacher in the Bethlehem School District and took a similar position at Phillipsburg when he was hired as head basketball coach. Additional information is included with his bio as head coach at Liberty.[88]

Pete Tomaino (1969-1973)

Pete Tomaino graduated from Murray State University in Kentucky in 1964. He took an English teacher position with Phillipsburg upon graduation. He assumed the head basketball coach position in 1968 with the resignation of Al Senavitis. He also was a very successful tennis coach at Phillipsburg, Northampton Area Community College, and Lafayette College.[89]

Mike Koury (1974-1975)

After eight years at Central Catholic, Mike Koury resigned to take a similar position at Phillipsburg High School. Additional information is included in his bio from his tenure at Central Catholic.[90]

Al Senavitis[18]

Pete Tomaino[91]

Mike Koury[36]

Pottstown

Carroll Bechtel (1926-1931)

Carroll "Mush" Bechtel served as both athletic director and coach at Pottstown High School from 1918-1931. In 1919, he opened Bechtel's Sport Shop in Pottstown and owned and operated it until his death in late 1962.

Carroll Bechtel[92]

Pottsville

Randolph Grimmett (1926)

Minton Randolph "Grub" Grimmett was born and raised in Palmyra, Illinois, and played sports at Palmyra HS. He attended Eureka College prior to transferring to Muhlenberg College. At Muhlenberg, he played right guard with J. Birney Crum, who also had transferred as quarterback, and first base on the baseball team with Crum as the catcher. After graduating, Grimmett was appointed commercial arithmetic teacher and football and basketball coach at Pottsville. He left Pottsville in 1926 to take similar positions in Conshohocken, PA. In 1939, he took a coaching position at Upper Darby High School. He served as secretary/treasurer of the PIAA Philadelphia District Officials from 1935 to 1957. He moved to Florida in 1970 and passed away in July 1985.[93, 94, 95]

William Stevens (1927)

William Stevens graduated from Coatesville High School in 1922 and Gettysburg College 1926. He taught commercial arithmetic at Pottsville High School in addition to his coaching duties.[96,]

Charles Williams (1928-1929)

Charles Williams served as athletic director and served as football and baseball coach in addition to his two years as head basketball coach. Williams was raised in Pottsville and graduated from Pottsville High School in 1920. He played football, basketball, and baseball at Pottsville. After graduating from the

University of Pennsylvania, he taught English and history at Pottsville in addition to coaching. He left Pottsville to join the faculty at the Chestnut Hill Academy. In 1935, he joined the Philadelphia school district and served as a high school principal for 27 years. He passed away in May 1982.[97, 133]

Ross Hufford (1930-1931)

Ross Hufford graduated from Penn State where he excelled as a football player for coach Hugo Bezdek, He played in the 1923 Rose Bowl when Penn State lost to Southern California 14-3 in the first game played in the current Rose Bowl. After graduation, he coached football and basketball at Sunbury High School for six seasons, Northumberland High School for two season, Pottsville High School for two seasons, and Lewistown High School for ten seasons. He died in April 1971 at the age of 72.[98]

Howard Flack (1932)

Howard Flack graduated from Doylestown High School in 1904 and Syracuse University in 1914. He taught at several schools and coached at Miami University of Ohio, Louisiana Tech, Oregon, University of Maine before assuming teaching positions. He died in April 1941.[99]

George Dimmerling (1933-1938,1959)

George Dimmerling led Pottsville to the East Penn League championship in the league's inaugural season and was a three-sport athlete. He graduated from Lafayette College where he starred and captained both the basketball and baseball teams. He played on the football team as a punter and kick specialist. After graduation, he coached at Blythe Township for several years before moving to Pottsville in 1933. He coached basketball and baseball at Pottsville until 1939. He served as a teacher in the Pottsville School District for 41 years. He served in the Army's Medical Corps in World War II. He passed away in September 1981 at the age of 75.[100, 101]

Alfred Sadusky (1939-1942)

Alfred Sadusky graduated from Mahanoy City High School in 1929. He then played football and basketball for four years at Western Maryland College graduating from the college in 1933. He came to Pottsville as a teacher and coach in 1936 and took over as Pottsville basketball coach for the 1939 season and coached the team through the 1941 season when he entered the Army to serve in World War II. He finished his coaching career at Bethesda-Chevy Chase High School as both football and basketball coach from 1953-1973. He passed away in March 1999.[102, 109]

Chet Rogowicz (1943-1946)

Chet Rogowicz graduated from Newport Township High School, near Wilkes-Barre, in 1919. He graduated from Susquehanna University in 1924 where he played football, basketball, and baseball. Before taking over at his high school alma mater Newport Township, he coached for a year at Pottsville in 1924. He came back to Pottsville in 1942, He also served as athletic director at Pottsville. He died in 1982.[103, 109]

Eddie Deitch (1947-1955)

Eddie Deitch began his teaching and coaching career at Pottsville in September 1946. Prior to Pottsville, Deitch taught and coached basketball at Freeland High School for six years and Berwick High School for a year. He graduated from Freeland MMI and St. Thomas University in Scranton. He left Pottsville in 1953 to take a position at Nutley, NJ, High School as a coach and teacher. He passed away in June 1997.[104, 105]

Charles Miller (1956-1958)

Charles "Daw" Miller resigned in March 1955 as basketball coach at St. Clair High School to assume the same position at Pottsville High School. He starred in basketball at Frackville High School in 1931 and Kutztown State Teachers College in 1935. He began his teaching and assistant coaching career at Frackville in the fall of 1935. He moved to St. Clair High School in 1945 and taught and served as the head basketball coach until his resignation to take the Pottsville position. He served as head basketball coach until December 1959 when he unexpectedly passed away at the age of 45. His overall coaching record at St. Clair and Pottsville was 319-109. He led St. Clair to four North Schuylkill League championships. In addition to his Bachelor's Degree from Kutztown, he received a Master's Degree from Lehigh University. He passed away on December 19, 1958.[106]

John Slegeski (1960)

John Slegeski was selected to succeed Charles Miller who passed away in December 1958. George Dimmerling served as the interim coach upon the sudden passing of Miller, Slegeski graduated from Freeland High School in 1941 and Bloomsburg State Teacher's College in 1947. He coached at Freeland Mining and Mechanical Institute from 1948 through 1952 and then entered the insurance business. He died in March 1985.[107]

Francis "Larry" Haberle (1961-1963)

Larry Haberle graduated from Frackville High School in 1944. After spending two years at Temple University, he served in the US Army in World War II. After his discharge he briefly attended Seton Hall University and finished college at East Stroudsburg State Teachers College in 1951. He served as a civics and physical education teacher at West Mahony Township High School from 1951-1958 prior to his arrival at Pottsville as the junior varsity coach. He moved into the head basketball coach position at Pottsville in 1960. He also coached baseball at Pottsville. In 1964, Haberle was selected to serve as athletic director at Pottsville. He served in the US Army during World War II. He passed away in August 2010.[108, 109]

Ken Kline (1964-1975)

Ken Kline attained all-state mention at Allentown High School and then was a four-year starter at Millersville State College. He began his basketball coaching career at Coplay High School as a junior varsity coach. Kline was named head basketball coach at Jim Thorpe and in his seven years there won a Class C state title and two second place finishes. He took the Pottsville head coach position in 1964 and spent 15 years before moving on to Mt. Carmel for two seasons. From 1981-84, Kline coached the Blue Mountain High School basketball team. He finished his coaching career at Panther Valley High school from 1989 through 1991. In 31 seasons as a varsity basketball coach, he compiled a record of 437 wins and 323 losses. He passed away in August 2022.[109, 134]

Minton Grimmett[110]

William Stevens[96]

Charles Williams[97]

Ross Hufford[111]

Howard Flack[112]

George Dimmerling[113]

Albert Sadusky[114]

Chet Rogowicz[115]

Eddie Deitch[116]

John Slegeski[118]

Larry Haberle[119]

Kenneth Kline[120]

Charles Miller[117]

Tamaqua

Hugh Hoke (1933-1934, 1962-1968)

Hugh Hoke was a three-sport star a Gettysburg College. In 1930, he was hired as football coach at Tamaqua. He coached the basketball team in 1933 and 1934. He also played professional basketball for several years. After leaving the teaching profession, he became an account executive with Motorola Communications and Electronics retiring in 1975. He died in May 1984 at the age of 75.[121]

Eli Purnell (1935-1942)

Eli "Pinky" Purnell, a 1922 Tamaqua alumnus who played basketball and baseball, graduated from Albright College in 1931. He was a US Coast Guard veteran serving in World War II. He taught bookkeeping and biology from 1934 through 1968. He served as Tamaqua's basketball coach for 26 years with an overall record of 284-270. He passed away in May 1995.[122, 135]

Harold "Hal" Carney (1943)

Hal Carney came to Tamaqua in 1940 as an assistant football coach for head coach Charles Schaeffer. Carney had been a teammate of Schaeffer's at Albright College. He graduated from Albright in 1931 and in 1934 served as an assistant football coach at Albright. He was also an assistant football coach at Muhlenberg College in 1936. Carney took over as head basketball coach for Eli Purnell when Purnell entered the Navy. He was assisted by Charles Schaeffer. He received a commission to serve in the US Navy in December 1942 and resigned from the Tamaqua staff at the same time. Unfortunately, while serving in the Navy, he collapsed and died of a heart attack at the age of 33 at Naval pre-flight school in Chapel Hill, NC.[123]

Charles Schaeffer (1943)

Charles "Ding" Schaeffer assumed the head coach position when Hal Carney entered the Navy. Carney had taken over for Eli Purnell when Purnell entered the Navy. He also served as head football coach at

Tamaqua from 1938 through 1943 when he resigned to join his Albright teammate as an assistant football coach at McKeesport High School. He passed away in June 1993.[124]

John Gildea (1944)

John Gildea served as an assistant football coach, physical education teacher, and head basketball coach at Tamaqua. He graduated from Coaldale High School and St. Bonaventure. At St. Bonaventure, Gildea was recognized nationally as a punter and played in the backfield. He played professional football and was a punter for the 1938 New York Giants world championship team. He only coached a year and returned to active duty in the Army in World War II. He passed away in November 1979.[125, 126]

Nicholas James "Nick" Young (1969-1971)

Nick Young graduated from Tamaqua High School in 1942. He served in World War II after having attended Kutztown State Teachers College for a year. While serving at the Battle of the Bulge, Young was captured and held as a prisoner by the German Army. After he was discharged, he attended East Stroudsburg State Teachers College and graduated in 1949. He joined the Tamaqua coaching staff as the junior high school basketball coach in 1950. After serving for 18 years as an assistant, he took over at head coach with the retirement of Eli Purnell. He also served as a guidance counselor at the high school. He and his wife both died in September 2012.[127, 128]

Hugh Hoke[129]

Eli Purnell[130]

Charles Schaeffer[131]

John Gildea[125]

Nick Young[132]

Footnotes

1921-24

1. The Morning Call (Allentown, PA), March 22, 1920, Page 5
2. The Morning Call (Allentown, PA), March 23, 1921, Page 11
3. The Morning Call (Allentown, PA), March 29, 1921, Page 11
4. The Morning Call (Allentown, PA), April 4, 1921, Page 11
5. The Morning Call (Allentown, PA), January 8, 1922, Page 13
6. The Morning Call (Allentown, PA), February 4, 1922, Page 17
7. The Morning Call (Allentown, PA), February 11, 1922, Page 13
8. The Morning Call (Allentown, PA), February 12, 1922, Page 11
9. The Morning Call (Allentown, PA), March 11, 1922, Page 16
10. The Morning Call (Allentown, PA), March 17, 1922, Page 22
11. The Morning Call (Allentown, PA), March 18, 1922, Page 16
12. The Morning Call (Allentown, PA), April 1, 1922, Page 17
13. The Morning Call (Allentown, PA), December 1, 1944, Page 36
14. The Morning Call (Allentown, PA), January 21, 1969, Page 19
15. The Morning Call (Allentown, PA), March 22, 1923, Page 16
16. The Morning Call (Allentown, PA), March 18, 1923, Page 11
17. The Morning Call (Allentown, PA), January 21, 1969, Page 19
18. The Morning Call (Allentown, PA), March 23, 1924, Page 11
19. The Morning Call (Allentown, PA), March 23, 1924, Page 13

1925

1. The Morning Call (Allentown, PA), March 20, 1925, Page 28.
2. The Morning Call (Allentown, PA), March 23, 1925, Page 14.
3. The Tribune (Scranton, PA), March 25, 1925, Page 18.
4. The Morning Call (Allentown, PA), January 12, 1925, Page 13.
5. The Morning Call (Allentown, PA), January 14, 1925, Page 17.
6. The Philadelphia Inquirer (Philadelphia, PA), September 27, 1925, Page 28.
7. The Morning Call (Allentown, PA), February 15, 1952, Page 5.
8. The Morning Call (Allentown, PA), August 4, 1960, Page 25.
9. The Morning Call (Allentown, PA), June 25, 1965, Page 42.
10. The Morning Call (Allentown, PA), November 7, 1945, Page 4.

1926

1. The Morning Call (Allentown, PA), April 15, 1925, Page 18.
2. The Morning Call (Allentown, PA), December 21, 1925, Page 15.
3. Lancaster New Era (Lancaster, PA), January 2, 1926, Page 8.
4. Pottsville Republican (Pottsville, PA), January 9, 1926, Page 11.
5. Lancaster New Era (Lancaster, PA). January 9, 1926, Page 9.
6. Lancaster New Era (Lancaster, PA), January 16, 1926, Page 15.
7. The Morning Call (Allentown, PA), January 16, page 19.
8. The Morning Call (Allentown, PA), January 23, page 15.
9. The Morning Call (Allentown, PA), January 28, page 15.

10. Pottsville Republican (Pottsville, PA), January 29, 1926, Page 11.
11. The Morning Call (Allentown, PA), January 30, 1926, Page 15.
12. The Morning Call (Allentown, PA), February 6, 1926, Page 15.
13. The Morning Call (Allentown, PA), February 13, page 15.
14. The Morning Call (Allentown, PA), February 13, 1926, Page 16.
15. Lancaster New Era (Lancaster, PA), February 13, 1926, Page 9.
16. The Lancaster New Era (Lancaster, PA), February 20, 1926, Page 8.
17. The Morning Call (Allentown, PA), February 20, 1926, Page 17.
18. Pottsville Republican (Pottsville, PA), February 27, 1926, Page 9.
19. The Morning Call (Allentown, PA), February 27, page 16.
20. Pottsville Republican (Pottsville, PA), March 6, 1926, Page 7.
21. The Morning Call (Allentown, PA), March 6, Page 17.
22. The Morning Call (Allentown, PA), March 6, Page 15.
23. The Morning Call (Allentown, PA), March 13, Page 18.
24. The Morning Call (Allentown, PA), March 19, 1926, Page 34.
25. The Morning Call (Allentown, PA), March 24, 1926, Page 19.
26. Reading Times (Reading, PA), April 3, 1926, Page 11.
27. The Daily News (Mt. Carmel, PA), April 2, 1926, Page 6.
28. Pottsville Republican (Pottsville, PA), February 6, 1926, Page 7.

1927

1. Lancaster New Era (Lancaster, PA), December 2, 1926, Page 18.
2. Evening Republican (Pottsville, PA), June 8, 1927, Page 11.
3. Lancaster New Era (Lancaster, PA), May 22, 1926, Page 9.
4. Lancaster New Era (Lancaster, PA), December 18, 1926, Page 9.
5. The Morning Call (Allentown, PA), December 18, 1926, Page 17.
6. Lancaster New Era (Lancaster, PA), January 8, 1927, Page 9.
7. The Morning Call (Allentown, PA), January 8, 1927, Page 17.
8. The Morning Call (Allentown, PA), January 15, 1927, Page 17.
9. Lancaster New Era (Lancaster, PA), January 15, 1927, Page 8.
10. The Morning Call (Allentown, PA), January 22, 1927, Page 16.
11. The Morning Call (Allentown, PA), January 22, 1927, Page 15.
12. The Morning Call (Allentown, PA), January 29, 1927, Page 17
13. The Morning Call (Allentown, PA), February 6, 1927, Page 9.
14. The Morning Call (Allentown, PA), February 5, 1927, Page 15.
15. The Morning Call (Allentown, PA), February 5, 1927, Page 16.
16. The Morning Call (Allentown, PA), February 12, 1927, Page 17.
17. The Morning Call (Allentown, PA), February 12, 1927, Page 16.
18. The Morning Call (Allentown, PA), February 19, 1927, Page 17
19. Lancaster New Era (Lancaster, PA), February 19, 1927, Page 15.
20. The Morning Call (Allentown, PA), February 26, 1927, Page 17.
21. The Morning Call (Allentown, PA), February 26, 1927, Page 18.
22. The Morning Call (Allentown, PA), March 5, 1927, Page 16.
23. The Morning Call (Allentown, PA), March 5, 1927, Page 18.
24. The Lancaster New Era (Lancaster, PA), March 5, 1927, Page 9.

25. The Morning Call (Allentown, PA), March 12, 1927, Page 17.
26. Lancaster New Era (Lancaster, PA), March 12, 1927, Page 11.
27. The Morning Call (Allentown, PA), January 1, 1927, Page 16.
28. The Morning Call (Allentown, PA), March 2, 1927, Page 21.
29. The Morning Call (Allentown, PA), March 20, 1927, Page 12.
30. The Morning Call (Allentown, PA), March 30, 1927, Page 19.
31. Pottstown High School – Troiad Yearbook – Class of 1927, Page 56.

1928

1. The Morning Call (Allentown, PA), April 2, 1927, Page 17.
2. The Morning Call (Allentown, PA), May 7. 1927, Page 17.
3. The Morning Call (Allentown, PA), December 17, 1927, Page 18.
4. The Standard-Sentinel (Hazleton, PA), December 17, 1927, Page 24.
5. The Morning Call (Allentown, PA), December 24, 1927, Page 33.
6. The Plain Speaker (Hazleton, PA), December 24, 1927, Page 18.
7. Lancaster New Era (Lancaster, PA), December 24, 1927, Page 21.
8. The Morning Call (Allentown, PA), January 7, 1928, Page 18.
9. Pottsville Republican (Pottsville, PA), January 7, 1928, Page 9.
10. The Morning Call (Allentown, PA), January 14, 1928, Page 19.
11. Lancaster New Era (Lancaster, PA), January 14, 1928, Page 15.
12. Pottsville Republican (Pottsville, PA), January 14, 1928, Page 11.
13. The Morning Call (Allentown, PA), January 14, 1928, Page 20.
14. The Morning Call (Allentown, PA), January 21, 1928, Page 18.
15. Pottsville Republican (Pottsville, PA), January 21, 1928, Page 9.
16. The Morning Call (Allentown, PA), January 21, 1928, Page 17.
17. Intelligencer Journal (Lancaster, PA), January 21, 1928, Page 14.
18. The Morning Call (Allentown, PA), January 25, 1928, Page 19.
19. The Morning Call (Allentown, PA), January 28, Page 18.
20. The Plain Speaker (Hazleton, PA), January 28, 1928, Page 8.
21. Lancaster New Era (Lancaster, PA), January 28, 1928, Page 12.
22. The Morning Call (Allentown, PA), February 4, 1928, Page 20.
23. The Plain Speaker (Hazleton, PA), February 4, 1928, Page 8.
24. The Morning Call (Allentown, PA), February 4, 1928, Page 13.
25. The Morning Call (Allentown, PA), February 6, Page 16.
26. Pottsville Republican (Pottsville, PA), February 9, 1928, Page 9.
27. The Plain Speaker (Hazleton, PA), February 11, 1928, Page 10.
28. The Morning Call (Allentown, PA), February 11, 1928, Page 20.
29. The Morning Call (Allentown, PA), February 12, 1928, Page 11.
30. The Morning Call (Allentown, PA), February 15, 1928, Page 23.
31. The Morning Call (Allentown, PA), February 18, 1928, Page 18.
32. The Pottsville Republican (Pottsville, PA), February 18, 1928, Page 9.
33. Lancaster New Era (Lancaster, PA) February 18, 1928, Page 14.
34. The Morning Call (Allentown, PA), February 25, 1928, Page 18.
35. Intelligencer Journal (Lancaster, PA), February 25, 1928, Page 15.
36. The Morning Call (Allentown, PA), February 25, 1928, Page 16.

37. The Pottsville Republican (Pottsville, PA), February 25, 1928, Page 11.
38. The Morning Call (Allentown, PA), March 3, 1928, Page 23.
39. The Pottsville Republican (Pottsville, PA), March 3, 1928, Page 9.
40. Standard Sentinel (Hazleton, PA), March 3, 1928, Page 18.
41. The Morning Call (Allentown, PA), March 4, 1928, Page 13.
42. The Morning Call (Allentown, PA), March 10, 1928, Page 21.
43. Intelligencer Journal (Lancaster, PA), March 10, 1928, Page 15.
44. The Morning Call (Allentown, PA), March 11, 1928, Page 13.
45. The Morning Call (Allentown, PA), March 11, 1928, Page 14.
46. Pottsville Republican (Pottsville, PA), March 12, 1928, Page 8.
47. Lancaster New Era (Lancaster, PA), March 12, 1928, Page 15.
48. The Plain Speaker (Hazleton, PA), March 12, 1928, Page 16.
49. The Plain Speaker (Hazleton, PA), March 13, 1928, Page 12.
50. The Morning Call (Allentown, PA), March 16, 1928, Page 31.
51. The Morning Call (Allentown, PA), March 18, 1928, Page 11.
52. Wilkes-Barre Times Leader, The Evening News (Wilkes-Barre, PA), March 21, 1928, Page 21.
53. The Plain Speaker (Hazleton, PA), March 24, 1928, Page 24.
54. The Morning Call (Allentown, PA), April 3, 1928, Page 19.
55. The Morning Call (Allentown, PA), March 13, 1928, Page 18.

1929

1. The Plain Speaker (Hazleton, PA), December 15, 1928, Page 10.
2. The Morning Call (Allentown, PA), December 15, 1928, Page 18.
3. The Plain Speaker (Hazleton, PA), December 22, 1928, Page 10.
4. The Morning Call (Allentown, PA), December 22, 1928, Page 17.
5. The Morning Call (Allentown, PA), December 23, 1928, Page 12.
6. The Morning Call (Allentown, PA), January 5, 1929, Page 17.
7. The Morning Call (Allentown, PA), January 5, 1929, Page 18.
8. The Morning Call (Allentown, PA), January 9, 1929, Page 19.
9. The Morning Call (Allentown, PA), January 12, 1929, Page 19.
10. The Standard-Sentinel (Hazleton, PA), January 12, 1929, Page 20.
11. The Morning Call (Allentown, PA), January 16, 1929, Page 20.
12. The Morning Call (Allentown, PA), January 18, 1929, Page 31.
13. The Morning Call (Allentown, PA), January 19, 1929, Page 17.
14. The Morning Call (Allentown, PA), January 19, 1929, Page 16.
15. The Standard-Sentinel (Hazleton, PA), January 19, 1929, Page 20.
16. The Morning Call (Allentown, PA), January 21, 1929, Page 18.
17. The Standard-Sentinel (Hazleton, PA), January 28, 1929, Pages 8 and 9.
18. The Morning Call (Allentown, PA), January 27, 1929, Page 15.
19. The Morning Call (Allentown, PA), January 27, 1929, Page 19.
20. Lancaster New Era (Lancaster, PA), January 29, 1929, Page 13.
21. The Morning Call (Allentown, PA), February 4, 1929, Page 18.
22. The Morning Call (Allentown, PA), February 2, 1929, Page 17.
23. The Morning Call (Allentown, PA), February 9, 1929, Page 18.
24. Pottsville Republican (Pottsville, PA), February 9, 1929, Page 9.

25. The Morning Call (Allentown, PA), February 10, 1929, Page 14.
26. The Morning Call (Allentown, PA), February 16, 1929, Page 20.
27. The Morning Call (Allentown, PA), February 16, 1929, Page 18.
28. The Morning Call (Allentown, PA), February 20, 1929, Page 20.
29. The Morning Call (Allentown, PA), February 23, 1929, Page 19.
30. The Morning Call (Allentown, PA), February 24, 1929, Page 11.
31. The Morning Call (Allentown, PA), March 1, 1929, Page 31.
32. The Morning Call (Allentown, PA), March 2, 1929, Page 17.
33. Pottsville Evening Republican (Pottsville, PA), March 9, 1929, Pages 9 and 10.
34. Pottsville Republican (Pottsville, PA), March 13, 1929, Page 9.
35. The Morning Call (Allentown, PA), March 16, 1929, Page 22.
36. The Morning Call) Allentown, PA), March 12, 1929, Page 26.
37. The Morning Call (Allentown, PA), March 14, 1929, Page 24.
38. The Morning Call (Allentown, PA), March 14, 1929, Page 25.
39. The Morning Call (Allentown, PA), March 17, 1929, Page 11.
40. The Morning Call (Allentown, PA), March 20, 1929, Page 21.
41. The Morning Call (Allentown, PA), March 23, 1929, Page 21.
42. The Morning Call (Allentown, PA), March 24, 1929, Page 13.
43. Hazleton High School-Janus Yearbook-Class of 1929. Page 148.

1930

1. Pittstown Gazette (Pittstown, PA), April 13, 1929, Page 7.
2. The Morning Call (Allentown, PA), December 14, 1929, Page 20.
3. The Morning Call (Allentown, PA), December 14, 1929, Page 18.
4. The Morning Call (Allentown, PA), December 21, 1929, Page 18.
5. The Morning Call (Allentown, PA), January 4, 1930, Page 14.
6. The Morning Call (Allentown, PA), January 4, 1930, Page 20.
7. The Morning Call (Allentown, PA), January11, 1930, Page 16.
8. The Morning Call (Allentown, PA), January 11, 1930, Page 18.
9. Pottsville Evening Republican (Pottsville, PA), January 11, 1930, Page 9.
10. The Morning Call (Allentown, PA), January 18, 1930, Page 18.
11. The Morning Call (Allentown, PA), January 19, 1930, Page 17.
12. The Morning Call (Allentown, PA), January 25, 1930, Page 15.
13. The Morning Call (Allentown, PA), January 25, 1930, Page 16.
14. Philadelphia Inquirer (Philadelphia, PA), January 25, 1930, Page 16.
15. The Morning Call (Allentown, PA), February 1, 1930, Page 17.
16. The Morning Call (Allentown, PA), February 1, 1930, Page 18.
17. The Morning Call (Allentown, PA), February 8, 1930, Page 18.
18. The Morning Call (Allentown, PA), February 8, 1930, Page 19.
19. The Standard Sentinel (Hazleton, PA), February 8, 1930, Page 16.
20. The Morning Call (Allentown, PA), February 15, 1930, Page 16
21. The Morning Call (Allentown, PA), February 15, 1930, Page 18.
22. Pottsville Evening Republican (Pottsville, PA), February 15, 1930, Page 9.
23. The Morning Call (Allentown, PA), February 22, 1930, Page 16.
24. The Morning Call (Allentown, PA), February 23, 1930, Page 9.

25. The Morning Call (Allentown, PA), February 24, 1930, Page 21.
26. The Morning Call (Allentown, PA), March 1, 1930, Page 19.
27. The Morning Call (Allentown, PA), March 1, 1930, Page 20.
28. The Morning Call (Allentown, PA), March 8, 1930, Page 19.
29. The Morning Call (Allentown, PA), March 8, 1930, Page 20.
30. The Morning Call (Allentown, PA), March 12, 1930, Pages 1 and 21.
31. The Morning Call (Allentown, PA), March 14, 1930, Page 1 and 28.
32. The Morning Call (Allentown, PA), March 16, 1930, Pages 1 and 9.
33. The Morning Call (Allentown, PA), March 4, 1930, Page 23.

1931

1. Standard-Sentinel (Hazleton, PA), November 11, 1930, Page 10.
2. The Morning Call (Allentown, PA), December 15, 1930, Page 14.
3. The Morning Call (Allentown, PA), December 13, 1930, Page 20.
4. The Morning Call (Allentown, PA), December 13, 1930, Page 15.
5. The Morning Call (Allentown, PA), December 20, 1930, Page 21.
6. The Morning Call (Allentown, PA), December 20, 1930, Page 22.
7. The Morning Call (Allentown, PA), December 19, 1930, Page 28.
8. The Morning Call (Allentown, PA), January 10, 1931, Page 15.
9. The Morning Call (Allentown, PA), January 10, 1931, Page 14.
10. The Morning Call (Allentown, PA), January 17, 1931, Page 14.
11. The Morning Call (Allentown, PA), January 21, 1931, Page 14.
12. The Morning Call (Allentown, PA), January 24, 1931, Page 15.
13. The Morning Call (Allentown, PA), January 24, 1931, Page 16.
14. The Morning Call (Allentown, PA), January 31, 1931, Page 14.
15. The Morning Call (Allentown, PA), February 7, 1931, Page 15.
16. The Morning Call (Allentown, PA), February 14, 1931, Page 16.
17. The Morning Call (Allentown, PA), February 21, 1931, Page 18.
18. The Morning Call (Allentown, PA), February 21, 1931, Page 17.
19. The Morning Call (Allentown, PA), February 25, 1931, Page 20.
20. The Morning Call (Allentown, PA), February 28, 1931, Page 19.
21. The Morning Call (Allentown, PA), February 28, 1931, Page 18.
22. The Morning Call (Allentown, PA), March 4, 1931, Page 21.
23. The Plain Speaker (Hazleton, PA), March 7, 1931, Page 9.
24. The Morning Call (Allentown, PA), March 7, 1931, Page 20.
25. The Morning Call (Allentown, PA), March 7, 1931, Page 22.
26. The Morning Call (Allentown, PA), March 8, 1931, Page 11.
27. The Morning Call (Allentown, PA), March 13, 1931, Page 30.
28. The Morning Call (Allentown, PA), March 14, 1931, Page 20.
29. The Morning Call (Allentown, PA), March 15, 1931, Page 9.
30. The Morning Call (Allentown, PA), March 18, 1931, Page 26.
31. The Morning Call (Allentown, PA), March 18, 1931, Page 27.
32. Standard-Speaker (Hazleton, PA), March 19, 1931, Page 16.
33. Allentown High School-Comus Yearbook-Class of 1931, Page 165.

1932

1. The Morning Call (Allentown, PA), May 11, 1931, Page 17.
2. The Morning Call (Allentown, PA), December 19, 1931, Page 18.
3. The Morning Call (Allentown, PA), December 19, 1931, Page 19.
4. The Morning Call (Allentown, PA), January 9, 1932, Page 18.
5. The Morning Call (Allentown, PA), January 9, 1932, Page 20.
6. The Plain Speaker (Hazleton, PA), January 16, 1932, Page 8.
7. The Morning Call (Allentown, PA), January 16, 1932, Page 18.
8. The Morning Call (Allentown, PA), January 23, 1932, Page 19.
9. The Morning Call (Allentown, PA), January 30, 1932, Page 18.
10. The Morning Call (Allentown, PA), February 6, 1932, Page 20.
11. The Morning Call (Allentown, PA), February 13, 1932, Page 18.
12. The Morning Call (Allentown, PA), February 20, 1932, Page 20.
13. The Morning Call (Allentown, PA), February 17, 1932, Page 17.
14. The Morning Call (Allentown, PA), February 20, 1932, Page 16.
15. The Morning Call (Allentown, PA), February 20, 1932, Page 20.
16. The Morning Call (Allentown, PA), February 25, 1932, Page 20.
17. The Morning Call (Allentown, PA), March 5, 1932, Page 18.
18. The Morning Call (Allentown, PA), March 5, 1932, Page 17.
19. Wilkes-Barre Times Leader, The Evening News (Wilkes-Barre, PA), March 10, 1932, Page 17.
20. The Morning Call (Allentown, PA), March 13, 1932, Page 20.
21. The Morning Call (Allentown, PA), March 10, 1932, Page 18.
22. The Standard Sentinel (Hazleton, PA), March 7, 1932, Page 8.
23. The Standard Sentinel (Hazleton, PA), March 14, 1932, Page 8.
24. The Plain Speaker (Hazleton, PA), March 19, 1932, Page 8.
25. Evening Republican (Pottsville, PA), April 14, 1932, Page 15.
26. The Plain Speaker (Hazleton, PA), February 5, 1932, Page 20.

1933

1. The Morning Call (Allentown, PA), April 2, 1932, Page 18.
2. The Morning Call (Allentown, PA), May 30, 1932, Page 15.
3. Chicago Tribune (Chicago, IL), April 10, 1932, Page 30.
4. The Standard Sentinel (Hazleton, PA), December 13, 1932, Page 16.
5. The Morning Call (Allentown, PA), December 17, 1932, Page 16.
6. The Morning Call (Allentown, PA), December 17, 1932, Page 17.
7. The Morning Call (Allentown, PA), December 24, 1932, Page 24.
8. The Morning Call (Allentown, PA), December 28, 1932, Page 14.
9. The Morning Call (Allentown, PA), January 7, 1933, Page 12.
10. The Morning Call (Allentown, PA), January 14, 1933, Page 14.
11. The Morning Call (Allentown, PA), January 21, 1933, Page 10.
12. The Plain Speaker (Hazleton, PA), January 21, 1933, Page 8.
13. The Morning Call (Allentown, PA), January 25, 1933, Page 10.
14. The Plain Speaker (Hazleton, PA), January 25, 1933, Page 10.
15. The Morning Call (Allentown, PA), January 25, 1933, Page 11.
16. The Morning Call (Allentown, PA), January 28, 1933, Page 11.

17. The Plain Speaker (Hazleton, PA), January 30, 1933, Page 10.
18. The Morning Call (Allentown, PA), February 4, 1933, Page 14.
19. The Morning Call (Allentown, PA), February 4, 1933, Page 13.
20. The Morning Call (Allentown, PA), February 11, 1933, Page 14.
21. The Morning Call (Allentown, PA), February 15, 1933, Page 14.
22. The Morning Call (Allentown, PA), February 18, 1933, Page 13.
23. The Morning Call (Allentown, PA), February 18, 1933, Page 14.
24. The Morning Call (Allentown, PA), February 25, 1933, Page 11.
25. The Morning Call (Allentown, PA), March 4, 1933, Page 12.
26. Standard Sentinel (Hazleton, PA), March 4, 1933, Page 16.
27. Pottsville Evening Republican (Pottsville, PA), March 4, 1933, Page 12.
28. The Morning Call (Allentown, PA), March 8, 1933, Page 13.
29. The Morning Call (Allentown, PA), March 11, 1933, Page 10.
30. The Morning Call (Allentown, PA), March 15, 1933, Page 11.
31. The Morning Call (Allentown, PA), March 6, 1933, Page 9.
32. The Morning Call (Allentown, PA), April 10, 1933, Page 9.
33. The Plain Speaker (Hazleton, PA), December 8, 1933, Page 24.
34. Allentown High School – Comus Yearbook – Class of 1933, Page 172

1934

1. The Morning Call (Allentown, PA), April 10, 1933, Page 9.
2. The Morning Call (Allentown, PA), May 7, 1933, Page 11.
3. The Morning Call (Allentown, PA), October 21, 1933, Page 20.
4. The Morning Call (Allentown, PA), December 5, 1933, Page 20.
5. The Morning Call (Allentown, PA), April 20, 1933, Page 15.
6. The Morning Call (Allentown, PA), December 16, 1933, Page 15.
7. The Morning Call (Allentown, PA), December 23, 1933, Page 14.
8. The Morning Call (Allentown, PA), December 23, 1933, Page 18.
9. The Morning Call (Allentown, PA), December 30, 1933, Page 16.
10. The Morning Call (Allentown, PA), January 6, 1934, Page 15.
11. The Morning Call (Allentown, PA), January 13, 1934, Page 15.
12. The Morning Call (Allentown, PA), January 13, 1934, Page 16.
13. Standard-Speaker (Hazleton, PA), January 20, Page 18.
14. The Morning Call (Allentown, PA), January 24, 1934, Page 16.
15. The Morning Call (Allentown, PA), January 27, 1934, Page 15.
16. The Morning Call (Allentown, PA), January 27, 1934, Page 16.
17. Standard-Speaker (Hazleton, PA), January 27, 1934, Page 20.
18. The Morning Call (Allentown, PA), January 31, 1934, Page 17.
19. The Morning Call (Allentown, PA), February 3, 1934, Page 15.
20. The Morning Call (Allentown, PA), February 3, 1934, Page 16.
21. The Morning Call (Allentown, PA), February 7, 1934, Page 25.
22. The Morning Call (Allentown, PA), February 8, 1934, Page 20.
23. The Morning Call (Allentown, PA), February 10, 1934, Page 16.
24. The Morning Call (Allentown, PA), February 14, 1934, Page 17.
25. The Morning Call (Allentown, PA), February 14, 1934, Page 18.

26. The Morning Call (Allentown, PA), February 17, 1934, Page 17.
27. The Morning Call (Allentown, PA), February 24, 1934, Page 16.
28. The Morning Call (Allentown, PA), February 26, 1934, Page 13.
29. The Morning Call (Allentown, PA), March 3, 1934, Page 15.
30. Standard-Sentinel (Hazleton, PA), March 3, 1934, Page 20.
31. The Morning Call (Allentown, PA), March 10, 1934, Page 17.
32. The Morning Call (Allentown, PA), March 14, 1934, Page 19.
33. The Morning Call (Allentown, PA), April 7, 1934, Page 8.
34. Liberty High School – Cauldron Yearbook – Class of 1934, Page 176

1935

1. The Morning Call (Allentown, PA), April 15, 1934, Page 14.
2. The Morning Call (Allentown, PA), May 5, 1934, Page 18.
3. The Morning Call (Allentown, PA), December 15, 1934, Page 18.
4. The Morning Call (Allentown, PA), December 22, 1934, Page 18.
5. The Morning Call (Allentown, PA), December 22, 1934, Page 19.
6. The Plain Speaker (Hazleton, PA), December 29, 1934, Pages 10 and 11.
7. The Morning Call (Allentown, PA), December 20, 1934, Page 20.
8. The Morning Call (Allentown, PA), January 5, 1935, Page 19.
9. The Morning Call (Allentown, PA), January 5, 1935, Page 18.
10. The Morning Call (Allentown, PA), January 12, 1935, Page 17.
11. The Plain Speaker (Hazleton, PA), January 19, 1935, Pages 10 and 11.
12. The Morning Call (Allentown, PA), January 19, 1935, Page 18.
13. The Morning Call (Allentown, PA), January 23, 1935, Page 20.
14. The Morning Call (Allentown, PA), January 23, 1935, Page 17.
15. The Morning Call (Allentown, PA), January 26, 1935, Page 15.
16. The Morning Call (Allentown, PA), January 26, 1935, Page 10.
17. The Morning Call (Allentown, PA), February 1, 1935, Page 21.
18. The Morning Call (Allentown, PA), February 2, 1935, Page 16.
19. Standard-Speaker (Hazleton, PA), February 6, 1935, Page 10.
20. The Morning Call (Allentown, PA), February 9, 1935, Page 18.
21. The Morning Call (Allentown, PA), February 13, 1935, Page 17.
22. The Morning Call (Allentown, PA), February 13, 1935, Page 18.
23. The Morning Call (Allentown, PA), February 16, 1935, Page 19.
24. The Morning Call (Allentown, PA), February 16, 1935, Page 20.
25. The Morning Call (Allentown, PA), February 23, 1935, Page 16.
26. The Morning Call (Allentown, PA), March 2, 1935, Page 16.
27. The Morning Call (Allentown, PA), March 3, 1935, Page 10.
28. The Morning Call (Allentown, PA), March 6, 1935, Page 20.
29. The Morning Call (Allentown, PA), March 9, 1935, Page 16.
30. The Morning Call (Allentown, PA), March 14, 1935, Page 21.
31. The Morning Call (Allentown, PA), March 17, 1935, Page 10.
32. The Morning Call (Allentown, PA), March 20, 1935, Page 20.
33. The Morning Call (Allentown, PA), March 24, 1935, Pages 1 and 10.
34. The Standard-Sentinel (Hazleton, PA), March 13, 1935, Page 33.

35. The Morning Call (Allentown, PA), April 8, 1935, Page 19.
36. The Morning Call (Allentown, PA), May 9, 1935, Page 2.
37. The Morning Call (Allentown, PA), March 20, 1935. Page 19.

1936

1. The Morning Call (Allentown, PA), November 12, 1935, Page 37.
2. The Evening Herald (Pottsville, PA), November 16, 1935, Page 8.
3. The Morning Call (Allentown, PA), December 14, 1935, Page 16.
4. The Morning Call (Allentown, PA), December 14, 1935, Page 11.
5. The Morning Call (Allentown, PA), December 21, 1935, Page 16.
6. The Morning Call (Allentown, PA), December 20, 1935, Page 38.
7. The Morning Call (Allentown, PA), December 28, 1935, Page 15.
8. The Morning Call (Allentown, PA), January 4, 1936, Page 15.
9. The Evening Republican, (Pottsville, PA, January 4, 1936, Pages 11 and 12.
10. The Morning Call (Allentown, PA), January 11, 1936, Page 15.
11. The Morning Call (Allentown, PA), January 18, 1936, Page 16.
12. The Morning Call (Allentown, PA), January 18, 1936, Page 17.
13. The Morning Call (Allentown, PA), January 22, 1936, Page 17.
14. Standard-Sentinel (Hazleton, PA), January 22, 1936, Page 13.
15. Standard-Sentinel (Hazleton, PA), January 25, 1936, Page 16.
16. The Morning Call (Allentown, PA), January 25, 1936, Page 17.
17. The Morning Call (Allentown, PA), February 1, 1936, Page 11.
18. The Morning Call (Allentown, PA), February 8, 1936, Page 17.
19. The Morning Call (Allentown, PA), February 12, 1936, Page 18.
20. The Morning Call (Allentown, PA), February 15, 1936, Page 15.
21. The Morning Call (Allentown, PA), February 19, 1936, Page 15.
22. The Morning Call (Allentown, PA), February 22, 1936, Page 15.
23. The Morning Call (Allentown, PA), February 29, 1936, Page 13.
24. The Morning Call (Allentown, PA), March 7, 1936, Page 1.
25. The Morning Call (Allentown, PA), March 8, 1936, Page 11.
26. The Morning Call (Allentown, PA), March 11, 1936, Page 21.
27. The Morning Call (Allentown, PA), March 14, 1936, Page 16.
28. The Morning Call (Allentown, PA), March 2, 1936, Page 15.
29. The Plain Speaker (Hazleton, PA), April 18, Page 12.
30. Tamaqua High School – Sphinx Yearbook – Class of 1936, Page 79

1937

1. The Morning Call (Allentown, PA), April 19, 1936, Page 17.
2. The Morning Call (Allentown, PA), December 10, 1936, Page 27.
3. The Morning Call (Allentown, PA), December 12, 1936, Page 16.
4. The Morning Call (Allentown, PA), December 19, 1936, Page 17.
5. The Morning Call (Allentown, PA), December 23, 1936, Page 23.
6. The Morning Call (Allentown, PA), December 23, 1936, Page 25.
7. The Morning Call (Allentown, PA), January 9, 1937, Page 17.
8. The Morning Call (Allentown, PA), January 16, 1937, Page 15.
9. The Morning Call (Allentown, PA), January 20, 1937, Page 17.

10. The Morning Call (Allentown, PA), January 23, 1937, Page 13.
11. The Morning Call (Allentown, PA), January 30, 1937, Page 17.
12. The Morning Call (Allentown, PA), February 6, 1937, Page 15.
13. The Morning Call (Allentown, PA), February 13, 1937, Page 15.
14. The Morning Call (Allentown, PA), February 20, 1937, Page 16.
15. The Morning Call (Allentown, PA), February 23, 1937, Page 22.
16. The Morning Call (Allentown, PA), February 23, 1937, Page 21.
17. The Morning Call (Allentown, PA), February 24, 1937, Page 16.
18. The Morning Call (Allentown, PA), February 27, 1937, Page 21.
19. The Morning Call (Allentown, PA), February 27, 1937, Page 20.
20. The Morning Call (Allentown, PA), March 3, 1937, Page 23.
21. Pottsville Evening Republican (Pottsville, PA), March 5, 1937, Page 25.
22. The Morning Call (Allentown, PA), March 5, 1937, Page 40.
23. The Morning Call (Allentown, PA), March 6, 1937, Page 15.
24. The Morning Call (Allentown, PA), March 10, 1937, Page 23.
25. The Morning Call (Allentown, PA), March 3, 1937, Page 23.
26. The Morning Call (Allentown, PA), April 15, 1937, Page 23.
27. Standard-Speaker (Hazleton, PA), February 22, 1937, Page 8.

1938

1. The Morning Call (Allentown, PA), April 15, 1937, Page 23.
2. The Morning Call (Allentown, PA), December 11, 1937, Page 15.
3. The Morning Call (Allentown, PA), December 18, 1937, Page 16.
4. The Morning Call (Allentown, PA), December 18, 1937, Page 15.
5. The Morning Call (Allentown, PA), December 22, 1937, Page 31.
6. Pottsville Evening Republican (Pottsville, PA), December 22, 1937, Pages 15 and 16.
7. The Morning Call (Allentown, PA), January 5, 1938, Page 16.
8. The Morning Call (Allentown, PA), January 8, 1938, Page 14.
9. The Morning Call (Allentown, PA), January 15, 1938, Page 14.
10. The Morning Call (Allentown, PA), January 19, 1938, Page 17.
11. The Morning Call (Allentown, PA), January 28, 1938, Page 38.
12. The Morning Call (Allentown, PA), January 29, 1938, Page 20.
13. The Morning Call (Allentown, PA), February 2, 1938, Page 18.
14. The Morning Call (Allentown, PA), February 5, 1938, Page 14.
15. The Morning Call (Allentown, PA), February 12, 1938, Page 15.
16. The Morning Call (Allentown, PA), February 16, 1938, Page 16.
17. The Morning Call (Allentown, PA), February 19, 1938, Page 13.
18. Pottsville Evening Republican (Pottsville, PA), February 19. 1938, Page 12.
19. The Morning Call (Allentown, PA), February 23, 1938, Page 18.
20. The Morning Call (Allentown, PA), February 26, 1938, Pages 1 and 13.
21. The Morning Call (Allentown, PA), March 6, 1938, Page 18.
22. The Morning Call (Allentown, PA), March 10, 1938, Page 19.
23. The Morning Call (Allentown, PA), March 13, 1938, Page 21.
24. The Morning Call (Allentown, PA), March 17, 1938, Page 17.
25. The Morning Call (Allentown, PA), March 20, 1938, Page 19.

26. The Morning Call (Allentown, PA), March 27, 1938, Page 18.
27. Standard-Sentinel (Hazleton, PA), March 2, 1938, Page 14.
28. The Morning Call (Allentown, PA), April 22, 1938, Page 9.
29. Standard-Speaker (Hazleton, PA), March 28, 1938, Page 12.

1939

1. The Morning Call (Allentown, PA), April 7, 1938, Page 8.
2. The Plain Speaker (Hazleton, PA), May 5, 1938, Page 17.
3. The Morning Call (Allentown, PA), April 22, 1938, Page 9.
4. The Morning Call (Allentown, PA), January 7, 1939, Page 13.
5. The Morning Call (Allentown, PA), January 7, 1939, Page 14.
6. The Morning Call (Allentown, PA), January 14, 1939, Page 12.
7. The Morning Call (Allentown, PA), January 14, 1939, Page 11.
8. The Morning Call (Allentown, PA), January 18, 1939, Page 12.
9. The Morning Call (Allentown, PA), January 21, 1939, Page 13.
10. The Morning Call (Allentown, PA), January 21, 1939, Page 14.
11. The Morning Call (Allentown, PA), January 28, 1939, Page 16.
12. The Morning Call (Allentown, PA), February 4, 1939, Page 14.
13. The Morning Call (Allentown, PA), February 11, 1939, Page 12.
14. The Morning Call (Allentown, PA), February 11, 1939, Page 7.
15. The Morning Call (Allentown, PA), February 15, 1939, Page 14.
16. The Morning Call (Allentown, PA), February 18, 1939, Page 12.
17. The Morning Call (Allentown, PA), February 25, 1939, Page 12.
18. The Morning Call (Allentown, PA), February 28, 1939, Page 20.
19. The Morning Call (Allentown, PA), March 12, 1939, Page 17.
20. The Morning Call (Allentown, PA), March 15, 1939, Page 12.
21. The Morning Call (Allentown, PA), March 18, 1939, Page 14.
22. Standard-Sentinel (Hazleton, PA), February 21, 1939, Page 13.
23. The Morning Call (Allentown, PA), March 30, 1939, Page 5.
24. Standard-Speaker (Hazleton, PA), February 28, 1939, Page 12.

1940

1. The Morning Call (Allentown, PA), March 30, 1939, Page 5.
2. The Plain Speaker (Hazleton, PA), December 27, 1939, Page 12.
3. The Morning Call (Allentown, PA), January 6, 1940, Page 11.
4. The Morning Call (Allentown, PA), January 6, 1940, Page 12.
5. The Morning Call (Allentown, PA), January 13, 1940, Page 12.
6. The Morning Call (Allentown, PA), January 13, 1940, Page 15.
7. The Morning Call (Allentown, PA), January 13, 1940, Page 12.
8. The Morning Call (Allentown, PA), January 17, 1940, Page 16.
9. The Morning Call (Allentown, PA), January 17, 1940, Page 11.
10. The Morning Call (Allentown, PA), January 20, 1940, Page 12.
11. The Standard-Sentinel (Hazleton, PA), January 20, 1940, Page 18.
12. The Morning Call (Allentown, PA), January 24, 1940, Page 16.
13. The Morning Call (Allentown, PA), January 24, 1940, Page 17.
14. The Morning Call (Allentown, PA), January 25, 1940, Page 15.

15. The Morning Call (Allentown, PA), January 26, 1940, Page 13 and 14.
16. The Morning Call (Allentown, PA), February 3, 1940, Page 12.
17. The Morning Call (Allentown, PA), February 3, 1940, Page 13.
18. The Morning Call (Allentown, PA), February 10, 1940, Page 12.
19. The Morning Call (Allentown, PA), February 10, 1940, Page 13.
20. The Morning Call (Allentown, PA), February 14, 1940, Page 7.
21. The Morning Call (Allentown, PA), February 17, 1940, Page 12.
22. The Morning Call (Allentown, PA), February 17, 1940, Page 32.
23. The Morning Call (Allentown, PA), February 21, 1940, Page 34.
24. The Morning Call (Allentown, PA), March 6, 1940, Page 16.
25. The Morning Call (Allentown, PA), March 9, 1940, Page 12.
26. The Morning Call (Allentown, PA), March 14, 1940, Page 16.
27. The Morning Call (Allentown, PA), March 17, 1940, Page 13.
28. Standard-Sentinel (Hazleton, PA), February 26, 1940, Page 10.
29. Standard-Sentinel (Hazleton, PA), April 5, 1940, Page 20.
30. Standard-Speaker (Hazleton, PA), February 22, 1940, Page 12.

1941

1. Standard-Sentinel (Hazleton, PA), April 5, 1940, Page 20.
2. The Morning Call (Allentown, PA), January 4, 1941, Page 10.
3. The Morning Call (Allentown, PA), January 4, 1941, Page 12.
4. The Morning Call (Allentown, PA), January 11, 1941, Page 12
5. The Morning Call (Allentown, PA), January 11, 1941, Page 10.
6. The Morning Call (Allentown, PA), January 18, 1941, Page 12.
7. The Morning Call (Allentown, PA), January 18, 1941, Page 19.
8. The Morning Call (Allentown, PA), January 22, 1941, Page 16.
9. The Morning Call (Allentown, PA), January 22, 1941, Page 17.
10. The Morning Call (Allentown, PA), January 25, 1941, Page 19.
11. The Morning Call (Allentown, PA), February 5, 1941, Page 14.
12. The Morning Call (Allentown, PA), February 8, 1941, Page 12.
13. The Morning Call (Allentown, PA), February 8, 1941, Page 10.
14. The Morning Call (Allentown, PA), February 15, 1941, Page 19.
15. The Morning Call (Allentown, PA), February 15, 1941, Page 20.
16. The Morning Call (Allentown, PA), February 22, 1941, Page 13.
17. The Morning Call (Allentown, PA), February 22, 1941, Page 12.
18. The Morning Call (Allentown, PA), February 22, 1941, Page 13.
19. The Morning Call (Allentown, PA), February 18, 1941, Page 28.
20. The Morning Call (Allentown, PA), March 1, 1941, Page 14.
21. The Morning Call (Allentown, PA), February 25, 1941, Page 18.
22. The Morning Call (Allentown, PA), March 5, 1941, Pages 1 and 14.
23. The Morning Call (Allentown, PA), March 8, 1941, Page 12.
24. The Morning Call (Allentown, PA), March 11, 1941, Page 20.
25. The Morning Call (Allentown, PA), March 14, 1941, Page 35.
26. The Morning Call (Allentown, PA), March 1, 1941, Page 12.
27. The Plain Speaker (Hazleton, PA), March 19, 1941, Page 12.

28. The Morning Call (Allentown, PA), April 10, 1941, Page 20.
29. The Morning Call (Allentown, PA), February 14, 1941, Page 32.

1942

1. The Morning Call (Allentown, PA), April 10, 1941, Page 21.
2. The Morning Call (Allentown, PA), January 10, 1942, Page 10.
3. The Morning Call (Allentown, PA), January 17, 1942, Page 10.
4. The Morning Call (Allentown, PA), January 21, 1942, Page 16.
5. The Morning Call (Allentown, PA), January 21, 1942, Page 17.
6. The Morning Call (Allentown, PA), January 24, 1942, Page 10.
7. The Morning Call (Allentown, PA), January 28, 1942, Page 16.
8. The Morning Call (Allentown, PA), January 31, 1942, Page 11.
9. The Morning Call (Allentown, PA), February 4, 1942, Page 14.
10. The Morning Call (Allentown, PA), February 7, 1942, Page 9.
11. The Morning Call (Allentown, PA), February 14, 1942, Page 9.
12. The Morning Call (Allentown, PA), February 21, 1942, Page 7.
13. The Morning Call (Allentown, PA), February 21, 1942, Page 8.
14. The Morning Call (Allentown, PA), February 25, 1942, Page 12.
15. The Morning Call (Allentown, PA), February 25, 1942, Page 13.
16. The Morning Call (Allentown, PA), February 28, 1942, Page 9.
17. The Morning Call (Allentown, PA), March 5, 1942, Page 15.
18. The Pottsville Republican (Pottsville, PA), March 11, 1942, Page 4.
19. The Pottsville Republican (Pottsville, PA), March 14, 1942, Page 8.
20. The Pottsville Republican (Pottsville, PA), March 18, 1942, Page 6.
21. Standard-Sentinel (Hazleton, PA), March 21, 1942, Page 19.
22. Pottsville Evening Republican (Pottsville, PA), March 2, 1942, Page 4.
23. The Morning Call (Allentown, PA), April 18, 1942, Page 10.
24. Pottsville High School – High School Yearbook – Class of 1942, Page 98

1943

1. The Morning Call (Allentown, PA), April 18, 1942, Page 10.
2. The Morning Call (Allentown, PA), January 9, 1943, Page 9.
3. The Morning Call (Allentown, PA), January 18, 1943, Page 12.
4. The Morning Call (Allentown, PA), January 20, 1943, Page 16.
5. The Morning Call (Allentown, PA), January 23, 1943, Page 12.
6. The Morning Call (Allentown, PA), January 27, 1943, Page 18.
7. The Morning Call (Allentown, PA), February 3, 1943, Page 11.
8. The Morning Call (Allentown, PA), February 6, 1943, Page 12.
9. The Morning Call (Allentown, PA), February 13, 1943, Page 7
10. The Morning Call (Allentown, PA), February 17, 1943, Page 16.
11. The Morning Call (Allentown, PA), February 20, 1943, Page 8.
12. The Morning Call (Allentown, PA), February 27, 1943, Page 7.
13. The Morning Call (Allentown, PA), March 3, 1943, Page 6.
14. The Morning Call (Allentown, PA), March 6, 1943, Page 7.
15. Standard-Sentinel (Hazleton, PA), March 10,1943, Pages 10 and 11.
16. The Morning Call (Allentown, PA), March 13, 1943, Page 7.

17. The Plain Speaker (Hazleton, PA), March 17, 1943, Page 12.
18. The Morning Call (Allentown, PA), March 21, 1943, Pages 9 and 10.
19. Standard-Sentinel (Hazleton, PA), March 24,1943, Pages 10.
20. The Plain Speaker (Hazleton, PA), February 15, 1943, Page 8.
21. The Morning Call (Allentown, PA), April 7, 1943, Page 5.
22. Standard-Sentinel (Hazleton, PA), April 6, 1943, Page 10.
23. Hazleton High School-Janus Yearbook-Class of 1943, Page 141.

1944

1. The Morning Call (Allentown, PA), May 1, 1943, Page 9.
2. The Morning Call (Allentown, PA), January 8, 1944, Page 9.
3. The Morning Call (Allentown, PA), January 15, 1944, Page 9.
4. The Morning Call (Allentown, PA), January 19, 1944, Page 14.
5. The Morning Call (Allentown, PA), January 22, 1944, Page 9.
6. The Morning Call (Allentown, PA), January 25, 1944, Page 14.
7. The Morning Call (Allentown, PA), January 26, 1944, Page 10.
8. The Morning Call (Allentown, PA), January 29, 1944, Page 9.
9. The Morning Call (Allentown, PA), January 28, 1944, Page 25.
10. The Morning Call (Allentown, PA), January 30, 1944, Page 9.
11. The Morning Call (Allentown, PA), February 5, 1944, Page 9
12. The Morning Call (Allentown, PA), February 12, 1944, Page 9.
13. The Morning Call (Allentown, PA), February 16, 1944, Page 10.
14. The Morning Call (Allentown, PA), February 19, 1944, Page 9.
15. The Morning Call (Allentown, PA), February 26, 1944, Page 9.
16. The Morning Call (Allentown, PA), March 1, 1944, Page 10.
17. The Morning Call (Allentown, PA), March 4, 1944, Page 9.
18. The Morning Call (Allentown, PA), March 8, 1944, Page 16.
19. The Morning Call (Allentown, PA), March 12, 1944, Page 9.
20. The Morning Call (Allentown, PA), March 15, 1944, Page 16.
21. The Morning Call (Allentown, PA), March 19, 1944, Page 9.
22. The Morning Call (Allentown, PA), March 25, 1944, Page 7.
23. The Morning Call (Allentown, PA), March 29, 1944, Page 9.
24. The Morning Call (Allentown, PA), April 2, 1944, Page 9.
25. The Morning Call (Allentown, PA), February 28, 1944, Page 9.
26. The Plain-Speaker (Hazleton, PA), April 4, 1944, Page 8.
27. Pittsburgh Post-Gazette (Pittsburgh, PA), March 31, 1944, Page 14.

1945

1. The Morning Call (Allentown, PA), April 14, 1944, Page 26.
2. The Morning Call (Allentown, PA), December 12, 1944, Page 20.
3. The Morning Call (Allentown, PA), January 10, 1945, Page 10.
4. The Morning Call (Allentown, PA), January 13, 1945, Page 9.
5. The Morning Call (Allentown, PA), January 17, 1945, Page 10.
6. The Morning Call (Allentown, PA), January 20, 1945, Page 9.
7. The Morning Call (Allentown, PA), January 25, 1945, Page 10.
8. The Morning Call (Allentown, PA), January 27, 1945, Page 9.

9. The Morning Call (Allentown, PA), February 1, 1945, Page 12.
10. The Morning Call (Allentown, PA), February 7, 1945, Page 16.
11. The Morning Call (Allentown, PA), February 10, 1945, Page 9.
12. The Morning Call (Allentown, PA), February 17, 1945, Page 9.
13. The Morning Call (Allentown, PA), February 21, 1945, Page 16.
14. The Morning Call (Allentown, PA), February 24, 1945, Page 9.
15. The Morning Call (Allentown, PA), March 3, 1945, Page 9.
16. The Morning Call (Allentown, PA), March 7, 1945, Page 16.
17. The Morning Call (Allentown, PA), March 11, 1945, Page 9.
18. The Morning Call (Allentown, PA), March 14, 1945, Page 9.
19. The Morning Call (Allentown, PA), March 21, 1945, Page 8
20. The Morning Call (Allentown, PA), March 25, 1945, Pages 9 and 10.
21. The Plain Speaker, (Hazleton, PA), March 28, 1945, Page 12.
22. Standard-Sentinel (Hazleton, PA), March 5, 1945, Page 7.
23. The Morning Call (Allentown, PA), April 2, 1945, Page 10.
24. The Morning Call (Allentown, PA), March 25, 1945, Page 5.

1946

1. The Morning Call (Allentown, PA), April 13, 1945, Page 18.
2. The Morning Call (Allentown, PA), January 5, 1946, Page 9.
3. The Morning Call (Allentown, PA), January 12, 1946, Page 9.
4. The Morning Call (Allentown, PA), January 19, 1946, Page 9.
5. The Morning Call (Allentown, PA), January 23, 1946, Page 14.
6. The Morning Call (Allentown, PA), January 24, 1946, Page 12.
7. The Morning Call (Allentown, PA), January 26, 1946, Page 9.
8. The Morning Call (Allentown, PA), February 2, 1946, Page 9.
9. The Morning Call (Allentown, PA), February 9, 1946, Page 9.
10. The Morning Call (Allentown, PA), February 16. 1946, Page 9.
11. The Morning Call (Allentown, PA), February 15, 1946, Page 20.
12. The Morning Call (Allentown, PA), February 23, 1946, Page 12.
13. The Morning Call (Allentown, PA), March 1, 1946, Page 24.
14. The Standard-Sentinel (Hazleton, PA), March 2, 1946, Page 16.
15. The Morning Call (Allentown, PA), March 13, 1946, Page 14.
16. The Morning Call (Allentown, PA), March 16, 1946, Page 9.
17. The Morning Call (Allentown, PA), March 23, 1946, Page 9.
18. The Morning Call (Allentown, PA), March 26, 1946, Page 13.
19. The Morning Call (Allentown, PA), March 31, 1946, Pages 1 and 15.
20. The Morning Call (Allentown, PA), April 14, 1946, Page 17.
21. The Plain Speaker (Hazleton, PA), March 12, 1946, Page 12.
22. Pottsville Republican (Pottsville, PA), March 8, 1946, Page 14.
23. The Morning Call (Allentown, PA), March 30, 1946, Page 9.

1947

1. The Morning Call (Allentown, PA), May 17, 1946, Page 22.
2. The Morning Call (Allentown, PA), June 13, 1946, Page 17.
3. The Morning Call (Allentown, PA), January 4, 1947, Page 9.

4. The Morning Call (Allentown, PA), January 4, 1947, Page 10.
5. The Morning Call (Allentown, PA), January 11, 1947, Page 9.
6. The Morning Call (Allentown, PA), January 15, 1947, Page 12.
7. The Morning Call (Allentown, PA), January 18, 1947, Page 9.
8. The Morning Call (Allentown, PA), January 25, 1947, Page 9.
9. The Morning Call (Allentown, PA), February 5, 1947, Pages 1 and 15.
10. The Morning Call (Allentown, PA), February 8, 1947, Page 9.
11. The Morning Call (Allentown, PA), February 15, 1947, Page 8.
12. The Morning Call (Allentown, PA), February 8, 1947, Page 11.
13. The Morning Call (Allentown, PA), February 22, 1947, Page 9.
14. The Morning Call (Allentown, PA), February 28, 1947, Page 18.
15. The Standard-Sentinel (Hazleton, PA), March 1, 1947, Page 19.
16. The Morning Call (Allentown, PA), March 4, 1947, Pages 1 and 14.
17. The Morning Call (Allentown, PA), March 6, 1947, Pages 1 and 16.
18. The Morning Call (Allentown, PA), March 9, 1947, Pages 17 and 20.
19. The Morning Call (Allentown, PA), March 14, 1947, Pages 1 and 30.
20. The Morning Call (Allentown, PA), March 18, 1947, Pages 1 and 14.
21. The Morning Call (Allentown, PA), March 26, 1947, Pages 1 and 16.
22. The Morning Call (Allentown, PA), March 30, 1947, Pages 17 and 21.
23. Plain Speaker (Hazleton, PA), March 8, 1947, Page 10.
24. Standard-Sentinel (Hazleton, PA), April 14, 1947, Page 10.
25. Plain Speaker (Hazleton, PA), March 11, 1947, Page 19.

1946 And 1947 Titles Vacated

1. Plain Speaker (Hazleton, PA), March 8, 1947, Page 10.
2. The Morning Call (Allentown, PA), May 15, 1947, Pages 1 and 22.

1948

1. The Morning Call (Allentown, PA), January 8, 1948, Page 20.
2. Pottsville Republican (Pottsville, PA), January 10, 1948, Page 8.
3. Pottsville Republican (Pottsville, PA), January 14, 1948, Page 10.
4. The Plain Speaker (Hazleton, PA), January 17, 1948, Pages 10 and 11.
5. The Morning Call (Allentown, PA), January 21, 1948, Page 16.
6. Standard-Sentinel (Hazleton, PA), January 21, 1948, Page 18.
7. The Morning Call (Allentown, PA), January 24, 1948, Page 9.
8. Pottsville Republican (Pottsville, PA), January 24, 1948, Page 7.
9. The Morning Call (Allentown, PA), January 28, 1948, Page 17.
10. The Plain Speaker (Hazleton, PA), February 4, 1948, Pages 12 and 13.
11. The Morning Call (Allentown, PA), February 4, 1948, Page 30.
12. The Morning Call (Allentown, PA), February 7, 1948, Page 9.
13. The Morning Call (Allentown, PA), February 11, 1948, Page 21.
14. Pottsville Republican (Pottsville, PA), January 17, 1948, Page 14.
15. The Plain Speaker (Hazleton, PA), February 18, 1948, Pages 12 and 13.
16. The Morning Call (Allentown, PA), February 21, 1948, Page 9.
17. The Morning Call (Allentown, PA), February 25, 1948, Page 16.

18. The Morning Call (Allentown, PA), February 28, 1948, Page 11.
19. The Morning Call (Allentown, PA), March 3, 1948, Page 20.
20. Standard-Sentinel (Hazleton, PA), March 6, 1948, Page 22.
21. The Morning Call (Allentown, PA), March 14, 1948, Pages 23 and 24.
22. The Morning Call (Allentown, PA), March 20, 1948, Page 11.
23. The Morning Call (Allentown, PA), March 8, 1948, Page 9.
24. The Morning Call (Allentown, PA), March 17, 1948, Page 22.
25. The Morning Call (Allentown, PA), March 23, 1948, Page 22.
26. The Morning Call (Allentown, PA), March 25, 1948, Page 30.
27. The Morning Call (Allentown, PA), April 1, 1948, Page 20.
28. Central Catholic High School – Glen Echoes Yearbook – Class of 1948, Page 90
29. The Morning Call (Allentown, PA), February 26, 1948, Page 24.
30. Altoona Tribune (Altoona, PA), April 14, 1948, Page 6.

1949

1. The Standard-Sentinel (Hazleton, PA), August 14, 1948, Page 22.
2. The Plain Speaker (Hazleton, PA), September 15, 1948, Page 8.
3. The Plain Speaker (Hazleton, PA), January 7, 1949, Page 24.
4. The Morning Call (Allentown, PA), January 12, 1949, Page 18.
5. The Morning Call (Allentown, PA), January 15, 1949, Page 11.
6. The Morning Call (Allentown, PA), January 15, 1949, Page 12.
7. The Morning Call (Allentown, PA), January 18, 1949, Page 18.
8. The Morning Call (Allentown, PA), January 18, 1949, Page 19.
9. The Morning Call (Allentown, PA), January 22, 1949, Page 11.
10. The Morning Call (Allentown, PA), January 29, 1949, Page 11.
11. The Morning Call (Allentown, PA), February 5, 1949, Page 9.
12. The Morning Call (Allentown, PA), February 5, 1949, Page 10.
13. The Morning Call (Allentown, PA), February 9, 1949, Page 18.
14. The Morning Call (Allentown, PA), February 16, 1949, Page 20.
15. The Morning Call (Allentown, PA), February 19, 1949, Page 11.
16. The Morning Call (Allentown, PA), February 23, 1949, Page 24.
17. The Morning Call (Allentown, PA), February 27, 1949, Page 25.
18. The Morning Call (Allentown, PA), March 2, 1949, Page 22.
19. The Plain Speaker (Hazleton, PA), March 2, 1949, Page 24.
20. The Morning Call (Allentown, PA), March 10, 1949, page 26.
21. The Morning Call (Allentown, PA), March 13, 1949, Page 25.
22. The Morning Call (Allentown, PA), March 17, 1949, Page 26.
23. The Morning Call (Allentown, PA), March 19, 1949, Page 11.
24. The Morning Call (Allentown, PA), March 26, 1949, Page 11.
25. Central Catholic High School – Glen Echoes Yearbook, Class of 1949, Page 78.
26. The Plain Speaker (Hazleton, PA), February 24, 1949, Page 19.
27. The Plain Speaker (Hazleton, PA), March 8, 1949, Page 24.
28. The Plain Speaker (Hazleton, PA), April 14, 1949, Page 25.

1950

1. The Morning Call (Allentown, PA), December 9, 1949, Page 45.

2. The Morning Call (Allentown, PA), December 13, 1949, Page 22.
3. The Morning Call (Allentown, PA), January 7, 1950, Page 11.
4. The Morning Call (Allentown, PA), January 14, 1950, Pages 11 and 12.
5. The Morning Call (Allentown, PA), January 18, 1950, Page 20.
6. The Morning Call (Allentown, PA), January 21, 1950, Page 11.
7. The Morning Call (Allentown, PA), January 28, 1950, Page 11.
8. The Morning Call (Allentown, PA), February 8, 1950, Page 23.
9. The Morning Call (Allentown, PA), February 11, 1950, Page 11.
10. The Morning Call (Allentown, PA), February 18, 1950, Page 11.
11. The Morning Call (Allentown, PA), February 22, 1950, Page 18.
12. The Morning Call (Allentown, PA), February 25, 1950, Page 11.
13. The Morning Call (Allentown, PA), March 1, 1950, Page 25.
14. The Plain Speaker (Hazleton, PA), March 16, 1950, Pages 24 and 25.
15. Hazleton High School – Janus Yearbook – Class of 1950, Page 142
16. The Morning Call (Allentown, PA), March 14, 1950, Page 24.
17. The Morning Call (Allentown, PA), March 19, 1950, Pages 35 and 36.
18. The Morning Call (Allentown, PA), March 26, 1950, Page 25.
19. The Morning Call (Allentown, PA), March 15, 1959, Page 26.
20. Standard Sentinel (Hazleton, PA0, March 1, 1950, Page 24.
21. The Plain Speaker (Hazleton, PA), March 20, Page 14.
22. The Plain Speaker (Hazleton, PA), April 18, Page 24.

1951

1. The Morning Call (Allentown, PA), December 13, 1950, Page 31.
2. The Morning Call (Allentown, PA), January 6, 1951, Page 16.
3. The Morning Call (Allentown, PA), January 6, 1951, Page 17.
4. The Morning Call (Allentown, PA), January 10, 1951, Page 26
5. The Morning Call (Allentown, PA), January 13, 1951, Page 8.
6. The Morning Call (Allentown, PA), January 17, 1951, Pages 24 and 25.
7. The Morning Call (Allentown, PA), January 20, 1951, Page 8.
8. The Morning Call (Allentown, PA), January 27, 1951, Page 8.
9. The Morning Call (Allentown, PA), February 7, 1951, Page 22.
10. The Morning Call (Allentown, PA), February 10, 1951, Page 13.
11. The Morning Call (Allentown, PA), February 17, 1951, Page 8.
12. The Morning Call (Allentown, PA), February 21, 1951, Page 24.
13. The Morning Call (Allentown, PA), February 21, 1951, Page 25.
14. The Standard-Sentinel (Hazleton, PA0, February 21, 1951, Page 24.
15. The Morning Call (Allentown, PA), February 24, 1951, Page 8.
16. The Morning Call (Allentown, PA), March 2, 1951, Page 38.
17. The Morning Call (Allentown, PA), March 10, 1951, Page 8.
18. The Morning Call (Allentown, PA), March 15, 1951, Pages 41 and 43.
19. The Morning Call (Allentown, PA), March 18, 1951, Pages 39 and 41.
20. The Morning Call (Allentown, PA), March 29, 1951, Pages 28 and 29.
21. The Morning Call (Allentown, PA), April 1, 1951, Pages 1 and 37.
22. Allentown High School -Comus Yearbook – Class of 1951, Page 226.

23. The Morning Call (Allentown, PA), February 24, 1951, Page 8.
24. The Morning Call (Allentown, PA), April 6, 1951, Page 38.

1952

1. The Morning Call (Allentown, PA), May 11, 1951, Page 35.
2. The Morning Call (Allentown, PA), December 14, 1951, Page 47.
3. The Morning Call (Allentown, PA), January 5, 1952, Page 8.
4. The Morning Call (Allentown, PA), January 12, 1952, Page 12.
5. The Morning Call (Allentown, PA), January 16, 1952, Page 3.
6. The Morning Call (Allentown, PA), January 19, 1952, Page 12.
7. The Morning Call (Allentown, PA), January 19, 1952, Page 13.
8. The Morning Call (Allentown, PA), January 26, 1952, Page 10.
9. The Morning Call (Allentown, PA), January 26, 1952, Page 11.
10. The Morning Call (Allentown, PA), February 2, 1952, Page 8.
11. The Morning Call (Allentown, PA), February 9, 1952, Page 12.
12. The Morning Call (Allentown, PA), February 13, 1952, Page 24.
13. The Morning Call (Allentown, PA), February 16, 1952, Page 13.
14. The Morning Call (Allentown, PA), February 16, 1952, Page 12.
15. The Morning Call (Allentown, PA), February 23, 1952, Page 13.
16. The Morning Call (Allentown, PA), February 23, 1952, Page 12.
17. The Morning Call (Allentown, PA), March 5, 1952, Pages 25 and 26.
18. The Morning Call (Allentown, PA), March 8, 1952, Pages 1 and 12.
19. The Morning Call (Allentown, PA), January 31, 1952, Page 26.
20. The Morning Call (Allentown, PA), March 12, 1952, Pages 1, 35 and 36.
21. The Morning Call (Allentown, PA), March 16, 1952, Pages 1, 41 and 42.
22. The Morning Call (Allentown, PA), March 7, 1952, Page 40.
23. The Morning Call (Allentown, PA), March 15, 1952, Page 12.
24. The Morning Call (Allentown, PA), March 21, 1952, Page 38,
25. The Morning Call (Allentown, PA), March 23, 1952, Pages 1 and 41.
26. Central Catholic High School -Glenn Echoes Yearbook-Class of 1952, Page 84.
27. The Morning Call (Allentown, PA), February 25, 1952, Page 11.
28. Plain Speaker (Hazleton, PA), March 14, 1952, Page 36.
29. The Evening Herald (Pottsville, PA), March 28, 1952, Page 18.

1953

1. The Morning Call (Allentown, PA), April 25, 1952, Page 26.
2. The Morning Call (Allentown, PA), December 16, 1952, Page 18.
3. The Morning Call (Allentown, PA), January 7, 1953, Page 21.
4. The Morning Call (Allentown, PA), January 10, 1953, Page 12.
5. The Morning Call (Allentown, PA), January 17, 1953, Page 12.
6. The Morning Call (Allentown, PA), January 21, 1953, Page 20.
7. The Morning Call (Allentown, PA), January 24, 1953, Page 12.
8. The Morning Call (Allentown, PA), January 31, 1953, Page 12.
9. The Morning Call (Allentown, PA), February 7, 1953, Page 12.
10. The Morning Call (Allentown, PA), February 14, 1953, Page 14.
11. The Morning Call (Allentown, PA), February 21, 1953, Page 12.

12. The Morning Call (Allentown, PA), February 28, 1953, Page 14.
13. The Morning Call (Allentown, PA), March 4, 1953, Page 7.
14. Allentown High School – Comus Yearbook – Class of 1953, Page 110.
15. The Morning Call (Allentown, PA), March 11, 1953, Page 30.
16. The Morning Call (Allentown, PA), March 14, 1953, Page 14.
17. The Morning Call (Allentown, PA), March 22, 1953, Pages 41 and 43.
18. The Morning Call (Allentown, PA), March 26, 1953, Pages 36 and 40.
19. The Morning Call (Allentown, PA), March 17, 1953, Page 20.
20. The Morning Call (Allentown, PA), March 19, 1953, Page 38.
21. The Morning Call (Allentown, PA), March 1, 1953, Page 44.
22. The Plain Speaker (Hazleton, PA), March 5, 1953, Page 24.
23. The Plain Speaker (Hazleton, PA), April 1, 1953, Page 21.

1954

1. The Morning Call (Allentown, PA), November 17, 1953, Page 24.
2. The Morning Call (Allentown, PA), December 10, 1953, Page 45.
3. The Morning Call (Allentown, PA), December 15, 1953, Page 23.
4. The Morning Call (Allentown, PA), January 9, 1954, Page 10.
5. The Morning Call (Allentown, PA), January 16, 1954, Page 10.
6. The Morning Call (Allentown, PA), January 20, 1954, Page 26.
7. The Morning Call (Allentown, PA), January 23, 1954, Page 10.
8. The Morning Call (Allentown, PA), January 30, 1954, Page 10.
9. The Morning Call (Allentown, PA), February 6, 1954, Page 10.
10. The Morning Call (Allentown, PA), February 13, 1954, Page 10.
11. The Morning Call (Allentown, PA), February 17, 1954, Page 28.
12. The Morning Call (Allentown, PA), February 20, 1954, Page 10.
13. The Morning Call (Allentown, PA), February 27, 1954, Page 10.
14. Allentown High School-Comus Yearbook-Class of 1954, Page 88.
15. The Morning Call (Allentown, PA), March 7, 1954, Pages 1 and 39.
16. The Morning Call (Allentown, PA), March 13, 1954, Page 10.
17. The Morning Call (Allentown, PA), March 19, 1954, Page 36.
18. The Morning Call (Allentown, PA), March 24, 1954, Page 26.
19. The Morning Call (Allentown, PA), March 26, 1954, Page 32.
20. The Morning Call (Allentown, PA), March 1, 1954, Page 16.
21. Pottsville Republican (Pottsville, PA), March17, 1954, Page 10.
22. Pottsville Republican (Pottsville, PA), April 7, 1954, Page 10.

1955

1. Plain Speaker (Hazleton, PA), April 2, 1954, Page 28.
2. The Morning Call (Allentown, PA), January 8, 1955, Page 10.
3. The Morning Call (Allentown, PA), January 15, 1955, Page 7.
4. The Morning Call (Allentown, PA), January 19, 1955, Page 23.
5. The Morning Call (Allentown, PA), January 19, 1955, Page 24.
6. The Morning Call (Allentown, PA), January 22, 1955, Page 16.
7. The Morning Call (Allentown, PA), January 29, 1955, Page 10.
8. The Morning Call (Allentown, PA), February 5, 1955, Page 10.

9. The Morning Call (Allentown, PA), February 12, 1955, Page 10.
10. The Morning Call (Allentown, PA), February 13, 1955, Pages 42 and 43.
11. The Morning Call (Allentown, PA), February 16, 1955, Page 26.
12. The Morning Call (Allentown, PA), February 19, 1955, Page 10.
13. Pottsville Republican (Pottsville, PA), February 24, 1955, Page 14.
14. The Plain Speaker (Hazleton, PA), February 26, 1955, Page 13.
15. The Morning Call (Allentown, PA), February 26, 1955, Page 10.
16. Allentown High School-Comus Yearbook-Class of 1955, Page 202.
17. The Morning Call (Allentown, PA), March 5, 1955, Page 8.
18. The Morning Call (Allentown, PA), March 12, 1955, Page 12.
19. The Morning Call (Allentown, PA), March 16, 1955, Page 34.
20. The Morning Call (Allentown, PA), March 12, 1955, Page 12.
21. The Morning Call (Allentown, PA), March 15, 1955, Page 18.
22. The Morning Call (Allentown, PA), March 18, 1955, Page 34.
23. The Standard-Sentinel (Hazleton, PA), March 11, 1955, Page 24.
24. The Standard-Sentinel (Hazleton, PA), March 31, 1955, Page 14.
25. Pottsville Republican (Pottsville, PA), April 7, 1955, Page 10.

1956

1. The Plain Speaker (Hazleton, PA), April 14, 1955, Page 24.
2. The Morning Call (Allentown, PA), January 7, 1956, Page 10.
3. The Morning Call (Allentown, PA), January 14, 1956, Page 9.
4. The Morning Call (Allentown, PA), January 18, 1956, Page 25.
5. The Morning Call (Allentown, PA), January 21, 1956, Page 7.
6. The Morning Call (Allentown, PA), January 28, 1956, Page 10.
7. The Morning Call (Allentown, PA), February 4, 1956, Page 10.
8. The Morning Call (Allentown, PA), February 11, 1956, Page 25.
9. The Morning Call (Allentown, PA), February 4, 1956, Page 22.
10. The Morning Call (Allentown, PA), February 4, 1956, Page 23.
11. The Morning Call (Allentown, PA), February 18, 1956, Page 10.
12. The Morning Call (Allentown, PA), February 22, 1956, Page 24.
13. The Morning Call (Allentown, PA), February 22, 1956, Page 25.
14. The Morning Call (Allentown, PA), March 11, 1956, Pages 41 and 43.
15. Allentown High School-Comus Yearbook-Class of 1956, Page 100.
16. The Morning Call (Allentown, PA), March 15, 1956, Pages 1 and 45.
17. The Morning Call (Allentown, PA), March 3, 1956, Page 18.
18. The Morning Call (Allentown, PA), March 6, 1956, Page 22.
19. The Morning Call (Allentown, PA), March 10, 1956, Page 8.
20. The Morning Call (Allentown, PA), March 14, 1956, Page 24.
21. The Morning Call (Allentown, PA), March 18, 1956, Pages 41 and 42.
22. The Morning Call (Allentown, PA), March 23, 1956, Page 11.
23. The Morning Call (Allentown, PA), March 24, 1956, Page 16.
24. The Morning Call (Allentown, PA), March 25, 1956, Page 41.
25. The Morning Call (Allentown, PA), February 24, 1956, Page 32.
26. The Plain Speaker (Hazleton, PA), March 13, 1956, Page 25.

27. The Morning Call (Allentown, PA), March 30, 1956, Page 25.

1957

1. Pottsville Republican (Pottsville, PA), April 14, 1956
2. The Morning Call (Allentown, PA), January 9, 1957, Page 23.
3. The Morning Call (Allentown, PA), January 9, 1957, Page 22.
4. The Morning Call (Allentown, PA), January 12, 1957, Page 11.
5. The Morning Call (Allentown, PA), January 12, 1957, Page 5.
6. The Morning Call (Allentown, PA), January 16, 1957, Page 24.
7. The Morning Call (Allentown, PA), January 19, 1957, Page 16.
8. The Morning Call (Allentown, PA), January 19, 1957, Page 17.
9. The Morning Call (Allentown, PA), January 26, 1957, Page 10.
10. The Morning Call (Allentown, PA), January 27, 1957, Page 39.
11. The Morning Call (Allentown, PA), February 2, 1957, Page 8.
12. The Morning Call (Allentown, PA), February 9, 1957, Page 10.
13. The Morning Call (Allentown, PA), February 13, 1957, Page 24.
14. The Morning Call (Allentown, PA), February 13, 1957, Page 25.
15. The Morning Call (Allentown, PA), February 16, 1957, Page 14.
16. The Morning Call (Allentown, PA), February 20, 1957, Page 25.
17. The Morning Call (Allentown, PA), February 22, 1957, Page 32.
18. The Morning Call (Allentown, PA), February 22, 1957, Page 33.
19. Allentown High School-Comus Yearbook-Class of 1957, Page 116.
20. The Morning Call (Allentown, PA), March 6, 1957, Page 24.
21. The Morning Call (Allentown, PA), March 15, 1957, Pages 1 and 35.
22. The Morning Call (Allentown, PA), March 23, 1957, Page 8.
23. The Morning Call (Allentown, PA), March 8, 1957, Page 30.
24. The Morning Call (Allentown, PA), March 11, 1957, Page 14.
25. The Morning Call (Allentown, PA), March 16, 1957, Page 10.
26. The Morning Call (Allentown, PA), March 20, 1957, Page 30.
27. The Morning Call (Allentown, PA), March 23, 1957, Page 8.
28. The Morning Call (Allentown, PA), March 9, 1957, Page 11.
29. The Morning Call (Allentown, PA), March 1, 1957, Page 27.
30. Standard Sentinel (Hazleton, PA), March 28, 1957, Page 16.

1958

1. Standard-Sentinel (Hazleton, PA), April 26, 1957, Page 28.
2. Pottsville Republican (Pottsville, PA), December 19, 1958.
3. The Morning Call (Allentown, PA), January 11, 1958, Page 10.
4. The Morning Call (Allentown, PA), January 15, 1958, Page 30.
5. The Morning Call (Allentown, PA), January 15, 1958, Page 28.
6. The Morning Call (Allentown, PA), January 18, 1958, Page 10.
7. The Morning Call (Allentown, PA), January 25, 1958, Page 10.
8. Pottsville Republican (Pottsville, PA), January 25, 1958, Page 6.
9. The Morning Call (Allentown, PA), January 25, 1958, Page 11.
10. The Morning Call (Allentown, PA), February 1, 1958, Page 10.
11. The Morning Call (Allentown, PA), February 8, 1958, Page 10.

12. The Morning Call (Allentown, PA), February 12, 1958, Page 26.
13. The Morning Call (Allentown, PA), February 12, 1958, Page 28.
14. Standard-Sentinel (Hazleton, PA), February 12, 1958, Page 20.
15. The Morning Call (Allentown, PA), February 15, 1958, Page 10.
16. The Morning Call (Allentown, PA), February 22, 1958, Page 10.
17. The Morning Call (Allentown, PA), February 26, 1958, Page 33.
18. The Plain Speaker (Hazleton, PA), February 26, 1958, Page 15.
19. The Morning Call (Allentown, PA), March 4, 1958, Page 24.
20. The Morning Call (Allentown, PA), March 7, 1958, Page 33.
21. Liberty High School-Cauldron Yearbook-Class of 1958, Page 212.
22. The Morning Call (Allentown, PA), March 11, 1958, Page 23.
23. The Morning Call (Allentown, PA), March 13, 1958, Page 14.
24. The Morning Call (Allentown, PA), March 19, 1958, Pages 25 and 26.
25. The Morning Call (Allentown, PA), March 8, 1958, Page 8.
26. The Morning Call (Allentown, PA), March 12, 1958, Page 24.
27. The Morning Call (Allentown, PA), March 15, 1958, Page 12.
28. The Morning Call (Allentown, PA), March 19, 1958, Page 26.
29. The Plain Speaker (Hazleton, PA), March 4, 1958, Page 20.
30. The Plain Speaker (Hazleton, PA), March 7, 1958, Page 24.
31. Pottsville Republican (Pottsville, PA), March 27, 1958, Page 14.

1959

1. Standard-Sentinel (Hazleton, PA), April 15, 1958, Page 16.
2. Standard-Sentinel (Hazleton, PA), December 18, 1958, Page 21.
3. The Morning Call (Allentown, PA), January 10, 1959, Page 11.
4. The Morning Call (Allentown, PA), January 10, 1959, Page 13.
5. The Morning Call (Allentown, PA), January 14, 1959, Page 26.
6. The Morning Call (Allentown, PA), January 17, 1959, Page 12.
7. The Morning Call (Allentown, PA), January 20, 1959, Page 23.
8. The Morning Call (Allentown, PA), January 24, 1959, Page 11.
9. The Morning Call (Allentown, PA), January 24, 1959, Page 13.
10. The Morning Call (Allentown, PA), January 31, 1959, Page 12.
11. The Morning Call (Allentown, PA), February 4, 1959, Page 22.
12. The Morning Call (Allentown, PA), February 7, 1959, Page 13.
13. The Morning Call (Allentown, PA), February 11, 1959, Page 11.
14. The Morning Call (Allentown, PA), February 11, 1959, Page 13.
15. The Morning Call (Allentown, PA), February 14, 1959, Page 12.
16. The Morning Call (Allentown, PA), February 14, 1959, Page 13.
17. The Morning Call (Allentown, PA), February 21, 1959, Page 13.
18. The Morning Call (Allentown, PA), February 21, 1959, Page 14.
19. The Morning Call (Allentown, PA), February 25, 1959, Page 26.
20. The Morning Call (Allentown, PA), February 25, 1959, Page 27.
21. The Morning Call (Allentown, PA), February 28, 1959, Pages 11 and 12.
22. Allentown High School-Comus Yearbook-Class of 1959, Page 124.
23. The Morning Call (Allentown, PA), March 5, 1959, Pages 45 and 46.

24. The Morning Call (Allentown, PA), March 7, 1959, Pages 13 and 14.
25. The Morning Call (Allentown, PA), March 4, 1959, Page 22.
26. The Morning Call (Allentown, PA), March 7, 1959, Page 14.
27. The Morning Call (Allentown, PA), March 10, 1959, Page 20.
28. The Morning Call (Allentown, PA), March 14, 1959, Page 14.
29. The Morning Call (Allentown, PA), March 21, 1959, Page 14.
30. The Morning Call (Allentown, PA), April 3, 1959, Page 26.
31. The Morning Call (Allentown, PA), April 4, 1959, Page 14.
32. The Morning Call (Allentown, PA), March 18, 1959, Page 21.
33. The Plain Speaker (Hazleton, PA), March 14, 1959, Page 14.
34. Standard-Sentinel (Hazleton, PA), March 11, 1959, Page 25.

1960

1. The Morning Call (Allentown, PA), April 14, 1959, Page 25.
2. The Plain Speaker (Hazleton, PA), December 19, 1959, Page 17.
3. The Morning Call (Allentown, PA), January 6, 1960, Page 18.
4. The Morning Call (Allentown, PA), January 9, 1960, Page 11.
5. The Morning Call (Allentown, PA), January 13, 1960, Page 21.
6. The Morning Call (Allentown, PA), January 16, 1960, Page 11.
7. The Morning Call (Allentown, PA), January 20, 1960, Page 22.
8. The Morning Call (Allentown, PA), January 23, 1960, Pages 11 and 12.
9. The Morning Call (Allentown, PA), January 27, 1960, Page 20.
10. The Morning Call (Allentown, PA), January 30, 1960, Pages 11 and 12.
11. The Morning Call (Allentown, PA), February 3, 1960, Page 20.
12. The Morning Call (Allentown, PA), February 6, 1960, Page 11.
13. The Morning Call (Allentown, PA), February 10, 1960, Pages 22 and 25.
14. The Morning Call (Allentown, PA), February 13, 1960, Pages 11.
15. The Morning Call (Allentown, PA), February 17, 1960, Page 25.
16. The Morning Call (Allentown, PA), February 20, 1960, Page 13.
17. The Morning Call (Allentown, PA), February 24, 1960, Page 20.
18. The Morning Call (Allentown, PA), February 27, 1960, Page 10.
19. Hazleton High School-Janus Yearbook-Class of 1960, Page 122.
20. The Morning Call (Allentown, PA), March 8, 1960, Page 13.
21. The Morning Call (Allentown, PA), March 10, 1960, Page 41.
22. The Morning Call (Allentown, PA), March 12, 1960, Pages 1 and 11.
23. The Morning Call (Allentown, PA), March 6, 1960, Pages 37 and 38.
24. The Morning Call (Allentown, PA), March 10, 1960, Pages 41 and 42.
25. Standard-Sentinel (Hazleton, PA), February 29, 1960, Page 12.
26. Pottsville Republican (Pottsville, PA), March 11, 1960, Page 6.
27. The Morning Call (Allentown, PA), March 30, 1960, Page 26.

1961

1. The Morning Call (Allentown, PA), April 12, 1960, Page 21.
2. Pottsville Republican (Pottsville, PA), December 23, 1960, Page 6.
3. The Plain Speaker (Hazleton, PA), January 4, 1961, Page 16.
4. Standard-Sentinel (Hazleton, PA), January 7, 1961, Page 16.

5. Standard-Sentinel (Hazleton, PA), January 7, 1961, Page 17.
6. Standard-Sentinel (Hazleton, PA), January 11, 1961, Page 20.
7. Standard-Sentinel (Hazleton, PA), January 14, 1961, Page 17.
8. Standard-Sentinel (Hazleton, PA), January 14, 1961, Page 16.
9. Standard-Sentinel (Hazleton, PA), January 18, 1961, Page 24.
10. The Plain Speaker (Hazleton, PA), January 23, 1961, Page 12.
11. Standard-Sentinel (Hazleton, PA), January 25, 1961, Page 21.
12. The Plain Speaker (Hazleton, PA), January 28, 1961, Page 19.
13. Standard-Sentinel (Hazleton, PA), February 1, 1961, Page 18.
14. Standard-Sentinel (Hazleton, PA), February 4, 1961, Page 16.
15. Standard-Sentinel (Hazleton, PA), February 1, 1961, Page 17.
16. The Plain Speaker (Hazleton, PA), February 8, 1961, Page 18.
17. The Plain Speaker (Hazleton, PA), February 11, 1961, Page 12.
18. Standard-Sentinel (Hazleton, PA), February 11, 1961, Page 17.
19. Standard-Sentinel (Hazleton, PA), February 15, 1961, Page 20.
20. The Plain Speaker (Hazleton, PA), February 15, 1961, Page 20.
21. Standard-Sentinel (Hazleton, PA), February 18, 1961, Page 18.
22. The Morning Call (Allentown, PA), February 22, 1961, Page 23.
23. The Morning Call (Allentown, PA), February 22, 1961, Page 24.
24. Standard-Sentinel (Hazleton, PA), February 24, 1961, Page 20.
25. The Morning Call (Allentown, PA), March 6, 1961, Page 19.
26. The Morning Call (Allentown, PA), March 8, 1961, Page 23.
27. The Morning Call (Allentown, PA), March 12, 1961, Pages 45 and 46.
28. The Morning Call (Allentown, PA), March 16, 1961, Page 45.
29. The Morning Call (Allentown, PA), March 4, 1961, Page 11.
30. The Morning Call (Allentown, PA), February 27, 1961, Page 15.
31. The Morning Call (Allentown, PA), March 9, 1961, Page 46.
32. The Morning Call (Allentown, PA), March 31, 1961, Page 24.

1962

1. The Morning Call (Allentown, PA), April 20, 1961, Page 15.
2. Standard-Speaker (Hazleton, PA), January 6, 1962. Page 17.
3. Standard-Speaker (Hazleton, PA), January 10, 1962. Page 17.
4. The Morning Call (Allentown, PA), January 13, 1962, Page 11.
5. Pottsville Republican (Pottsville, PA), January 17, 1962, Page 10.
6. The Morning Call (Allentown, PA), January 17, 1962, Page 22.
7. The Morning Call (Allentown, PA), January 20, 1962, Page 11.
8. The Morning Call (Allentown, PA), January 24, 1962, Page 28.
9. Standard-Speaker (Hazleton, PA), January 24, 1962. Page 12.
10. The Morning Call (Allentown, PA), January 27, 1962, Page 11.
11. The Morning Call (Allentown, PA), February 3, 1962, Page 11.
12. The Morning Call (Allentown, PA), February 7, 1962, Page 22.
13. The Morning Call (Allentown, PA), February 10, 1962, Page 11.
14. The Morning Call (Allentown, PA), February 14, 1962, Page 22.
15. Standard-Speaker (Hazleton, PA), February 24, 1962. Page 15.

16. The Morning Call (Allentown, PA), February 17, 1962, Page 11.
17. The Morning Call (Allentown, PA), February 18, 1962, Page 41.
18. The Morning Call (Allentown, PA), February 21, 1962, Page 47.
19. The Morning Call (Allentown, PA), February 23, 1962, Page 26.
20. The Morning Call (Allentown, PA), February 24, 1962, Page 17.
21. The Morning Call (Allentown, PA), February 24, 1962, Page 18.
22. The Morning Call (Allentown, PA), March 8, 1962, Page 42.
23. The Morning Call (Allentown, PA), March 11, 1962, Pages 37 and 42.
24. The Morning Call (Allentown, PA), March 3, 1962, Page 13.
25. The Morning Call (Allentown, PA), March 6, 1962, Page 24.
26. The Morning Call (Allentown, PA), March 10, 1962, Page 13.
27. The Morning Call (Allentown, PA), March 14, 1962, Page 30.
28. Pottsville Republican (Pottsville, PA), March 13, 1962, Page 11.
29. Standard-Speaker (Hazleton, PA), March 10, 1962, Page 15.
30. Philadelphia Inquirer (Philadelphia, PA), March 29, 1962, Page 37.

<u>1963</u>

1. The Morning Call (Allentown, PA), April 4, 1962, Page 33.
2. The Morning Call (Allentown, PA), January 5, 1963, Page 11.
3. The Morning Call (Allentown, PA), January 9, 1963, Page 23.
4. The Morning Call (Allentown, PA), January 9, 1963, Page 24.
5. Standard-Speaker (Hazleton, PA), January 9, 1963, Page 16.
6. The Morning Call (Allentown, PA), January 12, 1963, Page 11.
7. The Morning Call (Allentown, PA), January 16, 1963, Page 25.
8. The Morning Call (Allentown, PA), January 16, 1963, Page 26.
9. Republican and Herald (Pottsville, PA), January 24, 1963, Page 1.
10. The Morning Call (Allentown, PA), January 19, 1963, Page 11.
11. The Morning Call (Allentown, PA), January 23, 1963, Page 11.
12. The Morning Call (Allentown, PA), January 26, 1963, Page 13.
13. The Morning Call (Allentown, PA), January 30, 1963, Page 25.
14. The Morning Call (Allentown, PA), February 2, 1963, Page 9.
15. The Morning Call (Allentown, PA), February 6, 1963, Page 22.
16. The Morning Call (Allentown, PA), February 9, 1963, Page 13.
17. The Morning Call (Allentown, PA), February 13, 1963, Page 28.
18. The Morning Call (Allentown, PA), February 13, 1963, Page 29.
19. The Morning Call (Allentown, PA), February 14, 1963, Page 52.
20. The Morning Call (Allentown, PA), February 16, 1963, Page 13.
21. The Morning Call (Allentown, PA), February 20, 1963, Page 26.
22. The Morning Call (Allentown, PA), February 22, 1963, Page 34.
23. The Morning Call (Allentown, PA), March 1, 1963, Page 24.
24. The Morning Call (Allentown, PA), February 28, 1963, Page 52.
25. The Morning Call (Allentown, PA), March 6, 1963, Page 28.
26. The Morning Call (Allentown, PA), March 2, 1963, Page 11.
27. The Morning Call (Allentown, PA), March 6, 1963, Page 29.
28. The Morning Call (Allentown, PA), March 9, 1963, Page 13.

29. Standard-Speaker (Hazleton, PA) February 26, 1963, Page 20.
30. Pottsville Republican (Pottsville, PA), March 13, 1963, Page 10.
31. The Evening Herald (Pottsville, PA), March 20, 1963, Page 14.

1964

1. Pottsville Republican (Pottsville, PA), April 9, 1963, Page 6.
2. The Morning Call (Allentown, PA), December 18, 1963, Page 34.
3. The Morning Call (Allentown, PA), December 21, 1963, Page 11.
4. The Morning Call (Allentown, PA), January 4, 1964, Page 11.
5. The Morning Call (Allentown, PA), January 8, 1964, Page 23.
6. The Morning Call (Allentown, PA), January 10, 1964, Page 33.
7. The Morning Call (Allentown, PA), January 11, 1964, Page 11.
8. The Morning Call (Allentown, PA), January 16, 1964, Page 47.
9. The Morning Call (Allentown, PA), January 16, 1964, Page 48.
10. The Morning Call (Allentown, PA), January 18, 1964, Page 11.
11. The Morning Call (Allentown, PA), January 22, 1964, Page 24
12. The Morning Call (Allentown, PA), January 23, 1964, Page 47.
13. The Morning Call (Allentown, PA), January 25, 1964, Page 11.
14. The Morning Call (Allentown, PA), February 1, 1964, Page 22.
15. The Morning Call (Allentown, PA), February 8, 1964, Page 11.
16. The Morning Call (Allentown, PA), February 12, 1964, Page 11.
17. The Morning Call (Allentown, PA), February 15, 1964, Page 9.
18. The Morning Call (Allentown, PA), February 19, 1964, Page 30.
19. Pottsville Republican (Pottsville, PA), February 19, Page 10.
20. The Morning Call (Allentown, PA), February 22, 1964, Page 13.
21. The Morning Call (Allentown, PA), February 26, 1964, Page 27.
22. The Morning Call (Allentown, PA), February 28, 1964, Page 35.
23. The Morning Call (Allentown, PA), February 28, 1964, Page 36.
24. The Morning Call (Allentown, PA), March 1, 1964, Page 49.
25. The Morning Call (Allentown, PA), March 5, 1964, Page 50.
26. The Morning Call (Allentown, PA), March 7, 1964, Page 11.
27. The Morning Call (Allentown, PA), March 11, 1964, Page 32.
28. The Morning Call (Allentown, PA), March 18, 1964, Page 34.
29. The Morning Call (Allentown, PA), March 21, 1964, Page 11.
30. Standard-Speaker (Hazleton, PA), March 3, 1964, Page 20.
31. Standard-Speaker (Hazleton, PA), March 12, 1964, Page 28.
32. Standard-Speaker (Hazleton, PA), March 21, 1964, Page 20.

1965

1. The Morning Call (Allentown, PA), December 19, 1964, Page 15.
2. The Morning Call (Allentown, PA), December 23, 1964, Page 26.
3. The Morning Call (Allentown, PA), January 7, 1965, Page 46.
4. The Morning Call (Allentown, PA), January 6, 1965, Page 24.
5. The Morning Call (Allentown, PA), January 6, 1965, Page 25.
6. The Morning Call (Allentown, PA), January 9, 1965, Page 11.
7. The Morning Call (Allentown, PA), January 13, 1965, Page 28.

8. The Morning Call (Allentown, PA), January 16, 1965, Page 11.
9. The Morning Call (Allentown, PA), January 20, 1965, Page 26.
10. The Morning Call (Allentown, PA), January 20, 1965, Page 27.
11. The Morning Call (Allentown, PA), January 23, 1965, Page 11.
12. Standard-Speaker (Hazleton, PA), January 27, 1965, Page 19.
13. The Morning Call (Allentown, PA), January 27, 1965, Page 28.
14. The Morning Call (Allentown, PA), January 29, 1965, Page 27.
15. Standard-Speaker (Hazleton, PA), January 30, 1965, Page 19.
16. The Morning Call (Allentown, PA), January 30, 1965, Page 11.
17. The Morning Call (Allentown, PA), January 31, 1965, Page 45.
18. The Morning Call (Allentown, PA), February 3, 1965, Page 30.
19. The Morning Call (Allentown, PA), February 4, 1965, Page 45.
20. The Morning Call (Allentown, PA), February 6, 1965, Page 11.
21. The Morning Call (Allentown, PA), February 10, 1965, Page 32.
22. The Morning Call (Allentown, PA), February 12, 1965, Page 28.
23. The Morning Call (Allentown, PA), February 13, 1965, Page 13.
24. The Morning Call (Allentown, PA), February 17, 1965, Page 26.
25. Standard-Speaker (Hazleton, PA), February 17, 1965, Page 21.
26. The Morning Call (Allentown, PA), February 20, 1965, Page 13.
27. The Morning Call (Allentown, PA), February 20, 1965, Page 14.
28. The Morning Call (Allentown, PA), February 24, 1965, Page 26.
29. The Morning Call (Allentown, PA), February 26, 1965, Page 26.
30. The Morning Call (Allentown, PA), March 5, 1965, Page 30.
31. Central Catholic High School-Glen Echoes Yearbook-Class of 1965, Page 58.
32. The Morning Call (Allentown, PA), March 6, 1965, Page 13.
33. The Morning Call (Allentown, PA), March 10, 1965, Page 28.
34. The Morning Call (Allentown, PA), March 17, 1965, Page 32.
35. The Morning Call (Allentown, PA), March 20, 1965, Page 13.
36. Standard-Speaker (Hazleton, PA), March 2, 1965, Page 20.
37. The Morning Call (Allentown, PA), March 26, 1965, Page 33.

1966

1. The Morning Call (Allentown, PA), December 15, 1965, Page 34.
2. The Morning Call (Allentown, PA), December 16, 1965, Page 58.
3. The Morning Call (Allentown, PA), December 18, 1965, Page 13.
4. The Morning Call (Allentown, PA), December 22, 1965, Page 32.
5. The Morning Call (Allentown, PA), January 5, 1966, Page 11.
6. The Morning Call (Allentown, PA), January 8, 1966, Page 11.
7. Standard-Speaker (Hazleton, PA), January 8, 1966, Page 18.
8. The Morning Call (Allentown, PA), January 12, 1966, Page 11.
9. The Morning Call (Allentown, PA), January 15, 1966, Page 11.
10. Standard-Speaker (Hazleton, PA), January 19, 1966, Page 20.
11. The Morning Call (Allentown, PA), January 19, 1966, Page 26.
12. The Morning Call (Allentown, PA), January 22, 1966, Page 13.
13. The Morning Call (Allentown, PA), January 29, 1966, Page 15.

14. The Morning Call (Allentown, PA), February 3, 1966, Page 33.
15. The Morning Call (Allentown, PA), February 5, 1966, Page 13.
16. The Morning Call (Allentown, PA), February 8, 1966, Page 18.
17. The Morning Call (Allentown, PA), February 9, 1966, Page 26.
18. Pottsville Republican (Pottsville, PA), February 9, Page 26.
19. The Morning Call (Allentown, PA), February 12, 1966, Page 13.
20. The Morning Call (Allentown, PA), February 16, 1966, Page 30.
21. The Morning Call (Allentown, PA), February 18, 1966, Page 28.
22. The Morning Call (Allentown, PA), February 19, 1966, Page 13.
23. The Morning Call (Allentown, PA), February 23, 1966, Page 30.
24. The Morning Call (Allentown, PA), February 25, 1966, Page 29.
25. The Morning Call (Allentown, PA), February 26, 1966, Page 13.
26. Pottsville Republican (Pottsville, PA), February 26, Page 6.
27. Standard Speaker (Hazleton, A), February 28, 1966, Page 20.
28. The Morning Call (Allentown, PA), March 2, 1966, Page 26.
29. The Morning Call (Allentown, PA), March 9, 1966, Page 33.
30. The Morning Call (Allentown, PA), March 13, 1966, Pages 53 and 55.
31. The Morning Call (Allentown, PA), March 17, 1966, Page 57.
32. The Morning Call (Allentown, PA), March 5, 1966, Page 14.
33. Standard-Speaker (Hazleton, PA), March 1, 1966, Page 18.
34. The Morning Call (Allentown, PA), March 25, 1966, Page 39.
35. The Morning Call (Allentown, PA), March 22, 1966, Page 16.

1967

1. The Morning Call (Allentown, PA), April 8, 1965, Page 16.
2. The Morning Call (Allentown, PA), December 14, 1966, Page 41.
3. The Morning Call (Allentown, PA), December 17, 1966, Page 24.
4. Standard-Speaker (Hazleton, PA), December 17, 1966, Page 16.
5. The Morning Call (Allentown, PA), December 21, 1966, Page 13.
6. The Morning Call (Allentown, PA), December 23, 1966, Page 28.
7. The Morning Call (Allentown, PA), January 4, 1967, Page 27.
8. The Morning Call (Allentown, PA), January 5, 1967, Page 39.
9. The Morning Call (Allentown, PA), January 7, 1967, Page 21.
10. The Morning Call (Allentown, PA), January 11, 1967, Page 28.
11. The Morning Call (Allentown, PA), January 14, 1967, Page 23.
12. The Morning Call (Allentown, PA), January 18, 1967, Page 33.
13. The Morning Call (Allentown, PA), January 21, 1967, Page 13.
14. The Morning Call (Allentown, PA), January 25, 1967, Page 34.
15. The Morning Call (Allentown, PA), January 28, 1967, Page 15.
16. The Morning Call (Allentown, PA), January 28, 1967, Page 16.
17. The Morning Call (Allentown, PA), February 1, 1967, Page 31.
18. The Morning Call (Allentown, PA), February 3, 1967, Page 26.
19. The Morning Call (Allentown, PA), February 4, 1967, Page 23.
20. The Morning Call (Allentown, PA), February 9, 1967, Page 36.
21. The Morning Call (Allentown, PA), February 11, 1967, Page 16.

22. The Morning Call (Allentown, PA), February 14, 1967, Page 18.
23. The Morning Call (Allentown, PA), February 15, 1967, Page 33.
24. Standard-Speaker (Hazleton, PA), February 16, 1967, Page 28.
25. The Morning Call (Allentown, PA), February 18, 1967, Page 31.
26. The Morning Call (Allentown, PA), February 22, 1967, Page 32.
27. The Morning Call (Allentown, PA), February 24, 1967, Page 31.
28. The Morning Call (Allentown, PA), February 25, 1967, Page 33.
29. The Morning Call (Allentown, PA), February 26, 1967, Page 53.
30. The Morning Call (Allentown, PA), March 1, 1967, Page 36.
31. The Morning Call (Allentown, PA), March 5, 1967, Pages 13 and 14.
32. The Morning Call (Allentown, PA), March 9, 1967, Page 57.
33. The Morning Call (Allentown, PA), March 16, 1967, Page 59.
34. The Morning Call (Allentown, PA), March 4, 1967, Page 29.
35. The Morning Call (Allentown, PA), March 11, 1967, Page 12.
36. Standard-Speaker (Hazleton, PA), March 2, 1967, Page 28.
37. Pottsville Republican (Pottsville, PA), April 3, 1967, Page 7.
38. Pottsville Republican (Pottsville, PA), March 23, 1967, Page 10.

1968

1. The Morning Call (Allentown, PA), December 6, 1967, Page 53.
2. The Morning Call (Allentown, PA), December 13, 1967, Page 48.
3. The Morning Call (Allentown, PA), December 16, 1967, Page 21.
4. The Morning Call (Allentown, PA), December 20, 1967, Page 41.
5. The Morning Call (Allentown, PA), December 20, 1967, Page 42.
6. Evening Herald and Ashland Daily News (Pottsville, PA), December 23, 1967, Page 18.
7. The Morning Call (Allentown, PA), January 4, 1968, Page 41.
8. The Morning Call (Allentown, PA), January 6, 1968, Page 25.
9. The Morning Call (Allentown, PA), January 10, 1968, Page 34.
10. Standard-Speaker (Hazleton, PA), January 10, 1968, Page 20.
11. The Morning Call (Allentown, PA), January 13, 1968, Page 27.
12. The Morning Call (Allentown, PA), January 17, 1968, Page 32.
13. The Morning Call (Allentown, PA), January 17, 1968, Page 35.
14. The Morning Call (Allentown, PA), January 18, 1968, Page 43.
15. The Morning Call (Allentown, PA), January 20, 1968, Page 15.
16. The Morning Call (Allentown, PA), January 24, 1968, Page 32.
17. The Morning Call (Allentown, PA), January 27, 1968, Page 15.
18. The Morning Call (Allentown, PA), January 31, 1968, Page 30.
19. Pottsville Republican (Pottsville, PA), January 31, 1968, Page 10.
20. The Morning Call (Allentown, PA), February 3, 1968, Page 15.
21. The Morning Call (Allentown, PA), February 7, 1968, Page 30.
22. The Morning Call (Allentown, PA), February 7, 1968, Page 31.
23. The Morning Call (Allentown, PA), February 10, 1968, Page 15.
24. The Morning Call (Allentown, PA), February 14, 1968, Page 34.
25. Standard-Speaker (Hazleton, PA), February 16, Page 18.
26. The Morning Call (Allentown, PA), February 17, 1968, Page 17.

27. The Morning Call (Allentown, PA), February 21, 1968, Page 55.
28. The Morning Call (Allentown, PA), February 23, 1968, Page 30
29. The Morning Call (Allentown, PA), February 24, 1968, Page 15.
30. The Morning Call (Allentown, PA), February 27, 1968, Page 17.
31. The Morning Call (Allentown, PA), February 29, 1968, Page 53.
32. The Morning Call (Allentown, PA), March 7, 1968, Page 59.
33. The Morning Call (Allentown, PA), March 10, 1968, Pages 37 and 38.
34. The Morning Call (Allentown, PA), March 17, 1968, Pages 41 and 42.
35. The Morning Call (Allentown, PA), March 21, 1968, Page 55.
36. The Morning Call (Allentown, PA), March 6, 1968, Page 49.
37. The Morning Call (Allentown, PA), March 9, 1968, Page 16.
38. The Morning Call (Allentown, PA), February 27, 1968, Page 18.
39. Standard-Speaker (Hazleton, PA), April 5, 1968, Page 26.
40. The Morning Call (Allentown, PA), March 21, 1968, Page 56.

1969

1. The Morning Call (Allentown, PA), March 30, 1967, Page 52
2. The Morning Call (Allentown, PA), December 4, 1968, Page 42.
3. The Morning Call (Allentown, PA), December 7, 1968, Page 13.
4. The Morning Call (Allentown, PA), December 7, 1968, Page 14.
5. The Morning Call (Allentown, PA), December 10, 1968, Page 22.
6. The Morning Call (Allentown, PA), December 11, 1968, Page 35.
7. The Morning Call (Allentown, PA), December 14, 1968, Page 15.
8. The Morning Call (Allentown, PA), December 18, 1968, Page 38.
9. The Morning Call (Allentown, PA), December 21, 1968, Page 15.
10. Standard-Speaker (Hazleton, PA), January 3, 1969, Page 20.
11. The Morning Call (Allentown, PA), January 4, 1969, Page 13.
12. The Morning Call (Allentown, PA), January 8, 1969, Page 26.
13. The Morning Call (Allentown, PA), January 11, 1969, Page 13.
14. The Morning Call (Allentown, PA), January 15, 1969, Page 29.
15. Standard-Speaker (Hazleton, PA), January16, 1969, Page 22.
16. The Morning Call (Allentown, PA), January 18, 1969, Page 21.
17. The Morning Call (Allentown, PA), January 25, 1969, Page 18.
18. The Morning Call (Allentown, PA), January 29, 1969, Page 34.
19. Pottsville Republican (Pottsville, PA), January 29, 1969, Page 11.
20. Standard-Speaker (Hazleton, PA), January 31, 1969, Page 18.
21. The Morning Call (Allentown, PA), February 1, 1969, Page 13.
22. The Morning Call (Allentown, PA), February 1, 1969, Page 14.
23. The Morning Call (Allentown, PA), February 5, 1969, Page 34.
24. The Morning Call (Allentown, PA), February 7, 1969, Page 28.
25. The Morning Call (Allentown, PA), February 8, 1969, Page 12.
26. The Morning Call (Allentown, PA), February 12, 1969, Page 34.
27. Standard-Speaker (Hazleton, PA), February 13, 1969, Page 26.
28. Standard-Speaker (Hazleton, PA), February 15, 1969, Page 15.
29. The Morning Call (Allentown, PA), February 15, 1969, Page 11.

30. The Morning Call (Allentown, PA), February 19, 1969, Page 32.
31. The Morning Call (Allentown, PA), February 21, 1969, Page 51.
32. The Morning Call (Allentown, PA), February 22, 1969, Page 25.
33. The Morning Call (Allentown, PA), February 25, 1969, Page 17.
34. Pottsville Republican (Pottsville, PA), February 25, 1969, Page 6.
35. The Morning Call (Allentown, PA), February 27, 1969, Page 53.
36. The Morning Call (Allentown, PA), February 27, 1969, Page 54.
37. The Morning Call (Allentown, PA), March 1, 1969, Page 13.
38. The Morning Call (Allentown, PA), March 2, 1969, Pages 37 and 38.
39. The Morning Call (Allentown, PA), March 4, 1969, Page 10.
40. The Morning Call (Allentown, PA), March 6, 1969, Pages 59 and 60.
41. The Morning Call (Allentown, PA), March 9, 1969, Page 41.
42. The Morning Call (Allentown, PA), March 13, 1969, Page 23.
43. The Morning Call (Allentown, PA), March 5, 1969, Page 35.
44. The Morning Call (Allentown, PA), March 8, 1969, Page 10.
45. The Morning Call (Allentown, PA), March 12, 1969, Page 36.
46. The Morning Call (Allentown, PA), March 15, 1969, Page 15.
47. Standard-Speaker (Hazleton, PA), March 4, 1969, Page 21.
48. Standard-Speaker (Hazleton, PA), March 20, 1969, Page 28.
49. The Morning Call (Allentown, PA), March 19, 1969, Page 50.

1970

1. The Morning Call (Allentown, PA), December 3, 1969, Page 43.
2. The Morning Call (Allentown, PA), December 3, 1969, Page 44.
3. Standard-Speaker (Hazleton, PA), December 5, 1969, Page 26.
4. The Morning Call (Allentown, PA), December 6, 1969, Page 13.
5. The Morning Call (Allentown, PA), December 10, 1969, Page 38.
6. The Morning Call (Allentown, PA), December 13, 1969, Page 13.
7. The Morning Call (Allentown, PA), December 17, 1969, Page 43.
8. Standard-Speaker (Hazleton, PA), December 19, 1969, Page 26.
9. The Morning Call (Allentown, PA), December 20, 1969, Page 28.
10. The Morning Call (Allentown, PA), December 23, 1969, Page 20.
11. The Morning Call (Allentown, PA), December 24, 1969, Page 36.
12. Pottsville Republican (Pottsville, PA), December 30, Page 6.
13. The Morning Call (Allentown, PA), January 7, 1970, Page 30.
14. The Morning Call (Allentown, PA), January 10, 1970, Page 13.
15. The Morning Call (Allentown, PA), January 14, 1970, Page 38.
16. The Morning Call (Allentown, PA), January 17, 1970, Page 13.
17. The Morning Call (Allentown, PA), January 20, 1970, Page 13.
18. The Morning Call (Allentown, PA), January 22, 1970, Page 48.
19. The Morning Call (Allentown, PA), January 24, 1970, Page 13.
20. The Morning Call (Allentown, PA), January 28, 1970, Page 37.
21. The Morning Call (Allentown, PA), January 31, 1970, Page 13.
22. The Morning Call (Allentown, PA), February 4, 1970, Page 28.
23. The Morning Call (Allentown, PA), February 7, 1970, Page 25.

24. The Morning Call (Allentown, PA), February 11, 1970, Page 44.
25. The Morning Call (Allentown, PA), February 11, 1970, Page 45.
26. The Morning Call (Allentown, PA), February 14, 1970, Page 29.
27. The Morning Call (Allentown, PA), February 18, 1970, Page 32.
28. Standard-Speaker (Hazleton, PA), February 19, Page 28.
29. The Morning Call (Allentown, PA), February 20, 1970, Page 39.
30. The Morning Call (Allentown, PA), February 21, 1970, Page 13.
31. The Morning Call (Allentown, PA), February 24, 1970, Page 17.
32. The Morning Call (Allentown, PA), February 26, 1970, Page 46.
33. The Morning Call (Allentown, PA), February 28, 1970, Page 13.
34. The Morning Call (Allentown, PA), March 1, 1970, Pages 39 and 41.
35. The Morning Call (Allentown, PA), March 3, 1970, Page 22.
36. The Morning Call (Allentown, PA), March 5, 1970, Page 59.
37. The Morning Call (Allentown, PA), March 8, 1970, Pages 39 and 40.
38. The Morning Call (Allentown, PA), March 4, 1970, Page 34.
39. The Morning Call (Allentown, PA), March 11, 1970, Page 41.
40. The Morning Call (Allentown, PA), March 14, 1970, Page 12.
41. Standard-Speaker (Hazleton, PA), February 27, 1970, Page 19.
42. Evening Herald (Pottsville, PA), April 9, 1970, Page 20.
43. Standard-Speaker (Hazleton, PA), March 28, 1970, Page 14.

1971

1. The Morning Call (Allentown, PA), December 5, 1970, Page 25.
2. Standard-Speaker (Hazleton, PA), December 5, 1970, Page 25.
3. Standard-Speaker (Hazleton, PA), December 8, 1970, Page 24.
4. The Morning Call (Allentown, PA), December 9, 1970, Page 44.
5. The Morning Call (Allentown, PA), December 9, 1970, Page 45.
6. The Morning Call (Allentown, PA), December 12, 1970, Page 24.
7. Standard-Speaker (Hazleton, PA), December 14, 1970, Page 23.
8. The Morning Call (Allentown, PA), December 16, 1970, Page 14.
9. The Morning Call (Allentown, PA), December 16, 1970, Page 15.
10. The Morning Call (Allentown, PA), December 19, 1970, Page 16.
11. Standard-Speaker (Hazleton, PA) December 18, 1970, Page 26.
12. The Morning Call (Allentown, PA), December 23, 1970, Page 19.
13. The Morning Call (Allentown, PA), December 24, 1970, Page 40.
14. The Morning Call (Allentown, PA), December 29, 1970, Page 24.
15. The Morning Call (Allentown, PA), December 30, 1970, Page 8.
16. The Morning Call (Allentown, PA), December 31, 1970, Page 14.
17. The Morning Call (Allentown, PA), January 3, 1971, Pages 37 and 38.
18. The Morning Call (Allentown, PA), January 6, 1971, Page 25.
19. The Morning Call (Allentown, PA), January 6, 1971, Page 26.
20. The Morning Call (Allentown, PA), January 8, 1971, Page 26
21. The Morning Call (Allentown, PA), January 9, 1971, Page 13.
22. The Morning Call (Allentown, PA), January 12, 1971, Page 21.
23. The Morning Call (Allentown, PA), January 14, 1971, Page 43.

24. The Morning Call (Allentown, PA), January 16, 1971, Page 13.
25. The Morning Call (Allentown, PA), January 20, 1971, Page 32.
26. The Morning Call (Allentown, PA), January 20, 1971, Page 33.
27. The Morning Call (Allentown, PA), January 20, 1971, Page 34.
28. The Morning Call (Allentown, PA), January 23, 1971, Page 13.
29. The Morning Call (Allentown, PA), January 27, 1971, Page 30.
30. The Morning Call (Allentown, PA), January 30, 1971, Page 13.
31. The Morning Call (Allentown, PA), February 3, 1971, Page 28.
32. Standard-Speaker (Hazleton, PA), February 4, 1971, Page 20.
33. The Morning Call (Allentown, PA), February 6, 1971, Page 13.
34. The Morning Call (Allentown, PA), February 10, 1971, Page 36.
35. The Morning Call (Allentown, PA), February 13, 1971, Page 13.
36. The Morning Call (Allentown, PA), February 16, 1971, Page 18.
37. The Morning Call (Allentown, PA), February 18, 1971, Page 47.
38. The Morning Call (Allentown, PA), February 20, 1971, Page 13.
39. The Morning Call (Allentown, PA), February 26, 1971, Page 32.
40. The Morning Call (Allentown, PA), March 3, 1971, Page 51.
41. Standard-Speaker (Hazleton, PA), March 8, 1971, Pages 18 and 19.
42. Standard-Speaker (Hazleton, PA), March 11, 1971, Pag 16.
43. The Morning Call (Allentown, PA), March 14, 1971, Pages 37 and 38.
44. The Morning Call (Allentown, PA), March 21, 1971, Pages 35 and 36.
45. The Morning Call (Allentown, PA), March 3, 1971, Page 52.
46. The Morning Call (Allentown, PA), March 17, 1971, Page 35.
47. The Morning Call (Allentown, PA), March 20, 1971, Page 13.
48. Pottsville Republican (Pottsville, PA), February 27, 1971, Page 7.
49. The Morning Call (Allentown, PA), March 24, 1971, Page 39.

1972

1. The Morning Call (Allentown, PA), March 24, 1971, Page 39.
2. The Morning Call (Allentown, PA), December 11, 1971, Page 17.
3. The Morning Call (Allentown, PA), December 15, 1971, Page 49.
4. The Morning Call (Allentown, PA), December 15, 1971, Page 50.
5. The Morning Call (Allentown, PA), December 18, 1971, Page 17.
6. The Morning Call (Allentown, PA), December 22, 1971, Page 38.
7. The Morning Call (Allentown, PA), December 24, 1971, Page 21.
8. The Morning Call (Allentown, PA), January 5, 1972, Page 39.
9. The Morning Call (Allentown, PA), January 8, 1972, Page 13.
10. Pottsville Republican (Pottsville, PA), January 8, 1972, Page 7.
11. The Morning Call (Allentown, PA), January 12, 1972, Page 36.
12. The Morning Call (Allentown, PA), January 15, 1972, Page 13.
13. The Morning Call (Allentown, PA), January 19, 1972, Page 37.
14. The Morning Call (Allentown, PA), January 22, 1972, Page 15.
15. The Morning Call (Allentown, PA), January 28, 1972, Page 34.
16. Standard-Speaker (Hazleton, PA), January 22, 1972, Page 20.
17. The Morning Call (Allentown, PA), January 26, 1972, Page 38.

18. The Morning Call (Allentown, PA), January 29, 1972, Page 13.
19. The Morning Call (Allentown, PA), February 2, 1972, Page 38
20. Pottsville Republican (Pottsville, PA), February 2, 1972, Page 13.
21. The Morning Call (Allentown, PA), February 5, 1972, Page 24.
22. The Morning Call (Allentown, PA), February 9, 1972, Page 18.
23. Pottsville Republican (Pottsville, PA), February 9, 1972, Page 14.
24. The Morning Call (Allentown, PA), February 12, 1972, Page 13.
25. The Morning Call (Allentown, PA), February 16, 1972, Page 17.
26. The Morning Call (Allentown, PA), February 19, 1972, Page 20.
27. The Morning Call (Allentown, PA), February 24, 1972, Page 51.
28. The Morning Call (Allentown, PA), March 1, 1972, Page 57.
29. The Morning Call (Allentown, PA), March 4, 1972, Page 13.
30. The Morning Call (Allentown, PA), March 8, 1972, Page 43.
31. The Morning Call (Allentown, PA), March 9, 1972, Page 49.
32. The Morning Call (Allentown, PA), March 12, 1972, Pages 41 and 42.
33. The Morning Call (Allentown, PA), March 1, 1972, Page 58.
34. The Morning Call (Allentown, PA), March 8, 1972, Page 44.
35. The Morning Call (Allentown, PA), March 12, 1972, Pages 11 and 12.
36. The Morning Call (Allentown, PA), March 17, 1972, Page 45.
37. Pottsville Republican (Pottsville, PA), March 2, 1972, Page 11.
38. The Morning Call (Allentown, PA), April 12, 1972, Page 51.
39. The Morning Call (Allentown, PA), March 30, 1972, Page 50.

1973

1. The Morning Call (Allentown, PA), April 12, 1972, Page 51.
2. The Morning Call (Allentown, PA), December 9, 1972, Page 15.
3. The Morning Call (Allentown, PA), December 10, 1972, Page 11.
4. The Morning Call (Allentown, PA), December 13, 1972, Page 57.
5. Standard-Speaker (Hazleton, PA), December 13, 1972, Page 46.
6. The Morning Call (Allentown, PA), December 16, 1972, Page 20.
7. The Morning Call (Allentown, PA), December 20, 1972, Page 49.
8. The Morning Call (Allentown, PA), December 20, 1972, Pages 49 and 50.
9. The Morning Call (Allentown, PA), December 20, 1972, Page 50.
10. Evening Herald (Pottsville, PA), December 20, 1972, Page 20.
11. The Morning Call (Allentown, PA), December 23, 1972, Page 12.
12. The Morning Call (Allentown, PA), January 4, 1973, Page 49.
13. The Morning Call (Allentown, PA), January 4, 1973, Page 50.
14. The Morning Call (Allentown, PA), January 6, 1973, Page 15.
15. Evening Herald (Pottsville, PA), January 6, 1973, Page 10.
16. The Morning Call (Allentown, PA), January 10, 1973, Page 38.
17. The Morning Call (Allentown, PA), January 10, 1973, Page 39.
18. Pottsville Republican (Pottsville, PA), January 10, 1973, Page 12.
19. The Morning Call (Allentown, PA), January 13, 1973, Page 15.
20. The Morning Call (Allentown, PA), January 17, 1973, Page 50.
21. Standard-Speaker (Hazleton, PA), January 18, 1973, Page 22.

22. The Morning Call (Allentown, PA), January 18, 1973, Page 53.
23. The Morning Call (Allentown, PA), January 20, 1973, Page 22.
24. Pottsville Republican (Pottsville, PA), January 20, 1973, Page 7.
25. The Morning Call (Allentown, PA), January 24, 1973, Page 47.
26. Standard-Speaker (Hazleton, PA), January 24, 1973, Page 34.
27. The Morning Call (Allentown, PA), January 27, 1973, Page 11.
28. The Morning Call (Allentown, PA), January 31, 1973, Page 19.
29. The Morning Call (Allentown, PA), February 3, 1973, Page 20.
30. The Morning Call (Allentown, PA), February 7, 1973, Page 43.
31. The Morning Call (Allentown, PA), February 10, 1973, Page 19.
32. Standard-Speaker (Hazleton, PA), February 10, 1973, Page 22.
33. Evening Herald (Pottsville, PA), February 10, 1973, Page 15.
34. The Morning Call (Allentown, PA), February 14, 1973, Page 43.
35. The Morning Call (Allentown, PA), February 17, 1973, Page 24.
36. The Morning Call (Allentown, PA), February 21, 1973, Page 40.
37. The Morning Call (Allentown, PA), February 24, 1973, Page 15.
38. The Morning Call (Allentown, PA), March 3, 1973, Page 23.
39. The Morning Call (Allentown, PA), March 4, 1973, Pages 37 and 39.
40. The Morning Call (Allentown, PA), March 7, 1973, Page 57.
41. The Morning Call (Allentown, PA), March 8, 1973, Page 18.
42. The Morning Call (Allentown, PA), March 11, 1973, Page 46.
43. The Morning Call (Allentown, PA), March 11, 1973, Pages 45 and 46.
44. The Morning Call (Allentown, PA), March 15, 1973, Pages 61 and 62.
45. The Morning Call (Allentown, PA), March 18, 1973, Pages 45 and 46.
46. The Morning Call (Allentown, PA), March 22, 1973, Page 61.
47. Pottsville Republican (Pottsville, PA), April 4, 1973, Page 16.
48. The Morning Call (Allentown, PA), March 29, 1973, Page 62.

1974

1. The Morning Call (Allentown, PA), December 8, 1973, Page 18.
2. The Morning Call (Allentown, PA), December 12, 1973, Page 14,
3. The Morning Call (Allentown, PA), December 15, 1973, Page 18.
4. The Morning Call (Allentown, PA), December 19, 1973, Page 54.
5. The Morning Call (Allentown, PA), December 22, 1973, Page 17.
6. The Morning Call (Allentown, PA), January 3, 1974, Page 43.
7. The Morning Call (Allentown, PA), January 5, 1974, Page 13.
8. The Morning Call (Allentown, PA), January 9, 1974, Page 38.
9. The Morning Call (Allentown, PA), January 12, 1974, Page 17.
10. The Morning Call (Allentown, PA), January 16, 1974, Page 45.
11. The Morning Call (Allentown, PA), January 19, 1974, Page 43.
12. The Morning Call (Allentown, PA), January 23, 1974, Page 42.
13. The Morning Call (Allentown, PA), January 26, 1974, Page 13.
14. The Morning Call (Allentown, PA), January 30, 1974, Page 24.
15. The Morning Call (Allentown, PA), February 2, 1974, Page 13.
16. The Morning Call (Allentown, PA), February 6, 1974, Page 40.

17. The Morning Call (Allentown, PA), February 9, 1974, Page 13.
18. The Morning Call (Allentown, PA), February 13, 1974, Page 45.
19. The Morning Call (Allentown, PA), February 14, 1974, Page 44.
20. The Morning Call (Allentown, PA), February 16, 1974, Page 13.
21. The Morning Call (Allentown, PA), February 21, 1974, Page 13.
22. The Morning Call (Allentown, PA), March 2, 1974, Page 13.
23. The Morning Call (Allentown, PA), March 5, 1974, Page 24.
24. The Morning Call (Allentown, PA), March 6, 1974, Page 49.
25. The Morning Call (Allentown, PA), March 7, 1974, Page 51.
26. The Morning Call (Allentown, PA), March 9, 1974, Page 13.
27. The Morning Call (Allentown, PA), March 10, 1974, Page 41.
28. The Morning Call (Allentown, PA), March 14, 1974, Page 49.
29. The Morning Call (Allentown, PA), March 17, 1974, Pages 41 and 42.
30. The Morning Call (Allentown, PA), March 21, 1974, Page 42.
31. Standard-Speaker (Hazleton, PA), February 19, 1974, Page 18.
32. The Morning Call (Allentown, PA), April 14, 1974, Page 45.
33. The Morning Call (Allentown, PA), March 29, 1974, Page 20.

1975

1. The Morning Call (Allentown, PA), April 14, 1974, Page 45.
2. The Morning Call (Allentown, PA), December 7, 1974, Page 17.
3. The Morning Call (Allentown, PA), December 11, 1974, Page 64.
4. The Morning Call (Allentown, PA), December 14, 1974, Page 17.
5. The Morning Call (Allentown, PA), December 18, 1974, Page 64.
6. The Morning Call (Allentown, PA), December 21, 1974, Page 17.
7. The Morning Call (Allentown, PA), January 4, 1975, Page 12.
8. The Morning Call (Allentown, PA), January 8, 1975, Page 42.
9. The Morning Call (Allentown, PA), January 11, 1975, Page 13.
10. The Morning Call (Allentown, PA), January 15, 1975, Page 38.
11. The Morning Call (Allentown, PA), January 22, 1975, Page 31.
12. The Morning Call (Allentown, PA), January 25, 1975, Page 13.
13. The Morning Call (Allentown, PA), January 29, 1975, Page 36.
14. The Morning Call (Allentown, PA), February 1, 1975, Page 13.
15. The Morning Call (Allentown, PA), February 5, 1975, Page 50.
16. The Morning Call (Allentown, PA), February 8, 1975, Page 17.
17. The Morning Call (Allentown, PA), February 12, 1975, Page 54.
18. The Morning Call (Allentown, PA), February 15, 1975, Page 13.
19. The Morning Call (Allentown, PA), February 19, 1975, Page 49.
20. The Morning Call (Allentown, PA), February 21, 1975, Page 28.
21. The Morning Call (Allentown, PA), February 23, 1975, Page 41.
22. The Morning Call (Allentown, PA), February 27, 1975, Page 15.
23. The Morning Call (Allentown, PA), February 23, 1975, Page 48.
24. The Morning Call (Allentown, PA), March 1, 1975, Page 13.
25. The Morning Call (Allentown, PA), March 4, 1975, Page 30.
26. The Morning Call (Allentown, PA), March 6, 1975, Page 23.

27. The Morning Call (Allentown, PA), March 8, 1975, Page 13.
28. The Morning Call (Allentown, PA), March 9, 1975, Page 45.
29. Pottsville Republican (Pottsville, PA), March 13, 1975, Page 7.
30. The Morning Call (Allentown, PA), March 13, 1975, Page 61.
31. Pottsville Republican (Pottsville, PA), March 17, 1975, Page 15.
32. Pottsville Republican (Pottsville, PA), March 15, 1975, Page 12.
33. Pottsville Republican (Pottsville, PA), April 2, 1975, Page 15.

The Coaches

1. The Morning Call (Allentown, PA), December 26, 1981, Page 21
2. The Morning Call (Allentown, PA), July 12, 2003, Page 30.
3. The Morning Call (Allentown, PA), August 18, 2014, Page A12.
4. Allentown High School-Comus Yearbook-Class of 1940, Page 234.
5. Allentown High School-Comus Yearbook-Class of 1943, Page 238.
6. William Allen High School-Comus Yearbook-Class of 1982, Page 248.
7. The Morning Call (Allentown, PA), August 4, 1960, Page 25.
8. The Morning Call (Allentown, PA), April 6, 1927, Page 23.
9. The Morning Call (Allentown, PA), December 29, 2005, Page 49.
10. The Morning Call (Allentown, PA), August 14, 1980.
11. The Morning Call (Allentown, PA), August 10, 1985, Page 94.
12. The Morning Call (Allentown, PA), April 4, 2018, Page A10.
13. The Morning Call (Allentown, PA), November 5, 2010, Page 19.
14. The Morning Call (Allentown, PA), June 27, 1973, Page 57.
15. Bethlehem High School-Cauldron Yearbook-Class of 1954, Page 9.
16. Bethlehem High School - Cauldron Yearbook – Class of 1928, Page 136.
17. Bethlehem High School - Cauldron Yearbook – Class of 1960, Page 14.
18. Phillipsburg (NJ) High School-Karux Yearbook-Class of 1966, Page 41.
19. The Morning Call (Allentown, PA), December 18, 1980, Page 178.
20. The Morning Call (Allentown, PA), April 2, 2012, Page A11.
21. 1995 Via Classic Program
22. The Morning Call (Allentown, PA), June 12, 1998, Page B8.
23. The Morning Call (Allentown, PA), March 16, 1975, Page 18.
24. Citizen's Voice (Wilkes-Barre, PA), January 14, 2003, Page 35.
25. The Morning Call (Allentown, PA), July 21, 1953, Page 20.
26. The Morning Call (Allentown, PA), August 14, 1953, Page 41.
27. The Morning Call (Allentown, PA), January 12, 1984, Page 35.
28. The Morning Call (Allentown, PA), May 28, 1957, Page 35.
29. The Morning Call (Allentown, PA), February 3, 2018, Page A22.
30. The Morning Call (Allentown, PA), October 23, 1997, Page 32.
31. The Morning Call (Allentown, PA), June 30, 2012, Page A18.
32. Central Catholic High School-Glen Echoes Yearbook-Class of 1950, Page 88.
33. Central Catholic High School-Glen Echoes Yearbook-Class of 1951, Page 84.
34. Central Catholic High School-Glen Echoes Yearbook-Class of 1957, Page 12.
35. Central Catholic High School-Glen Echoes Yearbook-Class of 1958, Page 38.
36. 1987 LARC Classic Program

37. Intelligencer Journal (Lancaster, PA), March 4, 1972, Page 2.
38. The Mercury (Pottstown, PA), November 3, 1945, Page 5.
39. The Morning Press (Bloomsburg, PA), December 12, 1927, Page 2.
40. Bloomsburg University-Obiter Yearbook-Class of 1924, Page 101.
41. 1984 LARC Classic Program
42. The Morning Call (Allentown, PA), June 15, 2001, Page 25.
43. 1985 LARC Classic Program
44. Lebanon Daily News (Lebanon, PA), March 18, 1932, Page 20.
45. Lebanon Daily News (Lebanon, PA), April 20, 1957, Page 10.
46. Lebanon Daily News (Lebanon, PA), April 30, 1969, Page 2.
47. Central Bucks High School West – Antler Yearbook – Class of 1954, Page 80.
48. The Pocono Record (The Stroudsburgs, PA), July 9, 1965, Page 8.
49. West Schuylkill Express and Pine Grove Herald (Tremont, PA), March 6, 1936, Page 4
50. East Stroudsburg High School – Cavalier Yearbook – Class of 1945, Page 11.
51. East Stroudsburg High School – Cavalier Yearbook – Class of 1956, Page 95.
52. The Morning Call (Allentown, PA), December 31, 1975, Page 12.
53. The Morning Call (Allentown, PA), July 24, 1966, Page 24.
54. The Morning Call (Allentown, PA), February 25, 2001, page 30.
55. The Morning Call (Allentown, PA), March 27, 1935, Page 29.
56. The Orlando Sentinel (Orlando, FL), August 9, 1982, Page 18.
57. The Morning Call (Allentown, PA), April 15, 1942, Page 15.
58. The Morning Call (Allentown, PA), June 14, 1952, Page 11.
59. The Morning Call (Allentown, PA), July 22, 1954, Page 29.
60. The Morning Call (Allentown, PA), January 9, 1967, Page 9.
61. The Morning Call (Allentown, PA), April 24, 1956, Page 28.
62. Standard-Speaker (Hazleton, PA), August 11, 1958, Page 13.
63. 1995 Via Classic Program
64. Easton High School-Rechauffe Yearbook-Class of 1926, Page 88.
65. Easton High School-Rechauffe Yearbook-Class of 1942, Page 12.
66. Wilson Area High School-Les Memoirs Yearbook-Class of 1960, Page 137.
67. Easton High School-Rechauffe Yearbook-Class of 1942, Page 8.
68. Hazleton High School-Janus Yearbook-Class of 1942, Page 16.
69. Hellertown High School-Reflector yearbook-Class of 1944, Page 12.
70. Easton High School-Rechauffe Yearbook-Class of 1955, Page 83.
71. Easton High School-Rechauffe Yearbook-Class of 1955, Page 82.
72. 1982 LARC Classic Program
73. The Morning Call (Allentown, PA), May 16, 1970, Page 31.
74. The Morning Call (Allentown, PA), July 17, 1974, Page 54.
75. The Morning Call (Allentown, PA), February 24, 1989, Page 46.
76. The Morning Call (Allentown, PA), June 8, 1990, Page 44.
77. Republican and Herald (Pottsville, PA), August 18, 1948, Page 10.
78. The Morning Call (Allentown, PA), May 3, 1982, Page 27.
79. Standard-Speaker (Hazleton, PA), July 27, 1977. Page 2.
80. Standard-Speaker (Hazleton, PA), November 20, 2020, Page A2.

81. Times Leader (Wilkes-Barre, PA), January 10, 2010, Page 2.
82. Standard-Speaker (Hazleton, PA), July 18, 1969, Page 18.
83. Hazleton High School – Janus Yearbook – Class of 1948, Page 17.
84. Hazleton High School – Janus Yearbook – Class of 1959, Page 18.
85. Hazleton High School-Janus Yearbook-Class of 1969, Page 193.
86. Hazleton High School-Janus Yearbook-Class of 1970, Page 216.
87. Evening Herald (Shenandoah, PA), February 4, 1974, Page 1.
88. The Morning Call (Allentown, PA), October 22, 1963, Page 21.
89. The Morning Call (Allentown, PA), March 13, 1977, Page 48.
90. The Morning Call (Allentown, PA), May 15, 1973, Page 32.
91. Phillipsburg High School-Karux Yearbook-Class of 1975, Page 27.
92. The Mercury (Pottstown, PA), January 29, 1971, Page 31.
93. The Morning Call (Allentown, PA) November 8, 1922, Page 17.
94. Pottsville Republican (Pottsville, PA), September 21, 1925. Page 9.
95. Tampa Tribune (Tampa, FL), July 23, 1985, Page 33.
96. Gettysburg College-Spectrum Yearbook-Class of 1926, Page 108.
97. Pottsville High School-Hi S Potts Yearbook-Class of 1929, Page 83.
98. The Daily Item (Sunbury, PA), May 1, 1971, Page 14.
99. Mount Carmel Item (Mount Carmel, PA), May 16, 1931, Page 5.
100. Pottsville Republican (Pottsville, PA), September 26, 1981, Page 2.
101. Pottsville Republican (Pottsville, PA), August 7, 1981, Page 11.
102. The Plain-Speaker (Hazleton, PA), July 30, 1938, Page 11.
103. Pottsville Republican (Pottsville, PA), October 21, 1982, Page 2.
104. Pottsville Republican (Pottsville, PA), August 10, 1946, Page 1.
105. Standard-Speaker (Hazleton, PA), June 23, 1997, Page 2.
106. Pottsville Republican (Pottsville, PA), December 19, 1958.
107. Pottsville Republican (Pottsville, PA), May 19, 1959, Page 8.
108. Republican Herald (Pottsville, PA), September 2, 2010, Page A9.
109. Pottsville Republican (Pottsville, PA), August 7, 1981, Page 11.
110. Upper Darby High School Oak Yearbook, Class of 1940, Page 28.
111. Pottsville High School Yearbook – Class of 1930, Page 112.
112. Pottsville High School Yearbook – Class of 1932, Page 89.
113. Pottsville High School Yearbook – Class of 1938, Page 12.
114. Pottsville High School – High School Yearbook – Class of 1939, Page 96.
115. Pottsville High School – High School Yearbook – Class of 1945, Page 82.
116. Pottsville High School – High School Yearbook – Class of 1949, Page 12.
117. St. Clair High School-Clairian Yearbook-Class of 1955, Page 66.
118. Pottsville High School-High School Yearbook-Class of 1969, Page 96.
119. Pottsville High School-High School Yearbook-Class of 1960, Page 105.
120. Pottsville High School-High School Yearbook-Class of 1971, Page 13.
121. Pottsville Republican (Pottsville, PA), May 5, 1984, Page 2.
122. The Morning Call (Allentown, PA), June 3, 1993, Page 156.
123. The Morning Call (Allentown, PA), June 22, 1943, Page 5.
124. Pottsville Republican (Pottsville, PA), December 4, 1942, Page 18

125. The Morning Call (Allentown, PA), August 19, 1943, Page 14.
126. Republican and Herald (Pottsville, PA), November 21, 1979, Page 2.
127. The Morning Call (Allentown, PA), May 10, 1968, Page 16.
128. Standard-Speaker (Hazleton, PA), October 3, 2012, Page A2.
129. Tamaqua High School – Sphinx Yearbook – Class of 1935, Page 74.
130. Tamaqua High School – Sphinx Yearbook – Class of 1958, Page 11.
131. Tamaqua High School – Sphinx Yearbook – Class of 1942, Page 15.
132. East Stroudsburg University-Stroud Yearbook-Class of 1949, Page 91.
133. Pottsville Republican (Pottsville, PA), May 11, 1982, Page 2.
134. The Morning Call (Allentown, PA), August 31, 2022, Page A21.
135. Pottsville Republican (Pottsville, PA), May 15, 1995, Page 2.

Made in the USA
Middletown, DE
12 August 2025

12121048R00325